EMBRY-RIDDLE
Aeronautical University.
WORLDWIDE

Dear Student,

Welcome to the Master of Science in Management (MSM) program! This dynamic program will provide you with incredible insight into all aspects of management. Whether you have your sights set on a global, high-tech, Fortune 500 Company or you are looking for a promotion within your own organization, the MSM program will benefit you.

Along the way the faculty will use current events, case studies, provocative discussion, and recent literature to help you expand your managerial horizons. You will be challenged to think creatively and apply critical thinking and problem solving skills to a host of different management problems. Also, you will learn how to stay abreast of changes in management so you are always on the leading edge.

This course is designed to refresh your knowledge on a few key areas and help prepare you for success in the MSM program. The skills learned in MGMT 500 will be used in all other MSM courses and will make things like writing and research easier for you. In addition, you will be quickly brought up to speed on foundational concepts in management, preparing for the Capstone, and getting the most out of this program.

Finally, we hope you are as dedicated to the MSM program as we are. Through hard work and collaboration we will help you be successful.

Dr. Aaron M. Glassman
Program Chair
aaron.glassman@erau.edu

Dr. Rose Opengart
Assistant Program Chair
rose.opengart@erau.edu

600 S. Clyde Morris Blvd.
Daytona Beach, FL 32114-3900
800-862-2416

Business Foundations

MGMT 500

Embry-Riddle Aeronautical University

William M. Pride | Robert J. Hughes | Jack R. Kapoor
William G. Zikmund | Barry J. Babin | Jon C. Carr | Mitch Griffin
David R. Anderson | Dennis J. Sweeney | Thomas A. Williams |
Jeffrey D. Camm | James J. Cochran

CENGAGE
Learning·

Australia • Brazil • Japan • Korea • Mexico • Singapore • Spain • United Kingdom • United States

CENGAGE
Learning·

Business Foundations: MGMT 500, Embry-Riddle Aeronautical University

Senior Manager, Student Engagement:

Linda deStefano

Janey Moeller

Manager, Student Engagement:

Julie Dierig

Marketing Manager:

Rachael Kloos

Manager, Production Editorial:

Kim Fry

Manager, Intellectual Property Project Manager:

Brian Methe

Senior Manager, Production and Manufacturing:

Donna M. Brown

Manager, Production:

Terri Daley

Foundations of Business, Fourth Edition
William M. Pride | Robert J. Hughes | Jack R. Kapoor

© 2015 Cengage Learning. All rights reserved.

Business Research Methods
William G. Zikmund | Barry J. Babin | Jon C. Carr | Mitch Griffin

© 2013 Cengage Learning. All rights reserved.

Essentials of Statistics for Business and Economics
David R. Anderson | Dennis J. Sweeney | Thomas A. Williams | Jeffrey D. Camm | James J. Cochran

© 2014 Cengage Learning. All rights reserved.

For product information and technology assistance, contact us at
Cengage Learning Customer & Sales Support, 1-800-354-9706

For permission to use material from this text or product,
submit all requests online at **cengage.com/permissions**
Further permissions questions can be emailed to
permissionrequest@cengage.com

This book contains select works from existing Cengage Learning resources and was produced by Cengage Learning Custom Solutions for collegiate use. As such, those adopting and/or contributing to this work are responsible for editorial content accuracy, continuity and completeness.

Compilation © 2014 Cengage Learning

ISBN-13: 9781305028616

ISBN-10: 1305028619

WCN: 01-100-101

Cengage Learning

5191 Natorp Boulevard
Mason, Ohio 45040
USA

Cengage Learning is a leading provider of customized learning solutions with office locations around the globe, including Singapore, the United Kingdom, Australia, Mexico, Brazil, and Japan. Locate your local office at:
international.cengage.com/region.

Cengage Learning products are represented in Canada by Nelson Education, Ltd.
For your lifelong learning solutions, visit **www.cengage.com/custom.**
Visit our corporate website at **www.cengage.com.**

Brief Contents

Dear Student

From:
Foundations of Business, Fourth Edition
William M. Pride | Robert J. Hughes | Jack R. Kapoor

From:
Business Research Methods
William G. Zikmund | Barry J. Babin | Jon C. Carr | Mitch Griffin

From:

Essentials of Statistics for Business and Economics

David R. Anderson | Dennis J. Sweeney | Thomas A. Williams | Jeffrey D. Camm | James J. Cochran

© EDHAR/SHUTTERSTOCK.COM

Exploring the World of Business and Economics

Learning Objectives

What you will be able to do once you complete this chapter:

1 Discuss what you must do to be successful in the world of business.

2 Define *business* and identify potential risks and rewards.

3 Define *economics* and describe the two types of economic systems: capitalism and command economy.

4 Identify the ways to measure economic performance.

5 Examine the different phases in the typical business cycle.

6 Outline the four types of competition.

7 Summarize the factors that affect the business environment and the challenges that American businesses will encounter in the future.

Why Should You Care?

Studying business will help you to choose a career, become a successful employee or manager, start your own business, and become a more informed consumer and better investor.

How Starbucks Brews Up Global Profits

Starbucks was a small, decade-old business in 1981 when Howard Schultz happened to be in its store in Seattle's Pike Place Market and sipped the founder's freshly brewed coffee. Intrigued by the product and the possibilities, he soon joined the firm. Then he traveled to Italy and got a first hand taste of the robust espressos and the welcoming ambiance in local coffeehouses. Back home, Schultz decided to start his own company, opening European-style cafés serving premium coffees brewed to order. A few years later, he and a group of investors bought Starbucks and began opening cafés all across America. To raise millions of dollars for funding new cafés and creating new products, Starbucks sold stock and became a publicly traded corporation in 1992.

Now, after 25 years of aggressive growth, Starbucks has spread its unique brand of coffee culture around the country and around the world. The company's familiar green-and-white mermaid logo appears on its nearly 18,000 cafés in 60 countries, with future openings planned throughout Asia, Northern Europe, and beyond. The ever-expanding menu includes hot and iced coffees and teas, fruit juices and chilled drinks, and an assortment of pastries, wraps, and yogurts. Thanks to acquisitions and partnerships, the Starbucks empire also includes packaged coffee beans, coffee ice cream, coffee drinks, and fruit juices sold in supermarkets, as well as high-tech coffeemakers for home and office.

Starbucks is a company with a conscience. It provides health-care coverage to both full-time and part-time employees, a benefit that many companies offer to full-timers only. It also emphasizes environment-friendly practices such as composting coffee grounds, conserving water, and recycling paper, glass, and plastic. In addition, Starbucks is piloting the development of smaller, certified energy-efficient stores constructed from locally available materials. Looking ahead, how will Starbucks handle such critical challenges as intense competition and economic uncertainty?[1]

Did You Know?

Starbucks rings up more than $13 billion in annual revenue through nearly 18,000 cafés in 60 nations.

Wow! What a challenging world we live in. Just for a moment, think about how you would answer the question below.

In the future, which of the following is the most serious problem facing Americans?

    a. The national debt.
    b. The high unemployment rate.
    c. A volatile stock market.
    d. Consumer pessimism.
    e. An unstable economy and business environment.

Unfortunately there is no one best answer because all of the above options are serious problems facing you, American businesses, and the nation. Ask almost anyone, and they will tell you that they are worried about at least one or more of the above problems. At the time of the publication of your text, there are signs of economic improvement when compared to the last five years, but people still worry about their future and the future of the nation. Still, it is important to remember the old adage, "History is a great teacher." Both the nation and individuals should take a look at what went wrong to avoid making the same mistakes in the future.

In addition, it helps to keep one factor in mind: Our economy continues to adapt and change to meet the challenges of an ever-changing world and to provide opportunities for those who want to achieve success. Our economic system provides an amazing amount of freedom that allows businesses like Starbucks—the company profiled in the Inside Business opening case for this chapter—to adapt to changing business environments. Despite troubling economic times and a weak economy, Starbucks—and its employees—is a success because it was able to introduce new products, open new stores, meet the needs of its customers, earn a profit, and sell stock to the general public.

Within certain limits, imposed mainly to ensure public safety, the owners of a business can produce any legal good or service they choose and attempt to sell it at the price they set. This system of business, in which individuals decide what to produce, how to produce it, and at what price to sell it, is called **free enterprise**. Our free-enterprise system ensures, for example, that Amazon.com can sell everything from televisions, toys, and tools to computers, cameras, and clothing. Our system gives Amazon's owners and stockholders the right to make a profit from the company's success. It gives Amazon's management the right to compete with bookstore rival Barnes & Noble and electronics giant Sony. It also gives you—the consumer—the right to choose.

In this chapter, we look briefly at what business is and how it became that way. First, we discuss what you must do to be successful in the world of business and explore some important reasons for studying business. Then we define *business*, noting how business organizations satisfy their customers' needs and earn profits. Next, we examine how capitalism and command economies answer four basic economic questions. Then our focus shifts to how the nations of the world measure economic performance, the phases in a typical business cycle, and the four types of competitive situations. Next, we look at the events that helped shape today's business system, the current business environment, and the challenges that businesses face.

free enterprise the system of business in which individuals are free to decide what to produce, how to produce it, and at what price to sell it

YOUR FUTURE IN THE CHANGING WORLD OF BUSINESS

Learning Objective

1 Discuss what you must do to be successful in the world of business.

The key word in this heading is *changing*. When faced with both economic problems and increasing competition not only from firms in the United States but also from international firms located in other parts of the world, employees and managers began to ask the question: What do we do now? Although this is a fair question, it is difficult to answer. Certainly, for a college student taking business courses or an employee just starting a career, the question is even more difficult to answer. Yet there are still opportunities out there for people who are willing to work hard, continue to learn, and possess the ability to adapt to change. Let's begin our discussion in this section with three basic concepts.

- What do you want?
- Why do you want it?
- Write it down!

During a segment on a national television talk show, Joe Dudley, one of the world's most respected black business owners, gave the preceding advice to anyone who wanted to succeed in business. His advice can help you achieve success. What is so amazing about Dudley's success is that he started a manufacturing business in his own kitchen, with his wife and children serving as the new firm's only employees. He went on to develop his own line of hair-care and cosmetic products sold directly to cosmetologists, barbers, beauty schools, and consumers in the United States and 18 foreign countries. Today, Mr. Dudley has a multimillion-dollar empire—one of the most successful minority-owned companies in the nation. He is not only a successful business owner but also a winner of the Horatio Alger Award—an award given to outstanding individuals who have succeeded in the face of adversity.[2]

Although many people would say that Joe Dudley was just lucky or happened to be in the right place at the right time, the truth is that he became a success because he had a dream and worked hard to turn his dream into a reality. He would be the first to tell you that you have the same opportunities that he had. According to Mr. Dudley, "Success is a journey, not just a destination."[3]

Whether you want to obtain part-time employment to pay college and living expenses, begin your career as a full-time employee, or start a business, you must *bring* something to the table that makes you different from the next person. Employers and

No matter what career you choose, you'll be much more effective on the job if you use these five keys to higher productivity.

1. *Focus on one task at a time.* If you divide your attention, you can't apply as much mental muscle to complex projects or difficult challenges.

2. *Make your workload more manageable.* Divide large tasks into small steps so you won't feel as intimidated by all you have to accomplish. Just as important, you can determine which steps should be completed now and which can wait for another day.

3. *Organize your work space and your work day.* It's easier to focus and put your hands on the materials you need when you're not surrounded by clutter. Keep yourself on track by making notes (electronically or on paper) about what you plan to do and when. If you don't complete your daily or weekly "to do" list, check again to see what should take priority and what you can cut out or postpone.

4. *Structure your time.* Plan to avoid distractions and interruptions during some parts of every work day. Turn off your e-mail, close the web browser, and settle down to concentrate for a set period.

5. *Give your brain a break.* Treat yourself to a brief break every few hours. Stand up, stretch, walk around if you can, and think about something else for a couple of minutes. When you return to the task at hand, you'll feel more refreshed — and you may even have some fresh ideas.

Sources: Based on information in Daniel Bortz, "10 Ways to Be More Productive at Work," *U.S. News & World Report*, May 4, 2012, http://money.usnews.com; Sabah Karimi, "7 Ways to Jump-Start Your Productivity at Work," *U.S. News & World Report*, February 27, 2012, http://money.usnews.com; Eilene Zimmerman, "Distracted? It's Time to Hit the Reset Button," *New York Times*, November 19, 2011, www.nytimes.com; Daniel McGinn, "Being More Productive," *Harvard Business Review*, May 2011, http://hbr.org.

our economic system are more demanding than ever before. Ask yourself: What can I do that will make employers want to pay me a salary? What skills do I have that employers need? With these two questions in mind, we begin the next section with another basic question: Why study business?

Why Study Business?

The potential benefits of higher education are enormous. To begin with, there are economic benefits. Over their lifetimes, college graduates on average earn much more than high school graduates. Although lifetime earnings are substantially higher for college graduates, so are annual income amounts (see Figure 1-1). In addition to higher income, you will find at least five compelling reasons for studying business.

FOR HELP IN CHOOSING A CAREER What do you want to do with the rest of your life? Like many people, you may find it a difficult question to answer. This business course will introduce you to a wide array of employment opportunities. In private enterprise, these range from small, local businesses owned by one individual to large companies such as American Express and Marriott International that are owned by thousands of stockholders. There are also employment opportunities with federal, state, county, and local governments and with charitable organizations such as the Red Cross and Save the Children. For help in deciding which career might be right for you, read Appendix B: Careers in Business, which appears on the text website. To view this information:

1. Go to www.cengagebrain.com.
2. At the CengageBrain.com home page, search for the ISBN for your book (located on the back cover of your book) using the search box at the top of the page. This will take you to the product page where companion resources can be found.

FIGURE 1-1 Who Makes the Most Money?

Education makes a difference. Dollar amounts represent the median annual salary for full-time workers.

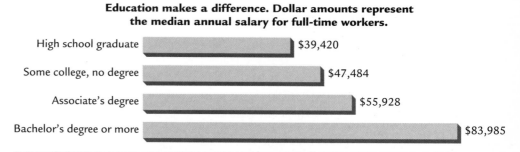

High school graduate	$39,420
Some college, no degree	$47,484
Associate's degree	$55,928
Bachelor's degree or more	$83,985

Source: "Educational Attainment of Householder—Households with Householder 25 Years Old and Over by Median and Mean Income," The U.S. Census Bureau at www.census.gov (accessed January 2, 2013).

In addition to career information in Appendix B, a number of additional websites provide information about career development. For more information, visit the following sites:

- Career Builder at www.careerbuilder.com
- Career One Stop at www.careeronestop.org
- Monster at www.monster.com

To click your career into high gear, you can also use online networking to advance your career. Websites like Facebook, Twitter, LinkedIn, and other social media sites can help you locate job openings, help prospective employers to find you, and make a good impression on current and future employers. To make the most of online networking, begin by identifying and joining sites where you can connect with potential employers, former classmates, and others who may have or may hear of job openings. Next, be sure your online profiles, photographs, and posts communicate your abilities and interests. Finally, be ready to respond quickly when you spot a job opening.

One thing to remember as you think about what your ideal career might be is that a person's choice of a career ultimately is just a reflection of what he or she values and holds most important. What will give one individual personal satisfaction may not satisfy another. For example, one person may dream of a career as a corporate executive and becoming a millionaire before the age of 30. Another may choose a career that has more modest monetary rewards but that provides the opportunity to help others. What you choose to do with your life will be based on what you feel is most important. And *you* are a very important part of that decision.

TO BE A SUCCESSFUL EMPLOYEE Deciding on the type of career you want is only the first step. To get a job in your chosen field and to be successful at it, you will have to develop a plan, or a road map, that ensures that you have the skills and knowledge the job requires. You will also be expected to have the ability to work well with many types of people in a culturally diverse workforce. **Cultural (or workplace) diversity** refers to the differences among people in a workforce owing to race, ethnicity, and gender. These skills and an appreciation for a culturally diverse workplace, can give you an inside edge when you are interviewing with a prospective employer.

This course, your instructor, and all of the resources available at your college or university can help you to acquire the skills and knowledge you will need for a successful career. But do not underestimate your part in making your dream a reality. In addition to the job-related skills and knowledge you'll need to be successful in a specific job, employers will also look for the following characteristics when hiring a new employee or promoting an existing employee:

- Honesty and integrity
- Willingness to work hard
- Dependability
- Time management skills
- Self-confidence
- Motivation
- Willingness to learn
- Communication skills
- Professionalism

Employers will also be interested in any work experience you may have had in cooperative work/school programs, during summer vacations, or in part-time jobs during the school year. These things can make a difference when it is time to apply for the job you really want.

Personal Apps

Sometimes you have to reach for success!

There's an old saying that if you choose a career you like, you never have to work a day in your life. For most people, the first decision is choosing a career. Then the material in the sections "To Be a Successful Employee" and "To Improve Your Management Skills" can help you achieve success.

© SPECTRAL-DESIGN/SHUTTERSTOCK.COM

cultural (or workplace) diversity differences among people in a workforce owing to race, ethnicity, and gender

© ALMAGAMI/SHUTTERSTOCK.COM

A life changing decision! Often the most important factor to consider when choosing a career is what you think is important. For some people, more responsibility, promotions, and money may be important. For others, more free time and the opportunity to help others may be more important. Ultimately, it's your choice—an important choice that can affect the rest of your life.

TO IMPROVE YOUR MANAGEMENT SKILLS Many employees want to become managers because managers often receive higher salaries and can earn promotions within an organization. Although management obviously can be a rewarding career, what is not so obvious is the amount of time and hard work needed to achieve the higher salaries and promotions. For starters, employers expect more from managers and supervisors than ever before. Typically, the heavy workload requires that managers work long hours, and most do not get paid overtime. They also face increased problems created by an unstable economy, increased competition, employee downsizing, the quest for improved quality, and the need for efficient use of the firm's resources.

To be an effective manager, managers must be able to perform four basic management functions: planning, organizing, leading and motivating, and controlling. All four topics are discussed in Chapter 6, Understanding the Management Process. To successfully perform these management functions, managers must possess four very important skills.

- *Interpersonal skills*—The ability to deal effectively with individual employees, other managers within the firm, and people outside the firm.
- *Analytic skills*—The ability to identify problems correctly, generate reasonable alternatives, and select the "best" alternatives to solve problems.
- *Technical skills*—The skill required to accomplish a specific kind of work being done in an organization. Although managers may not actually perform the technical tasks, they should be able to train employees and answer technical questions.
- *Conceptual skills*—The ability to think in abstract terms in order to see the "big picture." Conceptual skills help managers understand how the various parts of an organization or idea can fit together.

In addition to the four skills just described, a successful manager will need many of the same characteristics that an employee needs to be successful.

TO START YOUR OWN BUSINESS Some people prefer to work for themselves, and they open their own businesses. To be successful, business owners must possess many of the same characteristics that successful employees have, and they must be willing to work hard and put in long hours.

It also helps if your small business can provide a product or service that customers want. For example, Steve Demeter, the CEO and founder of the software development firm Demiforce, began his career by creating the *Trism* application for the Apple iPhone. *Trism* was an immediate sensation and sold 50,000 copies at $4.99 in its first two months on Apple's App Store. Now Demeter and the employees at Demiforce are working with a number of promising ideas in the works all with one goal in mind: to provide games and applications that people want.[4]

Unfortunately, many small-business firms fail: Approximately 70 percent of them fail within the first ten years. Typical reasons for business failures include undercapitalization (not enough money), poor business location, poor customer service, unqualified or untrained employees, fraud, lack of a proper business plan, and failure to seek outside professional help. The material in Chapter 5, Small Business, Entrepreneurship, and Franchises, and selected topics and examples throughout this text will help you to decide whether you want to open your own business. This material will also help you to overcome many of these problems.

TO BECOME A BETTER INFORMED CONSUMER AND INVESTOR The world of business surrounds us. You cannot buy a home, a new Ford Fusion Hybrid from the local Ford dealer, a pair of jeans at Gap Inc., or a hot dog from a street vendor without entering into a business transaction. Because you no doubt will engage in business transactions almost every day of your life, one very good reason for studying business is to become a more fully informed consumer.

Many people also rely on a basic understanding of business to help them to invest for the future. According to Julie Stav, Hispanic stockbroker-turned-author/radio personality, "Take $25, add to it drive plus determination and then watch it multiply into

Concept Check

- ✓ What reasons would you give if you were advising someone to study business?
- ✓ What factors affect a person's choice of careers?
- ✓ Once you have a job, what steps can you take to be successful?

an empire."[5] The author of *Get Your Share* believes that it is important to learn the basics about the economy and business, stocks, mutual funds, and other alternatives before investing your money. She also believes that it is never too early to start investing. Although this is an obvious conclusion, just dreaming of being rich does not make it happen. In fact, like many facets of life, it takes planning and determination to establish the type of investment program that will help you to accomplish your financial goals.

Special Note to Business Students

It is important to begin reading this text with one thing in mind: *This business course does not have to be difficult.* We have done everything possible to eliminate the problems that you encounter in a typical class. All of the features in each chapter have been evaluated and recommended by instructors with years of teaching experience. In addition, business students were asked to critique each chapter component. Based on this feedback, the text includes the following features:

- *Learning objectives* appear at the beginning of each chapter.
- *Inside Business* is a chapter-opening case that highlights how successful companies do business on a day-to-day basis.
- *Margin notes* are used throughout the text to reinforce both learning objectives and key terms.
- *Boxed features* in each chapter highlight how both employees and entrepreneurs can be ethical and successful.
- *Two Personal Apps* in each chapter provide special student-centered examples and explanations that help you immediately grasp and retain the material.
- *Sustaining the Planet* features provide information about companies working to protect the environment.
- *Social Media* features provide examples of how businesses and individuals are using social networking and social media sites.
- *Concept Checks* at the end of each major section within a chapter help you test your understanding of the major issues just discussed.
- *End-of-chapter materials* provide a chapter summary, a list of key terms, discussion questions, a Test Yourself Quiz, and a video case about a successful, real-world company.
- The last section of every chapter is entitled *Building Skills for Career Success* and includes exercises devoted to enhancing your social media skills, building team skills, and researching different careers.
- *End-of-part materials* provide a continuing video case about Graeter's Ice Cream, a company that operates a chain of retail outlets in the Cincinnati, Ohio, area and sells to Kroger Stores and other retailers throughout the country. Also, at the end of each major part is an exercise designed to help you to develop the components that are included in a typical business plan.

In addition to the text, a number of student supplements will help you to explore the world of business. We are especially proud of the website that accompanies this edition. There, you will find online study aids, such as interactive quizzes, key terms and definitions, student PowerPoint slides, crossword puzzles, and links to the videos for each chapter. If you want to take a look at the Internet support materials available for this edition of *Business,*

1. Go to www.cengagebrain.com.
2. At the CengageBrain.com home page, search for the ISBN for your book (located on the back cover of your book) using the search box at the top of the page. This will take you to the textbook website where companion resources can be found.

As authors, we want you to be successful. We know that your time is valuable and that your schedule is crowded with many different activities. We also appreciate the fact that textbooks are expensive. Therefore, we want you to use this text and get the most out of your investment. To help you get off to a good start, a number of suggestions for developing effective study skills and using this text are provided in Table 1-1.

TABLE 1-1 Seven Ways to Use This Text and Its Resources

1. Prepare before you go to class.	Early preparation is the key to success in many of life's activities. Certainly, early preparation for this course can help you to participate in class, ask questions, and improve your performance on examinations.
2. Read the chapter.	Although it may seem like an obvious suggestion, many students never take the time to really read the material. Find a quiet space where there are no distractions, and invest enough time to become a "content expert."
3. Underline or highlight important concepts.	Make this text yours. Do not be afraid to write on the pages of your text or highlight important material. It is much easier to review material if you have identified important concepts.
4. Take notes.	While reading, take the time to jot down important points and summarize concepts in your own words. Also, take notes in class.
5. Apply the concepts.	Learning is always easier if you can apply the content to your real-life situation. Think about how you could use the material either now or in the future.
6. Practice critical thinking.	Test the material in the text. Do the concepts make sense? To build critical-thinking skills, answer the discussion questions and the questions that accompany the cases at the end of each chapter. Also, many of the exercises in the Building Skills for Career Success require critical thinking.
7. Prepare for the examinations.	Allow enough time to review the material before the examinations. Check out the concept check questions at the end of each major section in the chapter and the summary at the end of the chapter. Then use the resources on the text website.

© CENGAGE LEARNING 2015

Because a text should always be evaluated by the students and instructors who use it, we would welcome and sincerely appreciate your comments and suggestions. Please feel free to contact us by using one of the following e-mail addresses:

Bill Pride: w-pride@tamu.edu

Bob Hughes: bhughes@dcccd.edu

Jack Kapoor: kapoorj@cod.edu

Learning Objective

2 Define *business* and identify potential risks and rewards.

business the organized effort of individuals to produce and sell, for a profit, the goods and services that satisfy society's needs

BUSINESS: A DEFINITION

Business is the organized effort of individuals to produce and sell, for a profit, the goods and services that satisfy society's needs. The general term *business* refers to all such efforts within a society (as in "American business"). However, *a business* is a particular organization, such as Kraft Foods, Inc., or Cracker Barrel Old Country Stores. To be successful, a business must perform three activities. It must be organized, it must satisfy needs, and it must earn a profit.

The Organized Effort of Individuals

For a business to be organized, it must combine four kinds of resources: material, human, financial, and informational. *Material* resources include the raw materials used in manufacturing processes as well as buildings and machinery. For example, Mrs. Fields Cookies needs flour, sugar, butter, eggs, and other raw materials to produce the food products it sells worldwide. In addition, this Colorado-based company needs human, financial, and informational resources. *Human* resources are the people who furnish their labor to the business in return for wages. The *financial* resource is the money required to pay employees, purchase materials, and generally keep the business operating. *Information* is the resource that tells the managers of the business how effectively the other three resources are being combined and used (see Figure 1-2).

Today, businesses are usually organized as one of three specific types. *Service businesses* produce services, such as haircuts, legal advice, or tax preparation. H&R Block provides tax preparation, retail banking, and software and digital products to both businesses and consumers in the United States, Canada, and Australia.

FIGURE 1-2 Combining Resources

A business must combine all four resources effectively to be successful.

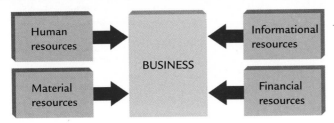

© CENGAGE LEARNING 2015

Manufacturing businesses process various materials into tangible goods, such as delivery trucks, towels, or computers. Intel, for example, produces computer chips that, in turn, are sold to companies that manufacture computers. Finally, some firms called *marketing intermediaries* buy products from manufacturers and then resell them. Sony Corporation is a manufacturer that produces stereo equipment, televisions, and other electronic products. These products may be sold to a marketing intermediary such as Best Buy or Walmart, which then resells the manufactured goods to consumers in their retail stores.

Satisfying Needs

The ultimate objective of every firm must be to satisfy the needs of its customers. People generally do not buy goods and services simply to own them; they buy goods and services to satisfy particular needs. Some of us may feel that the need for transportation is best satisfied by an air-conditioned BMW with navigation system, stereo system, heated and cooled seats, automatic transmission, power windows, and remote-control side mirrors. Others may believe that a Chevrolet Sonic with a stick shift will do just fine. Both products are available to those who want them, along with a wide variety of other products that satisfy the need for transportation.

When firms lose sight of their customers' needs, they are likely to find the going rough. However, when businesses understand their customers' needs and work to satisfy those needs, they are usually successful. Back in 1962, Sam Walton opened his first discount store in Rogers, Arkansas. Although the original store was quite different from the Walmart Superstores you see today, the basic ideas of providing customer service and offering goods that satisfied needs at low prices are part of the reason why this firm has grown to become the largest retailer in the world.

Business Profit

A business receives money (sales revenue) from its customers in exchange for goods or services. It must also pay out money to cover the expenses involved in doing business. If the firm's sales revenues are greater than its expenses, it has earned a profit. More specifically, as shown in Figure 1-3, **profit** is what remains after all business expenses have been deducted from sales revenue.

A negative profit, which results when a firm's expenses are greater than its sales revenue, is called a *loss*. A business cannot continue to operate at a loss for an indefinite period of time. Management and employees must find some way to increase sales revenues and reduce expenses to return to profitability. If some specific actions are not taken to eliminate losses, a firm may be forced to close

BLOOMBERG/GETTY IMAGES

Do you recognize these two entrepreneurs?
Although you may not recognize the two people in this photo, there's a good chance that you will recognize the businesses that they started. On the left is Jack Dorsey—one of the co-founders of Twitter and Square, Inc. On the right is Howard Schultz—the founder and CEO of Starbucks. Both are known for the ideas that helped make their companies a success.

profit what remains after all business expenses have been deducted from sales revenue

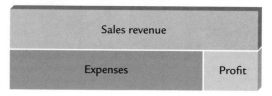

FIGURE 1-3 The Relationship Between Sales Revenue and Profit

Profit is what remains after all business expenses have been deducted from sales revenue.

© CENGAGE LEARNING 2015

stakeholders all the different people or groups of people who are affected by an organization's policies, decisions, and activities

its doors or file for bankruptcy protection. Although many people—especially stockholders and business owners—believe that profit is literally the bottom line or most important goal for a business, many stakeholders may be just as concerned about a firm's social responsibility record. The term **stakeholders** is used to describe all the different people or groups of people who are affected by an organization's policies, decisions, and activities. Many corporations, for example, are careful to point out their efforts to sustain the planet, participate in the green ecological movement, and help people to live better lives in an annual social responsibility report. In its latest social responsibility report, General Mills describes how it contributes $2 million each week to a wide variety of causes, including support for programs that feed the hungry and non profit organizations in the United States and around the globe.[6] Although stockholders and business owners sometimes argue that the money that a business contributes to charitable causes could have been used to pay larger dividends to stockholders or increase the return on the owners' investment, the fact is that most socially responsible business firms feel social responsibility is the right thing to do and is good for business.

The profit earned by a business becomes the property of its owners. Thus, in one sense, profit is the reward business owners receive for producing goods and services that customers want. Profit is also the payment that business owners receive for assuming the considerable risks of business ownership. One of these is the risk of not being paid. Everyone else—employees, suppliers, and lenders—must be paid before the owners.

A second risk that owners undertake is the risk of losing whatever they have invested into the business. A business that cannot earn a profit is very likely to fail, in which case the owners lose whatever money, effort, and time they have invested.

To satisfy society's needs and make a profit, a business must operate within the parameters of a nation's economic system. In the next section, we define economics and describe two different types of economic systems.

Concept Check

✓ Describe the four resources that must be combined to organize and operate a business.

✓ What is the difference between a manufacturing business, a service business, and a marketing intermediary?

✓ Explain the relationship among profit, business risk, and the satisfaction of customers' needs.

Learning Objective

3 Define *economics* and describe the two types of economic systems: capitalism and command economy.

economics the study of how wealth is created and distributed

TYPES OF ECONOMIC SYSTEMS

Economics is the study of how wealth is created and distributed. By *wealth*, we mean "anything of value," including the goods and services produced and sold by business. *How wealth is distributed* simply means "who gets what." Experts often use economics to explain the choices we make and how these choices change as we cope with the demands of everyday life. In simple terms, individuals, businesses, governments, and society must make decisions that reflect what is important to each group at a particular time. For example, suppose you want to take a week-end trip to some exotic vacation spot, and you also want to begin an investment program. Because of your financial resources, though, you cannot do both, so you must decide what is most important. Business firms, governments, and to some extent society face the same types of decisions. Each group must deal with scarcity when making important decisions. In this case, *scarcity* means "lack of resources"—money, time, natural resources, and so on—that are needed to satisfy a want or need.

Today, experts often study economic problems from two different perspectives: microeconomics and macroeconomics. **Microeconomics** is the study of the decisions made by individuals and businesses. Microeconomics, for example, examines how the prices of homes affect the number of homes individuals will buy. On the other hand, **macroeconomics** is the study of the national economy and the global economy. Macroeconomics examines the economic effect of national income, unemployment, inflation, taxes, government spending, interest rates, and similar factors on a nation and society.

Saving natural resources one bus at a time. While "green" used to refer to a color in a box of crayons, now it has taken on a whole new meaning. For consumers, the government, *and* businesses, green means a new way to save natural resources, to protect the environment, and often to reduce our dependence on oil from foreign countries.

The decisions that individuals, business firms, government, and society make, and the way in which people deal with the creation and distribution of wealth determine the kind of economic system, or **economy**, that a nation has.

Over the years, the economic systems of the world have differed in essentially two ways: (1) the ownership of the factors of production and (2) how they answer four basic economic questions that direct a nation's economic activity.

Factors of production are the resources used to produce goods and services. There are four such factors:

- *Land and natural resources*—elements that can be used in the production process to make appliances, automobiles, and other products. Typical examples include crude oil, forests, minerals, land, water, and even air.
- *Labor*—the time and effort that we use to produce goods and services. It includes human resources such as managers and employees.
- *Capital*—the money, facilities, equipment, and machines used in the operation of organizations. Although most people think of capital as just money, it can also be the manufacturing equipment in a Pepperidge Farm production facility or a computer used in the corporate offices of McDonald's.
- *Entrepreneurship*—the activity that organizes land and natural resources, labor, and capital. It is the willingness to take risks and the knowledge and ability to use the other factors of production efficiently. An **entrepreneur** is a person who risks his or her time, effort, and money to start and operate a business.

A nation's economic system significantly affects all the economic activities of its citizens and organizations. This far-reaching impact becomes more apparent when we consider that a country's economic system determines how the factors of production are used to meet the needs of society. Today, two different economic systems exist: capitalism and command economies. The way each system answers the four basic economic questions listed here determines a nation's economy.

1. *What* goods and services—and how much of each—will be produced?
2. *How* will these goods and services be produced?
3. *For whom* will these goods and services be produced?
4. *Who* owns and who controls the major factors of production?

microeconomics the study of the decisions made by individuals and businesses

macroeconomics the study of the national economy and the global economy

economy the way in which people deal with the creation and distribution of wealth

factors of production resources used to produce goods and services

entrepreneur a person who risks time, effort, and money to start and operate a business

Nick D'Aloisio, who lives in the south of London, England, created his first iPhone app when he was 12. Two apps later, teen entrepreneur D'Aloisio hit upon a new app idea that has brought him into the major leagues of the app business world.

D'Aloisio was searching the Internet for information for a term paper when he realized how much time it takes to determine the content of each web page. To speed things up, he developed an algorithm that summarizes the key points in a few words. He named this app Trimit, priced it at 99 cents per download, released it on Apple's App Store, and earned $1,600 within the first three days.

To accelerate Trimit's momentum, D'Aloisio decided to give it away free instead of charging for it. The app's download numbers skyrocketed, bringing it to the attention of Horizon Ventures, a firm that invests in businesses when they're in the early stages of growth. Horizon invested $250,000 to commercialize the app, which was renamed Summly and relaunched a few months later. As Summly, the app was downloaded 30,000 times in the first week alone, putting D'Aloisio squarely on the path toward his goal of building a $1 million app business.

Sources: Based on information in the Summly website at www.summly.com (accessed January 7, 2013), Jane Wakefield, "British Teenage Designer of Summly App Hits Jackpot," *BBC News*, December 28, 2011, www.bbc.co.uk; Parmy Olson, "Teen Programmer Hopes to Make a Million from A.I. App," *Forbes*, September 1, 2011, www.forbes.com; Kit Eaton, "The 15-year-old Creator of the Trimit App Makes Regular Old Entrepreneurs Seem Like Slackers," *Fast Company*, August 11, 2011, www.fastcompany.com.

capitalism an economic system in which individuals own and operate the majority of businesses that provide goods and services

invisible hand a term created by Adam Smith to describe how an individual's personal gain benefits others and a nation's economy

Capitalism

Capitalism is an economic system in which individuals own and operate the majority of businesses that provide goods and services. Capitalism stems from the theories of the 18th-century Scottish economist Adam Smith. In his book *Wealth of Nations*, published in 1776, Smith argued that a society's interests are best served when the individuals within that society are allowed to pursue their own self-interest. According to Smith, when individuals act to improve their own fortunes, they indirectly promote the good of their community and the people in that community. Smith went on to call this concept the "invisible hand." The **invisible hand** is a term created by Adam Smith to describe how an individual's own personal gain benefits others and a nation's economy. For example, the only way a small-business owner who produces shoes can increase personal wealth is to sell shoes to customers. To become even more prosperous, the small-business owner must hire workers to produce even more shoes. According to the invisible hand, people in the small-business owner's community not only would have shoes but also would have jobs working for the shoemaker. Thus, the success of people in the community and, to some extent, the nation's economy are tied indirectly to the success of the small-business owner.

Adam Smith's capitalism is based on the following fundamental issues—also see Figure 1-4.

1. The creation of wealth is properly the concern of private individuals, not the government.
2. Private individuals must own private property and the resources used to create wealth.
3. Economic freedom ensures the existence of competitive markets that allow both sellers and buyers to enter and exit the market as they choose.
4. The role of government should be limited to providing defense against foreign enemies, ensuring internal order, and furnishing public works and education.

One factor that Smith felt was extremely important was the role of government. He believed that government should act only as rule maker and umpire. The French term *laissez-faire* describes Smith's capitalistic system and implies that there should

FIGURE 1-4 Basic Assumptions of Adam Smith's Laissez-Faire Capitalism

Laissez-Faire capitalism

Right to create wealth

Right to own private property and resources

Right to economic freedom and freedom to compete

Right to limited government intervention

© CENGAGE LEARNING 2015

be no government interference in the economy. Loosely translated, this term means "let them do" (as they see fit).

Adam Smith's laissez-faire capitalism is also based on the concept of a market economy. A **market economy** (sometimes referred to as a *free-market economy*) is an economic system in which businesses and individuals decide what to produce and buy, and the market determines prices and quantities sold. The owners of resources should be free to determine how these resources are used and also to enjoy the income, profits, and other benefits derived from ownership of these resources.

market economy an economic system in which businesses and individuals decide what to produce and buy, and the market determines quantities sold and prices

Capitalism in the United States

Our economic system is rooted in the laissez-faire capitalism of Adam Smith. However, our real-world economy is not as laissez-faire as Smith would have liked because government participates as more than umpire and rule maker. Our economy is, in fact, a **mixed economy**, one that exhibits elements of both capitalism and socialism.

In a mixed economy, the four basic economic questions discussed at the beginning of this section (*what, how, for whom,* and *who*) are answered through the interaction of households, businesses, and governments. The interactions among these three groups are shown in Figure 1-5.

mixed economy an economy that exhibits elements of both capitalism and socialism

HOUSEHOLDS Households, made up of individuals, are the consumers of goods and services as well as owners of some of the factors of production. As *resource owners*, the members of households provide businesses with labor, capital, and other resources. In return, businesses pay wages, rent, and dividends and interest, which households receive as income.

FIGURE 1-5 The Circular Flow in Our Mixed Economy

Our economic system is guided by the interaction of buyers and sellers, with the role of government being taken into account.

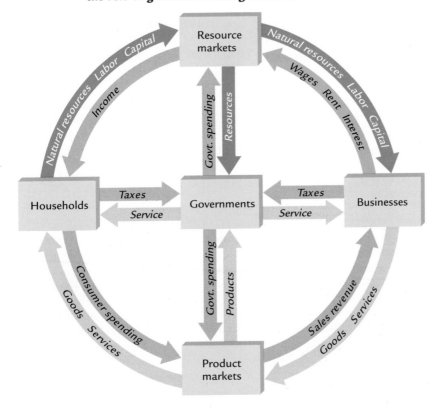

© CENGAGE LEARNING 2015

BLOOMBERG/GETTY IMAGES

Why is Apple successful? The answer: The company has a history of introducing state-of-the-art consumer products like the iPhone and iPad. In fact, consumers often line up and wait for hours to get Apple's latest products.

consumer products goods and services purchased by individuals for personal consumption

command economy an economic system in which the government decides what goods and services will be produced, how they will be produced, for whom available goods and services will be produced, and who owns and controls the major factors of production

As *consumers*, household members use their income to purchase the goods and services produced by business. Today, approximately 70 percent of our nation's total production consists of **consumer products**—goods and services purchased by individuals for personal consumption.[7] This means that consumers, as a group, are the biggest customers of American business.

BUSINESSES Like households, businesses are engaged in two different exchanges. They exchange money for natural resources, labor, and capital and use these resources to produce goods and services. Then they exchange their goods and services for sales revenue. This sales revenue, in turn, is exchanged for additional resources, which are used to produce and sell more goods and services.

Along the way, of course, business owners would like to remove something from the circular flow in the form of profits. When business profits are distributed to business owners, these profits become household income. (Business owners are, after all, members of households.) Households try to retain some income as savings. But are profits and savings really removed from the flow? Usually not! When the economy is running smoothly, households are willing to invest their savings in businesses. They can do so directly by buying stocks issued by businesses, by purchasing shares in mutual funds that purchase stocks in businesses, or by lending money to businesses. They can also invest indirectly by placing their savings in bank accounts. Banks and other financial institutions then invest these savings as part of their normal business operations. Thus, business profits, too, are retained in the business system, and the circular flow in Figure 1-5 is complete. How, then, does government fit in?

GOVERNMENTS The numerous government services are important but they (1) would either not be produced by private business firms or (2) would be produced only for those who could afford them. Typical services include national defense, police, fire protection, education, and construction of roads and highways. To pay for all these services, governments collect a variety of taxes from households (such as personal income taxes and sales taxes) and from businesses (corporate income taxes).

Figure 1-5 shows this exchange of taxes for government services. It also shows government spending of tax dollars for resources and products required to provide these services.

Actually, with government included, our circular flow looks more like a combination of several flows. In reality, it is. The important point is that together the various flows make up a single unit—a complete economic system that effectively provides answers to the basic economic questions. Simply put, the system works.

Command Economies

A **command economy** is an economic system in which the government decides *what* goods and services will be produced, *how* they will be produced, *for whom* available goods and services will be produced, and *who* owns and controls the major factors of production. The answers to all four basic economic questions are determined, at least to some degree, through centralized government planning. Today, two types of economic systems—*socialism* and *communism*—serve as examples of command economies.

SOCIALISM In a socialist economy, the key industries are owned and controlled by the government. Such industries usually include transportation, utilities, communications, banking, and industries producing important materials such as steel. Land, buildings, and raw materials may also be the property of the state in a socialist economy. Depending on the country, private ownership of smaller businesses is permitted to varying degrees. Usually, people may choose their own occupations, although many work in state-owned industries.

What to produce and how to produce it are determined in accordance with national goals, which are based on projected needs and the availability of resources. The distribution of goods and services—who gets what—is also controlled by the state to the extent that it controls taxes, rents, and wages. Among the professed aims of socialist countries are the equitable distribution of income, the elimination of poverty, and the distribution of social services (such as medical care) to all who need them. The disadvantages of socialism include increased taxation and loss of incentive and motivation for both individuals and business owners.

Today, many of the nations that have been labeled as socialist nations traditionally, including France, Sweden, and India, are transitioning to a free-market economy. Currently, many countries that were once thought of as communist countries are now often referred to as socialist countries. Examples of former communist countries often referred to as socialists (or even capitalists) include most of the nations that were formerly part of the Union of Soviet Socialist Republics, China, and Vietnam.

COMMUNISM If Adam Smith was the father of capitalism, Karl Marx was the father of communism. In his writings during the mid-19th century, Marx advocated a classless society whose citizens together owned all economic resources. All workers would then contribute to this *communist* society according to their ability and would receive benefits according to their need.

Since the breakup of the Soviet Union and economic reforms in China and most of the Eastern European countries, the best remaining examples of communism are North Korea and Cuba. Today these so-called communist economies seem to practice a strictly controlled kind of socialism. The basic four economic questions are answered through centralized government plans. Emphasis is placed on the production of goods the government needs rather than on the products that consumers might want, so there are frequent shortages of consumer goods.

MEASURING ECONOMIC PERFORMANCE

Consider for just a moment the following questions:

- Is the gross domestic product for the United States increasing or decreasing?
- Why is the unemployment rate important?
- Are U.S. workers as productive as workers in other countries?

The information needed to answer these questions is easily obtainable from many sources. More important, the answers to these and other questions can be used to gauge the economic health of the nation. For individuals, the health of the nation's economy can affect:

- the financing you need to continue your education;
- your ability to get a job; and
- the amount of interest you pay for credit card purchases, automobiles, homes, and other credit transactions.

The Importance of Productivity in the Global Marketplace

One way to measure a nation's economic performance is to assess its productivity. While there are other definitions of productivity, for our purposes, **productivity** is the average level of output per worker per hour.

Concept Check

✓ What are the four basic economic questions? How are they answered in a capitalist economy?

✓ Describe the four basic assumptions required for a laissez-faire capitalist economy.

✓ Why is the American economy called a mixed economy?

✓ How does capitalism differ from socialism and communism?

Learning Objective

4 Identify the ways to measure economic performance.

productivity the average level of output per worker per hour

One way to reduce costs is to manufacture products in a foreign country. In this photo, a Chinese worker assembles an electronic keyboard. To compete with foreign competition, manufacturers in the United States use sophisticated equipment and the latest technology to reduce costs, increase profits, *and* improve productivity.

An increase in productivity results in economic growth because a larger number of goods and services are produced by a given labor force. To see how productivity affects you and the economy, consider the following three questions:

Question: *How does productivity growth affect the economy?*

Answer: Because of increased productivity, it now takes fewer workers to produce more goods and services. As a result, employers have reduced costs, earned more profits, and sold their products for less. Finally, productivity growth helps American business to compete more effectively with other nations in a competitive world.

Question: *How does a nation improve productivity?*

Answer: Reducing costs and enabling employees to work more efficiently are at the core of all attempts to improve productivity. Methods that can be used to increase productivity are discussed in detail in Chapter 8, Producing Quality Goods and Services.

Question: *Is productivity growth always good?*

Answer: Fewer workers producing more goods and services can lead to higher unemployment rates. In this case, increased productivity is good for employers but not good for unemployed workers seeking jobs in a very competitive work environment.

The Nation's Gross Domestic Product

In the margin:

gross domestic product (GDP) the total dollar value of all goods and services produced by all people within the boundaries of a country during a one-year period

In addition to productivity, a measure called *gross domestic product* can be used to measure the economic well-being of a nation. **Gross domestic product (GDP)** is the total dollar value of all goods and services produced by all people within the boundaries of a country during a one-year period. For example, the values of automobiles produced by employees in an American-owned General Motors plant and a Japanese-owned Toyota plant in the United States are both included in the GDP for the United States. The U.S. GDP was $15.7 trillion in 2012.[8] (*Note:* At the time of publication, 2012 was the last year for which complete statistics were available.)

The GDP figure facilitates comparisons between the United States and other countries because it is the standard used in international guidelines for economic accounting. It is also possible to compare the GDP for one nation over several different time periods. This comparison allows observers to determine the extent to which a nation is experiencing economic growth. For example, government experts project that GDP will grow to $23.7 trillion by the year 2020.[9]

In the margin:

inflation a general rise in the level of prices

deflation a general decrease in the level of prices

unemployment rate the percentage of a nation's labor force unemployed at any time

To make accurate comparisons of the GDP for different years, we must adjust the dollar amounts for inflation. **Inflation** is a general rise in the level of prices. (The opposite of inflation is deflation.) **Deflation** is a general decrease in the level of prices. By using inflation-adjusted figures, we are able to measure the *real* GDP for a nation. In effect, it is now possible to compare the products and services produced by a nation in constant dollars—dollars that will purchase the same amount of goods and services. Figure 1-6 depicts the GDP of the United States in current dollars and the real GDP in inflation-adjusted dollars. Note that between 1990 and 2012, America's real GDP grew from $8 trillion to $13.6 trillion.[10]

Important Economic Indicators That Measure a Nation's Economy

In addition to productivity, GDP, and real GDP, other economic measures exist that can be used to evaluate a nation's economy. Because of the recent economic crisis, one very important statistic is the unemployment rate. The **unemployment rate** is the percentage of a nation's labor force unemployed at any time. Although the unemployment rate for the United States is typically about 4 to 6 percent, it peaked during the recent economic crisis. Despite both federal and state programs to reduce the unemployment rate for the United States, it is still hovering between 7 and 8 percent

Concept Check

✓ How does an increase in productivity affect business?

✓ Define gross domestic product. Why is this economic measure significant?

✓ How does inflation affect the prices you pay for goods and services?

✓ How is the producer price index related to the consumer price index?

FIGURE 1-6 GDP in Current Dollars and in Inflation-Adjusted Dollars

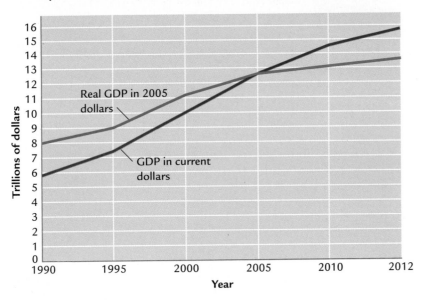

The change in GDP and real GDP for the United States from one year to another year can be used to measure economic growth.

Source: U.S. Bureau of Economic Analysis website at www.bea.gov (accessed January 30, 2013).

at the time of publication. This is an especially important statistic—especially if you are unemployed.

The **consumer price index (CPI)** is a monthly index that measures the changes in prices of a fixed basket of goods purchased by a typical consumer in an urban area. Goods listed in the CPI include food and beverages, transportation, housing, clothing, medical care, recreation, education, communication, and other goods and services. Economists often use the CPI to determine the effect of inflation on not only the nation's economy but also individual consumers. Another monthly index is the producer price index. The **producer price index (PPI)** measures prices that producers receive for their finished goods. Because changes in the PPI reflect price increases or decreases at the wholesale level, the PPI is an accurate predictor of both changes in the CPI and prices that consumers will pay for many everyday necessities.

Some additional economic measures are described in Table 1-2. Like the measures for GDP, real GDP, unemployment rate, and price indexes, these measures can be used to compare one economic statistic over different periods of time.

THE BUSINESS CYCLE

All industrialized nations of the world seek economic growth, full employment, and price stability. However, a nation's economy fluctuates rather than grows at a steady pace every year. In fact, if you were to graph the economic growth rate for a country like the United States, it would resemble a roller-coaster ride with peaks (high points) and troughs (low points). These fluctuations are generally referred to as the **business cycle**, that is, the recurrence of periods of growth and recession in a nation's economic activity.

At the time of publication, many experts believed that the U.S. economy was showing signs of improvement. However, the nation's unemployment rate is still high and people are reluctant to spend money on many consumer goods. Although the federal government has enacted a number of stimulus plans to help unemployed

consumer price index (CPI) a monthly index that measures the changes in prices of a fixed basket of goods purchased by a typical consumer in an urban area

producer price index (PPI) an index that measures prices that producers receive for their finished goods

Learning Objective

5 Examine the different phases in the typical business cycle.

business cycle the recurrence of periods of growth and recession in a nation's economic activity

TABLE 1-2 Common Measures Used to Evaluate a Nation's Economic Health

Economic Measure	Description
1. Balance of trade	The total value of a nation's exports minus the total value of its imports over a specific period of time.
2. Consumer confidence index	A measure of how optimistic or pessimistic consumers are about the nation's economy. This measure is usually reported on a monthly basis.
3. Corporate profits	The total amount of profits made by corporations over selected time periods.
4. Inflation rate	An economic statistic that tracks the increase in prices of goods and services over a period of time. This measure is usually calculated on a monthly or an annual basis.
5. National income	The total income earned by various segments of the population, including employees, self-employed individuals, corporations, and other types of income.
6. New housing starts	The total number of new homes started during a specific time period.
7. Prime interest rate	The lowest interest rate that banks charge their most credit-worthy customers.

© CENGAGE LEARNING 2015

recession two or more consecutive three-month periods of decline in a country's GDP

© ICONCEPT/SHUTTERSTOCK.COM

Just push the red button. Unfortunately, it's not that easy to stop a recession and restore a nation's economy. A recession— two or more consecutive three-month period of decline in a country's gross domestic products—can impact both what consumers buy and what businesses produce.

depression a severe recession that lasts longer than a typical recession and has a larger decline in business activity when compared to a recession

monetary policies Federal Reserve's decisions that determine the size of the supply of money in the nation and the level of interest rates

fiscal policy government influence on the amount of savings and expenditures; accomplished by altering the tax structure and by changing the levels of government spending

workers, to shore up the nation's financial system, and to reduce the number of home foreclosures, many experts still believe that we have serious financial problems. For one, the size of the national debt—a topic described later in this section— is a concern. To make matters worse, the recent economic crisis did not affect just the U.S. economy but also the economies of countries around the world.

The changes that result from either economic growth or economic downturn affect the amount of products and services that consumers are willing to purchase and, as a result, the amount of products and services produced by business firms. Generally, the business cycle consists of four phases: the peak (sometimes called prosperity), recession, the trough, and recovery (sometimes called expansion).

During the *peak period* (prosperity), the economy is at its highest point and unemployment is low. Total income is relatively high. As long as the economic outlook remains prosperous, consumers are willing to buy products and services. In fact, businesses often expand and offer new products and services during the peak period to take advantage of consumers' increased buying power.

Generally, economists define a **recession** as two or more consecutive three-month periods of decline in a country's GDP. Because unemployment rises during a recession, total buying power declines. The pessimism that accompanies a recession often stifles both consumer and business spending. As buying power decreases, consumers tend to become more value conscious and reluctant to purchase frivolous or nonessential items. And companies and government at all levels often postpone or go slow on major projects during a recession. In response to a recession, many businesses focus on producing the products and services that provide the most value to their customers.

Economists define a **depression** as a severe recession that lasts longer than a typical recession and has a larger decline in business activity when compared to a recession. A depression is characterized by extremely high unemployment rates, low wages, reduced purchasing power, lack of confidence in the economy, lower stock values, and a general decrease in business activity.

The third phase of the business cycle is the *trough*. The trough of a recession or depression is the turning point when a nation's production and employment bottom out and reach their lowest levels. To offset the effects of recession and depression, the federal government uses both monetary and fiscal policies. **Monetary policies** are the Federal Reserve's decisions that determine the size of the supply of money in the nation and the level of interest rates. Through **fiscal policy**, the government can influence the amount of savings and expenditures by altering the tax structure and changing the levels of government spending.

Although the federal government collects over $2 trillion in annual revenues, the government usually spends more than it receives, resulting in a **federal deficit**. For example, the government had a federal deficit for each year between 2002 and 2012. The total of all federal deficits is called the **national debt**. Today, the U.S. national debt is $16.4 trillion or approximately $52,000 for every man, woman, and child in the United States.[11]

Since World War II, business cycles have lasted from three to five years from one peak period to the next peak period. During the same time period, the average length of recessions has been 11 months.[12] Some experts believe that effective use of monetary and fiscal policies can speed up recovery and reduce the amount of time the economy is in recession. *Recovery* (or *expansion*) is the movement of the economy from recession or depression to prosperity. High unemployment rates decline, income increases, and both the ability and the willingness to buy rise.

At the time of publication, many business leaders, politicians, and consumers are still worried about the health and stability of the U.S. economy. Unfortunately, many of the problems that caused the recent economic crisis are still there, and they will take years to correct and resolve.

TYPES OF COMPETITION

Our capitalist system ensures that individuals and businesses make the decisions about what to produce, how to produce it, and what price to charge for the product. Mattel, Inc., for example, can introduce new versions of its famous Barbie doll, license the Barbie name, change the doll's price and method of distribution, and attempt to produce and market Barbie in other countries or over the Internet at www.mattel.com. Our system also allows customers the right to choose between Mattel's products and those produced by competitors.

As a consumer, you get to choose which products or services you want to buy. Competition like that between Mattel and other toy manufacturers is a necessary and extremely important by-product of capitalism. Business **competition** is essentially a rivalry among businesses for sales to potential customers. In a capitalistic economy, competition also ensures that a firm will survive only if it serves its customers well by providing products and services that meet needs. Economists recognize four different degrees of competition ranging from ideal, complete competition to no competition at all. These are perfect competition, monopolistic competition, oligopoly, and monopoly. For a quick overview of the different types of competition, including numbers of firms and examples for each type, look at Table 1-3.

Perfect Competition

Perfect (or pure) competition is the market situation in which there are many buyers and sellers of a product, and no single buyer or seller is powerful enough to affect the price of that product. For perfect competition to exist, there are five very important concepts.

- We are discussing the market for a single product, such as bushels of wheat.
- There are no restrictions on firms entering the industry.
- All sellers offer essentially the same product for sale.

Competition often gives consumers a choice. Often wonder why there are so many soap products? It's called competition. Different manufacturers use product differentiation to develop and promote the differences between their products and all similar products. Not only does product differentiation help their products stand out from the competition, it gives you—the consumer—a choice.

TABLE 1-3 Four Different Types of Competition

The number of firms determines the degree of competition within an industry.

Type of Competition	Number of Business Firms or Suppliers	Real-World Examples
1. Perfect	Many	Corn, wheat, peanuts
2. Monopolistic	Many	Clothing, shoes
3. Oligopoly	Few	Automobiles, cereals
4. Monopoly	One	Software protected by copyright, many local public utilities

© CENGAGE LEARNING 2015

- All buyers and sellers know everything there is to know about the market (including, in our example, the prices that all sellers are asking for their wheat).
- The overall market is not affected by the actions of any one buyer or seller.

When perfect competition exists, every seller should ask the same price that every other seller is asking. Why? Because if one seller wanted 50 cents more for his products than all the others, that seller would not be able to sell a single product. Buyers could—and would—do better by purchasing the same products from the competition. On the other hand, a firm willing to sell below the going price would sell all its products quickly. However, that seller would lose sales revenue (and profit) because buyers are actually willing to pay more.

In perfect competition, then, sellers—and buyers as well—must accept the going price. The price of each product is determined by the actions of all buyers and all sellers together through the forces of supply and demand.

supply the quantity of a product that producers are willing to sell at each of various prices

THE BASICS OF SUPPLY AND DEMAND The **supply** of a particular product is the quantity of the product that producers are willing to sell at each of various prices. Producers are rational people, so we would expect them to offer more of a product for sale at higher prices and to offer less of the product at lower prices, as illustrated by the supply curve in Figure 1-7.

FIGURE 1-7 Supply Curve and Demand Curve

The intersection of a supply curve and a demand curve is called the *equilibrium,* or *market price*. This intersection indicates a single price and quantity at which suppliers will sell products and buyers will purchase them.

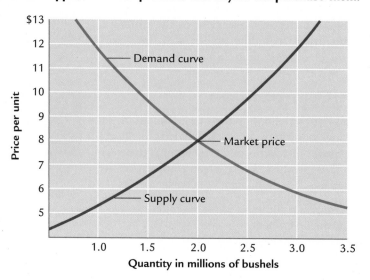

© CENGAGE LEARNING 2015

The **demand** for a particular product is the quantity that buyers are willing to purchase at each of various prices. Buyers, too, are usually rational, so we would expect them—as a group—to buy more of a product when its price is low and to buy less of the product when its price is high, as depicted by the demand curve in Figure 1-7.

THE EQUILIBRIUM, OR MARKET, PRICE There is always one certain price at which the demand for a product is exactly equal to the quantity of that product produced. Suppose that producers are willing to *supply* two million bushels of wheat at a price of $8 per bushel and that buyers are willing to *purchase* two million bushels at a price of $8 per bushel. In other words, supply and demand are in balance, or in equilibrium, at the price of $8. Economists call this price the *market price*. The **market price** of any product is the price at which the quantity demanded is exactly equal to the quantity supplied.

In theory and in the real world, market prices are affected by anything that affects supply and demand. The *demand* for wheat, for example, might change if researchers suddenly discovered that it offered a previously unknown health benefit. Then buyers would demand more wheat at every price. Or the *supply* of wheat might change if new technology permitted the production of greater quantities of wheat from the same amount of acreage. Other changes that can affect competitive prices are shifts in buyer tastes, the development of new products, fluctuations in income owing to inflation or recession, or even changes in the weather that affect the production of wheat.

Perfect competition is quite rare in today's world. Many real markets, however, are examples of monopolistic competition.

Monopolistic Competition

Monopolistic competition is a market situation in which there are many buyers along with a relatively large number of sellers. The various products available in a monopolistically competitive market are very similar in nature, and they are all intended to satisfy the same need. However, each seller attempts to make its product different from the others by providing unique product features, an attention-getting brand name, unique packaging, or services such as free delivery or a lifetime warranty.

Product differentiation is the process of developing and promoting differences between one's products and all competitive products. It is a fact of life for the producers of many consumer goods, from soaps to clothing to furniture to shoes. A furniture manufacturer such as Thomasville sees what looks like a mob of competitors, all trying to chip away at its share of the market. By differentiating each of its products from all similar products produced by competitors, Thomasville obtains some limited control over the market price of its product.

Oligopoly

An **oligopoly** is a market (or industry) situation in which there are few sellers. Generally, these sellers are quite large, and sizable investments are required to enter into their market. Examples of oligopolies are the automobile, airline, car rental, cereal, and farm implement industries.

Because there are few sellers in an oligopoly, the market actions of each seller can have a strong effect on competitors' sales and prices. If General Motors, for example, reduces its automobile prices, Ford, Honda, Toyota, and Nissan usually do the same to retain their market shares. In the absence of much price competition, product differentiation becomes the major competitive weapon; this is very evident in the advertising of the major automobile manufacturers. For instance, when Ford and General Motors began offering cash incentives to encourage consumers to

Personal Apps

Why do consumers choose one product instead of another?

The next time you go to the discount store, supermarket, or drug store, notice all the products competing for your dollars. No two canned vegetables, shampoos, or candies are exactly alike. Thanks to product differentiation, you have a lot of choices when you shop.

GERARD FRITZ/PHOTOGRAPHER'S CHOICE/GETTY IMAGES

demand the quantity of a product that buyers are willing to purchase at each of various prices

market price the price at which the quantity demanded is exactly equal to the quantity supplied

monopolistic competition a market situation in which there are many buyers along with a relatively large number of sellers who differentiate their products from the products of competitors

product differentiation the process of developing and promoting differences between one's products and all competitive products

oligopoly a market (or industry) in which there are few sellers

purchase a new automobile at the end of 2012, Chrysler, Honda, Nissan, and Toyota began offering similar incentives and for the same reason—to attract new-car buyers.

Monopoly

A **monopoly** is a market (or industry) with only one seller, and there are barriers to keep other firms from entering the industry. In a monopoly, there is no close substitute for the product or service. Because only one firm is the supplier of a product, it would seem that it has complete control over price. However, no firm can set its price at some astronomical figure just because there is no competition; the firm would soon find that it has no customers or sales revenue either. Instead, the firm in a monopoly position must consider the demand for its product and set the price at the most profitable level.

Classic examples of monopolies in the United States are public utilities, including companies that provide local gas, water, or electricity. Each utility firm operates in a *natural monopoly*, an industry that requires a huge investment in capital and within which any duplication of facilities would be wasteful. Natural monopolies are permitted to exist because the public interest is best served by their existence, but they operate under the scrutiny and control of various state and federal agencies. Although many public utilities are still classified as natural monopolies, there is increased competition in many areas of the country. For example, there have been increased demands for consumer choice when selecting a company that provides electrical service to both homes and businesses.

A legal monopoly—sometimes referred to as a *limited monopoly*—is created when a government entity issues a franchise, license, copyright, patent, or trademark. For example, a copyright exists for a specific period of time and can be used to protect the owners of written materials from unauthorized use by competitors that have not shared in the time, effort, and expense required for their development. Because Microsoft owns the copyright on its popular Windows software, it enjoys a legal-monopoly position. Except for natural monopolies and legal monopolies, federal antitrust laws prohibit both monopolies and attempts to form monopolies.

AMERICAN BUSINESS TODAY

Although our economic system is far from perfect, it provides Americans with a high standard of living compared with people in other countries throughout the world. **Standard of living** is a loose, subjective measure of how well off an individual or a society is, mainly in terms of want satisfaction through goods and services. Also, our economic system offers solutions to many of the problems that plague society and provides opportunities for people who are willing to work and to continue learning.

To understand the current business environment and the challenges ahead, it helps to understand how business developed.

Early Business Development

Our American business system has its roots in the knowledge, skills, and values that the earliest settlers brought to this country. The first settlers in the United States were concerned mainly with providing themselves with basic necessities—food, clothing, and shelter. Almost all families lived on farms, and the entire family worked at the business of surviving. They used their surplus for trading, mainly by barter, among themselves and with the English trading ships that called at the colonies. **Barter** is a system of exchange in which goods or services are traded directly for other goods or services without using money. As this trade increased, small businesses began to appear. Some settlers were able to use their skills and their excess time to work under the domestic system of production. The **domestic system** was a method of manufacturing in which an entrepreneur distributed raw materials to various homes, where families would process them into finished goods. The entrepreneur then offered the goods for sale.

Then, in 1793, a young English apprentice mechanic named Samuel Slater set up a textile factory in Pawtucket, Rhode Island, to spin raw cotton into thread. Slater's ingenuity resulted in America's first use of the **factory system** of manufacturing, in which all the materials, machinery, and workers required to manufacture a product are assembled in one place. The Industrial Revolution in America was born. A manufacturing technique called *specialization* was used to improve productivity. **Specialization** is the separation of a manufacturing process into distinct tasks and the assignment of the different tasks to different individuals.

The years from 1820 to 1900 were the golden age of invention and innovation in machinery. At the same time, new means of transportation greatly expanded the domestic markets for American products. Certainly, many basic characteristics of our modern business system took form during this time period.

Business Development in the 1900s

Industrial growth and prosperity continued well into the 20th century. Henry Ford's moving automotive assembly line, which brought the work to the worker, refined the concept of specialization and helped spur on the mass production of consumer goods. Fundamental changes occurred in business ownership and management as well. No longer were the largest businesses owned by one individual; instead, ownership was in the hands of thousands of corporate shareholders who were willing to invest in—but not to operate—a business.

The Roaring Twenties ended with the sudden crash of the stock market in 1929 and the near collapse of the economy. The Great Depression that followed in the 1930s was a time of misery and human suffering. People lost their faith in business and its ability to satisfy the needs of society without government involvement. After Franklin D. Roosevelt became president in 1933, the federal government devised a number of programs to get the economy moving again. In implementing these programs, the government got deeply involved in business for the first time.

To understand the major events that shaped the United States during the remainder of the 20th century, it helps to remember that the economy was compared to a roller-coaster ride earlier in this chapter—periods of economic growth followed by periods of economic slowdown. The following are major events that shaped the nation's economy during the period from 1940 to 2000:

- World War II, the Korean War, and the Vietnam War
- Rapid economic growth and higher standard of living during the 1950s and 1960s
- The social responsibility movement during the 1960s
- A shortage of crude oil and higher prices for most goods in the mid-1970s
- High inflation, high interest rates, and reduced business profits during the early 1980s
- Sustained economic growth in the 1990s

During the last part of the 20th century, the Internet became a major force in the economy. e-Business—a topic we will continue to explore throughout this text—became an accepted method of conducting business.

Unfortunately, by the last part of the 20th century, a larger number of business failures and declining stock values were initial signs that larger economic problems were on the way.

EVERETT COLLECTION/SUPERSTOCK

Gas shortages—could it happen again? For an industrialized economy like the United States, crude oil is an essential natural resource. When the nation experienced a shortage of crude oil during the mid-1970s, it was common to see signs like the one in this photo. Even now, both the supply and price for a gallon of gasoline are still concerns as the nation begins to rebound from the recent economic crisis.

factory system a system of manufacturing in which all the materials, machinery, and workers required to manufacture a product are assembled in one place

specialization the separation of a manufacturing process into distinct tasks and the assignment of the different tasks to different individuals

A New Century: 2000 and Beyond

According to many economic experts, the first part of the 21st century might be characterized as the best of times and the worst of times rolled into one package. On the plus side, technology became available at an affordable price. Both individuals and businesses could now access information with the click of a button. They also could buy and sell merchandise online.

In addition to information technology, the growth of service businesses also changed the way American firms do business in the 21st century. Because service businesses employ approximately 85 percent of the nation's workforce, we now have a service economy.[13] A **service economy** is an economy in which more effort is devoted to the production of services than to the production of goods. Typical service businesses include restaurants, laundries and dry cleaners, real estate, movie theaters, repair companies, and other services that we often take for granted. More information about how service businesses affect the economy is provided in Chapter 8, Producing Quality Goods and Services.

On the negative side, it is hard to watch television, surf the Web, listen to the radio, or read the newspaper without hearing some news about the economy. Because many of the economic indicators described in Table 1-2 on page 18 indicate troubling economic problems, there is still a certain amount of pessimism surrounding the economy.

service economy an economy in which more effort is devoted to the production of services than to the production of goods

The Current Business Environment

Before reading on, answer the following question:

In today's competitive business world, which of the following environments affects business?

a. The competitive environment
b. The global environment
c. The technological environment
d. The economic environment
e. All of the above

Correct Answer: e. All the environments listed in the above question affect business today.

THE COMPETITIVE ENVIRONMENT As noted earlier in this chapter, competition is a basic component of capitalism. Every day, business owners must figure out what makes their businesses successful and how the goods and services they provide are different from the competition. Often, the answer is contained in the basic definition of business provided on page 8. Just for a moment, review the definition:

Business is the organized effort of individuals to produce and sell, for a profit, the goods and services that satisfy society's needs.

In the definition of business, note the phrase *satisfy society's needs.* These three words say a lot about how well a successful firm competes with competitors. If you meet customer needs, then you have a better chance at success.

THE GLOBAL ENVIRONMENT Related to the competitive environment is the global environment. Not only do American businesses have to compete with other American businesses, but they also must compete with businesses from all over the globe. According to global experts, China is one of the fastest-growing economies in the world. And China is not alone. Other countries around the world also compete with U.S. firms. There was once a time when the label

OLEKSIY MARK/PHOTOS.COM

"Made in the United States" gave U.S. businesses an inside edge both at home and in the global marketplace. Today, because business firms in other countries manufacture and sell goods, the global marketplace has never been more competitive.

While many foreign firms are attempting to sell goods and services to U.S. customers, U.S. firms are also increasing both sales and profits by selling goods and services to customers in other countries. In fact there are many "potential" customers in developing nations that will buy goods and services manufactured by U.S. firms. For example, Procter & Gamble sells laundry detergent, soap, and diapers in Nigeria and has plans to do business in more than 50 African countries.[14] And Procter & Gamble is not alone. Unilever, DuPont, Johnson & Johnson, General Motors, and many more U.S. companies are also selling goods and services to customers in countries all over the globe.

THE TECHNOLOGY ENVIRONMENT Although increased global competition and technological innovation has changed the way we do business, the technology environment for U.S. businesses has never been more challenging. Changes in manufacturing equipment, distribution of products, and communication with customers are all examples of how technology has changed everyday business practices. For example, many businesses are now using social media to provide customers with information about products and services. If you ask different people, you will often find different definitions for social media, but for our purposes **social media** is defined as online interaction that allows people and businesses to communicate and share ideas, personal information, and information about products or services. To illustrate how popular social media is, consider that Facebook with over one billion active users was launched in 2004 and Twitter with approximately 200 million active users was launched in 2006. Because of rapid developments in social media and the increased importance of technology and information, businesses will need to spend additional money to keep abreast of an ever-changing technology environment and even more money to train employees to use the new technology.

social media the online interaction that allows people and businesses to communicate and share ideas, personal information, and information about products or services

THE ECONOMIC ENVIRONMENT The economic environment must always be considered when making business decisions. This fact is especially important when the nation's economy takes a nosedive or an individual firm's sales revenue and profits are declining. For example, both small and large business firms reduced both spending and hiring new employees over the last five years because of the nation's unstable economy.

In addition to economic pressures, today's socially responsible managers and business owners must be concerned about the concept of sustainability. According to the U.S. Environmental Protection Agency, **sustainability** means creating and maintaining the conditions under which humans and nature can exist in productive harmony while fulfilling the social, economic, and other requirements of present and future generations.[15] Although the word *green* used to mean a color in a box of crayons, today green means a new way of doing business. As a result, a combination of forces, including economic factors, growth in population, increased energy use, and concerns for the environment, is changing the way individuals live and businesses operate.

sustainability creating and maintaining the conditions under which humans and nature can exist in productive harmony while fulfilling the social, economic, and other requirements of present and future generations

When you look back at the original question we asked at the beginning of this section, clearly, each different type of environment—competitive, global, technological, and economic—affects the way a business does *business*. As a result, there are always opportunities for improvement and challenges that must be considered.

The Challenges Ahead

There it is—the American business system in brief.

When it works well, it provides jobs for those who are willing to work, a standard of living that few countries can match, and many opportunities for personal advancement for those willing to work hard and continue to learn. However, like every other system devised by humans, it is not perfect. Our business system may give us prosperity, but it also gave us the Great Depression of the 1930s, the economic problems of the 1970s and the early 1980s, and the recent economic crisis.

Obviously, the system can be improved. Certainly, there are plenty of people who are willing to tell us exactly what they think the American economy needs. However, these people often provide us only with conflicting opinions. Who is right and who is wrong? Even the experts cannot agree.

The experts do agree, however, that several key issues will challenge our economic system (and our nation) over the next decade. Some of the questions to be resolved include:

- How can we create a more stable economy and create new jobs for the unemployed?
- How do we reduce the national debt and still stimulate business growth?
- How do we restore investor confidence in the financial system?
- How can we use technology to make American workers more productive and American firms more competitive in the global marketplace?
- How can we preserve the benefits of competition and small business in our American economic system?
- How can we conserve natural resources and sustain our environment?
- How can we meet the needs of two-income families, single parents, older Americans, and the less fortunate who need health care and social programs to exist?
- How can we defeat terrorism and resolve conflict with Iran, North Korea, and other countries throughout the world?

The answers to these questions are anything but simple. In the past, Americans have always been able to solve their economic problems through ingenuity and creativity. Now, as we continue the journey through the 21st century, we need that same ingenuity and creativity not only to solve our current problems but also to compete in the global marketplace and build a nation and economy for future generations.

The American business system is not perfect by any means, but it does work reasonably well. We discuss some of its problems in Chapter 2 as we examine the topics of social responsibility and business ethics.

Concept Check

✓ How does your standard of living affect the products or services you buy?

✓ What is the difference between the domestic system and the factory system?

✓ Choose one of the environments that affect business and explain how it affects a small electronics manufacturer located in Portland, Oregon.

✓ What do you consider the most important challenge that will face people in the United States in the years ahead?

Looking for Success? *Get Flashcards, Quizzes, Games, Crosswords, and more @ www.cengagebrain.com.*

Summary

1 Discuss what you must do to be successful in the world of business.

For many years, people in business—both employees and managers—assumed that prosperity would continue. When faced with both economic problems and increased competition, a large number of these people began to ask the question: What do we do now? Although this is a fair question, it is difficult to answer. Certainly, for a college student taking business courses or an employee just starting a career, the question is even more difficult to answer. And yet there are still opportunities out there for people who are willing to work hard, continue to learn, and possess the ability to adapt to change. The kind of career you choose ultimately will depend on your own values and what you feel is most important in life. By studying business, you can become a better employee or manager or you may decide to start your own business. You can also become a better consumer and investor.

2 Define *business* and identify potential risks and rewards.

Business is the organized effort of individuals to produce and sell, for a profit, the goods and services that satisfy society's needs. Four kinds of resources—material, human, financial, and informational—must be combined to start and operate a business. The three general types of businesses are service businesses, manufacturers, and marketing intermediaries. Profit is what remains after all business expenses are deducted from sales revenue. It is the payment that owners receive for assuming the risks of business—primarily the risks of not receiving payment and of losing whatever has been invested in the firm. Although many people believe that profit is literally the bottom line or most important goal for a business, the ultimate objective of a successful business is to satisfy the needs of its customers. In addition to profit, many corporations are careful to point out their efforts to sustain the planet, participate in the green ecological movement, and help people to live better lives.

3 Define *economics* and describe the two types of economic systems: capitalism and command economy.

Economics is the study of how wealth is created and distributed. An economic system must answer four questions: *What* goods and services will be produced? *How* will they be produced? *For whom* will they be produced? *Who* owns and who controls the major factors of production? The factors of production are land and natural resources, labor, capital, and entrepreneurship. Capitalism (on which our economic system is based) is an economic system in which individuals own and operate the majority of businesses that provide goods and services. Capitalism stems from the theories of Adam Smith. Smith's pure laissez-faire capitalism is an economic system in which the factors of production are owned by private entities and all individuals are free to use their resources as they see fit; prices are determined by the workings of supply and demand in competitive markets; and the economic role of government is limited to rule maker and umpire.

Our economic system today is a mixed economy and exhibits elements of both capitalism and socialism. In the circular flow that characterizes our business system (see Figure 1-5), households and businesses exchange resources for goods and services, using money as the medium of exchange. In a similar manner, the government collects taxes from businesses and households and purchases products and resources with which to provide services.

In a command economy, government, rather than individuals, owns many of the factors of production and provides the answers to the three other economic questions. Socialist and communist economies are—at least in theory—command economies.

4 Identify the ways to measure economic performance.

One way to evaluate the performance of an economic system is to assess changes in productivity, which is the average level of output per worker per hour. Gross domestic product (GDP) can also be used to measure a nation's economic well-being and is the total dollar value of all goods and services produced by all people within the boundaries of a country during a one-year period. It is also possible to adjust GDP for inflation and thus to measure real GDP. In addition to GDP, other economic indicators include a nation's balance of trade, consumer confidence index, consumer price index (CPI), corporate profits, inflation rate, national income, new housing starts, prime interest rate, producer price index (PPI), and unemployment rate.

5 Examine the different phases in the typical business cycle.

A nation's economy fluctuates rather than grows at a steady pace every year. These fluctuations are generally referred to as the business cycle. Generally, the business cycle consists of four states: the peak (sometimes called prosperity), recession, the trough, and recovery (sometimes called expansion). Some experts believe that effective use of monetary policy (the Federal Reserve's decisions that determine the size of the supply of money and the level of interest rates) and fiscal policy (the government's influence on the amount of savings and expenditures) can speed up recovery.

A federal deficit occurs when the government spends more than it receives in taxes and other revenues. At the time of publication, the national debt is over $16.4 trillion or approximately $52,000 for every man, woman, and child in the United States.

6 Outline the four types of competition.

Competition is essentially a rivalry among businesses for sales to potential customers. In a capitalist economy, competition works to ensure the efficient and effective operation of business. Competition also ensures that a firm will survive only if it serves its customers well by providing products and services that meet their needs. Economists recognize four degrees of competition. Ranging from most to least competitive, the four degrees are perfect competition, monopolistic competition, oligopoly, and monopoly. The factors of supply and demand generally influence the price that customers pay producers for goods and services.

7 Summarize the factors that affect the business environment and the challenges that American businesses will encounter in the future.

From the beginning of the Industrial Revolution to the phenomenal expansion of American industry in the 19th and early 20th centuries, our government maintained an essentially laissez-faire attitude toward business. However, during the Great Depression of the 1930s, the federal government began to provide a number of social services to its citizens.

To understand the major events that shaped the United States during the remainder of the 20th and 21st century, it helps to remember that the economy was compared to a roller-coaster ride earlier in this chapter—periods of economic growth followed by periods of economic slowdown. Events and a changing business environment including wars, rapid economic growth, the social responsibility movement, a shortage of crude oil, high inflation, high interest rates, reduced business profits, increased use of technology, e-business, and social media all have shaped business and the economy.

Now more than ever before, the way a business operates is affected by the competitive environment, global environment, technological environment, and economic environment. As a result, business has a number of opportunities for improvement and challenges for the future.

Key Terms

You should now be able to define and give an example relevant to each of the following terms:

free enterprise (3)
cultural (or workplace)
    diversity (5)
business (8)
profit (9)
stakeholders (10)
economics (10)
microeconomics (11)
macroeconomics (11)
economy (11)
factors of
    production (11)
entrepreneur (11)
capitalism (12)

invisible hand (12)
market economy (13)
mixed economy (13)
consumer products (14)
command economy (14)
productivity (15)
gross domestic product
    (GDP) (16)
inflation (16)
deflation (16)
unemployment
    rate (16)
consumer price index
    (CPI) (17)

producer price index
    (PPI) (17)
business cycle (17)
recession (18)
depression (18)
monetary policies (18)
fiscal policy (18)
federal deficit (19)
national debt (19)
competition (19)
perfect (or pure)
    competition (19)
supply (20)
demand (21)

market price (21)
monopolistic
    competition (21)
product differentiation (21)
oligopoly (21)
monopoly (22)
standard of living (22)
barter (22)
domestic system (22)
factory system (23)
specialization (23)
service economy (24)
social media (25)
sustainability (25)

Discussion Questions

1. In what ways have the problems caused by the recent economic crisis affected business firms? In what ways have these problems affected employees and individuals?
2. What factors caused American business to develop into a mixed economic system rather than some other type of economic system?
3. Does an individual consumer really have a voice in answering the basic four economic questions?
4. Is gross domestic product a reliable indicator of a nation's economic health? What might be a better indicator?
5. Discuss this statement: "Business competition encourages improved product quality and increased customer satisfaction."
6. Is government participation in our business system good or bad? What factors can be used to explain your position.
7. Choose one of the challenges listed on page 26 and describe possible ways in which business and society could help to solve or eliminate the problem in the future.

Test Yourself

Matching Questions

1. _____ Materials, machinery, and workers are assembled in one place.
2. _____ The government spends more than it receives.
3. _____ System of exchange.
4. _____ The process of distinguishing Colgate from Crest toothpaste.
5. _____ The average level of output per worker per hour.
6. _____ A study of how wealth is created and distributed.
7. _____ An organized effort to produce and sell goods and services for a profit.
8. _____ A system where individuals own and operate the majority of businesses.
9. _____ A person who takes the risk and invests in a business.
10. _____ Value of all goods and services produced within a country during a one-year period.

a. capitalism
b. economics
c. federal deficit
d. productivity
e. product differentiation
f. business
g. factory system
h. entrepreneur
i. gross domestic product
j. barter

True False Questions

11. **T F** The majority of small business firms are successful at the end of ten years.

12. **T F** For a business to be organized, it must combine four types of resources: workers, natural resources, capital, and ownership.

13. **T F** The equilibrium price means that the supply and demand for a product are in balance.

14. **T F** Under communism, individual consumers determine what will be produced.

15. **T F** Hewlett-Packard Corporation and Dell Computer use product differentiation in the marketplace.

16. **T F** If a firm's sales revenues exceed its expenses, the firm has earned a profit.

17. **T F** Fiscal policy determines the level of interest rates.

18. **T F** The ultimate objective of business firms should be to satisfy the needs of their customers.

19. **T F** Adam Smith is the father of communism and advocated a classless society.

20. **T F** A business cycle consists of four states: peak, recession, trough, and recovery.

Multiple-Choice Questions

21. _____ Demand is a
    a. relationship between prices and the quantities purchased by buyers.
    b. relationship between prices and the quantities offered by producers.
    c. quantity of goods available for purchase.
    d. is measured by comparing the gross domestic product with supply.
    e. by-product of communism.

22. _____ The process of separating work into distinct tasks is called
    a. bartering.
    b. networking.
    c. specialization.
    d. a factory system.
    e. a domestic system.

23. _____ What term implies that there shall be no government interference in the economy?
    a. market economy
    b. free-market economy
    c. command economy
    d. laissez-faire
    e. socialism

24. _____ When the level of prices in an economy rise, it's called
    a. prosperity.
    b. recession.
    c. depression.
    d. recovery.
    e. inflation.

25. _____ The total of all federal deficits is called
    a. depression.
    b. fiscal policy.
    c. gross domestic product.
    d. national debt.
    e. business cycle.

26. _____ The ability to work well with many types of people in the workplace is referred to as
    a. workplace differentiation.
    b. cultural diversity.
    c. economic stability.
    d. career unity.
    e. employee magnification.

27. _____ Best Buy and Walmart are both examples of
    a. production intermediaries.
    b. manufacturing businesses.
    c. service businesses.
    d. marketing intermediaries.
    e. small businesses.

28. _____ The study of the national economy and the global economy is referred to as
    a. factors of the economy.
    b. microeconomics.
    c. macroeconomics.
    d. laissez-faire capitalism.
    e. a command economy.

29. _____ How well off an individual or a society is, mainly in terms of want satisfaction through goods and services is referred to as
    a. microeconomics.
    b. national satisfaction index.
    c. economic standard.
    d. standard of living.
    e. global comparison measure.

30. _____ A monthly index that measures changes in prices that consumers pay for goods is referred to as the
    a. prosperity index.
    b. producer's price index.
    c. prosperity price predictor.
    d. inflation rate index.
    e. consumer price index.

Answers to the Test Yourself questions appear at the end of the book on page TY-1.

Video Case

KlipTech Turns Recycled Paper into Products and Profits

Joel Klippert became an entrepreneur at the urging of his wife, LeeAnn Klippert, who believed in his unusual idea of turning recycled paper into a superstrong surface for skateboard ramps. For months he had tried, without success, to find a manufacturer willing to work with him in developing a durable composite ramp surface made from recycled and eco-friendly materials. Even his closest friends were skeptical. However, because Klippert and his wife were convinced that there was a viable market for this kind of sustainable product, they moved ahead to form KlipTech (http://kliptech.com) in 2000.

For the next two years, Klippert wrote and fine-tuned a business plan as he had manufacturing experts test various materials and production processes for transforming his invention from an idea to a reality. Despite unenthusiastic responses from most of the bankers he approached for possible financing, Klippert introduced his new skateboard ramp surface product in 2002. Later that same year, he pioneered yet another green product by introducing kitchen countertops made from a composite of recycled materials.

Despite ever-higher sales of these products, Klippert still faced the challenge of enhancing the aesthetic appearance of his paper-based composite countertops for home use. At the time, such composites were produced only in dark colors because of the resins used in the manufacturing process. Klippert recognized that a broader range of colors would make the countertops more appealing to more consumers. Working with a new supplier, he created an innovative countertop composite made with both recycled paper and bamboo and capable of being dyed in either light or dark colors. This new type of countertop attracted the attention of mainstream buyers, not just green-minded buyers, and gave KlipTech the edge it needed to compete more effectively with some of the biggest names in the industry.

KlipTech continues to build revenues and profits by introducing new products made from recycled paper. Most recently, it launched EcoClad, a line of composites used for exterior siding on commercial buildings and residences. Not only is EcoClad attractive and durable, it also helps buildings qualify as green under the U.S. Green Building Council's standards, confirming its environmentally-sound qualities.

Today, KlipTech is a profitable small business with multiple product lines, a global customer base, and a reputation for dedication to sustainability. What lessons has Joel Klippert learned in the years since becoming a successful entrepreneur? First, he found out first hand that an entrepreneur must have the confidence, patience, and perseverance to take the practical steps necessary to turn a good idea into an actual product that can meet customers' needs. It took many months of experimentation to perfect the skateboard ramp surface that gave KlipTech its start in the business world, but Klippert never gave up.

Second, the product must be unique so the company can, in effect, make its own market rather than go head-to-head with major competitors in an established market. When Klippert introduced his first skateboard ramp surface, no one else was making such products from recycled paper. The same was true for KlipTech's first kitchen counter surface, as well as its later products. KlipTech's innovations resulted in unique products that really fit the needs of its customers.

Third, Klippert learned that a nimble startup has an important advantage over large competitors. "The great part about being a small business is you're like a speed boat on the water," he explains. This means KlipTech can respond very quickly, "on the fly," to emerging trends in the business environment. In contrast, big rivals need more time to make and implement decisions about adapting to the same changes in the business environment.

Klippert also advises entrepreneurs to do their homework early on legal issues and financing possibilities, so they have experts and resources in place before problems arise. From experience, he knows that small business owners must understand finance and plan to pay vendors and employees before paying themselves. He's always thinking about how to improve one of his products or listening to customers talk about a new product they'd like to see. Succeeding in the global economy is far from easy, but Klippert remains enthusiastic about the opportunities he faces every day as the co-founder and co-owner of a successful small business.[16]

Questions

1. Joel Klippert says he pays himself last, after he pays his vendors and employees. Explain this decision in terms of the principle of business profit. Do you agree with his payment priorities?

2. When compared to larger manufacturing firms in the building products industry, what advantages have helped KlipTech become successful?

3. How have the competitive, global, technological, and economic environments helped KlipTech to become a successful small business? Which of the above environments might pose the most challenges in the next few years, and why?

Building Skills for Career Success

1. Social Media Exercise

Today, many companies have a social media presence on Facebook, Twitter, Flickr, and other sites beyond their corporate website. Think of three of your favorite car companies and conduct a quick search using a search engine like Google or Yahoo! Then answer the following:

1. Name the social networks for each company.
2. Compare each of their Facebook pages. How many "likes" does each company have? Are there multiple pages for the company? How much interaction (or engagement) is on each Facebook page?
3. What business goals do you think each company is trying to reach through their Facebook presence?

2. Building Team Skills

Over the past few years, employees have been expected to function as productive team members instead of working alone. People often believe that they can work effectively in teams, but many people find working with a group of people to be a challenge.

College classes that function as teams are more interesting and more fun to attend, and students generally learn more about the topics in the course. One way to begin creating a team is to learn something about each student in the class. This helps team members to feel comfortable with each other and fosters a sense of trust.

Assignment

1. Find a partner, preferably someone you do not know.
2. Each partner has two to three minutes to answer the following questions:
   a. What is your name, and where do you work?
   b. What interesting or unusual thing have you done in your life? (Do not talk about work or college; rather, focus on such things as hobbies, travel, family, and sports.)
   c. Why are you taking this course, and what do you expect to learn? (Satisfying a degree requirement is not an acceptable answer.)
3. Introduce your partner to the class. Use one to two minutes, depending on the size of the class.

3. Researching Different Careers

In this chapter, *entrepreneurship* is defined as the willingness to take risks and the knowledge and ability to use the other factors of production efficiently. An *entrepreneur* is a person who risks time, effort, and money to start and operate a business. Often, people believe that these terms apply only to small business. However, employees with entrepreneurial attitudes have recently advanced more rapidly in large companies as well.

Assignment

1. Go to the local library or use the Internet to research how large firms, especially corporations, are rewarding employees who have entrepreneurial skills.
2. Find answers to the following questions:
   a. Why is an entrepreneurial attitude important in large corporations today?
   b. What makes an entrepreneurial employee different from other employees?
   c. How are these employees being rewarded, and are the rewards worth the effort?
3. Write a two-page report that summarizes your findings.

Endnotes

1. Based on information in Lauren Torrisi, "Starbucks Unveils New Menu Items in Calif. Stores," *ABC News*, October 8, 2012, http://abcnews.go.com; "An Experimental New Starbucks Store," *Fast Company Design*, October 1, 2012, www.fastcodesign.com; James Callan, "Starbucks Adds Stores in Scandinavia to Spur European Sales," *Bloomberg*, September 26, 2012, www.bloomberg.com; "Starbucks: #73 *Fortune* 100 Best Companies to Work For," *Fortune*, February 6, 2012, http://money.cnn.com; Leslie Patton, "Starbucks Falls After Cutting Forecast Below Estimate," *Bloomberg*, August 14, 2012, www.bloomberg.com; www.starbucks.com.
2. The Horatio Alger website at www.horatioalger.org (accessed April 23, 2011).
3. Ibid.
4. The 66Apps website at www.66apps.com (accessed January 11, 2012).
5. Idy Fernandez, "Julie Stav," *Hispanic*, June–July 2005, 204.
6. The General Mills website at www.generalmills.com (accessed January 3, 2013).
7. The Bureau of Economic Analysis website at www.bea.gov (accessed January 3, 2013).
8. The Bureau of Economic Analysis website at www.bea.gov (accessed January 3, 2013).
9. The Bureau of Labor Statistics website at www.bls.gov (accessed January 7, 2013).
10. The Bureau of Economic Analysis website at www.bea.gov (accessed January 30, 2013).
11. The Treasury Direct website at www.treasurydirect.gov (accessed January 9, 2012) and the U.S. Census Bureau website at www.census.gov (accessed January 7, 2013).
12. The Investopedia website at www.investopedia.com (accessed January 3, 2013).
13. The Bureau of Labor Statistics website at www.bls.gov (accessed January 3, 2013).
14. Les Dlabay, "The Future of Global Business at 'Base of the Pyramid,'" *The Daily Herald Business Ledger*, November 29, 2011, p. 22.
15. The Environmental Protection Agency website at www.epa.gov (accessed January 3, 2013).
16. Sources: Based on information in "Editor's Choice: The Hot 50 Products 2012," *Green Builder*, February 2012, www.greenbuildermag.com/hot502012; Wanda Lau, "KlipTech EcoClad XP," *Architect*, January 2012, www.architectmagazine.com; Kevin O'Donnell, "Stories of Sustainability: KlipTech," *Current TV*, January 19, 2010, http://current.com; and the Cengage video, "The Entrepreneurial Life: KlipTech."

Being Ethical and Socially Responsible

Why Should You Care?

Business ethics and social responsibility issues have become extremely relevant in today's business world. Business schools teach business ethics to prepare managers to be more responsible. Corporations are developing ethics and social responsibility programs to help meet these needs in the work place.

Learning Objectives

Once you complete this chapter, you will be able to:

1 Understand what is meant by *business ethics.*

2 Identify the types of ethical concerns that arise in the business world.

3 Discuss the factors that affect the level of ethical behavior in organizations.

4 Explain how ethical decision making can be encouraged.

5 Describe how our current views on the social responsibility of business have evolved.

6 Explain the two views on the social responsibility of business and understand the arguments for and against increased social responsibility.

7 Discuss the factors that led to the consumer movement and list some of its results.

8 Analyze how present employment practices are being used to counteract past abuses.

9 Describe the major types of pollution, their causes, and their cures.

10 Identify the steps a business must take to implement a program of social responsibility.

Get Flashcards, Quizzes, Games, Crosswords, and more @ www.cengagebrain.com.

Chipotle Mexican Grill's "Food with Integrity"

When Steve Ells founded Chipotle Mexican Grill (www.chipotle.com) in 1993, most fast-food restaurants were competing on the basis of trendy new menu items and glitzy advertising. Ells, a trained chef, saw an opportunity for an entrepreneurial company to take fast food upscale. He developed recipes for boldly flavored burritos, tacos, and toppings, all made fresh from quality ingredients, and named his Denver restaurant after a smoked chili pepper. Customers crowded in, attracted by the authentic tastes and popular prices, and soon Ells was opening a couple of new Chipotle restaurants every year, with barely any menu changes and almost no advertising. By the end of 2006, Chipotle was a very successful publicly traded corporation, opening more than 100 new restaurants a year.

As the company grew and needed to buy larger quantities of fresh meats, vegetables, and beans, Ells took a closer look at where these ingredients come from. He became convinced that foods produced in a sustainable, humane way would be better for the planet and would taste better. Starting in 1999, Chipotle began buying naturally raised beef, later adding naturally raised pork and chicken as well as dairy products from pasture-raised cows. It's also become a big buyer of organic produce, preferring to work with local suppliers and family farms in particular.

Chipotle is so dedicated to the concept of "food with integrity" that it's trademarked the phrase, making ethical sourcing and sustainability the cornerstone of all customer communications. Not long ago, the company commissioned a two-minute animated video titled "Back to the Start," about a farmer who goes from family farming to large-scale industrial farming and finally chooses back-to-the-earth sustainable farming. The video was first released online, then aired as a commercial during the Grammy Awards. It reached tens of millions of viewers and made a big social media splash by putting the spotlight squarely on Chipotle's long-term commitment to ethics and social responsibility.[1]

Did You Know?

Serving "food with integrity," Chipotle has expanded beyond 1,300 restaurants worldwide and increased annual sales above $2 billion.

Obviously, organizations like Chipotle want to be recognized as responsible corporate citizens. Such companies recognize the need to harmonize their operations with environmental demands and other vital social concerns. Not all firms, however, have taken steps to encourage a consideration of social responsibility and ethics in their decisions and day-to-day activities. Some managers still regard such business practices as a poor investment, in which the cost is not worth the return. Other managers—indeed, most managers—view the cost of these practices as a necessary business expense, similar to wages or rent.

Most managers today, like those at Chipotle, are finding ways to balance a growing agenda of socially responsible activities with the drive to generate profits. This also happens to be a good way for a company to demonstrate its values and to attract like-minded employees, customers, and stockholders. In a highly competitive business environment, an increasing number of companies are, like Chipotle, seeking to set themselves apart by developing a reputation for ethical and socially responsible behavior.

We begin this chapter by defining *business ethics* and examining ethical issues. Next, we look at the standards of behavior in organizations and how ethical behavior can be encouraged. We then turn to the topic of social responsibility. We compare and contrast two present-day models of social responsibility and present arguments for and against increasing the social responsibility of business. We then examine the major elements of the consumer movement. We discuss how social responsibility in business has affected employment practices and environmental concerns. Finally, we consider the commitment, planning, and funding that go into a firm's program of social responsibility.

BUSINESS ETHICS DEFINED

Ethics is the study of right and wrong and of the morality of the choices individuals make. An ethical decision or action is one that is "right" according to some standard of behavior. **Business ethics** is the application of moral standards to business situations. Recent court cases involving unethical behavior have helped to make business ethics a matter of public concern. In one such case, Copley Pharmaceutical, Inc., pled guilty to federal criminal charges (and paid a $10.65 million fine) for falsifying drug manufacturers' reports to the Food and Drug Administration. In another much-publicized case, lawsuits against tobacco companies have led to $246 billion in settlements, although there has been only one class-action lawsuit filed on behalf of all smokers. The case, *Engle v. R. J. Reynolds*, could cost tobacco companies an estimated $500 billion. In yet another case, Adelphia Communications Corp., the nation's fifth-largest cable television company, agreed to pay $715 million to settle federal investigations stemming from rampant earnings manipulation by its founder John J. Rigas, and his son, Timothy J. Rigas. Prosecutors and government regulators charged that both father and son had misappropriated $2.3 billion of Adelphia funds for their own use and had failed to pay the corporation for securities they controlled. Consequently, investors lost more than $60 billion when Adelphia declared bankruptcy. The tax evasion charge against the Rigases was dismissed in early 2012. John Rigas and Timothy Rigas are serving 12 years and 17 years in prison, respectively. John Rigas applied for a presidential pardon in January 2009, but George W. Bush left office without making a decision on Rigas's request. Mr. Rigas is scheduled to be released from federal prison in 2018. The Rigases have appealed their convictions to the Second Court of Appeals and they are awaiting a date from the court for oral arguments.[2]

ETHICAL ISSUES

Ethical issues often arise out of a business's relationship with investors, customers, employees, creditors, or competitors. Each of these groups has specific concerns and usually exerts pressure on the organization's managers. For example, investors want management to make sensible financial decisions that will boost sales, profits, and returns on their investments. Customers expect a firm's products to be safe, reliable, and reasonably priced. Employees demand to be treated fairly in hiring, promotion, and compensation decisions. Creditors require accounts to be paid on time and the accounting information furnished by the firm to be accurate. Competitors expect the firm's competitive practices to be fair and honest. Consider TAP Pharmaceutical Products, Inc., whose sales representatives offered every urologist in the United States a big-screen TV, computers, fax machines, and golf vacations if the doctors prescribed TAP's new prostate cancer drug Lupron. Moreover, the sales representatives sold Lupron at cut-rate prices or gratis while defrauding Medicare. Recently, the federal government won an $875 million judgment against TAP when a former TAP vice president of sales, Douglas Durand, and Dr. Joseph Gerstein blew the whistle.[3]

In late 2006, Hewlett-Packard Co.'s chairman, Patricia Dunn, and general counsel, Ann Baskins, resigned amid allegations that the company used intrusive tactics in observing the personal lives of journalists and the company's directors, thus tarnishing Hewlett-Packard's reputation for integrity. According to Congressman John Dingell of Michigan, "We have before us witnesses from Hewlett-Packard to discuss a plunderers' operation that would make (former president) Richard Nixon blush were he still alive." Alternatively, consider Bernard Madoff, former stockbroker, financial advisor, and chairman of the NASDAQ

stock exchange. In 2009, he was convicted of securities and other frauds, including a Ponzi scheme that defrauded clients of $65 billion. Madoff was sentenced to 150 years in prison.

Businesspeople face ethical issues every day, and some of these issues can be difficult to assess. Although some types of issues arise infrequently, others occur regularly. Let's take a closer look at several ethical issues.

Fairness and Honesty

Fairness and honesty in business are two important ethical concerns. Besides obeying all laws and regulations, businesspeople are expected to refrain from knowingly deceiving, misrepresenting, or intimidating others. The consequences of failing to do so can be expensive. Recently, for example, Keith E. Anderson and Wayne Anderson, the leaders of an international tax shelter scheme known as Anderson's Ark and Associates, were sentenced to as many as 20 years in prison. The Andersons; Richard Marks, their chief accounting officer; and Karolyn Grosnickle, the chief administrative officer, were ordered to pay more than $200 million in fines and restitution.[4] More than 1,500 clients of Anderson's Ark and Associates lost about $31 million. In yet another case, the accounting firm PricewaterhouseCoopers LLP agreed to pay the U.S. government $42 million to resolve allegations that it made false claims in connection with travel reimbursements it collected for several federal agencies.[5]

Deere & Company requires each employee to deal fairly with its customers, suppliers, competitors, and employees. "No employee should take unfair advantage of anyone through manipulation, concealment, abuse of privileged information, misrepresentation of material facts or any other unfair dealing practice." Employees are encouraged to report possible violations of company ethics policies using a 24-hour hotline or anonymous e-mails. Reporting is not only encouraged; it is an accepted and protected behavior.[6]

Personal data security breaches have become a major threat to personal privacy in the new millennium. Can businesses keep your personal data secure?

Personal Apps

In some buying situations, the "right" thing to do isn't always clear, is it?

Business ethics applies to customers as well as to managers and employees. For example, should you buy from a retail store that has been found to be unfair to its employees? Read on for tips about recognizing and resolving ethical issues.

Organizational Relationships

A businessperson may be tempted to place his or her personal welfare above the welfare of others or the welfare of the organization. For example, in late 2002, former CEO of Tyco International, Ltd, Leo Dennis Kozlowski, was indicted for misappropriating $43 million in corporate funds to make philanthropic contributions in his own name, including $5 million to Seton Hall University, which named its new business-school building Kozlowski Hall. Furthermore, according to Tyco, the former CEO took $61.7 million in interest-free relocation loans without the board's permission. He allegedly used the money to finance many personal luxuries, including a $15 million yacht and a $3.9 million Renoir painting, and to throw a $2 million party for his wife's birthday. Mr. Kozlowski, currently serving up to 25 years in prison, paid $134 million in restitution to Tyco and criminal fines of $70 million. In 2009, the U.S. Supreme Court denied his petition for a judicial review.[7]

Relationships with customers and co-workers often create ethical problems. Unethical behavior in these areas includes taking credit for others' ideas or work, not meeting one's commitments in a mutual agreement, and pressuring others to behave unethically.

RJ CAPAK/WIREIMAGE/GETTY IMAGES

Conflict of Interest

Conflict of interest results when a businessperson takes advantage of a situation for his or her own personal interest rather than for the employer's interest. Such conflict may occur when payments and gifts make their way into business deals. A wise rule to remember is that anything given to a person that might unfairly influence that person's business decision is a bribe, and all bribes are unethical.

For example, at Procter & Gamble Company (P&G), all employees are obligated to act at all times solely in the best interests of the company. A conflict of interest arises when an employee has a personal relationship or financial or other interest that could interfere with this obligation, or when an employee uses his or her position with the company for personal gain. P&G requires employees to disclose all potential conflicts of interest and to take prompt actions to eliminate a conflict when the company asks them to do so. Generally, it is not acceptable to receive gifts, entertainment, or other gratuities from people with whom P&G does business because doing so could imply an obligation on the part of the company and potentially pose a conflict of interest.

Communications

Business communications, especially advertising, can present ethical questions. False and misleading advertising is illegal and unethical, and it can infuriate customers. Sponsors of advertisements aimed at children must be especially careful to avoid misleading messages. Advertisers of health-related products also must take precautions to guard against deception when using such descriptive terms as *low fat*, *fat free*, and *light*. In fact, the Federal Trade Commission has issued guidelines on the use of these labels.

Learning Objective

3 Discuss the factors that affect the level of ethical behavior in organizations.

FACTORS AFFECTING ETHICAL BEHAVIOR

Is it possible for an individual with strong moral values to make ethically questionable decisions in a business setting? What factors affect a person's inclination to make either ethical or unethical decisions in a business organization? Although the answers to these questions are not entirely clear, three general sets of factors do appear to influence the standards of behavior in an organization. As shown in Figure 2-1, the sets consist of individual factors, social factors, and opportunities.

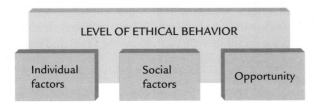

Source: Based on O. C. Ferrell and Larry Gresham, "A Contingency Framework for Understanding Ethical Decision Making in Marketing," *Journal of Marketing* (Summer 1985), 89.

Individual Factors Affecting Ethics

Several individual factors influence the level of ethical behavior in an organization.

- *Individual knowledge of an issue.* How much an individual knows about an issue is one factor. A decision maker with a greater amount of knowledge regarding a situation may take steps to avoid ethical problems, whereas a less-informed person may take action unknowingly that leads to an ethical quagmire.
- *Personal values.* An individual's moral values and central, value-related attitudes also clearly influence his or her business behavior. Most people join organizations to accomplish personal goals.
- *Personal goals.* The types of personal goals an individual aspires to and the manner in which these goals are pursued have a significant impact on that individual's behavior in an organization. The actions of specific individuals in scandal-plagued companies, such as Adelphia, Arthur Anderson, Enron, Halliburton, Qwest, and WorldCom, often raise questions about individuals' personal character and integrity.

Social Factors Affecting Ethics

Many social factors can affect ethical behavior within a firm, including cultural norms, actions and decisions of co-workers, values and attitudes of "significant others," and the use of the Internet.

- *Cultural norms.* A person's behavior in the workplace, to some degree, is determined by cultural norms, and these social factors vary from one culture to another. For example, in some countries it is acceptable and ethical for customs agents to receive gratuities for performing ordinary, legal tasks that are a part of their jobs, whereas in other countries these practices would be viewed as unethical and perhaps illegal.
- *Co-workers.* The actions and decisions of co-workers constitute another social factor believed to shape a person's sense of business ethics. For example, if your co-workers make long-distance telephone calls on company time and at company expense, you might view that behavior as acceptable and ethical because everyone does it.
- *Significant others.* The moral values and attitudes of "significant others"—spouses, friends, and relatives, for instance—also can affect an employee's perception of what is ethical and unethical behavior in the workplace.

- *Use of the Internet.* Even the Internet presents new challenges for firms whose employees enjoy easy access to sites through convenient high-speed connections at work. An employee's behavior online can be viewed as offensive to co-workers and possibly lead to lawsuits against the firm if employees engage in unethical behavior on controversial websites not related to their job. Interestingly, one recent survey of employees found that most workers assume that their use of technology at work will be monitored. A large majority of employees approved of most monitoring methods such as monitoring faxes and e-mail, tracking Web use, and even recording telephone calls.

"Opportunity" as a Factor Affecting Ethics

Several "opportunity" factors affect ethics in an organization.

- *Presence of opportunity. Opportunity* refers to the amount of freedom an organization gives an employee to behave unethically if he or she makes that choice. In some organizations, certain company policies and procedures reduce the opportunity to be unethical. For example, at some fast-food restaurants, one employee takes your order and receives your payment, and another fills the order. This procedure reduces the opportunity to be unethical because the person handling the money is not dispensing the product, and the person giving out the product is not handling the money.
- *Ethical codes.* The existence of an ethical code and the importance management places on this code are other determinants of opportunity (codes of ethics are discussed in more detail in the next section).
- *Enforcement.* The degree of enforcement of company policies, procedures, and ethical codes is a major force affecting opportunity. When violations are dealt with consistently and firmly, the opportunity to be unethical is reduced.

Do you make personal telephone calls on company time? Many individuals do. Although most employees limit personal calls to a few minutes, some make personal calls in excess of 30 minutes. Whether you use company time and equipment to make personal calls is an example of a personal ethical decision.

Now that we have considered some of the factors believed to influence the level of ethical behavior in the workplace, let us explore what can be done to encourage ethical behavior and to discourage unethical behavior.

Concept Check

✓ Describe several individual factors that influence the level of ethical behavior in an organization.

✓ Explain several social factors that affect ethics in an organization.

✓ How does "opportunity" influence the level of ethical behavior in the workplace?

Learning Objective

4 **Explain how ethical decision making can be encouraged.**

ENCOURAGING ETHICAL BEHAVIOR

Most authorities agree that there is room for improvement in business ethics. A more problematic question is: Can business be made more ethical in the real world? The majority opinion on this issue suggests that government, trade associations, and individual firms indeed can establish acceptable levels of ethical behavior.

Government's Role in Encouraging Ethics

Sarbanes–Oxley Act of 2002 provides sweeping new legal protection for employees who report corporate misconduct

The government can encourage ethical behavior by legislating more stringent regulations. For example, the landmark **Sarbanes–Oxley Act of 2002** provides sweeping new legal protection for those who report corporate misconduct. At the signing ceremony, President George W. Bush stated, "The act adopts tough new provisions to deter and punish corporate and accounting fraud and corruption, ensure justice for wrongdoers, and protect the interests of workers and shareholders." Among other things, the law deals with corporate responsibility, conflicts of interest, and corporate accountability. However, rules require enforcement, and the unethical businessperson frequently seems to "slip something by" without getting caught. Increased regulation may help, but it surely cannot solve the entire ethics problem.

Trade Associations' Role in Encouraging Ethics

Trade associations can and often do provide ethical guidelines for their members. These organizations, which operate within particular industries, are in an excellent position to exert pressure on members who stoop to questionable business practices. For example, recently, a pharmaceutical trade group adopted a new set of guidelines to halt the extravagant dinners and other gifts sales representatives often give to physicians. However, enforcement and authority vary from association to association. Because trade associations exist for the benefit of their members, harsh measures may be self-defeating.

Individual Companies' Role in Encouraging Ethics

Codes of ethics that companies provide to their employees are perhaps the most effective way to encourage ethical behavior. A **code of ethics** is a written guide to acceptable and ethical behavior as defined by an organization; it outlines uniform policies, standards, and punishments for violations. Because employees know what is expected of them and what will happen if they violate the rules, a code of ethics goes a long way toward encouraging ethical behavior. However, codes cannot possibly cover every situation. Companies also must create an environment in which employees recognize the importance of complying with the written code. Managers must provide direction by fostering communication, actively modeling and encouraging ethical decision making, and training employees to make ethical decisions.

During the 1980s, an increasing number of organizations created and implemented ethics codes. In a recent survey of *Fortune* 1000 firms, 93 percent of the companies that responded reported having a formal code of ethics. Some companies are now even taking steps to strengthen their codes. For example, to strengthen its accountability, the Healthcare Financial Management Association recently revised its code to designate contact persons who handle reports of ethics violations, to clarify how its board of directors should deal with violations of business ethics, and to guarantee a fair hearing process. S. C. Johnson & Son, makers of Pledge®,

code of ethics a guide to acceptable and ethical behavior as defined by the organization

Meet Senators Sarbanes and Oxley. The Sarbanes-Oxley Act of 2002 adopted tough new provisions to deter and punish corporate and accounting fraud and corruption. The legislation passed with near unanimous support.

Drano®, Windex®, and many other household products, is another firm that recognizes that it must behave in ways the public perceives as ethical; its code includes expectations for employees and its commitment to consumers, the community, and society in general. As shown in Figure 2-2, the ethics code of electronics giant Texas

FIGURE 2-2 Defining Acceptable Behavior: Texas Instruments' Code of Ethics

Texas Instruments encourages ethical behavior through an extensive training program and a written code of ethics and shared values.

TEXAS INSTRUMENTS CODE OF ETHICS

"Integrity is the foundation on which TI is built. There is no other characteristic more essential to a TIer's makeup. It has to be present at all levels. Integrity is expected of managers and individuals when they make commitments. They are expected to stand by their commitments to the best of their ability.

One of TI's greatest strengths is its values and ethics. We had some early leaders who set those values as the standard for how they lived their lives. And it is important that TI grew that way. It's something that we don't want to lose. At the same time, we must move more rapidly. But we don't want to confuse that with the fact that we're ethical and we're moral. We're very responsible, and we live up to what we say."

Tom Engibous, President and CEO
Texas Instruments, 1997

We Respect and Value People By:

Treating others as we want to be treated.

- Exercising the basic virtues of respect, dignity, kindness, courtesy and manners in all work relationships.
- Recognizing and avoiding behaviors that others may find offensive, including the manner in which we speak and relate to one another and the materials we bring into the workplace, both printed and electronically.
- Respecting the right and obligation of every TIer to resolve concerns relating to ethics questions in the course of our duties without retribution and retaliation.
- Giving all TIers the same opportunity to have their questions, issues and situations fairly considered while understanding that being treated fairly does not always mean that we will all be treated the same.
- Trusting one another to use sound judgment in our use of TI business and information systems.
- Understanding that even though TI has the obligation to monitor its business information systems activity, we will respect privacy by prohibiting random searches of individual TIers' communications.
- Recognizing that conduct socially and professionally acceptable in one culture and country may be viewed differently in another.

We Are Honest By:

Representing ourselves and our intentions truthfully.

- Offering full disclosure and withdrawing ourselves from discussions and decisions when our business judgment appears to be in conflict with a personal interest.
- Respecting the rights and property of others, including their intellectual property. Accepting confidential or trade secret information only after we clearly understand our obligations as defined in a nondisclosure agreement.
- Competing fairly without collusion or collaboration with competitors to divide markets, set prices, restrict production, allocate customers or otherwise restrain competition.
- Assuring that no payments or favors are offered to influence others to do something wrong.
- Keeping records that are accurate and include all payments and receipts.
- Exercising good judgment in the exchange of business courtesies, meals and entertainment by avoiding activities that could create even the appearance that our decisions could be compromised.
- Refusing to speculate in TI stock through frequent buying and selling or through other forms of speculative trading.

Source: Courtesy of Texas Instruments, http://www.ti.com/corp/docs/csr/corpgov/ethics (accessed February 3, 2013).

Instruments (TI) includes issues relating to policies and procedures; laws and regulations; relationships with customers, suppliers, and competitors; conflicts of interest; handling of proprietary information; and code enforcement.

Assigning an ethics officer who coordinates ethical conduct gives employees someone to consult if they are not sure of the right thing to do. An ethics officer meets with employees and top management to provide ethical advice, establishes and maintains an anonymous confidential service to answer questions about ethical issues, and takes action on ethics code violations.

Sometimes even employees who want to act ethically may find it difficult to do so. Unethical practices can become ingrained in an organization. Employees with high personal ethics may then take a controversial step called *whistle-blowing*. **Whistle-blowing** is informing the press or government officials about unethical practices within one's organization.

Whistle-blowing could have averted disaster and prevented needless deaths in the *Challenger* space shuttle disaster, for example. How could employees have known about life-threatening problems and let them pass? Whistle-blowing, however, can have serious repercussions for employees: Those who "blow whistles" sometimes lose their jobs. However, the Sarbanes–Oxley Act of 2002 protects whistle-blowers who report corporate misconduct. Any executive who retaliates against a whistle-blower can be held criminally liable and imprisoned for up to ten years.

The Whistleblower Protection Act of 1989 protects federal employees who report an agency's misconduct. The Obama administration is attempting to pass a law that would further protect the government whistle-blowers.[8]

When firms set up anonymous hotlines to handle ethically questionable situations, employees actually may be more likely to engage in whistle-blowing. When firms instead create an environment that educates employees and nurtures ethical behavior, fewer ethical problems arise. Ultimately, the need for whistle-blowing is greatly reduced.

It is difficult for an organization to develop ethics codes, policies, and procedures to deal with all relationships and every situation. When no company policies or procedures exist or apply, a quick test to determine if a behavior is ethical is to see if others—co-workers, customers, and suppliers—approve of it. Ethical decisions will always withstand scrutiny. Openness and communication about choices will often build trust and strengthen business relationships. Table 2-1 provides some general guidelines for making ethical decisions.

whistle-blowing informing the press or government officials about unethical practices within one's organization

TABLE 2-1 Guidelines for Making Ethical Decisions

1. Listen and learn.	Recognize the problem or decision-making opportunity that confronts your company, team, or unit. Don't argue, criticize, or defend yourself—keep listening and reviewing until you are sure that you understand others.
2. Identify the ethical issues.	Examine how co-workers and consumers are affected by the situation or decision at hand. Examine how you feel about the situation, and attempt to understand the viewpoint of those involved in the decision or in the consequences of the decision.
3. Create and analyze options.	Try to put aside strong feelings such as anger or a desire for power and prestige and come up with as many alternatives as possible before developing an analysis. Ask everyone involved for ideas about which options offer the best long-term results for you and the company. Then decide which option will increase your self-respect even if, in the long run, things don't work out the way you hope they will.
4. Identify the best option from your point of view.	Consider it and test it against some established criteria, such as respect, understanding, caring, fairness, honesty, and openness.
5. Explain your decision and resolve any differences that arise.	This may require neutral arbitration from a trusted manager or taking "time out" to reconsider, consult, or exchange written proposals before a decision is reached.

Source: Based on information in Tom Rusk with D. Patrick Miller, "Doing the Right Thing," *Sky* (Delta Airlines), August 1993, 18–22.

SOCIAL RESPONSIBILITY

social responsibility the recognition that business activities have an impact on society and the consideration of that impact in business decision making

Social responsibility is the recognition that business activities have an impact on society and the consideration of that impact in business decision making. In the first few days after Hurricane Sandy hit the East Coast, Walmart pledged $1.5 million to help with the relief efforts in the hardest hit areas. In addition to providing food and personal care products, the company delivered about one million bottles of water in New York City and to the state of New Jersey. Obviously, social responsibility costs money. It is perhaps not so obvious—except in isolated cases—that social responsibility is also good business. Customers eventually find out which firms act responsibly and which do not. Just as easily as they can purchase a product made by a company that is socially responsible, they can choose against buying from the firm that is not.

Consider the following examples of organizations that are attempting to be socially responsible:

- Social responsibility can take many forms—including flying lessons. Through Young Eagles, underwritten by S. C. Johnson, Phillips Petroleum, Lockheed Martin, Jaguar, and other corporations, 22,000 volunteer pilots have taken a half million youngsters on free flights designed to teach flying basics and inspire excitement about flying careers. Young Eagles is just one of the growing number of education projects undertaken by businesses building solid records as good corporate citizens.

- The General Mills Foundation, created in 1954, is one of the nation's largest company-sponsored foundations. Since the General Mills Foundation was created, it has awarded more than $1 billion to its communities.

  Since its inception in the mid-1990s, General Mills Box Tops for Education has raised more than $400 million to provide schools with funding for whatever students need, everything from playground equipment to paint, computers to clarinets.[9]

- As part of Dell's commitment to the community, the Dell Foundation contributes significantly to the quality of life in communities where Dell employees live and work. The Dell Foundation supports innovative and effective programs that provide fundamental prerequisites to equip youth to learn and excel in a world driven by the digital economy. The Dell Foundation supports a wide range of programs that benefit children from newborn to 17 years of age in Dell's principal U.S. locations and welcomes proposals from nonprofit organizations that address health and human services, education, and technology access for youth. In partnership with the University of Texas, Dell invites college students from around the world to join its strong community of support and to present their innovative ideas for solving social problems into the Dell Social Innovation Challenge.

  Globally, the Michael and Susan Dell Foundation has contributed more than $850 million to improve student performance and increase access to education so that all children have the opportunity to achieve their dreams.[10]

- Improving public schools around the world continues to be IBM's top social priority. Its efforts are focused on preparing the next generation of leaders and workers. Through Reinventing Education and other strategic efforts, IBM is solving education's toughest problems with solutions that draw on advanced information technologies and the best minds IBM can apply. Its programs are paving the way for reforms in school systems around the world.

  IBM launched the World Community Grid in November 2004. It combines excess processing power from thousands of computers into a virtual supercomputer. This grid enables researchers to gather and analyze unprecedented quantities of data aimed at advancing research on genomics, diseases, and natural disasters. The first project, the Human Proteome Folding Project, assists in identifying cures for diseases such as malaria and tuberculosis and has registered more than 150,000 devices around the world to date.[11]

Social responsibility is good business. When Hurricane Sandy hit the East Coast, Walmart provided food, personal care products, and delivered about one million bottles of water in New York City and to the state of New Jersey.

- General Electric Company (GE) has a long history of supporting the communities where its employees work and live through GE's unique combination of resources, equipment, and employees' and retirees' hearts and souls. Today GE's responsibility extends to communities around the world.

  For example, the GE Foundation matches GE employee and retiree gifts to disaster relief organizations such as the International Red Cross, UNICEF, AmeriCares, and Save the Children. Recently, the GE employees and retirees around the world contributed 1.3 million hours through company-sponsored programs. GE's network of more than 220 Volunteer Councils in 51 countries completed 6,200 projects of support and tutoring, cleanups, and paint-and-fix.[12]

- With the help of dedicated Schwab volunteers, the Charles Schwab Foundation provides programs and funding to help individuals fill the information gap. For example, Schwab MoneyWise helps adults teach—and children learn—the basics of financial literacy. Interactive tools are available at http://schwabmoneywise.com, and local workshops cover topics such as getting kids started on a budget. In addition to these efforts, widely distributed publications and news columns by foundation President Carrie Schwab Pomerantz promote financial literacy on a wide range of topics—from saving for a child's education to bridging the health insurance gap for retirees. Since its founding in 1993, Charles Schwab Foundation has made contributions averaging $4 million a year to more than 2,300 nonprofit organizations.[13]

- ExxonMobil's commitment to education spans all levels of achievement. One of its corporate primary goals is to support basic education and literacy programs in the developing world. In areas of the world where basic education levels have been met, ExxonMobil supports education programs in science, technology, engineering, and mathematics.

  In recognition of 2011 International Women's Day, ExxonMobil granted $6 million to support economic opportunities for women around the world. In announcing the grant, Suzanne McCarron, president of ExxonMobil Foundation said, "Research tells us that the success of women entrepreneurs is key to building communities. When women thrive economically, entire societies are transformed by becoming healthier, more stable and more prosperous." Recently, ExxonMobil Corporation, its employees, retirees, and the ExxonMobil Foundation provided $278.4 million in cash, goods, and services around the world.[14]

- AT&T has built a tradition of supporting education, health and human services, the environment, public policy, and the arts in the communities it serves since Alexander Graham Bell founded the company over a century ago. Since 1984, AT&T has invested more than $900 million in support of education. Currently, more than half the company's contribution dollars, employee volunteer time, and community-service activities are directed toward education. Since 1911, AT&T has been a sponsor to the Telephone Pioneers of America, the world's largest industry-based volunteer organization consisting of nearly 620,000 employees and retirees from the telecommunications industry. Each year, the Pioneers volunteer millions of hours and raise millions of dollars for health and human services and the environment. In schools and neighborhoods, the Pioneers strengthen connections and build communities.

  In 2012, AT&T developed the "Texting and Driving: 'It Can Wait'" Simulator to show the dangers of texting behind the wheel. AT&T and its 240,000 employees urge all drivers to go to www.itcanwait.com to take the no-texting-and-driving pledge and then share their promise with others via Twitter (# itcanwait) and Facebook. According to AT&T Chairman and CEO, Randall Stephenson, "More than 100,000 times each year an automobile crashes and people are injured or die while a driver was texting and driving. Our goal is to save lives." In 2013, AT&T was developing preload no-texting-while-driving technology for all AT&T smartphones. Many manufacturers, including Samsung and HTC, have plans to preload DriveMode onto future smartphones in 2013.[15]

- At Merck & Co., Inc., the Patient Assistance Program makes the company's medicines available to low-income Americans and their families at no cost. When patients do not have health insurance or a prescription drug plan and are unable to afford the Merck medicines their doctors prescribe, they can work with their physicians to contact the Merck Patient Assistance Program. For more than 50 years, Merck has provided its medicines completely free of charge to people in need through this program. Patients can get information through www.merck.com; by calling a toll-free number, 1-800-727-5400; or from their physician's office. For eligible patients, the medicines are shipped directly to their home or the prescribing physician's office. Each applicant may receive up to one year of medicines, and patients may reapply to the program if their need continues. In its annual survey of philanthropic giving by U.S. corporations, *The Chronicle of Philanthropy* ranked Merck third in corporate donations of cash and products among some of the country's largest corporations.

  Education programs often link social responsibility with corporate self-interest. For example, Bayer and Merck, two major pharmaceuticals firms, promote science education as a way to enlarge the pool of future employees. Students who visit the Bayer Science Forum in Elkhart, Indiana, work alongside scientists conducting a variety of experiments. Workshops created by the Merck Institute for Science Education show teachers how to put scientific principles into action through hands-on experiments.

These are just a few illustrations from the long list of companies, big and small, that attempt to behave in socially responsible ways. In general, people are more likely to want to work for and buy from such organizations.

Concept Check

✓ How can the government encourage the ethical behavior of organizations?

✓ What is trade associations' role in encouraging ethics?

✓ What is whistle-blowing? Who protects the whistle-blowers?

✓ What is social responsibility? How can business be socially responsible?

Learning Objective

5 Describe how our current views on the social responsibility of business have evolved.

THE EVOLUTION OF SOCIAL RESPONSIBILITY IN BUSINESS

Business is far from perfect in many respects, but its record of social responsibility today is much better than that in past decades. In fact, present demands for social responsibility have their roots in outraged reactions to the abusive business practices of the early 1900s.

Historical Evolution of Business Social Responsibility

During the first quarter of the 20th century, businesses were free to operate pretty much as they chose. Government protection of workers and consumers was minimal. As a result, people either accepted what business had to offer or they did without. Working conditions often were deplorable by today's standards. The average workweek in most industries exceeded 60 hours, no minimum-wage law existed, and employee benefits were almost nonexistent. Work areas were crowded and unsafe, and industrial accidents were the rule rather than the exception. To improve working conditions, employees organized and joined labor unions. During the early 1900s, however, businesses—with the help of government—were able to use court orders, brute force, and even the few existing antitrust laws to defeat union attempts to improve working conditions.

During this period, consumers generally were subject to the doctrine of **caveat emptor**, a Latin phrase meaning "let the buyer beware." In other words, "what you see is what you get," and if it is not what you expected, too bad. Although victims of unscrupulous business practices could take legal action, going to court was very expensive, and consumers rarely won their cases. Moreover, no consumer groups or government agencies existed to publicize their consumers' grievances or to hold sellers accountable for their actions.

caveat emptor a Latin phrase meaning "let the buyer beware"

Before the 1930s, most people believed that competition and the action of the marketplace would, in time, correct abuses. Government, therefore, became involved in day-to-day business activities only in cases of obvious abuse of the free-market system. Six of the most important business-related federal laws passed between 1887 and 1914 are described in Table 2-2. As you can see, these laws were aimed more at encouraging competition than at correcting abuses, although two of them did deal with the purity of food and drug products.

The collapse of the stock market on October 29, 1929, triggered the Great Depression and years of dire economic problems for the United States. Factory production fell by almost half, and up to 25 percent of the nation's workforce was unemployed. Before long, public pressure mounted for the government to "do something" about the economy and about worsening social conditions.

Soon after Franklin D. Roosevelt became president in 1933, he instituted programs to restore the economy and improve social conditions. The government passed laws to correct what many viewed as the monopolistic abuses of big business, and

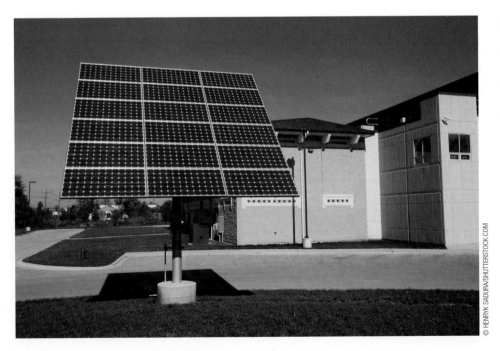

Breaking away from fossil fuels. Today's businesses (and consumers) are more open to alternative sources of energy, such as the solar energy, because they are concerned about the negative impact of conventional energy sources.

© HENRYK SADURA/SHUTTERSTOCK.COM

TABLE 2-2 Early Government Regulations That Affected American Business

Government Regulation	Major Provisions
Interstate Commerce Act (1887)	First federal act to regulate business practices; provided regulation of railroads and shipping rates
Sherman Antitrust Act (1890)	Prevented monopolies or mergers where competition was endangered
Pure Food and Drug Act (1906)	Established limited supervision of interstate sales of food and drugs
Meat Inspection Act (1906)	Provided for limited supervision of interstate sales of meat and meat products
Federal Trade Commission Act (1914)	Created the Federal Trade Commission to investigate illegal trade practices
Clayton Antitrust Act (1914)	Eliminated many forms of price discrimination that gave large businesses a competitive advantage over smaller firms

© CENGAGE LEARNING 2015

provided various social services for individuals. These massive federal programs became the foundation for increased government involvement in the dealings between business and society.

As government involvement has increased, so has everyone's awareness of the social responsibility of business. Today's business owners are concerned about the return on their investment, but at the same time most of them demand ethical behavior from employees. In addition, employees demand better working conditions, and consumers want safe, reliable products. Various advocacy groups echo these concerns and also call for careful consideration of Earth's delicate ecological balance. Therefore, managers must operate in a complex business environment—one in which they are just as responsible for their managerial actions as for their actions as individual citizens. Interestingly, today's high-tech and Internet-based firms fare relatively well when it comes to environmental issues, worker conditions, the representation of minorities and women in upper management, animal testing, and charitable donations.

Concept Check

✓ Outline the historical evolution of business social responsibility.

✓ What is the doctrine of caveat emptor?

✓ What are the six important business-related federal laws passed between 1887 and 1914?

Learning Objective

6 Explain the two views on the social responsibility of business and understand the arguments for and against increased social responsibility.

TWO VIEWS OF SOCIAL RESPONSIBILITY

Government regulation and public awareness are *external* forces that have increased the social responsibility of business. However, business decisions are made within the firm—there, social responsibility begins with the attitude of management. Two contrasting philosophies, or models, define the range of management attitudes toward social responsibility.

The Economic Model

According to the traditional concept of business, a firm exists to produce quality goods and services, earn a reasonable profit, and provide jobs. In line with this concept, the **economic model of social responsibility** holds that society will benefit most when business is left alone to produce and market profitable products that society needs. The economic model has its origins in the 18th century, when businesses were owned primarily by entrepreneurs or owner-managers. Competition was vigorous among small firms, and short-run profits and survival were the primary concerns.

To the manager who adopts this traditional attitude, social responsibility is someone else's job. After all, stockholders invest in a corporation to earn a return

economic model of social responsibility the view that society will benefit most when business is left alone to produce and market profitable products that society needs

on their investment, not because the firm is socially responsible, and the firm is legally obligated to act in the economic interest of its stockholders. Moreover, profitable firms pay federal, state, and local taxes that are used to meet the needs of society. Thus, managers who concentrate on profit believe that they fulfill their social responsibility indirectly through the taxes paid by their firms. As a result, social responsibility becomes the problem of the government, various environmental groups, charitable foundations, and similar organizations.

The Socioeconomic Model

In contrast, some managers believe that they have a responsibility not only to stockholders but also to customers, employees, suppliers, and the general public. This broader view is referred to as the **socioeconomic model of social responsibility**, which places emphasis not only on profits but also on the impact of business decisions on society.

> **socioeconomic model of social responsibility** the concept that business should emphasize not only profits but also the impact of its decisions on society

Recently, increasing numbers of managers and firms have adopted the socioeconomic model, and they have done so for at least three reasons. First, business is dominated by the corporate form of ownership, and the corporation is a creation of society. If a corporation does not perform as a good citizen, society can and will demand changes. Second, many firms have begun to take pride in their social responsibility records, among them Starbucks Coffee, Hewlett-Packard, Colgate-Palmolive, and Coca-Cola. Each of these companies is a winner of a Corporate Conscience Award in the areas of environmental concern, responsiveness to employees, equal opportunity, and community involvement. Of course, many other corporations are much more socially responsible today than they were ten years ago. Third, many businesspeople believe that it is in their best interest to take the initiative in this area. The alternative may be legal action brought against the firm by some special-interest group; in such a situation, the firm may lose control of its activities.

The Pros and Cons of Social Responsibility

Business owners, managers, customers, and government officials have debated the pros and cons of the economic and socioeconomic models for years. Each side seems to have four major arguments to reinforce its viewpoint.

ARGUMENTS FOR INCREASED SOCIAL RESPONSIBILITY Proponents of the socioeconomic model maintain that a business must do more than simply seek profits. To support their position, they offer the following arguments:

1. Because business is a part of our society, it cannot ignore social issues.
2. Business has the technical, financial, and managerial resources needed to tackle today's complex social issues.
3. By helping resolve social issues, business can create a more stable environment for long-term profitability.
4. Socially responsible decision making by firms can prevent increased government intervention, which would force businesses to do what they fail to do voluntarily.

These arguments are based on the assumption that a business has a responsibility not only to its stockholders but also to its customers, employees, suppliers, and the general public.

ARGUMENTS AGAINST INCREASED SOCIAL RESPONSIBILITY Opponents of the socioeconomic model argue that business should do what it does best: earn a profit by manufacturing and marketing products that people want. Those who support this position argue as follows:

1. Business managers are responsible primarily to stockholders, so management must be concerned with providing a return on owners' investments.
2. Corporate time, money, and talent should be used to maximize profits, not to solve society's problems.

TABLE 2-3 A Comparison of the Economic and Socioeconomic Models of Social Responsibility as Implemented in Business

Economic Model Primary Emphasis		Socioeconomic Model Primary Emphasis
1. Production		1. Quality of life
2. Exploitation of natural resources		2. Conservation of natural resources
3. Internal, market-based decisions	Middle ground	3. Market-based decisions, with some community controls
4. Economic return (profit)		4. Balance of economic return and social return
5. Firm's or manager's interest		5. Firm's and community's interests
6. Minor role for government		6. Active government

Source: Adapted from Keith Davis, William C. Frederick, and Robert L. Blomstron, *Business and Society: Concepts and Policy Issues* (New York: Mcgraw-Hill, 1980), 9. Used by permission of Mcgraw-Hill Book Company.

3. Social problems affect society in general, so individual businesses should not be expected to solve these problems.
4. Social issues are the responsibility of government officials who are elected for that purpose and who are accountable to the voters for their decisions.

These arguments obviously are based on the assumption that the primary objective of business is to earn profits and that government and social institutions should deal with social problems.

Table 2-3 compares the economic and socioeconomic viewpoints in terms of business emphasis. Today, few firms are either purely economic or purely socioeconomic in outlook; most have chosen some middle ground between the two extremes. However, our society generally seems to want—and even to expect—some degree of social responsibility from business. Thus, within this middle ground, businesses are leaning toward the socioeconomic view. In the next several sections, we look at some results of this movement in four specific areas: consumerism, employment practices, concern for the environment, and implementation of social responsibility programs.

Learning Objective

7 Discuss the factors that led to the consumer movement and list some of its results.

consumerism all activities undertaken to protect the rights of consumers

CONSUMERISM

Consumerism consists of all activities undertaken to protect the rights of consumers. The fundamental issues pursued by the consumer movement fall into three categories: environmental protection, product performance and safety, and information disclosure. Although consumerism has been with us to some extent since the early 19th century, the consumer movement became stronger in the 1960s. It was then that President John F. Kennedy declared that the consumer was entitled to a new "Bill of Rights."

The Six Basic Rights of Consumers

President Kennedy's Consumer Bill of Rights asserted that consumers have a right to safety, to be informed, to choose, and to be heard. Two additional rights added since 1975 are the right to consumer education and the right to courteous service. These six rights are the basis of much of the consumer-oriented legislation passed during the last 45 years. These rights also provide an effective outline of the objectives and accomplishments of the consumer movement.

THE RIGHT TO SAFETY The consumers' right to safety means that the products they purchase must be safe for their intended use, must include thorough and explicit directions for proper use, and must be tested by the manufacturer to ensure product quality and reliability. There are several reasons why American business firms must be concerned about product safety.

Corrective Actions Can Be Expensive. Federal agencies, such as the Food and Drug Administration and the Consumer Product Safety Commission, have the power to force businesses that make or sell defective products to take corrective actions. Such actions include offering refunds, recalling defective products, issuing public warnings, and reimbursing consumers—all of which can be expensive.

Increasing Number of Lawsuits. Business firms also should be aware that consumers and the government have been winning an increasing number of product-liability lawsuits against sellers of defective products. Moreover, the amount of the awards in these suits has been increasing steadily. Fearing the outcome of numerous lawsuits filed around the nation, tobacco giants Philip Morris and R. J. Reynolds, which for decades had denied that cigarettes cause illness, began negotiating in 1997 with state attorneys general, plaintiffs' lawyers, and antismoking activists. The tobacco giants proposed sweeping curbs on their sales and advertising practices and the payment of hundreds of billions of dollars in compensation.

Consumer Demand. Yet another major reason for improving product safety is consumers' demand for safe products. People simply will stop buying a product they believe is unsafe or unreliable.

THE RIGHT TO BE INFORMED The right to be informed means that consumers must have access to complete information about a product before they buy it. Detailed information about ingredients and nutrition must be provided on food containers, information about fabrics and laundering methods must be attached to clothing, and lenders must disclose the true cost of borrowing the money they make available to customers who purchase merchandise on credit.

In addition, manufacturers must inform consumers about the potential dangers of using their products. Manufacturers that fail to provide such information can be held responsible for personal injuries suffered because of their products. For example, Maytag provides customers with a lengthy booklet that describes how they should use an automatic clothes washer. Sometimes such warnings seem excessive, but they are necessary if user injuries (and resulting lawsuits) are to be avoided.

THE RIGHT TO CHOOSE The right to choose means that consumers must have a choice of products, offered by different manufacturers and sellers, to satisfy a particular need. The government has done its part by encouraging competition through antitrust legislation. The greater the competition, the greater is the choice available to consumers.

Competition and the resulting freedom of choice provide additional benefits for customers by reducing prices. For example, when personal computers were introduced, they cost more than $5,000. Thanks to intense competition and technological advancements, personal computers today can be purchased for less than $500.

THE RIGHT TO BE HEARD This fourth right means that someone will listen and take appropriate action when customers complain. Actually, management began to listen to consumers after World War II, when competition between businesses that manufactured and sold consumer goods increased. One way that firms got a competitive edge was to listen to consumers and provide the products they said they wanted and needed. Today, businesses are listening even more attentively, and many larger firms have consumer relations departments that can be contacted easily via toll-free telephone numbers.

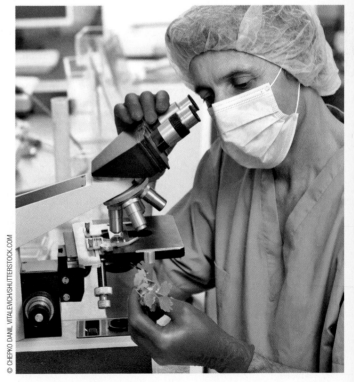

The right to safety. The Consumer Bill of Rights asserts consumers' basic rights. The right to safety means that products must be safe for their intended use and must be tested by the processor to ensure product quality and safety.

Keep these consumer rights in mind when you shop around for goods or services, buy something, or have a problem with a purchase. You're entitled to be informed, to have choices, to be heard, to buy safe products, to have responsive service, and to know your rights.

Other groups listen, too. Most large cities and some states have consumer affairs offices to act on citizens' complaints.

ADDITIONAL CONSUMER RIGHTS In 1975, President Gerald Ford added to the Consumer Bill of Rights the right to consumer education, which entitles people to be fully informed about their rights as consumers. In 1994, President Bill Clinton added a sixth right, the right to service, which entitles consumers to convenience, courtesy, and responsiveness from manufacturers and sellers of consumer products.

Major Consumerism Forces

The major forces in consumerism are individual consumer advocates and organizations, consumer education programs, and consumer laws. Consumer advocates, such as Ralph Nader, take it on themselves to protect the rights of consumers. They band together into consumer organizations, either independently or under government sponsorship. Some organizations, such as the National Consumers' League and the Consumer Federation of America, operate nationally, whereas others are active at state and local levels. They inform and organize other consumers, raise issues, help businesses to develop consumer-oriented programs, and pressure lawmakers to enact consumer protection laws. Some consumer advocates and organizations encourage consumers to boycott products and businesses to which they have objections. Today, the consumer movement has adopted corporate-style marketing and addresses a broad range of issues. Current campaigns include efforts (1) to curtail the use of animals for testing purposes, (2) to reduce liquor and cigarette billboard advertising in low-income, inner-city neighborhoods, and (3) to encourage recycling.

Educating consumers to make wiser purchasing decisions is perhaps one of the most far-reaching aspects of consumerism. Increasingly, consumer education is becoming a part of high school and college curricula and adult-education programs. These programs cover many topics—for instance, what major factors should be considered when buying specific products, such as insurance, real estate, automobiles, appliances and furniture, clothes, and food; the provisions of certain consumer-protection laws; and the sources of information that can help individuals become knowledgeable consumers.

Major advances in consumerism have come through federal legislation. Some laws enacted in the last 50 years to protect your rights as a consumer are listed and described in Table 2-4.

Most businesspeople now realize that they ignore consumer issues only at their own peril. Managers know that improper handling of consumer complaints can result in lost sales, bad publicity, and lawsuits.

Concept Check

✓ Describe the six basic rights of consumers.

✓ What are the major forces in consumerism today?

✓ What are some of the federal laws enacted in the last 50 years to protect your rights as a consumer?

Learning Objective

8 Analyze how present employment practices are being used to counteract past abuses.

EMPLOYMENT PRACTICES

Managers who subscribe to the socioeconomic view of a business's social responsibility, together with significant government legislation enacted to protect the buying public, have broadened the rights of consumers. The last five decades have seen similar progress in affirming the rights of employees to equal treatment in the workplace.

Everyone should have the opportunity to land a job for which he or she is qualified and to be rewarded on the basis of ability and performance. This is an important issue for society, and it also makes good business sense. Yet, over the years, this opportunity

TABLE 2-4 Major Federal Legislation Protecting Consumers Since 1960

Legislation	Major Provisions
Federal Hazardous Substances Labeling Act (1960)	Required warning labels on household chemicals if they were highly toxic
Kefauver–Harris Drug Amendments (1962)	Established testing practices for drugs and required manufacturers to label drugs with generic names in addition to trade names
Cigarette Labeling Act (1965)	Required manufacturers to place standard warning labels on all cigarette packages and advertising
Fair Packaging and Labeling Act (1966)	Called for all products sold across state lines to be labeled with net weight, ingredients, and manufacturer's name and address
Motor Vehicle Safety Act (1966)	Established standards for safer cars
Truth in Lending Act (1968)	Required lenders and credit merchants to disclose the full cost of finance charges in both dollars and annual percentage rates
Credit Card Liability Act (1970)	Limited credit-card holder's liability to $50 per card and stopped credit-card companies from issuing unsolicited cards
Fair Credit Reporting Act (1971)	Required credit bureaus to provide credit reports to consumers regarding their own credit files; also provided for correction of incorrect information
Consumer Product Safety Commission Act (1972)	Established an abbreviated procedure for registering certain generic drugs
Fair Credit Billing Act (1974)	Amended the Truth in Lending Act to enable consumers to challenge billing errors
Equal Credit Opportunity Act (1974)	Provided equal credit opportunities for males and females and for married and single individuals
Magnuson–Moss Warranty–Federal Trade Commission Act (1975)	Provided for minimum disclosure standards for written consumer-product warranties for products that cost more than $15
Amendments to the Equal Credit Opportunity Act (1976, 1994)	Prevented discrimination based on race, creed, color, religion, age, and income when granting credit
Fair Debt Collection Practices Act (1977)	Outlawed abusive collection practices by third parties
Nutrition Labeling and Education Act (1990)	Required the Food and Drug Administration to review current food labeling and packaging focusing on nutrition label content, label format, ingredient labeling, food descriptors and standards, and health messages
Telephone Consumer Protection Act (1991)	Prohibited the use of automated dialing and prerecorded-voice calling equipment to make calls or deliver messages
Consumer Credit Reporting Reform Act (1997)	Placed more responsibility for accurate credit data on credit issuers; required creditors to verify that disputed data are accurate and to notify a consumer before reinstating the data
Children's Online Privacy Protection Act (2000)	Placed parents in control over what information is collected online from their children younger than 13 years; required commercial website operators to maintain the confidentiality, security, and integrity of personal information collected from children
Do Not Call Implementation Act (2003)	Directed the FCC and the FTC to coordinate so that their rules are consistent regarding telemarketing call practices including the Do Not Call Registry and other lists, as well as call abandonment
Credit Card Accountability, Responsibility, and Disclosure Act (2009)	Provided the most sweeping changes in credit card protections since the Truth in Lending Act of 1968
Dodd–Frank Wall Street Reform and Consumer Protection Act of 2010	Promoted the financial stability of the United States by improving accountability and responsibility in the financial system; established a new Consumer Financial Protection Agency to regulate home mortgages, car loans, and credit cards; became Public Law on July 21, 2010

© CENGAGE LEARNING 2015

minority a racial, religious, political, national, or other group regarded as different from the larger group of which it is a part and that is often singled out for unfavorable treatment

has been denied to members of various minority groups. A **minority** is a racial, religious, political, national, or other group regarded as different from the larger group of which it is a part and that is often singled out for unfavorable treatment.

The federal government responded to the outcry of minority groups during the 1960s and 1970s by passing a number of laws forbidding discrimination in the workplace. (These laws are discussed in Chapter 9 in the context of human resources management.) Now, almost 50 years after passage of the first of these (the Civil Rights Act of 1964), abuses still exist. An example is the disparity in income levels for whites, blacks, Hispanics, and Asians, as illustrated in Figure 2-3. Lower incomes and higher unemployment rates also characterize Native Americans, handicapped persons, and women. Responsible managers have instituted a number of programs to counteract the results of discrimination.

Affirmative Action Programs

affirmative action program a plan designed to increase the number of minority employees at all levels within an organization

An **affirmative action program** is a plan designed to increase the number of minority employees at all levels within an organization. Employers with federal contracts of more than $50,000 per year must have written affirmative action plans. The objective of such programs is to ensure that minorities are represented within the organization in approximately the same proportion as in the surrounding community. If 25 percent of the electricians in a geographic area in which a company is located are African Americans, then approximately 25 percent of the electricians it employs also should be African Americans. Affirmative action plans encompass all areas of human resources management: recruiting, hiring, training, promotion, and pay.

Unfortunately, affirmative action programs have been plagued by two problems. The first involves quotas. In the beginning, many firms pledged to recruit and hire a certain number of minority members by a specific date. To achieve this goal, they were forced to consider only minority applicants for job openings; if they

FIGURE 2-3 Comparative Income Levels

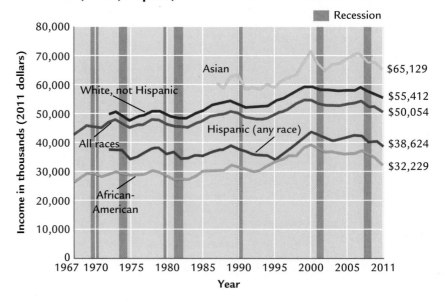

This chart shows the median household incomes of Asian, white, Hispanic, and African-American workers in 2011.

Source: U.S. Census Bureau, Current Population Report, 1968 to 2012 Annual Social and Economic Supplements, *Income, Poverty, and Health Insurance Coverage in the United States: 2012*, issued September 2012, U.S. Census Bureau, U.S. Department of Commerce, 5, http://www.census.gov/prod/2012pubs/p60-243pdf (accessed February 4, 2013).

hired nonminority workers, they would be defeating their own purpose. However, the courts have ruled that such quotas are unconstitutional even though their purpose is commendable. They are, in fact, a form of discrimination called *reverse discrimination*.

The second problem is that although most such programs have been reasonably successful, not all businesspeople are in favor of affirmative action programs. Managers not committed to these programs can "play the game" and still discriminate against workers. To help solve this problem, Congress created (and later strengthened) the **Equal Employment Opportunity Commission (EEOC)**, a government agency with the power to investigate complaints of employment discrimination and sue firms that practice it.

The threat of legal action has persuaded some corporations to amend their hiring and promotional policies, but the discrepancy between men's and women's salaries still exists, as illustrated in Figure 2-4. For more than 50 years, women have consistently earned only about 77 cents for each dollar earned by men.

Training Programs for the Hard-Core Unemployed

For some firms, social responsibility extends far beyond placing a help-wanted advertisement in the local newspaper. These firms have assumed the task of helping the **hard-core unemployed,** workers with little education or vocational training and a long history of unemployment. For example, a few years ago, General Mills helped establish Siyeza, a frozen soul-food processing plant in North Minneapolis. Through the years, Siyeza has provided stable, high-quality full-time jobs for a permanent core of 80 unemployed or underemployed minority inner-city residents. In addition, groups of up to 100 temporary employees are called in when needed. In the past, such workers often were turned down routinely by personnel managers, even for the most menial jobs.

Meet Sam's Club president and CEO.
In early 2012, Rosalind Brewer became the first African-American woman to hold a CEO position at one of the company's business units.

Equal Employment Opportunity Commission (EEOC) a government agency with the power to investigate complaints of employment discrimination and the power to sue firms that practice it

hard-core unemployed workers with little education or vocational training and a long history of unemployment

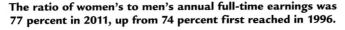

FIGURE 2-4 Relative Earnings of Male and Female Workers

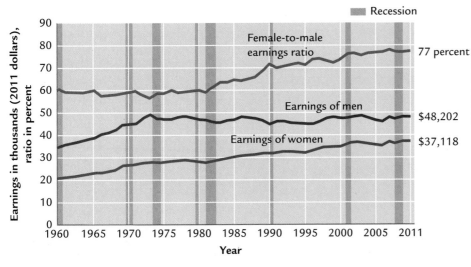

The ratio of women's to men's annual full-time earnings was 77 percent in 2011, up from 74 percent first reached in 1996.

Source: U.S. Census Bureau, Current Population Survey, 1960 to 2011 Annual Social and Economic Supplements, *Income, Poverty, and Health Insurance Coverage in the United States: 2011*, issued September 2012, U.S. Census Bureau, U.S. Department of Commerce, 9, http://www.census.gov/prod/2012pubs/p60-243.pdf (accessed February 4, 2013).

Concept Check

✓ What is an affirmative action program? What is its purpose?

✓ Why did Congress create (and later strengthen) the Equal Employment Opportunity Commission?

Learning Objective

9 Describe the major types of pollution, their causes, and their cures.

CONCERN FOR THE ENVIRONMENT

pollution the contamination of water, air, or land through the actions of people in an industrialized society

The social consciousness of responsible business managers, the encouragement of a concerned government, and an increasing concern on the part of the public have led to a major effort to reduce environmental pollution, conserve natural resources, and reverse some of the worst effects of past negligence in this area. **Pollution** is the contamination of water, air, or land through the actions of people in an industrialized society. For several decades, environmentalists have been warning us about the dangers of industrial pollution. Unfortunately, business and government leaders either ignored the problem or were not concerned about it until pollution became a threat to life and health in America. Today, Americans expect business and government leaders to take swift action to clean up our environment—and to keep it clean.

Effects of Environmental Legislation

As in other areas of concern to our society, legislation and regulations play a crucial role in pollution control. The laws outlined in Table 2-5 reflect the scope of current environmental legislation: laws to promote clean air, clean water, and even quiet work and living environments. Of major importance was the creation of the Environmental Protection Agency (EPA), the federal agency charged with enforcing laws designed to protect the environment.

TABLE 2-5 Summary of Major Environmental Laws

Legislation	Major Provisions
National Environmental Policy Act (1970)	Established the Environmental Protection Agency (EPA) to enforce federal laws that involve the environment
Clean Air Amendment (1970)	Provided stringent automotive, aircraft, and factory emission standards
Water Quality Improvement Act (1970)	Strengthened existing water pollution regulations and provided for large monetary fines against violators
Resource Recovery Act (1970)	Enlarged the solid-waste disposal program and provided for enforcement by the EPA
Water Pollution Control Act Amendment (1972)	Established standards for cleaning navigable streams and lakes and eliminating all harmful waste disposal by 1985
Noise Control Act (1972)	Established standards for major sources of noise and required the EPA to advise the Federal Aviation Administration on standards for airplanes
Clean Air Act Amendment (1977)	Established new deadlines for cleaning up polluted areas; also required review of existing air-quality standards
Resource Conservation and Recovery Act (1984)	Amended the original 1976 act and required federal regulation of potentially dangerous solid-waste disposal
Clean Air Act Amendment (1987)	Established a national air-quality standard for ozone
Oil Pollution Act (1990)	Expanded the nation's oil-spill prevention and response activities; also established the Oil Spill Liability Trust Fund
Clean Air Act Amendments (1990)	Required that motor vehicles be equipped with onboard systems to control about 90 percent of refueling vapors
Food Quality Protection Act (1996)	Amended the Federal Insecticide, Fungicide and Rodenticide Act and the Federal Food Drug and Cosmetic Act; the requirements included a new safety standard—reasonable certainty of no harm—that must be applied to all pesticides used on foods
American Recovery and Reinvestment Act (2009)	Provided $7.22 billion to the EPA to protect and promote "green" jobs and a healthier environment

When they are aware of a pollution problem, many firms respond to it rather than wait to be cited by the EPA. Other owners and managers, however, take the position that environmental standards are too strict. (Loosely translated, this means that compliance with present standards is too expensive.) Consequently, it often has been necessary for the EPA to take legal action to force firms to install antipollution equipment and to clean up waste storage areas.

Experience has shown that the combination of environmental legislation, voluntary compliance, and EPA action can succeed in cleaning up the environment and keeping it clean. However, much still remains to be done.

WATER POLLUTION The Clean Water Act has been credited with greatly improving the condition of the waters in the United States. This success comes largely from the control of pollutant discharges from industrial and wastewater treatment plants. Although the quality of our nation's rivers, lakes, and streams has improved significantly in recent years, many of these surface waters remain severely polluted. Currently, one of the most serious water-quality problems results from the high level of toxic pollutants found in these waters.

Among the serious threats to people posed by water pollutants are respiratory irritation, cancer, kidney and liver damage, anemia, and heart failure. Toxic pollutants also damage fish and other forms of wildlife. In fish, they cause tumors or reproductive problems; shellfish and wildlife living in or drinking from toxin-laden waters also have suffered genetic defects. Recently, the Pollution Control Board of Kerala in India ordered Coca-Cola to close its major bottling plant. For years, villagers in the nearby areas had accused Coke of depleting local groundwater and producing other local pollution. The village council president said, "We are happy that the government is finally giving justice to the people who are affected by the plant."

The task of water cleanup has proved to be extremely complicated and costly because of pollution runoff and toxic contamination. Yet, improved water quality is not only necessary, it is also achievable. Consider Cleveland's Cuyahoga River. A few years ago, the river was so contaminated by industrial wastes that it burst into flames one hot summer day! Now, after a sustained community cleanup effort, the river is pure enough for fish to thrive in.

Another serious issue is acid rain, which is contributing significantly to the deterioration of coastal waters, lakes, and marine life in the eastern United States. Acid rain forms when sulfur emitted by smokestacks in industrialized areas combines with moisture in the atmosphere to form acids that are spread by winds. The acids eventually fall to Earth in rain, which finds its way into streams, rivers, and lakes. The acid-rain problem has spread rapidly in recent years, and experts fear that the situation will worsen if the nation begins to burn more coal to generate electricity. To solve the problem, investigators first must determine where the sulfur is being emitted. The costs of this vital investigation and cleanup are going to be high. The human costs of having ignored the problem so long may be higher still.

AIR POLLUTION Aviation emissions are a potentially significant and growing percentage of greenhouse gases that contribute to global warming. Aircraft emissions are significant for several reasons. First, jet aircraft are the main source of human emissions deposited directly into the upper atmosphere, where they may have a greater warming

Sustain the Planet

Social Responsibility at Xerox

Over the past 40 years, Xerox has demonstrated leadership in sustainability and corporate citizenship by designing waste-free products built in waste-free plants, investing in innovations that benefit the environment, supporting community projects, and many other initiatives. Take a look at its 2012 Report on Global Citizenship, which details its environmental sustainability initiatives, corporate donations, volunteerism, and more.

http://www.xerox.com/about-xerox/citizenship/enus.html

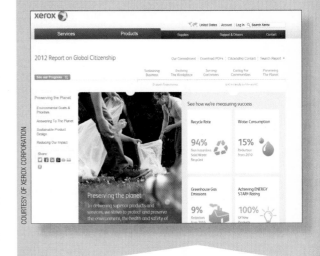

Worsening water and land pollution problem. Land pollution is still a serious problem in many parts of the country. It is not just the manufacturers and service businesses that produce millions of tons of waste! We, the individuals in the United States, contribute to the waste-disposal problem, too.

effect than if they were released at Earth's surface. Second, carbon dioxide—the primary aircraft emission—is the main focus of international concern. For example, it survives in the atmosphere for nearly 100 years and contributes to global warming, according to the Intergovernmental Panel on Climate Change. The carbon dioxide emissions from worldwide aviation roughly equal those of some industrialized countries. Third, carbon dioxide emissions combined with other gases and particles emitted by jet aircraft could have two to four times as great an effect on the atmosphere as carbon dioxide alone. Fourth, the Intergovernmental Panel recently concluded that the rise in aviation emissions owing to the growing demand for air travel would not be fully offset by reductions in emissions achieved solely through technological improvements.

How effective is air pollution control? The EPA estimates that the Clean Air Act and its amendments will eventually result in the removal of 56 billion of pollution from the air each year, thus measurably reducing lung disease, cancer, and other serious health problems caused by air pollution. Other authorities note that we have already seen improvement in air quality. A number of cities have cleaner air today than they did 30 years ago. Even in southern California, bad air-quality days have dropped to less than 40 days a year, about 60 percent lower than that observed just a decade ago. Numerous chemical companies have recognized that they must take responsibility for operating their plants in an environmentally safe manner; some now devote considerable capital to purchasing antipollution devices. For example, 3M's pioneering Pollution Prevention Pays (3P) program, designed to find ways to avoid the generation of pollutants, marked its 30th anniversary in 2005. Since 1975, more than 5,600 employee-driven 3P projects have prevented the generation of more than 2.2 billion pounds of pollutants and produced first-year savings of nearly $1 billion.

LAND POLLUTION Air and water quality may be improving, but land pollution is still a serious problem in many areas. The fundamental issues are (1) how to restore damaged or contaminated land at a reasonable cost and (2) how to protect unpolluted land from future damage.

The land pollution problem has been worsening over the past few years because modern technology has continued to produce increasing amounts of chemical and radioactive waste. U.S. manufacturers produce an estimated 40 to 60 million tons of contaminated oil, solvents, acids, and sludge each year. Service businesses, utility companies, hospitals, and other industries also dump vast amounts of wastes into the environment.

Individuals in the United States contribute to the waste-disposal problem, too. A shortage of landfills, owing to stricter regulations, makes garbage disposal a serious problem in some areas. Incinerators help to solve the landfill-shortage problem, but they bring with them their own problems. They reduce the amount of garbage but also leave tons of ash to be buried—ash that often has a higher concentration of toxicity than the original garbage. Other causes of land pollution include strip mining of coal, nonselective cutting of forests, and development of agricultural land for housing and industry.

To help pay the enormous costs of cleaning up land polluted with chemicals and toxic wastes, Congress created a $1.6 billion Superfund in 1980. Originally, money was to flow into the Superfund from a tax paid by 800 oil and chemical companies that produce toxic waste. The EPA was to use the money in the Superfund to finance the cleanup of hazardous waste sites across the nation. To replenish the Superfund, the EPA had two options: It could sue companies guilty of dumping chemicals at specific waste sites, or it could negotiate with guilty companies and thus completely avoid the legal system. During the 1980s, officials at the EPA came under fire because they preferred negotiated settlements. Critics referred to these settlements as "sweetheart deals" with industry. They felt that the EPA should be much more aggressive in reducing land pollution. Of course, most corporate executives believe that cleanup efficiency and quality might be improved if companies were more involved in the process.

NOISE POLLUTION Excessive noise caused by traffic, aircraft, and machinery can do physical harm to human beings. Research has shown that people who are exposed to loud noises for long periods of time can suffer permanent hearing loss. The Noise Control Act of 1972 established noise emission standards for aircraft and airports, railroads, and interstate motor carriers. The act also provided funding for noise research at state and local levels.

Noise levels can be reduced by two methods. The source of noise pollution can be isolated as much as possible. (Thus, many metropolitan airports are located outside the cities.) Engineers can also modify machinery and equipment to reduce noise levels. If it is impossible to reduce industrial noise to acceptable levels, workers should be required to wear earplugs to guard them against permanent hearing damage.

Entrepreneurial Success

Social Entrepreneurs of Tomorrow

A growing number of young entrepreneurs are starting businesses with the goal of using their skills for a socially responsible purpose: to improve the quality of life for people all over the world. Many of these social entrepreneurs are focusing on different ways to bring reliable, inexpensive sources of electricity to poverty-stricken areas.

For example, Alan Hurt, John Harkness, Jason Schwebke, and Mike Sutarik are members of Team Light Up Africa, which won $10,000 in the first Northern Illinois University Social Venture Business Plan Competition. Their Zoom Box, currently in development, is a low-cost, lightweight generator suitable for powering electric lights and charging cell phones in Africa. "We're more than a company and more than a passing idea," says Hurt. "We're a movement."

Teenage inventor Eden Full created a rotating solar panel, the SunSaluter, that turns to follow the sun throughout the day. The improved efficiency increases the amount of solar power that can be generated in an earth-friendly manner. Her SunSaluter panels are already lighting up two villages in Kenya, with more installations on the way. Full's ingenuity has won her social enterprise additional funding to refine and manufacture the product on a larger scale.

Sources: Based on information in Jack McCarthy, "NIU Students Generate Winning Idea," *Chicago Tribune*, December 11, 2011, www.chicagotribune.com; Zachary Sniderman, "4 Young Social Good Entrepreneurs to Watch," *Mashable*, December 6, 2011, http://mashable.com; "Class Launches Social Entrepreneurs," *NIU Today (Northern Illinois University)*, December 20, 2011, www.niutoday.info; Anya Kamenetz, "Peter Thiel Gives Whiz Kids $100K to Quit College, Start Businesses," *Fast Company*, May 25, 2011, www.fastcompany.com.

Who Should Pay for a Clean Environment?

Governments and businesses are spending billions of dollars annually to reduce pollution—more than $45 billion to control air pollution, $33 billion to control water pollution, and $12 billion to treat hazardous wastes. To make matters worse, much of the money required to purify the environment is supposed to come from already depressed industries, such as the chemical industry. A few firms have discovered that it is cheaper to pay a fine than to install expensive equipment for pollution control.

Who, then, will pay for the environmental cleanup? Many business leaders offer one answer—tax money should be used to clean up the environment and to keep it clean. They reason that business is not the only source of pollution, so business should not be forced to absorb the entire cost of the cleanup. Environmentalists disagree. They believe that the cost of proper treatment and disposal of industrial wastes is an expense of doing business. In either case, consumers probably will pay a large part of the cost—either as taxes or in the form of higher prices for goods and services.

Concept Check

✓ Describe the major types of pollution? What are their causes and their cures?

✓ Summarize major provisions of federal environmental laws enacted since 1970?

✓ Who should pay for a clean environment?

Learning Objective

10 Identify the steps a business must take to implement a program of social responsibility.

IMPLEMENTING A PROGRAM OF SOCIAL RESPONSIBILITY

A firm's decision to be socially responsible is a step in the right direction—but only the first step. The firm then must develop and implement a program to reach this goal. The program will be affected by the firm's size, financial resources, past record in the area of social responsibility, and competition. Above all, however, the program must have the firm's total commitment or it will fail.

Developing a Program of Social Responsibility

An effective program for social responsibility takes time, money, and organization. In most cases, developing and implementing such a program will require four steps: securing the commitment of top executives, planning, appointing a director, and preparing a social audit.

COMMITMENT OF TOP EXECUTIVES Without the support of top executives, any program will soon falter and become ineffective. For example, the Boeing Company's Ethics and Business Conduct Committee is responsible for the ethics program. The committee is appointed by the Boeing board of directors, and its members include the company chairman and CEO, the president and chief operating officer, the presidents of the operating groups, and senior vice presidents. As evidence of their commitment to social responsibility, top managers should develop a policy statement that outlines key areas of concern. This statement sets a tone of positive support and later will serve as a guide for other employees as they become involved in the program.

PLANNING Next, a committee of managers should be appointed to plan the program. Whatever form their plan takes, it should deal with each of the issues described in the top managers' policy statement. If necessary, outside consultants can be hired to help develop the plan.

APPOINTMENT OF A DIRECTOR After the social responsibility plan is established, a top-level executive should be appointed to implement the organization's plan. This individual should be charged with recommending specific policies and helping individual departments to understand and live up to the social responsibilities the firm has assumed. Depending on the size of the firm, the director may require a staff to handle the program on a day-to-day basis. For example, at the Boeing Company, the director of ethics and business conduct administers the ethics and business conduct program.

THE SOCIAL AUDIT At specified intervals, the program director should prepare a social audit for the firm. A **social audit** is a comprehensive report of what an organization has done and is doing with regard to social issues that affect it. This document provides the information the firm needs to evaluate and revise its social responsibility program. Typical subject areas include human resources, community involvement, the quality and safety of products, business practices, and efforts to reduce pollution and improve the environment. The information included in a social audit should be as accurate and as quantitative as possible, and the audit should reveal both positive and negative aspects of the program.

Today, many companies listen to concerned individuals within and outside the company. For example, the Boeing Ethics Line listens to and acts on concerns expressed by employees and others about possible violations of company policies, laws, or regulations, such as improper or unethical business practices, as well as health, safety, and environmental issues. Employees are encouraged to communicate their concerns, as well as ask questions about ethical issues. The Ethics Line is available to all Boeing employees, including Boeing subsidiaries. It is also available to concerned individuals outside the company.

social audit a comprehensive report of what an organization has done and is doing with regard to social issues that affect it

Funding the Program

We have noted that social responsibility costs money. Thus, just like any other corporate undertaking, a program to improve social responsibility must be funded. Funding can come from three sources:

1. Management can pass the cost on to consumers in the form of higher prices.
2. The corporation may be forced to absorb the cost of the program if, for example, the competitive situation does not permit a price increase. In this case, the cost is treated as a business expense, and profit is reduced.
3. The federal government may pay for all or part of the cost through tax reductions or other incentives.

Concept Check

✓ What steps must a business take to implement a program of social responsibility?

✓ What is the social audit? Who should prepare a social audit for the firm?

✓ What are the three sources of funding for a social responsibility program?

Looking for Success? *Get Flashcards, Quizzes, Games, Crosswords, and more @ www.cengagebrain.com.*

Summary

1 Understand what is meant by business ethics.

Ethics is the study of right and wrong and of the morality of choices. Business ethics is the application of moral standards to business situations.

2 Identify the types of ethical concerns that arise in the business world.

Ethical issues arise often in business situations out of relationships with investors, customers, employees, creditors, or competitors. Businesspeople should make every effort to be fair, to consider the welfare of customers and others within the firm, to avoid conflicts of interest, and to communicate honestly.

3 Discuss the factors that affect the level of ethical behavior in organizations.

Individual, social, and opportunity factors all affect the level of ethical behavior in an organization. Individual factors include knowledge level, moral values and attitudes, and personal goals. Social factors include cultural norms and the actions and values of co-workers and significant others. Opportunity factors refer to the amount of leeway that exists in an organization for employees to behave unethically if they choose to do so.

4 Explain how ethical decision making can be encouraged.

Governments, trade associations, and individual firms can establish guidelines for defining ethical behavior. Governments can pass stricter regulations. Trade associations provide ethical guidelines for their members.

Companies provide codes of ethics—written guides to acceptable and ethical behavior as defined by an organization—and create an atmosphere in which ethical behavior is encouraged. An ethical employee working in an unethical environment may resort to whistle-blowing to bring a questionable practice to light.

5 Describe how our current views on the social responsibility of business have evolved.

In a socially responsible business, management realizes that its activities have an impact on society and considers that impact in the decision-making process. Before the 1930s, workers, consumers, and government had very little influence on business activities; as a result, business leaders gave little thought to social responsibility. All this changed with the Great Depression. Government regulations, employee demands, and consumer awareness combined to create a demand that businesses act in socially responsible ways.

6 Explain the two views on the social responsibility of business and understand the arguments for and against increased social responsibility.

The basic premise of the economic model of social responsibility is that society benefits most when business is left alone to produce profitable goods and services. According to the socioeconomic model, business has as much responsibility to society as it has to its owners. Most managers adopt a viewpoint somewhere between these two extremes.

7 Discuss the factors that led to the consumer movement and list some of its results.

Consumerism consists of all activities undertaken to protect the rights of consumers. The consumer movement generally has demanded—and received—attention from business in the areas of product safety, product information, product choices through competition, and the resolution of complaints about products and business practices. Although concerns over consumer rights have been around to some extent since the early 19th century, the movement became more powerful in the 1960s when President John F. Kennedy initiated the Consumer Bill of Rights. The six basic rights of consumers include the right to safety, the right to be informed, the right to choose, the right to be heard, and the rights to consumer education and courteous service.

8 Analyze how present employment practices are being used to counteract past abuses.

Legislation and public demand have prompted some businesses to correct past abuses in employment practices—mainly with regard to minority groups. Affirmative action and training of the hard-core unemployed are two types of programs that have been used successfully.

9 Describe the major types of pollution, their causes, and their cures.

Industry has contributed to noise pollution and pollution of our land and water through the dumping of wastes, and to air pollution through vehicle and smoke-stack emissions. This contamination can be cleaned up and controlled, but the big question is: Who will pay? Present cleanup efforts are funded partly by government tax revenues, partly by business, and in the long run by consumers.

10 Identify the steps a business must take to implement a program of social responsibility.

A program to implement social responsibility in a business begins with total commitment by top management. The program should be planned carefully, and a capable director should be appointed to implement it. Social audits should be prepared periodically as a means of evaluating and revising the program. Programs may be funded through price increases, reduction of profit, or federal incentives.

Key Terms

You should now be able to define and give an example relevant to each of the following terms:

ethics (34)
business ethics (34)
Sarbanes–Oxley Act of 2002 (38)
code of ethics (39)
whistle-blowing (41)

social responsibility (42)
caveat emptor (45)
economic model of social responsibility (46)
socioeconomic model of social responsibility (47)

consumerism (48)
minority (52)
affirmative action program (52)
Equal Employment Opportunity Commission (EEOC) (53)

hard-core unemployed (53)
pollution (54)
social audit (58)

Discussion Questions

1. When a company acts in an ethically questionable manner, what types of problems are caused for the organization and its customers?
2. How can an employee take an ethical stand regarding a business decision when his or her superior already has taken a different position?
3. Overall, would it be more profitable for a business to follow the economic model or the socioeconomic model of social responsibility?
4. Why should business take on the task of training the hard-core unemployed?
5. To what extent should the blame for vehicular air pollution be shared by manufacturers, consumers, and government?
6. Why is there so much government regulation involving social responsibility issues? Should there be less?

Test Yourself

Matching Questions

1. _____ An application of moral standards to business situations.

2. _____ Provides legal protection for employees who report corporate misconduct.

3. _____ A guide to acceptable and ethical behavior as defined by the organization.

4. _____ All activities undertaken to protect the rights of consumers.

5. _____ Informing the press or government officials about unethical practices within one's organization.

6. _____ A Latin phrase meaning "let the buyer beware."

7. _____ A racial, religious, political, national, or other group regarded as different from the larger group of which it is a part.

8. _____ A plan designed to increase the number of minority employees at all levels within an organization.

9. _____ Workers with little education or vocational training and a long history of unemployment.

10. _____ The contamination of water, air, or land.

    a. whistle-blowing
    b. pollution
    c. social audit
    d. minority
    e. code of ethics
    f. hard-core unemployed
    g. Sarbanes–Oxley Act of 2002
    h. economic model of social responsibility
    i. affirmative action program
    j. business ethics
    k. consumerism
    l. caveat emptor

True False Questions

11. **T F** The field of business ethics applies moral standards to business situations.

12. **T F** Business ethics rarely involves the application of moral standards to the business activity of a normal company.

13. **T F** The economic model of social responsibility emphasizes the effect of business decisions on society.

14. **T F** Consumerism consists of all activities undertaken to protect the rights of consumers.

15. **T F** Manufacturers are not required by law to inform consumers about the potential dangers of using their products.

16. **T F** Affirmative-action plans encompass all areas of human resources management, including recruiting, hiring, training, promotion, and pay.

17. **T F** Hard-core unemployed workers are those with little education or vocational training.

18. **T F** The EPA was created by the government to develop new improved ways to clean and improve the environment.

19. **T F** Consumers will probably pay in large part for cleaning up our environment through increased taxes or increased product cost.

20. **T F** A key step in developing and implementing a social responsibility program is the environmental audit.

Multiple-Choice Questions

21. _____ Business ethics
    a. is laws and regulations that govern business.
    b. is the application of moral standards to business situations.
    c. do not vary from one person to another.
    d. is most important for advertising agencies.
    e. is well-defined rules for appropriate business behavior.

22. _____ Customers expect a firm's products to
    a. boost sales.
    b. be profitable.
    c. earn a reasonable return on investment.
    d. be available everywhere.
    e. be safe, reliable, and reasonably priced.

23. _____ Some AIG executives were aware of the financial problems the company was facing and yet failed to reveal this information to the public.

These actions taken by AIG executives were
    a. moral.
    b. normal.
    c. in the best interests of shareholders.
    d. unethical.
    e. in the best interests of the employees.

24. _____ Bribes are
    a. unethical.
    b. ethical only under certain circumstances.
    c. uncommon in many foreign countries.
    d. economic returns.
    e. ethical.

25. _____ What are three sets of factors that influence the standards of behavior in an organization?
   a. Organizational norms, circumstances, morals
   b. Peer pressure, attitudes, social factors
   c. Historical factors, management attitudes, opportunity
   d. Opportunity, individual factors, social factors
   e. Financial factors, opportunity, morals

26. _____ Informing the press or government officials about unethical practices within one's organization is called
   a. unethical behavior.
   b. whistling.
   c. whistle-blowing.
   d. trumpeting.
   e. a company violation.

27. _____ Social responsibility
   a. has little or no associated costs.
   b. can be extremely expensive and provides very little benefit to a company.
   c. has become less important as businesses become more competitive.
   d. is generally a crafty scheme to put competitors out of business.
   e. is costly but provides tremendous benefits to society and the business.

28. _____ *Caveat emptor*
   a. is a French term that implies laissez-faire.
   b. implies disagreements over peer evaluations.
   c. is a Latin phrase meaning "let the buyer beware."
   d. is a Latin phrase meaning "let the seller beware."
   e. is a Latin phrase meaning "the cave is empty."

29. _____ Where does social responsibility of business have to begin?
   a. Government
   b. Management
   c. Consumers
   d. Consumer protection groups
   e. Society

30. _____ Primary emphasis in the economic model of social responsibility is on
   a. quality of life.
   b. conservation of resources.
   c. market-based decisions.
   d. production.
   e. firm's and community's interests.

Answers to the Test Yourself questions appear at the end of the book on page TY-1.

Video Case
PortionPac Chemical Is People-Friendly, Planet-Friendly

When Marvin Klein and Syd Weisberg founded PortionPac Chemical Corporation (www.portionpaccorp.com) in 1964, they were thinking "green" long before the word came to describe an international environmental movement. The partners shared the belief that cleaning solutions didn't have to be toxic or caustic to be effective. They also realized that both water and packaging went to waste when manufacturers poured premixed cleaning liquids into spray bottles that customers would throw away when empty. One more thing the cofounders agreed on: They wanted to do business with integrity, dealing with employees, suppliers, and customers in an ethical way.

With commercial customers in mind, Weisberg tested and developed concentrated cleaning formulas that did away with grease and dirt in offices, kitchens, and bathrooms without endangering people or the planet. He and Klein prepared small packages of concentrate to be mixed with water for full-strength cleaning in elementary schools, companies, factories, and correctional facilities. To be sure the cleaning solution wasn't too strong or too weak, the entrepreneurs gave custodians, janitors, and other cleaning staff careful instructions about exactly how to dilute the concentrate. And to avoid mountains of empty bottles piling up in local landfills, they had customers use refillable spray bottles.

Chicago-based PortionPac's core principles of safety and sustainability were way ahead of their time. Now that environmental issues are in the public eye, the company is thriving, with $20 million in annual sales, 84 employees, and an ever-expanding customer base. Unlike most businesses, however, PortionPac rewards its salespeople for selling only the amount of cleaning products that customers need. This policy reflects its respect for the environment as well as its emphasis on ethical business practices. If customers buy too much, they may use too much and put their staff or the environment at risk, not to mention spending more than they should. PortionPac also provides customers with on-site and online training about the proper use of cleaning products and timesaving ways to get the job done. No wonder so many of PortionPac's customers remain loyal buyers year after year.

PortionPac pays just as much attention to the needs of its employees as it does to the needs of its customers and the planet. Machines in the company's Chicago factory have been designed to operate with minimal noise, so that employees can talk or listen to music as they work. Sunshine streams through large skylights, potted plants brighten the factory floor, and thoughtful sculptures follow the themes of plumbing and cleaning. Rather than operate three shifts around the clock, PortionPac arranges family-friendly work schedules that allow managers and employees to balance their personal and professional obligations.

Once every year, on Front to Back Day, top executives and all non production managers and employees go into the factory to work side by side with frontline employees. This experience gives them a better understanding of everyday challenges and conditions on the factory floor, which, in turn, helps senior managers make more informed decisions about production. At the end of the day, the entire workforce joins in a barbecue that reinforces the company's close-knit family feeling. It's not surprising that turnover is exceptionally low. More than half the workforce has been with PortionPac for more than a decade. On the few occasions when positions do open up, employees encourage their brothers, sisters, or adult children to apply. Recognizing the company's commitment to its employees, *Inc.* magazine has named PortionPac to its list of Winning Workplaces.

Marvin Klein, who now serves as chairman, stresses that PortionPac's dedication to business ethics and integrity is actually a matter of common sense. It's also a two-way street: He wants to do business with suppliers and customers that do the right thing. As PortionPac celebrates its 50th anniversary, Klein and the entire management team are planning for a people-friendly, planet-friendly future.[16]

Questions

1. PortionPac is family-owned. How does this private ownership affect the company's ability to follow the socioeconomic model of social responsibility?
2. If you were appointed to conduct a social audit of PortionPac, what type of information would you collect? What questions would you ask? Explain your answer.
3. Do you agree with Marvin Klein's assessment of business ethics as a matter of common sense? Why or why not?

Building Skills for Career Success

1. Social Media Exercise

In 2010, Pepsi decided to develop a new social media–based project, called Pepsi Refresh Project, aimed at Millennials and allowing consumers to post ideas for improving their communities. This replaced the $20 million they spent on Superbowl advertising. The project received more than 57 million votes. Visit the website at http://www.refresheverything.com/.

1. Do you think this was an effective strategy for Pepsi? Do you think this resonated with the Millennial generation?
2. Do you think this is a good example of corporate social responsibility (CSR)? Why or why not?
3. How does this CSR example for Pepsi compare with that of its main rival Coca-Cola (see http://www.thecoca-colacompany.com/citizenship/index.html)?

2. Building Team Skills

A firm's code of ethics outlines the kinds of behaviors expected within the organization and serves as a guideline for encouraging ethical behavior in the workplace. It reflects the rights of the firm's workers, shareholders, and consumers.

Assignment

1. Working in a team of four, find a code of ethics for a business firm. Start the search by asking firms in your community for a copy of their codes, by visiting the library, or by searching and downloading information from the Internet.

2. Analyze the code of ethics you have chosen, and answer the following questions:
   a. What does the company's code of ethics say about the rights of its workers, shareholders, consumers, and suppliers? How does the code reflect the company's attitude toward competitors?
   b. How does this code of ethics resemble the information discussed in this chapter? How does it differ?
   c. As an employee of this company, how would you personally interpret the code of ethics? How might the code influence your behavior within the workplace? Give several examples.

3. Researching Different Careers

Business ethics has been at the heart of many discussions over the years and continues to trouble employees and shareholders. Stories about dishonesty and wrongful behavior in the workplace appear on a regular basis in newspapers and on the national news.

Assignment

Prepare a written report on the following:

1. Why can it be so difficult for people to do what is right?
2. What is your personal code of ethics? Prepare a code outlining what you believe is morally right. The document should include guidelines for your personal behavior.
3. How will your code of ethics affect your decisions about:
   a. The types of questions you should ask in a job interview?
   b. Selecting a company in which to work?

Endnotes

1. Based on information in Hosea Sanders, "Less Is More for Green Business," *ABC WLS-TV*, January 21, 2011, http://abclocal.go.com; Leigh Buchanan, "A Look Inside the Un-Factory," *Inc.*, June 8, 2010, www.inc.com; "Top Workplaces: PortionPac Chemical," *Inc.*, June 1, 2010, www.inc.com; Nicole J. Bowman, "PortionPac Chemical Corp.," *ISSA*, March 23, 2010, http://current.issa.com; www.portionpaccorp.com.

2. Official John Rigas website, http://johnrigas.com/AdelphiaLitigation.html (accessed February 2, 2013), http://www.time.com/time/specials/packages/articles/0,288 (accessed April 24, 2012), and the U.S. Department of Justice website at http://www.justice.gov/usao/pam/news/2012/Rigas_01_25 (accessed February 2, 2013).

3. The U.S. Department of Justice website at http://www.justice.gov/opa/pr/2001/October/513civ.htm, and http://www.justice.gov/opa/pr/2003/June/03_civ_371.htm (accessed February 2, 2013).

4. The U.S. Department of Justice website at http://www.justice.gov/tax/txdv05268.htm, and http://www.justice.gov/tax/usaopress/2007/txdv072007-122 (Creasia).pdf (accessed February 3, 2013).

5. *Frontlines* (Washington, DC: U.S. Agency for International Development, September 2005), 16.

6. Deere & Company website at http://search.deere.com/wps/dcom/en_US/corporate/our_company/investor accessed February 3, 2013.

7. U.S. Securities and Exchange Commission website at http://www.sec.gov/litigation/litre-leases/2009/lr21129.htm and http://http://www.sec.gov/litigation/complaints/complr17722.htm (accessed February 2, 2013).

8. U.S. Department of Labor website at http://www.dol.gov/compliance/laws/comp-whistleblower.htm and http://www.sec.gov/news/press/2011/2011-116.htm (accessed February 5, 2013).

9. The General Mills website at http://www.generalmills.com/~/media/Files/CSR/global_resp_summary_2012 (accessed February 5, 2013).

10. The Michael and Susan Dell Foundation website at http://www.msdf.org/about/ and The Dell Corporate Responsibility Report at http://www.dell.com (accessed February 2, 2013).

11. The IBM website at http://www.ibm.com/ibm/g10/us/en/world.wcgrid.html (accessed February 3, 2013).

12. The GE website at http://www.gecitizenship.com/community-engagement/volunteering/ (accessed February 5, 2013).

13. The Charles Schwab Foundation website at http://www.aboutschwab.com/about/overview/charles_schwab/foundation (accessed February 2, 2013).

14. The ExxonMobil website at http://www.exxonmobil.com/corporate/community_wwgiving.aspx (accessed February 1, 2013).

15. The AT&T website at http://www.att.com/gen/press-room?pid=2964 (accessed February 4, 2013).

16. Based on information in "NIST Visit to Chicago Spotlights Manufacturing Success," *Department of Commerce*, July 20, 2012, http://www.commerce.gov Hosea; Sanders, "Less Is More for Green Business," *ABC WLS-TV*, January 21, 2011, http://abclocal.go.com; Leigh Buchanan, "A Look Inside the Un-Factory," *Inc.*, June 8, 2010, http://www.inc.com; "Top Workplaces: PortionPac Chemical," *Inc.*, June 1, 2010, http://www.inc.com; Nicole J. Bowman, "PortionPac Chemical Corp.," *ISSA*, March 23, 2010, http://current.issa.com; http://www.portionpaccorp.com.

Exploring Global Business

Learning Objectives

Once you complete this chapter, you will be able to:

1 Explain the economic basis for international business.

2 Discuss the restrictions nations place on international trade, the objectives of these restrictions, and their results.

3 Outline the extent of international business and the world economic outlook for trade.

4 Discuss international trade agreements and international economic organizations working to foster trade.

5 Define the methods by which a firm can organize for and enter into international markets.

6 Describe the various sources of export assistance.

7 Identify the institutions that help firms and nations finance international business.

Why Should You Care?

Free trade—are you for or against it? Most economists support free-trade policies, but public support can be lukewarm, and certain groups are adamantly opposed, alleging that "trade harms large segments of U.S. workers," "degrades the environment," and "exploits the poor."

Coca-Cola

The Coca-Cola Company has been an international success story in soft drinks for more than 100 years. With $46.5 billion in annual revenues and 146,000 employees worldwide, the company sells beverages under well-known brands such as Coca-Cola, Diet Coke, Minute Maid, Sprite, and Dasani. In fact, 15 of Coca-Cola's global brands ring up $1 billion or more in annual sales.

Founded in Atlanta in 1886, Coca-Cola first expanded across the country and then looked beyond our borders for more profit opportunity. By 1912, the company's familiar hourglass bottles were on store shelves in Canada, the Caribbean, Central America, and the Philippines. Today, more than half of Coca-Cola's sales are made outside the United States. It operates in more than 200 nations and is investing $30 billion to open new bottling plants and other facilities in Africa, South America, Russia, Asia, and the Middle East.

Doing business around the world presents Coca-Cola with both opportunities and challenges. For example, aiming for higher market share in China, where soft-drink consumption is on the rise, the company created the Minute Maid Pulpy fruit drink to suit local taste preferences. The product became so popular that Coca-Cola quickly introduced it in 18 countries. On the other hand, because a high percentage of company sales come from non-U.S. markets, changes in the value of world currencies can significantly affect both revenues and profits. Moreover, Coca-Cola has to be creative in dealing with frequent power outages or unpaved roads in some developing nations.

To more effectively manage its activities, Coca-Cola has established three distinct divisions responsible for specific parts of the business: Coca-Cola Americas (covering North and South America), Coca-Cola International (covering Africa, Europe, Eurasia, and the Pacific), and the Bottling Investments Group (covering bottling units outside of North America). Looking ahead, Coca-Cola aims to build on its global success by doubling worldwide revenues by 2020.[1]

Did You Know?

Coca-Cola rings up $46.5 billion in annual revenue around the world.

Coca-Cola is just one of a growing number of companies, large and small, that are doing business with firms in other countries. Some companies, such as General Electric, sell to firms in other countries; others, such as Pier 1 Imports, buy goods around the world to import into the United States. Whether they buy or sell products across national borders, these companies are all contributing to the volume of international trade that is fueling the global economy.

Theoretically, international trade is every bit as logical and worthwhile as interstate trade between, say, California and Washington. Yet, nations tend to restrict the import of certain goods for a variety of reasons. For example, in the early 2000s, the United States restricted the import of Mexican fresh tomatoes because they were undercutting price levels of domestic fresh tomatoes.

Despite such restrictions, international trade has increased almost steadily since World War II. Many of the industrialized nations have signed trade agreements intended to eliminate problems in international business and to help less-developed nations participate in world trade. Individual firms around the world have seized the opportunity to compete in foreign markets by exporting products and increasing foreign production, as well as by other means.

Signing the Trade Act of 2002, President George W. Bush remarked, "Trade is an important source of good jobs for our workers and a source of higher growth for our economy. Free trade is also a proven strategy for building global prosperity and adding to the momentum of political freedom. Trade is an engine of economic growth. In our lifetime, trade has helped lift millions of people and whole nations out of poverty and put them on the path of prosperity."[2] In his national best seller, *The World Is Flat*, Thomas L. Friedman states, "The flattening of the world has presented us with new opportunities, new challenges, new partners but, also, alas new dangers, particularly as Americans it is imperative that we be the best global citizens that we can be—because in a flat world, if you don't visit a bad neighborhood, it might visit you."

We describe international trade in this chapter in terms of modern specialization, whereby each country trades the surplus goods and services it produces most efficiently for products in short supply. We also explain the restrictions nations place on products and services from other countries and present some of the possible advantages and disadvantages of these restrictions. We then describe the extent of international trade and identify the organizations working to foster it. We describe several methods of entering international markets and the various sources of export assistance available from the federal government. Finally, we identify some of the institutions that provide the complex financing necessary for modern international trade.

THE BASIS FOR INTERNATIONAL BUSINESS

Learning Objective

1 Explain the economic basis for international business.

International business encompasses all business activities that involve exchanges across national boundaries. Thus, a firm is engaged in international business when it buys some portion of its input from, or sells some portion of its output to, an organization located in a foreign country. (A small retail store may sell goods produced in some other country. However, because it purchases these goods from American distributors, it is not engaged in international trade.)

International business all business activities that involve exchanges across national boundaries

Absolute and Comparative Advantage

Some countries are better equipped than others to produce particular goods or services. The reason may be a country's natural resources, its labor supply, or even customs or a historical accident. Such a country would be best off if it could specialize in the production of such products so that it can produce them most efficiently. The country could use what it needed of these products and then trade the surplus for products it could not produce efficiently on its own.

Saudi Arabia thus has specialized in the production of crude oil and petroleum products; South Africa, in diamonds; and Australia, in wool. Each of these countries is said to have an absolute advantage with regard to a particular product. An **absolute advantage** is the ability to produce a specific product more efficiently than any other nation.

One country may have an absolute advantage with regard to several products, whereas another country may have no absolute advantage at all. Yet it is still worthwhile for these two countries to specialize and trade with each other. To see why this is so, imagine that you are the president of a successful manufacturing firm and that you can accurately type 90 words per minute. Your assistant can type 80 words per minute but would run the business poorly. Thus, you have an absolute advantage over your assistant in both typing and managing. However, you cannot afford to type your own letters because your time is better spent in managing the business. That is, you have a **comparative advantage** in managing. A comparative advantage is the ability to produce a specific product more efficiently than any other product.

Your assistant, on the other hand, has a comparative advantage in typing because he or she can do that better than managing the business. Thus, you spend your time managing, and you leave the typing to your assistant. Overall, the business is run as efficiently as possible because you are each working in accordance with your own comparative advantage.

absolute advantage the ability to produce a specific product more efficiently than any other nation

comparative advantage the ability to produce a specific product more efficiently than any other product

© KLETR/SHUTTERSTOCK.COM

Exploiting an American advantage. The United States has long specialized in the production of wheat. Because of its natural resource, the United States and some other countries enjoy an absolute advantage—their ability to produce wheat more efficiently than countries in other parts of the world.

The same is true for nations. Goods and services are produced more efficiently when each country specializes in the products for which it has a comparative advantage. Moreover, by definition, every country has a comparative advantage in some product. The United States has many comparative advantages—in research and development, high-technology industries, and identifying new markets, for instance.

Exporting and Importing

Suppose that the United States specializes in producing corn. It then will produce a surplus of corn, but perhaps it will have a shortage of wine. France, on the other hand, specializes in producing wine but experiences a shortage of corn. To satisfy both needs—for corn and for wine—the two countries should trade with each other. The United States should export corn and import wine. France should export wine and import corn.

Exporting is selling and shipping raw materials or products to other nations. The Boeing Company, for example, exports its airplanes to a number of countries for use by their airlines. Figure 3-1 shows the top ten merchandise-exporting states in the United States.

Importing is purchasing raw materials or products in other nations and bringing them into one's own country. Thus, buyers for Macy's department stores may purchase rugs in India or raincoats in England and have them shipped back to the United States for resale.

Importing and exporting are the principal activities in international trade. They give rise to an important concept called the *balance of trade*. A nation's **balance of trade** is the total value of its exports minus the total value of its imports over some period of time. If a country imports more than it exports, its balance of trade is negative and is said to be *unfavorable*. (A negative balance of trade is unfavorable because the country must export money to pay for its excess imports.)

In 2012, the United States imported $2,736 billion worth of goods and services and exported $2,196 billion worth. It thus had a trade deficit of $540 billion. A **trade deficit** is a negative balance of trade (see Figure 3.2). However, the United States has

exporting selling and shipping raw materials or products to other nations

importing purchasing raw materials or products in other nations and bringing them into one's own country

balance of trade the total value of a nation's exports minus the total value of its imports over some period of time

trade deficit a negative balance of trade

FIGURE 3-1 The Top Ten Merchandise-Exporting States

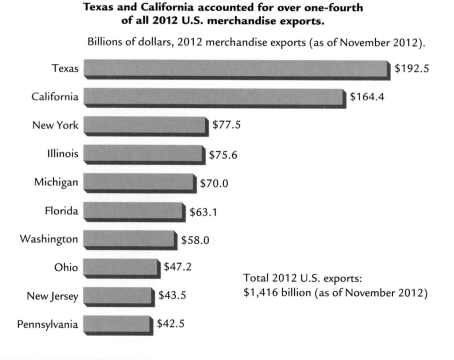

Texas and California accounted for over one-fourth of all 2012 U.S. merchandise exports.

Billions of dollars, 2012 merchandise exports (as of November 2012).

Texas	$192.5
California	$164.4
New York	$77.5
Illinois	$75.6
Michigan	$70.0
Florida	$63.1
Washington	$58.0
Ohio	$47.2
New Jersey	$43.5
Pennsylvania	$42.5

Total 2012 U.S. exports: $1,416 billion (as of November 2012)

Source: www.census.gov/foreign-trade/statistics/state/zip/2012/11/zipstate.pdf (accessed February 6, 2013).

FIGURE 3-2 U.S. International Trade in Goods and Services

If a country imports more goods than it exports, the balance of trade is negative, as it was in the United States from 1987 to 2012.

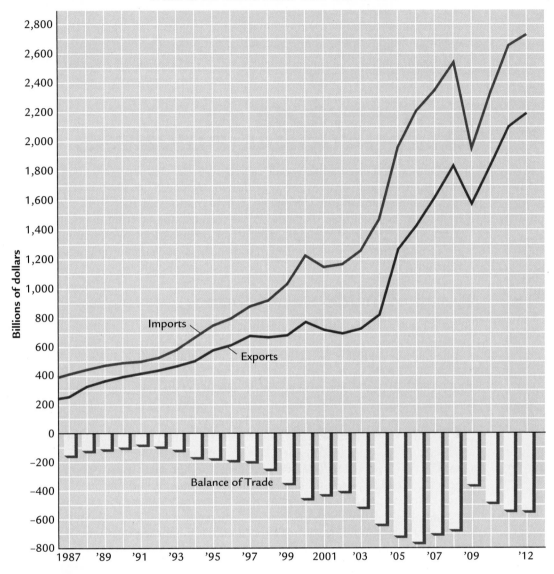

Source: U.S. Department of Commerce, International Trade Administration, U.S. Bureau of Economic Analysis, www.trade.gov/press/press-releases/2013 /export-factsheet-february2013-020813.pdf (accessed August 26, 2013).

consistently enjoyed a large and rapidly growing surplus in services. For example, in 2012, the United States imported $437 billion worth of services and exported $632 billion worth, thus creating a favorable balance of $195 billion.[3]

Question: *Are trade deficits bad?*

Answer: In testimony before the Senate Finance Committee, Daniel T. Griswold, associate director of the Center for Trade Policy at the Cato Institute, remarked, "The trade deficit is not a sign of economic distress, but of rising domestic demand and investment. Imposing new trade barriers will only make Americans worse off while leaving the trade deficit virtually unchanged."

On the other hand, when a country exports more than it imports, it is said to have a favorable balance of trade. This has consistently been the case for Japan over the last two decades or so.

Concept Check

✓ Why do firms engage in international trade?

✓ What is the difference between an absolute advantage and a comparative advantage?

✓ What is the difference between balance of trade and balance of payments?

A nation's **balance of payments** is the total flow of money into a country minus the total flow of money out of that country over some period of time. Balance of payments, therefore, is a much broader concept than balance of trade. It includes imports and exports, of course. However, it also includes investments, money spent by foreign tourists, payments by foreign governments, aid to foreign governments, and all other receipts and payments.

A continual deficit in a nation's balance of payments (a negative balance) can cause other nations to lose confidence in that nation's economy. Alternatively, a continual surplus may indicate that the country encourages exports but limits imports by imposing trade restrictions.

Learning Objective

2 Discuss the restrictions nations place on international trade, the objectives of these restrictions, and their results.

RESTRICTIONS TO INTERNATIONAL BUSINESS

Specialization and international trade can result in the efficient production of want-satisfying goods and services on a worldwide basis. As we have noted, international business generally is increasing. Yet the nations of the world continue to erect barriers to free trade. They do so for reasons ranging from internal political and economic pressures to simple mistrust of other nations. We examine first the types of restrictions that are applied and then the arguments for and against trade restrictions.

Types of Trade Restrictions

Nations generally are eager to export their products. They want to provide markets for their industries and to develop a favorable balance of trade. Hence, most trade restrictions are applied to imports from other nations.

import duty (tariff) a tax levied on a particular foreign product entering a country

TARIFFS Perhaps the most commonly applied trade restriction is the customs (or import) duty. An **import duty** (also called a **tariff**) is a tax levied on a particular foreign product entering a country. For example, the United States imposes a 2.2 percent import duty on fresh Chilean tomatoes, an 8.7 percent duty if tomatoes are dried and packaged, and nearly 12 percent if tomatoes are made into ketchup or salsa. The two types of tariffs are revenue tariffs and protective tariffs; both have the effect of raising the price of the product in the importing nations, but for different reasons. *Revenue tariffs* are imposed solely to generate income for the government. For example, the United States imposes a duty on Scotch whiskey solely for revenue purposes. *Protective tariffs*, on the other hand, are imposed to protect a domestic industry from competition by keeping the price of competing imports level with or higher than the price of similar domestic products. Because fewer units of the product will be sold at the increased price, fewer units will be imported. The French and Japanese agricultural sectors would both shrink drastically if their nations abolished the protective tariffs that keep the price of imported farm products high. Today, U.S. tariffs are the lowest in history, with average tariff rates on all imports under 3 percent.

Some countries rationalize their protectionist policies as a way of offsetting an international trade practice called *dumping*. **Dumping** is the exportation of large quantities of a product at a price lower than that of the same product in the home market.

dumping exportation of large quantities of a product at a price lower than that of the same product in the home market

Thus, dumping drives down the price of the domestic item. Recently, for example, the Pencil Makers Association, which represents eight U.S. pencil manufacturers, charged that low-priced pencils from Thailand and the People's Republic of China were being sold in the United States at less than fair value prices. Unable to compete with these inexpensive imports, several domestic manufacturers had to shut down. To protect themselves, domestic manufacturers can obtain an anti-dumping duty through the government to offset the advantage of the foreign product. Recently, for example, the U.S. Department of Commerce imposed antidumping duties of up to 99 percent on a variety of steel products imported from China, following allegations by U.S. Steel Corp. and other producers that the products were being dumped at unfair prices.

NONTARIFF BARRIERS A **nontariff barrier** is a nontax measure imposed by a government to favor domestic over foreign suppliers. Nontariff barriers create obstacles to the marketing of foreign goods in a country and increase costs for exporters. The following are a few examples of government-imposed nontariff barriers:

Restricting the trade: The Russian style. In early 2012, Russian foreign minister Sergey Lavrov speaks at a news conference in Moscow, Russia. Mr. Lavrov threatens that Moscow will not abide by its World Trade Organization's commitments in trade with the United States unless it scraps a Cold War trade law.

- An **import quota** is a limit on the amount of a particular good that may be imported into a country during a given period of time. The limit may be set in terms of either quantity (so many pounds of beef) or value (so many dollars' worth of shoes). Quotas also may be set on individual products imported from specific countries. Once an import quota has been reached, imports are halted until the specified time has elapsed.
- An **embargo** is a complete halt to trading with a particular nation or of a particular product. The embargo is used most often as a political weapon. At present, the United States has import embargoes against Iran and North Korea—both as a result of extremely poor political relations.
- A **foreign-exchange control** is a restriction on the amount of a particular foreign currency that can be purchased or sold. By limiting the amount of foreign currency importers can obtain, a government limits the amount of goods importers can purchase with that currency. This has the effect of limiting imports from the country whose foreign exchange is being controlled.
- A nation can increase or decrease the value of its money relative to the currency of other nations. **Currency devaluation** is the reduction of the value of a nation's currency relative to the currencies of other countries.

Devaluation increases the cost of foreign goods, whereas it decreases the cost of domestic goods to foreign firms. For example, suppose that the British pound is worth $2. In this case, an American-made $2,000 computer can be purchased for £1,000. However, if the United Kingdom devalues the pound so that it is worth only $1, that same computer will cost £2,000. The increased cost, in pounds, will reduce the import of American computers—and all foreign goods—into England.

On the other hand, before devaluation, a £500 set of English bone china will cost an American $1,000. After the devaluation, the set of china will cost only $500. The decreased cost will make the china—and all English goods—much more attractive to U.S. purchasers. Bureaucratic red tape is more subtle than the other forms of nontariff barriers. Yet it can be the most frustrating trade barrier of all. A few examples are the unnecessarily restrictive application of standards and complex requirements related to product testing, labeling, and certification.

CULTURAL BARRIERS Another type of nontariff barrier is related to cultural attitudes. Cultural barriers can impede acceptance of products in foreign countries. For example, illustrations of feet are regarded as despicable in Thailand. Even so simple a thing as the color of a product or its package can present a problem. In Japan, black and white are the colors of mourning, so they should not be used in packaging. In Brazil, purple is the color of death. And in Egypt, green is never used on a package because it is the national color. When customers are unfamiliar

nontariff barrier a nontax measure imposed by a government to favor domestic over foreign suppliers

import quota a limit on the amount of a particular good that may be imported into a country during a given period of time

embargo a complete halt to trading with a particular nation or in a particular product

foreign-exchange control a restriction on the amount of a particular foreign currency that can be purchased or sold

currency devaluation the reduction of the value of a nation's currency relative to the currencies of other countries

Would your reaction be the same if the product had been made elsewhere? Clearly, cultural attitudes can influence how people feel about goods in the global marketplace.

© STEPHEN MARQUES/SHUTTERSTOCK.COM

with particular products from another country, their general perceptions of the country itself affect their attitude toward the product and help to determine whether they will buy it. Because Mexican cars have not been viewed by the world as being quality products, Volkswagen, for example, may not want to advertise that some of its models sold in the United States are made in Mexico. Many retailers on the Internet have yet to come to grips with the task of designing an online shopping site that is attractive and functional for all global customers.

Gifts to authorities—sometimes quite large ones—may be standard business procedure in some countries. In others, including the United States, they are called bribes or payoffs and are strictly illegal.

Reasons for Trade Restrictions

Various reasons are given for trade restrictions either on the import of specific products or on trade with particular countries. We have noted that political considerations usually are involved in trade embargoes. Other frequently cited reasons for restricting trade include the following:

- *To equalize a nation's balance of payments.* This may be considered necessary to restore confidence in the country's monetary system and in its ability to repay its debts.
- *To protect new or weak industries.* A new, or infant, industry may not be strong enough to withstand foreign competition. Temporary trade restrictions may be used to give it a chance to grow and become self-sufficient. The problem is that once an industry is protected from foreign competition, it may refuse to grow, and "temporary" trade restrictions will become permanent. For example, a recent report by the Government Accountability Office (GAO), the congressional investigative agency, has accused the federal government of routinely imposing quotas on foreign textiles without "demonstrating the threat of serious damage" to U.S. industry. The GAO said that the Committee for the Implementation of Textile Agreements sometimes applies quotas even though it cannot prove the textile industry's claims that American companies have been hurt or jobs have been eliminated.
- *To protect national security.* Restrictions in this category generally apply to technological products that must be kept out of the hands of potential enemies. For example, strategic and defense-related goods cannot be exported to unfriendly nations.
- *To protect the health of citizens.* Products may be embargoed because they are dangerous or unhealthy (e.g., farm products contaminated with insecticides).
- *To retaliate for another nation's trade restrictions.* A country whose exports are taxed by another country may respond by imposing tariffs on imports from that country.
- *To protect domestic jobs.* By restricting imports, a nation can protect jobs in domestic industries. However, protecting these jobs can be expensive. For example, protecting 9,000 jobs in the U.S. carbon-steel industry costs $6.8 billion, or $750,000 per job. In addition, Gary Hufbauer and Ben Goodrich, economists at the Institute for International Economics, estimate that the tariffs could temporarily save 3,500 jobs in the steel industry, but at an annual cost to steel users of $2 billion, or $584,000 per job saved. Yet recently the United States imposed tariffs of up to 616 percent on steel pipes imported from China, South

Korea, and Mexico. Similarly, it is estimated that we spent more than $100,000 for every job saved in the apparel manufacturing industry—jobs that seldom paid more than $35,000 a year.

Reasons Against Trade Restrictions

Trade restrictions have immediate and long-term economic consequences—both within the restricting nation and in world trade patterns. These include the following:

- *Higher prices for consumers.* Higher prices may result from the imposition of tariffs or the elimination of foreign competition, as described earlier. For example, imposing quota restrictions and import protections adds $25 billion annually to U.S. consumers' apparel costs by directly increasing costs for imported apparel.
- *Restriction of consumers' choices.* Again, this is a direct result of the elimination of some foreign products from the marketplace and of the artificially high prices that importers must charge for products that are still imported.
- *Misallocation of international resources.* The protection of weak industries results in the inefficient use of limited resources. The economies of both the restricting nation and other nations eventually suffer because of this waste.
- *Loss of jobs.* The restriction of imports by one nation must lead to cutbacks—and the loss of jobs—in the export-oriented industries of other nations. Furthermore, trade protection has a significant effect on the composition of employment. U.S. trade restrictions—whether on textiles, apparel, steel, or automobiles—benefit only a few industries while harming many others. The gains in employment accrue to the protected industries and their primary suppliers, and the losses are spread across all other industries. A few states gain employment, but many other states lose employment.

Career Success

The Global Economy Creates Jobs at Home, Too

Today's global economy is actually creating new job opportunities for you within the United States. If you're interested in a career with an international accent, consider applying to a non-U.S. company that's expanding within the 50 states. Companies like Lenovo and Electrolux want to stay close to their American customers and promote "made in America" products. Lenovo, the Chinese company that purchased IBM's personal computer division years ago, decided to build a factory in North Carolina so it could speed custom-ordered computers to U.S. customers. Electrolux, the Swedish-owned appliance manufacturer, opened a high-tech U.S. design center to develop new products for the North American market.

Or you might go to work for a U.S. company that's increasing its U.S. workforce because of strong global demand for its goods or services. Ford, for example, is expanding U.S. production as vehicle sales increase in other nations. Chinese buyers see Ford's luxury made-in-America Lincoln cars as status symbols, which is why Ford is adding jobs to produce more vehicles for export to China. Another possibility is to look for openings at U.S. businesses opening new branches abroad, because they often hire headquarters personnel to support expansion plans.

Finally, you might get a career boost from the emerging trend toward "reverse outsourcing." As labor costs rise in other countries and international shipping costs edge upward, companies that once sent work to overseas suppliers or facilities are starting to add U.S. jobs instead. The multinational firms at the leading edge of this trend seek to save time, improve coordination, and control expenses.

Sources: Based on information in Alisa Priddle, "Ford Bringing New Lincolns, Jobs, and Long Future to Flat Rock," *Detroit Free Press*, October 21, 2012, www.freep.com; Erik Sherman, "More Jobs Return to the U.S.: Is It a Trend?" CBS News MoneyWatch, October 15, 2012, www.cbsnews.com; Ely Portillo, "After 2 Years, Electrolux Grows into Charlotte," *Charlotte Observer (North Carolina)*, October 23, 2012, www.charlotteobserver.com.

THE EXTENT OF INTERNATIONAL BUSINESS

Learning Objective

3 Outline the extent of international business and the world economic outlook for trade.

Restrictions or not, international business is growing. Although the worldwide recessions of 1991 and 2001–2002 slowed the rate of growth, and the 2008–2009 global economic crisis caused the sharpest decline in more than 75 years, globalization is a reality of our time. In the United States, international trade now accounts for over one-fourth of Gross Domestic Product (GDP). As trade barriers decrease, new competitors enter the global marketplace, creating more choices for consumers and new opportunities for job seekers. International business will grow along with the expansion of commercial use of the Internet.

The World Economic Outlook for Trade

Although the global economy continued to grow robustly until 2007, economic performance was not equal: growth in the advanced economies slowed and then stopped in 2009, whereas emerging and developing economies continued to grow. Looking ahead, the International Monetary Fund (IMF), an international bank with 188 member nations, expected a gradual global growth to continue in 2013 and 2014 in both advanced and emerging developing economies.[4]

CANADA AND WESTERN EUROPE Our leading export partner, Canada, is projected to show a growth rate of 1.8 percent in 2013 and 2.3 percent in 2014. The euro area, which was projected to decline by 0.2 percent in 2013 is expected to grow 1.0 percent in 2014. The United Kingdom is expected to grow 1.0 percent and 1.9 percent in 2013 and 2014, respectively.

MEXICO AND LATIN AMERICA Our second-largest export customer, Mexico, suffered its sharpest recession ever in 1995, and experienced another major setback in 2009. However, its growth rate in 2013 and 2014 is expected to be 3.5 percent. Growth of about 3.5 percent and 4 percent is expected in 2013 and 2014, respectively. In general, the Latin American and the Caribbean economies are recovering at a robust pace.

JAPAN Japan's economy is regaining some momentum after suffering from an earthquake, tsunami, and nuclear plant disaster in 2011. Stronger consumer demand and business investment make Japan less reliant on exports for growth. The IMF estimates the growth for Japan at 1.2 percent in 2013 and 0.7 percent in 2014.

OTHER ASIAN COUNTRIES The economic growth in Asia remained strong in 2011 and 2012 despite the global recession. Growth was led by China, where its economy expanded by 7.8 percent in 2012, and is expected to grow at 8.2 percent and 8.5 percent in 2013 and 2014, respectively. Growth in India was 4.5 percent in 2012, and is predicted to grow at 5.9 percent and 6.4 percent in 2013 and 2014, respectively. Growth in ASEAN-5 countries—Indonesia, Malaysia, the Philippines, Thailand, and Vietnam—is expected at 5.5 percent and 5.7 percent in 2013 and 2014, respectively. In short, the key emerging economies in Asia are leading the global recovery.

China's emergence as a global economic power has been among the most dramatic economic developments of recent decades. From 1980 to 2004, China's economy averaged a real GDP growth rate of 9.5 percent and became the world's sixth-largest economy. By 2004, China had become the third-largest trading nation in dollar terms, behind the United States and Germany and just ahead of Japan. Today, China, the world's second-largest economy, generates 10 to 15 percent of world GDP, and in 2011, accounted for about 25 percent of world GDP growth. The United States now imports more goods from China than any other nation in the world. In fact, China, with almost $1.9 trillion in exports, is the world's number-one exporter.

Caterpillar in South Africa. Restrictions or not, international business is booming. Globalization is the reality of our time. As trade barriers decrease, ever increasing number of U.S. companies, such as Caterpillar, are selling in the global marketplace.

IMAGEBROKER/ALAMY

In 2012, China took steps to promote the international use of its currency, the renminbi.[5]

COMMONWEALTH OF INDEPENDENT STATES The growth in this region is expected to be 3.8 percent in 2013 and 4.1 percent in 2014. Strong growth is expected to continue in Azerbaijan and Armenia, whereas growth is projected to remain stable in Moldova, Tajikistan, and Uzbekistan. Table 3-1 shows the growth rate from 2011 to 2014 for most regions of the world.

EXPORTS AND THE U.S. ECONOMY In 2008, U.S. exports supported more than 10.3 million full- and part-time jobs during a historic time, when exports as a percentage of GDP reached the highest levels since 1916. The new record, 13.8 percent of GDP in 2011, shows that U.S. businesses have great opportunities in the global marketplace. Even though the global economic crisis caused the number of jobs supported by exports to decline sharply to 8.5 million in 2009, globalization represents a huge opportunity for all countries—rich or poor. Indeed, in 2011, for the first time, the U.S. exports exceeded $2.15 trillion and supported 9.7 million jobs, an increase of 1.2 million jobs since 2009.[6] The 15-fold increase in trade volume over the past 65 years has been one of the most important factors in the rise of living standards around the world. During this time, exports have become increasingly important to the U.S. economy. Exports as a percentage of U.S. GDP have increased steadily since 1985, except in the 2001 and 2008 recessions. Our exports to developing

TABLE 3-1 Global Growth Is Picking Up Gradually

Growth has been led by developing countries and emerging markets.

	Annual Percent Change			
	2011	2012	Projected 2013	Projected 2014
World	3.9	3.2	3.5	4.1
United States	1.8	2.3	2.0	3.0
Euro area	1.4	−0.4	−0.2	1.0
United Kingdom	0.9	−0.2	1.0	1.9
Japan	−0.6	2.0	1.2	0.7
Canada	2.6	2.0	1.8	2.3
Other advanced economies	3.3	1.9	2.7	3.3
Newly industrialized Asian economies	4.0	1.8	3.2	3.9
Emerging markets and developing countries	6.3	5.1	5.5	5.9
Developing Asia	8.0	6.6	7.1	7.5
Commonwealth of Independent States	4.9	3.6	3.8	4.1
Middle East and North Africa	3.5	5.2	3.4	3.8
Latin America and the Caribbean	4.5	3.0	3.6	3.9

Source: *International Monetary Fund: World Economic Outlook* by International Monetary Fund. Copyright 2013 by International Monetary Fund. Reproduced with permission of International Monetary Fund via Copyright Clearance Center. www.imf.org/external/pubs/ft/weo/2013/update/01/index.htm (accessed August 26, 2013).

TABLE 3-2 Value of U.S. Merchandise Exports and Imports, 2012 (as of November 2012)

Rank/Trading Partner	Exports ($ billions)	Rank/Trading Partner	Imports ($ billions)
1) Canada	270.1	1) China	390.8
2) Mexico	199.9	2) Canada	298.4
3) China	100.2	3) Mexico	257.3
4) Japan	64.0	4) Japan	134.6
5) United Kingdom	50.8	5) Germany	99.3
6) Germany	45.0	6) South Korea	54.3
7) Brazil	40.2	7) Saudi Arabia	52.0
8) South Korea	38.9	8) United Kingdom	50.6
9) Netherlands	36.8	9) France	38.3
10) France	28.4	10) India	37.7

Source: U.S. Census Bureau website, http://www.census.gov/foreign-trade/statistics/highlights/toppartners.html (accessed February 5, 2013).

Concept Check

✓ According to the IMF, what are the world economic growth projections for 2013 and 2014?

✓ What is the importance of exports to the U.S. economy?

✓ Which nations are the principal trading partners of the United States? What are the major U.S. imports and exports?

and newly industrialized countries are on the rise. Table 3-2 shows the value of U.S. merchandise exports to, and imports from, each of the nation's ten major trading partners. Note that Canada and Mexico are our best partners for our exports; China and Canada, for imports.

Figure 3-3 shows the U.S. goods export and import shares in 2012. Major U.S. exports and imports are manufactured goods, agricultural products, and mineral fuels.

FIGURE 3-3 U.S. Goods Export and Import Shares in 2012

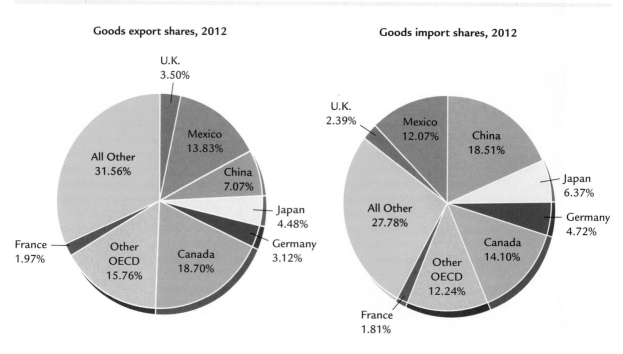

Source: Federal Reserve Bank of St. Louis, *National Economic Trends*, May 2013, p.18.

INTERNATIONAL TRADE AGREEMENTS

The General Agreement on Tariffs and Trade and the World Trade Organization

Learning Objective

4 Discuss international trade agreements and international economic organizations working to foster trade.

At the end of World War II, the United States and 22 other nations organized the body that came to be known as GATT. The **General Agreement on Tariffs and Trade (GATT)** is an international organization of 159 nations dedicated to reducing or eliminating tariffs and other barriers to world trade. These 159 nations accounted for more than 97 percent of the world's merchandise trade (see Figure 3-4). GATT, headquartered in Geneva, Switzerland, provided a forum for tariff negotiations and a means for settling international trade disputes and problems. Most-favored-nation status (MFN) was the famous principle of GATT. It meant that each GATT member nation was to be treated equally by all contracting nations. Therefore, MFN ensured that any tariff reductions or other trade concessions were extended automatically to all GATT members. From 1947 to 1994, the body sponsored eight rounds of negotiations to reduce trade restrictions. Three of the most fruitful were the Kennedy Round, the Tokyo Round, and the Uruguay Round.

General Agreement on Tariffs and Trade (GATT) an international organization of 159 nations dedicated to reducing or eliminating tariffs and other barriers to world trade

THE KENNEDY ROUND (1964–1967) In 1962, the United States Congress passed the Trade Expansion Act. This law gave President John F. Kennedy the authority to negotiate reciprocal trade agreements that could reduce U.S. tariffs by as much as 50 percent. Armed with this authority, which was granted for a period of five years, President Kennedy called for a round of negotiations through GATT.

These negotiations, which began in 1964, have since become known as the Kennedy Round. They were aimed at reducing tariffs and other barriers to trade in

FIGURE 3-4 WTO Members Share in World Merchandise Trade, 2011

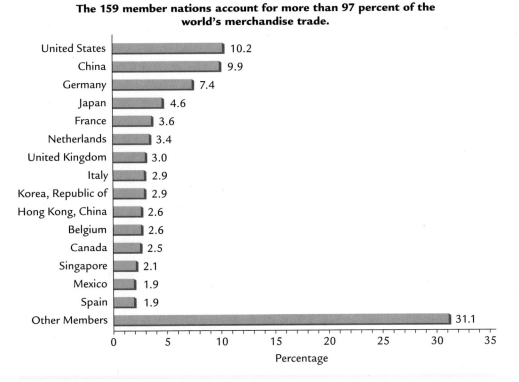

The 159 member nations account for more than 97 percent of the world's merchandise trade.

Nation	Percentage
United States	10.2
China	9.9
Germany	7.4
Japan	4.6
France	3.6
Netherlands	3.4
United Kingdom	3.0
Italy	2.9
Korea, Republic of	2.9
Hong Kong, China	2.6
Belgium	2.6
Canada	2.5
Singapore	2.1
Mexico	1.9
Spain	1.9
Other Members	31.1

Source: www.wto.org/english/res_e/Statis_e/its2012_e/its12_charts_e.htm (accessed February 7, 2013).

both industrial and agricultural products. The participants succeeded in reducing tariffs on these products by an average of more than 35 percent. However, they were less successful in removing other types of trade barriers.

THE TOKYO ROUND (1973–1979) In 1973, representatives of approximately 100 nations gathered in Tokyo for another round of GATT negotiations. The *Tokyo Round* was completed in 1979. The participants negotiated tariff cuts of 30 to 35 percent, which were to be implemented over an eight-year period. In addition, they were able to remove or ease such nontariff barriers as import quotas, unrealistic quality standards for imports, and unnecessary red tape in customs procedures.

THE URUGUAY ROUND (1986–1993) In 1986, the *Uruguay Round* was launched to extend trade liberalization and widen the GATT treaty to include textiles, agricultural products, business services, and intellectual-property rights. This most ambitious and comprehensive global commercial agreement in history concluded overall negotiations on December 15, 1993, with delegations on hand from 109 nations. The agreement included provisions to lower tariffs by greater than one-third, to reform trade in agricultural goods, to write new rules of trade for intellectual property and services, and to strengthen the dispute-settlement process. These reforms were expected to expand the world economy by an estimated $200 billion annually.

The Uruguay Round also created the **World Trade Organization (WTO)** on January 1, 1995. The WTO was established by GATT to oversee the provisions of the Uruguay Round and resolve any resulting trade disputes. Membership in the WTO obliges 159 member nations to observe GATT rules. The WTO has judicial powers to mediate among members disputing the new rules. It incorporates trade in goods, services, and ideas and exerts more binding authority than GATT. Its main function is to ensure that trade flows as smoothly, predictably, and freely as possible.

THE DOHA ROUND (2001) On November 14, 2001, in Doha, Qatar, the WTO members agreed to further reduce trade barriers through multilateral trade negotiations over the next three years. This new round of negotiations focuses on industrial tariffs and nontariff barriers, agriculture, services, and easing trade rules. The Doha Round has set the stage for WTO members to take an important step toward significant new multilateral trade liberalization. It is a difficult task, but the rewards—lower tariffs, more choices for consumers, and further integration of developing countries into the world trading system—are sure to be worth the effort. Some experts suggest that U.S. exporters of industrial and agricultural goods and services should have improved access to overseas markets, whereas others disagree. Negotiations between the developed and developing countries continued in 2013.

World Trade and the Global Economic Crisis

After the sharpest decline in more than 72 years, world trade was set to rebound in 2010 by growing at 9.5 percent, according to the WTO economists. In a 2012 speech, WTO Director-General Pascal Lamy stated, "The multilateral trading system has been instrumental in maintaining trade openness during the crisis, thereby avoiding even worse outcomes. Members must remain vigilant. This is not the time for go-it-alone measures. This is the time to strengthen and preserve the global trading system so that it keeps performing this vital function in the future."[7]

International Economic Organizations Working to Foster Trade

The primary objective of the WTO is to remove barriers to trade on a worldwide basis. On a smaller scale, an **economic community** is an organization of nations formed to promote the free movement of resources and products among its members and to create common economic policies. A number of economic communities now exist.

World Trade Organization (WTO) powerful successor to GATT that incorporates trade in goods, services, and ideas

economic community an organization of nations formed to promote the free movement of resources and products among its members and to create common economic policies

THE EUROPEAN UNION The European Union (EU), also known as the European Economic Community and the Common Market, was formed in 1957 by six countries—France, the Federal Republic of Germany, Italy, Belgium, the Netherlands, and Luxembourg. Its objective was freely conducted commerce among these nations and others that might later join. As shown in Figure 3-5, many more nations have joined the EU since then.

On January 1, 2007, the 25 nations of the EU became the EU27 as Bulgaria and Romania became new members. The EU, with a population of nearly 504 million, is now an economic force with a collective economy larger than much of the United States or Japan.

In celebrating the EU's 50th anniversary in 2007, the president of the European Commission, José Manuel Durão Barroso, declared, "Let us first recognize 50 years of achievement. Peace, liberty, and prosperity, beyond the dreams of even the most optimistic founding fathers of Europe. In 1957, 15 of our 27 members were either under dictatorship or were not allowed to exist as independent countries. Now we are all prospering democracies. The EU of today is around 50 times more prosperous and with three times the population of the EU of 1957."

Since January 2002, 17 member nations of the EU have been participating in the new common currency, the euro. The euro is the single currency of the European Monetary Union nations. However, three EU members, Denmark, the United Kingdom, and Sweden, still maintain their own currencies.

THE NORTH AMERICAN FREE TRADE AGREEMENT The North American Free Trade Agreement (NAFTA) joined the United States with its first- and second-largest export trading partners, Canada and Mexico. Implementation of

FIGURE 3-5 The Evolving European Union

The evolving European Union: The European Union is now an economic force, with a collective economy larger than that of the United States or Japan.

Source: http://europa.eu/abc/european_countries/index_en.htm (accessed February 4, 2013).

NAFTA on January 1, 1994, created a market of more than 469 million people. This market consists of Canada (population 35 million), the United States (317 million), and Mexico (117 million). According to the Office of the U.S. Trade Representative, after 19 years, NAFTA has achieved its core goals of expanding trade and investment between the United States, Canada, and Mexico. For example, from 1993 to 2011, trade among the NAFTA nations more than tripled, from $297 billion to $1,058 billion.

NAFTA is built on the Canadian Free Trade Agreement, signed by the United States and Canada in 1989, and on the substantial trade and investment reforms undertaken by Mexico since the mid-1980s. Initiated by the Mexican government, formal negotiations on NAFTA began in June 1991 among the three governments. The support of NAFTA by President Bill Clinton, former Presidents Ronald Reagan and Jimmy Carter, and Nobel Prize–winning economists provided the impetus for U.S. congressional ratification of NAFTA in November 1993. By 2008, NAFTA had gradually eliminated all tariffs and quotas on goods produced and traded among Canada, Mexico, and the United States to provide for a totally free-trade area. Chile is expected to become the fourth member of NAFTA, but political forces may delay its entry into the agreement for several years.

However, NAFTA is not without its critics. Critics maintain that NAFTA

- has not achieved its goals
- has resulted in job losses
- hurts workers by eroding labor standards and lowering wages
- undermines national sovereignty and independence
- does nothing to help the environment, and
- hurts the agricultural sector

The proponents of NAFTA call the agreement a remarkable economic success story for all three partners. They maintain that NAFTA

- has contributed to significant increases in trade and investment
- has benefited companies in all three countries
- has resulted in increased sales, new partnerships, and new opportunities
- has created high-paying export-related jobs, and
- better prices and selection in consumer goods

THE CENTRAL AMERICAN FREE TRADE AGREEMENT The Central American Free Trade Agreement (CAFTA) was created in 2003 by the United States and four Central American countries—El Salvador, Guatemala, Honduras, and Nicaragua. The CAFTA became CAFTA-DR when the Dominican Republic joined the group in 2007. On January 1, 2009, Costa Rica joined CAFTA-DR as the sixth member. CAFTA-DR creates the third-largest U.S. export market in Latin America, behind only Mexico and Brazil.

THE ASSOCIATION OF SOUTHEAST ASIAN NATIONS The Association of Southeast Asian Nations, with headquarters in Jakarta, Indonesia, was established in 1967 to promote political, economic, and social cooperation among its seven member countries: Indonesia, Malaysia, the Philippines, Singapore, Thailand, Brunei, and Vietnam. With the three new members, Cambodia, Laos, and Myanmar, this region of more than 600 million people is already our fifth-largest trading partner.

THE COMMONWEALTH OF INDEPENDENT STATES The Commonwealth of Independent States was established in December 1991 by the newly independent states as an association of 11 republics of the former Soviet Union.

TRANS-PACIFIC PARTNERSHIP (TPP) On November 12, 2011, the leaders of the nine countries—Australia, Brunei Darussalam, Chile, Malaysia, New Zealand, Peru, Singapore, Vietnam, and the United States—formed the Trans-Pacific Partnership. This partnership will boost economies of the member countries, lower barriers to trade and investment, increase exports, and create more jobs. Together, these eight economies would be America's fifth-largest trading partner. According to President Obama, "We already do more than $200 billion in trade with them every year, and with nearly 500 million consumers between us, there's so much more that we can do together." The Asia-Pacific region is one of the fastest growing areas in the world and TPP will open more markets to American businesses and exports.[8]

THE COMMON MARKET OF THE SOUTHERN CONE (MERCOSUR) Headquartered in Montevideo, Uruguay, the Common Market of the Southern Cone (MERCOSUR) was established in 1991 under the Treaty of Asuncion to unite Argentina, Brazil, Paraguay, and Uruguay as a free-trade alliance; Colombia, Ecuador, Peru, Bolivia, and Chile joined later as associates. In 2012, Venezuela, an associate member since 2004, became a full member of MERCOSUR. The alliance represents more than 267 million consumers—67 percent of South America's population, making it the third-largest trading block behind NAFTA and the EU. Like NAFTA, MERCOSUR promotes "the free circulation of goods, services, and production factors among the countries" and established a common external tariff and commercial policy.

THE ORGANIZATION OF PETROLEUM EXPORTING COUNTRIES The Organization of Petroleum Exporting Countries was founded in 1960 in response to reductions in the prices that oil companies were willing to pay for crude oil. The organization was conceived as a collective bargaining unit to provide oil-producing nations with some control over oil prices.

Concept Check

✓ Define and describe the major objectives of the World Trade Organization (WTO) and the international economic communities.

✓ What is the North American Free Trade Agreement (NAFTA)? What is its importance for the United States, Canada, and Mexico?

METHODS OF ENTERING INTERNATIONAL BUSINESS

A firm that has decided to enter international markets can do so in several ways. We will discuss several different methods. These different approaches require varying degrees of involvement in international business. Typically, a firm begins its international operations at the simplest level. Then, depending on its goals, it may progress to higher levels of involvement.

Learning Objective

5 Define the methods by which a firm can organize for and enter into international markets.

licensing a contractual agreement in which one firm permits another to produce and market its product and use its brand name in return for a royalty or other compensation

Licensing

Licensing is a contractual agreement in which one firm permits another to produce and market its product and use its brand name in return for a royalty or other compensation. For example, Yoplait yogurt is a French yogurt licensed for production in the United States. The Yoplait brand maintains an appealing French image, and in return, the U.S. producer pays the French firm a percentage of its income from sales of the product.

Licensing is especially advantageous for small manufacturers wanting to launch a well-known domestic brand internationally. For example, all Spalding sporting products are licensed worldwide. The licensor, the Questor Corporation, owns the Spalding name but produces no goods itself. Licensing thus provides a simple method for expanding into a foreign market with virtually no investment. On the other hand, if the licensee does not maintain the licensor's product standards, the product's image may be damaged. Another possible disadvantage is that a licensing arrangement may not provide the original producer with any foreign marketing experience.

© STUART MILES/SHUTTERSTOCK.COM

Exporting

A firm also may manufacture its products in its home country and export them for sale in foreign markets. As with licensing, exporting can be a relatively low-risk method of entering foreign markets. Unlike licensing, however, it is not a simple method; it opens up several levels of involvement to the exporting firm.

At the most basic level, the exporting firm may sell its products outright to an *export–import merchant*, which is essentially a merchant wholesaler. The merchant assumes all the risks of product ownership, distribution, and sale. It may even purchase the goods in the producer's home country and assume responsibility for exporting the goods. An important and practical issue for domestic firms dealing with foreign customers is securing payment. This is a two-sided issue that reflects the mutual concern rightly felt by both parties to the trade deal: The exporter would like to be paid before shipping the merchandise, whereas the importer obviously would prefer to know that it has received the shipment before releasing any funds. Neither side wants to take the risk of fulfilling its part of the deal only to discover later that the other side has not. The result would lead to legal costs and complex, lengthy dealings that would waste everyone's resources. This mutual level of mistrust, in fact, makes good business sense and has been around since the beginning of trade centuries ago. The solution then was the same as it still is today—for both parties to use a mutually trusted go-between who can ensure that the payment is held until the merchandise is in fact delivered according to the terms of the trade contract. The go-between representatives employed by the importer and exporter are still, as they were in the past, the local domestic banks involved in international business.

EXPORTING TO INTERNATIONAL MARKETS American companies may manufacture their products in the United States and export them for sale in foreign markets. Exporting can be a relatively low-risk method of entering foreign markets.

Here is a simplified version of how it works. After signing contracts detailing the merchandise sold and terms for its delivery, an importer will ask its local bank to issue a **letter of credit** for the amount of money needed to pay for the merchandise. The letter of credit is issued "in favor of the exporter," meaning that the funds are tied specifically to the trade contract involved. The importer's bank forwards the letter of credit to the exporter's bank, which also normally deals in international transactions. The exporter's bank then notifies the exporter that a letter of credit has been received in its name, and the exporter can go ahead with the shipment. The carrier transporting the merchandise provides the exporter with evidence of the shipment in a document called a **bill of lading**. The exporter signs over title to the merchandise (now in transit) to its bank by delivering signed copies of the bill of lading and the letter of credit.

In exchange, the exporter issues a **draft** from the bank, which orders the importer's bank to pay for the merchandise. The draft, bill of lading, and letter of credit are sent from the exporter's bank to the importer's bank. Acceptance by the importer's bank leads to return of the draft and its sale by the exporter to its bank, meaning that the exporter receives cash and the bank assumes the risk of collecting the funds from the foreign bank. The importer is obliged to pay its bank on delivery of the merchandise, and the deal is complete.

In most cases, the letter of credit is part of a lending arrangement between the importer and its bank. Of course, both banks earn fees for issuing letters of credit and drafts and for handling the import–export services for their clients. Furthermore, the process incorporates the fact that both importer and exporter will have different local currencies and might even negotiate their trade in a third currency. The banks look after all the necessary exchanges. For example, the vast majority of international business is negotiated in U.S. dollars, even though the trade may be between countries other than the United States. Thus, although the importer may end up paying for the merchandise in its local currency and the exporter may receive payment

letter of credit issued by a bank on request of an importer stating that the bank will pay an amount of money to a stated beneficiary

bill of lading document issued by a transport carrier to an exporter to prove that merchandise has been shipped

draft issued by the exporter's bank, ordering the importer's bank to pay for the merchandise, thus guaranteeing payment once accepted by the importer's bank

in another local currency, the banks involved will exchange all necessary foreign funds in order to allow the deal to take place.

Alternatively, the exporting firm may ship its products to an *export–import agent*, which arranges the sale of the products to foreign intermediaries for a commission or fee. The agent is an independent firm—like other agents—that sells and may perform other marketing functions for the exporter. The exporter, however, retains title to the products during shipment and until they are sold.

An exporting firm also may establish its own *sales offices*, or *branches*, in foreign countries. These installations are international extensions of the firm's distribution system. They represent a deeper involvement in international business than the other exporting techniques we have discussed—and thus they carry a greater risk. The exporting firm maintains control over sales, and it gains both experience in and knowledge of foreign markets. Eventually, the firm also may develop its own sales force to operate in conjunction with foreign sales offices.

Exporting to international markets. American companies may manufacture their products in the United States and export them for sale in foreign markets. Exporting can be a relatively risk-free method of entering foreign markets.

Joint Ventures

A *joint venture* is a partnership formed to achieve a specific goal or to operate for a specific period of time. A joint venture with an established firm in a foreign country provides immediate market knowledge and access, reduced risk, and control over product attributes. However, joint-venture agreements established across national borders can become extremely complex. As a result, joint-venture agreements generally require a very high level of commitment from all the parties involved.

A joint venture may be used to produce and market an existing product in a foreign nation or to develop an entirely new product. Recently, for example, Archer Daniels Midland Company (ADM), one of the world's leading food processors, entered into a joint venture with Gruma SA, Mexico's largest corn flour and tortilla company. Besides a 22 percent stake in Gruma, ADM also received stakes in other joint ventures operated by Gruma. One of them will combine both companies' U.S. corn flour operations, which account for about 25 percent of the U.S. market. ADM also has a 40 percent stake in a Mexican wheat flour mill. ADM's joint venture increased its participation in the growing Mexican economy, where ADM already produces corn syrup, fructose, starch, and wheat flour.

Totally Owned Facilities

At a still deeper level of involvement in international business, a firm may develop *totally owned facilities,* that is, its own production and marketing facilities in one or more foreign nations. This *direct investment* provides complete control over operations, but it carries a greater risk than the joint venture. The firm is really establishing a subsidiary in a foreign country. Most firms do so only after they have acquired some knowledge of the host country's markets.

Direct investment may take either of two forms. In the first, the firm builds or purchases manufacturing and other facilities in the foreign country. It uses these facilities to produce its own established products and to market them in that country and perhaps in neighboring countries. Firms such as General Motors, Union Carbide, and Colgate-Palmolive are multinational companies with worldwide manufacturing facilities. Colgate-Palmolive factories are becoming *Eurofactories,* supplying neighboring countries as well as their own local markets.

A second form of direct investment in international business is the purchase of an existing firm in a foreign country under an arrangement that allows it to operate

Services Team Up to Enter India

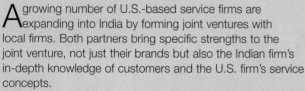

A growing number of U.S.-based service firms are expanding into India by forming joint ventures with local firms. Both partners bring specific strengths to the joint venture, not just their brands but also the Indian firm's in-depth knowledge of customers and the U.S. firm's service concepts.

For example, Cigna, which markets health insurance, has teamed up with TTK Group to sell insurance policies in India. TTK Group operates 1,500 retail stores and sells a variety of goods and services, including insurance. The joint venture will enable Cigna to reach consumers without creating a separate network of insurance agents—and TTK Group gains another product line to diversify its offerings.

CBS and its partner in India, Reliance Broadcast Networks, recently launched English-language channels to tap into the country's burgeoning market for television entertainment. CBS provides the content (including hit programs such as CSI) and Reliance provides its expertise in distribution and advertising sales for this joint venture, known as Big CBS.

Dunkin' Donuts has a joint venture with Jubilant Foodworks to open shops featuring an all-day menu of coffee, donuts, and other foods adapted to Indian tastes. In this partnership, "Dunkin' provides flexibility in localizing recipes, and we have strengths in food and culinary which we intend to leverage," explains Jubilant's chairman.

Sources: Based on information in Vikas Bajaj, "Cigna in Deal to Sell Health Insurance in India," *New York Times*, November 21, 2011, www.nytimes.com; Sanjeev Choudhary, "Dunkin' Donuts to Enter India with Jubilant Foodworks," *Reuters*, February 25, 2011, www.reuters.com; Nyay Bhushan, "Reliance, RTL Group Plan Joint Venture for English, Local-Language Channels," *Hollywood Reporter*, March 11, 2011, www.hollywoodreporter.com.

independently of the parent company. When Sony Corporation (a Japanese firm) decided to enter the motion picture business in the United States, it chose to purchase Columbia Pictures Entertainment, Inc., rather than start a new motion picture studio from scratch.

Strategic Alliances

strategic alliance a partnership formed to create competitive advantage on a worldwide basis

A **strategic alliance**, the newest form of international business structure, is a partnership formed to create competitive advantage on a worldwide basis. Strategic alliances are very similar to joint ventures. The number of strategic alliances is growing at an estimated rate of about 20 percent per year. In fact, in the automobile and computer industries, strategic alliances are becoming the predominant means of competing. International competition is so fierce and the costs of competing on a global basis are so high that few firms have all the resources needed to do it alone. Thus, individual firms that lack the internal resources essential for international success may seek to collaborate with other companies.

An example of such an alliance is the New United Motor Manufacturing, Inc. (NUMMI), formed by Toyota and General Motors to make automobiles of both firms. This enterprise united the quality engineering of Japanese cars with the marketing expertise and market access of General Motors.

Trading Companies

trading company provides a link between buyers and sellers in different countries

A **trading company** provides a link between buyers and sellers in different countries. A trading company, as its name implies, is not involved in manufacturing or owning assets related to manufacturing. It buys products in one country at the lowest price consistent with quality and sells to buyers in another country. An important function of trading companies is taking title to products and performing all the activities necessary to move the products from the domestic country to a foreign country. For example, large grain-trading companies operating out of home offices both in the United States and overseas control a major portion of the world's trade in basic food commodities. These trading companies sell homogeneous agricultural commodities that can be stored and moved rapidly in response to market conditions.

Countertrade

In the early 1990s, many developing nations had major restrictions on converting domestic currency into foreign currency. Therefore, exporters had to resort to barter agreements with importers. **Countertrade** is essentially an international barter transaction in which goods and services are exchanged for different goods and services. Examples include Saudi Arabia's purchase of ten 747 jets from Boeing with payment in crude oil and Philip Morris's sale of cigarettes to Russia in return for chemicals used to make fertilizers.

Multinational Firms

A **multinational enterprise** is a firm that operates on a worldwide scale without ties to any specific nation or region. The multinational firm represents the highest level of involvement in international business. It is equally "at home" in most countries of the world. In fact, as far as the operations of the multinational enterprise are concerned, national boundaries exist only on maps. It is, however, organized under the laws of its home country.

Table 3-3 shows the ten largest foreign and U.S. public multinational companies; the ranking is based on a composite score reflecting each company's best three out of four rankings for sales, profits, assets, and market value. Table 3-4 describes steps in entering international markets.

According to the chairman of the board of Dow Chemical Company, a multinational firm of U.S. origin, "The emergence of a world economy and of the multinational corporation has been accomplished hand in hand." He sees multinational enterprises moving toward what he calls the "anational company," a firm that has no nationality but belongs to all countries. In recognition of this movement, there already have been international conferences devoted to the question of how such enterprises would be controlled.

countertrade an international barter transaction

multinational enterprise a firm that operates on a worldwide scale without ties to any specific nation or region

Concept Check

✓ Two methods of engaging in international business may be categorized as either direct or indirect. How would you classify each of the methods described in this chapter? Why?

✓ What is a letter of credit? A bill of lading? A draft?

✓ In what ways is a multinational enterprise different from a large corporation that does business in several countries?

✓ What are the steps in entering international markets?

TABLE 3-3 The Ten Largest Foreign and U.S. Multinational Corporations

2012 Rank	Company	Business	Country	Revenue ($ millions)
1	Royal Dutch/Shell Group	Energy	Netherlands	484,489
2	ExxonMobil	Energy	United States	452,926
3	Walmart Stores	General merchandiser	United States	446,950
4	BP	Energy	United Kingdom	386,463
5	Sinopec Group	Energy	China	375,214
6	China Natural Petroleum	Energy	China	352,338
7	State Grid	Power grids	China	259,142
8	Chevron	Energy	United States	245,621
9	Conoco Phillips	Energy	United States	237,272
10	Toyota Motor	Automobiles	Japan	235,364

Source: http://money.cnn.com/magazine/fortune/global500/2012/snapshots/6388.html (accessed February 6, 2013).

TABLE 3-4 Steps in Entering International Markets

Step	Activity	Marketing Tasks
1	Identify exportable products.	Identify key selling features. Identify needs that they satisfy. Identify the selling constraints that are imposed.
2	Identify key foreign markets for the products.	Determine who the customers are. Pinpoint what and when they will buy. Do market research. Establish priority, or "target," countries.
3	Analyze how to sell in each priority market (methods will be affected by product characteristics and unique features of country/market).	Locate available government and private-sector resources. Determine service and backup sales requirements.
4	Set export prices and payment terms, methods, and techniques.	Establish methods of export pricing. Establish sales terms, quotations, invoices, and conditions of sale. Determine methods of international payments, secured and unsecured.
5	Estimate resource requirements and returns.	Estimate financial requirements. Estimate human resources requirements (full- or part-time export department or operation). Estimate plant production capacity. Determine necessary product adaptations.
6	Establish overseas distribution network.	Determine distribution agreement and other key marketing decisions (price, repair policies, returns, territory, performance, and termination). Know your customer (use U.S. Department of Commerce international marketing services).
7	Determine shipping, traffic, and documentation procedures and requirements.	Determine methods of shipment (air or ocean freight, truck, rail). Finalize containerization. Obtain validated export license. Follow export-administration documentation procedures.
8	Promote, sell, and be paid.	Use international media, communications, advertising, trade shows, and exhibitions. Determine the need for overseas travel (when, where, and how often?). Initiate customer follow-up procedures.
9	Continuously analyze current marketing, economic, and political situations.	Recognize changing factors influencing marketing strategies. Constantly re-evaluate.

Source: U.S. Department of Commerce, International Trade Administration, Washington, DC.

Learning Objective

6 Describe the various sources of export assistance.

SOURCES OF EXPORT ASSISTANCE

In August 2010, President Obama announced the *National Export Initiative* (NEI) to revitalize U.S. exports. Under the NEI, many federal agencies assist U.S. firms in developing export-promotion programs. The export services and programs of these agencies can help American firms to compete in foreign markets and create new jobs in the United States. For example, recently the International Trade Administration coordinated 77 trade missions to 38 countries. More than 1,120 companies secured over $1.25 billion in export sales during these missions. Table 3-5 provides an overview of selected export assistance programs.

These and other sources of export information enhance the business opportunities of U.S. firms seeking to enter expanding foreign markets. Another vital energy factor is financing.

Concept Check

✓ List some key sources of export assistance. How can these sources be useful to small business firms?

TABLE 3-5 U.S. Government Export Assistance Programs

1	U.S. Export Assistance Centers, www.sba.gov/oit/export/useac.html	Provides assistance in export marketing and trade finance
2	International Trade Administration, www.ita.doc.gov/	Offers assistance and information to exporters through its domestic and overseas commercial officers
3	U.S. and Foreign Commercial Services, www.export.gov/	Helps U.S. firms compete more effectively in the global marketplace and provides information on foreign markets
4	Advocacy Center, www.ita.doc.gov/advocacy	Facilitates advocacy to assist U.S. firms competing for major projects and procurements worldwide
5	Trade Information Center, www.ita.doc.gov/td/tic/	Provides U.S. companies information on federal programs and activities that support U.S. exports
6	STAT-USA/Internet, www.stat-usa.gov/	Offers a comprehensive collection of business, economic, and trade information on the Web
7	Small Business Administration, www.sba.gov/oit/	Publishes many helpful guides to assist small- and medium-sized companies
8	National Trade Data Bank, www.stat-usa.gov/tradtest.nsf	Provides international economic and export-promotion information supplied by more than 20 U.S. agencies

© CENGAGE LEARNING 2015

FINANCING INTERNATIONAL BUSINESS

Learning Objective

7 **Identify the institutions that help firms and nations finance international business.**

International trade compounds the concerns of financial managers. Currency exchange rates, tariffs and foreign exchange controls, and the tax structures of host nations all affect international operations and the flow of cash. In addition, financial managers must be concerned both with the financing of their international operations and with the means available to their customers to finance purchases.

Fortunately, along with business in general, a number of large banks have become international in scope. Many have established branches in major cities around the world. Thus, like firms in other industries, they are able to provide their services where and when they are needed. In addition, financial assistance is available from U.S. government and international sources.

Several of today's international financial organizations were founded many years ago to facilitate free trade and the exchange of currencies among nations. Some, such as the Inter-American Development Bank, are supported internationally and focus on developing countries. Others, such as the Export-Import Bank, are operated by one country but provide international financing.

The Export-Import Bank of the United States

The **Export-Import Bank of the United States**, created in 1934, is an independent agency of the U.S. government whose function is to assist in financing the exports of American firms. *Ex-Im Bank*, as it is commonly called, extends and guarantees credit to overseas buyers of American goods and services and guarantees short-term financing for exports. It also cooperates with commercial banks in helping American exporters to offer credit to their overseas customers. For example, in early 2013, the Ex-Im Bank guaranteed a $500 million loan to finance export of Boeing 777 jets to Aeroflot Russian Airlines. This loan created approximately 3,200 U.S. jobs.

According to Fred P. Hochberg, chairman and president of Ex-Im Bank, "Working with private lenders we are helping U.S. exporters put Americans to work producing the high quality goods and services that foreign buyers prefer. As part of President Obama's National Export Initiative, Ex-Im Bank's export financing is contributing to the goal of doubling of U.S. exports within the next five years."

Export-Import Bank of the United States an independent agency of the U.S. government whose function is to assist in financing the exports of American firms

Multilateral Development Banks

A **multilateral development bank (MDB)** is an internationally supported bank that provides loans to developing countries to help them grow. The most familiar is the World Bank, a cooperative of 188 member countries, which operates worldwide. Established in 1944 and headquartered in Washington, DC, the bank provides low-interest loans, interest-free credits, and grants to developing countries. The loans and grants help these countries to:

- supply safe drinking water
- build schools and train teachers
- increase agricultural productivity
- expand citizens' access to markets, jobs, and housing
- improve health care and access to water and sanitation
- manage forests and other natural resources
- build and maintain roads, railways, and ports, and
- reduce air pollution and protect the environment.[9]

Four other MDBs operate primarily in Central and South America, Asia, Africa, and Eastern and Central Europe. All five are supported by the industrialized nations, including the United States.

THE INTER-AMERICAN DEVELOPMENT BANK The Inter-American Development Bank (IDB), the oldest and largest regional bank, was created in 1959 by 19 Latin American countries and the United States. The bank, which is headquartered in Washington, DC, makes loans and provides technical advice and assistance to countries. Today, the IDB is owned by 48 member states.

THE ASIAN DEVELOPMENT BANK With 67 member nations, the Asian Development Bank (ADB), created in 1966 and headquartered in the Philippines, promotes economic and social progress in Asian and Pacific regions. The U.S. government is the second-largest contributor to the ADB's capital, after Japan.

multilateral development bank (MDB) an internationally supported bank that provides loans to developing countries to help them grow

THE AFRICAN DEVELOPMENT BANK The African Development Bank (AFDB), also known as *Banque Africaines de Development*, was established in 1964 with headquarters in Abidjan, Ivory Coast. Its members include 53 African and 24 non-African countries from the Americas, Europe, and Asia. The AFDB's goal is to foster the economic and social development of its African members. The bank pursues this goal through loans, research, technical assistance, and the development of trade programs.

EUROPEAN BANK FOR RECONSTRUCTION AND DEVELOPMENT Established in 1991 to encourage reconstruction and development in the Eastern and Central European countries, the London-based *European Bank for Reconstruction and Development* is owned by 64 countries and 2 intergovernmental institutions. Its loans are geared toward developing market-oriented economies and promoting private enterprise.

The International Monetary Fund

International Monetary Fund (IMF) an international bank with 188 member nations that makes short-term loans to developing countries experiencing balance-of-payment deficits

The **International Monetary Fund (IMF)** is an international bank with 188 member nations that makes short-term loans to developing countries experiencing balance-of-payment deficits. This financing is contributed by member nations, and it must be repaid with interest. Loans are provided primarily to fund international trade. Created in 1945 and headquartered in Washington, DC, the bank's main goals are to:

- promote international monetary cooperation
- facilitate the expansion and balanced growth of international trade

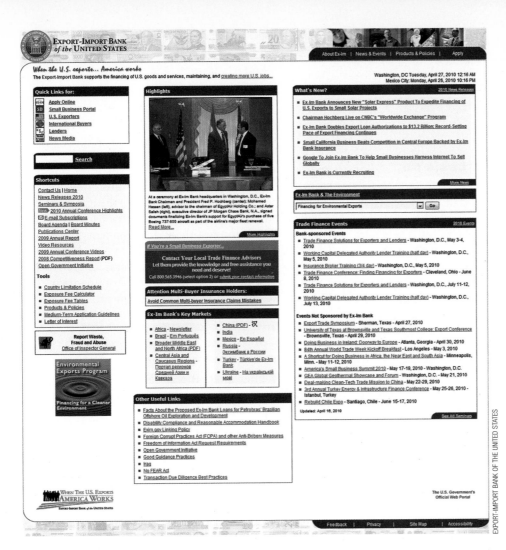

Mission possible. The Export-Import Bank of the United States (Ex-Im Bank) is the official export credit agency of the United States. Ex-Im Bank's mission is to assist in financing U.S. goods and services to international markets. With more than 78 years of experience, Ex-Im Bank has supported more than $400 billion of U.S. exports, primarily to developing markets worldwide.

- promote exchange rate stability
- assist in establishing a multilateral system of payments, and
- make resources available to members experiencing balance-of-payment difficulties.

The Challenges Ahead

In a 2012 speech at Oxford University, Pascal Lamy, Director-General of the World Trade Organization stated, "We live in a world of ever-growing independence and interconnectedness. Our interdependence has grown beyond anyone's imagination. The world of today is virtually unrecognizable from the world in which we lived one generation ago." The most striking example of globalization is Apple. Apple's iPod is designed in the United States, manufactured with components from Japan, Korea, and several other Asian countries, and assembled in China by a company from Chinese Taipei. Nowadays, most products are not "Made in the UK" or "Made in France"; they are in fact "Made in the World."[10]

In 2013, the global economic recovery remained sluggish. Financial challenges in some euro-area economies slowed the economic growth. However, WTO rules and principles have assisted governments in keeping markets open and they now provide a platform for which the trade can grow as the global economy improves. According to Mr. Lamy, "We see the light at the end of the tunnel and trade promises to be an important part of the recovery. But we must avoid derailing any economic revival through protectionism."

Concept Check

✓ What is the Export-Import Bank of the United States? How does it assist U.S. exporters?

✓ What is a multilateral development bank (MDB)? Who supports these banks?

✓ What is the International Monetary Fund? What types of loans does the IMF provide?

Summary

1 Explain the economic basis for international business.

International business encompasses all business activities that involve exchanges across national boundaries. International trade is based on specialization, whereby each country produces the goods and services that it can produce more efficiently than any other goods and services. A nation is said to have a comparative advantage relative to these goods. International trade develops when each nation trades its surplus products for those in short supply.

A nation's balance of trade is the difference between the value of its exports and the value of its imports. Its balance of payments is the difference between the flow of money into and out of the nation. Generally, a negative balance of trade is considered unfavorable.

2 Discuss the restrictions nations place on international trade, the objectives of these restrictions, and their results.

Despite the benefits of world trade, nations tend to use tariffs and nontariff barriers (import quotas, embargoes, and other restrictions) to limit trade. These restrictions typically are justified as being needed to protect a nation's economy, industries, citizens, or security. They can result in the loss of jobs, higher prices, fewer choices in the marketplace, and the misallocation of resources.

3 Outline the extent of international business and the world economic outlook for trade.

World trade is generally increasing. Trade between the United States and other nations is increasing in dollar value but decreasing in terms of our share of the world market. Exports as a percentage of U.S. GDP have increased steadily since 1985, except in the 2001 and 2008 recessions.

4 Discuss international trade agreements and international economic organizations working to foster trade.

The General Agreement on Tariffs and Trade (GATT) was formed to dismantle trade barriers and provide an environment in which international business can grow. Today, the World Trade Organization (WTO) and various economic communities carry on this mission. These world economic communities include the European Union, the NAFTA, the CAFTA, the Association of Southeast Asian Nations, the Pacific Rim, the Commonwealth of Independent States, the Caribbean Basin Initiative, the Common Market of the Southern Cone, the Organization of Petroleum Exporting Countries, and the Organization for Economic Cooperation and Development.

5 Define the methods by which a firm can organize for and enter into international markets.

A firm can enter international markets in several ways. It may license a foreign firm to produce and market its products. It may export its products and sell them through foreign intermediaries or its own sales organization abroad, or it may sell its exports outright to an export–import merchant. It may enter into a joint venture with a foreign firm. It may establish its own foreign subsidiaries, or it may develop into a multinational enterprise.

Generally, each of these methods represents an increasingly deeper level of involvement in international business, with licensing being the simplest and the development of a multinational corporation the most involved.

6 Describe the various sources of export assistance.

Many government and international agencies provide export assistance to U.S. and foreign firms. Sources of export assistance include U.S. Export Assistance Centers, the International Trade Administration, U.S. and Foreign Commercial Services, Export Legal Assistance Network, Advocacy Center, National Trade Data Bank, and other government and international agencies.

7 Identify the institutions that help firms and nations finance international business.

The financing of international trade is more complex than that of domestic trade. Institutions such as the Ex-Im Bank and the International Monetary Fund have been established to provide financing and ultimately to increase world trade for American and international firms.

Key Terms

You should now be able to define and give an example relevant to each of the following terms:

international business (67)
absolute advantage (67)
comparative advantage (67)
exporting (68)
importing (68)
balance of trade (68)
trade deficit (68)
balance of payments (70)
import duty (tariff) (70)

dumping (70)
nontariff barrier (71)
import quota (71)
embargo (71)
foreign-exchange control (71)
currency devaluation (71)
General Agreement on
  Tariffs and Trade
  (GATT) (77)

World Trade Organization
  (WTO) (78)
economic community (78)
licensing (81)
letter of credit (82)
bill of lading (82)
draft (82)
strategic alliance (84)
trading company (84)

countertrade (85)
multinational enterprise (85)
Export-Import Bank of the
  United States (87)
multilateral development
  bank (MDB) (88)
International Monetary
  Fund (IMF) (88)

Discussion Questions

1. The United States restricts imports but, at the same time, supports the WTO and international banks whose objective is to enhance world trade. As a member of Congress, how would you justify this contradiction to your constituents?

2. What effects might the devaluation of a nation's currency have on its business firms, its consumers, and the debts it owes to other nations?

3. Should imports to the United States be curtailed by, say, 20 percent to eliminate our trade deficit? What might happen if this were done?

4. When should a firm consider expanding from strictly domestic trade to international trade? When should it consider becoming further involved in international trade? What factors might affect the firm's decisions in each case?

5. How can a firm obtain the expertise needed to produce and market its products in, for example, the EU?

Test Yourself

Matching Questions

1. _____ The total value of a nation's exports minus the total value of its imports over some period of time.

2. _____ The ability to produce a specific product more efficiently than any other nation.

3. _____ Selling and shipping raw materials or products to other nations.

4. _____ The ability to produce a specific product more efficiently than any other product.

5. _____ All business activities that involve exchanges across national boundaries.

6. _____ The total flow of money into a country minus the total flow of money out of that country over the same period of time.

7. _____ A tax levied on a particular foreign product entering a country.

8. _____ A complete halt to trading with a particular nation or in a particular product.

9. _____ An international barter transaction.

10. _____ An internationally supported bank that provides loans to developing countries to help them grow.

a. countertrade
b. foreign exchange control
c. multilateral development bank (MDB)
d. absolute advantage
e. import duty
f. embargo
g. exporting
h. international business
i. balance of trade
j. comparative advantage
k. Export-Import
l. balance of payments

True False Questions

11. **T F** The United States has enjoyed a trade surplus during the last two decades.

12. **T F** Tariff is a tax levied on a particular foreign product entering a country.

13. **T F** Quotas may be set on worldwide imports or on imports from a specific country.

14. **T F** The participants in the Kennedy Round have succeeded in reducing tariffs by less than 20 percent.

15. **T F** Licensing and exporting can be considered relatively low-risk methods of entering foreign markets.

16. **T F** A letter of credit is issued in favor of the importer.

17. **T F** A letter of credit is issued by the transport carrier to the exporter to prove that merchandise has been shipped.

18. **T F** Strategic alliances are partnerships formed to create competitive advantage on a worldwide basis.

19. **T F** A firm that has no ties to a specific nation or region and operates on a worldwide scale is called a national enterprise.

20. **T F** The International Monetary Fund (IMF) makes short-term loans to developing countries experiencing balance-of-payment deficits.

Multiple-Choice Questions

21. _____ By definition, every country has a(n) advantage in some product.
 a. relative
 b. absolute
 c. comparative
 d. superior
 e. inferior

22. _____ Purchasing products or materials in other nations and bringing them into one's own country is
 a. trading.
 b. balancing.
 c. exporting.
 d. importing.
 e. dumping.

23. _____ General Motors and Ford products produced in the United States are found around the world. The United States is these automobiles.
 a. tariffing
 b. importing
 c. exporting
 d. releasing
 e. dumping

24. _____ is the exportation of large quantities of a product at a price lower than that of the same product in the home market.
 a. Embargo
 b. Duty
 c. Dumping
 d. Export quota
 e. Dropping

25. _____ A complete halt to trading with a particular nation or in a particular product is called a(n)
 a. embargo.
 b. stoppage.
 c. stay.
 d. closure.
 e. barricade.

26. _____ Because it has not been around long enough to establish itself, the Russian automobile industry could be classified as a(n)
 a. hopeless industry.
 b. soft industry.
 c. infant industry.
 d. protected industry.
 e. toddler industry.

27. _____ The World Trade Organization was created by the
 a. Kennedy Round.
 b. United Nations.
 c. League of Nations.
 d. Tokyo Round.
 e. Uruguay Round.

28. _____ CAFTA, NAFTA, OECD, and OPEC are all examples of
 a. political organizations.
 b. peace treaties.
 c. international economic communities.
 d. World Trade Organization members.
 e. democratic organizations.

29. _____ Foreign licensing is similar to
 a. starting from scratch.
 b. franchising.
 c. wholesaling.
 d. establishing a subsidiary in another country.
 e. establishing a sales office in a foreign country.

30. _____ Established in 1944 and headquartered in Washington, D.C., the World Bank is an example of
 a. Eximbank
 b. IMF
 c. MDB
 d. EFTA
 e. LAFTA

Answers to the Test Yourself questions appear at the end of the book on page TY-1.

Video Case

Keeping Brazil's Economy Hot

It's been hot in Brazil. No, we're not talking about the country's temperature: We're talking about its economy, which has been growing at a heated pace. In 2010, the country's GDP grew by 7.5 percent. That's a growth rate developed countries such as the United States haven't experienced for years, if not decades. Although Brazil's growth rate slowed considerably in 2011 and 2012 due to the global economic crisis, it has fared better than many other nations. Recently it surpassed the United Kingdom as the sixth-largest economy in the world.

Why has Brazil done so well economically? Increased world trade is one reason why. The country has an abundant amount of natural resources firms in other countries around the world are eager to buy—especially companies in the fast-growing nation of China. Greater exports have also helped 40 million Brazilians rise up out of poverty and into the middle class. Their massive spending power is creating new markets for multinational companies ranging from McDonald's and Whirlpool to Nestlé, Avon, and Volkswagen. Brazil has become Avon's largest market. Volkswagen now sells more cars in Brazil than it does Germany, where the company is headquartered. "China may have over a billion inhabitants, but Brazil has 200,000 consumers," explains Ivan Zurita, the president of Nestle's Brazil division.

Clouds on the horizon threaten to cool off Brazil's growth, however. To begin with, the country is concerned that its trade with China is out of balance. Although China purchases more natural resources from Brazil than any other nation, it doesn't purchase near as many manufactured goods from Brazil as it exports to it.

A bigger issue is the appreciation of Brazil's currency, the real. Massive amounts of money have been flowing into Brazil to take advantage of the nation's high interest rates and growth opportunities. This has increased the demand for the real, causing its value to rise by nearly 50 percent relative to other currencies. The good news is that the stronger real has made imported products cheaper for Brazilians to buy. The bad news is that products made in Brazil have become more expensive for the rest of the world to purchase, slowing the country's exports and growth.

Businesses in Brazil have lobbied the government to weaken the real so their products are better able to compete against imports. Their efforts appear to have paid off. Recently, Guido Mantega, Brazil's minister of finance, said the country will take steps "as needed" to weaken the real. The government has also imposed tariffs on a number of imported products, including cars, shoes, chemicals, and textiles, and signed a trade deal with Mexico that put a quota on the number of automobiles imported from that country.

Imports and the value of the real are not the only clouds threatening Brazil, though. Businesses in the country face a great deal of bureaucratic red tape, heavy regulations, and tax rates that are some of the highest in the world. To deal with these problems, Brazilian President Dilma Rousseff has announced that her administration will eliminate payroll taxes for employers in industries hardest hit by imports. To further ease the nation's growing pains, Brazil's development bank, BDM, will subsidize business loans to boost the production of many products, including tablets and off-shore oil rigs. The goal is to stimulate technological innovations that will enable manufacturers to produce higher-value products so Brazil doesn't have to rely on natural resources to fuel its growth. "Look, a government isn't made on the second or third day," Rousseff has said about her administration's incremental efforts to keep Brazil's emerging economy moving forward. "It's made over time. Things mature."[1]

Questions

1. Do you think the efforts of Brazil's government to keep the economy growing will be successful? Why or why not?
2. What downsides might Brazil experience by implementing quotas, tariffs, and measures to devalue its currency?

Building Skills for Career Success

1. Social Media Exercise

Although Nike was founded in the Pacific Northwest and still has its corporate headquarters near Beaverton, Oregon, the company has become a multinational enterprise. The firm employs more than 35,000 people across six continents and is now a global marketer of footwear, apparel, and athletic equipment.

Because it operates in 160 countries around the globe and manufactures products in over 900 factories in 47 different countries, sustainability is a big initiative for Nike. Today, Nike uses the YouTube social media site to share its sustainability message with consumers, employees, investors, politicians, and other interested stakeholders. To learn about the company's efforts to sustain the planet, follow these steps:

- Make an Internet connection and go to the YouTube website (www.youtube.com).
- Enter the words "Nike" and "Sustainability" in the search window and click the search button.

1. View at least three different YouTube videos about Nike's sustainability efforts.
2. Based on the information in the videos you watched, do you believe that Nike is a good corporate citizen because of its efforts to sustain the planet? Why or why not?
3. Prepare a one to two page report that describes how Nike is taking steps to reduce waste, improve the environment, and reduce its carbon footprint while manufacturing products around the globe.

2. Building Team Skills

The North American Free Trade Agreement among the United States, Mexico, and Canada went into effect on January 1, 1994. It has made a difference in trade among the countries and has affected the lives of many people.

Assignment
1. Working in teams and using the resources of your library, investigate NAFTA. Answer the following questions:
   a. What are NAFTA's objectives?
   b. What are its benefits?
   c. What impact has NAFTA had on trade, jobs, and travel?
   d. Some Americans were opposed to the implementation of NAFTA. What were their objections? Have any of these objections been justified?
   e. Has NAFTA influenced your life? How?
2. Summarize your answers in a written report. Your team also should be prepared to give a class presentation.

3. Researching Different Careers

Today, firms around the world need employees with special skills. In some countries, such employees are not always available, and firms then must search abroad for qualified applicants. One way they can do this is through global workforce databases. As business and trade operations continue to grow globally, you may one day find yourself working in a foreign country, perhaps for an American company doing business there or for a foreign company. In what foreign country would you like to work? What problems might you face?

Assignment
1. Choose a country in which you might like to work.
2. Research the country. The National Trade Data Bank is a good place to start. Find answers to the following questions:
   a. What language is spoken in this country? Are you proficient in it? What would you need to do if you are not proficient?
   b. What are the economic, social, and legal systems like in this nation?
   c. What is its history?
   d. What are its culture and social traditions like? How might they affect your work or your living arrangements?
3. Describe what you have found out about this country in a written report. Include an assessment of whether you would want to work there and the problems you might face if you did.

Running a Business
Part 1

Let's Go Get a Graeter's!

Only a tiny fraction of family-owned businesses are still growing four generations after their founding, but happily for lovers of premium-quality ice cream, Graeter's is one of them.

Now a $30 million firm with national distribution, Graeter's was founded in Cincinnati in 1870 by Louis Charles Graeter and his wife, Regina Graeter. The young couple made ice cream and chocolate candies in the back room of their shop, sold them in the front room, and lived upstairs. Ice cream was a special treat in this era before refrigeration, and the Graeters started from scratch every day to make theirs from the freshest, finest ingredients. Even after freezers were invented, the Graeters continued to make ice cream in small batches to preserve the quality, texture, and rich flavor.

After her husband's death, Regina's entrepreneurial leadership became the driving force behind Graeter's expansion from 1920 until well into the 1950s. At a time when few women owned or operated a business, Regina opened 20 new Graeter's stores in the Cincinnati area and added manufacturing capacity to support this ambitious—and successful—growth strategy. Her sons and grandchildren followed her into the business and continued to open ice-cream shops all around Ohio and beyond. Today, three of Regina's great-grandsons run Graeter's with the same attention to quality that made the firm famous. In her honor, the street in front of the company's ultramodern Cincinnati factory is named Regina Graeter Way.

The Scoop on Graeter's Success

Graeter's fourth-generation owners are Richard Graeter II (CEO), Robert (Bob) Graeter (vice president of operations), and Chip Graeter (vice president of retail operations). They grew up in the business, learning through hands-on experience how to do everything from packing a pint of ice cream to locking up the store at night. They also absorbed the family's dedication to product quality, a key reason for the company's enduring success. "Our family has always been contented to make a little less profit in order to ensure our long-term survival," explains the CEO.

Throughout its history, Graeter's has used a unique, time-consuming manufacturing process to produce its signature ice creams in small batches. "Our competition is making thousands and thousands of gallons a day," says Chip Graeter. "We are making hundreds of gallons a day at the most. All of our ice cream is packed by hand, so it's a very laborious process." Graeter's "French pot" manufacturing method ensures that very little air gets into the product. As a result, the company's ice cream is dense and creamy, not light and fluffy—so dense, in fact, that each pint weighs nearly a pound.

Another success factor is the use of simple, fresh ingredients like high-grade chocolate, choice seasonal fruits, and farm-fresh cream. Graeter's imports some ingredients, such as vanilla from Madagascar, and buys other ingredients from U.S. producers known for their quality. "We use a really great grade of chocolate," says Bob Graeter. "We don't cut corners on that … Specially selected great black raspberries, strawberries, blueberries, and cherries go into our ice cream because we feel that we want to provide flavor not from artificial or unnatural ingredients but from really quality, ripe, rich fruits." Instead of tiny chocolate chips, Graeter's products contain giant chunks formed when liquid chocolate is poured into the ice-cream base just before the mixture is frozen and packed into pints.

Maintaining the Core of Success

Graeter's "fanatical devotion to product quality" and its time-tested recipes have not changed over the years. The current generation of owners is maintaining this core of the company's success while mixing in a generous dash of innovation. "If you just preserve the core," Bob Graeter says, "ultimately you stagnate. And if you are constantly stimulating progress and looking for new ideas, well, then you risk losing what was important. . . . Part of your secret to long-term success is knowing what your core is and holding to that. Once you know what you're really all about and what is most important to you, you can change everything else."

One of those "important" things is giving back to the community and its families via local charities and other initiatives. "Community involvement is just part of being a good corporate citizen," observes Richard Graeter. When Graeter's celebrated a recent new store opening, for example, it made a cash donation to the neighborhood public library. It is also a major sponsor of The Cure Starts Now Foundation, a research foundation seeking a cure for pediatric brain cancer. In line with its focus on natural goodness, Graeter's has been doing its part to preserve the environment by recycling and by boosting production efficiency to conserve water, energy, and other resources.

Graeter's Looks to the Future

Even though Graeter's recipes reflect its 19th-century heritage, the company is clearly a 21st-century operation. It has 150,000 Facebook "likes," connects with brand fans on Twitter, and invites customers to subscribe to its e-mail newsletter. The company sells its products online and ships orders via United Parcel Service to ice-cream lovers across the continental United States. Its newly-opened production facility uses state-of-the-art refrigeration, storage, and sanitation—yet the ice cream is still mixed by hand rather than by automated equipment. With an eye toward future growth, Graeter's is refining its information system to provide managers with all the details they need to make timely decisions in today's fast-paced business environment.

Graeter's competition ranges from small, local businesses to international giants such as Unilever, which owns Ben & Jerry's, and Nestle, which owns Haagen-Dazs. Throughout the economic ups and downs of recent years, Graeter's has continued to expand, and its ice creams are now distributed through 6,200 stores in 43 states. Oprah Winfrey and other celebrities have praised its products in public. But the owners are just as proud of their home-town success. "Graeter's in Cincinnati is synonymous with ice cream," says Bob Graeter. "People will say, 'Let's go get a Graeter's.' "[12]

Questions

1. How have Graeter's owners used the four factors of production to build the business over time?
2. Which of Graeter's stakeholders are most affected by the family's decision to take a long-term view of the business rather than aiming for short-term profit? Explain your answer.
3. Knowing that Graeter's competes with multinational corporations as well as small businesses, would you recommend that Graeter's expand by licensing its brand to a company in another country? Why or why not?

Building a Business Plan: Part 1

A *business plan* is a carefully constructed guide for a person starting a business. The purpose of a well-prepared business plan is to show how practical and attainable the entrepreneur's goals are. It also serves as a concise document that potential investors can examine to see if they would like to invest or assist in financing a new venture. A business plan should include the following 12 components:

- Introduction
- Executive summary
- Benefits to the community
- Company and industry
- Management team
- Manufacturing and operations plan
- Labor force
- Marketing plan
- Financial plan
- Exit strategy
- Critical risks and assumptions
- Appendix

A brief description of each of these sections is provided in Chapter 5 (see also Table 5-3 on page 139).

This is the first of seven exercises that appear at the ends of each of the seven major parts in this textbook. The goal of these exercises is to help you work through the preceding components to create your own business plan. For example, in the exercise for this part, you will make decisions and complete the research that will help you to develop the introduction for your business plan and the benefits to the community that your business will provide. In the exercises for Parts 2 through 6, you will add more components to your plan and eventually build a plan that actually could be used to start a business. The flowchart shown in Figure 3.6 gives an overview of the steps you will be taking to prepare your business plan.

The First Step: Choosing Your Business

One of the first steps for starting your own business is to decide what type of business you want to start. Take some time to think about this decision. Before proceeding, answer the following questions:

- Why did you choose this type of business?
- Why do you think this business will be successful?
- Would you enjoy owning and operating this type of business?

Warning: Do not rush this step. This step often requires much thought, but it is well worth the time and effort. As an added bonus, you are more likely to develop a quality business plan if you really want to open this type of business.

Now that you have decided on a specific type of business, it is time to begin the planning process. The goal for this part is to complete the introduction and benefits-to-the-community components of your business plan.

Before you begin, it is important to note that the business plan is not a document that is written and then set aside. It is a living document that an entrepreneur should refer to continuously in order to ensure that plans are being carried through appropriately. As the entrepreneur begins to execute the plan, he or she should monitor the business environment continuously and make changes to the plan to address any challenges or opportunities that were not foreseen originally.

Throughout this course, you will, of course, be building your knowledge about business. Therefore, it will be appropriate for you to continually revisit parts of the plan that you have already written in order to refine them based on your more comprehensive knowledge. You will find that writing your plan is not a simple matter of starting at the beginning and moving chronologically through to the end. Instead, you probably will find yourself jumping around the various components, making refinements as you go. In fact, the second component—the executive summary—should be written last, but because of its comprehensive nature and its importance to potential investors, it appears after the introduction in the final business plan. By the end of this course, you should be able to put the finishing touches on your plan, making sure that all the parts create a comprehensive and sound whole so that you can present it for evaluation.

The Introduction Component

1.1. Start with the cover page. Provide the business name, street address, telephone number, Web address (if any), name(s) of owner(s) of the business, and the date the plan is issued.

1.2. Next, provide background information on the company and include the general nature of the business: retailing, manufacturing, or service; what your product or service is; what is unique about it; and why you believe that your business will be successful.

FIGURE 3-6 Business Plan

Steps in creating a business plan

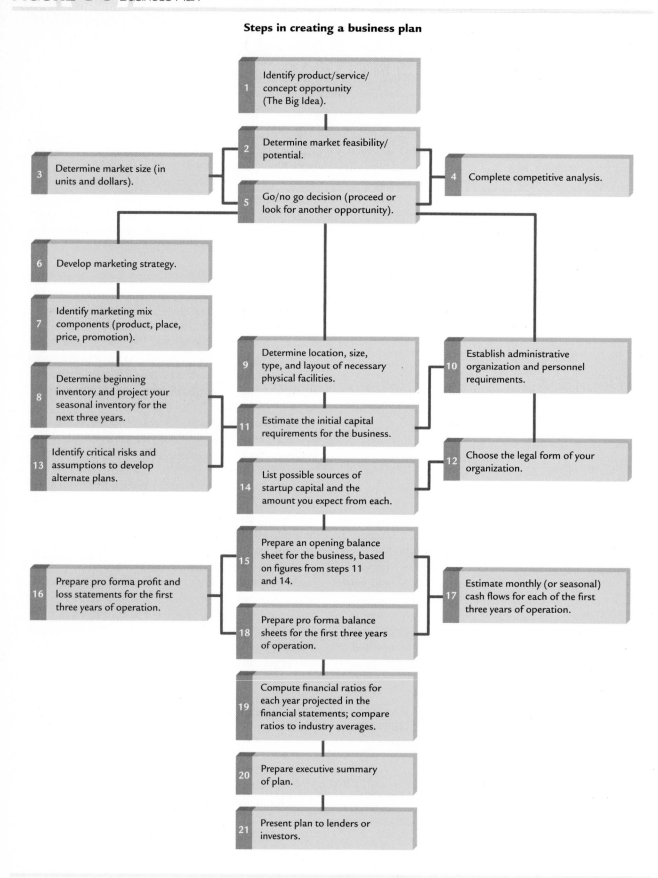

1. Identify product/service/concept opportunity (The Big Idea).
2. Determine market feasibility/potential.
3. Determine market size (in units and dollars).
4. Complete competitive analysis.
5. Go/no go decision (proceed or look for another opportunity).
6. Develop marketing strategy.
7. Identify marketing mix components (product, place, price, promotion).
8. Determine beginning inventory and project your seasonal inventory for the next three years.
9. Determine location, size, type, and layout of necessary physical facilities.
10. Establish administrative organization and personnel requirements.
11. Estimate the initial capital requirements for the business.
12. Choose the legal form of your organization.
13. Identify critical risks and assumptions to develop alternate plans.
14. List possible sources of startup capital and the amount you expect from each.
15. Prepare an opening balance sheet for the business, based on figures from steps 11 and 14.
16. Prepare pro forma profit and loss statements for the first three years of operation.
17. Estimate monthly (or seasonal) cash flows for each of the first three years of operation.
18. Prepare pro forma balance sheets for the first three years of operation.
19. Compute financial ratios for each year projected in the financial statements; compare ratios to industry averages.
20. Prepare executive summary of plan.
21. Present plan to lenders or investors.

Source: Hatten, Timothy, *Small Business Management*, Fifth Edition. Copyright © 2012 Cengage Learning.

1.3. Then include a summary statement of the business's financial needs, if any. You probably will need to revise your financial needs summary after you complete a detailed financial plan later in Part 6.

1.4. Finally, include a statement of confidentiality to keep important information away from potential competitors.

The Benefits-to-the-Community Component

In this section, describe the potential benefits to the community that your business could provide. Chapter 2 in your textbook, "Being Ethical and Socially Responsible," can help you in answering some of these questions. At the very least, address the following issues:

1.5. Describe the number of skilled and nonskilled jobs the business will create, and indicate how purchases of supplies and other materials can help local businesses.

1.6. Next, describe how providing needed goods or services will improve the community and its standard of living.

1.7. Finally, state how your business can develop new technical, management, or leadership skills; offer attractive wages; and provide other types of individual growth.

Review of Business Plan Activities

Read over the information that you have gathered. Because the Building a Business Plan exercises at the end of Parts 2 through 7 are built on the work you do in Part 1, make sure that any weaknesses or problem areas are resolved before continuing. Finally, write a brief statement that summarizes all the information for this part of the business plan.

Endnotes

1. Based on information in "Strong Dollar Dents Coca-Cola's Profits," *New York Times*, October 16, 2012, www.nytimes.com; Leon Stafford, "Coca-Cola to Spend $30 Billion to Grow Globally," *Atlanta Journal-Constitution*, September 9, 2012, www.ajc.com; Melanie Lee, "Exclusive: Coke Adds Billion Dollar Brand from China to Portfolio," *Reuters*, February 1, 2011, www.reuters.com; Lara O'Reilly, "Coke Restructures Global Businesses," *Marketing Week*, July 31, 2012, www.marketingweek.co.uk; www.coca-cola.com.
2. The White House, Office of the Press Secretary, Press Release, August 6, 2002.
3. International Trade Administration website at www.trade.gov/press /press-releases/2013/export-factsheet-february2013-020813.pdf (accessed May 26, 2013).
4. This section draws heavily from the *World Economic Outlook* International Monetary Fund website at www.imf.org/external/pubs/ft /weo/2013/update/01/index.htm (accessed February 5, 2013).
5. Ibid.
6. U.S. Department of Commerce, International Trade Administration, "Jobs Supported by Exports: An Update," March 12, 2012, www.trade .gov/mas/ian/index.asp (accessed February 6, 2013), and The White House Fact Sheet at www.whitehouse.gov/blog/2012/05/30/president (accessed February 6, 2013).
7. The World Trade Organization website at www.wto.org/english/news_e /pres11_e/pres11_e.htm (accessed February 5, 2013).
8. Office of the United States Trade Representative website at www.ustr. gov/tpp (accessed February 4, 2013).
9. The World Trade Organization at www.wto.org/english/news_e/sppl_e /spp1220_htm, (accessed February 6, 2013).
10. Ibid.
11. Sources: Andre Soliani, "Surge," *Bloomberg BusinessWeek*, April 3, 2012, www.businessweek.com; "Invigorated Roussef Shifts Focus to 'Brazil Cost,'" *Reuters*, April 2, 2012, www.reuters.com; Komal Sri-Kumar, "Brazil Should Embrace a Freer Market," *Financial Times*, March 6, 2012, www .ft.com; "Multinationals Choose Brazilian Investment," *Obelisk Investment News*, May 4, 2011, www.obeliskinternational.com.
12. Sources: Based on information from Kimberly L. Jackson, "Graeter's Premium Chocolate Chip Ice Cream Lands at Stop & Shop," *Newark Star-Ledger (NJ)*, April 4, 2012, www.nj.com; "Graeter's Ice Cream Debuts in Bay Area," *Tampa Bay Times (St. Petersburg, FL)*, January 10, 2012, p. 4B; Jim Carper, "Graeter's Runs a Hands-on Ice Cream Plant," *Dairy Foods*, August 2011, pp. 36+; Jim Carper, "The Greater Good," *Dairy Foods*, August 2011, pp. 95+; "Graeter's Unveils New 'Mystery Flavor,'" *Dayton Daily News*, March 29, 2012, www.daytondailynews. com; Bob Driehaus, "A Cincinnati Ice Cream Maker Aims Big," *New York Times*, September 11, 2010, www.nytimes.com; Lucy May, "Graeter's Northern Kentucky Franchisee Puts Stores on the Block," *Business Courier*, August 6, 2010, http://cincinnati.bizjournals.com; www.graeters .com; interviews with company staff and Cengage videos about Graeter's.

Chapter 5

Small Business, Entrepreneurship, and Franchises

Learning Objectives

Once you complete this chapter, you will be able to:

1 Define what a small business is and recognize the fields in which small businesses are concentrated.

2 Identify the people who start small businesses and the reasons why some succeed and many fail.

3 Assess the contributions of small businesses to our economy.

4 Describe the advantages and disadvantages of operating a small business.

5 Explain how the Small Business Administration helps small businesses.

6 Explain the concept and types of franchising.

7 Analyze the growth of franchising and its advantages and disadvantages.

Why Should You Care?

America's small businesses drive the U.S. economy. Small businesses represent 99.7 percent of all employer firms, and there is a good probability that you will work for a small business or perhaps even start your own business. This chapter can help you to become a good employee or a successful entrepreneur.

Get Flashcards, Quizzes, Games, Crosswords, and more @ www.cengagebrain.com.

Dunkin' Brands Helps Franchisees Brew up Sales

Massachusetts-based Dunkin' Brands (www.dunkinbrands.com) is in the middle of a growth spurt that will bring thousands of new Dunkin' Donuts coffee shops and Baskin-Robbins ice-cream shops under the control of local entrepreneurs worldwide. As a franchisor, Dunkin' Brands works with entrepreneurs who want to own their own business backed by the advantages of a well-known brand and proven methods of operation. Currently, franchisees operate a total of nearly 17,000 Dunkin' Donuts and Baskin-Robbins stores and, in all, ring up global revenues of $8.3 billion each year.

Baskin-Robbins, famous for its wide variety of ice-cream flavors, is especially strong outside the United States. Franchisees have signed to launch new shops across Asia and in other regions where economic growth is boosting personal income. Meanwhile, Dunkin' Donuts has an aggressive growth strategy for increasing the number of U.S. franchised stores to 15,000 by 2030. Brewing up this level of expansion means building on its track record of success in the Eastern states, where Dunkin' Donuts has long been popular, to help franchisees open shops in the Western states, where the brand has been less visible—until now.

Westward expansion will put Dunkin' Donuts into some areas dominated by powerful rivals like Starbucks (which doesn't offer franchises) as well as independent coffee shops that have already carved out a loyal customer base. To give franchise owners even more competitive strength, Dunkin' Donuts has stepped up its introduction of new menu items, including non-breakfast foods and beverages to attract customers throughout the day. It's also increased efficiency through cutting-edge technology that streamlines customer transactions and store operations procedures. Finally, the company is giving the Dunkin' Donuts brand a bigger boost nationwide through advertising, social media, online promotions, mobile communications, and marketing alliances with major sports teams.[1]

Did You Know?

Dunkin' Donuts has 10,000 franchised locations worldwide and its sister company, Baskin-Robbins, has nearly 7,000 franchised locations worldwide.

Most businesses start small and those that survive usually stay small. However, they provide a solid foundation for our economy—as employers, as suppliers and purchasers of goods and services, and as taxpayers.

In this chapter, we do not take small businesses for granted. Instead, we look closely at this important business sector—beginning with a definition of small business, a description of industries that often attract small businesses, and a profile of some of the people who start small businesses. Next, we consider the importance of small businesses in our economy. We also present the advantages and disadvantages of smallness in business. We then describe services provided by the Small Business Administration, a government agency formed to assist owners and managers of small businesses. We conclude the chapter with a discussion of the pros and cons of franchising, an approach to small-business ownership that has become very popular in the last 55 years.

Learning Objective

1 Define what a small business is and recognize the fields in which small businesses are concentrated.

small business one that is independently owned and operated for profit and is not dominant in its field

SMALL BUSINESS: A PROFILE

The Small Business Administration (SBA) defines a **small business** as "one which is independently owned and operated for profit and is not dominant in its field." How small must a firm be not to dominate its field? That depends on the particular industry it is in. The SBA has developed the following specific "smallness" guidelines for the various industries, as shown in Table 5-1.[2] The SBA periodically revises and simplifies its small-business size regulations.

Annual sales in millions of dollars may not seem very small. However, for many firms, profit is only a small percentage of total sales. Thus, a firm may earn only $50,000 or $60,000 on yearly sales of $1 million—and that is small in comparison

TABLE 5-1 Industry Group–Size Standards

Small-business size standards are usually stated in number of employees or average annual sales. In the United States, 99.7 percent of all businesses are considered small.

Industry Group	Size Standard
Manufacturing, mining industries	500 employees
Wholesale trade	100 employees
Agriculture	$750,000
Retail trade	$7 million
General and heavy construction (except dredging)	$33.5 million
Dredging	$20 million
Special trade contractors	$14 million
Travel agencies	$3.5 million (commissions and other income)
Business and personal services except	$7 million
• Architectural, engineering, surveying, and mapping services	$4.5 million
• Dry cleaning and carpet cleaning services	$4.5 million

Source: www.sbaonline.sba.gov/contractingopportunities/owners/basics/what (accessed June 5, 2013).

with the profits earned by most medium-sized and large firms. Moreover, most small firms have annual sales well below the maximum limits in the SBA guidelines.

Small businesses are very important to the U.S. economy. For example, small businesses

- represent 99.7 percent of all employer firms;
- employ about half of all private sector employees;
- pay 43 percent of total U.S. private payroll;
- have generated 64 percent of net new jobs over the past 18 years;
- create more than half of the nonfarm private GDP;
- hire 43 percent of high-tech workers (scientists, engineers, computer programmers, and others);
- are 52 percent home-based and 2 percent franchises;
- made up 97.5 percent of all identified exporters and produced 31 percent of export value; and
- produced 16.5 times more patents per employee than large patenting firms.[3]

The Small-Business Sector

In the United States, it typically takes less than a week and $600 to establish a business as a legal entity. The steps include registering the name of the business, applying for tax IDs, and setting up unemployment and workers' compensation insurance. In Japan, however, a typical entrepreneur spends more than $3,500 and 31 days to follow 11 different procedures.

A surprising number of Americans take advantage of their freedom to start a business. There are, in fact, about 27.9 million businesses in this country. Only just 18,500 of these employ more than 500 workers—enough to be considered large.

Interest in owning or starting a small business has never been greater than it is today. During the last decade, the number of small businesses in the United States has increased 49 percent. For the last few years, new-business formation in the United States has broken successive records, except during the 2001–2002 and 2008 recessions.

Have you worked for a small business?

Sometime in your career, you're likely to have a job in a small business. You might work in a store, in a service business, or in production. If you're thinking of starting your own business, be sure to watch how these entrepreneurs manage their companies.

Recently, 533,945 new businesses were incorporated. Furthermore, part-time entrepreneurs have increased fivefold in recent years; they now account for one-third of all small businesses.[4]

According to a recent study, 69 percent of new businesses survive at least two years, about 50 percent survive at least five years, and 31 percent survive at least ten years.[5] The primary reason for these failures is mismanagement resulting from a lack of business know-how. The makeup of the small-business sector thus is constantly changing. Despite the high failure rate, many small businesses succeed modestly. Some, like Apple Computer, Inc., are extremely successful—to the point where they can no longer be considered small. Taken together, small businesses are also responsible for providing a high percentage of the jobs in the United States. According to some estimates, the figure is well over 50 percent.

Industries That Attract Small Businesses

Some industries, such as auto manufacturing, require huge investments in machinery and equipment. Businesses in such industries are big from the day they are started—if an entrepreneur or group of entrepreneurs can gather the capital required to start one.

By contrast, a number of other industries require only a low initial investment and some special skills or knowledge. It is these industries that tend to attract new businesses. Growing industries, such as outpatient-care facilities, are attractive because of their profit potential. However, knowledgeable entrepreneurs choose areas with which they are familiar, and these are most often the more established industries.

Small enterprise spans the gamut from corner newspaper vending to the development of optical fibers. The owners of small businesses sell gasoline, flowers, and coffee to go. They publish magazines, haul freight, teach languages, and program computers. They make wines, movies, and high-fashion clothes. They build new homes and restore old ones. They fix appliances, recycle metals, and sell used cars. They drive cabs and fly planes. They make us well when we are ill, and they sell us the products of corporate giants. In fact, 74 percent of real estate, rental, and leasing industries; 61 percent of the businesses in the leisure and hospitality services; and 86 percent of the construction industries are dominated by small businesses. The various kinds of businesses generally fall into three broad categories of industry: distribution, service, and production.

DISTRIBUTION INDUSTRIES This category includes retailing, wholesaling, transportation, and communications—industries concerned with the movement of goods from producers to consumers. Distribution industries account for approximately 33 percent of all small businesses. Of these, almost three-quarters are involved in retailing, that is, the sale of goods directly to consumers. Clothing and jewelry stores, pet shops, bookstores, and grocery stores, for example, are all retailing firms. Slightly less than one-quarter of the small distribution firms are wholesalers. Wholesalers purchase products in quantity from manufacturers and then resell them to retailers.

SERVICE INDUSTRIES This category accounts for more than 48 percent of all small businesses. Of these, about three-quarters provide such nonfinancial services as medical and dental care; watch, shoe, and TV repairs; haircutting and styling; restaurant meals; and dry cleaning. About 8 percent of the small service firms offer financial services, such as accounting, insurance, real estate, and investment counseling. An increasing number of self-employed Americans are running service businesses from home.

Concept Check

✓ What information would you need to determine whether a particular business is small according to SBA guidelines?

✓ Which two areas of business generally attract the most small business? Why are these areas attractive to small business?

✓ Distinguish among service industries, distribution industries, and production industries

PRODUCTION INDUSTRIES This last category includes the construction, mining, and manufacturing industries. Only about 19 percent of all small businesses are in this group, mainly because these industries require relatively large initial investments. Small firms that do venture into production generally make parts and subassemblies for larger manufacturing firms or supply special skills to larger construction firms.

THE PEOPLE IN SMALL BUSINESSES: THE ENTREPRENEURS

Learning Objective

2 Identify the people who start small businesses and the reasons why some succeed and many fail.

The entrepreneurial spirit is alive and well in the United States. One study revealed that the U.S. population is quite entrepreneurial when compared with those of other countries. More than 70 percent of Americans would prefer being an entrepreneur to working for someone else. This compares with 46 percent of adults in Western Europe and 58 percent of adults in Canada. Another study on entrepreneurial activity found that of 36 countries studied, the United States was in the top third in entrepreneurial activity and was the leader when compared with Japan, Canada, and Western Europe.[6]

Small businesses typically are managed by the people who started and own them. Most of these people have held jobs with other firms and still could be so employed if they wanted. Yet owners of small businesses would rather take the risk of starting and operating their own firms, even if the money they make is less than the salaries they otherwise might earn.

Researchers have suggested a variety of personal factors as reasons why people go into business for themselves. These are discussed next.

Characteristics of Entrepreneurs

Entrepreneurial spirit is the desire to create a new business. For example, Nikki Olyai always knew that she wanted to create and develop her own business. Her father, a successful businessman in Iran, was her role model. She came to the United States at the age of 17 and lived with a host family in Salem, Oregon, attending high school there. Undergraduate and graduate degrees in computer science led her to start Innovision Technologies while she held two other jobs to keep the business going and took care of her four-year-old son. Recently, Nikki Olyai's business was honored by the Women's Business Enterprise National Council's "Salute to Women's Business Enterprises" as one of 11 top successful firms. For three consecutive years, her firm was selected as a "Future 50 of Greater Detroit Company."

Other Personal Factors

Other personal factors in small-business success include

- independence;
- a desire to determine one's own destiny;
- a willingness to find and accept a challenge;
- family background (in particular, researchers think that people whose families have been in business, successfully or not, are most apt to start and run their own businesses); and
- age (those who start their own businesses also tend to cluster around certain ages—more than 70 percent are between 24 and 44 years of age; see Figure 5-1).

AP IMAGES/NATI HARNIK

Meet Sam Altman, co-founder and CEO of Loopt. In 2004, Altman co-founded a location-based social networking mobile application when he was a sophomore majoring in computer science at Stanford University. *BusinessWeek* named him one of the "Best Young Entrepreneurs in Technology" and *Inc.* magazine ranked him number 4 among the top 30 entrepreneurs under the age of 30. In 2012, prepaid money card issuer Green Dot Corp. agreed to acquire Loopt Inc. for $43.4 million.

FIGURE 5-1 How Old Is the Average Entrepreneur?

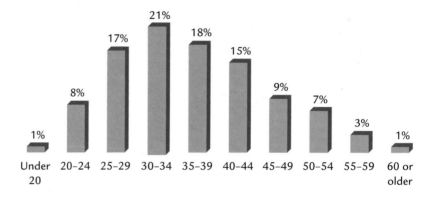

People in all age groups become entrepreneurs, but more than 70 percent are between 25 and 44 years of age.

Source: Data developed and provided by the National Federation of Independent Business Foundation and sponsored by the American Express Travel Related Services Company, Inc.

Motivation

There must be some motivation to start a business. A person may decide that he or she simply has "had enough" of working and earning a profit for someone else. Another may lose his or her job for some reason and decide to start the business he or she has always wanted rather than to seek another job. Still another person may have an idea for a new product or a new way to sell an existing product. Or the opportunity to go into business may arise suddenly, perhaps as a result of a hobby. For example, Cheryl Strand started baking and decorating cakes from her home while working full time as a word processor at Clemson University. Her cakes became so popular that she soon found herself working through her lunch breaks and late into the night to meet customer demand.

Victor "Beau" Shell, a child entrepreneur. This 9-year old boy co-owns and operates a small ice cream truck business in Athens, Georgia. In 2013, Shell celebrated his first anniversary and joined the Athens Area Chamber of Commerce. His mother says, "He is a natural business owner. I am so proud of his entrepreneurial spirit."

Women as Small-Business Owners

According to the latest 2013 data available from the SBA

- Women are 51 percent of the U.S. population, and according to the SBA, they owned at least 30 percent of all small businesses in 2012.
- Women already own 66 percent of the home-based businesses in this country, and the number of men in home-based businesses is growing rapidly.
- About 7.8 million women-owned businesses in the United States provide almost 7.6 million jobs and generate $1.2 trillion in sales.
- Women-owned businesses in the United States have proven that they are more successful; more than 40 percent have been in business for 12 years or more.
- Women-owned businesses are financially sound and credit-worthy, and their risk of failure is lower than average.
- Compared to other working women, self-employed women are older, better educated, and have more managerial experience.

- Just over one-half of small businesses are home based, and 91 percent have no employees. About 60 percent of home-based businesses are in service industries, 16 percent in construction, 14 percent in retail trade, and the rest in manufacturing, finance, transportation, communications, wholesaling, and other industries.[7]

Teenagers as Small-Business Owners

High-tech teen entrepreneurship is definitely exploding. "There's not a period in history where we've seen such a plethora of young entrepreneurs," comments Nancy F. Koehn, associate professor of business administration at Harvard Business School. Still, teen entrepreneurs face unique pressures in juggling their schoolwork, their social life, and their high-tech workload. Some ultimately quit school, whereas others quit or cut back on their business activities. Consider Brian Hendricks at Winston Churchill High School in Potomac, Maryland. He is the founder of StartUpPc and VB Solutions, Inc. StartUpPc, founded in 2001, sells custom-built computers and computer services for home users, home offices, small businesses, and students. Brian's services include design, installation of systems, training, networking, and on-site technical support. A year later, Brian founded VB Solutions, Inc., which develops and customizes websites and message boards. The firm sets up advertising contracts and counsels website owners on site improvements. The company has designed corporate ID kits, logos, and websites for clients from all over the world. Brian learned at a very young age that working for yourself is one of the best jobs available. According to Brian, a young entrepreneur must possess "the five P's of entrepreneurship"—planning, persistence, patience, people, and profit. Brian knows what it takes to be a successful entrepreneur. His accolades include Junior Achievement's "National Youth Entrepreneur of the Year" and SBA's "Young Entrepreneur of the Year" awards.[8]

In some people, the motivation to start a business develops slowly as they gain the knowledge and ability required for success as a business owner. Knowledge and ability—especially, management ability—are probably the most important factors involved. A new firm is very much built around the entrepreneur. The owner must be able to manage the firm's finances, its personnel (if there are any employees), and its day-to-day operations. He or she must handle sales, advertising, purchasing, pricing, and a variety of other business functions. The knowledge and ability to do so are acquired most often through experience working for other firms in the same area of business.

Why Some Entrepreneurs and Small Businesses Fail

Small businesses are prone to failure. Capital, management, and planning are the key ingredients in the survival of a small business, as well as the most common reasons for failure. Businesses can experience a number of money-related problems. It may take

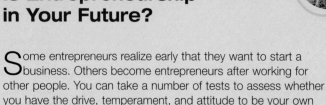

Career Success

Is Entrepreneurship in Your Future?

Some entrepreneurs realize early that they want to start a business. Others become entrepreneurs after working for other people. You can take a number of tests to assess whether you have the drive, temperament, and attitude to be your own boss. No test can tell whether your business will be successful, but you can get a sense of your own skills and capabilities as a future entrepreneur.

Stop by the career center on campus, which may offer an entrepreneurship self-test. For another perspective on your entrepreneurial potential, take at least one more test. For example, the informal questions on the Isenberg Entrepreneur Test, created by Professor Daniel Isenberg of Babson College, are designed to get you thinking about what you like and why. Do you like to challenge yourself? Would you prefer to fail at something you've chosen rather than succeed at something chosen by someone else?

The U.S. SBA (www.sba.gov) offers an online self-assessment to determine whether you're ready to start your own business. In addition, compare what you know about yourself to the SBA's listing of entrepreneur characteristics to see how well you match up. Similarly, the Business Development Bank of Canada's online test shows whether your attitudes, aptitudes, and motivations would be a good fit with the entrepreneurial life.

Sources: Based on information in Daniel Isenberg, "Should You Be an Entrepreneur? Take This Test," *Harvard Business Review*, February 12, 2010, www.hbr.org; U.S. Small Business Administration, www.sba.gov; Business Development Bank of Canada, www.bdc.ca.

TABLE 5-2 U.S. Business Start-ups, Closures, and Bankruptcies

	New	Closures	Bankruptcies
2011	781,000	752,000	47,806
2010	781,000	752,000	56,282
2009	518,500	680,716	60,837
2008	597,074	641,400	43,546
2007	668,395	592,410	28,322
2006	670,058	599,333	19,695
2005	644,122	565,745	39,201

NA = Not available.

Source: U.S. Small Business Administration, Office of Advocacy, *Small Business Economy 2012*, www.sba.gov/advocacy/849/6282 (accessed June 5, 2013).

several years before a business begins to show a profit. Entrepreneurs need to have not only the capital to open a business but also the money to operate it in its possibly lengthy start-up phase. One cash flow obstacle often leads to others. Moreover, a series of cash flow predicaments usually ends in a business failure. This scenario is played out all too often by small and not-so-small start-up Internet firms that fail to meet their financial backers' expectations and so are denied a second wave of investment dollars to continue their drive to establish a profitable online firm. According to Maureen Borzacchiello, co-owner of Creative Display Solutions, a trade show products company, "Big businesses such as Bear Stearns, Fannie Mae and Freddie Mac, and AIG can get bailouts, but small-business owners are on their own when times are tough and credit is tight."

Many entrepreneurs lack the management skills required to run a business. Money, time, personnel, and inventory all need to be managed effectively if a small business is to succeed. Starting a small business requires much more than optimism and a good idea.

Success and expansion sometimes lead to problems. Frequently, entrepreneurs with successful small businesses make the mistake of overexpansion. Fast growth often results in dramatic changes in a business. Thus, the entrepreneur must plan carefully and adjust competently to new and potentially disruptive situations.

Every day, and in every part of the country, people open new businesses. For example, 781,000 new businesses recently opened their doors. At the same time, however, 752,000 businesses closed their business and 47,806 businesses declared bankruptcy (see Table 5-2).[9] Although many fail, others represent well-conceived ideas developed by entrepreneurs who have the expertise, resources, and determination to make their businesses succeed. As these well-prepared entrepreneurs pursue their individual goals, our society benefits in many ways from their work and creativity. Billion-dollar companies such as Apple Computer, McDonald's Corporation, and Procter & Gamble are all examples of small businesses that expanded into industry giants.

Concept Check

✓ What kinds of factors encourage certain people to start new businesses?

✓ What are the major causes of small-business failure? Do these causes also apply to larger businesses?

Learning Objective

3 Assess the contributions of small businesses to our economy.

THE IMPORTANCE OF SMALL BUSINESSES IN OUR ECONOMY

This country's economic history abounds with stories of ambitious men and women who turned their ideas into business dynasties. The Ford Motor Company started as a one-man operation with an innovative method for industrial production. L.L.Bean, Inc., can trace its beginnings to a basement shop in Freeport, Maine. Both Xerox and Polaroid began as small firms with a better way to do a job. Indeed, every year since 1963, the president of the United States has proclaimed National Small Business Week to recognize the contributions of small businesses to the economic well-being of America.

Providing Technical Innovation

Invention and innovation are part of the foundations of our economy. The increases in productivity that have characterized the past 200 years of our history are all rooted in one principal source: new ways to do a job with less effort for less money. Studies show that the incidence of innovation among small-business workers is significantly higher than among workers in large businesses. Small firms produce two-and-a-half times as many innovations as large firms relative to the number of persons employed. In fact, small firms employ 43 percent of all high-tech workers such as scientists, engineers, and computer specialists. No wonder small firms produce 16 to 17 times more patents per employee than large patenting firms.

Consider Waymon Armstrong, the owner of a small business that uses computer simulations to help government and other clients prepare for and respond to natural disasters, medical emergencies, and combat. In presenting the 2010 National Small Business Person of the Year award, Karen Mills, Administrator of the U.S. Small Business Administration, said, "Waymon Armstrong is a perfect example of the innovation, inspiration, and determination that exemplify America's most successful entrepreneurs. He believed in his brainchild to the point where he deferred his own salary for three years to keep it afloat. When layoffs loomed for his staff after 9/11, their loyalty and belief in the company was so great that they were willing to work without pay for four months.

"Waymon's commitment to his employees and to his business—Engineering & Computer Simulations, Inc.—demonstrates the qualities that make small businesses such a powerful force for job creation in the American economy and in their local communities," said Mills. "It's the same qualities that will lead us to economic recovery. We are especially proud that his company benefited from two grants under SBA's Small Business Innovation and Research Program."[10]

According to the U.S. Office of Management and Budget, more than half the major technological advances of the 20th century originated with individual inventors and small companies. Even just a sampling of those innovations is remarkable:

- Air-conditioning
- Airplane
- Automatic transmission
- FM radio
- Heart valve
- Helicopter
- Instant camera
- Insulin
- Jet engine
- Penicillin
- Personal computer
- Power steering

Perhaps even more remarkable—and important—is that many of these inventions sparked major new U.S. industries or contributed to an established industry by adding some valuable service.

MICHAEL BRYANT/NEWSCOM

Providing technical innovation. Lutron Electronics invented a dimmer switch for CFL lighting; Allure energy has integrated home energy management with entertainment; Blu Homes took some cues from the "Transformers" franchise to build high-tech prefab homes; and Tremont Electric has built a wearable kinetic energy generator.

Providing Employment

Small firms traditionally have added more than their proportional share of new jobs to the economy. Seven out of the ten industries that added the most new jobs were small-business-dominated industries. Small businesses creating the most new jobs recently included business services, leisure and hospitality services, and special trade contractors. Small firms hire a larger proportion of employees who are younger workers, older workers, women, or workers who prefer to work part time.

Furthermore, small businesses provide 67 percent of workers with their first jobs and initial on-the-job training in basic skills. According to the SBA, small businesses represent 99.7 percent of all employers, employ more than 50 percent of the private workforce, and provide about two-thirds of the net new jobs added to our economy.[11] Small businesses thus contribute significantly to solving unemployment problems.

Providing Competition

Small businesses challenge larger, established firms in many ways, causing them to become more efficient and more responsive to consumer needs. A small business cannot, of course, compete with a large firm in all respects. However, a number of small firms, each competing in its own particular area and its own particular way, together have the desired competitive effect. Thus, several small janitorial companies together add up to reasonable competition for the no-longer-small ServiceMaster.

Filling Needs of Society and Other Businesses

Small firms also provide a variety of goods and services to each other and to much larger firms. Sears, Roebuck & Co. purchases merchandise from approximately 12,000 suppliers—and most of them are small businesses. General Motors relies on more than 32,000 companies for parts and supplies and depends on more than 11,000 independent dealers to sell its automobiles and trucks. Large firms generally buy parts and assemblies from smaller firms for one very good reason: It is less expensive than manufacturing the parts in their own factories. This lower cost eventually is reflected in the price that consumers pay for their products.

It is clear that small businesses are a vital part of our economy and that, as consumers and as members of the labor force, we all benefit enormously from their existence. Now let us look at the situation from the viewpoint of the owners of small businesses.

Concept Check

✓ Briefly describe four contributions of small business to the American economy.

✓ Give examples of how small businesses fill needs of society and other businesses.

Learning Objective

4 Describe the advantages and disadvantages of operating a small business.

THE PROS AND CONS OF SMALLNESS

Do most owners of small businesses dream that their firms will grow into giant corporations—managed by professionals—while they serve only on the board of directors? Or would they rather stay small, in a firm where they have the opportunity (and the responsibility) to do everything that needs to be done? The answers depend on the personal characteristics and motivations of the individual owners. For many, the advantages of remaining small far outweigh the disadvantages.

Advantages of Small Business

Small-business owners with limited resources often must struggle to enter competitive new markets. They also have to deal with increasing international competition. However, they enjoy several unique advantages.

PERSONAL RELATIONSHIPS WITH CUS-TOMERS AND EMPLOYEES For those who like dealing with people, small business is the place to be. The owners of retail shops get to know many of their customers by name and deal with them on a personal basis. Through such relationships, small-business owners often become involved in the social, cultural, and political life of the community.

Relationships between owner-managers and employees also tend to be closer in smaller businesses. In many cases, the owner is a friend and counselor as well as the boss.

These personal relationships provide an important business advantage. The personal service small businesses offer to customers is a major competitive weapon—one that larger firms try to match but often cannot. In addition, close relationships with employees often help the small-business owner to keep effective workers who might earn more with a larger firm.

ABILITY TO ADAPT TO CHANGE Being his or her own boss, the owner-manager of a small business does not need anyone's permission to adapt to change. An owner may add or discontinue merchandise or services, change store hours, and experiment with various price strategies in response to changes in market conditions. And through personal relationships with customers, the owners of small businesses quickly become aware of changes in people's needs and interests, as well as in the activities of competing firms.

Getting personal. For those who like dealing with people, small business is the place to be. Here a business owner provides personalized service to a happy customer.

SIMPLIFIED RECORD KEEPING Many small firms need only a simple set of records. Record keeping might consist of a checkbook, a cash-receipts journal in which to record all sales, and a cash-disbursements journal in which to record all amounts paid out. Obviously, enough records must be kept to allow for producing and filing accurate tax returns.

INDEPENDENCE Small-business owners do not have to punch in and out, bid for vacation times, take orders from superiors, or worry about being fired or laid off. They are the masters of their own destinies—at least with regard to employment. For many people, this is the prime advantage of owning a small business.

OTHER ADVANTAGES According to the SBA, the most profitable companies in the United States are small firms that have been in business for more than ten years and employ fewer than 20 people. Small-business owners also enjoy all the advantages of sole proprietorships, which were discussed in Chapter 4. These include being able to keep all profits, the ease and low cost of going into business and (if necessary) going out of business, and being able to keep business information secret.

Disadvantages of Small Business

Personal contacts with customers, closer relationships with employees, being one's own boss, less cumbersome record-keeping chores, and independence are the bright side of small business. In contrast, the dark side reflects problems unique to these firms.

RISK OF FAILURE As we have noted, small businesses (especially new ones) run a heavy risk of going out of business—about 50 percent survive at least five years. Older, well-established small firms can be hit hard by a business recession mainly because they do not have the financial resources to weather an extended difficult period.

Students by Day, Entrepreneurs by Night

A growing number of students are becoming entrepreneurs even before they graduate, gaining valuable business experience and taking advantage of the many resources on campus. Brandt Page, who started a company while at Brigham Young University and has since founded or co-founded two more, explains that as a student entrepreneur, "you have free access to libraries, free access to mentors, to professors, to business competitions, to really being recognized and mentored."

Corinne Prevot had already earned $8,000 from her ski apparel business, Skida, before she entered college. After taking an entrepreneurship course as a freshman at Middlebury College, she rethought her approach to business. She researched competitors, looked at distribution, repriced her products, and formalized her branding. Now Skida's yearly sales are more than $100,000, and Prevot is ready to expand.

Partners Noah Chilton, Harry Kelley, Jackson Kroopf, and Misha Epstein like gourmet coffee, so they created a rolling cart to bring their favorite brews to classmates at Vassar through a business they called Tree City. The entrepreneurs buy from growers who use eco-friendly agricultural methods and they discuss good coffee while they brew a fresh cup for each customer. "Part of what we love about coffee is the way it brings people together," Kroopf says.

Sources: Based on information in Rebecca Palmer, "The College of Hard Knocks," *Utah Business*, January 11, 2012, www.utahbusiness.com; Joanna Hamer, "Tree City Serves Up Ethical Coffee, Enticing Conversation," *Miscellany News* (Poughkeepsie, New York), October 25, 2011, www.miscellanynews.com; Helen Coster, "All Star Student Entrepreneurs," *Forbes*, August 3, 2011, www.forbes.com; Brian Nichols, "Know-How for Hire," *New York Times Education Life*, November 6, 2011, p. 34.

LIMITED POTENTIAL Small businesses that survive do so with varying degrees of success. Many are simply the means of making a living for the owner and his or her family. The owner may have some technical skill—as a hair stylist or electrician, for example—and may have started a business to put this skill to work. Such a business is unlikely to grow into big business. In addition, employees' potential for advancement is limited.

LIMITED ABILITY TO RAISE CAPITAL Small businesses typically have a limited ability to obtain capital. Figure 5-2 shows that most small-business financing comes out of the owner's pocket. Personal loans from lending institutions provide only about one-fourth of the capital required by small businesses. About 50 percent of all new firms begin with less than $30,000 in total capital, according to Census Bureau and Federal Reserve surveys. In fact, almost 36 percent of new firms begin with less than $20,000, usually provided by the owner or family members and friends.[12] According to the SBA, average capital for starting a new business is $80,000.

Although every person who considers starting a small business should be aware of the hazards and pitfalls we have noted, a well-conceived business plan may help to avoid the risk of failure. The U.S. government is also dedicated to helping small businesses make it. It expresses this aim most actively through the SBA.

The Importance of a Business Plan

Lack of planning can be as deadly as lack of money to a new small business. Planning is important to any business, large or small, and never should be overlooked or taken lightly. A **business plan** is a carefully constructed guide for the person starting a business. Consider it as a tool with three basic purposes: communication, management, and planning. As a communication tool, a business plan serves as a concise document that potential investors can examine to see if they would like to invest or assist in financing a new venture. It shows whether a business has the potential to make a profit. As a management tool, the business plan helps to track, monitor, and evaluate the progress. The business plan is a living document; it is modified as the entrepreneur gains knowledge and experience. It also serves to establish time lines and milestones and allows comparison of growth projections against actual accomplishments. Finally, as a planning tool, the business plan guides a businessperson through the various phases of business. For example, the plan helps to identify obstacles to avoid and to establish alternatives. According to Robert Krummer, Jr., chairman of First Business Bank in Los Angeles, "The business plan is a necessity. If the person who wants to start a small business can't put a business plan together, he or she is in trouble."

business plan a carefully constructed guide for the person starting a business

Components of a Business Plan

Table 5-3 shows the 12 sections that a business plan should include. Each section is further explained at the end of each of the seven major parts in the text. The goal of each end-of-the-part exercise is to help a businessperson create his or her

FIGURE 5-2 Sources of Capital for Entrepreneurs

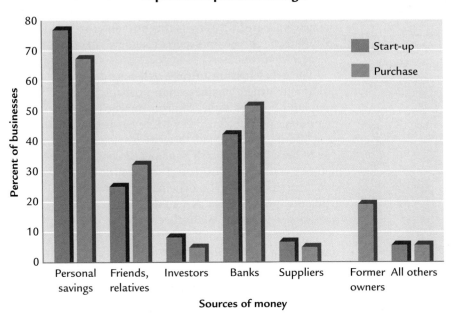

Small businesses get financing from various sources; the most important is personal savings.

Source: Data developed and provided by the National Federation of Independent Business Foundation and sponsored by the American Express Travel Related Services Company, Inc.

TABLE 5-3 Components of a Business Plan

1. *Introduction.* Basic information such as the name, address, and phone number of the business; the date the plan was issued; and a statement of confidentiality to keep important information away from potential competitors.

2. *Executive Summary.* A one- to two-page overview of the entire business plan, including a justification why the business will succeed.

3. *Benefits to the Community.* Information on how the business will have an impact on economic development, community development, and human development.

4. *Company and Industry.* The background of the company, choice of the legal business form, information on the products or services to be offered, and examination of the potential customers, current competitors, and the business's future.

5. *Management Team.* Discussion of skills, talents, and job descriptions of management team, managerial compensation, management training needs, and professional assistance requirements.

6. *Manufacturing and Operations Plan.* Discussion of facilities needed, space requirements, capital equipment, labor force, inventory control, and purchasing requirement.

7. *Labor Force.* Discussion of the quality of skilled workers available and the training, compensation, and motivation of workers.

8. *Marketing Plan.* Discussion of markets, market trends, competition, market share, pricing, promotion, distribution, and service policy.

9. *Financial Plan.* Summary of the investment needed, sales and cash flow forecasts, breakeven analysis, and sources of funding.

10. *Exit Strategy.* Discussion of a succession plan or going public. Who will take over the business?

11. *Critical Risks and Assumptions.* Evaluation of the weaknesses of the business and how the company plans to deal with these and other business problems.

12. *Appendix.* Supplementary information crucial to the plan, such as résumés of owners and principal managers, advertising samples, organization chart, and any related information.

Source: From HATTEN, *Small Business Management*, 5E. © 2012 Cengage Learning.

A business plan is a great idea!

Although writing a business plan won't guarantee your success, it will help you think through many of the issues that can trip up entrepreneurs. And if you work for a big company, you may find yourself writing a kind of business plan for a product or project.

own business plan. When constructing a business plan, the businessperson should strive to keep it easy to read, uncluttered, and complete. Like other busy executives, officials of financial institutions do not have the time to wade through pages of extraneous data. The business plan should answer the four questions banking officials and investors are most interested in: (1) What exactly is the nature and mission of the new venture? (2) Why is this new enterprise a good idea? (3) What are the businessperson's goals? (4) How much will the new venture cost?

The great amount of time and consideration that should go into creating a business plan probably will end up saving time later. For example, Sharon Burch, who was running a computer software business while earning a degree in business administration, had to write a business plan as part of one of her courses. Burch has said, "I wish I'd taken the class before I started my business. I see a lot of things I could have done differently. But it has helped me since because I've been using the business plan as a guide for my business." Table 5-4 provides a business plan checklist. Accuracy and realistic expectations are crucial to an effective business plan. It is unethical to deceive loan officers, and it is unwise to deceive yourself.

TABLE 5-4 Business Plan Checklist

1. Does the executive summary grab the reader's attention and highlight the major points of the business plan?

2. Does the business-concept section clearly describe the purpose of the business, the customers, the value proposition, and the distribution channel and convey a compelling story?

3. Do the industry and market analyses support acceptance and demand for the business concept in the marketplace and define a first customer in depth?

4. Does the management team plan persuade the reader that the team could implement the business concept successfully? Does it assure the reader that an effective infrastructure is in place to facilitate the goals and operations of the company?

5. Does the product/service plan clearly provide details on the status of the product, the time line for completion, and the intellectual property that will be acquired?

6. Does the operations plan prove that the product or service could be produced and distributed efficiently and effectively?

7. Does the marketing plan successfully demonstrate how the company will create customer awareness in the target market and deliver the benefit to the customer?

8. Does the financial plan convince the reader that the business model is sustainable—that it will provide a superior return on investment for the investor and sufficient cash flow to repay loans to potential lenders?

9. Does the growth plan convince the reader that the company has long-term growth potential and spin-off products and services?

10. Does the contingency and exit-strategy plan convince the reader that the risk associated with this venture can be mediated? Is there an exit strategy in place for investors?

Source: From ALLEN, *Launching New Ventures*, 6E. © 2012 Cengage Learning.

Concept Check

✓ What are the major advantages and disadvantages of smallness in business?

✓ What are the major components of a business plan? Why should an individual develop a business plan?

THE SMALL BUSINESS ADMINISTRATION

Learning Objective

5 Explain how the Small Business Administration helps small businesses.

The **Small Business Administration (SBA)**, created by Congress in 1953, is a governmental agency that assists, counsels, and protects the interests of small businesses in the United States. It helps people get into business and stay in business. The agency provides assistance to owners and managers of prospective, new, and established small businesses. Through more than 1,000 offices and resource centers throughout the nation, the SBA provides both financial assistance and management counseling. Recently, the SBA provided training, technical assistance, and education to more than 3 million small businesses. It helps small firms to bid for and obtain government contracts, and it helps them to prepare to enter foreign markets.

Small Business Administration (SBA) a governmental agency that assists, counsels, and protects the interests of small businesses in the United States

SBA Management Assistance

Statistics show that most failures in small business are related to poor management. For this reason, the SBA places special emphasis on improving the management ability of the owners and managers of small businesses. The SBA's Management Assistance Program is extensive and diversified. It includes free individual counseling, courses, conferences, workshops, and a wide range of publications. Recently, the SBA provided management and technical assistance to nearly 1 million small businesses through its 900 Small Business Development Centers and 13,000 volunteers from the Service Corps of Retired Executives.[13]

MANAGEMENT COURSES AND WORKSHOPS The management courses offered by the SBA cover all the functions, duties, and roles of managers. Instructors may be teachers from local colleges and universities or other professionals, such as management consultants, bankers, lawyers, and accountants. Fees for these courses are quite low. The most popular such course is a general survey of eight to ten different areas of business management. In follow-up studies, businesspeople may concentrate in depth on one or more of these areas depending on their particular strengths and weaknesses. The SBA occasionally offers one-day conferences. These conferences are aimed at keeping owner-managers up-to-date on new management developments, tax laws, and the like. The Small Business Training Network (SBTN) is an online training network consisting of 23 SBA-run courses, workshops, and resources. Some of the most requested courses include Entrepreneurship, Starting and Managing Your Own Business, Developing a Business Plan, Managing the Digital Enterprise, Identify Your Target Market, and Analyze Profitability. Find out more at www.sba.gov/training. Recently, more than 240,000 small-business owners benefited from SBA's free online business courses.

SCORE The **Service Corps of Retired Executives (SCORE)**, Counselors to America's Small Business, created in 1964, is a group of more than 13,000 retired and active businesspeople, including more than 2,000 women who volunteer their services to small businesses through the SBA. The collective experience of SCORE volunteers spans the full range of American enterprise. These volunteers have worked for such notable companies as Eastman Kodak, General Electric, IBM, and Procter & Gamble. Experts in areas of accounting, finance, marketing, engineering, and retailing provide counseling and mentoring to entrepreneurs.

Service Corps of Retired Executives (SCORE) a group of businesspeople who volunteer their services to small businesses through the SBA

A small-business owner who has a particular problem can request free counseling from SCORE. An assigned counselor visits the owner in his or her establishment and, through careful observation, analyzes the business situation and the problem. If the problem is complex, the counselor may call on other volunteer experts to assist. Finally, the counselor offers a plan for solving the problem and helping the owner through the critical period.

Minority-owned businesses. Are you ready to start your business, but don't know where to start or what opportunities are available to minority groups? The SBA provides information on federal government programs and services that help members of the minority groups start their own businesses.

Consider the plight of Elizabeth Halvorsen, a mystery writer from Minneapolis. Her husband had built up the family advertising and graphic arts firm for 17 years when he was called in 1991 to serve in the Persian Gulf War. The only one left behind to run the business was Mrs. Halvorsen, who admittedly had no business experience. Enter SCORE. With a SCORE management expert at her side, she kept the business on track. Recently, SCORE volunteers served more than 523,800 small-business people like Mrs. Halvorsen through its 348 offices. Since its inception, SCORE has assisted more than 10 million small-business people with online and face-to-face small business counseling.[14]

Help for Minority-Owned Small Businesses

Americans who are members of minority groups have had difficulty entering the nation's economic mainstream. Raising money is a nagging problem for minority business owners, who also may lack adequate training. Members of minority groups are, of course, eligible for all SBA programs, but the SBA makes a special effort to assist those minority groups who want to start small businesses or expand existing ones. For example, the Minority Business Development Agency awards grants to develop and increase business opportunities for members of racial and ethnic minorities.

Helping women become entrepreneurs is also a special goal of the SBA. Emily Harrington, one of nine children, was born in Manila, the Philippines. She arrived in the United States in 1972 as a foreign-exchange student. Convinced that there was a market for hard-working, dedicated minorities and women, she launched Qualified Resources, Inc., a professional staffing services firm. *Inc.* magazine selected her firm as one of "America's Fastest Growing Private Companies" just six years later. Harrington credits the SBA with giving her the technical support that made her first loan possible. Finding a SCORE counselor to work directly with her, she refined her business plan until she got a bank loan. Before contacting the SBA, Harrington was turned down for business loans "by all the banks I approached," even though she worked as a manager of loan credit and collection for a bank. Later, Emily Harrington was SBA's winner of the local, regional, and national Small Business Entrepreneurial Success Award for Rhode Island, the New England region, and the nation! For several years in a row, Qualified Resources, Inc., was named one of the fastest growing private companies in Rhode Island. Now with more than 100 Women's Business Centers, entrepreneurs like Harrington can receive training and technical assistance, access to credit and capital, federal contracts, and international markets. The SBA's Online Women's Business Center (www.sba.gov/aboutsba/sbaprograms/onlinewbc/index.html) is a state-of-the-art Internet site to help women expand their businesses. This free, interactive website offers women information about business principles and practices, management techniques, networking, industry news, market research and technology training, online counseling, and hundreds of links to other sites, as well as information about the many SBA services and resources available to them.

small-business institutes (SBIs) groups of senior and graduate students in business administration who provide management counseling to small businesses

SMALL-BUSINESS INSTITUTES small-business institutes (SBIs), created in 1972, are groups of senior and graduate students in business administration who provide management counseling to small businesses. SBIs have been set up on more than 520 college campuses as another way to help business owners. The students work in small groups guided by faculty advisers and SBA management-assistance experts. Like SCORE volunteers, they analyze and help solve the problems of small-business owners at their business establishments.

SMALL-BUSINESS DEVELOPMENT CENTERS small-business development centers (SBDCs) are university-based groups that provide individual counseling and practical training to owners of small businesses. SBDCs draw from the resources of local, state, and federal governments, private businesses, and universities. These groups can provide managerial and technical help, data from research studies, and other types of specialized assistance of value to small businesses. In 2012, there were more than 900 SBDC locations, primarily at colleges and universities, assisting people such as Kathleen DuBois. After scribbling a list of her abilities and the names of potential clients on a napkin in a local restaurant, Kathleen DuBois decided to start her own marketing firm. Beth Thornton launched her engineering firm after a discussion with a colleague in the ladies room of the Marriott. When Richard Shell was laid off after 20 years of service with Nisource (Columbia Gas), he searched the Internet tirelessly before finding the right franchise option. Introduced by mutual friends, Jim Bostic and Denver McMillion quickly connected, built a high level of trust, and combined their diverse professional backgrounds to form a manufacturing company. Although these entrepreneurs took different routes in starting their new businesses in West Virginia, all of them turned to the West Virginia Small Business Development Center for the technical assistance to make their dreams become a reality.

SBA PUBLICATIONS The SBA issues management, marketing, and technical publications dealing with hundreds of topics of interest to present and prospective managers of small firms. Most of these publications are available from the SBA free of charge. Others can be obtained for a small fee from the U.S. Government Printing Office.

SBA Financial Assistance

Small businesses seem to be constantly in need of money. An owner may have enough capital to start and operate the business. But then he or she may require more money to finance increased operations during peak selling seasons, to pay for required pollution control equipment, to finance an expansion, or to mop up after a natural disaster such as a flood or a terrorist attack. For example, the Supplemental Terrorist Activity Relief program has made more than $3.7 billion in loans to 8,202 small businesses harmed or disrupted by the September 11 terrorist attacks. In early 2013, 90 days after Hurricane Sandy hit the Northeast, the SBA guaranteed over $1 billion loans to more than 16,800 businesses, homeowners, and renters.[15] Earlier, the SBA offered economic injury loans to fishing and fishing-dependent small businesses as a result of the Deepwater BP spill that shut down commercial and recreational fishing waters. According to the SBA Administrator, "SBA remains committed to taking every step to help small businesses deal with the financial challenges they are facing as a result of the Deepwater BP oil spill."[16] The SBA offers special financial-assistance programs that cover all these situations. However, its primary financial function is to guarantee loans to eligible businesses.

REGULAR BUSINESS LOANS Most of the SBA's business loans are actually made by private lenders such as banks, but repayment is partially guaranteed by the agency. That is, the SBA may guarantee that it will repay the lender up to 90 percent of the loan if the borrowing firm cannot repay it. Guaranteed loans approved on or after October 1, 2002, may be as large as $2.0 million (this loan limit may be increased in the future). The average size of an SBA-guaranteed business loan is about $300,000, and its average duration is about eight years.

small-business development centers (SBDCs) university-based groups that provide individual counseling and practical training to owners of small businesses

SMALL-BUSINESS INVESTMENT COMPANIES Venture capital is money that is invested in small (and sometimes struggling) firms that have the potential to become very successful. In many cases, only a lack of capital keeps these firms from rapid and solid growth. The people who invest in such firms expect that their investments will grow with the firms and become quite profitable.

The popularity of these investments has increased over the past 30 years, but most small firms still have difficulty obtaining venture capital. To help such businesses, the SBA licenses, regulates, and provides financial assistance to **small-business investment companies (SBICs)**.

An SBIC is a privately owned firm that provides venture capital to small enterprises that meet its investment standards. Such firms as America Online, Apple Computer, Costco, Jenny Craig, Federal Express, Compaq Computer, Intel Corporation, Outback Steakhouse, and Staples, Inc., all were financed through SBICs during their initial growth period. More than 300 SBICs are intended to be profit-making organizations. The aid that SBA offers allows them to invest in small businesses that otherwise would not attract venture capital. Since Congress created the program in 1958, SBICs have financed more than 107,000 small businesses for a total of about $60 billion. In 2012, SBICs benefited 1,339 businesses, and 34 percent of these firms were owned by women or other minorities.[17]

We have discussed the importance of the small-business segment of our economy. We have weighed the advantages and drawbacks of operating a small business as compared with a large one. But is there a way to achieve the best of both worlds? Can one preserve one's independence as a business owner and still enjoy some of the benefits of "bigness"? Let's take a close look at franchising.

FRANCHISING

A **franchise** is a license to operate an individually owned business as if it were part of a chain of outlets or stores. Often, the business itself is also called a *franchise*. Among the most familiar franchises are McDonald's, H&R Block, AAMCO Transmissions, GNC (General Nutrition Centers), and Dairy Queen. Many other franchises carry familiar names; this method of doing business has become very popular in the last 55 years or so. It is an attractive means of starting and operating a small business.

What Is Franchising?

Franchising is the actual granting of a franchise. A **franchisor** is an individual or organization granting a franchise. A **franchisee** is a person or organization purchasing a franchise. The franchisor supplies a known and advertised business name, management skills, the required training and materials, and a method of doing business. The franchisee supplies labor and capital, operates the franchised business, and agrees to abide by the provisions of the franchise agreement. Table 5-5 lists the basic franchisee rights and obligations that would be covered in a typical franchise agreement.

Types of Franchising

Franchising arrangements fall into three general categories. In the first approach, a manufacturer authorizes a number of retail stores to sell a certain brand-name item. This type of franchising arrangement, one of the oldest, is prevalent in sales of passenger cars and trucks, farm equipment, shoes, paint, earth-moving equipment, and petroleum. About 90 percent of all gasoline is sold through franchised, independent retail service stations, and franchised dealers handle virtually all sales of new cars and trucks. In the second type of franchising arrangement, a

TABLE 5-5 Basic Rights and Obligations Delineated in a Franchise Agreement

Franchisee rights include:

1. use of trademarks, trade names, and patents of the franchisor;

2. use of the brand image and the design and decor of the premises developed by the franchisor;

3. use of the franchisor's secret methods;

4. use of the franchisor's copyrighted materials;

5. use of recipes, formulae, specifications, processes, and methods of manufacture developed by the franchisor;

6. conducting the franchised business upon or from the agreed premises strictly in accordance with the franchisor's methods and subject to the franchisor's directions;

7. guidelines established by the franchisor regarding exclusive territorial rights; and

8. rights to obtain supplies from nominated suppliers at special prices.

Franchisee obligations include:

1. to carry on the business franchised and no other business upon the approved and nominated premises;

2. to observe certain minimum operating hours;

3. to pay a franchise fee;

4. to follow the accounting system laid down by the franchisor;

5. not to advertise without prior approval of the advertisements by the franchisor;

6. to use and display such point-of-sale advertising materials as the franchisor stipulates;

7. to maintain the premises in good, clean, and sanitary condition and to redecorate when required to do so by the franchisor;

8. to maintain the widest possible insurance coverage;

9. to permit the franchisor's staff to enter the premises to inspect and see if the franchisor's standards are being maintained;

10. to purchase goods or products from the franchisor or his designated suppliers;

11. to train the staff in the franchisor's methods to ensure that they are neatly and appropriately clothed; and

12. not to assign the franchise contract without the franchisor's consent.

Source: Excerpted from the SBA's "Is Franchising for Me?" www.sba.gov (accessed August 26, 2013).

producer licenses distributors to sell a given product to retailers. This arrangement is common in the soft drink industry. Most national manufacturers of soft drink syrups—The Coca-Cola Company, Dr. Pepper/Seven-Up Companies, PepsiCo, Royal Crown Companies, Inc.—franchise independent bottlers who then serve retailers. In a third form of franchising, a franchisor supplies brand names, techniques, or other services instead of a complete product. Although the franchisor may provide certain production and distribution services, its primary role is the careful development and control of marketing strategies. This approach to franchising, which is the most typical today, is used by Avis, Hampton Hotels, 7-Eleven Inc., Anytime Fitness, Denny's Inc., Pizza Hut Inc., McDonald's, and SUBWAY, to name but a few.

Concept Check

✓ Explain the relationships among a franchise, the franchisor, and the franchisee.

✓ Describe the three general categories of franchising arrangements.

Learning Objective

7 Analyze the growth of franchising and its advantages and disadvantages.

THE GROWTH OF FRANCHISING

Franchising, which began in the United States around the time of the Civil War, was used originally by large firms, such as the Singer Sewing Company, to distribute their products. Franchising has been increasing steadily in popularity since the early 1900s, primarily for filling stations and car dealerships; however, this retailing strategy has experienced enormous growth since the mid-1970s. The franchise proliferation generally has paralleled the expansion of the fast-food industry.

Of course, franchising is not limited to fast foods. Hair salons, tanning parlors, and dentists and lawyers are expected to participate in franchising arrangements in growing numbers. Franchised health clubs, pest exterminators, and campgrounds are already widespread, as are franchised tax preparers and travel agencies. The real estate industry also has experienced a rapid increase in franchising.

Also, franchising is attracting more women and minority business owners in the United States than ever before. One reason is that special outreach programs designed to encourage franchisee diversity have developed. Consider Angela Trammel, a young mother of two. She had been laid off from her job at the Marriott after 9/11. Since she was a member of a Curves Fitness Center and liked the concept of empowering women to become physically fit, she began researching the cost of purchasing a Curves franchise and ways to finance the business. "I was online looking for financing, and I linked to Enterprise Development Group in Washington, DC. I knew that they had diverse clients." The cost for the franchise was $19,500, but it took $60,000 to open the doors to her fitness center. "Applying for a loan to start the business was much harder than buying a house," said Trammel. Just three years later, Angela and her husband, Ernest, own three Curves Fitness Centers with 12 employees. Recently, since giving birth to her third child, she has found the financial freedom and flexibility needed to care for her busy family. In fact, within a three-year period, the Trammels grew their annual household income from $80,000 to $250,000.[18] Franchisors such as Wendy's, McDonald's, Burger King, and Church's Chicken all have special corporate programs to attract minority and women franchisees. Just as important, successful women and minority franchisees are willing to get involved by offering advice and guidance to new franchisees.

Getting ad value from your car. Joe McGuinness founded Signs By Tomorrow in 1986. Today, with over 180 locations nationwide, the Columbia, Maryland-based franchise company turns hundreds of autos into rolling billboards each year, much like this one for 1-800-GOT-JUNK. Some companies may compensate your gas costs to use your car.

Herman Petty, the first African-American McDonald's franchisee, remembers that the company provided a great deal of help while he worked to establish his first units. In turn, Petty traveled to help other black franchisees, and he invited new franchisees to gain hands-on experience in his Chicago restaurants before starting their own establishments. In 1972, Petty also organized a support group, the National Black McDonald's Operators Association, to help black franchisees in other areas. Today, members of this association own nearly 1,300 McDonald's restaurants throughout the United States, South Africa, and the Caribbean with annual sales of more than $2.7 billion. "By staying together, we will realize the dream that our forefathers envisioned: an organization of successful African-American entrepreneurs who did not forget their humble beginnings," says Roland G. Parrish, the McDonald's franchisee who leads the group.

Dual-branded franchises, in which two franchisors offer their products together, are a new small-business trend. For example, in 1993, pleased with the success of its first co-branded restaurant with Texaco in Beebe, Arkansas, McDonald's now has more than 400 co-branded restaurants in the United States. Also, an agreement between franchisors Doctor's Associates, Inc., and TCBY Enterprises, Inc., now allows franchisees to sell SUBWAY sandwiches and TCBY yogurt in the same establishment.

Are Franchises Successful?

Franchising is designed to provide a tested formula for success, along with ongoing advice and training. The success rate for businesses owned and operated by franchisees is significantly higher than the success rate for other independently owned small businesses. In a recent nationwide Gallup poll of 944 franchise owners, 94 percent of franchisees indicated that they were very or somewhat successful, only 5 percent believed that they were very unsuccessful or somewhat unsuccessful, and 1 percent did not know. Despite these impressive statistics, franchising is not a guarantee of success for either franchisees or franchisors. Too rapid expansion, inadequate capital or management skills, and a host of other problems can cause failure for both franchisee and franchisor. Thus, for example, the Dizzy Dean's Beef and Burger franchise is no longer in business. Timothy Bates, a Wayne State University economist, warns, "Despite the hype that franchising is the safest way to go when starting a new business, the research just doesn't bear that out." Just consider Boston Chicken, which once had more than 1,200 restaurants before declaring bankruptcy in 1998.

Advantages of Franchising

Franchising plays a vital role in our economy and soon may become the dominant form of retailing. Why? Because franchising offers advantages to both the franchisor and the franchisee.

TO THE FRANCHISOR The franchisor gains fast and well-controlled distribution of its products without incurring the high cost of constructing and operating its own outlets. The franchisor thus has more capital available to expand production and to use for advertising. At the same time, it can ensure, through the franchise agreement, that outlets are maintained and operated according to its own standards.

The franchisor also benefits from the fact that the franchisee—a sole proprietor in most cases—is likely to be very highly motivated to succeed. The success of the franchise means more sales, which translate into higher royalties for the franchisor.

TO THE FRANCHISEE The franchisee gets the opportunity to start a business with limited capital and to make use of the business experience of others. Moreover, an outlet with a nationally advertised name, such as RadioShack, McDonald's, or Century 21, has guaranteed customers as soon as it opens.

If business problems arise, the franchisor gives the franchisee guidance and advice. This counseling is primarily responsible for the very high degree of success enjoyed by franchises. In most cases, the franchisee does not pay for such help.

The franchisee also receives materials to use in local advertising and can take part in national promotional campaigns sponsored by the franchisor. McDonald's and its franchisees, for example, constitute one of the nation's top 20 purchasers of advertising. Finally, the franchisee may be able to minimize the cost of advertising, supplies, and various business necessities by purchasing them in cooperation with other franchisees.

The growth of franchising. Franchising is designed to provide a tested formula for success, along with ongoing advice and training. The franchisor, such as Wendy's or Burger King, supplies a known and advertised business name, management skills, the required training and materials, and a method of doing business. Franchising, however, is not a guarantee of success for either franchisees or franchisors.

Disadvantages of Franchising

The main disadvantage of franchising affects the franchisee, and it arises because the franchisor retains a great deal of control. The franchisor's contract can dictate every aspect of the business: decor, design of employee uniforms, types of signs, and all the details of business operations. All Burger King French fries taste the same because all Burger King franchisees have to make them the same way.

Contract disputes are the cause of many lawsuits. For example, Rekha Gabhawala, a Dunkin' Donuts franchisee in Milwaukee, alleged that the franchisor was forcing her out of business so that the company could profit by reselling the downtown franchise to someone else; the company, on the other hand, alleged that Gabhawala breached the contract by not running the business according to company standards. In another case, Dunkin' Donuts sued Chris Romanias, its franchisee in Pennsylvania, alleging that Romanias intentionally underreported gross sales to the company. Romanias, on the other hand, alleged that Dunkin' Donuts, Inc., breached the contract because it failed to provide assistance in operating the franchise. Other franchisees claim that contracts are unfairly tilted toward the franchisors. Yet others have charged that they lost their franchise and investment because their franchisor would not approve the sale of the business when they found a buyer.

To arbitrate disputes between franchisors and franchisees, the National Franchise Mediation Program was established in 1993 by 30 member firms, including Burger King Corporation, McDonald's Corporation, and Wendy's International, Inc. Negotiators have since resolved numerous cases through mediation. Recently, Carl's Jr. brought in one of its largest franchisees to help set its system straight, making most franchisees happy for the first time in years. The program also helped PepsiCo settle a long-term contract dispute and renegotiate its franchise agreements.

Because disagreements between franchisors and franchisees have increased in recent years, many franchisees have been demanding government regulation of franchising. In 1997, to avoid government regulation, some of the largest franchisors proposed a new self-policing plan to the Federal Trade Commission.

Franchise holders pay for their security, usually with a one-time franchise fee and continuing royalty and advertising fees, collected as a percentage of sales. A SUBWAY franchisee pays an initial franchise fee of $15,000 and an annual fee of 8 percent of gross sales. In some fields, franchise agreements are not uniform. One franchisee may pay more than another for the same services.

Even success can cause problems. Sometimes a franchise is so successful that the franchisor opens its own outlet nearby, in direct competition—although franchisees may fight back. For example, a court recently ruled that Burger King could not enter into direct competition with the franchisee because the contract was not specific on the issue. A spokesperson for one franchisor contends that the company "gives no geographical protection" to its franchise holders and thus is free to move in on them. Franchise operators work hard. They often put in 10- and 12-hour days, six days a week. The International Franchise Association advises prospective franchise purchasers to investigate before investing and to approach buying a franchise cautiously. Franchises vary widely in approach as well as in products. Some, such as Dunkin' Donuts and Baskin-Robbins, demand long hours. Others, such as Great Clips and SportClips hair salons, are more appropriate for those who do not want to spend many hours at their stores.

© MARK LAMOYNE/SHUTTERSTOCK.COM

GLOBAL PERSPECTIVES IN SMALL BUSINESS

For small American businesses, the world is becoming smaller. National and international economies are growing more and more interdependent as political leadership and national economic directions change and trade barriers diminish or disappear. Globalization and instant worldwide communications are rapidly shrinking distances at the same time that they are expanding business opportunities. According to a recent study, the Internet is increasingly important to small-business strategic thinking, with more than 50 percent of those surveyed indicating that the Internet represented their most favored strategy for growth. This was more than double the next-favored choice, strategic alliances reflecting the opportunity to reach both global and domestic customers. The Internet and online payment systems enable even very small businesses to serve international customers. In fact, technology now gives small businesses the leverage and power to reach markets that were once limited solely to large corporations. According to the U.S. Commercial Service, "More than 70 percent of the world's purchasing power is outside of the United States and over the next five years, 85 percent of the world's economic growth will be overseas."[19]

The SBA offers help to the nation's small-business owners who want to enter the world markets. The SBA's efforts include counseling small firms on how and where to market overseas, matching U.S. small-business executives with potential overseas customers, and helping exporters to secure financing. The agency brings small U.S. firms into direct contact with potential overseas buyers and partners. The SBA International Trade Loan program provides guarantees of up to $5 million in loans to small-business owners. These loans help small firms in expanding or developing new export markets. The U.S. Commercial Service, a Commerce Department division, aids small- and medium-sized businesses in selling overseas. The division's global network includes more than 100 offices in the United States and 151 others in 75 countries around the world.[20]

Consider Daniel J. Nanigian, president of Nanmac Corporation in Framingham, Massachusetts. This company manufactures temperature sensors used in a wide range of industrial applications. With an export strategy aimed at growing revenues in diverse foreign markets including China, the Nanmac Corporation experienced explosive growth in 2009. The company nearly doubled its sales from $2.7 million in 2008 to $5.1 million in 2009. The company's international sales, at $300,000 in 2004, reached $700,000 in 2009 and $1.7 million in 2010. Its administrative, sales, and manufacturing employees have increased by 80 percent.

The company has a strong presence in China and is expanding in other markets, as well, including Latin America, Singapore, and Russia. Under Nanigian's guidance, the company has developed creative solutions and partnerships to help maximize its presence internationally. As part of its China strategy, Nanmac partners with distributors, recruits European and in-country sales representatives, uses a localized Chinese website, and relies for advice on the export assistance programs of the Massachusetts Small Business Development Center Network's Massachusetts Export Center. The strategy, along with travel to China to conduct technical training seminars and attend trade shows and technical conferences, has helped to grow Nanmac's Chinese client list from 1 in 2003 to more than 30 accounts today. Mr. Nanigian received SBA's Small Business Exporter of the Year Award.[21]

International trade will become more important to small-business owners as they face unique challenges in the new century. Small businesses, which are expected to remain the dominant form of organization in this country, must be prepared to adapt to significant demographic and economic changes in the world marketplace.

This chapter ends our discussion of American business today. From here on, we shall be looking closely at various aspects of business operations. We begin, in the next chapter, with a discussion of management—what management is, what managers do, and how they work to coordinate the basic economic resources within a business organization.

Concept Check

✓ What does the franchisor receive in a franchising agreement? What does the franchisee receive? What does each provide?

✓ Cite one major benefit of franchising for the franchisor. Cite one major benefit of franchising for the franchisee.

✓ How does the SBA help small business-owners who want to enter the world markets?

Summary

1 Define what a small business is and recognize the fields in which small businesses are concentrated.

A small business is one that is independently owned and operated for profit and is not dominant in its field. There are about 27.9 million businesses in this country, and 99.7 percent of them are small businesses. Small businesses employ more than half the nation's workforce. About 69 percent of small businesses survive at least two years and about 50 percent survive at least five years. More than half of all small businesses are in retailing and services.

2 Identify the people who start small businesses and the reasons why some succeed and many fail.

Such personal characteristics as independence, desire to create a new enterprise, and willingness to accept a challenge may encourage individuals to start small businesses. Various external circumstances, such as special expertise or even the loss of a job, also can supply the motivation to strike out on one's own. Poor planning and lack of capital and management experience are the major causes of small-business failures.

3 Assess the contributions of small businesses to our economy.

Small businesses have been responsible for a wide variety of inventions and innovations, some of which have given rise to new industries. Historically, small businesses have created the bulk of the nation's new jobs. Further, they have mounted effective competition to larger firms. They provide things that society needs, act as suppliers to larger firms, and serve as customers of other businesses, both large and small.

4 Describe the advantages and disadvantages of operating a small business.

The advantages of smallness in business include the opportunity to establish personal relationships with customers and employees, the ability to adapt to changes quickly, independence, and simplified record keeping. The major disadvantages are the high risk of failure, the limited potential for growth, and the limited ability to raise capital.

5 Explain how the Small Business Administration helps small businesses.

The Small Business Administration (SBA) was created in 1953 to assist and counsel the nation's millions of small-business owners. The SBA offers management courses and workshops; managerial help, including one-to-one counseling through SCORE; various publications; and financial assistance through guaranteed loans and SBICs. It places special emphasis on aid to minority-owned businesses, including those owned by women.

6 Explain the concept and types of franchising.

A franchise is a license to operate an individually owned business as though it were part of a chain. The franchisor provides a known business name, management skills, a method of doing business, and the training and required materials. The franchisee contributes labor and capital, operates the franchised business, and agrees to abide by the provisions of the franchise agreement. There are three major categories of franchise agreements.

7 Analyze the growth of franchising and its advantages and disadvantages.

Franchising has grown tremendously since the mid-1970s. The franchisor's major advantage in franchising is fast and well-controlled distribution of products with minimal capital outlay. In return, the franchisee has the opportunity to open a business with limited capital, to make use of the business experience of others, and to sell to an existing clientele. For this, the franchisee usually must pay both an initial franchise fee and a continuing royalty based on sales. He or she also must follow the dictates of the franchise with regard to operation of the business.

Worldwide business opportunities are expanding for small businesses. The SBA assists small-business owners in penetrating foreign markets. The next century will present unique challenges and opportunities for small-business owners.

Key Terms

You should now be able to define and give an example relevant to each of the following terms:

small business (128)
business plan (138)
Small Business
    Administration (SBA)
    (141)

Service Corps of Retired
    Executives (SCORE)
    (141)
small-business institutes
    (SBIs) (142)

small-business development
    centers (SBDCs) (143)
venture capital (144)
small-business investment
    companies (SBICs) (144)

franchise (144)
franchising (144)
franchisor (144)
franchisee (144)

Discussion Questions

1. Most people who start small businesses are aware of the high failure rate and the reasons for it. Why, then, do some take no steps to protect their firms from failure? What steps should they take?
2. Are the so-called advantages of small business really advantages? Wouldn't every small-business owner like his or her business to grow into a large firm?
3. Do average citizens benefit from the activities of the SBA, or is the SBA just another way to spend our tax money?
4. Would you rather own your own business independently or become a franchisee? Why?

Test Yourself

Matching Questions

1. _____ A carefully constructed guide for the person starting a business.
2. _____ A group of retired and active business people who volunteer their services to small businesses through the SBA.
3. _____ A government agency that assists, counsels, and protects the interests of small businesses in the United States.
4. _____ Money that is invested in small (and sometimes struggling) firms that have the potential to become very successful.
5. _____ Group of senior and graduate students in business administration who provide management counseling to small businesses.
6. _____ A business that is independently owned and operated for profit and is not dominant in its field.
7. _____ A person or organization purchasing a franchise.

8. _____ A license to operate an individually owned business as though it were a part of a chain of outlets or stores.
9. _____ The actual granting of a franchise.
10. _____ An individual or organization granting a franchise.

    a. venture capital
    b. franchisee
    c. joint venture
    d. Small-Business Institutes (SBIs)
    e. SCORE
    f. small business
    g. franchise
    h. strategic alliance
    i. business plan
    j. franchising
    k. SBA
    l. franchisor

True False Questions

11. **T F** The SBA has defined a small business as one independently owned, operated for profit, and not dominant in its field.
12. **T F** The various types of businesses attracting small business are generally grouped into service industries, distribution industries, and financial industries.
13. **T F** Small businesses are generally managed by professional managers.
14. **T F** Small firms have traditionally added more than their proportional share of new jobs to the economy.
15. **T F** Economically, the U.S government is not concerned with whether or not small businesses make it.
16. **T F** SCORE is a group of active business executives offering their services to small businesses for a fee.
17. **T F** A small-business investment company (SBIC) is a government agency that provides venture capital to small enterprises.

18. **T F** The purchaser of a franchise is called the franchisor.

19. **T F** An agreement between two franchisors in which the two franchisors offer their products together is called double franchising.

20. **T F** International trade will become more important to small-business owners in the new century.

Multiple-Choice Questions

21. _____ What is the primary reason that so many new businesses fail?
    a. Owner does not work hard enough
    b. Mismanagement resulting from lack of business know-how
    c. Low employee quality for new businesses
    d. Lack of brand-name recognition
    e. Inability to compete with well-established brand names

22. _____ Businesses such as flower shops, restaurants, bed and breakfasts, and automobile repair are good candidates for entrepreneurs because they
    a. do not require any skills.
    b. are the most likely to succeed.
    c. can obtain financing easily.
    d. require no special equipment.
    e. have a relatively low initial investment.

23. _____ An individual's desire to create a new business is referred to as
    a. the entrepreneurial spirit.
    b. the desire for ownership.
    c. self-determination.
    d. self-evaluation.
    e. the *laissez-faire* spirit.

24. _____ What is a common mistake that small-business owners make when their businesses begin growing?
    a. They sell more goods and services.
    b. They put too much money in advertising.
    c. They move beyond their local area.
    d. They over-expand without proper planning.
    e. They invest too much of their own money.

25. _____ The fact that insulin and power steering both originated with individual inventors and small companies is testimony to the power of small businesses as providers of
    a. employment.
    b. competition.
    c. technical innovation.
    d. capital.
    e. quality products.

26. _____ In her small retail shop, Jocelyn knows most of her best customers by name and knows their preferences in clothing and shoes. This demonstrates which advantage of a small business?
    a. Ability to adapt to change
    b. Independence from customer's desires
    c. Simplified record keeping
    d. Personal relationships with customers
    e. Small customer base

27. _____ Shonta started a graphic design firm a year ago. The business has done well, but it needs a lot more equipment, computers, and employees to continue expanding. Shonta thinks she can get all the money she will need from her bank. What advice might you give to her?
    a. She is right—the bank is likely to lend her as much as she needs because banks primarily focus on supporting small businesses.
    b. She is crazy—banks do not lend money to small businesses but only to well-known, well-established organizations.
    c. She should sell her business immediately before it fails because most small businesses fail during the first five years.
    d. She should not accept any new clients so that she can end the need to add additional equipment and employees.
    e. She should consider alternative sources of financing because banks provide only a portion of the total capital to small businesses.

28. _____ Volunteers for SCORE are
    a. mostly university business professors.
    b. active executives from large corporations.
    c. generally either lawyers or accountants.
    d. graduate business students working on projects.
    e. retired and active businesspeople from different industries.

29. _____ An individual or organization granting a license to operate an individually owned business as though it were part of a chain of outlets or stores is a(n)
    a. franchise.
    b. franchisor.
    c. franchisee.
    d. venture capitalist.
    e. entrepreneur.

30. _____ Manju asks for your advice in opening a new business. She plans to provide tax-related services to individuals and small-business owners in her community. Of course, she wants an attractive means of starting and operating her business with a reasonable hope of succeeding in it. What will be your advice?
    a. Start your own independent business.
    b. Form a partnership with a CPA.
    c. Consider purchasing a franchise.
    d. Forget about opening the business because it is too risky.
    e. First secure a loan from the Small Business Administration.

Answers to the Test Yourself questions appear at the end of the book on page TY-1.

Video Case

From Two Men and a Truck to 220 Franchises and 1,400 Trucks

Two Men and a Truck (www.twomenandatruck.com) began in the 1980s as a way for brothers Brig and Jon Sorber to make money while in high school. They started with one old pickup truck, placed a newspaper ad promoting their moving services in and around Lansing, Michigan, and charged $25 per hour to transport household goods. Their mother Mary Ellen Sheets created the hand-drawn logo of stick-figure men inside a truck, which has been part of the company's business identity since the beginning.

When the brothers left for college, their mother took over to keep the moving business on the move. Demand was so strong, in fact, that Sheets decided to buy a larger used truck for $350, hire two more men, and undertake even larger moving jobs. During school breaks, the brothers came home and earned extra spending money by climbing into one of the trucks and helping homeowners move.

Two Men and a Truck continued to attract so many customers that Sheets finally quit her job to operate the business as a full-time entrepreneur. In 1985, she hired more people, purchased a new truck, and set a tone of superior customer service embodied by the "Grandma Rule"—treat every customer with the same care and respect you would show your own grandmother. Within two years, Two Men and a Truck had earned its first profit, which Sheets donated to community charities. This was only the first of many efforts driven by the entrepreneur's core value of taking care of people—the community as well as the customers.

One day, Sheets was part of a panel about entrepreneurship and met a woman who had successfully franchised her business. With this woman's encouragement, Sheets looked into the idea of franchising Two Men and a Truck. She asked her daughter Melanie Bergeron to join the family business as head of the franchising division. Thanks to a grant, Bergeron was able to learn about franchising through weekly consultations with experts at the accounting firm of Deloitte & Touche. Two Men and a Truck started to offer franchises and as its aggressive growth continued, Bergeron's brothers returned to work in the family business a few years later.

Over time, each family member has found ways to apply his or her own strengths to the challenges and opportunities faced by the company, and to function effectively as business partners when they're all in the office dealing with a problem. Today, Brig Sorber is the CEO, Jon Sorber is the executive vice president, and Melanie Bergeron serves as chair of Two Men and a Truck. Looking ahead, the company has a structured succession plan in place for an orderly transition if the next generation chooses to become part of the business. Alicia Sorber, Brig's daughter, is already involved, working for a franchisee and learning from her father's experiences and ideas.

Two Men and a Truck now has 220 franchisees and 1,400 trucks across the United States and is expanding into Europe. The company's annual revenue is $275 million and it handles more than 400,000 moves every year. Franchisees have adopted the company's credo of caring, using their trucks and employees for the benefit of local causes. For example, some have moved boxes of donated food from collection points to food banks for distribution to needy families. Others have delivered cleaning supplies, food, and personal care items to areas hit hard by natural disasters. No matter what cause they support, local franchisees show how Two Men and a Truck cares for its communities as well as its customers.[22]

Questions

1. Which advantages of small business helped Mary Ellen Sheets establish and grow Two Men and a Truck?
2. Which disadvantages of small business did Two Men and a Truck have to overcome? If you had been part of the business at the start, what suggestions would you have offered for overcoming these issues?
3. Do you think it's a good idea for Two Men and a Truck to offer franchises outside of North America? Why or why not? What kinds of questions would international franchisees be likely to ask the company?

Building Skills for Career Success

1. Social Media Exercise

American Express's "Open Forum" is a website that is designed for small-business owners (www.openforum.com). Do a search using a search engine like Google or Bing and you will also find its presence on Tumblr and Pinterest. Take a look at the Open Forum website and answer the following questions.

1. What questions can Open Forum answer for business owners?
2. Develop a list of five issues or topics that you feel illustrates how American Express does an effective job of presenting information on this website.

2. Building Team Skills

A business plan is a written statement that documents the nature of a business and how that business intends to achieve its goals. Although entrepreneurs should prepare a business plan *before* starting a business, the plan also serves as an effective guide later on. The plan should concisely describe the business's mission, the amount of capital it requires, its target market, competition, resources, production plan, marketing plan, organizational plan, assessment of risk, and financial plan.

Assignment

1. Working in a team of four students, identify a company in your community that would benefit from using a business plan, or create a scenario in which a hypothetical entrepreneur wants to start a business.
2. Using the resources of the library or the Internet and/or interviews with business owners, write a business plan incorporating the information in Table 5-3.
3. Present your business plan to the class.

3. Researching Different Careers

Many people dream of opening and operating their own businesses. Are you one of them? To be successful, entrepreneurs must have certain characteristics; their profiles generally differ from those of people who work for someone else. Do you know which personal characteristics make some entrepreneurs succeed and others fail? Do you fit the successful entrepreneur's profile? What is your potential for opening and operating a successful small business?

Assignment

1. Use the resources of the library or the Internet to establish what a successful entrepreneur's profile is and to determine whether your personal characteristics fit that profile. Internet addresses that can help you are www.smartbiz.com/sbs/arts/ieb1.html and www.sba.gov (see "Start your Business" and "FAQ"). These sites have quizzes online that can help you to assess your personal characteristics. The SBA also has helpful brochures.
2. Interview several small-business owners. Ask them to describe the characteristics they think are necessary for being a successful entrepreneur.
3. Using your findings, write a report that includes the following:
   a. A profile of a successful small-business owner
   b. A comparison of your personal characteristics with the profile of the successful entrepreneur
   c. A discussion of your potential as a successful small-business owner

Running a Business
Part 2

Graeter's: A Fourth-Generation Family Business

Independent and family-owned for more than 140 years, Graeter's has successfully made the transition from a 19th-century mom-and-pop ice cream business to a 21st-century corporation with three manufacturing facilities, dozens of ice cream shops, and hundreds of employees. Much of the company's success over the years has been due to the family's strong and enduring entrepreneurial spirit.

Small Business, Big Ambitions

The road to small-business success started with co-founder Louis Charles Graeter, who developed the startup's first flavors, insisted on only the finest ingredients, and made all his ice cream by hand in small batches to ensure freshness and quality. After his death, his wife and co-founder Regina maintained the same high level of quality as she led the company through three decades of aggressive growth. Her great-grandson, CEO Richard Graeter II, says that "without her strength, fortitude, and foresight, there would be no Graeter's ice cream today."

Richard, Bob, and Chip, great-grandsons of the founders, are the fourth generation to own and operate Graeter's. They grew up in the business, and now they share responsibility for the firm's day-to-day management and for determining its future direction. Bob worked his way up to vice president of operations, starting with a management position in one of the Graeter's ice-cream shops. Chip, currently vice president of retail operations, handled all kinds of jobs in Graeter's stores as a teenager. He uses this first-hand knowledge of customer relations to fine-tune every store function.

Richard Graeter became the company's CEO in 2007. "Even though I have the title of CEO, in a family business titles don't mean a whole lot," he comments. "The functions that I am doing now as CEO, I was doing as executive vice president for years . . . It really was and remains a partnership with my two cousins . . . Our fathers brought us into the business at an early age . . . I think most important is we saw our fathers and their dedication and the fact that, you know, they came home later, they came home tired, they got up early and went to work before we ever got up to go to school in the morning, and you see that dedication and appreciate that—that is what keeps your business going."

Graeter continues, "It can be challenging to work with your family. My father and I didn't always see things the same

way. But on the other hand, there is a lot of strength in the family relationship . . . we certainly had struggles, and family businesses do struggle, especially with transition . . . but we found people to help us, including lawyers, accountants, and a family-business psychologist."

Growing Beyond Cincinnati

To expand beyond Cincinnati without diverting resources from the existing stores and factory, the third generation of Graeter's family owners decided to license a handful of franchise operators. One franchise operation was so successful that it even opened its own factory. A few years ago, however, the fourth generation switched gears on growth and repurchased all the stores of its last remaining franchisee. "When you think about Graeter's," says the CEO, "the core of Graeter's is the quality of the product. You can't franchise your core. So by franchising our manufacturing, that created substantial risk for the organization, because the customer doesn't know that it is a franchise. . . . They know it is Graeter's. . . . You really have to rely on the intention and goodwill of the individual franchisees to make the product the way you would make it, and that is not an easy thing to guarantee."

After working with consultants to carefully analyze the situation and evaluate alternative paths to future growth, the founder's great-grandsons decided against further franchising. Instead, they pursued nationwide distribution through a large network of grocery stores and supermarket chains. They also built a new facility to increase production capacity and hired experienced executives to help manage the expanded business.

As a private company, Graeter's can take actions like these without worrying about the reaction of the stock market. Specifically, Graeter's is an S-corporation, which allows it limited-liability protection coupled with the benefit of not being taxed as a corporation. Instead, the three owners—who are the stockholders—pay only personal income taxes on the corporation's profits. In the event of significant legal or tax code changes, Graeter's owners do have the option of choosing a different form of corporate organization.[23]

© ISTOCKPHOTO.COM/LUIO

Questions

1. Graeter's current management team bought the business from their parents, who did not have a formal succession plan in place to indicate who would do what. Do you think the current team should have such a plan specifying who is to step into the business, when, and with what responsibilities? Why or why not?

2. Graeter's hired management consultants to help improve its training procedures and expand distribution. "I think my cousins and I all have come to realize we can't do it alone," says the CEO. Why do you think the management team made this decision? Does the involvement of outside consultants move Graeter's further from its roots as a family business?

3. Do you agree with Graeter's decision to stop franchising? Explain your answer.

Building a Business Plan: Part 2

After reading Part 2, "Business Ownership and Entrepreneurship," you should be ready to tackle the company and industry component of your business plan. In this section, you will provide information about the background of the company, choice of the legal business form, information on the product or services to be offered, and descriptions of potential customers, current competitors, and the business's future. This chapter and the previous chapter (Chapter 4) in your textbook, "Choosing a Form of Business Ownership," and Chapter 5, "Small Business, Entrepreneurship, and Franchises," can help you to answer some of the questions in this part of the business plan.

The Company and Industry Component

The company and industry analysis should include the answers to at least the following questions:

2.1. What is the legal form of your business? Is your business a sole proprietorship, a partnership, or a corporation?

2.2. What licenses or permits will you need, if any?

2.3. Is your business a new independent business, a take-over, an expansion, or a franchise?

2.4. If you are dealing with an existing business, how did your company get to the point where it is today?

2.5. What does your business do, and how does it satisfy customers' needs?

2.6. How did you choose and develop the products or services to be sold, and how are they different from those currently on the market?

2.7. What industry do you operate in, and what are the industry-wide trends?

2.8. Who are the major competitors in your industry?

2.9. Have any businesses recently entered or exited? Why did they leave?

2.10. Why will your business be profitable, and what are your growth opportunities?

2.11. Does any part of your business involve e-business?

Review of Business Plan Activities

Make sure to check the information you have collected, make any changes, and correct any weaknesses before beginning Part 3. *Reminder:* Review the answers to questions in the preceding part to make sure that all your answers are consistent throughout the business plan. Finally, write a summary statement that incorporates all the information for this part of the business plan.

Endnotes

1. Based on information in Leslie Patton, "Seattle's Best to Take on Dunkin' with Drive-Throughs," *Bloomberg*, November 14, 2012, www.bloomberg.com; Jenn Abelson and Todd Wallack, "Dunkin' Donuts Lays Claim to 'Best Coffee in America' Trademark," *Boston Globe*, October 4, 2012, www.bostonglobe.com; Lisa Baertlein, "Dunkin' Brands Raises 2012 View as Competition Brews," *Reuters*, October 25, 2012, www.reuters.com.

2. U.S. Small Business Administration website at www.sbaonline.sba.gov/contractingopportunities/owners/basic/what (accessed June 5, 2013).

3. U.S. Small Business Administration, Office of Advocacy, *Frequently Asked Questions*, updated September 2012, www.sba.gov/advo (accessed June 5, 2013).

4. Ibid.

5. Ibid.

6. Thomas A. Garrett, "Entrepreneurs Thrive in America," *Bridges*, Federal Reserve Bank of St. Louis, Spring 2005, 2.

7. U.S. Small Business Administration, Office of Advocacy, *Frequently Asked Questions*, updated September 2012, www.sba.gov/advo (accessed February 8, 2013), and the SBA website at sba.gov/about-sba-services/7367/432861 (accessed June 5, 2013).

8. U.S. Small Business Administration, *News Release*, Number 05–53, September 13, 2005, www.sba.gov/teens/brian_hendricks.html (accessed February 8, 2013).

9. U.S. Small Business Administration, Office of Advocacy, *Frequently Asked Questions*, updated September 2012, www.sba.gov/advo (accessed June 5, 2013).

10. SBA Press Release, "Computer Simulation Company from Florida Is National Small Business of the Year," May 25, 2010, www.sba.gov/news (accessed March 15, 2012).

11. U.S. Small Business Administration, Office of Advocacy, *Frequently Asked Questions*, September 2012, www.sba.gov/advo (accessed June 5, 2013).

12. Timothy S. Hatten, *Small Business Management: Entrepreneurship and Beyond*, 5th ed., Copyright © 2012 by Cengage Learning. Reprinted with permission.

13. SCORE website at www.score.org/about-score (accessed February 8, 2013).

14. SCORE website at score.org (accessed February 8, 2013).

15. The SBA website at www.sba.gov (accessed February 8, 2013).

16. U.S. Small Business Administration, *News Release*, Release Number 10–33, May 26, 2010, www.sba.gov/news (accessed March 18, 2012).

17. SBIC Program Overview, website at http://archive.sba.gov/idc/groups/public/documents/sba_program_office/inv_sbic; Small Business Investor Alliance website at www.nabic.org (accessed March 23, 2012); sba.gov/INV (accessed February 8, 2013) and the SBA website at sba.gov/content/sbc-program-overview-0 (accessed February 8, 2013).

18. Cindy Elmore, "Putting the Power into the Hands of Small Business Owners," *Marketwise*, Federal Reserve Bank of Richmond, Issue II, 2005, 13.

19. U.S. Commercial Service, U.S. Department of Commerce 2011 Annual Report, accessed at trade.gov/cs/cs_annualreport12.pdf (accessed February 9, 2013).

20. SBA Press Release 12-12, "SBA Announces a New Partnership to Connect Small Businesses With Corporate Supply Chains," March 22, 2012, www.sba.gov/news (accessed March 23, 2012); and International Trade website at www.trade.gov/CS/ (accessed March 23, 2012); and trade.gov/cs/cs_annualreport12.pdf (accessed February 9, 2013).

21. SBA Press Release, "SBA 2010 Small Business Exporter of the Year," www.sba.gov/news (accessed March 20, 2012); and NANMAC Corporation website at http://nanmac.com/press-sba.html (accessed February 9, 2013).

22. Sources: Based on information in Joe Boomgaard, "Mother Knows Best: Mary Ellen Sheets Helps Foster Culture for Two Men and a Truck Moving Company," *MiBiz (Grand Rapids, Michigan)*, May 13, 2012, www.mibiz.com; "Janelle Dowley Distinction: President and Franchisee of Two Men and a Truck," *Palm Beach Post (Florida)*, February 20, 2012, p. 2D; "In the Classroom: ABC Academy, Two Men and a Truck Join Forces in Thanksgiving Food Collection," *Michigan Live*, November 19, 2012, www.mlive.com; J. Patrick Pepper, "Woodhaven: From Downriver to Sandy's Downtrodden, a Special Delivery," *News Herald (Downriver, Michigan)*, November 16, 2012, www.thenewsherald.com; www.twomenandatruck.com.

23. Sources: Based on information from Kimberly L. Jackson, "Graeter's Premium Chocolate Chip Ice Cream Lands at Stop & Shop," *Newark Star-Ledger (NJ)*, April 4, 2012, www.nj.com; "Graeter's Ice Cream Debuts in Bay Area," *Tampa Bay Times (St. Petersburg, FL)*, January 10, 2012, p. 4B; Jim Carper, "Graeter's Runs a Hands-on Ice Cream Plant," *Dairy Foods*, August 2011, pp. 36+; Jim Carper, "The Greater Good," *Dairy Foods*, August 2011, pp. 95+; "Graeter's Unveils New 'Mystery Flavor,'" *Dayton Daily News*, March 29, 2012, www.daytondailynews.com; Bob Driehaus, "A Cincinnati Ice Cream Maker Aims Big," *New York Times*, September 11, 2010, www.nytimes.com; Lucy May, "Graeter's Northern Kentucky Franchisee Puts Stores on the Block," *Business Courier*, August 6, 2010, http://cincinnati.bizjournals.com; www.graeters.com; interviews with company staff and Cengage videos about Graeter's.

© PRESSMASTER/SHUTTERSTOCK.COM

Understanding the Management Process

Learning Objectives

Once you complete this chapter, you will be able to:

1 Define what management is.

2 Describe the four basic management functions: planning, organizing, leading and motivating, and controlling.

3 Distinguish among the various kinds of managers in terms of both level and area of management.

4 Identify the key management skills of successful managers.

5 Explain the different types of leadership.

6 Discuss the steps in the managerial decision-making process.

7 Describe how organizations benefit from total quality management.

Why Should You Care?

Most of the people who read this chapter will advance upward and become managers. Thus an overview of the field of management is essential.

Amazon's Customer First Philosophy

Ever since the online retailer Amazon.com (www.amazon.com) opened its virtual doors in 1995, founder and CEO Jeff Bezos has put long-term customer satisfaction at the top of his list when planning for the future. Amazon.com is an Internet success story, graduating from a scrappy, garage-based startup to a well-managed retail power player and a trusted provider of information services. Its mission is to "be earth's most customer centric company." When executives face a decision about creating a new product or buying a business, the first question they ask is whether it will be good for Amazon's customers. If not, they don't move ahead.

Bezos is known for his big-picture view of business and his long-range planning expertise. He looks ahead five to seven years and has the patience to give innovations enough time to establish themselves. For example, when Amazon introduced the Kindle e-book reader in 2007, digital books were not yet mainstream. By making the Kindle easy to use and pricing it lower than competing products, Amazon attracted millions of buyers. Then, after Apple launched the iPad in 2010, Amazon responded with a popularly priced tablet version of the Kindle. By this time, people were routinely downloading books, movies, music, and other content.

Despite the Kindle's enormous success, the product line itself is not profitable—all according to plan. Bezos wants Amazon to profit when customers *use* their Kindles, not when they buy their Kindles. In fact, customers with a Kindle read four times as many books as before they bought the Kindle, and they continue buying printed books while buying digital books as well, which means Amazon benefits in the long run.

Looking ahead to Amazon's e-commerce future, Bezos has acquired a firm that makes robots to move merchandise inside order fulfillment centers. The robots aren't intended to displace employees, but to make them more productive as Amazon opens new facilities to keep up with the orders its customers will place next month, next year, and beyond.[1]

Did You Know?

Amazon rings up more than $48 billion in annual revenue from retailing and information services.

The leadership employed at Amazon, which creates the company's unique culture, illustrates that management can be one of the most exciting and rewarding professions available today. Depending on its size, a firm may employ a number of specialized managers who are responsible for particular areas of management, such as marketing, finance, and operations. That same organization also includes managers at several levels within the firm. In this chapter, we define *management* and describe the four basic management functions of planning, organizing, leading and motivating, and controlling. Then we focus on the types of managers with respect to levels of responsibility and areas of expertise. Next, we focus on the skills of effective managers and the different roles managers must play. We examine several styles of leadership and explore the process by which managers make decisions. We also describe how total quality management can improve customer satisfaction.

Learning Objective

1 Define what management is.

management the process of coordinating people and other resources to achieve the goals of an organization

WHAT IS MANAGEMENT?

Management is the process of coordinating people and other resources to achieve the goals of an organization. As we saw in Chapter 1, most organizations make use of four kinds of resources: material, human, financial, and informational (see Figure 6-1).

Material resources are the tangible, physical resources an organization uses. For example, General Motors uses steel, glass, and fiberglass to produce cars and trucks on complex machine-driven assembly lines. A college or university uses books, classroom buildings, desks, and computers to educate students. And the Mayo Clinic uses operating room equipment, diagnostic machines, and laboratory tests to provide health care.

Perhaps the most important resources of any organization are its *human resources*—people. In fact, some firms live by the philosophy that employees are their most important assets. Some managers believe that the way employees are developed and managed has more impact on an organization than other vital components such as marketing, financial decisions, production, or technology. Research supports this belief. It shows that prioritizing human resources and working to ensure that employees are happy can greatly affect productivity and customer relationships. For example, taking steps to put employees in a good mood early in the day can positively impact company performance.[2]

Financial resources are the funds an organization uses to meet its obligations to investors and creditors. A 7-Eleven convenience store obtains money from customers at the checkout counter and uses a portion to pay its suppliers. Your college obtains money in the form of tuition, income from endowments, and state and federal grants. It uses the money to pay bills, insurance premiums, and salaries.

Increasingly, organizations are finding that they cannot afford to ignore *information*. External environmental conditions—the economy, consumer markets, technology, politics, and cultural forces—are all changing so rapidly that a business must adapt to survive. To adapt to change, the business must gather information about competitors and changes to the industry in order to learn from the failures and successes of others.

It is important to realize that the four types of resources described earlier are only general categories. Within each category are hundreds or thousands of more specific resources. It is this complex mix of specific resources—which varies between companies and industries—that managers must coordinate to produce goods and services.

Another way to look at management is in terms of the different functions managers perform, which are planning, organizing, leading and motivating employees, and controlling. We look at each of these management functions in the next section.

Concept Check

✓ What is management?

✓ What are the four kinds of resources?

FIGURE 6-1 The Four Main Resources of Management

Managers coordinate an organization's resources to achieve the organization's goals.

MANAGEMENT

Material resources — Human resources — Financial resources — Informational resources → Organizational goals

© CENGAGE LEARNING 2015

Learning Objective

2 Describe the four basic management functions: planning, organizing, leading and motivating, and controlling.

BASIC MANAGEMENT FUNCTIONS

After years of declining profits and the near destruction of the auto industry in the wake of the recent economic crisis, Ford analyzed its situation and restructured to respond to changes in the industry and cut costs. This plan involved hiring new managers, including a new Chief Operating Officer. It also physically restructured by closing plants in Europe, moving manufacturing operations closer to major markets such as Brazil, and adding new car models adapted to the needs of growing target markets.[3]

Management functions do not occur according to some rigid, preset timetable. Managers do not plan in January, organize in February, lead and motivate in March, and control in April. At any given time, managers may engage in a number of functions simultaneously. However, each function tends to lead naturally to others. Figure 6-2 provides a visual framework for a more detailed discussion of the four basic management functions. How well managers perform these key functions determines whether a business is successful.

Planning

planning establishing organizational goals and deciding how to accomplish them

mission a statement of the basic purpose that makes an organization different from others

strategic planning process the establishment of an organization's major goals and objectives and the allocation of resources to achieve them

goal an end result that an organization is expected to achieve over a one- to ten-year period

objective a specific statement detailing what an organization intends to accomplish over a shorter period of time

Planning, in its simplest form, is establishing organizational goals and deciding how to accomplish them. It is often referred to as the "first" management function because all other management functions depend on planning. Organizations such as Twitter, Amazon, and Facebook base the planning process on a mission statement.

An organization's **mission** is a statement of the basic purpose that makes that organization different from others. Starbucks mission statement, for example, is "to inspire and nurture the human spirit—one person, one cup, and one neighborhood at a time." Amazon.com's mission is "to be earth's most customer-centric company; to build a place where people can come to find and discover anything they might want to buy online." Facebook's mission statement is "to give people the power to share and make the world more open and connected."[4] Once a mission has been stated, the next step is to engage in strategic planning.

STRATEGIC PLANNING PROCESS The **strategic planning process** involves establishing an organization's major goals and objectives and allocating resources to achieve them. Top management is responsible for strategic planning, although customers, products, competitors, and company resources all factor into the process.

In today's rapidly changing business environment, constant internal or external changes may necessitate changes in a company's goals, mission, or strategy. The timeline for strategic plans is generally one to two years, but can be much longer. Strategic plans should be flexible and include action items, such as outlining how plans will be implemented.

ESTABLISHING GOALS AND OBJECTIVES A **goal** is an end result that an organization is expected to achieve over a one- to ten-year period. An **objective** is a specific statement detailing what the organization intends to accomplish over a shorter period of time.

Goals and objectives can involve a variety of factors, such as sales, company growth, costs, customer satisfaction, and employee morale. Whereas a small manufacturer may focus primarily on sales objectives for the next six months, a large firm may be more interested in goals that will impact the firm for several years. While many

Human Resources. Superior human resources management can set a firm apart. Do you have a great business plan or product? A competitor can easily copy both. Great employees, however, are much harder to duplicate. That's why being able to attract, train, and retain talented workers can give a firm a competitive advantage over its rivals.

© KONSTANTIN CHAGIN/SHUTTERSTOCK.COM

FIGURE 6-2 The Management Process

Note that management is not a step-by-step procedure but a process with a feedback loop that represents a flow.

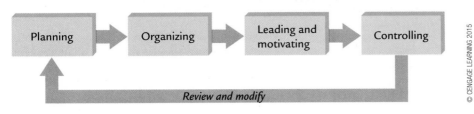

Planning → Organizing → Leading and motivating → Controlling

Review and modify

© CENGAGE LEARNING 2015

retailers have scaled back in recent years, Starbucks has set ambitious growth targets through opening new stores and acquiring new businesses, such as the Evolution Fresh juice chain, La Boulange bakery, and the Teavana tea chain. The company aims to open around 1,000 new stores annually, to achieve 20,000 global outlets within the next few years.[5] Finally, goals are set at every level of an organization. Every member of an organization—the president of the company, the head of a department, and an operating employee at the lowest level—has a set of goals that he or she hopes to achieve.

It is likely that some conflicts will arise among levels within the organization, but goals must be made consistent across an organization. A production department, for example, may have a goal of minimizing costs. One way to do this is to produce only one type of product and limited customer service. Marketing may have a goal of maximizing sales, which might be achieved by offering a wide range of products and options. As part of goal-setting, the manager responsible for *both* departments must strike a balance between conflicting goals. This balancing process is called *optimization*.

The optimization of conflicting goals requires insight and ability. Faced with the marketing-versus-production conflict just described, most managers would find a middle ground through offering a moderately diverse product line featuring only the most popular products. Such a compromise would be best for the whole organization.

SWOT ANALYSIS SWOT analysis is the identification and evaluation of a firm's strengths, weaknesses, opportunities, and threats. Strengths and weaknesses are internal factors that affect a company's capabilities. Strengths refer to a firm's favorable characteristics and core competencies. **Core competencies** are approaches and processes that a company performs well that may give it an advantage over its competitors. These core competencies may help the firm attract financial and human resources that increase the firm's capacity to produce products that satisfy customers. Weaknesses refer to internal limitations a company faces in developing or implementing plans. At times, managers have difficulty identifying and understanding the negative effects of weaknesses in their organizations.

External opportunities and threats exist independently of the firm. Opportunities refer to favorable conditions in the environment that could benefit the organization if properly exploited. Threats, on the other hand, are conditions or barriers that may prevent the firm from reaching its objectives. Opportunities and threats can stem

© KURHAN/SHUTTERSTOCK.COM

General Motors Mission Statement

"G.M. is a multinational corporation engaged in socially responsible operations, worldwide. It is dedicated to provide products and services of such quality that our customers will receive superior value while our employees and business partners will share in our success and our stock-holders will receive a sustained superior return on their investment."

General Motors

What is your organization's purpose? How is it different than other organizations? Those are the questions a firm's mission statement like the one shown here should answer. Mission statements are meant for multiple audiences, including a company's customers, investors, the general public, and employees. Most firms familiarize their personnel with their mission statements so they know what's expected of them and what they should strive for.

SWOT analysis the identification and evaluation of a firm's strengths, weaknesses, opportunities, and threats

core competencies approaches and processes that a company performs well that may give it an advantage over its competitors

Are you ready to be a manager? Start now to inventory your personal and professional strengths, weaknesses, opportunities, and threats so you can identify areas for improvement and prepare for future success.

- *What are your strengths?* Think about the skills, training, and experiences that successful managers need. For example, are you a top-notch communicator? Do you have excellent technical skills? Do you know how to get along with people at all levels? Are you following developments in your industry and in the business world?

- *What are your weaknesses?* Are your skills and training up to date? Do you know how to make a good impression with potential employers? Do you have the enthusiasm, commitment, confidence, and patience you need for success in management? Are you ready for more responsibility? How can you acquire the education or experience you need for your chosen field?

- *What opportunities do you see?* Are businesses looking for the capabilities, education, and job experience that you count among your strengths? Are you involved in volunteer activities, hobbies, or internships that help you develop your management capabilities? Can your personal or professional contacts provide ideas or guidance about moving into management?

- *What threats might affect you?* What unfavorable trends might affect your ability to advance into management? Which developments in the business world are likely to be most challenging to you as a manager? What steps can you take today to be ready for tomorrow's threats and opportunities?

Sources: Based on information in Ron Ashkenas, "The Case for Growing Your Own Senior Leaders," *Harvard Business Review Blog Network*, October 30, 2012, http://blogs.hbr.org; Michael Mink, "Develop and Maximize Strengths to Lead Effectively," *Investor's Business Daily*, October 2, 2012, http://news.investors.com; Peter Whitehead, "A Tough Test of Leadership Ability," *Financial Times*, March 29, 2012, p. 1; Glenn Llopis, "Five Most Effective Ways to Invest in Your Career," *Forbes*, October 22, 2012, www.forbes.com.

plan an outline of the actions by which an organization intends to accomplish its goals and objectives

strategic plan an organization's broadest plan, developed as a guide for major policy setting and decision making

tactical plan a smaller scale plan developed to implement a strategy

operational plan a type of plan designed to implement tactical plans

from many sources within the business environment. Because environmental factors vary between firms and industries, threats for some firms may be opportunities for others. Examples of strengths, weaknesses, opportunities, and threats are shown in Figure 6-3.

TYPES OF PLANS Once goals and objectives have been set for the organization, managers must develop plans for achieving them. A **plan** is an outline of the actions by which an organization intends to accomplish its goals and objectives. The organization develops several types of plans, as shown in Figure 6-4.

An organization's **strategic plan** is its broadest plan, developed as a guide during the strategic planning process for major policy setting and decision making. Strategic plans are set by the board of directors and top management and are generally designed to achieve the organization's long-term goals. Thus, a firm's strategic plan defines what business the company is in or wants to be in and the kind of company it is or wants to be. After decades of being one of the dominant video game companies in the world, Nintendo faces stiff competition from free or low-cost games, such as Angry Birds, that can be played on smartphones and tablets. Sharply sagging sales prompted the company to revise its strategic plan to focus more on product innovation and adapting to the new ways users play games. Its Wii U console, for example, combines aspects of an iPad with traditional gaming controls.[6]

In addition to strategic plans, most organizations also employ several narrower kinds of plans. A **tactical plan** is a smaller scale plan developed to implement a strategy. Most tactical plans cover a one- to three-year period. If a strategic plan will take five years to complete, the firm may develop five tactical plans, one covering each year. Tactical plans may be updated periodically as dictated by conditions and experience. Their more limited scope permits them to be changed more easily than strategies. As part of its tactical plan to improve revenue, Best Buy's CEO is fighting slumping sales with a reinvention effort called "Renew Blue." This plan involves more emphasis on online sales through bestbuy.com and improving distribution so that stores do not run out of popular items.[7]

An **operational plan** is a type of plan designed to implement tactical plans. Operational plans are usually established for one year or less and deal with how to accomplish the organization's specific objectives.

Regardless of how hard managers try, sometimes business activities do not go as planned. Today, most corporations also develop contingency plans along with strategies, tactical plans, and operational plans. A **contingency plan** is a plan that outlines alternative courses of action that may be taken if an organization's other plans are disrupted or become ineffective. As the European Union struggles with debt, fiscal austerity measures, and Greece's possible exit from the Euro zone,

FIGURE 6-3 Elements and Examples of SWOT Analysis

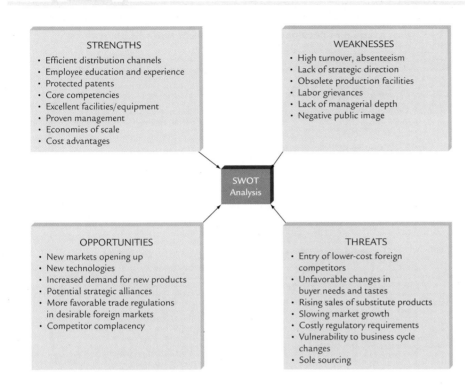

STRENGTHS
- Efficient distribution channels
- Employee education and experience
- Protected patents
- Core competencies
- Excellent facilities/equipment
- Proven management
- Economies of scale
- Cost advantages

WEAKNESSES
- High turnover, absenteeism
- Lack of strategic direction
- Obsolete production facilities
- Labor grievances
- Lack of managerial depth
- Negative public image

SWOT Analysis

OPPORTUNITIES
- New markets opening up
- New technologies
- Increased demand for new products
- Potential strategic alliances
- More favorable trade regulations in desirable foreign markets
- Competitor complacency

THREATS
- Entry of lower-cost foreign competitors
- Unfavorable changes in buyer needs and tastes
- Rising sales of substitute products
- Slowing market growth
- Costly regulatory requirements
- Vulnerability to business cycle changes
- Sole sourcing

© CENGAGE LEARNING 2015

contingency plan a plan that outlines alternative courses of action that may be taken if an organization's other plans are disrupted or become ineffective

organizing the grouping of resources and activities to accomplish some end result in an efficient and effective manner

leading the process of influencing people to work toward a common goal

motivating the process of providing reasons for people to work in the best interests of an organization

companies have developed contingency plans to ensure that production continues, distribution is unaffected, and workers are paid. Most companies have plans for different scenarios.[8]

Organizing the Enterprise

After goal-setting and planning, the manager's second major function is organization. **Organizing** is the grouping of resources and activities to accomplish some end result in an efficient and effective manner. Consider the case of an inventor who creates a new product and goes into business to sell it. At first, the inventor will do everything on his or her own—purchase raw materials, make the product, advertise it, sell it, and keep business records. Eventually, as business grows, the inventor will need help. To begin with, he or she might hire a professional sales representative and a part-time bookkeeper. Later, it also might be necessary to hire sales staff, people to assist with production, and an accountant. As the inventor hires new personnel, he or she must decide what each person will do, to whom each person will report, and how each person can best take part in the organization's activities. We discuss these and other facets of the organizing function in much more detail in Chapter 7.

Leading and Motivating

The leading and motivating function is concerned with an organization's human resources. Specifically, **leading** is the process of influencing people to work toward a common goal. **Motivating** is the process of providing reasons for

C.W. GRIFFIN/MCT/LANDOV

Tearing down the walls at Burger King. Burger King's top-level executives no longer have closed door offices, and employees no longer work in cubicles. The new physical arrangement facilitates better communication and collaboration among employees at all levels.

FIGURE 6-4 Types of Plans

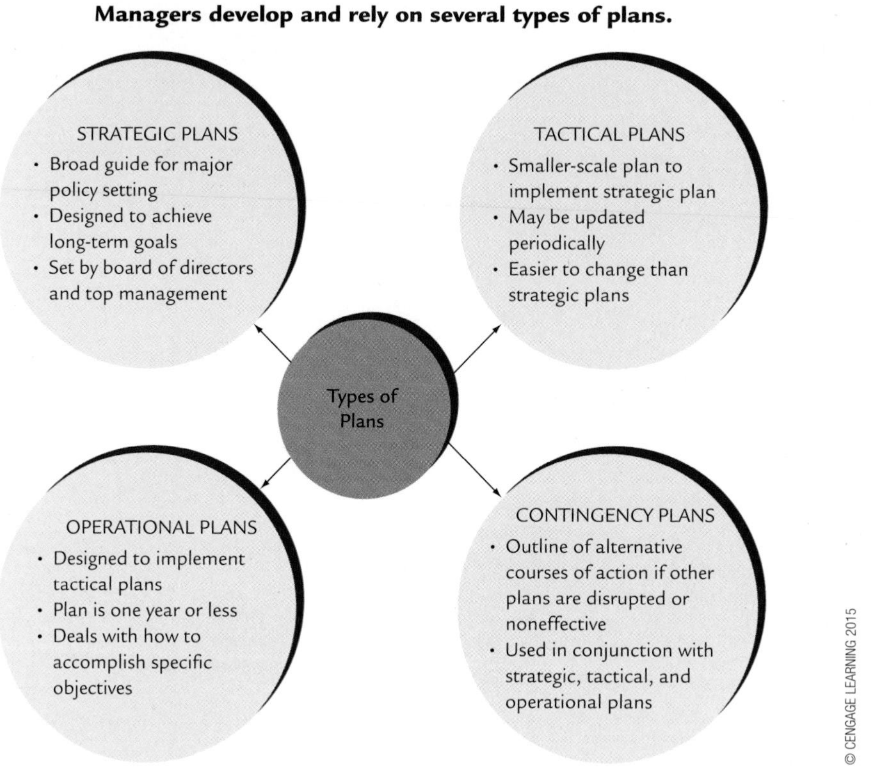

Managers develop and rely on several types of plans.

STRATEGIC PLANS
- Broad guide for major policy setting
- Designed to achieve long-term goals
- Set by board of directors and top management

TACTICAL PLANS
- Smaller-scale plan to implement strategic plan
- May be updated periodically
- Easier to change than strategic plans

Types of Plans

OPERATIONAL PLANS
- Designed to implement tactical plans
- Plan is one year or less
- Deals with how to accomplish specific objectives

CONTINGENCY PLANS
- Outline of alternative courses of action if other plans are disrupted or noneffective
- Used in conjunction with strategic, tactical, and operational plans

directing the combined processes of leading and motivating

people to work in the best interests of an organization. Together, leading and motivating are often referred to as **directing**.

Leading and motivating are critical activities because of the importance of an organization's human resources. Obviously, different people do things for different reasons—that is, they have different *motivations*. Some are interested primarily in earning as much money as they can. Others may be spurred on by opportunities to get promoted. Part of a manager's job, then, is to determine what factors motivate workers and to try to provide those incentives to encourage effective performance. Many people choose to work at Amazon because it is the largest online retailer, worth over $100 billion, and they want to be part of a major international company with tremendous market share. Jeff Bezos, CEO of Amazon, is the top CEO in America and has guided Amazon to success through his model leadership. While other companies pay more (no executive earns over $175,000), he motivates his employees through keeping the workplace fast-paced and exciting, providing benefits like restricted stock options, and maintaining a tight focus on customer satisfaction and needs.[9] A lot of research has been done on both motivation and leadership. As you will see in Chapter 10, research on motivation has yielded very useful information. However, research on leadership has been less successful. Despite decades of study, no one has discovered a general set of personal traits or characteristics that makes a good leader. Later in this chapter, we discuss leadership in more detail.

Controlling Ongoing Activities

controlling the process of evaluating and regulating ongoing activities to ensure that goals are achieved

Controlling is the process of evaluating and regulating ongoing activities to ensure that goals are achieved. Honeywell Aerospace, for example, makes employee and product safety a priority goal. Because of the intricacy of its products, the company

FIGURE 6-5 The Control Function

The control function includes three steps: setting standards, measuring actual performance, and taking corrective action.

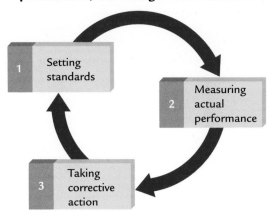

© CENGAGE LEARNING 2015

upholds rigorous quality standards in their design, manufacture, and distribution through the application of its Honeywell Quality Value program.

The control function includes three steps (see Figure 6-5). The first is *setting standards* against which performance can be compared. The second is *measuring actual performance* and comparing it with the standard. The third is *taking corrective action* as necessary. Notice that the control function is circular in nature. The steps in the control function must be repeated periodically until the goal is achieved. For example, suppose that Southwest Airlines establishes a goal of increasing profits by 12 percent. Southwest's management will monitor its profit on a monthly basis to ensure success. After three months, if profit has increased by 3 percent, management may assume that plans are effective. In this case, no action will likely be taken. However, if profit has increased only 1 percent, some corrective action will be needed to get the firm on track. The action that is required depends on the reason for the less-than-expected increase.

KINDS OF MANAGERS

Managers can be classified in two ways: according to their level within an organization and according to their area of management. In this section, we use both perspectives to explore the various types of managers.

Levels of Management

For the moment, think of an organization as a three-story structure (as illustrated in Figure 6-6). Each story corresponds to one of the three general levels of management: top managers, middle managers, and first-line managers.

TOP MANAGERS A **top manager** is an upper-level executive who guides and controls an organization's overall fortunes. Top managers represent the smallest of the three groups. In terms of planning, they are generally responsible for developing the organization's mission. They also determine the firm's strategy. It takes years of hard work, long hours, and perseverance, talent, and no small share of good luck to reach the ranks of top management in large companies. Common job titles associated with top managers are president, vice president, chief executive officer (CEO), and chief operating officer (COO).

Concept Check

✓ Why is planning sometimes referred to as the "first" management function?

✓ What is a plan? Differentiate between the major types of plans.

✓ What kind of motivations do different employees have?

✓ What are the three steps of controlling?

Learning Objective

3 **Distinguish among the various kinds of managers in terms of both level and area of management.**

top manager an upper-level executive who guides and controls the overall fortunes of an organization

FIGURE 6-6 Management Levels Found in Most Companies

The coordinated effort of all three levels of managers is required to implement the goals of any company.

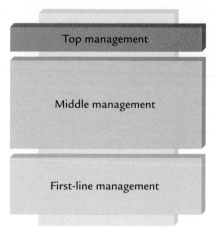

Top management

Middle management

First-line management

© CENGAGE LEARNING 2015

middle manager a manager who implements the strategy and major policies developed by top management

first-line manager a manager who coordinates and supervises the activities of operating employees

financial manager a manager who is primarily responsible for an organization's financial resources

operations manager a manager who manages the systems that convert resources into goods and services

MIDDLE MANAGERS Middle managers make up the largest group of managers in most organizations. A **middle manager** is a manager who implements the strategy and major policies developed by top management. Middle managers develop tactical and operational plans, and they coordinate and supervise the activities of first-line managers. Titles at the middle-management level include division manager, department head, plant manager, and operations manager.

FIRST-LINE MANAGERS A **first-line manager** is a manager who coordinates and supervises the activities of operating employees. First-line managers spend most of their time working with and motivating their employees, answering questions, and solving day-to-day problems. Most first-line managers are former operating employees who were promoted into management. Many of today's middle and top managers began their careers on this first management level. Common titles for first-line managers include office manager, supervisor, and foreman.

AP IMAGES/MARK LENNIHAN

A top manager's out-of-this-world business strategy. At the age of 16, Richard Branson, the CEO and founder of the Virgin Group, started his first business venture: a magazine called *The Student*. Today, the Virgin Group consists of over 400 companies, including Virgin Telecommunications, Virgin Radio, Virgin Cola, Virgin Wine, Virgin Spa, Virgin Airlines—and the list goes on. In the near future, Virgin Galactic, one of Branson's newest companies, aims to launch paying customers into space.

Areas of Management Specialization

Organizational structure can also be divided into areas of management specialization (see Figure 6-7). The most common areas are finance, operations, marketing, human resources, and administration. Depending on its mission, goals, and objectives, an organization may include other areas as well—research and development (R&D), for example.

FINANCIAL MANAGERS A **financial manager** is primarily responsible for an organization's financial resources. Accounting and investment are specialized areas within financial management. Because financing

FIGURE 6-7 Areas of Management Specialization

Other areas may have to be added, depending on the nature of the firm and the industry.

| Finance | Operations | Marketing | Human resources | Administration | Others (e.g., research and development) |

© CENGAGE LEARNING 2015

affects the operation of the entire firm, many CEOs and presidents of large companies are people who were first trained as financial managers.

OPERATIONS MANAGERS An **operations manager** manages the systems that convert resources into goods and services. Traditionally, operations management has been equated with manufacturing—the production of goods. However, in recent years, many of the techniques and procedures of operations management have been applied to the production of services and to a variety of nonbusiness activities. As with financial management, operations management has produced a large percentage of today's company CEOs and presidents.

MARKETING MANAGERS A **marketing manager** is responsible for facilitating the exchange of products between an organization and its customers or clients. Specific areas within marketing are marketing research, product management, advertising, promotion, sales, and distribution. A sizable number of today's company presidents have risen from marketing management.

HUMAN RESOURCES MANAGERS A **human resources manager** is charged with managing an organization's human resources programs. He or she engages in human resources planning, designs systems for hiring, training, and evaluating the performance of employees, and ensures that the organization follows government regulations concerning employment practices. There are many technological tools to help human resources managers. For example, Workday, Inc. produces a suite of software and tools for human resources departments, including a program to streamline the recruiting and hiring process and tools that help HR managers collect and process information.

ADMINISTRATIVE MANAGERS An **administrative manager** (also called a *general manager*) is not associated with any specific functional area, but provides overall administrative guidance and leadership. A hospital administrator is an example of an administrative manager. He or she does not specialize in operations, finance, marketing, or human resources management but instead coordinates the activities of specialized managers in all these areas. In many respects, most top managers are really administrative managers.

Whatever their level and specialization in the organization, successful managers generally exhibit certain key skills and are able to play a variety of managerial roles. However, as we shall see, some skills are likely to be more critical at one level of management than at another.

marketing manager a manager who is responsible for facilitating the exchange of products between an organization and its customers or clients

human resources manager a person charged with managing an organization's human resources programs

administrative manager a manager who is not associated with any specific functional area but who provides overall administrative guidance and leadership

Concept Check

✓ Describe the three levels of management.

✓ Identify the various areas of management specialization, and describe the responsibilities of each.

© AUREMAR/SHUTTERSTOCK.COM

Harnessing the cooperation of an organization's specialized managers. Imagine the managers of different departments as a team of horses. If they—and their employees—don't all work together and pull in the same direction, the organization won't get to the destination it's trying to reach.

KEY SKILLS OF SUCCESSFUL MANAGERS

As shown in Figure 6-8, managers need a variety of skills, including conceptual, analytic, interpersonal, technical, and communication skills.

Conceptual Skills

conceptual skills the ability to think in abstract terms

Conceptual skills involve the ability to think in abstract terms. Conceptual skills allow a manager to see the "big picture" and understand how the various parts of an organization or idea can fit together. Jack Dorsey, creator of Twitter, is a master at seeing large trends and developing products that address needs. In 2009, he created a product called Square, which lets small businesses run credit transactions using their smartphones. Even Starbucks is on board. Square handles all credit and debit card transactions at its 7,000 stores.[10] Conceptual skills are useful in a wide range of situations, including the optimization of goals described earlier.

Analytic Skills

analytic skills the ability to identify problems correctly, generate reasonable alternatives, and select the "best" alternatives to solve problems

interpersonal skills the ability to deal effectively with other people

technical skills specific skills needed to accomplish a specialized activity

communication skills the ability to speak, listen, and write effectively

Employers expect managers to use **analytic skills** to identify problems correctly, generate reasonable alternatives, and select the "best" alternatives to solve problems. Top-level managers especially need these skills because they must discern the important issues from the less important ones, as well as recognize the underlying reasons for different situations. Managers who use these skills not only address a situation but also correct the initial event or problem that caused it to occur. Thus, these skills are vital to running a business efficiently and logically.

FIGURE 6-8 Key Skills of Successful Managers

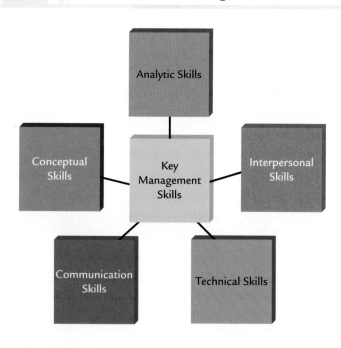

© CENGAGE LEARNING 2015

Concept Check

✓ What are the key skills that successful managers should have?

✓ For each skill, provide two reasons why a successful manager should have that skill.

Interpersonal Skills

Interpersonal skills involve the ability to deal effectively with other people, both inside and outside an organization. Examples of interpersonal skills are the ability to relate to people, understand their needs and motives, and show genuine compassion. After the incoming chief was ousted for having an improper relationship with a subordinate, Lockheed Martin chose Marillyn Hewson as its new CEO. Hewson was selected not only for her dedicated performance and competence, but also for her strong interpersonal skills and humility. Employees appreciate her willingness to listen to them. Her polite and gracious personality is also a strength in an industry that regularly interacts with the government.[11]

Technical Skills

Technical skills involve specific skills needed to accomplish a specialized activity. For example, engineers and machinists need technical skills to do their jobs. First-line managers (and, to a lesser extent, middle managers) need to understand the technical skills relevant to the activities they manage in order to train subordinates, answer questions, and provide guidance, even though the managers may not perform the technical tasks themselves. In general, top managers do not rely on technical skills as heavily as managers at other levels. Still, understanding the technical side of a business is an aid to effective management at every level.

Communication Skills

Communication skills, both oral and written, involve the ability to speak, listen, and write effectively. Managers need both oral and written communication skills. Because a large part of a manager's day is spent conversing with others, the ability to speak *and* listen is critical. Oral communication skills are used when a manager makes sales presentations, conducts interviews, and holds press conferences. Written communication skills are important because a manager's ability to prepare letters, e-mails, memos, sales reports, and other written documents may spell the difference between success and failure. Computers, smartphones, and other high-tech devices make communication in today's businesses easier and faster. To manage an organization effectively and to stay informed, it is very important that managers understand how to use and maximize the potential of digital communication devices.

CEO Dilemma: To Blog or Not to Blog?

At the advertising agency Saatchi & Saatchi, the hotel company Marriott International, and the online retailer Zappos.com, the chief executive officer is also the chief blogger. CEOs who blog not only share ideas with customers, employees, and the public, but also encourage dialogue, build relationships, and add a personal touch to corporate communication. Yet most CEOs don't blog, because of time constraints, legal issues, or the potential for misunderstanding. Should blogging be a high priority for CEOs?

Saatchi & Saatchi's CEO blogs frequently on a wide range of topics, from creativity and pop culture to leadership and global business. See the blog at http://krconnect.blogspot.com.

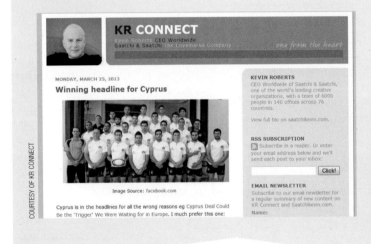

How good are your managerial skills? To be successful, managers must master and simultaneously utilize a number of skills. These include technical skills that aid with specialized work, conceptual skills that foster abstract thinking, and interpersonal skills to help manage and motivate their employees. Which of these skills will you need to work on as you build your career?

leadership the ability to influence others

autocratic leadership task-oriented leadership style in which workers are told what to do and how to accomplish it without having a say in the decision-making process

participative leadership leadership style in which all members of a team are involved in identifying essential goals and developing strategies to reach those goals

entrepreneurial leadership personality-based leadership style in which the manager seeks to inspire workers with a vision of what can be accomplished to benefit all stakeholders

LEADERSHIP

Leadership has been defined broadly as the ability to influence others. Leadership is different from management in that a leader strives for voluntary cooperation, whereas a manager may have to depend on coercion to change employee behavior.

Formal and Informal Leadership

Some experts make distinctions between formal leadership and informal leadership. Formal leaders have legitimate power of position. They have *authority* within an organization to influence others to work toward the organization's objectives. Informal leaders usually have no such authority and may or may not exert their influence in support of the organization. Both formal and informal leaders make use of several kinds of power, including the ability to grant rewards or impose punishments, the possession of expert knowledge, and personal attraction or charisma. Informal leaders who identify with the organization's goals are a valuable asset to any organization. However, a business can be greatly hampered by informal leaders who turn work groups against management.

Styles of Leadership

For many years, finding a consensus on the most important leadership traits was difficult. Leadership was viewed as a combination of personality traits, such as self-confidence, concern for people, intelligence, and dependability. In recent years, the emphasis has been on styles of leadership. Several styles have emerged, including *autocratic*, *participative*, and *entrepreneurial*.

Autocratic leadership is very task-oriented. Decisions are made unilaterally, with little concern for employee opinions. Employees are told exactly what is expected from them and given specific guidelines, rules, and regulations on how to achieve their tasks.

Participative leadership is common in today's business organizations. Participative leaders consult workers before making decisions. This helps workers understand which goals are important and fosters a sense of ownership and commitment to reach them. Participative leaders can be classified into three groups: consultative, consensus, and democratic. *Consultative leaders* discuss issues with workers but retain the final authority for decision making. *Consensus leaders* seek input from almost all workers and make final decisions based on their support. *Democratic leaders* give final authority to the group. They collect opinions and base their decisions on the vote of the group. New Belgium Brewing frequently appears on lists of best places to work in part because of the company's "high involvement, ownership culture" and participative leader, CEO Kim Jordan. She encourages employees to own stock and make important business decisions.[12] Communication is open up and down the hierarchy. Coaching, collaborating, and negotiating are important skills for participative leaders.

Entrepreneurial leadership is personality dependent. Although each entrepreneur is different, this leadership style is generally task-oriented, driven, charismatic, and enthusiastic.[13] The entrepreneurial personality tends to take initiative, be visionary, and be forward-looking. Their enthusiasm energizes and inspires employees. Entrepreneurial leaders tend to be very invested in their businesses, working long hours to ensure

Personal Apps

Who do you admire?

AP IMAGES/MARK LENNIHAN

Think of a leader you admire—someone in the business world or an entertainer raising awareness for a social cause, for example. Why does this person inspire you or make you want to take action? What can you learn from his or her leadership that will help you become a leader in *your* life?

success. They may not understand why their employees do not have the same level of passion for their work. Hamdi Ulukaya, President and CEO of yogurt company Chobani, was recognized by Ernst & Young as a top entrepreneur. He beat out thousands of others for this distinction through his tireless commitment to the success of the company and its mission, delivering a high-quality product, and focusing on developing loyal customers.[14]

LAURA CIOCCARELLI/LANDOV

A CEO who leads by example. Bill Gates's leadership style and technological know-how have helped him foster an environment at Microsoft in which top-notch products can be created. Gates's leadership style includes dimensions of both autocratic and participative leadership.

Which Leadership Style Is the Best?

Today, most management experts agree that no "best" managerial leadership style exists. Each of the styles described—autocratic, participative, and entrepreneurial—has advantages and disadvantages. For example, participative leadership can motivate employees to work effectively because they have a sense of ownership in decision making. However, the decision-making process in participative leadership takes time that subordinates could be devoting to the work itself.

Although hundreds of research studies have been conducted to prove which leadership style is best, there are no definite conclusions. Each of the leadership styles can be highly effective in the right situation. The *most* effective style depends on the right balance between interaction among employees, characteristics of the work situation, and the manager's personality.

Concept Check

✓ Describe the major leadership styles.

✓ Which one is best?

MANAGERIAL DECISION MAKING

Learning Objective

6 Discuss the steps in the managerial decision-making process.

Decision making is the act of choosing one alternative from a set of alternatives.[15] In ordinary situations, decisions are made casually and informally. We encounter a problem, mull it over, settle on a solution, and go on. Managers, however, require a more systematic method for solving complex problems. As shown in Figure 6-9, managerial decision-making process involves four steps: (1) identifying the problem or opportunity, (2) generating alternatives, (3) selecting an alternative, and (4) implementing and evaluating the solution.

decision making the act of choosing one alternative from a set of alternatives

Identifying the Problem or Opportunity

A **problem** is the discrepancy between an actual condition and a desired condition—the difference between what is occurring and what one wishes would occur. For example, a marketing manager at Campbell's Soup Company has a problem if sales revenues for its Pepperidge Farm Goldfish crackers are declining (the actual condition). To solve this problem,

© ISTOCKPHOTO.COM/KUPICOO

problem the discrepancy between an actual condition and a desired condition

FIGURE 6-9 Major Steps in the Managerial Decision-Making Process

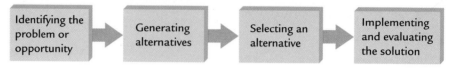

Managers require a systematic method for solving problems in a variety of situations.

Identifying the problem or opportunity → Generating alternatives → Selecting an alternative → Implementing and evaluating the solution

© CENGAGE LEARNING 2015

the marketing manager must take steps to increase sales revenues (desired condition). Most people consider a problem to be "negative," but a problem also can be "positive." Some problems can be viewed as "opportunities."

Although accurate identification of a problem is essential before it can be solved or turned into an opportunity, this stage of decision making creates many difficulties for managers. Sometimes managers' preconceptions of the problem prevent them from seeing the actual situation. They produce an answer before the proper question has been asked, leading him or her to focus on insignificant issues. Also, managers may mistakenly analyze problems in terms of symptoms rather than underlying causes.

Effective managers learn to look ahead so that they are prepared when decisions must be made. They clarify situations and examine the causes of problems, asking whether the presence or absence of certain variables alters a situation. Finally, they consider how individual behaviors and values affect the way problems or opportunities are defined.

Generating Alternatives

After a problem has been defined, the next task is to generate alternatives. The more important the decision, the more attention must be devoted to this stage. Managers should be open to fresh, innovative ideas as well as obvious answers.

Certain techniques can aid in the generation of creative alternatives. Brainstorming, commonly used in group discussions, encourages participants to produce many new ideas. During brainstorming, other group members are not permitted to criticize or ridicule. Another approach, developed by the U.S. Navy, is called "Blast! Then Refine." Group members tackle a recurring problem by erasing all previous solutions and procedures. The group then re-evaluates its original objectives, modifies them if necessary, and devises new solutions. Other techniques—including trial and error—are also useful in this stage of decision making.

Selecting an Alternative

Final decisions are influenced by a number of considerations, including financial constraints, human and informational resources, time limits, legal obstacles, and political factors. Managers must select the alternative that will be most effective and practical. When publishing giant, Meredith Corporation (*Family Circle and Every Day with Rachel Ray*), acquired *Eating Well* magazine, managers had to decide what focus it would have. For example, it could emphasize comfort food or health food. After analyzing the alternatives and the competition, managers decided to focus on healthy meals on a shoestring, a choice that has paid off.[16]

At times, two or more alternatives or some combination of alternatives will be equally appropriate. Managers may choose solutions to problems on several levels. The word *satisfice* describes solutions that are only adequate and not ideal. When lacking time or information, managers often make decisions that "satisfice." Whenever possible, managers should try to investigate alternatives carefully and select the ideal solution.

Concept Check

✓ Describe the major steps in the managerial decision-making process.

✓ Why does a manager need to evaluate the solution and look for problems after a solution has been implemented?

Implementing and Evaluating the Solution

Implementation of a decision requires time, planning, preparation of personnel, and evaluation of results. Managers usually deal with unforeseen consequences even when they have carefully considered the alternatives.

The final step in managerial decision making entails evaluating a decision's effectiveness. If the alternative that was chosen removes the difference between the actual condition and the desired condition, the decision is considered effective. If the problem still exists, managers may select one of the following choices:

- Decide to give the chosen alternative more time to work.
- Adopt a different alternative.
- Start the problem identification process all over again.

Managers should be aware that failure to evaluate decisions adequately may have negative consequences.

MANAGING TOTAL QUALITY

The management of quality is a high priority in many organizations today. Major reasons for a greater focus on quality include foreign competition, more demanding customers who have the ability to comparison shop online, and poor financial performance resulting from reduced market shares and higher costs. Over the last few years, several U.S. firms have lost the dominant competitive positions they had held for decades.

Total quality management is a much broader concept than just controlling the quality of the product itself (which is discussed in Chapter 8). **Total quality management (TQM)** is the coordination of efforts directed at improving customer satisfaction, increasing employee participation, strengthening supplier partnerships, and facilitating an organizational atmosphere of continuous quality improvement. For TQM programs to be effective, management must address each of the following components:

- *Customer satisfaction.* Ways to improve include producing higher-quality products, providing better customer service, and showing customers that the company cares.
- *Employee participation.* This can be increased by allowing employees to contribute to decisions, develop self-managed work teams, and assume responsibility for improving the quality of their work.
- *Strengthening supplier partnerships.* Developing good working relationships with suppliers can ensure that the right supplies and materials will be delivered on time at lower costs.
- *Continuous quality improvement.* A program based on continuous improvement has proven to be the most effective long-term approach.

One tool that is used for TQM is called benchmarking. **Benchmarking** is the process of evaluating the products, processes, or management practices of another organization for the purpose of improving quality. The benchmark should be superior in safety, customer service, productivity, innovation, or in some other way.

For example, competitors' products might be disassembled and evaluated, or wage and benefit plans might be surveyed to measure compensation packages against the labor market. The four basic steps of benchmarking are identifying

total quality management (TQM) the coordination of efforts directed at improving customer satisfaction, increasing employee participation, strengthening supplier partnerships, and facilitating an organizational atmosphere of continuous quality improvement

benchmarking a process used to evaluate the products, processes, or management practices of another organization that is superior in some way in order to improve quality

Learning Objective

7 Describe how organizations benefit from total quality management.

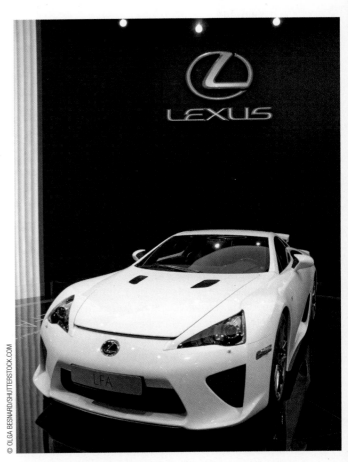

© OLGA BESNARD/SHUTTERSTOCK.COM

Total Quality Management. Prior to the 1970s, products "Made in Japan" were often considered shoddy. Not anymore. Toyota Motor Company, the maker of Lexus, worked hard to change that image by pioneering the use of total quality management practices. As a part of its total quality management practices, Toyota meticulously inspects its products and continuously strives to improve them.

objectives, forming a benchmarking team, collecting and analyzing data, and acting on the results. Best practices may be discovered in any industry or organization.

Although many factors influence the effectiveness of a TQM program, two issues are crucial. First, top management must make a strong commitment to a TQM program by treating quality improvement as a top priority and giving it frequent attention. Firms that establish a TQM program but then focus on other priorities will find that their quality-improvement initiatives will fail. Second, management must coordinate the specific elements of a TQM program so that they work in harmony with each other.

Although not all U.S. companies have TQM programs, they provide many benefits. Overall financial benefits include lower operating costs, higher return on sales and on investments, and an improved ability to use premium pricing rather than competitive pricing. Firms that do not implement TQM are sometimes afraid that the costs of doing so will be prohibitive. While implementing TQM can be high initially, the savings from preventing future problems and integrating systems usually make up for the expense. The long-term costs of not implementing TQM can involve damage to a company's reputation and lost productivity and time spent fixing mistakes after they have happened.[17]

Concept Check

✓ Why does top management need to be strongly committed to TQM programs?

✓ Describe the major components of a TQM program.

Looking for Success? *Get Flashcards, Quizzes, Games, Crosswords and more at @ www.cengagebrain.com.*

Summary

1 Define what management is.

Management is the process of coordinating people and other resources to achieve an organization's goals. Managers are concerned with four types of resources—material, human, financial, and informational.

2 Describe the four basic management functions: planning, organizing, leading and motivating, and controlling.

Managers perform four basic functions, which do not occur according to a rigid, preset timetable. At any time, managers may engage in a number of functions simultaneously. However, each function tends to lead naturally to the next. Managers engage in planning—determining where the firm should be going and how best to get there. One method of planning that can be used is SWOT analysis, which identifies and evaluates a firm's strengths, weaknesses, opportunities, and threats. Three types of plans, from the broadest to the most specific, are strategic, tactical, and operational. Managers also organize resources and activities to accomplish results in an efficient and effective manner, and they lead and motivate others to work in the best interests of the organization. In addition, managers control ongoing activities to keep the organization on course. There are three steps in the control function: setting standards, measuring actual performance, and taking corrective action.

3 Distinguish among the various kinds of managers in terms of both level and area of management.

Managers—or management positions—may be classified from two different perspectives. From the perspective of level within the organization, there are top managers, who control the organization as a whole, middle managers, who implement strategies and major policies, and first-line managers, who supervise the activities of operating employees. From the viewpoint of area of management, managers most often deal with the areas of finance, operations, marketing, human resources, and administration.

4 Identify the key management skills of successful managers.

Managers need a variety of skills in order to run a successful and efficient business. Conceptual skills are used to think in abstract terms or see the "big picture." Analytic skills are used to identify problems correctly, generate reasonable alternatives, and select the "best" alternatives to solve problems. Interpersonal skills are used to deal effectively with other people, both inside and outside an organization. Technical skills are needed to accomplish a specialized activity, whether they are used to actually do the task or to train and assist employees. Communication skills are used to speak, listen, and write effectively.

5 Explain the different types of leadership.

Managers' effectiveness often depends on their styles of leadership—that is, their ability to influence others, either formally or informally. Autocratic leaders are very task oriented; they tell their employees exactly what is expected from them and give them specific instructions on how to do their assigned tasks. Participative leaders consult their employees before making decisions and can be classified into three groups: consultative, consensus, and democratic. Entrepreneurial leaders are different depending on their personalities, but they are generally enthusiastic and passionate about their work and tend to take the initiative.

6 Discuss the steps in the managerial decision-making process.

Decision making, an integral part of a manager's work, is the process of developing a set of possible alternative solutions to a problem and choosing one alternative from among the set. Managerial decision making involves four steps: Managers must accurately identify problems, generate several possible solutions, choose the solution that will be most effective under the circumstances, and implement and evaluate the chosen course of action.

7 Describe how organizations benefit from total quality management.

Total quality management (TQM) is the coordination of efforts directed at improving customer satisfaction, increasing employee participation, strengthening supplier partnerships, and facilitating an organizational atmosphere of continuous quality improvement. Another tool used for TQM is benchmarking, which involves comparing and evaluating the products, processes, or management practices of another organization that is superior in some way in order to improve quality. The five basic steps in benchmarking are identifying objectives, forming a benchmarking team, collecting data, analyzing data, and acting on the results. To have an effective TQM program, top management must make a strong, sustained commitment to the effort and must be able to coordinate all the program's elements so that they work in harmony. Benefits of TQM include lower operating costs, higher return on sales and on investment, and an improved ability to use premium pricing rather than competitive pricing.

Key Terms

You should now be able to define and give an example relevant to each of the following terms:

management (160)
planning (162)
mission (162)
strategic planning process (162)
goal (162)
objective (162)
SWOT analysis (163)
core competencies (163)
plan (164)
strategic plan (164)

tactical plan (164)
operational plan (164)
contingency plan (165)
organizing (165)
leading (165)
motivating (165)
directing (166)
controlling (166)
top manager (167)
middle manager (168)
first-line manager (168)

financial manager (168)
operations manager (168)
marketing manager (169)
human resources manager (169)
administrative manager (169)
conceptual skills (170)
analytic skills (170)
interpersonal skills (170)
technical skills (170)

communication skills (170)
leadership (172)
autocratic leadership (172)
participative leadership (172)
entrepreneurial leadership (172)
decision making (173)
problem (173)
total quality management (TQM) (175)
benchmarking (175)

Discussion Questions

1. Define the word *manager* without using the word *management* in your definition.
2. Does a healthy firm (one that is doing well) have to worry about effective management? Explain.
3. What might be the mission of a neighborhood restaurant? Of the Salvation Army? What might be reasonable objectives for these organizations?
4. What are the major elements of SWOT analysis?
5. How do a strategic plan, a tactical plan, and an operational plan differ? What do they all have in common?
6. Why are leadership and motivation necessary in a business in which people are paid for their work?
7. Compare and contrast the major styles of leadership.

8. According to this chapter, the leadership style that is most effective depends on interaction among the employees, characteristics of the work situation, and the manager's personality. Do you agree or disagree? Explain your answer.

9. What are the major benefits of a total quality management program?

10. Do you think that people are really as important to an organization as this chapter seems to indicate?

11. Discuss what happens during each of the four steps of the managerial decision-making process.

12. As you learned in this chapter, managers often work long hours at a hectic pace. Would this type of career appeal to you? Explain.

Test Yourself

Matching Questions

1. _____ The process of accomplishing objectives through people.

2. _____ The process of establishing an organization's goals and objectives.

3. _____ Its purpose is to implement a strategy.

4. _____ Its purpose is to outline alternative courses of action.

5. _____ The process of influencing people to work.

6. _____ It is a combination of leading and motivating.

7. _____ A vast amount of time is spent motivating employees.

8. _____ Specific skills needed to work a computer.

9. _____ The ability to influence others.

10. _____ Improving customer satisfaction and increasing employee participation are two objectives of this process.

a. conceptual skills
b. contingency plan
c. directing
d. first-line manager
e. leadership
f. leading
g. management
h. operations manager
i. strategic planning
j. tactical plan
k. technical skills
l. total quality management (TQM)

True False Questions

11. **T F** Management functions occur according to a rigid, preset timetable.

12. **T F** As managers carry out their functions, the first step is to control, the second to organize, and the third to plan.

13. **T F** An organization's mission is the means by which it fulfills its purpose.

14. **T F** SWOT analysis is the identification and evaluation of a firm's strengths and weaknesses and external opportunities

15. **T F** Operational plans aimed at increasing sales would include specific advertising activities.

16. **T F** Measuring actual performance is the first step in the control process.

17. **T F** Top managers rely on technical skills more than managers at other levels.

18. **T F** A democratic leader makes all the decisions and tells subordinates what to do.

19. **T F** Brainstorming is a common technique used to generate alternatives in solving problems.

20. **T F** Implementation of a decision requires time, planning, preparation of personnel, and evaluation of results.

Multiple-Choice Questions

21. _____ The process of developing a set of goals and committing an organization to them is called
a. organizing.
b. planning.
c. motivating.
d. controlling.
e. directing.

22. _____ Grouping resources and activities to accomplish some goal is called
a. motivating.
b. directing.
c. leading.
d. planning.
e. organizing.

23. _____ Acme Houseware established a goal to increase its sales by 20 percent in the next year. To ensure that the firm reaches its goal, the sales reports are monitored on a weekly basis. When sales show a slight decline, the sales manager takes actions to correct the problem. Which management function is the manager using?
   a. Leading
   b. Controlling
   c. Directing
   d. Organizing
   e. Planning

24. _____ Who is responsible for developing a firm's mission?
   a. Top managers
   b. First-level managers
   c. Operations managers
   d. Middle managers
   e. Supervisors

25. _____ The chief executive officer of Southwest Airlines provides the company with leadership and overall guidance and is responsible for developing its mission and establishing its goals. Which area of management is being used?
   a. Human resources
   b. Operations
   c. Financial
   d. Administrative
   e. Marketing

26. _____ This manager is responsible for facilitating the exchange of products between an organization and its customers or clients.
   a. Human resources manager
   b. Marketing manager
   c. Operations manager
   d. Financial manager
   e. Administrative manager

27. _____ These types of skills allow a manager to see the "big picture" and understand how the various parts of an organization or idea can fit together.
   a. Interpersonal skills
   b. Conceptual skills
   c. Technical skills
   d. Communication skills
   e. Analytical skills

28. _____ Because a large part of the manager's day is spent conversing with others, it is important for the managers to have
   a. conceptual skills.
   b. analytical skills.
   c. technical skills.
   d. communication skills.
   e. interpersonal skills

29. _____ Which leadership style is task-oriented, driven, charismatic, and enthusiastic?
   a. Autocratic leadership
   b. Participative leadership
   c. Entrepreneurial leadership
   d. Democratic leadership

30. _____ Which of the following statements is correct about TQM?
   a. Top management must make a strong commitment to a TQM program by treating quality improvement as a top priority.
   b. Employees should be aware of TQM movement, not necessarily involved in it.
   c. Managers need to ask for input occasionally in order to practice TQM.
   d. The top administration should appear to be interested in TQM.
   e. In order for TQM to function effectively, you need a lot of resources.

Answers to the Test Yourself questions appear at the end of the book on page TY-1.

Video Case
L.L.Bean Relies on Its Core Values and Effective Leadership

L.L.Bean's first product was a waterproof boot, designed by Maine outdoorsman Leon Leonwood Bean, who promised complete customer satisfaction. One hundred pairs were sold—and 90 pairs were returned because of a defect. Bean refunded the customers' money and went to work perfecting the product, now one of the most popular in the firm's long and successful history.

L.L.Bean began in 1912 as a tiny mail-order company and has grown to include 14 retail stores in ten states, an online store, and a popular catalog showcasing many of the company's 20,000 items, including high-quality clothing, accessories, outdoor gear, luggage, linens, and furniture. It

is still privately owned and family run and has had just three presidents in its history—L.L.Bean himself, his grandson Leon Gorman, and now Chris McCormick, the first nonfamily member to lead the firm. New England is the core of L.L.Bean's market, and its selling cycle accelerates sharply every year around the winter holidays. Headquartered in Freeport, Maine, near its original store, the company reports annual sales of over $1.5 billion.

Managers at L.L.Bean today have many opportunities for using their planning, organizing, leading, and controlling skills. During the preholiday selling season, for instance, temporary workers hired to handle the increased workload bring the regular staff of about 4,600 to almost double its size, so managers have to reorganize the teams of 25 to 30 front-line employees who work in the call centers. Regular employees not currently in leadership positions are asked to head the teams of temps, ensuring they have an experienced person to help them develop their skills and perform to expectations. This organizing strategy works so well that many temps return year after year.

Planning skills come to the fore when top management decides when and where to open new retail stores, whether to expand the number of outlet stores offering discontinued items and overstocks, and how much to invest in ensuring that L.L.Bean buildings meet the highest standards of environmental stewardship. One recent strategic planning project resulted in the creation of a new clothing and accessories collection called L.L.Bean Signature, featuring updated versions of classic items from the company's 100-year heritage.

With respect to the control function, managers assess employee performance with a continuous evaluation process. Corporate-level goals are broken down to the level of the individual store and employee. If something isn't on track, the supervisor is expected to let the employee know and help figure out a solution. However, control at L.L.Bean is not entirely a top-down process. Employees are encouraged to develop their own personal goals, such as learning a new skill or gaining a better appreciation of the way L.L.Bean makes business decisions. Managers help them find ways to meet these personal objectives as well, through a temporary reassignment within the firm or participation in a special company project.

L.L.Bean has a strong collaborative work culture in which it is equally important to work through your supervisor, your co-workers, and your subordinates. That means everyone is a leader to some extent. Formal management candidates are asked to demonstrate both analytical and interpersonal skills and to model the company's six core values: outdoor heritage, integrity, service, respect, perseverance, and safe and healthy living. In the early days of the company, L.L.Bean lived above the store and would come downstairs in the middle of the night to help a customer who rang the bell. "A customer is the most important person ever in this office—in person or by mail," he was fond of saying. So, true to his beliefs, leadership style continues to revolve around serving the customer's needs. As one L.L.Bean manager said, the company is all about salespeople and customer service representatives so that they can better serve customers.[18]

Questions

1. What style of leadership do you think most L.L.Bean managers probably employ?
2. To produce hot water in L.L.Bean's flagship store, the company recently installed a solar hot water system that will offset almost 11,000 pounds of carbon dioxide emissions every year. Suggest some of the questions the company's managers might have asked at each level of planning (strategic, tactical, operational, and contingency) for this project.
3. Which managerial role or roles do you think the leaders of L.L.Bean's temp teams fill?

Building Skills for Career Success

1. Social Media Exercise

Crowdsourcing is a set of principles, processes, and platforms to get things done that includes putting out an open call to a group and managing the responses and output. Crowdsourcing can be like outsourcing in a bigger way because instead of contracting to one known entity, you are putting a call out to a bigger group, often a global online community, to either get many to participate or to find the person you need by casting a much wider net.

There are crowdsourcing companies that perform specific types of work such as translations (MyGengo, Smartling), transcription (CastingWords), keyword marketing (Trada), even design and marketing work (Prova, 99Designs, CrowdSpring). Each company operates differently. In the case of transcription or translation, you give work to a company like CastingWords or MyGengo, and they in turn put the job out to their "crowd" of workers from around

the world. They are like the middleman to helping you get the work done, and their distributed workforce can be less costly to them so they pass on their savings to your organization.

1. Check out a few of these crowdsourcing companies. What are your thoughts? Do you think they are effective? Why or why not?
2. Which type of leadership is most likely to include the use of crowdsourcing?
3. Can you think of other areas in businesses that can benefit from the use of crowdsourcing? What are they?

2. Building Team Skills

Over the past few years, an increasing number of employees, stockholders, and customers have demanded to know more about their companies. As a result, more companies have been taking the time to analyze their operations and to prepare mission statements that focus on the purpose of the company. The mission statement is becoming a critical planning tool for successful companies. To make effective decisions, employees must understand the purpose of their company.

Assignment

1. Divide into teams and write a mission statement for one of the following types of businesses:

   Food service, restaurant
   Banking
   Airline
   Auto repair
   Cabinet manufacturing

2. Discuss your mission statement with other teams. How did the other teams interpret the purpose of your company? What is the mission statement saying about the company?

3. Write a one-page report on what you learned about developing mission statements.

3. Researching Different Careers

A successful career requires planning. Without a plan, or roadmap, you will find it very difficult, if not impossible, to reach your desired career destination. The first step in planning is to establish your career goal. You then must set objectives and develop plans for accomplishing those objectives. This kind of planning takes time, but it will pay off later.

Assignment

Complete the following statements:

1. My career objective is to
   *
   *
   *
   *

This statement should encapsulate what you want to accomplish over the long run. It may include the type of job you want and the type of business or industry you want to work in. Examples include the following:

* My career goal is to work as a top manager in the food industry.
* My career goal is to supervise aircraft mechanics.
* My career goal is to win the top achievement award in the advertising industry.

2. My career objectives are to
   *
   *
   *
   *

Objectives are benchmarks along the route to a career destination. They are more specific than a career goal. A statement about a career objective should specify what you want to accomplish, when you will complete it, and any other details that will serve as criteria against which you can measure your progress. Examples include the following:

* My objective is to enroll in a management course at Main College in the spring semester 2014.
* My objective is to earn an A in the management course at Main College in the spring semester 2014.
* My objective is to be promoted to supervisor by January 1, 2016.
* My objective is to prepare a status report by September 30 covering the last quarter's activities by asking Charlie in Quality Control to teach me the procedures.

3. Exchange your goal and objectives statements with another class member. Can your partner interpret your objectives correctly? Are the objectives concise and complete? Do they include criteria against which you can measure your progress? If not, discuss the problem and rewrite the objective.

Endnotes

1. Based on information in "Kindle Fire HD and Paperwhite Sales Make Amazon No Profit", *BBC News,* October 11, 2012, www.bbc.co.uk; Erika Andersen, "The Shift that Will Save Your Business—and 3 Ways to Make It Happen," *Forbes,* October 29, 2012, www.forbes.com; John Letzing, "Amazon Adds that Robotic Touch," *Wall Street Journal,* March 20, 2012, www.wsj.com; James B. Stewart, "Amazon Says Long Term and Means It," *New York Times,* December 16, 2011, www.nytimes .com; www.amazon.com.

2. Nancy Rothbard. "Put on a Happy Face, Seriously," *Wall Street Journal,* October 24, 2011, http://online.wsj.com/article/SB1000142240529702033 8880457661294373851699.html.

3. Mike Ramsey, "Ford Names COO, Revamps Regional Chiefs," *Wall Street Journal,* November 1, 2012, http://online.wsj.com/article/SB1000 14240529702048463045780925421022359974.html; Mike Ramsey, "Ford Pledges New Focus in South America," *Wall Street Journal,* November 14, 2012, http://online.wsj.com/article/SB10001424127887324556304578111 9193988515894.html.

4. Twitter, https://twitter.com/ (accessed November 17, 2012); Amazon.com, http://phx.corporate-ir.net/phoenix.zhtml?c=97664& p=irol-faq#14296 (accessed November 17, 2012); Facebook, https:// www.facebook.com/facebook?v=info (accessed November 17, 2012).

5. Lisa Jennings, "Starbucks to Accelerate Growth in 2013," *Nation's Restaurant News,* November 2, 2012, http://nrn.com/news/starbucks -accelerate-growth-2013.

6. Nick Wingfield, "Nintendo Confronts a Changed Video Game World," *New York Times,* November 24, 2012, http://www.nytimes .com/2012/11/25/technology/nintendos-wii-u-takes-aim-at-a-changed -video-game-world.html.

7. Ann Zimmerman and Joan E. Solsman, "Best Buy's Turnaround Plan Models Unlikely Set of Retailers," *Wall Street Journal,* November 15, 2012, http://online.wsj.com/article/SB10001424127887324556304578111 9321442547426.html.

8. Nelson D. Schwartz, "U.S. Companies Brace for an Exit From the Euro by Greece," *New York Times,* September 2, 2012, http://www.nytimes.com/2012/09/03/business/economy/us-companies-prepare-in-case-greece-exits-euro.html.

9. Adam Lashinsky, "Amazon's Jeff Bezos: The ultimate disrupter," *Fortune*, November 16, 2012, http://management.fortune.cnn.com/2012/11/16/jeff-bezos-amazon/.

10. Seth Stevenson, "Simplicity and Order for All," *Wall Street Journal,* October 26, 2012, http://online.wsj.com/article/SB10001424052970204425904578072640691246804.html.

11. Christopher Drew, "Lockheed's Incoming Chief Forced Out Over Ethics Violation," *New York Times*, November 9, 2012, http://www.nytimes.com/2012/11/10/business/lockheed-citing-ethics-violation-says-incoming-chief-has-quit.html; Loren Thompson, "Lockheed's New CEO is the Right Mix of Tough and Sensible," *Forbes*, November 13, 2012, http://www.forbes.com/sites/lorenthompson/2012/11/13/lockheed-martins-new-ceo-is-the-right-mix-of-tough-and-sensible/.

12. Bryan Simpson, "New Belgium Brewing: How Intangibles Keep Employees Coming Back for More," *Sustainable Brands*, July 2012, http://www.sustainablebrands.com/news_and_views/jul2012/new-belgium-brewing-how-intangibles-keep-employees-coming-back-more.

13. Andrew J. Dubrin, *Leadership: Research Findings, Practice and Skills*, 7th ed. (Mason, OH: South-Western/Cengage Learning, 2013).

14. Anthony Volastro, "Who is the Entrepreneur of the Year?" *CNBC*, November 26, 2012, http://www.cnbc.com/id/49967727.

15. Ricky Griffin, *Management*, 11th ed. (Mason, OH: South-Western Cengage, 2012), 7.

16. Christine Haughney, "A Sale Gives a Magazine on Healthy Eating a New Lease on Life," *New York Times*, October 21, 2012, http://www.nytimes.com/2012/10/22/business/media/eating-well-magazines-new-lease-on-life.html.

17. Martin Murray, "Total Quality Management (TQM)," http://logistics.about.com/od/qualityinthesupplychain/a/TQM.htm (accessed March 23, 2012).

18. Based on information on the company website www.llbean.com (accessed January 20, 2011); company news release, "L.L.Bean Installs a Solar Hot Water System to Its Flagship Store in Freeport," www.llbean.com, June 15, 2010; interviews with L.L.Bean employees, and the video, "L.L.Bean Relies on Its Core Values and Effective Leadership."

Chapter 7

Creating a Flexible Organization

Learning Objectives

Once you complete this chapter, you will be able to:

1 Understand what an organization is and identify its characteristics.

2 Explain why job specialization is important.

3 Identify the various bases for departmentalization.

4 Explain how decentralization follows from delegation.

5 Understand how the span of management describes an organization.

6 Describe the four basic forms of organizational structure.

7 Describe the effects of corporate culture.

8 Understand how committees and task forces are used.

9 Explain the functions of the informal organization and the grapevine in a business.

Why Should You Care?

To operate a successful business, those in charge must create an organization that operates efficiently and is able to attract employees.

© CANDYBOX IMAGES/SHUTTERSTOCK.COM

Autonomy Fosters Innovation and Success at W.L. Gore

At W.L. Gore & Associates (www.gore.com), the Delaware-based multinational firm best known for its durable Gore-Tex water-shedding fabric, CEO Terri Kelly is among the few employees with an official job title. The 55-year-old company operates in 30 nations and rings up $3 billion in annual revenue from its portfolio of 1,000 products, ranging from specialized fibers and turbine filters to fiber optic cables and pharmaceutical hoses. Every one of Gore's 10,000 employees (called "associates") is responsible for defining his or her own responsibilities, and because everyone is a part-owner, all have a real stake in the company's long-term success.

Rather than reporting to a manager and referring decisions to higher levels, associates form teams on their own and make decisions with the input of anyone in the organization with the relevant knowledge and expertise. This unconventional "lattice" structure encourages internal communication, commitment, cooperation, and creativity. Coming to agreement on a major decision takes more time at Gore than in traditionally structured organizations. However, because associates are involved every step of the way and healthy debate is part of the process, their ideas and contributions improve the end result.

When new associates are hired, they work with a sponsor to learn how to be effective within the lattice organization and how to chart a rewarding career path. Turnover is low because associates thrive on the challenges, opportunities, experimentation, and teamwork. Even during the recent economic downturn, Gore continued to expand and build on the technological breakthroughs pioneered by its talented and motivated associates.

Thanks to its innovative organization and positive workplace environment, Gore has been named numerous times to *Fortune's* annual list of "100 Best Companies to Work For." Associates have the freedom to develop their capabilities, authority to make things happen through teamwork, and individual accountability for a job well done.[1]

Did You Know?

W.L. Gore employs 10,000 people and rings up $3 billion in annual sales from more than 1,000 products.

To survive and to grow, companies such as W.L. Gore must constantly look for ways to improve their methods of doing business. Managers at W.L. Gore, like those at many organizations, maintain an organizational structure that best achieves company goals and creates products that foster long-term customer relationships.

When firms are organized, or reorganized, the focus is sometimes on achieving low operating costs. Other firms, such as Nike, emphasize providing high-quality products to ensure customer satisfaction. The issue of a firm's organizational structure is important because it can influence performance.

We begin this chapter by examining the business organization—what it is and how it functions in today's business environment. Next, we focus one by one on five characteristics that shape an organization's structure. We discuss job specialization within a company, the grouping of jobs into manageable units or departments, the delegation of power from management to workers, the span of management, and establishment of a chain of command. Then we step back for

ANDREY POPOV/PHOTOS.COM

an overall view of organizational structure, describe the effects of corporate culture, and focus in on how committees and task forces are used. Finally, we look at the network of social interactions—the informal organization—that operates within the formal business structure.

WHAT IS AN ORGANIZATION?

We used the term *organization* throughout Chapter 6 without really defining it, mainly because its everyday meaning is close to its business meaning. Here, however, let us agree that an **organization** is a group of two or more people working together to achieve a common set of goals. A neighborhood dry cleaner owned and operated by a husband-and-wife team is an organization. IBM and Home Depot, which employ thousands of workers worldwide, are also organizations. Although each corporation's organizational structure is more complex than the dry-cleaning establishment, all must be organized to achieve their goals.

An inventor who goes into business to produce and market a new invention hires people, decides what each will do, determines who will report to whom, and so on. These activities are the essence of organizing, or creating, the organization. An organization chart helps to illustrate the shape of an organization.

Developing Organization Charts

An **organization chart** is a diagram that represents the positions and relationships within an organization. An example of an organization chart is shown in Figure 7-1. Each rectangle represents a particular position or person in the organization. At the top is the president, next are the vice presidents, and so on. The solid vertical lines connecting each level of the hierarchy indicate who is in the chain of command. The **chain of command** is the line of authority that extends from the highest to the lowest levels of the organization. You can see that each vice president reports directly to the president. Similarly, the plant managers, regional sales managers, and accounting department manager report to the vice presidents. An organization's chain of command can be short or long. A small local restaurant may have a very short chain of command consisting of the owner at the top and employees below. Large multinational corporations, on the other hand, may have very long chains of command. No matter what the length of the chain of command, organizations must ensure that communication along the chain is clear. Not everyone who works for an organization is part of the direct chain of command. In the chart these positions are represented by broken lines, as you can see with the directors of legal services, public affairs, and human resources. Instead, they hold *advisory*, or *staff*, positions. This difference will be examined later in the chapter when we discuss line-and-staff positions.

Most smaller organizations find organization charts useful. They clarify positions and relationships for everyone in the organization, and they help managers to track growth and change in the organizational structure. However, many large organizations, such as ExxonMobil, Kellogg's, and Procter & Gamble, do not maintain complete, detailed charts. There are two reasons for this. First, it is difficult to chart even a few dozen positions accurately, much less the thousands that characterize larger firms. Second, larger organizations are almost always changing parts of their structure. An organization chart would be outdated before it was completed. Increasingly, technology can help even large and complicated organizations implement up-to-date organization charts.

Major Considerations for Organizing a Business

When a firm is started, management must decide how to organize the firm. These decisions focus on job design, departmentalization, delegation, span of management, and chain of command. In the next several sections, we discuss major issues associated with these dimensions.

Concept Check

✓ How do large and small organizations use organizational charts differently?

✓ Identify the major considerations when organizing a business.

FIGURE 7-1 A Typical Corporate Organization Chart

A Company's organization chart represents the positions and relationships within the organization and shows the managerial chains of command.

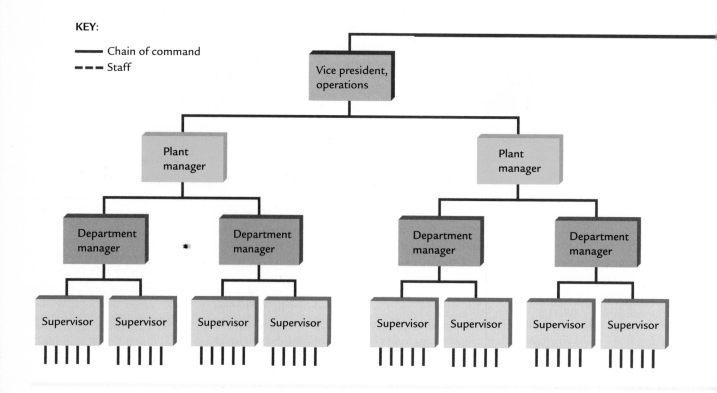

KEY:

—— Chain of command
- - - Staff

JOB DESIGN

In Chapter 1, we defined *specialization* as the separation of a manufacturing process into distinct tasks and the assignment of different tasks to different people. Here we are extending that concept to *all* the activities performed within an organization.

Job Specialization

job specialization the separation of all organizational activities into distinct tasks and the assignment of different tasks to different people

Job specialization is the separation of all organizational activities into distinct tasks and the assignment of different tasks to different people. Adam Smith, the 18th-century economist whose theories gave rise to capitalism, was the first to emphasize the power of specialization in his book, *The Wealth of Nations*. According to Smith, the various tasks in a particular pin factory were arranged so that one worker drew the wire for the pins, another straightened the wire, a third

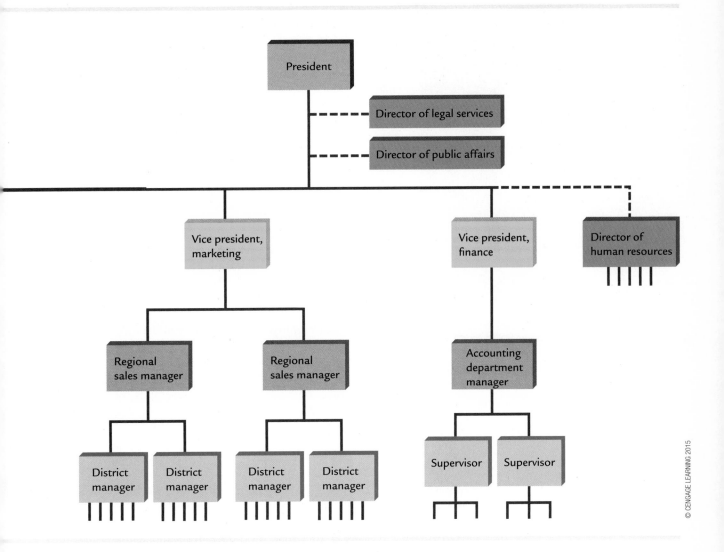

cut it, a fourth ground the point, and a fifth attached the head. Smith claimed that 10 men were able to produce 48,000 pins per day. Before specialization, they could produce only 200 pins per day because each worker had to perform all five tasks!

The Rationale for Specialization

For a number of reasons, some job specialization is necessary in every organization because the "job" of most organizations is too large for one person to handle. In a firm such as Ford Motor Company, thousands of people are needed to manufacture automobiles. Others are needed to sell the cars, control the firm's finances, and so on.

Second, when a worker has to learn one specific, highly specialized task, that individual can learn it quickly and perform it efficiently. Third, a worker repeating the same job does not lose time changing operations, as the pin workers did when producing complete pins. Fourth, the more specialized the job, the easier it is to

Concept Check

✓ What are the positive and negative effects of specialization?

✓ What are three ways to reduce the negative effects of specialization?

design specialized equipment. And finally, the more specialized the job, the easier the job training.

Alternatives to Job Specialization

Unfortunately, specialization can have negative consequences. The most significant drawback is the boredom and dissatisfaction employees may feel when repeating the same job. Bored employees may be absent from work frequently, not put much effort into their work, and even sabotage the company's efforts to produce quality products.

To combat these problems, managers often turn to job rotation. **Job rotation** is the systematic shifting of employees from one job to another. For example, a worker may be assigned a different job every week for a four-week period and then return to the first job in the fifth week. Job rotation provides a variety of tasks so that workers are less likely to become bored and dissatisfied. Intel, for instance, encourages job rotation as a means of sharing ideas, perspectives, and best practices across the company. Job rotation helps workers stay interested in their jobs, develop new skills, and identify new roles where they may want to focus their energies in the future. According to the Society for Human Resource Management, around 38 percent of employers offer some kind of cross-training for their workers.[2]

Two other approaches—job enlargement and job enrichment—also can provide solutions to the problems caused by job specialization. These topics, along with other methods used to motivate employees, are discussed in Chapter 10.

Specialization has its drawbacks. This employee has a specialized job that includes cutting out leather components that will be used to produce handbags. Specialization is efficient for the firm, but it can leave employees bored and dissatisfied. What do you think a firm can do to offset these problems?

© OLAF SPEIER/SHUTTERSTOCK.COM

Learning Objective

3 **Identify the various bases for departmentalization.**

job rotation the systematic shifting of employees from one job to another

departmentalization the process of grouping jobs into manageable units

departmentalization by function grouping jobs that relate to the same organizational activity

departmentalization by product grouping activities related to a particular product or service

DEPARTMENTALIZATION

After jobs are designed, they must be grouped together into "working units," or departments. This process is called **departmentalization**, which is the process of grouping jobs into manageable units. Today, the most common bases for organizing a business into effective departments are by function, by product, by location, and by customer.

By Function

Departmentalization by function groups jobs that relate to the same organizational activity. Under this scheme, all marketing personnel are grouped together in the marketing department, all production personnel in the production department, and so on.

Most smaller and newer organizations departmentalize by function. Supervision is simplified because everyone is involved in the same activities and coordination is easy. The disadvantages of this method of grouping jobs are that it can lead to slow decision making and it tends to emphasize the department over the organization as a whole.

By Product

Departmentalization by product groups activities related to a particular good or service. This approach is used often by older and larger firms that produce and sell a variety of products. Each department handles its own marketing, production, financial management, and human resources activities.

Departmentalization by product makes decision making easier and provides for the integration of all activities associated with each product. However, it causes some duplication of specialized activities—such as finance—between departments. Moreover, the emphasis is placed on the product rather than on the whole organization.

By Location

Departmentalization by location groups activities according to the defined geographic area in which they are performed. Departmental areas may range from whole countries (for international firms) to regions within countries (for national firms) to areas of several city blocks (for police departments organized into precincts). For example, Ford has divisions for the Americas, Europe, Asia Pacific and Africa, and China. Departmentalization by location allows the organization to respond readily to the unique demands or requirements of different locations. Nevertheless, a large administrative staff and an elaborate control system may be needed to coordinate operations across many locations.

By Customer

Departmentalization by customer groups activities according to the needs of various customer populations. The advantage of this approach is that it allows the firm to deal efficiently with unique customers or customer groups. The biggest drawback is that a larger-than-usual administrative staff is needed.

Combinations of Bases

Many organizations use a combination of departmentalization bases. PepsiCo, for instance, is divided by product and location. It has product divisions such as Beverages, Frito-Lay, Quaker, and Latin American Foods, as well as divisions based on location such as Asia, Europe, the Middle East, and Africa.[3]

Take a moment to examine Figure 7-2. Notice that departmentalization by customer is used to organize New-Wave Fashions, Inc., into three major divisions: Men's,

How is your school organized? These call center employees are organized by their function. Some businesses are organized by more than their functions, though. For example, if your university has more than one campus, they are organized by location but also by function such as by their business, social sciences, and math departments. Your school also might be organized by customer such as by undergraduate, graduate, and continuing education students.

departmentalization by location grouping activities according to the defined geographic area in which they are performed

departmentalization by customer grouping activities according to the needs of various customer populations

Concept Check

✓ What are the four most common bases for departmentalization?

✓ Give an example of each.

FIGURE 7-2 Multibase Departmentalization for New-Wave Fashions, Inc.

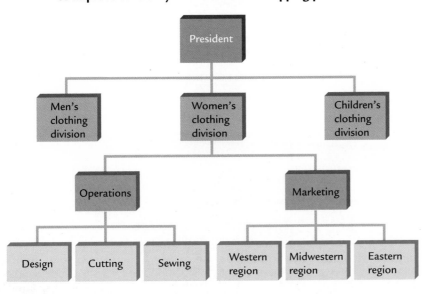

Most firms use more than one basis for departmentalization to improve efficiency and to avoid overlapping positions.

Women's, and Children's clothing. Then functional departmentalization is used to distinguish the firm's production and marketing activities. Finally, location is used to organize the firm's marketing efforts.

Learning Objective

4 Explain how decentralization follows from delegation.

delegation assigning part of a manager's work and power to other workers

responsibility the duty to do a job or perform a task

authority the power, within an organization, to accomplish an assigned job or task

accountability the obligation of a worker to accomplish an assigned job or task

decentralized organization an organization in which management consciously attempts to spread authority widely in the lower levels of the organization

centralized organization an organization that systematically works to concentrate authority at the upper levels of the organization

DELEGATION, DECENTRALIZATION, AND CENTRALIZATION

The third major step in the organizing process is to distribute power in the organization. **Delegation** assigns work and power to other workers. The degree of centralization or decentralization of authority is determined by the overall pattern of delegation within the organization.

Delegation of Authority

Because no manager can do everything, delegation is vital to completion of a manager's work. Delegation is also important in developing the skills and abilities of subordinates. It allows those who are being groomed for higher-level positions to play increasingly important roles in decision making.

STEPS IN DELEGATION The delegation process generally involves three steps (see Figure 7-3). First, the manager must *assign responsibility*. **Responsibility** is the duty to do a job or perform a task. In most job settings, a manager simply gives the worker a job to do. Typical job assignments might range from preparing a report on the status of a new quality control program to being put in charge of a task force. Second, the manager must *grant authority*. **Authority** is the power, within the organization, to accomplish an assigned job or task. This might include the power to obtain specific information, order supplies, authorize relevant expenditures, or make certain decisions. Finally, the manager must *create accountability*. **Accountability** is the obligation of a worker to accomplish an assigned job or task.

FIGURE 7-3 Steps in the Delegation Process

To be successful, a manager must learn how to delegate. No one can do everything alone.

THE DELEGATION PROCESS

© CENGAGE LEARNING 2015

Note that accountability is created but it cannot be delegated. Suppose that you are an operations manager for Target and are responsible for performing a specific task. You, in turn, delegate this task to someone else. You nonetheless remain accountable to your immediate supervisor for getting the task done properly. If the other person fails to complete the assignment, you—not the person to whom you delegated the task—will be held accountable.

BARRIERS TO DELEGATION For several reasons, managers may be unwilling to delegate work. This may be because the manager does not trust the employee to complete the task, or because the manager fears the employee will perform exceptionally and attract the notice of higher level managers. Finally, some managers do not delegate because they are disorganized and they are not able to plan and assign work effectively.

Decentralization of Authority

The pattern of delegation throughout an organization determines the extent to which that organization is decentralized or centralized. In a **decentralized organization**, management consciously attempts to spread authority widely across various organization levels. A **centralized organization**, on the other hand, systematically works to concentrate authority at the upper levels. For example, shipping companies like UPS, tend to be centralized, with shipping dispatches coordinated by upper management. Large organizations may have characteristics of both decentralized and centralized organizations. Random House and Penguin Books merged to become the largest consumer book publishing house in the world. Yet, the merged company hopes to maintain the flexibility and creativity of a smaller and more decentralized company while taking advantage of the benefits of large scale.[4]

A number of factors can influence the extent to which a firm is decentralized. One is the external environment in which the firm operates. The more complex and unpredictable this environment, the more likely it is that top management will let lower-level managers make important decisions because lower-level managers are closer to the problems. Another factor is the nature of the decision itself. The riskier or more important the decisions that have to be made, the greater the tendency to centralize decision making. A third factor is the abilities

Entrepreneurial Success

Successful Leaders Are Successful Delegators

Starting a business? This is a good time to learn to delegate, because as the business grows, you'll need help getting everything done. Lifelong entrepreneur Sir Richard Branson, who heads the Virgin Group, realized the importance of delegation early in his business career. He found that by hiring enthusiastic, capable employees to handle his fledgling firm's daily operations, he would have more time to focus on strategy and on problem solving. Branson also gave his employees the flexibility to develop their own skills and contribute their own ideas to improve the business, making delegation a win–win for all.

Another tip for effective delegation: Understand which tasks must be done and which must be done by *you*, and divide the work accordingly. Although somebody has to buy office supplies, it doesn't necessarily have to be added to your to-do list. On the other hand, you may not want to delegate a few small or unimportant tasks that give you satisfaction, as long as you don't allow them to take up too much of your day.

Finally, agree on specific goals, set deadlines, and communicate regularly after you delegate—and then resist the impulse to manage too closely. You can be supportive and provide guidance without hovering over an employee's shoulder or undermining the employee's authority. Unless a major problem arises, step back and allow the assigned person to assume responsibility instead of rushing in to take charge before you're needed.

Sources: Based on information in Erica Quin-Easter, "From Entrepreneur to Manager: Managing for Growth," *Bangor Daily News (Maine)*, October 11, 2012, www.bangordailynews.com; "Richard Branson on the Art of Delegation," *Entrepreneur*, July 19, 2011, www.entrepreneur.com; Jeffrey R. Cornwall, "When Starting a Business, Delegate, Delegate, Delegate," *Christian Science Monitor*, March 14, 2012, www.csmonitor.com; Adelaide Lancaster, "Get the Job You Love: An Entrepreneur's Guide to Delegating," *Forbes*, May 15, 2012, www.forbes.com.

Delegate, delegate, delegate. The industrialist Andrew Carnegie once said, "No person will make a great business who wants to do it all himself or get all the credit." Delegating gives employees different tasks to do, which can enrich and enlarge their jobs. It also enables both employees and their superiors to learn new skills required for higher-level positions.

of lower-level managers. If these managers do not have strong decision-making skills, top managers will be reluctant to decentralize. Finally, a firm that has practiced centralization or decentralization is likely to maintain that same posture in the future.

In principle, neither decentralization nor centralization is right. What works for one organization may or may not work for another. Every organization must assess its own situation and choose the level of centralization or decentralization that will work best.

Learning Objective

5 Understand how the span of management describes an organization.

span of management (or **span of control**) the number of workers who report directly to one manager

THE SPAN OF MANAGEMENT

The fourth major step in organizing a business is establishing the **span of management** (or **span of control**), which is the number of workers who report directly to one manager. Hundreds of years of research has shown that there is no perfect ratio of subordinates to managers. More recently, theorists have focused on the width of the span of management. This issue is complicated because the span of management may change by department within the same organization. A highly mechanized factory where all operations are standardized may allow for a wide span of management. An advertising agency, where new problems and opportunities arise every day and where teamwork is a constant necessity, will have a much narrower span of management.

Wide and Narrow Spans of Management

A *wide* span of management exists when a manager has a larger number of subordinates. A *narrow* span exists when the manager has only a few subordinates. Several factors determine the span that is best for a particular manager (see Figure 7-4). Generally, the span of management may be wide when (1) the manager and the subordinates are very competent, (2) the organization has a well-established set of

FIGURE 7-4 The Span of Management

Several criteria determine whether a firm uses a wide span of management, in which a number of workers report to one manager, or a narrow span, in which a manager supervises only a few workers.

WIDE SPAN

- High level of competence in managers and workers
- Standard operating procedures
- Few new problems

NARROW SPAN

- Physical dispersion of subordinates
- Manager has additional tasks
- High level of interaction required between manager and workers
- High frequency of new problems

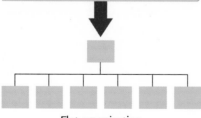

Flat organization

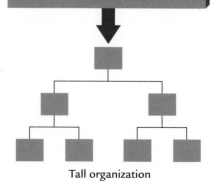

Tall organization

© CENGAGE LEARNING 2015

standard operating procedures, and (3) few new problems are expected to arise. The span should be narrow when (1) workers are physically located far from one another, (2) the manager has much work to do in addition to supervising workers, (3) a great deal of interaction is required between supervisor and workers, and (4) new problems arise frequently.

Organizational Height

The span of management has an obvious impact on relations between managers and workers. It has a more subtle, but equally important, impact on the height of the organization. **Organizational height** is the number of layers, or levels, of management in a firm. The span of management plays a direct role in determining the height of the organization (see Figure 7-4). If the span of management is wide, fewer levels are needed, and the organization is *flat*. If the span of management is narrow, more levels are needed, and the resulting organization is *tall*.

In a tall organization, administrative costs are higher because more managers are needed. Communication may become distorted because information has to pass up and down through more levels. When companies are cutting costs, one option is to decrease organizational height in order to reduce related administrative expenses. For example, in the wake of fallout from the 2008 financial crisis and stricter rules on risky forms of investing, major Swiss bank UBS laid off 10,000 employees (15 percent of staff) and scrapped its risky fixed income business. These steps were meant to simplify the company's structure and help it return to its roots as a private banker.[5] Although flat organizations avoid these problems, their managers may perform more administrative duties simply because there are fewer managers. Wide spans of management also may require managers to spend considerably more time supervising and working with subordinates.

Narrow versus wide spans of management: Which is better? The manager on the right side of the photo supervises only a handful of employees. Consequently, he has a narrow span of management. Companies are constantly searching for the ideal number of employees their supervisors should manage.

organizational height the number of layers, or levels, of management in a firm

Concept Check

✓ Describe the two spans of management.

✓ What are problems associated with each one?

FORMS OF ORGANIZATIONAL STRUCTURE

Up to this point, we have focused our attention on the major characteristics of organizational structure. In many ways, this is like discussing the parts of a jigsaw puzzle one by one. It is now time to put the puzzle together. We will next discuss four basic forms of organizational structure: line, line-and-staff, matrix, and network.

Learning Objective

6 Describe the four basic forms of organizational structure.

The Line Structure

The simplest and oldest form of organizational structure is the **line structure**, in which the chain of command goes directly from person to person throughout the organization. Thus, a straight line could be drawn down through the levels of management, from the chief executive down to the lowest level in the organization. In a small retail store, for example, an hourly employee might report to an assistant manager, who reports to a store manager, who reports to the owner.

Managers within a line structure, called **line managers**, make decisions and give orders to subordinates to achieve the organization's goals. A line structure's simplicity and clear chain of command allow line managers to make decisions quickly with direct accountability because the decision maker only has one supervisor to report to.

The downside of a line structure is that line managers are responsible for many activities, and therefore must have a wide range of knowledge about all of them. While this may not be a problem for small organizations with a lower volume of

line structure an organizational structure in which the chain of command goes directly from person to person throughout the organization

line managers a position in which a person makes decisions and gives orders to subordinates to achieve the organization's goals

If you're looking to move up, try to get some advice from co-workers in both line and staff positions. Not only will this broaden your understanding of the organization, it will also help you bridge the gaps between line and staff and connect with both groups.

line-and-staff structure an organizational structure that utilizes the chain of command from a line structure in combination with the assistance of staff managers

staff managers a position created to provide support, advice, and expertise within an organization

activities, in a larger organization, activities are more numerous and complex, thus making it more difficult for line managers to fully understand what they are in charge of. Therefore, line managers in a larger organization would have a hard time making an educated decision without expert advice from outside sources. As a result, line structures are not very effective in medium- or large-sized organizations, but are very popular in small organizations.

The Line-and-Staff Structure

A **line-and-staff structure** not only utilizes the chain of command from a line structure but also provides line managers with specialists, called staff managers. Therefore, this structure works much better for medium- and large-sized organizations than line management alone. **Staff managers** provide support, advice, and expertise to line managers, thus eliminating the major drawback of line structures. Staff managers are not part of the chain of command like line managers are, but they do have authority over their assistants (see Figure 7-5).

Both line and staff managers are needed for effective management, but the two positions differ in important ways. Most importantly, line managers have *line authority*, which means that they can make decisions and issue directives relating to the organization's goals. Staff managers seldom have this kind of authority. Instead, they usually have either advisory authority or functional authority. *Advisory authority* is the expectation that line managers will consult the appropriate staff manager when

FIGURE 7-5 Line and Staff Managers

A line manager has direct responsibility for achieving the company's goals and is in the direct chain of command. A staff manager supports and advises the line managers.

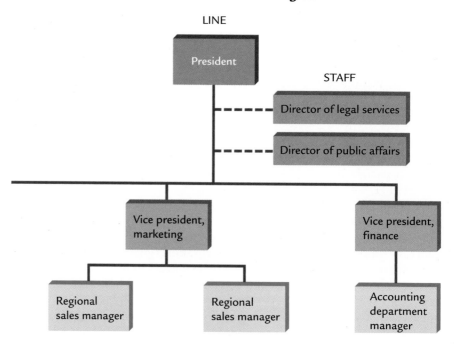

making decisions. *Functional authority* is a stronger form. It is the authority of staff managers to make decisions and issue directives about their areas of expertise. For example, a legal adviser for Nike can decide whether to retain a particular clause in a contract but not product pricing.

Staff managers in a line-and-staff structure tend to have more access to information than line managers. This means that line managers must rely on the staff managers for information. This is usually not an issue, unless the staff manager makes a wrong decision and there is no one else to catch his or her mistake.[6] For a variety of reasons, conflict between line managers and staff managers is fairly common in business. Staff managers often have more formal education and sometimes are younger (and perhaps more ambitious) than line managers. Line managers may perceive staff managers as a threat to their own authority and thus may resent them. For their part, staff managers may become annoyed or angry if their expert recommendations are not adopted by line management.

Fortunately, there are several ways to minimize the likelihood of such conflict. One way is to integrate line and staff managers into one team. Another is to ensure that the areas of responsibility of line and staff managers are clearly defined. Finally, line and staff managers both can be held accountable for the results of their activities.

Line-and-staff organization structure. Ronald McDonald occupies a staff position and does not have direct authority over other employees at McDonald's. The other individuals shown here occupy line positions and do have direct authority over some of the other McDonald's employees.

The Matrix Structure

The **matrix structure** combines vertical and horizontal lines of authority, forming a matrix shape in the organizational chart. The matrix structure occurs when product departmentalization is superimposed on a functionally departmentalized organization. In a matrix organization, authority flows both down and across and individuals report to more than one superior at the same time.

To understand the structure of a matrix organization, consider the usual functional arrangement, with people working in departments such as engineering, finance, and marketing. Now suppose that we assign people from these departments to a special group that is working on a new project as a team—a cross-functional team. A **cross-functional team** consists of individuals with varying specialties, expertise, and skills that are brought together to achieve a common task. Frequently, cross-functional teams are charged with the responsibility of developing new products. The manager in charge of a team is usually called a *project manager.* Any individual who is working with the team reports to *both* the project manager and the individual's superior in the functional department (see Figure 7-6).

Cross-functional team projects may be temporary, in which case the team is disbanded once the mission is accomplished, or they may be permanent. As the world becomes more connected, many companies require managers to have had cross-functional team experience. Major corporations such as GE, Whirlpool, Procter & Gamble all utilize the diverse viewpoints that come out of cross-functional teams.

These teams often are empowered to make major decisions. When a cross-functional team is employed, prospective team members may receive special training because effective teamwork can require different skills. For cross-functional teams to be successful, team members must be given specific information on the job each performs. The team must also develop a sense of cohesiveness and maintain good communications among its members.

Matrix structures offer advantages over other organizational forms, added flexibility probably being the most obvious one. The matrix structure also can increase productivity, raise morale, and nurture creativity and innovation. In addition, employees experience personal development through doing a variety of jobs.

matrix structure an organizational structure that combines vertical and horizontal lines of authority, usually by superimposing product departmentalization on a functionally departmentalized organization

cross-functional team a team of individuals with varying specialties, expertise, and skills that are brought together to achieve a common task

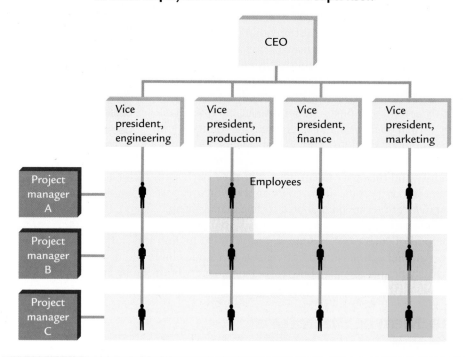

FIGURE 7-6 A Matrix Structure

A matrix is usually the result of combining product departmentalization with function departmentalization. It is a complex structure in which employees have more than one supervisor.

Source: Ricky W. Griffin, *Management*, 11th ed. Copyright © 2012 by South-Western/Cengage Learning, Mason, OH. Adapted with permission.

The matrix structure also has disadvantages. Having employees report to more than one supervisor can cause confusion about who is in charge. Like committees, teams may take longer to resolve problems and issues than individuals working alone. Other difficulties include personality clashes, poor communication, undefined individual roles, unclear responsibilities, and difficulties in finding ways to reward individual and team performance simultaneously. Because more managers and support staff may be needed, a matrix structure may be more expensive to maintain.

The Network Structure

network structure an organizational structure in which administration is the primary function, and most other functions are contracted out to other firms

In a **network structure** (sometimes called a *virtual organization*), administration is the primary function performed, and other functions such as engineering, production, marketing, and finance are contracted out to other organizations. Frequently, a network organization does not manufacture the products it sells. This type of organization has a few permanent employees consisting of top management and hourly clerical workers. Leased facilities and equipment, as well as temporary workers, are increased or decreased as the organization's needs change. Thus, there is limited formal structure associated with a network organization.

An obvious strength of a network structure is flexibility that allows the organization to adjust quickly to changes. Network structures consist of a lot of teams working together, rather than relying on one centralized leader. This also means that network structures may be more likely to survive if an important leader or member leaves because there is no power vacuum left at the top.[7] Some of the challenges faced by managers in network-structured organizations include controlling the quality of work performed by other organizations, low morale and high turnover among hourly workers, and a lack of a clear hierarchy.

Concept Check

✓ Describe the four forms of organizational structure.

✓ Give an example of each form.

CORPORATE CULTURE

Most managers function within a corporate culture. A **corporate culture** is generally defined as the inner rites, rituals, heroes, and values of a firm. An organization's culture has a powerful influence on how employees think and act. It also can determine public perception of the organization.

corporate culture the inner rites, rituals, heroes, and values of a firm

Corporate culture generally is thought to have a very strong influence on a firm's performance over time. Hence, it is useful to be able to assess a firm's corporate culture. Common indicators include the physical setting (building or office layouts), what the company says about its corporate culture (in advertising or news releases), how the company greets guests (formal or informal reception areas), and how employees spend their time (working alone in an office or working with others).

Goffee and Jones identified four distinct types of corporate cultures (see Figure 7-7). One is called the *networked culture*, characterized by a base of trust and friendship among employees, a strong commitment to the organization, and an informal environment. A small nonprofit organization may seek to build a networked culture where employees look out for each other and believe strongly in the organizational mission. Building a networked culture in such an organization is important because employees may have to work long hours for relatively little pay, and a strong sense of community and commitment helps to keep productivity high and turnover low.

The phrase *mercenary culture* may have a negative connotation, but it also involves a high degree of passion, energy, sense of purpose, and excitement for one's work. Large banks and investment firms often have mercenary cultures because the environment is fast-paced, the stakes are high, and winning is important. This kind of culture can be very stressful for an employee with an incompatible personality. The term *mercenary* does not imply that employees are motivated to work only for the money, although financial gain does play a role. In this culture, employees are very intense, focused, and determined to win. For example, years after the 2008 economic crisis, Barclays, a major financial company, is still being criticized by regulators for its mercenary culture. Accusations include excessive risk-taking culture and encouraging employees to win by any means.[8]

FIGURE 7-7 Types of Corporate Cultures

Which corporate culture would you choose?

	High	
Sociability	**Networked Culture** • Extrovert energized by relationships • Tolerant of ambiguities and have low needs for structure • Can spot politics and act to stop "negative" politics • Consider yourself easygoing, affable, and loyal to others	**Communal Culture** • You consider yourself passionate • Strong need to identify with something bigger than yourself • You enjoy being in teams • Prepared to make sacrifices for the greater good
	Fragmented Culture • Are a reflective and self-contained introvert • Have a high autonomy drive and strong desire to work independently • Have a strong sense of self	**Mercenary Culture** • Goal-oriented and have an obsessive desire to complete tasks • Thrive on competitive energy • Keep "relationships" out of work—develop them

Source: "Types of Corporate Culture," in Rob Goffee and Gareth Jones, *The Character of a Corporation* (New York: HarperCollins, 1998). Copyright © 1998 by Rob Goffee and Gareth Jones. Permission granted by Rob Goffee and Gareth Jones.

Dell Restructures to Jump-Start Innovation

With more than $60 billion in global revenue from computers, cloud computing, and other high-tech offerings, Dell is hardly a scrappy startup. To recapture market share and create the hot new products of tomorrow, the Texas-based company is decentralizing to encourage speedier innovation. As an example, it maintains a separate research-and-development group in Silicon Valley to identify, develop, and market new offerings in networking and other technologies.

As another example, one of Dell's business units—located just eight miles from headquarters—comes up with its own designs for data storage centers. The business acts like a firm founded in somebody's garage, rather than one of many units in a multinational corporation's portfolio. In fact, one of its engineers actually built a piece of equipment in his garage when the unit was young. The head of this unit says "you need a crayon drawing on a napkin," not layers of bureaucracy and strict guidelines, to fuel entrepreneurial innovation. In just five years, this unit has blossomed into a $1 billion business with 500 employees—and more growth is on the horizon.

Restructuring to nurture innovation doesn't guarantee a product hit, as Dell knows from its unsuccessful first experience with a separate smartphone division. Still, decentralization is giving Dell an opportunity to recapture the nimble, innovative spirit of its early days.

Sources: Based on information in Shara Tibken, "Dell Plans to Expand Silicon Valley Staff for R&D," *Marketwatch*, January 31, 2012, http://marketwatch.com/story/dell-plans-to-expand-silicon-valley-staff-for-rd-2012-01-31; Christopher Calnan, "Dell to Up Staff in Santa Clara, Calif.," *Austin Business Journal*, January 31, 2011, http://bizjournals.com/austin/news/2012/01/31/dell-to-up-staff-in-santa-clara-calif.html; Anne VanderMey, "Dell Gets in Touch with Its Inner Entrepreneur," *Fortune*, December 12, 2011, p. 58.

Corporate Culture. Corporate culture can influence an employee's attitudes toward fitness and health. Some organizations have gyms and complimentary healthy snacks such as fruit.

Concept Check

✓ What is corporate culture?

✓ Explain the four types of corporate cultures.

In the *fragmented culture*, employees do not become friends, and they work "at" the organization, not "for" it. Employees have a high degree of autonomy, flexibility, and equality.

The *communal culture* combines the positive traits of the networked culture and the mercenary culture—those of friendship, commitment, high focus on performance, and high energy. People's lives revolve around the product in this culture, and success by anyone in the organization is celebrated by all.[9]

Some experts believe that cultural change is needed when a company's environment changes, such as when the industry becomes more competitive, the company's performance is mediocre, or when the company is growing. It is not uncommon that companies feel they must adjust their culture in order to attract top talent. For example, many companies have formally come out in favor of same-sex marriage, including General Mills, Alcoa, and Aetna. Having a nondiscriminatory culture is seen as important for maintaining a strong workforce for many corporations.[10]

Organizations in the future will look quite different, as technology allows more to be done in small, flexible work groups that are coordinated by computers and held together by strong corporate cultures. Businesses operating in fast-changing industries will require leadership that supports trust and risk taking. Creating a culture of trust in an organization can lead to increases in growth, profit, productivity, and job satisfaction. A culture of trust can help an organization to retain the best people, inspire customer loyalty, develop new markets, and increase creativity.

Another area where corporate culture plays a vital role is the integration of two or more companies. Business leaders often cite the role of corporate cultures in the integration process as one of the primary factors affecting the success of a merger or acquisition. Experts note that corporate culture is a way of conducting business both within the company and externally. If two merging companies do not address differences in corporate culture, they are setting themselves up for missed opportunities and possibly failure.

COMMITTEES AND TASK FORCES

Learning Objective

8 Understand how committees and task forces are used.

Today, business firms use several types of committees that affect organizational structure. An **ad hoc committee** is created for a specific short-term purpose, such as reviewing the firm's employee benefits plan. Once its work is finished, the ad hoc committee disbands. A **standing committee** is a relatively permanent committee charged with performing a recurring task. A firm might establish a budget review committee, for example, to review departmental budget requests on an ongoing basis. Finally, a **task force** is a committee established to investigate a major problem or pending decision. A firm contemplating a merger with another company might form a task force to assess the pros and cons of the merger.

Committees offer some advantages over individual action. Their several members are able to bring information and knowledge to the task at hand. Furthermore, committees tend to make more accurate decisions and to transmit their results through the organization more effectively. However, committee deliberations take longer than individual actions. In addition, unnecessary compromise may take place within the committee, or the opposite may occur, as one person dominates (and thus negates) the committee process.

ad hoc committee a committee created for a specific short-term purpose

standing committee a relatively permanent committee charged with performing some recurring task

task force a committee established to investigate a major problem or pending decision

Concept Check

✓ What is the difference between a committee and a task force?

✓ What are the advantages and disadvantages of using committees?

THE INFORMAL ORGANIZATION AND THE GRAPEVINE

Learning Objective

9 Explain the functions of the informal organization and the grapevine in a business.

So far, we have discussed the organization as a formal structure consisting of interrelated positions. This is the organization that is shown on an organization chart. There is another kind of organization, however, that does not appear on any chart. We define this **informal organization** as the pattern of behavior and interaction that stems from personal rather than official relationships. Embedded within every informal organization are informal groups and the notorious grapevine.

An **informal group** is created by the group members themselves to accomplish goals that may or may not be relevant to the organization. Workers may create an informal group to go bowling, form a union, get a particular manager fired or transferred, or meet for lunch. The group may last for several years or a few hours.

informal organization the pattern of behavior and interaction that stems from personal rather than official relationships

informal group a group created by the members themselves to accomplish goals that may or may not be relevant to an organization

There is power in numbers. It's common for employees to befriend one another and form informal groups within an organization. The groups provide their members with camaraderie and information, but can create both challenges and benefits for the organization.

Concept Check

✓ In what ways can informal groups affect a business?

✓ How is the grapevine used in a business organization?

Informal groups can be powerful forces in organizations. They can restrict output, or they can help managers through tight spots. They can cause disagreement and conflict, or they can help to boost morale and job satisfaction. They have the power to improve or worsen employee performance and productivity. Clearly, managers should be aware of informal groups and determine how to utilize them.

The **grapevine** is the informal communications network within an organization. It is completely separate from—and sometimes much faster than—the organization's formal channels of communication. Formal communications usually follow a path that parallels the organizational chain of command. Information can be transmitted through the grapevine in any direction—up, down, diagonally, or horizontally across the organizational structure. Subordinates may pass information to their bosses, an executive may relay something to a maintenance worker, or there may be an exchange of information between people who work in totally unrelated departments. Information gleaned from the grapevine can run the gamut from the latest management decisions to gossip.

How should managers treat the grapevine? Certainly, it would be a mistake to try to eliminate it. People working together, day in and day out, are bound to communicate. A more rational approach is to recognize its existence. For example, managers should respond promptly and aggressively to inaccurate grapevine information to minimize the damage that such misinformation might do. Moreover, the grapevine can come in handy when managers are on the receiving end of important communications from the informal organization.

In the next chapter, we apply these and other management concepts to an extremely important business function: the production of goods and services.

Summary

1 Understand what an organization is and identify its characteristics.

An organization is a group of two or more people working together to achieve a common set of goals. The relationships among positions within an organization can be illustrated by means of an organization chart. Five elements—job design, departmentalization, delegation, span of management, and chain of command—help to determine what an organization chart and the organization itself look like.

2 Explain why job specialization is important.

Job specialization is the separation of all the activities within an organization into smaller components and

the assignment of those different components to different people. Several factors combine to make specialization a useful technique for designing jobs, but high levels of specialization may cause employee dissatisfaction and boredom. One technique for overcoming these problems is job rotation.

3 Identify the various bases for departmentalization.

Departmentalization is the grouping of jobs into manageable units. Typical bases for departmentalization are by function, product, location, or customer. Because each of these bases provides particular advantages, most firms—especially larger ones—use a combination of different bases to address different organizational situations.

4 Explain how decentralization follows from delegation.

Delegation is giving part of a manager's work to other workers. It involves the following three steps: (1) assigning responsibility, (2) granting authority, and (3) creating accountability. A decentralized firm is one that delegates as much power as possible to people in the lower management levels. In a centralized firm, on the other hand, power is retained at the upper levels.

5 Understand how the span of management describes an organization.

The span of management is the number of workers who report directly to a manager. Spans generally are characterized as wide (many workers per manager) or narrow (few workers per manager). Wide spans generally result in flat organizations (few layers of management); narrow spans generally result in tall organizations (many layers of management).

6 Describe the four basic forms of organizational structure.

There are four basic forms of organizational structure. The line structure is the oldest and simplest structure, in which the chain of command moves in a straight line from person to person down through the levels of management. The line-and-staff structure is similar to the line structure, but adds specialists called staff managers to assist the line managers in decision making. The line structure works most efficiently for smaller organizations, whereas the line-and-staff structure is used by medium- and large-sized organizations. The matrix structure may be depicted as product departmentalization superimposed on functional departmentalization. With the matrix structure, an employee on a cross-functional team reports to both the project manager and the individual's supervisor in a functional department. In an organization with a network structure, the primary function performed internally is administration, and other functions are contracted out to other firms.

7 Describe the effects of corporate culture.

Corporate culture has both internal and external effects on an organization. An organization's culture can influence the way employees think and act, and it can also determine the public's perception of the organization. Corporate culture can affect a firm's performance over time, either negatively or positively. Creating a culture of trust, for example, can lead to increased growth, profits, productivity, and job satisfaction, while retaining the best employees, inspiring customer loyalty, developing new markets, and increasing creativity. In addition, when two or more companies undergo the integration process, their different or similar corporate cultures can affect the success of a merger or acquisition.

8 Understand how committees and task forces are used.

Committees and task forces are used to develop organizational structure within an organization. An ad hoc committee is created for a specific short-term purpose, whereas a standing committee is relatively permanent. A task force is created to investigate a major problem or pending decision.

9 Explain the functions of the informal organization and the grapevine in a business.

Informal groups are created by group members to accomplish goals that may or may not be relevant to the organization, and they can be very powerful forces. The grapevine—the informal communications network within an organization—can be used to transmit information (important or gossip) through an organization much faster than through the formal communication network. Information transmitted through the grapevine can go in any direction across the organizational structure, skipping up or down levels of management and even across departments.

Key Terms

You should now be able to define and give an example relevant to each of the following terms:

organization (185)
organization chart (185)
chain of command (185)
job specialization (186)
job rotation (188)
departmentalization (188)
departmentalization by function (188)
departmentalization by product (188)

departmentalization by location (189)
departmentalization by customer (189)
delegation (190)
responsibility (190)
authority (190)
accountability (190)
decentralized organization (190)

centralized organization (190)
span of management (or span of control) (192)
organizational height (193)
line structure (193)
line manager (193)
line-and-staff structure (194)
staff manager (194)
matrix structure (195)

cross-functional team (195)
network structure (196)
corporate culture (197)
ad hoc committee (199)
standing committee (199)
task force (199)
informal organization (199)
informal group (199)
grapevine (200)

Discussion Questions

1. In what way do organization charts create a picture of an organization?
2. What determines the degree of specialization within an organization?
3. Describe how job rotation can be used to combat the problems caused by job specialization.
4. Why do most firms employ a combination of departmentalization bases?
5. What three steps are involved in delegation? Explain each.
6. How does a firm's top management influence its degree of centralization?
7. How is organization height related to the span of management?
8. Contrast line-and-staff and matrix forms of organizational structure.
9. How does the corporate culture of a local Best Buy store compare to that of a local McDonald's?
10. Which kinds of firms probably would operate most effectively as centralized firms? As decentralized firms?
11. How do decisions concerning span of management and the use of committees affect organizational structure?

Test Yourself

Matching Questions

1. _____ Line of authority from the highest to lowest levels.
2. _____ Two or more people working toward a common goal.
3. _____ Grouping jobs into manageable units.
4. _____ Assigns part of the manager's work to others.
5. _____ The power to accomplish an assigned task.
6. _____ The duty to do a job or perform a task.
7. _____ Combines vertical and horizontal lines of authority.
8. _____ Charged with the responsibility of developing new products.
9. _____ An informal communications network.
10. _____ Committee that investigates major problems or pending decisions.

   a. ad hoc committee
   b. authority
   c. chain of command
   d. cross-functional team
   e. delegation
   f. departmentalization
   g. grapevine
   h. matrix structure
   i. network structure
   j. organization
   k. responsibility
   l. task force
   m. span of management

True False Questions

11. **T   F** A benefit of specialization is improved efficiency and increased productivity.
12. **T   F** Job rotation involves assigning an employee more tasks and greater control.
13. **T   F** The power to make decisions is granted through authority.
14. **T   F** Accountability is created, not delegated.
15. **T   F** The span of management should be wide when a great deal of interaction is required between the supervisor and worker.
16. **T   F** Line positions support staff positions in decision making.
17. **T   F** Many firms find that by using matrix organization, the motivation level is lowered, and personal growth of employees is limited.
18. **T   F** In the mercenary culture, employees work "at" the organization, not "for" it.
19. **T   F** Creating a culture of trust can lead to decreased productivity and job satisfaction.
20. **T   F** Ad hoc committees can be used effectively to review a firm's employee benefits plan.

Multiple-Choice Questions

21. _____ The process of dividing work to be done by an entire organization into separate parts and assigning the parts to positions within the organization is called _____

   a. departmentalization.
   b. delegation.
   c. job design.
   d. specialization.
   e. organizing.

22. _____ Who was the first to recognize the power of specialization?
   a. Karl Marx
   b. Max Weber
   c. John Kenneth Galbraith
   d. Adam Smith
   e. Thomas Friedman

23. _____ ABC Distributors is reorganizing to better control costs. The company decided to group hospitals, schools, and churches together into one department. Which departmentalization base is the company using?
   a. Location
   b. Function
   c. Employees
   d. Product
   e. Customer

24. _____ Older and larger firms that produce and sell a variety of products tend to organize by _____
   a. location.
   b. product.
   c. customer.
   d. function.
   e. executive decisions.

25. _____ A supervisor assigned to Wendy, the most proficient employee in the accounting department, a project on cost control that was due in three weeks. For Wendy to be accountable for the project, what must Wendy be given?
   a. Responsibility
   b. Power
   c. Authority
   d. Training
   e. Control

26. _____ Many managers are reluctant to delegate. Which one of the following is not one of the reasons they are reluctant to do so?
   a. They want to be sure that the work gets done.
   b. They fear that workers will do the work well and attract the approving notice of higher-level managers.

   c. They are so disorganized that they simply are not able to plan and assign work.
   d. Most managers are workaholics.
   e. Most subordinates are reluctant to accept delegated tasks.

27. _____ A narrow span of management works best when _____
   a. subordinates are located close together.
   b. the manager has few responsibilities outside of supervision.
   c. little interaction is required between the manager and the worker.
   d. new problems arise frequently.
   e. few problems arise on a daily basis.

28. _____ A relatively permanent committee charged with performing some recurring task is called _____
   a. an ad hoc committee.
   b. a standing committee.
   c. a task force.
   d. a managerial committee.
   e. a permanent committee.

29. _____ A committee is organized to review applications for scholarships. The group will award two scholarships to recent high school graduates. What type of committee would work best?
   a. Ad hoc committee
   b. Task force
   c. Liaison committee
   d. Standing committee
   e. Self-managed team

30. _____ In order to best handle the grapevine, managers should _____
   a. try to eliminate it.
   b. respond slowly to inaccurate information.
   c. respond aggressively to accurate information.
   d. recognize its existence.
   e. reprimand employees who pass on important information.

Answers to the Test Yourself questions appear at the end of the book on page TY-1.

Video Case
Zappos Wants to Make Customers (and Employees) Happy

Zappos (www.zappos.com) doesn't want to simply satisfy its customers—it wants to make them happy, a major reason for its success as an Internet retailer. Founded in 1999 to sell shoes online, the business soon earned a reputation for delivering personalized, responsive customer service. Top executives didn't pressure call-center employees (known internally as members of the Customer Loyalty Team) to follow a script or end conversations quickly. In fact, they encouraged employees to stay on the phone as long as needed to answer customers' questions, discuss merchandise, add a little chit-chat, and provide a "wow" shopping experience. Delighted customers would tell their friends and click or call back for more "wow" the next time they're in the market for new shoes.

By 2009, when it was purchased by the pioneering web giant Amazon, Las Vegas-based Zappos was beginning to branch out into clothing, handbags, and other merchandise. Today, with annual sales surpassing $1 billion, the website features outerwear, beauty products, sporting goods, and many other items, as well as shoes and clothing for the whole family. In addition, the company has established an Insights division to help other companies understand and adapt the unique corporate culture that has given Zappos a vital competitive edge in the dynamic world of e-commerce.

Zappos is so famous for its upbeat, can-do culture—not to mention the many opportunities for advancement available in a fast-growing firm—that it attracts 55,000 job applications every year. During interviews, managers ask offbeat questions such as, "On a scale of one to ten, how weird are you?" The purpose is to determine whether an applicant has the personality and temperament to fit into a corporate culture where fun, change, teamwork, creativity, transparency, and personal growth are highly valued. All newly hired employees have to sign a statement confirming that they understand these core values and are committed to applying them on the job.

Delivering superior service with a virtual smile requires careful behind-the-scenes coordination. Every Zappos employee is responsible for performing specific tasks, supported by regular training plus optional courses to build new skills. Because so many orders come in by phone, the entire workforce (including the CEO) receives a month of call-center training, along with a week of training in the warehouse, to get a first-hand taste of the challenges of customer contact and order fulfillment.

In line with the corporate culture, Zappos provides the tools and the opportunities for employees to become the best they can be. For example, employees are invited to meet with an on-site life coach for assistance in setting and meeting both personal and professional goals. They can sign up to shadow a manager or employee elsewhere in the organization as a way to explore new career possibilities. Work hard, play hard is the rule at Zappos, where holiday parties, picnics, parades, and other special events bring employees together for a bit of fun. These are only some of the ways that Zappos makes the workplace a "Wow" experience for its workforce.

To keep the organization running smoothly, Zappos holds an "all hands" meeting every three months. Videotaped and available online for repeat viewing, these meetings update everyone on the latest departmental and company news, serve as team-building events, and keep employees excited and inspired about working at Zappos. In addition, the firm monitors key performance statistics and posts them at headquarters to inform employees about what's happening to the business, day by day.

Now Zappos is taking on a leadership role in Las Vegas, using its new headquarters in the former city hall as the corporate linchpin in an ambitious plan to revitalize the downtown area. Will Zappos succeed in making its community as happy as its employees and customers?[11]

Questions

1. Do you think Zappos is a decentralized or centralized organization? Do you think it should change? Explain your answer.
2. Of the four types of corporate culture, which most closely describes the culture of Zappos? What are the implications for the organization and for managers and employees?
3. What effect are quarterly meetings and daily posting of performance statistics likely to have on the grapevine inside Zappos?

Building Skills for Career Success

1. Social Media Exercise

Zappos has a reputation for being customer-centered, meaning it embraces the notion that customers come first. One of the ways that it allows employees to communicate with customers is through its blog www.zapposinsights.com/blog.

1. Take a look at this blog. What can you tell about the corporate culture of Zappos?
2. How do they approach customer service? Do you think it works? Why or why not?

2. Building Team Skills

An organization chart is a diagram showing how employees and tasks are grouped and how the lines of communication and authority flow within an organization. These charts can look very different depending on a number of factors, including the nature and size of the business, the way it is departmentalized, its patterns of delegating authority, and its span of management.

Assignment

1. Working in a team, use the following information to draw an organization chart: The KDS Design Center works closely with two home-construction companies, ACME Homebuilders and Highmass. KDS's role is to help customers select materials for their new homes and to ensure that their selections are communicated accurately to the builders. The company is also a retailer of wallpaper, blinds, and drapery. The retail department, the ACME Homebuilders accounts, and the Highmass accounts make up KDS's

three departments. The company has the following positions: president, executive vice president, managers, two appointment coordinators, two ACME Homebuilders coordinators, two Highmass coordinators, two consultants/designers for the Amex and Highmass accounts, 15 retail positions, and four payroll and billing personnel.

2. After your team has drawn the organization chart, discuss the following:
   a. What type of organizational structure does your chart depict? Is it a bureaucratic, matrix, cluster, or network structure? Why?
   b. How does KDS use departmentalization?
   c. To what extent is authority in the company centralized or decentralized?
   d. What is the span of management within KDS?
   e. Which positions are line positions and which are staff? Why?
3. Prepare a three-page report summarizing what the chart revealed about relationships and tasks at the KDS Design Center and what your team learned about the value of organization charts. Include your chart in your report.

3. Researching Different Careers

In the past, company loyalty and the ability to assume increasing job responsibility usually ensured advancement within an organization. While the reasons for seeking advancement (the desire for a better-paying position, more prestige, and job satisfaction) have not changed, the qualifications for career advancement have. In today's business environment, climbing the corporate ladder requires packaging and marketing yourself. To be promoted within your company or to be considered for employment with another company, it is wise to improve your skills continually. By taking workshops and seminars or enrolling in community college courses, you can keep up with the changing technology in your industry.

Networking with people in your business or community can help you to find a new job. Most jobs are filled through personal contacts, proving that who you know can be important.

A list of your accomplishments on the job can reveal your strengths and weaknesses. Setting goals for improvement helps to increase your self-confidence.

Be sure to recognize the signs of job dissatisfaction. If you are feeling unhappy in your job, it may be time to move to another position or company.

Assignment

Are you prepared to climb the corporate ladder? Do a self-assessment by analyzing the following areas and summarize the results in a two-page report.

1. Skills
   * What are your most valuable skills?
   * What skills do you lack?
   * Describe your plan for acquiring new skills and improving your existing skills.
2. Networking
   * How effective are you at using a mentor?
   * Are you a member of a professional organization?
   * In which community, civic, or church groups are you participating?
   * Whom have you added to your contact list in the last six weeks?
3. Accomplishments
   * What achievements have you reached in your job?
   * What would you like to accomplish? What will it take for you to reach your goal?
4. Promotion or new job
   * What is your likelihood for getting a promotion?
   * Are you ready for a change? What are you doing or willing to do to find another job?

Endnotes

1. Based on information in Robert Safian, "Terry Kelly, The 'Un-CEO' of W.L. Gore, on How to Deal with Chaos: Grow Up," Fast Company, October 29, 2012. www.fastcompany.com; Gary Hamel, "W.L. Gore: Lessons from a Management Revolutionary, Part 1," Wall Street Journal, March 18, 2010, www.wsj.com; Gary Hamel, "W.L. Gore: Lessons from a Management Revolutionary, Part 2," Wall Street Journal, April 2, 2010, www.wsj.com.
2. Jennifer Alsever, "Job Swaps: Are They for You?" Fortune, October 29, 2012, http://management.fortune.cnn.com/2012/10/24/job-swaps/.
3. PepsiCo Corporate Profile, www.pepsico.com/Investors/Corporate-Profile.html (accessed November 17, 2012).
4. Eric Pfanner and Any Chozick, "Random House and Penguin Merger Creates Global Giant," New York Times, October 29, 2012, http://www.nytimes.com/2012/10/30/business/global/random-house-and-penguin-to-be-combined.html.
5. "Francesco Guerrera, "UBS Tells Why it Cut off a Limb," Wall Street Journal, November 12, 2012, http://online.wsj.com/article/SB10001424127887323894704578114863817976002.html.
6. Dana Griffin, "Disadvantages of a Line & Staff Organization Structure," Small Business, http://smallbusiness.chron.com/disadvantages-line-staff-organization-structure-2762.html (accessed November 17, 2012).
7. John Kotter, "Can Your Organization Handle Losing a Leader?" Forbes, March 21, 2012, www.forbes.com/sites/johnkotter/2012/03/21/can-your-organization-handle-losing-a-leader/.
8. Peter J. Henning, "A Triple Whammy for Barclays," New York Times, November 5, 2012, http://dealbook.nytimes.com/2012/11/05/a-triple-whammy-for-barclays/.
9. Rob Goffee and Gareth Jones, "The Character of a Corporation: How Your Company's Culture Can Make or Break Your Business," Jones Harper Business, December 2003, 182.
10. Leslie Kwoh, "To Snag Top Talent, Companies Come out For Gay Rights," New York Times, November 13, 2012, http://blogs.wsj.com/atwork/2012/11/13/to-snag-top-talent-companies-come-out-for-gay-rights/.
11. Sources: Based on information in Rhymer Rigby, "The Benefits of Workplace Levity," Financial Times, December 19, 2012, www.ft.com; Carmine Gallo, "America's Happiest Employee," Forbes, December 26, 2012, www.forbes.com; Mig Pascual, "Zappos: 5 Out-of-the-Box Ideas for Keeping Employees Engaged," U.S. News & World Report, October 30, 2012, http://money.usnews.com; Lisa V. Gillespie, "Workplace Culture: Targeting Soft Skills Yields Hard Returns for Employers," Employee Benefit News, April 15, 2012, p. 18; Priya de Langen, "The Right Fit at Zappos," HRM Asia, January 5, 2012, www.hrmasia.com; www.zappos.com; Cengage "Zappos" video; www.zappos.com.

© MICHAELJUNG/SHUTTERSTOCK.COM

Producing Quality Goods and Services

Why Should You Care?

Think for a moment about the products and services you bought in the past week. Those products and services could not be produced if it weren't for the production activities described in this chapter and that means consumers like you would not be able to purchase the products and services they need or want.

Learning Objectives

Once you complete this chapter, you will be able to:

1 Explain the nature of production.

2 Outline how the conversion process transforms raw materials, labor, and other resources into finished goods or services.

3 Understand the importance of service businesses to consumers, other business firms, and the nation's economy.

4 Describe how research and development leads to new products and services.

5 Discuss the components involved in planning the production process.

6 Explain how purchasing, inventory control, scheduling, and quality control affect production.

7 Summarize how technology can make American firms more productive and competitive in the global marketplace.

ntel Invests in State-of-the-Art Production

How do you create gigantic state-of-the-art production facilities to make products that get tinier and more sophisticated day by day? That's only one of the manufacturing challenges facing California-based Intel (www.intel.com), which has $54 billion in sales revenues and 82,500 employees worldwide. Intel is a pioneer of the microprocessor, the chips that now provide computing power in laptops, servers, smartphones, even cars. Three-quarters of its products come from company factories in Arizona, New Mexico, Oregon, and Massachusetts. Intel also operates factories in China, Ireland, and Israel.

Intel begins its research on new chips a decade in advance, identifying the kinds of products that will need new chips and planning to pack more processing capability into each chip. Engineers and manufacturing experts work together to perfect the new chip design and fine-tune its production at one of the Oregon plants. Following a "copy exactly" strategy, Intel then duplicates the production process at its other factories, to ensure high chip quality, minimize mistakes, and meet market demand.

Every year, Intel spends more than $10 billion to build or expand plants, overhaul the production process, and install cutting-edge equipment to boost efficiency. While some chipmakers partner with outside manufacturers to keep costs down, Intel sees its investment in production as vital to maintaining its competitive edge. Given the fast pace of technological change, Intel needs to be able to switch to an innovative product or process quickly—which it can do because it owns its manufacturing facilities.

The newly opened Intel factory in Hillsboro, Oregon, cost $3 billion and is 60 percent larger than the massive Intel facility next door. Another giant Intel chip plant in Arizona cost $5 billion to build. This extra space gives Intel more flexibility in adapting to future needs and using the latest tools and technology. No one knows what the best-selling chip of 2020 will be, but Intel stands ready to design and produce it.[1]

Did You Know?

Intel invests more than $10 billion every year to build new production facilities and upgrade existing facilities and equipment.

Back in 1968, two scientists, Robert Noyce and Gordon Moore, founded Intel with a vision for semiconductor memory products. Their efforts to develop and manufacture the world's first microprocessor paid off, and today Intel—the company profiled in the Inside Business feature for this chapter—is one of the world's largest and most important chip manufacturers. Now, the company is making a real difference because without the chips the company manufacturers, many of the electronic products and gadgets we often take for granted could not be produced. And while the products you buy may not have the Intel logo on the actual product, Intel chips may be inside making everything work the way it is supposed to work. Looking ahead, the company's chips and technology products will be even more important as new products require more processing capability for the next generation of technology products. In fact, that's why Intel invest billions of dollars each year to research new chips and build or expand plants in order to make sure it has the capacity to produce the chips that are needed years in the future. Today, Intel is an excellent example of what this chapter's content—the production of quality goods and services—is all about.

We begin this chapter with an overview of operations management—the activities required to produce goods and services that meet the needs of customers. In this section, we also discuss the role of manufacturing in the U.S. economy, competition in the global marketplace, and careers in operations management. Next, we describe the conversion process that makes production possible and also note the growing role of services in our economy. Then we examine more closely three important aspects of operations management: developing ideas for new products, planning for production, and effectively controlling operations after production has begun. We close the chapter with a look at the productivity trends and the ways that manufacturing can be improved through the use of technology.

WHAT IS PRODUCTION?

Have you ever wondered where a new pair of Levi's jeans comes from? Or an Apple iPad Mini, or a Uniroyal tire for your car? Even factory service on a Maytag clothes dryer would be impossible if it weren't for the activities described in this chapter. In fact, these products and services and millions of others like them would not exist if it weren't for production activities.

Let's begin this chapter by reviewing what an operating manager does. In Chapter 6, we described an *operations manager* as a person who manages the systems that convert resources into goods and services. This area of management is usually referred to as **operations management**, which consists of all the activities required to produce goods and services.

operations management all the activities required to produce goods and services

To produce a product or service successfully, a business must perform a number of specific activities. For example, suppose that Toyota (the parent company of Lexus automobiles) has an idea for a new, sport version of the Lexus GS 350 that will cost approximately $50,000. Marketing research must determine not only if customers are willing to pay the price for this product but also what special features they want. Then Toyota's operations managers must turn the idea into reality.

Toyota's managers cannot just push the "start button" and immediately begin producing the new automobile. As you will see, planning takes place both *before* anything is produced and *during* the production process.

Managers also must concern themselves with the control of operations to ensure that the organization's goals are achieved. For a product such as the Lexus GS 350, control of operations involves a number of important issues, including product quality, performance standards, the amount of inventory of both raw materials and finished products, and production costs.

We discuss each of the major activities of operations management later in this chapter. First, however, let's take a closer look at American manufacturers and how they compete in the global marketplace.

How American Manufacturers Compete in the Global Marketplace

After World War II, the United States became the most productive country in the world. For almost 30 years, until the late 1970s, its leadership was never threatened. By then, however, manufacturers in Japan, Germany, Taiwan, Korea, Singapore, Sweden, and other industrialized nations were offering U.S. firms increasing competition. Now the Chinese are manufacturing everything from sophisticated electronic equipment and automobiles to less expensive everyday items. And yet, in the face of increasing competition, there is both good and bad news for U.S. manufacturers. First the bad news.

THE BAD NEWS FOR MANUFACTURERS The number of Americans employed in the manufacturing sector has decreased. Currently, approximately 12 million U.S. workers are employed in manufacturing jobs—down from just over 19 million back in 1979.[2] While there are many additional factors, three major factors explain why employment in this economic sector has declined.

AP IMAGES/APPLE

Why is the product in this photo important? While it may be hard to tell at this stage of production, the product at this work station is one of the most successful products in recent history—the Apple iPhone. On the left, the man in the yellow coat is Apple CEO Tim Cook who is talking with lab technicians that produce the product in this Chinese factory.

- Many of the manufacturing jobs that were lost were outsourced to low-wage workers in nations where there are few labor and environmental regulations.
- It costs about 20 percent more to manufacture goods in the United States than it does anywhere else in the world.[3]

- The number of unemployed factory workers increased during the recent economic crisis because of decreased consumer demand for manufactured goods.

As a result, manufacturing accounts for only about 9 percent of the current workforce.[4] Since 1979, 7 million jobs have been lost, and many of those jobs aren't coming back.

THE GOOD NEWS FOR MANUFACTURERS The United States remains one of the largest manufacturing countries in the world. While some people would argue that "Made in America" doesn't mean what it used to mean, consider the following:

- U.S. manufacturers produce approximately 18 percent of total global manufacturing output.[5]
- Every year, manufacturing contributes about 12 percent of the gross domestic product and approximately $2 trillion to the U.S. economy.[6]
- Manufacturing exports are nearly 60 percent of all U.S. exports.[7]
- Between now and 2018, it is anticipated that there will be 2 million job openings for skilled workers in manufacturing.[8]
- For every new manufacturing job created, there are another three new jobs created in the supply chain, the trucking industry, and other related areas of the economy.[9]

As a result, the manufacturing sector is still a very important part of the U.S. economy. Although the number of manufacturing jobs has declined, productivity has increased. At least two very important factors account for increases in productivity: First, innovation—finding a better way to produce products—is the key factor that has enabled American manufacturers to compete in the global marketplace. Second, today's workers in the manufacturing sector are highly skilled in order to operate sophisticated equipment. Simply put, Americans are making more goods, but with fewer employees.

Even more good news is that many American manufacturers that outsourced work to factories in foreign nations are once again beginning to manufacture goods in the United States. For our purposes, the term **reshoring** (sometimes referred to as onshoring or insourcing) describes a situation where U.S. manufacturers bring manufacturing jobs back to the United States. For example, General Electric, Ford, Apple, Caterpillar, Honda, Intel, and Master Lock and many other U.S. firms are involved in reshoring. The primary reasons why U.S. firms are "coming back home" include increasing labor costs in foreign nations, higher shipping costs, significant quality and safety issues, faster product development when goods are produced in the United States, and federal and state subsidies to encourage manufactures to produce products in the United States.

Although there are many challenges facing U.S. manufacturers, experts predict that there could be a significant resurgence for manufacturers that can meet current

reshoring a situation in which U.S. manufacturers bring manufacturing jobs back to the United States

Entrepreneurial Success

Profit from Demand for "Made in America"

Quality goods made in America are increasingly in demand worldwide, a trend that's boosting sales and profits for entrepreneurial manufacturers. Cabot Hosiery Mills, located in Vermont, was struggling to compete with overseas producers of socks when the founder and his son had a flash of insight. Rather than continue to make everyday socks, they believed Cabot had the experience and expertise to design and manufacture high-performance socks for the high end of the market. After some experimentation, they came up with Darn Tough socks: durable, well-cushioned, and backed by a lifetime replacement guarantee. Now Cabot sells 4 million Darn Tough socks every year. Although only a few hundred pairs have ever been returned, Cabot examines each one carefully for clues to making Darn Tough even tougher.

Watermark Designs, a manufacturer in Brooklyn, New York, has earned a global reputation for stylish, hand-crafted plumbing fixtures. Because Watermark's designers are based in the factory, they can consult with production managers while they develop a new product, and then have a prototype made or refined within days. For quality control purposes, workers test every faucet before it's shipped to Michigan, Manitoba, Macau, or beyond.

A growing number of U.S. stores, markets, and websites are devoted to made-in-America products, giving manufacturers more opportunities to reach new customers and demonstrate their quality credentials. Entrepreneurs are showcasing everything from boots to bicycles, explaining where their raw materials come from and highlighting the quality and care built into every product.

Sources: Based on information in Jim Dwyer, "In Manufacturing Shift, Made in U.S. but Sold in China," *New York Times*, September 20, 2012, www.nytimes.com; Emanuella Grinberg, "Made in America Markets Create Communities of Like-Minded Consumers," *CNN*, November 5, 2012, www.cnn.com; Jim Motavalli, "To Make Socks in Vermont, You Have to Be Darn Tough," *Success*, September 2011, p. 42.

and future challenges. The bottom line: The global marketplace has never been more competitive and successful U.S. firms will focus on the following:

1. Meeting the needs of customers and improving product quality.
2. Motivating employees to cooperate with management and improve productivity.
3. Reducing costs by selecting suppliers that offer higher quality raw materials and components at reasonable prices.
4. Using computer-aided and flexible manufacturing systems that allow a higher degree of customization.
5. Improving control procedures to help ensure lower manufacturing costs.
6. Using green manufacturing to conserve natural resources and sustain the planet.

For most firms, competing in the global marketplace is not only profitable but also an essential activity that requires the cooperation of everyone within the organization.

Careers in Operations Management

Although it is hard to provide information about specific career opportunities in operations management, some generalizations do apply to this management area. A basic understanding of mass production and the difference between an analytical process and a synthetic process is essential. **Mass production** is a manufacturing process that lowers the cost required to produce a large number of identical or similar products over a long period of time. An **analytical process** breaks raw materials into different component parts. For example, a barrel of crude oil refined by Marathon Oil Corporation—a Texas-based oil and energy exploration company—can be broken down into gasoline, oil, lubricants, and many other petroleum by-products. A **synthetic process** is just the opposite of the analytical one; it combines raw materials or components to create a finished product. Black & Decker uses a synthetic process when it combines plastic, steel, rechargeable batteries, and other components to produce a cordless drill.

Once you understand that operations managers are responsible for producing tangible goods or services that customers want, you must determine how you fit into the production process. Today's successful operations managers must:

1. Be able to motivate and lead people.
2. Understand how technology can make a manufacturer more productive.
3. Appreciate the control processes that help lower production costs and improve product quality.
4. Understand the relationship between the customer, the marketing of a product, and the production of a product.

If operations management seems like an area you might be interested in, why not do more career exploration?

THE CONVERSION PROCESS

The purpose of manufacturing or a service business is to provide utility to customers. **Utility** is the ability of a good or service to satisfy a human need. Although there are four types of utilities—form, place, time, and possession—operations management focuses primarily on form utility. **Form utility** is created by people converting raw materials, finances, and information into finished products. The other types of utility—place, time, and possession—are discussed in Chapter 11.

But how does the conversion take place? How does Kellogg's convert corn, sugar, salt, and other ingredients; money from previous sales and stockholders' investments; production workers and managers; and economic and marketing forecasts into Frosted Flakes cereal products? How does H&R Block employ more than 100,000 tax preparers and convert retail locations, computers and software, and advertising and promotion into tax services for its clients. They do so through the

Concept Check

✓ List the major activities in operations management.

✓ What steps have U.S. firms taken to regain a competitive edge in the global marketplace?

✓ What is the difference between an analytical and a synthetic manufacturing process? Give an example of each type of process.

Learning Objective

2 Outline how the conversion process transforms raw materials, labor, and other resources into finished goods or services.

utility the ability of a good or service to satisfy a human need

form utility utility created by people converting raw materials, finances, and information into finished products

use of a conversion process like the one illustrated in Figure 8-1. As indicated by our H&R Block example, the conversion process can be used to produce services.

Manufacturing Using a Conversion Process

The conversion of resources into products and services can be described in several ways. We limit our discussion here to three: the focus or major resource used in the conversion process, its magnitude of change, and the number of production processes employed.

FOCUS By the *focus* of a conversion process, we mean the resource or resources that make up the major or most important *input*. The resources are financial, material, information, and people—the same resources discussed in Chapters 1 and 6. For a bank such as Citibank, financial resources are the major resource. A chemical and energy company such as Chevron concentrates on material resources. Your college or university is concerned primarily with information. And temporary employment services, such as Manpower, focus on the use of human resources.

MAGNITUDE OF CHANGE The *magnitude* of a conversion process is the degree to which the resources are physically changed. At one extreme lie such processes as the one by which the Glad Products Company produces Glad® Cling Wrap. Various chemicals in liquid or powder form are combined to produce long, thin sheets of plastic Glad Cling Wrap. Here, the original resources are totally unrecognizable in the finished product. At the other extreme, Southwest Airlines produces no physical change in its original resources. The airline simply provides a service and transports people from one place to another.

NUMBER OF PRODUCTION PROCESSES A single firm may employ one production process or many. In general, larger firms that make a variety of products use multiple production processes. For example, GE

FIGURE 8-1 The Conversion Process

The conversion process converts ideas and resources into useful goods and services.

PRODUCTION INPUTS
- Concept or idea for a new good or service
- Human, financial, material, and informational resources

↓

CONVERSION
- Plan necessary production activities to create a good or service
- Design the good or service
- Execute the plan to produce the good or service
- Evaluate the quality of the good or service
- Improve the good or service based on evaluation
- Redesign the good or service if necessary

↓

OUTPUTS
- Completed good or service

© CENGAGE LEARNING 2015

© DUSTIN MUDRY/SHUTTERSTOCK.COM

What does it take to make a home? It is often said that a home must have people in order to be a real home. And yet, a lot of different materials—concrete, lumber, sheet rock, flooring, roofing, etc. must be combined to produce the finished product—a home that people can live in.

Concept Check

✓ Explain how utility is related to form utility.

✓ In terms of focus, magnitude of change, and number, characterize the production processes used by a local pizza parlor, a dry-cleaning establishment, and an automobile repair shop.

Learning Objective

3 Understand the importance of service businesses to consumers, other business firms, and the nation's economy.

service economy an economy in which more effort is devoted to the production of services than to the production of goods

manufactures some of its own products, buys other merchandise from suppliers, and operates multiple divisions including a finance division, a lighting division, an appliance division, a healthcare division, and other divisions responsible for the products and services that customers associate with the GE name. Smaller firms, by contrast, may use one production process. For example, Texas-based Advanced Cast Stone, Inc., manufactures one basic product: building materials made from concrete.

THE INCREASING IMPORTANCE OF SERVICES

The application of the basic principles of operations management to the production of services has coincided with a dramatic growth in the number and diversity of service businesses. In 1900, only 28 percent of American workers were employed in service firms. By 1950, this figure had grown to 40 percent, and by the beginning of 2013, it had risen to 87 percent.[10] In fact, the American economy is now characterized as a service economy (see Figure 8-2). A **service economy** is one in which more effort is devoted to the production of services than to the production of goods.

Planning Quality Services

Today, the managers of restaurants, laundries, real estate agencies, banks, movie theaters, airlines, travel bureaus, and other service firms have realized that they can benefit from the experience of manufacturers. And while service firms are different from manufacturing firms, both types of businesses must complete many of the same activities in order to be successful. For example, as illustrated in the middle section of Figure 8-1, service businesses must plan, design, execute, evaluate, improve, and redesign their services in order to provide the services that their customers want.

For a service firm, planning often begins with determining who the customer is and what needs the customer has. After customer needs are identified, the next step for successful service firms is to develop a plan that will enable the firm to deliver the services that their customers want or need. For example, a swimming pool repair business must develop a business plan that includes a process for hiring and training qualified employees, obtaining necessary parts and supplies, marketing the

FIGURE 8-2 Service Industries

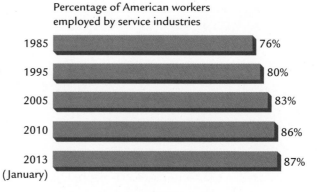

The growth of service firms has increased so dramatically that we now live in what is referred to as a service economy.

Percentage of American workers employed by service industries

Year	Percentage
1985	76%
1995	80%
2005	83%
2010	86%
2013 (January)	87%

Source: U.S. Bureau of Labor Statistics website, www.bls.gov (accessed February 15, 2013).

firm's services, and creating management and accounting systems to control the firm's activities. Once the firm provides a service to a customer, successful firms evaluate their operating systems and measure customer satisfaction. And if necessary, redesign their operating systems and their services to improve the customer's experience.

Evaluating the Quality of a Firm's Services

The production of services is very different from the production of manufactured goods in the following five ways:

1. When compared to manufactured goods, customers are much more involved in obtaining the service they want or need.
2. Services are consumed immediately and, unlike manufactured goods, cannot be stored. For example, a hair stylist cannot store completed haircuts.
3. Services are provided when and where the customer desires the service. In many cases, customers will not travel as far to obtain a service.
4. Services are usually labor-intensive because the human resource is often the most important resource used in the production of services.
5. Services are intangible, and it is therefore more difficult to evaluate customer satisfaction.[11]

Compared with manufacturers, service firms often listen more carefully to customers and respond more quickly to the market's changing needs. For example, Maggiano's Little Italy restaurant is a chain of eating establishments owned by Brinker International. In order to continuously improve customer service, the restaurant encourages diners to complete online surveys that prompt diners to evaluate the food, atmosphere, service, and other variables. The information from the surveys is then used to fine-tune the way Maggiano's meets its customers' needs.

In addition, many service firms are now using social media to build relationships with their customers. Coldwell Banker, one of the largest real estate companies in the United States sponsors an Internet blog that can be used not only to provide information about the current housing market, but also as a method to encourage comments and questions from customers.

Now that we understand something about the production process that is used to transform resources into goods and services, we can consider three major activities involved in operations management: research and development, planning for production, and operations control.

Concept Check

✓ How is the production of services similar to the production of manufactured goods?

✓ How is the production of services different from the production of manufactured goods?

✓ How can service firms measure customer satisfaction?

WHERE DO NEW PRODUCTS AND SERVICES COME FROM?

Learning Objective

4 Describe how research and development leads to new products and services.

No firm can produce a product or service until it has an idea. Both Apple's iPad Mini and Ford's Electric Focus automobile began as an idea and as a result of a company's research and development activities.

Research and Development

How did we get the Apple iPad Mini or the Electric Ford Focus automobile? We got them as a result of people working with new ideas that developed into useful products. These activities generally are referred to as research and development. For our purposes, **research and development (R&D)** involves a set of activities intended to identify new ideas that have the potential to result in new goods and services.

Today, business firms use three general types of R&D activities. *Basic research* consists of activities aimed at uncovering new knowledge. The goal of basic research is scientific advancement, without regard for its potential use in the development of goods and services. *Applied research*, in contrast, consists

research and development (R&D) a set of activities intended to identify new ideas that have the potential to result in new goods and services

Your idea for a new good or service may be your ticket to a small business of your own, if you have entrepreneurial spirit. But don't forget that big corporations also value people with new product ideas.

of activities geared toward discovering new knowledge with some potential use. *Development and implementation* involves research activities undertaken specifically to put new or existing knowledge to use in producing goods and services. For many companies, R&D is a very important part of their business operations. The 3M company, for example, has always been known for its development and implementation research activities. Currently, 3M employs 7,900 researchers worldwide and has invested more than $7 billion over the last five years to develop new products designed to make people's lives easier and safer.[12]

Product Extension and Refinement

If a firm sells only one product or service, when customers quit buying the product or service, the firm will die. To stay in business, the firm must, at the very least, find ways to refine or extend the want-satisfying capability of its product or service. Consider television sets. Since they were introduced in the late 1930s, television sets have been constantly *refined* so that they now provide clearer, sharper pictures with less dial adjusting. During the same time, television sets also were *extended*. There are basic flat-screen televisions without added features, and many others that include DVD or Blu-Ray players and Apps that can be used to access the Internet. The latest development—high-definition television—has already become the standard.

For most firms, extension and refinement are expected results of their research, development, and implementation activities. Each refinement or extension results in an essentially "new" product whose sales make up for the declining sales of a product that was introduced earlier. When consumers were introduced to the original five varieties of Campbell's Soup, they discovered that these soups were of the highest quality,

Concept Check

✓ Describe how research and development leads to new products.

✓ What is the difference between basic research, applied research, and development and implementation?

✓ Explain why product extension and refinement are important.

There are no guarantees when developing new products and services! Although a firm's research and development activities can make the difference between success and failure, developing new products and services is not a perfect science. In fact, the search for new products and services that have the potential to be successful often begins in the laboratory where scientists work to turn ideas into actual products.

as well as inexpensive, and the soups were an instant success. Although one of the most successful companies at the beginning of the 1900s, Campbell's had to continue to innovate, refine, and extend its product line. For example, many consumers in the United States live in what is called an on-the-go society. To meet this need, Campbell's Soup has developed ready-to-serve products that can be popped into a microwave at work or school.

HOW DO MANAGERS PLAN PRODUCTION?

Learning Objective

5 Discuss the components involved in planning the production process.

Only a few of the many ideas for new products ever reach the production stage. For those ideas that do, however, the next step is planning for production. Once a new idea for a product or service has been identified, planning for production involves three different phases: design planning, facilities planning, and operational planning (see Figure 8-3).

Design Planning

When the R&D staff at Samsung recommended to top management that the firm manufacture and market a "Smart Fridge" with a touch screen, Wi-Fi connectivity, and apps that allow consumers to update their calendars, leave notes to family members, or even provide recipe suggestions, the company could not simply swing into production the next day. Instead, a great deal of time and energy had to be invested in determining what the new refrigerator would look like, where and how it would be produced, and what options would be included. These decisions are a part of design planning. **Design planning** is the development of a plan for converting an idea into an actual product or service. The major decisions involved in design planning deal with product line, required capacity, and use of technology.

design planning the development of a plan for converting an idea into an actual product or service

PRODUCT LINE A **product line** is a group of similar products that differ only in relatively minor characteristics. During the design-planning stage, a manufacturer like Samsung must determine how many different models to produce and what major options to offer. Likewise, a restaurant chain such as Pizza Hut must decide how many menu items to offer.

product line a group of similar products that differ only in relatively minor characteristics

FIGURE 8-3 Planning for Production

Once research and development identifies an idea that meets customer needs, three additional steps are used to convert the idea to an actual good or service.

Research and development identifies an idea for a new good or service.

1 Design planning develops a plan to convert the idea into a new good or service.

2 Facilities planning identifies a site where the good or service can be produced.

3 Operational planning decides on the amount of goods or services that will be produced within a specific time period.

© CENGAGE LEARNING 2015

An important issue in deciding on the product line is to balance customer preferences and production requirements. Typically, marketing personnel want a "long" product line that offers customers many options. Because a long product line with more options gives customers greater choice, it is easier to sell products that meet the needs of individual customers. On the other hand, production personnel generally want a "short" product line with fewer options because products are easier to produce.

Once the product line has been determined, each distinct product within the product line must be designed. **Product design** is the process of creating a set of specifications from which a product can be produced. For example, product engineers for Samsung must make sure that their new "Smart Fridge" keeps food frozen in the freezer compartment. At the same time, they must make sure that lettuce and tomatoes do not freeze in the crisper section of the refrigerator. The need for a complete product design is fairly obvious; products that work cannot be manufactured without it. But services should be designed carefully as well—and *for the same reason.*

Question: Why do people buy Apple products? Answer: One "big" reason why people buy Apple products is the firm's research and development efforts to design products that actually work. Although many people often underestimate the importance of product design, even small details can make a big difference—especially when selling products in the very competitive technology industry.

© JOCIC/SHUTTERSTOCK.COM

product design the process of creating a set of specifications from which a product can be produced

capacity the amount of products or services that an organization can produce in a given time

labor-intensive technology a process in which people must do most of the work

capital-intensive technology a process in which machines and equipment do most of the work

REQUIRED PRODUCTION CAPACITY Capacity is the amount of products or services that an organization can produce in a given period of time. (For example, the capacity of a Panasonic assembly plant might be 1.3 million high-definition televisions per year.) Operations managers—again working with the firm's marketing managers—must determine the required capacity. This, in turn, determines the size of the production facility. If the facility is built with too much capacity, valuable resources (plant, equipment, and money) will lie idle. If the facility offers insufficient capacity, additional capacity may have to be added later when it is much more expensive than in the initial building stage.

Capacity means about the same thing to service businesses. For example, the capacity of a restaurant such as the Hard Rock Cafe in Nashville, Tennessee, is the number of customers it can serve at one time.

USE OF TECHNOLOGY During the design-planning stage, management must determine the degree to which *automation* and *technology* will be used to produce a product or service. Here, there is a trade-off between high initial costs and low operating costs (for automation) and low initial costs and high operating costs (for human labor). Ultimately, management must choose between a labor-intensive technology and a capital-intensive technology. A **labor-intensive technology** is a process in which people must do most of the work. Housecleaning services and the New York Yankees baseball team, for example, are labor-intensive. A **capital-intensive technology** is a process in which machines and equipment do most of the work. A Sony automated assembly plant is capital intensive because there are fewer workers that operate automated machinery.

Site Selection and Facilities Planning

Generally, a business will choose to produce a new product in an existing factory as long as (1) the existing factory has enough capacity to handle customer demand for both the new product and established products and (2) the cost of refurbishing an existing factory is less than the cost of building a new one.

After exploring the capacity of existing factories, management may decide to build a new production facility. In determining where to locate production facilities, management must consider a number of variables, including the following:

- Locations of major customers and suppliers.
- Availability and cost of skilled and unskilled labor.

- Quality of life for employees and management in the proposed location.
- The cost of land and building costs.
- Local and state taxes, environmental regulations, and zoning laws.
- The amount of financial support and subsidies, if any, offered by local and state governments.
- Special requirements, such as great amounts of energy or water used in the production process.

Before making a final decision about where a proposed plant will be located and how it will be organized, two other factors—human resources and plant layout—should be examined.

HUMAN RESOURCES Several issues involved in site selection and facilities planning fall within the province of human resources managers. When Nestlé built its new 900,000-square-foot production facility to make liquid Nesquik® and Coffee-Mate® products in Anderson, Indiana, human resources managers were involved to make sure the necessary managers and employees needed to staff the plant were available. And when a company decides to build a new facility in a foreign country, again human resources managers are involved. For example, suppose that a U.S. firm like AT&T wants to lower labor costs by importing products from China. It has two choices. It can build its own manufacturing facility in a foreign country or it can outsource production to local firms. In either case, human resources become involved in the decision. If the decision is made to build its own plant, human resources managers will have to recruit managers and employees with the appropriate skills who are willing to relocate to a foreign country, develop training programs for local Chinese workers, or both. On the other hand, if the decision is made to outsource production to local suppliers, human resources managers must make sure that local suppliers are complying with the U.S. company's human rights policies and with all applicable national and local wage and hour laws.

Sustain the Planet

Saving Energy—And the Environment

The industrial sector uses approximately 40% of the world's total delivered energy, so it's fertile ground for energy optimization efforts. By working with their customers on energy resource management and reducing emissions and waste, Rockwell Automation, a manufacturer of industrial automation control and information solutions, is helping make their customers' operations cleaner, more energy efficient, and more competitive. In short, they're showing their customers ways they can save money and energy while saving the environment. Take a closer look at how Rockwell is helping their customers meet their lean objectives while still meeting their green objectives at www.rockwellautomation.com.

Sources: "Sustainable Production," The Rockwell Automation website at www.rockwellautomation.com, accessed February 15, 2013; Presher, A. (August 8, 2011), "Energy Optimization as Productivity Enhancer," *DesignNews*. Retrieved from www.designnews.com/document.asp?doc_id=231868; "Rockwell Automation named to Dow Jones Sustainability North America Index," *ReliablePlant*, retrieved February 22, 2012 from www.reliableplant.com/Read/26680/Rockwell-Automation-sustainability-index.

COURTESY OF ROCKWELL AUTOMATION, INC.

PLANT LAYOUT **Plant layout** is the arrangement of machinery, equipment, and personnel within a production facility. Three general types of plant layout are used (see Figure 8-4).

The *process layout* is used when different operations are required for creating small batches of different products or working on different parts of a product. The plant is arranged so that each operation is performed in its own particular area. An auto repair facility at a local automobile dealership provides an example of a process layout. The various operations may be engine repair, bodywork, wheel alignment, and safety inspection. If you take your Lincoln Navigator for a wheel alignment, your car "visits" only the area where alignments are performed.

A *product layout* (sometimes referred to as an *assembly line*) is used when all products undergo the same operations in the same sequence. Workstations are arranged to match the sequence of operations, and work flows from station to station.

plant layout the arrangement of machinery, equipment, and personnel within a production facility

FIGURE 8-4 Facilities Planning

The process layout is used when small batches of different products are created or when working on different parts of a product. The product layout (assembly line) is used when all products undergo the same operations in the same sequence. The fixed-position layout is used in producing a product too large to move.

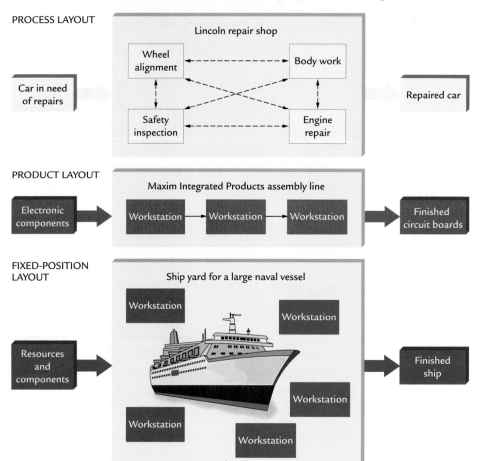

PROCESS LAYOUT

Lincoln repair shop

Car in need of repairs → Wheel alignment ⇄ Body work / Safety inspection ⇄ Engine repair → Repaired car

PRODUCT LAYOUT

Maxim Integrated Products assembly line

Electronic components → Workstation → Workstation → Workstation → Finished circuit boards

FIXED-POSITION LAYOUT

Ship yard for a large naval vessel

Resources and components → Workstation / Workstation / Workstation / Workstation → Finished ship

© CENGAGE LEARNING 2015

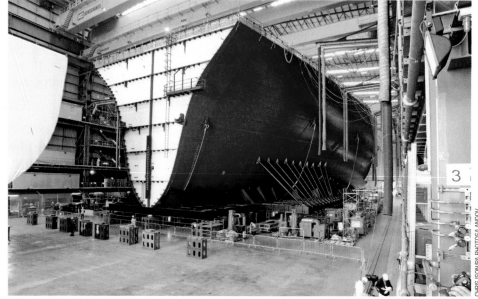

A big product! The British Royal Navy's aircraft carrier HMS Queen Elizabeth was constructed using a fixed-position layout. To see how large the ship is, compare its size with the people at the bottom of this photo. When a product is this large, it is easier to move people, machinery, and parts to where they are needed instead of moving the ship.

CHRIS ISON/PA PHOTOS/LANDOV

An assembly line is the best example of a product layout. For example, California-based Maxim Integrated Products, Inc., uses a product layout to manufacture components for consumer and business electronic products. A *fixed-position layout* is used when a very large product is produced. Shipbuilders apply this method because of the difficulty of moving a large product such as an ocean liner. The product remains stationary, and people and machines are moved as needed to assemble the product.

Operational Planning

The objective of operational planning is to decide on the amount of products or services each facility will produce during a specific period of time. Four steps are required.

STEP 1: SELECTING A PLANNING HORIZON A **planning horizon** is simply the time period during which an operational plan will be in effect. A common planning horizon for production plans is one year. Then, before each year is up, management must plan for the next. A planning horizon of one year generally is long enough to average out seasonal increases and decreases in sales. At the same time, it is short enough for planners to adjust production to accommodate long-range sales trends.

STEP 2: ESTIMATING MARKET DEMAND The *market demand* for a product is the quantity that customers will purchase at the going price. This quantity must be estimated for the time period covered by the planning horizon. Sales projections developed by marketing managers are the basis for market-demand estimates.

STEP 3: COMPARING MARKET DEMAND WITH CAPACITY The third step in operational planning is to compare the estimated market demand with the facility's capacity to satisfy that demand. (Remember that capacity is the amount of products or services that an organization can produce in a given time period.) One of three outcomes may result: Demand may exceed capacity, capacity may exceed demand, or capacity and demand may be equal. If they are equal, the facility should be operated at full capacity. However, if market demand and capacity are not equal, adjustments may be necessary.

STEP 4: ADJUSTING PRODUCTS OR SERVICES TO MEET DEMAND The biggest reason for changes to a firm's production schedule is changes in the amount of products or services that a company sells to its customers. For example, Indiana-based Berry Plastics produces all kinds of plastic products. One particularly successful product line for Berry Plastics is drink cups that can be screen-printed to promote a company or its products or services.[13] If Berry Plastics obtains a large contract to provide promotional cups to a large fast-food chain such as Whataburger or McDonald's, the company may need to work three shifts a day, seven days a week, until the contract is fulfilled. Unfortunately, the reverse is also true. If the company's sales force does not generate new sales, there may be only enough work for the employees on one shift.

When market demand exceeds capacity, several options are available to a firm. Production of products or services may be increased by operating the facility overtime with existing personnel or by starting a second or third work shift. For manufacturers, another response is to subcontract or outsource a portion of the work to other manufacturers. If the excess demand is likely to be permanent, the firm may expand the current facility or build another facility.

Fruit tarts that taste as good as they look. For just a moment, assume you are the production manager of a large bakery that must produce thousands of fruit tarts each week. What would your factory look like? How could plant layout improve your firm's productivity? How would you manage human resources, purchasing, and quality control? All good questions that should be answered before a single fruit tart is produced.

planning horizon the period during which an operational plan will be in effect

Concept Check

✓ What are the major elements of design planning?

✓ Define capacity. Why is it important for a manufacturing business or a service business?

✓ What factors should be considered when selecting a site for a new manufacturing facility?

✓ What is the objective of operational planning? What four steps are used to accomplish this objective?

What happens when capacity exceeds market demand? Again, there are several options. To reduce output temporarily, workers may be laid off or the facility may be operated on a shorter-than-normal workweek. To adjust to a permanently decreased demand, management may shift the excess capacity of a manufacturing facility to the production of other goods or services. The most radical adjustment is to eliminate the excess capacity by selling unused manufacturing facilities.

Learning Objective

6 Explain how purchasing, inventory control, scheduling, and quality control affect production.

OPERATIONS CONTROL

We have discussed the development of an idea for a product or service and the planning that translates that idea into the reality. Now we are ready to begin the actual production process. In this section, we examine four important areas of operations control: purchasing, inventory control, scheduling, and quality control (see Figure 8-5).

Purchasing

purchasing all the activities involved in obtaining required materials, supplies, components, and parts from other firms

Purchasing consists of all the activities involved in obtaining required materials, supplies, components (or subassemblies), and parts from other firms. Levi Strauss, for example, must purchase denim cloth, thread, and zippers before it can produce a single pair of jeans.

The objective of purchasing is to ensure that required materials are available when they are needed, in the proper amounts, and at minimum cost. Generally, the company with purchasing needs and suppliers must develop a working relationship built on trust. In addition, many companies believe that purchasing is one area where they can promote diversity. For example, AT&T developed a Supplier Diversity Program in 1968. Today, more than 45 years later, goals for the AT&T program include purchasing a total of 21.5 percent of all products and services from minorities, women, and disabled veteran business enterprises.[14]

Purchasing personnel should constantly be on the lookout for new or backup suppliers, even when their needs are being met by their present suppliers, because problems such as strikes and equipment breakdowns can cut off the flow of purchased materials from a primary supplier at any time.

The choice of suppliers should result from careful analysis of a number of factors. The following are especially critical:

- *Price.* Comparing prices offered by different suppliers is always an essential part of selecting a supplier.
- *Quality.* Purchasing specialists always try to buy materials at a level of quality in keeping with the type of product being manufactured. The lowest acceptable quality is usually specified by product designers.
- *Reliability.* An agreement to purchase high-quality materials at a low price is the purchaser's dream. However, the dream becomes a nightmare if the supplier does not deliver.

FIGURE 8-5 Four Aspects of Operations Control

Implementing the operations control system in any business requires the effective use of purchasing, inventory control, scheduling, and quality control.

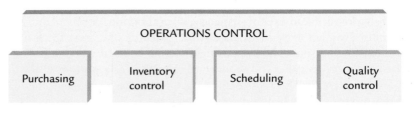

© CENGAGE LEARNING 2015

- *Credit terms.* Purchasing specialists should determine if the supplier demands immediate payment or will extend credit.
- *Shipping costs.* The question of who pays the shipping costs should be answered before any supplier is chosen.

Inventory Control

Can you imagine what would happen if a Coca-Cola manufacturing plant ran out of the company's familiar red-and-white aluminum cans? It would be impossible to complete the manufacturing process and ship the cases of Coke to retailers. Management would be forced to shut the assembly line down until the next shipment of cans arrived from a supplier. The simple fact is that shutdowns are expensive because costs such as wages, rent, utilities, insurance, and other expenses still must be paid.

Operations managers are concerned with three types of inventories. A *raw-materials inventory* consists of materials that will become part of the product during the production process. The *work-in-process inventory* consists of partially completed products. The *finished-goods inventory* consists of completed goods. Each type of inventory also has a *holding cost*, or storage cost, and a *stock-out cost,* the cost of running out of inventory. **Inventory control** is the process of managing inventories in such a way as to minimize inventory costs, including both holding costs and potential stock-out costs.

Today, computer systems are being used to keep track of inventories and alert managers to impending stock-outs. One of the most sophisticated methods of inventory control used today is materials requirements planning. **Materials requirements planning (MRP)** is a computerized system that integrates production planning and inventory control. One of the great advantages of an MRP system is its ability to juggle delivery schedules and lead times effectively. For a complex product such as an automobile with 4,000 or more individual parts, it is virtually impossible for individual managers to oversee the hundreds of parts that go into the finished product. However, a manager using an MRP system can arrange both order and delivery schedules so that materials, parts, and supplies arrive when they are needed.

Because large firms can incur huge inventory costs, much attention has been devoted to inventory control. The just-in-time system being used by some businesses is one result of all this attention. A **just-in-time inventory system** is designed to ensure that materials or supplies arrive at a facility just when they are needed so that storage and holding costs are minimized. For example, managers using a just-in-time inventory system at a Toyota assembly plant determine the number of automobiles that will be assembled in a specified time period. Then Toyota purchasing personnel order just the parts needed to produce those automobiles. In turn, suppliers deliver the parts in time or when they are needed on the assembly line.

Without proper inventory control, it is impossible for operations managers to schedule the work required to produce goods and services that can be sold to customers.

Scheduling

Scheduling is the process of ensuring that materials and other resources are at the right place at the right time. The materials and resources may be moved from a warehouse to the workstations, they may move from station to station along an assembly line, or they may arrive at workstations "just in time" to be made part of the work-in-process there.

inventory control the process of managing inventories in such a way as to minimize inventory costs, including both holding costs and potential stock-out costs

materials requirements planning (MRP) a computerized system that integrates production planning and inventory control

just-in-time inventory system a system designed to ensure that materials or supplies arrive at a facility just when they are needed so that storage and holding costs are minimized

scheduling the process of ensuring that materials and other resources are at the right place at the right time

© SPLAJUM/SHUTTERSTOCK.COM

Tracking inventory can be a tedious, but necessary chore.
For a wholesaler or retailer, running out of inventory means a business has nothing to sell. For a manufacturer, no inventory can lead to shutting down a production facility and no finished products. In either case, no inventory equals no sales and can lead to no profits.

As our definition implies, both place and time are important to scheduling. The *routing* of materials is the sequence of workstations that the materials will follow. Assume that Drexel Heritage—one of America's largest and oldest furniture manufacturers—is scheduling production of an oval coffee table made from cherry wood. Operations managers route the needed materials (wood, screws, packaging materials, etc.) through a series of individual workstations along an assembly line. At each workstation, a specific task is performed, and then the partially finished coffee table moves to the next workstation. When routing materials, operations managers are especially concerned with the sequence of each step of the production process. For the coffee table, the top and legs must be cut to specifications before the wood is finished. (If the wood were finished before being cut, the finish would be ruined, and the coffee table would have to be stained again.)

When scheduling production, managers also are concerned with timing. The *timing* function specifies when the materials will arrive at each station and how long they will remain there. For the cherry coffee table, it may take workers 30 minutes to cut the table top and legs and another 30 minutes to drill the holes and assemble the table. Before packaging the coffee table for shipment, it must be finished with cherry stain and allowed to dry. This last step may take as long as three days depending on weather conditions and humidity.

Regardless of whether the finished product requires a simple or complex production process, operations managers are responsible for monitoring schedules—called *follow-up*—to ensure that the work flows according to the schedule.

Quality Control

Over the years, more and more managers have realized that quality is an essential "ingredient" of the good or service being produced. This view of quality provides several benefits. The number of defects decreases, which causes profits to increase. Furthermore, making products or completing services right the first time reduces many of the rejects and much of the rework.

As mentioned earlier in this chapter, American business firms that compete in the very competitive global marketplace have taken another look at the importance of improving quality. Today, there is even a national quality award. The **Malcolm Baldrige National Quality Award** is given by the President of the United States to organizations judged to be outstanding in specific managerial tasks that lead to improved quality for both products and services. Past winners include Mesa Products, Ritz-Carlton Hotels, Boeing Aerospace, Motorola, Nestlé Purina Petcare, Cargill Corn Milling North America, and Richland Community College (part of the Dallas Community College District), among many others. All Baldrige winners have one factor in common: They use quality control to improve their firm's products or services.

Quality control is the process of ensuring that goods and services are produced in accordance with design specifications. The major objective of quality control is to see that the organization lives up to the standards it has set for itself on quality. Some firms, such as Mercedes-Benz, have built their reputations on quality. Other firms adopt a strategy of emphasizing lower prices along with reasonable (but not particularly high) quality. Today, many firms use the techniques described in Table 8-1 to gather information and statistics that can be used to improve the quality of a firm's products or services.

Although the techniques described in Table 8-1 can provide information and statistics, it is people who must act on the information and make changes to improve the production process. And the firm's employees are often the most important component needed to improve quality.

Quality matters! In this photo, an employee inspects a custom-made shoe to make sure small details like the quality of leather and stitching meet the company's design specifications. Products that are not within design specifications and don't pass inspection are removed from production.

© TORANICO/SHUTTERSTOCK.COM

TABLE 8-1 Four Widely Used Techniques to Improve the Quality of a Firm's Products.

Technique	Description
Benchmarking	A process of comparing the way a firm produces products or services to the methods used by organizations known to be leaders in an industry in order to determine the "best practices" that can be used to improve quality.
Continuous Improvement	Continuous improvement is a never-ending effort to eliminate problems and improve quality. Often this method involves many small changes or steps designed to improve the production process on an ongoing basis.
Statistical Process Control (SPC)	Sampling to obtain data that are plotted on control charts and graphs to see if the production process is operating as it should and to pinpoint problem areas.
Statistical Quality Control (SQC)	A detailed set of specific statistical techniques used to monitor all aspects of the production process to ensure that both work-in-process and finished products meet the firm's quality standards.

© CENGAGE LEARNING 2015

IMPROVING QUALITY THROUGH EMPLOYEE PARTICIPATION One of the first steps needed to improve quality is employee participation. Simply put: Successful firms encourage employees to accept full responsibility for the quality of their work. When Toyota, once the role model for world-class manufacturing, faced a quality crisis, the company announced a quality-improvement plan based on its famous "Toyota Way." One tenet of the Toyota Way is the need to solve problems at their source, which allows factory workers to stop the production line if necessary to address a problem. Another tenet that enabled Toyota to resolve quality problems was the use of quality circles designated to deal with difficulties as they arise. A **quality circle** is a team of employees who meet on company time to solve problems of product quality. Quality circles have also been used successfully in companies such as IBM, Northrop Grumman Corporation, Lockheed Martin, and GE.

Increased effort is also being devoted to **inspection**, which is the examination of the quality of work-in-process. Employees perform inspections at various times during production. Purchased materials may be inspected when they arrive at the production facility. Subassemblies and manufactured parts may be inspected before they become part of a finished product. In addition, finished goods may be inspected before they are shipped to customers. Items that are within design specifications continue on their way. Those that are not within design specifications are removed from production.

Total quality management (TQM) can also be used to improve quality of a firm's products or services. As noted in Chapter 6, a TQM program coordinates the efforts directed at improving customer satisfaction, increasing employee participation, strengthening supplier partnerships, and facilitating an organizational atmosphere of continuous quality improvement. Firms such as American Express, AT&T, Motorola, and Hewlett-Packard all have used TQM to improve product quality and, ultimately, customer satisfaction.

Another technique that businesses may use to improve not only quality but also overall performance is Six Sigma. **Six Sigma** is a disciplined approach that relies on statistical data and improved methods to eliminate defects for a firm's products and services. Although many experts agree that Six Sigma is similar to TQM, Six Sigma often has more top-level support, much more teamwork, and a new corporate attitude or culture.[15] The companies that developed, refined, and have the most experience with Six Sigma are Motorola, GE, Ford, and Honeywell. Although each of these companies is a corporate giant, the underlying principles of Six Sigma can be used by any firm, regardless of size.

WORLD QUALITY STANDARDS: ISO 9000 AND ISO 14000 Without a common standard of quality, customers may be at the mercy of manufacturers and vendors. As the number of companies competing in the global marketplace

quality circle a team of employees who meet on company time to solve problems of product quality

inspection the examination of the quality of work-in-process

Six Sigma a disciplined approach that relies on statistical data and improved methods to eliminate defects for a firm's products and services

Nobody likes complaints!

You don't want to buy a shoddy product, and any company you work for doesn't want to gain a reputation for poor quality. That's why strict quality control is so important.

International Organization for Standardization (ISO) a network of national standards institutes and similar organizations from over 160 different countries that is charged with developing standards for quality products and services that are traded throughout the globe

Concept Check

✓ Why is selecting a supplier important? What factors should be considered when selecting a supplier?

✓ What costs must be balanced and minimized through inventory control?

✓ Explain in what sense scheduling is a control function of operations managers.

✓ How can a business firm improve the quality of its products or services?

has increased, so has the seriousness of this problem. To deal with the problem of standardization, the International Organization for Standardization, a nongovernmental organization with headquarters in Geneva, Switzerland, was created. The **International Organization for Standardization (ISO)** is a network of national standards institutes and similar organizations from over 160 different countries that is charged with developing standards for quality products and services that are traded throughout the globe. According to the organization,

> ISO's work makes a positive difference to the world we live in. ISO standards add value to all types of business operations. They contribute to making the development, manufacturing and supply of products and services more efficient, safer and cleaner. They make trade between countries easier and fairer. ISO standards also serve to safeguard consumers and users of products and services in general, as well as making their lives simpler.[16]

Standardization is achieved through consensus agreements between national delegations representing all the economic stakeholders—suppliers, customers, and often governments. The member organization for the United States is the American National Standards Institute located in Washington, D.C.

Although certification is not a legal requirement to conduct business globally, the organization's member countries have approved the ISO standards. In fact, ISO standards are so prevalent around the globe that many customers refuse to do business with noncertified companies. As an added bonus, companies completing the certification process often discover new, cost-efficient ways to improve their existing quality-control programs.

In 1987, the panel published ISO 9000 (*iso* is Greek for "equal"), which sets the guidelines for quality management procedures that manufacturers and service providers must use to receive certification. Certification by independent auditors and laboratory testing services serves as evidence that a company meets the standards for quality control procedures in design, production processes, and product testing.

As a continuation of this standardization process, the ISO has developed many different standards for businesses that provide goods and services to customers around the globe. For example, the ISO 14000 is a family of international standards for incorporating environmental concerns into operations and product standards. ISO standards are also updated periodically. For example, ISO 9001:2008 includes important clarifications and addresses issues of compatibility with ISO's other quality standards.

Production Planning: A Summary

In this chapter, the activities that firms use to produce products and services have been described. And yet, it is often hard to determine how the individual activities fit together in a logical sequence. Now, toward the end of the chapter, it may help to look at a table to see how all of the "pieces of the puzzle" fit together. At the top of Table 8-2, planning for production begins with research and development, design planning, site selection and facilities planning, and operational planning—all topics described in this chapter. In the middle of Table 8-2, activities that were described in the Operations Control section (purchasing, inventory control, scheduling, and quality control) are summarized. The goal of all the planning activities in the top section and operations control activities in the middle section is to create and produce a successful product or service. Of course, the steps for planning production and operations control should always be evaluated to determine if the firm's activities can be improved in order to meet the needs of its customers and to increase the firm's productivity.

TABLE 8-2 Production Planning: A Summary

Both planning for production and operations control are necessary if a firm is to produce a successful product or service.

The Process Begins with Planning for Production
1. *Research and Development* identifies ideas for a product or service.
2. *Design Planning* develops a plan for producing a product or service.
3. *Site Selection and Facilities Planning* identifies a production site, a plant layout, and if human resources are available.
4. *Operational Planning* decides on the amount of products or services that will be produced.

Then Four Operations Control Steps Are Used to Produce a Product or Service
1. *Purchasing* obtains required materials, supplies, and parts from other firms.
2. *Inventory Control* ensures that materials, supplies, and parts are available when needed.
3. *Scheduling* ensures that materials and other resources are at the right place and at the right time in the production process.
4. *Quality Control* determines if the firm has lived up to the standards it has set for itself on the quality of its products or services.

The End Result: A Successful Product or Service

© CENGAGE LEARNING 2015

IMPROVING PRODUCTIVITY WITH TECHNOLOGY

Learning Objective

7 Summarize how technology can make American firms more productive and competitive in the global marketplace.

No coverage of operations management would be complete without a discussion of productivity and technology. Productivity concerns all managers, but it is especially important to operations managers, the people who must oversee the creation of a firm's goods or services. In Chapter 1, *productivity* was defined as the average level of output per worker per hour. Hence, if each worker at plant A produces 75 units per day and each worker at plant B produces only 70 units per day, the workers at plant A are more productive. If one bank teller serves 25 customers per hour and another serves 28 per hour, the second teller is more productive.

Productivity Trends

For U.S. businesses, overall productivity growth for output per hour averaged 4.2 percent for the period 1979–2011.[17] More specifically, 2011 output per hour for U.S. firms increased 2 percent.[18] (*Note:* At the time of publication, 2011 was the last year that complete statistics were available.) While the 2 percent increase in output per hour in 2011 was lower when compared with our average productivity growth, 11 other nations that the U.S. Bureau Labor Statistics tracks each year had larger growth in productivity than the United States—as illustrated in Figure 8-6.[19]

Improving Productivity Growth

Many U.S. firms are using a number of techniques to improve productivity. For example, a large number of business firms are adopting the concept of lean manufacturing. **Lean manufacturing** is a concept built on the idea of eliminating waste from all of the activities required to produce a product or service. Benefits of lean manufacturing include a reduction in the amount of resources required to produce a product or service, more efficient use of employee time, improved quality, and

lean manufacturing a concept built on the idea of eliminating waste from all of the activities required to produce a product or service

FIGURE 8-6 Productivity Growth Rates

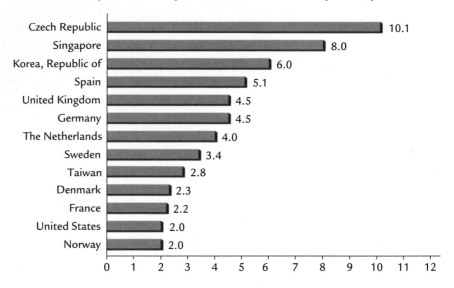

This graph identifies nations with the largest increase in output per hour in 2011—the last year that complete results were available prior to publication.

Source: Based on information in "International Comparisons of Manufacturing Productivity and Unit Labor Cost Trends, 2011," The Bureau of Labor Statistics website at www.bls.gov (accessed December 6, 2012).

increased profits. In addition to lean manufacturing, several other factors must be considered if U.S. firms are going to increase productivity *and* their ability to compete in the global marketplace. For example:

- The United States must stabilize its economy so that firms will invest more money in new facilities, equipment, technology, and employee training.
- Managers and executives must cooperate with employees to increase employee motivation and participation in the workplace.
- All government policies must be examined to ensure that unreasonable regulations that may be hindering productivity growth are eliminated.
- Successful techniques that have been used in manufacturing firms must be used to increase productivity in the service industry.
- Increased use of automation, robotics, and computer manufacturing systems must be used to lower production costs.
- There must be more emphasis on satisfying the customer's needs with quality goods and services.

Finally, innovation and research and development efforts to create new products and services must be increased in order for U.S. firms to compete in the global marketplace.

The Impact of Automation, Robotics, and Computers on Productivity

automation the total or near-total use of machines to do work

Automation is the total or near-total use of machines to do work. The rapid increase in automated procedures has been made possible by the microprocessor, a silicon chip that led to the production of desktop computers for businesses, homes, and schools. In factories, microprocessors are used in robotics and in computer manufacturing systems.

Robotics Robotics is the use of programmable machines to perform a variety of tasks by manipulating materials and tools. Robots work quickly, accurately, and steadily. For example, Illumina, Inc., a San Diego company, sells robotic equipment that performs medical laboratory tests. As an added bonus, Illumina's robotic equipment can work 24 hours a day at much lower costs than if human lab workers performed the same tests.[20]

Robots are especially effective in tedious, repetitive assembly-line jobs, as well as in handling hazardous materials. Lincoln Electric, for example, provides robotic arc welders that eliminate the hot, dirty job of welding, which is key to many manufacturing tasks. As an added bonus, robotic arc welders are often quicker and are more precise than old-fashioned welding machines.

Robots are also useful as artificial "eyes" that can check the quality of products as they are being processed on assembly lines. To date, the automotive industry has made the most extensive use of robotics, but robots also have been used to mine coal, inspect the inner surfaces of pipes, assemble computer components, provide certain kinds of patient care in hospitals, and clean and guard buildings at night.

Robotics can be a manufacturer's best friend. One of the first industries to use robotics to increase the number of products produced and improve employee productivity was the automobile industry. In this photo, robotics is used to move the right side of a sport utility vehicle (SUV) from one workstation on an assembly line to the next station.

robotics the use of programmable machines to perform a variety of tasks by manipulating materials and tools

COMPUTER MANUFACTURING SYSTEMS People are quick to point out how computers have changed their everyday lives, but most people do not realize the impact computers have had on manufacturing. In simple terms, the factory of the future has already arrived. For most manufacturers, the changeover began with the use of computer-aided design and computer-aided manufacturing. **Computer-aided design (CAD)** is the use of computers to aid in the development of products. Ford speeds up car design, Canon designs new photocopiers, and American Greetings creates new birthday cards by using CAD.

Computer-aided manufacturing (CAM) is the use of computers to plan and control manufacturing processes. A well-designed CAM system allows manufacturers to become much more productive. Not only are a greater number of products produced, but speed and quality also increase. Using CAM systems, Toyota produces automobiles, Hasbro manufactures toys, and Apple Computer creates electronic products.

If you are thinking that the next logical step is to combine the CAD and CAM computer systems, you are right. Today, the most successful manufacturers use CAD and CAM together to form a computer-integrated manufacturing system. Specifically, **computer-integrated manufacturing (CIM)** is a computer system that not only helps to design products but also controls the machinery needed to produce the finished product. For example, Fifth & Pacific Companies (formerly Liz Claiborne) uses CIM to design clothing, to establish patterns for new fashions, and then to cut the cloth needed to produce the finished product. Other advantages of using CIM include improved flexibility, more efficient scheduling, and higher product quality—all factors that make a production facility more competitive in today's global economy.

computer-aided design (CAD) the use of computers to aid in the development of products

computer-aided manufacturing (CAM) the use of computers to plan and control manufacturing processes

computer-integrated manufacturing (CIM) a computer system that not only helps to design products but also controls the machinery needed to produce the finished product

FLEXIBLE MANUFACTURING SYSTEMS Manufacturers have known for a number of years that the mass-production and traditional assembly lines used to manufacture products present a number of problems. For example, although traditional assembly lines turn out extremely large numbers of identical products economically, the system requires expensive, time-consuming retooling of equipment whenever a new product is to be manufactured. This type of manufacturing is often referred to as a continuous process. **Continuous process** is a manufacturing process in which a firm produces the same product(s) over a long period of time. Now it is possible to use flexible manufacturing systems to solve such problems. A **flexible manufacturing system (FMS)** combines electronic machines and CIM in a single production system. Instead of having to spend large amounts of time and effort to retool the traditional mechanical equipment on an assembly line for each new product, an FMS is rearranged simply by reprogramming electronic machines. Because FMSs require less time and expense to reprogram than traditional systems, manufacturers can produce smaller batches of a variety of products without raising the production cost. Flexible manufacturing is sometimes referred to as an intermittent process. An **intermittent process** is a manufacturing process in which a firm's manufacturing machines and equipment are changed to produce different products.

For most manufacturers, the driving force behind FMSs is the customer. In fact, the term *customer-driven production* is often used to describe a manufacturing system that is driven by customer needs and what customers want to buy. For example, advanced software and a flexible manufacturing system have enabled Dell Computer to change to a more customer-driven manufacturing process. Although the costs of designing and installing an FMS such as this are high, the electronic equipment is used more frequently and efficiently than the machinery on a traditional assembly line.

Sustainability and Technological Displacement

In Chapter 1, *sustainability* was defined as creating and maintaining the conditions under which humans and nature can exist in productive harmony while fulfilling the social, economic, and other requirements of present and future generations. While sustainability affects all aspects of a nation, its people, and the economy, the concept is especially important for manufacturers and service providers. Because of the amount of resources required to produce goods and services, these businesses must conserve resources whenever possible. As an added bonus, efforts to reduce waste and sustain the planet can often improve a firm's bottom-line profit amount.

Today, many countries around the globe produce goods and services and compete with U.S. manufacturers. And yet, U.S. producers are known for quality and innovation—especially for products that are more expensive or more complicated to manufacture. As a result, most experts agree that, because U.S. manufacturers will continue to innovate, workers who have manufacturing jobs will be highly skilled and can work with the automated and computer-aided manufacturing systems. Those that don't possess high-tech skills will be dispensable and unemployed. Many workers will be faced with the choice of retraining for new jobs or seeking jobs in other sectors of the economy. Government, business, and education will have to cooperate to prepare workers for new roles in an automated workplace.

The next chapter discusses many of the issues caused by technological displacement. In addition, a number of major components of human resources management are described, and we see how managers use various reward systems to boost motivation, productivity, and morale.

continuous process a manufacturing process in which a firm produces the same product(s) over a long period of time

flexible manufacturing system (FMS) a single production system that combines electronic machines and CIM

intermittent process a manufacturing process in which a firm's manufacturing machines and equipment are changed to produce different products

© ISTOCKPHOTO.COM/PHOTOVIDEOSTOCK

Concept Check

✓ How might productivity be measured in a restaurant? In a department store? In a public school system?

✓ How can robotics, computer manufacturing systems, and flexible manufacturing systems help a manufacturer to produce products?

Summary

1 Explain the nature of production.

Operations management consists of all the activities that managers engage in to create goods and services. Operations are as relevant to service organizations as to manufacturing firms. Today, U.S. companies are forced to compete in an ever-smaller world to meet the needs of more-demanding customers. As a result, U.S. manufacturers have used innovation to improve productivity. Because of innovation, fewer workers are needed, but those workers who are needed possess the skills to use automation and technology. In an attempt to regain a competitive edge, manufacturers have taken another look at the importance of improving quality and meeting the needs of their customers. They also have used new techniques to motivate employees, reduced costs, used computer-aided and flexible manufacturing systems, improved control procedures, and used green manufacturing. Competing in the global economy is not only profitable but also an essential activity that requires the cooperation of everyone within an organization. A number of career options are available for employees in operations management.

2 Outline how the conversion process transforms raw materials, labor, and other resources into finished goods or services.

A business transforms resources into goods and services in order to provide utility to customers. Utility is the ability of a good or service to satisfy a human need. Form utility is created by people converting raw materials, finances, and information into finished products. Conversion processes vary in terms of the major resources used to produce goods and services (focus), the degree to which resources are changed (magnitude of change), and the number of production processes that a business uses.

3 Understand the importance of service businesses to consumers, other business firms, and the nation's economy.

The application of the basic principles of operations management to the production of services has coincided with the growth and importance of service businesses in the United States. Today 87 percent of American workers are employed in the service industry. In fact, the American economy is now characterized as a service economy. For a service firm, planning often begins with determining who the customer is and what needs the customer has. After customer needs are identified the next step is to develop a plan that will enable the firm to deliver the services that their customers want or need. Although it is often more difficult to measure customer satisfaction, today's successful service firms work hard at providing the services customers want. For example, compared with manufacturers, service firms often listen more carefully to customers and respond more quickly to the market's changing needs.

4 Describe how research and development leads to new products and services.

Operations management often begins with product research and development and often referred to as R&D. The results of R&D may be entirely new products or services or extensions and refinements of existing products or services. R&D activities are classified as basic research (aimed at uncovering new knowledge), applied research (discovering new knowledge with some potential use), and development and implementation (using new or existing knowledge to produce goods and services). If a firm sells only one product or provides only one service, when customers quit buying the product or service, the firm will die. To stay in business, the firm must, at the very least, find ways to refine or extend the want-satisfying capability of its product or service.

5 Discuss the components involved in planning the production process.

Planning for production involves three major phases: design planning, site selection and facilities planning, and operational planning. First, design planning is undertaken to address questions related to the product line, required production capacity, and the use of technology. Then production facilities, human resources, and plant layout must be considered. Operational planning focuses on the use of production facilities and resources. The steps for operational planning include (1) selecting a planning horizon, (2) estimating market demand, (3) comparing market demand with capacity, and (4) adjusting production of products or services to meet demand.

6 Explain how purchasing, inventory control, scheduling, and quality control affect production.

The major areas of operations control are purchasing, inventory control, scheduling, and quality control.

Purchasing involves selecting suppliers. The choice of suppliers should result from careful analysis of a number of factors, including price, quality, reliability, credit terms, and shipping costs. Inventory control is the management of stocks of raw materials, work-in-process, and finished goods to minimize the total inventory cost. Scheduling ensures that materials and other resources are at the right place at the right time. Quality control guarantees that products and services are produced in accordance with design specifications. The major objective of quality control is to see that the organization lives up to the standards it has set for itself on quality. A number of different activities including quality circles, inspection, total quality management, and six sigma can be used to encourage employee participation and to improve quality.

7 Summarize how technology can make American firms more productive and competitive in the global marketplace.

Productivity is the average level of output per worker per hour. From 1979 to 2011, U.S. productivity growth averaged a 4.2 percent increase. More specifically,

productivity in 2011 increased 2 percent. Although a 2 percent increase was lower when compared to our average productivity growth over the 1979 to 2011 time period, 11 other nations that the U.S. Bureau of Labor Statistics tracks each year had larger growth in productivity than the United States. Several factors must be considered if U.S. firms are going to increase productivity and their ability to compete in the global marketplace.

Automation, the total or near-total use of machines to do work, has for some years been changing the way work is done in factories. A growing number of industries are using programmable machines called robots. Computer-aided design, computer-aided manufacturing, and computer-integrated manufacturing use computers to help design and manufacture products. A flexible manufacturing system (FMS) combines electronic machines and CIM to produce smaller batches of products more efficiently than on the traditional assembly line. Instead of having to spend vast amounts of time and effort to retool the traditional mechanical equipment on an assembly line for each new product, an FMS is rearranged simply by reprogramming electronic machines. An FMS is sometimes referred to as an intermittent process.

Key Terms

You should now be able to define and give an example relevant to each of the following terms:

operations management (208)
reshoring (209)
mass production (210)
analytical process (210)
synthetic process (210)
utility (210)
form utility (210)
service economy (212)
research and development (R&D) (213)
design planning (215)
product line (215)

product design (216)
capacity (216)
labor-intensive technology (216)
capital-intensive technology (216)
plant layout (217)
planning horizon (219)
purchasing (220)
inventory control (221)
materials requirements planning (MRP) (221)

just-in-time inventory system (221)
scheduling (221)
Malcolm Baldrige National Quality Award (222)
quality control (222)
quality circle (223)
inspection (223)
Six Sigma (223)
International Organization for Standardization (ISO) (224)
lean manufacturing (225)
automation (226)

robotics (227)
computer-aided design (CAD) (227)
computer-aided manufacturing (CAM) (227)
computer-integrated manufacturing (CIM) (227)
continuous process (228)
flexible manufacturing system (FMS) (228)
intermittent process (228)

Discussion Questions

1. Why would Rubbermaid—a successful U.S. company—need to expand and sell its products to customers in foreign countries?
2. What steps have U.S. firms taken to regain a competitive edge in the global marketplace?
3. Do certain kinds of firms need to stress particular areas of operations management? Explain.

4. Is it really necessary for service firms to engage in research and development? In planning for production and operations control?
5. How are the four areas of operations control interrelated?
6. Is operations management relevant to nonbusiness organizations such as colleges and hospitals? Why or why not?

Test Yourself

Matching Questions

1. _____ It is a plan for converting a product idea into an actual product or service.

2. _____ Raw materials are broken into different components.

3. _____ Its focus is minimizing holding costs and potential stock-out costs.

4. _____ It is created by people converting materials, finances and information into finished goods.

5. _____ A manufacturing process in which a firm's manufacturing machines and equipment are changed to produce different products.

6. _____ Work is accomplished mostly by equipment.

7. _____ Input from workers is used to improve the workplace.

8. _____ The average level of output per worker per hour.

9. _____ Computers are the main tool used in the development of products.

10. _____ The time period during which an operational plan will be in effect.

a. analytical process
b. capital-intensive technology
c. product line
d. computer-aided design
e. design planning
f. form utility
g. inventory control
h. plant layout
i. planning horizon
j. productivity
k. quality circle
l. intermittent process

True False Questions

11. **T F** Capacity is the degree to which input resources are physically changed by the conversion process.

12. **T F** Reshoring is sometimes referred to as onshoring or insourcing.

13. **T F** Operations management is the process of creating a set of specifications from which the product can be produced.

14. **T F** A purchasing agent need not worry about a tiny difference in price when a large quantity is being bought.

15. **T F** A synthetic process combines raw materials or components to create a finished product.

16. **T F** When work stations are arranged to match the sequence of operations, a process layout is being used.

17. **T F** Work-in-process inventories are raw materials and supplies waiting to be processed.

18. **T F** The purpose of research and development is to identify new ideas that have the potential to result in new goods and services.

19. **T F** For a food-processing plant such as Kraft Foods, capacity refers to the number of employees working on an assembly line.

20. **T F** Labor-intensive technology is accompanied by low initial costs and high operating costs.

Multiple-Choice Questions

21. _____ One worker in Department A produces 45 units of work per day on a computer, whereas a co-worker produces only 40 units of work per day on a computer. Since the first worker produces more units, that worker has a
   a. lower capacity to use technology.
   b. higher productivity rate.
   c. desire to help the co-worker.
   d. computer-integrated system.
   e. computer-aided system

22. _____ Services differ from the production of manufactured goods in all ways except that services
   a. are consumed immediately and cannot be stored.
   b. aren't as important as manufactured products to the U.S. economy.
   c. are provided when and where the customer desires the service.
   d. are usually labor-intensive.
   e. are intangible, and it's more difficult to evaluate customer service.

23. _____ The goal of basic research is to
   a. uncover new knowledge without regard for its potential use.
   b. discover new knowledge with regard for potential use in development.
   c. discover knowledge for potential use.
   d. put new or existing knowledge to use.
   e. combine ideas.

24. _____ Two important components of scheduling are
   a. lead time and planning.
   b. designing and arranging.
   c. monitoring and controlling.
   d. place and time.
   e. logistics and flow.

25. _____ A common planning horizon for production activities is
    a. one day.
    b. a week.
    c. a month.
    d. six months.
    e. one year.

26. _____ A _____ manufacturing system combines electronic machines and computer-integrated manufacturing in a single-production system.
    a. continuous
    b. analytic
    c. synthetic
    d. flexible
    e. automation

27. _____ The process of acquiring materials, supplies, components, and parts from other firms is known as
    a. acquisition.
    b. planning.
    c. purchasing.
    d. inventory requisition.
    e. materials requirements planning.

28. _____ Procter & Gamble uses _____ production to produce household products.
    a. efficient order
    b. demand
    c. supply order
    d. mass
    e. effective

29. _____ If a good or service satisfies a human need, it has
    a. form.
    b. value.
    c. focus.
    d. magnitude.
    e. utility.

30. _____ The American economy is now characterized as a(n) _____ economy.
    a. civilized
    b. stagnant
    c. service
    d. bureaucratic
    e. industrialized

Answers to the Test Yourself questions appear at the end of the book on page TY-1.

Video Case
Chobani Gives the World a Taste for Greek Yogurt

Entrepreneur Hamdi Ulukaya, founder of fast-growing Chobani, needed less than five years to transform a defunct yogurt factory in rural South Edmeston, New York into the U.S. capitol of Greek yogurt production. He came up with the idea of making Greek yogurt in the United States in 2005, when he bought the factory with the help of a Small Business Administration loan from its former owner, Kraft Foods. Ulukaya spent the next 18 months experimenting with recipes while upgrading the factory, arranging a steady supply of milk and other fresh ingredients, and working out the details of what the yogurt cup would look like.

By 2007, Ulukaya had perfected his recipe and was churning out the first cases of Chobani yogurt for an ever-larger list of supermarket customers. His Greek yogurt, thicker and tangier than traditional yogurts, took the industry by storm. Ulukaya originally projected that Chobani would break even if it produced 20,000 cases of yogurt every week. By 2009, the company was getting weekly orders for 200,000 cases—ten times the founder's estimate.

Suddenly, Chobani's Greek yogurt wasn't a tiny, niche product that multinational competitors like Dannon and Yoplait could ignore. Although Ulukaya considered enlarging the factory to accommodate weekly production capacity of 400,000 cases, he decided on the much more ambitious strategy of planning for weekly production capacity of 1 million cases. This huge expansion required new equipment and an around-the-clock production schedule. At the newly enlarged plant, employees would operate machines for 10 hours, followed by a cleaning period of 4 hours to ensure product purity.

By 2012, Chobani was ringing up $1 billion in annual sales throughout North America, and the South Edmeston factory was turning out 12 million yogurt cups every day, making it the country's center of Greek yogurt production. However, Chobani was having difficulty obtaining sufficient quantities of fresh milk to further boost production in the New York plant. Whereas one cup of regular yogurt is made from one cup of milk, one cup of Greek yogurt requires three cups of milk. Ulukaya's $450 million solution to the challenge of milk availability: Build a cavernous new production facility in Twin Falls, Idaho, where Chobani can draw on an abundant local supply of milk. This plant opened in December, 2012, with a weekly production capacity of more than 2 million cases of yogurt. It serves Western states, while the original New York plant ships to Eastern states.

Even as Chobani gears up for higher production and higher market share in North America, it's also getting ready for growth halfway around the world. Ulukaya purchased a dairy near Melbourne, Australia, and invested millions of dollars to upgrade and expand yogurt production at the site. From this facility, Chobani will serve Australia and export its popular Greek yogurt to new markets in Asia. In addition, it maintains a sales office in Europe to support expansion on the continent.

Today, Chobani—a company that didn't even exist a decade ago—dominates the U.S. market for Greek yogurt. It has expanded its product line to include Greek yogurt for children and various sizes and flavors of Greek yogurt for adults. Not long ago, Ulukaya opened a specialty yogurt shop in a trendy part of New York City. New flavor combinations that prove especially popular there may soon be transferred to the production lines in New York, Idaho, and beyond.[21]

Questions

1. Do you agree with Ulukaya's decision to open a production facility in Idaho instead of buying milk and trucking it to Chobani's New York plant? In addition to the cost of transporting the milk, are there other factors that might have influenced Ulukaya's decision to build a second plant?

2. What can Chobani do to gauge market demand for Greek yogurt and for particular flavors and products in its own product line? Identify at least three specific ideas.

3. Chobani's equipment runs for 10 hours and must be idle for four hours while being cleaned. Its plants operate day and night, all week long. What are the implications for the company's purchasing, inventory control, scheduling, and quality control functions?

Building Skills for Career Success

1. Social Media Exercise

Starbucks has taken an innovative approach to improving their products and the customer experience in their stores. Their entire purpose is to create a "third place" beyond home and work where people can congregate and socialize (while having a nice cup of coffee). To engage customers, they created a website called My Starbucks Idea (http://mystarbucksidea.com) that allows customers to post their ideas and then allows customers to also vote on them.

1. Visit the http://mystarbucksidea.com site. Do you have an idea for Starbucks? If so, post it. Do you have a feeling about one of the current ideas? If so, then vote for it.

2. Do you think this is an effective way to gain customer ideas for new products? Why or why not?

3. Can you think of other ways that corporate executives at Starbucks can gauge customer interest in their products and in-store experience using social media?

2. Building Team Skills

Suppose that you are planning to build a house in the country. It will be a brick, one-story structure of approximately 2,000 square feet, centrally heated and cooled. It will have three bedrooms, two bathrooms, a family room, a dining room, a kitchen with a breakfast nook, a study, a utility room, an entry foyer, a two-car garage, a covered patio, and a fireplace. Appliances will operate on electricity and propane fuel. You have received approval and can be connected to the cooperative water system at any time. Public sewerage services are not available; therefore, you must rely on a septic system. You want to know how long it will take to build the house.

Assignment

1. In a group, identify the major activities involved in the project and sequence them in the proper order.

2. Estimate the time required for each activity.

3. Present your list of activities to the class and ask for comments and suggestions.

3. Researching Different Careers

Because service businesses are now such a dominant part of our economy, job seekers sometimes overlook the employment opportunities available in production. Two positions often found in manufacturing and production are quality-control inspector and purchasing agent.

Assignment

1. Using the *Occupational Outlook Handbook* at your local library or on the Internet (http://stats.bls.gov/oco/home.htm), find the following information for the jobs of quality-control inspector and purchasing agent:

   Nature of work, including main activities and responsibilities
   Job outlook
   Earnings
   Training, qualifications, and advancement.

2. Look for other production jobs that may interest you and compile the same sort of information about them.

3. Summarize in a two-page report the key things you learned about jobs in production.

Running a Business
Part 3

Graeter's Grows Through Good Management, Organization, and Quality

Graeter's began as a tiny Cincinnati business and now enjoys a national reputation for the quality of its premium ice cream. Even though the $30 million company recently opened a new factory to support its expansion plans, it still clings fiercely to its original small-batch production method for making creamy ice cream from fresh ingredients. CEO Richard Graeter emphasizes that profits are important, but "staying true to who you are and investing in your business is what makes sure that your business is going to be here tomorrow." That's why Graeter's still makes all of its ice cream by hand, ensuring that the texture and taste meet its high standards batch after batch, year after year.

More than a Family Affair

Graeter's top-management team includes the CEO and his two cousins, Bob and Chip Graeter. As vice president of operations, Bob is responsible for manufacturing, as well as for developing new products and finding suppliers to provide ingredients such as fresh fruits, cream, eggs, and chocolates. His brother Chip oversees all of the company's ice cream shops. Rounding out the management team is a chief operating officer, a controller, a vice president of sales and marketing, and a candy production manager.

"Every major decision, we make on a consensus basis," Richard says, describing the equal partnership among the three family members. "That doesn't mean we don't have a different point of view from time to time, but . . . we learn to see each other's view and discuss, debate, and get down to a decision that all of us support. The other thing that we have learned to do, something that is a little different than our parents' generation [did], is bring in outside people into the . . . executive level of the management team. . . . We now work with a couple of consultants to help us plan our strategy to look for a new vision, to develop training programs . . . all those systems that big companies have." Managers stay in close contact with employees at all levels and don't hesitate to ask for their input when solving problems and making decisions.

Inside the Org Chart

Graeter's formalized its organization structure over the years as it opened more stores and expanded beyond Cincinnati.

Today, the store managers report to a group manager, who in turn reports to the vice president of retail operations. At the company's recently opened 28,000 square foot production facility, employees in each of three shifts are supervised by a shift manager, who reports to the vice president of operations. The first and third shifts are responsible for ice cream production, while the second shift is in charge of cleaning and sanitizing the facility.

Because so many Graeter's stores are located miles from headquarters, two managers "shop" each store every month, checking on quality and service. These management visits are supplemented by two monthly visits from "mystery shoppers" who buy ice cream on different days, observing what employees are doing and taking note of what else is happening in the store. Their written reports give Graeter's top managers another view of the business, this time from the customer's perspective.

What's the plan?

Change has come quickly to Graeter's, not all of it anticipated. The company was constructing its second factory to support the drive for nationwide distribution when an unexpected opportunity arose: to buy out the last franchise company operating Graeter's retail stores and take over its factory as well. The management team jumped at the chance. "A few months ago our strategy was just operate one plant," says Richard. "Now our strategy is, adapt to the opportunity that came along . . . we are operating three plants. The goal is to keep all of your assets deployed productively, so if we have these three plants, what is the most we can do out of those plants to be generating product and profit? One example would be supplying restaurants in other cities, which we really weren't considering originally because our new plant was really geared for pints, but if we have this excess capacity, the smart thing to do is figure out what we can do with that."

The newest Graeter's facility, on Regina Graeter Way in Cincinnati, was built to produce as much as 1 million gallons of ice cream per year, although the current annual output is about 625,000 gallons. Many steps, such as putting lids on

© ISTOCKPHOTO.COM/LUXO

packages and moving them into refrigerated storage, are handled by automated equipment. Yet all of the ice cream is still made in small batches and by hand. Experienced technicians wield a paddle to gradually mix in ingredients such as molten chocolate, which have been pasteurized on the premises to comply with government regulations. Once the ice cream reaches the right temperature and texture, another employee hand-packs it into individual packages, which are then automatically capped, stamped with a date code, sealed, and whisked away to be kept cold until being loaded onto trucks for delivery to supermarket customers. Ice cream samples from every shift's output are tested to ensure purity and quality.

Graeter's sets weekly and monthly sales goals for its stores, based on each unit's location and other factors that affect demand. If a store doesn't meet its goals, the group manager acts quickly to find out why and help the store get back on track. As the company explores the possibility of opening Graeter's stores as far away as Los Angeles and New York, the management team is planning carefully and assessing the potential challenges and advantages of coast-to-coast operations.[22]

Questions

1. Based on this case and the two previous Graeter's cases, what are the company's most important strengths? Can you identify any weaknesses that might affect its ability to grow?

2. How would you describe the departmentalization and the organizational structure at Graeter's? Do you think Graeter's is centralized or decentralized, and what are the implications for its plans for growth?

3. The newest Graeter's plant can produce far more ice cream than is needed today. The company also makes ice cream at its original plant and at the plant formerly owned by a franchisee. What are the implications for Graeter's strategy and for its operational planning?

Using Management and Accounting Information

Why Should You Care?

Question: How important is management and accounting information for a successful business? Answer: It would be extremely difficult to manage even a small business without management and accounting information.

Learning Objectives

Once you complete this chapter, you will be able to:

1 Examine how information can reduce risk when making a decision.

2 Discuss management's information requirements.

3 Outline the five functions of an information system.

4 Explain why accurate accounting information and audited financial statements are important.

5 Read and interpret a balance sheet.

6 Read and interpret an income statement.

7 Describe business activities that affect a firm's cash flow.

8 Summarize how managers evaluate the financial health of a business.

Get Flashcards, Quizzes, Games, Crosswords, and more @ www.cengagebrain.com.

Intuit Takes Technology into the Future

When Intuit (www.intuit.com) first introduced Quicken software in 1983 to help consumers and small businesses manage their money, the IBM PC was only two years old, software was sold on diskettes, and the World Wide Web hadn't even been invented. Now, three decades later, Intuit uses cloud computing, mobile apps, and other cutting-edge technologies to deliver specialized software and services that help small businesses handle accounting, finance, payroll, and other functions. It also offers a variety of products for consumers, including tax preparation software (TurboTax) and a free personal finance website (www.mint.com).

Worldwide, Intuit rings up over $4 billion in annual sales and invests hundreds of millions of dollars yearly to research and develop new software and new services. The company has also been acquiring other companies and products to expand the high-tech tools it offers for small businesses. For example, it recently purchased Demandforce, which provides systems for managing marketing and communications data and programs. By integrating Demandforce's marketing systems with its best-selling QuickBooks accounting system, Intuit enables small businesses to analyze historical transaction data and make more informed decisions about implementing customer-outreach programs.

Today, Intuit delivers most of its services on demand, via the Internet. As a result, small businesses have the option of using desktop computers, smart phones, or tablet computers to upload data, check trends, create reports, or schedule financial transactions in the office or on the go. In the coming years, Intuit plans to expand its in-the-cloud services through partnerships with other companies. Once these connections are in place, customers will be able to log in once for access to any of the partners' systems and services, and receive a single bill for all the services they utilize. This added efficiency will allow small businesses more time to focus on serving *their* customers, while helping Intuit increase profits and strengthen customer relationships for continued success.[1]

Did You Know?

Intuit rings up over $4 billion in annual sales worldwide and invests hundreds of millions of dollars each year to research and develop new products and technology.

Information—that's what this chapter is all about! We begin this chapter with information about Intuit—the company profiled in the Inside Business feature. For this financial software firm, one of its most important goals is to provide information that enables both business clients and consumers to manage their finances. Although Intuit was founded back in 1983, today the firm has evolved into a global leader in the financial software industry because of its investment in research to develop not only software but also the latest technology. With software for desktop computers and apps for both smart phones and tablet computers, Intuit makes it easy for its customers to obtain the information they need.

In this chapter, we begin by describing why employees need information. The first three major sections in this chapter answer the following questions:

- How can information reduce risk when making a decision?
- What is a management information system?
- How do employees use a management information system?

Next, we look at why accounting information is important, attempts to improve financial reporting, and careers in the accounting industry. Then we examine the basic accounting equation and the three most important financial statements: the balance sheet, the income statement, and the statement of cash flows. Finally, we take a look at how managers evaluate the firm's financial health.

Learning Objective

1 Examine how information can reduce risk when making a decision.

HOW CAN INFORMATION REDUCE RISK WHEN MAKING A DECISION?

As we noted in Chapter 1, information is one of the four major resources (along with material, human, and financial resources) managers must have to operate a business. Although a successful business uses all four resources efficiently, it is information that helps managers reduce risk when making a decision.

Information and Risk

To improve the decision-making process and reduce risk, the information used by individuals and business firms must be relevant or useful to meet a specific need. Using relevant information results in better decisions.

Relevant information → Better intelligence and knowledge → Better decisions

For businesses, better intelligence and knowledge that lead to better decisions are especially important because they can provide a *competitive edge* over competitors and improve a firm's *profits*.

Theoretically, with accurate and complete information, there is no risk whatsoever. On the other hand, a decision made without any information is a gamble. These two extreme situations are rare in business. For the most part, business decision makers see themselves located someplace between the extremes. As illustrated in Figure 15-1, when the amount of available information is high, there is less risk; when the amount of available information is low, there is more risk.

Suppose that a marketing manager for Procter & Gamble (P&G) responsible for the promotion of a well-known shampoo such as Pantene Pro-V has called a meeting of key people within her department to consider the selection of a new magazine advertisement. The company's advertising agency has submitted two new advertisements in sealed envelopes. Neither the manager nor any of her team has seen them before. Only one selection will be made for the new advertising campaign. Which advertisement should be chosen?

Without any further information, the team might as well make the decision by flipping a coin. If, however, team members were allowed to open the envelopes and examine the advertisements, they would have more information. If, in addition to allowing them to examine the advertisements, the marketing manager circulated a report containing the reactions of a group of target consumers to each of the two advertisements, the team would have even more information with which to work. Thus, information, when understood properly, produces knowledge and empowers managers and employees to make better decisions.

FIGURE 15-1 The Relationship Between Information and Risk

When the amount of available information is high, managers tend to make better decisions. On the other hand, when the amount of information is low, there is a high risk of making a poor decision.

© CENGAGE LEARNING 2015

Information Rules

Marketing research continues to show that discounts influence almost all car buyers. Simply put, if dealers lower their prices, they will sell more cars. This relationship between buyer behavior and price can be thought of as an information rule that usually will guide the marketing manager correctly. An information rule emerges when research confirms the same results each time that it studies the same or a similar set of circumstances.

Because of the volume of information they receive each day and their need to make decisions on a daily basis, businesspeople try to accumulate information rules to shorten the time they spend analyzing choices. Information rules are the "great simplifiers" for all decision makers. Business research is continuously looking for new rules that can be put to good use and looking to discredit old ones that are no longer valid. This ongoing process is necessary because business conditions rarely stay the same for very long.

The Difference Between Data and Information

Many people use the terms *data* and *information* interchangeably, but the two differ in important ways. **Data** are numerical or verbal descriptions that usually result from some sort of measurement. Your current wage level, the amount of last year's after-tax profit for ExxonMobil Corporation, and the current retail prices of Honda automobiles are all data. Most people think of data as being numerical only, but they can be nonnumerical as well. A description of an individual as a "tall, athletic person with short, dark hair" certainly would qualify as data.

Information is data presented in a form that is useful for a specific purpose. Suppose that a human resources manager wants to compare the wages paid to male and female employees over a period of five years. The manager might begin with a stack of computer printouts listing every person employed by the firm, along with

More Knowledge = Better Decisions

You can reduce the risk in any decision you make—a decision about school, a decision about work, or a decision about buying something expensive—by doing your homework. The more you know about the situation and your alternatives, the better your decision will be.

data numerical or verbal descriptions that usually result from some sort of measurement

information data presented in a form that is useful for a specific purpose

Technology giant! Cisco Systems is a company known for transforming how people connect, communicate, and collaborate. The technology giant is also a respected innovator that develops state-of-the-art equipment needed by employees, managers, and individuals to manage knowledge and information.

each employee's current and past wages. The manager would be hard pressed to make any sense of all the names and numbers. Such printouts consist of data rather than information.

Now suppose that the manager uses a computer to graph the average wages paid to men and to women in each of the five years. The result is information because the manager can use it to compare wages paid to men with those paid to women over the five-year period. For a manager, information presented in a practical, useful form, such as a graph, simplifies the decision-making process.

Knowledge Management

The average company maintains a great deal of data that can be transformed into information. Typical data include records pertaining to personnel, inventory, sales, and accounting. Often each type of data is stored in individual departments within an organization. However, the data can be used more effectively when they are organized into a database. A **database** is a single collection of data and information stored in one place that can be used by people throughout an organization to make decisions. Although databases are important, the way the data and information are used is even more important—and more valuable to the firm. As a result, management information experts now use the term **knowledge management (KM)** to describe a firm's procedures for generating, using, and sharing the data and information. Typically, data, information, databases, and KM all become important parts of a firm's management information system.

WHAT IS A MANAGEMENT INFORMATION SYSTEM?

A **management information system (MIS)** is a system that provides managers and employees with the information they need to perform their jobs as effectively as possible. The purpose of an MIS (sometimes referred to as an information technology system or simply IT system) is to distribute timely and useful information from both internal and external sources to the managers and employees who need it.

A Firm's Information Requirements

Employees and managers have to plan for the future, implement their plans in the present, and evaluate results against what has been accomplished in the past. Of course, the specific types of information they need depend on their work area and on their level within the firm.

Today, many firms are organized into five areas of management: *finance*, *operations*, *marketing*, *human resources*, and *administration*. Managers in each of these areas need specific information in order to make decisions (see Figure 15-2).

- *Financial managers* are obviously most concerned with a firm's finances. They must ensure that the firm's managers and employees, lenders and suppliers, stockholders and potential investors, and government agencies have the information they need to measure the financial health of the firm.
- *Operations managers* are concerned with present and future sales levels, current inventory levels of work in process and finished goods, and the availability and cost of the resources required to produce products and services.
- *Marketing managers* need to have detailed information about a firm's products and services and those offered by competitors. Such information includes pricing strategies, new promotional campaigns, and products that competitors are test marketing. Information concerning the firm's customers, current and projected market share, and new and pending product legislation is also important to marketing managers.
- *Human resources managers* must be aware of anything that pertains to a firm's employees. Key examples include current wage levels and benefits packages

FIGURE 15-2 Management Information System (MIS)

After an MIS is installed, employers and managers can get information directly from the MIS without having to go through other people in the organization.

MANAGEMENT INFORMATION SYSTEM

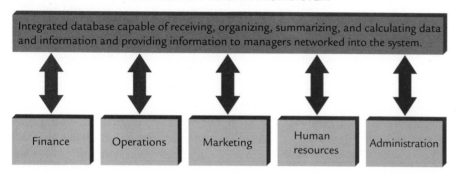

Integrated database capable of receiving, organizing, summarizing, and calculating data and information and providing information to managers networked into the system.

| Finance | Operations | Marketing | Human resources | Administration |

Source: Adapted from Ricky W. Griffin, *Management* (Mason, OH: Cengage Learning, 2013). Reprinted with permission.

both within the firm and in firms that compete for valuable employees, current legislation and court decisions that affect employment practices, and the firm's plans for growth, expansion, or mergers.

- *Administrative managers* are responsible for the overall management of the organization. Thus, they are concerned with the coordination of information—just as they are concerned with the coordination of material, human, and financial resources.

Administrative managers must ensure that the information is used in a consistent manner throughout the firm. Suppose, for example, that General Electric (GE) is designing a new plant in China to manufacture energy-efficient light bulbs that will open in five years. GE's management will want answers to many questions: Is the capacity of the plant consistent with marketing plans based on sales projections? Will human resources managers be able to recruit U.S. employees with the appropriate skills who are willing to relocate to a foreign country and hire and train Chinese workers to staff the plant? And do sales projections indicate enough income to cover the expected cost of the plant? Next, administrative managers must make sure that all managers and employees are able to use the information technology that is available. Certainly, this requires that all employees receive the skills training required to access the information. Finally, administrative managers must commit to the costs of updating the firm's MIS and providing additional training when necessary.

Costs and Limits of the System

Can employees, managers, and executives have too much information? The answer is yes. The truth is that each group needs relevant information that helps them make better decisions.

Is all this information really necessary? Today, we live in an information society—that is, a society in which large groups of individuals, employees, and managers generate or depend on information to perform everyday tasks. As a result, all three groups often complain that they have too much information. For many, the problem is not lack of information, but how to determine what information is really needed?

And yet, too much information that must be analyzed can lead to information overload. Another problem related to information overload is the amount of worthless information, junk e-mails, and advertising that contribute to information overload. Just for a moment, think about the time employees spend reading e-mails that have been sent to everyone in a firm instead of the one or two people who really need to receive the e-mail. Unfortunately, there are other misuses of information technology that do nothing but rob employees of time that could be devoted to more productive activities. In addition to lower employee productivity, the cost of computers, software, and related equipment can be staggering. Although it would be nice for all employees to have new computers and the latest software applications, in reality, even the largest and most profitable business firms cannot afford to waste money on unnecessary computer hardware and software. One of the main goals of a firm's information technology officer is to make sure that a firm has the equipment necessary to provide information the employees need to make effective decisions—*at a reasonable cost*.

In reality, an MIS must be tailored to the needs of the organization it serves. In some firms, a tendency to save on initial costs may result in a system that is too small or overly simple. Such a system generally ends up serving only one or two management levels or a single department. Managers in other departments "give up" on the system as soon as they find that it cannot process their data.

Almost as bad is an MIS that is too large or too complex for the organization. Unused capacity and complexity do nothing but increase the cost of owning and operating the system. In addition, a system that is difficult to use probably will not be used at all.

Concept Check

✓ How do the information requirements of managers differ by management area?

✓ What happens if a business has a management information system that is too large?

✓ What happens if a business has a management information system that is too small?

Learning Objective

3 Outline the five functions of an information system.

HOW DO EMPLOYEES USE A MANAGEMENT INFORMATION SYSTEM?

To provide information, an MIS must perform five specific functions. It must (1) collect data, (2) store the data, (3) update the data, (4) process the data into information, and (5) present the information to users (see Figure 15-3).

Step 1: Collecting Data

A firm's employees, with the help of an MIS system, must gather the data and information needed to establish the firm's *database*. The database should include all past and current data that may be useful in managing the firm. Clearly, the data entered into the system must be *relevant* to the needs of the firm's managers. And perhaps most important, the data must be *accurate*. Irrelevant data are simply useless; inaccurate data can be disastrous. There are two data sources: *internal* and *external*.

Typically, most of the data gathered for an MIS come from internal sources. The most common internal sources of information are managers and employees, company records and reports, accounting data, and minutes of meetings.

External sources of data include customers, suppliers, financial institutions and banks, trade and business publications, industry conferences, online computer services, lawyers, government sources, and firms that specialize in gathering marketing research for organizations.

Whether the source of the data is internal or external, always remember the following three cautions:

1. The cost of obtaining data from some external sources, such as marketing research firms, can be quite high.
2. Outdated or incomplete data usually yield inaccurate information.
3. Although computers generally do not make mistakes, the people who use them can make or cause errors. When data (or information) and your judgment disagree, always check the data.

FIGURE 15-3 Five Management Information System Functions

Every MIS must be tailored to the organization it serves and must perform five functions.

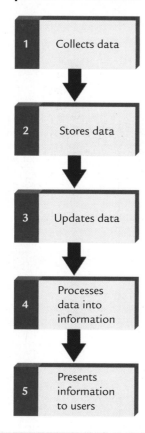

© CENGAGE LEARNING 2015

Step 2: Storing Data

An MIS must be capable of storing data until they are needed. Typically, the method chosen to store data depends on the size and needs of the organization. Small businesses may enter data and then store them directly on an employee's computer. Generally, medium-sized to large businesses store data in a larger computer system and provide access to employees through a computer network.

Step 3: Updating Data

Today, an MIS must be able to update stored data regularly to ensure that the information presented to managers and employees is accurate, complete, and up-to-date. The frequency with which the data are updated depends on how fast they change and how often they are used. When it is vital to have current data, updating may occur as soon as the new data are available. For example, Macy's, a national retailer that sells a wide range of merchandise including apparel and accessories for men, women, and children, cosmetics, home furnishing, and other consumer goods, has cash registers that automatically transmit data on each item sold in each store to a central computer. The computer adjusts the store's inventory records accordingly. In addition to maintaining accurate inventory records, sales representatives can tell customers where they can obtain merchandise if the store where they are shopping is out of the merchandise they want. Data and information may also be entered into a firm's data bank at certain intervals—every 24 hours, weekly, or monthly.

How Much Should Businesses Know About Internet Users?

When you click to conduct an online search or to download a digital coupon, businesses can follow your electronic movements. Tracking online behavior helps businesses make better decisions about targeting communications and tailoring offers to an individual's needs and interests. Yet the public may not always understand what information is being gathered, how long it will be held, how it will be used, or who can see it. This raises questions about how much data should businesses be able to collect about Internet users—and whether consumers should be able to avoid or minimize tracking of their online movements.

Privacy advocates worry about the potential for identity theft and the possibility that data may be shared without consent. They also express concern that businesses might restrict access to some products based on what consumers do or say online. For example, would a bank consider a consumer's history of visiting Internet gambling sites when determining which financial services products to offer or approve? Businesses point out the benefits of collecting data to personalize website functionality

based on each user's preferences and previous visits. They also look at behavioral data when planning new products and services.

The controversy has become even more heated as people flock to social media. As experts debate the limits of online privacy, regulators are formulating new privacy protections, makers of Web browsers are adding anti-tracking features, and industry groups are discussing ways to allow consumers to opt out of tracking if they choose. So how much should businesses be able to find out about what consumers say or do online?

Sources: Based on information in Natasha Singer, "Mediator Joins Contentious Effort to Add a 'Do Not Track' Option to Web Browsing," *New York Times*, November 28, 2012, www.nytimes.com; Julia Angwin, "A Search for Privacy in a Nonprivate Age," *Wall Street Journal*, November 16, 2012, www.wsj.com; Julia Angwin, Scott Thurm, and Michael Hickins, "Lawmaker Introduces New Privacy Bill," *Wall Street Journal*, February 11, 2011, www.wsj.com; Wendy Davis, "Report: Marketers Limit Behavioral Targeting Due to Privacy Worries," *Media Post*, May 2, 2010, www.mediapost.com; Emily Steel and Julia Angwin, "The Web's Cutting Edge, Anonymity in Name Only," *Wall Street Journal*, August 3, 2010, www.wsj.com.

Step 4: Processing Data

data processing the transformation of data into a form that is useful for a specific purpose

Some data are used in the form in which they are stored, whereas other data require processing to extract, highlight, or summarize the information they contain. **Data processing** is the transformation of data into a form that is useful for a specific purpose.

For verbal data, this processing consists mainly of extracting the pertinent material from storage and combining it into a report. Most business data, however, are in the form of numbers—large groups of numbers, such as daily sales totals or production costs for a specific product. Fortunately, computers can be programmed to process such large volumes of numbers quickly. While such groups of numbers may be difficult to handle and to comprehend, their contents can be summarized through the use of statistics. A **statistic** is a measure that summarizes a particular characteristic of an entire group of numbers.

statistic a measure that summarizes a particular characteristic of an entire group of numbers

Step 5: Presenting Information

An MIS must be capable of presenting information in a usable form. That is, the method of presentation—reports, tables, graphs, or charts, for example—must be appropriate for the information itself and for the uses to which it will be put.

BUSINESS REPORTS Verbal information may be presented in list or paragraph form. Employees often are asked to prepare formal business reports. A typical business report includes

- An introduction
- The body of the report
- The conclusions
- The recommendations

The *introduction*, which sets the stage for the remainder of the report, describes the problem to be studied in the report, identifies the research techniques that were used, and previews the material that will be presented in the report. The *body* of the report should objectively describe the facts that were discovered in the process of completing the report. The body also should provide a foundation for the conclusions and the recommendations. The *conclusions* are statements of fact that describe the findings contained in the report. Conclusions should be specific, practical, and based on the evidence in the report. The *recommendations* section presents suggestions on how the problem might be solved. Like the conclusions, the recommendations should be specific, practical, and based on the evidence.

VISUAL DISPLAYS AND TABLES A visual display can also be used to present information and may be a diagram that represents several items of information in a manner that makes comparison easier. Figure 15-4 illustrates examples of visual displays including graphs, bar charts, and pie charts generated by a computer.

A tabular display is used to present verbal or numerical information in columns and rows. It is most useful in presenting information about two or more related variables. A table, for example, can be used to illustrate the number of salespeople in each region of the country, sales for different types of products, and total sales for all products (see Table 15-1). Information that is to be manipulated—for example, to calculate loan payments—is usually displayed in tabular form.

Tabular displays generally have less impact than visual displays. However, displaying the information that could be contained in a multicolumn table such as the one shown in Table 15-1 would require several bar or pie charts.

PATRICK LA ROQUE/ALAMY

Who are the people who use information? Although the primary users of information are a firm's managers and employees, parties outside the organization—lenders, suppliers, stockholders, and government agencies—are also interested in the firm's information. In fact, both managers and employees and outside groups often examine a firm's annual report to determine the financial health of a firm.

Making Smart Decisions

How do managers and employees sort out relevant and useful information from the spam, junk mail, and useless data? In addition to the steps described in the last section (collecting data, storing data, updating data, processing data, and presenting information) three different software applications can actually help to improve and speed the decision-making process for people at different levels within an organization. First, a **decision-support system (DSS)** is a type of software program that provides relevant data and information to help a firm's employees make decisions. It also can be used to determine the effect of changing different variables and answer "what if" type questions. For example, a manager at Michigan-based Pulte Homes may use a DSS to determine prices for new homes built in an upscale, luxury subdivision. By entering the number of homes that will be built along with different costs associated with land, labor, materials, building permits, promotional costs, and all other costs, a DSS can help to determine a base price for each new home. It is also possible to increase or decrease the building costs and determine new home prices for each set of assumptions with a DSS. Although similar to a DSS, an **executive information system (EIS)** is a computer-based system that facilitates and supports the decision-making needs of top managers and senior executives by providing easy access to both internal and external information.

decision-support system (DSS) a type of software program that provides relevant data and information to help a firm's employees make decisions

executive information system (EIS) a computer-based system that facilitates and supports the decision-making needs of top managers and senior executives by providing easy access to both internal and external information

FIGURE 15-4 Typical Visual Displays Used in Business Presentations

Visual displays help businesspeople present information in a form that can be understood easily.

GRAPH

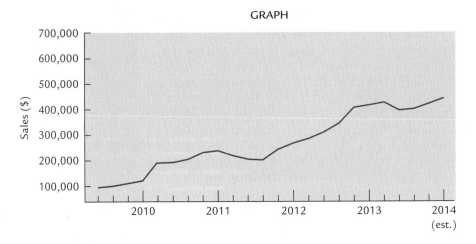

BAR CHART

Profits for the period 2009–2014, in millions

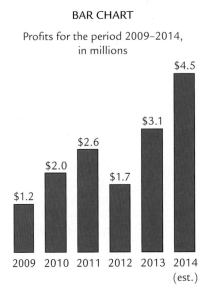

PIE CHART

Sales figures for selected products of Martin Manufacturing

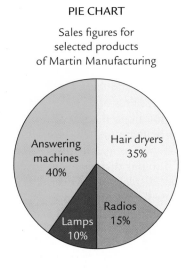

© CENGAGE LEARNING 2015

TABLE 15-1 Typical Three-Column Table Used in Business Presentations

Tables are most useful for displaying information about two or more variables.

All-Star Technology Projected Sales

Section of the Country	Number of Salespeople	Consumer Products ($)	Industrial Products ($)
Eastern territory	15	1,500,000	3,500,000
Midwestern territory	20	2,000,000	5,000,000
Western territory	10	1,000,000	4,000,000
TOTAL	45	4,500,000	12,500,000

© CENGAGE LEARNING 2015

TABLE 15-2 Current Business Application Software Used to Improve Productivity

Word processing	Users can prepare and edit written documents and store them in the computer or on a memory device.
Desktop publishing	Users can combine text and graphics in professional reports, newsletters, and pamphlets.
Accounting	Users can record routine financial transactions and prepare financial reports at the end of the accounting period.
Database management	Users can electronically store large amounts of data and transform the data into information.
Graphics	Users can display and print pictures, drawings, charts, and diagrams.
Spreadsheets	Users can organize numerical data into a grid of rows and columns.

© CENGAGE LEARNING 2015

An **expert system** is a type of computer program that uses artificial intelligence to imitate a human's ability to think. An expert system uses a set of rules that analyze information supplied by the user about a particular activity or problem. Based on the information supplied, the expert system then provides recommendations or suggests specific actions in order to help make decisions. Expert systems, for example, have been used to schedule manufacturing tasks, diagnose illnesses, determine credit limits for credit card customers, evaluate loan applications, and develop electronic games.

Business Application Software

Early software typically performed a single function. Today, however, *integrated* software combines many functions in a single package. Integrated packages allow for the easy linking of text, numerical data, graphs, photographs, and even audiovisual clips. A business report prepared using the Microsoft Office package, for instance, can include all these components.

Integration offers at least two other benefits. Once data have been entered into an application in an integrated package, the data can be used in another integrated package without having to reenter the data. In addition, once a user learns one application, it is much easier to learn another application in an integrated package. From a career standpoint, you should realize that employers will assume that you possess, or will possess after training, a high degree of working comfort with several of the software applications described in Table 15-2.

Concept Check

✓ List the five functions of an MIS.

✓ What are the components of a typical business report?

✓ What types of information could be illustrated in a visual display? In a tabular display?

✓ Describe the three types of computer applications that help employees, managers, and executives make smart decisions.

WHY ACCOUNTING INFORMATION IS IMPORTANT

Learning Objective

4 Explain why accurate accounting information and audited financial statements are important.

In today's competitive business environment, all successful firms use information to make decisions. In order to obtain needed information, firms use an MIS like the one described in the first part of this chapter. Executives, managers, and employees also rely on the firm's accounting system to provide needed financial information. **Accounting** is the process of systematically collecting, analyzing, and reporting financial information. Just for a moment, think about the following three questions:

1. How much profit did a business earn last year?
2. How much tax does a business owe the Internal Revenue Service?
3. How much cash does a business have to pay lenders and suppliers?

In each case, the firm's accountants and its accounting system provide the answers to these questions and many others. Although accounting information can be used to answer questions about what has happened in the past, it can also be used to help make decisions about the future.

Because the information provided by a firm's accountants and its accounting system is so important, managers and other groups interested in a business firm's financial records must be able to "trust the numbers." To improve the accuracy of a firm's accounting information and its financial statements, businesses rely on audits conducted by accountants employed by public accounting firms.

audit an examination of a company's financial statements and the accounting practices that produced them

generally accepted accounting principles (GAAPs) an accepted set of guidelines and practices for U.S. companies reporting financial information and for the accounting profession

Why Audited Financial Statements Are Important?

An **audit** is an examination of a company's financial statements and the accounting practices that produced them. The purpose of an audit is to make sure that a firm's financial statements have been prepared in accordance with **generally accepted accounting principles (GAAPs)**. GAAPs have been developed to provide an accepted set of guidelines and practices for U.S. companies reporting financial information and the accounting profession. At the time of publication, the Financial Accounting Standards Board (FASB), which establishes and improves accounting standards for U.S. companies, is working toward establishing a new set of standards that combines GAAPs with the International Financial Reporting Standards (IFRS) to create one set of accounting standards that can be used by both U.S. and multinational firms. Created by the International Accounting Standards Board, IFRS are now used in more than 100 different countries around the world. For multinational firms like Royal Dutch Shell, ExxonMobil, Walmart, and Toyota, the benefits of global accounting standards are huge because preparing financial statements and accounting records that meet global standards saves both time and money. According to many accounting experts, the United States is on a path toward the adoption of IFRS, the question is when.[2]

If an accountant determines that a firm's financial statements present financial information fairly and conform to GAAPs, then he or she will issue the following statement:

> *In our opinion, the financial statements . . . present fairly, in all material respects the financial position of the company . . . in conformity with generally accepted accounting principles.*

Although an audit and the resulting report do not *guarantee* that a company has not "cooked" the books, it does imply that, on the whole, the company has followed GAAPs. Bankers, creditors, investors, and government agencies are willing to rely on an auditor's opinion because of the historically ethical reputation and independence of auditors and accounting firms. Finally, it should be noted that without the audit function and GAAPs, there would be very little oversight or supervision. The validity of a firm's financial statements and its accounting records would drop quickly, and firms would find it difficult to obtain debt financing, acquire goods and services from suppliers, find investor financing, or prepare documents requested by government agencies.

COMSTOCK IMAGES/GETTY IMAGES

Does this executive trust the numbers? Good question! A firm's managers and employees must have accurate accounting information to make decisions and plan for the future. Other groups including investors, lenders, and suppliers also must "trust" accounting information to determine the financial health of a company. In fact, without accurate accounting information, the numbers are just that numbers.

Accounting Fraud, Ethical Behavior, and Reform

Which of the following firms has been convicted or accused of accounting fraud?

a. Lehman Brothers (Banking in the United States)
b. Sino-Forest (Forestry Operations in China)
c. Fannie Mae (Home Mortgages in United States)
d. Autonomy Software (Software Development in Britain)
e. All of the above

Unfortunately, the answer to the question is e—all of the above. Each company is a large business that has been plagued by accounting problems. In some cases, the accounting problems led to bankruptcy for Lehman Brothers and Sino-Forest Corporation. In other cases, the value of the corporation's stock plummeted because the firm had inflated sales or underreported expenses. And as you can tell from the options to the above question, the companies can operate in any industry and be located any place on the globe. The bottom line: The accounting problems at these companies—and similar problems at even more companies—have forced many investors, lenders and suppliers, and government regulators to question the motives behind fraudulent and unethical accounting practices.

Today, much of the pressure on corporate executives to "cook" the books is driven by the desire to look good to Wall Street analysts and investors. If a company reports sales and profit figures that are lower than expected, the company's stock value can drop dramatically. Greed—especially when executive salaries and bonuses are tied to a company's stock value—is another factor that can lead some corporate executives to use unethical accounting methods to inflate a firm's sales revenues and profit amount.

Unfortunately, the ones hurt when companies (and their accountants) report inaccurate or misleading accounting information often are not the high-paid corporate executives. In many cases, it's the employees who lose their jobs when the company files for bankruptcy, as well as the money they invested in the company's retirement program. In addition, investors, lenders, and suppliers who relied on fraudulent accounting information in order to make a decision to invest in or lend money to the company also usually experience a loss.

To help ensure that corporate financial information is accurate and to prevent the type of accounting scandals that have occurred in the past, Congress enacted the Sarbanes–Oxley Act in 2002. Key components include the following:[3]

- The Securities and Exchange Commission (SEC) is required to establish a full-time five-member federal oversight board that will police the accounting industry.
- Chief executive and financial officers are required to certify periodic financial reports and are liable for intentional violations of securities reporting requirements.
- Accounting firms are prohibited from providing many types of nonaudit and consulting services to the companies they audit.
- Auditors must maintain financial documents and audit work papers for five years.
- Auditors, accountants, and employees can be imprisoned for up to 20 years and subject to fines for destroying financial documents and willful violations of the securities laws.
- A public corporation must change its lead auditing firm every five years.
- There is added protection for whistle-blowers who report violations of the Sarbanes–Oxley Act.

Although most people welcome the Sarbanes–Oxley Act, complex rules make compliance more expensive and time-consuming for corporate management and more difficult for accounting firms. Yet, most people agree that the cost of compliance is justified.

Different Types of Accounting

Although many people think that all accountants do the same tasks, there are special areas of expertise within the accounting industry. In fact, accounting is usually broken down into two broad categories: managerial and financial.

Managerial accounting provides managers and employees within the organization with the information needed to make decisions about a firm's financing, investing, marketing, and operating activities. By using managerial accounting information, both managers and employees can evaluate how well they have done in the past and what they can expect in the future.

Financial accounting, on the other hand, generates financial statements and reports for interested people outside of an organization. Typically, stockholders, financial analysts, bankers, lenders, suppliers, government agencies, and other interested groups use the information provided by financial accounting to determine how well a business firm has achieved its goals. In addition to managerial and financial accounting, additional special areas of accounting include the following:

© OPOLJA/SHUTTERSTOCK.COM

managerial accounting
provides managers and employees with the information needed to make decisions about a firm's financing, investing, marketing, and operating activities

financial accounting generates financial statements and reports for interested people outside an organization

- *Cost accounting*—determining the cost of producing specific products or services;
- *Tax accounting*—planning tax strategy and preparing tax returns for firms or individuals;
- *Government accounting*—providing basic accounting services to ensure that tax revenues are collected and used to meet the goals of state, local, and federal agencies; and
- *Not-for-profit accounting*—helping not-for-profit organizations to account for all donations and expenditures.

Careers in Accounting

What is the typical day like for accountants? While each day may be different than the next and depending on if they are self-employed, work for a business firm, or work for an accounting firm, accountants typically do the following:

- Inspect a firm's accounting systems to ensure the business is using generally accepted accounting procedures.
- Examine financial statements to be sure that they are accurate.
- Calculate the amount of taxes owed, prepare tax returns, and ensure that taxes are paid properly and on time.
- Organize and maintain financial records.
- Assist employees, managers, and owners to improve financial decisions.
- Suggest ways to reduce costs, enhance revenues, and improve profits.

According to the *Occupational Outlook Handbook*, published by the Department of Labor, job opportunities for accountants, as well as auditors in the accounting area, are expected to experience a 16 percent increase or about average employment growth between now and the year 2020.[4] And more good news: Starting salaries for employees in the accounting industry are often higher than the starting salaries for other entry-level positions.

Accounting can be an exciting and rewarding career. To be successful in the accounting industry, employees must

- be responsible, honest, and ethical;
- have a strong background in financial management;
- know how to use a computer and software to process data into accounting information; and
- be able to communicate with people who need accounting information.

Today, accountants generally are classified as either private accountants or public accountants. A *private accountant* is employed by a specific organization. On the other hand, a *public accountant* works on a fee basis for clients and may be self-employed or be the employee of an accounting firm. Accounting firms range in size from one-person operations to huge international firms with hundreds of accounting partners and thousands of employees. Today, the largest accounting firms, sometimes referred to as the "Big Four," are PricewaterhouseCoopers (PwC), Ernst & Young, KPMG, and Deloitte Touche Tohmatsu.

Typically, public accounting firms include on their staffs at least one **certified public accountant (CPA)**, an individual who has met state requirements for accounting education and experience and has passed a rigorous accounting examination. More information about general requirements and the CPA profession can be obtained by contacting the American Institute of CPAs (AICPA) at www.aicpa.org. State requirements usually include a college degree or a specified number of hours of college course work and generally from one to three years of on-the-job experience. Details regarding specific state requirements for practice as a CPA can be obtained by contacting the state's board of accountancy.

Certification as a CPA brings both status and responsibility. Publicly traded corporations, for example, must hire an independent CPA to audit their financial statements. Fees for the services provided by CPAs generally range from $50 to $300 an hour.

THE ACCOUNTING EQUATION AND THE BALANCE SHEET

At the beginning of this chapter, *information* was defined as data presented in a form that is useful for a specific purpose. Now, we examine how financial *data* is transformed into financial *information* and reported on three very important financial statements—the balance sheet, income statement, and statement of cash flows. We begin by describing why the fundamental accounting equation is the basis for a firm's balance sheet.

The Accounting Equation

The accounting equation is a simple statement that forms the basis for the accounting process. This equation shows the relationship between a firm's assets, liabilities, and owners' equity.

- **Assets** are the resources a business owns—cash, inventory, equipment, and real estate.
- **Liabilities** are the firm's debts—borrowed money it owes to others that must be repaid.
- **Owners' equity** is the difference between total assets and total liabilities—what would be left for the owners if the firm's assets were sold and the money used to pay off its liabilities.

The relationship between assets, liabilities, and owners' equity is shown by the following **accounting equation:**

$$\text{Assets} = \text{Liabilities} + \text{Owners' equity}$$

The dollar total of all of a firm's assets cannot equal more than the total funds obtained by borrowing money (liabilities) and the investment of the owner(s).

double-entry bookkeeping system a system in which each financial transaction is recorded as two separate accounting entries to maintain the balance shown in the accounting equation

Whether a business is a small corner grocery store or a global giant like Procter & Gamble, the total dollar amount for assets must equal the sum of its liabilities and owners' equity. To use this equation, a firm's accountants must record raw data—that is, the firm's day-to-day financial transactions—using the double-entry system of bookkeeping. The **double-entry bookkeeping system** is a system in which each financial transaction is recorded as two separate accounting entries to maintain the balance shown in the accounting equation. At the end of a specific accounting period, all of the financial transactions can now be summarized in the firm's financial statements. This information is presented in a standardized format to make the statements as accessible as possible to the various people who may be interested in the firm's financial affairs—managers, employees, lenders, suppliers, stockholders, potential investors, and government agencies. In fact, the form of the financial statements is pretty much the same for all businesses, from a neighborhood video store or small dry cleaner to giant conglomerates such as Home Depot, Boeing, and Bank of America. A firm's financial statements are prepared at least once a year and included in the firm's annual report. An **annual report** is a report distributed to stockholders and other interested parties that describes a firm's operating activities and its financial condition. Most firms also have financial statements prepared semiannually, quarterly, or monthly.

annual report a report distributed to stockholders and other interested parties that describes the firm's operating activities and its financial condition

The Balance Sheet

Question: *Where could you find the total amount of assets, liabilities, and owners' equity for Hershey Foods Corporation?*

Answer: The firm's balance sheet.

balance sheet (or statement of financial position) a summary of the dollar amounts of a firm's assets, liabilities, and owners' equity accounts at the end of a specific accounting period

A **balance sheet** (sometimes referred to as a **statement of financial position**) is a summary of the dollar amounts of a firm's assets, liabilities, and owners' equity accounts at the end of a specific accounting period. The balance sheet must demonstrate that assets are equal to liabilities plus owners' equity, and the accounting equation is still in balance. Most people think of a balance sheet as a statement that reports the financial condition of a business firm such as the Hershey Foods Corporation, but balance sheets apply to individuals, too. For example, Marty Campbell graduated from college three years ago and obtained a position as a sales representative for an office supply firm. After going to work, he established a checking and savings account and purchased an automobile, stereo, television, and furniture for his apartment. Marty paid cash for some purchases, but he had to borrow money to pay for the larger ones. Figure 15-5 shows Marty's current personal balance sheet.

Marty Campbell's assets total $26,500, and his liabilities amount to $10,000. Although the difference between total assets and total liabilities is referred to as *owners' equity* or *stockholders' equity* for a business, it is normally called *net worth* for an individual. As reported on Marty's personal balance sheet, net worth is $16,500. The total assets ($26,500) and the total liabilities *plus* net worth ($26,500) are equal. Thus, the accounting equation (Assets = Liabilities + Owners' equity) is still in balance.

Figure 15-6 shows the balance sheet for Northeast Art Supply, a small corporation that sells picture frames, paints, canvases, and other artists' supplies to retailers in New England. Note that assets are reported on the left side of the statement, and liabilities and stockholders' equity are reported on the right side. Let's work through the different accounts in Figure 15-6.

Assets

liquidity the ease with which an asset can be converted into cash

On a balance sheet, assets are listed in order from the *most liquid* to the *least liquid*. The **liquidity** of an asset is the ease with which it can be converted into cash.

FIGURE 15-5 Personal Balance Sheet

Often, individuals determine their net worth, or owners' equity, by subtracting the value of their liabilities from the value of their assets.

Marty Campbell
Personal Balance Sheet
December 31, 20XX

ASSETS		LIABILITIES	
Cash	$ 2,500	Automobile loan	$ 9,500
Savings account	5,000	Credit card balance	500
Automobile	15,000	TOTAL LIABILITIES	$10,000
Stereo	1,000		
Television	500		
Furniture	2,500	NET WORTH (Owners' Equity)	16,500
TOTAL ASSETS	$26,500	TOTAL LIABILITIES AND NET WORTH	$26,500

© CENGAGE LEARNING 2015

FIGURE 15-6 Business Balance Sheet

A balance sheet (sometimes referred to as a statement of financial position) summarizes a firm's assets, liabilities, and owners' equity. Note that assets ($340,000) equal liabilities plus owners' equity ($340,000) and the accounting equation is still in balance.

NORTHEAST ART SUPPLY, INC.

Balance Sheet
December 31, 20XX

ASSETS				LIABILITIES AND STOCKHOLDERS' EQUITY		
Current assets				**Current liabilities**		
Cash		$ 59,000		Accounts payable	$ 35,000	
Marketable securities		10,000		Notes payable	25,675	
Accounts receivable	$ 40,000			Salaries payable	4,000	
Less allowance for doubtful accounts	2,000	38,000		Taxes payable	5,325	
Notes receivable		32,000		Total current liabilities		$ 70,000
Merchandise inventory		41,000				
Prepaid expenses		2,000				
Total current assets			$182,000	**Long-term liabilities**		
				Mortgage payable on store equipment	$ 40,000	
Fixed assets				Total long-term liabilities		$ 40,000
Delivery equipment	$110,000			TOTAL LIABILITIES		$110,000
Less accumulated depreciation	20,000	$ 90,000				
Furniture and store equipment	$62,000					
Less accumulated depreciation	15,000	47,000		**Stockholders' equity**		
Total fixed assets			137,000	Common stock (25,000×$6)	$ 150,000	
				Retained earnings	80,000	
Intangible assets						
Patents		$ 21,000				
Total intangible assets			21,000	TOTAL OWNERS' EQUITY		230,000
TOTAL ASSETS			$340,000	TOTAL LIABILITIES AND OWNERS' EQUITY		$340,000

© CENGAGE LEARNING 2015

Checking it once, checking it twice. . . . Before determining the total value of a firm's assets, accountants must determine the value of each type of inventory a firm has on hand to meet customer demand. Accurate accounting procedures for inventory can also determine when it is time to order more inventory.

current assets assets that can be converted quickly into cash or that will be used in one year or less

CURRENT ASSETS Current assets are assets that can be converted quickly into cash or that will be used in one year or less. Because cash is the most liquid asset, it is listed first. Next are *marketable securities*—stocks, bonds, and other investments—that can be converted into cash in a matter of days.

Next are the firm's receivables. Its *accounts receivable*, which result from allowing customers to make credit purchases, generally are paid within 30 to 60 days. However, the firm expects that some of these debts will not be collected. Thus, it has reduced its accounts receivables by a 5 percent *allowance for doubtful accounts*. The firm's *notes receivable* are receivables for which customers have signed promissory notes. They generally are repaid over a longer period of time than the firm's accounts receivable.

Northeast's *merchandise inventory* represents the value of goods on hand for sale to customers. Since Northeast Art Supply is a wholesale operation, the inventory listed in Figure 15-6 represents finished goods ready for sale to retailers. For a manufacturing firm, merchandise inventory also may represent raw materials that will become part of a finished product or work that has been partially completed but requires further processing.

Northeast Art's last current asset is *prepaid expenses*, which are assets that have been paid for in advance but have not yet been used. An example is insurance premiums. They are usually paid at the beginning of the policy year. The unused portion (say, for the last four months of the time period covered by the policy) is a prepaid expense. For Northeast Art, all current assets total $182,000.

fixed assets assets that will be held or used for a period longer than one year

depreciation the process of apportioning the cost of a fixed asset over the period during which it will be used

FIXED ASSETS Fixed assets are assets that will be held or used for a period longer than one year. They generally include land, buildings, and equipment used in the continuing operation of the business. Although Northeast Art owns no land or buildings, it does own delivery equipment that originally cost $110,000. It also owns furniture and store equipment that originally cost $62,000.

Note that the values of both fixed assets are decreased by their *accumulated depreciation*. **Depreciation** is the process of apportioning the cost of a fixed asset over the period during which it will be used, that is, its useful life. The depreciation amount allotted to each year is an expense for that year, and the value of the asset must be reduced by the amount of depreciation expense. In the case of Northeast's delivery equipment, $20,000 of its value has been depreciated since it was purchased. Its value at this time is thus $110,000 less $20,000, or $90,000. In a similar fashion, the original value of furniture and store equipment ($62,000) has been

Concept Check

✓ How are current assets distinguished from fixed assets?

✓ Why are fixed assets depreciated on a firm's balance sheet?

✓ How do you determine the dollar amount of owners' equity for a sole proprietorship, or a partnership, or a corporation?

✓ If a business firm has assets worth $170,000 and liabilities that total $40,000, what is the value of the owners' equity?

reduced by depreciation totaling $15,000. Furniture and store equipment now has a reported value of $47,000. For Northeast Art, all fixed assets total $137,000.

INTANGIBLE ASSETS Intangible assets are assets that do not exist physically but that have a value based on the rights or privileges they confer on a firm. They include patents, copyrights, trademarks, and goodwill. By their nature, intangible assets are long-term assets—they are of value to the firm for a number of years.

Northeast Art Supply lists a *patent* for a special oil paint that the company purchased from the inventor. The firm's accountants estimate that the patent has a current market value of $21,000. The firm's intangible assets total $21,000. Now it is possible to total all three types of assets for Northeast Art. As calculated in Figure 15-6, total assets are $340,000.

Liabilities and Owners' Equity

The liabilities and the owners' equity accounts complete the balance sheet. The firm's liabilities are separated into two categories—current and long-term liabilities.

CURRENT LIABILITIES A firm's **current liabilities** are debts that will be repaid in one year or less. Northeast Art Supply purchased merchandise from its suppliers on credit. Thus, its balance sheet includes an entry for accounts payable. *Accounts payable* are short-term obligations that arise as a result of a firm making credit purchases.

Notes payable are obligations that have been secured with promissory notes. They are usually short-term obligations, but they may extend beyond one year. Only those that must be paid within the year are listed under current liabilities.

Northeast Art also lists *salaries payable* and *taxes payable* as current liabilities. These are both expenses that have been incurred during the current accounting period but will be paid in the next accounting period. For Northeast Art, current liabilities total $70,000.

LONG-TERM LIABILITIES **Long-term liabilities** are debts that need not be repaid for at least one year. Northeast Art lists only one long-term liability—a $40,000 *mortgage payable* for store equipment. As you can see in Figure 15-6, Northeast Art's current and long-term liabilities total $110,000.

OWNERS' OR STOCKHOLDERS' EQUITY For a sole proprietorship or partnership, the owners' equity is shown as the difference between assets and liabilities. In a partnership, each partner's share of the ownership is reported separately in each owner's name. For a corporation, the owners' equity usually is referred to as *stockholders' equity*. The dollar amount reported on the balance sheet is the total value of stock plus retained earnings that have accumulated to date. **Retained earnings** are the portion of a business's profits not distributed to stockholders.

The original investment by the owners of Northeast Art Supply was $150,000 and was obtained by selling 25,000 shares at $6 per share. In addition, $80,000 of Northeast Art's earnings have been reinvested in the business since it was founded. Thus, owners' equity totals $230,000.

As the two grand totals in Figure 15-6 show, Northeast Art's assets and the sum of its liabilities and owners' equity are equal—at $340,000. The accounting equation (Assets = Liabilities + Owners' equity) is still in balance.

Personal Apps

Smart Career Moves

Before you accept a company's job offer or buy its stock, check financials and its business situation. Are profits increasing or decreasing? How is it handling its debt? What are its plans for expansion?

intangible assets assets that do not exist physically but that have a value based on the rights or privileges they confer on a firm

current liabilities debts that will be repaid in one year or less

long-term liabilities debts that need not be repaid for at least one year

retained earnings the portion of a business's profits not distributed to stockholders

THE INCOME STATEMENT

Question: *Where can you find the profit or loss amount for Apple, Inc.?*

Answer: The firm's income statement.

An **income statement** is a summary of a firm's revenues and expenses during a specified accounting period—one month, three months, six months, or a year. The income statement is sometimes called the *earnings statement* or *the statement of income and expenses*. Let's begin our discussion by constructing a personal income statement for Marty Campbell. Having worked as a sales representative for an office supply firm for the past three years, Marty now earns $33,600 a year, or $2,800 a month. After deductions, his take-home pay is $1,900 a month. As illustrated in Figure 15-7, Marty's typical monthly expenses include payments for an automobile loan, credit card purchases, apartment rent, utilities, food, clothing, and recreation and entertainment.

Although the difference between income and expenses is referred to as *profit* or *loss* for a business, it is normally referred to as a *cash surplus* or *cash deficit* for an individual. Fortunately for Marty, he has a surplus of $250 at the end of each month. He can use this surplus for savings, investing, or paying off debts. It is also possible to use the information from a personal income statement to construct a personal budget. A *personal budget* is a specific plan for spending your income—over the next month, for example.

Figure 15-8 shows the income statement for Northeast Art Supply. For a business,

Revenues *less* Cost of goods sold *less* Operating expenses equals Net income

FIGURE 15-7 Personal Income Statement

By subtracting expenses from income, anyone can construct a personal income statement and determine if he or she has a surplus or deficit at the end of each month.

Marty Campbell
Personal Income Statement
For the month ended December 31, 20XX

INCOME (Take-home pay)		$1,900
LESS MONTHLY EXPENSES		
Automobile loan	$ 250	
Credit card payment	100	
Apartment rent	500	
Utilities	200	
Food	250	
Clothing	100	
Recreation & entertainment	250	
TOTAL MONTHLY EXPENSES		1,650
CASH SURPLUS (or profit)		$ 250

Comparing Financial Data

Many firms compare their financial results with those of competing firms, with industry averages, and with their own financial results. Comparisons are possible as long as accountants follow GAAPs. Except for minor differences in format and terms, the balance sheet, income statement, and statement of cash flows of Procter & Gamble, for example, will be similar to those of other large corporations, such as Clorox, Colgate-Palmolive, and Unilever, in the consumer goods industry. Comparisons among firms give executives, managers, and employees a general idea of a firm's relative effectiveness and its standing within the industry. Competitors' financial statements can be obtained from their annual reports—if they are public corporations. Industry averages are published by reporting services such as D&B (formerly Dun & Bradstreet) and Hoover's, Inc., as well as by some industry trade associations.

Today, most corporations include in their annual reports comparisons of the important elements of their financial statements for recent years. For example, Figure 15-10 shows such comparisons—of revenue, research and development (R&D), operating income, and sales and marketing expenses—for Microsoft Corporation, a world leader in the computer software industry. By examining these data, an operating

FIGURE 15-10 Comparisons of Present and Past Financial Statements for Microsoft Corporation

Most corporations include in their annual reports comparisons of the important elements of their financial statements for recent years.

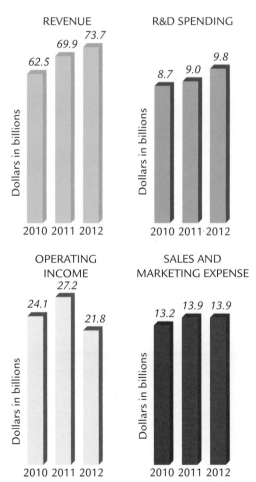

Source: Adapted from the Microsoft Corporation 2012 Annual Report, www.microsoft.com (accessed January 24, 2013).

Financial Audit

Accounting · Assurance · Control · Report · Risks · Legal · Tax

Evaluating financial statements is serious business. Even after a firm's financial statements are prepared, accountants often dig deeper and prepare audits to make sure that accounting information is accurate. They also calculate financial ratios to measure a firm's profitability, its ability to pay its debts, and how well it manages inventory.

manager can tell whether R&D expenditures have been increasing or decreasing over the past three years. The vice president of marketing can determine if the total amount of sales and marketing expenses is changing. Stockholders and potential investors, on the other hand, may be more concerned with increases or decreases in Microsoft's revenues and operating income over the same time period. Still another type of analysis of a firm's financial health involves computation of financial ratios.

Financial Ratios

A **financial ratio** is a number that shows the relationship between two elements of a firm's financial statements. While it is possible to calculate many different financial ratios, we'll only discuss three different ratios that are used to measure a firm's profitability, its ability to pay its debts, and how often it sells its inventory. Like the individual elements in financial statements, these ratios can be compared with those of competitors, with industry averages, and with the firm's past ratios from previous accounting periods. The information required to form these ratios is found in a firm's balance sheet, income statement, and statement of cash flows (in our examples for Northeast Art Supply, Figures 15-6, 15-8, and 15-9).

financial ratio a number that shows the relationship between two elements of a firm's financial statements

return on sales (or profit margin) a financial ratio calculated by dividing net income after taxes by net sales

MEASURING A FIRM'S ABILITY TO EARN PROFITS A firm's net income after taxes indicates whether the firm is profitable. It does not, however, indicate how effectively the firm's resources are being used. For this latter purpose, a return on sales ratio can be computed. **Return on sales (or profit margin)** is a financial ratio calculated by dividing net income after taxes by net sales. For Northeast Art Supply,

$$\text{Return on sales} = \frac{\text{Net income after taxes}}{\text{Net sales}} = \frac{\$30,175}{\$451,000}$$
$$= 0.067, \text{ or } 6.7 \text{ percent}$$

The return on sales indicates how effectively the firm is transforming sales into profits. A higher return on sales is better than a low one. Today, the average return on sales for all business firms is between 4 and 5 percent. With a return on sales of 6.7 percent, Northeast Art Supply is above average. A low return on sales can be increased by reducing expenses, increasing sales, or both.

current ratio a financial ratio computed by dividing current assets by current liabilities

MEASURING A FIRM'S ABILITY TO PAY ITS DEBTS A current ratio can be used to evaluate a firm's ability to pay its current liabilities. A firm's **current ratio** is computed by dividing current assets by current liabilities. For Northeast Art Supply,

$$\text{Current ratio} = \frac{\text{Current assets}}{\text{Current liabilities}} = \frac{\$182,000}{\$70,000} = 2.6$$

This means that Northeast Art Supply has $2.60 of current assets for every $1 of current liabilities. The average current ratio for all industries is 2.0, but it varies greatly from industry to industry. A high current ratio indicates that a firm can pay its current liabilities. A low current ratio can be improved by repaying current liabilities, by reducing dividend payments to stockholders to increase the firm's cash balance, or by obtaining additional cash from investors.

MEASURING HOW WELL A FIRM MANAGES ITS INVENTORY A firm's **inventory turnover** is the number of times the firm sells its merchandise inventory in one year. It is approximated by dividing the cost of goods sold in one year by the average value of the inventory.

The average value of the inventory can be found by adding the beginning inventory value and the ending inventory value (given on the income statement) and dividing the sum by 2. For Northeast Art Supply, average inventory is $40,500. Thus

$$\text{Inventory turnover} = \frac{\text{cost of goods sold}}{\text{average inventory}} = \frac{\$334,000}{\$40,500}$$

$$= 8.2 \text{ times per year}$$

Northeast Art Supply sells its merchandise inventory 8.2 times each year, or about once every 45 days. The average inventory turnover for all firms is about 9 times per year, but turnover rates vary widely from industry to industry. For example, supermarkets may have inventory turnover rates of 20 or higher, whereas inventory turnover rates for furniture stores are generally well below the national average. The quickest way to improve inventory turnover is to order merchandise in smaller quantities at more frequent intervals.

Like the three ratios described in this section, the calculations for other financial ratios, including return on owners' equity, earnings per share, working capital, and debt-to-equity, are based on the information contained in a firm's balance sheet, income statement, and statement of cash flows. For more detailed information on ratio analysis, you may want to read more on the topic in an accounting or finance textbook or use an Internet search engine.

This chapter ends our discussion of management and accounting information. In Chapter 16, we see why firms need financing, how they obtain it, and how they ensure that funds are used effectively in keeping with the organization's goals.

> **inventory turnover** a financial ratio calculated by dividing the cost of goods sold in one year by the average value of the inventory

Concept Check

✓ What are the benefits of comparing a firm's current financial information with information for previous accounting periods, with industry averages, and with financial information for competitors?

✓ Explain the calculation procedures for and significance of each of the following:

   a. Return on sales.

   b. The current ratio.

   c. Inventory turnover.

Looking for Success? *Get Flashcards, Quizzes, Games, Crosswords, and more @ www.cengagebrain.com.*

Summary

1 Examine how information can reduce risk when making a decision.

The more information a manager has, the less risk there is that a decision will be incorrect. Information produces knowledge and empowers managers and employees to make better decisions. Because of the volume of information they receive each day and their need to make decisions on a daily basis, businesspeople use information rules to shorten the time spent analyzing choices. Information rules emerge when business research confirms the same results each time it studies the same or a similar set of circumstances. Although many people use the terms *data* and *information* interchangeably, there is a difference. Data are numerical or verbal descriptions that usually result from some sort of measurement. Information is data presented in a form that is useful for

a specific purpose. A database is a single collection of data and information stored in one place that can be used by people throughout an organization to make decisions. Although databases are important, the way the data and information are used is even more important. As a result, management information experts now use the term *knowledge management* (KM) to describe a firm's procedures for generating, using, and sharing the data and information.

2 Discuss management's information requirements.

A management information system (MIS) is a means of providing managers with the information they need to perform their jobs as effectively as possible. The purpose of an MIS (sometimes referred to as an information technology system or simply IT system) is to distribute timely and useful information from both internal and external sources to the decision makers who need it. The specific types of information managers need depend on their area of management and level within the firm. The size and complexity of an MIS must be tailored to the information needs of the organization it serves.

3 Outline the five functions of an information system.

The five functions performed by an MIS system are collecting data, storing data, updating data, processing data into information, and presenting information. Data may be collected from internal sources and external sources. An MIS must be able to store data until they are needed and to update them regularly to ensure that the information presented to managers and employees is accurate, complete, and timely. Data processing is the MIS function that transforms stored data into a form useful for a specific purpose. Finally, the processed data (which now can be called information) must be presented for use. Verbal information generally is presented in the form of a report. Numerical information most often is displayed in graphs, charts, or tables. In addition to the five basic functions performed by an MIS, managers and employees can use a decision-support system (DSS), an executive information system (EIS), expert system, and business application software to make decisions and to report data and information.

4 Explain why accurate accounting information and audited financial statements are important.

Accounting is the process of systematically collecting, analyzing, and reporting financial information. It can be used to answer questions about what has happened in the past; it also can be used to help make decisions about the future. The purpose of an audit is to make sure that a firm's financial statements have been prepared in accordance with generally accepted accounting principles. To help ensure that corporate financial information is accurate and in response to the accounting scandals that surfaced in the last few years, the Sarbanes–Oxley Act was signed into law. This law contains a number of provisions designed to restore public confidence in the accounting industry. Although many people think all accountants do the same thing, typical areas of expertise include managerial, financial, cost, tax, government, and not-for-profit. A private accountant is employed by a private firm. A public accountant performs accounting work for various individuals or firms on a fee basis. Most accounting firms include on their staffs at least one CPA.

5 Read and interpret a balance sheet.

A balance sheet (sometimes referred to as a statement of financial position) is a summary of a firm's assets, liabilities, and owners' equity accounts at the end of an accounting period. This statement must demonstrate that the accounting equation is in balance. On the balance sheet, assets are categorized as current, fixed, or intangible. Similarly, liabilities can be divided into current liabilities and long-term liabilities. For a sole proprietorship or partnership, owners' equity is shown as the difference between assets and liabilities. For corporations, the owners' equity section reports the values of stock and retained earnings.

6 Read and interpret an income statement.

An income statement is a summary of a firm's financial operations during the specified accounting period. On the income statement, the company's gross profit is computed by subtracting the cost of goods sold from net sales. Operating expenses and interest expense then are deducted to compute net income before taxes. Finally, income taxes are deducted to obtain the firm's net income after taxes.

7 Describe business activities that affect a firm's cash flow.

Since 1987, the Securities and Exchange Commission (SEC) and the Financial Accounting Standards Board (FASB) have required all publicly traded companies to include a statement of cash flows in their annual reports. This statement illustrates how the company's operating, investing, and financing activities affect cash during an accounting period. Together, the cash flow statement, balance sheet, and income statement illustrate the results of past decisions and the business's ability to pay debts and dividends as well as to finance new growth.

8 Summarize how managers evaluate the financial health of a business.

The firm's financial statements and its accounting information become more meaningful when compared with information for competitors, for the industry in which the firm operates, and corresponding information for previous years. Such comparisons permit managers, employees, lenders, investors, and other interested people to pick out trends in growth, borrowing, income, and other business variables and to determine whether the firm is on the way to accomplishing its long-term goals. A number of financial ratios can be computed from the information in a firm's financial statements. These ratios provide a picture of a firm's profitability, its ability to pay its debts, and how often it sells its inventory. Like the information on the firm's financial statements, these ratios can and should be compared with information for competitors, for the industry in which the firm operates, and corresponding information for previous years.

Key Terms

You should now be able to define and give an example relevant to each of the following terms:

data (429)
information (429)
database (430)
knowledge management (KM) (430)
management information system (MIS) (430)
data processing (434)
statistic (434)
decision-support system (DSS) (435)
executive information system (EIS) (435)
expert system (437)

accounting (437)
audit (438)
generally accepted accounting principles (GAAPs) (438)
managerial accounting (440)
financial accounting (440)
certified public accountant (CPA) (441)
assets (441)
liabilities (441)
owners' equity (441)
accounting equation (441)

double-entry bookkeeping system (442)
annual report (442)
balance sheet (or statement of financial position) (442)
liquidity (442)
current assets (444)
fixed assets (444)
depreciation (444)
intangible assets (445)
current liabilities (445)
long-term liabilities (445)
retained earnings (445)
income statement (446)

revenues (447)
gross sales (447)
net sales (447)
cost of goods sold (448)
gross profit (449)
operating expenses (449)
net income (449)
net loss (449)
statement of cash flows (449)
financial ratio (452)
return on sales (or profit margin) (452)
current ratio (452)
inventory turnover (453)

Discussion Questions

1. Do managers really need all the kinds of information discussed in this chapter? If not, which kinds can they do without?
2. How can confidential data and information (such as the wages of individual employees) be kept confidential and yet still be available to managers who need them?
3. Bankers usually insist that prospective borrowers submit audited financial statements along with a loan application. Why should financial statements be audited by a CPA?
4. What can be said about a firm whose owners' equity is a negative amount? How could such a situation come about?
5. Do the balance sheet, income statement, and statement of cash flows contain all the information you might want as a potential lender or stockholder? What other information would you like to examine?
6. Of the three financial ratios discussed in this chapter, which do you think is the most important financial ratio? Why?

Test Yourself

Matching Questions

1. _____ Data that have been processed.
2. _____ A term for the debts of a firm.
3. _____ It is the difference between a firm's assets and its liabilities.
4. _____ It transforms data into useful information.
5. _____ Inventories are an example.
6. _____ The ease with which assets can be converted into cash.
7. _____ This statement reveals the financial position of the firm.
8. _____ It illustrates how operating, investing, and financing activities affect cash.
9. _____ It incorporates a firm's procedures for generating, using, and sharing the data and information contained in the firm's database.
10. _____ The result of dividing current assets by current liabilities.

a. assets
b. balance sheet
c. cost of goods sold
d. current ratio
e. data processing
f. information
g. liabilities
h. liquidity
i. knowledge management
j. owners' equity
k. public accountant
l. statement of cash flows

True False Questions

11. **T F** The more information a manager has, the less risk there is that a decision will be incorrect.

12. **T F** A single collection of data stored in one place is called a data center.

13. **T F** Information is defined as numerical or verbal descriptions that usually result from sort of measurement.

14. **T F** In a business report, the conclusions present suggestions on how the problem might be solved.

15. **T F** An expert system uses artificial intelligence to imitate a human's ability to think.

16. **T F** There is added protection for whistle-blowers who report violations of the Sarbanes–Oxley Act.

17. **T F** A private accountant is an accountant whose services may be hired on a fee basis by individuals or business firms.

18. **T F** The accounting equation is assets + liabilities = owners' equity.

19. **T F** Marketable securities can be converted into cash in a matter of days.

20. **T F** Stockholders' equity represents the total value of a corporation's stock plus retained earnings that have accumulated to date.

Multiple-Choice Questions

21. _____ Which statement is not true about a balance sheet?
    a. It provides proof that Assets = Liabilities + Owners' equity.
    b. It lists the current, fixed, and intangible assets.
    c. It summarizes the firm's revenues and expenses during one accounting period.
    d. It gives the liabilities of the firm.
    e. It shows the owners' equity in the business.

22. _____ The board of directors decided to pay 50 percent of the firm's $460,000 earnings in dividends to the stockholders. The firm has retained earnings of $680,000 on the books. After the dividends are paid, which of the following statements is true about the firm's retained earnings account?
    a. The new value of the firm's retained earnings is $910,000.
    b. The new value of the firm's retained earnings is $450,000.
    c. The firm failed to reach its profit goal.
    d. Each shareholder will receive more than he or she received last year.
    e. The firm's retained earnings are too high.

23. _____ A firm had gross profits from sales in the amount of $180,000, operating expenses of $90,000, and federal incomes taxes of $20,000. What was the firm's net income after taxes?
    a. $10,000
    b. $20,000
    c. $70,000
    d. $90,000
    e. $200,000

24. _____ The Sarbanes–Oxley Act
    a. requires the SEC to establish a federal oversight board for the accounting industry.
    b. requires CEOs to certify periodic financial statements.
    c. subjects auditors, accountants, and employees to imprisonment for destroying financial documents.
    d. prohibits many types of consulting services by accounting firms.
    e. All of the above are true.

25. _____ You are a purchasing manager in a large firm and are responsible for deciding on and ordering the appropriate software program that allows the user to prepare and edit letters and store them on a computer memory stick. Which type of program will you order?
    a. Spreadsheet
    b. Word processing
    c. Graphics
    d. Communications
    e. Database

26. _____ An income statement is sometimes called the
    a. statement of financial position.
    b. owners' equity statement.
    c. earnings statement.
    d. statement of cash inflow.
    e. statement of revenues.

27. _____ When a company reports financial numbers that are lower than expected, generally
    a. the company's stock value will increase.
    b. the company's stock value will decrease.
    c. the company will restate its earnings amount.
    d. the stockholders' will immediately ask for an audit.
    e. the corporate officers will resign and new officers will be appointed.

28. _____ An audit is
    a. performed by the firm's private bookkeepers.
    b. not necessary if the firm used accepted bookkeeping procedures.
    c. required by many lenders who are trying to validate a firm's accounting statements.
    d. a waste of the firm's resources.
    e. a guarantee that a firm hasn't "cooked" the books.

29. _____ Management information systems
    a. collect data, hire personnel, and evaluate workers.
    b. store data, present data to users, and make final decisions.
    c. collect, store, update, process, and present data.
    d. supervise personnel, reprimand workers, and conduct follow-up evaluations.
    e. collect relevant information.

30. _____ As an administrative manager, you must ensure that
    a. information is protected from employees.
    b. information is used in a consistent manner.
    c. the smart group receives the data first.
    d. the promotional campaigns are aired on time.
    e. new product planning is on schedule.

Answers to the Test Yourself questions appear at the end of the book on page TY-2.

Video Case
Making the Numbers or Faking the Numbers?

Will sales and profits meet the expectations of investors and Wall Street analysts? Managers at public corporations must answer this important question quarter after quarter, year after year. In an ideal world—one in which there is never an economic crisis, expenses never go up, and customers never buy competing products—the corporation's price for a share of its stock would soar, and investors would cheer as every financial report showed ever-higher sales revenues, profit margins, and earnings.

In the real world, however, many uncontrollable and unpredictable factors can affect a corporation's performance. Customers may buy fewer units or postpone purchases, competitors may introduce superior products, expenses may rise, interest rates may climb, and buying power may plummet. Faced with the prospect of releasing financial results that fall short of Wall Street's expectations, managers may feel intense pressure to "make the numbers" using a variety of accounting techniques.

For example, executives and board members at Groupon—the premier source for consumers who want to take advantage of daily deals—found itself having to answer difficult questions about how it reported revenues, expenses, and its internal accounting controls. What's worse, the questions came just a few months after it sold stock to the public. As a result of increased scrutiny by both regulators and investors, the company was forced to reexamine its accounting practices and tighten its audit procedures.

Under the Sarbanes–Oxley Act, the CEO and CFO now must certify the corporation's financial reports. (For more information about Sarbanes–Oxley, visit www.aicpa.org, the website of the American Institute of Certified Public Accountants.) Immediately after this legislation became effective, hundreds of companies restated their earnings, a sign that stricter accounting controls were having the intended effect. "I don't mean to sugarcoat the figure on restatements," says Steve Odland, the former CEO of Office Depot, "but I think it is positive—it shows a healthy system." Yet not all earnings restatements are due to accounting irregularities. "The general impression of the public is that accounting rules are black and white," he adds. "They are often anything but

that, and in many instances the changes in earnings came after new interpretations by the chief accountant of the SEC."

Now that stricter regulation has been in force for some time, fewer and fewer corporations are announcing restatements. In fact, the number of corporations restating earnings has declined since it peaked in 2006. The chief reason for the decline is that corporations and their accounting firms have learned to dig deeper and analyze the process used to produce the figures for financial statements, as well as checking the numbers themselves.

Because accounting rules are open to interpretation, managers sometimes find themselves facing ethical dilemmas when a corporation feels pressure to live up to Wall Street's expectations. Consider the hypothetical situation at Commodore Appliances, a fictional company that sells to Home Depot, Lowe's, and other major retail chains. Margaret, the vice president of sales, has told Rob, a district manager, that the company's sales are down 10 percent in the current quarter. She points out that sales in Rob's district are down 20 percent and states that higher-level managers want him to improve this month's figures using "book and hold," which means recording future sales transactions in the current period.

Rob hesitates, saying that the company is gaining market share and that he needs more time to get sales momentum going. He thinks "book and hold" is not a good business practice, even if it is legal. Margaret hints that Rob will lose his job if his sales figures don't look better and stresses that he will need the book-and-hold approach for one month only. Rob realizes that if he doesn't go along, he won't be working at Commodore for very much longer.

Meeting with Kevin, one of Commodore's auditors, Rob learns that book and hold meets GAAPs. Kevin emphasizes that customers must be willing to take title to the goods before they're delivered or billed. Any book-and-hold sales must be real, backed by documentation such as e-mails to and from buyers, and the transactions must be completed in the near future.

Rob is at a crossroads: His sales figures must be higher if Commodore is to achieve its performance targets, yet he doesn't know exactly when (or if) he actually would complete any book-and-hold sales he might report this month. He doesn't want to mislead anyone, but he also doesn't want to lose his job or put other people's jobs in jeopardy by refusing to do what he is being asked to do. Rob is confident that he can improve his district's sales over the long term. However, Commodore's executives are pressuring Rob to make the sales figures look better right now. What should he do?[5]

Questions

1. What are the ethical and legal implications of using accounting practices such as the book-and-hold technique to accelerate revenues and inflate corporate earnings?
2. Why would Commodore's auditor insist that Rob document any sales booked under the book-and-hold technique?
3. If you were in Rob's situation, would you agree to use the book-and-hold technique this month to accelerate revenues? Justify your decision.
4. Imagine that Commodore has taken out a multimillion-dollar loan that must be repaid next year. How might the lender react if it learned that Commodore was using the book-and-hold method to make revenues look higher than they really are?

Building Skills for Career Success

1. Using Social Media

All of the Big Four accounting firms are active on Twitter, as well as posting messages, content, and photos on Facebook, listing job openings on LinkedIn, and posting videos on YouTube. The idea is to connect with clients and potential job candidates, interact with clients and potential clients, engage employees, showcase the firm's expertise, and polish their reputations.

Assignment

1. Choose one of the Big Four accounting firms and take a look at its Twitter, Facebook, LinkedIn, or YouTube websites.
2. How does the accounting firm you chose use social media? Are they trying to reach potential job candidates, existing clients and potential clients, or employees?
3. Do you think that social media is an effective way for an accounting firm to reach the target audience?

2. Building Team Skills

This has been a bad year for Miami-based Park Avenue Furniture. The firm increased sales revenues to $1,400,000, but total expenses ballooned to $1,750,000. Although management realized that some of the firm's expenses were out of control, including cost of goods sold ($700,000), salaries ($450,000), and advertising costs ($140,000), it could not contain expenses. As a result, the furniture retailer lost $350,000. To make matters worse, the retailer applied for a $350,000 loan at Fidelity National Bank and was turned down. The bank officer, Mike Nettles, said that the firm already had too much debt. At that time, liabilities totaled $420,000; owners' equity was $600,000.

Assignment

1. In groups of three or four, analyze the financial condition of Park Avenue Furniture.
2. Discuss why you think the bank officer turned down Park Avenue's loan request.
3. Prepare a detailed plan of action to improve the financial health of Park Avenue Furniture over the next 12 months.

3. Researching Different Careers

To improve productivity, employers expect employees to use computers and computer software. Typical business applications include e-mail, word processing, spreadsheets, and graphics. By improving your skills in these areas, you can increase your chances not only of being employed but also of being promoted once you are employed.

Assignment

1. Assess your computer skills by placing a check in the appropriate column in the following table:

Software	Skill Level			
	None	Low	Average	High
e-Mail				
Word processing				
Desktop publishing				
Accounting				
Database management				
Graphics				
Spreadsheet				
Internet research				

2. Describe your self-assessment in a written report. Specify the skills in which you need to become more proficient, and outline a plan for doing this.

Endnotes

1. Based on information in Doug Tsuruoka, "Intuit on Track for Double-Digit FY '13 Growth: CFO," *Investor's Business Daily*, November 19, 2012, http://investors.com; R. Wang, "How Intuit Uses Cloud Computing," *Forbes*, February 9, 2012, www.forbes.com; Chris Kanaracus, "Intuit Ties QuickBooks to Demandforce marketing software," *PC World*, November 1, 2012, www.pcworld.com; www.intuit.com.

2. John Smith, EU's McCreevy, IASB's Smith on Financial Reporting in a Changing World FEI Financial Reporting Blog website at http://financailexecutives.blogspot.com, accessed May 8, 2009.

3. "Summary of the Provisions of the Sarbanes–Oxley Act of 2002," the AICPA website at www.aicpa.org, accessed January 23, 2013.

4. *Occupational Outlook Handbook*, The U.S. Bureau of Labor Statistics website at www.bls.gov/oco/ocos001.htm, accessed January 23, 2013.

5. Based on information from Jonathon Weil, "Groupon IPO Scandal Is the Sleaze that's Legal," the Bloomberg website at www.bloomberg.com, accessed April 4, 2012; Walter Pavlo, "Groupon Accounting Scandal, and We're Surprised," the Forbes website at www.forbes.com, accessed April 3, 2012; The Office Depot website at www.officedepot.com, accessed April 12, 2012; Matt Krantz, "Companies Are Making Fewer Accounting Mistakes," *USA Today*, March 1, 2010, www.usatoday.com; Jane Sasseen, "White-Collar Crime: Who Does Time?" *BusinessWeek*, February 6, 2006, www.businessweek.com; Stephen Labaton, "Four Years Later, Enron's Shadow Lingers as Change Comes Slowly," *New York Times*, January 5, 2006, C1; *Making the Numbers at Commodore Appliance* (Cengage video).

© RED-FENIKS/SHUTTERSTOCK.COM

Chapter 16

Mastering Financial Management

Why Should You Care?

The old saying goes, "Money makes the world go around." For business firms, this is true. It's hard to operate a business without money. In this chapter, we discuss how financial management is used to obtain money and ensure that it is used effectively.

Learning Objectives

Once you complete this chapter, you will be able to:

1 Understand why financial management is important in today's uncertain economy.

2 Identify a firm's short- and long-term financial needs.

3 Summarize the process of planning for financial management.

4 Identify the services provided by banks and financial institutions for their business customers.

5 Describe the advantages and disadvantages of different methods of short-term debt financing.

6 Evaluate the advantages and disadvantages of equity financing.

7 Evaluate the advantages and disadvantages of long-term debt financing.

How Cisco Finances Future Growth

Founded in 1984 to make switches and routers for computer systems, Cisco Systems (www.cisco.com) approaches its fourth decade in business with billions of dollars on hand to fuel plans for future growth. The company sells networking gear, software, and services in over 160 countries, employing 67,000 people and ringing up $46 billion in annual revenue.

One way Cisco maintains its market leadership in the fast-paced technology industry is by investing more than $5 billion, year after year, to research and develop innovative products and processes for Internet-based communication and collaboration. As a result, Cisco files for hundreds of patents each year, a key element in its strategy for ongoing success. The company also buys companies to strengthen or complement its position in key areas. Not long ago, it acquired NDS Group, to profit from the boom in digital delivery of television programming across multiple devices. Earlier, it had acquired WebEx, which offers web-based conferencing services, to accelerate expansion in the fast-growing market for online collaboration.

How does Cisco find the billions it needs for R&D and acquisitions every year? First, it always keeps money in the bank, as well as marketable securities it can convert into cash on short notice as needed. Second, the company sometimes uses long-term debt financing to raise money. Since it became a publicly traded corporation in 1990, Cisco has issued corporate bonds only four times. Most recently, it sold $4 billion worth of unsecured bonds at historically low interest rates, knowing that the cost of borrowing was inexpensive enough to justify taking on repayments for up to six years. The company used some of that money to buy back shares of its common stock, which were trading at low prices during the recent period of economic turmoil. By taking good care of its financial situation today, Cisco will be ready for the challenges and opportunities of growth in the future.[1]

Did You Know?

Cisco is a global powerhouse in networking technology, with $46 billion in annual revenue and 67,000 employees in over 160 countries.

Question: How important is financial management for a business firm like Cisco Systems—the company profiled in the Inside Business feature for this chapter?

Answer: Very Important! Without financial management the company would not be able to pay its bills, fund the research needed to develop new products and services, and acquire other companies to maintain its market leadership. And without financial management, a business firm would not be able to borrow money (debt capital) or obtain money from stockholders (equity capital). The fact is that finances are necessary for the efficient operation of any business firm. Without money, creditors and lenders can't be paid, employees don't get paychecks, and the business may close its doors and cease to exist. On the other hand, when a company—like Cisco Systems—manages its finances it can not only pay its bills and employees, but can grow and expand in order to meet the needs of its customers and society.

In this chapter we examine why financial management is important. Then, we discuss how firms find the financing required to meet two needs of all business organizations: the need for money to start a business and keep it going, and the need to manage that money effectively. We also look at how firms develop financial plans and evaluate financial performance. Then we examine typical banking services and compare various methods of obtaining short-term and long-term financing.

WHY FINANCIAL MANAGEMENT?

Learning Objective

1 Understand why financial management is important in today's uncertain economy.

Financial management can make the difference between success and failure for both large and small businesses. For example, executives at Ford used aggressive financial planning to anticipate the automaker's need for financing during the recent economic crisis. To avoid the same fate as General Motors and Chrysler—bankruptcy—Ford's financial managers borrowed money in anticipation

CHRIS HOWES/WILD PLACES PHOTOGRAPHY/ALAMY

How do managers decide how much inventory is needed? One of the most perplexing problems financial managers must deal with is the amount of inventory a retail store needs. If a retailer has too much inventory, then too much money is tied up in merchandise that is not selling. If a retailer has too little inventory, it may not have enough merchandise to meet consumer demand.

of a downturn in the company's sales and profits. Ford also sold both stocks and bonds to raise the money it needed to keep the company operating during the crisis and even build for the future. Did that financial plan work? The answer: A definite yes! Today, Ford is selling more cars, developing environmentally friendly engines, creating concept cars for the future, and has returned to profitability.

Managers and employees must find the money needed to keep a business operating and pay lenders and suppliers, employees, and fund all the goals and objectives that a successful business wants to achieve. A business that cannot pay its bills may have to close its doors and even be forced to file for bankruptcy protection. Fortunately, the number of business firms filing for bankruptcy has decreased when compared to the large number of firms filing bankruptcy during the worst part of the recent economic crisis, as illustrated in Figure 16-1. And now that the nation's economy is improving, the number of bankruptcies should continue to decline.

The Need for Financial Management

financial management all the activities concerned with obtaining money and using it effectively

Financial management consists of all the activities concerned with obtaining money and using it effectively. To some extent, financial management can be viewed as a two-sided problem. On one side, the uses of funds often dictate the type or types of financing needed by a business. On the other side, the activities a business can undertake are determined by the types of financing available. Financial managers must ensure that funds are available when needed, that they are obtained at the lowest

FIGURE 16-1 Business Bankruptcies in the United States

The number of businesses that filed for bankruptcy increased during the economic crisis. (*Note*: At the time of publication, 2012 was the most recent year for which complete statistics were available.)

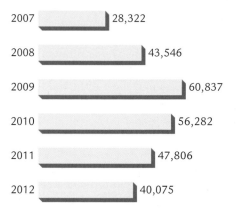

Year	
2007	28,322
2008	43,546
2009	60,837
2010	56,282
2011	47,806
2012	40,075

Source: Based on The American Bankruptcy Institute website at www.abiworld.org (accessed June 11, 2013).

possible cost, and that they are used as efficiently as possible. In addition, proper financial management must also ensure that:

- Financing priorities are established in line with organizational goals and objectives.
- Spending is planned and controlled.
- Sufficient financing is available when it is needed, both now and in the future.
- A firm's credit customers pay their bills on time, and the number of past due accounts is reduced.
- Bills are paid promptly to protect the firm's credit rating and its ability to borrow money.
- The funds required for paying the firm's taxes are available when needed to meet tax deadlines.
- Excess cash is invested in certificates of deposit (CDs), government securities, or conservative, marketable securities.

Financial Reform After the Economic Crisis

The job of financial managers became a bit easier as the economy stabilized. Still, it became apparent that something needed to be done to stabilize the financial system and prevent future economic meltdowns. In the wake of the crisis that affected both business firms and individuals, a cry for more regulations and reforms became a high priority. To meet this need, President Obama signed the Dodd–Frank Wall Street Reform and Consumer Protection Act into law on July 21, 2010. Even with the new regulations, some experts say the law did not go far enough while others argue it went too far. Although the U.S. Senate and House of Representatives debate additional regulations, the goals are to hold Wall Street firms accountable for their actions, end taxpayer bailouts, tighten regulations for major financial firms, and increase government oversight. There has also been debate about limiting the amount of executive pay and bonuses, limiting the size of the largest financial firms, and curbing speculative investment techniques that were used by banks before the crisis.

New regulations will also protect American families from unfair, abusive financial and banking practices. For business firms, the impact of new regulations could increase the time and cost of obtaining both short- and long-term financing.

Careers in Finance

A career in finance can be rewarding. As an added bonus, the Bureau of Labor Statistics projects there will be about a 9 percent increase in the number of jobs in the financial sector of the economy between now and 2020.[2]

Today, there are many different types of positions in finance. At the executive level, most large business firms have a chief financial officer for financial management. A **chief financial officer (CFO)** is a high-level corporate executive who manages a firm's finances and reports directly to the company's chief executive officer or president. Some firms prefer to use the titles vice president of financial management, treasurer, or controller instead of the CFO title for executive-level positions in the finance area.

Although some executives in finance do make $300,000 a year or more, many entry-level and lower-level positions that pay quite a bit less are available. Banks, insurance companies, and investment firms obviously have a need for workers who can manage and analyze financial data. So do businesses involved in manufacturing, services, and marketing. Colleges and universities, not-for-profit organizations, and government entities at all levels also need finance workers.

People in finance must have certain traits and skills. One of the most important priorities for someone interested in a finance career is honesty. Be warned: Investors, lenders, and other corporate executives expect financial managers to be above

chief financial officer (CFO) a high-level corporate executive who manages a firm's finances and reports directly to the company's chief executive officer or president

reproach. Moreover, both federal and state government entities have enacted legislation to ensure that corporate financial statements reflect the "real" status of a firm's financial position. In addition to honesty, managers and employees in the finance area must:

1. Have a strong background in accounting or mathematics.
2. Know how to use a computer to analyze data.
3. Be an expert at both written and oral communication.

Typical job titles in finance include bank officer, consumer credit officer, financial analyst, financial planner, loan officer, insurance analyst, and investment account executive. Depending on qualifications, work experience, and education, starting salaries generally begin at $25,000 to $35,000 a year, but it is not uncommon for college graduates to earn higher salaries. In addition to salary, many employees have attractive benefits and other perks that make a career in financial management attractive.

Concept Check

✓ For a business firm, what type of activities does financial management involve?

✓ How has financial management changed after the recent economic crisis?

✓ To be successful, what traits and skills does an employee in the finance industry need?

Learning Objective

2 **Identify a firm's short- and long-term financial needs.**

short-term financing money that will be used for one year or less

cash flow the movement of money into and out of an organization

THE NEED FOR FINANCING

Money is needed both to start a business and to keep it going. The original investment of the owners, along with money they may have borrowed, should be enough to open the doors. After that, ideally sales revenues should be used to pay the firm's expenses and provide a profit as well.

This is exactly what happens in a successful firm—over the long run. However, income and expenses may vary from month to month or from year to year. Temporary financing may be needed when expenses are high or sales are low. Then, too, situations such as the opportunity to purchase a new facility or expand an existing plant may require more money than is currently available within a firm.

Short-Term Financing

Short-term financing is money that will be used for one year or less. As illustrated in Table 16-1, there are many short-term financing needs, but three deserve special attention. First, certain business practices may affect a firm's cash flow and create a need for short-term financing. **Cash flow** is the movement of money into and out of an organization. The goal is to have sufficient money coming into the firm in any period to cover the firm's expenses during that period. This goal, however, is not always achieved. For example, California-based Callaway Golf offers credit to retailers and wholesalers that carry the firm's golf clubs, balls, clothing, and golf accessories. Credit purchases made by Callaway's retailers generally are not paid until 30 to 60 days (or more) after the transaction. Callaway therefore may need short-term financing to pay its bills until its customers have paid theirs.

A second major need for short-term financing is speculative production. **Speculative production** refers to the time lag between the actual production of goods and when the goods are sold. Consider what happens when a firm such as Connecticut-based Stanley Black & Decker begins to manufacture power and small hand tools for sale during the Christmas season. Manufacturing begins in

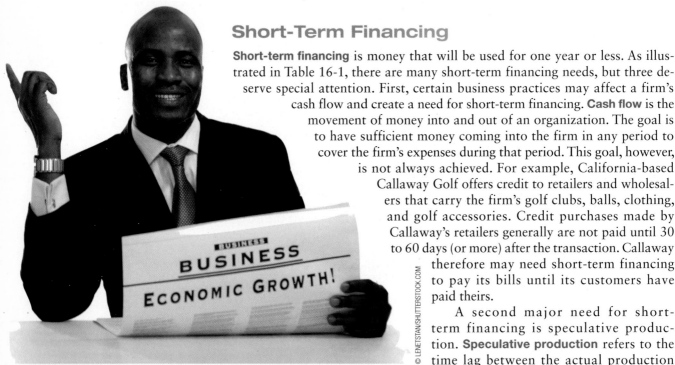

© LENETSTAN/SHUTTERSTOCK.COM

A career in finance can mean more than money! While most people think a job in finance is all about "money," there are other attractive perks and benefits. According to the U.S. Bureau of Labor Statistics, jobs in finance are expected to increase about 9 percent between now and the year 2020. And there are finance jobs in all-types of companies, schools and universities, not-for-profit organizations, and government entities. You could even become a financial planner and help people manage their money.

TABLE 16-1 Comparison of Short- and Long-Term Financing

Whether a business seeks short- or long-term financing depends on what the money will be used for.	
Corporate Cash Needs	
Short-Term Financing Needs	**Long-Term Financing Needs**
Cash-flow problems	Business start-up costs
Speculative production	Mergers and acquisitions
Current inventory needs	New product development
Monthly expenses	Long-term marketing activities
Short-term promotional needs	Replacement of equipment
Unexpected emergencies	Expansion of facilities

© CENGAGE LEARNING 2015

March, April, and May, and the firm negotiates short-term financing to buy materials and supplies, to pay wages and rent, and to cover inventory costs until its products eventually are sold to wholesalers and retailers later in the year. Take a look at Figure 16-2. Although Stanley Black & Decker manufactures and sells finished products all during the year, expenses peak during the first part of the year. During this same period, sales revenues are low. Once the firm's finished products are shipped to retailers and wholesalers and payment is received (usually within 30 to 60 days), sales revenues are used to repay short-term financing.

A third need for short-term financing is to increase inventory. Retailers that range in size from Walmart to the neighborhood drugstore need short-term financing to build up their inventories before peak selling periods. For example, Dallas-based Bruce Miller Nurseries must increase the number of shrubs, trees, and flowering plants that it makes available for sale during the spring and

speculative production the time lag between the actual production of goods and when the goods are sold

FIGURE 16-2 Cash Flow for a Manufacturing Business

Manufacturers such as Stanley Black & Decker often use short-term financing to pay expenses during the production process. Once goods are shipped to retailers and wholesalers and payment is received, sales revenues are used to repay short-term financing.

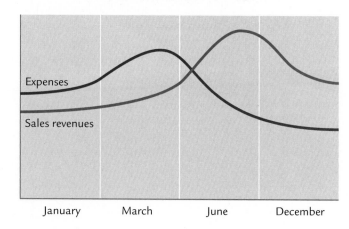

© CENGAGE LEARNING 2015

long-term financing money that will be used for longer than one year

Business success often begins with a financial plan. Before the merchandise in this IKEA warehouse can be sold, it must be purchased from manufacturers or suppliers and then stored until it is needed in the retailer's stores. *Successful* businesses often use sound financial planning built on the firm's goals and objectives, different types of budgets, and available sources of funds to make sure financing is available to purchase inventory and other necessities needed to operate a business.

summer growing seasons. To obtain this merchandise inventory from growers or wholesalers, it uses short-term financing and repays the loans when the merchandise is sold.

Long-Term Financing

Long-term financing is money that will be used for longer than one year. Long-term financing obviously is needed to start a new business. As Table 16-1 shows, it is also needed for business mergers and acquisitions, new product development, long-term marketing activities, replacement of equipment that has become obsolete, and expansion of facilities.

The amounts of long-term financing needed by large firms can seem almost unreal. The 3M Company—a large multinational corporation known for research and development—spent $1.6 billion in 2012 and has invested more than $7 billion over the last five years to develop new products designed to make people's lives easier and safer.[3]

The Risk–Return Ratio

According to financial experts, business firms will find it more difficult to raise both short- and long-term financing in the future for two reasons. First, financial reform and increased regulations will lengthen the process required to obtain financing. Second, both lenders and investors are more cautious about who receives financing. As a result of these two factors, financial managers must develop a strong financial plan that describes how the money will be used and how it will be repaid.

RANDY DUCHAINE/ALAMY

When developing a financial plan for a business, a financial manager must also consider the risk–return ratio when making decisions that affect the firm's finances. The **risk–return ratio** is based on the principle that a high-risk decision should generate higher financial returns for a business. On the other hand, more conservative decisions (with less risk) often generate lesser returns. Although financial managers want higher returns, they often must strive for a balance between risk and return. For example, Ohio-based American Electric Power may consider investing millions of dollars to fund research into new solar technology that could enable the company to use the sun to generate electrical power. Yet, financial managers (along with other managers throughout the organization) must determine the potential return before committing to such a costly research project.

Concept Check

✓ How does short-term financing differ from long-term financing? Give two business uses for each type of financing.

✓ What is speculative production? How is it related to a firm's cash-flow problems?

PLANNING—THE BASIS OF SOUND FINANCIAL MANAGEMENT

Learning Objective

3 Summarize the process of planning for financial management.

In Chapter 6, we defined a *plan* as an outline of the actions by which an organization intends to accomplish its goals and objectives. A **financial plan**, then, is a plan for obtaining and using the money needed to implement an organization's goals and objectives.

risk–return ratio a ratio based on the principle that a high-risk decision should generate higher financial returns for a business and more conservative decisions often generate lower returns

Developing the Financial Plan

Financial planning (like all planning) begins with establishing a set of valid goals and objectives. Financial managers must then determine how much money is needed to accomplish each goal and objective. Finally, financial managers must identify available sources of financing and decide which to use. The three steps involved in financial planning are illustrated in Figure 16-3.

financial plan a plan for obtaining and using the money needed to implement an organization's goals and objectives

FIGURE 16-3 The Three Steps of Financial Planning

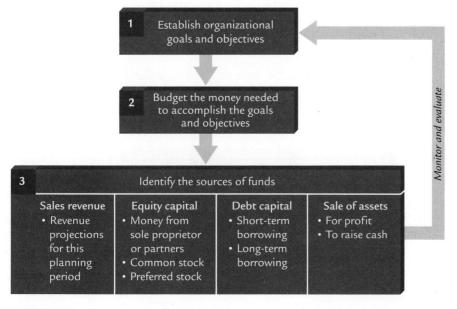

After a financial plan has been developed, it must be monitored continually to ensure that it actually fulfills the firm's goals.

1. Establish organizational goals and objectives

2. Budget the money needed to accomplish the goals and objectives

3. Identify the sources of funds

Sales revenue	Equity capital	Debt capital	Sale of assets
• Revenue projections for this planning period	• Money from sole proprietor or partners • Common stock • Preferred stock	• Short-term borrowing • Long-term borrowing	• For profit • To raise cash

Monitor and evaluate

© CENGAGE LEARNING 2015

ESTABLISHING ORGANIZATIONAL GOALS AND OBJECTIVES As pointed out in Chapter 6, a *goal* is an end result that an organization expects to achieve over a one- to ten-year period. An *objective* was defined in Chapter 6 as a specific statement detailing what an organization intends to accomplish over a shorter period of time. If goals and objectives are not specific and measurable, they cannot be translated into dollar costs, and financial planning cannot proceed. For large corporations, both goals and objectives can be expensive. For example, have you ever wondered how much McDonald's spends on advertising? Well, to reach the nearly 69 million customers it serves each day in 119 countries, the world's most famous fast-food restaurant chain spends over $768 million each year.[4]

budget a financial statement that projects income, expenditures, or both over a specified future period

cash budget a financial statement that estimates cash receipts and cash expenditures over a specified period

BUDGETING FOR FINANCIAL NEEDS Once planners know what the firm's goals and objectives are for a specific period—say, the next calendar year—they can construct a budget that projects the costs the firm will incur and the sales revenues it will receive. Specifically, a **budget** is a financial statement that projects income, expenditures, or both over a specified future period.

Usually, the budgeting process begins with the construction of departmental budgets for sales and various types of expenses. Financial managers can easily combine each department's budget for sales and expenses into a company-wide cash budget. A **cash budget** estimates cash receipts and cash expenditures over a specified period. Notice in the cash budget for Stars and Stripes Clothing, shown in Figure 16-4, cash sales and collections are listed at the top for each calendar quarter. Payments for purchases and routine expenses are listed in the middle section. Using this information, it is possible to calculate the anticipated cash gain or loss at the end of each quarter for this retail clothing store.

Most firms today use one of two approaches to budgeting. In the *traditional* approach, each new budget is based on the dollar amounts contained in the budget for the preceding year. These amounts are modified to reflect any revised goals, and managers are required to justify only new expenditures. The problem with this approach is that it leaves room for padding budget items to protect the (sometimes selfish) interests of the manager or his or her department.

FIGURE 16-4 Cash Budget for Stars and Stripes Clothing

A company-wide cash budget projects sales, collections, purchases, and expenses over a specified period to anticipate cash surpluses and deficits.

STARS AND STRIPES CLOTHING
Cash Budget   From January 1, 2013 to December 31, 2013

	First Quarter ($)	Second Quarter ($)	Third Quarter ($)	Fourth Quarter ($)	Total ($)
Cash sales and collections	150,000	160,000	150,000	185,000	645,000
Less payments					
Purchases	110,000	80,000	90,000	60,000	340,000
Wages/salaries	25,000	20,000	25,000	30,000	100,000
Rent	10,000	10,000	12,000	12,000	44,000
Other expenses	4,000	4,000	5,000	6,000	19,000
Taxes	8,000	8,000	10,000	10,000	36,000
Total payments	157,000	122,000	142,000	118,000	539,000
Cash gain or (loss)	(7,000)	38,000	8,000	67,000	106,000

This problem is essentially eliminated through zero-base budgeting. **Zero-base budgeting** is a budgeting approach in which every expense in every budget must be justified.

To develop a plan for long-term financing needs, managers often construct a capital budget. A **capital budget** estimates a firm's expenditures for major assets, including new product development, expansion of facilities, replacement of obsolete equipment, and mergers and acquisitions. For example, 3G Capital Management and Berkshire Hathaway purchased Heinz—a company known for manufacturing ketchup. Berkshire Hathaway, a company known for purchasing well-managed and innovative companies, constructed a capital budget to determine the best way to finance its part of the $28 billion 2013 acquisition.[5]

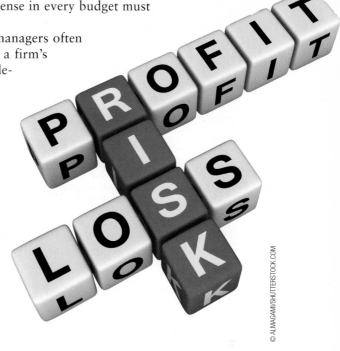

© ALMAGAMI/SHUTTERSTOCK.COM

IDENTIFYING SOURCES OF FUNDS The four primary sources of funds, listed in Figure 16-3, are sales revenue, equity capital, debt capital, and proceeds from the sale of assets. Future sales revenue generally provides the greatest part of a firm's financing. Figure 16-4 shows that for Stars and Stripes Clothing, sales for the year are expected to cover all expenses and to provide a cash gain of $106,000. However, Stars and Stripes has a problem in the first quarter, when sales are expected to fall short of expenses by $7,000. In fact, one of the primary reasons for financial planning is to provide management with adequate lead time to solve this type of cash-flow problem.

A second type of funding is **equity capital**. For a sole proprietorship or partnership, equity capital is provided by the owner or owners of the business. For a corporation, equity capital is money obtained from the sale of shares of ownership in the business. Equity capital is used almost exclusively for long-term financing.

A third type of funding is **debt capital**, which is borrowed money. Debt capital may be borrowed for either short- or long-term use—and a short-term loan seems made to order for Stars and Stripes Clothing's shortfall problem. The firm probably would borrow the needed $7,000 (or perhaps a bit more) at some point during the first quarter and repay it from second-quarter sales revenue.

Proceeds from the sale of assets are the fourth type of funding. Selling assets is a drastic step. However, it may be a reasonable last resort when sales revenues are declining and equity capital or debt capital cannot be found. Assets also may be sold to increase a firm's cash balance or when they are no longer needed or do not "fit" with the company's core business. In 2012, Citigroup, one of the world's largest financial institutions, agreed to sell its part in India's Housing Development Finance Corporation for $2 billion. Citigroup will use the cash it receives from the sale to meet increased capital requirements required by government regulators.[6]

Monitoring and Evaluating Financial Performance

It is important to ensure that financial plans are implemented properly and to catch potential problems before they become major ones. Despite efforts to raise additional financing, reduce expenses, increase sales to become profitable, and negotiate a new labor agreement with the union representing employees, Hostess Brands—the maker of Twinkies and Wonder Bread—shut down all operations in late 2012. Eventually, the firm's assets were sold in order to pay creditors and lenders.[7]

zero-base budgeting a budgeting approach in which every expense in every budget must be justified

capital budget a financial statement that estimates a firm's expenditures for major assets and its long-term financing needs

equity capital money received from the owners or from the sale of shares of ownership in a business

debt capital borrowed money obtained through loans of various types

Concept Check

✓ What is the function of a cash budget? A capital budget?

✓ What is the difference between equity capital and debt capital?

✓ Describe the four sources of funds for a business.

✓ How does a financial manager monitor and evaluate a firm's financing?

To prevent such problems, financial managers should establish a means of monitoring financial performance. Interim budgets (weekly, monthly, or quarterly) may be prepared for comparison purposes. These comparisons point up areas that require additional or revised planning—or at least areas calling for a more careful investigation. Budget comparisons can also be used to improve the firm's future budgets.

Learning Objective

4 Identify the services provided by banks and financial institutions for their business customers.

FINANCIAL SERVICES PROVIDED BY BANKS AND OTHER FINANCIAL INSTITUTIONS

For a business owner, it helps to know your banker. Banking services can be divided into three broad categories: traditional services, electronic banking services, and international services.

Traditional Banking Services for Business Clients

Traditional services provided by banks and other financial institutions include savings and checking accounts, loans, processing credit- and debit-card transactions, and providing professional advice.

SAVINGS AND CHECKING ACCOUNTS Savings accounts provide a safe place to store money and a very conservative means of investing. The usual *passbook savings account* earns between 0.10 and 0.50 percent in banks and savings and loan associations (S&Ls) and slightly more in credit unions. A business with excess cash it is willing to leave on deposit with a bank for a set period of time can earn a higher rate of interest. To do so, the business firm buys a certificate of deposit. A **certificate of deposit (CD)** is a document stating that the bank will pay the depositor a guaranteed interest rate on money left on deposit for a specified period of time. At the time of publication, CDs were paying between 0.30 and 1 percent. The rate can vary depending on the financial institution and the amount of time until maturity.

Business firms (and individuals) also deposit money in checking accounts so that they can write checks to pay for purchases. A **check** is a written order for a bank or other financial institution to pay a stated dollar amount to the business or person indicated on the face of the check. For businesses, monthly charges are based on the average daily balance in the checking account and/or the number of checks written.

BUSINESS LOANS Banks, savings and loan associations, credit unions, and other financial institutions provide short- and long-term loans to businesses. *Short-term business loans* must be repaid within one year or less. Typical uses for the money obtained through short-term loans include solving cash-flow problems, purchasing inventory, and meeting unexpected emergencies. To help ensure that short-term money will be available when needed, many firms establish a line of credit. A **line of credit** is a loan that is approved before the money is actually needed. Because all the necessary paperwork is already completed and the loan is preapproved, the business can obtain the money later without delay, as soon as it is required. Even with a line of credit, a firm may not be able to borrow money if the bank does not have sufficient funds available. For this reason, some firms prefer a **revolving credit agreement**, which is a guaranteed line of credit. Under this type of agreement, the bank guarantees that the money will be available when the borrower needs it. In return for the guarantee, the bank charges a commitment fee ranging from 0.25 to

certificate of deposit (CD) A document stating that the bank will pay the depositor a guaranteed interest rate on money left on deposit for a specified period of time

check a written order for a bank or other financial institution to pay a stated dollar amount to the business or person indicated on the face of the check

line of credit a loan that is approved before the money is actually needed

revolving credit agreement a guaranteed line of credit

1.0 percent of the *unused* portion of the revolving credit agreement. The usual interest is charged for the portion that *is* borrowed.

Long-term business loans are repaid over a period of years. The average length of a long-term business loan is generally 3 to 7 years but sometimes as long as 15 to 20 years. Long-term loans are used most often to finance the expansion of buildings and retail facilities, mergers and acquisitions, replacement of equipment, or product development. Most lenders require some type of collateral for long-term loans. **Collateral** is real estate or property (e.g., stocks, bonds, equipment, or any other asset of value) pledged as security for a loan.

Repayment terms and interest rates for both short- and long-term loans are arranged between the lender and the borrower. For businesses, repayment terms may include monthly, quarterly, semiannual, or annual payments.

THE BASICS OF GETTING A LOAN According to many financial experts, preparation is the key when applying for a business loan. In reality, preparation begins before you ever apply for the loan. To begin the process, you should get to know potential lenders before requesting debt financing. Although there may be many potential lenders that can provide the money you need, the logical place to borrow money is where your business does its banking. This fact underscores the importance of maintaining adequate balances in the firm's bank accounts. Before applying for a loan, you may also want to check your firm's credit rating with a national credit bureau such as D&B (formerly known as Dun & Bradstreet). Typically, business owners will be asked to fill out a loan application. In addition to the loan application, the lender will also want to see your current business plan. Be sure to explain what your business is, how much funding you require to accomplish your goals, and how the loan will be repaid. Most lenders insist that you submit current financial statements that have been prepared by an independent certified public accountant. Then compile a list of references that includes your suppliers, other lenders, or the professionals with whom you are associated. You may also be asked to discuss the loan request with a loan officer. Hopefully, your loan request will be approved. If not, try to determine why your loan request was rejected. Think back over the loan process and determine what you could do to improve your chances of getting a loan the next time you apply.

RICHARD LEVINE/ALAMY

Even "big" banks want more customers. Bank of America, one of the largest bank in the United States, still wants your business. Like many competitors, the bank offers cash back, competitive rates for savings and loans, online banking, and many other services to attract new customers. Check out the latest promotions at www.bankofamerica.com.

collateral real estate or property pledged as security for a loan

Why Has the Use of Credit Transactions Increased?

At the beginning of 2013, it was estimated that 160 million Americans use their credit cards to pay for everything from tickets on American Airlines to Zebco fishing gear.[8] Why have credit cards become so popular? For a merchant, the answer is obvious. By depositing charge slips in a bank or other financial institution, the merchant can convert credit-card sales into cash. In return for processing the merchant's credit-card transactions, the financial institution charges a fee that generally ranges between 1.5 and 4 percent. Typically, small, independent businesses pay more than larger stores or chain stores. Let's assume that you use a Visa credit card to purchase a microwave oven for $300 from Gold Star Appliances, a small retailer in Richardson, Texas. At the end of the day, the retailer deposits your charge slip, along with other charge slips, checks, and currency collected during the day, at its bank. If the bank charges Gold Star Appliances 4 percent to process each credit-card transaction, the bank deducts a processing fee of $12 ($300 × 0.04 = $12) for the customer's credit-card transaction and immediately deposits the remainder ($288) in Gold Star Appliances' account. The number of credit-card transactions, the total dollar amount of credit sales, and how well the merchant can negotiate the fees the financial institution charges determine actual fees.

Do not confuse debit cards with credit cards. Although they may look alike, there are important differences. A **debit card** electronically subtracts the amount of a customer's purchase from her or his bank account at the moment the purchase is made. (By contrast, when you use your credit card, the credit-card company extends short-term financing, and you do not make payment until you receive your next statement.) At the beginning of 2013, approximately 190 million Americans had at least one debit card.[9] Debit cards are used most commonly to obtain cash at automatic teller machines (ATMs) and to purchase products and services from retailers.

Electronic Banking Services

An **electronic funds transfer (EFT) system** is a means of performing financial transactions through a computer terminal. The following four EFT applications are changing how banks help firms do business:

1. *Automatic teller machines (ATMs).* An ATM is an electronic bank teller—a machine that provides almost any service a human teller can provide. Once the customer is properly identified, the machine dispenses cash from the customer's checking or savings account or makes a cash advance charged to a credit card. ATMs are located in bank parking lots, supermarkets, drugstores, and even gas stations. Customers have access to them at all times of the day or night. There may be a fee for each transaction.

2. *Automated clearinghouses (ACHs).* Designed to reduce the number of paper checks, automated clearinghouses process checks, recurring bill payments, Social Security benefits, and employee salaries. For example, large companies use the ACH network to transfer wages and salaries directly into their employees' bank accounts, thus eliminating the need to make out individual paychecks.

3. *Point-of-sale (POS) terminals.* A POS terminal is a computerized cash register located in a retail store and connected to a bank's computer. Assume you want to pay for purchases at a Walmart Supercenter. You begin the process by pulling your bank credit or debit card through a magnetic card reader. A central processing center notifies a computer at your bank that you want to make a purchase. The bank's computer immediately adds the amount to your account for a credit-card transaction. In a similar process, the bank's computer deducts the amount of the purchase from your bank account if you use a debit card. Finally, the amount of your purchase is added to the store's account. The Walmart store then is notified that the transaction is complete, and the cash register prints out your receipt.

4. *Electronic check conversion (ECC).* Electronic check conversion is a process used to convert information from a paper check into an electronic payment for merchandise, services, or bills. When you give your completed check to a store cashier at a Best Buy store, the check is processed through an electronic system that captures your banking information and the dollar amount of the check. Once the check is processed, you are asked to sign a receipt, and you get a voided (canceled) check back for your records. Finally, the funds to pay for your transaction are transferred into the business firm's account. ECC also can be used for checks you mail to pay for a purchase or to pay on an account.

Bankers and business owners generally are pleased with EFT systems. EFTs are fast, and they eliminate the costly processing of checks. However, some customers are reluctant to use online banking or EFT systems. Some simply do not like "the technology," whereas others fear that the computer will garble their accounts.

debit card a card that electronically subtracts the amount of a customer's purchase from her or his bank account at the moment the purchase is made

electronic funds transfer (EFT) system a means of performing financial transactions through a computer terminal

Early on, in 1978, Congress responded to such fears by passing the Electronic Funds Transfer Act, which protects the customer in case the bank makes an error or the customer's credit or debit card is stolen.

International Banking Services

For international businesses, banking services are extremely important. Depending on the needs of an international firm, a bank can help by providing a letter of credit or a banker's acceptance.

A **letter of credit** is a legal document issued by a bank or other financial institution guaranteeing to pay a seller a stated amount for a specified period of time—usually thirty to sixty days. (With a letter of credit, certain conditions, such as delivery of the merchandise, may be specified before payment is made.)

A **banker's acceptance** is a written order for a bank to pay a third party a stated amount of money on a specific date. (With a banker's acceptance, no conditions are specified. It is simply an order to pay without any strings attached.)

Both a letter of credit and a banker's acceptance are popular methods of paying for import and export transactions. Imagine that you are a business owner in the United States who wants to purchase some leather products from a small business in Florence, Italy. You offer to pay for the merchandise with your company's check drawn on an American bank, but the Italian business owner is worried about payment. To solve the problem, your bank can issue either a letter of credit or a banker's acceptance to guarantee that payment will be made. In addition to a letter of credit and a banker's acceptance, banks also can use EFT technology to speed international banking transactions.

One other international banking service should be noted. Banks and other financial institutions provide for currency exchange. If you place an order for Japanese merchandise valued at $50,000, how do you pay for the order? Do you use U.S. dollars or Japanese yen? To solve this problem, you can use the bank's currency-exchange service. To make payment, you can use either currency, and if necessary, the bank will exchange one currency for the other to complete your transaction.

letter of credit a legal document issued by a bank or other financial institution guaranteeing to pay a seller a stated amount for a specified period of time

banker's acceptance a written order for a bank to pay a third party a stated amount of money on a specific state

Concept Check

✓ Describe the traditional banking services provided by financial institutions.

✓ What are the major advantages of electronic banking services?

✓ How can a bank or other financial institution help American businesses to compete in the global marketplace?

SOURCES OF SHORT-TERM DEBT FINANCING

The decision to borrow money does not necessarily mean that a firm is in financial trouble. On the contrary, astute financial management often means regular, responsible borrowing of many different kinds to meet different needs. In this section, we examine the sources of *short-term debt financing* available to businesses. In the next two sections, we look at long-term financing options: equity capital and debt capital.

Learning Objective

5 **Describe the advantages and disadvantages of different methods of short-term debt financing.**

Sources of Unsecured Short-Term Financing

Short-term debt financing is usually easier to obtain than long-term debt financing for three reasons:

1. For the lender, the shorter repayment period means less risk of nonpayment.
2. The dollar amounts of short-term loans are usually smaller than those of long-term loans.
3. A close working relationship normally exists between the short-term borrower and the lender.

Most lenders do not require collateral for short-term financing. If they do, it is usually because they are concerned about the size of a particular loan, the borrowing firm's poor credit rating, or the general prospects of repayment. Remember in the last section that *collateral* was defined as real estate or property pledged as security for a loan.

Unsecured financing is financing that is not backed by collateral. A company seeking unsecured short-term financing has several options.

TRADE CREDIT Manufacturers and wholesalers often provide financial aid to retailers by allowing them 30 to 60 days (or more) in which to pay for merchandise. This delayed payment, known as **trade credit**, is a type of short-term financing extended by a seller who does not require immediate payment after delivery of merchandise. It is the most popular form of short-term financing, because most manufacturers and wholesalers do not charge interest for trade credit. In fact, from 70 to 90 percent of all transactions between businesses involve some trade credit.

Let us assume that Discount Tire Stores receives a shipment of tires from a manufacturer. Along with the merchandise, the manufacturer sends an invoice that states the terms of payment. Discount Tire now has two options for payment. First, the retailer may pay the invoice promptly and take advantage of any cash discount the manufacturer offers. Cash-discount terms are specified on the invoice. For instance, "2/10, net 30" means that the customer—Discount Tire—may take a "2" percent discount if it pays the invoice within ten days of the invoice date. Let us assume that the dollar amount of the invoice is $200,000. In this case, the cash discount is $4,000 ($200,000 × 0.02 = $4,000). If the cash discount is taken, Discount Tire only has to pay the manufacturer $196,000 ($200,000 − $4,000 = $196,000).

A second option is to wait until the end of the credit period before making payment. If payment is made between 11 and 30 days after the date of the invoice, Discount Tire must pay the entire amount. As long as payment is made before the end of the credit period, the retailer maintains the ability to purchase additional merchandise using the trade-credit arrangement.

PROMISSORY NOTES ISSUED TO SUPPLIERS A **promissory note** is a written pledge by a borrower to pay a certain sum of money to a creditor at a specified future date. Suppliers uneasy about extending trade credit may be less reluctant to offer credit to customers who sign promissory notes. Unlike trade credit, however, promissory notes usually require the borrower to pay interest. Although repayment periods may extend to one year, most short-term promissory notes are repaid in 60 to 180 days.

A promissory note offers two important advantages to the firm extending the credit.

1. A promissory note is legally binding and an enforceable contract.
2. A promissory note is a negotiable instrument.

Because a promissory note is negotiable, the manufacturer, wholesaler, or company extending credit may be able to discount, or sell, the note to its own bank. If the note is discounted, the dollar amount received by the company extending credit is slightly less than the maturity value because the bank charges a fee for the service. The supplier recoups most of its money immediately, and the bank collects the maturity value when the note matures.

Entrepreneurs can always use more capital. Even though Body Rest Mattress Company in St. Petersburg, Florida, was successful, Carl and Emma Calhoun found that obtaining short-term financing was difficult during the economic crisis. Traditional sources of financing—banks and other financial institutions—tightened the requirements for obtaining unsecured loans or in many cases rejected loan requests.

unsecured financing financing that is not backed by collateral

trade credit a type of short-term financing extended by a seller who does not require immediate payment after delivery of merchandise

promissory note a written pledge by a borrower to pay a certain sum of money to a creditor at a specified future date

UNSECURED BANK LOANS Banks and other financial institutions offer unsecured short-term loans to businesses at interest rates that vary with each borrower's credit rating. The **prime interest rate** is the lowest rate charged by a bank for a short-term loan. Figure 16-5 traces the fluctuations in the average prime rate charged by U.S. banks from 1990 to February 2013. This lowest rate generally is reserved for large corporations with excellent credit ratings. Organizations with good to high credit ratings may pay the prime rate plus "2" percent. Firms with questionable credit ratings may have to pay the prime rate plus "4" percent. (The fact that a banker charges a higher interest rate for a higher-risk loan is a practical application of the risk–return ratio discussed earlier in this chapter.) Of course, if the banker believes that loan repayment may be a problem, the borrower's loan application may well be rejected.

prime interest rate the lowest rate charged by a bank for a short-term loan

When a business obtains a short-term bank loan, interest rates and repayment terms may be negotiated. As a condition of the loan, a bank may require that a *compensating balance* be kept on deposit at the bank. Compensating balances, if required, are typically 10 to 20 percent of the borrowed funds. The bank may also require that every commercial borrower *clean up* (pay off completely) its short-term loans at least once each year and not use it again for a period of 30 to 60 days.

COMMERCIAL PAPER Large firms with excellent credit reputations like Microsoft, Procter & Gamble, and Caterpillar can raise large sums of money quickly by issuing commercial paper. **Commercial paper** is a short-term promissory note issued by a large corporation. The maturity date for commercial paper is normally 270 days or less.

commercial paper a short-term promissory note issued by a large corporation.

Commercial paper is secured only by the reputation of the issuing firm; no collateral is involved. The interest rate a corporation pays when it sells commercial paper is tied to its credit rating and its ability to repay the commercial paper. In most cases, corporations selling commercial paper pay interest rates slightly below the interest rates charged by banks for short-term loans. Thus, selling commercial paper is cheaper than getting short-term financing from a bank.

Although it is possible to purchase commercial paper in smaller denominations, larger amounts—$100,000 or more—are quite common. Money obtained by selling commercial paper is most often used to purchase inventory, finance a firm's accounts receivable, pay salaries and other necessary expenses, and solve cash-flow problems.

FIGURE 16-5 Average Prime Interest Rate Paid by U.S. Businesses, 1990–February 2013

The prime rate is the interest rate charged by U.S. banks when businesses with the "best" credit ratings borrow money. All other businesses pay higher interest rates than the prime rate.

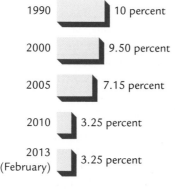

1990	10 percent
2000	9.50 percent
2005	7.15 percent
2010	3.25 percent
2013 (February)	3.25 percent

Source: Federal Reserve Bank website, www.federalreserve.gov (accessed March 7, 2013).

Sources of Secured Short-Term Financing

If a business cannot obtain enough money through unsecured financing, it must put up collateral to obtain additional short-term financing. Almost any asset can serve as collateral. However, *inventories* and *accounts receivable* are the assets most commonly pledged for short-term financing. Even when it is willing to pledge collateral to back up a loan, a firm that is financially weak may have difficulty obtaining short-term financing.

LOANS SECURED BY INVENTORY Normally, manufacturers, wholesalers, and retailers have large amounts of money invested in finished goods. In addition, manufacturers carry raw materials and work-in-process inventories. All three types of inventory may be pledged as collateral for short-term loans. However, lenders prefer the much more salable finished merchandise to raw materials or work-in-process inventories.

A lender may insist that inventory used as collateral be stored in a public warehouse. In such a case, the receipt issued by the warehouse is retained by the lender. Without this receipt, the public warehouse will not release the merchandise. The lender releases the warehouse receipt—and the merchandise—to the borrower when the borrowed money is repaid. In addition to paying the interest on the loan, the borrower must pay for storage in the public warehouse. As a result, this type of loan is more expensive than an unsecured short-term loan.

LOANS SECURED BY RECEIVABLES As defined in Chapter 15, *accounts receivable* are amounts owed to a firm by its customers. A firm can pledge its accounts receivable as collateral to obtain short-term financing. A lender may advance 70 to 80 percent of the dollar amount of the receivables. First, however, it conducts a thorough investigation to determine the *quality* of the receivables. (The quality of the receivables is the credit standing of the firm's customers, coupled with the customers' ability to repay their credit obligations when they are due.) If a favorable determination is made, the loan is approved. When the borrowing firm collects from a customer whose account has been pledged as collateral, generally it must turn the money over to the lender as partial repayment of the loan. An alternative approach is to notify the borrowing firm's credit customers to make their payments directly to the lender.

Factoring Accounts Receivable

Accounts receivable may be used in one other way to help raise short-term financing: They can be sold to a factoring company (or factor). A **factor** is a firm that specializes in buying other firms' accounts receivable. The factor buys the accounts receivable for less than their face value; however, it collects the full dollar amount when each account is due. The factor's profit thus is the difference between the face value of the accounts receivable and the amount the factor has paid for them. Generally, the amount of profit the factor receives is based on the risk the factor assumes. Risk, in this case, is the probability that the accounts receivable will not be repaid when they mature.

Even though the firm selling its accounts receivable gets less than face value, it does receive needed cash immediately. Moreover, it has shifted both the task of collecting and the risk of nonpayment to the factor, which now owns the accounts receivable. Generally, customers whose accounts receivable have been factored are given instructions to make their payments directly to the factor.

Cost Comparisons

Table 16-2 compares the various types of short-term financing. As you can see, trade credit is the least expensive. Factoring of accounts receivable is typically the highest-cost method shown.

For many purposes, short-term financing suits a firm's needs perfectly. At other times, however, long-term financing may be more appropriate. In this case, a business may try to raise equity capital or long-term debt capital.

Concept Check

✓ How important is trade credit as a source of short-term financing?

✓ Why would a supplier require a customer to sign a promissory note?

✓ What is the prime rate? Who gets the prime rate?

✓ Explain how factoring works. Of what benefit is factoring to a firm that sells its receivables?

TABLE 16-2 Comparison of Short-Term Financing Methods

Type of Financing	Cost	Repayment Period	Businesses That May Use It	Comments
Trade credit	Low, if any	30–60 days	All businesses with good credit	Usually no finance charge
Promissory note issued to suppliers	Moderate	One year or less	All businesses	Usually unsecured but requires legal document
Unsecured bank loan	Moderate	One year or less	All businesses	Promissory note is required and compensating balance may be required
Commercial paper	Moderate	270 days or less	Large corporations with high credit ratings	Available only to large firms
Secured loan	High	One year or less	Firms with questionable credit ratings	Inventory or accounts receivable often used as collateral
Factoring	High	None	Firms that have large numbers of credit customers	Accounts receivable sold to a factor

© CENGAGE LEARNING 2015

SOURCES OF EQUITY FINANCING

Learning Objective

6 Evaluate the advantages and disadvantages of equity financing.

initial public offering (IPO)
occurs when a corporation sells common stock to the general public for the first time

Sources of long-term financing vary with the size and type of business. As mentioned earlier, a sole proprietorship or partnership acquires equity capital (sometimes referred to as *owners' equity*) when the owner or partners invest money in the business. For corporations, equity-financing options include the sale of stock and the use of profits not distributed to owners. All three types of businesses can also obtain venture capital and use long-term debt capital (borrowed money) to meet their financial needs.

Selling Stock

Some equity capital is used to start every business—sole proprietorship, partnership, or corporation. In the case of corporations, stockholders who buy shares in the company provide equity capital.

INITIAL PUBLIC OFFERING AND THE PRIMARY MARKET An **initial public offering (IPO)** occurs when a corporation sells common stock to the general public for the first time. In mid-2012, Facebook used an IPO to raise capital, and it was one of the largest IPOs in recent history. And at the time of the publication of your text, there are more social media and technology companies using IPOs to raise capital. Corporations in other industries also use IPOs to raise money. In fact, as illustrated in Figure 16-6, the largest IPOs—Visa, Facebook, General Motors, AT&T Wireless, and Kraft Foods—for U.S. companies involve companies from a number of different industries.

© TUPUNGATO/SHUTTERSTOCK.COM

Just a piece of paper—or is it? In fact, a piece of paper can be worth a lot of money when it is a stock certificate. A corporation sells stock to raise needed financing for expansion and to pay for other long-term financial needs. On the other hand, investors purchase stock because they can profit from their investment if the price of the corporation's stock increases and a corporation pays dividends.

These five corporations raised billions of dollars by selling stock. Visa—the record holder for U.S. companies—raised almost $18 billion when it sold stock for the first time in 2008.

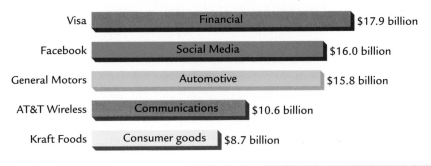

Visa	Financial	$17.9 billion
Facebook	Social Media	$16.0 billion
General Motors	Automotive	$15.8 billion
AT&T Wireless	Communications	$10.6 billion
Kraft Foods	Consumer goods	$8.7 billion

Source: Renaissance Capital, Greenwich, CT (www.renaissancecapital.com), (accessed March 7, 2013).

Established companies that plan to raise capital by selling subsidiaries to the public can also use IPOs. In 2013, Pfizer sold shares in its animal health division and raised over $2 billion. Monies from the IPO will be used to increase the parent company's cash balance, allow Pfizer to concentrate on its core business, and provide funding for growth opportunities and expansion.[10] In addition to using an IPO to increase the cash balance for the parent company, corporations often sell shares in a subsidiary when shares can be sold at a profit or when the subsidiary no longer fits with its current business plan. Finally, some corporations will sell a subsidiary that is growing more slowly than the rest of the company's operating divisions.

When a corporation uses an IPO to raise capital, the stock is sold in the primary market. The **primary market** is a market in which an investor purchases financial securities (via an investment bank) directly from the issuer of the securities. An **investment banking firm** is an organization that assists corporations in raising funds, usually by helping to sell new issues of stocks, bonds, or other financial securities.

Although a corporation can have only one IPO, it can sell additional stock after the IPO, assuming that there is a market for the company's stock. Even though the cost of selling stock (often referred to as *flotation costs*) is high, the *ongoing* costs associated with this type of equity financing are low for two reasons. First, the corporation does not have to repay money obtained from the sale of stock because the corporation is under no legal obligation to do so. If you purchase corporate stock and later decide to sell your stock, you may sell it to another investor—not the corporation.

A second advantage of selling stock is that a corporation is under no legal obligation to pay dividends to stockholders. As noted in Chapter 4, a *dividend* is a distribution of earnings to the stockholders of a corporation. For any reason (e.g., if a company has a bad year), the board of directors can vote to omit dividend payments. Earnings then are retained for use in funding business operations. Of course, corporate management may hear from unhappy stockholders if expected dividends are omitted too frequently.

THE SECONDARY MARKET Although a share of corporate stock is only sold one time in the primary market, the stock can be sold again and again in the secondary market. The **secondary market** is a market for existing financial securities that are traded between investors. Although a corporation does not receive money each time its stock is bought or sold in the secondary market, the ability to obtain cash

primary market a market in which an investor purchases financial securities (via an investment bank) directly from the issuer of those securities

investment banking firm an organization that assists corporations in raising funds, usually by helping to sell new issues of stocks, bonds, or other financial securities

secondary market a market for existing financial securities that are traded between investors

Investor Relations in the Social Media Era

Tweeting about earnings? Increasingly, public corporations are communicating with their investors via Twitter, Facebook, YouTube, LinkedIn, and other social media. Companies still publish annual reports (in print and online) and hold annual meetings (in person and via webcast). In addition, because stockholders and potential investors want easy access to the latest financial news, companies like Alcoa, Dell, and eBay now use social media to provide official updates. Although the timing and content of these messages must comply with regulatory requirements, the ability to connect quickly and directly with investors is vital at a time when rumors can fly around the world at the click of a mouse.

Alcoa, for example, uses its Facebook page to announce quarterly earnings figures and link to executive webcasts. It also uses its Twitter account to call attention to specific results and invite comments from its followers. For investors who want to dig deeper into quarterly or annual financial reports, the investor relations department shares its electronic presentations on SlideShare.

Thanks to Twitter, YouTube, a dedicated investor relations blog, and other social media, Dell reaches more than five million people when it presents its quarterly financial results. And the online auction site eBay live-tweets earnings results as the CEO announces them. Watch for corporate investor relations departments to become even more social in the years ahead.

Sources: Based on information in Rachel Koning Beals, "Investors Increasingly Tap Social Media for Stock Tips," *U.S. News & World Report*, January 31, 2012, http://money.usnews.com/money; Dominic Jones, "Social Media Investor Relations Reaches Tipping Point," *IR Web Report*, April 14, 2011, http://irwebreport.com; Dave Hogan, "Investor Relations and Social Media: Together at Last," *PR News Online*, May 9, 2011, www.prnewsonline.com; Jennifer Van Grove, "Investor Relations Tool Helps Fortune 500 Companies Get Social," *Mashable*, June 8, 2011, www.mashable.com.

by selling stock investments is one reason why investors purchase corporate stock. Without the secondary market, investors would not purchase stock in the primary market because there would be no way to sell shares to other investors. Usually, secondary-market transactions are completed through a securities exchange or the over-the-counter (OTC) market.

A **securities exchange** is a marketplace where member brokers meet to buy and sell securities. Generally, securities issued by larger corporations are traded at the New York Stock Exchange (NYSE) (now owned by the NYSE Euronext), or at regional exchanges located in different parts of the country. The securities of very large corporations may be traded at more than one of these exchanges. Securities of firms also may be listed on foreign securities exchanges—in Tokyo or London, for example.

Stocks issued by several thousand companies are traded in the OTC market. The **over-the-counter (OTC) market** is a network of dealers who buy and sell the stocks of corporations that are not listed on a securities exchange. The term *over-the-counter* was coined more than 100 years ago when securities actually were sold "over the counter" in stores and banks. Many stocks are traded through an *electronic* exchange called the Nasdaq (pronounced "nazzdack"). The Nasdaq is now one of the largest securities markets in the world. Today, the Nasdaq is known for its forward-looking, innovative, growth companies, including Intel, Microsoft, Cisco Systems, and Dell Computer.

There are two types of stock: common and preferred. Each type has advantages and drawbacks as a means of long-term financing.

COMMON STOCK A share of **common stock** represents the most basic form of corporate ownership. In return for the financing provided by selling common stock, management must make certain concessions to stockholders that may restrict or change corporate policies. Every corporation must hold an annual meeting, at which the holders of common stock may vote for the board of directors. Often, stockholders are also asked to approve or disapprove of major corporate actions.

securities exchange a marketplace where member brokers meet to buy and sell securities

over-the-counter (OTC) market a network of dealers who buy and sell the stocks of corporations that are not listed on a securities exchange

common stock stock whose owners may vote on corporate matters but whose claims on profits and assets are subordinate to the claims of others

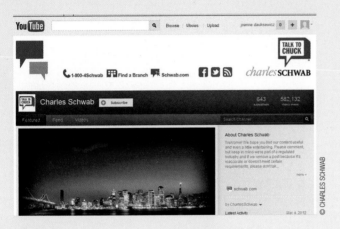
Few investors will buy common stock unless they believe that their investment will increase in value. As already mentioned, stockholders may receive dividends if the corporation's board of directors approves a dividend distribution. Additional information on the reasons why investors purchase stocks and how to evaluate stock investments is provided in Appendix A, "Understanding Personal Finances and Investments."

PREFERRED STOCK As noted in Chapter 4, the owners of **preferred stock** must receive their dividends before holders of common stock receive theirs. Also, preferred stockholders know the dollar amount of their dividend because it is stated on the stock certificate. When compared to common stockholders, preferred stockholders also have first claim (after creditors) on assets if the corporation is dissolved or declares bankruptcy. Even so, as with common stock, the board of directors must approve dividends on preferred stock, and this type of financing does not represent a debt that must be legally repaid. In return for preferential treatment, preferred stockholders generally give up the right to vote at a corporation's annual meeting.

Although a corporation usually issues only one type of common stock, it may issue many types of preferred stock with varying dividends or dividend rates. For example, New York–based Consolidated Edison has one common-stock issue but three preferred-stock issues.[11]

Retained Earnings

Most large corporations distribute only a portion of their after-tax earnings to stockholders. The portion of a corporation's profits *not* distributed to stockholders is called **retained earnings**. Because they are undistributed profits, retained earnings are considered a form of equity financing.

The amount of retained earnings in any year is determined by corporate management and approved by the board of directors. Most small and growing corporations pay no cash dividend—or a very small dividend—to their stockholders. All or most earnings are reinvested in the business for research and development, expansion, or the funding of major projects. Reinvestment tends to increase the value of the firm's stock while it provides essentially cost-free financing for the business. More mature corporations may distribute 40 to 60 percent of their after-tax profits as dividends. Utility companies and other corporations with very stable earnings often pay out as much as 80 to 90 percent of what they earn. For a large corporation, retained earnings can amount to a hefty bit of financing. For example, as reported in its last annual report, the total amount of retained earnings for General Electric was over $144 billion.[12]

Venture Capital and Private Placements

To establish a new business or expand an existing one, an entrepreneur may try to obtain venture capital. In Chapter 5, we defined *venture capital* as money invested in small (and sometimes struggling) firms that have the potential to become very successful. Most venture capital firms do not invest in the typical small business—a

preferred stock stock whose owners usually do not have voting rights but whose claims on dividends and assets are paid before those of common-stock owners

retained earnings the portion of a corporation's profits not distributed to stockholders

neighborhood convenience store or a local dry cleaner—but in firms that have the potential to become extremely profitable. Today, most venture capital firms are investing in companies that build the nation's infrastructure, develop computer software, or provide consumer information or social media services. For example, Zynga—the fast-growing company behind such popular games as FarmVille—received venture capital before selling stock to the public.[13]

Generally, a venture capital firm consists of a pool of investors, a partnership established by a wealthy family, or a joint venture formed by corporations with money to invest. In return for financing, these investors generally receive an equity or ownership position in the business and share in its profits. Although venture capital firms are willing to take chances, they have also been more selective about where they invest their money after the recent economic crisis.

Another method of raising capital is through a private placement. A **private placement** occurs when stock and other corporate securities are sold directly to insurance companies, pension funds, or large institutional investors. When compared with selling stocks and other corporate securities to the public, there are often fewer government regulations and the cost is generally less when the securities are sold through a private placement. Typically, terms between the buyer and seller are negotiated when a private placement is used to raise capital.

private placement occurs when stock and other corporate securities are sold directly to insurance companies, pension funds, or large institutional investors

Concept Check

✓ What are the advantages of financing through the sale of stock?

✓ From a corporation's point of view, how does preferred stock differ from common stock?

✓ What is venture capital?

SOURCES OF LONG-TERM DEBT FINANCING

As pointed out earlier in this chapter, businesses borrow money on a short-term basis for many valid reasons other than desperation. There are equally valid reasons for long-term borrowing. In addition to using borrowed money to meet the long-term needs listed in Table 16-1, successful businesses often use the financial leverage it creates to improve their financial performance. **Financial leverage** is the use of borrowed funds to increase the return on owners' equity. The principle of financial leverage works as long as a firm's earnings are larger than the interest charged for the borrowed money.

To understand how financial leverage can increase a firm's return on owners' equity, study the information for Texas-based Cypress Springs Plastics presented in Table 16-3. Pete Johnston, the owner of the firm, is trying to decide how best to finance a $100,000 purchase of new high-tech manufacturing equipment.

- He could borrow the money and pay 7 percent annual interest.
- He could invest an additional $100,000 in the firm.

Assuming that the firm earns $95,000 a year and that annual interest for this loan totals $7,000 ($100,000 × 0.07 = $7,000), the return on owners' equity for Cypress Springs Plastics would be higher if the firm borrowed the additional financing. Return on owners' equity is determined by dividing a firm's profit by the dollar amount of owners' equity. Based on the calculations illustrated in Table 16-3, Cypress Springs Plastics' return on owners' equity equals 17.6 percent if Johnston borrows the additional $100,000. The firm's return on owners' equity would decrease to 15.8 percent if Johnston invests an additional $100,000 in the business.

The most obvious danger when using financial leverage is that the firm's earnings may be lower than expected. If this situation occurs, the fixed interest charge actually works to reduce or eliminate the return on owners' equity. Of course, borrowed money eventually must be repaid.

For a small business, long-term debt financing is generally limited to loans. Large corporations have the additional option of issuing corporate bonds.

Learning Objective

7 **Evaluate the advantages and disadvantages of long-term debt financing.**

financial leverage the use of borrowed funds to increase the return on owners' equity

Long-Term Loans

Many businesses satisfy their long-term financing needs, such as those listed in Table 16-1, with loans from commercial banks and other financial institutions. Manufacturers and suppliers of heavy machinery may also provide long-term debt financing by granting credit to their customers.

Additional Debt		Additional Equity	
Owners' equity	$500,000	Owners' equity	$500,000
Additional equity	+0	Additional equity	+100,000
Total owner's equity	$500,000	Total owner's equity	$600,000
Loan (@ 7%)	+100,000	No loan	+0
Total capital	$600,000	Total capital	$600,000
Year-End Earnings			
Gross profit	$95,000	Gross profit	$95,000
Less loan interest	−7,000	No interest	−0
Profit	$88,000	Profit	$95,000
Return on owners' equity	17.6%	Return on owners' equity	15.8%
($88,000 ÷ $500,000 = 17.6%)		($95,000 ÷ $600,000 = 15.8%)	

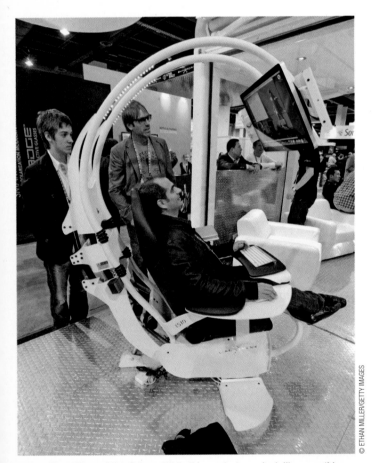

The office of the future. While this product may look like something that should be on the next spaceship to the moon, it is a state-of-the-art office chair designed for people who spend long hours in front of computer monitors. The chair was created by Modern Work Environment (MWE) Lab. Companies that develop innovative products like this one need financing, and they generally have two choices. They can obtain financing from owners and investors or they can borrow money.

TERM-LOAN AGREEMENTS A **term-loan agreement** is a promissory note that requires a borrower to repay a loan in monthly, quarterly, semiannual, or annual installments. As discussed earlier in this chapter, repayment may be as long as 15 to 20 years, but long-term business loans normally are repaid in 3 to 7 years.

Assume that Pete Johnston, the owner of Cypress Springs Plastics, decides to borrow $100,000 and take advantage of the principle of financial leverage illustrated in Table 16-3. Although the firm's return on owners' equity does increase, interest must be paid each year and, eventually, the loan must be repaid. To pay off a $100,000 loan over a three-year period with annual payments, Cypress Springs Plastics must pay $33,333 on the loan balance plus $7,000 annual interest, or a total of $40,333 the first year. Although the amount of interest decreases each year because of the previous year's payment on the loan balance, annual payments of this amount are still a large commitment for a small firm such as Cypress Springs Plastics.

The interest rate and repayment terms for term loans often are based on factors such as the reasons for borrowing, the borrowing firm's credit rating, and the value of collateral. Although long-term loans occasionally may be unsecured, the lender usually requires some type of collateral. Acceptable collateral includes real estate, stocks, bonds, equipment, or any asset with value. Lenders may also require that borrowers maintain a minimum amount of working capital.

Corporate Bonds

In addition to loans, large corporations may choose to issue bonds in denominations of $1,000 to $50,000. Although the usual face value for corporate bonds is

$1,000, the total face value of all the bonds in an issue usually amounts to millions of dollars. In fact, one of the reasons why corporations sell bonds is so that they can borrow a lot of money from a lot of different bondholders and raise larger amounts of money than could be borrowed from one lender. A **corporate bond** is a corporation's written pledge that it will repay a specified amount of money with interest. Interest rates for corporate bonds vary with the financial health of the company issuing the bond. Specific factors that increase or decrease the interest rate that a corporation must pay when it issues bonds include

- The corporation's ability to pay interest each year until maturity.
- The corporation's ability to repay the bond at maturity.

For bond investors, the interest rate on corporate bonds is an example of the risk–return ratio discussed earlier in this chapter. Simply put: Investors expect more interest if there is more risk with more speculative bond issues—see Figure 16-7. As a result, corporations must pay higher interest if investors are concerned about continued interest payments or eventual repayment of a corporate bond.

The **maturity date** is the date on which the corporation is to repay the borrowed money. Today, most corporate bonds are registered bonds. A **registered bond** is a bond registered in the owner's name by the issuing company. Many corporations do not issue actual bonds. Instead, the bonds are recorded electronically, and the specific details regarding the bond issue, along with the current owner's name and address, are maintained by computer. Computer entries are safer because they cannot be stolen, misplaced, or destroyed, and make it easier to transfer when a bond is sold.

Until a bond's maturity, a corporation pays interest to the bond owner at the stated rate. For example, owners of American & Foreign Power Company bonds that mature in 2030 receive 5 percent per year for each bond. For each $1,000 bond issued, the corporation must pay bondholders $50 ($1,000 × 0.05 = $50) each year. Because interest for corporate bonds is usually paid semiannually, the owner of an American & Foreign Power bond will receive a $25 payment every six months for each bond they own. On the maturity date, a registered owner will receive cash equaling the face value of the bond.

term-loan agreement a promissory note that requires a borrower to repay a loan in monthly, quarterly, semiannual, or annual installments

corporate bond a corporation's written pledge that it will repay a specified amount of money with interest

maturity date the date on which a corporation is to repay borrowed money

registered bond a bond registered in the owner's name by the issuing company

FIGURE 16-7 The Risk–Return Ratio for Corporate Bond Investors

High-quality corporate bonds pay less interest when compared to bonds that are more speculative.

LESS RISK
Bonds with less risk have lower interest rates

lower **Interest rates** *higher*

MORE RISK
Bonds with more risk have higher interest rates

© CENGAGE LEARNING 2015

TYPES OF BONDS Corporate bonds are generally classified as debentures, mortgage bonds, or convertible bonds. Most corporate bonds are debenture bonds. A **debenture bond** is a bond backed only by the reputation of the issuing corporation. To make its bonds more appealing to investors, a corporation may issue mortgage bonds. A **mortgage bond** is a corporate bond secured by various assets of the issuing firm. Typical corporate assets that are used as collateral for a mortgage bond include real estate, machinery, and equipment that is not pledged as collateral for other debt obligations. The corporation can also issue convertible bonds. A **convertible bond** can be exchanged, at the owner's option, for a specified number of shares of the corporation's common stock. An Advanced Micro Devices (AMD) bond that matures in 2015 is convertible: Each bond can be converted to 35.6125 shares of AMD common stock.[14] A corporation can gain in three ways by issuing convertible bonds. First, convertibles usually carry a lower interest rate than nonconvertible bonds. Second, the conversion feature attracts investors who are interested in the speculative gain that conversion to common stock may provide. Third, if the bondholder converts to common stock, the corporation no longer has to redeem the bond at maturity.

REPAYMENT PROVISIONS FOR CORPORATE BONDS Maturity dates for bonds generally range from 10 to 30 years after the date of issue. Some bonds are callable before the maturity date; that is, a corporation can buy back, or redeem, them. For these bonds, the corporation may pay the bond owner a call premium. The amount of the call premium, if any, is specified, along with other provisions, in the bond indenture. The **bond indenture** is a legal document that details all the conditions relating to a bond issue.

A corporation may use one of three methods to ensure that it has sufficient funds available to redeem a bond issue. First, it can issue the bonds as **serial bonds**, which are bonds of a single issue that mature on different dates. For example, a company may use a 25-year $50 million bond issue to finance its expansion. None of the bonds mature during the first 15 years. Thereafter, 10 percent of the bonds mature each year until all the bonds are retired at the end of the 25th year. Second, the corporation can establish a sinking fund. A **sinking fund** is a sum of money to which deposits are made each year for the purpose of redeeming a bond issue. When Union Pacific Corporation sold a $275 million bond issue, the company agreed to contribute to a sinking fund until the bond's maturity in the year 2025.[15] Third, a corporation can pay off an old bond issue by selling new bonds. Although this may appear to perpetuate the corporation's long-term debt, a number of utility companies and railroads use this repayment method.

A corporation that issues bonds must also appoint a **trustee**, an individual or an independent firm that acts as the bond owner's representative. A trustee's duties are handled most often by a commercial bank or other large financial institution. The corporation must report to the trustee periodically regarding its ability to make interest payments and eventually redeem the bonds. In turn, the trustee transmits this information to the bond owners, along with its own evaluation of the corporation's ability to pay.

Cost Comparisons

Table 16-4 compares some of the methods that can be used to obtain long-term equity *and* debt financing. Although the initial flotation cost of issuing stock is high, selling common stock is generally a popular option for most financial managers. Once the stock is sold and upfront costs are paid, the *ongoing* costs of using stock to finance a business are low. The type of long-term financing that generally has the highest *ongoing* costs is a long-term loan (debt).

To a great extent, firms are financed through the investments of individuals—money that people have deposited in banks or have used to purchase stocks, mutual funds, and bonds. In Appendix A, we look at how you can invest your money in business.

---

debenture bond a bond backed only by the reputation of the issuing corporation

mortgage bond a corporate bond secured by various assets of the issuing firm

convertible bond a bond that can be exchanged, at the owner's option, for a specified number of shares of the corporation's common stock

bond indenture a legal document that details all the conditions relating to a bond issue

serial bonds bonds of a single issue that mature on different dates

sinking fund a sum of money to which deposits are made each year for the purpose of redeeming a bond issue

trustee an individual or an independent firm that acts as a bond owner's representative

---

Concept Check

✓ Describe how financial leverage can increase return on owners' equity.

✓ For a corporation, what are the advantages of corporate bonds over long-term loans?

✓ Describe the three methods used to ensure that funds are available to redeem corporate bonds at maturity.

TABLE 16-4 Comparison of Long-Term Financing Methods

Type of Financing	Repayment	Repayment Period	Cost/Dividends Interest	Businesses That May Use It
Equity				
Common stock	No	None	High initial cost; low ongoing costs because dividends not required	All corporations that sell stock to investors
Preferred stock	No	None	Dividends not required but must be paid before common stockholders receive any dividends	Large corporations that have an established investor base of common stockholders
Debt				
Long-term loan	Yes	Usually 3–7 years	Interest rates between 3.50 and 12 percent depending on economic conditions, the financial stability of the company requesting the loan, and the amount of the loan	All firms that can meet the lender's repayment and collateral requirements
Corporate bond	Yes	Usually 10–30 years	Interest rates between 3 and 9 percent depending on the financial stability of the company issuing the bonds and economic conditions	Large corporations that are financially healthy

Looking for Success? *Get Flashcards, Quizzes, Games, Crosswords, and more @ www.cengagebrain.com.*

Summary

1 Understand why financial management is important in today's uncertain economy.

Financial management consists of all activities concerned with obtaining money and using it effectively. Financial management can be viewed as a two-sided problem. On one side, the uses of funds often dictate the type or types of financing needed by a business. On the other side, the activities a business can undertake are determined by the types of financing available. Financial managers must ensure that funds are available when needed, that they are obtained at the lowest possible cost, and that they are used as efficiently as possible. In the wake of the economic crisis, the Dodd–Frank Wall Street Reform and Consumer Protection Act was signed into law. And today, there is an ongoing debate if more regulations are needed. Still, there are a number of rewarding jobs in finance for qualified job applicants.

2 Identify a firm's short- and long-term financial needs.

Short-term financing is money that will be used for one year or less. There are many short-term needs, but cash flow, speculative production, and inventory are three for which financing is often required. Long-term financing is money that will be used for more than one year. Such financing may be required for a business start-up, for a merger or an acquisition, for new product development, for long-term marketing activities, for replacement of equipment, or for expansion of facilities. According to financial experts, business firms will find it more difficult to raise both short- and long-term financing in the future because of increased regulations and more cautious lenders. Financial managers must also consider the risk–return ratio when making financial decisions. The risk–return ratio is based on the principle that a high-risk decision should generate higher financial returns for a business. On the other hand, more conservative decisions generate lesser returns.

3 Summarize the process of planning for financial management.

A financial plan begins with an organization's goals and objectives. Next, a firm's goals and objectives are "translated" into departmental budgets that detail expected income and expenses. From these budgets, which may be combined into an overall cash budget, the financial manager determines what funding will be needed and where it may be obtained. Whereas departmental and cash budgets emphasize short-term financing needs, a capital budget can be used to estimate a firm's expenditures for major assets and its long-term financing needs. The four principal sources of financing are sales revenues, equity capital, debt capital, and proceeds from the sale of assets. Once the needed funds have been obtained, the financial manager is responsible for monitoring and evaluating the firm's financial activities.

4 Identify the services provided by banks and financial institutions for their business customers.

Banks and other financial institutions offer today's business customers a tempting array of services. Among the most important and attractive banking services are savings accounts and certificates of deposit, checking accounts, short- and long-term loans, and credit-card and debit-card processing. Increased use of electronic funds transfer systems (automated teller machines, automated clearinghouse systems, point-of-sale terminals, and electronic check conversion) also will change the way that business firms bank and conduct typical business transactions. For firms in the global marketplace, a bank can provide letters of credit and banker's acceptances that will reduce the risk of nonpayment for sellers. Banks and financial institutions also can provide currency exchange to reduce payment problems for import or export transactions.

5 Describe the advantages and disadvantages of different methods of short-term debt financing.

Most short-term financing is unsecured; that is, no collateral is required. Sources of unsecured short-term financing include trade credit, promissory notes issued to suppliers, unsecured bank loans, and commercial paper. Sources of secured short-term financing include loans secured by inventory and accounts receivable. A firm may also sell its receivables to factors. Trade credit is the least-expensive source of short-term

financing. The cost of financing through other sources generally depends on the source and on the credit rating of the firm that requires the financing. Factoring is generally the most expensive approach.

6 Evaluate the advantages and disadvantages of equity financing.

The first time a corporation sells stock to the general public is referred to as an initial public offering (IPO). With an IPO, the stock is sold in the primary market. Once sold in the primary market, investors buy and sell stock in the secondary market. Usually, secondary market transactions are completed through a securities exchange or the over-the-counter market. Common stock is voting stock; holders of common stock elect the corporation's directors and often must approve changes to the corporate charter. Holders of preferred stock must be paid dividends before holders of common stock are paid any dividends. Another source of equity funding is retained earnings, which is the portion of a business's profits *not* distributed to stockholders. Venture capital—money invested in small (and sometimes struggling) firms that have the potential to become very successful—is yet another source of equity funding. Finally, a private placement can be used to sell stocks and other corporate securities.

7 Evaluate the advantages and disadvantages of long-term debt financing.

For a small business, debt financing is generally limited to loans. Large corporations have the additional option of issuing corporate bonds. Regardless of whether the business is small or large, it can take advantage of financial leverage. Financial leverage is the use of borrowed funds to increase the return on owners' equity. The rate of interest for long-term loans usually depends on the financial status of the borrower, the reason for borrowing, and the kind of collateral pledged to back up the loan. Long-term business loans are normally repaid in 3 to 7 years but can be as long as 15 to 20 years. Money realized from the sale of corporate bonds must be repaid when the bonds mature. In addition, the corporation must pay interest on that money from the time the bonds are sold until maturity. The interest rate the corporation must pay often depends on the financial health of the firm issuing bonds. Maturity dates for bonds generally range from 10 to 30 years after the date of issue. Three types of bonds—debentures, mortgage bonds, and convertible bonds—are sold to raise debt capital. When comparing the cost of long-term financing, the ongoing costs of using stock (equity) to finance a business are low. The most expensive is a long-term loan (debt).

Key Terms

You should now be able to define and give an example relevant to each of the following terms:

financial management (462)
chief financial officer
(CFO) (463)
short-term financing (464)
cash flow (464)
speculative production
(465)
long-term financing (466)
risk–return ratio (467)
financial plan (467)
budget (468)
cash budget (468)
zero-base budgeting (469)
capital budget (469)
equity capital (469)

debt capital (469)
certificate of deposit
(470)
check (470)
line of credit (470)
revolving credit agreement
(470)
collateral (471)
debit card (472)
electronic funds transfer
system (EFT) (472)
letter of credit (473)
banker's acceptance (473)
unsecured financing (474)
trade credit (474)

promissory note (474)
prime interest rate (475)
commercial paper (475)
factor (476)
initial public offering
(IPO) (477)
primary market (478)
investment banking
firm (478)
secondary market (478)
securities exchange (479)
over-the-counter (OTC)
market (479)
common stock (479)
preferred stock (480)

retained earnings (480)
private placement (481)
financial leverage (481)
term-loan agreement
(483)
corporate bond (483)
maturity date (483)
registered bond (483)
debenture bond (484)
mortgage bond (484)
convertible bond (484)
bond indenture (484)
serial bonds (484)
sinking fund (484)
trustee (484)

Discussion Questions

1. During the recent economic crisis, many financial managers and corporate officers have been criticized for (a) poor decisions, (b) lack of ethical behavior, (c) large salaries, (d) lucrative severance packages worth millions of dollars, and (e) extravagant lifestyles. Is this criticism justified? Justify your opinion.
2. If you were the financial manager of Stars and Stripes Clothing, what would you do with the excess cash that the firm expects in the second and fourth quarters? (See Figure 16-4.)
3. Develop a *personal* cash budget for the next six months. Explain what you would do if there are budget shortfalls or excess cash amounts at the end of any month during the six-month period.
4. Why would a lender offer unsecured short-term loans when it could demand collateral?
5. How can a small-business owner or corporate manager use financial leverage to improve the firm's profits and return on owners' equity?
6. In what circumstances might a large corporation sell stock rather than bonds to obtain long-term financing? In what circumstances would it sell bonds rather than stock?

Test Yourself

Matching Questions

1. _____ It is the movement of money into and out of a business organization.
2. _____ Determining a firm's financial needs is one of its important functions.
3. _____ A loan that is approved before the money is actually needed.
4. _____ Funding that comes from the sale of stock.
5. _____ Payments are usually made in 30 to 60 days from the invoice date.
6. _____ Must receive dividends before common stockholders.
7. _____ It is pledged as security for a loan.
8. _____ A method of financing that is a legally binding and enforceable and often issued to suppliers.

9. _____ The deposits are used for redeeming a bond issue.

10. _____ This investment is backed by the reputation of the issuing corporation.

a. cash flow
b. collateral
c. debenture bond
d. equity capital

e. financial management
f. letter of credit
g. line of credit
h. preferred stock
i. private placement
j. promissory note
k. sinking fund
l. trade credit

True False Questions

11. **T** **F** Long-term financing is generally used to open new businesses.

12. **T** **F** A budget is a historical record of the previous year's financial activities.

13. **T** **F** When you use a debit card to make a purchase, a financial institution is extending credit to you and expects to be paid in the future.

14. **T** **F** With a banker's acceptance, certain conditions, such as delivery of the merchandise, may be specified before payment is made.

15. **T** **F** Most lenders do not require collateral for short-term financing.

16. **T** **F** A revolving credit agreement is a guaranteed line of credit.

17. **T** **F** Factoring of accounts receivable typically is the highest cost method of short-term financing.

18. **T** **F** Normally, the usual repayment period for a long-term loan is three to seven years.

19. **T** **F** The usual face value for most corporate bonds is $5,000.

20. **T** **F** A capital budget estimates a firm's expenditures for labor costs and other monthly expenses.

Multiple Choice Questions

21. _____ A written order for a bank or other financial institution to pay a stated dollar amount to a specified business or person is called a
a. check.
b. deposit slip.
c. notes receivable.
d. receipt.
e. debit memorandum.

22. _____ Judy Martinez, owner of Judy's Fashions, received a $12,000 tax refund. She deposited the money in Chase Bank. The terms of the agreement are that she must leave the money on deposit for three years and the bank will pay her 1 percent interest. Her account is a
a. line of credit.
b. certificate of deposit.
c. checking account.
d. commercial paper agreement.
e. savings account.

23. _____ An invoice in the amount of $200 carries cash terms of "2/10, net 30." If the buyer takes advantage of the discount terms, how much will the buyer pay?
a. $100
b. $120
c. $140
d. $160
e. $196

24. _____ When a firm sells its accounts receivable to raise short-term cash, it is engaging in a strategy called

a. factoring.
b. financial planning.
c. equity financing
d. debt financing.
e. drafting.

25. _____ Retained earnings, as a form of equity financing, are
a. gross earnings.
b. profits before taxes.
c. profits after taxes.
d. undistributed profits.
e. total owners' equity.

26. _____ Since prices are extremely low, the Pipeline Supply Company wants to purchase a special line of pipes from a company going out of business. Pipeline, however, will need to borrow money to make this deal. Which assets will Pipeline most commonly pledge as collateral for this short-term loan?
a. delivery equipment
b. notes payable
c. manufacturing equipment
d. owners' equity
e. inventory

27. _____ The most basic form of corporate ownership that has voting rights is
a. preferred stock.
b. common stock.
c. retained stock.
d. deferred value stock.
e. treasury stock.

28. _____ A short-term promissory note issued by large corporations is known as
   a. debenture agreement.
   b. equity agreement.
   c. commercial paper.
   d. draft agreement.
   e. loan commitment.

29. _____ Each of the following causes a cash flow problem except
   a. embezzlement of company funds.
   b. an unexpected slow selling season.
   c. a large number of credit sales.
   d. slow-paying customers.
   e. customers who pay on time.

30. _____ The primary sources of funds available to a business include all of the following *except*
   a. debt capital.
   b. equity capital.
   c. sales revenue.
   d. government grants.
   e. sale of assets.

Answers to the Test Yourself questions appear at the end of the book on page TY-2.

Video Case
Financial Planning Equals Profits for Nederlander Concerts

Nederlander Concerts is in the business of booking, promoting, and producing live music shows in the western United States. The company presents artists ranging from James Taylor to Flogging Molly, Bruce Springsteen, Bonnie Raitt, and the Allman Brothers Band. But, according to Adam Friedman, Nederlander's former CEO, "We're not trying to be necessarily a national player or an international player. We seek out opportunities that fit within and leverage our existing portfolio of small- to mid-size venues. . . . It's one of the few remaining family-run entertainment enterprises worldwide. . . . What this means for us on a day-to-day basis is that we can focus on running the business. We're not as guided by Wall Street, we don't have the same constraints, we don't have the same reporting responsibilities, and it allows us to focus on . . . our business strategy for development."

Of course, being a privately owned company and not needing to respond to shareholders (Wall Street) doesn't mean that Nederlander has *no* reporting responsibilities. As Friedman explains, "We assess at the beginning of the year not only concert revenue and expenses but also special event revenue." Nederlander owns some theaters, amphitheaters, and arenas, and it sometimes rents space for concerts and events along the West Coast. "When we rent the facilities to, for example, movie premieres here in Los Angeles, what kind of revenue are we going to see? What kind of expenses are attended to generating that revenue? What's our fixed overhead for the year? Who's on the payroll, whether full-time, or part-time, or seasonal, and how much does it cost us to run the business on a day-to-day basis in order to secure those revenues and pay those expenses? That's wrapped up into an annual budget at the beginning of every year, which is kind of a guideline for me to know how we achieve growth. It also allows me to communicate to our owners what our growth orientation is for that given year. . . . Every event has its own profit and loss statement . . . which is a mini version of that annual plan," says Friedman.

In addition to daily, weekly, and quarterly event reports, Nederlander's financial team generates daily and weekly reports of ticket sales. Monthly reports on company-wide performance feed into quarterly and annual reports. Each annual report is compared to that year's budget. The finance department tallies hundreds of transactions in order to arrive at some of these annual numbers, which are reported to the company's owners to ensure that the company is running as profitably as it can be.

Nederlander's managers say growth in the concert industry must be measured in the long term because the business is cyclical and the cost of real estate is so high that short-term profit is hard to generate. Still, the company is in a strong financial position (it is part of a profitable global theater-ownership company called the Nederlander Organization), so it can afford to fund its own growth and expansion, or it can borrow on favorable terms. "We're very fortunate to have an ownership that is very well capitalized with over 80 years in the business," says Friedman. "Our balance sheet is so strong that we have the ability to tap into debt financing if it makes the most sense. . . . or [use] the corporate treasury. . . . If it makes more sense to borrow the money, we will, and we're typically able to do that on very favorable rates because of very long-term banking relationships."

It can be thrilling to meet some of the artists the company books. "But at the end of the day, it's a business," Friedman points out. "If we're not successful in growing our revenue and managing our expense, ultimately we won't be profitable, and our ownership will not be happy with those results."[16]

Questions

1. Here's what Nederlander's chief operating officer has to say about its business model: "A show has a short lifetime. You go and sell two months out, and the tickets have no value on any day but the day of the show. So it's a very interesting model in that sense." How do you think the short life of the company's products affects its financial planning?

2. The company uses its own arenas and theaters about 90 percent of the time. What are some of the possible advantages and disadvantages of owning its own venues?

3. Why would Nederlander choose to sometimes borrow funds for expansion if it has capital of its own?

Building Skills for Career Success

1. Social Media Exercise

Turbo Tax is probably one of the best-known tax preparation services in the world. One of the reasons for its popularity is that it provides software that small business firms and individuals really need to make financial decisions and prepare tax returns. Another reason for its popularity is the company's use of social media through various platforms that include building an online community of users, using Twitter, and developing a YouTube channel. Each video on the TurboTax channel illustrates how a company can use social media to provide valuable information to customers. You can check out Turbo Tax videos at www.youtube.com/user/TurboTax.

1. Visit the YouTube channel for Turbo Tax (www.youtube .com/user/TurboTax). Do you think social media is an effective method of obtaining the tax information you might need to prepare your taxes?
2. Can you think of other companies that could use videos on a YouTube channel to share information that their customers could use?

2. Building Team Skills

Suppose that for the past three years you have been repairing lawn mowers in your garage. Your business has grown steadily, and you recently hired two part-time workers. Your garage is no longer adequate for your business; it is also in violation of the city code, and you have already been fined for noncompliance. You have decided that it is time to find another location for your shop and that it also would be a good time to expand your business. If the business continues to grow in the new location, you plan to hire a full-time employee to repair small appliances. You are concerned, however, about how you will get the money to move your shop and get it established in a new location.

Assignment

1. With all class members participating, use brainstorming to identify the following:
   a. The funds you will need to accomplish your business goals

   b. The sources of short-term financing available to you
   c. Problems that might prevent you from getting a short-term loan
   d. How you will repay the money if you get a loan
2. Have a classmate write the ideas on the board.
3. Discuss how you can overcome any problems that might hamper your current chances of getting a loan and how your business can improve its chances of securing short-term loans in the future.
4. Summarize what you learned from participating in this exercise.

3. Researching Different Careers

Financial managers are responsible for determining the best way to raise funds, for ensuring that the funds are used to accomplish their firm's goals and objectives, and for developing and implementing their firm's financial plan. Their decisions have a direct impact on the firm's level of success.

Assignment

1. Investigate the job of financial manager by searching the library or Internet, by interviewing a financial manager, or both.
2. Find answers to the following questions:
   a. What skills do financial managers need?
   b. How much education is required?
   c. What is the starting salary? Top salary?
   d. What will the job of financial manager be like in the future?
   e. What opportunities are available?
   f. What types of firms are most likely to hire financial managers? What is the employment potential?
3. Prepare a report on your findings.

Running a Business
Part 6

Graeter's Recipe for Growth: New Systems, Social Media, and Financing

Graeter's still makes ice cream by hand, just like the founders did in 1870. But in every other respect, it's a very different business from the mom-and-pop firm founded by the great-grandparents of Richard, Robert, and Chip Graeter. With the rise of communication technologies such as social media, Graeter's can stay in touch with customers and see what people say about its brand. Technology is also a factor in the new systems Graeter's recently installed to keep the business running smoothly as it pursues fast-paced growth. Just as important, the company has arranged financing to support its long-term plans for national expansion.

Graeter's Social Side

Even a small business can have a big presence in social media. Graeter's has designated an employee to manage all of the company's activities on Facebook, Twitter, and YouTube. With 155,000 Facebook "likes," Graeter's engages its brand fans in conversations about new or favorite flavors, the size of its chocolate chunks, and more. It posts a new message or photo every few days, and reveals the names of mystery flavors on Facebook in advance of other publicity. As a result, fans return to its Facebook page often. In addition, Graeter's tweets frequently and periodically posts videos on its YouTube channel. Graeter's also monitors "mentions" of its brand on other social-media sites. For example, hundreds of consumers have shared images of Graeter's ice cream on the Pinterest site. As other people add their comments and click to "like," the conversation continues and the word of mouth builds buzz for Graeter's.

New Growth, New Systems

Paul Porcino, a consultant working with the Graeter family, observes that small, entrepreneurial firms often have only "a very small amount of information, and . . . it hasn't been pulled together in any meaningful way." The first step was to define what Graeter's executives needed to know to run the business. For example, they needed to be able to track unit sales online, in each store, and to each wholesale customer, and to measure both costs and profitability by product and distribution channel.

Despite some technical challenges during implementation, Graeter's has already experienced some of the benefits of collecting better information. When management noticed that overall bakery sales weren't up to par, "we had to adjust," comments Porcino. The remedy was surprising: "We actually reduced the number of products we were selling in the store. . . . It wasn't very clear exactly how much we were selling, but at least [we had] the good-enough gut sense in terms of the ones that were not selling, and we . . . adjusted the total inventory line."

Counting on Accounting

Graeter's controller, David Blink, is responsible for preparing "all financial statements, all reports, payroll, [and] any ad hoc reports that any of the managers would need. I handle a lot of the reporting for the retail side as well as the manufacturing side," he says. With these reports in hand, the Graeter's team can make informed decisions about how many seasonal employees to hire, which products to keep, how much to invest in new equipment, and other issues that arise day by day. Although an outside payroll company actually prints the employees' checks, Blink's department collects and analyzes payroll data as input for management decisions.

Money Matters

With expansion on the menu, the Graeter's recognized they needed a new production facility. After scouting possible locations, Graeter's signed a 20-year deal with Cincinnati, paying a token amount for land and borrowing $10 million from the city to pay for construction of a new 28,000-square-foot factory. The loan carried low interest rates and would be repaid over 20 years. In turn, Cincinnati issued $10 million in bonds to provide Graeter's with this funding. The package of financial incentives that Graeter's received toward its new Bond Hill factory was worth $3.3 million. In exchange, Graeter's committed to "stay and grow" in Cincinnati for at least 20 years, creating dozens of new jobs when the facility opened in 2010 and additional jobs as Graeter's growth continued.

© ISTOCKPHOTO.COM/LUVO

As opening day for the Bond Hill facility approached, Graeter's was presented with an unexpected opportunity. Its largest franchisee wanted to sell the franchise operation, complete with stores and an ice-cream factory, and Graeter's had the right to buy the franchise back. "That was not planned, not part of our strategic vision," explains Richard Graeter, "but the opportunity came up, and we had to look at it." After examining what the business had done in the past and where it was going in the future, the three great-grandsons of Graeter's founders put together the financing to buy the stores and factory from the franchisee. Now Graeter's has the right combination of ingredients for expanding from coast to coast and beyond.[17]

Questions

1. Suppose you were writing a social media plan for Graeter's, with two objectives: to improve brand awareness in new markets and to build online orders during holiday periods. What quantitative and qualitative measurements would you use to evaluate the results of your plan?

2. Graeter's uses information to track cash, sales revenue, and expenses on a daily basis. How does this type of accounting system facilitate effective decision making?

3. What kinds of questions do you think Cincinnati officials asked Graeter's owners before agreeing to loan the company $10 million? Why would Graeter's go with this financing arrangement rather than borrowing from a bank to pay for the Bond Hill factory?

Building a Business Plan: Part 6

Now that you have a marketing plan, the next big and important step is to prepare an information and financial plan. One of the biggest mistakes an entrepreneur makes when faced with a need for financing is not being prepared. The information contained in Chapter 14 (Exploring Social Media and e-Business), Chapter 15 (Using Management and Accounting Information), and Chapter 16 (Mastering Financial Management) will help you prepare this section of the business plan and determine the amount of financing you need to start your business. With the help of information in the last three chapters of the text, the task may be easier than you think.

In this last section, you should also provide some information about your exit strategy, and discuss any potential trends, problems, or risks that you may encounter. Now is also the time to go back and prepare the executive summary, which should be placed at the beginning of the business plan.

The Information and Accounting Plan Component

Information and accounting systems are important if your business is to succeed. Your information plan should answer at least the following questions:

6.1. How will you gather information about competitors, their products, and the prices that they charge for their products and services?

6.2. Explain how you will develop a management information system to collect, store, update, process data, and present information.

6.3. Will your business have an e-business component? If so, explain how you sell your products or services online.

6.4. Are there ways that you can use social media to promote products and services and reach out to your customers?

6.5. Who will create and maintain the accounting system that you use to record routine business transactions for your business?

6.6. Will you hire an accountant to prepare financial statements for your firm?

The Financial Plan Component

Your financial plan should answer at least the following questions about the investment needed, sales and cash-flow forecasts, breakeven analysis, and sources of funding:

6.7. What is the actual amount of money you need to open your business (start-up budget) and the amount needed to keep it open (operating budget)? Prepare a realistic budget.

6.8. How much money do you have, and how much money will you need to start your business and stay in business?

6.9. Prepare a projected income statement by month for the first year of operation and by quarter for the second and third years.

6.10. Prepare projected balance sheets for each of the first three years of operation.

6.11. Prepare a breakeven analysis. How many units of your products or service will have to be sold to cover your costs?

6.12. Reinforce your final projections by comparing them with industry averages for your chosen industry.

The Exit Strategy Component

Your exit strategy component should at least include answers to the following questions:

6.13. How do you intend to get yourself (and your money) out of the business?

6.14. Will your children take over the business, or do you intend to sell it later?

6.15. Do you intend to grow the business to the point of an IPO?

6.16. How will investors get their money back?

The Critical Risks and Assumptions Component

Your critical risks and assumptions component should answer at least the following questions:

6.17. What will you do if your market does not develop as quickly as you predicted? What if your market develops too quickly?

6.18. What will you do if your competitors underprice or make your product obsolete?

6.19. What will you do if there is an unfavorable industry-wide trend?

6.20. What will happen if trained workers are not available as predicted?

6.21. What will you do if there is an erratic supply of products or raw materials?

The Appendix Component

Supplemental information and documents often are included in an appendix. Here are a few examples of some documents that can be included:

- Résumés of owners and principal managers
- Advertising samples and brochures
- An organization chart
- Floor plans

Review of Business Plan Activities

As you have discovered, writing a business plan involves a long series of interrelated steps. As with any project involving a number of complex steps and calculations, your business plan should be reviewed carefully and revised before you present it to potential investors.

Remember, there is one more component you need to prepare after your business plan is completed: The executive summary should be written last, but because of its importance, it appears after the introduction.

The Executive Summary Component

In the executive summary, give a one- to two-page overview of your entire business plan. This is the most important part of the business plan and is of special interest to busy bankers, investors, and other interested parties. Remember, this section is a summary; more detailed information is provided in the remainder of your business plan.

Make sure that the executive summary captures the reader's attention instantly in the first sentence by using a key selling point or benefit of the business.

Your executive summary should include answers to at least the following:

6.22. *Company information*. What product or service do you provide? What is your competitive advantage? When will the company be formed? What are your company objectives? What is the background of you and your management team?

6.23. *Market opportunity*. What is the expected size and growth rate of your market, your expected market share, and any relevant market trends?

Once again, review your answers to all the questions in the preceding parts to make sure that they are all consistent throughout the entire business plan.

Although many would-be entrepreneurs are excited about the prospects of opening their own business, remember that it takes a lot of hard work, time, and in most cases a substantial amount of money. While the business plan provides an enormous amount of information about your business, it is only the first step. Once it is completed, it is now your responsibility to implement the plan. Good luck in your business venture.

The information contained in "Building a Business Plan" will also assist you in completing the online *Interactive Business Plan*.

Endnotes

1. Based on information in Jeffrey Burt, "Cisco Sees Revenue Jump 6 percent as It Expands Business Reach," *eWeek*, November 13, 2012, www.eweek.com; Quentin Hardy, "Cisco's Net Income Climbs, Beating Wall St. Forecasts," *New York Times*, November 13, 2012, www.nytimes .com; Noah Buhayar, "Cisco Adds to Technology Issuance with $4 Billion Debt Sale," *Bloomberg*, March 9, 2011, www.bloomberg.com; www.cisco.com.
2. The U.S. Bureau of Labor Statistics at http://bls.gov (accessed March 5, 2013).
3. The 3M Corporation website at www.3m.com (accessed March 5, 2013).
4. The McDonald's Corporate website at www.aboutmcdonalds.com (accessed March 4, 2013).
5. Dan Primack, "Buffettt: Heinz Is Not a 'Private Equity' Deal," The CNNMoney website at http://finance.fortune.cnn.com (accessed March 5, 2013).
6. Kenneth Rapozza, "Looking for Cash, Citigroup Selling India Bank Position," the Forbes website at www.forbes.com (accessed February 23, 2012).
7. "Hostess Brands Is Closed," The Hostess Brands website at www .hostessbrands.com (accessed November 21, 2012).
8. U.S. Census Bureau, Statistical Abstract of the United States, 2012 (Washington, D.C.: U.S. Government Printing Office, p. 740).
9. Ibid.
10. Steve Schaefer, "Puppies Over Pills: Pfizer Spinout Zoetisshines in Biggest IPO Since Facebook," the Forbes website at www.forbes.com (accessed February 1, 2013).
11. The Consolidated Edison Company of New York website at www .conedison.com (accessed March 8, 2013).
12. The General Electric website at www.ge.com (accessed September 7, 2013).
13. Russ Garland, "Zynga Inc: Venture Capital Investment Up Despite Fund-Raising Constraints," the 4-Traders.com website at www.4-traders.com (accessed January 20, 2012).
14. The Advanced Micro Devices corporate website at www.amd.com (accessed March 8, 2013).
15. *Mergent Transportation Manual* (New York: Mergent, Inc., 2009), 64.
16. Based on information from the company website www.nederlander concerts.com (accessed March 9, 2013); Nederlander Organization company overview, *BusinessWeek*, www.businessweek.com (accessed August 20, 2010); Hannah Heineman, "Moving Forward on Capital Improvement Projects," *Santa Monica Mirror*, July 28, 2010, www .smmirror.com; Steve Knopper, "Tour Biz Strong in Weak Economy," *Rolling Stone*, October 2, 2008, 11–12; Ray Waddell, "Nederlander/ Viejas Deal Offers Touring Opportunities," *Billboard*, January 10, 2008, www.billboard.com; interviews with Nederlander employees and the video "Financial Planning and Budgets Equal Profits for Nederlander Concerts."
17. Sources: Based on information from the Graeter's company website at www.graeter.com (accessed March 10, 2013); Kimberly L. Jackson, "Graeter's Premium Chocolate Chip Ice Cream Lands at Stop & Shop," *Newark Star-Ledger (NJ)*, April 4, 2012, www.nj.com; "Graeter's Ice Cream Debuts in Bay Area," *Tampa Bay Times (St. Petersburg, FL)*, January 10, 2012, p. 4B; Jim Carper, "Graeter's Runs a Hands-on Ice Cream Plant," *Dairy Foods*, August 2011, pp. 36+; Jim Carper, "The Greater Good," *Dairy Foods*, August 2011, pp. 95+; "Graeter's Unveils New 'Mystery Flavor,'" *Dayton Daily News*, March 29, 2012, www .daytondailynews.com; Bob Driehaus, "A Cincinnati Ice Cream Maker Aims Big," *New York Times*, September 11, 2010, www.nytimes.com; Lucy May, "Graeter's Northern Kentucky Franchisee Puts Stores on the Block," *Business Courier*, August 6, 2010, http://cincinnati.bizjournals .com; www.graeters.com; interviews with company staff and Cengage videos about Graeter's.

Answer Key

CHAPTER 1

1. g	2. c	3. j	4. e	5. d	6. b
7. f	8. a	9. h	10. i	11. F	12. F
13. T	14. F	15. T	16. T	17. F	18. T
19. F	20. T	21. a	22. c	23. d	24. e
25. d	26. b	27. d	28. c	29. d	30. e

CHAPTER 2

1. j	2. g	3. e	4. k	5. a	6. l
7. d	8. i	9. f	10. b	11. T	12. F
13. F	14. T	15. F	16. T	17. T	18. F
19. T	20. F	21. b	22. e	23. d	24. a
25. d	26. c	27. e	28. c	29. b	30. d

CHAPTER 3

1. i	2. d	3. g	4. j	5. h	6. l
7. e	8. f	9. a	10. c	11. F	12. T
13. T	14. F	15. T	16. F	17. F	18. T
19. F	20. T	21. c	22. d	23. c	24. c
25. a	26. c	27. e	28. c	29. b	30. c

CHAPTER 6

1. g	2. i	3. j	4. b	5. f	6. c
7. d	8. k	9. e	10. l	11. F	12. F
13. T	14. F	15. T	16. F	17. F	18. F
19. T	20. T	21. b	22. e	23. b	24. a
25. d	26. b	27. b	28. d	29. c	30. a

CHAPTER 7

1. c	2. j	3. f	4. e	5. b	6. k
7. h	8. d	9. g	10. l	11. T	12. F
13. T	14. T	15. F	16. T	17. F	18. F
19. F	20. T	21. d	22. d	23. e	24. b
25. a	26. c	27. d	28. b	29. a	30. d

CHAPTER 8

1. e	2. a	3. g	4. f	5. l	6. b
7. k	8. j	9. d	10. i	11. f	12. t
13. f	14. f	15. t	16. f	17. f	18. t
19. f	20. t	21. b	22. b	23. a	24. d
25. e	26. d	27. c	28. d	29. e	30. c

CHAPTER 15

1. f	2. g	3. j	4. e	5. a	6. h
7. b	8. l	9. i	10. d	11. T	12. F
13. F	14. F	15. T	16. T	17. F	18. F
19. T	20. T	21. c	22. a	23. c	24. e
25. b	26. c	27. b	28. c	29. c	30. b

CHAPTER 16

1. a	2. e	3. g	4. d	5. l	6. h
7. b	8. j	9. k	10. c	11. T	12. F
13. F	14. F	15. T	16. T	17. T	18. T
19. F	20. F	21. a	22. b	23. e	24. a
25. d	26. e	27. b	28. c	29. e	30. d

Glossary

A

absolute advantage the ability to produce a specific product more efficiently than any other nation.

accessory equipment standardized equipment used in a firm's production or office activities.

accountability the obligation of a worker to accomplish an assigned job or task.

accounting the process of systematically collecting, analyzing, and reporting financial information.

accounting equation the basis for the accounting process: assets = liabilities + owners' equity.

ad hoc committee a committee created for a specific short-term purpose.

administrative manager a manager who is not associated with any specific functional area but who provides overall administrative guidance and leadership.

advertising a paid nonpersonal message communicated to a select audience through a mass medium.

advertising agency an independent firm that plans, produces, and places advertising for its clients.

affirmative action program a plan designed to increase the number of minority employees at all levels within an organization.

agent a middleman that expedites exchanges, represents a buyer or a seller, and often is hired permanently on a commission basis.

alien corporation a corporation chartered by a foreign government and conducting business in the United States.

analytic skills the ability to identify problems correctly, generate reasonable alternatives, and select the "best" alternatives to solve problems.

analytical process a process in operations management in which raw materials are broken into different component parts.

annual report a report distributed to stockholders and other interested parties that describes the firm's operating activities and its financial condition.

assets the resources that a business owns.

audit an examination of a company's financial statements and the accounting practices that produced them.

authority the power, within an organization, to accomplish an assigned job or task.

autocratic leadership task-oriented leadership style in which workers are told what to do and how to accomplish it without having a say in the decision-making process.

automatic vending the use of machines to dispense products.

automation the total or near-total use of machines to do work.

B

balance of payments the total flow of money into a country minus the total flow of money out of that country over some period of time.

balance of trade the total value of a nation's exports minus the total value of its imports over some period of time.

balance sheet (or statement of financial position) a summary of the dollar amounts of a firm's assets, liabilities, and owners' equity accounts at the end of a specific accounting period.

banker's acceptance a written order for a bank to pay a third party a stated amount of money on a specific state.

barter a system of exchange in which goods or services are traded directly for other goods or services without using money.

behavior modification a systematic program of reinforcement to encourage desirable behavior.

benchmarking a process used to evaluate the products, processes, or management practices of another organization that is superior in some way in order to improve quality.

bill of lading document issued by a transport carrier to an exporter to prove that merchandise has been shipped.

blog a website that allows a company to share information in order to not only increase the customer's knowledge about its products and services but also to build trust.

board of directors the top governing body of a corporation, the members of which are elected by the stockholders.

bond indenture a legal document that details all the conditions relating to a bond issue.

brand a name, term, symbol, design, or any combination of these that identifies a seller's products as distinct from those of other sellers.

brand equity marketing and financial value associated with a brand's strength in a market.

brand extension using an existing brand to brand a new product in a different product category.

brand loyalty extent to which a customer is favorable toward buying a specific brand.

brand mark the part of a brand that is a symbol or distinctive design.

brand name the part of a brand that can be spoken.

breakeven quantity the number of units that must be sold for the total revenue (from all units sold) to equal the total cost (of all units sold).

broker a middleman that specializes in a particular commodity, represents either a buyer or a seller, and is likely to be hired on a temporary basis.

budget a financial statement that projects income, expenditures, or both over a specified future period.

bundle pricing packaging together two or more complementary products and selling them for a single price.

business the organized effort of individuals to produce and sell, for a profit, the goods and services that satisfy society's needs.

business buying behavior the purchasing of products by producers, resellers, governmental units, and institutions.

business cycle the recurrence of periods of growth and recession in a nation's economic activity.

business ethics the application of moral standards to business situations.

business model represents a group of common characteristics and methods of doing business to generate sales revenues and reduce expenses.

business plan a carefully constructed guide for the person starting a business.

business product a product bought for resale, for making other products, or for use in a firm's operations.

business service an intangible product that an organization uses in its operations.

business-to-business (or B2B) model a model used by firms that conduct business with other businesses.

business-to-consumer (or B2C) model a model used by firms that focus on conducting business with individual consumers.

buying allowance a temporary price reduction to resellers for purchasing specified quantities of a product.

buying behavior the decisions and actions of people involved in buying and using products.

C

capacity the amount of products or services that an organization can produce in a given time.

capital budget a financial statement that estimates a firm's expenditures for major assets and its long-term financing needs.

capital-intensive technology a process in which machines and equipment do most of the work.

capitalism an economic system in which individuals own and operate the majority of businesses that provide goods and services.

captioned photograph a picture accompanied by a brief explanation.

captive pricing pricing the basic product in a product line low, but pricing related items at a higher level.

carrier a firm that offers transportation services.

cash budget a financial statement that estimates cash receipts and cash expenditures over a specified period.

cash flow the movement of money into and out of an organization.

catalog marketing a type of marketing in which an organization provides a catalog from which customers make selections and place orders by mail, telephone, or the Internet.

category killer a very large specialty store that concentrates on a single product line and competes on the basis of low prices and product availability.

caveat emptor a Latin phrase meaning "let the buyer beware."

centralized organization an organization that systematically works to concentrate authority at the upper levels of the organization.

certificate of deposit (CD) a document stating that the bank will pay the depositor a guaranteed interest rate on money left on deposit for a specified period of time.

certified public accountant (CPA) an individual who has met state requirements for accounting education and experience and has passed a rigorous accounting examination.

chain of command the line of authority that extends from the highest to the lowest levels of an organization.

chain retailer a company that operates more than one retail outlet.

check a written order for a bank or other financial institution to pay a stated dollar amount to the business or person indicated on the face of the check.

chief financial officer (CFO) a high-level corporate executive who manages a firm's finances and reports directly to the company's chief executive officer or president.

closed corporation a corporation whose stock is owned by relatively few people and is not sold to the general public.

cloud computing a type of computer usage in which services stored on the Internet is provided to users on a temporary basis.

code of ethics a guide to acceptable and ethical behavior as defined by the organization.

collateral real estate or property pledged as security for a loan.

command economy an economic system in which the government decides what goods and services will be produced, how they will be produced, for whom available goods and services will be produced, and who owns and controls the major factors of production.

commercial paper a short-term promissory note issued by a large corporation..

commission a payment that is a percentage of sales revenue.

common stock stock owned by individuals or firms who may vote on corporate matters but whose claims on profits and assets are subordinate to the claims of others.

communication skills the ability to speak, listen, and write effectively.

community shopping center a planned shopping center that includes one or two department stores and some specialty stores, along with convenience stores.

comparable worth a concept that seeks equal compensation for jobs requiring about the same level of education, training, and skills.

comparative advantage the ability to produce a specific product more efficiently than any other product.

comparison discounting setting a price at a specific level and comparing it with a higher price.

compensation the payment employees receive in return for their labor.

competition rivalry among businesses for sales to potential customers.

compensation system the policies and strategies that determine employee compensation.

component part an item that becomes part of a physical product and is either a finished item ready for assembly or a product that needs little processing before assembly.

computer-aided design (CAD) the use of computers to aid in the development of products.

computer-aided manufacturing (CAM) the use of computers to plan and control manufacturing processes.

computer-integrated manufacturing (CIM) a computer system that not only helps to design products but also controls the machinery needed to produce the finished product.

conceptual skills the ability to think in abstract terms.

consumer buying behavior the purchasing of products for personal or household use, not for business purposes.

consumerism all activities undertaken to protect the rights of consumers.

consumer price index (CPI) a monthly index that measures the changes in prices of a fixed basket of goods purchased by a typical consumer in an urban area.

consumer product a product purchased to satisfy personal and family needs.

consumer sales promotion method a sales promotion method designed to attract consumers to particular retail stores and to motivate them to purchase certain new or established products.

contingency plan a plan that outlines alternative courses of action that may be taken if an organization's other plans are disrupted or become ineffective.

continuous process a manufacturing process in which a firm produces the same product(s) over a long period of time.

controlling the process of evaluating and regulating ongoing activities to ensure that goals are achieved.

convenience product a relatively inexpensive, frequently purchased item for which buyers want to exert only minimal effort.

convenience store a small food store that sells a limited variety of products but remains open well beyond normal business hours.

convertible bond a bond that can be exchanged, at the owner's option, for a specified number of shares of the corporation's common stock.

cookie a small piece of software sent by a website that tracks an individual's Internet use.

cooperative advertising an arrangement whereby a manufacturer agrees to pay a certain amount of a retailer's media cost for advertising the manufacturer's products.

core competencies approaches and processes that a company performs well that may give it an advantage over its competitors.

corporate bond a corporation's written pledge that it will repay a specified amount of money with interest.

corporate culture the inner rites, rituals, heroes, and values of a firm.

corporate officers the chairman of the board, president, executive vice presidents, corporate secretary, treasurer, and any other top executive appointed by the board of directors.

corporation an artificial person created by law with most of the legal rights of a real person, including the rights to start and operate a business, to buy or sell property, to borrow money, to sue or be sued, and to enter into binding contracts.

cost of goods sold the dollar amount equal to beginning inventory plus net purchases less ending inventory.

countertrade an international barter transaction.

coupon reduces the retail price of a particular item by a stated amount at the time of purchase.

creative selling selling products to new customers and increasing sales to present customers.

cross-functional team a team of individuals with varying specialties, expertise, and skills that are brought together to achieve a common task.

crowdsourcing outsourcing tasks to a group of people in order to tap into the ideas of the crowd.

cultural (workplace) diversity differences among people in a workforce owing to race, ethnicity, and gender.

currency devaluation the reduction of the value of a nation's currency relative to the currencies of other countries.

current assets assets that can be converted quickly into cash or that will be used in one year or less.

current liabilities debts that will be repaid in one year or less.

current ratio a financial ratio computed by dividing current assets by current liabilities.

customary pricing pricing on the basis of tradition.

customer lifetime value a measure of a customer's worth (sales minus costs) to a business over one's lifetime.

customer relationship management (CRM) using information about customers to create marketing strategies that develop and sustain desirable customer relationships.

D

data numerical or verbal descriptions that usually result from some sort of measurement.

database a single collection of data and information stored in one place that can be used by people throughout an organization to make decisions.

data mining the practice of searching through data records looking for useful information.

data processing the transformation of data into a form that is useful for a specific purpose.

debenture bond a bond backed only by the reputation of the issuing corporation.

debit card a card that electronically subtracts the amount of a customer's purchase from her or his bank account at the moment the purchase is made.

debt capital borrowed money obtained through loans of various types.

decentralized organization an organization in which management consciously attempts to spread authority widely in the lower levels of the organization.

decision making the act of choosing one alternative from a set of alternatives.

decision-support system (DSS) a type of software program that provides relevant data and information to help a firm's employees make decisions.

deflation a general decrease in the level of prices.

delegation assigning part of a manager's work and power to other workers.

demand the quantity of a product that buyers are willing to purchase at each of various prices.

departmentalization the process of grouping jobs into manageable units.

departmentalization by customer grouping activities according to the needs of various customer populations.

departmentalization by function grouping jobs that relate to the same organizational activity.

departmentalization by location grouping activities according to the defined geographic area in which they are performed.

departmentalization by product grouping activities related to a particular product or service.

department store a retail store that (1) employs 25 or more persons and (2) sells at least home furnishings, appliances, family apparel, and household linens and dry goods, each in a different part of the store.

depreciation the process of apportioning the cost of a fixed asset over the period during which it will be used.

depression a severe recession that lasts longer than a typical recession and has a larger decline in business activity when compared to a recession.

design planning the development of a plan for converting an idea into an actual product or service.

directing the combined processes of leading and motivating.

direct marketing the use of the telephone, Internet, and nonpersonal media to introduce products to customers, who then can purchase them via mail, telephone, or the Internet.

direct-response marketing a type of marketing in which a retailer advertises a product and makes it available through mail, telephone, or online orders.

direct selling the marketing of products to customers through face-to-face sales presentations at home or in the workplace.

discount a deduction from the price of an item.

discount store a self-service general-merchandise outlet that sells products at lower-than-usual prices.

discretionary income disposable income less savings and expenditures on food, clothing, and housing.

disposable income personal income less all additional personal taxes.

distribution channel (or marketing channel) a sequence of marketing organizations that directs a product from the producer to the ultimate user.

dividend a distribution of earnings to the stockholders of a corporation.

domestic corporation a corporation in the state in which it is incorporated.

domestic system a method of manufacturing in which an entrepreneur distributes raw materials to various homes, where families process them into finished goods to be offered for sale by the merchant entrepreneur.

double-entry bookkeeping system a system in which each financial transaction is recorded as two separate accounting entries to maintain the balance shown in the accounting equation.

draft issued by the exporter's bank, ordering the importer's bank to pay for the merchandise, thus guaranteeing payment once accepted by the importer's bank.

dumping exportation of large quantities of a product at a price lower than that of the same product in the home market.

E

e-business (electronic business) the organized effort of individuals to produce and sell, for a profit, the products and services that satisfy society's needs through the facilities available on the Internet.

economic community an organization of nations formed to promote the free movement of resources and products among its members and to create common economic policies.

economic model of social responsibility the view that society will benefit most when business is left alone to produce and market profitable products that society needs.

economy the way in which people deal with the creation and distribution of wealth.

electronic funds transfer (EFT) system a means of performing financial transactions through a computer terminal.

embargo a complete halt to trading with a particular nation or in a particular product.

employee benefit a reward in addition to regular compensation that is provided indirectly to employees.

employee ownership a situation in which employees own the company they work for by virtue of being stockholders.

employee training the process of teaching operations and training employees how to do their present jobs more effectively and efficiently.

empowerment making employees more involved in their jobs by increasing their participation in decision making.

entrepreneur a person who risks time, effort, and money to start and operate a business.

entrepreneurial leadership personality-based leadership style in which the manager seeks to inspire workers with a vision of what can be accomplished to benefit all stakeholders.

Equal Employment Opportunity Commission (EEOC) a government agency with the power to investigate complaints of employment discrimination and the power to sue firms that practice it.

equity capital money received from the owners or from the sale of shares of ownership in a business.

equity theory a theory of motivation based on the premise that people are motivated to obtain and preserve equitable treatment for themselves.

esteem needs our need for respect, recognition, and a sense of our own accomplishment and worth.

ethics the study of right and wrong and of the morality of the choices individuals make.

everyday low prices (EDLPs) setting a low price for products on a consistent basis.

exclusive distribution the use of only a single retail outlet for a product in a large geographic area.

executive information system (EIS) a computer-based system that facilitates and supports the decision-making needs of top managers and senior executives by providing easy access to both internal and external information.

expectancy theory a model of motivation based on the assumption that motivation depends on how much we want something and on how likely we think we are to get it.

expert system a type of computer program that uses artificial intelligence to imitate a human's ability to think.

Export-Import Bank of the United States an independent agency of the U.S. government whose function is to assist in financing the exports of American firms.

exporting selling and shipping raw materials or products to other nations.

express warranty a written explanation of the producer's responsibilities in the event that a product is found to be defective or otherwise unsatisfactory.

external recruiting the attempt to attract job applicants from outside an organization.

F

factor a firm that specializes in buying other firms' accounts receivable.

factors of production resources used to produce goods and services.

factory system a system of manufacturing in which all the materials, machinery, and workers required to manufacture a product are assembled in one place.

family branding the strategy in which a firm uses the same brand for all or most of its products.

feature article a piece (of up to 3,000 words) prepared by an organization for inclusion in a particular publication.

federal deficit a shortfall created when the federal government spends more in a fiscal year than it receives.

financial accounting generates financial statements and reports for interested people outside an organization.

financial leverage the use of borrowed funds to increase the return on owners' equity.

financial management all the activities concerned with obtaining money and using it effectively.

financial manager a manager who is primarily responsible for an organization's financial resources.

financial plan a plan for obtaining and using the money needed to implement an organization's goals and objectives.

financial ratio a number that shows the relationship between two elements of a firm's financial statements.

first-line manager a manager who coordinates and supervises the activities of operating employees.

fiscal policy government influence on the amount of savings and expenditures; accomplished by altering the tax structure and by changing the levels of government spending.

fixed assets assets that will be held or used for a period longer than one year.

fixed cost a cost incurred no matter how many units of a product are produced or sold.

flexible benefit plan compensation plan whereby an employee receives a predetermined amount of benefit dollars to spend on a package of benefits he or she has selected to meet individual needs.

flexible manufacturing system (FMS) a single production system that combines electronic machines and CIM.

flextime a system in which employees set their own work hours within employer-determined limits.

foreign corporation a corporation in any state in which it does business except the one in which it is incorporated.

foreign-exchange control a restriction on the amount of a particular foreign currency that can be purchased or sold.

form utility utility created by people converting raw materials, finances, and information into finished products.

forum an interactive version of a community bulletin board that focuses on threaded discussions.

franchise a license to operate an individually owned business as though it were part of a chain of outlets or stores.

franchisee a person or organization purchasing a franchise.

franchising the actual granting of a franchise.

franchisor an individual or organization granting a franchise.

free enterprise the system of business in which individuals are free to decide what to produce, how to produce it, and at what price to sell it.

frequent-user incentive a program developed to reward customers who engage in repeat (frequent) purchases.

full-service wholesaler a middleman that performs the entire range of wholesaler functions.

functional middleman a middleman that helps in the transfer of ownership of products but does not take title to the products.

G

General Agreement on Tariffs and Trade (GATT) an international organization of 158 nations dedicated to reducing or eliminating tariffs and other barriers to world trade.

generally accepted accounting principles (GAAPs) an accepted set of guidelines and practices for companies reporting financial information and for the accounting profession.

general-merchandise wholesaler a middleman that deals in a wide variety of products.

general partner a person who assumes full or shared responsibility for operating a business.

generic product (or brand) a product with no brand at all.

goal an end result that an organization is expected to achieve over a one- to ten-year period.

goal-setting theory a theory of motivation suggesting that employees are motivated to achieve goals that they and their managers establish together.

grapevine the informal communications network within an organization.

green IT a term used to describe all of a firm's activities to support a healthy environment and sustain the planet.

gross domestic product (GDP) the total dollar value of all goods and services produced by all people within the boundaries of a country during a one-year period.

gross profit a firm's net sales less the cost of goods sold.

gross sales the total dollar amount of all goods and services sold during the accounting period.

H

hard-core unemployed workers with little education or vocational training and a long history of unemployment.

hostile takeover a situation in which the management and board of directors of a firm targeted for acquisition disapprove of the merger.

hourly wage a specific amount of money paid for each hour of work.

human resources management (HRM) all the activities involved in acquiring, maintaining, and developing an organization's human resources.

human resources manager a person charged with managing an organization's human resources programs.

human resources planning the development of strategies to meet a firm's future human resources needs.

hygiene factors job factors that reduce dissatisfaction when present to an acceptable degree but that do not necessarily result in high levels of motivation.

I

import duty (tariff) a tax levied on a particular foreign product entering a country.

importing purchasing raw materials or products in other nations and bringing them into one's own country.

import quota a limit on the amount of a particular good that may be imported into a country during a given period of time.

inbound marketing a marketing term that describes new ways of gaining attention and ultimately customers by creating content on a website that pulls customers in.

incentive payment a payment in addition to wages, salary, or commissions.

income statement a summary of a firm's revenues and expenses during a specified accounting period.

independent retailer a firm that operates only one retail outlet.

individual branding the strategy in which a firm uses a different brand for each of its products.

inflation a general rise in the level of prices.

informal group a group created by the members themselves to accomplish goals that may or may not be relevant to an organization.

informal organization the pattern of behavior and interaction that stems from personal rather than official relationships.

information data presented in a form that is useful for a specific purpose.

initial public offering (IPO) occurs when a corporation sells common stock to the general public for the first time.

inspection the examination of the quality of work-in-process.

institutional advertising advertising designed to enhance a firm's image or reputation.

intangible assets assets that do not exist physically but that have a value based on the rights or privileges they confer on a firm.

integrated marketing communications coordination of promotion efforts to ensure maximal informational and persuasive impact on customers.

intensive distribution the use of all available outlets for a product.

intermittent process a manufacturing process in which a firm's manufacturing machines and equipment are changed to produce different products.

internal recruiting considering present employees as applicants for available positions.

International business all business activities that involve exchanges across national boundaries.

International Monetary Fund (IMF) an international bank with 188 member nations that makes short-term loans to developing countries experiencing balance-of-payment deficits.

International Organization for Standardization (ISO) a network of national standards institutes and similar organizations from over 160 different countries that is charged with developing standards for quality products and services that are traded throughout the globe.

interpersonal skills the ability to deal effectively with other people.

inventory control the process of managing inventories in such a way as to minimize inventory costs, including both holding costs and potential stock-out costs.

inventory turnover a financial ratio calculated by dividing the cost of goods sold in one year by the average value of the inventory.

investment banking firm an organization that assists corporations in raising funds, usually by helping to sell new issues of stocks, bonds, or other financial securities.

invisible hand a term created by Adam Smith to describe how an individual's personal gain benefits others and a nation's economy.

J

job analysis a systematic procedure for studying jobs to determine their various elements and requirements.

job description a list of the elements that make up a particular job.

job enlargement expanding a worker's assignments to include additional but similar tasks.

job enrichment a motivation technique that provides employees with more variety and responsibility in their jobs.

job evaluation the process of determining the relative worth of the various jobs within a firm.

job redesign a type of job enrichment in which work is restructured to cultivate the worker-job match.

job rotation the systematic shifting of employees from one job to another.

job sharing an arrangement whereby two people share one full-time position.

job specialization the separation of all organizational activities into distinct tasks and the assignment of different tasks to different people.

job specification a list of the qualifications required to perform a particular job.

joint venture an agreement between two or more groups to form a business entity in order to achieve a specific goal or to operate for a specific period of time.

just-in-time inventory system a system designed to ensure that materials or supplies arrive at a facility just when they are needed so that storage and holding costs are minimized.

K

key performance indicators (KPIs) measurements that define and measure the progress of an organization toward achieving its objectives.

knowledge management (KM) a firm's procedures for generating, using, and sharing the data and information.

L

labeling the presentation of information on a product or its package.

labor-intensive technology a process in which people must do most of the work.

leadership the ability to influence others.

leading the process of influencing people to work toward a common goal.

lean manufacturing a concept built on the idea of eliminating waste from all of the activities required to produce a product or service.

letter of credit issued by a bank on request of an importer stating that the bank will pay an amount of money to a stated beneficiary.

liabilities a firm's debts and obligations.

licensing a contractual agreement in which one firm permits another to produce and market its product and use its brand name in return for a royalty or other compensation.

lifestyle shopping center an open-air-environment shopping center with upscale chain specialty stores.

limited liability a feature of corporate ownership that limits each owner's financial liability to the amount of money that he or she has paid for the corporation's stock.

limited-liability company (LLC) a form of business ownership that combines the benefits of a corporation and a partnership while avoiding some of the restrictions and disadvantages of those forms of ownership.

limited-line wholesaler a middleman that stocks only a few product lines but carries numerous product items within each line.

limited partner a person who invests money in a business but has no management responsibility or liability for losses beyond the amount he or she invested in the partnership.

line-and-staff structure an organizational structure that utilizes the chain of command from a line structure in combination with the assistance of staff managers.

line extension development of a new product that is closely related to one or more products in the existing product line but designed specifically to meet somewhat different customer needs.

line managers a position in which a person makes decisions and gives orders to subordinates to achieve the organization's goals.

line of credit a loan that is approved before the money is actually needed.

line structure an organizational structure in which the chain of command goes directly from person to person throughout the organization.

liquidity the ease with which an asset can be converted into cash.

long-term financing money that will be used for longer than one year.

long-term liabilities debts that need not be repaid for at least one year.

lump-sum salary increase an entire pay raise taken in one lump sum.

M

macroeconomics the study of the national economy and the global economy.

major equipment large tools and machines used for production purposes.

Malcolm Baldrige National Quality Award an award given by the President of the United States to organizations judged to be outstanding in specific managerial tasks that lead to improved quality for both products and services.

malware a general term that describes software designed to infiltrate a computer system without the user's consent.

management the process of coordinating people and other resources to achieve the goals of an organization.

management by objectives (MBO) a motivation technique in which managers and employees collaborate in setting goals.

management development the process of preparing managers and other professionals to assume increased responsibility in both present and future positions.

management information system (MIS) a system that provides managers and employees with the information they need to perform their jobs as effectively as possible.

managerial accounting provides managers and employees with the information needed to make decisions about a firm's financing, investing, marketing, and operating activities.

manufacturer (or producer) brand a brand that is owned by a manufacturer.

market a group of individuals or organizations, or both, that need products in a given category and that have the ability, willingness, and authority to purchase them.

market economy an economic system in which businesses and individuals decide what to produce and buy, and the market determines quantities sold and prices.

marketing the activity, set of institutions, and processes for creating, communicating, delivering, and exchanging offerings that have value for customers, clients, partners, and society at large.

marketing concept a business philosophy that a firm should provide goods and services that satisfy customers' needs through a coordinated set of activities that allow the firm to achieve its objectives.

marketing information system a system for managing marketing information that is gathered continually from internal and external sources.

marketing manager a manager who is responsible for facilitating the exchange of products between an organization and its customers or clients.

marketing mix a combination of product, price, distribution, and promotion developed to satisfy a particular target market.

marketing plan a written document that specifies an organization's resources, objectives, strategy, and implementation and control efforts to be used in marketing a specific product or product group.

market price the price at which the quantity demanded is exactly equal to the quantity supplied.

market segment a group of individuals or organizations within a market that share one or more common characteristics.

market segmentation the process of dividing a market into segments and directing a marketing mix at a particular segment or segments rather than at the total market.

marketing research the process of systematically gathering, recording, and analyzing data concerning a particular marketing problem.

marketing strategy a plan that will enable an organization to make the best use of its resources and advantages to meet its objectives.

markup the amount a seller adds to the cost of a product to determine its basic selling price.

Maslow's hierarchy of needs a sequence of human needs in the order of their importance.

mass production a manufacturing process that lowers the cost required to produce a large number of identical or similar products over a long period of time.

materials handling the actual physical handling of goods, in warehouses as well as during transportation.

materials requirements planning (MRP) a computerized system that integrates production planning and inventory control.

matrix structure an organizational structure that combines vertical and horizontal lines of authority, usually by superimposing product departmentalization on a functionally departmentalized organization.

maturity date the date on which a corporation is to repay borrowed money.

media sharing sites allow users to upload photos, videos, and podcasts.

merchant middleman a middleman that actually takes title to products by buying them.

merchant wholesaler a middleman that purchases goods in large quantities and sells them to other wholesalers or retailers and to institutional, farm, government, professional, or industrial users.

merger the purchase of one corporation by another.

microeconomics the study of the decisions made by individuals and businesses.

middleman (or marketing intermediary) a marketing organization that links a producer and user within a marketing channel.

middle manager a manager who implements the strategy and major policies developed by top management.

Millennials tech-savvy digital natives born after 1980.

minority a racial, religious, political, national, or other group regarded as different from the larger group of which it is a part and that is often singled out for unfavorable treatment.

mission a statement of the basic purpose that makes an organization different from others.

missionary salesperson a salesperson—generally employed by a manufacturer—who visits retailers to persuade them to buy the manufacturer's products.

mixed economy an economy that exhibits elements of both capitalism and socialism.

monetary policies Federal Reserve's decisions that determine the size of the supply of money in the nation and the level of interest rates.

monopolistic competition a market situation in which there are many buyers along with a relatively large number of sellers who differentiate their products from the products of competitors.

monopoly a market (or industry) with only one seller, and there are barriers to keep other firms from entering the industry.

morale an employee's feelings about the job, about superiors, and about the firm itself.

mortgage bond a corporate bond secured by various assets of the issuing firm.

motivating the process of providing reasons for people to work in the best interests of an organization.

motivation the individual internal process that energizes, directs, and sustains behavior; the personal "force" that causes you or me to behave in a particular way.

motivation factors job factors that increase motivation, although their absence does not necessarily result in dissatisfaction.

motivation-hygiene theory the idea that satisfaction and dissatisfaction are separate and distinct dimensions.

multilateral development bank (MDB) an internationally supported bank that provides loans to developing countries to help them grow.

multinational enterprise a firm that operates on a worldwide scale without ties to any specific nation or region.

multiple-unit pricing the strategy of setting a single price for two or more units.

N

national debt the total of all federal deficits.

need a personal requirement.

negotiated pricing establishing a final price through bargaining.

neighborhood shopping center a planned shopping center consisting of several small convenience and specialty stores.

net income occurs when revenues exceed expenses.

net loss occurs when expenses exceed revenues.

net sales the actual dollar amounts received by a firm for the goods and services it has sold after adjustment for returns, allowances, and discounts.

network structure an organizational structure in which administration is the primary function, and most other functions are contracted out to other firms.

news release a typed page of about 300 words provided by an organization to the media as a form of publicity.

non-price competition competition based on factors other than price.

nonstore retailing a type of retailing whereby consumers purchase products without visiting a store.

nontariff barrier a nontax measure imposed by a government to favor domestic over foreign suppliers.

not-for-profit corporation a corporation organized to provide a social, educational, religious, or other service rather than to earn a profit.

O

objective a specific statement detailing what an organization intends to accomplish over a shorter period of time.

odd-number pricing the strategy of setting prices using odd numbers that are slightly below whole-dollar amounts.

off-price retailer a store that buys manufacturers' seconds, overruns, returns, and off-season merchandise for resale to consumers at deep discounts.

oligopoly a market (or industry) in which there are few sellers.

online retailing retailing that makes products available to buyers through computer connections.

open corporation a corporation whose stock can be bought and sold by any individual.

operating expenses all business costs other than the cost of goods sold.

operational plan a type of plan designed to implement tactical plans.

operations management all the activities required to produce goods and services.

operations manager a manager who manages the systems that convert resources into goods and services.

order getter a salesperson who is responsible for selling a firm's products to new customers and increasing sales to present customers.

order processing activities involved in receiving and filling customers' purchase orders.

order taker a salesperson who handles repeat sales in ways that maintain positive relationships with customers.

organization a group of two or more people working together to achieve a common set of goals.

organizational height the number of layers, or levels, of management in a firm.

organization chart a diagram that represents the positions and relationships within an organization.

organizing the grouping of resources and activities to accomplish some end result in an efficient and effective manner.

orientation the process of acquainting new employees with an organization.

outsourcing the process of finding outside vendors and suppliers that provide professional help, parts, or materials at a lower cost.

over-the-counter (OTC) market a network of dealers who buy and sell the stocks of corporations that are not listed on a securities exchange.

owners' equity the difference between a firm's assets and its liabilities.

P

packaging all the activities involved in developing and providing a container with graphics for a product.

participative leadership leadership style in which all members of a team are involved in identifying essential goals and developing strategies to reach those goals.

partnership a voluntary association of two or more persons to act as co-owners of a business for profit.

part-time work permanent employment in which individuals work less than a standard work week.

penetration pricing the strategy of setting a low price for a new product.

perfect (or pure) competition the market situation in which there are many buyers and sellers of a product, and no single buyer or seller is powerful enough to affect the price of that product.

performance appraisal the evaluation of employees' current and potential levels of performance to allow managers to make objective human resources decisions.

periodic discounting temporary reduction of prices on a patterned or systematic basis.

personal income the income an individual receives from all sources less the Social Security taxes the individual must pay.

personal selling personal communication aimed at informing customers and persuading them to buy a firm's products.

physical distribution all those activities concerned with the efficient movement of products from the producer to the ultimate user.

physiological needs the things we require for survival.

piece-rate system a compensation system under which employees are paid a certain amount for each unit of output they produce.

place utility utility created by making a product available at a location where customers wish to purchase it.

plan an outline of the actions by which an organization intends to accomplish its goals and objectives.

planning establishing organizational goals and deciding how to accomplish them.

planning horizon the period during which an operational plan will be in effect.

plant layout the arrangement of machinery, equipment, and personnel within a production facility.

podcasts digital audio or video files that people listen to or watch online on tablets, computers, MP3 players, or smartphones.

point-of-purchase display promotional material placed within a retail store.

pollution the contamination of water, air, or land through the actions of people in an industrialized society.

possession utility utility created by transferring title (or ownership) of a product to a buyer.

preferred stock stock owned by individuals or firms who usually do not have voting rights but whose claims on dividends are paid before those of common-stock owners.

premium a gift that a producer offers a customer in return for buying its product.

premium pricing pricing the highest-quality or most-versatile products higher than other models in the product line.

press conference a meeting at which invited media personnel hear important news announcements and receive supplementary textual materials and photographs.

price the amount of money a seller is willing to accept in exchange for a product at a given time and under given circumstances.

price competition an emphasis on setting a price equal to or lower than competitors' prices to gain sales or market share.

price leaders products priced below the usual markup, near cost, or below cost.

price lining the strategy of selling goods only at certain predetermined prices that reflect definite price breaks.

price skimming the strategy of charging the highest possible price for a product during the introduction stage of its life-cycle.

primary-demand advertising advertising whose purpose is to increase the demand for all brands of a product within a specific industry.

primary market a market in which an investor purchases financial securities (via an investment bank) directly from the issuer of those securities.

prime interest rate the lowest rate charged by a bank for a short-term loan.

private placement occurs when stock and other corporate securities are sold directly to insurance companies, pension funds, or large institutional investors.

problem the discrepancy between an actual condition and a desired condition.

problem-solving team a team of knowledgeable employees brought together to tackle a specific problem.

process material a material that is used directly in the production of another product but is not readily identifiable in the finished product.

producer price index (PPI) an index that measures prices that producers receive for their finished goods.

product everything one receives in an exchange, including all tangible and intangible attributes and expected benefits; it may be a good, a service, or an idea.

product deletion the elimination of one or more products from a product line.

product design the process of creating a set of specifications from which a product can be produced.

product differentiation the process of developing and promoting differences between one's product and all similar products.

productivity the average level of output per worker per hour.

product life-cycle a series of stages in which a product's sales revenue and profit increase, reach a peak, and then decline.

product line a group of similar products that differ only in relatively minor characteristics.

product mix all the products a firm offers for sale.

product modification the process of changing one or more of a product's characteristics.

profit what remains after all business expenses have been deducted from sales revenue.

profit-sharing the distribution of a percentage of a firm's profit among its employees.

promissory note a written pledge by a borrower to pay a certain sum of money to a creditor at a specified future date.

promotion communication about an organization and its products that is intended to inform, persuade, or remind target-market members.

promotion mix the particular combination of promotion methods a firm uses to reach a target market.

proxy a legal form listing issues to be decided at a stockholders' meeting and enabling stockholders to transfer their voting rights to some other individual or individuals.

proxy fight a technique used to gather enough stockholder votes to control a targeted company.

publicity communication in news-story form about an organization, its products, or both.

public relations communication activities used to create and maintain favorable relationships between an organization and various public groups, both internal and external.

purchasing all the activities involved in obtaining required materials, supplies, components, and parts from other firms.

Q

qualitative social media measurement the process of accessing the opinions and beliefs about a brand and primarily uses sentiment analysis to categorize what is being said about a company.

quality circle a team of employees who meet on company time to solve problems of product quality.

quality control the process of ensuring that goods and services are produced in accordance with design specifications.

quantitative social media measurement using numerical measurements, such as counting the number of website visitors, number of fans and followers, number of leads generated, and the number of new customers.

R

random discounting temporary reduction of prices on an unsystematic basis.

raw material a basic material that actually becomes part of a physical product; usually comes from mines, forests, oceans, or recycled solid wastes.

rebate a return of part of the purchase price of a product.

recession two or more consecutive three-month periods of decline in a country's GDP.

recruiting the process of attracting qualified job applicants.

reference pricing pricing a product at a moderate level and positioning it next to a more expensive model or brand.

regional shopping center a planned shopping center containing large department stores, numerous specialty stores, restaurants, movie theaters, and sometimes even hotels.

registered bond a bond registered in the owner's name by the issuing company.

reinforcement theory a theory of motivation based on the premise that rewarded behavior is likely to be repeated, whereas punished behavior is less likely to recur.

relationship marketing establishing long-term, mutually satisfying buyer–seller relationships.

replacement chart a list of key personnel and their possible replacements within a firm.

research and development (R&D) a set of activities intended to identify new ideas that have the potential to result in new goods and services.

reshoring a situation in which U.S. manufacturers bring manufacturing jobs back to the United States.

responsibility the duty to do a job or perform a task.

retailer a middleman that buys from producers or other middlemen and sells to consumers.

retained earnings the portion of a corporation's profits not distributed to stockholders.

return on sales (or profit margin) a financial ratio calculated by dividing net income after taxes by net sales.

revenues the dollar amounts earned by a firm from selling goods, providing services, or performing business activities.

revenue stream a source of revenue flowing into a firm.

revolving credit agreement a guaranteed line of credit.

risk-return ratio a ratio based on the principle that a high-risk decision should generate higher financial returns for a business and more conservative decisions often generate lower returns.

Robotics the use of programmable machines to perform a variety of tasks by manipulating materials and tools.

S

safety needs the things we require for physical and emotional security.

salary a specific amount of money paid for an employee's work during a set calendar period, regardless of the actual number of hours worked.

sales forecast an estimate of the amount of a product that an organization expects to sell during a certain period of time based on a specified level of marketing effort.

sales promotion the use of activities or materials as direct inducements to customers or salespersons.

sales support personnel employees who aid in selling but are more involved in locating prospects, educating customers, building goodwill for the firm, and providing follow-up service.

sample a free product given to customers to encourage trial and purchase.

Sarbanes-Oxley Act of 2002 provides sweeping new legal protection for employees who report corporate misconduct.

scheduling the process of ensuring that materials and other resources are at the right place at the right time.

scientific management the application of scientific principles to management of work and workers.

S-corporation a corporation that is taxed as though it were a partnership.

secondary market a market for existing financial securities that are traded between investors.

secondary-market pricing setting one price for the primary target market and a different price for another market.

securities exchange a marketplace where member brokers meet to buy and sell securities.

selection the process of gathering information about applicants for a position and then using that information to choose the most appropriate applicant.

selective-demand (or brand) advertising advertising that is used to sell a particular brand of product.

selective distribution the use of only a portion of the available outlets for a product in each geographic area.

self-actualization needs the need to grow and develop and to become all that we are capable of being.

self-managed teams groups of employees with the authority and skills to manage themselves.

sentiment analysis a measurement that uses technology to detect the moods, attitudes, or emotions of people who experience a social media activity.

serial bonds bonds of a single issue that mature on different dates.

Service Corps of Retired Executives (SCORE) a group of businesspeople who volunteer their services to small businesses through the SBA.

service economy an economy in which more effort is devoted to the production of services than to the production of goods.

shopping product an item for which buyers are willing to expend considerable effort on planning and making the purchase.

short-term financing money that will be used for one year or less.

sinking fund a sum of money to which deposits are made each year for the purpose of redeeming a bond issue.

Six Sigma a disciplined approach that relies on statistical data and improved methods to eliminate defects for a firm's products and services.

skills inventory a computerized data bank containing information on the skills and experience of all present employees.

small business one that is independently owned and operated for profit and is not dominant in its field.

Small Business Administration (SBA) a governmental agency that assists, counsels, and protects the interests of small businesses in the United States.

small-business development centers (SBDCs) university-based groups that provide individual counseling and practical training to owners of small businesses.

small-business institutes (SBIs) groups of senior and graduate students in business administration who provide management counseling to small businesses.

small-business investment companies (SBICs) privately owned firms that provide venture capital to small enterprises that meet their investment standards.

social audit a comprehensive report of what an organization has done and is doing with regard to social issues that affect it.

social content sites allow companies to create and share information about their products and services.

social game a multiplayer, competitive, goal-oriented activity with defined rules of engagement and online connectivity among a community of players.

social media the online interaction that allows people and businesses to communicate and share ideas, personal information, and information about products or services.

social media communities social networks based on the relationships among people.

social media marketing the utilization of social media technologies, channels, and software to create, communicate, deliver, and exchange offerings that have value for an organization.

social needs the human requirements for love and affection and a sense of belonging.

social responsibility the recognition that business activities have an impact on society and the consideration of that impact in business decision making.

socioeconomic model of social responsibility the concept that business should emphasize not only profits but also the impact of its decisions on society.

sole proprietorship a business that is owned (and usually operated) by one person.

span of management (or span of control) the number of workers who report directly to one manager.

special-event pricing advertised sales or price cutting linked to a holiday, season, or event.

specialization the separation of a manufacturing process into distinct tasks and the assignment of the different tasks to different individuals.

specialty-line wholesaler a middleman that carries a select group of products within a single line.

specialty product an item that possesses one or more unique characteristics for which a significant group of buyers is willing to expend considerable purchasing effort.

speculative production the time lag between the actual production of goods and when the goods are sold.

staff managers a position created to provide support, advice, and expertise within an organization.

stakeholders all the different people or groups of people who are affected by an organization's policies, decisions, and activities.

standard of living a loose, subjective measure of how well off an individual or a society is, mainly in terms of want satisfaction through goods and services.

standing committee a relatively permanent committee charged with performing some recurring task.

statement of cash flows a statement that illustrates how the company's operating, investing, and financing activities affect cash during an accounting period.

statistic a measure that summarizes a particular characteristic of an entire group of numbers.

stock the shares of ownership of a corporation.

stockholder a person who owns a corporation's stock.

store (or private brand) a brand that is owned by an individual wholesaler or retailer.

strategic alliance a partnership formed to create competitive advantage on a worldwide basis.

strategic plan an organization's broadest plan, developed as a guide for major policy setting and decision making.

strategic planning process the establishment of an organization's major goals and objectives and the allocation of resources to achieve them.

supermarket a large self-service store that sells primarily food and household products.

superstore a large retail store that carries not only food and nonfood products ordinarily found in supermarkets but also additional product lines.

supply an item that facilitates production and operations but does not become part of a finished product.

supply the quantity of a product that producers are willing to sell at each of various prices.

supply-chain management long-term partnership among channel members working together to create a distribution system that reduces inefficiencies, costs, and redundancies while creating a competitive advantage and satisfying customers.

sustainability creating and maintaining the conditions under which humans and nature can exist in productive harmony while fulfilling the social, economic, and other requirements of present and future generations.

SWOT analysis the identification and evaluation of a firm's strengths, weaknesses, opportunities, and threats.

syndicate a temporary association of individuals or firms organized to perform a specific task that requires a large amount of capital.

synthetic process a process in operations management in which raw materials or components are combined to create a finished product.

T

tactical plan a smaller scale plan developed to implement a strategy.

target market a group of individuals or organizations, or both, for which a firm develops and maintains a marketing mix suitable for the specific needs and preferences of that group.

task force a committee established to investigate a major problem or pending decision.

team two or more workers operating as a coordinated unit to accomplish a specific task or goal.

technical salesperson a salesperson who assists a company's current customers in technical matters.

technical skills specific skills needed to accomplish a specialized activity.

telecommuting working at home all the time or for a portion of the work week.

telemarketing the performance of marketing-related activities by telephone.

television home shopping a form of selling in which products are presented to television viewers, who can buy them by calling a toll-free number and paying with a credit card.

tender offer an offer to purchase the stock of a firm targeted for acquisition at a price just high enough to tempt stockholders to sell their shares.

term-loan agreement a promissory note that requires a borrower to repay a loan in monthly, quarterly, semiannual, or annual installments.

Theory X a concept of employee motivation generally consistent with Taylor's scientific management; assumes that employees dislike work and will function only in a highly controlled work environment.

Theory Y a concept of employee motivation generally consistent with the ideas of the human relations movement; assumes responsibility and work toward organizational goals, and by doing so they also achieve personal rewards.

Theory Z the belief that some middle ground between type A and type J practices is best for American business.

time utility utility created by making a product available when customers wish to purchase it.

top manager an upper-level executive who guides and controls the overall fortunes of an organization.

total cost the sum of the fixed costs and the variable costs attributed to a product.

total quality management (TQM) the coordination of efforts directed at improving customer satisfaction, increasing employee participation, strengthening supplier partnerships, and facilitating an organizational atmosphere of continuous quality improvement.

total revenue the total amount received from the sales of a product.

trade credit a type of short-term financing extended by a seller who does not require immediate payment after delivery of merchandise.

trade deficit a negative balance of trade.

trade name the complete and legal name of an organization.

trade salesperson a salesperson—generally employed by a food producer or processor—who assists customers in promoting products, especially in retail stores.

trade sales promotion method a sales promotion method designed to encourage wholesalers and retailers to stock and actively promote a manufacturer's product.

trademark a brand name or brand mark that is registered with the U.S. Patent and Trademark Office and thus is legally protected from use by anyone except its owner.

trade show an industry-wide exhibit at which many sellers display their products.

trading company provides a link between buyers and sellers in different countries.

traditional specialty store a store that carries a narrow product mix with deep product lines.

transfer pricing prices charged in sales between an organization's units.

transportation the shipment of products to customers.

trustee an individual or an independent firm that acts as a bond owner's representative.

U

undifferentiated approach directing a single marketing mix at the entire market for a particular product.

unemployment rate the percentage of a nation's labor force unemployed at any time.

unlimited liability a legal concept that holds a business owner personally responsible for all the debts of the business.

unsecured financing financing that is not backed by collateral.

utility the ability of a good or service to satisfy a human need.

V

variable cost a cost that depends on the number of units produced.

venture capital money that is invested in small (and sometimes struggling) firms that have the potential to become very successful.

virtual team a team consisting of members who are geographically dispersed but communicate electronically.

W

wage survey a collection of data on prevailing wage rates within an industry or a geographic area.

warehouse club a large-scale members-only establishment that combines features of cash-and-carry wholesaling with discount retailing.

warehouse showroom a retail facility in a large, low-cost building with a large on-premises inventory and minimal service.

warehousing the set of activities involved in receiving and storing goods and preparing them for reshipment.

whistle-blowing informing the press or government officials about unethical practices within one's organization.

wholesaler a middleman that sells products to other firms.

wiki a collaborative online working space that enables members to contribute content that can be shared with other people.

World Trade Organization (WTO) powerful successor to GATT that incorporates trade in goods, services, and ideas.

Z

zero-base budgeting a budgeting approach in which every expense in every budget must be justified.

Name Index

Subject Index

A

absolute advantage, 67–68
accessibility, transportation mode, 370, 371
accessory equipment, 325
accountability, creating, 190
accounting
  careers in, 440–441
  defined, 437
  equation, 441–442
  fraud, 439
  types of, 440
accounts payable, 445
accounts receivable, 444
  factoring, 476
  of a firm, 444
  pledged for short-term financing, 476
accumulated depreciation, 444
acid rain, 55
acquisition, 119–120
  of people, 239–240
  trends for the future, 121
adaptations, 331
ad hoc committee, 199
adjourning stage, of team development, 286
administrative managers, 169, 431
advertising, 372
  campaign, execution of, 376
  campaign, major steps in developing, 374–376
  defined, 372
  false and misleading, 37
  social and legal considerations, 377
  types of, 373–374
advertising agency, 376
advertising appropriation, 374
advertising e-business model, 415
advertising message, 375
advertising money, shifting to digital marketing, 403
advertising objectives, 374
advertising platform, 374
advisory authority, 194
advisory positions, 185
aesthetic modifications, of existing products, 329
affirmative action, 52–53, 259

Affordable Care Act (2010), 258
Age Discrimination in Employment Act (1967-1986), 258
agent, 362
aircraft emissions, 55, 56
air pollution, 56, 57
air transport, 370–371
alien corporation, 111
allocator, price serving function of, 339
allowance, 348
  for doubtful accounts, 444
alternatives, 174
American Recovery and Reinvestment Act (2009), 54
Americans with Disabilities Act (ADA) (1990), 258, 259–260
analytical process, in operations management, 210
analytic skills, of managers, 6, 170
anational company, 85
annual meetings, 479, 480
annual reports, 442, 479, 489
app business, building a million-dollar, 12
applied research, 213
appraisal errors, avoiding, 256
Armenia, economic growth, 75
articles of incorporation, 111
articles of partnership, 106, 107
ASEAN-5 countries, 74
Asian countries, economic growth, 89
assembly line, 217, 218
assessment centers, 249
assets, 441, 442–445
  proceeds from the sale of, 469
Association of Southeast Asian Nations, 80
associations, of brand, 335
attrition, cutbacks through, 242
audit, 438
authority
  within an organization, 172
  decentralization of, 191–192
  delegation of, 190–191
  granting, 190
authors, e-mail addresses of, 8
autocratic leadership, 172
automatic vending, 366
automation, 216, 226–228
Azerbaijan, economic growth, 75

B

balance of payments, 70
balance of trade, 18, 68, 69
balance sheet, 442, 443
bar chart, example, 436
barter, 22
basic research, 213
basis, for segmentation, 306
B2B firms, types of, 413–414
"Be a Star" campaign, 409
behavior modification, 280
benchmarking, 175, 223
benchmarks, setting, 409
benefits, 240
benefits-to-the-community component, of a business plan, 99
bilingual skills, from cultural diversity, 244
bill of lading, 82
"Blast! Then Refine,", 174
blogs, 398–399, 409
board of directors, 112–113
Boeing Ethics Line, 58
bond indenture, 484
bonds
  types of, 484
"book and hold," 457–458
brainstorming, 174
branches, of an exporting firm, 82–83
brand awareness, 335
brand equity, 335
brand extensions, 337
branding, 333–337
  benefits of, 334–335
  strategies, 336
brand insistence, 335
brand loyalty, 334
brand mark, 333
brand names, 333, 336
brand preference, 334–335
brand recognition, 334
brands, 333
  choosing and protecting, 335–336
  top ten most valuable, 335
  types of, 333–334
Brazil, 93
breakeven quantity, 342, 343
bribes, as unethical, 36
broker, 362

brokerage e-business model, 415
budget, 468
budgeting, approaches to, 468–469
bundle pricing, 346
business
  activities of, 8–10
  changing world of, 3–8
  considerations for organizing, 186
  defined, 410
  defined, 8
  filing for bankruptcy, 462
  in a mixed economy, 13
  reasons to study, 4–7
  selecting type of, 97
  starting your own, 6
  start-ups, closures, and bankruptcies
    in the U.S. from 2005, 134
  today in the U.S., 22–26
business analysis, of new products, 332
business application software, 437
business buying behavior, 314, 316
business communications, presenting
    ethical questions, 36
business cycle, 17–19
business development, 23
business environment, current, 24–25
business ethics, defined, 33
business loans, 470–471
  SBA's, 143
business markets, discounts listed
    for, 348
business model, 413
business ownership, special types of,
    116–118
business plan
  components of, 97, 99, 138–140
  defined, 97
  purposes of, 138
  steps in creating, 98
business products. See also business-
    to-business products
  classifications, 325
  pricing, 347–348
business profits, 9–10
business reports, 434–435
business service, 325
business skills and knowledge, of
    partners, 109
business-to-business markets, 303
business-to-business (B2B) model, 413
business-to-business products, 324
business-to-consumer (B2C) model, 415
buyers' purchasing behavior, 324
buying allowance, 382
buying behavior, 314–316

C

CAD. See computer-aided design (CAD)
CAFTA. See Central American Free
    Trade Agreement (CAFTA)
CAFTA-DR, 80

CAM. See computer-aided
    manufacturing (CAM)
Canada, 74, 76
Canadian Free Trade Agreement, 80
capacity
  defined, 216
  exceeding market demand, 219
  of a production facility, 216
capital, 11
  available to partnerships, 106, 107
  ease or raising for corporations, 114
  limited ability to raise, 138
  main ingredient in growth, 119
  sources for entrepreneurs, 139
capital budget, 469
capital-intensive technology, 216
capitalism, 12–14
captioned photograph, 382
captive pricing, 346
carbon dioxide, primary aircraft
    emission, 56
careers
  in accounting, 440–441
  in business, viewing, 4
  choosing, 4–5
  in finance, 463–464
  in operations management, 210
carrier, 369
cash budget, 468
cash deficit, 446
cash discounts, 348
cash flow, 464
cash flows from financing activities, 449
cash flows from investing activities, 449
cash flows from operating activities, 449
cash rewards, for "going green," 282
cash surplus, 446
catalog marketing, 365
category killers, 365
category management, 360
caveat emptor, 45
C-corporation, 115
Central American Free Trade Agreement
    (CAFTA), 80
centralized government planning, 14
centralized organization, 190, 191
certificate of deposit (CD), 470
certification, as a CPA, 441
certified public accountant (CPA), 441
chain of command, 185
chain retailer, 363
Challenger space shuttle disaster, 41
change, ability to adapt to in a small
    business, 137
characteristics, of entrepreneurs, 131
check, 470
chief diversity officer (CDO), 243
chief executive officer (CEO), 167
chief financial officer (CFO), 463
chief operating officer (COO), 167
Children's Online Privacy Protection Act
    (2000), 51

China
  economic growth, 74–75
  steel products imported from, 71
Cigarette Labeling Act (1965), 51
CIM. See computer-integrated
    manufacturing (CIM)
circular flow, in a mixed economy, 13
Civil Rights Act (1964), 52
Civil Rights Act (1991), 257, 258
classification, of products, 325
classroom teaching and lectures, 254
Clayton Antitrust Act (1914), 46
Clean Air Act, 56
Clean Air Act Amendments, 54
clean environment, paying for, 57
cleaning up, short-term loans, 475
Clean Water Act, 55
closed corporation, 110
cloud computing, 417
code of ethics, 39, 40
cohesiveness, of teams, 287
collaborative work, at L.L.Bean, 180
collateral, defined, 471
Columbus, Ohio, popular test marketing
    location, 332
command economies, 14–15
commercial databases, 312
commercialization, of new products, 332
commercial paper, 475, 477
commissions, 251
committees, 199
common carrier, 369
Common Market, 79, 81
Common Market of the Southern Cone
    (MERCOSUR), 81
common stock, 111, 479–480, 485
Commonwealth of Independent
    States, 80
communal culture, 197, 198
communication skills, of
    managers, 171
communications, presenting ethical
    questions, 36
communism, 15
communist countries, former, 15
communities, building in social media,
    400–401
community involvement, as being a
    good corporate citizen, 95
community shopping center, 367
companies, role in encouraging ethics,
    39–41
comparable worth, 250
comparative advantage, 67–68
comparative advertising, 373
comparison discounting, 347
comparison other, 276
compensating balance, 475
compensation, 240
  decisions, 249–250
  defined, 249
  types of, 251

competition
  encouraging, 49
  small businesses providing, 136
  types of, 19–21
competition-based pricing, 343
competitive environment, effects on
    business, 24
competitive forces, in the marketing
    environment, 309
competitors, 161, 162, 163
  concerns of, 34
component part, 325
compromises, 287
computer-aided design (CAD), 227
computer-aided manufacturing
    (CAM), 227
computer-integrated manufacturing
    (CIM), 227
computer manufacturing systems, 227
computer technology, challenges for,
    417–419
computer virus, 417
concentrated market segmentation,
    305, 306
concept testing, of new products,
    331–332
conceptual skills, of managers, 6, 170
conferences and seminars, 254
confidentiality, threats to, 417
conflict, between two or more team
    members, 287
conflict of interest, 36
conglomerate merger, 120–121
consensus basis, for decisions, 234
consensus leaders, 172
constant dollars, 16
consultative leaders, 172
consumer advocates, 50
Consumer Bill of Rights, 48, 49, 50
consumer buying behavior, 314–316
consumer complaints, important source
    of data, 313
consumer confidence index, 18
consumer convenience, packaging
    offering, 337
Consumer Credit Reporting Reform Act
    (1997), 51
consumer demand, for safe
    products, 49
consumer education, 48, 50
consumerism, 48–50
consumer markets, 303
consumer price index (CPI), 17
consumer products, 14, 324
Consumer Product Safety Commission
    Act (1972), 51
consumers
  becoming better informed, 6–7
  buying behavior, 314–316
  household members as, 14
  protecting the rights of, 48, 50
  restriction of choices, 73

consumer sales promotion
    method, 380
consumer-to-consumer model, 415
contingency plan, 164, 165
continual collection, of marketing
    data, 311
continual reinforcement, 275
continuity, lack of, 122
continuous improvement, 223
continuous process, 228
continuous quality improvement, 175
contract carriers, 369
control function, 167
controlling, ongoing activities,
    166–167
convenience product, 324
convenience store, 364
conversion process, 210–212
convertible bond, 484
cookie, 416
cooperative advertising, 382
core competencies, 163
core time, 280
corporate bonds, 482–484, 485
corporate charter, 112
corporate culture, 197–198
Corporate Gifts and Rewards Program,
    at Apple, 280
corporate growth, 119–121
corporate officers, appointed by board
    of directors, 113
corporate profits, 18
corporate raider, 119
corporate structure, 112–113
corporations
  advantages and disadvantages of,
      113–116
  as artificial persons, 109, 111
  conflict within, 122
  forming, 115–116
  performing as good citizens, 47
  restating earnings, 457
corrective actions
  expense of, 49
  taking, 167
cost accounting, 440
cost-based pricing, 341–342
cost comparisons, 476–477, 484–485
cost of goods sold, 448
cost savings, from cultural diversity,
    243, 244
cost, transportation mode, 370, 371
countertrade, 85
coupon, 380
co-workers, affecting ethics, 37
CPA. See certified public accountant
    (CPA)
CPI. See consumer price index (CPI)
creative selling, 377
creativity, from cultural diversity, 244
credit
  available to partnership, 105

Credit Card Accountability,
    Responsibility, and Disclosure Act
    (2009), 51
Credit Card Liability Act (1970), 51
creditors, concerns of, 34
crisis management, 401–402
critical path, 220
cross-functional teams, 195, 284–285
cross-training, for workers, 188
crowdsourcing, 404
crowd voting, 404
Cuba, 15
cultural barriers, 71
cultural diversity, 5
  advantages of, 244
  in human resources, 243–244
cultural norms, affecting ethics, 37
culture, of trust, 198
currency devaluation, 71
current assets, 444
current liabilities, 445
current ratio, 452
customary pricing, 346
customer-driven production, 228
customer lifetime value (CLV), 300
customer orientation, adopting, 302
customer relationship management
    (CRM), 299
customer relationships, managing,
    298–300
customers
  concerns of, 34
  departmentalization by, 189
  firing, 300
  more involved in obtaining
      services, 213
  targeting, 402
customer satisfaction, improving, 175
customer satisfaction scores, 410
customer service, personalized, 125
Cuyahoga River, Cleveland's, 55

D

data
  collecting, 432–433
  compared to information, 429
  defined, 429
  external sources of, 432
  internal sources of, 432
  processing, 434
  storing, 433
  updating, 433
database, 312, 430, 432
data mining, 417
data processing, 434
debenture bond, 484
debt capital, 469, 473, 476, 477
debt financing, sources of short-term,
    473–477
debts, 452–453
decentralized organization, 190, 191

expectancy theory, 276–277
expenses, reducing, 413
expert system, 437
export assistance, sources of, 86, 87
export-import agent, 83
export-import merchant, 82
exporting, 82–83
exports, U.S., 76
express warranty, 339
extension, of products, 214–215
external environmental forces, affecting
    an e-business, 418
external environment, influencing
    decentralization, 191
external recruiting, 246
external sources
    of data, 432
    marketing data from, 311
extinction, managers relying on, 275

F

facilitating functions, of marketing, 299
facilities planning, 216–219
factoring, 477
factors, 476
    of production, 11
factory system, of manufacturing, 23
Fair Credit Billing Act (1974), 51
Fair Credit Reporting Act (1971), 51
Fair Debt Collection Practices Act
    (1977), 51
Fair Labor Standards Act (1938),
    257, 258
fairness, in business, 35
Fair Packaging and Labeling Act
    (1966), 51
Family and Medical Leave Act (1993),
    258
family branding, 336
family packaging, 338
family time, increased demand for, 281
FASB. See Financial Accounting
    Standards Board (FASB)
feature article, 382
Federal deficit, 19
Federal Hazardous Substances Labeling
    Act (1960), 51
federal regulations, specifying
    information for labeling, 338–339
Federal Trade Commission Act (1914), 46
finance, careers in, 463–464
financial accounting, 440
Financial Accounting Standards Board
    (FASB), 438
financial assistance, SBA's, 143–144
financial benefits, of TQM
    programs, 176
financial data, 441, 451–452
financial leverage, 481
financial management, 461–464
financial managers, 168–169, 430

financial needs, budgeting for, 468–469
financial performance, monitoring and
    evaluating, 469–470
financial plan, 467–469
financial ratios, 452–453
financial resources, 8, 161, 168–169, 411
financial security, need for, 268
financial statements, evaluating, 450–453
financing activities, cash flows from, 449
financing, need for, 464–467
finished-goods inventory, 221
firing, unnecessary employees, 242–243
firms, information requirements, 430–431
first-line managers, 168
fiscal policy, 18
fixed assets, 444–445
fixed cost, 342
fixed-position layout, 218, 219
flat organization, 192, 193
flexibility, from cultural diversity, 244
flexible benefit plans, 252
flexible manufacturing system
    (FMS), 228
flextime, 280–281
flotation costs, 478
FMS. See flexible manufacturing system
    (FMS)
FOB destination, 348
FOB origin pricing, 348
focus, of a conversion process, 211
follow-up, monitoring schedules, 222
Food Quality Protection Act (1996), 54
foreign corporation, 111
foreign-exchange control, 71
formal leadership, 172
formation, difficulty and expense for
    corporations, 122
forming stage, of team development, 286
form utility, 210, 300, 301
forums, 401
fragmented culture, 197, 198
France, quotas for women directors, 113
franchise agreement, typical, 145
franchise, 144
    advantages to, 147
    defined, 144
    obligations, 145
    rights, 145
franchising, 144
    advantages and disadvantages of,
        147–148
    growth of, 146–148
    types of, 144–145
franchisor, 144
free enterprise, 3
free-market economy, 13
free trade, 66
freight forwarders, 370
"French pot" manufacturing method, at
    Graeter's, 95
frequency, transportation mode,
    370, 371

frequent-user incentive, 381
full-service wholesaler, 362
functional authority, 195
functional middleman, 358
functional modifications, of existing
    products, 329
function, departmentalization by, 188
funds, identifying sources of, 469

G

GAAPs. See generally accepted
    accounting principles (GAAPs)
gain sharing, 251
gamification
    of motivation, 276
    of social media, 400
GATT. See General Agreement on Tariffs
    and Trade (GATT)
GDP (gross domestic product)
    comparisons of, 16
    U.S. economy, 75
GE Foundation Developing Futures in
    Education program, 43
General Agreement on Tariffs and Trade
    (GATT), 77–78
general expenses, 448
generally accepted accounting principles
    (GAAPs), 438, 451
general-merchandise wholesaler, 362
general partners, 105
    unlimited liability of, 104
generic brand, 334
generic product, 334
generic terms, 336
geographic pricing strategies, 348
Get Your Share (Stav), 7
global economic crisis, world trade
    and, 78
global economic growth, 74
global environment, 24–25
globalization
    Apple as an example of, 89
    expanding business opportunities, 149
    reality of our time, 73, 74
    representing a huge opportunity for all
        countries, 75
global marketplace, 208–210
global perspectives, in small
    business, 149
goal, defined, 162
goal-setting theory, 277–278
going price, accepting, 20
goods, 323
government
    accounting, 440
    role in a mixed economy, 13
    role in capitalism, 13–14
    role in encouraging ethics, 38
governmental markets, 303–304
government export assistance
    programs, U.S., 87

government involvement, increasing, 46
government regulation, of
  corporations, 115
grapevine, 199–200
graph, example, 436
Great Depression, 23, 45
green IT, 418
green, saving natural resources, 11
gross domestic product (GDP), 16, 73
gross profit, 448, 449
gross sales, 447
growth
  from within, 119
  of business, 119–121
  through mergers and acquisitions, 121
growth stage, of the product
    life-cycle, 326

H

hard-core unemployed, training
    programs for, 53
Hawthorne Studies, 269–270
health-care benefits, working full- or
    part-time, 281
health of citizens, protecting with trade
    restrictions, 72
Herzberg's motivation-hygiene theory,
    271–273
higher prices, from imposition of
    tariffs, 73
holding costs, 221, 368
honesty, in business, 35
Horatio Alger Award, 3
horizontal merger, 120
hostile takeover, 119
hourly wage, 251
households, in a mixed economy, 13–14
HRM. See human resources
    management (HRM)
human factors, responsible for
    experiment results, 270
Human Proteome Folding Project, 42
human relations movement, in
    management, 270
human resource managers, 169,
    430–431
human resources, 8, 161, 217, 410, 411
  cultural diversity in, 243–244
  importance of an organization's, 165
  maintaining, 239
human resources demand,
    forecasting, 241
human resources management (HRM)
  activities, 240
  legal environment of, 257–260
  phases of, 240
  responsibility for, 240–241
human resources planning, 240,
    241–243
human resources supply, forecasting,
    241–242

The Human Side of Enterprise
    (McGregor), 273
hygiene factors, 272

I

idea generation, 331
identity theft, 417
IMF. *See* International Monetary Fund
    (IMF)
imitations, 330–331
immediate-response advertising, 373
import duty, 70
importing, 68–70
import quota, 71
inbound marketing, 404
incentive payments, 251
income levels, for whites, blacks,
    Hispanics, and Asians, 52
income statement, 446–449
income, types of, 315–316
incorporation process, beginning by
    consulting a lawyer, 110, 111
independence, in a small business, 137
independent retailer, 363
India, 68, 84
individual branding, 336
individual factors, affecting ethics, 37
individual knowledge, affecting ethics, 37
individual wages, 250
industrial markets, 303
industrial products, 324. *See also*
    business-to-business products
industries
  attracting small businesses, 146
  protecting new or weak with trade
    restrictions, 72
inflation, 16
inflation rate, 18
informal groups, 199
informal leadership, 172
informal organization, 199
information, 8, 161
  defined, 429, 441
  described, 427
  presenting, 434–435
  risk and, 428
  rules, 429
informational resources, 410, 411
information technology system (IT
    system), 430
infringement, on an existing brand, 336
initial public offering (IPO), 477–478
innovations, 23, 135, 226, 331
inputs, contributed to the
    organization, 275
input-to-outcome ratio, 275–276
inside order takers, 377
insourcing, 209
inspection, of work-in-process, 223
institutional advertising, 374
institutional markets, 304

insurance packages, 252
intangible assets, 445
integrated marketing communications,
    371–372
intensive distribution, 360
Intergovernmental Panel on Climate
    Change, 56
intermediaries, 338, 348
intermittent process, 228
internal environmental forces, in an
    e-business, 418
internal recruiting, 246–247
internal sources
  of data, 432
  marketing data from, 311
International Accounting Standards
    Board, 438
international business
  basis for, 67–70
  extent of, 73–76
  financing, 87–89
  methods of entering, 81–86
  restrictions to, 70–73
international economic organizations,
    working to foster trade, 77, 90
International Financial Reporting
    Standards (IFRS), 438
International Franchise Association, 148
international markets
  exporting to, 83
  steps in entering, 86
International Monetary Fund (IMF), 74,
    88–89
international resources, misallocation
    of, 73
international trade, 77–81
international trade agreements, 90
International Trade Loan program,
    SBA's, 149
Internet
  affecting ethics, 38
  creating new customer needs, 411
  crime, 417
  ethics on, 416–417
  growth potential, 416
  as a major force in economy, 23
  relationship marketing and, 299
  selling merchandise on, 412
  social responsibility on, 416–417
Internet business, starting a new, 414
interpersonal skills, of managers, 6, 171
Interstate Commerce Act (1887), 48
interviews, 248–249
intranets, 313
introduction component, of a business
    plan, 97, 99
introduction stage, of the product life-
    cycle, 325–326
inventories, 221, 476
  pledged for short-term financing, 476
inventory control, 221
inventory management, 368

inventory turnover, 453
investing activities, cash flows from, 449
investment banking firms, 478
investments
    frozen in a partnership, 109
    return on, 341
investor relations, in social media era, 479
investors, 34
invisible hand, 12
Iran, embargoes against, 71
Isenberg Entrepreneur Test, 133
ISO 9000, 223–224
ISO 14000, 223–224
issue resolution rate, 410

J

Japan, projected growth, 74
jet aircraft, carbon monoxide and
        hydrocarbon emitted by, 56
job analysis, 240, 245
job applicants, attracting qualified, 246
jobbers, 362
job description, 245
job design, 186–188
job enlargement, 279
job enrichment, 279–280
job evaluation, 250
job posting, 247
job redesign, 279–280
job rotation, 188
job sharing, 281–282
jobs, loss of from trade restrictions, 73
job specialization, 186–187
job specification, 245
joint ventures, 83, 118
judgmental appraisal methods, 255–256
just-in-time (JIT) inventory system, 221

K

Kefauver-Harris Drug Amendments
        (1962), 51
Kennedy Round (1964-1967), 77–78
key performance indicators (KPIs), 409
Kindle, inventing, 160
knowledge management (KM), 430

L

label, 338
labeling, 338–339
labor, 11
labor-intensive technology, 216
Labor-Management Relations Act
        (1947), 257, 258
labor unions, 45
laid off, employees, 242
laissez faire capitalism, 12, 13
land and natural resources, 11
land pollution, 56–57
Latin America, projected growth
        rates, 74

"lattice" structure, 184
lawsuits, product liability, 49
leadership, 172–173
leading, 165
lean manufacturing, 225
legal and regulatory forces, in the
        marketing environment, 309
legal monopoly, 22
letter of credit, 82
liabilities, 441, 445
licensing, 81
lifestyle shopping center, 367
limited liability
    of corporations, 114
    for malpractice of other partners, 108
limited-liability company (LLC)
    advantages and disadvantages of,
        108
    taxed like a partnership, 116
limited-liability partnership (LLP), 108
limited-line retailers, 364
limited-line wholesaler, 362
limited monopoly, 22
limited partners, 106
limited partnerships, 106
limited potential, of small
        businesses, 138
line-and-staff structure, 194–195
line authority, 194
line extensions, 330, 337
line managers, 193
line of credit, 470
line structure, 193–194
liquidity
    of an asset, 442
LLC. See limited-liability
        company (LLC)
LLP. See limited-liability partnership
        (LLP)
load flexibility, transportation mode,
        370, 371
loans
    basics of getting, 471
    by inventory, 476
    receivables, 476
location, departmentalization by, 189
"long" product line, 216
long-term debt financing, sources of,
        481–485
long-term financing, 465, 466
long-term liabilities, 445
long-term loans, 481–482, 485
loss, 9, 446
lower-level managers, abilities of, 191
lump-sum salary increases, 251
Lupron cancer drug, 34

M

macroeconomics, 11
"Made in America,", 72, 73, 209
"Made in the United States" label, 25

magnitude
    of a conversion process, 211
Magnuson-Moss Warranty-Federal
        Trade Commission Act (1975), 51
major equipment, 325
major events, shaping nation's economy
        from 1940 to 2000, 23
Malcolm Baldrige National Quality
        Award, 222
male and female workers, relative
        earnings of, 53
malware, 417
management, 160
    areas of, 430–431
    defined, 160–161
    functions, 162–167
    levels of, 167–168
    resources of, 161
    span of, 192–193
Management Assistance Program,
        SBA's, 141
management by objectives (MBO),
        278–279
management courses, offered by
        SBA, 141
management development, 253
management disagreement, in
        partnerships, 122
management functions, 6
management information system
        (MIS), 430–432
    costs and limits of, 431–432
    employees using, 432–437
management process, functions of,
        162–167
management skills
    improving, 6
    limited for sole proprietors, 104
management specialization, areas of,
        168–169
managerial accounting, 440
managerial decision making, 173–175
managers
    coordinated effort of all three levels
        of, 168
    kinds of, 167–169
    skills of, 7
    skills of successful, 170–171
managing, total quality, 175–176
manufacturers, 333
    U.S., 208–210
manufacturer's agents, 362
manufacturing businesses, 9
marketable securities, 444
market coverage, level of, 360
market demand
    comparing with capacity, 219
    estimating, 219
    exceeding capacity, 219
market economy, 13
marketing channel, 357
marketing-communications mix, 372

online applications, 247
online information services, 313
online marketing, areas of, 404
online networking, 5
online presence, building for an existing
　　business, 413, 414
online retailing, 366
onshoring, 209
on-the-job training methods, 254
OPEC (Organization of Petroleum
　　Exporting Countries), 81
open corporation, 110
operating activities, cash flows from, 449
operating expenses, 448–449
operational planning, 164, 219–220
operations control, 220–225
operations management, 208, 210
operations managers, 168, 169, 208,
　　216, 430
opportunities
　　as factors affecting ethics,
　　　36–37
　　identifying, 173–174
　　listening for on social media, 406
　　in a SWOT analysis, 163–164
optimization, of conflicting goals, 163
oral communication skills, 171
order getter, 377
order processing, 368
order taker, 377
organizational goals and objectives,
　　establishing, 468
organizational height, 193
organizational meeting, to form a
　　corporation, 111
organizational relationships, creating
　　ethical problems, 35
organizational structure, forms of,
　　193–196
organization charts, developing,
　　185–186
organization, defined, 185
Organization of Petroleum Exporting
　　Countries (OPEC), 81
organized effort of individuals, in a
　　business, 8
organizing, 165
orientation, of new employees, 240, 249
outcomes, rewards from the
　　organization, 275–276
output per hour, nations with largest
　　increase in, 225, 226
output quota, 269
outside (or field) order takers, 377
outsourcing, 411
over-the-counter (OTC) market, 479
owners' equity, 441, 442, 445
ownership
　　ease of transfer of for a corporation, 113
　　of factors of production, 11
　　sole proprietor's pride in, 103
owners, risk of not being paid, 10

P

package design, considerations, 337–338
packaging, 337–338
participative decision making, emphasis
　　on, 274
participative leadership, 172
partnership agreement, 106, 107
partnerships, 102, 105–106
partners, types of, 105–106
part-time work, 281
pass-through taxation, for an LLC, 116
patent, as an asset, 445
pay for time not worked, 252
pay-per-view e-business model, 415
peak period (prosperity), 18
penetration pricing, 344
pension and retirement programs, 252
People's Republic of China, 70
perfect (pure) competition, 19
performance appraisal, 254–257
performance, factors affecting a
　　corporation's, 457
performance feedback, 256–257
performance feedback interview, 256
performing stage, of team
　　development, 286
periodic discounting, 345
perpetual life, of a corporation, 122
personal budget, 446
personal goals, affecting ethics, 37
personal income, 315–316
personal relationships, with customers
　　and employees, 137
personal selling, 372, 377–379
personal values, affecting ethics, 37
personnel management, 239
photo sharing, by companies, 399
physical distribution, 368
physical distribution functions, 299
physiological needs, 270
piece-rate system, 269
pie chart, example, 436
piggyback, 370
pipelines, 371
place utility, 300–301
planned shopping center, 367
planning
　　as basis of financial management,
　　　467–470
　　by managers, 162–167
planning horizon, selecting, 219
planning skills, at L.L. Bean, 180
plans
　　defined, 164, 467
　　types of, 164–165, 166
plant layout, 217–219
podcasts, 399
point-of-purchase display, 381
poison pills, 119
political forces, in the marketing
　　environment, 309

pollution, 54
Pollution Control Board of Kerala in
　　India, 55
Pollution Prevention Pays (3P)
　　program, 56
porcupine provisions, 119
positive reinforcement, 274–275
possession utility, 301
preferred stock, 111, 480, 485
premium, 381
premium pricing, 347
prepaid expenses, 444
presentation
　　of information, 434–435
　　personal-selling process, 378
press conference, 382
price
　　buyers' perceptions of, 340
　　definition, 339
　　meaning and use of, 339
price competition, 339–340
　　in oligopoly, 21–22
price differentiation, 342
price floor, establishing, 341
price leaders, 347
price lining, 347
price skimming, 344
pricing
　　business products, 347–348
　　cost-based, 341–342
　　demand-based, 342–343
　　methods, 341–343
　　products, 339–340
　　strategies, 344–347
pricing ingredient, of the marketing mix,
　　307, 308
pricing objectives, 340–341
pride of ownership, in a partnership,
　　107, 108
primary-demand advertising, 373
primary market, 478
prime interest rate, 18, 475
privacy, threats to, 417
private accountant, 441
private brand, 334
private carrier, 369
private placement, 480–481
private warehouse, 369
problem, identifying, 173–174
problem-solving
　　approach, 256
problem solving, from cultural
　　diversity, 244
problem-solving teams, 284
processing, data, 434
process layout, for a plant, 219
process material, 325
producer markets, 303
producer price index (PPI), 17
product deletion, 330
product, departmentalization
　　by, 188

product design, 216
product development phase, 332
product differentiation, 21, 340
product ideas, generating new, 404–405
product ingredient, of the marketing mix, 307, 308
production, 208–210
production capacity, required, 215
production industries, 131
production orientation, of business, 302
production processes, number of, 211–212
productivity
    defined, 15
    improving, 225–228
    improving, 15–16
    increases in, 209
    trends, 225
productivity growth, improving, 225–226
product layout, 217
product-liability lawsuits, 49
product life-cycle, 325–328
product line, 215–216, 328
product-line pricing, 344, 346–347
product mix, 328–333
product modifications, 329
products, 323
    adjusting to meet demand, 219–220
    classification of, 324
    developing new, 330–332
    extension and refinement, 214–215
    failure of, 332–333
    managing existing, 329–330
    pricing, 339–340
product safety, reasons for concern about, 48, 49
profit, 9–10
profit margin, 452
profit maximization, pricing for, 341
profit-sharing, 251
profits, retention, 108
project manager, 195, 196
promissory note, 474, 477
promotion, 372
    to higher-level positions, 246–247
promotional pricing, 344, 347
promotional role, of packages, 338
promotion ingredient, of the marketing mix, 307, 308
promotion mix, 372–373
prospect, personal selling, 378
protective tariffs, 70
proxy fight, 119
proxy, voting by, 112
psychological factors, buying process influenced by, 315
psychological pricing, 344, 345–346
public accountant, 441
publications, SBA's, 143
publicity, 382

public relations
    defined, 373
    tools, types of, 382–383
    uses of, 383
public utilities, 22
public warehouses, 369
punishment, 275
purchasing, 220–221
Pure Food and Drug Act (1906), 46
purpose statement, 109

Q

qualified individual, with a disability, 259
qualitative social media measurement, 409–410
quality
    techniques to improve, 223
quality circles, 223
quality control, 222–224
quality modifications, of existing products, 329
quality services, planning, 212–213
quantitative measurements, for selected social media Web sites, 409
quantitative social media measurement, 409
quantity discounts, 348
quotas, as unconstitutional, 53

R

railroad, 370
random discounting, 345
rating scale, for employee appraisals, 255
raw materials, 8, 325
raw-materials inventory, 221
real (currency), appreciation of Brazil's, 93
real GDP, measuring, 16–17
reasonable accommodation, 260
rebate, 380
receivables
    of a firm, 444
    loans secured by, 476
recession, 18
recognition
    need for, 268
    pay increased as a form of, 272–273
record keeping, simplified in a small business, 137
recovery (expansion), 19
recruiting, 246–247
    employees, 405–406
    for positions, 246
reference pricing, 345
references, furnished by job candidates, 249
refinement, of products, 214–215
reform, 439

regional shopping center, 367
registered bond, 483
registered trademark symbol®, 336
registration, protecting trademarks, 335–336
regular corporation, 117
reinforcement theory, 274–275
reinventing, a company, 164
reinvestment, of earnings, 480
relationship marketing, 298–299
relevancy, of data, 432
reminder advertising, 373
replacement chart, for personnel, 242
reports, required for corporations, 116
reputation management, 401–402
research and development (R&D), 213–214
reseller markets, 303
reshoring, 209
resolution time, 410
Resource Conservation and Recovery Act (1984), 54
Resource Recovery Act (1970), 54
resources
    kinds of, 8, 160, 161
    used by businesses, 411
responsibility, assigning, 190
restrictions, to international business, 70–73
résumés, submitting, 247
retailer, 358
retained earnings, 445, 480
return on investment (ROI), 341
return on sales (or profit margin), 452
revenues, 447, 448
revenue stream, 412
revenue tariffs, 70
reverse discrimination, 53
revolving credit agreement, 470–471
right to be heard, 60
right to be informed, 49
right to choose, 49
right to safety, 48–49
risk
    of failure for small businesses, 137
    information and, 428
risk-return ratio, 466–467
robotics, 227
role-playing, 254
roles, within a team, 286–287
routing, of materials, 222

S

safety
    right to, 48–49
safety needs, 270
salaries, 53, 251
salaries payable, 445
sales agents, 362
sales forecast, 310–311
sales management tasks, 379

sales offices, of an exporting firm, 83
sales orientation, of business, 302
salespersons, kinds of, 377–378
sales promotion, 373, 379
  methods, 380
  objectives, 379–380
  selection of methods, 380–382
sales revenue
  exchanged for additional resources, 14
  increasing, 412–413
  relationship with profit, 10
sales support personnel, 377–378
sample, 381
Sarbanes-Oxley Act (2002), 38, 41,
  439, 457
satisfaction, of employees, 271–272
"satisfice," making decisions that, 174
satisfiers, 272
Saudi Arabia, 67, 74
savings accounts, 470
SBA. *See* Small Business
  Administration (SBA)
SBDCs. *See* small-business
  development centers (SBDCs)
SBICs. *See* small-business investment
  companies (SBICs)
SBIs. *See* Small-business institutes
  (SBIs)
SBTN. *See* Small Business Training
  Network (SBTN)
scarcity, dealing with, 11
scheduling, materials and resources,
  221–222
scientific management, 268–269
SCORE. *See* Service Corps of Retired
  Executives (SCORE)
S-corporations
  advantages and disadvantages
    of, 117
  Graeter's as, 155
  taxed like a partnership, 122
screening, of new products, 331
search engines
  optimization, 404
seasonal discounts, 348
secondary information, sources of,
  313, 314
secondary market, 478–480
secondary-market pricing, 345
secrecy, lack of for open
  corporations, 116
secured loan, 477
securities exchange, 479
segmentation bases, variety of, 307
selection, 240, 247–249
selective-demand (or brand) advertising,
  373, 374
selective distribution, 360
self-actualization needs, 271
self-managed teams, 284
selling expenses, 448
sense of involvement, of workers, 270

sentiment analysis, 409–410
serial bonds, 484
service businesses, 8
Service Corps of Retired Executives
  (SCORE), 141–142
service economy, 24, 212
service industries, 130
service, right to, 50
services, 323
  adjusting to meet demand, 219–220
  consumed immediately, 213
  evaluating the quality of a firm's, 213
  increasing importance of, 212–213
  labor-intensive, 216
setting standards, 167
shares of ownership, of a
  corporation, 110
shark repellents, 119
Sherman Antitrust Act (1890), 46
shopping product, 324
"short" product line, 216
short-term financing, 464–466, 473–477
  comparison of methods, 477
  sources of secured, 476
  sources of unsecured, 473–475
significant others, affecting ethics, 37
simulations, 254
single line retailers, 364–365
sinking fund, 484
site selection, 216–219
situational factors, buying process
  influenced by, 315
Six Sigma, 223
skills inventory, 242
Skype/gotomeeting.com, for
  interviewing, 248
Small Business Administration (SBA),
  128, 141–144
small-business development centers
  (SBDCs), 143
small businesses
  advantages of remaining small, 136–137
  defined, 131
  disadvantages of, 137–138
  failure of, 6
  global perspectives, 149
  importance in U.S. economy, 129
  industries attracting, 130–131
  minority-owned, 142–143
  prone to failure, 133
  during the recession, 129
  size standards, 129
  solving unemployment problems, 136
Small-business institutes (SBIs), 142
small-business investment companies
  (SBICs), 144
small-business owners, teenagers
  as, 133
small-business sector, 129–130
Small Business Training Network
  (SBTN), 141
smart decisions, making, 435–437

social acceptance, of a group, 270
social audit, 58
social content sites, 398
social customer, segmenting and
  targeting, 406–407
social entrepreneurs, 57
social factors, 37–38, 315
social games, 400
socialism, 14–15
socialist nations, transitioning to a free-
  market economy, 15
social media
  achieving business objectives
    through, 400–406
  advancing your career, 5
  building relationships with
    customers, 213
  businesses using, 397–398
  challenges for, 417–419
  communities, 400–401
  defined, 25
  described, 396–397
  employee use of, 171
  importance of, 395–398
  making a good impression, 405
  policy, 253
  Raleigh active in, 320
  reasons for using, 397–398
  reviews and ratings on, 399–400
  small businesses marketing on, 336
  timeline of, 396
  tools for business use, 398–400
social media marketing, 403–404
social media measurement, types of,
  408–410
social media objectives, establishing, 406
social media plan
  cost of maintaining, 410
  developing, 406–408
  implementing and integrating,
    407–408
  measuring and adapting, 408–410
  steps to building, 406–408
social media sites
  for professionals, 253
social media tools, selecting, 407
social needs, 271
social responsibility, 42–48
  arguments for/against increased, 47
  developing a program of, 58
  evolution of in business, 45–46
  funding the program, 59
  historical evolution of business,
    45–46
  implementing a program of, 58–59
  on the Internet, 416–417
  pros and cons of, 47–48
  views of, 46–48
social responsibility record, of a firm, 10
Social Security account, 252
society, impact of business decisions
  on, 47

PART ONE

Introduction

© Songquan Deng/Shutterstock

CHAPTER 1

The Role of Business Research

LEARNING OUTCOMES

After studying this chapter, you should be able to

1. Understand how research contributes to business success
2. Know how to define business research
3. Understand the difference between basic and applied business research
4. Understand how research activities can be used to address business decisions
5. Know when business research should and should not be conducted
6. Appreciate the way that technology and internationalization are changing business research

Chapter Vignette:

ESPN Hits a Home Run by Leveraging the Power of its Business Research

To many people, the abbreviation ESPN says it all when you are thinking about sports programming. The Entertainment and Sports Programming Network was launched in 1979, with its famous SportsCenter broadcast followed by a presentation of a slow pitch softball game. Over time, ESPN has become a media juggernaut, expanding its sports content and programming globally, and is a media presence in every possible outlet, including television, video, and the Internet. In fact, ESPN.com has long been one of the most visited sites on the World Wide Web.

It is the passionate sports fan that makes ESPN's success possible. Over the years, information about the people who watch and interact with ESPN content had been slowly accumulating across their different media outlets. This information included not just web clicks and television viewership, but also purchases from ESPN and its affiliated advertising partners. Since this information was located in separate databases and across different operating units, it had become difficult to know just who the fan was, and what they were truly interested in. What could be done with this considerable business information? Could ESPN become more knowledgeable (and more profitable) by learning more about the sports fans who use their content?

The answer was a resounding "Yes!" ESPN partnered with Quaero, a business research company that specializes in customer intelligence, to integrate their numerous databases and begin to learn more about how fans use their media, and what specifically they were looking for. They learned that enhancing the fan's experience, regardless of the media, had bottom-line implications for their own revenue, and the revenue of their advertisers. ESPN realized that based upon their customer research, cross-network promotions and individualized

advertising content could be built for their sports fans, and that seeing the sports fan as a core asset of the company was critical to success. In fact, the activities associated with the business research they conducted on their customers were not viewed as a cost, but in fact served as a revenue driver to their firm's profitability.

It was business research that made this possible. Gaining intelligence on a critical business function, a function that had global implications, helped create a profitable solution for ESPN. The value of this research for ESPN and its millions of sports fans created a "win-win" for all. ESPN had, in fact, hit a "home run" through the use of business research.[1]

Introduction

The recent history of ESPN demonstrates the need for information in making informed decisions addressing key issues faced by all competitive businesses. Research can provide that information. Without it, business decisions involving both tactics and strategies are made in the dark.

We open with two examples illustrating how business decisions require intelligence and how research can provide that intelligence. The following examples focus specifically on how research can lead to innovation in the form of new products, improvements in existing goods and services, or enhancements in employee relationships. Imagine yourself in the role of business manager as you read these examples and think about the information needs you may have in trying to build success for your company.

The coffee industry, after years of the "daily grind," has proved quite dynamic over the past decade. After years of steady decline, research on consumers' beverage purchases show that coffee sales began rebounding around 1995. Telephone interviews with American consumers estimated that there were 80 million occasional coffee drinkers and 7 million daily upscale coffee drinkers in 1995. By 2001, estimates suggested there were 161 million daily or occasional U.S. coffee drinkers and 27 million daily upscale coffee drinkers.[2]

Coffee drinking habits have also changed. In 1991 there were fewer than 450 coffeehouses in the United States. Today, it seems like places such as Starbucks, Second Cup, The Coffee Bean & Tea Leaf, and Gloria Jean's are virtually everywhere in the United States and Canada. There are more than 17,000 Starbucks locations around the world with the majority of these being wholly owned stores.[3] While locating these outlets requires significant formal research, Starbucks also is researching new concepts aimed at other ways a coffee shop can provide value to consumers. One concept that has survived testing thus far is the addition of free, in-store high-speed wireless Internet access. Thus, you can have hot coffee in a hotspot! After Starbucks baristas began reporting that customers were asking clerks what music was playing in the stores, Starbucks began testing the sales of CDs containing their in-store music. In 2009, Starbucks began a bundled pricing promotion offering a breakfast sandwich or pastry and a tall coffee drink for $3.95 in response to the declining economy. The research that underlies the introduction of these value-added concepts could first include simply asking a consumer or a small group of consumers for their reaction to the concept. Survey research and then actual in-store tests may follow. So, the research underlying such decisions can be multilayered.

Often, business research is directed toward an element of an organization's internal operations. For example, DuPont utilizes research techniques to better understand their employees' needs. DuPont has 94,000 employees worldwide and 54,000 in the United States.[4] The company has conducted four comprehensive work/life needs assessment surveys of its employees since 1985. This business research provides the company with considerable insight into employee work/life behavior and allows DuPont to identify trends regarding employee needs.

The most recent survey found that, as the company's work force is aging, employees' child care needs are diminishing, but elder care needs are emerging. The survey found that 88 percent of respondents identified themselves as baby boomers. About 50 percent of the employees say that they have—or expect to have—elder care responsibilities in the next three to four years, up from 40 percent in 1995.

The surveys have shown that DuPont employees want to balance work and family responsibilities, feeling deeply committed to both aspects of their lives. The latest research shows that company efforts to satisfy these desires have been successful. Employee perception of support from management for work/life issues improved from the 1995 study and the results indicate employees feel

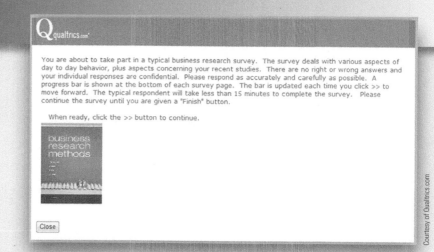
less stress. Support from colleagues is rated high, and women indicated they now have more role models. The study also reported that the feeling of management support is directly connected to employees' efforts to make the company successful. Employees who use the work/life programs are willing to "go the extra mile."

These examples illustrate the need for information in making informed business decisions. The statistics about coffee demonstrate how research can track trends that may lead to new business opportunities. Starbucks's research also illustrates how research can be used to examine new concepts in progressively more complex stages, setting the stage for a more successful product introduction. DuPont's ability to track employee attitudes allows them to adjust employee benefit packages to maximize satisfaction and reduce employee turnover. These are only the tip of the iceberg when it comes to the types of business research that are conducted every day. This chapter introduces basic concepts of business research and describes how research can play a crucial role in creating and managing a successful business.

The Nature of Business Research

Business research covers a wide range of phenomena. For managers, the purpose of research is to provide knowledge regarding the organization, the market, the economy, or another area of uncertainty. A financial manager may ask, "Will the environment for long-term financing be better two years from now?" A personnel manager may ask, "What kind of training is necessary for production employees?" or "What is the reason for the company's high employee turnover?" A marketing manager may ask, "How can I monitor my retail sales and retail trade activities?" Each of these questions requires information about how the environment, employees, customers, or the economy will respond to executives' decisions. Research is one of the principal tools for answering these practical questions.

Within an organization, a business researcher may be referred to as a marketing researcher, an organizational researcher, a director of financial and economic research, or one of many other titles. Although business researchers are often specialized, the term business research encompasses all of these functional specialties. While researchers in different functional areas may investigate different phenomena, they are similar to one another because they share similar research methods.

It's been said that "every business issue ultimately boils down to an information problem."[5] Can the right information be delivered? The ultimate goal of research is to supply accurate information that reduces the uncertainty in managerial decision making. Very often, decisions are made with little information for various reasons, including cost considerations, insufficient time to conduct research, or management's belief that enough is already known. Relying on seat-of-the-pants decision making—decision making without research—is like betting on a long shot at the race-track because the horse's name is appealing. Occasionally there are successes, but in the long run, intuition without research leads to losses. Business research helps decision makers shift from intuitive information gathering to systematic and objective investigation.

Business Research Defined

Business research is the application of the scientific method in searching for the truth about business phenomena. These activities include defining business opportunities and problems, generating and evaluating alternative courses of action, and monitoring employee and organizational performance. Business research is more than conducting surveys.[6] This process includes idea and theory development, problem definition, searching for and collecting information, analyzing data, and communicating the findings and their implications.

This definition suggests that business research information is not intuitive or haphazardly gathered. Literally, research (re-search) means "to search again." The term connotes patient study and scientific investigation wherein the researcher takes another, more careful look at the data to discover all that is known about the subject. Ultimately, all findings are tied back to the underlying theory.

The definition also emphasizes, through reference to the scientific method, that any information generated should be accurate and objective. The nineteenth-century American humorist Artemus Ward claimed, "It ain't the things we don't know that gets us in trouble. It's the things we know that ain't so." In other words, research isn't performed to support preconceived ideas but to test them. The researcher must be personally detached and free of bias in attempting to find truth. If bias enters into the research process, the value of the research is considerably reduced. We will discuss this further Chapter 12.

Our definition makes it clear that business research is designed to facilitate the managerial decision-making process for all aspects of the business: finance, marketing, human resources, and so on. Business research is an essential tool for management in virtually all problem-solving and decision-making activities. By providing the necessary information on which to base business decisions, research can decrease the risk of making a wrong decision in each area. However, it is important to note that research is an aid to managerial decision making, never a substitute for it.

Finally, this definition of business research is limited by one's definition of business. Certainly, research regarding production, finance, marketing, and management in for-profit corporations like DuPont is business research. However, business research also includes efforts that assist non-profit organizations such as the American Heart Association, the San Diego Zoo, the Boston Pops Orchestra, or a parochial school. Further, governmental agencies such as the Federal Emergency Management Agency (FEMA) and the Department of Homeland Security (DHS) perform many functions that are similar, if not identical, to those of for-profit business organizations. For instance, the Food and Drug Administration (FDA) is an important user of research, employing it to address the way people view and use various food and drugs. One such study commissioned and funded research to address the question of how consumers used the risk summaries that are included with all drugs sold in the United States.[7] Therefore, not-for-profits and governmental agencies can use research in much the same way as managers at Starbucks or DuPont. While the focus is on for-profit organizations, this book explores business research as it applies to all institutions.

Applied and Basic Business Research

One useful way to describe research is based on the specificity of its purpose. **Applied business research** is conducted to address a specific business decision for a specific firm or organization. The opening vignette describes a situation in which ESPN used applied research to decide how to best create knowledge of its sports fans and their preferences.

Basic business research (sometimes referred to as pure research) is conducted without a specific decision in mind, and it usually does not address the needs of a specific organization. It attempts to expand the limits of knowledge in general, and as such it is not aimed at solving a particular pragmatic

business research

The application of the scientific method in searching for the truth about business phenomena. These activities include defining business opportunities and problems, generating and evaluating ideas, monitoring performance, and understanding the business process.

applied business research

Research conducted to address a specific business decision for a specific firm or organization.

basic business research

Research conducted without a specific decision in mind that usually does not address the needs of a specific organization. It attempts to expand the limits of knowledge in general and is not aimed at solving a particular pragmatic problem.

problem. Basic research can be used to test the validity of a general business theory (one that applies to all businesses) or to learn more about a particular business phenomenon. For instance, a great deal of basic research addresses employee motivation. How can managers best encourage workers to dedicate themselves toward the organization's goals? From such research, we can learn the factors that are most important to workers and how to create an environment where employees are most highly motivated. This basic research does not examine the problem from any single organization's perspective. However, Starbucks' or DuPont's management may become aware of such research and use it to design applied research studies examining questions about their own employees. Thus, the two types of research are not completely independent, as basic research often provides the foundation for later applied research.

While the distinction between basic and applied is useful in describing research, there are very few aspects of research that apply only to basic or only to applied research. We will use the term business research more generally to refer to either type of research. The focus of this text is more on applied research—studies that are undertaken to answer questions about specific problems or to make decisions about particular courses of action or policies. Applied research is emphasized in this text because most students will be oriented toward the day-to-day practice of management, and most students and researchers will be exposed to short-term, problem-solving research conducted for businesses or nonprofit organizations.

The Scientific Method

the scientific method

The way researchers go about using knowledge and evidence to reach objective conclusions about the real world.

All research, whether basic or applied, involves the scientific method. **The scientific method** is the way researchers go about using knowledge and evidence to reach objective conclusions about the real world. The scientific method is the same in social sciences, such as business, as in physical sciences, such as physics. In this case, it is the way we come to understand business phenomena.

Exhibit 1.1 briefly illustrates the scientific method. In the scientific method, there are multiple routes to developing ideas. When the ideas can be stated in researchable terms, we reach the hypothesis stage. The next step involves testing the hypothesis against empirical evidence (facts from observation or experimentation). The results either support a hypothesis or do not support a hypothesis. From these results, new knowledge is generated.

EXHIBIT 1.1

A Summary of the Scientific Method

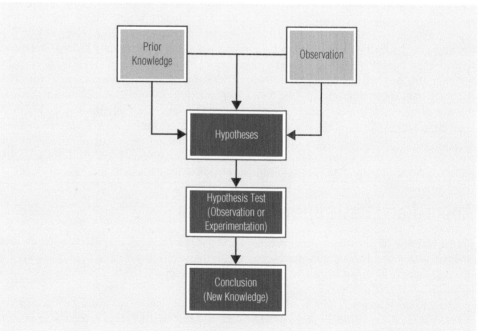

In basic research, testing these prior conceptions or hypotheses and then making inferences and conclusions about the phenomena leads to the establishment of general laws about the phenomena. Use of the scientific method in applied research ensures objectivity in gathering facts and testing creative ideas for alternative business strategies. The essence of research, whether basic or applied, lies in the scientific method. Much of this book deals with scientific methodology. Thus, the techniques of basic and applied research differ largely in degree rather than in substance.

Managerial Value of Business Research

In all of business strategy, there are only a few business orientations (see Exhibit 1.2). A firm can be **product-oriented**. A product-oriented firm prioritizes decision making in a way that emphasizes technical superiority in the product. Thus, research that gathers information from technicians and experts in the field is very important in making critical decisions. A firm can be **production-oriented**. A production-oriented firm prioritizes the efficiency and effectiveness of production processes in making decisions. Here, research providing input from workers, engineers, finance, and accounting becomes important as the firm seeks to drive costs down. Production-oriented firms are usually very large firms manufacturing products in very large quantities. The third orientation is **marketing-oriented**, which focuses more on how the firm provides value to customers than on the physical product or production process. With a marketing-oriented organization the majority of research focuses on the customer. Research addressing consumer desires, beliefs, and attitudes becomes essential.

We have argued that research facilitates effective management. For example, Yoplait Go-Gurt illustrates the benefit of business research. The company's consumer research about eating regular yogurt at school showed that moms and kids in their "tweens" wanted convenience and portability. Some brands, like Colombo Spoon in a Snap, offered the convenience of having a utensil as part of the packaging/delivery system. However, from what Yoplait learned about consumers, they thought kids would eat more yogurt if they could "lose the spoon" and eat yogurt anywhere, anytime. Moms and kids participating in a taste test were invited to sample different types of on-the-go packaging shapes—long tubes, thin tubes, fat tubes, and other shapes—without being told how to handle the packaging. One of the company's researchers said, "It was funny to see the moms fidget around, then daintily pour the product onto a spoon, then into their mouths. The kids instantly

product-oriented

Describes a firm that prioritizes decision making in a way that emphasizes technical superiority in the product.

production-oriented

Describes a firm that prioritizes efficiency and effectiveness of the production processes in making decisions.

marketing-oriented

Describes a firm in which all decisions are made with a conscious awareness of their effect on the customer.

EXHIBIT **1.2**
Business Orientations

Product-Oriented Firm	Example
Prioritizes decision making that emphasizes physical product design, trendiness, or technical superiority	The fashion industry makes clothes in styles and sizes that few can adopt.

Research focuses on technicians and experts in the field.

Production-Oriented Firm	Example
Prioritizes efficiency and effectiveness of production processes in making decisions	The U.S. auto industry's assembly-line process is intent on reducing costs of production as low as possible.

Research focuses on line employees, engineers, accountants, and other efficiency experts.

Marketing-Oriented Firm	Example
Focuses on how the firm provides value to customers	Well-known hotel chains are designed to address the needs of travelers, particularly business travelers.

Research focuses on customers.

jumped on it. They knew what to do."[8] Squeezing Go-Gurt from the tube was a big plus. The kids loved the fact that the packaging gave them permission to play with their food, something parents always tell them not to do. Based on their research, Yoplait introduced Go-Gurt in a three-sided tube designed to fit in kids' lunchboxes. The results were spectacular, with more than $100 million in sales its first year on the market. Yoplait realized that knowledge of consumers' needs, coupled with product research and development, leads to successful business strategies.

As the Yoplait example shows, the prime managerial value of business research is that it provides information that improves the decision-making process. The decision-making process associated with the development and implementation of a business strategy involves four interrelated stages:

1. Identifying problems or opportunities
2. Diagnosing and assessing problems or opportunities
3. Selecting and implementing a course of action
4. Evaluating the course of action

Business research, by supplying managers with pertinent information, may play an important role by reducing managerial uncertainty in each of these stages.

Identifying Problems or Opportunities

Before any strategy can be developed, an organization must determine where it wants to go and how it will get there. Business research can help managers plan strategies by determining the nature of situations or by identifying the existence of problems or opportunities present in the organization. Business research may be used as a scanning activity to provide information about what is occurring within an organization or in its environment. The mere description of some social or economic activity may familiarize managers with organizational and environmental occurrences and help them understand a situation. Consider these two examples:

■ The description of the dividend history of stocks in an industry may point to an attractive investment opportunity. Information supplied by business research may also indicate problems.
■ Employee interviews undertaken to characterize the dimensions of an airline reservation clerk's job may reveal that reservation clerks emphasize competence in issuing tickets over courtesy and friendliness in customer contact.

Once business research indicates a problem or opportunity, managers may feel that the alternatives are clear enough to make a decision based on their experience or intuition. However, often they decide that more business research is needed to generate additional information for a better understanding of the situation.

Diagnosing and Assessing Problems or Opportunities

After an organization recognizes a problem or identifies a potential opportunity, business research can help clarify the situation. Managers need to gain insight about the underlying factors causing the situation. If there is a problem, they need to specify what happened and why. If an opportunity exists, they may need to explore, refine, and quantify the opportunity. If multiple opportunities exist, research may be conducted to set priorities.

Selecting and Implementing a Course of Action

After the alternative courses of action have been clearly identified, business research is often conducted to obtain specific information that will aid in evaluating the alternatives and in selecting the best course of action. For example, suppose Harley-Davidson is considering establishing a dealer network in either China or India. In this case, business research can be designed to gather the relevant information necessary to determine which, if either, course of action is best for the organization.

Opportunities may be evaluated through the use of various performance criteria. For example, estimates of market potential allow managers to evaluate the revenue that will be generated by each of the possible opportunities. A good forecast supplied by business researchers is among the most useful pieces of planning information a manager can have. Of course, complete accuracy in forecasting the future is not possible, because change is constantly occurring in the business environment. Nevertheless, objective information generated by business research to forecast environmental occurrences may be the foundation for selecting a particular course of action.

Even the best plan is likely to fail if it is not properly implemented. Business research may be conducted to indicate the specific tactics required to implement a course of action.

Evaluating the Course of Action

After a course of action has been implemented, business research may serve as a tool to tell managers whether or not planned activities were properly executed and if they accomplished what they were expected to accomplish. In other words, managers may use evaluation research to provide feedback for evaluation and control of strategies and tactics.

Evaluation research is the formal, objective measurement and appraisal of the extent to which a given activity, project, or program has achieved its objectives or whether continuing programs are presently performing as projected. Evaluation research may also provide information about the major factors influencing the observed performance levels.

In addition to business organizations, nonprofit organizations and governmental agencies frequently conduct evaluation research. Every year thousands of federal evaluation studies are undertaken to systematically assess the effects of public programs. For example, the U.S. General Accounting Office has been responsible for measuring outcomes of the Employment Opportunity Act, the Job Corps program, and Occupational and Safety and Health Administration (OSHA) programs.

Performance-monitoring research is a specific type of evaluation research that regularly, perhaps routinely, provides feedback for the evaluation and control of recurring business activity. For example, most firms continuously monitor wholesale and retail activity to ensure early detection of sales declines and other anomalies. In the grocery and retail drug industries, sales research may use the Universal Product Code (UPC) for packages, together with computerized cash registers and electronic scanners at checkout counters, to provide valuable market-share information to store and brand managers interested in the retail sales volume of specific products.

United Airlines' Omnibus in-flight survey provides a good example of performance-monitoring research for quality management. United routinely selects sample flights and administers a questionnaire about in-flight service, food, and other aspects of air travel. The Omnibus survey is conducted quarterly to determine who is flying and for what reasons. It enables United to track demographic changes and to monitor customer ratings of its services on a continuing basis, allowing the airline to gather vast amounts of information at low cost. The information relating to customer reaction to services can be compared over time. For example, suppose United decided to change its menu for in-flight meals. The results of the Omnibus survey might indicate that,

evaluation research

The formal, objective measurement and appraisal of the extent a given activity, project, or program has achieved its objectives or whether continuing programs are presently performing as projected.

performance-monitoring research

Refers to research that regularly, sometimes routinely, provides feedback for evaluation and control of business activity.

● ● ● ● ● ● ●

Fun in the snow depends on weather trends, economic outlook, equipment, and clothing—all subjects for a business researcher.

© Agefotostock/SuperStock

Harley-Davidson Goes Abroad

Before Harley-Davidson goes overseas, it must perform considerable research on that market. It may find that consumers in some countries, such as France or Italy, have a strong preference for more economical and practical motorbikes. There, people may prefer a Vespa Wasp to a Harley Hog! Other times, they may find that consumers have a favorable attitude toward Harley-Davidson and that it could even be a product viewed as very prestigious. Harley recently considered doing business in India based on trend analysis showing a booming economy. Favorable consumer opinion and a booming economy were insufficient to justify distributing Harleys in India. The problem? Luxury imports would be subject to very high duties that would make them cost-prohibitive to nearly all Indian consumers and India has strict emission rules for motorbikes. Thus, although research on the market was largely positive, Harley's research on the political operating environment eventually determined its decision. Even after considerable negotiation, India refused to budge on tariffs although they were willing to give on emission standards. Instead, Harley may direct its effort more toward the U.S. women's market for bikes. Research shows that motorcycle ownership among U.S. women has nearly doubled since 1990 to approximately 10 percent. Product research suggests that Harley may need to design smaller and sportier bikes to satisfy this market's desires. Perhaps these new products would also be easier to market in India. Research will tell.

Sources: "Harley Davidson Rules Out India Foray for Near Future," *Asia-Africa Intelligence Wire* (September 2, 2005); "Women Kick It into Gear," *Akron Beacon Journal* (May 22, 2005); "No Duty Cut on Harley Davidson Bikes, India to US," *The Financial Express* (February 24, 2008), www.financialexpress.com/news/No-duty-cut-on-Harley-Davidson-bikes-India-to-US/276635, accessed August 2, 2011.

> **"The secret of success is to know something nobody else knows."**
>
> —ARISTOTLE ONASSIS

shortly after the menu changed, the customers' rating of the airline's food declined. Such information about product quality is extremely valuable, as it allows management to quickly spot trends among passengers in many aspects of air travel, such as airport lounges, gate-line waits, or cabin cleanliness. Then managers can rapidly take action to remedy such problems.

When Is Business Research Needed?

The need to make intelligent, informed decisions ultimately motivates an organization to engage in business research. Not every decision requires research. Thus, when confronting a key decision, a manager must initially decide whether or not to conduct business research. The determination of the need for research centers on (1) time constraints, (2) the availability of data, (3) the nature of the decision to be made, and (4) the value of the research information in relation to costs.

Time Constraints

Systematic research takes time. In many instances, management believes that a decision must be made immediately, allowing no time for research. Decisions sometimes are made without adequate information or thorough understanding of the business situation. Although making decisions without researching a situation is not ideal, sometimes the urgency of a situation precludes the use of research. The urgency with which managers usually want to make decisions conflicts with researchers' desire for rigor in following the scientific method.

Availability of Data

Often managers already possess enough data, or information, to make sound decisions without additional research. When they lack adequate information, however, research must be considered. This means that data need to be collected from an appropriate source. If a potential source of data exists, managers will want to know how much it will cost to get the data.

© Lars Lindblad/Shutterstock

Business Class Success?

If you've ever checked the price of business-class airfare on a flight overseas, you were probably surprised at the price. A discounted round-trip coach ticket from Atlanta to Paris in peak season often costs just over one thousand dollars. That same business-class ticket would often cost between five and ten thousand-dollars! Typically, these flights take place in larger passenger aircraft such as a Boeing 747 or a Boeing 777. A Boeing 777 can seat up to 450 passengers. However, by including three dozen business-class seats, the capacity drops to under 400 passengers.

Thus, it is easy to see that a great deal of research must assess both the product design (what service and product attributes make up a business-class experience) and pricing (in both coach and business class) to determine the best configuration of the aircraft. Research shows that business-class travelers prioritize the comfort of the seat and the ability to be able to lie flat during the flight, the quality of food, and the convenience of boarding as attributes that make up the business-class experience.

In the past few years, a few start-up airlines have been trying to capitalize on this concept by starting "discount" business-class-only airlines. Maxjet estimated that consumers will exchange a little comfort for a reduction in price. They configured Boeing 737s (smaller than typical trans-ocean carriers) with 102 business-class seats that will not quite lie flat—and no

coach seats! The result is a business-class-only airline with cross-Atlantic fares ranging between $1,600 and $3,800, less than half of traditional business-class fares. Taking the concept to an even smaller scale, Eos configured Boeing 757s into 48-seat all-business-class planes.

Both Maxjet and Eos received positive reviews, along with some criticisms. For example, Maxjet did not provide power outlets for laptops at their seats, considered by some to be a "fatal flaw" as far as business-class service is considered. Despite the apparent appeal, both Maxjet (December 2007) and Eos (April 2008) declared bankruptcy.

Could more effective business research have determined these were not feasible business ventures? Or, could Maxjet's "fatal flaw" of a lack of power outlets been identified? Sound business research may have enhanced the chance of success of these airlines.

Sources: McCarnety, Scott, "Start-Up Airlines Fly Only Business Class," *The Wall Street Journal* (September 20, 2005), D1; Pitock, Todd, "Getting There," *Forbes* 176 (September 2005), 30–32; Robertson, David, "Eos Bankruptcy Filing Signals End to Cheap Executive Travel," *The Times* (April 28, 2008).

If the data cannot be obtained, or it cannot be obtained in a timely fashion, this particular research project should not be conducted. For example, many African nations have never conducted a population census. Organizations engaged in international business often find that data about business activity or population characteristics that are readily available in the United States are nonexistent or sparse in developing countries. Imagine the problems facing researchers who wish to investigate market potential in places like Uzbekistan, Macedonia, or Rwanda.

Nature of the Decision

The value of business research will depend on the nature of the managerial decision to be made. A routine tactical decision that does not require a substantial investment may not seem to warrant a substantial expenditure for research. For example, a computer company must update its operator's instruction manual when it makes minor product modifications. The research cost of determining the proper wording to use in the updated manual is likely to be too high for such a minor decision. The nature of the decision is not totally independent of the next issue to be considered: the benefits versus the costs of the research. In general, however, the more strategically or tactically important the decision, the more likely it is that research will be conducted.

Benefits versus Costs

Earlier we discussed some of the managerial benefits of business research. Of course, conducting research to obtain these benefits requires an expenditure of money. In any decision-making situation, managers must identify alternative courses of action and then weigh the value of each alternative against its cost. Business research can be thought of as an investment alternative. When deciding whether to make a decision without research or to postpone the decision in order to conduct research, managers should ask three questions:

1. Will the payoff or rate of return be worth the investment?
2. Will the information gained by business research improve the quality of the managerial decision enough to warrant the expenditure?
3. Is the proposed research expenditure the best use of the available funds?

For example, TV-Cable Week was not test-marketed before its launch. Although the magazine had articles and stories about television personalities and events, its main feature was program listings, channel by channel, showing the exact programs a particular subscriber could receive. To produce a custom magazine for each individual cable television system in the country required developing a costly computer system. Because that development necessitated a substantial expenditure, one that could not be scaled down by research, conducting research was judged to be an unwise investment. The value of the potential research information was not positive because its cost exceeded its benefits. Unfortunately, pricing and distribution problems became so compelling after the magazine was launched that the product was a failure. Nevertheless, without the luxury of hindsight, managers made a reasonable decision not to conduct research. They analyzed the cost of the information relative to the potential benefits of the information. Exhibit 1.3 outlines the criteria for determining when to conduct business research.

EXHIBIT 1.3

Determining When to Conduct Business Research

Time Constraints		Availability of Data		Nature of the Decision		Benefits versus Costs		
Is sufficient time available before a decision will be made?	Yes →	Is it feasible to obtain the data?	Yes →	Is the decision of considerable strategic or tactical importance?	Yes →	Does the value of the research information exceed the cost of conducting research?	Yes →	Conduct Business Research
No ↓		No ↓		No ↓		No ↓		
			Do Not Conduct Business Research					

© Cengage Learning 2013

Business Research in the Twenty-First Century

Business research, like all business activity, continues to change. Changes in communication technologies and the trend toward an ever more global marketplace have played a large role in many of these changes.

Communication Technologies

Virtually everyone is "connected" today. Increasingly, many people are "connected" nearly all the time. Within the lifetime of the typical undergraduate college senior, the way information is exchanged, stored, and gathered has been revolutionized completely. Today, the amount of information formally contained in an entire library can rest easily in a single personal computer.

The speed with which information can be exchanged has also increased tremendously. During the 1970s, exchanging information overnight through a courier service from anywhere in

© Susan Van Etten

"Jacques" Daniels

Sales of U.S. distilled spirits have declined over the last 10 to 15 years as more Americans turn to wine or beer as their beverage of choice. As a result, companies like Bacardi and Brown-Forman, producers of Jack Daniels, have pursued business development strategies involving increased efforts to expand into international markets. The Brown-Forman budget for international ventures includes a significant allocation for research. By doing research before launching the product, Brown-Forman can learn product usage patterns within a particular culture. Some of the findings from this research indicate:

1. Japanese consumers use Jack Daniels (JD) as a dinner beverage. A party of four or five consumers in a restaurant will order and drink a bottle of JD with their meal.
2. Australian consumers mostly consume distilled spirits in their homes. Also in contrast to Japanese consumers, Australians prefer to mix JD with soft drinks or other mixers. As a result of this research, JD launched a mixture called "Jack and Cola" sold in 12-ounce bottles all around Australia. The product has been very successful.
3. British distilled spirit consumers also like mixed drinks, but they usually partake in bars and restaurants.
4. In China and India, consumers more often choose counterfeit or "knock-offs" to save money. Thus, innovative research approaches have addressed questions related to the way the black market works and how they can better educate consumers about the differences between the real thing and the knock-offs.

The result is that Jack Daniels is now sold extensively, in various forms, and with different promotional campaigns, outside of the United States.

Sources: Swibel, Mathew, "How Distiller Brown-Forman Gets Rich by Exploiting the Greenback's Fall—and Pushing Its Brands Abroad," *Forbes* 175, no. 8 (2005), 152–155.

the continental United States was heralded as a near miracle of modern technology. Today, we can exchange information from nearly anywhere in the world to nearly anywhere in the world almost instantly. Internet connections are now wireless, so one doesn't have to be tethered to a wall to access the World Wide Web. Our mobile phones and handheld data devices can be used not only to converse, but also as a means of communication that can even involve business research data. In many cases, technology also has made it possible to store or collect data at a lower cost than in the past. Electronic communications are usually less costly than regular mail—and certainly less costly than a face-to-face interview—and cost about the same amount no matter how far away a respondent is from a researcher. Thus, the expressions "time is collapsing" and "distance is disappearing" capture the tremendous revolution in the speed and reach of our communication technologies.

Changes in computer technology have made for easier data collection and data analysis. As we discuss in Chapter 10, many consumer household panels now exist and can be accessed via the Internet. Thus, there is less need for the time and expense associated with regular mail survey approaches. Furthermore, the computing power necessary to solve complicated statistical problems is now easily accessible. Again, as recently as the 1970s, such computer applications required expensive mainframe computers found only in very large corporations, major universities, and large governmental/military institutions. Researchers could expect to wait hours or even longer to get results from a statistical program involving 200 respondents. Today, even the most basic laptop computers can solve complicated statistical problems involving thousands of data points in practically a nanosecond.

Global Business Research

Like all business activities, business research has become increasingly global as more and more firms operate with few, if any, geographic boundaries. Some companies have extensive international research operations. Upjohn conducts research in 160 different countries. ACNielsen International, known for its television ratings, is the world's largest research company. Two-thirds of its business comes from outside the United States.[9] Starbucks can now be found in nearly every developed country on the Earth. ESPN offers its programming on multiple continents. DuPont has a significant presence in all regions of the world.

Companies that conduct business in foreign countries must understand the nature of those particular markets and judge whether they require customized business strategies. For example, although the 15 nations of the European Union share a single formal market, research shows that Europeans do not share identical tastes for many consumer products. Business researchers have found no such thing as a "typical" European consumer; language, religion, climate, and centuries of tradition divide the nations of the European Union. Scantel Research, a British firm that advises companies on color preferences, found inexplicable differences in Europeans' preferences in medicines. The French prefer to pop purple pills, but the English and Dutch favor white ones. Consumers in all three countries dislike bright red capsules, which are big sellers in the United States. This example illustrates that companies that do business in Europe must research throughout Europe to adapt to local customs and buying habits.[10]

Even companies that produce brands that are icons in their own country are now doing research internationally. The Research Snapshot "'Jacques' Daniels" discusses how Brown-Forman, the parent company of Jack Daniels (the classic American "sour mash" or Bourbon whiskey), is now interviewing consumers in the far corners of the world.[11] The internationalization of research places greater demands on business researchers and heightens the need for research tools that allow us to **cross-validate** research results, meaning that the empirical findings from one culture also exist and behave similarly in another culture. The development and application of these international research tools are an important topic in basic business research.[12]

cross-validate

To verify that the empirical findings from one culture also exist and behave similarly in another culture.

Overview

The business research process is often presented as a linear, sequential process, with one specific step following another. In reality, this is not the case. For example, the time spent on each step varies, overlap between steps is common, some stages may be omitted, occasionally we need to backtrack, and the order sometimes changes. Nonetheless, some structure for the research process is necessary.

The book is organized to provide this structure, both within each chapter and in the order of the chapters. Each chapter begins with a set of specific learning objectives. Each chapter then opens with a Chapter Vignette—a glimpse of a business research situation that provides a basis of reference for that chapter. Each chapter also contains multiple Research Snapshots—specific business research scenarios that illustrate key points. Finally, each chapter concludes with a review of the learning objectives.

The book is organized into seven parts. Part One is the Introduction, which includes this chapter and four others. This chapter provided an introduction to business research. The next three chapters of the book give students a fuller understanding of the business research environment. Part Two, Beginning Stages of the Research Process, provides the foundation for business research, discussing problem definition and qualitative and secondary research. The third section of the book, Research Designs for Collecting Primary Data, introduces survey research, discusses observation as a research technique, and provides an overview of experimental research. Measurement Concepts, Part Four of the book, discusses the measurement of research constructs and questionnaire design. Part Five, Sampling and Fieldwork, describes the process involved in selecting a research sample and collecting data. Part Six, Data Analysis and Presentation, explains the various approaches to analyzing the data and describes methods of presentation. The book concludes with Part Seven, Comprehensive Cases with Computerized Databases, which will be integrated throughout the first six parts. Exhibit 1.4 provides an overview of the book and the research process.

An Overview of Business Research

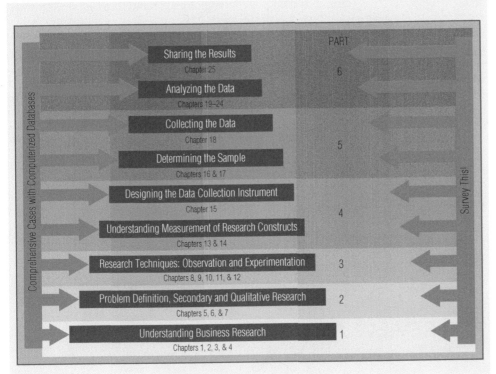

© Cengage Learning 2013

∴ SUMMARY

There were six learning objectives in this chapter. After reading the chapter, the student should be competent in each area described by a learning objective.

1. **Understand how research contributes to business success.** While many business decisions are made "by the seat of the pants" or based on a manager's intuition, this type of decision making carries with it a large amount of risk. By first researching an issue and gathering the appropriate information (from employees, customers, competitors, and the market) managers can make a more informed decision. The result is less risky decision making.

Research is the intelligence-gathering function in business. The intelligence includes information about customers, competitors, economic trends, employees, and other factors that affect business success. This intelligence assists in decisions ranging from long-range planning to near-term tactical decisions.

2. **Know how to define business research.** Business research is the application of the scientific method in searching for truth about business phenomena. The research must be conducted systematically, not haphazardly. It must be objective to avoid the distorting effects of personal bias. Business research should be rigorous, but the rigor is always traded off against the resource and time constraints that go with a particular business decision.

3. **Understand the difference between basic and applied business research.** Applied business research seeks to facilitate managerial decision making. It is directed toward a specific managerial decision in a particular organization. Basic or pure research seeks to increase knowledge of theories and concepts. Both are important, but applied research is more often the topic in this text.

4. **Understand how research activities can be used to address business decisions.** Businesses can make more accurate decisions about dealing with problems and/or the opportunities to pursue and how to best pursue them. The chapter provides examples of studies involving several dimensions of managerial decision making. Thus, business research is useful both in a strategic and in a tactical sense.

5. Know when business research should and should not be conducted. Managers determine whether research should be conducted based on (1) time constraints, (2) availability of data, (3) the nature of the decision to be made, and (4) the benefit of the research information versus its cost.

6. Appreciate the way that technology and internationalization are changing business research. Technology has changed almost every aspect of business research. Modern computer and communications technology makes data collection, study design, data analysis, data reporting, and practically all other aspects of research easier and better. Furthermore, as more companies do business outside their own borders, companies are conducting research globally. This places a greater emphasis on research that can assess the degree to which research tools can be applied and interpreted the same way in different cultures. Thus, research techniques often must cross-validate results.

:: KEY TERMS AND CONCEPTS

applied business research, *5*
basic business research, *5*
business research, *5*
cross-validate, *14*

evaluation research, *9*
marketing-oriented, *7*
performance-monitoring research, *9*
product-oriented, *7*

production-oriented, *7*
the scientific method, *6*

:: QUESTIONS FOR REVIEW AND CRITICAL THINKING

1. Is it possible to make sound managerial decisions without business research? What advantages does research offer to the decision maker over seat-of-the-pants decision making?
2. Define a marketing orientation and a product orientation. Under which strategic orientation is there a greater need for business research?
3. Name some products that logically might have been developed with the help of business research.
4. Define business research and describe its task.
5. Which of the following organizations are likely to use business research? Why? How?
   a. Manufacturer of breakfast cereals
   b. Manufacturer of nuts, bolts, and other fasteners
   c. The Federal Trade Commission
   d. A hospital
   e. A company that publishes business textbooks
6. An automobile manufacturer is conducting research in an attempt to predict the type of car design consumers will desire in the year 2020. Is this basic or applied research? Explain.

7. Comment on the following statements:
   a. Managers are paid to take chances with decisions. Researchers are paid to reduce the risk of making those decisions.
   b. A business strategy can be no better than the information on which it is formulated.
   c. The purpose of research is to solve business problems.
8. List the conditions that help a researcher decide when research should or should not be conducted.
9. How have technology and internationalization affected business research?
10. 'NET How do you believe the Internet has facilitated research? Try to use the Internet to find the total annual sales for Starbucks and for DuPont.
11. What types of tools does the researcher need to use more given the ever increasing internationalization of business?

:: RESEARCH ACTIVITIES

1. 'NET Suppose you owned a jewelry store in Denton, Texas. You are considering opening a second store just like your current store. You are undecided on whether to locate the new store in another location in Denton, Texas, or in Birmingham, Alabama. Why would you decide to have some research done before making the decision? Should the research be conducted? Go to **http://www.census.gov**. Do you think any of this information would be useful in the research?

2. 'NET Find recent examples of news articles involving the use of business research in making decisions about different aspects of business.
3. 'NET Find an article illustrating an example of an applied research study involving some aspect of technology. How does it differ from a basic research study also focusing on a similar aspect of technology?

Information Systems and Knowledge Management

LEARNING OUTCOMES

After studying this chapter, you should be able to

1. Know and distinguish the concepts of data, information, and intelligence
2. Understand the four characteristics that describe data
3. Know the purpose of research in assisting business operations
4. Know what a decision support system is and does
5. Recognize the major categories of databases

Chapter Vignette:

Delivery, Data, and UPS

When it comes to package delivery, United Parcel Service (UPS) beats them all. UPS is the largest package delivery company in the world, both in terms of the number of packages it delivers (almost four billion packages per year), and the revenue that it generates (almost 45 billion dollars in 2010). While it may be easy to think about UPS as a company focused on the U.S. market, it is actually a global corporation that delivers more packages per day in international markets than in the U.S. How does a company of this size combine both global services with local delivery? The answer is through an intense investment in data management and integration, with the goal of leveraging data to meet its core global business goals, namely timely and accurate package delivery.

With a yearly technology investment of over one billion dollars a year, UPS succeeds by making sure data management is a key driver of its business processes. Using a global ground and air network, the company has the only integrated data collection and management system that incorporates all levels of services, both global and domestic, in one pickup and delivery system. With 3,200 network sites across the globe, and a presence in over 220 countries,

© Bill Aron/PhotoEdit

UPS leverages its data intelligence to create real-world, real-time information throughout its global delivery network.

It is important to remember that technology investment in data and information services never stops for a company such as UPS. From information and tracking applications for computers and smartphones, to the use of telematics (which incorporates global positioning systems with package information),

UPS sees information systems as a core component of its business success.

So, the next time you meet the UPS driver dropping off a package to you, realize that there is another "driver" with them—the data behind the driver that helps makes sure that you got the right package, at the right time.[1]

Introduction

UPS's focus (and investment) in information illustrates the sometimes sophisticated way in which modern businesses integrate data into their decision processes. Many of the decisions that used to be made with guesswork are now supplemented with "intelligence" either automatically delivered by some computer software or drawn from a data warehouse.

Global delivery companies certainly aren't alone in this effort. Imagine all the information that passes through a single Home Depot store each day. Every customer transaction, every empty shelf, every employee's work schedule—right down to the schedule to clean restrooms—creates potentially valuable information that can be used by researchers and decision makers. Considering that Home Depot operates thousands of stores, obviously, Home Depot needs a data depot!

While UPS controls its data storage and management, Home Depot has outsourced the storage and management of data inventories. In this case, IBM manages the data, allowing it to be integrated into management strategy and tactics. Data from cash registers, time clocks, shelf counts, and much more are all compiled, analyzed, and either fed automatically into management systems or supplied in the form of a research report. In a way, this type of business research is automatic![2]

This chapter discusses knowledge management and the role decision support systems play in helping firms make informed business decisions. The chapter also introduces the concept of global information systems and sources of data that exist beyond the walls of any business. Modern data technology allows businesses to more easily integrate research into strategy and operations.

Information, Data, and Intelligence

data

Facts or recorded measures of certain phenomena (things).

information

Data formatted (structured) to support decision making or define the relationship between two facts.

business intelligence

The subset of data and information that actually has some explanatory power enabling effective decisions to be made.

In everyday language, terms like information and data are often used interchangeably. Researchers use these terms in specific ways that emphasize how useful each can be. **Data** are simply facts or recorded measures of certain phenomena (things or events). **Information** is data formatted (structured) to support decision making or to define the relationship between two facts. **Business intelligence** is the subset of data and information that actually has some explanatory power enabling effective managerial decisions to be made. So, there is more data than information, and more information than intelligence.

Think again about the thousands upon thousands of unsummarized facts recorded by Home Depot each day. Each time a product is scanned at checkout, that fact is recorded and becomes data. Each customer's transactions are simultaneously entered into the store's computerized inventory system. The inventory system structures the data in such a way that a stock report can be generated and orders for that store can be placed. Thus, the automated inventory system turns data into information. Further, the information from each store's sales and inventory records may be harvested by analysts. The analysts may analyze the trends and prepare reports that help Home Depot buyers get the right products into each store or even suggest places for new Home Depot locations. Thus, the analyst has now completed the transformation of data into intelligence. Exhibit 2.1 helps to illustrate the distinction between data, information, and intelligence.

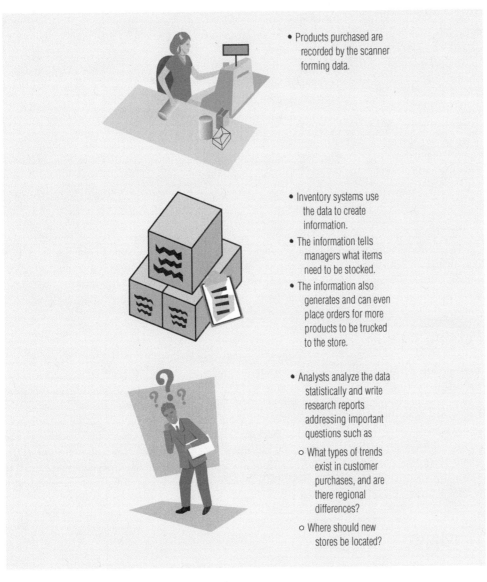

© Cengage Learning 2013

EXHIBIT **2.1**
Data, Information, Intelligence

The Characteristics of Valuable Information

Not all data are valuable to decision makers. Useful data become information and help a business manager make decisions, and can also become intelligence. Four characteristics help determine how useful data may be: relevance, quality, timeliness, and completeness.

Relevance

Relevance is a characteristic of data reflecting how pertinent these particular facts are to the situation at hand. Put another way, the facts are logically connected to the situation. Unfortunately, irrelevant data and information often creep into decision making. One particularly useful way to distinguish relevance from irrelevance is to think about how things change. Relevant data are facts about things that can be changed, and if they are changed, it will materially alter the situation. So, this simple question becomes important:

Will a change in the data coincide with a change in some important outcome?

relevance

A characteristic of data reflecting how pertinent these particular facts are to the situation at hand.

Please respond to each question based on how much you agree with it using the scale provided.

	Strongly Disagree	Disagree	Neither Agree nor Disagree	Agree	Strongly Agree
I am energetically pursuing my goals	◎	◎	◎	◎	◎
I really can't see any way around my problems	◎	◎	◎	◎	◎
I am meeting the goals I set for myself	◎	◎	◎	◎	◎
I am simply not being very successful these days	◎	◎	◎	◎	◎
I know there are many ways to achieve my goals	◎	◎	◎	◎	◎
My life could hardly be any better	◎	◎	◎	◎	◎

Courtesy of Qualtrics.com

For example, businesses across the globe are changing the amount and degree of information they need concerning their shipped packages, information trends that are very relevant to UPS. If companies become more Internet-focused with this information, than UPS must revise its own service offerings to incorporate these changing preferences in their business model.

Quality

data quality

The degree to which data represent the true situation.

Data quality is the degree to which data represent the true situation. High-quality data are accurate, valid, and reliable, issues we discuss in detail in later chapters. High-quality data represent reality faithfully. If a consumer were to replace the product UPC from one drill at Home Depot with one from a different drill, not only would the consumer be acting unethically, but it would also mean that the data collected at the checkout counter would be inaccurate. Therefore, to the extent that the cash register is not actually recording the products that consumers take out of the stores, its quality is lowered. Sometimes, researchers will try to obtain the same data from multiple data sources as one check on its quality.[3] Data quality is a critical issue in business research, and it will be discussed throughout this text.

Timeliness

timeliness

Means that the data are current enough to still be relevant.

Business is a dynamic field in which out-of-date information can lead to poor decisions. Business information must be timely—that is, provided at the right time. Computerized information systems can record events and dispense relevant information soon after the event. A great deal of business information becomes available almost at the moment that a transaction occurs. **Timeliness** means that the data are current enough to still be relevant.

Computer technology has redefined standards for timely information. For example, if a business executive at Home Depot wishes to know the sales volume of any store worldwide, detailed information about any of thousands of products can be instantly determined. At Home Depot, the point-of-sale checkout system uses UPC scanners and satellite communications to link individual stores to the headquarters' computer system, from which managers can retrieve and analyze up-to-the-minute sales data on all merchandise in each store.

Completeness

information completeness

Having the right amount of information.

Information completeness refers to having the right amount of information. Managers must have sufficient information about all aspects of their decisions. For example, a company considering establishing a production facility in Eastern Europe may plan to analyze four former Soviet-bloc countries. Population statistics, GDP, and information on inflation rates may be available on all four

RFID Technology Gets Cheaper—Business Knowledge Grows

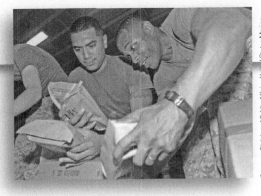

Radio frequency identification (RFID) tags have been used by large organizations for several years now. The U.S. military makes great use of RFIDs in tracking the whereabouts of virtually all kinds of products both big and small. Logistics officers can instantly track the whereabouts of Humvees and MREs (Meals Ready to Eat). Information from the tag is transmitted to computer servers and then directly into a GTN (Global Tracking Network). Equipment and supplies can then be ordered and dispatched to needed locations with minimal human contact. Product consumption (ammunition, food, water, computer printers, and so forth) can also be tracked in real time. The Marines can know in real time if personnel in a desert use more food and water than personnel in a jungle.

Walmart is pushing suppliers to adopt the technology. Not only can Walmart use RFIDs in logistical operations, but the potential exists to "go into" consumers' homes and track how much and the way consumers actually consume products. Potentially, decision support systems (DSS) could tie ordering to customer consumption. However, the costs of RFIDs make them impractical for many suppliers.

Alien Technology Corporation recently announced a drop in the price of RFID tags. Now, when a company orders a million or more, the unit cost for an RFID is 12.9¢. Although this is a "basic" RFID tag, it still can store 96 bits of information. Analysts predict that the price of RFID tags will continue to drop. By 2011, the cost for a passive RFID tag continues to range from 9¢ to 25¢, which points to the possibility that the use of RFID technology in business research and operations should continue to soar.

Sources: Clark, Don, "Alien Cuts Radio ID Tag Price to Spur Adoption by Retailers," *The Wall Street Journal* (September 12, 2005), D4; Fergueson, R. B., "Marines Deploy RFID," *e-Week* 21 (November 15, 2004), 37; >; http://rfid.net/best-practices/43-best-practices/135-passive-rfid-smart-label-buyers-guide downloaded August 17, 2011.

countries. However, information about unemployment levels may be available for only three of the countries. If information about unemployment or other characteristics cannot be obtained, the information is incomplete. Often incomplete information leads decision makers to conduct their own business research.

Knowledge Management

Who has the best pizza in town? The answer to this question requires knowledge. Indeed, you, as a consumer, have stored knowledge about many products. You know the best restaurants, best theaters, best bars, and so forth. All of this knowledge helps you make decisions as a consumer. Much of it is based on personal research involving product trials or searches for information. From an individual's perspective, knowledge is simply what you have stored in memory. It helps you make decisions about a variety of things in your life.

Organizations can use knowledge in a similar way. Knowledge is accumulated not just from a single individual, however, but from many sources. Financial managers, human resource managers, sales managers, customer reports, economic forecasts, and custom-ordered research all contribute to an organization's knowledge base. All of this data forms the organization's memory. From a company's perspective, **knowledge** is a blend of previous experience, insight, and data that forms organizational memory. It provides a framework that can be thoughtfully applied when assessing a business problem. Business researchers and decision makers use this knowledge to help create solutions to strategic and tactical problems. Thus, knowledge is a key resource and a potential competitive advantage.[4]

Knowledge management is the process of creating an inclusive, comprehensive, easily accessible organizational memory, which can be called the organization's intellectual capital.[5] The purpose of knowledge management is to organize the intellectual capital of an organization in a formally structured way for easy use. Knowledge is presented in a way that helps managers comprehend and

knowledge

A blend of previous experience, insight, and data that forms organizational memory.

knowledge management

The process of creating an inclusive, comprehensive, easily accessible organizational memory, which is often called the organization's intellectual capital.

Are Businesses Clairvoyant?

A business traveler checks into a Wyndham hotel and finds his favorite type of pillow, favorite snacks, and one of his favorite types of wine waiting upon arrival. Another customer daydreams of a recent golf vacation to Hawaii and wishes she could do it again. Later that day, an e-mail from Travelocity arrives with a great package deal to visit the same resort. Yet another consumer visits BarnesandNoble.com and a pop-up displays a new novel by his favorite author. Using a system called active data warehousing, the companies integrate data with research results that allow them to predict consumer preferences and even cyclical usage patterns quite accurately. Modern technology gives these firms a big advantage in the marketplace. Firms that don't

adapt the technology may have a much harder time serving their customers. The latest technologies even provide ways for customers to voluntarily enter data or block certain data from being transmitted to the companies they do business with.

Sources: Dewey, A., Rudolf, P., Woolfork, M., Berman, R., Bee, S., Partridge, P., & Hotchkiss, D., "The Active Data Warehouse: Where Agile Retailers Win by Capitalizing on Time," Teradata Corporation (EB-4923); Watson, Richard T., "I Am My Own Database," *Harvard Business Review* 82 (November 2004), 18–19.

act on that information and make better decisions in all areas of business. Knowledge management systems are particularly useful in making data available across the functional areas of the firm. Thus, marketing, management, and financial knowledge can be integrated. Recent research demonstrates how knowledge management systems are particularly useful in new product development and introduction.[6]

The firm's sales force plays a particularly useful role in the knowledge management process. Salespeople are in a key position to have a lot of knowledge about customers and the firm's capabilities. Thus, they are tools both for accumulating knowledge and for turning it into useful information.[7] Market-oriented organizations generally provide both formal and informal methods through which the knowledge gained by salespeople can be entered into a data warehouse to assist all decision makers, not just the sales force.

Global Information Systems

global information system

An organized collection of computer hardware, software, data, and personnel designed to capture, store, update, manipulate, analyze, and immediately display information about worldwide business activity.

Increased global competition and technological advances in interactive media have given rise to global information systems. A **global information system** is an organized collection of computer hardware, software, data, and personnel designed to capture, store, update, manipulate, analyze, and immediately display information about worldwide business activities. It is a tool for providing past, present, and projected information on internal operations and external activity. Using satellite communications, high-speed microcomputers, electronic data interchanges, fiber optics, data storage devices, and other technological advances in interactive media, global information systems are changing the nature of business.

Consider the chapter vignette presented earlier. At any moment, UPS can track the status of any shipment around the world. UPS drivers use handheld electronic clipboards called delivery information acquisition devices (DIADs) to record appropriate data about each pickup or delivery. The data are then entered into the company's main computer for record-keeping and analysis. A satellite telecommunications system allows UPS to track any shipment for a customer.

Also, as noted in the Research Snapshot "RFID Technology Gets Cheaper—Business Knowledge Grows", RFIDs can be used to track products and greatly assist a company's global information system.[8]

With so much diverse information available in a global information system, organizations have found it necessary to determine what data, information, and knowledge are most useful to particular business units.

Decision Support Systems

Business research can be described in many ways. One way is to categorize research based on the four possible functions it serves in business:

1. Foundational—answers basic questions. What business should we be in?
2. Testing—addresses things like new product concepts or promotional ideas. How effective will they be?
3. Issues—examines how specific issues impact the firm. How does organizational structure impact employee job satisfaction and turnover?
4. Performance—monitors specific metrics including financial statistics like profitability and delivery times. This type of research is critical in real-time management and in "what-if" types of analyses examining the potential impact of a change in policy.

Of these, it is the performance category that is of most interest to decision support systems. The metrics that are monitored can be fed into automated decision-making systems, or they can trigger reports that are delivered to managers. These form the basis of a decision support system and best typify the way business research assists managers with day-to-day operational decisions.

A **decision support system (DSS)** is a system that helps decision makers confront problems through direct interaction with computerized databases and analytical software programs. The purpose of a decision support system is to store data and transform them into organized information that is easily accessible to managers. Doing so saves managers countless hours so that decisions that might take days or even weeks otherwise can be made in minutes using a DSS.

Modern decision support systems greatly facilitate **customer relationship management (CRM)**. A CRM system is the part of the DSS that addresses exchanges between the firm and its customers. It brings together information about customers including sales data, market trends, marketing promotions and the way consumers respond to them, customer preferences, and more. A CRM system describes customer relationships in sufficient detail so that financial directors, marketing managers, salespeople, customer service representatives, and perhaps the customers themselves can access information directly, match customer needs with satisfying product offerings, remind customers of service requirements, and know what other products a customer has purchased.

Casinos track regular customers' behavior via "players' cards" that are swiped each time a consumer conducts a transaction. This information is fed automatically into a CRM system that creates tailor-made promotional packages. The promotion may be unique to a specific customer's preferences as tracked by their own pattern of behavior. You may notice when visiting certain websites that they seem to be able to predict your behavior. The Research Snapshot "Are Businesses Clairvoyant?" explains how a CRM may be behind this clairvoyance.

Exhibit 2.2 provides a basic illustration of a decision support system. Raw, unsummarized data are input to the DSS. Data collected in business research projects are a major source of this input, but the data may be purchased or collected by accountants, financial officers, sales managers, production managers, or company employees other than business researchers. Effective businesses spend a great deal of time and effort collecting information for input into the decision support

decision support system (DSS)

A computer-based system that helps decision makers confront problems through direct interaction with databases and analytical software programs.

customer relationship management (CRM)

The part of the DSS that addresses exchanges between the firm and its customers.

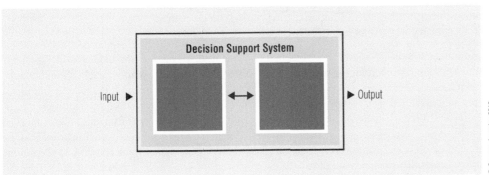

© Cengage Learning 2013

EXHIBIT **2.2**
Decision Support System

system. Useful information is the output of a DSS. A decision support system requires both databases and software. For firms operating across national borders, the DSS becomes part of its global information system.

Databases and Data Warehousing

database

A collection of raw data arranged logically and organized in a form that can be stored and processed by a computer.

A **database** is a collection of raw data arranged logically and organized in a form that can be stored and processed by a computer. A customer mailing list is one type of database. Population characteristics may be recorded by state, county, and city in another database. Production figures and costs can come from internal company records. Modern computer technology makes both the storage and retrieval of this information easy and convenient. Twenty years ago, retrieving the population data needed to do a retail site analysis may have required days, possibly weeks, in a library. Today, the information is just a few clicks away.

data warehousing

The process allowing important day-to-day operational data to be stored and organized for simplified access.

data warehouse

The multitiered computer storehouse of current and historical data.

Data warehousing is the process allowing important day-to-day operational data to be stored and organized for simplified access. More specifically, a **data warehouse** is the multitiered computer storehouse of current and historical data. Data warehouse management requires that the detailed data from operational systems be extracted, transformed, placed into logical partitions (for example, daily data, weekly data, etc.), and stored in a consistent manner. Organizations with data warehouses may integrate databases from both inside and outside the company. Managing a data warehouse effectively requires considerable computing power and expertise. As a result, data warehouse companies exist that provide this service for companies in return for a fee.[9] Data warehousing allows for sophisticated analysis, such as data mining, discussed more in Chapter 8.

Input Management

How does data end up in a data warehouse where it can be used by a decision support system? In other words, how is the input managed? Input includes all the numerical, text, voice, and image data that enter the DSS. Systematic accumulation of pertinent, timely, and accurate data is essential to the success of a decision support system.

DSS managers, systems analysts, and programmers are responsible for the decision support system as a whole, but many functions within an organization provide input data. Business researchers, accountants, corporate librarians, personnel directors, salespeople, production managers, and many others within the organization help to collect data and provide input for the DSS. Input data can also come from external sources.

Exhibit 2.3 shows five major sources of data input: internal records, proprietary business research, salesperson input, behavioral tracking, and outside vendors and external distributors of data. Each source can provide valuable input.

Internal Records

Internal records, such as accounting reports of production costs and sales figures, provide considerable data that may become useful information for managers. An effective data collection system establishes orderly procedures to ensure that data about costs, shipments, inventory, sales, and other aspects of regular operations are routinely collected and entered into the computer.

Proprietary Business Research

proprietary business research

The gathering of new data to investigate specific problems.

Business research has already been defined as a broad set of procedures and methods. To clarify the DSS concept, consider a narrower view of business research. **Proprietary business research** emphasizes the company's gathering of new data. Few proprietary research procedures and methods are conducted regularly or continuously. Instead, research projects conducted to study specific company problems generate data; this is proprietary business research. Providing managers with nonroutine data that otherwise would not be available is a major function of proprietary business research. Earlier, we discussed four categories of research. Proprietary research often involves either the testing and/or issues types of research.

EXHIBIT **2.3**

Six Major Sources of Input for Decision Support Systems

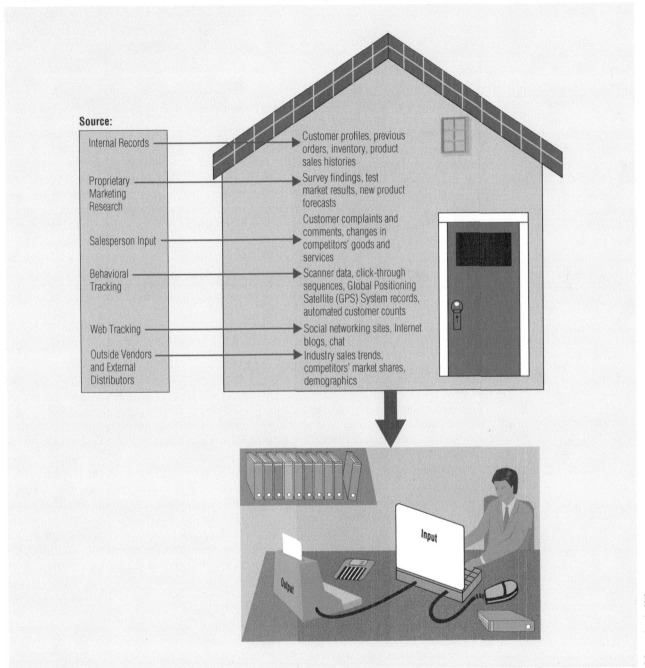

Source:

Internal Records	Customer profiles, previous orders, inventory, product sales histories
Proprietary Marketing Research	Survey findings, test market results, new product forecasts
Salesperson Input	Customer complaints and comments, changes in competitors' goods and services
Behavioral Tracking	Scanner data, click-through sequences, Global Positioning Satellite (GPS) System records, automated customer counts
Web Tracking	Social networking sites, Internet blogs, chat
Outside Vendors and External Distributors	Industry sales trends, competitors' market shares, demographics

Input

Output

© Cengage Learning 2013

Salesperson Input

Salespeople are typically a business's boundary spanners, the link between the organization and external environments. Since they are in touch with these outside entities, they commonly provide essential business data. Sales representatives' reports frequently alert managers to changes in competitors' prices and new product offerings. They also may involve the types of complaints salespeople are hearing from customers. As trends become evident, this data may become business intelligence, leading to a change in product design or service delivery.

Staying Home at Home Depot

The DSS of any organization is no better than the quality of the data input to its data warehouse. How can firms make sure that the input remains relevant and retains a "high-touch" component in a "high-tech" world?

Home Depot has always tried to make sure its executives "stay in touch" by requiring them to spend a substantial amount of time on the sales floor of a Home Depot store, which means that one of the folks in the bright orange apron helping you choose the right flush valve may well be a six-figure executive. When Jack VanWoerkom was named new executive vice president, general counsel, and corporate secretary in 2007, his first tasks were not at the corporate headquarters in Atlanta, but rather working in the aisles of a store. Therefore, the people who decide what should go into the data warehouse and how the DSS will use it maintain an appreciation for the types of decisions faced by Home Depot store managers each and every day. Home Depot even asks outside suppliers who may be involved in information technology (IT) design to spend a

few days in an actual Home Depot store. Thus, as Home Depot implements key innovations in its data networks, the people helping it to do so understand what the information needs of employees really are. Even Home Depot's outside directors meet with middle managers and conduct store visits so that they can provide more meaningful advice to senior executives. Part of this advice concerns the data needs of Home Depot managers.

Do you think such a plan would be similarly successful for a company like UPS? How?

Sources: Lublin, Joanne, "Home Depot Board Gains Insight from Trenches," *The Wall Street Journal* (October 10, 2005), B3; Tucker, Katheryn Hayes, "New Home Depot GC Learns Ropes at Store" *Fulton County Daily Report* (July 18, 2007).

Behavioral Tracking

Modern technology provides new ways of tracking human behavior. Global positioning satellite (GPS) systems allow management to track the whereabouts of delivery personnel at all times. This is the same system that provides directions through an automobile's navigation system. For example, if your delivery person takes a quick break for nine holes of golf at Weaver Ridge or decides to stop at Gorman's Pub for a couple of beers mid-afternoon, management can spot these as deviations from the appropriate delivery route. Thus, it can help track which employees are doing their jobs well.

Technology also allows firms to track actual customer behavior. While it's true that GPS tracking of customers physical location is also possible, as the photograph suggests, the Internet also greatly facilitates customer behavior tracking. For instance, Google tracks the "click-through" sequence of customers. Therefore, if a customer is searching for information on refrigerators, and then goes to BestBuy.com, Google can track this behavior and use the information to let Best Buy know how important it is to advertise on Google and even automate pricing for advertisers.[10]

scanner data

The accumulated records resulting from point-of-sale data recordings.

Purchase behavior can also be tracked at the point of sale. **Scanner data** refers to the accumulated records resulting from point-of-sale data recordings. In other words, each time products are scanned at a checkout counter, the information can be stored. The term single-source data refers to a system's ability to gather several types of interrelated data, such as type of purchase, use of a sales promotion, or advertising frequency data, from a single source in a format that will facilitate integration, comparison, and analysis.

Outside Vendors and External Distributors

Outside vendors and external distributors market information as their products. Many organizations specialize in the collection and publication of high-quality information. One outside vendor, Nielsen, provides television program ratings, audience counts, and information about the demographic composition of television viewer groups. Other vendors specialize in the distribution of information. Public libraries have always purchased information, traditionally in the form of books, and they have served as distributors of this information.

Media representatives often provide useful demographic and lifestyle data about their audiences. Advertising Age, The Wall Street Journal, Sales and Marketing Management, and other business-oriented publications are important sources of information. These publications keep managers up-to-date about the economy, competitors' activities, and other aspects of the business environment.

Companies called data specialists record and store certain business information. Computer technology has changed the way many of these organizations supply data, favoring the development of computerized databases.

Computerized Data Archives

Historically, collections of organized and readily retrievable data were available in printed form at libraries. The Statistical Abstract of the United States, which is filled with tables of statistical facts, is a typical example. As with many resources, the Statistical Abstract is now available electronically. Users can purchase it via CD-ROM or access it via the Internet. The entire 2000 U.S. Census, the 2007 Economic Census, as well as projections through the current year are available at **http://www.census.gov**.
More and more data are available in digitized form every day.

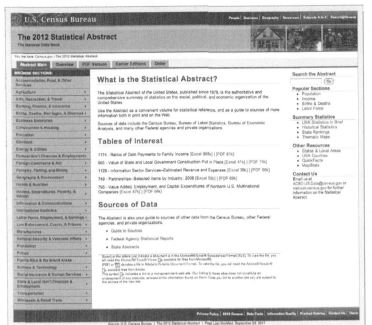

In the past, data archives were only available in print form. Today, online data is becoming the most common way to access business research data.

Numerous computerized search and retrieval systems and electronic databases are available as subscription services or in libraries. Just as a student can query the school library to find information for a term paper without leaving home, data acquisition for businesses has also become far more convenient in recent years. Today, business people access online information search and retrieval services, such as Dow Jones News Retrieval and Bloomberg Financial Markets, without leaving their offices. In fact, an increasing range of information services can be accessed from remote locations via digital wireless devices.

Modern library patrons can command a computer to search indexes and retrieve databases from a range of vendors. Just as wholesalers collect goods from manufacturers and offer them for sale to retailers who then provide them to consumers, many information firms serve as data wholesalers. **Data wholesalers** put together consortia of data sources into packages that are offered to municipal, corporate, and university libraries for a fee. Information users then access the data through these libraries. Some of the better known databases include Wilson Business Center, Hoovers, PROQUEST, INFOTRAC, DIALOG (Dialog Information Services, Inc.), LEXIS-NEXIS, and Dow Jones News Retrieval Services. These databases provide all types of information including recent news stories and data tables charting statistical trends.

data wholesalers

Companies that put together consortia of data sources into packages that are offered to municipal, corporate, and university libraries for a fee.

DIALOG, for example, maintains more than 600 databases. A typical database may have a million or more records, each consisting of a one- or two-paragraph abstract that summarizes the major points of a published article along with bibliographic information. One of the DIALOG databases, ABI/INFORM, abstracts significant articles in more than one thousand current business and management journals. Many computerized archives provide full-text downloads of published articles about companies and various research topics.

Exhibit 2.4 illustrates the services provided by two popular vendors of information services that electronically index numerous databases. For a more extensive listing, see the Gale Directory of Databases.[11]

Several types of databases from outside vendors and external distributors are so fundamental to decision support systems that they deserve further explanation. The following sections discuss statistical databases, financial databases, and video databases in slightly more detail.

Statistical Databases

Statistical databases contain numerical data for analysis and forecasting. Often demographic, sales, and other relevant business variables are recorded by geographical area. Geographic information systems use these geographical databases and powerful software to prepare computer maps of relevant

EXHIBIT **2.4**

Vendors of Information
Services and Electronic
Indexing

Vendors	Selected Databases	Type of Data
DIALOG	ABI/INFORM	Summaries and citations from over 1,000 academic management, marketing, and general business journals with full text of more than 500 of these publications
	ASI (American Statistics Index)	Abstracts and indexes of federal government statistical publications
	PROMT (The Predicast Overview of Markets and Technologies)	Summaries and full text from 1,000 U.S. and international business and trade journals, industry newsletters, newspapers, and business research studies; information about industries and companies, including the products and technologies they develop and the markets in which they compete
	Investext	Full text of over 2 million company, industry, and geographic research reports written by analysts at more than 600 leading investment banks, brokerage houses, and consulting firms worldwide
Dow Jones News Retrieval	Business Newsstand	Articles from *New York Times, Los Angeles Times, Washington Post*, and other leading newspapers and magazines
	Historical Data Center	Historical data on securities, dividends, and exchange rates
	Web Center	Information obtained from searches of corporate, industry, government, and news websites

variables. Companies such as Claritas, Urban Decision Systems, and CACI all offer geographic/demographic databases that are widely used in industry.

One source for these huge data warehouses is scanner data. Substituting electronic record-keeping like optical scanners for human record-keeping results in greater accuracy and more rapid feedback about store activity.

One weakness of scanner data is that not all points of sale have scanner technology. For instance, many convenience stores lack scanner technology, as do most vending machines. Thus, those purchases go unrecorded. The Universal Product Code, or UPC, contains information on the category of goods, the manufacturer, and product identification based on size, flavor, color, and so on. This is what the optical scanner actually reads. If a large percentage of a brand's sales occur in environments without the ability to read the UPC code, the business should be aware that the scanner data may not be representative.

Financial Databases

Competitors' and customers' financial data, such as income statements and balance sheets, are of obvious interest to business managers. These are easy to access in financial databases. CompuStat publishes an extensive financial database on thousands of companies, broken down by industry and other criteria. To illustrate the depth of this pool of information, CompuStat Global offers extensive data on 6,650 companies in more than 30 countries in Europe, the Pacific Rim, and North America.

Video Databases

Video databases and streaming media are having a major impact on many goods and services. For example, movie studios provide clips of upcoming films and advertising agencies put television commercials on the Internet (see **http://www.adcritic.com**). McDonald's maintains a digital archive of television commercials and other video footage to share with its franchisees around the world. The video database enables franchisees and their advertising agencies to create local advertising without the need for filming the same types of scenes already archived. Just imagine the value of digital video databases to advertising agencies' decision support systems!

Networks and Electronic Data Interchange

Individual personal computers can be connected through networks to other computers. Networking involves linking two or more computers to share data and software.

Electronic data interchange (EDI) systems integrate one company's computer system directly with another company's system. Much of the input to a company's decision support system may come through networks from other companies' computers. Companies such as GXS (GXS.com) allow corporations to exchange business information with suppliers or customers. For example, every evening Walmart transmits millions of characters of data about the day's sales to its apparel suppliers. Wrangler, a supplier of blue jeans, shares the data and a model that interprets the data. Wrangler also shares software applications that act to replenish stock in Walmart stores. This DSS lets Wrangler's managers know when to send specific quantities of specific sizes and colors of jeans to specific stores from specific warehouses. The result is a learning loop that lowers inventory costs and leads to fewer stockouts.

electronic data interchange (EDI)
Type of exchange that occurs when one company's computer system is integrated with another company's system.

The Internet and Research

When most readers of this book were born, the Internet had yet to enter the everyday vocabulary. In fact, few people outside of a small number of universities and the U.S. Department of Defense had any clue as to what the Internet might be. In the 1960s, mainframe computers revolutionized research by allowing researchers to use research techniques involving large numbers of mathematical computations that previously would have been impossible or, at the least, impractical. In the 1980s, the mainframe computing power of the 1960s, which was available primarily in large universities, government agencies, and very large companies, was transformed into something that could go on nearly every businessperson's desktop. The personal computer (PC) and simple operating systems like DOS and eventually Windows revolutionized many business applications by making computing power relatively inexpensive and convenient. Today, the widespread usage of the Internet is perhaps the single biggest change agent in business research. Since most readers are no

Internet
A worldwide network of computers that allows users access to information from distant sources.

● ● ● ● ● ● ●

Electronic data storage is revolutionizing some research tasks. Thousands of television commercials and employee training films are available for analysis by just searching the right electronic video database.

doubt experienced in using the Internet, we highlight a few terms and facts about the Internet that are especially useful in understanding business research.

In the following pages we discuss the World Wide Web and how to use the Internet for research. However, keep in mind that the Internet is constantly changing. The description of the Internet, especially home page addresses, may be out of date by the time this book is published. Be aware that the Internet of today will not be the Internet of tomorrow.

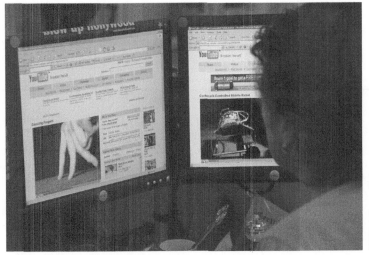

© AP Photo/Cameron Bloch

What Exactly Is the Internet?

The **Internet** is a worldwide network of computers that allows users access to data, information, and feedback from distant sources. It functions as the world's largest public library, providing access to a seemingly endless range of data. Many people believe the Internet is the most important communications medium since television.

The Internet began in the 1960s as an experimental connection between computers at Stanford University, the University of California at Santa Barbara, the University of California at Los Angeles, and the University of Utah, in conjunction with the Department of Defense.[12] The Department of Defense was involved because it wanted to develop a communications network that could survive nuclear war. The Internet gradually grew into a nationwide network of connected computers, and now it is a worldwide network often referred to as the "information superhighway."

The Internet has no central computer; instead, each message sent bears an address code that lets a sender forward a message to a desired destination from any computer linked to the Net. Many benefits of the Internet arise because the Internet is a collection of thousands of small networks, both domestic and foreign, rather than a single computer operation.

host

Where the content for a particular website physically resides and is accessed.

A domain is typically a company name, institutional name, or organizational name associated with a host computer. A **host** is where the content for a particular website physically resides and is accessed. For example, Forbes magazine's Internet edition is located at **http://forbes.com**. The "com" indicates this domain is a commercial site. Educational sites end in "edu"—Louisiana Tech can be reached at **http://www.latech.edu** and Bradley University can be accessed at **http://www.bradley .edu**. The United States Marine Corps can be found at **http://www.marines.mil** (the "mil" indicating military) and many government sites, such as the U.S. House of Representatives, end with "gov," as in **http://www.house.gov** and **http://www.census.gov**. Many nonprofit organizations end in "org" or "net" as in **http://www.ams-web.org**, the web home for the Academy of Marketing Science. Web addresses outside the United States often end in abbreviations for their country such as "ca," "de," or "uk" for Canada, Germany (Deutschland), and the United Kingdom, respectively.

How Is the Internet Useful in Research?

The Internet is useful to researchers in many ways. In fact, more and more applications become known as the technology grows and is adopted by more and more users. The Internet is particularly useful as a source for accessing available data and as a way of collecting data.

Accessing Available Data

The Internet allows instantaneous and effortless access to a great deal of information. Noncommercial and commercial organizations make a wealth of data and other resources available on the Internet. For example, the U.S. Library of Congress provides the full text of all versions of House and Senate legislation and the full text of the Congressional Record. The Internal Revenue Service makes it possible to obtain information and download a variety of income tax forms. Cengage Learning (**www.cengage.com**) and its college divisions (**www.cengage.com/highered/**) have online directories that allow college professors to access information about the company and its textbooks. The Gale Research Database provides basic statistics and news stories on literally thousands of companies worldwide. Thus, information that formerly took a great deal of time and effort to obtain is now available with a few clicks. Further, since it can often be electronically downloaded or copied, it isn't necessary for a person to transcribe the data. Therefore, it is available in a more error-free form.

Collecting Data

The Internet is also revolutionizing the way researchers collect data. Later in this text, we discuss in more detail the use of web-based surveys. In short, questionnaires can be posted on a website and respondents can be invited to go to the particular URL and participate in the survey. This cuts down on the expense associated with traditional mail surveys and also reduces error since the data can be automatically recorded rather than transcribed from a paper form into an electronic format.

Furthermore, when a consumer uses the World Wide Web, his or her usage leaves a record that can be traced and observed. For instance, Zappos.com can determine how many pages were visited at their shopping site before a purchase was made. They can see if products were abandoned in the "virtual shopping cart" without a purchase being made. Online auctions provide another mechanism to track consumers' behavior. Prototype products can be offered for sale in an online auction to help assist with product design, forecasting demand, and setting an appropriate price.[13]

Navigating the Internet

The **World Wide Web (WWW)** refers specifically to that portion of the Internet made up of servers that support a retrieval system that organizes information into documents called web pages. World Wide Web documents, which may include graphic images, video clips, and sound clips, are formatted in programming languages, such as HTML (HyperText Markup Language) and XML (Extensible Markup Language) that allow for displaying, linking, and sharing of information on the Internet.

Parties that furnish information on the World Wide Web are called **content providers**. Content providers maintain websites. A website consists of one or more web pages with related information about a particular topic; for example, Bradley University's website includes pages about its mission, courses, athletics, admissions, and faculty (see **http://www.bradley.edu**). The introductory page or opening screen is called the home page because it provides basic information about the purpose of the document along with a menu of selections or links that lead to other screens with more specific information. Thus, each page can have connections, or hyperlinks, to other pages, which may be on any computer connected to the Internet. People using the World Wide Web may be viewing information that is stored on a host computer or on a machine halfway around the world.

Most web browsers also allow the user to enter a **uniform resource locator (URL)** into the program. The URL is really just a website address that web browsers recognize. Many websites allow any user or visitor access without previous approval. However, many commercial sites require that the user have a valid account and password before access is granted.

One of the most basic research tools available via the Internet is a search engine. A **search engine** is a computerized directory that allows anyone to search the World Wide Web for information based on a keyword search. A **keyword search** takes place as the search engine searches through millions of web pages for documents containing the keywords. Some of the most comprehensive and accurate search engines are:

Yahoo!	http://www.yahoo.com
Google	http://www.google.com
Hotbot	http://www.hotbot.com
Go.com	http://www.go.com
Excite	http://www.excite.com
Bing!	http://www.bing.com
Ask.com	http://www.ask.com
WebCrawler	http://www.webcrawler.com

Google revolutionized search engines by changing the way the search was actually conducted. It searches based on a mathematical theory known as graph theory.[14] Google greatly improved the accuracy and usefulness of the search results obtained from a keyword search. In fact, "google" is now included as a word in many dictionaries, meaning "to search for information on the World Wide Web." Exhibit 2.5 illustrates the Google interface and expanded Google options. For instance, if one clicks on Google Scholar, a search of citations for a particular author or basic research papers on any given topic indicated by the keywords can be performed.

Interactive Media and Environmental Scanning

The Internet is an **interactive medium** because users click commands and often get customized responses. So the user and equipment can have a continuing conversation. Two or more individuals who communicate one-to-one via e-mail using an Internet service provider are also using interactive media. So are individuals who communicate with many senders and receivers via bulletin boards or chat rooms. Because of its vastness, the Internet is an especially useful source for

World Wide Web (WWW)

A portion of the Internet that is a system of computer servers that organize information into documents called web pages.

content providers

Parties that furnish information on the World Wide Web.

uniform resource locator (URL)

A website address that web browsers recognize.

search engine

A computerized directory that allows anyone to search the World Wide Web for information using a keyword search.

keyword search

Takes place as the search engine searches through millions of web pages for documents containing the keywords.

interactive medium

A medium, such as the Internet, that a person can use to communicate with and interact with other users.

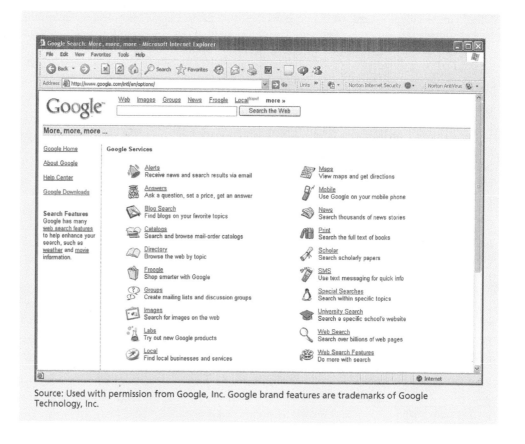

Source: Used with permission from Google, Inc. Google brand features are trademarks of Google Technology, Inc.

environmental scanning

Entails all information gathering designed to detect changes in the external operating environment of the firm.

scanning many types of environmental changes. **Environmental scanning** entails all information gathering designed to detect changes in the external operating environment of the firm. These things are usually beyond the control of the firm, but they still can have a significant impact on firm performance.

Ford Motor Company maintains an Internet-based relationship marketing program that, among other things, helps the automaker scan its environment using the Internet. Its dealer website creates a centralized communication service linking dealers via an Internet connection. Its buyer website allows prospective buyers to visit a virtual showroom and to get price quotes and financial information. Its owner website allows an owner who registers and supplies pertinent vehicle information to get free e-mail and other ownership perks. A perk might be a free Hertz upgrade or an autographed photo of one of the Ford-sponsored NASCAR drivers. In return, Ford collects data at all levels, which allow managers to scan for trends and apply what they learn at a local level.

pull technology

Consumers request information from a web page and the browser then determines a response; the consumer is essentially asking for the data.

push technology

Sends data to a user's computer without a request being made; software is used to guess what information might be interesting to consumers based on the pattern of previous responses.

Information Technology

Data and information can be delivered to consumers or other end users via either **pull technology** or **push technology**. Conventionally, consumers request information from a web page and the browser then determines a response. Thus, the consumer is essentially asking for the data. In this case, it is said to be pulled through the channel. The opposite of pull is push. Push technology sends data to a user's computer without a request being made. In other words, software is used to guess what information might be interesting to consumers based on the pattern of previous responses.

Smart information delivery (known by a variety of technical names, including push phase technology) allows a website, such as the Yahoo! portal, to become a one-on-one medium for each individual user. Today's information technology uses "smart agents" or "intelligent agents" to deliver customized content to a viewer's desktop. **Smart agent software** is capable of learning an Internet user's preferences and automatically searching out information and distributing the information to a user's computer. My Yahoo! and My Excite are portal services that personalize web pages. Users can get stock quotes relevant to their portfolios, news about favorite sports teams, local weather, and other personalized information. Users can customize the sections of the service they want delivered. With push technology, pertinent content is delivered to the viewer's desktop without the user having to do the searching.

Cookies, in computer terminology, are small computer files that record a user's web usage history. If a person looks up a weather report by keying a zip code into a personalized web page, the fact that the user visited the website and the zip code entered are recorded in the cookie. This is a clue that tells where the person lives (or maybe where he or she may be planning to visit). Websites can then direct information to that consumer based on information in the cookie. So, someone in Hattiesburg, Mississippi, may receive pop-up ads for restaurants in Hattiesburg. Information technology is having a major impact on the nature of business research. We will explore this topic in several places throughout this book.

Intranets

An **intranet** is a company's private data network that uses Internet standards and technology.[15] The information on an intranet—data, graphics, video, and voice—is available only inside the organization or to those individuals whom the organization deems as appropriate participants. Thus, a key difference between the Internet and an intranet is that security software programs, or "firewalls," are installed to limit access to only those employees authorized to enter the system. Intranets then serve as secure knowledge portals that contain substantial amounts of organizational memory and can integrate it with information from outside sources. For example, Caterpillar has an intranet that includes their knowledge network, a portal that provides Caterpillar employees and dealership personnel with a vast array of information about the company and its product offering. The challenge in designing an intranet is making sure that it is capable of delivering relevant data to decision makers. Research suggests that relevance is a key in getting knowledge workers to actually make use of company intranets.[16]

An intranet can be extended to include key consumers as a source of valuable research. Their participation in an intranet can lead to new product developments. Texas Instruments successfully established an intranet that integrated communications between customers and researchers, leading to the introduction of new calculators and modification of existing calculators.[17] An intranet lets authorized users, possibly including key customers, look at product drawings, employee newsletters, sales figures, and other kinds of company information.

Internet2

As we mentioned earlier, information technology changes rapidly. As sophisticated as the Internet and intranets are today, new technologies, such as Internet2, will dramatically enhance researchers' ability to answer business problems in the future.

Internet2 (**http://www.internet2.edu/**) is a collaborative effort involving about 250 universities, government entities (including the military), and corporate organizations. The project hopes to recreate some of the cooperative spirit that created the Internet originally. Internet2 users are limited to those involved with the affiliate organizations. The hope is to create a faster, more powerful Internet by providing multimodal access, employing more wireless technologies, and building in global trading mechanisms. Internet2 began as a research tool for the universities and organizations involved in its development.[18]

smart agent software

Software capable of learning an Internet user's preferences and automatically searching out information in selected websites and then distributing it.

cookies

Small computer files that a content provider can save onto the computer of someone who visits its website.

intranet

A company's private data network that uses Internet standards and technology.

● ● ● ● ● ● ●

The iPhone offers one example of how modern technology makes it possible to store and deliver information, providing cellular communication and contacts, e-mail capabilities, calendar functions, GPS mapping, and music downloads, among a host of other capabilities.

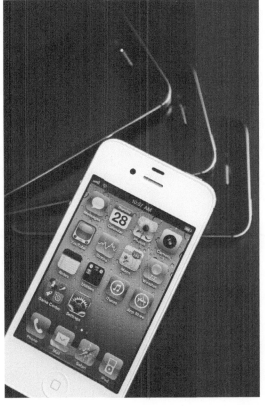

© Bloomberg via Getty Images

∴ SUMMARY

1. Know and distinguish between the concepts of data, information, and intelligence. Increased global competition and technological advances in interactive media have spurred development of global information systems. A global information system is an organized collection of computer hardware, software, data, and personnel designed to capture, store, update, manipulate, analyze, and immediately display information about worldwide business activity.

From a research perspective, there is a difference between data, information, and intelligence. Data are simply facts or recorded measures of certain phenomena (things); information is data formatted (structured) to support decision making or define the relationship between two facts. Business intelligence is the subset of data and information that actually has some explanatory power enabling effective decisions to be made.

2. Understand the four characteristics that describe data. The usefulness of data to management can be described based on four characteristics: relevance, quality, timeliness, and completeness. Relevant data have the characteristic of pertinence to the situation at hand. The information is useful. The quality of information is the degree to which data represent the true situation. High-quality data are accurate, valid, and reliable. High-quality data represent reality faithfully and present a good picture of reality. Timely information is obtained at the right time. Computerized information systems can record events and present information as a transaction takes place, improving timeliness. Complete information is the right quantity of information. Managers must have sufficient information to relate all aspects of their decisions together.

3. Know the purpose of research in assisting business operations. A computer-based decision support system helps decision makers confront problems through direct interactions with databases and analytical models. A DSS stores data and transforms them into organized information that is easily accessible to managers.

4. Know what a decision support system is and does. A database is a collection of raw data arranged logically and organized in a form that can be stored and processed by a computer. Business data come from four major sources: internal records, proprietary business research, business intelligence, and outside vendors and external distributors. Each source can provide valuable input. Because most companies compile and store many different databases, they often develop data warehousing systems. Data warehousing is a process that allows important day-to-day operational data to be stored and organized for simplified access. More specifically, a data warehouse is the multitiered computer storehouse of current and historical data. Data warehouse management requires that the detailed data from operational systems be extracted, transformed, and stored (warehoused) so that the various database tables from both inside and outside the company are consistent. All of this feeds into the decision support system that automates or assists business decision making.

Numerous database search and retrieval systems are available by subscription or in libraries. Computer-assisted database searching has made the collection of external data faster and easier. Managers refer to many different types of databases.

Although personal computers work independently, they can connect to other computers in networks to share data and software. Electronic data interchange (EDI) allows one company's computer system to join directly to another company's system.

5. Recognize the major categories of databases. The Internet is a worldwide network of computers that allows users access to information and documents from distant sources. It is a combination of a worldwide communication system and the world's largest public library. The World Wide Web is a system of thousands of interconnected pages or documents that can be easily accessed with web browsers and search engines.

An intranet is a company's private data network that uses Internet standards and technology. The information on an intranet—data, graphics, video, and voice—is available only inside the organization. Thus, a key difference between the Internet and an intranet is that "firewalls," or security software programs, are installed to limit access to only those employees authorized to enter the system.

A company uses Internet features to build its own intranet. Groupware and other technology can facilitate the transfer of data, information, and knowledge. In organizations that practice knowledge management, intranets function to make the knowledge of company experts more accessible throughout their organizations.

:: KEY TERMS AND CONCEPTS

business intelligence, *18*
content providers, *31*
cookies, *33*
customer relationship management
    (CRM), *23*
data quality, *20*
data warehouse, *24*
data warehousing, *24*
data wholesalers, *27*
data, *18*
database, *24*
decision support system (DSS), *23*

electronic data interchange
    (EDI), *29*
environmental scanning, *32*
global information system, *22*
host, *30*
information completeness, *20*
information, *18*
interactive medium, *31*
Internet, *29*
intranet, *33*
keyword search, *31*
knowledge management, *21*

knowledge, *21*
proprietary business research, *24*
pull technology, *32*
push technology, *32*
relevance, *19*
scanner data, *26*
search engine, *31*
smart agent software, *33*
timeliness, *20*
uniform resource locator
    (URL), *31*
World Wide Web (WWW), *31*

:: QUESTIONS FOR REVIEW AND CRITICAL THINKING

1. What is the difference between data, information, and intelligence?
2. What are the characteristics of useful information?
3. What is the key question distinguishing relevant data from irrelevant data?
4. Define knowledge management. What is its purpose within an organization?
5. What types of databases might be found in the following organizations?
    a. Holiday Inn
    b. A major university's athletic department
    c. Anheuser-Busch
6. What type of operational questions could a delivery firm like FedEx expect to automate with the company's decision support system?
7. What makes a decision support system successful?
8. What is data warehousing?
9. 'NET How does data warehousing assist decision making? Visit **http://www.kbb.com**. While there, choose two cars that you might consider buying and compare them. Which do you like the best? What would you do now? What are at least three pieces of data that should be stored in a data

warehouse somewhere based on your interaction with Kelley Blue Book?
10. 'NET Give three examples of computerized databases that are available at your college or university library.
11. What is the difference between the Internet and an intranet?
12. Suppose a retail firm is interested in studying the effect of lighting on customer purchase behavior. Which of the following pieces of information is the least relevant and why?
    a. Amount of natural light in the store
    b. The compensation system for store salespeople
    c. The color of the walls in the store
    d. The type of lighting: fluorescent or incandescent
13. 'NET Imagine the data collected by eBay each day. List at least five types of data that are collected through its daily operations. Describe each in terms of it illustrating data, information, or intelligence. Make sure you list at least one of each.
14. How could New Balance, a maker of athletic shoes, use RFID technology to collect data?
15. 'NET The Spider's Apprentice is a website that provides many useful tips about using search engines. Go to **http://www .monash.com/spidap.html**, then click on Search Engine FAQ to learn the ins and outs of search engines.

:: RESEARCH ACTIVITIES

1. 'NET To learn more about data warehousing, go to **http:// www.datawarehousing.org**.
2. 'NET Use the Internet to see if you can find information to answer the following questions:

a. What is the weather in Angers, France, today?
b. What are four restaurants in the French Quarter in New Orleans?
c. What is the population of Brazil?

Harvard Cooperative Society

CASE 2.1

From his office window overlooking the main floor of the Harvard Cooperative Society, CEO Jerry Murphy can glance down and see customers shopping.[19] They make their way through the narrow aisles of the crowded department store, picking up a sweatshirt here, trying on a baseball cap there, checking out the endless array of merchandise that bears the Harvard University insignia.

Watching Murphy, you can well imagine the Co-op's founders, who started the store in 1882, peering through the tiny window-panes to keep an eye on the shop floor. Was the Harvard Square store attracting steady traffic? Were the college students buying enough books and supplies for the Co-op to make a profit? Back then, it was tough to answer those questions precisely. The owners had to watch and wait, relying only on their gut feelings to know how things were going from minute to minute.

Now, more than a hundred years later, Murphy can tell you, down to the last stock-keeping unit, how he's doing at any given moment. His window on the business is the PC that sits on his desk. All day long it delivers up-to-the-minute, easy-to-read electronic reports on what's selling and what's not, which items are running low in inventory and which have fallen short of forecast. In a matter of seconds, the computer can report gross margins for any product or supplier, and Murphy can decide whether the margins are fat enough to justify keeping the supplier or product on board. "We were in the 1800s, and we had to move ahead," he says of the $55 million business.

Questions

1. What is a decision support system? What advantages does a decision support system have for a business like the Harvard Cooperative Society?
2. How would the decision support system of a business like the Harvard Cooperative Society differ from that of a major corporation?
3. Briefly outline the components of the Harvard Cooperative Society's decision support system.

Theory Building

LEARNING OUTCOMES

After studying this chapter, you should be able to

1. Define the meaning of theory
2. Understand the goals of theory
3. Understand the terms concepts, propositions, variables, and hypotheses
4. Discuss how theories are developed
5. Understand the scientific method

Chapter Vignette:

Theory and Practice

W hat if you went home tonight and turned on the light switch and nothing happened? Most of us would immediately start seeking a logical explanation: "Is the bulb burnt out?" "Did my roommate forget to pay the electric bill?" "Is the electricity out?" "Did a fuse blow?" These are common thoughts that would race through our minds. The order would probably depend on our past experience and we would try to determine the cause through a logical thought sequence. Attribution theory is one framework that helps us explain the world and determine the cause of an event (the light bulb not working) or behavior (why my girlfriend is mad at me). Simply put, this theory helps us make sense of events by providing a systematic method to assess and evaluate why things occur. Attribution theory is just one of many theoretical models that are useful to business researchers.

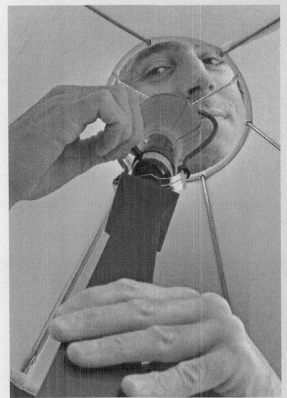

© OmniTerra Images

Introduction

The purpose of science concerns the expansion of knowledge and the search for truth. Theory building is the means by which basic researchers hope to achieve this purpose.

Students sometimes think their classes or course material are "too theoretical" or lacking "practical application." However, this should certainly not be the case. Theories are simply generalizations that help us better understand reality. Furthermore, theories allow us to understand the logic behind things we observe. If a theory does not hold true in practice, then that theory holds no value. This chapter will provide a fundamental knowledge of theory, theory development, and some terminology regarding theory necessary for business researchers.

What Is a Theory?

Like all abstractions, the word "theory" has been used in many different ways, in many different contexts, at times so broadly as to include almost all descriptive statements about a class of phenomena, and at other times so narrowly as to exclude everything but a series of terms and their relationships that satisfies certain logical requirements.[1]

theory

A formal, logical explanation of some events that includes predictions of how things relate to one another.

A theory consists of a coherent set of general propositions that offer an explanation of some phenomena by describing the way other things correspond to this phenomena. So, a **theory** is a formal, testable explanation of some events that includes explanations of how things relate to one another. A simpler way to think of a theory is to consider it a model of reality, a simplification that helps us better understand the logic and relationships among different factors.

You are probably already familiar with many business theories. For example, one of the most basic theories in the business world is the theory of supply and demand commonly discussed in economics classes. The differing amount of a product or service that a producer is willing to provide at different prices is termed supply. The quantity of the good or service that customers are willing to purchase at differing prices is termed demand. The law of demand states that demand for a product or service will decrease as price increases. While we accept this as common knowledge today, this is actually a theory largely attributed to Alfred Marshall, who recognized that customers played a role in the determination of prices, rather than simply relying on the classical approach of determining prices solely on costs.

A theory can be built through a process of reviewing previous findings of similar studies, simple logical deduction, and/or knowledge of applicable theoretical areas. For example, if a web designer is trying to decide what color background is most effective in increasing online sales, he may first consult previous studies examining the effects of color on package design and retail store design. He may also find theories that deal with the wavelength of different colors, affective response to colors, or those that explain retail atmospherics. This may lead to the specific prediction that blue is the most effective background color for a website.[2]

While it may seem that theory is only relevant to academic or basic business research, theory plays a role in understanding practical research as well. Before setting research objectives, the researcher must be able to describe the business situation in some coherent way. Without this type of explanation, the researcher would have little idea of where to start. Ultimately, the logical explanation helps the researcher know what variables need to be included in the study and how they may relate to one another. The Research Snapshot "Social Network Theory" illustrates how theory is applied to virtually every situation, including social networking.

What Are the Goals of Theory?

Suppose a researcher investigating business phenomena wants to know what caused the financial crisis. Another person wants to know if organizational structure influences leadership style. Both of these individuals want to gain a better understanding of the environment and be able to predict behavior; to be able to say that if we take a particular course of action we can expect a specific outcome to occur. These two issues—understanding and predicting—are the two purposes of theory.[3]

Go online to the Internet survey you completed for the Chapter 1 assignment. Please go back and review all the questions included on the survey. Following our discussion of theory in this chapter, you should have a solid foundation in understanding theory development and the importance of theory in business research. Considering the questions asked in the survey, build a theory about the relationship among at least four questions. How do you think the responses to these questions should relate? Why? Provide a theoretical explanation for the relationships you are proposing.

Accomplishing the first goal allows the theorist to gain an understanding of the relationship among various phenomena. For example, a financial advisor may believe, or theorize, that older investors tend to be more interested in investment income than younger investors. This theory, once verified, would then allow her to predict the importance of expected dividend yield based on the age of her customer. Thus a theory enables us to predict the behavior or characteristics of one phenomenon from the knowledge of another phenomenon. The value of understanding and anticipating future conditions in the environment or in an organization should be obvious. In most situations, of course, understanding and prediction go hand in hand. To predict phenomena, we must have an explanation of why variables behave as they do. Theories provide these explanations.

concept (or construct)

A generalized idea about a class of objects that has been given a name; an abstraction of reality that is the basic unit for theory development.

Research Concepts, Constructs, Propositions, Variables, and Hypotheses

Theory development is essentially a process of describing phenomena at increasingly higher levels of abstraction. In other words, as business researchers, we need to be able to think of things in a very abstract manner, but eventually link these abstract concepts to observable reality. To understand theory and the business research process, it will be useful to know different terminology and how these terms relate.

Research Concepts and Constructs

A **concept** or **construct** is a generalized idea about a class of objects, attributes, occurrences, or processes that has been given a name. If you, as an organizational theorist, were to describe phenomena such as supervisory behavior or risk aversion, you would categorize empirical events or real things into concepts. Concepts are the building blocks of theory. In organizational theory, leadership, productivity, and morale are concepts. In the theory of finance, gross national product, risk aversion, and inflation are frequently used concepts. Accounting concepts include assets, liabilities, and depreciation. In marketing, customer satisfaction, market share, and loyalty are important concepts.

Social Network Theory

Researchers have developed theories about the links and structure of social networks, complete with constructs and propositions about how linkages are formed. Each separate entity (individuals or organizations) is referred to as a node. The relationships among nodes are referred to as ties. When nodes become linked they yield social contacts.

What creates ties? How do the nodes become linked? Many factors have been indentified, including family relationships, friendship, professional association, common interest and activities, sexual relationships, and shared beliefs. When linked together with ties these nodes form a social network.

Network theory is used to examine social networks. The links between and among nodes can be simple or complex. They can be as simple as a single family or so complex as to operate on a national or international level. The network can play an important role in the success of an individual, how a family functions, and how a business makes decisions. The value derived from the social network is termed social capital.

While electronic social networking is a relatively recent development, businesses are already examining ways to utilize social networks to spread information, better serve their customers, and grow profits. The next few years will be exciting as the theory of social networks develops and businesses continue to explore how they can gain social capital from engaging in social networking.

Source: http://www.facebook.com/pages/Social-network-theory/112159215470744, accessed August 3, 2011.

© Annette Shaff/Shutterstock

EXHIBIT **3.1**

A Ladder of Abstraction for Concepts

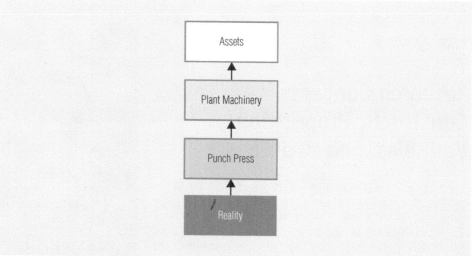

© Cengage Learning 2013

ladder of abstraction

Organization of concepts in sequence from the most concrete and individual to the most general.

abstract level

In theory development, the level of knowledge expressing a concept that exists only as an idea or a quality apart from an object.

empirical level

Level of knowledge that is verifiable by experience or observation.

latent construct

A concept that is not directly observable or measurable, but can be estimated through proxy measures.

Concepts abstract reality. That is, concepts express in words various events or objects. Concepts, however, may vary in degree of abstraction. For example, the concept of an asset is an abstract term that may, in the concrete world of reality, refer to a wide variety of things, including a specific punch press machine in a production shop. The abstraction ladder in Exhibit 3.1 indicates that it is possible to discuss concepts at various levels of abstraction. Moving up the **ladder of abstraction**, the basic concept becomes more general, wider in scope, and less amenable to measurement.

The basic or scientific business researcher operates at two levels: on the **abstract level** of concepts (and propositions) and on the empirical level of variables (and hypotheses). At the **empirical level**, we "experience" reality—that is, we observe, measure, or manipulate objects or events. For example, we commonly use the term job performance, but this is an abstract term that can mean different things to different people or in different situations. To move to the empirical level, we must more clearly define this construct and identify actual measures that we can assess and measure to represent job performance as shown in Exhibit 3.2. In research, we use the term **latent construct** to refer to a concept that is not directly observable or measurable, but can be estimated through proxy measures.[4] Job performance, customer satisfaction, and risk aversion are just three examples of the many latent constructs in business research. While we cannot directly see these latent constructs, we can measure them, and doing so is one of the greatest challenges for business researchers.

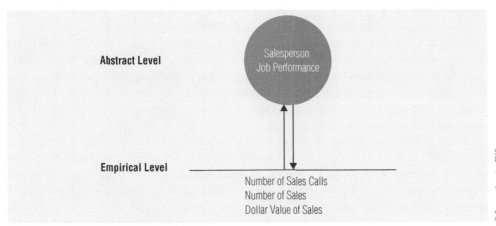

© Cengage Learning 2013

EXHIBIT 3.2
Concepts Are Abstractions of Reality

If an organizational researcher says, "Older workers prefer different rewards than younger workers," two concepts—age of worker and reward preference—are the subjects of this abstract statement. If the researcher wishes to test this relationship, Jason, age 25, Angela, age 42, and Ed, age 62—along with other workers—may be questioned about their preferences for salary, retirement plans, intrinsic job satisfaction, and so forth. Recording their ages and assessing their reward preferences are activities that occur at the empirical level. In this example, we can see that researchers have a much easier time assessing and measuring age than the latent construct of reward preference.

In the end, researchers are concerned with the observable world, or what we shall loosely term reality. Theorists translate their conceptualization of reality into abstract ideas. Thus, theory deals with abstraction. Things are not the essence of theory; ideas are.[5] Concepts in isolation are not theories. To construct a theory we must explain how concepts relate to other concepts as discussed below.

> **"Reality is merely an illusion, albeit a very persistent one."**
> —ALBERT EINSTEIN

Research Propositions and Hypotheses

As we just mentioned, concepts are the basic units of theory development. However, theories require an understanding of the relationship among concepts. Thus, once the concepts of interest have been identified, a researcher is interested in the relationship among these concepts. **Propositions** are statements concerned with the relationships among concepts. A proposition explains the logical linkage among certain concepts by asserting a universal connection between concepts. For example, we might propose that treating our employees better will make them more loyal employees. This is certainly a logical link between managerial actions and employee reactions, but is quite general and not really testable in its current form.

A **hypothesis** is a formal statement explaining some outcome. In its simplest form, a hypothesis is a guess. A sales manager may hypothesize that the salespeople who are highest in product knowledge will be the most productive. An advertising manager may hypothesize that if consumers' attitudes toward a product change in a positive direction, there will be an increase in consumption of the product. A human resource manager may hypothesize that job candidates with certain majors will be more successful employees.

A hypothesis is a proposition that is empirically testable. In other words, when one states a hypothesis, it should be written in a manner that can be supported or shown to be wrong through an empirical test. For example, using the color of the background for a website discussed previously, the researcher may use theoretical reasoning to develop the following hypothesis:

H1: A website with a blue background will generate more sales than an otherwise identical website with a red background.

We often apply statistics to data to empirically test hypotheses. **Empirical testing** means that something has been examined against reality using data. The abstract proposition, "Treating our employees better will make them more loyal employees" may be tested empirically with a hypothesis. Exhibit 3.3 shows that the hypothesis, "Increasing retirement benefits will reduce intention to leave the organization" is an empirical counterpart of this proposition. Retirement benefits

propositions
Statements explaining the logical linkage among certain concepts by asserting a universal connection between concepts.

hypothesis
Formal statement of an unproven proposition that is empirically testable.

empirical testing
Examining a research hypothesis against reality using data.

EXHIBIT 3.3

Hypotheses Are the Empirical Counterparts of Propositions

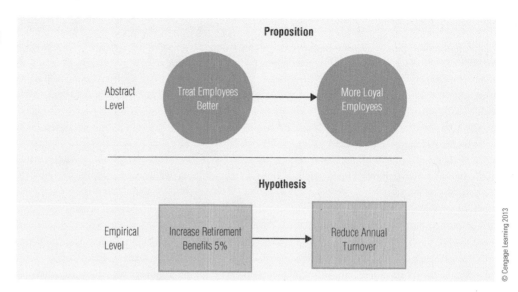

variables

Anything that may assume different numerical values; the empirical assessment of a concept.

and intention to leave are **variables**, reflecting the concepts of employee treatment and employee loyalty. When the data are consistent with a hypothesis, we say the hypothesis is supported. When the data are inconsistent with a hypothesis, we say the hypothesis is not supported. We are often tempted to say that we prove a hypothesis when the data conform to the prediction, but this isn't really true. Because our result is based on statistics, there is always the possibility that our conclusion is wrong. Now, at times we can be very, very confident in our conclusion, but from an absolute perspective, statistics cannot prove a hypothesis is true.

Because variables are at the empirical level, variables can be measured. In this case, retirement benefits might be measured quite easily and precisely (e.g., the actual percentage change in matching retirement funds), while the latent construct of intention to leave would be more challenging for the researcher. This step is known as **operationalizing** our variables—the process of identifying the actual measurement scales to assess the variables of interest. We will discussion operationalization in more detail in Chapter 13.

operationalizing

The process of identifying the actual measurement scales to assess the variables of interest.

Thus, the scientific inquiry has two basic levels:

> . . . the empirical and the abstract, conceptual. The empirical aspect is primarily concerned with the facts of the science as revealed by observation and experiments. The abstract or theoretical aspect, on the other hand, consists in a serious attempt to understand the facts of the science, and to integrate them into a coherent, i.e., a logical, system. From these observations and integrations are derived, directly or indirectly, the basic laws of the science.[6]

Understanding Theory

Exhibit 3.4 is a simplified portrayal of a theory to explain voluntary job turnover—the movement of employees to other organizations. Two concepts—(1) the perceived desirability of movement to another organization and (2) the perceived ease of movement from the present job—are expected to be the primary determinants of intention to quit. This is a proposition. Further, the concept intention to quit is expected to be a necessary condition for the actual voluntary job turnover behavior to occur. This is a second proposition that links concepts together in this theory. In the more elaborate theory, job performance is another concept considered to be the primary determinant influencing both perceived ease of movement and perceived desirability of movement. Moreover, perceived ease of movement is related to other concepts such as labor market conditions, number of organizations visible to the individual, and personal characteristics. Perceived desirability of movement is influenced by concepts such as equity of pay, job complexity, and participation in decision making. A complete explanation of this theory is not possible; however, this example should help you understand the terminology used by theory builders.

"If facts conflict with a theory, either the theory must be changed or the facts."

—BENEDICT SPINOZA

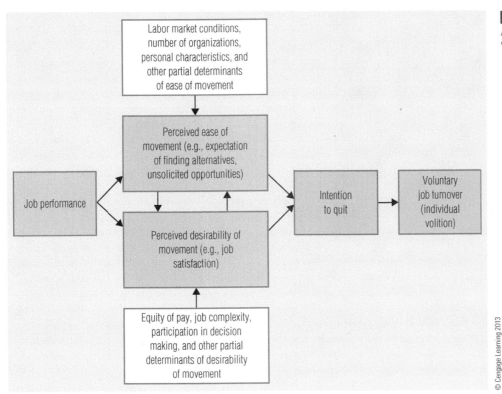

EXHIBIT 3.4
A Basic Theory Explaining
Voluntary Job Turnover[7]

Verifying Theory

In most scientific situations there are alternative theories to explain certain phenomena. To determine which is the better theory, researchers make observations or gather empirical data to verify the theories.

    Maslow's hierarchical theory of motivation offers one explanation of human behavior. Maslow theorizes that individuals will attempt to satisfy physiological needs before self-esteem needs. An alternative view of motivation is provided by Freudian (psychoanalytic) theory, which suggests that unconscious, emotional impulses are the basic influences on behavior. One task of science is to determine if a given theoretical proposition is false or if there are inconsistencies between competing theories. Just as records are made to be broken, theories are made to be tested.

> *It must be possible to demonstrate that a given proposition or theory is false. This may at first glance appear strange. Why "false" rather than "true"? Technically, there may be other untested theories which could account for the results we obtained in our study of a proposition. At the very least, there may be a competing explanation which could be the "real" explanation for a given set of research findings. Thus, we can never be certain that our proposition or theory is the correct one. The scientist can only say, "I have a theory which I have objectively tested with data and the data are consistent with my theory." If the possibility of proving an idea false or wrong is not inherent in our test of an idea, then we cannot put much faith in the evidence that suggests it to be true. No other evidence was allowed to manifest itself.[9]*

"Every genuine test of a theory is an attempt to falsify it, or to refute it.[8]"

—KARL POPPER

Theory Building

You may be wondering, "Where do theories come from?" Although this is not an easy question to answer in a short chapter on theory in business research, we will explore this topic briefly. In this chapter, theory has been explained at the abstract, conceptual level and at the empirical level. Theory generation may occur at either level.

    At the abstract, conceptual level, a theory may be developed with deductive reasoning by going from a general statement to a specific assertion. **Deductive reasoning** is the logical process

deductive reasoning

The logical process of deriving a conclusion about a specific instance based on a known general premise or something known to be true.

Noting a link between changes in gold prices and political instability could be the foundation for a basic theory.

inductive reasoning

The logical process of establishing a general proposition on the basis of observation of particular facts.

scientific method

A set of prescribed procedures for establishing and connecting theoretical statements about events, for analyzing empirical evidence, and for predicting events yet unknown; techniques or procedures used to analyze empirical evidence in an attempt to confirm or disprove prior conceptions.

of deriving a conclusion about a specific instance based on a known general premise or something known to be true. For example, while you might occasionally have doubts, we know that all business professors are human beings. If we also know that Barry Babin is a business professor, then we can deduce that Barry Babin is a human being.

At the empirical level, a theory may be developed with inductive reasoning. **Inductive reasoning** is the logical process of establishing a general proposition on the basis of observation of particular facts. All business professors that have ever been seen are human beings; therefore, all business professors are human beings.

Suppose a stockbroker with 15 years' experience trading on the New York Stock Exchange repeatedly notices that the price of gold and the price of gold stocks rise whenever there is a hijacking, terrorist bombing, or military skirmish. In other words, similar patterns occur whenever a certain type of event occurs. The stockbroker may induce from these empirical observations the more general situation that the price of gold is related to political stability. Thus, the stockbroker states a proposition based on his or her experience or specific observations: "Gold prices will increase during times of political instability." The stockbroker has constructed a basic theory.

Over the course of time, theory construction is often the result of a combination of deductive and inductive reasoning. Our experiences lead us to draw conclusions that we then try to verify empirically by using the scientific method.

The Scientific Method

The **scientific method** is a set of prescribed procedures for establishing and connecting theoretical statements about events, for analyzing empirical evidence, and for predicting events yet unknown. It is useful to look at the analytic process of scientific theory building as a series of stages. While there is not complete consensus concerning exact procedures for the scientific method, we suggest seven operations may be viewed as the steps involved in the application of the scientific method:

1. Assessment of relevant existing knowledge of a phenomenon
2. Formulation of concepts and propositions
3. Statement of hypotheses
4. Design of research to test the hypotheses
5. Acquisition of meaningful empirical data
6. Analysis and evaluation of data
7. Proposal of an explanation of the phenomenon and statement of new problems raised by the research[10]

An excellent overview of the scientific method is presented in Robert Pirsig's book Zen and the Art of Motorcycle Maintenance:

Actually I've never seen a cycle-maintenance problem complex enough really to require full-scale formal scientific method. Repair problems are not that hard. When I think of formal scientific method an image sometimes comes to mind of an enormous juggernaut, a huge bulldozer—slow, tedious, lumbering, laborious, but invincible. It takes twice as long, five times as long, maybe a dozen times as long as informal mechanic's techniques, but you know in the end you're going to get it. There's no fault isolation problem in motorcycle maintenance that can stand up to it. When you've hit a really tough one, tried everything, racked your brain and nothing works, and you know that this time Nature has really decided to be difficult, you say, "Okay, Nature, that's the end of the nice guy," and you crank up the formal scientific method.

For this you keep a lab notebook. Everything gets written down, formally, so that you know at all times where you are, where you've been, where you're going and where you want to get. In scientific work and electronics technology this is necessary because otherwise the problems get so complex you get lost in them and confused and forget what you know and what you don't know and have to give up. In cycle maintenance things are not that involved, but when confusion starts it's a good idea to hold it down by making everything formal and exact. Sometimes just the act of writing down the problems straightens out your head as to what they really are.

The logical statements entered into the notebook are broken down into six categories: (1) statement of the problem, (2) hypotheses as to the cause of the problem, (3) experiments designed to test each hypothesis, (4) predicted results of the experiments, (5) observed results of the experiments, and (6) conclusions from the results of the experiments. This is not different from the formal arrangement of many college and high-school lab notebooks but the purpose here is no longer just busywork. The purpose now is precise guidance of thoughts that will fail if they are not accurate.

The real purpose of scientific method is to make sure Nature hasn't misled you into thinking you know something you don't actually know. There's not a mechanic or scientist or technician alive who hasn't suffered from that one so much that he's not instinctively on guard. That's the main reason why so much scientific and mechanical information sounds so dull and so cautious. If you get careless or go romanticizing scientific information, giving it a flourish here and there, Nature will soon make a complete fool out of you. It does it often enough anyway even when you don't give it opportunities. One must be extremely careful and rigidly logical when dealing with Nature: one logical slip and an entire scientific edifice comes tumbling down. One false deduction about the machine and you can get hung up indefinitely.

In Part One of formal scientific method, which is the statement of the problem, the main skill is in stating absolutely no more than you are positive you know. It is much better to enter a statement "Solve Problem: Why doesn't cycle work?" which sounds dumb but is correct, than it is to enter a statement "Solve Problem: What is wrong with the electrical system?" when you don't absolutely know the trouble is in the electrical system. What you should state is "Solve Problem: What is wrong with cycle?" and then state as the first entry of Part Two: "Hypothesis Number One: The trouble is in the electrical system." You think of as many hypotheses as you can, then you design experiments to test them to see which are true and which are false.

This careful approach to the beginning questions keeps you from taking a major wrong turn which might cause you weeks of extra work or can even hang you up completely. Scientific questions often have a surface appearance of dumbness for this reason. They are asked in order to prevent dumb mistakes later on.

Part Three, that part of formal scientific method called experimentation, is sometimes thought of by romantics as all of science itself because that's the only part with much visual surface. They see lots of test tubes and bizarre equipment and people running around making discoveries. They do not see the experiment as part of a larger intellectual process and so they often confuse experiments with demonstrations, which look the same. A man conducting a gee-whiz science show with fifty thousand dollars' worth of Frankenstein equipment is not doing anything scientific if he knows beforehand what the results of his efforts are going to be. A motorcycle mechanic, on the other hand, who honks the horn to see if the battery works is informally conducting a true scientific experiment. He is testing a hypothesis by putting the question to nature. The TV scientist who mutters sadly, "The experiment is a failure; we have failed to achieve what we had hoped for," is suffering mainly from a bad scriptwriter. An experiment is never a failure solely because it fails to achieve predicted results. An experiment is a failure only when it also fails adequately to test the hypothesis in question, when the data it produces don't prove anything one way or another.

Skill at this point consists of using experiments that test only the hypothesis in question, nothing less, nothing more. If the horn honks, and the mechanic concludes that the whole electrical system is working, he is in deep trouble. He has reached an illogical

● ● ● ● ● ● ●

A motorcycle mechanic … who honks the horn to see if the battery works is informally conducting a true scientific experiment. He is testing a hypothesis by putting the question to nature.

— Robert M. Pirsig

© dbimages/Alamy

conclusion. The honking horn only tells him that the battery and horn are working. To design an experiment properly he has to think very rigidly in terms of what directly causes what. This you know from the hierarchy. The horn doesn't make the cycle go. Neither does the battery, except in a very indirect way. The point at which the electrical system directly causes the engine to fire is at the spark plugs, and if you don't test here, at the output of the electrical system, you will never really know whether the failure is electrical or not.

To test properly the mechanic removes the plug and lays it against the engine so that the base around the plug is electrically grounded, kicks the starter lever and watches the spark-plug gap for a blue spark. If there isn't any he can conclude one of two things: (a) there is an electrical failure or (b) his experiment is sloppy. If he is experienced he will try it a few more times, checking connections, trying every way he can think of to get that plug to fire. Then, if he can't get it to fire, he finally concludes that (a) is correct, there's an electrical failure, and the experiment is over. He has proved that his hypothesis is correct.

In the final category, conclusions, skill comes in stating no more than the experiment has proved. It hasn't proved that when he fixes the electrical system the motorcycle will start. There may be other things wrong. But he does know that the motorcycle isn't going to run until the electrical system is working and he sets up the next formal question: "Solve problem: What is wrong with the electrical system?"

He then sets up hypotheses for these and tests them. By asking the right questions and choosing the right tests and drawing the right conclusions the mechanic works his way down the echelons of the motorcycle hierarchy until he has found the exact specific cause or causes of the engine failure, and then he changes them so that they no longer cause the failure.

An untrained observer will see only physical labor and often get the idea that physical labor is mainly what the mechanic does. Actually the physical labor is the smallest and easiest part of what the mechanic does. By far the greatest part of his work is careful observation and precise thinking. That is why mechanics sometimes seem so taciturn and withdrawn when performing tests. They don't like it when you talk to them because they are concentrating on mental images, hierarchies, and not really looking at you or the physical motorcycle at all. They are using the experiment as part of a program to expand their hierarchy of knowledge of the faulty motorcycle and compare it to the correct hierarchy in their mind. They are looking at underlying form.[11]

Practical Value of Theories

As the above excerpt makes evident, theories allow us to generalize beyond individual facts or isolated situations. Theories provide a framework that can guide managerial strategy by providing insights into general rules of behavior. When different incidents may be theoretically comparable in some way, the scientific knowledge gained from theory development may have practical value. A good theory allows us to generalize beyond individual facts so that general patterns may be understood and predicted. For this reason it is often said there is nothing so practical as a good theory.

∷ SUMMARY

1. **Define the meaning of theory.** Theories are simply models designed to help us better understand reality and to understand the logic behind things we observe. A theory is a formal, logical explanation of some events that includes predictions of how things relate to one another.

2. **Understand the goals of theory.** There are two primary goals of theory. The first is to understand the relationships among various phenomena. A theory provides a picture of the linkages among different concepts, allowing us to better comprehend how they affect one another. The second goal is to predict. Once we have an understanding of the relationships among concepts, we can then predict what will happen if we change one factor. For example, if we understand the relationship between advertising expenditures and retail sales, we can then predict the impact of decreasing or increasing our advertising expenditures.

3. **Understand the terms concepts, propositions, variables, and hypotheses.** A concept or construct is a generalized idea about a class of objects, attributes, occurrences, or processes that has been given a name. Leadership style, employee turnover, and customer satisfaction are all

concepts. Concepts express in words various events or objects. Propositions are statements concerned with the relationships among concepts. A proposition explains the logical linkage among certain concepts by asserting a universal connection between concepts: "Leadership style is related to employee turnover." A hypothesis is a formal statement explaining some outcome regarding variables of interest. Variables are the empirical reflection of a concept and a hypothesis is a proposition stated in a testable format. So, concepts and propositions are at the abstract level, while variables and hypotheses are at the empirical level.

4. Discuss how theories are developed. A theory can be built through a process of reviewing previous findings of similar studies or knowledge of applicable theoretical areas. A theory may be developed with deductive reasoning by going from a general statement to a specific assertion. Deductive reasoning is the logical process of deriving a conclusion about a specific instance based on a known general premise or something known to be true. Inductive reasoning is the logical process of establishing a general proposition on the basis of observation of particular facts.

5. Understand the scientific method. The scientific method is a set of prescribed procedures for establishing and connecting theoretical statements about events, for analyzing empirical evidence, and for predicting events yet unknown. It is useful to look at the analytic process of scientific theory building as a series of stages. We mentioned that seven operations may be viewed as the steps involved in the application of the scientific method: (1) assessment of relevant existing knowledge of a phenomenon, (2) formulation of concepts and propositions, (3) statement of hypotheses, (4) design of research to test the hypotheses, (5) acquisition of meaningful empirical data, (6) analysis and evaluation of data, and (7) proposal of an explanation of the phenomenon and statement of new problems raised by the research. In sum, the scientific method guides us from the abstract nature of concepts and propositions, to the empirical variables and hypotheses, and to the testing and verification of theory.

:: KEY TERMS AND CONCEPTS

abstract level, *40*

concept (or construct), *39*

deductive reasoning, *43*

empirical level, *40*

empirical testing, *41*

hypothesis, *41*

inductive reasoning, *44*

ladder of abstraction, *40*

latent construct, *40*

operationalizing, *42*

propositions, *41*

scientific method, *44*

theory, *38*

variables, *42*

:: QUESTIONS FOR REVIEW AND CRITICAL THINKING

1. What are some theories offered to explain aspects of your field of business?
2. Reflect on your own social network. How are the nodes in your social network linked? What social capital do you gain from your social network?
3. How do propositions and hypotheses differ?
4. How do concepts differ from variables?
5. What does the statement, "There is nothing so practical as a good theory" mean? Do you agree with this statement?
6. The seventeenth-century Dutch philosopher Benedict Spinoza said, "If the facts conflict with a theory, either the theory must be changed or the facts." What is the practical meaning of this statement?
7. Compare and contrast deductive logic with inductive logic. Give an example of both.
8. Find another definition of theory. How is the definition you found similar to this book's definition? How is it different?

:: RESEARCH ACTIVITIES

1. 'NET The Chapter Vignette briefly introduced attribution theory. Do a Web search regarding attribution theory and identify the key characteristics of this theory.
2. 'NET The Merriam-Webster dictionary definition of theory can be found at **http://www.merriam-webster.com/dictionary/theory**. What is the definition of theory given at this site? How does it compare to the definition given in this chapter?
3. 'NET The Logic of Scientific Discovery is an important theoretical work. Visit The Karl Popper Web at **http://elm.eeng.dcu.ie/~tkpw/** to learn about its author and his work.

The Business Research Process
An Overview

LEARNING OUTCOMES

After studying this chapter, you should be able to

1. Define decision making and understand the role research plays in making decisions

2. Classify business research as either exploratory research, descriptive research, or causal research

3. List the major phases of the research process and the steps within each

4. Explain the difference between a research project and a research program

Chapter Vignette:

Getting (and Keeping) Up to Speed: Hoover's Helps HP

L ike most global companies, Hewlett-Packard (HP) must continue to innovate, develop new technology-based products and services, and engage end users, other businesses, and even governmental institutions across the globe. And, it must do this in a continuously changing environment, with time pressures and other competitors seeking to exploit technology advances that they bring to these same customers. Finally, HP is hiring new sales staff, and changing their market territories, on a continuous basis. Business opportunities in information technology are hard-fought, and hard-won. How can HP help their sales staff with data and analyses to keep them up to speed with new companies, new territories, and new technologies?

The solution to HP's data and analysis support problems was found with Hoovers, a division of the Dun & Bradstreet Corporation. Hoover's provides detailed company information, including industry data and news, to HP's sales staff in a real-time format. Hoover's assists with account planning and engagement, executive information, and up-to-the-minute industry information that HP sales reps can use to quickly and efficiently engage existing and new customers around the globe. In some instances, Hoover's

is an integral part of HP's customer relationship management (CRM) strategy, with "data plug-in" capabilities that give sales reps real-time information to assist them in their decision-making.

Through the use of Hoover's data and analysis tools, HP's sales staff can now help manage their sales contacts in the intensely complicated and time-intensive information technology environment. Clearly, Hoovers helps HP get (and keep) up to speed.[1]

Source: "Hewlett-Packard Makes Hoover's Part of Global CRM Strategy and End-to-End Sales Process" (http://www.hoovers.com/about/case-studies/100000292-1.html).

Introduction

This chapter focuses on the relationship between business research and managerial decision making. Business success is determined directly by the quality of decisions made by key personnel. Researchers contribute to decision making in several key ways. These include:

1. Helping to better define the current situation
2. Defining the firm—determining how consumers, competitors, and employees view the firm
3. Providing ideas for enhancing current business practices
4. Identifying new strategic directions
5. Testing ideas that will assist in implementing business strategies for the firm
6. Examining how correct a certain business theory is in a given situation

The chapter introduces the types of research that allow researchers to provide input to key decision makers. Causality and the conditions for establishing causality are presented. Last but not least, the chapter discusses stages in the business research process.

Decision Making

Businesses, such as Hewlett-Packard, face decisions that shape the future of the organization, its employees, and its customers. In each case, the decisions are brought about as the firm either seeks to capitalize on some opportunity or to reduce any potential negative impacts related to some business problem. A **business opportunity** is a situation that makes some potential competitive advantage possible. The discovery of some underserved segment presents such an opportunity. For example, eBay capitalized on a business opportunity presented by technological advances to do much the same thing that is done at a garage sale but on a very, very large scale.

A **business problem** is a situation that makes some significant negative consequence more likely. A natural disaster can present a problem for many firms as they face potential loss of property and personnel and the possibility that their operations, and therefore their revenue, will be interrupted. Most business problems, however, are not nearly as obvious. In fact, many are not easily observable. Instead, problems are commonly inferred from **symptoms**, which are observable cues that serve as a signal of a problem because they are caused by that problem. An increase in employee turnover is generally only a symptom of a business problem, rather than the problem itself. Research may help identify what is causing this symptom so that decision makers can actually attack the problem, not just the symptom. Patients don't usually go to the doctor and point out their problem (such as an ulcer). Instead, they point out the symptoms (upset stomach) they are experiencing. Similarly, decision makers usually hear about symptoms and often need help from research to identify and attack problems. Whether facing an opportunity or a problem, businesses need quality information to deal effectively with these situations.

Formally defined, **decision making** is the process of developing and deciding among alternative ways of resolving a problem or choosing from among alternative opportunities. A decision maker must recognize the nature of the problem or opportunity, identify how much information is currently available and how reliable it is, and determine what additional information is needed to better deal with the situation. Every decision-making situation can be classified based on whether it best represents a problem or an opportunity and where the situation falls on a continuum from absolute ambiguity to complete certainty.

business opportunity

A situation that makes some potential competitive advantage possible.

business problem

A situation that makes some significant negative consequence more likely.

symptoms

Observable cues that serve as a signal of a problem because they are caused by that problem.

decision making

The process of developing and deciding among alternative ways of resolving a problem or choosing from among alternative opportunities.

Certainty

Complete certainty means that the decision maker has all information needed to make an optimal decision. This includes the exact nature of the business problem or opportunity. For example, an advertising agency may need to know the demographic characteristics of subscribers to magazines in which it may place a client's advertisements. The agency knows exactly what information it needs and where to find the information. If a manager is completely certain about both the problem or opportunity and future outcomes, then research may not be needed at all. However, perfect certainty, especially about the future, is rare.

SURVEY
THIS!

Review the online survey we are using for this course. Based on the data that the survey gathers, what business problems or opportunities do you feel can be addressed from the information? Specify at least three research questions that can be answered by the information gathered by this survey. Do you think this survey is most representative of an exploratory research, descriptive research, or causal research design? Justify your answer.

| My Surveys | Create Survey | Edit Survey | Distribute Survey | View Results | Polls | Library | Panels | Administration |

View Reports   Responses   Download Data   Cross Tabulation

Get Help   Ask a Question

Courtesy of Qualtrics.com

Uncertainty

Uncertainty means that the manager grasps the general nature of desired objectives, but the information about alternatives is incomplete. Predictions about forces that shape future events are educated guesses. Under conditions of uncertainty, effective managers recognize that spending additional time to gather data that clarify the nature of a decision is needed. For instance, a firm needing operating capital may consider an initial public offering, but is not certain of demand for the stock or how to establish the price of the IPO. Business decisions generally involve uncertainty, particularly when a company is seeking new opportunities.

Ambiguity

Ambiguity means that the nature of the problem itself is unclear. Objectives are vague and decision alternatives are difficult to define. This is by far the most difficult decision situation, but perhaps the most common.

Managers face a variety of problems and decisions. Complete certainty and predictable future outcomes may make business research a waste of time. However, under conditions of uncertainty or ambiguity, business research becomes more attractive to the decision makers. Decisions also vary in terms of importance, meaning that some may have great impact on the welfare of the firm and others may have negligible impact. The more important, ambiguous, or uncertain a situation is, the more likely it is that additional time must be spent on business research.

• • • • • • •

Can you identify symptoms that may indicate problems for these businesses? What business problems might they signify?

© Susan Van Etten

Problems and Opportunities

Exhibit 4.1 depicts decision situations characterized by the nature of the decision and the degree of ambiguity.[2] Under problem-focused decision making and conditions of high ambiguity, symptoms may not clearly point to some problem. Indeed, they may be quite vague or subtle, indicating only small deviations from normal conditions. For instance, a fast-food restaurant may be experiencing small changes in the sales of its individual products, but no change in overall sales. Such a symptom may not easily point to a problem such as a change in consumer tastes. As ambiguity is lessened, the symptoms are clearer and are better indicators of a problem. A large and sudden drop in overall sales may suggest the problem that

EXHIBIT **4.1**
Describing Decision-Making
Situations

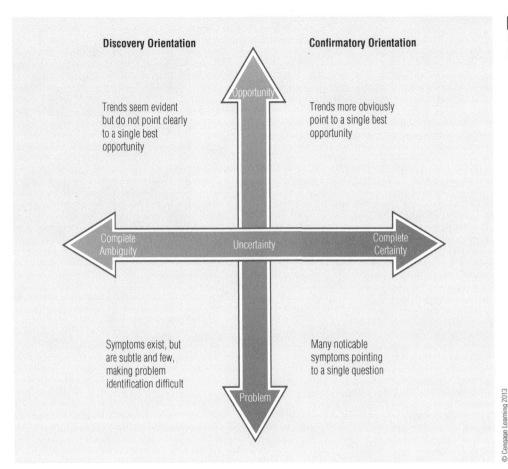

the restaurant's menu does not fare well compared to competitors' menus. Thus, a menu change may be in order. However, it is also possible the drop in sales is due to new competition, or a competitor's price drop or new promotional campaign. Thus, research is needed to clarify the situation.

Similarly, in opportunity-oriented research, ambiguity is characterized by environmental trends that do not suggest a clear direction. As the trends become larger and clearer, they are more diagnostic, meaning they point more clearly to a single opportunity.

Types of Business Research

Business research is undertaken to reduce uncertainty and focus decision making. In more ambiguous circumstances, management may be totally unaware of a business problem. Alternatively, someone may be scanning the environment for opportunities. For example, an entrepreneur may have a personal interest in softball and baseball. She is interested in converting her hobby into a profitable business venture and hits on the idea of establishing an indoor softball and baseball training facility and instructional center. However, the demand for such a business is unknown. Even if there is sufficient demand, she is not sure of the best location, actual services offered, desired hours of operation, and so forth. Some preliminary research is necessary to gain insights into the nature of such a situation. Without it, the situation may remain too ambiguous to make more than a seat-of-the-pants decision. In this situation, business research is almost certainly needed.

Cute, Funny, or Sexy? What Makes a Mascot Tick?

Has the Pillsbury Doughboy ever changed? How old should the Brawny (paper towel) man be? What should the M&Ms characters be named? These questions all have many possible answers. In truth, a lot of research goes into answering these kinds of questions. It often begins with exploratory research. For instance, focus groups involving female consumers revealed a considerable amount of intimate discussion about the Brawny man. Thus, it seemed that a sexy Brawny man would yield a better response than a humorous or intelligent Brawny man.

Mr. Peanut, the icon for Planters Peanuts, has actually changed very little since his introduction in the 1920s. He looks good for his age! Again, exploratory research suggests generally positive comments about Mr. Peanut, so only minor changes in the color scheme have been introduced. A few years ago, exploratory research led to some further tests of a Mr. Peanut in Bermuda shorts, but the tests proved overwhelmingly negative, sending Planters back to a more original peanut.

Similarly, exploratory research asked a few consumers for their reactions to the Mars M&Ms characters. Mars was interested in discovering names for the characters. They found that most consumers simply referred to them by their colors. This piece of information became useful in shaping future research and business strategy.

Sources: Voight, Joan, "Mascot Makeover: The Risky Business of Tampering with Brand Icons," *Adweek* (July 7, 2003), 20–26; Elliot, Stuart, "Updating a Venerable Character, or Tarnishing a Sterling Reputation?" *The New York Times* (March 19, 2004), C5; "Advertising Mascots—People," TV Acres, http://www.tvacres.com/admascots_brawny.htm, accessed August 3, 2011.

In other situations, researchers know exactly what their problems are and can design careful studies to test specific hypotheses. For example, an organization may face a problem regarding health care benefits for their employees. Awareness of this problem could be based on input from human resource managers, recruiters, and current employees. The problem could be contributing to difficulties in recruiting new employees. How should the organization's executive team address this problem? They may devise a careful test exploring which of three different health plans are judged the most desirable. This type of research is problem-oriented and seems relatively unambiguous. This process may culminate with researchers preparing a report suggesting the relative effect of each alternative plan on employee recruitment. The selection of a new health plan should follow relatively directly from the research.

Business research can be classified on the basis of either technique or purpose. Experiments, surveys, and observational studies are just a few common research techniques. Classifying research by its purpose, such as the situations described above, shows how the nature of a decision situation influences the research methodology. The following section introduces the three types of business research:

1. Exploratory
2. Descriptive
3. Causal

Matching the particular decision situation with the right type of research is important in obtaining useful research results.

Exploratory Research

exploratory research

Conducted to clarify ambiguous situations or discover ideas that may be potential business opportunities.

Exploratory research is conducted to clarify ambiguous situations or discover potential business opportunities. As the name implies, exploratory research is not intended to provide conclusive evidence from which to determine a particular course of action. In this sense, exploratory research is not an end unto itself. Usually exploratory research is a first step, conducted with the expectation that additional research will be needed to provide more conclusive evidence. Exploratory research is often used to guide and refine these subsequent research efforts. The Research Snapshot "Cute, Funny, or Sexy? What Makes a Mascot Tick?" illustrates a use of exploratory research. For example, rushing into detailed surveys before it is clear exactly what decisions need to be made can waste time, money, and effort by providing irrelevant information. This is a common mistake in business research programs.

Exploratory research is particularly useful in new product development.[3] Sony and Honda have each been instrumental in developing robot technology.[4] Making a functional robot that can move around, perform basic functions, carry out instructions, and even carry on a conversation isn't really a problem. What Sony and Honda have to research is what business opportunities may exist based on robot technology. Exploratory research allowing consumers to interact with robots suggests that consumers are more engaged when the robot has human qualities, such as the ability to walk on two legs. Researchers noticed that people will actually talk to the robot (which can understand basic oral commands) more when it has human qualities. In addition, consumers do seem entertained by a walking, talking, dancing robot. These initial insights have allowed each company to form more specific research questions focusing on the relative value of a robot as an entertainment device or as a security guard, and identifying characteristics that may be important to consumers.

Descriptive Research

As the name implies, the major purpose of **descriptive research** is to describe characteristics of objects, people, groups, organizations, or environments. In other words, descriptive research tries to "paint a picture" of a given situation by addressing who, what, when, where, and how questions. For example, every month the Bureau of Labor Statistics (BLS) conducts descriptive research in the form of the Current Population Survey. Official statistics on a variety of characteristics of the labor force are derived from this survey (the Current Population Survey can be found at **http://www.bls.gov/CPS/**). This research describes the who, what, when, where, and how regarding the current economic and employment situation.

Unlike exploratory research, descriptive studies are conducted after the researcher has gained a firm grasp of the situation being studied. This understanding, which may have been developed in part from exploratory research, directs the study toward specific issues. Later, we will discuss the role of research questions and hypotheses. These statements help greatly in designing and implementing a descriptive study. Without these, the researcher would have little or no idea of what questions to ask. The Research Snapshot "Taking a Swing at Business Success" illustrates an application of descriptive research.

Descriptive research often helps describe market segments. For example, researchers used descriptive surveys to describe consumers who are heavy consumers (buy a lot) of organic food products. The resulting report showed that these consumers tend to live in coastal cities with populations over 500,000, with the majority residing on the West Coast. The most frequent buyers of organic foods are affluent men and women ages 45–54 (36 percent) and 18–34 (35 percent).[5] Interestingly, consumers who buy organic foods are not very brand-oriented—81 percent of them cannot name a single organic brand. Research such as this helps high-quality supermarkets such as Whole Foods make location decisions. Over half of Whole Foods' food products are organic.

Similarly, the university considering the addition of an online MBA program might benefit from descriptive research profiling current and potential customers. Online customers are not identical to the traditional MBA student. They tend to be older than the average 24-year-old traditional student, averaging about 30 years of age. Also, they tend to live in rural communities, be more introverted, and expect a higher workload than traditional students. Another key statistic is that the dropout rate for online students is significantly higher than for traditional MBA students. Nearly

descriptive research

Describes characteristics of objects, people, groups, organizations, or environments; tries to "paint a picture" of a given situation.

● ● ● ● ● ● ●

Descriptive research about consumers who buy organic food has paid off for the Whole Foods chain of stores.

Taking a Swing at Business Success

Greg Norman is best known for performance on the golf course. However, he is also one of the most successful businesspeople to come out of sports. Among his many ventures, Norman is a well-respected vintner. Norman Estates gained fame in the wine trade with Australian wines that offered considerable quality at a fair price. More recently, Norman Estates is expanding its portfolio by purchasing vineyard properties and production capacity in California. As Norman Estates and other wineries consider diversifying production beyond their traditional boundaries, descriptive research can be vital in making these key decisions.

Descriptive research details what wine consumers like to drink in terms of where the wine is from and where the consumers are located. Consumers around the world form geographic segments with preferences for wines from certain areas. American consumers, for instance, have contributed to the growing slump in French wine sales by switching increasingly from French wines to Australian- and American-made wines. In particular, French wines at low and moderate prices have suffered, whereas higher price French wine sales remain steady.

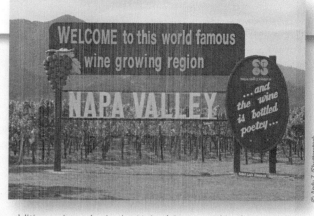

In addition, wine sales in the United States and in the United Kingdom are relatively strong compared to wine sales in France and Germany.

All of these descriptive results may allow Greg Norman a better understanding of the international wine market and therefore allow him to make better decisions about where to grow and produce wine. Do you think the choice to expand to California rather than France seems like a good decision?

Sources: Orth, U. R., M. M. Wolf, and T. Dodd, "Dimensions of Wine Region Equity and Their Impact on Consumer Preferences," *Journal of Product and Brand Management* 14, no. 2 (2005), 88–97; "Swings and Roundabouts: An Analysis of Consumption Trends," *AIM-Digest* (2008), http://www .aimdigest.com/gateway/pages/s&p%20drinking%20patterns/articles/ trends%202005.htm.

14 percent of online students drop before completing a course as compared to 7.2 percent for traditional in-class students. For this and other reasons, online students are much more costly to serve.[6]

Accuracy is critically important in descriptive research. If a descriptive study incorrectly estimates a university's demand for its MBA offering by even a few students, it can mean the difference between the program sustaining itself or being a drain on already scarce resources. For instance, if a cohort group of 25 students is predicted, but only 15 students actually sign up, the program will likely not generate enough revenue to sustain itself. Therefore, it is easy to see that descriptive research forecasting sales revenue and costs or describing consumer attitudes, satisfaction, and commitment must be accurate or decision making will suffer.

Survey research typifies a descriptive study. For example, state societies of certified public accountants (CPAs) conduct annual practice management surveys that ask questions such as, "Do you charge clients for travel time at regular rates?" "Do you have a program of continuing education on a regular basis for professional employees?" "Do you pay incentive bonuses to professional staff?" Although the researcher may have a general understanding of the business practices of CPAs, conclusive evidence in the form of answers to questions of fact must be collected to determine the actual activities.

diagnostic analysis

Seeks to diagnose reasons for business outcomes and focuses specifically on the beliefs and feelings consumers have about and toward competing products.

A **diagnostic analysis** seeks to diagnose reasons for business outcomes and focuses specifically on the beliefs and feelings respondents have about and toward specific issues. A research study trying to diagnose slumping French wine sales might ask consumers their beliefs about the taste of French, Australian, and American wines. The results might indicate a deficiency in taste, suggesting that consumers do not believe French wines taste as fruity as do the others. Descriptive research can sometimes provide an explanation by diagnosing differences among competitors, but descriptive research does not provide direct evidence of causality.

Causal Research

causal research

Allows causal inferences to be made; seeks to identify cause-and-effect relationships.

If a decision maker knows what causes important outcomes like sales, stock price, and employee satisfaction, then he or she can shape firm decisions in a positive way. Causal inferences are very powerful because they lead to greater control. **Causal research** seeks to identify cause-and-effect relationships. When something causes an effect, it means it brings it about or makes it happen. The effect is the outcome. Rain causes grass to get wet. Rain is the cause and wet grass is the effect.

The different types of research discussed here are often building blocks—exploratory research builds the foundation for descriptive research, which usually establishes the basis for causal research. Thus, before causal studies are undertaken, researchers typically have a good understanding of the phenomena being studied. Because of this, the researcher can make an educated prediction about the cause-and-effect relationships that will be tested. Although greater knowledge of the situation is a good thing, it doesn't come without a price. Causal research designs can take a long time to implement. Also, they often involve intricate designs that can be very expensive. Even though managers may often want the assurance that causal inferences can bring, they are not always willing to spend the time and money it takes to get them.

Causality

Ideally, managers want to know how a change in one event will change another event of interest. As an example, how will implementing a new employee training program change job performance? Causal research attempts to establish that when we do one thing, another thing will follow. A **causal inference** is just such a conclusion. While we use the term "cause" frequently in our everyday language, scientifically establishing something as a cause is not so easy. A causal inference can only be supported when very specific evidence exists. Three critical pieces of causal evidence are:

causal inference
A conclusion that when one thing happens, another specific thing will follow.

1. Temporal Sequence
2. Concomitant Variance
3. Nonspurious Association

TEMPORAL SEQUENCE

Temporal sequence deals with the time order of events. In other words, having an appropriate causal order of events, or temporal sequence, is one criterion for causality. Simply put, the cause must occur before the effect. It would be difficult for a restaurant manager to blame a decrease in sales on a new chef if the drop in sales occurred before the new chef arrived. If a change in the CEO causes a change in stock prices, the CEO change must occur before the change in stock values.

temporal sequence
One of three criteria for causality; deals with the time order of events—the cause must occur before the effect.

CONCOMITANT VARIATION

Concomitant variation occurs when two events "covary" or "correlate," meaning they vary systematically. In causal terms, concomitant variation means that when a change in the cause occurs, a change in the outcome also is observed. A correlation coefficient, which we discuss in Chapter 23, is often used to represent concomitant variation. Causality cannot possibly exist when there is no systematic variation between the variables. For example, if a retail store never changes its employees' vacation policy, then the vacation policy cannot possibly be responsible for a change in employee satisfaction. There is no correlation between the two events. On the other hand, if two events vary together, one event may be causing the other. If a university increases its number of online MBA course offerings and experiences a decrease in enrollment in its traditional in-class MBA offerings, the online course offerings may be causing the decrease. But the systematic variation alone doesn't guarantee it.

concomitant variation
One of three criteria for causality; occurs when two events "covary," meaning they vary systematically.

NONSPURIOUS ASSOCIATION

Nonspurious association means any covariation between a cause and an effect is true, rather than due to some other variable. A spurious association is one that is not true. Often, a causal inference cannot be made even though the other two conditions exist because both the cause and effect have some common cause; that is, both may be influenced by a third variable. For instance, there is a strong, positive correlation between ice cream purchases and murder rates—as ice cream purchases increase, so do murder rates.[7] When ice cream sales decline, murder rates also drop. Do people become murderers after eating ice cream? Should we outlaw the sale of ice cream? This would be silly because the concomitant variation observed between ice cream consumption and murder

nonspurious association
One of three criteria for causality; means any covariation between a cause and an effect is true and not simply due to some other variable.

rates is spurious. A third variable is actually important here. People purchase more ice cream when the weather is hot. People are also more active and likely to commit a violent crime when it is hot. The weather, being associated with both may actually cause both. Exhibit 4.2 illustrates the concept of spurious association.

EXHIBIT **4.2**

The Spurious Effect of Ice Cream

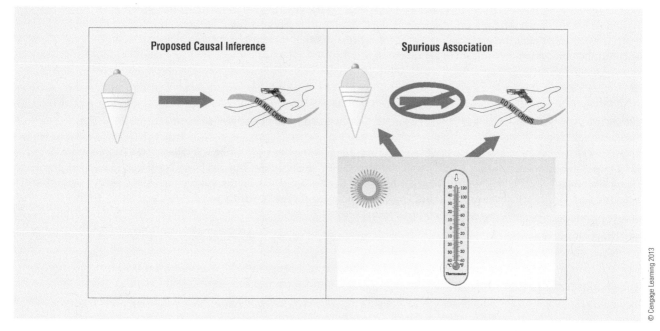

© Cengage Learning 2013

Establishing evidence of nonspuriousness can be difficult. If a researcher finds a third variable that is related to both the cause and effect, which causes a significant drop in the correlation between the cause and effect, then a causal inference becomes difficult to support. Although the researcher would like to rule out the possibility of any alternative causes, it is impossible to observe the effect of every variable on the correlation between the cause and effect. Therefore, the researcher must use logic, or a theory, to identify the most likely "third" variables that would relate significantly to both the cause and effect. The researcher must control for these variables in some way. In addition, the researcher should use theory to make sure the assumed cause-and-effect relationship truly makes sense.

In summary, causal research should do all of the following:

1. Establish the appropriate causal order or sequence of events
2. Measure the concomitant variation between the presumed cause and the presumed effect
3. Examine the possibility of spuriousness by considering the presence of alternative plausible causal factors

Degrees of Causality

absolute causality

Means the cause is necessary and sufficient to bring about the effect.

conditional causality

Means that a cause is necessary but not sufficient to bring about an effect.

In everyday language, we often use the word "cause" in an absolute sense. For example, a warning label used on cigarette packages claims "smoking causes cancer." Is this true in an absolute sense? **Absolute causality** means the cause is necessary and sufficient to bring about the effect. Thus, if we find only one smoker who does not eventually get cancer, the claim is false. Although this is a very strong inference, it is impractical to think that we can establish absolute causality in the behavioral sciences.

Why do we continue to do causal research then? Well, although managers may like to be able to draw absolute conclusions, they can often make very good decisions based on less powerful inferences. **Conditional causality** means that a cause is necessary but not sufficient to bring about an effect. This is a weaker causal inference. One way to think about conditional causality is that the cause can bring about the effect, but it cannot do so alone. If other conditions are right, the cause can bring about the effect. We know there are other medical factors that contribute to cancer. For instance, genetics, lifestyle, and diet are also plausible causes of cancer. Thus, if one smokes and has a genetic disposition, diet, and lifestyle that promote cancer, smoking could be considered a conditional cause of cancer. However, if we can find someone who has contracted cancer and never smoked, the causal inference would be proven wrong.

Contributory causality is the weakest form of causality, but it is still a useful concept. A cause need be neither necessary nor sufficient to bring about an effect. However, causal evidence can be established using the three factors discussed. For any outcome, there may be multiple causes. So, an event can be a contributory cause of something so long as the introduction of the other possible causes does not eliminate the correlation between it and the effect. This will become clearer when we discuss ways to test relationships in Chapters 23 and 24. Smoking then can be a contributory cause of cancer so long as the introduction of other possible causes does not cause both smoking and cancer.

contributory causality

Means that a cause need be neither necessary nor sufficient to bring about an effect.

Experiments

Business experiments hold the greatest potential for establishing cause-and-effect relationships. An **experiment** is a carefully controlled study in which the researcher manipulates a proposed cause and observes any corresponding change in the proposed effect. An **experimental variable** represents the proposed cause and is controlled by the researcher by manipulating it. **Manipulation** means that the researcher alters the level of the variable in specific increments.

For example, consider a manager who needs to make decisions about the price and distribution of a new video game console called the Wee Box. She understands that both the price level and the type of retail outlet in which the product is placed are potential causes of sales. A study can be designed which manipulates both the price and distribution. The price can be manipulated by offering it for $100 among some consumers and $200 among others. Retail distribution may be manipulated by selling the Wee Box at discount stores in some consumer markets and at specialty electronics stores in others. The retailer can examine whether price and distribution cause sales by comparing the sales results in each of the four conditions created. Exhibit 4.3 illustrates this study.

experiment

A carefully controlled study in which the researcher manipulates a proposed cause and observes any corresponding change in the proposed effect.

experimental variable

Represents the proposed cause and is controlled by the researcher by manipulating it.

manipulation

Means that the researcher alters the level of the variable in specific increments.

EXHIBIT **4.3**
Testing for Causes with an Experiment

	Wee Box Sales by Condition	
	High Price	**Low Price**
Specialty Distribution	**Peoria, Illinois:** Retail Price: $200 Retail Store: Best Buy	**Des Moines, Iowa:** Retail Price: $100 Retail Store: Best Buy
General Distribution	**St. Louis, Missouri:** Retail Price: $200 Retail Store: Big Cheap-Mart	**Kansas City, Missouri:** Retail Price: $100 Retail Store: Big Cheap-Mart

Assuming that Wee Box consumers are the same in each of these cities, the extent to which price and distribution cause sales can be examined by comparing the sales results in each of these four conditions.

© Cengage Learning 2013

An experiment like the one described above may take place in a test-market. Test-marketing is a frequently used form of business experimentation. A **test-market** is an experiment that is conducted within actual business conditions. McDonald's restaurants have a long-standing tradition of test-marketing new product concepts by introducing them at selected stores and monitoring sales and customer feedback. Recently, McDonald's extensively test-marketed McCafé

test-market

An experiment that is conducted within actual market conditions.

specialty coffees and beverages. These products were sold at a group of McDonald's outlets and feedback was used to refine the offering including the size of the cups, prices, and what types of extras to add to the drink (including sprinkles of chocolate, whipped cream, steamed milk, and chocolate, vanilla, and caramel shots). McDonald's could then monitor the effect on overall sales, as well as cannibalization of regular coffee sales, in a real-world setting. Earlier, McDonald's had test-marketed Wi-Fi service in some outlets. Three different rival Wi-Fi service providers (the manipulation) were used in different locations and the cost, service, and customer feedback were used to select the best provider for use in McDonald's restaurants.

Most basic scientific studies in business (for example, the development of theories about employee motivation or consumer behavior) ultimately seek to identify cause-and-effect relationships. In fact, we often associate science with experiments. To predict a relationship between, say, price and perceived quality of a product, causal studies often create statistical experiments with controls that establish contrast groups.

Uncertainty Influences the Type of Research

So, which form of research—exploratory, descriptive, or causal—is appropriate for the current situation? The most appropriate type and the amount of research needed are largely a function of how much uncertainty surrounds the situation motivating the research. Exhibit 4.4 contrasts the types of research and illustrates that exploratory research is conducted during the early stages of decision making. At this point, the decision situation is usually highly ambiguous and management is very uncertain about what actions should, or even could, be taken. When management is aware of the problem but lacks some knowledge, descriptive research is usually conducted. Causal research requires sharply defined problems.

Each type of research also produces a different type of result. In many ways, exploratory research is the most productive since it should yield large numbers of ideas. It is part of the "domain of discovery," and as such, unstructured approaches can be very successful. Too much structure in this type of research may lead to more narrowly focused types of responses that could

EXHIBIT 4.4

Characteristics of Different Types of Business Research

	Exploratory Research	Descriptive Research	Causal Research
Amount of Uncertainty Characterizing Decision Situation	Highly ambiguous	Partially defined	Clearly defined
Key Research Statement	Research question	Research question	Research hypothesis
When Conducted?	Early stage of decision making	Later stages of decision making	Later stages of decision making
Usual Research Approach	Unstructured	Structured	Highly structured
Examples	"Our sales are declining for no apparent reason." "What kinds of new products are fast-food customers interested in?"	"What kind of people patronize our stores compared to our primary competitor?" "What product features are most important to our customers?"	"Will consumers buy more products in a blue package?" "Which of two advertising campaigns will be more effective?"
Nature of Results	Discovery oriented, productive, but still speculative. Often in need of further research.	Can be confirmatory although more research is sometimes still needed. Results can be managerially actionable.	Confirmatory oriented. Fairly conclusive with managerially actionable results often obtained.

© Cengage Learning 2013

stifle creativity. Thus, although it is productive, exploratory research results usually need further testing and evaluation before they can be made actionable. At times, however, managers do take action based only on exploratory research results. Sometimes, management may not be able or may not care to invest the time and resources needed to conduct further research. Decisions made based only on exploratory research can be more risky, since exploratory research does not test ideas among a scientific sample.[8] For instance, a business school professor may ask a class of current MBA students for ideas about an online program. Although the students may provide many ideas that sound very good, even the best of them has not been tested on a sample of potential online MBA students.

Descriptive research is typically focused around one or more fairly specific research questions. It is usually much more structured and, for many common types of business research, can yield managerially actionable results. For example, descriptive research is often used to profile a customer segment both demographically and psychographically. Results like this can greatly assist firms in deciding when and where to offer their goods or services for sale.

Causal research is usually very focused around a small number of research hypotheses. Experimental methods require tight control of research procedures. Thus, causal research is highly structured to produce specific results. Causal research results are often managerially actionable since they suggest that if management changes the value of a "cause," some desirable effect will come about. So, by changing the training program, the cause, an increase in employee productivity, can result.

Stages in the Research Process

Business research, like other forms of scientific inquiry, involves a sequence of highly interrelated activities. The stages of the research process overlap continuously, and it is clearly an oversimplification to state that every research project has exactly the same ordered sequence of activities. Nevertheless, business research often follows a general pattern. We offer the following research business stages:

1. Defining the research objectives
2. Planning a research design
3. Planning a sample
4. Collecting the data
5. Analyzing the data
6. Formulating the conclusions and preparing the report

Exhibit 4.5 portrays these six stages as a cyclical or circular-flow process. The circular-flow concept is used because conclusions from research studies can generate new ideas and knowledge that can lead to further investigation. Thus, there is a dashed connection between conclusions and reporting and defining the research objectives. Notice also that management is in the center of the process. The research objectives cannot be properly defined without managerial input. After all, it is the manager who ultimately has to make the decision. It is also the manager who may ask for additional research once a report is given.

In practice, the stages overlap somewhat from a timing perspective. Later stages sometimes can be completed before earlier ones. The terms forward linkage and backward linkage reflect the interrelationships between stages. **Forward linkage** implies that the earlier stages influence the later stages. Thus, the research objectives outlined in the first stage affect the sample selection and the way data are collected. The sample selection question affects the wording of questionnaire items. For example, if the research concentrates on respondents with low educational levels, the questionnaire wording will be simpler than if the respondents were college graduates.

Backward linkage implies that later steps influence earlier stages of the research process. If it is known that the data will be collected via e-mail, then the sampling must include those with e-mail access. A very important example of backward linkage is the knowledge that the executives who will read the research report are looking for specific information. The professional researcher anticipates executives' needs for information throughout the planning process, particularly during the analysis and reporting.

forward linkage

Implies that the earlier stages of the research process influence the later stages.

backward linkage

Implies that later steps influence earlier stages of the research process.

EXHIBIT **4.5**
Stages of the Research
Process

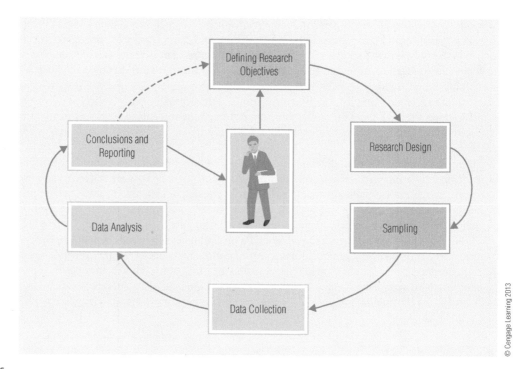

research objectives

The goals to be achieved by
conducting research.

deliverables

The term used often in
consulting to describe research
objectives to a research client.

● ● ● ● ● ● ●

Research is sometimes directly
actionable. The results may also
suggest ideas for new studies.

Alternatives in the Research Process

The researcher must choose among a number of alternatives during each stage of the research process. The research process can be compared to a map. It is important to remember that there is no single "right" path for all journeys. The road one takes depends on where one wants to go and the resources (money, time, labor, and so on) available for the trip. The map analogy is useful for the business researcher because there are several paths that can be followed at each stage. When there are severe time constraints, the quickest path may be most appropriate. When money and human resources are plentiful, more options are available and the appropriate path may be quite different.

Chapter 1 introduced the research process. Here, we briefly describe the six stages of the research process. Later, each stage is discussed in greater depth. Exhibit 4.6 shows the decisions that researchers must make in each stage. This discussion of the research process begins with research objectives, because most research projects are initiated to remedy managers' uncertainty about some aspect of the firm's business program.

Defining the Research Objectives

Exhibit 4.6 shows that the research process begins with **research objectives**. Research objectives are the goals to be achieved by conducting research. In consulting, the term **deliverables** is often used to describe the objectives to a research client. The genesis of the research objectives lies in the type of decision situation faced. The objectives may involve exploring the possibilities of entering a new market. Alternatively, they may involve testing the effect of some policy change on employee job satisfaction. Different types of objectives lead to different types of research designs.

EXHIBIT **4.6**
Flowchart of the Business Research Process

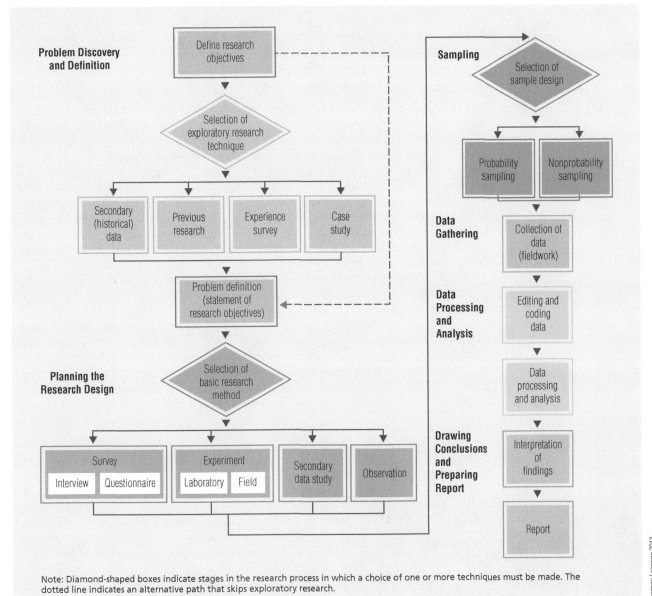

Note: Diamond-shaped boxes indicate stages in the research process in which a choice of one or more techniques must be made. The dotted line indicates an alternative path that skips exploratory research.

© Cengage Learning 2013

In applied business research, the objectives cannot really be determined until there is a clear understanding of the managerial decision to be made. This understanding must be shared between the actual decision maker and the lead researcher. We often describe this understanding as a problem statement. In general usage, the word problem suggests that something has gone wrong. This isn't always the case before research gets started. Actually, the research objective may be to simply clarify a situation, define an opportunity, or monitor and evaluate current business operations. The research objectives cannot be developed until managers and researchers have agreed on the actual business "problem" that will be addressed by the research. Thus, they set out to "discover" this problem through a series of interviews and through a document called a research proposal.

It should be noted that this process is oriented more toward discovery than confirmation or justification. Managers and researchers alike may not have a clear-cut understanding of the situation at the outset of the research process. Managers may only be able to list symptoms that could indicate a problem. For example, employee turnover is increasing, but management may not know the exact nature of the problem. Thus, the problem statement often is made only in general terms; what is to be investigated is not yet specifically identified.

Defining the Managerial Decision Situation

In business research, the adage "a problem well defined is a problem half solved" is worth remembering. Similarly, Albert Einstein noted that "the formulation of a problem is often more essential than its solution."[9] These phrases emphasize that an orderly definition of the research problem provides direction to the investigation. Careful attention to problem definition allows the researcher to set the proper research objectives. When the purpose of the research is clear, the chances of collecting the necessary and relevant information, and not collecting surplus information, will be much greater.

Managers often are more concerned with finding the right answer rather than asking the right question. They also want one solution quickly, rather than having to spend time considering many possible solutions. However, properly defining a problem can be more difficult than actually solving it. In business research, if data are collected before the nature of the problem is carefully thought out, they probably will not yield useful information.

Thus, defining the decision situation must precede the research objectives. Frequently the researcher will not be involved until the management team has discovered that some information about a particular aspect of the business is needed. Even at this point the exact nature of the situation may be poorly defined. Once a problem area has been discovered, the researcher and management together can begin the process of precisely defining it.

Much too often research is conducted without a clear definition of the objectives. Researchers forget that the best place to begin a research project is at the end. In other words, knowing what is to be accomplished determines the research process. An error or omission in specifying objectives is likely to be a costly mistake that cannot be corrected in later stages of the research process.

The library contains a wealth of information. Studies forming a literature review can be found in the library.

© Digital Vision/Getty Images

Exploratory Research

Exploratory research can be used to help identify and clarify the decisions that need to be made. These preliminary research activities can narrow the scope of the research topic and help transform ambiguous problems into well-defined ones that yield specific research objectives. By investigating any existing studies on the subject, talking with knowledgeable individuals, and informally investigating the situation, the researcher can progressively sharpen the focus of the research. After such exploration, the researcher should know exactly which data to collect during the formal phases of the project and how to conduct the project. Exhibit 4.6 indicates that managers and researchers must decide whether to use one or more exploratory research techniques. As Exhibit 4.6 indicates, this stage is optional.

The business researcher can employ techniques from four basic categories to obtain insights and gain a clearer idea of the problem: previous research, pilot studies, case studies, and experience surveys. These are discussed in detail in later chapters. This section will briefly discuss previous research and focus group interviews, the most popular type of pilot study.

PREVIOUS RESEARCH

As a general rule, researchers should first investigate previous research to see whether or not others may have already addressed similar research problems. Initially, internal research reports should be searched within the company's archives. In addition, some firms, such as Hoover's in the chapter vignette, specialize in providing various types of research reports, such as economic forecasts. The Census of Population and the Survey of Current Business are each examples of previous research conducted by an outside source.

Previous research may also exist in the public domain. The first place researchers will likely look today is online. The Internet and modern electronic search engines available through most university libraries have made literature reviews simpler and faster to conduct. A **literature review** is a directed search of published works, including periodicals and books, that discusses theory and presents empirical results that are relevant to the topic at hand. While a literature survey is common in applied research studies, it is a fundamental requirement of a basic research report.

Suppose, for example, that a bank is interested in determining the best site for additional automated teller machines. A logical first step would be to investigate the factors that bankers in other parts of the country consider important. By reading articles in banking journals, management might quickly discover that the best locations are inside supermarkets located in residential areas where people are young, highly educated, and earning higher-than-average incomes. These data might lead the bank to investigate census information to determine where in the city such people live. Reviewing and building on the work already compiled by others is an economical starting point for most research.

PILOT STUDIES

Almost all consumers take a test drive before buying a car. A pilot study serves a similar purpose for the researcher. A **pilot study** is a small-scale research project that collects data from respondents similar to those that will be used in the full study. It can serve as a guide for a larger study or examine specific aspects of the research to see if the selected procedures will actually work as intended. Pilot studies are critical in refining survey questions and reducing the risk that the full study will be fatally flawed. This is particularly true for experimental research, which depends critically on valid manipulations of experimental variables.[10] Pilot studies also often are useful in fine-tuning research objectives. Pilot studies are sometimes referred to as pretests. A **pretest** is a very descriptive term indicating a small-scale study in which the results are preliminary and intended only to assist in design of a subsequent study.

Focus group interviews are sometimes used as a pilot study. A **focus group** interview brings together six to twelve people in a loosely structured format. The technique is based on the assumption that individuals are more willing to talk about things when they are able to do so within a group discussion format. Focus group respondents sometimes feed on each other's comments to develop ideas that would be difficult to express in a different interview format.

For example, suppose a consultant is hired by Carrefour to research the way consumers react to sales promotions. Carrefour began in France over 50 years ago and pioneered the discount hypermarket format. Carrefour is now the second largest retailer in the world (behind Walmart), operating nearly 11,000 stores in 29 countries. Specifically, the researcher is asked to help Carrefour executives decide whether or not the size of promotional discounts should vary with national culture. In other words, the basic research question is whether or not culture influences consumer perceptions of sales promotions.[11] A pretest may be needed to examine whether or not differences in currency might interfere with these perceptions, or whether or not the different terms that refer to promotions and discounts can be translated into the languages of each culture. For example, is a discount expressed in Korean won interpreted the same way as a discount expressed in euros? Each euro equals about $1.43 U.S., whereas a single U.S. dollar is worth about 1,057 won.[12]

Exploratory research need not always follow a structured design. Because the purpose of exploratory research is to gain insights and discover new ideas, researchers may use considerable creativity and flexibility. Some companies perform exploratory research routinely as part of environmental scanning. If the conclusions made during this stage suggest business opportunities, the researcher is in a position to begin planning a formal, quantitative research project.

Stating Research Objectives

After identifying and clarifying the problem, with or without exploratory research, the researcher must formally state the research objectives. This statement delineates the type of research that is needed and what intelligence may result that would allow the decision maker to make informed

---

literature review

A directed search of published works, including periodicals and books, that discusses theory and presents empirical results that are relevant to the topic at hand.

pilot study

A small-scale research project that collects data from respondents similar to those to be used in the full study.

pretest

A small-scale study in which the results are only preliminary and intended only to assist in design of a subsequent study.

focus group

A small group discussion about some research topic led by a moderator who guides discussion among the participants.

choices. The statement of research objectives culminates the process of clarifying the managerial decision into something actionable.

A written decision statement expresses the business situation to the researcher and makes sure that managers and researchers are on the same page. The research objectives try to directly address the decision statement or statements, as the case may be. As such, the research objectives represent a contract of sorts that commits the researcher to producing the needed research. This is why they are expressed as deliverables in applied business research. These research objectives drive the rest of the research process. Indeed, before proceeding, the researcher and managers must agree that the objectives are appropriate and will produce relevant information.

Linking Decision Statements, Objectives, and Hypotheses

In Chapter 3 we discussed the role of theory and research hypotheses. Our hypotheses should be logically derived from and linked to our research objectives. For example, consider a person who is interested in pursuing an MBA from their local university. Since this same prospective student also needs to work, the researcher may use theoretical reasoning to develop the following hypothesis:

H1: The more hours per week a prospective student works, the more favorable the attitude toward online MBA class offerings.

Exhibit 4.7 illustrates how decision statements are linked to research objectives, which are linked to research hypotheses. Although the first two objectives each have one hypothesis, notice that the third has two. In reality, most research projects will involve more than one research objective, and each of these may often involve more than one hypothesis. Think about how you might go about trying to test the hypothesis listed in Exhibit 4.7.

EXHIBIT **4.7**

Example Decision Statements, Research Objectives, and Research Hypotheses

Decision Statement	Research Objectives	Hypotheses
What should be the retail price for product X?	Forecast sales for product X at three different prices.	Sales will be higher at $5.00 than at $4.00 or at $6.99.
In what ways can we improve our service quality?	Identify the top factors that contribute to customers' perceptions.	Cleanliness is related positively to customers' service quality service perceptions. Crowding is related negatively to customers' service quality perceptions.
Should we invest in a training program to reduce role conflict among our employees?	Determine how much role conflict influences employee job satisfaction.	Role conflict is related positively to job satisfaction.

© Cengage Learning 2013

Planning the Research Design

research design

A master plan that specifies the methods and procedures for collecting and analyzing the needed information.

After the researcher has formulated the research problem, he or she must develop the research design as part of the research design stage. A **research design** is a master plan that specifies the methods and procedures for collecting and analyzing the needed information. A research design provides a framework or plan of action for the research. Objectives of the study determined during the early stages of research are included in the design to ensure that the information collected is appropriate for solving the problem. The researcher also must determine the sources of information, the design technique (survey or experiment, for example), the sampling methodology, and the schedule and cost of the research.

Selection of the Basic Research Method

Here again, the researcher must make a decision. Exhibit 4.6 shows four basic design techniques for descriptive and causal research: surveys, experiments, secondary data, and observation. The objectives of the study, the available data sources, the urgency of the decision, and the cost of obtaining the data will determine which method should be chosen. The managerial aspects of selecting the research design will be considered later.

In business research, the most common method of generating primary data is the survey. Most people have seen the results of political surveys by Gallup or Harris Online, and some have been respondents (members of a sample who supply answers) to research questionnaires. A **survey** is a research technique in which a sample is interviewed in some form or the behavior of respondents is observed and described in some way. The term surveyor is most often reserved for civil engineers who describe some piece of property using a transit. Similarly, business researchers describe some group of interest (such as executives, employees, customers, or competitors) using a questionnaire. The task of writing a list of questions and designing the format of the printed or written questionnaire is an essential aspect of the development of a survey research design.

Research investigators may choose to contact respondents by telephone or mail, on the Internet, or in person. An advertiser spending $3 million for 30 seconds of commercial time during the Super Bowl may telephone people to quickly gather information concerning their responses to the advertising. The economic development director for a city trying to determine the most important factors in attracting new businesses might choose a mail questionnaire because the appropriate executives are hard to reach by telephone. A manufacturer of a birth control device for men might determine the need for a versatile survey method wherein an interviewer can ask a variety of personal questions in a flexible format. While personal interviews are expensive, they are valuable because investigators can use visual aids and supplement the interviews with observations. Each of these survey methods has advantages and disadvantages. A researcher's task is to find the most appropriate way to collect the needed information in a particular situation.

The objective of many research projects is merely to record what can be observed—for example, the number of automobiles that pass by a proposed site for a gas station. This can be mechanically recorded or observed by humans. Research personnel known as mystery shoppers may act as customers to observe actions of sales personnel or do comparative shopping to learn prices at competing outlets. A mystery shopper is paid to pretend to be a customer and gather data about the way employees behave and the way they are treated in general. How often are store policies followed? Are they treated courteously? Mystery shoppers can be valuable sources for observational data.

The main advantage of the observation technique is that it records behavior without relying on reports from respondents. Observational data are often collected unobtrusively and passively without a respondent's direct participation. For instance, Nielsen Media Research uses a "people meter" attached to television sets to record the programs being watched by each household member. This eliminates the possible bias of respondents stating that they watched the president's State of the Union address rather than Gossip Girl on another station.

Observation is more complex than mere "nose counting," and the task is more difficult than the inexperienced researcher would imagine. While observation eliminates potential bias from interviewer interaction, several things of interest, such as attitudes, opinions, motivations, and other intangible states of mind, simply cannot be observed.

survey

A research technique in which a sample is interviewed in some form or the behavior of respondents is observed and described in some way.

❝You cannot put the same shoe on every foot.❞

—PUBLIUS SYRUS

The "Best" Research Design

It is argued that there is no single best research design. As such, the researcher often has several alternatives that can accomplish the stated research objectives. Consider the researcher who must forecast sales for the upcoming year. Some commonly used forecasting methods are surveying executive opinion, collecting sales force composite opinions, surveying user expectations, projecting trends, and analyzing environmental factors. Any one of these may yield a reliable forecast.

The ability to select the most appropriate research design develops with experience. Inexperienced researchers often jump to the conclusion that a survey methodology is usually the best design because they are most comfortable with this method. When Chicago's Museum of Science

© PR Newsfoto/Rolling Rock

Rolling Rock

Making a mark in the U.S. beer market can be difficult. American consumers tend to favor milder beers at lower price points. Some argue that most beers taste very similar. Taste tests do reveal that similarly positioned beers do taste very much the same. However, the taste rankings do not correspond to market share. For instance, Stroh's fared very well in the taste tests, but it is hardly a market leader. Rolling Rock rated 12th out of 12 beers tasted. Tasters said it tasted a bit like canned corn. Clearly, there is something more to a successful beer than taste.

For many years Rolling Rock beer was a regional brand in western Pennsylvania. Its signature package was a longneck green bottle with a white painted label featuring icons such as a horse head, a steeplechase, the number 33, and a legend about the beer being brought to you "from the glass-lined tanks of Old Latrobe." The brand, now sold by Labatt USA, expanded nationally during the 1980s by focusing on core consumers who purchased specialty beers for on-premise consumption and who were willing to pay higher prices than for national brands such as Budweiser.

As years went by, packaging options expanded to include bottles with ordinary paper labels for take-home consumption, often packaged in 12-packs. In the mid-1990s, in response to a competitive explosion from microbrews, Rolling Rock offered a number of line extensions, such as Rock Bock and amber Rock Ice. They failed. Sales stagnated. In New York and other crucial markets, price reductions to the level of Budweiser and Miller became inhibiting aspects of its marketing program. Business executives held the view that the longneck painted bottle was the heart of the brand. However, earlier efforts to develop cheaper imitations of the painted-label look had not achieved success.

Rolling Rock executives decided to conduct a massive consumer study, recruiting consumers at shopping malls and other venues to view "live" shelf sets of beer—not just specialty beer, but beer at every price range from subpremiums and up. Consumers given money to spend in the form of chips were exposed to "old-bundle" packages (the old graphics and the paper-label stubbies) and "new-bundle" packages (two new graphics approaches, including the one ultimately selected, and painted-label longnecks) at a variety of price points and asked to allocate chips to their next ten purchases. Some were even invited to take the "new-bundle" packages home with them for follow-up research.

As the business executives had hoped, the results did not leave any room for interpretation: Not only did the new packages meet with consumers' strong approval, but consumers consistently indicated that they would be willing to pay more for the brand in those packages. In fact, not only were they willing to pay more; they expected to pay more, particularly among consumers already familiar with the Rock. In three regions, the Northeast, Southeast, and West, purchase intent among users increased dramatically both at prices 20 cents higher per 12-pack and at prices 40 cents higher per 12-pack. The increase in purchase intent was milder in the Midwest, but there Rock already commanded a solid premium over Bud and other premium beers. The sole exception to that trend was in the brand's core markets in Pennsylvania and Ohio, where Rock has never entirely escaped its shot-and-a-beer origins, but even there, purchase intent declined by only 2 percent at each of the higher prices.

Sources: Gerry Khermouch, "Sticking Their Neck Out," *BrandWeek* (November 9, 1998) 25–34, © 2006 VNU Business Media, Inc. Used with permission from Brandweek. © 1998–1999 VNU Business Media Inc.; "Which Brew for You?" *Consumer Reports* (August 2001), 10–17.

---

and Industry wanted to determine the relative popularity of its exhibits, it could have conducted a survey. Instead, a creative researcher familiar with other research designs suggested a far less expensive alternative: an unobtrusive observation technique. The researcher suggested that the museum merely keep track of the frequency with which the floor tiles in front of the various exhibits had to be replaced, indicating where the heaviest traffic occurred. When this was done, the museum found that the chick-hatching exhibit was the most popular. This method provided the same results as a survey but at a much lower cost. Take a look at the research design used by Rolling Rock illustrated in the Research Snapshot "Rolling Rock."

Sampling

sampling

Involves any procedure that draws conclusions based on measurements of a portion of the population.

Although the sampling plan is outlined in the research design, the sampling stage is a distinct phase of the research process. For convenience, however, we will treat the sample planning and the actual sample generation processes together in this section.

If you take your first bite of shrimp po-boy and conclude that it needs Tabasco, you have just conducted a sample. **Sampling** involves any procedure that draws conclusions based on measurements of a portion of the population. In other words, a sample is a subset from a larger population. If certain statistical procedures are followed, a researcher need not select every item in a population because the results of a good sample should have the same characteristics as the population as a whole. Of course, when errors are made, samples do not give reliable estimates of the population.

A famous example of error due to sampling is the 1936 Literary Digest fiasco. The magazine conducted a survey and predicted that Republican Alf Landon would win over Democrat Franklin D. Roosevelt by a landslide in that year's presidential election. This prediction was wrong—and the error was due to sample selection. The post-mortems showed that Literary Digest had sampled its readers and names drawn from telephone books and auto registrations. In 1936, not everyone had a telephone or a car; thus the sample was biased toward people with means. In reality, Roosevelt received over 60 percent of the popular vote.

In 2004, early exit polls led many to believe that John Kerry would win the U.S. presidential election.[13] The exit polls were performed early on election day and done mostly in highly urban areas in the Northeast, areas that are predominantly Democratic. The resulting sample of voters responding to the early exit polls did not represent the entire U.S. population, and Kerry lost to Bush by over 3 million votes, or about 3 percent of all votes cast. Thus, the accuracy of predictions from research depends on getting a sample that really matches the population.

The first sampling question to ask is, "Who is to be sampled?" The answer to this primary question requires the identification of a target population. Who do we want the sample to reflect? Defining this population and determining the sampling units may not be so easy. If, for example, a savings and loan association surveys people who already have accounts for answers to image questions, the selected sampling units may represent current customers but will not represent potential customers. Specifying the target population is a crucial aspect of the sampling plan.

The next sampling issue concerns sample size. How big should the sample be? Although management may wish to examine every potential buyer of a product or service, doing so may be unnecessary as well as unrealistic. Other things equal, larger samples are more precise than smaller ones. However, proper probability sampling can allow a small proportion of the total population to give a reliable measure of the whole. A later discussion will explain how large a sample must be in order to be truly representative of the universe or population. Essentially, this is a question of how much variance exists in the population.

The final sampling decision is how to select the sampling units. Simple random sampling may be the best known type, in which every unit in the population has an equal and known chance of being selected. However, this is only one type of sampling. For example, if members of the population are found in close geographical clusters, a cluster sampling procedure (one that selects area clusters rather than individual units in the population) will reduce costs. Rather than selecting 1,000 individuals throughout the United States, it may be more economical to first select 25 counties and then sample within those counties. This will substantially reduce travel, hiring, and training costs. In determining the appropriate sampling plan, the researcher will have to select the most appropriate sampling procedure for meeting the established study objectives.

Gathering Data

The data gathering stage begins once the sampling plan has been formalized. Data gathering is the process of gathering or collecting information. Data may be gathered by human observers or interviewers, or they may be recorded by machines as in the case of scanner data and web-based surveys.

Obviously, the many research techniques involve many methods of gathering data. Surveys require direct participation by research respondents. This may involve filling out a questionnaire or interacting with an interviewer. In this sense, they are obtrusive. **Unobtrusive methods** of data gathering are those in which the subjects do not have to be disturbed for data to be collected. They may even be unaware that research is going on at all. For instance, a simple count of motorists driving past a proposed franchising location is one kind of data gathering method. However the data are collected, it is important to minimize errors in the process. For example, the data gathering should be consistent in all geographical areas. If an interviewer phrases questions incorrectly or records a respondent's statements inaccurately (not verbatim), major data collection errors will result.

unobtrusive methods

Methods in which research respondents do not have to be disturbed for data to be gathered.

Processing and Analyzing Data

Editing and Coding

After the fieldwork has been completed, the data must be converted into a format that will answer the manager's questions. This is part of the data processing and analysis stage. Here, the information content will be mined from the raw data. Data processing generally begins with editing and coding the data. Editing involves checking the data collection forms for omissions, legibility, and consistency in classification. The editing process corrects problems such as interviewer errors (an answer recorded on the wrong portion of a questionnaire, for example) before the data are transferred to the computer.

Before data can be tabulated, meaningful categories and character symbols must be established for groups of responses. The rules for interpreting, categorizing, recording, and transferring the data to the data storage media are called codes. This coding process facilitates computer or hand tabulation. If computer analysis is to be used, the data are entered into the computer and verified. Computer-assisted (online) interviewing is an example of the impact of technological change on the research process. Telephone interviewers, seated at computer terminals, read survey questions displayed on the monitor. The interviewer asks the questions and then types in the respondents' answers. Thus, answers are collected and processed into the computer at the same time, eliminating intermediate steps that could introduce errors.

Data Analysis

data analysis

The application of reasoning to understand the data that have been gathered.

Data analysis is the application of reasoning to understand the data that have been gathered. In its simplest form, analysis may involve determining consistent patterns and summarizing the relevant details revealed in the investigation. The appropriate analytical technique for data analysis will be determined by management's information requirements, the characteristics of the research design, and the nature of the data gathered. Statistical analysis may range from portraying a simple frequency distribution to more complex multivariate analyses approaches, such as multiple regression. Part 6 of this text will discuss three general categories of statistical analysis: univariate analysis, bivariate analysis, and multivariate analysis.

Drawing Conclusions and Preparing a Report

One of the most important jobs that a researcher performs is communicating the research results. This is the final stage of the research project, but it is far from the least important. The conclusions and report preparation stage consists of interpreting the research results, describing the implications, and drawing the appropriate conclusions for managerial decisions. These conclusions should fulfill the deliverables promised in the research proposal. In addition, it's important that the researcher consider the varying abilities of people to understand the research results. The report shouldn't be written the same way to a group of PhDs as it would be to a group of line managers.

All too many applied business research reports are overly complicated statements of technical aspects and sophisticated research methods. Frequently, management is not interested in detailed reporting of the research design and statistical findings, but wishes only a summary of the findings. If the findings of the research remain unread on the manager's desk, the study will have been useless. The importance of effective communication cannot be overemphasized. Research is only as good as its applications.

Now that we have outlined the research process, note that the order of topics in this book follows the flowchart of the research process presented in Exhibit 4.4. Keep this flowchart in mind while reading later chapters.

The Research Program Strategy

research project

A single study that addresses one or a small number of research objectives.

Our discussion of the business research process began with the assumption that the researcher wished to collect data to achieve a specific organizational objective. When the researcher has only one or a small number of research objectives that can be addressed in a single study that study is referred to as a **research project**. We have emphasized the researcher's need to select specific techniques for solving one-dimensional problems, such as identifying customer segments, selecting the most desirable employee insurance plan, or determining an IPO stock price.

However, if you think about a firm's business activities in a given period of time (such as a year), you'll realize that business research is not a one-shot activity—it is a continuous process. An exploratory research study may be followed by a survey, or a researcher may conduct a specific research project for each business tactical decision. If a new product is being developed, the different types of research might include studies to identify the size and characteristics of the market; product usage testing to record consumers' reactions to prototype products; brand name and packaging research to determine the product's symbolic connotations; and test-marketing the new product. Thus, when numerous related studies come together to address issues about a single company, we refer to this as a **research program**. Because research is a continuous process, management should view business research at a strategic planning level. The program strategy refers to a firm's overall plan to use business research. It is a planning activity that places a series of research projects in the context of the company's strategic plan.

The business research program strategy can be likened to a term insurance policy. Conducting business research minimizes risk and increases certainty. Each research project can be seen as a series of term insurance policies that makes the manager's job a bit safer.

research program

Numerous related studies that come together to address multiple, related research objectives.

:: SUMMARY

1. Define decision making and understand the role research plays in making decisions. Decision making occurs when managers choose among alternative ways of resolving problems or pursuing opportunities. Decision makers must recognize the nature of the problem or opportunity, identify how much information is available, and recognize what information they need. Every business decision can be classified on a continuum ranging from complete certainty to absolute ambiguity. Research is a way that managers can become informed about different alternatives and make an educated guess about which alternative, if any, is the best to pursue.

2. Classify business research as either exploratory research, descriptive research, or causal research. Exploratory, descriptive, and causal research are three major types of business research projects. The clarity with which the decision situation is defined determines whether exploratory, descriptive, or causal research is most appropriate. When the decision is very ambiguous, or the interest is on discovering new ideas, exploratory research is most appropriate. Descriptive research attempts to paint a picture of the given situation by describing characteristics of objects, people, or organizations. Causal research identifies cause-and-effect relationships. Or, in other words, what change in "Y" will occur when there is some change in "X"? Three conditions must be satisfied to establish evidence of causality: 1) temporal sequence—the cause must occur before the effect; 2) concomitant variation—a change in the cause is associated (correlated) with a change in the effect; and 3) nonspurious association—the cause is true and not eliminated by the introduction of another potential cause.

3. List the major phases of the business research process and the steps within each. The six major phases of the research process discussed here are 1) defining the research objectives, 2) planning the research design, 3) sampling, 4) data gathering, 5) data processing and analysis, and 6) drawing conclusions and report preparation. Each stage involves several activities or steps. For instance, in planning the research design, the researchers must decide which type of study will be done and, if needed, recruit participants and design and develop experimental stimuli. Quite often research projects are conducted together as parts of a research program. Such programs can involve successive projects that monitor different elements of a firm's operations.

4. Explain the difference between a research project and a research program. A research project addresses one of a small number of research objectives that can be included in a single study. In contrast, a research program represents a series of studies addressing multiple research objectives. Many business activities require an ongoing research task of some type.

:: KEY TERMS AND CONCEPTS

absolute causality, *56*
backward linkage, *59*
business opportunity, *49*
business problem, *49*
causal inference, *55*
causal research, *54*
concomitant variation, *55*
conditional causality, *56*
contributory causality, *57*
data analysis, *68*
decision making, *49*
deliverables, *60*

descriptive research, *53*
diagnostic analysis, *54*
experiment, *57*
experimental variable, *57*
exploratory research, *52*
focus group, *63*
forward linkage, *59*
literature review, *63*
manipulation, *57*
nonspurious association, *55*
pilot study, *63*
pretest, *63*

research design, *64*
research objectives, *60*
research program, *69*
research project, *68*
sampling, *66*
survey, *65*
symptoms, *49*
temporal sequence, *55*
test-market, *57*
unobtrusive methods, *67*

:: QUESTIONS FOR REVIEW AND CRITICAL THINKING

1. List five ways that business research can contribute to effective business decision making.
2. Define business opportunity, business problem, and symptoms. Give an example of each as it applies to a university business school.
3. Consider the following list, and indicate and explain whether each best fits the definition of a problem, opportunity, or symptom:
    a. A 12.5 percent decrease in store traffic for a children's shoe store in a medium-sized city mall.
    b. Walmart's stock price has decreased 25 percent between 2007 and 2009.
    c. A furniture manufacturer and retailer in North Carolina reads a research report indicating consumer trends toward Australian Jarrah and Karri wood. The export of these products is very limited and very expensive.
    d. Marlboro reads a research report written by the U.S. FDA. It indicates that the number of cigarette smokers in sub-Saharan Africa is expected to increase dramatically over the next decade.
4. What are the three types of business research? Indicate which type each item in the list below illustrates. Explain your answers.
    a. Establishing the relationship between advertising and sales in the beer industry
    b. Ranking the key factors new college graduates are seeking in their first career position
    c. Estimating the five-year sales potential for CAT scan machines in the Ark-La-Tex (Arkansas, Louisiana, and Texas) region of the United States
    d. Testing the effect of "casual day" on employee job satisfaction
    e. Discovering the ways that people who live in apartments actually use vacuum cleaners, and identifying cleaning tasks for which they do not use a vacuum
5. Describe the type of research evidence that allows one to infer causality.
6. What is an experimental manipulation? A business researcher is hired by a specialty retail firm. The retailer is trying to decide what level of lighting and what temperature it should maintain in its stores to maximize sales. How can the researcher manipulate these experimental variables within a causal design?
7. A business researcher gives a presentation to a music industry executive. After considering the results of a test-market

examining whether or not lowering the price of in-store CDs will lower the number of illicit downloads of the same music, the executive claims: "The test-market was conducted in eight cities. In two of the cities, lowering the price did not decrease illicit downloading. Therefore, lowering the price does not decrease this behavior, and we should not decide to lower prices based on this research." Comment on the executive's conclusion. What type of inference is being made? Will the decision not to lower prices be a good one?

8. We introduced the scientific method in Chapter 3. Do the stages in the research process discussed here seem to follow the scientific method?
9. Why is the "defining the research objectives" phase of the research process probably the most important stage?
10. Suppose Auchan (**http://www.auchan.fr**), a hypermarket chain based out of France, was considering opening three hypermarkets in the midwestern United States. What role would theory play in designing a research study to track how the shopping habits of consumers from the United States differ from those in France and from those in Japan? What kind of hypothesis might be examined in a study of this topic?
11. Define research project and research program. Referring to the question immediately above, do you think a research project or a research program is needed to provide useful input to the Auchan decision makers?
12. What type of research design would you recommend in the situations below? For each applied business research project, what might be an example of a "deliverable"? Which do you think would involve actually testing a research hypothesis?
    a. The manufacturer of flight simulators and other pilot training equipment wishes to forecast sales volume for the next five years.
    b. A local chapter of the American Lung Association wishes to identify the demographic characteristics of individuals who donate more than $500 per year.
    c. Caterpillar Inc. is concerned about increasing inventory costs and is considering going completely to a just-in-time inventory system.
    d. A food company researcher wishes to know what types of food are carried in brown-bag lunches to learn if the company can capitalize on this phenomenon.
    e. A researcher wishes to identify who plays bingo.

:: RESEARCH ACTIVITIES

1. **'NET** Look up information about the online MBA programs at the University of Phoenix (**http://www.mba-online-program. com/university_of_phoenix_online_mba.html**). Compare it to the traditional MBA program at your university. Suppose each was looking to expand the numbers of students in their programs. How might the research design differ for each?

2. **'NET** Use a web browser to go to the Gallup Organization's home page at (**http://www.gallup.com**). The Gallup home page changes regularly. However, it should provide an opportunity to read the results of a recent poll. For example, a poll might break down Americans' sympathies toward Israel or the Palestinians based on numerous individual characteristics such as political affiliation or religious involvement. After reading the results of a Gallup poll of this type, learn how polls are conducted. You may need to click "About Gallup" and/or Frequently Asked Questions (FAQs) to find this information on how the polls are conducted. List the various stages of the research process and how they were (or were not) followed in Gallup's project.

3. Any significant business decision requires input from a research project. Write a brief essay either defending this statement or refuting it.

CASE 4.1

A New "Joe" on the Block

Joe Brown is ready to start a new career. After spending 30 years as a market researcher and inspired by the success of Starbucks, he is ready to enter the coffee shop business. However, before opening his first shop, he realizes that a great deal of research is needed. He has some key questions in mind.

- What markets in the United States hold the most promise for a new coffee shop?
- What type of location is best for a coffee shop?
- What is it that makes a coffee shop popular?
- What coffee do Americans prefer?

A quick trip to the Internet reveals more previous research on coffee, markets, and related materials than he expected. Many studies address taste. For example, he finds several studies that in one way or another compare the taste of different coffee shop coffees. Most commonly, they compare the taste of coffee from Starbucks against coffee from McDonald's, Dunkin' Donuts, Burger King, and sometimes a local competitor. However, it becomes difficult to draw a conclusion as the results seem to be inconsistent.

- One study had a headline that poked fun at Starbucks' high-priced coffee. The author of this study personally purchased coffee to go at four places, took them to his office, tasted them, made notes and then drew conclusions. All the coffee was tasted black with no sugar. Just cups of joe. He reached the conclusion that McDonald's Premium Coffee (at about $1.50 a cup), tasted nearly as good as Starbucks House Blend (at about $1.70 a cup), both of which were much better than either Dunkin' Donuts (at about $1.20) or Burger King (less than $1). This study argued that McDonald's was best, all things considered.
- Another study was written up by a good critic who was simply interested in identifying the best-tasting coffee. Again, he tasted them all black with nothing added. Each cup of coffee was consumed in an urban location near the inner city center in which he lived. He reached the conclusion that Starbucks' coffee had the best flavor although it showed room for improvement.

McDonald's Premium Coffee was not as good, but it was better than the other two. Dunkin' Donuts coffee had reasonably unobjectionable taste but was very weak and watery. The Burger King coffee was simply not very good.

- Yet another study talked about Starbucks becoming a huge company and how it had lost touch with the common coffee shop customer. The researchers stood outside a small organic specialty shop and interviewed 100 consumers as they exited the shop. They asked, "Which coffee do you prefer?" The results showed a preference for a local coffee, tea, and incense shop, and otherwise put Starbucks last behind McDonald's, Burger King, and Dunkin' Donuts.
- Still another study compared the coffee-drinking experience. A sample of 50 consumers in St. Louis, Missouri, were interviewed and asked to list the coffee shop they frequented most. Starbucks was listed by more consumers than any other place. A small percentage listed Dunkin' Donuts but none listed McDonald's, despite their efforts at creating a premium coffee experience. The study did not ask consumers to compare the tastes of the coffee across the different places.

Joe also wants to find data showing coffee consumption patterns and the number of coffee shops around the United States, so he spends time looking for data on the Internet. His searches don't reveal anything satisfying.

As Joe ponders how to go about starting "A Cup of Joe," he wonders about the relevance of this previous research. Is it useful at all? He even questions whether he is capable of doing any primary research himself and considers hiring someone to do a feasibility study for him. Maybe doing research is easier than using research.

Sources: Shiver, J., "Taste Test: The Little Joes Take on Starbucks," *USA Today* (March 26, 2008), http://www.usatoday.com/money/industries/food/2006-03-26-coffee_x.htm, accessed August 3, 2011; Associated Press, "McDonald's Coffee Beats Starbucks, Says Consumer Reports," *The Seattle Times* (February 2, 2007), http://seattletimes.nwsource.com/html/businesstechnology/2003553322_webcoffeetest02.html, accessed August 3, 2011; "Coffee Wars: Starbucks v McDonald's," *The Economist* 386 (January 10, 2008), 58.

(Continued)

Case 4.1 (*Continued*)

Questions

1. What are the top three key decisions faced by Joe?
2. What are the key deliverables that an outside researcher should produce to help Joe with the key decisions?
3. How relevant are the coffee taste studies cited above? Explain.
4. What flaws in the coffee taste studies should Joe consider in trying to weigh the merits of their results?
5. Briefly relate this situation to each of the major stages of the marketing research process.
6. Try to do a quick search to explore the question: "Are American consumer preferences the same all across the United States?"
7. Would it be better for Joe to do the research himself or have a consultant perform the work?
8. If a consultant comes in to do the job, what are three key deliverables that would likely be important to Joe in making a decision to launch the "A Cup of Joe" coffee shop.

The Human Side of Business Research
Organizational and Ethical Issues

LEARNING OUTCOMES

After studying this chapter, you should be able to

1. Know when research should be conducted externally and when it should be done internally

2. Be familiar with the types of jobs, job responsibilities, and career paths available within the business research industry

3. Understand the often conflicting relationship between management and researchers

4. Define ethics and understand how it applies to business research

5. Know and appreciate the rights and obligations of a) research respondents—particularly children, b) business researchers, and c) research clients or sponsors

6. Know how to avoid a conflict of interest in performing business research

Chapter Vignette:

I Can't Share This Report!

J ohn Harris has been senior research analyst for Delavan Insurance Group (DIG), a large insurance company, for the past 10 years. The consumer insurance industry has changed drastically in the past few years with the growing acceptance of Internet-based insurance providers and traditional insurance companies expanding their web presence. John's company had long based their reputation and business model on developing close personal relationships between the company's insurance agents and their customers. DIG's management feared that offering insurance direct to consumers online would harm this relationship and undermine their agent system. However, when Scott Jeckel was hired as the new CEO, that all changed. Scott was determined to make Delavan Insurance Group "a 21st century insurance provider" and demanded that the company push forward with a new website and introduce online insurance quotes and sales. Scott hired his cousin, Doug Jeckel, to develop and launch the new corporate web system.

John's latest project was to assess consumer perceptions of the company's new website. The study focused on the information provided, ease of use, and compared DIG's website to the

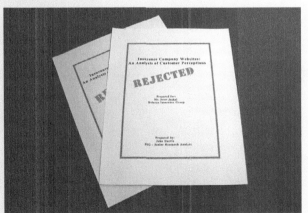

© Susan Van Etten

leading Internet insurance providers. His analyses and results were clear—the new website was not viewed as favorably as the competition on any dimension. In fact, of the six insurance companies included in the study, DIG was rated the very lowest. John carefully reviewed the research methodology and double-checked the analysis. There was no doubt that the new website was a failure.

John presented the results of the study to Scott Jeckel the week before the scheduled meeting of DIG's board of directors. Scott was furious! "I have my entire reputation riding on this website. We have invested millions of dollars on our new system. There is no way I am presenting the results of this study to our board. You must have made some mistake." John told Scott that he was very careful in carrying out the study and double-checked every step of the process. Scott pushed the report back across his desk to John and firmly stated, "I am certain you have made a mistake. I expect to see a new report with the correct results on my desk tomorrow; a report that we will all be excited to share with the board. Your career is riding on that." John picked up the report from Scott's desk and walked out of the office. What was he supposed to do?

Introduction

outside agency

An independent research firm contracted by the company that actually will benefit from the research.

in-house research

Research performed by employees of the company that will benefit from the research.

The vignette described above involves a researcher who faces a challenge in what is learned from the research process. Many companies have their own employees perform research projects and research programs. Thus, research is sometimes performed in-house, meaning that employees of the company that will benefit from the research project actually perform the research. In other cases, the research is performed by an **outside agency**, meaning that the company that will benefit from the research results hires an independent, outside firm to perform a research project.

While it would seem that **in-house research** would usually be of higher quality because of the increased knowledge of the researchers conducting the studies, there are several reasons why employees of the firm may not always be the best people to do the job (see Exhibit 5.1). When the firm facing a decision encounters one of the following situations, they should consider having the research performed by an outside agency:

EXHIBIT **5.1**

Should Research Be Done In-House or by an Outside Agency?

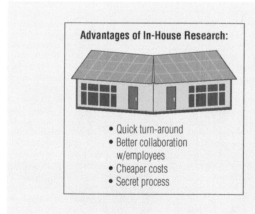
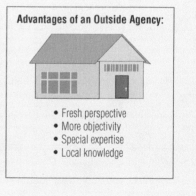

Advantages of In-House Research:
- Quick turn-around
- Better collaboration w/employees
- Cheaper costs
- Secret process

Advantages of an Outside Agency:
- Fresh perspective
- More objectivity
- Special expertise
- Local knowledge

© Cengage Learning 2013

"To manage a business is to manage its future; and to manage the future is to manage information."

—MARION HARPER

■ An outside agency often can provide a fresh perspective. Creativity is often hindered by too much knowledge. When a firm is seeking new ideas, particularly in discovery-oriented research, an outsider is not constrained by the groupthink that often affects a company employee. In other words, employees who spend so much time together in their day-to-day work activities begin to act and think alike to a large degree. For example, history is filled with stories of products that remained unsuccessful commercially for years until someone from outside the company discovered a useful application. The technology for a microwave oven was invented in the 1940s by a company called Raytheon. Raytheon worked on radar systems for the Allied military in World War II. Not until someone from another company, Amana, had the creativity to test the concept of using microwaves in a kitchen appliance did it become a commercial success. For a glimpse at some of the research organizations perceived as creative, take a look at the websites of the "Top 10 Most Innovative Research Organizations" shown in Exhibit 5.2.

Rank	Company	Website	Number of Mentions
1	Brainjuicer	http://www.brainjuicer.com/	60
2	TNS Global	http://www.tnsglobal.com/	32
3	Vision Critical	http://www.visioncritical.com/	32
4	Synovate	http://www.synovate.com/	31
5	Ipsos	http://www.ipsos-na.com/	25
6	Nielsen	http://www.nielsen.com/	25
7	Anderson Analytics	http://www.andersonanalytics.com/	21
8	Itracks	http://www.itracks.com/	18
9	GFK	http://www.gfk.com/	17
10	Peanut Labs	http://www1.peanutlabs.com/	16

EXHIBIT **5.2**
"Top 10" Most Innovative Research Organizations

Source: "Top 10 Market Research Companies Perceived to be Innovative," posted by Leonard Murphy, Tuesday, February 15, 2011, 15:53 pm at http://www.greenbookblog.org/2011/02/15/top-10-companies-perceived-to-be-innovative-grit-2010-sneak-peek/, accessed April 30, 2011.

■ An outside agency often can be more objective. When a firm is facing a particularly sensitive situation that may even impact a large number of jobs within the company, it may be difficult for researchers to be objective. Alternatively, as depicted in our opening vignette, if a chief executive within the firm is in love with some new idea, researchers may feel a great deal of pressure to present results that are supportive of the concept. In these cases, outside researchers may be a good choice. Since they don't have to work for the company and interact with the players involved on a daily basis, they are less concerned about presenting results that may not be truly welcome.

■ An outside agency may have special skills. When a firm needs research requiring a particular expertise that some outside agency specializes in, it may be a good idea to use that firm to conduct the research. For example, if a company is searching for new ideas about how to use its website, an online focus group interview may be needed. While this is a skill that may not be prevalent within the company, there are several research firms that specialize in this particular type of research. Thus, the outside agency may have greater competency in this specific area.

■ An outside agency often has local expertise allowing it to specialize in research from its home area or other global regions. When a company needs research conducted in a particular country or even from a specific area of a country, an outside agency may be advantageous because of its knowledge of the local customs and values. The company probably also knows acceptable ways to get information from citizens in that particular area. For example, a research agency based here in the United States would probably not strongly consider a door-to-door survey for consumer research. However, in other parts of the world,

By now, you are becoming familiar with the student questionnaire that accompanies this book. Examine the items in the questionnaire and the questionnaire overall for the following issues.

1. Were you required to identify yourself by name in completing the survey?
2. Can the results (you can access the results through your instructor) be linked to respondents by name?
3. Do any items need to be tied to a name to be useful to the researcher?
4. Consider the portion of the survey shown here. What if another instructor asked for the results from this particular section of the survey but was only interested in them if the names of the students also can be provided? The instructor believes that he can use the results to encourage particular students to change their study habits. Take the role of the researchers who implemented this research. Should you provide the information this instructor is asking for? Why or why not?

Courtesy of Qualtrics.com

particularly with a less developed communication infrastructure, door-to-door interviews may be a viable option. Thus, the outside agency may have greater competency in this specific area.

Likewise, there are conditions that make in-house research more attractive as well, as in the following situations:

- If the research project needs to be completed very quickly, chances are that in-house researchers can get started more quickly and get quicker or better access to internal resources that can help get the project done in short order.
- If the research project will require the close collaboration of many other employees from diverse areas of the organization, then in-house research may be preferable. The in-house research team can usually gain cooperation and more quickly ascertain just who needs to be interviewed and where those people can be found.
- A third reason for doing a project in-house has to do with economy. In-house research can almost always be done more cheaply than that done by an outside research firm.
- If secrecy is a major concern, then the research is best done in-house. Even though the outside firm might be trusted, it may take slightly less care in disguising its research efforts. Thus, other companies may pick up on signals in the marketplace that suggest the area of research for a firm.

This chapter focuses on the human side of research. We first discuss the internal working of a research unit within a large company. We then turn to the different types of options that exist when dealing with an outside agency. Some of the most creative research companies are presented in Exhibit 5.2. All of this is wrapped up by a discussion of the many ways in which ethics and research come together.

Organizational Structure of Business Research

The placement of business research within a firm's organizational structure and the structure of the research department itself vary substantially, depending on the firm's acceptance of the concept of internal research and its stage of research sophistication. A research department can easily become isolated with poor organizational placement. Researchers may lack a voice in executive committees when they have no continuous relationship with management. This can occur when the research department is positioned at an inappropriately low level. Given the critically important nature of the intelligence coming out of a research department, it should be placed relatively high in the organizational structure to ensure that senior management is well informed. Research departments should also be linked with a broad spectrum of other units within the organization. Thus, they should be positioned to provide credible information both upstream and downstream within the organization.

© AP Photo/Gene J. Puskar

Research departments that perform a staff function must wait for management to request assistance. Similar to John's situation in the opening vignett, often the term "client" or "internal consultant" is used by the research department to refer to management for whom services are being performed. The research department responds to clients' requests and is responsible for the design and execution of all research. It should function like an internal consulting organization that develops action-oriented, data-based recommendations.

● ● ● ● ● ● ● ●

When research departments grow, they begin to specialize by product or business unit. This happened in the Marriott Corporation, which now has a specific director of research for its lodging facilities.

Business Research Jobs

Research organizations themselves consist of layers of employees. Each employee has certain specific functions to perform based on his or her area of expertise and experience. A look at these jobs not only describes the potential structure of a research organization, but it also provides insight into the types of careers available as a business research specialist.

Small Firms

While it is difficult to precisely define the boundaries between small firms, midsized firms, and large firms, generally speaking, government statistics usually consider firms with fewer than 100 employees to be small. In small firms, the vice president of marketing may be in charge of all significant internal research projects. This officer may focus on organizational research projects that relate to staffing or stakeholder relations, or may be a sales manager who collects and analyzes sales histories, trade association statistics, and other internal data. Small companies usually have few resources and special competencies to conduct large-scale, sophisticated research projects. An advertising agency or a business consulting firm that specializes in research will be contracted if a large-scale survey is needed. At the other extreme, a large company like Procter & Gamble may staff its research departments with more than 100 people.

Midsized Firms

Midsized firms can be thought of as those with between 100 and 500 employees. In a midsized firm, the research department may reside in the organization under the director of marketing research, as shown in Exhibit 5.3. This person provides leadership in research efforts and

© Cengage Learning 2013

EXHIBIT 5.3

Organization of the Marketing Research Department in a Large Firm

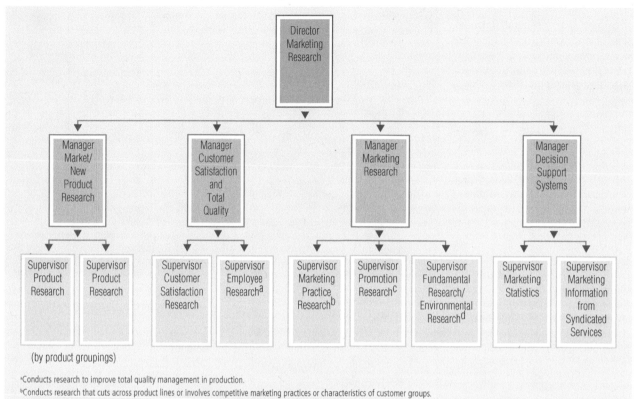

(by product groupings)

[a]Conducts research to improve total quality management in production.
[b]Conducts research that cuts across product lines or involves competitive marketing practices or characteristics of customer groups.
[c]Conducts research that cuts across product lines to measure the effectiveness of promotional activities.
[d]Conducts research aimed at gaining a basic understanding of various elements of the marketing process.

research analyst

A person responsible for client contact, project design, preparation of proposals, selection of research suppliers, and supervision of data collection, analysis, and reporting activities.

research assistants

Research employees who provide technical assistance with questionnaire design, data analyses, and similar activities.

manager of decision support systems

Employee who supervises the collection and analysis of sales, inventory, and other periodic customer relationship management (CRM) data.

forecast analyst

Employee who provides technical assistance such as running computer programs and manipulating data to generate a sales forecast.

integrates all staff-level research activities. (This position will be discussed in greater detail in the next section.)

A **research analyst** is responsible for client contact, project design, preparation of proposals, selection of research suppliers, and supervision of data collection, analysis, and reporting activities. Normally, the research analyst is responsible for several projects simultaneously covering a wide spectrum of the firm's organizational activities. He or she works with product or division management and makes recommendations based on analysis of collected data.

Research assistants (or associates) provide technical assistance with questionnaire design, data analyses, and so forth. Another common name for this position is junior analyst. The **manager of decision support systems** supervises the collection and analysis of sales, inventory, and other periodic customer relationship management (CRM) data. Sales forecasts for product lines usually are developed using analytical and quantitative techniques. Sales information is provided to satisfy the planning, analysis, and control needs of decision makers. The manager of decision support systems may be assisted by a **forecast analyst** who provides technical assistance, such as running computer programs and manipulating data to forecast sales for the firm.

Personnel within a planning department may perform the research function in a midsized firm. At times, they may outsource some research functions, depending on the size of the project and the degree of sophistication. The planner may design research studies and then contract with outside firms that supply research services such as interviewing or data processing. They can combine the input from these outside agencies with their own work to write research reports.

Large Research Firms

As research departments grow, they tend to specialize by product or strategic business unit. Major firms can be thought of as those with over 500 employees. Marriott Corporation has a director of research for lodging (for example, Marriott Hotels and Resorts, Courtyard by Marriott, and Fairfield Inn) and a director of research for contract services and restaurants (for example, Roy Rogers, Big Boy, and Senior Living Services). Each business unit's research director reports to the vice president of corporate marketing services. Many large organizations have managers of customer quality research who specialize in conducting surveys to measure consumers' satisfaction with product quality.

In many instances, business research units are located within a firm's marketing function. Exhibit 5.3 illustrates the organization of a typical major firm's marketing research department. Within this organization, the centralized research department conducts research for all the division's product groups. This is typical of a large research department that conducts much of its own research, including fieldwork.

Other positions within a major firm's research department may include director of data collection (field supervisor), manager of quantitative research, focus group moderator, and manager of data processing. These are not shown in Exhibit 5.3. Even large firms sometimes outsource some research functions or even an entire project from time to time. For now, we turn our attention to the job of director of research and the interface between the research department and other departments.

> *"The longer the title, the less important the job."*
> —GEORGE McGOVERN

The Director of Research as a Manager

A director of research plans, executes, and controls the firm's research function. This person typically serves on company executive committees that identify competitive opportunities and formulate strategies that involve customers or other organizational stakeholders. The various directors from each functional area generally make up this committee (such as finance, sales, production, and so forth). The director of research provides the research perspective during meetings. For instance, the researcher can provide input as to what types of business intelligence can be feasibly obtained given the decision being discussed. Research directors typically face problems like these:

- Skilled research professionals may like conducting research better than managing people. They pride themselves on being hands-on researchers. However, a director is a manager and spends more time in meetings and managing than actually conducting research.
- The research management role often is not formally recognized.
- Outstanding research professionals often have trouble delegating responsibility. The pride that comes with being a knowledgeable researcher makes it difficult to give up control. They may genuinely feel "I can do it better myself." As a result, they delegate only elementary or tedious tasks to subordinates. The subordinates can sometimes become disenchanted and thus become unhappy with their work.
- Finally, research is often seen as a hodgepodge of techniques available to answer individual, unrelated questions. According to this view, a research operation encompasses an array of more or less equal projects, each handled by a project director. Hence, many firms view a full-time director as unnecessary.[1]

Sources of Conflict between Senior Management and Research

In principle, the functions of research should merge harmoniously with the objectives of management for the benefit of both parties. In practice, the relationship between a research department and the users of research frequently is characterized by misunderstanding and conflict.

© Bloomberg via Getty Images

The True Power of Research

The customer's voice is powerful in many ways. How can a company harness that power? Many companies turn to J. D. Power to find powerful research results. J. D. Power rates competing company's products and services in many industries. For instance, do you want to know what tires make consumers the happiest? This might be an important question for retail dealers considering product lines and for auto manufacturers looking to enhance the value of their new cars by using quality OEM component parts. A sample of 30,000 consumers ranks Michelin highest based on good wear and the smallest number of problems. However, Pirelli tire owners thought their tires looked the best! Value comes in many forms. J. D. Power also breaks results down by region. In the southern

U.S., consumers rate Bright House Networks as the highest performing cable company based on customer service, price, and product offerings. However, in the Upper Midwest, WideOpenWest (WOW) is the leading provider. Perhaps the cable companies or even competitors like DirecTV will find information like this full of power.

Sources: Robuck, Mike "Cable operators fare well in J. D. Power study," CedMagazine.com - September 15, 2010; "Michelin, Pirelli Brands Top J. D. Power OE Tire Consumer Satisfaction Study," *Tire Business* 28 (May 10, 2010), 22–23.

Research That Implies Criticism

As we saw in the chapter vignette, a manager who requests information on customer reactions to a new website may not be happy when the results are unfavorable. Similarly, a sales manager who informally projects a 5 percent increase in sales will not like hearing from the research department that the market potential indicates sales volume should be up by 20 percent. In each of these situations, the research presents information that implies criticism of a line executive's decision. In personal life, a sure way to lose a friend is to be openly critical of him or her. Things are no different in business.

Money

Research budgets are a source of conflict between management and researchers. Financial managers often see research as a cost rather than as an investment or a way of lowering risk. Successful decisions that are supported by research are seldom attributed to the researcher. Thus, as is often true in many areas of business, managers often want to spend as little as possible on research. In contrast, researchers often vigorously resist cutting corners in conducting research. For instance, they may feel that a large random sample is necessary to adequately address a research question using descriptive research. This approach can be very expensive and sometimes time consuming. Inevitably, management's desire to save money and the researcher's desire to conduct rigorous research conflict. Successful research projects often are those that are based on compromise. This may involve working within a budget that will produce meaningful results and sacrifice precision and rigor minimally.

Time

Researchers say, "Good research takes time!" Managers say, "Time is money!" Like oil and water, these two views do not go together easily. A look back at the research process in the last chapter makes it clear that it can take some time to complete a research project. Simply planning one can involve days, if not weeks, of study and preparation. For instance, conducting a literature review or a review of previous studies can take weeks. Without them, the researcher may not be able to develop specific research hypotheses that would direct the project very specifically toward the current issue. Other times, the researcher may wish to interview more people than time can allow or take the time to use a more sophisticated data analysis approach.

When Your Brain "Trips Up"

Business researchers provide analyses and reports, but do decision makers always listen and use that information? Recent research provides evidence that regardless of the "facts," senior executives can make bad judgments, even when they are seeking to improve their company.

An Wang, CEO of Wang Laboratories, headed a company that dominated the computer word processing market. Despite clear and convincing evidence, he felt compelled to build a computer using a proprietary operating system, despite the IBM PC's dominance at the time, and the fact that Microsoft had developed the primary operating system and not IBM. What drove this decision? Wang had a long distrust of IBM, which dated back to his own personal dislike for the company years before. This had perhaps clouded his judgment, which ultimately led to the demise of the company.

Scientists recognize that any decision maker is a victim of their own mental biases and stereotypes. Some of the biases include making decisions based upon an overattachment to a particular plan, or even to a particular person. Other biases can include stereotypes about the importance of speed in making decisions, and an overreliance on emotion in making a decision. When making judgments, your brain can "trip you up," by causing you to see patterns in the results that are not there, or when you use your past experiences to see the results you wish to see. Recognizing your own cognitive shortcomings can be an important step towards avoiding a bad decision.

Source: Campbell, Andrew, Jo Whitehead, and Syndey Finkelstein, "Why Good Leaders Make Bad Decisions," *Harvard Business Review* (February 2009), 60–66.

Oftentimes, the more quickly the research project is done, the less likely it is to be successful. This doesn't mean it can't provide valuable information. It simply is not as certain that a quickly put together study will provide answers as valuable as a more deliberately planned project. When studies are rushed, the following sources of error become more prominent than they would be otherwise:

- Conducting a study that is needed. Taking more time to perform a literature search, including through company and industry reports, may have provided the needed intelligence without a new study.
- Addressing the wrong issue. Taking more time to make sure the decision statement is well defined and that the research questions that follow will truly address relevant issues can lessen the chance that the research goes in the wrong direction.
- Sampling difficulties. Correctly defining, identifying, and contacting a truly representative sample is a difficult and time consuming task. However, in some types of research, the quality of results depends directly on the quality of the sample.
- Inadequate data analysis. The researcher may analyze the data quickly and without the rigor that would otherwise be taken. Therefore, certain assumptions may not be considered, and important information within the data is simply not discovered.

Sometimes a researcher will have to submit to the time pressure and do a quick-and-dirty study. A sudden event can make it necessary to acquire data quickly—but rush jobs can sometimes be avoided with proper planning of the research program. If it is necessary to conduct a study under severe time limitations, the researcher is obligated to point this out to management. The research report and presentation should include all the study limitations, including those that resulted from a shortage of time or money.

"Someone's sitting in the shade today because someone planted a tree a long time ago."
—WARREN BUFFETT

Intuitive Decision Making

The fact of the matter is that managers are decision makers. They are action-oriented, and they often rely on gut reaction and intuition. Many times their intuition serves them well, so it isn't surprising that they sometimes do not believe a research project will help improve their decision making. At other times, they resist research because it just may provide information that is counter to their intuition or their desires. They particularly abhor being held back while waiting for some research report.

If managers do use research, they often request simple projects that will provide concrete results with certainty. Researchers tend to see problems as complex questions that can be answered only within probability ranges. One aspect of this conflict is the fact that a research report provides findings, but cannot make decisions. Decision-oriented executives may unrealistically expect research to make decisions for them or provide some type of guarantee that the action they take will be correct. While research provides information for decision making, it does not always remove all the uncertainties involved in complex decisions. Certain alternatives may be eliminated, but the research may reveal new aspects of a problem. Although research is a valuable decision-making tool, it does not relieve the executive of the decision-making task.

Presentation of the right facts can be extremely useful. However, decision makers often believe that researchers collect the wrong facts. Many researchers view themselves as technicians who generate numbers using sophisticated mathematical and statistical techniques; they may spend more time on technical details than on satisfying managerial needs. Each person who has a narrow perspective of another's job is a partial cause of the problem of generating limited or useless information.

Consider this situation: An Internet retailer (Send.com) used a television ad to try to stimulate more gift purchasing among its customers. The spot centers on several men on the golf course drinking champagne. The "punch line" comes when one of the guys is hit in the groin. The voice over exclaims, "He just got hit in the little giver!"

A male executive may like punch lines like this. However, the audience for these ads is not all male. Had research been used to test these ideas prior to spending the money to produce the ads and buy the spots, it would have revealed that men didn't respond as favorably as expected to these ads and women found them boorish.[2] Thus, intuition has its limits as a replacement for informed research intelligence.[3]

Future Decisions Based on Past Experience

Managers wish to predict the future, but researchers measure only current or past events. In 1957, Ford introduced the Edsel, one of the classic business failures of all time. One reason for the Edsel's failure was that the research conducted several years before the car's introduction indicated a strong demand for a medium-priced car for the "man on his way up." By the time the car was introduced, however, consumer preference had shifted to two cars, one being a small import for the suburban wife. Not all research information is so dated, but all research describes what people have done in the past. In this sense, researchers use the past to predict the future. As seen in the Research Snapshot "When Your Brain 'Trips Up' ", experiences can affect how decision makers see results.

Reducing the Conflict between Management and Researchers

Given the conflicting goals of management and research, it is probably impossible to completely eliminate the conflict. However, when researchers and decision makers work more closely together, there will be less conflict. The more closely they work together, the better the communication between decision makers and researchers. In this way, business decision makers will better understand the information needs and work requirements of researchers. It will allow for better planning of research projects and a greater appreciation for the role that research plays in minimizing the riskiness of business decision making. Exhibit 5.4 lists some common areas of conflict between research and management. Many of these can be avoided through improved understanding of the other's position.

With closer cooperation, managers are more involved with projects from the beginning. Early involvement increases the likelihood that managers will accept and act on the results. Researchers' responsibility should be made explicit by a formal job description. Better planning and an annual statement of the research program for the upcoming year will help minimize emergency assignments, which usually waste resources and demoralize personnel.

Business researchers likewise will come to understand management's perspective better. Researchers enhance company profits by encouraging better decisions. The closer together

EXHIBIT 5.4

Areas of Conflict between Top Management and Marketing Researchers

Area of Potential Conflict	Top Management's Position	Business Researcher's Position
Research responsibility	Researchers lack a sense of accountability. The sole function of the researcher is to provide information.	The responsibility for research should be explicitly defined, and this responsibility should be consistently followed. The researcher should be involved with top management in decision making.
Research personnel	Researchers are generally poor communicators who lack enthusiasm, skills, and imagination.	Top managers are anti-intellectual. Researchers should be hired, judged, and compensated on the basis of their research capabilities.
Budget	Research costs too much. Since the research department's contribution is difficult to measure, budget cuts in the department are defensible.	"You get what you pay for." Research must have a continuing, long-term commitment from top management.
Assignments	Projects tend to be overengineered and not executed with a sense of urgency. Researchers have a ritualized, staid approach.	Top managers make too many nonresearchable or emergency requests and do not allocate sufficient time or money.
Problem definition	The researcher is best equipped to define the problem; it is sufficient for the top manager to give general direction. Top managers cannot help it if circumstances change. The researcher must appreciate this and be willing to respond to changes.	Researchers are often not given all the relevant facts about situations, which often change after research is under way. Top managers are generally unsympathetic to this widespread problem.
Research reporting	Most reports are dull, use too much jargon and too many qualifiers, and are not decision oriented. Reports too often are presented after a decision has been made.	Top managers treat research reports superficially. Good research demands thorough reporting and documentation. Top managers give insufficient time to prepare good reports.
Use of research	Top managers should be free to use research as they see fit. Changes in the need for and timing of research are sometimes unavoidable.	Top managers' use of research to support a predetermined position or to confirm or excuse past decisions represents misuse. Also, it is wasteful to request research and then not use it after it has been conducted.

Source: Based on John G. Keane, "Some Observations on Marketing Research in Top Management Decision Making," *Journal of Marketing*, October 1969, p. 13. Reprinted with permission from the Journal of Marketing, published by the American Marketing Association.

managers and researchers work, the more researchers realize that managers sometimes need information urgently. Thus, they should try to develop cost-saving research alternatives and realize that sometimes a quick-and-dirty study is necessary, even though it may not be as scientifically rigorous as might be desired. Sometimes, quick-and-dirty studies still provide usable and timely information. In other words, they should focus on results.

Perhaps most important is more effective communication of the research findings and research designs. The researchers must understand the interests and needs of the users of the research. If the researchers are sensitive to the decision-making orientation of management and can translate research performance into management language, organizational conflict will diminish.

A **research generalist** can effectively serve as a link between management and the research specialist. The research generalist acts as a problem definer, an educator, a liaison, a communicator, and a friendly ear. This intermediary could work with specialists who understand management's needs and demands. The student with research skills who has a business degree seems most suited for this coordinating function.

Several strategies for reducing the conflict between management and research are possible. Managers generally should plan the role of research better, and researchers should become more decision-oriented and improve their communication skills (see Exhibit 5.5).[4]

research generalist

An employee who serves as a link between management and research specialists. The research generalist acts as a problem definer, an educator, a liaison, a communicator, and a friendly ear.

EXHIBIT 5.5
Improving Two-Way
Communication to Reduce
Conflict

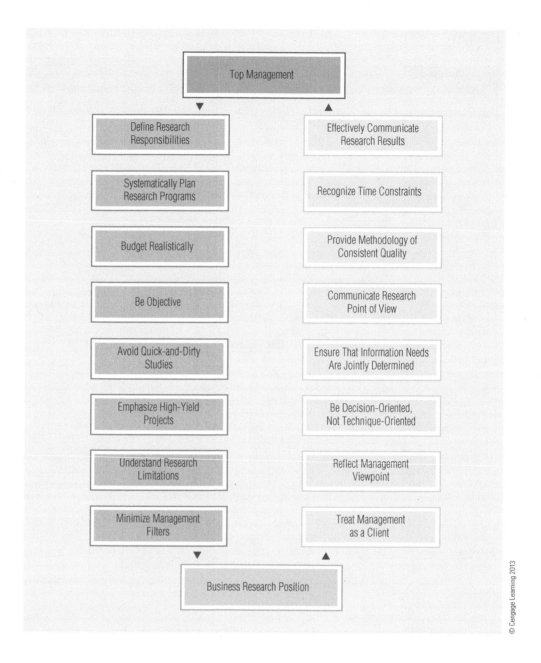

© Cengage Learning 2013

Cross-Functional Teams

The ability to develop a successful decision making approach is often a function of the input of many different stakeholders. With improved communication, a more focused solution is possible. One way to encourage this is through cross-functional teams.

cross-functional teams

Employee teams composed of individuals from various functional areas such as engineering, production, finance, and marketing who share a common purpose.

Cross-functional teams are composed of individuals from various functional areas such as engineering, production, finance, and marketing who share a common purpose. Cross-functional teams help organizations focus on a core business process, such as customer service or new-product development. Working in teams reduces the tendency for employees to focus single-mindedly on an isolated functional activity. Cross-functional teams help employees increase customer value since communication about their specific desires and opinions are better communicated across the firm.

At trendsetting organizations, many research directors are members of cross-functional teams. New product development, for example, may be done by a cross-functional team of engineers, finance executives, production personnel, marketing managers, and staff researchers who take an integrated approach to solve a problem or exploit opportunities. In the old days, research may not have been involved in developing new products until long after many key decisions about product specifications and manufacturing had been made. Now researchers' input is part of an integrated team effort. Researchers act both as business consultants and as providers of technical services. Researchers working in teams are more likely to understand the broad purpose of their research and less likely to focus exclusively on research methodology.

The effective cross-functional team is a good illustration of the business research concept in action. It reflects an effort to satisfy customers by using all the organization's resources. Cross-functional teams are having a dramatic impact on views of the role of business research within the organization.

Research Suppliers and Contractors

As mentioned in the beginning of the chapter, there are times when it makes good sense to obtain business research from an outside organization. In these cases, managers must interact with **research suppliers**, who are commercial providers of business and marketing research services. Business research is carried out by firms that may be variously classified as marketing and business research consulting companies, such as Burke, Market Facts, Inc., or The Freedonia Group; suppliers of syndicated research services, such as Experian Simmons as well as interviewing agencies, universities, and government agencies.

research suppliers

Commercial providers of research services.

Syndicated Service

No matter how large a firm's research department is, some projects are too expensive to perform in-house. A **syndicated service** is a research supplier that provides standardized information for many clients in return for a fee. They serve as a sort of supermarket for standardized research results. For example, J. D. Power and Associates sells research about customers' ratings of automobile quality and their reasons for satisfaction. Most automobile manufacturers and their advertising agencies subscribe to this syndicated service because the company provides important industry-wide information it gathers from a national sample of thousands of car buyers. By specializing in this type of customer satisfaction research, J. D. Power gains certain economies of scale.

syndicated service

A research supplier that provides standardized information for many clients in return for a fee.

Syndicated services can provide expensive information economically to numerous clients because the information is not specific to one client but interests many. Such suppliers offer standardized information to measure media audiences, wholesale and retail distribution data, and other forms of data.

Standardized Research Services

Standardized research service companies develop a unique methodology for investigating a business specialty area. Several research firms, such as Verdict Research (**http://www.verdict.co.uk/**), provide location services for retail firms. The Research Snapshot "Finding Häagen-Dazs in China" illustrates an interesting application for which an outside location service company may be particularly useful. Research suppliers conduct studies for multiple, individual clients using the same methods.

standardized research service

Companies that develop a unique methodology for investigating a business specialty area.

Nielsen (**http://www.nielsen.com**) collects information throughout the new product development process, from initial concept screening through test-marketing. The BASES system can evaluate initiatives relative to other products in the competitive environment. For example, a client can compare its day-after recall scores with average scores for a product category.

Finding Häagen-Dazs in China

Ice cream lovers needn't worry if they are sent on a business trip to China. Häagen-Dazs ice cream shops first appeared in Shanghai, China, in 1996 and now there are dozens of Häagen-Dazs ice cream shops in coastal China, with plans for hundreds more. Clearly, many firms would like to follow Häagen-Dazs into China. China is expected to be the world's largest consumer market by 2020. However, where should an ice cream shop be located in China? While location decisions can be difficult enough within the borders of one's own country, imagine trying to decide where to put a shop in a huge, unfamiliar country.

Fortunately, standardized research companies have resources deployed all around the world that can synthesize geographic information system (GIS) information with survey research and other information to assist firms with location decisions in China and in other developing countries. Since U.S.-based retail firms may lack the necessary connections and knowledge (expertise) to efficiently conduct research in faraway places, the use of an

outside research provider not only saves time and money, but also yields higher quality results than an in-house study. Imagine how difficult language barriers could be when dealing with the Chinese consumer market.

And, as difficult as identifying good retail locations seems in China, other top emerging retail nations include India, Russia, and the Ukraine. As in China, American and European firms may find that using a research supplier to help with retail location issues in these countries is wiser than doing the research themselves.

Sources: "Häagen-Dazs in China," *China Business Review* 31 (Jul/Aug 2004), 22; Hall, Cecily, "Spanning the Retail Globe," *WWD: Women's Wear Daily* 190 (July 21, 2005), 11.

---

custom research

Research projects that are tailored specifically to a client's unique needs.

• • • • • • • •

Research in a foreign country is often better done by an outside agency with resources in those places.

Even when a firm could perform the research task in-house, research suppliers may be able to conduct the project at a lower cost, faster, and relatively more objectively. A company that wishes to quickly evaluate a new advertising strategy may find an ad agency's research department is able to provide technical expertise on copy development research that is not available within the company itself. Researchers may be well advised to seek outside help when conducting research in a foreign country in which the necessary human resources and knowledge to effectively collect data are lacking. The Research Snapshot "Finding Häagen-Dazs in China" illustrates this situation.

Limited Research Service Companies and Custom Research

Limited-service research suppliers specialize in particular research activities, such as syndicated service, field interviewing, data warehousing, or data processing. Full-service research suppliers sometimes contract these companies for ad hoc research projects. The client usually controls these agencies or management consulting firms, but the research supplier handles most of the operating details of **custom research** projects. These are projects that are tailored specifically to a client's unique needs. A custom research supplier may employ individuals with titles that imply relationships with clients, such as account executive or account group manager, as well as functional specialists with titles such as statistician, librarian, director of field services, director of tabulation and data processing, and interviewer.

Largest Research Organizations

Exhibit 5.6 lists the top 15 suppliers of global research and their statistics from 2010. Just a few decades ago, the list would comprise solely firms based in the United States. Large research firms now base their operations in places around the globe including London, Tokyo, and Neuremberg. The explosion in global data availability will only add to the growth in the industry.

EXHIBIT **5.6**
Top 15 Global Research Firms

Rank	Organization	Headquarters	Home Country	Website	Employees (Full-Time)	Number of Countries	Approximate Revenue ($ millions)
1	The Nielsen Co.	New York	USA	nielson.com	33,100	100	4,628
2	Kantar	London	UK	kantar.com	19,400	80	2,823
3	IMS Health Inc.	Norwalk, CT	USA	imshealth.com	7,300	75	2,190
4	GfK	Neuremberg	Germany	gfk.com	10,100	59	1,622
5	Ipsos	New York	USA	ipsos.com	8,800	64	1,315
6	Westat Inc.	Rockville, MD	USA	wesstat.com	2,100	1	1,000
7	Synovate	London	UK	synovate.com	6,000	62	817
8	Symphony IRI	Chicago, IL	USA	symphonyiri.com	700	8	706
9	Arbitron Inc.	Columbia, MD	USA	arbitron.com	1,029	2	385
10	JD Power	Westlake Village, CA	USA	jdpower.com	800	8	370
11	INTAGE, Inc.	Tokyo	Japan	intage.co.jp	2,000	3	369
12	NPD Group Inc.	Port Washington, NY	USA	npd.com	1,000	12	226
13	dunnhumbyUSA	Cincinnati, OH	USA	dunnhumby.com	1,100	18	203
14	Video Research Ltd.	Tokyo	Japan	videor.co.jp	400	3	201
15	Harris Interactive	New York	USA	harrisinteractive.com	800	8	167

Source: Data taken from Honomichl, J., "Global Top 25: 2010 Honomichl Report," Marketing News, (August 30, 2010), 16.

Most of these organizations provide various services ranging from designing activities to fieldwork. The services they can provide are not covered in detail here because they are discussed throughout the book, especially in the sections on fieldwork. However, here we briefly consider some managerial and human aspects of dealing with research suppliers. Clearly, the exhibit reveals that research is big business. Its growth will continue as data availability increases and as businesses desire more precision in their decision making. Therefore, attractive career opportunities are numerous for those with the right skills and desires.

Ethical Issues in Business Research

As in all human interactions, ethical issues exist in research. Our earlier discussion of potential organizational politics and the implication of different goals or perspectives introduced a situation where ethics can come into play. This book considers various ethical issues concerning fair business dealings, proper research techniques, and appropriate use of research results in other chapters. The remainder of this chapter addresses society's and managers' concerns about the ethical implications of business research.

Ethical Questions Are Philosophical Questions

Ethical questions are philosophical questions. There are several philosophical theories that address how one develops a moral philosophy and how behavior is affected by morals. These include theories about cognitive moral development, the bases for ethical behavioral intentions, and opposing moral values.[5] While ethics remain a somewhat elusive topic, what is clear is that not everyone involved in business, or in fact involved in any human behavior, comes to the table with the same ethical standards or orientations.[6]

business ethics

The application of morals to behavior related to the exchange environment.

moral standards

Principles that reflect beliefs about what is ethical and what is unethical.

ethical dilemma

Refers to a situation in which one chooses from alternative courses of actions, each with different ethical implications.

relativism

A term that reflects the degree to which one rejects moral standards in favor of the acceptability of some action. This way of thinking rejects absolute principles in favor of situation-based evaluations.

idealism

A term that reflects the degree to which one bases one's morality on moral standards.

Business ethics is the application of morals to behavior related to the business environment or context. Generally, good ethics conforms to the notion of "right," and a lack of ethics conforms to the notion of "wrong." Highly ethical behavior can be characterized as being fair, just, and acceptable.[7] Ethical values can be highly influenced by one's moral standards. **Moral standards** are principles that reflect beliefs about what is ethical and what is unethical. More simply, they can be thought of as rules distinguishing right from wrong. The Golden Rule, "Do unto others as you would have them do unto you," is one such ethical principle.

An **ethical dilemma** simply refers to a situation in which one chooses from alternative courses of actions, each with different ethical implications. Each individual develops a philosophy or way of thinking that is applied to resolve the dilemmas they face. Many people use moral standards to guide their actions when confronted with an ethical dilemma. Others adapt an ethical orientation that rejects absolute principles. Their ethics are based more on the social or cultural acceptability of behavior. If it conforms to social or cultural norms, then it is ethical. **Relativism** is a term that reflects the degree to which one rejects moral standards in favor of the acceptability of some action. This way of thinking rejects absolute principles in favor of situation-based evaluations. Thus, an action that is judged ethical in one situation can be deemed unethical in another. In contrast, **idealism** is a term that reflects the degree to which one bases one's morality on moral standards. Someone who is an ethical idealist will try to apply ethical principles like the Golden Rule in all ethical dilemmas.

For example, a student may face an ethical dilemma when taking a test. Another student may arrange to exchange multiple choice responses to a test via electronic text messages. This represents an ethical dilemma because there are alternative courses of action each with differing moral implications. An ethical idealist may apply a rule that cheating is always wrong and therefore would not be likely to participate in the behavior. An ethical relativist may instead argue that the behavior is acceptable because a lot of the other students will be doing the same. In other words, the consensus is that this sort of cheating is acceptable, so this student would be likely to go ahead and participate in the behavior. Researchers and business stakeholders face ethical dilemmas practically every day. The following sections describe how this can occur.

General Rights and Obligations of Concerned Parties

Everyone involved in business research can face an ethical dilemma. For this discussion, we can divide those involved in research into three parties:

1. The people actually performing the research, who can also be thought of as the "doers"
2. The research client, sponsor, or the management team requesting the research, who can be thought of as the "users" of research
3. The research participants, meaning the actual research respondents or subjects

Each party has certain rights and obligations toward the other parties. Exhibit 5.7 diagrams these relationships.

Like the rest of business, research works best when all parties act ethically. Each party depends on the other to do so. A client depends on the researcher to be honest in presenting research results. The researcher depends on the client to be honest in presenting the reasons for doing the research and in describing the business situation. Each is also dependent on the research participant's honesty

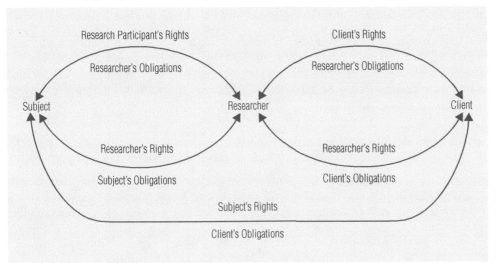

© Cengage Learning 2013

EXHIBIT **5.7**
Interaction of Rights and
Obligations between Parties

in answering questions during a research study. Thus, each is morally obligated toward the other. Likewise, each also has certain rights. The following section elaborates on the obligations and rights of each party.

Rights and Obligations of the Research Participant

Most business research is conducted with the research participant's consent. In other words, the participation is active. Traditional survey research requires that a respondent voluntarily answer questions in one way or another. This may involve answering questions on the phone, responding to an e-mail request, or even sending a completed questionnaire by regular mail. In these cases, **informed consent** means that the individual understands what the researcher wants him or her to do and consents to the research study. In other cases, research participants may not be aware that they are being monitored in some way. For instance, a research firm may monitor superstore purchases via an electronic scanner. The information may assist in understanding how customers respond to promotions. However, no consent is provided since the participant is participating passively. The ethical responsibilities vary depending on whether participation is active or passive.

informed consent

When an individual understands what the researcher wants him or her to do and consents to the research study.

The Obligation to Be Truthful

When someone willingly consents to participate actively, it is generally expected that he or she will provide truthful answers. Honest cooperation is the main obligation of the research participant. In return for being truthful, the subject has the right to expect confidentiality. **Confidentiality** means that information involved in the research will not be shared with others. When the respondent truly believes that confidentiality will be maintained, then it becomes much easier to respond truthfully, even about potentially sensitive topics. Likewise, the researcher and the research sponsor also may expect the respondent to maintain confidentiality. For instance, if the research involves a new food product from Nabisco, then they may not want the respondent to discuss the idea for fear that the idea may fall into the competition's hands. Thus, confidentiality is a tool to help ensure truthful responses.

confidentiality

The information involved in a research study will not be shared with others.

Participant's Right to Privacy

ACTIVE RESEARCH

Most people relish their privacy. Hence, the right to privacy is an important issue in business research. This issue involves the participant's freedom to choose whether to comply with the investigator's request. Traditionally, researchers have assumed that individuals make an informed choice.

However, critics have argued that the old, the poor, the poorly educated, and other underprivileged individuals may be unaware of their right to choose. They have further argued that an interviewer may begin with some vague explanation of a survey's purpose, initially ask questions that are relatively innocuous, and then move to questions of a highly personal nature. It has been suggested that subjects be informed of their right to be left alone or to break off the interview at any time. Researchers should not follow the tendency to "hold on" to busy respondents. However, this view definitely is not universally accepted in the research community.

The privacy issue is illustrated by these questions:

■ Is a telephone call that interrupts family dinner an invasion of privacy?
■ Is an e-mail requesting response to a 30-minute survey an invasion of privacy?

Generally, interviewing firms practice common courtesy by trying not to interview late in the evening or at other inconvenient times. However, the computerized random phone number interview has stimulated increased debate over the privacy issue. As a practical matter, respondents may feel more relaxed about privacy issues if they know who is conducting the survey. Thus, it is generally recommended that field interviewers indicate that they are legitimate researchers and name the company they work for as soon as someone answers the phone. For in-person surveys, interviewers should wear official name tags and provide identification giving their name and the names of their companies.

Research companies should adhere to the principles of the "do-not-call" policy and should respect consumers' "Internet privacy." **Do-not-call legislation** restricts any telemarketing effort from calling consumers who either register with a no-call list in their state or who request not to be called. Legislators aimed these laws at sales-related calls. However, legislation in several states, including California, Louisiana, and Rhode Island, has extended this legislation to apply to "those that seek marketing information." Thus, the legislation effectively protects consumers' privacy from researchers as well as salespeople.[8]

Consumers often are confused about the difference between telemarketing efforts and true marketing or business research. Part of this is because telemarketers sometimes disguise their sales efforts by opening the conversation by saying they are doing research. The resulting confusion contributes to both increased refusal rates and lower trust. In 1980, a public opinion poll found that 19 percent of Americans reported having refused to participate in a marketing survey within the past year. Today, that number approaches 50 percent. In 2001, only 40 percent of Americans either agreed or strongly agreed that marketers will protect their privacy. That number is down from 50 percent in 1995.[9]

Companies using the Internet to conduct research also face legislative changes. Much of this legislation is aimed at making sure consumers are properly notified about the collection of data and to whom it will be distributed. Researchers should make sure that consumers are given a clear and easy way to either consent to participation in active research or to easily opt out. Furthermore, companies should ensure that the information consumers send via the Internet is secure.[10]

do-not-call legislation

Restricts any telemarketing effort from calling consumers who either register with a no-call list or who request not to be called.

PASSIVE RESEARCH

Passive research involves different types of privacy issues. Generally, it is believed that unobtrusive observation of public behavior in places such as stores, airports, and museums is not a serious invasion of privacy. This belief is based on the fact that the consumers are indeed anonymous in that they are never identified by name nor is any attempt made to identify them. They are "faces in the crowd." As long as the behavior observed is typical of behavior commonly conducted in public, then there is no invasion of privacy. In contrast, recording behavior that is not typically conducted in public would be a violation of privacy. For example, hidden cameras recording people (without consent) taking showers at a health club, even if ultimately intended to gather information to help improve the shower experience, would be considered inappropriate.

Technology has also created new ways of collecting data passively that have privacy implications. Researchers are very interested in consumers' online behavior. For instance, the paths that consumers take while browsing the Internet can be extremely useful in understanding what kinds of information are most valued by consumers. Much of this information can be harvested and entered into a data warehouse. Researchers sometimes have legitimate reasons to use this data, which can improve consumers' ability to make wise decisions. In these cases, the researcher should gain the consumers' consent in some form before harvesting information from their web usage patterns. Furthermore, if the information will be shared with other companies, a specific consent agreement is needed. This can come in the form of a question to which consumers respond yes or no, as in the following example:

> *From time to time, the opportunity to share your information with other companies arises and this could be very helpful in offering you desirable product choices. We respect your privacy, however, and if you do not wish us to share this information, we will not. Would you like us to share your information with other companies?*

- *Yes, you can share the information*
- *No, please keep my information private*

Not all of these attempts are legitimate. Most readers have probably encountered spyware on their home computer. **Spyware** is software that is placed on your computer without consent or knowledge while using the Internet. This software then tracks your usage and sends the information back through the Internet to the source. Then, based on these usage patterns, the user will receive push technology advertising, usually in the form of pop-up ads. Sometimes, the user will receive so many pop-up ads that the computer becomes unusable. The use of spyware is illegitimate because it is done without consent and therefore violates the right to privacy and confidentiality.

spyware
Software placed on a computer without consent or knowledge of the user.

Legislators are increasingly turning their attention to privacy issues in data collection. When children are involved, researchers have a special obligation to insure their safety. COPPA, the Children's Online Privacy Protection Act, was enacted into U.S. federal law on April 12, 2000. It defines a child as anyone under the age of 13. Anyone engaging in contact with a child through the Internet is obligated to obtain parental consent and notification before any personal information or identification can be provided by a child. Therefore, a researcher collecting a child's name, phone number, or e-mail address without parental consent is violating the law. While the law and ethics do not always correspond, in this case, it is probably pretty clear that a child's personal information shouldn't be collected. The Research Snapshot "Crazy Good! Have Fun, Play Games (and Buy Pop-Tarts)!" further explains how conducting research with children is ethically complex.

Deception in Research Designs and the Right to Be Informed

EXPERIMENTAL DESIGNS

Experimental manipulations often involve some degree of deception. In fact, without some deception, a researcher would never know if a research subject was responding to the actual manipulation or to their perception of the experimental variable. This is why researchers sometimes use a placebo.

A **placebo** is a false experimental effect used to create the perception of a true effect. Imagine two consumers, each participating in a study of the effect of a new herbal supplement on hypertension. One consumer receives a packet containing the citrus-flavored supplement, which is meant to be mixed in water and consumed with breakfast. The other also receives a packet, but in this case the packet contains a mixture that will simply color the water and provide a citrus flavor. The second consumer also believes he or she is drinking the actual supplement. In this way, the psychological effect is the same on both consumers, and any actual difference in hypertension must be due to the actual herbs contained in the supplement. Interestingly, experimental subjects often display some placebo effect in which the mere belief that some treatment has been applied causes some effect.

placebo
A false experimental effect used to create the perception that some effect has been administered.

This type of deception can be considered ethical. Primarily, researchers conducting an experiment must generally (1) gain the willful cooperation of the research subject and (2) fully explain the actual experimental variables applied following the experiment's completion. Every experiment should include a **debriefing** session in which research subjects are fully informed and provided a chance to ask any questions that they may have about the experiment.

debriefing
Research subjects are fully informed and provided with a chance to ask any questions they may have about the experiment.

Crazy Good! Have Fun, Play Games (and Buy Pop-Tarts)!

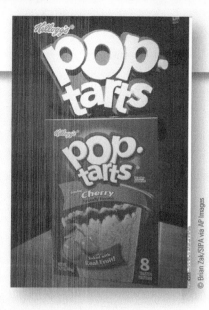

The online marketing of products and services to children has expanded exponentially. In the past, television was the primary advertising medium used to attract kids' interest. The idea behind marketing to children on television was simple. Children would see advertised food as fun, which would encourage them to get their parents to buy the product. Several studies examining the ethical aspects of television advertising to children have challenged whether this was an appropriate way to sell food.

With the advent of the Internet and electronic gaming, advertising food products to children through online websites has reached new levels of sophistication. For example, at PopTarts.com kids can enter PopTartsWorld.com and can play online games, enter the "store," and interactively create images and put their photo on a PopTarts box. Is this simply an online entertainment site, or something more?

Recent research indicates that these online sites contain "entertainment" that is also designed to communicate a careful message—and that children may not recognize that they are being exposed to a sophisticated marketing tool that seeks to influence them (and ultimately their parents) into buying food products. Some ethical challenges in particular are the direct inducement to buy product, and the challenges of privacy protection for children. Long term, the benefits and downsides of online entertainment and the marketing of products and services to children are only now being understood.

Source: Moore, E. S. and V. J. Rideout, "The Online Marketing of Food to Children: Is It Just Fun and Games?" *Journal of Public Policy & Marketing* 26, no. 2 (2007), 202–220. Reprinted by permission.

DESCRIPTIVE RESEARCH

Researchers sometimes will even withhold the actual research questions from respondents in simple descriptive research. A distinction can thus be made between deception and discreet silence. For instance, sometimes providing the actual research question to respondents is simply providing them more information than they need to give a valid response. A researcher may ask questions about the perceived price of a product when his or her real interest is in how consumers form quality impressions.

Protection from Harm

Researchers should do everything they can to make sure that research participants are not harmed by participating in research. Most types of research do not expose participants to any harm. However, the researcher should consider every possibility. For example, if the research involves tasting food or drink, the possibility exists that a research participant could have a severe allergic reaction. Similarly, researchers studying retail and workplace atmospherics often manipulate odors by injecting certain scents into the air.[11] The researcher is sometimes in a difficult situation. He or she has to somehow find out what things the subject is allergic to, without revealing the actual experimental conditions. One way this may be done is by asking the subjects to provide a list of potential allergies ostensibly as part of a separate research project.

Other times, research may involve some potential psychological harm. This may come in the form of stress or in the form of some experimental treatment that questions some strongly held conviction. For instance, a researcher studying helping behavior may lead a subject to believe that another person is being harmed in some way. In this way, the researcher can see how much a subject can withstand before doing something to help another person. In reality, the other person is usually a research confederate simply pretending to be in pain. Three key questions that can determine whether a research participant is being treated unethically as a result of experimental procedures are:

1. Has the research subject provided consent to participate in an experiment?
2. Is the research subject exposed to substantial physical or psychological trauma?
3. Can the research subject be easily returned to his or her initial state?

The issue of consent is tricky in experiments because the researcher cannot reveal exactly what the research is about ahead of time or the validity of the experiment will be threatened. In addition, experimental research subjects are usually provided some incentive to participate. We will have more on this in Chapter 12, but ethically speaking, the incentives should always be noncoercive. In other words, a faculty member seeking volunteers should not withhold a student's grade if he or she does not participate in an experiment. Thus, the volunteer should provide consent without fear of harm for saying no and with some idea about any potential risk involved.

If the answer to the second question is yes, then the research should not be conducted. If the answer to the second question is no and consent is obtained, then the manipulation does not present an ethical problem, and the researcher can proceed.

The third question is helpful in understanding how far one can go in applying manipulations to a research subject. If the answer to the third question is no, then the research should not be conducted. For example, researchers who seek to use hypnosis as a means of understanding preferences may be going too far in an effort to arrive at an answer. If the hypnotic state would cause the participant severe trauma, or if he or she cannot be easily returned to the prehypnotic state, then the research procedure should not be used. If, for instance, the consumer makes a large number of purchases under hypnosis, going deeply into debt, returning him or her to the original state may be difficult. If so, the application of hypnosis is probably inappropriate. If the answer to this question is yes, then the manipulation is ethical.

Many research companies and practically all universities now maintain a **human subjects review committee**. This is a committee that carefully reviews a proposed research design to try to make sure that no harm can come to any research participant. A side benefit of this committee is that it can also review the procedures to make sure no legal problems are created by implementing the particular design. This committee may go by some other name such as internal review board, but despite the name difference, the function remains to protect the company from doing harmful research.

human subjects review committee
Carefully reviews proposed research designs to try to make sure that no harm can come to any research participant.

Rights and Obligations of the Researcher

Research staff and research support firms should practice good business ethics. Researchers are often the focus of discussions of business ethics because of the necessity that they interact with the public. Several professional organizations have written and adopted codes of ethics for their researchers, including the American Marketing Association (AMA), the European Society for Opinion and Market Research (ESOMAR), the Marketing Research Society (MRS), and the Council of American Survey Research Organizations (CASRO). In reaction to the growing use of online surveying techniques, CASRO has provided guidelines for those conducting and participating in online research, presented in Exhibit 5.8.

In addition, the researchers have rights. In particular, once a research consulting firm is hired to conduct some research, they have the right to cooperation from the sponsoring client. In addition, the researchers have the right to be paid for the work they do as long as it is done professionally. Sometimes, the client may not like the results. But not liking the results is no basis for not paying. In addition, the client should pay the researcher in full and in a timely manner.

Research That Isn't Research

MIXING SALES OR FUND-RAISING WITH RESEARCH

Consumers sometimes agree to participate in an interview that is purported to be pure research, but it eventually becomes obvious that the interview is really a sales pitch in disguise. The research industry refers to this practice as **sugging**, meaning "selling under the guise of research." Closely related is the concept of **frugging**, or "fund-raising under the guise of research." These are unprofessional at best and fraudulent at worst. The Federal Trade Commission (FTC) has indicated that it is illegal to use any plan, scheme, or ruse that misrepresents the true status of a person seeking admission to a prospect's home, office, or other establishment. No research firm should engage in any sales or fund-raising attempts. Applied market researchers working for the sponsoring company should also avoid overtly mixing research and sales. However, the line is becoming less clear with increasing technology.

sugging
Selling under the guise of research.

frugging
Fund-raising under the guise of research.

EXHIBIT **5.8**
CASRO Online Survey Standards

Guidelines for Participating in Online Surveys
Use of the internet to conduct surveys has surged in recent years, and riding this trend are some dishonest or fraudulent research "pretenders." These "companies" make empty promises of "earning high income as a survey respondent," or worse, they may attempt to steal your money or your personal identity.

It is important to remember that the vast majority of online surveys are managed by legitimate companies and that your participation in these surveys is important—and they can also be a fun way to win prizes. The Council of American Survey Research Organizations (CASRO) offers the following guidelines to the public in an effort to help you recognize a legitimate and professional online survey and thereby avoid the potential risk to your money and your privacy from dishonest practitioners.

Legitimate Survey Research Companies Will:
1. Have contact information on their website, and a representative available to answer questions/concerns
2. Limit the number of surveys you can take
3. Ask participants to answer screening questions to see if they meet demographic requirements needed for their research sample

4. Value the time you take to complete a survey by offering modest incentives and "thank yous" such as sweepstakes entries, coupons or a nominal monetary reward. Remember, if the incentive seems too good to be true - it probably is.
5. Generally affiliate themselves with a trade group. (Most associations require members to meet certain ethical standards)
6. Have accessible terms and conditions and a privacy policy
7. Honor your request to discontinue sending e-mail invitations for surveys or to remove you from their online research panel

Legitimate Companies Won't:
1. Request credit card or bank account information or your Social Security number
2. Try to sell or promote a product
3. Request payment for anything
4. Try to recruit you with a one-question survey (e.g., "What's your favorite color?") in a pop-up ad or unsolicited e-mail
5. Contact or seek personal information from any child under the age of 13 without a parent's prior, verifiable consent

Source: http://www.casro.org/survandyou-guide.cfm, accessed April 30, 2011.

PSEUDO-RESEARCH

pseudo-research

Conducted not to gather information for marketing decisions but to bolster a point of view and satisfy other needs.

Consider the vignette that opened this chapter. Despite his best efforts, John is clearly feeling pressure to justify certain results obtained from his study. In fact, it is easy to see what is actually going on. The CEO really wants research that will justify and support a decision and investment that already has been made. If the customer perceptions contradict the decision, a manager will often disregard the research. This isn't really research so much as it is **pseudo-research** because it is conducted not to gather information for decisions but to bolster a point of view and satisfy other needs.

© Jose Luis Pelaez Inc./Getty Images

The most common type of pseudo-research is performed to justify a decision that has already been made or that management is already strongly committed to. A media company may wish to sell advertising space on Internet search sites. Even though they strongly believe that the ads will be worth the rates they will charge advertisers, they may not have the hard evidence to support this view. For example, an advertiser's sales force may provide feedback indicating customer resistance to moving their advertising from local radio to the Internet. The advertising company may then commission a study for which the only result they care to find is that the Internet ads will be effective. In this situation, a researcher should walk away from the project if it appears that management strongly desires the research to support a predetermined opinion only. While it is a fairly

© LeeCelano/Reuters/Landov

Is It Right, or Is It Wrong?

Sometimes, the application of research procedures to research participants can present significant ethical issues that cannot be easily dismissed by a single researcher alone. This is where a peer review process takes place. A human subjects research committee consists of a panel of researchers (and sometimes a legal authority) who carefully review the proposed procedures to identify any obvious or nonobvious ethical or legal issues. In fact, any research supported by U.S. federal funds must be subject to a peer review of this type. The peer review process for grants is described at this website: **http://grants.nih.gov/grants/peer/peer.htm**.

Most business research is innocuous and affords little opportunity for substantial physical or psychological trauma. However, companies involved in food marketing, dietary supplements or programs, and exercise physiology and pharmaceuticals, among others, do conduct consumer research with such possibilities. Academic researchers also sometimes conduct research with significant risks for participants. Consider research examining how some dietary supplement might make exercise more enjoyable, thus creating a better overall health and psychological effect. Clearly, a peer review by knowledgeable researchers is needed before proceeding with such research.

As it isn't possible to completely eliminate risk from research, a human subjects review is a good safety net. Deaths have been attributed to lack of or the breakdown of the human subjects review. Some of these have brought negative publicity to well-known universities including the University of Pennsylvania and Johns Hopkins University. At other times,

the risk to research participants is not obvious. For example, recently several researchers were interested in surveying through personal interviews victims of Hurricane Katrina. The results of the research may help public entities better serve victims, allow companies to respond with more appropriate goods and services, and help build psychological theory about how consumers make decisions under conditions of high personal trauma and stress. However, is it ethical to survey participants standing in the rubble of their home? Is it ethical to survey participants who are in the process of searching for or burying relatives that did not survive the disaster? Clearly, a thorough review of the procedures involved in such situations is called for.

Corporate human subjects committees are also becoming common. These reviews also consider the possibility of legal problems with experimental or survey procedures. In addition, as technology blurs the line between research and sales, they also should review the ethics of "research" that may somehow blend with sales. In addition, research conducted on animals also needs a critical review.

Sources: Glenn, David, "Lost (and Found) in the Flood," *Chronicle of Higher Education* 52 (October 7, 2005), A14–A19; Putney, S. B. and S. Gruskin, "Time, Place and Consciousness: Three Dimensions of Meaning for U.S. Institutional Review Boards," *American Journal of Public Health* 92 (July 2002), 1067–1071.

---

easy matter for an outside researcher to walk away from such a job, it is another matter for an in-house researcher to refuse such a job. Thus, avoiding pseudo-research is a right of the researcher but an obligation for the manager.

Occasionally, research is requested simply to pass blame for failure to another area. A human resource manager may request a research study with no intention of paying attention to the findings and recommendations. The manager may know that the new health care plan is not desirable, but plays the standard game to cover up for his or her mismanagement. If the project fails, marketing research will become the scapegoat. The ruse may involve a statement something like: "Well, research should have identified the problem earlier!"

Also, technology is making the line between research and sales less clear. It is very likely that research data collected by companies we transact with online could be used to push products toward us that we may truly like. This is the point of push technology. What makes this ethical or not ethical? With consent, it is clearly ethical. What other ethical challenges may be faced as the technology to collect consumer information continues to develop?

PUSH POLLS

Politicians concocted and specialize in a particular type of pseudo-research. A **push poll** is telemarketing under the guise of research intended to "sell" a particular political position or point of view. The purpose of the poll is to push consumers into a predetermined response. For instance, a polling organization calls thousands of potential voters inviting each to participate in a survey.

push poll

Telemarketing under the guise of research.

The interviewer then may ask loaded questions that put a certain spin on a candidate. "Do you think that candidate X, who is involved with people known to be linked to scandal and crime, can be trusted with the responsibility of office?" This is a push poll. An honest question may simply ask how much candidate X can be trusted.

Push polling doesn't always involve political candidates. Residents do not always welcome new Walmart locations based on factors including the impact on existing businesses and the increase in traffic and congestion that the store can bring to an area. In 2009, residents of Chicago received a polling call that went something like this:

> Mayor Daley says that the proposed Walmart would bring over 400 jobs to this area and allow neighborhood residents access to fresh food. Do you support the new Walmart store's construction?

The results indicated that over 70 percent of residents supported the new store.[12] However, the framing of the question by referencing the mayor and the mention of jobs, without mentioning potential problems, almost certainly swayed the results.

SERVICE MONITORING

Occasionally, the line between research and customer service isn't completely clear. For instance, Toyota may survey all of its new car owners after the first year of ownership. While the survey appears to be research, it may also provide information that could be used to correct some issue with the customer. For example, if the research shows that a customer is dissatisfied with the way the car handles, Toyota could follow up with the specific customer. The follow-up could result in changing the tires of the car, resulting in a smoother and quieter ride, as well as a more satisfied customer. Should a pattern develop showing other customers with the same opinion, Toyota may need to switch the original equipment tires used on this particular car.

In this case, both research and customer service is involved. Since the car is under warranty, there would be no selling attempt. Researchers are often asked to design satisfaction surveys. These may identify the customer so they may be contacted by the company. Such practice is acceptable as long as the researcher allows the consumer the option of either being contacted or not being contacted. In other words, the customer should be asked whether it is okay for someone to follow up in an effort to improve their satisfaction.

Selling under the guise of research, fund-raising under the guise of research, pseudo-research, and push polls are all misrepresentations of the true purpose of research and should be avoided. It is important that researchers understand the only accepted purpose of research is research.

Objectivity

The need for objective scientific investigation to ensure accuracy is stressed throughout this book. Researchers should maintain high standards to be certain that their data are accurate. Furthermore, they must not intentionally try to prove a particular point for political purposes.

Misrepresentation of Research

It should go without saying, but research results should not be misrepresented. This means, for instance, that the statistical accuracy of a test should be stated precisely and the meaning of findings should not be understated or overstated. Both the researcher and the client share this obligation. There are many ways that research results can be reported in a less than full and honest way. For example, a researcher may present results showing a relationship between advertising spending and sales. However, the researcher may also discover that this relationship disappears when the primary competitors' prices are taken into account. In other words, the relationship between advertising spending and sales is made spurious by the competitors' prices. Thus, it would be questionable to say the least to report a finding suggesting that sales could be increased by increasing ad spending without also mentioning the spurious nature of this finding.

HONESTY IN PRESENTING RESULTS

Misrepresentation can also occur in the way results are presented. For instance, charts can be created that make a very small difference appear very big. Likewise, they can be altered to make a meaningful difference seem small. Exhibit 5.9 illustrates this effect. Each chart presents exactly the same data. The data represent consumer responses to service quality ratings and satisfaction ratings. Both quality and satisfaction are collected on a five-point strongly-disagree-to-strongly-agree scale. In frame A, the chart appears to show meaningful differences between men and women, particularly for the service-quality rating. However, notice that the scale range is shown as 4 to 5. In frame B, the researcher presents the same data but shows the full scale range (1 to 5). Now, the differences are reported as trivial.

All charts and figures should reflect fully the relevant range of values reported by respondents. If the scale range is from 1 to 5, then the chart should reflect a 1 to 5 range unless there is some value that is simply not used by respondents. If no or only a very few respondents had reported a 1 for their service quality or satisfaction rating, then it may be appropriate to show the range as 2 to 5. However, if there is any doubt, the researcher should show the full scale range.

EXHIBIT **5.9**

How Results Can Be Misrepresented in a Report or Presentation

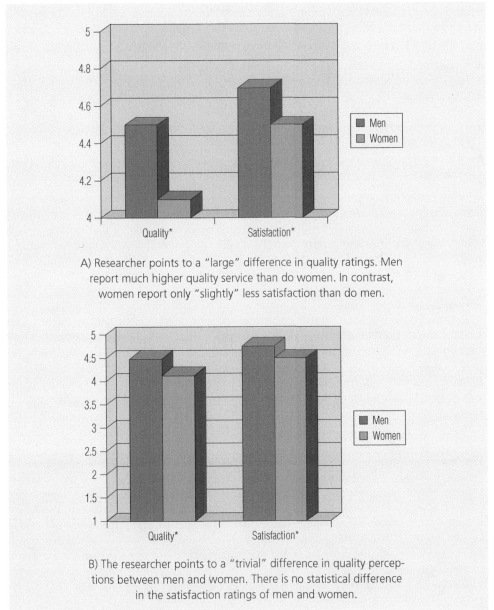

A) Researcher points to a "large" difference in quality ratings. Men report much higher quality service than do women. In contrast, women report only "slightly" less satisfaction than do men.

B) The researcher points to a "trivial" difference in quality perceptions between men and women. There is no statistical difference in the satisfaction ratings of men and women.

HONESTY IN REPORTING ERRORS

Likewise, any major error that has occurred during the course of the study should not be kept secret from management or the sponsor. Hiding errors or variations from the proper procedures tends to distort or shade the results. Similarly, every research design presents some limitations. For instance, the sample size may be smaller than ideal. The researcher should point out the key limitations in the research report and presentation. In this way, any factors that qualify the findings can be understood. The decision maker needs this information before deciding on any risky course of action.

Confidentiality

Confidentiality comes into play in several ways. The researcher often is obligated to protect the confidentiality of both the research sponsor and the research participant. In fact, business clients value researchers' confidentiality more than any other attribute of a research firm.[13] Imagine a researcher conducting a test-market for a new high-tech Apple iPod device that allows interactive video. Just after conducting the research, the same researcher is contacted by Samsung. Samsung, which has yet to develop video capability, wants research that addresses whether or not there is a market for iPod video of any type. The researcher is now in a difficult position. Certainly, an ethical dilemma exists presenting multiple choices to the researcher, including:

- Agreeing to do the research for Samsung and using some results from the Apple study to prepare a report and recommendation for Samsung
- Agreeing to sell the new concept to Samsung without doing any additional research. In other words, provide Apple's company secrets to Samsung
- Conducting an entirely new project for Samsung without revealing any of the results or ideas from the Apple study
- Turning down the chance to do the study without revealing any information about Apple to Samsung

Which is the best choice? Obviously, both of the first two options violate the principle of maintaining client confidentiality. Thus, both are unethical. The third choice, conducting an entirely new study, may be an option. However, it may prove nearly impossible to do the entire project as if the Apple study had never been done. Even with the best of intentions, the researcher may inadvertently violate confidentiality with Apple. The last choice is the best option from a moral standpoint. It avoids any potential **conflict of interest**. In other words, actions that would best serve one client, Samsung, would be detrimental to another client, Apple. Generally, it is best to avoid working for two direct competitors.

conflict of interest
Occurs when one researcher works for two competing companies.

Likewise, the researcher must also predict any confidentiality agreement with research participants. For instance, a researcher conducting a descriptive research survey may have identified each participant's e-mail address in the course of conducting the research. After seeing the results, the client may ask for the e-mail addresses as a logical prospect list. However, as long as the researcher assured each participant's confidentiality, the e-mail addresses cannot ethically be provided to the firm. Indeed, a commitment of confidentiality also helps build trust among survey respondents.[14]

Dissemination of Faulty Conclusions

"He uses statistics as a drunken man uses a lamppost—for support rather than illumination."

—ANDREW LANG

The American Marketing Association's marketing research Code of Ethics states that "a user of research shall not knowingly disseminate conclusions from a given research project or service that are inconsistent with or not warranted by the data." A dramatic example of a violation of this principle occurred in an advertisement of a cigarette smoker study. The advertisement compared two brands and stated that "of those expressing a preference, over 65 percent preferred" the advertised brand to a competing brand. The misleading portion of this reported result was that most of the respondents did not express a preference; they indicated that both brands tasted about the same. Thus, only a very small percentage of those studied actually revealed a preference, and the results were somewhat misleading. Such shading of results violates the obligation to report accurate findings.

Rights and Obligations of the Client Sponsor (User)

Ethical Behavior between Buyer and Seller

The general business ethics expected between a purchasing agent and a sales representative should hold in a marketing research situation. For example, if a purchasing agent has already decided to purchase a product from a friend, it would be unethical for that person to solicit competitive bids from others because they have no chance of being accepted. Similarly, a client seeking research should only seek bids from firms that have a legitimate chance of actually doing the work. In addition, any section on the ethical obligation of a research client would be remiss not to mention that the user is obligated to pay the provider the agreed upon wage and pay within the agreed upon time.

An Open Relationship with Research Suppliers

The client sponsor has the obligation to encourage the research supplier to objectively seek out the truth. To encourage this objectivity, a full and open statement of the decision situation, a full disclosure of constraints in time and money, and any other insights that assist the researcher should be provided. This means that the researcher will be provided adequate access to key decision makers. These decision makers should agree to openly and honestly discuss matters related to the situation. Finally, this means that the client is open to actually using the research results. Time is simply too valuable to ask a researcher to perform a project when the results will not be used.

An Open Relationship with Interested Parties

Conclusions should be based on data—not conjecture. Users should not knowingly disseminate conclusions from a research project in a manner that twists them into a position that cannot be supported by the data. Twisting the results in a self-serving manner or to support some political position poses serious ethical questions. A user may also be tempted to misrepresent results while trying to close a sale. Obviously, this is also morally inappropriate.

Advocacy research—research undertaken to support a specific claim in a legal action or to represent some advocacy group—puts a client in a unique situation. Researchers often conduct advocacy research in their role as an expert witness. For instance, a researcher may be deposed to present evidence showing that a "knock-off" brand diminishes the value of a better known name brand. In conventional research, attributes such as sample size, profile of people actually interviewed, and number of questions asked are weighed against cost in traditional research. However, a court's opinion on whether research results are reliable may be based exclusively on any one specific research aspect. Thus, the slightest variation from technically correct procedures may be magnified by an attorney until a standard research result or project no longer appears adequate in a judge's eyes. How open should the client be in the courtroom?

The ethics of advocacy research present a number of serious issues that can lead to an ethical dilemma:

- Attorneys' first responsibility is to represent their clients. Therefore, they might not be interested as much in the truth as they are in evidence that supports their client's position. Presenting accurate research results may harm the client.
- A researcher should be objective. However, he or she runs the risk of conducting research that does not support the desired position. In this case, the lawyer may ask the researcher if the results can somehow be interpreted in another manner.
- Should the attorney (in this case a user of research) ask the researcher to take the stand and present an inaccurate picture of the results?

Ethically, the attorney should certainly not put the researcher on the stand and encourage an act of perjury. The attorney may hope to ask specific questions that are so limited that taken alone, they may appear to support the client. However, this is risky because the opposing attorney likely also

advocacy research

Research undertaken to support a specific claim in a legal action or represent some advocacy group.

has an expert witness that can suggest questions for cross-examination. Returning to our branding example, if the research does not support an infringement of the known brand's name, then the brand name's attorney should probably not have the researcher take the stand.

Advocacy researchers do not necessarily bias results intentionally. However, attorneys rarely submit advocacy research evidence that does not support their clients' positions.

The question of advocacy research is one of objectivity: Can the researcher seek out the truth when the sponsoring client wishes to support its position at a trial? The ethical question stems from a conflict between legal ethics and research ethics. Although the courts have set judicial standards for research methodology, perhaps only the client and individual researcher can resolve this question.

Privacy

People believe the collection and distribution of personal information without their knowledge is a serious violation of their privacy. The privacy rights of research participants create a privacy obligation on the part of the research client. Suppose a database marketing company is offering a mailing list compiled by screening millions of households to obtain brand usage information. The information would be extremely valuable to your firm, but you suspect those individuals who filled out the information forms were misled into thinking they were participating in a survey. Would it be ethical to purchase the mailing list? If respondents have been deceived about the purpose of a survey and their names subsequently are sold as part of a user mailing list, this practice is certainly unethical. The client and the research supplier have the obligation to maintain respondents' privacy.

Consider another example. Sales managers know that a research survey of their business-to-business customers' buying intentions includes a means to attach a customer's name to each questionnaire. This confidential information could be of benefit to a sales representative calling on a specific customer. A client wishing to be ethical must resist the temptation to identify those accounts (that is, those respondents) that are the hottest prospects.

Privacy on the Internet

Privacy on the Internet is a controversial issue. A number of groups question whether website questionnaires, registration forms, and other means of collecting personal information will be kept confidential. Many business researchers argue that their organizations don't need to know who the user is because the individual's name is not important for their purposes. However, they do want to know certain information (such as demographic characteristics or product usage) associated with an anonymous profile. For instance, a web advertiser could reach a targeted audience without having access to identifying information. Of course, unethical companies may violate anonymity guidelines. Research shows that consumers are sensitive to confidentiality notices before providing information via a website. Over 80 percent of consumers report looking for specific privacy notices before they will exchange information electronically. In addition, over half believe that companies do not do enough to ensure the privacy of personal information.[15] Thus, research users should not disclose private information without permission from the consumers who provided that information.

A Final Note on Ethics

Certainly, there are researchers who would twist results for a client or who would fabricate results for personal gain. However, these are not professionals. When one is professional, one realizes that one's actions not only have implications for oneself but also for one's field. Indeed, just a few unscrupulous researchers can give the field a bad name. Thus, researchers should maintain the highest integrity in their work to protect our industry. Research participants should also play their role, or else the data they provide will not lead to better products for all consumers. Finally, the research users must also follow good professional ethics in their treatment of researchers and research results.

∷ SUMMARY

1. **Know when research should be conducted externally and when it should be done internally.** The company that needs the research is not always the best company to actually perform the research. Sometimes it is better to use an outside supplier of some form. An outside agency is better when a fresh perspective is needed, when it would be difficult for inside researchers to be objective, and when the outside firm has some special expertise. In contrast, it is better to do the research in-house when it needs to be done very quickly, when the project requires close collaboration of many employees within the company, when the budget for the project is limited, and when secrecy is a major concern. The decision to go outside or stay inside for research depends on these particular issues.

2. **Be familiar with the types of jobs, job responsibilities, and career paths available within the business research industry.** The business research function may be organized in any number of ways depending on a firm's size, business, and stage of research sophistication. Business research managers must remember they are managers, not just researchers.

Research offers many career opportunities. Entry-level jobs may involve simple tasks such as data entry or performing survey research. A research analyst may be the next step on the career path. This position may involve project design, preparation of proposals, data analysis, and interpretation. Whereas there are several intermediate positions that differ depending on whether one works for a small or large firm, the director of research is the chief information officer in charge of marketing information systems and other research projects. The director plans, executes, and controls the research function for the firm.

3. **Understand the often conflicting relationship between management and researchers.** Researchers and managers have different and often conflicting goals. Some of the key sources of conflict include money, time, intuition, and experience. Managers want to spend the least amount of money on research possible, have it done in the shortest period of time conceivable, and believe that intuition and experience are good substitutes for research. Researchers will exchange greater expense for more precision in the research, would like to take more time to be more certain of results, and are hesitant to rely on intuition and experience. Better communication is a key to reducing this conflict. One tool that can be useful is the implementation of cross-functional teams.

4. **Define ethics and understand how it applies to business research.** Business ethics is the application of morals to behavior related to the exchange environment. Generally, good ethics conforms to the notion of "right" and a lack of ethics conforms to the notion of "wrong." Those involved in research face numerous ethical dilemmas. Researchers serve clients or, put another way, the doers of research serve the users. It is often easy for a doer to compromise professional standards in an effort to please the user. After all, the user pays the bills. Given the large number of ethical dilemmas involved in research, ethics is highly applicable to business research.

5. **Know and appreciate the rights and obligations of a) research respondents—particularly children, b) business researchers, and c) research clients or sponsors.** Each party involved in research has certain rights and obligations. These are generally interdependent in the sense that one party's right often leads to an obligation for another party. While the rights and obligations of all three parties are important, the obligation of the researcher to protect research participants is particularly important. Experimental manipulations can sometimes expose subjects to some form of harm or involve them in a ruse. The researcher must be willing to fully inform the subjects of the true purpose of the research during a debriefing. The researcher must also avoid subjecting participants to undue physical or psychological trauma. In addition, it should be reasonably easy to return an experimental subject to his or her original, pre-experiment condition.

6. **Know how to avoid a conflict of interest in performing research.** A conflict of interest occurs when a researcher is faced with doing something to benefit one client at the expense of another client. One good way to avoid a conflict of interest is to avoid getting involved with multiple projects involving competing firms.

∴ KEY TERMS AND CONCEPTS

advocacy research, *99*

business ethics, *88*

confidentiality, *89*

conflict of interest, *98*

cross-functional teams, *84*

custom research, *86*

debriefing, *91*

do-not-call legislation, *90*

ethical dilemma, *88*

forecast analyst, *78*

frugging, *93*

human subjects review committee, *93*

idealism, *88*

in-house research, *74*

informed consent, *89*

manager of decision support systems, *78*

moral standards, *88*

outside agency, *74*

placebo, *91*

pseudo-research, *94*

push poll, *95*

relativism, *88*

research analyst, *78*

research assistants, *78*

research generalist, *83*

research suppliers, *85*

spyware, *91*

standardized research service, *85*

sugging, *93*

syndicated service, *85*

∴ QUESTIONS FOR REVIEW AND CRITICAL THINKING

1. What are the conditions that make in-house research preferable? What are the conditions that make outside research preferable?

2. Read a recent news article from the Wall Street Journal or other key source that deals with a new product introduction. Would you think it would be better for that firm to do research in-house or to use an outside agency? Explain.

3. What might the organizational structure of the research department be like for the following organizations?
   a. A large advertising agency
   b. A founder-owned company that operates a 20-unit restaurant chain
   c. Your university
   d. An industrial marketer with four product divisions
   e. A large consumer products company

4. What problems do research directors face in their roles as managers?

5. What are some of the basic causes of conflict between management and research?

6. Comment on the following situation: A product manager asks the research department to forecast costs for some basic ingredients (raw materials) for a new product. The researcher asserts that this is not a research job; it is a production forecast.

7. What is the difference between research and pseudo-research? Cite several examples of each.

8. ETHICS What are business ethics? How are ethics relevant to research?

9. ETHICS What is the difference between ethical relativism and ethical idealism? How might a person with an idealist ethical philosophy and a person with a relativist ethical philosophy differ with respect to including a sales pitch at the end of a research survey?

10. ETHICS What obligations does a researcher have with respect to confidentiality?

11. How should a researcher help top management better understand the functions and limitations of research?

12. ETHICS List at least one research obligation for research participants (respondents), researchers, and research clients (sponsors)?

13. ETHICS What is a conflict of interest in a research context? How can such conflicts of interest be avoided?

14. ETHICS What key questions help resolve the question of whether or not research participants serving as subjects in an experiment are treated ethically?

15. Identify a research supplier in your area and determine what syndicated services and other functions are available to clients.

16. 'NET Use the Internet to find at least five research firms that perform survey research. List and describe each firm briefly.

17. What actions might the business research industry take to convince the public that research is a legitimate activity and that firms that misrepresent their intentions and distort findings to achieve their aims are not true research companies?

18. ETHICS Comment on the ethics of the following situations:
   a. A food warehouse club advertises "savings up to 30 percent" after a survey showed a range of savings from 2 to 30 percent below average prices for selected items.
   b. A radio station broadcasts the following message during a syndicated rating service's rating period: "Please fill out your diary" (which lists what media the consumer has been watching or listening to).
   c. A furniture retailer advertises a market test and indicates that prices will be 50 percent off for three days only.
   d. A researcher tells a potential respondent that an interview will last 10 minutes rather than the 30 minutes he or she actually anticipates.
   e. A respondent tells an interviewer that she wishes to cooperate with the survey, but her time is valuable and, therefore, she expects to be paid for the interview.
   f. When you visit your favorite sports team's home page on the web, you are asked to fill out a registration questionnaire before you enter the site. The team then sells your information (team allegiance, age, address, and so on) to a company that markets sports memorabilia via catalogs and direct mail.

19. **ETHICS** Comment on the following interview:

Interviewer:	*Good afternoon, sir. My name is Mrs. Johnson, and I am with Counseling Services. We are conducting a survey concerning perceptions of Memorial Park Cemetery. Please answer the following questions with "yes" or "no."*
Respondent:	*(pauses)*
Interviewer:	*Are you familiar with Memorial Park?*
Respondent:	*Yes.*
Interviewer:	*Do you consider Memorial Park to be one of the best maintained cemeteries in this area?*
Respondent:	*Yes.*
Interviewer:	*You do own a funeral plot?*
Respondent:	*No.*
Interviewer:	*Would you mind if I sent you a letter concerning Memorial Park and the availability of funeral plots? Would you please give me your address?*

20. **ETHICS** Try to participate in a survey at a survey website such as **http://www.mysurvey.com** or **http://www.themsrgroup.com**. Write a short essay response about your experience with particular attention paid to how the sites have protections in place to prevent children from providing personal information.

:: RESEARCH ACTIVITIES

1. Find the mission statement of Burke, Inc. (**http://www.burke.com**). What career opportunities exist at Burke? Would you consider it a small, midsized, or large firm?
2. **'NET—ETHICS** One purpose of the United Kingdom's Market Research Society is to set and enforce the ethical standards to be observed by research practitioners. Go to its website at **www.mrs.org.uk**. Click on its code of conduct and evaluate it in light of the AMA's code.

CASE 5.1

Global Eating

Barton Boomer, director of marketing research for a large research firm, has a bachelor's degree in marketing from Michigan State University. He joined the firm nine years ago after a one-year stint as a research trainee at the corporate headquarters of a western packing corporation. Barton has a wife and two children. He earns $60,000 a year and owns a home in the suburbs. He is a typical research analyst. He is asked to interview an executive with a local restaurant chain, Eats-R-Wee. Eats-R-Wee is expanding internationally. The logical two choices for expansion are either to expand first to other nations that have values similar to those in the market area of Eats-R-Wee or to expand to the nearest geographical neighbor. During the initial interviews, Mr. Big, Vice President of Operations for Eats-R-Wee, makes several points to Barton.

- "Barton, we are all set to move across the border to Ontario and begin our international expansion with our neighbor to the north, Canada. Can you provide some research that will support this position?"

- "Barton, we are in a hurry. We can't sit on our hands for weeks waiting to make this decision. We need a comprehensive research project completed by the end of the month."
- "We are interested in how our competitors will react. Have you ever done research for them?"
- "Don't worry about the fee; we'll pay you top money for a 'good' report."

Marla Madam, Barton's Director of Research, encourages Barton to get back in touch with Mr. Big and tell him that the project will get underway right away.

Question

1. Critique this situation with respect to Barton's job. What recommendations would you have for him? Should the company get involved with the research? Explain your answers.

Big Brother Is Watching?

CASE 5.2

Technology is making our behavior more and more difficult to keep secret. Right at this very moment, there is probably some way that your location can be tracked in a way that researchers could use the information. Do you have your mobile phone with you? Is there an RFID tag in your shirt, your backpack, or some other personal item? Are you in your car, and does it have a GPS (Global Positioning Satellite) device? All of these are ways that your location and movements might be tracked.

For instance, rental cars can be tracked using GPS. Suppose a research firm contracts with an insurance firm to study the way people drive when using a rental car. A customer's every movement is then tracked. So, if the customer stops at a fast-food restaurant, the researcher knows. If the customer goes to the movie when he or she should be on a sales call, the researcher knows. If the customer is speeding, the researcher knows.

Clearly, modern technology is making confidentiality more and more difficult to maintain. While legitimate uses of this type of technology may assist in easing traffic patterns and providing better locations for service stations, shopping developments, and other retailers, at what point does the collection of such information become a concern? When would you become concerned about having your whereabouts constantly tracked?

Question

1. Suppose a GIS research firm is approached by the state legislature and asked to provide data about vehicle movement within the state for all cars with a satellite tracking mechanism. Based on the movement of the cars over a certain time, the police can decide when a car was speeding. They intend to use this data to send speeding tickets to those who moved too far, too fast. If you are the research firm, would you supply the data? Discuss the ethical implications of the decision.

Problem Definition
The Foundation of Business Research

LEARNING OUTCOMES

After studying this chapter, you should be able to

1. Explain why proper "problem definition" is essential to useful business research
2. Know how to recognize problems
3. Translate managerial decision statements into relevant research objectives
4. Translate research objectives into research questions and/or research hypotheses
5. Outline the components of a research proposal
6. Construct tables as part of a research proposal

Chapter Vignette:

Deland Trucking Has a "Recruitment" Problem

David Deland, who has owned his trucking business for 20 years, struggles with the spreadsheet in front of him. His recruitment specialist sits glumly across from his desk, pondering what kind of response to give to the inevitable question, "Why are our recruitment costs so high?" Next to the specialist sits James Garrett, a business research consultant who has been hired by the Deland Trucking Company to get a handle on the recruitment expenses the company has seen skyrocket over the last six months.

"I just don't get it," David sighs in frustration. "We have seen a 45 percent increase in our trucker recruitment advertising costs, and our driver intake and orientation expenses are killing us! James, I just don't understand what is happening here."

James and the specialist have had some initial discussions, but there is no easy way to reduce those costs without reducing the number of truckers that Deland hires. "Perhaps we can find a more efficient way of advertising our openings," suggests the recruiting specialist. "Maybe we can reduce the number of orientation sessions or travel expenses associated with the hiring process." David counters, "Well, I don't see how we are any different from our competitors. We use the same recruitment and orientation approach that they use. I have no handle on

their expenses, but the fact that our expenses are skyrocketing must mean something is going on."

James stares at his copy of the spreadsheet. "There is no easy way to do this, without hurting your ability to keep drivers in your trucks," he says. "Is it that the costs for driver selection and recruitment have gone up?" "No, the costs have been the same,"

© David Jones/iStockphoto

responds the recruiter. "It's just that we have had to do so many orientation and hiring sessions since the first of the year."

"David, it might be best if I get a look at some of your hiring statistics, as well as your driver census over the last year," comments James. Turning to the recruiter, James asks, "Can you give me some of your driver data to look through?"

"Sure," says the recruiter. "We have lots of info about our drivers, and the driver census is updated monthly. We even have some exit data we have gathered from a few drivers who have left us. I don't know exactly what the trend is with those drivers who leave, since we haven't had a chance to really analyze the data. I will send it to you through e-mail this afternoon."

James drives back to his office, reflecting on his meeting. As he passes by trucks on the way, he peeks at the drivers who are going in the same direction as he is. What do they think about their company? Would they see Deland as a great place to work? What would make Deland Trucking's recruitment costs go so high?

At his office, the e-mail with the trucker census and the hiring data has already arrived. Opening the numerous spreadsheets, James continues to wonder. Does Deland Trucking have a recruitment problem? Is it a training problem? Is retention too low? Is the problem the company itself? What is going on?

As he examines the hiring worksheet, he compares it to the driver census figures for the last six months. "There is the problem!" he exclaims. "I think I need to put together a proposal for David on this. I'm sure he will be surprised about what his company's problem really is."

Introduction

Importance of Starting with a Good Problem Definition

The first stage of the research process introduced in the early chapters and highlighted in Chapter 4 involves translating the business decision situation into specific research objectives. While it is tempting to skip this step and go directly to designing a research project, the chances that a research project will prove useful are directly related to how well the research objectives correspond to the true business "problem." Clearly, the easiest thing for James to do in the opening vignette is to start designing a study of Deland Trucking's recruitment effectiveness. This seems to be what David and his recruitment specialist want. But is it what they really need?

This chapter looks at this important step in the research process more closely. Some useful tools are described that can help translate the business situation into relevant, actionable research objectives. Research too often takes the blame for business failures when the real failure was really management's view of its own company's situation. The Research Snapshot "Good Answers, Bad Questions?" describes some classic illustrations involving companies as big and successful as Coca-Cola, R.J. Reynolds, and Ford. While the researcher certainly has some say in what is actually studied, we must remember that the client (either the firm's management team or an outside sponsor) is the research customer and the researcher is serving the client's needs. In other words, when the client fails to understand their situation or insists on studying an irrelevant problem, the research is very likely to fail, even if it is technically performed perfectly.

Translating a business situation into something that can be researched is somewhat like translating one language into another. It begins by coming to a consensus on a decision statement or question. A **decision statement** is a written expression of the key question(s) that a research user wishes to answer. It is the reason that research is being considered. It must be well stated and relevant. As discussed in Chapter 4, the researcher translates this into research terms by rephrasing the decision statement into one or more research objectives. These are expressed as deliverables in the research proposal. The researcher then further expresses these in precise and scientific research terminology by creating research hypotheses from the research objectives.

In this chapter, we use the term **problem definition**. Realize that sometimes this is really opportunity seeking rather than truly problem solving. Nonetheless, for simplicity, the term problem definition is adapted here to refer to the process of defining and developing a decision statement and the steps involved in translating it into more precise research terminology, including a set of research objectives. If this process breaks down at any point, the research will almost certainly be useless or even harmful. It will be useless if it presents results that simply are deemed irrelevant and do not assist in decision making. It can be harmful both because of the wasted resources and because it may misdirect the company in a poor direction.

decision statement

A written expression of the key question(s) that the research user wishes to answer.

problem definition

The process of defining and developing a decision statement and the steps involved in translating it into more precise research terminology, including a set of research objectives.

Review the survey you are using for this course. Consider the questions shown here and the other sections of the survey.

- Based on the survey you have completed, identify at least three decision statements that might have driven the construction of this questionnaire.
- Translate each of the decision statements from above into a research question and the related research hypothesis or hypotheses.
- What would a dummy table (see Exhibit 6.10) look like that would contain the data from the survey that addresses each of these hypotheses?
- What types of companies might be interested in this information?
- Would any nonprofit institutions be interested in this data?

Reflecting on your experience with your Business School (studies), how satisfied are you with each of the following aspects?

	Completely Dissatisfied	Dissatisfied	Somewhat Dissatisfied	Neutral	Somewhat Satisfied	Satisfied	Completely Satisfied
Overall Experience	☐	☐	☐	☐	☐	☐	☐
Teacher's Knowledge of Topics	☐	☐	☐	☐	☐	☐	☐
Schedule Times for your classes	☐	☐	☐	☐	☐	☐	☐
Your Test Scores	☐	☐	☐	☐	☐	☐	☐
Your Homework Load	☐	☐	☐	☐	☐	☐	☐
Class Discussion	☐	☐	☐	☐	☐	☐	☐
Instructor Enthusiasm	☐	☐	☐	☐	☐	☐	☐
Your Development as a Business Student	☐	☐	☐	☐	☐	☐	☐
Your Overall Academic Performance	☐	☐	☐	☐	☐	☐	☐

Close

Courtesy of Qualtrics.com

Ultimately, it is difficult to say that any one step in the research process is most important. However, formally defining the problem to be attacked by developing decision statements and translating them into actionable research objectives must be done well or the rest of the research process is misdirected. Even a good road map is useless unless you know where you are going! All of the roads can be correctly drawn, but they still don't get you where you want to be. Similarly, even the best research procedures will not overcome poor problem definition.

Problem Complexity

Simply put, the quality of business research is limited by the quality of the problem definition stage. While certainly critically important to the success of the project, this is far from the easiest stage of the research process. In fact, it can often be the most complex. Exhibit 6.1 helps to illustrate factors that influence how complex the process can be.

EXHIBIT 6.1

Defining Problems Can Be Difficult

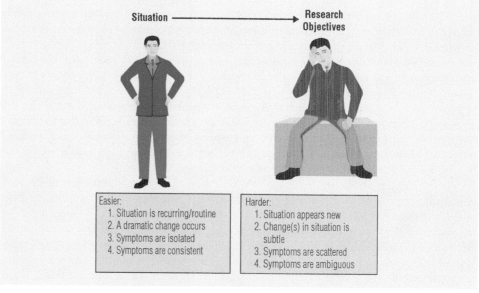

Situation → Research Objectives

Easier:
1. Situation is recurring/routine
2. A dramatic change occurs
3. Symptoms are isolated
4. Symptoms are consistent

Harder:
1. Situation appears new
2. Change(s) in situation is subtle
3. Symptoms are scattered
4. Symptoms are ambiguous

© Cengage Learning 2013

Good Answers, Bad Questions?

It's amazing, but sometimes even the most successful companies make huge research blunders. These mistakes often are based on a misunderstanding of exactly what the brand and/or product means to consumers. Some of the famous, or infamous, examples of such blunders include RJR's introduction of Premier "Smokeless" Cigarettes, Ford's introduction of the Edsel in the 1950s, and most famous (or infamous) of all, Coca-Cola's introduction of New Coke as a replacement for regular "old" Coke.

Volumes have been written about each of these episodes. One does have to wonder, how did these great companies do such apparently dumb things? The blame is often placed at the foot of the decision makers: "Research should have revealed that product was a loser." However, researchers address the questions they are asked to address by management. Certainly, the researchers play a role in framing any decision situation into something that can be addressed by a pointed research question. The decision makers almost always start the process by asking for input from their staff, or from research consultants they have hired. Hopefully, the dialogue that results will lead to a productive research question that will provide useful results. However it isn't always the case that such research questions are self-evident.

The "New Coke" saga is well worth repeating. In hindsight, it seems almost unthinkable that Coke could have made its decision to replace a product with a century-long success record without considering the emotional meaning that goes along with drinking a "Coke." However, management considered Coke to be a beverage, not a brand. Thus, the focus was on the taste of Coke. Thus, researchers set about trying to decide if New Coke, which was more similar to Pepsi, tasted better than the original Coke. A great deal of very careful research suggested clearly that it did taste better. If the key question was taste, New Coke was preferred over old Coke by more consumers. In fact, there was considerable evidence that already showed a taste preference for Pepsi over old Coke. Interestingly, Coke appeared to view itself as its primary competitor. At least two very important questions were never asked or were addressed insufficiently:

1. Do consumers prefer New Coke over Pepsi?
2. When people know what they are drinking, do they still prefer New Coke to old Coke?

For a taste test to be valid, it is should be done "blindly," meaning that the taster doesn't know what he or she is drinking.

Only then can one assess taste without being psychologically influenced by knowing the brand. So, Coke conducted a blind taste test. This is certainly

Does a name change always make sense? We must ask the correct research questions to be sure.

a good research practice—if the question is taste. The Coke research correctly answered the taste question. The big problem is that since management didn't realize that most of the meaning of Coke is psychological, and since they were so convinced that their old product was "inferior," the dialogue between management and researchers never produced more useful questions.

In the case of Ford's Edsel, a postmortem analysis suggests that research actually indicated many of the problems that ultimately led to its demise. The name, Edsel, was never tested by research, even though hundreds of other possibilities were.

Similarly, the idea of a smokeless cigarette seemed appealing. Research addressed the question, "What is the attitude of smokers and nonsmokers toward a smokeless cigarette?" Nonsmokers loved the idea. Smokers, particularly those who lived with a nonsmoker, also indicated a favorable attitude. However, as we know, the product failed miserably. If you take the "smoke" out of "smoking," is it still the same thing? This question was never asked. Would someone who would try a smokeless cigarette replace their old brand with this new brand? Again, this wasn't asked.

It is possible that some famous company could be making a very similar mistake today? Consider Macy's. Macy's has acquired many regional and local department stores around the country over the past few years. Clearly, Macy's is a very recognizable name brand that brings with it considerable "brand equity." How important is it for Macy's to ask, "What is the best name for this department store?" If the acquisition involves taking over a local retail "icon" such as Chicago's Marshall Field's, is a name change a good thing? These seem to be relevant questions to which research could probably provide good answers!

Sources: "New Coke: A 'Classic' Marketing Research Blunder?", http://imcetys.files.wordpress.com/2006/12/caso-newcoke.pdf, accessed May 8, 2011; "Is Macy's the New Coke?" Advertising Age 76 (September 26, 2005), 24, http://www.fieldsfanschicago.org/, accessed May 8, 2011.

Situation Frequency

Many business situations are cyclical, leading to recurring business problems. These problems can even become routine. In these cases, it is typically easy to define problems and identify the types of research that are needed. In some cases, problems are so routine that they can be solved without any additional research, such as when recurring problems can be automated through a company's decision support system (DSS).

For example, pricing problems often occur routinely. Just think about how the price of gas fluctuates when several stations are located within sight of each other. One station's prices definitely affect the sales of the other stations as well as of the station itself. Similarly, automobile companies, airline companies, and computer companies, to name just a few, face recurring pricing issues. Because these situations recur so frequently, addressing them becomes routine. Decision makers know how to communicate them to researchers and researchers know what data are needed.

Most pricing decisions in the airline industry are automated based on sophisticated demand models. The models take into account fluctuations in travel patterns based on the time of the year, time of the day, degree of competition for that particular route, and many other factors. At one time, these decisions were based on periodic research reports. Now, the information is simply fed into a decision support system that generates a pricing schedule. You can see how quickly information is analyzed and used for pricing decisions by simply checking prices for a specific flight online over the period of a few days. It is interesting that one factor that is not very important in many of these pricing decisions is the cost involved in flying someone from point A to point B. Indeed, some passengers pay a fare much higher than the actual costs and others pay a fare much lower than the actual costs involved in getting them to their desired destination.

Dramatic Changes

When a sudden change in the business situation takes place, it can be easier to define the problem. For example, if Deland Trucking's recruiting expenses had increased sharply at the beginning of the year, the key factors to study could be isolated by identifying other factors that changed in that same time period. It could be that a very large trucking contract had been obtained, a current customer dramatically increased their distribution needs, or a new competitor entered the market.

In contrast, when changes are very subtle and take effect over a long period of time, it can be more difficult to define the actual decision and research problems. Detecting trends that would permanently affect the recruitment challenges that Deland faces can be difficult. It may be difficult to detect the beginning of such a trend and even more difficult to know whether such a trend is relatively permanent or simply a temporary occurrence.

How Widespread Are the Symptoms?

The more scattered any symptoms are, the more difficult it is to put them together into some coherent problem statement. In contrast, firms may sometimes face situations in which multiple symptoms exist, but they are all pointing to some specific business area. For instance, an automobile manufacturing company may exhibit symptoms such as increased complaints about a car's fit and finish, increased warranty costs, higher labor costs, and lower performance ratings by consumer advocates such as Consumer Reports. All of these symptoms point to production as a likely problem area. This may lead to research questions that deal with supplier-manufacturer relationships, job performance, job satisfaction, supervisory support, and performance. Although having a lot of problems in one area may not sound very positive, it can be very helpful in pointing out the direction that is most in need of attention and improvement.

In contrast, when the problems are more widespread, it can be very difficult to develop useful research questions. If consumer complaints dealt with the handling and the appearance of the car, and these were accompanied by symptoms including consumer beliefs that gas mileage could be better and that dealerships did not have a pleasant environment, it may be more difficult to put these scattered symptoms together into one or a few related research questions. Later in the chapter, we'll discuss some tools for trying to analyze symptoms in an effort to find some potential common cause.

Symptom Ambiguity

Ambiguity is almost always unpleasant. People simply are uncomfortable with the uncertainty that comes with ambiguity. Similarly, an environmental scan of a business situation may lead to many symptoms, none of which seem to point in a clear and logical direction. In this case, the problem area remains vague and the alternative directions are difficult to ascertain.

A retail store may face a situation in which sales and traffic are up, but margins are down. They may have decreased employee turnover, but lower job satisfaction. In addition, there may be several issues that arise with their suppliers, none of which is clearly positive or negative. In this case, it may be very difficult to sort through the evidence and reach a definitive decision statement or list of research objectives.

The Problem-Definition Process

Problems Mean Gaps

A **problem** occurs when there is a difference between the current conditions and a more preferable set of conditions. In other words, a gap exists between the way things are now and a way that things could be better. The gap can come about in a number of ways:[1]

problem

Occurs when there is a difference between the current conditions and a more preferable set of conditions.

1. Business performance is worse than expected business performance. For instance, sales, profits, and margins could be below targets set by management. Or, employee turnover is higher than expected. This is a very typical type of problem analysis. Think of all the new products that fail to meet their targeted goals. Trend analysis would also be included in this type of problem. Management is constantly monitoring key performance variables. Previous performance usually provides a benchmark forming expectations. Sales, for example, are generally expected to increase a certain percentage each year. When sales fall below this expectation, or particularly when they fall below the previous year's sales, management usually recognizes that they have a potential problem on their hands. The Research Snapshot "Poor Questions Result in Poor Research in Japan!" illustrates this point.
2. Actual business performance is less than possible business performance. Realization of this gap first requires that management have some idea of what is possible. This may form a research problem in and of itself. Opportunity-seeking often falls into this type of problem-definition process. Many American and European Union companies have redefined what possible sales levels are based upon the expansion of free markets around the world. China's Civil Aviation Administration has relaxed requirements opening the Chinese air travel market to private airlines.[2] Suddenly, the possible market size for air travel has increased significantly, creating opportunities for growth.
3. Expected business performance is greater than possible business performance. Sometimes, management has unrealistic views of possible performance levels. One key problem with new product introductions involves identifying realistic possibilities for sales. While you may have heard the old adage that 90 percent of all new products fail, how many of the failures had a realistic sales ceiling? In other words, did the company know the possible size of the market? In this case, the problem is not with the product but with the plan. Some product "failures" may actually have been successful if management had a more accurate idea of the total market potential. Management can close this gap through decision making.

The Problem-Definition Process Steps

The problem-definition process involves several interrelated steps, as shown in Exhibit 6.2. Sometimes, the boundaries between each step aren't exactly clear. But generally, completing one step leads to the other and by the time the problem is defined, each of these steps has been addressed in some way. The steps are:

1. Understand the business situation—identify key symptoms
2. Identify key problem(s) from symptoms
3. Write managerial decision statement and corresponding research objectives
4. Determine the unit of analysis
5. Determine the relevant variables
6. Write research questions and/or research hypotheses

A separate section deals with each stage below.

Poor Questions Result in Poor Research in Japan!

French conglomerate BSN (Groupe Danone) is among the largest food manufacturers in the world. When the firm noted that the Japanese were becoming more Westernized, BSN decided to target Japan as a priority market for its yogurts. BSN knew better than to enter a new market without conducting marketing research, so they launched a market survey in Japan. The study reported that Japanese consumers were indeed becoming more Westernized in their food choices and eating habits and appeared to be offer a strong potential market for yogurts.

BSN rolled out their products in Japan, complete with extensive distribution and a well-financed promotional campaign. Sales, however, were disappointing, failing to meet company expectations.

After the fact, BSN conducted further research to understand what went wrong. The follow-up research indicated that the "Yes/No" questions asked were too simplistic to actually gather accurate responses. The Japanese consumers were simply too polite to reply "No" to a question. Furthermore, the respondents did not want to offend the researchers by criticizing advertisements featuring a spoon as an eating utensil. As a result the data was very misleading and presented an overly optimistic picture of the size, value, and potential of the Japanese market for yogurts.

Source: The Higher Education Academy: Teaching Resource Exchange, Hospitality, Leisure, Sport and Tourism Network, "Examples of Pitfalls and Mistakes," http://www.heacademy.ac.uk/assets/hlst/documents/heinfe_exchange/pitfalls.doc, accessed May 8, 2011.

EXHIBIT **6.2**
The Problem-Definition Process

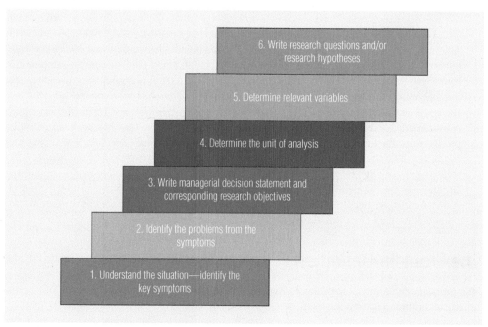

6. Write research questions and/or research hypotheses

5. Determine relevant variables

4. Determine the unit of analysis

3. Write managerial decision statement and corresponding research objectives

2. Identify the problems from the symptoms

1. Understand the situation—identify the key symptoms

© Cengage Learning 2013

Understand the Business Decision

situation analysis

The gathering of background information to familiarize researchers and managers with the decision-making environment.

A **situation analysis** involves the gathering of background information to familiarize researchers and managers with the decision-making environment. The situation analysis can be written up as a way of documenting the problem-definition process. Gaining an awareness of the relevant conditions and an appreciation of the situation often requires exploratory research. Researchers sometimes apply qualitative research as discussed in the next chapter with the objective of better problem definition. The situation analysis usually begins with an interview between the researcher and management.

Interview Process

The researcher must enter a dialogue with the key decision makers in an effort to fully understand the situation that has motivated a research effort. This process is critical and the researcher should be granted access to all individuals who have specific knowledge of or insight into this situation. Researchers working with managers who want the information "yesterday" often get little assistance when they ask, "What are your objectives for this study?" Nevertheless, even decision makers who have only a gut feeling that the research might be a good idea benefit greatly if they work with the researcher to articulate precise research objectives.[3] Even when there is strong cooperation, seldom can key decision makers express the situation in research terms:

> *Despite a popular misconception to the contrary, objectives are seldom clearly articulated and given to the researcher. The decision maker seldom formulates his objectives accurately. He is likely to state his objectives in the form of platitudes which have no operational significance. Consequently, objectives usually have to be extracted by the researcher. In so doing, the researcher may well be performing his most useful service to the decision maker.*[4]

Researchers may often be tempted to accept the first plausible problem statement offered by management. For instance, in the opening vignette, it is clear that David believes there is a recruitment problem. However, it is very important that the researcher not blindly accept a convenient problem definition for expediency's sake. In fact, research demonstrates that people who are better problem solvers generally reject problem definitions as given to them. Rather, they take information provided by others and reassociate it with other information in a creative way. This allows them to develop more innovative and more effective decision statements.[5]

There are many ways to discover problems and spot opportunities. Often there is as much art as science involved in translating scattered pieces of evidence about some business situation into relevant problem statements and then relevant research objectives. While there are other sources that address creative thinking in detail, some helpful hints that can be useful in the interview process include:

1. Develop several alternative problem statements. These can emerge from the interview material or from simply rephrasing decision statements and problem statements.
2. Think about potential solutions to the problem.[6] Ultimately, for the research to be actionable, some plausible solution must exist. After pairing decision statements with research objectives, think about the solutions that might result. This can help make sure any research that results is useful.
3. Make lists. Use free-association techniques to generate lists of ideas. At this stage of the research process, it is fair to say "the more ideas, the better." Use interrogative techniques to generate lists of potential questions that can be used in the interview process. **Interrogative techniques** simply involve asking multiple what, where, who, when, why, and how questions. They can also be used to provoke introspection, which can assist with problem definition.
4. Be open-minded. It is very important to consider all ideas as plausible in the beginning stages of problem solving. One sure way to stifle progress is to think only like those intimately involved in the business situation or only like those in other industries. Analogies can be useful in thinking more creatively.

interrogative techniques
Asking multiple what, where, who, when, why, and how questions.

Identifying Symptoms

Interviews with key decision makers also can be one of the best ways to identify key problem symptoms. Recall that all problems have symptoms just as human disease is diagnosed through symptoms. Once symptoms are identified, then the researcher must probe to identify possible

probing

An interview technique that tries to draw deeper and more elaborate explanations from the discussion.

causes of these changes. **Probing** is an interview technique that tries to draw progressively deeper and more elaborate explanations from the discussion. This discussion may involve potential problem causes. This probing process will likely be very helpful in identifying key variables that are prime candidates for study.

One of the most important questions the researcher can ask during these interviews is, "What has changed?" Then, the researcher should probe to identify potential causes of the change. At the risk of seeming repetitive, it is important that the researcher repeat this process to make sure that any important changes have not been left out.

In addition, the researcher should look for changes in company documents, including financial statements and operating reports. Changes may also be identified by tracking down news about competitors and customers. Exhibit 6.3 provides a summary of this approach.

EXHIBIT **6.3**
What Has Changed?

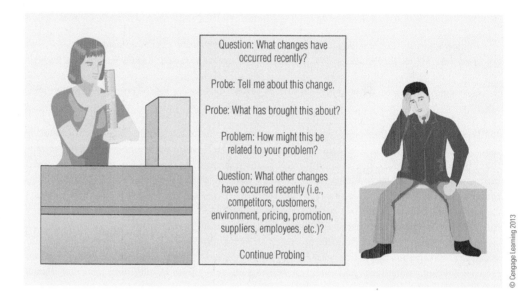

Think back to the opening vignette. Often, multiple interviews are necessary to identify all the key symptoms and gain a better understanding of the actual business situation. On a follow-up interview, the dialogue between James and David may proceed as follows:

James: *David, it is clear that your recruitment costs have been increasing since the start of the year. What other changes have occurred inside of your business within the past year?*

David: *Just a few things. We have had pressures on our bottom line, so we held back on raising the cents per mile that we give our drivers. Also, we have had to extend our long-haul trucking needs, so our drivers are on the road for a much longer period of time for each trip.*

James (probing): *Tell me, what led to this decision to extend the driver's time on the road?*

David: *It just worked out that way. Our contract just changed to allow us to do this, and our operations manager felt we could make more money per load this way.*

James: *Have you noticed changes in your customers?*

David: *We do see that they are a little irritated due to some of the problems of getting their freight delivered successfully.*

James: *Has there been a change in personnel?*

David: *Yes, we've had more than the usual share of turnover. I've turned over most personnel decisions to our new human resources manager. We've had trouble maintaining a person in that role.*

Opportunity Is a "Fleeting" Thing

Have non-European automotive companies missed out on European opportunities? Europe represents a nearly 14 million unit annual market for new automobiles. Traditionally, the thinking is that European's prefer smaller or "light-cars." Thus, European car companies like BMW and Audi were slow to enter the SUV market. Mercedes entered the SUV market rather early on, but the emphasis was on the American market. American and Japanese companies offered little more than a token effort at selling SUVs in Europe. Thus, the SUV wars were fought in America where total volume reached 4 million shortly after 2000. Europeans were left with fewer choices if an SUV struck their fancy.

As a result, pre-2000 SUV sales in Europe were almost non-existent. However, SUV sales in Europe have increased dramatically since then. By 2004, about 1 in 20 of all new autos sold in Europe. Today, Nissan, Toyota, Land Rover, and Suzuki are major players in the European SUV market. However, sales expectations for new entries from Opel, Renault, Volkswagen, Mercedes, and Audi are sluggish through 2008 with so many SUVs to choose from coupled with high fuel prices. In hindsight, could it be that several prominent automobile companies missed opportunities in Europe because they failed to know how big the market truly was?

Looking at this from the opposite direction, the tiny (by U.S. standards) two-seater SMART (http://www.smartusa.com) car has been introduced in the United States. SMART got off to a fast start in the United States, selling 24,622 cars in 2008. However sales fell to 5,927 units in 2010. SMART may now be poised to take advantage of an opportunity created by the current $4.00 a gallon gas prices. U.S. producers are also turning production away from large SUVs like HUMMER toward new entries like the Chevrolet Volt. The relative success of these new entries against European minis like the SMART may also depend on the exchange rate, which presently makes European entries expensive in the United States. Word is there may even be a SMART SUV—a miniature version of an American icon. What is the SMART future?

Sources: "The Business Week," *Business Week* (June 16, 2008), 6–10; Crain, K. C., "Analyst Sees Sales Decline for Light Vehicles in 2005," *Automotive News* 79 (January 24, 2005), 111; Meiners, Jena, "SUV Sales in Europe Will Peak in 2008," *Automotive News Europe* 9 (June 28, 2004); Marquand, R., "Euorpe's Little Smart Car to Hit U.S. Streets," *Christian Science Monitor* (2008), http://www.csmonitor.com/2008/0109/p01s01-woeu.html, accessed August 3, 2011; "Mercedes-Benz to Control Smart Car Distribution in the US - Penske Relieved of Duties," February 15, 2011, http://altenergyautos.blogspot.com/2011/02/mercedes-benz-to-control-smart-car.html, accessed May 8, 2011.

In the change interview, the researcher is trying to identify possible changes in the customers, the competitors, the internal conditions of the company, and the external environment. The interplay between things that have changed and things that have stayed the same can often lead to key research factors. Before preparing the proposal, James and David agree that the real decision faced is not as narrow as a recruiting problem. In this case, James is beginning to suspect that one key factor is that the increase in recruitment costs is a reflection of increased driver turnover. If driver retention could be increased, the need for larger recruitment expenses would stabilize, or even go down.

Almost any situation can be framed from a number of different perspectives. A pricing problem may be rephrased as a brand image problem. People expect high quality products to have higher prices. A quality problem may be rephrased as a packaging problem. For example, a potato chip company thought that a quality differential between their potatoes and their competitor's was the cause for the symptom showing sliding market share. However, one of the research questions that eventually resulted dealt with consumer preferences for packaging. In the end, research suggested that consumers prefer a foil package because it helps the chips stay fresher longer. Thus, the key gap turned out to be a package gap![7]

Researchers should make sure that they have uncovered all possible relevant symptoms and considered their potential causes. Perhaps more interview time with key decision makers asking why people choose Coke would have helped identify some of the less tangible aspects of the Coke-Pepsi-New Coke battle. Similarly, as seen in the Research Snapshot "Opportunity Is a 'Fleeting' Thing," the makers of automobiles in the United States should examine more carefully the possible ways that consumers make choices about the vehicles they buy. It can help avoid mistakes later.

Identifying the Relevant Issues from the Symptoms

"The real voyage of discovery consists not in seeking new landscapes, but in having new eyes."

—MARCEL PROUST

Anticipating the many influences and dimensions of a problem is impossible for any researcher or executive. The preceding interview is extremely useful in translating the decision situation into a working problem definition by focusing on symptoms. The probing process discussed on pages 113–115 begins this process. However, the researcher needs to be doubly certain that the research attacks real problems and not superficial symptoms.

For instance, when a firm has a problem with advertising effectiveness, the possible causes of this problem may be low brand awareness, the wrong brand image, use of the wrong media, or perhaps too small a budget. Certain occurrences that appear to be the problem may be only symptoms of a deeper problem. Exhibit 6.4 illustrates how symptoms can be translated into a problem and then a decision statement.

EXHIBIT 6.4
Symptoms Can Be Confusing

	Firm's Situation	Symptoms	Likely Problem (s)	Decision Statement
Research Action	Conduct situation analysis including interviews with key decision makers	Consider results of probing and apply creative processes	Express in actionable terms and make sure decision makers are in agreement
Situation 1	22-year-old neighborhood swimming association seeks research help	• Declining membership for six years • Increased attendance at new water park • Less frequent usage among members	Swim facility is outdated and does not appeal to younger families. Younger families and children have a negative image of pool. Their "old market" is aging.	What things can be done to energize new markets and create a more favorable attitude toward the association?
Situation 2	Manufacturer of palm-sized computer with wireless Internet access believes B2B sales are too low	• Distributors complain prices are too high • Business users still use larger computers for displaying information to customers or smartphones for other purposes	Business users do not see the advantages of smaller units. The advantages are not outweighed by costs. The transition costs may be a drawback for B2B customers more than for B2C customers	What things can be done to improve competitive positioning of the new product in B2B markets?
Situation 3	A new microbrewery is trying to establish itself	• Consumers seem to prefer national brands over the local microbrew products • Many customers order national brands within the microbrew itself • Some customers hesitant to try new microbrew flavors	Is there a negative flavor gap? Do consumers appreciate the microbrew approach and the full beer tasting (as opposed to drinking) experience?	How can we encourage more consumers to come to the microbrew and try our products? Should we redesign the brewery to be more inviting?

© Cengage Learning 2013

Writing Managerial Decision Statements and Corresponding Research Objectives

The situation analysis ends once researchers have a clear idea of the managerial objectives from the research effort. Decision statements capture these objectives in a way that invites multiple solutions. Multiple solutions are encouraged by using plural nouns to describe solutions. In other words, a decision statement that says in what "ways" a problem can be solved is better than one that says in what "way" a problem can be solved. Ultimately, research may provide evidence showing results of several ways a problem can be attacked.

Decision statements must be translated into research objectives. At this point, the researcher is starting to visualize what will need to be measured and what type of study will be needed. Exhibit 6.5 extends the examples from Exhibit 6.4, showing research objectives that correspond to each decision statement. Note that each research objective states a corresponding potential result(s) of the research project. Thus, in some ways, it is stating the information that is needed to help make the decision. Once the decision statement is written, the research essentially answers the question, "What information is needed to address this situation?"

EXHIBIT **6.5**
Translating Decision Statements

	Decision Statement	Research Objectives	Research Questions	Research Hypotheses
Research Action	Express in actionable terms and make sure decision makers are in agreement	Expresses potential research results that should aid decision-making	Ask a question that corresponds to each research objective	Specific statement explaining relationships, usually involving two variables, and including the direction of the relationship
Situation 1	What things can be done to energize new markets and create a more favorable attitude toward the association?	Determine reasons why families may choose to join or not join a "swim club."	How do the type of facilities and pricing relate to family attitudes toward a swim facility?	Child-friendly *pool designs* are positively related to *attitudes toward the facility.* Flexible *pricing policies* are positively related to *attitudes toward the facility.*
Situation 2	What product features can be improved and emphasized to improve competitive positioning of the new product in B2B markets?	List actions that may overcome the objections (switching costs) of B2B customers toward adoption of the new product.	What are the factors that most lead to perceptions of high switching costs?	*Perceived difficulty* in learning how to use the new device is related to *switching costs.* *Price* is positively related to *switching costs.* *Knowledge* of new product is positively related to *switching costs.*
Situation 3	How can we encourage more consumers to come to the microbrew and try our products? Should we redesign the brewery to be more inviting?	Describe how situational factors influence beer consumption and consumer attitudes toward beer products. List factors that will improve attitudes toward the microbrewery.	Do situational factors (such as time of day, food pairings, or environmental factors) relate to taste perceptions of beer?	Microbrew beer is *preferred* when consumed *with food.* An exciting *atmosphere* will improve consumer *attitudes toward the microbrew.*

© Cengage Learning 2013

Referring back to the opening vignette, the analysis of the symptoms has led to the conclusion that there is an employee retention problem. Perhaps drivers are dissatisfied with being away from their families for so long and this is leading to higher levels of driver turnover. Or, perhaps it is the cents per mile that is leading to driver frustration and a desire to go to a higher-paying competitor. David and James eventually agree on the following decision statement:

In what ways can Deland Trucking build driver loyalty so that retention increases and subsequent recruitment costs decrease?

What information or data will be needed to help answer this question? Obviously, we'll need to study the driver census and the number of hires needed to fill open positions. James needs to find out what might cause employee dissatisfaction and cause turnover to increase. Thinking back to the interview, James knows that there have been several changes in the company itself, many related to saving costs. Saving costs sounds like a good idea; however, if it harms driver loyalty even slightly, it probably isn't worthwhile. Thus, the corresponding research objectives are stated as follows:

- Determine what key variables relate to driver loyalty within the company, meaning (1) how does the lower level of pay impact driver retention and (2) what does the increase in long-haul trucking do to Deland Trucking's ability to increase retention?
- Assess the impact of different intervention strategies on driver satisfaction.

These research objectives are the deliverables of the research project. A research study will be conducted that (1) shows how much each of several key variables relates to loyalty and retention and (2) provides a description of likelihood of different intervention strategies on driver satisfaction.

The researcher should reach a consensus agreement with the decision maker regarding the overall decision statement(s) and research objectives. If the decision maker agrees that the statement captures the situation well and understands how the research objectives, if accomplished, will help address the situation, then the researcher can proceed. The researcher should make every effort to ensure that the decision maker understands what a research project can deliver. If there is no agreement on the decision statement or research objectives, more dialogue between decision makers and researchers is needed.

Determine the Unit of Analysis

unit of analysis

A study indicates what or who should provide the data and at what level of aggregation.

The **unit of analysis** for a study indicates what or who should provide the data and at what level of aggregation. Researchers specify whether an investigation will collect data about individuals (such as customers, employees, and owners), households (families, extended families, and so forth), organizations (businesses and business units), departments (sales, finance, and so forth), geographical areas, or objects (products, advertisements, and so forth). For example, for clothing purchases, individuals are likely to be the appropriate level of analysis. In studies of home buying, however, the husband/wife dyad typically is the best unit of analysis since this purchase decision would be made jointly by husband and wife.

Researchers who think carefully and creatively about situations often discover that a problem can be investigated at more than one level of analysis. For example, a lack of worker productivity could be due to problems that face individual employees or it could reflect problems that are present in entire business units. Determining the unit of analysis should not be overlooked during the problem-definition stage of the research.

Determine Relevant Variables

What Is A Variable?

variable

Anything that varies or changes from one instance to another; can exhibit differences in value, usually in magnitude or strength, or in direction.

constant

Something that does not change; is not useful in addressing research questions.

What things should be studied to address a decision statement? Researchers answer this question by identifying key variables. A **variable** is anything that varies or changes from one instance to another. Variables can exhibit differences in value, usually in magnitude or strength, or in direction. In research, a variable is either observed or manipulated, in which case it is an experimental variable.

The converse of a variable is a **constant**. A constant is something that does not change. Constants are not useful in addressing research questions. Since constants don't change, management isn't very interested in hearing the key to the problem is something that won't or can't be changed. In causal research, it can be important to make sure that some potential variable is actually held constant while studying the cause and effect between two other variables. In this way, a spurious relationship can be ruled out. This issue is discussed in detail in Chapter 12. At this point, the notion of a constant is more important in helping to understand how it differs from a variable.

Types of Variables

There are several key terms that help describe types of variables. The variance in variables is captured either with numerical differences or by an identified category membership. In addition, different terms describe whether a variable is a potential cause or an effect.

A **continuous variable** is one that can take on a range of values that correspond to some quantitative amount. Consumer attitude toward different airlines is a variable that would generally be captured by numbers, with higher numbers indicating a more positive attitude than lower numbers. Each attribute of airlines' services, such as safety, seat comfort, and baggage handling can be numerically scored in this way. Sales volume, profits, and margin are common business metrics that represent continuous variables.

A **categorical variable** is one that indicates membership in some group. The term **classificatory variable** is sometimes also used and is generally interchangeable with categorical variable. Categorical variables sometimes represent quantities that take on only a small number of values (one, two, or three). However, categorical variables more often simply identify membership.

For example, people can be categorized as either male or female. A variable representing biological sex describes this important difference. The variable values can be an "M" for membership in the male category and an "F" for membership in the female category. Alternatively, the researcher could assign a 0 for men and a 1 for women. In either case, the same information is represented.

A common categorical variable in consumer research is adoption, meaning the consumer either did or did not purchase a new product. Thus, the two groups, purchase or not purchase, comprise the variable. Similarly, turnover, or whether an employee has quit or not, is a common organizational variable.

In descriptive and causal research, the terms dependent variable and independent variable describe different variable types. This distinction becomes very important in understanding how business processes can be modeled by a researcher. The distinction must be clear before one can correctly apply certain statistical procedures like multiple regression analysis. In some cases, however, such as when only one variable is involved in a hypothesis, the researcher need not make this distinction.

A **dependent variable** is a process outcome or a variable that is predicted and/or explained by other variables. An **independent variable** is a variable that is expected to influence the dependent variable in some way. Such variables are independent in the sense that they are determined outside of the process being studied. That is another way of saying that dependent variables do not change independent variables.

For example, average customer loyalty may be a dependent variable that is influenced or predicted by an independent variable such as perceptions of restaurant food quality, service quality, and customer satisfaction. Thus, a process is described by which several variables together help create and explain how much customer loyalty exists. In other words, if we know how a customer rates the food quality, service quality, and satisfaction with a restaurant, then we can predict that customer's loyalty toward that restaurant. Note that this does not mean that we can predict food quality or service quality with customer loyalty.

Dependent variables are conventionally represented by the letter Y. Independent variables are conventionally represented by the letter X. If research involves two dependent variables and two or more independent variables, subscripts may also be used to indicate Y_1, Y_2 and X_1, X_2, and so on.

Ultimately, theory is critical in building processes that include both independent and dependent variables (see Chapter 4). Managers and researchers must be careful to identify relevant and actionable variables. Relevant means that a change in the variable matters and actionable means that a variable can be controlled by managerial action. Superfluous variables are those that are neither relevant nor actionable and should not be included in a study. Theory should help distinguish relevant from superfluous variables.

continuous variable

A variable that can take on a range of values that correspond to some quantitative amount.

categorical variable

A variable that indicates membership in some group.

classificatory variable

Another term for a categorical variable because it classifies units into categories.

dependent variable

A process outcome or a variable that is predicted and/or explained by other variables.

independent variable

A variable that is expected to influence the dependent variable in some way.

● ● ● ● ● ● ●

Several variables describe child consumers. Their biological sex is a categorical variable; their age or how often they go out to the mall are continuous variables.

The process of identifying the relevant variables overlaps with the process of determining the research objectives. Typically, each research objective will mention a variable or variables to be measured or analyzed. As the translation process proceeds through research objectives, research questions, and research hypotheses, it is usually possible to emphasize the variables that should be included in a study (as in Exhibit 6.5 and Exhibit 6.6).

EXHIBIT **6.6**

Example Business Decision Situations, Corresponding Research Hypotheses, and Variable Descriptions Example Business Decision Situations, Corresponding Research

Managerial Decision	Research Question(s)	Research Hypotheses	Categorical Variable(s)	Continuous Variable(s)
Retail grocer considering web-based delivery service	Is there sufficient demand? How much should delivery personnel be paid? Will delivery service (new retail form) cannibalize current business?	*Projected sales volume* will exceed $5 million annually. *Delivery personnel* can be paid less than cashiers and achieve the same *job satisfaction*. Web customers express lower *intentions to visit store* than other customers.	Type of employee (delivery, cashier, etc.) Retail form (independent variable): classifies respondents based on whether they shopped (1) in store or (2) via the web (delivery)	Sales volume: dollar amount based on a test trial in one geographic market (i.e., Phoenix/ Scottsdale) Hourly wages and satisfaction with pay Intentions to visit store (dependent variable): the percentage likelihood that a survey respondent would visit the store within the next seven days.
What market segments should be served?	Does nationality matter? Will French and German consumers express interest in our product? Does the attitude toward Korean companies influence purchase intentions?	*French* consumers have more *interest* in purchasing our *product* than *German* consumers. *Attitude toward Korean companies* is related positively to *product purchase interest*.	Nationality (independent variable): represents which country a survey respondent lives in: (1) France (2) Germany	Attitude toward Korean companies (independent variable): ratings scale that describes how favorably survey respondents view Korean companies (quality, reputation, value—higher scores mean better attitude) Product purchase interest: ratings scale that shows how interested a consumer is in buying the Korean product (higher scores = more interest)

© Cengage Learning 2013

Exhibit 6.6 includes some common business research hypotheses and a description of the key variables involved in each. In the first case, a regional grocery chain is considering offering a delivery service that would allow consumers to purchase groceries via the store website. They have conducted a trial of this in one market and have conducted a survey in that area. In the second case, a Korean automobile company is considering offering one of its models for sale in Europe. The company has also conducted a survey in two key European auto markets.

Write Research Objectives and Questions

Both managers and researchers expect problem-definition efforts to result in statements of research questions and research objectives. At the end of the problem-definition stage, the researcher should prepare a written statement that clarifies any ambiguity about what the research hopes to accomplish. This completes the translation process.

research questions

Express the research objectives in terms of questions that can be addressed by research.

Research questions express the research objectives in terms of questions that can be addressed by research. For example, one of the key research questions involved in the opening vignette is "Are wages and long-haul distance related to driver loyalty and retention?" Hypotheses are more specific than research questions. One key distinction between research questions and hypotheses is that hypotheses can generally specify the direction of a relationship. In other words, when an

Pricing Turbulence

A heavy equipment distributor sought out research because it believed there was an opportunity to increase revenues by raising prices. After several weeks of discussion, interviews, and proposal reviews, they settled on a decision statement that asked, "In what ways could revenues be increased by altering pricing policies across customers?" A research project was conducted that offered the following deliverables: (1) demonstrate how much customer characteristics and environmental characteristics influence price elasticity and (2) identify market segments based on price elasticity. This led to several hypotheses including the following:

H1: The desired delivery time for equipment is negatively related to price sensitivity.
H2: The degree of market turbulence is negatively related to price sensitivity.

In addition, a research question specifically addressing market segments was asked:

RQ1: Are there market segments that can be identified based on customers' desired benefits or environmental characteristics?

In other words, the more critical a piece of heavy equipment is to a company, the less concerned they are with the price. Similarly, customers are less concerned with price in markets that are more turbulent, meaning there are ever-changing environmental, competitive, and political pressures.

A study of heavy equipment purchasers around the world supported both hypotheses. For business segments where delivery time is of critical importance, higher prices can be charged without the fear of losing business. Similarly, in turbulent international markets, customers have other important concerns that make them less sensitive to equipment price and more sensitive to reliability and service. In the end, the heavy equipment company was able to build customer characteristics data into a DSS system that automated prices.

Interestingly, management did not express any concerns about either market segments or market turbulence in the initial interviews. Thus, this research succeeded because good research objectives, questions, and hypotheses were developed before any study was implemented.

Sources: Smith, M. F., I. Sinha, R. Lancianai, and H. Forman, "Role of Market Turbulence in Shaping Pricing," *Industrial Marketing Management* 28 (November 1999), 637–649; Peters, G., "Combating Too Much Information," *Industrial Distribution* 94 (December 2005), 22.

independent variable goes up, we have sufficient knowledge to predict that the dependent variable should also go up (or down as the case may be). One key research hypothesis for Deland Trucking is:

Higher cents per mile are related positively to driver loyalty.

At times, a researcher may suspect that two variables are related but have insufficient theoretical rationale to support the relationship as positive or negative. In this case, hypotheses cannot be offered. At times in research, particularly in exploratory research, a proposal can only offer research questions. Research hypotheses are much more specific and therefore require considerably more theoretical support. In addition, research questions are interrogative, whereas research hypotheses are declarative.

> *"I don't know the key to success, but the key to failure is trying to please everybody."*
>
> —BILL COSBY

Clarity in Research Questions and Hypotheses

Research questions make it easier to understand what is perplexing managers and to indicate what issues have to be resolved. A research question is the researcher's translation of the marketing problem into a specific inquiry.

A research question can be too vague and general, such as "Is advertising copy 1 better than advertising copy 2?" Advertising effectiveness can be variously measured by sales, recall of sales message, brand awareness, intention to buy, recognition, or knowledge, to name a few possibilities. Asking a more specific research question (such as, "Which advertisement has a higher day-after recall score?") helps the researcher design a study that will produce useful results, as seen in the Research Snapshot "Pricing Turbulence." Research question answers should provide input that can be used as a standard for selecting from among alternative solutions. Problem definition seeks to state research questions clearly and to develop well-formulated, specific hypotheses.

A sales manager may hypothesize that salespeople who show the highest job satisfaction will be the most productive. An advertising manager may believe that if consumers' attitudes toward a product are changed in a positive direction, consumption of the product also will increase. Hypotheses are statements that can be empirically tested.

A formal hypothesis has considerable practical value in planning and designing research. It forces researchers to be clear about what they expect to find through the study, and it raises crucial questions about data required. When evaluating a hypothesis, researchers should ensure that the information collected will be useful in decision making. Notice how the following hypotheses express expected relationships between variables:

■ There is a positive relationship between the presence of *younger children* in the home and *buying on the Internet*.
■ Regions that receive less *advertising support* will report *lower sales* for salespeople.
■ Consumers will experience *cognitive dissonance* after the decision to *purchase* a 3D television.
■ *Opinion leaders* are more affected by mass media communication *sources* than are nonleaders.
■ Among nonexporters, the degree of *perceived importance* of overcoming barriers to exporting is related positively to *general interest* in exporting (export intentions).[8]

Management is often faced with a "go/no go" decision. In such cases, a research question or hypothesis may be expressed in terms of a meaningful barrier that represents the turning point in such a decision. In this case, the research involves a **managerial action standard** that specifies a specific performance criterion upon which a decision can be based. If the criterion to be measured (for example, sales or attitude changes) turns out to be higher than some predetermined level, management will do A; if it is lower, management will do B.[9] In Exhibit 6.6, the specified sales volume of $5 million represents a managerial action standard for the retail grocery chain.

Research objectives also should be limited to a manageable number. Fewer study objectives make it easier to ensure that each will be addressed fully. It becomes easy to lose focus with too many research objectives.

Exhibit 6.7 summarizes how a decision statement (corresponding to a business research problem) leads to research objectives that become a basis for the research design. Once the research has been conducted, the results may show an unanticipated aspect of the problem and suggest a need for additional research to satisfy the main objective. Accomplished researchers who have had the experience of uncovering additional aspects of a particular research problem after finishing fieldwork recommend designing studies that include questions designed to reveal the unexpected.

managerial action standard

A specific performance criterion upon which a decision can be based.

EXHIBIT 6.7

Influence of Decision Statement of Marketing Problem on Research Objectives and Research Designs

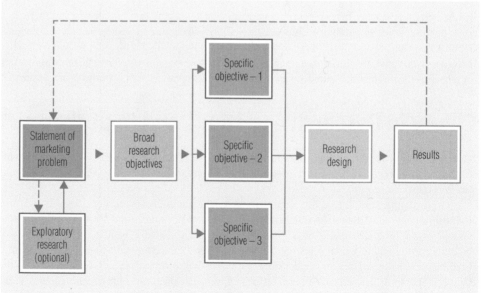

© Cengage Learning 2013

CHAPTER 6   Problem Definition: The Foundation of Business Research   ●   123

How Much Time Should Be Spent on Problem Definition?

Like almost every other decision in business research, budget constraints usually influence how much effort is spent on problem definition. Business situations can be complex and numerous variables may be relevant. Searching for every conceivable cause and minor influence is impractical. The more important the decision faced by management, the more resources should be allocated toward problem definition. While not a guarantee, allowing more time and spending more money will help make sure the research objectives that result are relevant and can demonstrate which influences management should focus on.

Managers, being responsible for decision making, may wish the problem-definition process to proceed quickly. Researchers who take a long time to produce a set of research objectives can frustrate managers. However, the time taken to identify the correct problem is usually time well spent.

The Research Proposal

The **research proposal** is a written statement of the research design. It always includes a statement explaining the purpose of the study (in the form of research objectives or deliverables) and a definition of the problem, often in the form of a decision statement. A good proposal systematically outlines the particular research methodology and details procedures that will be used during each stage of the research process. Normally a schedule of costs and deadlines is included in the research proposal. The research proposal becomes the primary communication document between the researcher and the research user.

Exhibit 6.8 illustrates an abbreviated proposal for a short research project conducted for the Internal Revenue Service (IRS) that explores public attitudes toward a variety of tax-related issues.

research proposal

A written statement of the research design.

The Proposal As a Planning Tool

Preparation of a research proposal forces the researcher to think critically about each stage of the research process. Vague plans, abstract ideas, and sweeping generalizations about problems or procedures must become concrete and precise statements about specific events. Data requirements and research procedures must be specified clearly so others may understand their exact implications. All ambiguities about why and how the research will be conducted must be clarified before the proposal is complete.

The researcher submits the proposal to management for acceptance, modification, or rejection. Research clients (management) evaluate the proposed study with particular emphasis on whether or not it will provide useful information, and whether it will do so within a reasonable resource budget. Initial proposals are almost always revised after the first review.

The proposal helps managers decide if the proper information will be obtained and if the proposed research will accomplish what is desired. If the problem has not been adequately translated into a set of specific research objectives and a research design, the client's assessment of the proposal will help ensure that the researchers revise it to meet the client's information needs.

An effective proposal communicates exactly what information will be obtained, where it will be obtained, and how it will be obtained. For this reason, it must be explicit about sample selection, measurement, fieldwork, and data analysis. For instance, most proposals involving descriptive research include a proposed questionnaire (or at least some sample questions).

The format for a research proposal follows the stages in the research process outlined in Chapter 4. At each stage, one or more questions must be answered before the researcher can select one of the various alternatives. For example, before a proposal can be completed, the researcher needs to know what is to be measured. A simple statement like "market share" may not be enough;

EXHIBIT 6.8

An Abbreviated Version of a Research Proposal for the IRS

Current Situation
Public perception of the IRS appears to be extremely negative. The IRS is the brunt of jokes, and the public avoids contact with any IRS entity. As a result, taxpayers are more inclined to cheat on their returns and many services provided by the IRS to assist taxpayers in preparing their tax returns and to help them understand ways they can avoid paying unnecessary taxes and penalties go unused. In addition, negative attitude lessens the Service's ability to effectively lobby for policy changes. The key decision faced by the IRS due to this situation can be stated as,

What steps could be taken to effectively improve consumer perceptions of the IRS and help design more user-friendly services?

Purpose of the Research
The general purpose of the study is to determine the taxpaying public's perceptions of the role of the IRS in administering the tax laws. In defining the limits of this study, the IRS identified the study areas to be addressed. A careful review of those areas led to the identification of the following specific research objectives:

1. To identify the extent to which taxpayers cheat on their returns, their reasons for doing so, and approaches that can be taken to deter this kind of behavior
2. To determine taxpayers' experience and level of satisfaction with various IRS services
3. To determine what services taxpayers need
4. To develop an accurate profile of taxpayers' behavior relative to the preparation of their income tax returns
5. To assess taxpayers' knowledge and opinions about various tax laws and procedures

Research Design
The survey research method will be the basic research design. Each respondent will be interviewed in his or her home. The personal interviews are generally expected to last between 35 and 45 minutes, although the length will vary depending on the previous tax-related experiences of the respondent. For example, if a respondent has never been audited, questions on audit experience will not be addressed. Or, if a respondent has never contacted the IRS for assistance, certain questions concerning reactions to IRS services will be skipped.

Some sample questions that will be asked are

Did you or your spouse prepare your federal tax return for (year)?
■ Self
■ Spouse
■ Someone else

Did the federal income tax package you received in the mail contain all the forms necessary for you to fill out your return?
■ Yes
■ No

■ Didn't receive one in the mail
■ Don't know

If you were calling the IRS for assistance and no one was able to help you immediately, would you rather get a busy signal or be asked to wait on hold?
■ Busy signal
■ Wait on hold
■ Neither
■ Don't know

During the interview a self-administered questionnaire will be given to the taxpayer to ask certain sensitive questions, such as

Have you ever claimed a dependent on your tax return that you weren't really entitled to?
■ Yes
■ No

Sample Design
A survey of approximately 5,000 individuals located in 50 counties throughout the country will provide the database for this study. The sample will be selected on a probability basis from all households in the continental United States.

Eligible respondents will be adults over the age of 18. Within each household an effort will be made to interview the individual who is most familiar with completing the federal tax forms. When there is more than one taxpayer in the household, a random process will be used to select the taxpayer to be interviewed.

Data Gathering
The fieldworkers of a consulting organization will conduct the interviews.

Data Processing and Analysis
Standard editing and coding procedures will be utilized. Simple tabulation and cross-tabulations will be utilized to analyze the data.

Report Preparation
A written report will be prepared, and an oral presentation of the findings will be made by the research analyst at the convenience of the IRS.

Budget and Time Schedule
Any complete research proposal should include a schedule of how long it will take to conduct each stage of the research and a statement of itemized costs.

Based on *A General Taxpayer Opinion Survey*, Office of Planning and Research, Internal Revenue Service, March 1980.

Source: Based on A General Taxpayer Opinion Survey, "Office of Planning and Research," *Internal Revenue Service*, March 1980.

market share may be measured by auditing retailers' or wholesalers' sales, using trade association data, or asking consumers what brands they buy. What is to be measured is just one of many important questions that must be answered before setting the research process in motion. Exhibit 6.9 presents an overview of some of the basic questions that managers and researchers typically must answer when planning a research design.

EXHIBIT **6.9**
Basic Points Addressed by Research Proposals

Decisions to Make	Basic Questions
Problem definition	What is the purpose of the study? How much is already known? Is additional background information necessary? What is to be measured? How? Can the data be made available? Should research be conducted? Can a hypothesis be formulated?
Selection of basic research design	What types of questions need to be answered? Are descriptive or causal findings required? What is the source of the data? Can objective answers be obtained by asking people? How quickly is the information needed? How should survey questions be worded? How should experimental manipulations be made?
Selection of sample	Who or what is the source of the data? Can the target population be identified? Is a sample necessary? How accurate must the sample be? Is a probability sample necessary? Is a national sample necessary? How large a sample is necessary? How will the sample be selected?
Data gathering	Who will gather the data? How long will data gathering take? How much supervision is needed? What procedures will data collectors need to follow?
Data analysis and evaluation	Will standardized editing and coding procedures be used? How will the data be categorized? Will computer or hand tabulation be used? What is the nature of the data? What questions need to be answered? How many variables are to be investigated simultaneously? What are the criteria for evaluation of performance? What statistical tools are appropriate?
Type of report	Who will read the report? Are managerial recommendations requested? How many presentations are required? What will be the format of the written report?
Overall evaluation	How much will the study cost? Is the time frame acceptable? Is outside help needed? Will this research design attain the stated research objectives? When should the research begin?

© Cengage Learning 2013

The Proposal as a Contract

When the research will be conducted by a consultant or an outside research supplier, the written proposal serves as that person's bid to offer a specific service. Typically, a client solicits several competitive proposals, and these written offers help management judge the relative quality of alternative research suppliers.

A wise researcher will not agree to do a research job for which no written proposal exists. The proposal also serves as a contract that describes the product the research user will buy. In fact, the proposal is in many ways the same as the final research report without the actual results. Misstatements and faulty communication may occur if the parties rely only on each individual's memory

Congress fights about everything ... including how to spend taxpayers' money on federal research grants.

of what occurred at a planning meeting. The proposal creates a record, which greatly reduces conflicts that might arise after the research has been conducted. Both the researcher and the research client should sign the proposal indicating agreement on what will be done.

The proposal then functions as a formal, written statement of agreement between marketing executives and researchers. As such, it protects the researcher from criticisms such as, "Shouldn't we have had a larger sample?" or "Why didn't you use a focus group approach?" As a record of the researcher's obligation, the proposal also provides a standard for determining whether the actual research was conducted as originally planned.

Suppose in our Deland Trucking case, following the research, David is unhappy with the nature of the results because they indicate that higher cents per mile do, in fact, impact driver loyalty. This is something that David may not wish to face. In his despair, he complains to James saying,

"What I really wanted was a recruitment expense study, yet you provide results indicating my wages are too low! Why should I pay you?"

James can refer back to the research proposal, which is signed by David. He can point right to the deliverables described above showing that David agreed to a study involving driver loyalty and the organizational characteristics that lead to loyalty. The proposal certainly protects the researcher in this case. In most cases like this, after the initial emotional reaction to unflattering results, the client comes around and realizes the report contents include information that will be helpful. Realize too that the proposal protects David in case James produced a study that failed to address the research objectives included in the proposal.

funded business research

Refers to basic research usually performed by academic researchers that is financially supported by some public or private institution, as in federal government grants.

In basic research efforts, a formal proposal serves much the same purpose. **Funded business research** generally refers to basic research usually performed by academic researchers and supported by some public or private institution. Most commonly, researchers pursue federal government grants. A very detailed proposal is usually needed for federal grants, and the agreement for funding is predicated on the research actually delivering the results described in the proposal.

One important comment needs to be made about the nature of research proposals. Not all proposals follow the same format. A researcher can adapt his or her proposal to the target audience or situation. An extremely brief proposal submitted by an organization's internal research department to its own executives bears little resemblance to a complex proposal submitted by a university professor to a federal government agency to research a basic business issue.

Anticipating Outcomes

As mentioned above, the proposal and the final research report will contain much of the same information. The proposal describes the data collection, measurement, data analysis, and so forth, in future tense. In the report, the actual results are presented. In this sense, the proposal anticipates the research outcome.

Experienced researchers know that research often fails because the problem-definition process breaks down or because the research client never truly understood what a research project could or couldn't do. While it probably seems as though the proposal should make this clear, any shortcoming in the proposal can contribute to a communication failure. Thus, any tool that helps communication become as clear as can be is valued very highly.

Dummy Tables

One such tool that is perhaps the best way to let management know exactly what kind of results will be produced by research is the dummy table. **Dummy tables** are placed in research proposals and are exact representations of the actual tables that will show results in the final report with one exception: the results are hypothetical. They get the name because the researcher fills in, or "dummies up," the tables with likely but fictitious data. Dummy tables include the tables that will present hypothesis test results. In this way, they are linked directly to research objectives.

A research analyst can present dummy tables to the decision maker and ask, "Given findings like these, will you be able to make a decision?" If the decision maker says yes, the proposal may be accepted. However, if the decision maker cannot see how results like those in the dummy tables will help make the needed decision(s), it may be back to the drawing board. In other words, the client and researcher need to rethink what research results are necessary to solve the problem. Sometimes, examining the dummy tables may reveal that a key variable is missing or that some dependent variable is really not relevant. In other words, the problem is clarified by deciding on action standards or performance criteria and recognizing the types of research findings necessary to make specific decisions.

dummy tables

Tables placed in research proposals that are exact representations of the actual tables that will show results in the final report with the exception that the results are hypothetical (fictitious).

Example Dummy Table

Exhibit 6.10 shows a dummy table taken from the research proposal for David Deland's trucking company. From it, David can see that it shows what things most determine driver loyalty. If the results turn out as shown in the dummy table, it would suggest that David needs to perhaps increase his compensation or reduce the number of long-haul routes that his drivers must conduct.

Regression Table: Results Showing Which Variables Determine Driver Loyalty

EXHIBIT **6.10**
A Dummy Table for David Deland

	Standardized Regression Coefficient	Rank (Importance)
Increase cents/mile	.50**	1
Number of long-haul routes (per month)	−.45**	2
Days off (per month)	.30**	3
Vehicle quality	.25*	4
Benefits provided	.15	5

* p-value < .01
** p-value < .05

© Cengage Learning 2013

While some tables may require some additional explanation from the researcher, every effort should be made to allow tables to stand alone and be interpreted by someone who is not an experienced researcher. In other words, the user should be able to understand the results and surmise implications that the results imply. When the final report is compiled, these tables will be included with the dummy results replaced with the actual research results.

::SUMMARY

1. **Explain why proper "problem definition" is essential to useful business research.** Problem definition is the process of defining and developing a decision statement and the steps involved in translating it into more precise research terminology, including a set of research objectives. While it is difficult to point to any particular research stage as the most important, a strong case can be made for this, the first stage. If this step falls apart, the entire research design is misguided. Effective problem definition helps make sure the research objectives are relevant and useful—meaning the results will actually be used. If problem definition is glossed over or done poorly, the results are likely irrelevant and potentially harmful.

2. **Know how to recognize problems.** Problems and opportunities are usually associated with differences. The differences can occur because of changes in some situation, or they can occur because expectations were unrealistic. Problems occur when there is a difference, or gap, between the current situation and a more ideal situation. One very common type of gap is when business performance does not match the expectations of performance in that dimension. In addition, opportunities exist when actual performance in some area does not match the potential performance. Research can supply information to help close the gap. Thus, problems are noticed by spotting these gaps. While many of these gaps may just be symptoms, further steps are taken to make sure that research addresses relevant issues, not just symptoms.

3. **Translate managerial decision statements into relevant research objectives.** The problem-definition process outlined in the chapter can help make sure that the research objectives are relevant. A situation analysis is helpful in this regard. In particular, interviews that identify symptoms and then probe the respondent for potential causes of these symptoms are helpful. One tool to help in this process is the "What has changed?" technique. The research objectives, once written, also indicate what variables are likely needed in the study.

4. **Translate research objectives into research questions and/or research hypotheses.** Research questions simply restate the research objectives in the form of a question. When the researcher has sufficient theoretical reasoning to make a more specific prediction that includes the direction of any predicted relationship, the research question can be translated into one or more research hypotheses.

5. **Outline the components of a research proposal.** The research proposal is a written statement of the research design that will be followed in addressing a specific problem. The research proposal allows managers to evaluate the details of the proposed research and determine if alterations are needed. Most research proposals include the following sections: decision description, purpose of the research including the research objectives, research design, sample design, data gathering and/or fieldwork techniques, data processing and analysis, budget, and time schedule.

6. **Construct dummy tables as part of a research proposal.** Dummy tables are included in research proposals and look exactly like the real tables that will be included in the final research report. However, they cannot actually contain results since the study has not yet been done. So, they include hypothetical results that look as much as possible like the actual results. These tables are a very good tool for communicating the value of a research project to management because they provide a real sense for implications that may result from the research.

::KEY TERMS AND CONCEPTS

:: QUESTIONS FOR REVIEW AND CRITICAL THINKING

1. What is a decision statement? How does the focus on an irrelevant decision affect the research process?
2. Define problem recognition. How is this process like translating text from one language into another? What role does "probing" play in this process?
3. List and describe four factors that influence how difficult the problem-definition process can be.
4. What are three types of gaps that exist, indicating that research may be needed to assist a business in making some decision?
5. Examine an article in the Wall Street Journal or a similar source that discusses a business situation of a company in the electronics or defense industry. Identify a problem that exists with the company. Develop some research objectives that you believe correspond to the problem.
6. What is a situation analysis? How can it be used to separate symptoms from actual problems?
7. Define unit of analysis in a marketing research context.
8. Find some business journal articles that deal with culture and international expansion. Find one that lists some hypotheses. What kinds of decisions might be assisted by the results of testing these hypotheses?
9. List and describe at least four terms that can describe the nature of a variable.
10. For each of the following variables, explain why it should be considered either continuous or categorical:
    a. Whether or not a university played in a football bowl game during 2011
    b. The average wait time a customer has before being served in a full-service restaurant
    c. Letter grades of A, B, C, D, or F
    d. The job satisfaction of a company's salespeople
    e. A consumer's age
11. Write at least three examples of hypotheses that involve a managerial action statement. Provide a corresponding decision statement for each.
12. What are the major components of a research proposal? How does a research proposal assist the researcher?
13. The chapter provides an example dummy table for the Deland Trucking vignette. Provide another example dummy table that corresponds to this same situation.
14. Evaluate the following statements of business research problems. For each provide a decision statement and corresponding research objectives:
    a. A farm implement manufacturer: Our objective is to learn the most effective form of advertising so we can maximize product line profits.

    b. An employees' credit union: Our problem is to determine the reasons why employees join the credit union, determine members' awareness of credit union services, and measure attitudes and beliefs about how effectively the credit union is operated.
    c. The producer of a television show: We have a marketing problem. The program's ratings are low. We need to learn how we can improve our ratings.
    d. A soft-drink manufacturer: The marketing problem is that we do not know if our bottlers are more satisfied with us than our competitors' bottlers are with them.
    e. A women's magazine: Our problem is to document the demographic changes that have occurred in recent decades in the lives of women and to put them in historical perspective; to examine several generations of American women through most of this century, tracking their roles as students, workers, wives, and mothers and noting the changes in timing, sequence, and duration of these roles; and to examine at what age and for how long a woman enters various stages of her life: school, work, marriage, childbearing, divorce. This will be accomplished by analyzing demographic data over several generations.
    f. A manufacturer of fishing boats: The problem is to determine sales trends over the past five years by product category and to determine the seasonality of unit boat sales by quarters and by region of the country.
    g. The inventor of a tension-headache remedy (a cooling pad that is placed on the forehead for up to four hours): The purpose of this research is (1) to identify the market potential for the product, (2) to identify what desirable features the product should possess, and (3) to determine possible advertising strategies/channel strategies for the product.
15. Comment on the following statements and situations:
    a. "The best researchers are prepared to rethink and rewrite their proposals."
    b. "The client's signature is an essential element of the research proposal."
16. You have been hired by a group of hotel owners, restaurant owners, and other people engaged in businesses that benefit from tourism on South Padre Island, Texas. They wish to learn how they can attract a large number of college students to their town during spring break. Define the marketing decision statement.
17. You have been hired by a local Big Brothers and Big Sisters organization to learn how they can increase the number of males who volunteer to become Big Brothers to fatherless boys. Define your research objectives.

:: RESEARCH ACTIVITIES

1. 'NET Examine the website for International Communications Research (http://icrsurvey.com).[10] What services do they seem to offer that fall into the problem-definition process?
2. Consider the current situation within your local university music department. Assuming it stages musical productions to

which audiences are invited and for which tickets are sold, describe the marketing situation it faces. Prepare a research proposal that would help it address a key decision. Make sure it includes at least one dummy table.

E-ZPass

In the 1990s, a task force was formed among executives of seven regional transportation agencies in the New York–New Jersey area.[11] The mission of the task force was to investigate the feasibility and desirability of adopting electronic toll collection (ETC) for the interregional roadways of the area. Electronic toll collection is accomplished by providing commuters with small transceivers (tags) that emit a tuned radio signal. Receivers placed at tollbooths are able to receive the radio signal and identify the commuter associated with the particular signal. Commuters establish ETC accounts that are debited for each use of a toll road or facility, thus eliminating the need for the commuter to pay by cash or token. Because the radio signal can be read from a car in motion, ETC can reduce traffic jams at toll plazas by allowing tag holders to pass through at moderate speeds.

At the time the New York and New Jersey agencies were studying the service, electronic toll collection was already being used successfully in Texas and Louisiana. Even though several of the agencies had individually considered implementing ETC, they recognized that independent adoption would fall far short of the potential benefits achievable with an integrated interregional system.

The task force was most interested in identifying the ideal configuration of service attributes for each agency's commuters and determining how similar or different these configurations might be across agencies. The task force identified a lengthy list of attributes that was ultimately culled to six questions:

- How many accounts are necessary and what statements will be received?
- How and where does one pay for E-ZPass?
- What lanes are available for use and how are they controlled?
- Is the tag transferable to other vehicles?
- What is the price of the tag and possible service charge?
- What are other possible uses for the E-ZPass tag (airport parking, gasoline purchases, and so forth)?

From a researcher's perspective, it also seemed important to assess commuter demand for the service. However, the task force was not convinced that it needed a projection of demand, because it was committed to implementing ETC regardless of initial commuter acceptance. The task force considered its primary role to be investigating commuters' preferences for how the service should be configured ideally.

Questions

1. Evaluate the problem-definition process. Has the problem been defined adequately so that a relevant decision statement can be written?
2. What type of research design would you recommend for this project?
3. What research questions might be tested?
4. What might a dummy table include in this research proposal?

Cane's Goes International

Raising Cane's is a fast-food chicken finger establishment based in Baton Rouge, Louisiana. Cane's restaurants are popular throughout the Gulf South. Cane's recently has been approached by people interested in opening Cane's restaurants in other countries. The best contact is an Australian. However, Cane's has also been approached about outlets in Montreal, Quebec, and in Monterrey, Mexico. Cane's prepares high-quality fried chicken fingers and has a limited menu consisting of fingers, fries, slaw, and lemonade (http://www.raisingcanes.com).

Questions

1. Write a decision statement for Raising Cane's.
2. Write corresponding research objectives and research questions.
3. What role would a proposal play in assisting this research effort and in assisting Cane's in improving their business situation?

Deland Trucking

Based on the case scenario described throughout this chapter, prepare a research proposal that addresses this situation.

Qualitative Research Tools

LEARNING OUTCOMES

After studying this chapter, you should be able to

1. List and understand the differences between qualitative research and quantitative research
2. Understand the role of qualitative research in exploratory research designs
3. Describe the basic qualitative research orientations
4. Prepare a focus group interview outline
5. Recognize technological advances in the application of qualitative research approaches
6. Recognize common qualitative research tools and know the advantages and limitations of their use
7. Know the risks associated with acting on only exploratory results

Chapter Vignette:

What's in the Van?

I
s this shoe too cool? That was really the question asked by VF Corporation when they acquired Vans, the company that makes the shoe shown here.[1] Vans traditionally are synonymous with skateboarding and skateboard culture. Readers that are unfamiliar with skateboarding may well have never heard of the company. However, a reader that is part of the skateboard culture is probably looking down at his or her Vans right now!

Former Vans CEO Gary Schoenfeld points out that a decade before the acquisition (a $396 million deal), Vans was practically a dead brand.[2] However, the last 10 years have seen a revival in skateboard interest and Vans has remained the number one skateboard shoe provider. Now, the incoming management team has been given the task of deciding how to raise Vans sales to $500 million per year.

Where will the growth come from? Should the company define itself as a "skateboard footwear" company, a "lifestyle" company, or as the icon for the skate culture? Answering this question will require a deeper interpretation of the meaning of the "Van."

Skateboarding is a dynamic activity. A study by Board-Trac suggests that today over one in four skateboarders is female, as opposed to fewer than one in ten as recently as 2000.[3]

So, what exactly is in the mind and heart of a "boarder"? Two important research questions involve "What is the meaning of a pair of Vans?" and "What things define the skateboarding experience?"

Questions like these call for qualitative research methods.[4] Not just any researcher is "fit" for this job. One way to collect this data is to hire young, energetic research employees to become "boarders" and immerse themselves into the culture.

They may have to "Casper" like a "flatland techer" while probing for meaning among the discussion and activities of the other boarders. Here, Vans may find that their brand helps identify a boarder and make them feel unique in some ways. If so, Vans may want to investigate increasing their product line beyond shoes and simple apparel.

Courtesy Vans Classic Slip-on

Depth interviews of Vans wearers in which people describe in detail why they wear Vans will also be useful. Vans shouldn't be surprised if they find a significant portion of their shoes are sold to people like Mr. Samuel Teel, a retired attorney from Toledo, Ohio. Sam is completely unaware of the connection between Vans and skateboarding. He likes them because he doesn't have to bend to tie his shoes! Maybe there are some secondary segments that could bring growth to Vans. But marketing to them could complicate things—who knows?

Introduction

Chemists sometimes use the term qualitative analysis to mean research that determines what some compound is made of. In other words, the focus is on the inner meaning of the chemical—its qualities. As the word implies, qualitative research is interested more in qualities than quantities. Therefore, qualitative research is not about applying specific numbers to measure variables or using statistical procedures to numerically specify a relationship's strength.

What Is Qualitative Research?

qualitative business research

Research that addresses business objectives through techniques that allow the researcher to provide elaborate interpretations of phenomena without depending on numerical measurement; its focus is on discovering true inner meanings and new insights.

Qualitative business research is research that addresses business objectives through techniques that allow the researcher to provide elaborate interpretations of market phenomena without depending on numerical measurement. Its focus is on discovering true inner meanings and new insights. Qualitative research is very widely applied in practice. There are many research firms that specialize in qualitative research.

Qualitative research is less structured than most quantitative approaches. It does not rely on self-response questionnaires containing structured response formats. Instead, it is more **researcher-dependent** in that the researcher must extract meaning from unstructured responses, such as text from a recorded interview or a collage representing the meaning of some experience, such as skateboarding. The researcher interprets the data to extract its meaning and converts it to information.

researcher-dependent

Research in which the researcher must extract meaning from unstructured responses such as text from a recorded interview or a collage representing the meaning of some experience.

Uses of Qualitative Research

Mechanics can't use a hammer to fix everything that is broken. Instead, the mechanic has a toolbox from which a tool is matched to a problem. Business research is the same. The researcher has many tools available and the research design should try to match the best tool to the research objective. Also, just as a mechanic is probably not an expert with every tool, each researcher usually has special expertise with a small number of tools. Not every researcher has expertise with tools that would comprise qualitative research.

Generally, the less specific the research objective, the more likely that qualitative research tools will be appropriate. Also, when the emphasis is on a deeper understanding of motivations or on developing novel concepts, qualitative research is often very appropriate. The following list represents common situations that often call for qualitative research:[5]

1. When it is difficult to develop specific and actionable problem statements or research objectives. For instance, if after several interviews with the research client the researcher still can't determine exactly what needs to be measured, then qualitative research approaches may help with problem definition. Qualitative research is often useful to gain further insight and crystallize the research problem.

2. When the research objective is to develop an understanding of some phenomena in great detail and in much depth. Qualitative research tools are aimed at discovering the primary themes indicating human motivations and the documentation of activities is usually very complete. Often qualitative research provides richer information than quantitative approaches.

Qqualtrics.com

What recommendations can you offer to improve the quality of business education at your school?

Close

We have been working with the online survey in this class. This survey primarily deals with quantitative information rather than qualitative information. However, the question that asks the respondent to provide suggestions about improving the quality of business education at your school is qualitative in nature. Look over the comments provided by the students in your class. First, read through all the comments. Then, identify the major themes or issues that are present. You should be able to identify a small number of issues that are mentioned by multiple respondents. Based on these comments, what suggestion would you offer administrators at your school for improving the educational environment?

Each of these describes a scenario that may require an exploratory orientation. Previously, we defined exploratory research as appropriate in ambiguous situations or when new insight is needed. We indicated that exploratory research approaches are sometimes needed just to reach the appropriate problem statement and research objectives. While equating qualitative research with exploratory research is an oversimplification, the application of qualitative tools can help clear up ambiguity and provide innovative ideas.

3. When the research objective is to learn how a phenomena occurs in its natural setting or to learn how to express some concept in colloquial terms. For example, how do consumers actually use a product? Or, exactly how does the accounting department process invoices? While a survey can probably ask many useful questions, observing a product in use or watching the invoice process will usually be more insightful. Qualitative research produces many product and process improvement ideas.

4. When some behavior the researcher is studying is particularly context dependent—meaning the reasons something is liked or some behavior is performed depend very much on the particular situation surrounding the event. Understanding why Vans are liked is probably difficult to determine correctly outside the skating environment.

5. When a fresh approach to studying some problem is needed. This is particularly the case when quantitative research has yielded less than satisfying results. Qualitative tools can yield unique insights, many of which may lead the organization in new directions.

Qualitative researchers can learn about the skating experience by becoming immersed in the culture.

Qualitative "versus" Quantitative Research

In social science, one can find many debates about the superiority of qualitative research over quantitative research or vice versa.[6] We'll begin by saying that this is largely a superfluous argument in either direction. The truth is that qualitative research can accomplish research objectives that quantitative research cannot. Similarly truthful, but no more so, quantitative research can accomplish objectives that qualitative research cannot. The key to successfully using either is to match the right approach to the right research context.

Many good research projects combine both qualitative and quantitative research. For instance, developing valid survey measures requires first a deep understanding of the concept to be measured and a description of the way these ideas are expressed in everyday language. Both of these are tasks best suited for qualitative research. However, validating the measure formally to make sure it can reliably capture the intended concept will likely require quantitative research.[7] Also, qualitative research may be needed to separate symptoms from problems and then quantitative research can follow up to test relationships among relevant variables. The Research Snapshot "Discoveries at P&G!" describes one such situation.[8]

Discoveries at P&G!

With literally thousands of products to manage, Procter & Gamble (P&G) finds itself in the situation to conduct qualitative research almost daily. P&G doesn't introduce a product that hasn't been reviewed from nearly every possible angle. Likewise, before taking a product to a new country, you can be confident that the product has been "focus grouped" in that environment.

P&G often uses qualitative research techniques to discover potential problems or opportunities for the company's products. For example, focus groups played a major role in Herbal Essences hair care's new logo, advertising copy, reformulated ingredients, and new bottle design. The redesigned bottles for shampoo and conditioner bottles are curved in a yin and yang fashion so they can fit together.

At times, P&G seeks outside help for its research. Such was the case when P&G wanted a study of its own business problems. The researchers selected began by applying qualitative research techniques including depth interviews, observational

techniques (shadowing), and focus groups on P&G managers and marketing employees. These interviews gave the researchers the idea that perhaps P&G was suffering more from a management problem than from a marketing problem. It helped form a general research question that asked whether business problems were really due to low morale among the employees. After a lot of qualitative interviews with dozens and dozens of P&G employees, a quantitative study followed up these findings and supported this idea, leading to suggestions for improving employee morale!

Sources: Nelson, Emily, "Focus Groupies: P&G Keeps Cincinnati Busy with All Its Studies," *Wall Street Journal* 239 (January 24, 2002), A1, Eastern Edition; Stengel, J. R., A. L. Dixon, and C. T. Allen, "Listening Begins at Home," *Harvard Business Review* (November 2003), 106–116.

quantitative business research

Business research that addresses research objectives through empirical assessments that involve numerical measurement and analysis.

Quantitative business research can be defined as business research that addresses research objectives through empirical assessments that involve numerical measurement and analysis approaches. Qualitative research is more apt to stand on its own in the sense that it requires less interpretation. For example, quantitative research is quite appropriate when a research objective involves a managerial action standard. For example, a salad dressing company considered changing its recipe.[9] The new recipe was tested with a sample of consumers. Each consumer rated the product using numeric scales. Management established a rule that a majority of consumers rating the new product higher than the old product would have to be established with 90 percent confidence before replacing the old formula. A project like this can involve both quantitative measurement in the form of numeric rating scales and quantitative analysis in the form of applied statistical procedures.

Contrasting Qualitative and Quantitative Methods

Exhibit 7.1 illustrates some differences between qualitative and quantitative research. Certainly, these are generalities and exceptions may apply. However, it covers some of the key distinctions. The Research Snapshot "Discoveries at P&G!" also introduces qualitative research.

subjective

Results are researcher-dependent, meaning different researchers may reach different conclusions based on the same interview.

intersubjective certifiability

Different individuals following the same procedure will produce the same results or come to the same conclusion.

Quantitative researchers direct a considerable amount of activity toward measuring concepts with scales that either directly or indirectly provide numeric values. The numeric values can then be used in statistical computations and hypothesis testing. As will be described in detail later, this process involves comparing numbers in some way. In contrast, qualitative researchers are more interested in observing, listening, and interpreting. As such, the researcher is intimately involved in the research process and in constructing the results. For these reasons, qualitative research is said to be more **subjective**, meaning that the results are researcher-dependent. Different researchers may reach different conclusions based on the same interview. In that respect, qualitative research lacks **intersubjective certifiability** (sometimes called intersubjective verifiability), the ability of different individuals following the same procedures to produce the same results or come to the same conclusion. This should not necessarily be considered a weakness of qualitative research; rather it is simply a characteristic that yields differing insights. In contrast, when a survey respondent provides

EXHIBIT **7.1**

Comparing Qualitative and Quantitative Research

Qualitative Research	Research Aspect	Quantitative Research
Discover Ideas, Used in Exploratory Research with General Research Objects	Common Purpose	Test Hypotheses or Specific Research Questions
Observe and Interpret	Approach	Measure and Test
Unstructured, Free-Form	Data Collection Approach	Structured Response Categories Provided
Researcher Is Intimately Involved. Results Are Subjective.	Researcher Independence	Researcher Uninvolved Observer. Results Are Objective.
Small Samples—Often in Natural Settings	Samples	Large Samples to Produce Generalizable Results (Results That Apply to Other Situations)
Exploratory Research Designs	Most Often Used	Descriptive and Causal Research Designs

© Cengage Learning 2013

a commitment score on a quantitative scale, it is thought to be more objective because the number will be the same no matter what researcher is involved in the analysis.

Qualitative research seldom involves samples with hundreds of respondents. Instead, a handful of people are usually the source of qualitative data. This is perfectly acceptable in discovery-oriented research. All ideas would still have to be tested before adopted. Does a smaller sample mean that qualitative research is cheaper than quantitative? Perhaps not. Although fewer respondents have to be interviewed, the greater researcher involvement in both the data collection and analysis can drive up the costs of qualitative research.

Given the close relationship between qualitative research and exploratory designs, it should not be surprising that qualitative research is most often used in exploratory designs. Small samples, interpretive procedures that require subjective judgments, and the unstructured interview format all make traditional hypotheses testing difficult with qualitative research. Thus, these procedures are not best suited for drawing definitive conclusions, as would be expected from causal designs involving experiments. These disadvantages for drawing inferences, however, become advantages when the goal is to draw out potential explanations because the researcher spends more time with each respondent and is able to explore much more ground due to the flexibility of the procedures.

Contrasting Exploratory and Confirmatory Research

Philosophically, research can be considered as either exploratory or confirmatory. Most exploratory research designs produce **qualitative data**. Exploratory designs do not usually produce **quantitative data**, which represent phenomena by assigning numbers in an ordered and meaningful way. Rather than numbers, the focus of qualitative research is on stories, visual portrayals, meaningful characterizations, interpretations, and other expressive descriptions. Often, exploratory

qualitative data

Data that are not characterized by numbers, and instead are textual, visual, or oral; focus is on stories, visual portrayals, meaningful characterizations, interpretations, and other expressive descriptions.

quantitative data

Represent phenomena by assigning numbers in an ordered and meaningful way.

● ● ● ● ● ● ●

Netflix is one of the few companies that reported higher sales and revenue for the fourth quarter of 2008.

"The cure for boredom is curiosity. There is no cure for curiosity."

—DOROTHY PARKER

research may be needed to develop the ideas that lead to research hypotheses. In other words, in some situations the outcome of exploratory research is a testable research hypothesis. Confirmatory research then tests these hypotheses with quantitative data. The results of these tests help decision making by suggesting a specific course of action.

For example, an exploratory researcher is more likely to adopt a qualitative approach that might involve trying to develop a deeper understanding of how families are impacted by changing economic conditions, investigating how people suffering economically spend scarce resources. This may lead to the development of a hypothesis that during challenging economic times consumers seek low-cost entertainment such as movie rentals, but would not test this hypothesis. In contrast, a quantitative researcher may search for numbers that indicate economic trends. This may lead to hypothesis tests concerning how much the economy influences rental movie consumption.

Some types of qualitative studies can be conducted very quickly. Others take a very long time. For example, a single focus group analysis involving a large bottling company's sales force can likely be conducted and interpreted in a matter of days. This would provide faster results than most descriptive or causal designs. However, other types of qualitative research, such as a participant-observer study aimed at understanding skateboarding, could take months to complete. A qualitative approach can, but does not necessarily, save time.

In summary, when researchers have limited experience or knowledge about a research issue, exploratory research is a useful step. Exploratory research, which often involves qualitative methods, can be an essential first step to a more conclusive, confirmatory study by reducing the chance of beginning with an inadequate, incorrect, or misleading set of research objectives.

Orientations to Qualitative Research

Qualitative research can be performed in many ways using many techniques. Orientations to qualitative research are very much influenced by the different fields of study involved in research. These orientations are each associated with a category of qualitative research. The major categories of qualitative research include

1. Phenomenology—originating in philosophy and psychology
2. Ethnography—originating in anthropology
3. Grounded theory—originating in sociology
4. Case studies—originating in psychology and in business research

Precise lines between these approaches are difficult to draw and there are clearly links among these orientations. In addition, a particular qualitative research study may involve elements of two or more approaches. However, each category does reflect a somewhat unique approach to human inquiry and approaches to discovering knowledge. Each will be described briefly below.

Phenomenology

phenomenology

A philosophical approach to studying human experiences based on the idea that human experience itself is inherently subjective and determined by the context in which people live.

What Is a Phenomenological Approach to Research?

Phenomenology represents a philosophical approach to studying human experiences based on the idea that human experience itself is inherently subjective and determined by the context in which people live.[10] The phenomenological researcher focuses on how a person's behavior is shaped by the relationship he or she has with the physical environment, objects, people, and situations. Phenomenological inquiry seeks to describe, reflect upon, and interpret experiences.

"When Will I Ever Learn?"

A hermeneutic approach can be used to provide insight into car shopping experiences. The approach involves a small number of consumers providing relatively lengthy stories about recent car shopping experiences. The goal is trying to discover particular reasons why certain car models are eliminated from consideration. The consumer tells a story of comparing a Ford and a GM (General Motors) minivan. She describes the two vehicles in great detail and ultimately concludes, "We might have gone with the Ford instead because it was real close between the Ford and the GM." The Ford was cheaper, but the way the door opened suggested difficulties in dealing with kids and groceries and the like, and so she purchased the GM model. The researcher in this story goes on to interpret the plotline of the story as having to do with the consumer's responsibility for poor consumption outcomes. Consider the following passage.

"It has got GM defects and that is really frustrating. I mean the transmission had to be rebuilt after about 150 miles …and it had this horrible vibration problem. We took a long vacation where you couldn't go over 60 miles an hour because the thing started shaking so bad …. I told everybody, 'Don't buy one of these things.' We should have known because our Buick—the

© AP Photo/Lenny Igneiz

Buick that is in the shop right now—its transmission lasted about 3,000 miles. My husband's parents are GM people and they had one go bad. I keep thinking, When I am going to learn? I think this one has done it. I don't think I will ever go back to GM after this."[11]

The research concludes that a hermeneutic link exists between the phrase "When I am going to learn?" and the plot of self-responsibility. The resulting behavior including no longer considering GM products and the negative word-of-mouth behavior are ways of restoring esteem given the events.

Source: *Journal of Marketing Research* by Winer, Russ. Copyright 1997 by American Marketing Association (AMA) (CHIC). Reproduced with permission of American Marketing Association (AMA) (CHIC) in the format Textbook via Copyright Clearance Center; Thompson, Craig J., "Interpreting Consumers: A Hermeneutical Framework for Deriving Marketing Insights from the Tests of Consumers' Consumption Stories," *Journal of Marketing Research*, 34 (November 1997), 438–455 (see pp. 443–444 for quotation).

Researchers with a phenomenological orientation rely largely on conversational interview tools. When conversational interviews are face to face, they are recorded either with video or audiotape and then interpreted by the researcher. The phenomenological interviewer is careful to avoid asking direct questions when at all possible. Instead, the research respondent is asked to tell a story about some experience. In addition, the researcher must do everything possible to make sure a respondent is comfortable telling his or her story. One way to accomplish this is to become a member of the group (for example, becoming a skateboarder in the scenario described earlier in this chapter). Another way may be to avoid having the person use his or her real name. This might be particularly necessary in studying potentially sensitive topics such as smoking, drug usage, shoplifting, or employee theft.

Therefore, a phenomenological approach to studying the meaning of Vans may require considerable time. The researcher may first spend weeks or months fitting in with the person or group of interest to establish a comfort level. During this time, careful notes of conversations are made. If an interview is sought, the researcher would likely not begin by asking a skateboarder to describe his or her shoes. Rather, asking for favorite skateboard incidents or talking about what makes a skateboarder unique may generate productive conversation. Generally, the approach is very unstructured as a way of avoiding leading questions and to provide every opportunity for new insights.

What Is Hermeneutics?

The term hermeneutics is important in phenomenology. **Hermeneutics** is an approach to understanding phenomenology that relies on analysis of texts in which a person tells a story about him or herself.[12] Meaning is then drawn by connecting text passages to one another or to themes expressed outside the story. These connections are usually facilitated by coding the key meanings expressed in the story. While a full understanding of hermeneutics is beyond the scope of this text, some of the terminology is used when applying qualitative tools. For instance, a **hermeneutic unit** refers to a text

hermeneutics

An approach to understanding phenomenology that relies on analysis of texts through which a person tells a story about him or herself.

hermeneutic unit

Refers to a text passage from a respondent's story that is linked with a key theme from within this story or provided by the researcher.

passage from a respondent's story that is linked with a key theme from within this story or provided by the researcher.[13] These passages are an important way in which data are interpreted.

Computerized software exists to assist in coding and interpreting texts and images. ATLAS.ti is one such software package that adopts the term hermeneutic unit in referring to groups of phrases that are linked with meaning. Hermeneutic units and computerized software are also very appropriate in grounded theory approaches. One useful component of computerized approaches is a word counter. The word counter will return counts of how many times words were used in a story. Often, frequently occurring words suggest a key theme. The Research Snapshot "When Will I Ever Learn?" demonstrates the use of hermeneutics in interpreting a story about a consumer shopping for a car.

Ethnography

What Is Ethnography?

ethnography
Represents ways of studying cultures through methods that involve becoming highly active within that culture.

participant-observation
Ethnographic research approach where the researcher becomes immersed within the culture that he or she is studying and draws data from his or her observations.

Ethnography represents ways of studying cultures through methods that involve becoming highly active within that culture. **Participant-observation** typifies an ethnographic research approach. Participant-observation means the researcher becomes immersed within the culture that he or she is studying and draws data from his or her observations. A culture can be either a broad culture, like American culture, or a narrow culture, like urban gangs, Harley-Davidson owners, or skateboarding enthusiasts.[14]

Organizational culture would also be relevant for ethnographic study.[15] At times, researchers have actually become employees of an organization for an extended period of time. In doing so, they become part of the culture and over time other employees come to act quite naturally around the researcher. The researcher may observe behaviors that the employee would never reveal otherwise. For instance, a researcher investigating the ethical behavior of salespeople may have difficulty getting a car salesperson to reveal any potentially deceptive sales tactics in a traditional interview. However, ethnographic techniques may result in the salesperson letting down his or her guard, resulting in more valid discoveries about the car-selling culture.

"I never predict. I just look out the window and see what is visible—but not yet seen".
—PETER DRUCKER

● ● ● ● ● ● ● ●

Ethnographic (participant-observation) approaches may be useful to understanding how children obtain value from their experiences with toys.

Observation In Ethnography

Observation plays a key role in ethnography. Researchers today sometimes ask households for permission to place video cameras in their home. In doing so, the ethnographer can study the consumer in a "natural habitat" and use the observations to test new products, develop new product ideas, and develop strategies in general.[16]

Ethnographic study can be particularly useful when a certain culture is comprised of individuals who cannot or will not verbalize their thoughts and feelings. For instance, ethnography has advantages for discovering insights among children since it does not rely largely on their answers to questions. Instead, the researcher can simply become part of the environment, allow the children to do what they do naturally, and record their behavior.[17]

The opening vignette describing a participant-observer approach to learning about skateboarding culture represents an ethnographic approach. Here, the researcher would draw insight from observations and personal experiences with the culture.

© Taxi/Getty Images

Grounded Theory

What Is Grounded Theory?

Grounded theory is probably applied less often in business research than is either phenomenology or ethnography.[18]

Grounded theory represents an inductive investigation in which the researcher poses questions about information provided by respondents or taken from historical records. The researcher asks the questions to him or herself and repeatedly questions the responses to derive deeper explanations. Grounded theory is particularly applicable in highly dynamic situations involving rapid and significant change. Two key questions asked by the grounded theory researcher are "What is happening here?" and "How is it different?"[19] The distinguishing characteristic of grounded theory is that it does not begin with a theory but instead extracts one from whatever emerges from an area of inquiry.[20]

How Is Grounded Theory Used?

Consider a company that approaches a researcher to study whether or not its sales force is as effective as it was five years ago. The researcher uses grounded theory to discover a potential explanation. A theory is inductively developed based on text analysis of dozens of sales meetings that had been recorded over the previous five years. By questioning the events discussed in the sales interviews and analyzing differences in the situations that may have led to the discussion, the researcher is able to develop a theory. The theory suggests that with an increasing reliance on e-mail and other technological devices for communication, the salespeople do not communicate with each other informally as much as they did five years previously. As a result, the salespeople had failed to bond into a close-knit "community."[21]

Computerized software also can be useful in developing grounded theory. In our Vans example, the researcher may interpret skateboarders' stories of good and bad skating experiences by questioning the events and changes described. These may yield theories about the role that certain brands play in shaping a good or bad experience. Alternatively, grounded theorists often rely on visual representations. Thus, the skateboarder could develop collages representing good and bad experiences. Just as with the text, questions can be applied to the visuals in an effort to develop theory.

Case Studies

What Are Case Studies?

Case studies simply refer to the documented history of a particular person, group, organization, or event. Typically, a case study may describe the events of a specific company as it faces an important decision or situation, such as introducing a new product or dealing with some management crisis. Textbook cases typify this kind of case study. Clinical interviews of managers, employees, or customers can represent a case study.

The case studies can then be analyzed for important themes. **Themes** are identified by the frequency with which the same term (or a synonym) arises in the narrative description. The themes may be useful in discovering variables that are relevant to potential explanations.

How Are Case Studies Used?

Case studies are commonly applied in business. For instance, case studies of brands that sell "luxury" products helped provide

grounded theory

Represents an inductive investigation in which the researcher poses questions about information provided by respondents or taken from historical records; the researcher asks the questions to him or herself and repeatedly questions the responses to derive deeper explanations.

case studies

The documented history of a particular person, group, organization, or event.

themes

Identified by the frequency with which the same term (or a synonym) arises in the narrative description.

● ● ● ● ● ● ●

Qualitative research reveals that products that are perceived as "authentic" offer more value for consumers.

© Lawton/Photo Cuisine

A Sensory Safari Provides Play Time (and Good Research) for Time Warner Cable

Traditional focus groups are used by businesses for a variety of reasons, most notably for the opportunity to see how potential consumers will react to new products or new services. But new focus group techniques are bringing this experience to another level. Welcome to the world of Spark, a New York-based market research firm that seeks to engage all of the senses of consumers as a way to understand potential products or services. Consumers are put in rooms with all kinds of materials, including Styrofoam, toys, fresh flowers, and even coffee beans and asked to build collages that reflect how they feel regarding a new product. They may create any montage they feel, and are encouraged to get as messy as they want. This signature program, the Sensory Safari, gives a new meaning to "play time."

When Time Warner Cable, a company that provides computer communication and cable television content to residential users, wished to see the impact of a new ad campaign, the company let Spark take some potential users on a Sensory Safari. Prior to the ads, users provided collages that included such images as knots of rope and roller coasters, with associated negative imagery and discussions. Subsequent to the ads, the users provided different collages, including a heart-shaped image with technology in the middle of it.

This nonverbal information proved to be critically important to Time Warner, which realized that it can be hard to "talk about how you feel" concerning technology in a traditional focus group. When people are allowed to fully engage all of their senses, they can "say a lot." Who knew play time could be so profitable?

Source: Spark-NYC, www.spark-nyc.com; Vega, Tanzina, "Focus Groups That Look Like Play Groups," *The New York Times* (May 30, 2011, Page B1).

insight into what makes up a prestigious brand. A business researcher carefully conducted case (no pun intended) studies of higher end wine labels (such as Penfold's Grange) including the methods of production and distribution. This analysis suggested that a key ingredient to a prestige brand may well be authenticity. When consumers know something is authentic, they attach more esteem to that product or brand.[22]

Case studies often overlap with one of the other categories of qualitative research. The Research Snapshot "A Sensory Safari Provides Play Time (and Good Research) for Time Warner Cable" illustrates how observation was useful in discovering insights leading to important business changes.

A primary advantage of the case study is that an entire organization or entity can be investigated in depth with meticulous attention to detail. This highly focused attention enables the researcher to carefully study the order of events as they occur or to concentrate on identifying the relationships among functions, individuals, or entities. Conducting a case study often requires the cooperation of the party whose history is being studied. This freedom to search for whatever data an investigator deems important makes the success of any case study highly dependent on the alertness, creativity, intelligence, and motivation of the individual performing the case analysis.

Common Techniques Used in Qualitative Research

Qualitative researchers apply a nearly endless number of techniques. These techniques overlap more than one of the orientations previously discussed, although each category may display a preference for certain techniques. Exhibit 7.2 lists characteristics of some common qualitative research techniques. Each is then described.

EXHIBIT 7.2
Four Common Qualitative Research Tools

Tool	Description	Type of Approach (Category)	Key Advantages	Key Disadvantages
Focus Group Interviews	Small group discussions led by a trained moderator	Ethnography, case studies	• Can be done quickly • Gain multiple perspectives • Flexibility	• Results dependent on moderator • Results do not generalize to larger population • Difficult to use for sensitive topics • Expensive
Depth Interviews	One-on-one, probing interview between a trained researcher and a respondent	Ethnography, grounded theory, case studies	• Gain considerable insight from each individual • Good for understanding unusual behaviors	• Result dependent on researcher's interpretation • Results not meant to generalize • Very expensive
Conversations	Unstructured dialogue recorded by a researcher	Phenomenology, grounded theory	• Gain unique insights from enthusiasts • Can cover sensitive topics • Less expensive than depth interviews or focus groups	• Easy to get off course • Interpretations are very researcher-dependent
Semistructured Interviews	Open-ended questions, often in writing, that ask for short essay-type answers from respondents	Grounded theory, ethnography	• Can address more specific issues • Results can be easily interpreted • Cost advantages over focus groups and depth interviews	• Lack the flexibility that is likely to produce truly creative or novel explanations
Word Association/ Sentence Completion	Records the first thoughts that come to a consumer in response to some stimulus	Grounded theory, case studies	• Economical • Can be done quickly	• Lack the flexibility that is likely to produce truly creative or novel explanations
Observation	Recorded notes describing observed events	Ethnography, grounded theory, case studies	• Can be unobtrusive • Can yield actual behavior patterns	• Can be very expensive with participant-observer series
Collages	Respondent assembles pictures that represent their thoughts/feelings	Phenomenology, grounded theory	• Flexible enough to allow novel insights	• Highly dependent on the researcher's interpretation of the collage
Thematic Apperception/ Cartoon Tests	Researcher provides an ambiguous picture and respondent tells about the story	Phenomenology, grounded theory	• Projective, allows to get at sensitive issues • Flexible	• Highly dependent on the researcher's interpretation

What Is a Focus Group Interview?

The focus group interview is so widely used that many advertising and research companies do nothing but focus group interviews. In that sense, it is wrongly synonymous with qualitative research. Nonetheless, focus groups are a very important qualitative research technique and deserve considerable discussion.

focus group interview

An unstructured, free-flowing interview with a small group of around six to ten people. Focus groups are led by a trained moderator who follows a flexible format encouraging dialogue among respondents.

A **focus group interview** is an unstructured, free-flowing interview with a small group of people, usually between six and ten. Focus groups are led by a trained moderator who follows a flexible format encouraging dialogue among respondents. Common focus group topics include employee programs, employee satisfaction, brand meanings, problems with products, advertising themes, or new product concepts.

The group meets at a central location at a designated time. Participants may range from consumers talking about hair coloring, petroleum engineers talking about problems in the "oil patch," children talking about toys, or employees talking about their jobs. A moderator begins by providing some opening statement to broadly steer discussion in the intended direction. Ideally, discussion topics emerge at the group's initiative, not the moderator's. Consistent with phenomenological approaches, moderators should avoid direct questioning unless absolutely necessary.

Advantages of Focus Group Interviews

Focus groups allow people to discuss their true feelings, anxieties, and frustrations, as well as the depth of their convictions, in their own words. While other approaches may also do much the same, focus groups offer several advantages:

1. Relatively fast
2. Easy to execute
3. Allow respondents to piggyback off each other's ideas
4. Provide multiple perspectives
5. Flexibility to allow more detailed descriptions
6. High degree of scrutiny

piggyback

A procedure in which one respondent stimulates thought among the others; as this process continues, increasingly creative insights are possible.

SPEED AND EASE

In an emergency situation, three or four group sessions can be conducted, analyzed, and reported in a week or so. The large number of research firms that conduct focus group interviews makes it easy to find someone to host and conduct the research. Practically every state in the United States contains multiple research firms that have their own focus group facilities. Companies with large research departments likely have at least one qualified focus group moderator so that they need not outsource the focus group.

PIGGYBACKING AND MULTIPLE PERSPECTIVES

Furthermore, the group approach may produce thoughts that would not be produced otherwise. The interplay between respondents allows them to **piggyback** off of each other's ideas. In other words, one respondent stimulates thought among the others and, as this process continues, increasingly creative insights are possible. A comment by one individual often triggers a chain of responses from the other participants. The social nature of the focus group also helps bring out multiple views as each person shares a particular perspective.

● ● ● ● ● ● ●

Focus group facilities typically include a comfortable room for respondents, recording equipment, and a viewing room via a two-way mirror.

FLEXIBILITY

The flexibility of focus group interviews is advantageous, especially when compared with the more structured and rigid survey format. Numerous topics can be discussed and many insights can be gained, particularly with regard to the variations in consumer behavior in different situations. Responses that would be unlikely to emerge in a survey often come out in group interviews: "If the day is hot and I have to serve the whole neighborhood, I make Kool-Aid; otherwise, I give them Dr Pepper or Coke" or "Usually I work on my projects at home in the evenings, but when it is a team project we set aside time on Monday morning and all meet in the conference room."

If a researcher is investigating a target group to determine who consumes a particular beverage or why a consumer purchases a certain brand, situational factors must be included in any interpretations of respondent comments. For instance, in the preceding situation, the fact that a particular beverage is consumed must be noted. It would be inappropriate to say that Kool-Aid is preferred in general. The proper interpretation is situation specific. On a hot day the whole neighborhood gets Kool-Aid. When the weather isn't hot, the kids may get nothing, or if only a few kids are around, they may get lucky and get Dr Pepper. Thus, Kool-Aid can be interpreted as appropriate for satisfying large numbers of hot kids while Dr Pepper is a treat for a select few. Similarly, individual assignments are worked on at home in the evenings, while team projects are worked on in the morning in the conference room.

SCRUTINY

A focus group interview allows closer scrutiny in several ways. First, the session can be observed by several people, as it is usually conducted in a room containing a two-way mirror. The respondents and moderator are on one side, and an invited audience that may include both researchers and decision makers is on the other. If the decision makers are located in another city or country, the session may be shown via a live video hookup. Either through live video or a two-way mirror, some check on the eventual interpretations is provided through the ability to actually watch the research being conducted. If the observers have questions that are not being asked or want the moderator to probe on an issue, they can send a quick text message with instructions to the moderator. Second, focus group sessions are generally recorded on audio or videotape. Later, detailed examination of the recorded session can offer additional insight and help clear up disagreements about what happened.

Focus Group Illustration

Focus groups often are used for concept screening and concept refinement. The concept may be continually modified, refined, and retested until management believes it is acceptable. While RJR's initial attempts at smokeless cigarettes failed in the United States, Philip Morris is developing a smokeless cigarette for the U.K. market. Focus groups are being used to help understand how the product will be received and how it might be improved.[23] The voluntary focus group respondents are presented with samples of the product and then they discuss it among themselves. The interview results suggest that the key product features that must be conveyed are the fact that it produces no ashes, no side smoke, and very little odor. These beliefs are expected to lead to a positive attitude. Focus group respondents show little concern about how the cigarette actually functioned. Smokers believe they will use the product if nonsmokers are not irritated by being near someone using the "electronic cigarette." Thus, the focus groups are useful in refining the product and developing a theory of how it should be marketed.

Group Composition

The ideal size of the focus group is six to ten people. If the group is too small, one or two members may intimidate the others. Groups that are too large may not allow for adequate participation by each group member.

Homogeneous groups seem to work best because they allow researchers to concentrate on consumers with similar lifestyles, experiences, and communication skills. The session does not become rife with too many arguments and different viewpoints stemming from diverse backgrounds. Also, from an ethnographic perspective, the respondents should all be members of a unique and identifiable culture. Vans may benefit from a focus group interview comprised only of skateboard enthusiasts. Perhaps participants can be recruited from a local skate park. However, additional group(s) of participants that are not boarders might be useful in gaining a different perspective.

● ● ● ● ● ● ● ●

Imagine the differences in reactions to legislation further restricting smoking behavior that would be found among a group of smokers compared to a group of nonsmokers.

When the Centers for Disease Control and Prevention tested public service announcements about AIDS through focus groups, it discovered that single-race groups and racially diverse groups reacted differently. By conducting separate focus groups, the organization was able to gain important insights about which creative strategies were most appropriate for targeted versus broad audiences.

For example, for focus groups regarding employee satisfaction, we might want to recruit homogeneous groups based on position in the organization. The researcher may find that entry-level employees have very different perspectives and concerns than those of middle or upper-level management. Also, it is fully understandable that employees might be hesitant to criticize their supervisors. Therefore, researchers may consider interviewing different levels of employees in separate groups.

Finding quality focus group participants can also be a challenge and can lead to issues as well. For example, a research client observed a focus group interview being conducted by a research supplier that had previously performed several other projects for the client, each dealing with a quite unique topic. During the interview, the client noticed that some focus group respondents looked familiar.

A few days later, the client reviewed video recordings of the session alongside videotapes from two previous focus groups outsourced to the same company. She found that eight of the ten respondents in the latest focus group had appeared in one of the previous interviews as well. She was furious and considered whether or not she should pay for the interview or bother having a report prepared.

The focus group researcher had taken this approach to make sure the session went smoothly. The moderator solicited subjects who in the past had been found to be very articulate and talkative. In this case, the focus group respondents are more or less "professional," paid participants. It is questionable whether such "professional respondents" can possibly offer relevant opinions on all these topics. The question is, has the research firm acted in an ethical manner?

Researchers who wish to collect information from different types of people should conduct several focus groups. A diverse overall sample may be obtained by using different groups even though each group is homogeneous. For instance, in discussing household chores, four groups might be used:

- Married men
- Married women
- Single men
- Single women

Although each group is homogeneous, by using four groups, researchers obtain opinions from a wide degree of respondents.

Environmental Conditions

A focus group session may typically take place at the research agency in a room specifically designed for this purpose. Research suppliers that specialize in conducting focus groups operate from commercial facilities that have videotape cameras in observation rooms behind two-way mirrors and microphone systems connected to tape recorders and speakers to allow greater scrutiny as discussed previously. Refreshments are provided to help create a more relaxed atmosphere conducive to a free exchange of ideas. More open and intimate reports of personal experiences and sentiments can be obtained under these conditions.

The Focus Group Moderator

The **moderator** essentially runs the focus group and plays a critical role in its success. There are several qualities that a good moderator must possess:

1. The moderator must be able to develop rapport with the group to promote interaction among all participants. The moderator should be someone who is really interested in people, who listens carefully to what others have to say, and who can readily establish rapport, gain people's confidence, and make them feel relaxed and eager to talk.

2. The moderator must be a good listener. Careful listening is especially important because the group interview's purpose is to stimulate spontaneous responses. Without good listening skills, the moderator may direct the group in an unproductive direction.

3. The moderator must try not to interject his or her own opinions. Good moderators usually say less rather than more. They can stimulate productive discussion with generalized follow-ups such as, "Tell us more about that incident," or "How are your experiences similar or different from the one you just heard?" The moderator must be particularly careful not to ask leading questions such as "You are happy to work at Acme, aren't you?"

4. The moderator must be able to control discussion without being overbearing. The moderator's role is also to focus the discussion on the areas of concern. When a topic is no longer generating fresh ideas, the effective moderator changes the flow of discussion. The moderator does not give the group total control of the discussion, but he or she normally has prepared questions on topics that concern management. However, the timing of these questions in the discussion and the manner in which they are raised are left to the moderator's discretion. The term focus group thus stems from the moderator's task. He or she starts out by asking for a general discussion but usually focuses in on specific topics during the session.

Planning the Focus Group Outline

Focus group researchers use a discussion guide to help control the interview and guide the discussion into product areas. A **discussion guide** includes written introductory comments informing the group about the focus group purpose and rules and then outlines topics or questions to be addressed in the group session. Thus, the discussion guide serves as the focus group outline. Some discussion guides will have only a few phrases in the entire document. Others may be more detailed. The amount of content depends on the nature and experience of the researcher and the complexity of the topic.

A cancer center that wanted to warn the public about the effects of the sun used the discussion guide in Exhibit 7.3. The business researchers had several objectives for this discussion guide:

■ The first question was very general, asking that respondents describe their feelings about being out in the sun. This opening question aimed to elicit the full range of views within the group. Some individuals might view being out in the sun as a healthful practice, whereas others view the sun as deadly. The hope is that by exposing the full range of opinions, respondents would be motivated to fully explain their own position. This was the only question asked specifically of every respondent. Each respondent had to give an answer before free discussion began. In this way, individuals experience a nonthreatening environment encouraging their free and full opinion. A general question seeking a reaction serves as an effective icebreaker.

■ The second question asks whether participants could think of any reason they should be warned about sunlight exposure. This question was simply designed to introduce the idea of a warning label.

■ Subsequent questions were asked and became increasingly specific. They were first asked about possible warning formats that might be effective. Respondents are allowed to react to any formats suggested by any other respondent. After this discussion, the moderator will introduce some specific formats the cancer center personnel have in mind.

moderator

A person who leads a focus group interview and ensures that everyone gets a chance to speak and contribute to the discussion.

discussion guide

A focus group outline that includes written introductory comments informing the group about the focus group purpose and rules and then outlines topics or questions to be addressed in the group session.

EXHIBIT **7.3**
Discussion Guide for a Focus Group Interview

Thank you very much for agreeing to help out with this research. We call this a focus group; let me explain how it works, and then please let me know if something isn't clear.

This is a discussion, as though you were sitting around just talking. You can disagree with each other, or just comment. We do ask that just one person talk at a time, because we tape-record the session to save me from having to take notes. Nothing you say will be associated with you or your church—this is just an easy way for us to get some people together.

The subject is health risk warnings. Some of you may remember seeing a chart in a newspaper that gives a pollen count or a pollution count. And you've heard on the radio sometimes a hurricane watch or warning. You've seen warnings on cigarette packages or cigarette advertising, even if you don't smoke. And today we're going to talk about warnings about the sun. Before we start, does anybody have a question?

1. OK, let's go around and talk about how often you spend time in the sun, and what you're likely to be doing. (FOR PARENTS): What about your kids—do you like them to be out in the sun?

2. OK, can you think of any reason that somebody would give you a warning about exposure to the sun?

(PROBE: IS ANY SUN EXPOSURE BAD, OR ONLY A CERTAIN DEGREE OF EXPOSURE, AND IF SO, WHAT IS IT? OR IS THE SUN GOOD FOR YOU?)

3. What if we had a way to measure the rays of the sun that are associated with skin problems, so that you could find out which times of the day or which days are especially dangerous? How could, say, a radio station tell you that information in a way that would be useful?

4. Now let me ask you about specific ways to measure danger. Suppose somebody said, "We monitored the sun's rays at noon, and a typical fair-skinned person with unprotected skin will burn after 40 minutes of direct exposure." What would you think?

5. Now let me ask you about another way to say the same kind of thing. Suppose somebody said, "The sun's rays at noon today measured 10 times the 8:00 A.M. baseline level of danger." What would you think?

6. OK, now suppose that you heard the same degree of danger expressed this way: "The sun's rays at noon today measured '8' on a sun danger scale that ranges from one to ten." What would you think?

7. What if the danger scale wasn't in numbers, but words? Suppose you heard, "The sun's rays at noon showed a moderate danger reading," or "The sun's rays showed a high danger reading." What would you think?

8. And here's another possibility: What if you heard "Here's the sun danger reading at noon today—the unprotected skin of a typical fair-skinned person will age the equivalent of one hour in a ten-minute period."

9. OK, what if somebody said today is a day to wear long sleeves and a hat, or today is a day you need sunscreen and long sleeves? What would you think?

10. OK, here's my last question. There are really three things you can do about sun danger: You can spend less time in the sun, you can go out at less dangerous times of day, like before 10:00 in the morning or after 4:00 in the afternoon, and you can cover your skin by wearing a hat or long sleeves, or using protective sunscreen lotion. Thinking about yourself listening to the radio, what kind of announcement would make you likely to do one or more of those things? (PARENTS: WHAT WOULD MAKE YOU BE SURE THAT YOUR CHILD WAS PROTECTED?)

11. And what would you be most likely to do to protect yourself? (YOUR CHILD?)

12. Before we break up, is there anything else you think would be useful for M. D. Anderson's people to know? Do you have any questions about any aspect of this interview?

OK, thank you very much for your help.

Source: Gelb, Betsy D. and Michael P. Eriksen, "Market Research May Help Prevent Cancer," *Marketing Research* (September 1991), 46. Published by American Marketing Association. Reprinted with permission.

■ Finally, the "bottom-line" question is asked: "What format would be most likely to induce people to take protective measures?" There would be probing follow-ups of each opinion so that a respondent couldn't simply say something like, "The second one." All focus groups finish up with a catchall question asking for any comments including any thoughts they wanted passed along to the sponsor (which in this case was only then revealed as the Houston-based cancer center).

Researchers who planned the outline established certain objectives for each part of the focus group. The initial effort was to break the ice and establish rapport within the group. The logical flow of the group session then moved from general discussion about sunbathing to more focused discussion of types of warnings about danger from sun exposure.

In general, the following steps should be used to conduct an effective focus group discussion guide:

1. Welcome and introductions should take place first.
2. Begin the interview with a broad icebreaker that does not reveal too many specifics about the interview. Sometimes, this may even involve respondents providing some written story or their reaction to some stimulus like a photograph, film, product, or advertisement.

3. Questions become increasingly more specific as the interview proceeds. However, the moderator will notice that a good interview will cover the specific question topics before they have to be asked. This is preferable as respondents are clearly not forced to react to the specific issue; it just emerges naturally.

4. If there is a very specific objective to be accomplished, such as explaining why a respondent would either buy or not buy a product, that question should probably be saved for last.

5. A debriefing statement should provide respondents with the actual focus group objectives and answer any questions they may have. This is also a final shot to gain some insight from the group.

Focus Group As Diagnostic Tools

Focus groups are perhaps the predominant means by which business researchers implement exploratory research designs. Focus groups also can be helpful in later stages of a research project, particularly when the findings from surveys or other quantitative techniques raise more questions than they answer. Managers who are puzzled about the meaning of survey research results may use focus groups to better understand what survey results indicate. In such a situation, the focus group supplies diagnostic help after quantitative research has been conducted.

Focus groups are also excellent diagnostic tools for spotting problems with ideas. For instance, idea screening is often done with focus groups. An initial concept is presented to the group and then they are allowed to comment on it in detail. This usually leads to lengthy lists of potential product problems and some ideas for overcoming them. Mature products can also be "focus-grouped" in this manner.

Videoconferencing and Focus Groups

With the widespread utilization of videoconferencing, the number of companies using these systems to conduct focus groups has increased. With videoconference focus groups, managers can stay home and watch on television rather than having to take a trip to a focus group facility.

FocusVision (**http://www.focusvision.com/**) is a business research company that provides videoconferencing equipment and services. The FocusVision system is modular, allowing for easy movement and an ability to capture each group member close up. The system operates via a remote keypad that allows observers in a far-off location to pan the focus group room or zoom in on a particular participant. Managers viewing at remote locations can send the moderator messages during the interview.

Interactive Media and Online Focus Groups

Internet applications of qualitative exploratory research are growing rapidly and involve both formal and informal applications. Formally, the term **online focus group** refers to a qualitative research effort in which a group of individuals provides unstructured comments by entering their remarks into an electronic Internet display board of some type, such as a chat-room session or in the form of a blog. Because respondents enter their comments into the computer, transcripts of verbatim responses are available immediately after the group session. Online groups can be quick and cost-efficient. However, because there is less personal interaction between participants, group synergy and snowballing of ideas may be diminished.

Several companies have established a form of informal, "continuous" focus group by establishing an Internet blog for that purpose.[24] We might call this technique a **focus blog** when the intention is to mine the site for business research purposes. General Motors, American Express, and Lego all have used ideas harvested from their focus blogs. When operating, the Lego blog can be found at **http://legoisfun.blogspot.com**. While traditional focus group respondents are generally paid $100 or more to show up and participate for 90 minutes, bloggers and online focus group respondents often participate for absolutely no fee at all! Thus, technology provides some cost advantages over traditional focus group approaches.[25]

online focus group

A qualitative research effort in which a group of individuals provides unstructured comments by entering their remarks into an electronic Internet display board of some type.

focus blog

A type of informal, "continuous" focus group established as an Internet blog for the purpose of collecting qualitative data from participant comments.

Online Versus Face-to-Face Focus Group Techniques

A research company can facilitate a formal online focus group by setting up a private chat room for that purpose. Participants in formal and informal online focus groups feel that their anonymity is very secure. Often respondents will say things in this environment that they would never say otherwise. For example, a lingerie company was able to get insights into how it could design sexy products for larger women. Online, these women freely discussed what it would take "to feel better about being naked."[26] One can hardly imagine how difficult such a discussion might be face to face. Increased anonymity can be a major advantage for a company investigating sensitive or embarrassing issues.

Because participants do not have to be together in the same room at a research facility, the number of participants in online focus groups can be larger than in traditional focus groups. Twenty-five participants or more is not uncommon for the simultaneous chat-room format. Participants can be at widely separated locations since the Internet does not have geographical restrictions. Of course, a major disadvantage is that often the researcher does not exercise as much control in precisely who participates. In other words, a person could very easily not match the desired profile or even answer screening questions in a misleading way simply to participate.

A major drawback with online focus groups is that moderators cannot see body language and facial expressions (bewilderment, excitement, boredom, interest, and so forth). Thus, they cannot fully interpret how people are reacting. Also, moderators' ability to probe and ask additional questions on the spot is reduced in online focus groups. Research that requires focus group members to actually touch something (such as a new easy-opening packaging design) or taste something is not generally suitable for an online format.

Disadvantages of Focus Groups

Focus groups offer many advantages as a form of qualitative research. Like practically every other research technique, the focus group has some limitations and disadvantages as well. Problems with focus groups include those discussed below.

First, focus groups require objective, sensitive, and effective moderators. It is very difficult for a moderator to remain completely objective about most topics. In large research firms, the moderator may be provided only enough information to effectively conduct the interview, no more. The focus group interview obviously shouldn't reduce to, or even be influenced by, the moderator's opinion. Also, without a good moderator, one or two participants may dominate a session, yielding results that are really the opinion of one or two people, not the group. The moderator has to try very hard to make sure that all respondents feel comfortable giving their opinions and even a timid respondent's opinion is given due consideration. While many people, even some with little or no background to do so, conduct focus groups, good moderators become effective through a combination of naturally good people skills, training (in qualitative research), and experience.

Second, some unique sampling problems arise with focus groups. Researchers often select focus group participants because they have similar backgrounds and experiences or because screening indicates that the participants are more articulate or gregarious than the typical consumer. Such participants may not be representative of the entire target market. Thus, focus group results are not intended to be representative of a larger population.

Third, although not so much an issue with online formats where respondents can remain anonymous, traditional face-to-face focus groups may not be useful for discussing sensitive topics. A focus group is a social setting and usually involves people with little to no familiarity with each other. Therefore, issues that people normally do not like to discuss in public may also prove difficult to discuss in a focus group.

Fourth, focus groups do cost a considerable amount of money, particularly when they are not conducted by someone employed by the company desiring the focus group. As research projects go, there are many more expensive approaches, including a full-blown mail survey using a national random sample. This may cost thousands of dollars to conduct and thousands of dollars to analyze and disseminate. Focus group prices vary regionally, but the following figures provide a rough guideline:

Renting facilities and equipment	$500
Recruiting of respondents ($75 person)	$750
Paying respondents ($100/person)	$1,000
Researcher costs	
■ Preparation	$750
■ Moderating	$1,000
■ Analysis and report preparation	$1,500
Miscellaneous expenses	$250

Thus, a client can expect a professional focus group to cost over $5,000 in most situations. Further, most business topics will call for multiple focus groups. There is some cost advantage in this, as some costs will not change proportionately just because there are multiple interviews. Preparation costs may be the same for one or more interviews; the analysis and report preparation will likely only increase slightly because two or three interviews are included instead of one.

Depth Interviews

An alternative to a focus group is a depth interview. A **depth interview** is a one-on-one interview between a professional researcher and a research respondent. Depth interviews are much the same as a psychological, clinical interview, but with a different purpose. The researcher asks many questions and follows up each answer with probes for additional elaboration. An excerpt from a depth interview is given in Exhibit 7.4.

Like focus group moderators, the interviewer's role is critical in a depth interview. He or she must be a highly skilled individual who can encourage the respondent to talk freely without influencing the direction of the conversation. Probing questions are critical.

Laddering is a term used for a particular approach to probing, asking respondents to compare differences between brands at different levels. What usually results is that the first distinctions are

depth interview

A one-on-one interview between a professional researcher and a research respondent conducted about some relevant business or social topic.

laddering

A particular approach to probing, asking respondents to compare differences between brands at different levels that produces distinctions at the attribute level, the benefit level, and the value or motivation level.

EXHIBIT **7.4**

Excerpt from a Depth Interview

An interviewer (I) talks with Marsha (M) about furniture purchases. Marsha indirectly indicates she delegates the buying responsibility to a trusted antique dealer. She has already said that she and her husband would write the dealer telling him the piece they wanted (e.g., bureau, table). The dealer would then locate a piece that he considered appropriate and would ship it to Marsha from his shop in another state.

M: ... We never actually shopped for furniture since we state what we want and (the antique dealer) picks it out and sends it to us. So we never have to go looking through stores and shops and things.

I: You depend on his (the antique dealer's) judgment?

M: Uh, huh. And, uh, he happens to have the sort of taste that we like and he knows what our taste is and always finds something that we're happy with.

I: You'd rather do that than do the shopping?

M: Oh, much rather, because it saves so much time and it would be so confusing for me to go through stores and stores looking for things, looking for furniture. This is so easy that I just am very fortunate.

I: Do you feel that he's a better judge than ...

M: Much better.

I: Than you are?

M: Yes, and that way I feel confident that what I have is very, very nice because he picked it out and I would be doubtful if I picked it out. I have confidence in him, (the antique dealer) knows everything about antiques, I think. If he tells me something, why I know it's true—no matter what I think. I know he is the one that's right.

This excerpt is most revealing of the way in which Marsha could increase her feeling of confidence by relying on the judgment of another person, particularly a person she trusted. Marsha tells us quite plainly that she would be doubtful (i.e., uncertain) about her own judgment, but she "knows" (i.e., is certain) that the antique dealer is a good judge, "no matter what I think." The dealer once sent a chair that, on first inspection, did not appeal to Marsha. She decided, however, that she must be wrong, and the dealer right, and grew to like the chair very much.

Source: From Cox, Donald F., Ed. *Risk Taking and Information Handling in Consumer Behavior* (Boston: Division of Research, Harvard Business School, © 1967), 65–66. Reprinted with permission.

attribute-level distinctions, the second are benefit-level distinctions, and the third are at the value or motivation level. Laddering can then distinguish two brands of skateboarding shoes based on a) the materials they are made of, b) the comfort they provide, and c) the excitement they create.

Each depth interview may last more than an hour. Thus, it is a time-consuming process if multiple interviews are conducted. Not only does the interview have to be conducted, but each interview produces about the same amount of text as does a focus group interview. This has to be analyzed and interpreted by the researcher. A third major issue stems from the necessity of recording both surface reactions and subconscious motivations of the respondent. Analysis and interpretation of such data are highly subjective, and it is difficult to settle on a true interpretation.

Depth interviews provide more insight into a particular individual than do focus groups. In addition, since the setting isn't really social, respondents are more likely to discuss sensitive topics than are those in a focus group. Depth interviews are particularly advantageous when some unique or unusual behavior is being studied. For instance, depth interviews have been usefully applied to reveal characteristics of adolescent behavior, ranging from the ways they get what they want from their parents to shopping, smoking, and shoplifting.[27]

Depth interviews are similar to focus groups in many ways. The costs are similar if only a few interviews are conducted. However, if a dozen or more interviews are included in a report, the costs are higher than focus group interviews due to the increased interviewing and analysis time.

Conversations

conversations

An informal qualitative data-gathering approach in which the researcher engages a respondent in a discussion of the relevant subject matter.

Holding **conversations** in qualitative research is an informal data-gathering approach in which the researcher engages a respondent in a discussion of the relevant subject matter. This approach is almost completely unstructured and the researcher enters the conversation with few expectations. The goal is to have the respondent produce a dialogue about his or her lived experiences. Meaning will be extracted from the resulting dialogue.

A conversational approach to qualitative research is particularly appropriate in phenomenological research and for developing grounded theory. In our Vans experience, the researcher may simply tape-record a conversation about becoming a "skater." The resulting dialogue can then be analyzed for themes and plots. The result may be some interesting and novel insight into the consumption patterns of skaters, for example, if the respondent said,

> "I knew I was a real skater when I just had to have Vans, not just for boarding, but for wearing."

This theme may connect to a rite-of-passage plot and show how Vans play a role in this process.

Technology is also influencing conversational research. Online communications such as the reviews posted about book purchases at **http://www.barnesandnoble.com** can be treated as a conversation. Companies may discover product problems and ideas for overcoming them by analyzing these computer-based consumer dialogues.[28]

A conversational approach is advantageous because each interview is usually inexpensive to conduct. Respondents often need not be paid. They are relatively effective at getting at sensitive issues once the researcher establishes a rapport with them. Conversational approaches, however, are prone to produce little relevant information since little effort is made to steer the conversation. Additionally, the data analysis is very much researcher-dependent.

Semistructured Interviews

Semistructured interviews usually come in written form and ask respondents for short essay responses to specific open-ended questions. Respondents are free to write as much or as little as they want. The questions would be divided into sections, typically, and within each section, the opening question would be followed by some probing questions. When these are performed face to face, there is room for less structured follow-ups.

The advantages to this approach include an ability to address more specific issues. Responses are usually easier to interpret than other qualitative approaches. Since the researcher can simply prepare the questions in writing ahead of time, and if in writing, the questions are administered without the presence of an interviewer, semistructured interviews can be relatively cost-effective.

Some researchers interested in studying car salesperson stereotypes used qualitative semistructured interviews to map consumers' cognitions (memory). The semistructured interview began with a free-association task:

List the first five things that come into your mind when you think of a "car salesman."

This was followed up with a probing question:

Describe the way a typical "car salesman" looks.

This was followed with questions about how the car salesperson acts and how the respondent feels in the presence of a car salesperson. The results led to research showing how the information that consumers process differs in the presence of a typical car salesperson, as opposed to a less typical car salesperson.[29]

Social Networking

Social networking is one of the most impactful trends in recent times. For many consumers, particularly younger generations, social networking sites like Facebook and MySpace have become the primary tool for communicating with friends both far and near and known and unknown. Social networking has replaced large volumes of e-mail and, many would say, face-to-face communications as well. While the impact that social networking will eventually have on society is an interesting question, what is most relevant to marketing research is the large portion of this information that discusses marketing and consumer related information.

Companies can assign research assistants to monitor these sites for information related to their particular brands. The information can be coded as either positive or negative. When too much negative information is being spread, the company can try to react to change the opinions. In addition, many companies like P&G and Ford maintain their own social networking sites for the purpose of gathering research data. In a way, these social networking sites are a way that companies can eavesdrop on consumer conversations and discover key information about their products. The textual data that consumers willingly put up becomes like a conversation. When researchers get the opportunity to react with consumers or employees through a social network site, they can function much like an online focus group or interview.

Free-Association/Sentence Completion Method

Free-association techniques simply record a respondent's first cognitive reactions (top-of-mind) to some stimulus. The Rorschach or inkblot test typifies the free-association method. Respondents view an ambiguous figure and are asked to say the first thing that comes to their mind. Free-association techniques allow researchers to map a respondent's thoughts or memory.

free-association techniques

Record respondents' first (top-of-mind) cognitive reactions to some stimulus.

The sentence completion method is based on free-association principles. Respondents simply are required to complete a few partial sentences with the first word or phrase that comes to mind. For example:

People who drink beer are _____.
A man who drinks a dark beer is _____.
Imported beer is most liked by _____.
The woman drinking beer in the commercial _____.

Answers to sentence-completion questions tend to be more extensive than responses to word-association tests. Although the responses lack the ability to probe for meaning as in other qualitative techniques, they are very effective in finding out what is on a respondent's mind. They can also do so in a quick and very cost-effective manner. Free-association and sentence-completion tasks are sometimes used in conjunction with other approaches. For instance, they can sometimes be used as effective icebreakers in focus group interviews.

Observation

field notes

The researcher's descriptions of what actually happens in the field; these notes then become the text from which meaning is extracted.

Observation can be a very important qualitative tool. The participant-observer approach typifies how observation can be used to explore various issues. Meaning is extracted from field notes. **Field notes** are the researchers' descriptions of what actually happens in the field. These notes then become the text from which meaning is extracted.

Observation may also take place in visual form. Researchers may observe employees in their workplace, consumers in their home, or try to gain knowledge from photographic records of one type or another. Observation can either be very inexpensive, such as when a research associate sits and simply observes behavior, or it can be very expensive, as in most participant-observer studies. Observational research is keenly advantageous for gaining insight into things that respondents cannot or will not verbalize. Observation research is a common method of data collection and is the focus of Chapter 11.

Collages

As seen in the Research Snapshot on Spark-NYC, business researchers sometimes have respondents prepare a collage to represent their experiences. The collages are then analyzed for meaning much in the same manner as text dialogues are analyzed. Computer software can even be applied to help develop potential grounded theories from the visual representations.

Harley-Davidson commissioned research in which collages depicting feelings about Harley-Davidson were compared based on whether the respondent was a Harley owner or an owner of a competitor's brand. The collages of "Hog" owners revealed themes of artwork and the freedom of the great outdoors. These themes did not emerge in the non-Hog groups. This led to confirmatory research that helped Harley continue its growth, appealing more specifically to its diverse market segments.[30]

Like sentence completion and word association, collages are often used within some other approach, such as a focus group or a depth interview. Collages offer the advantage of flexibility but are also very much subject to the researcher's interpretations.

Projective Research Techniques

projective technique

An indirect means of questioning enabling respondents to project beliefs and feelings onto a third party, an inanimate object, or a task situation.

A **projective technique** is an indirect means of questioning enabling respondents to project beliefs and feelings onto a third party, an inanimate object, or a task situation. Projective techniques usually encourage respondents to describe a situation in their own words with little prompting by the interviewer. Individuals are expected to interpret the situation within the context of their own experiences, attitudes, and personalities and to express opinions and emotions that may be hidden from others and possibly themselves. Projective techniques are particularly useful in studying sensitive issues.

There is an old story about asking a man why he purchased a Mercedes-Benz. When asked directly why he purchased a Mercedes, he responds that the car holds its value and does not depreciate much, that it gets better gas mileage than you'd expect, or that it has a comfortable ride. If you ask the same person why a neighbor purchased a Mercedes, he may well answer, "Oh, that status seeker!" This story illustrates that individuals may be more likely to give true answers (consciously or unconsciously) to disguised questions, and a projective technique provides a way of disguising just who is being described.

Thematic Apperception Test (TAT)

thematic apperception test (TAT)

A test that presents subjects with an ambiguous picture(s) in which consumers and products are the center of attention; the investigator asks the subject to tell what is happening in the picture(s) now and what might happen next.

A **thematic apperception test (TAT)**, sometimes called the picture interpretation technique, presents subjects with an ambiguous picture(s) and asks the subject to tell what is happening in the picture(s) now and what might happen next. Hence, themes (thematic) are elicited on the basis of the perceptual-interpretive (apperception) use of the pictures. The researcher then analyzes the contents of the stories that the subjects relate. A TAT represents a projective research technique.

Frequently, the TAT consists of a series of pictures with some continuity so that stories may be constructed in a variety of settings. The first picture might portray a person working at their desk; in the second picture, a person that could be a supervisor is talking to the worker; the final picture

© Cengage Learning 2013

EXHIBIT 7.5
An Example of a TAT Picture

might show the original employee and another having a discussion at the water cooler. A Vans TAT might include several ambiguous pictures of a skateboarder and then show him or her heading to the store. This might reveal ideas about the brands and products that fit the role of skateboarder.

The picture or cartoon stimulus must be sufficiently interesting to encourage discussion but ambiguous enough not to disclose the nature of the research project. Clues should not be given to the character's positive or negative predisposition. A pretest of a TAT investigating why men might purchase chainsaws used a picture of a man looking at a very large tree. The research respondents were homeowners and weekend woodcutters. They almost unanimously said that they would get professional help from a tree surgeon to deal with this situation. Thus, early in pretesting, the researchers found out that the picture was not sufficiently ambiguous. The tree was too large and did not allow respondents to identify with the tree-cutting task. If subjects are to project their own views into the situation, the environmental setting should be a well-defined, familiar problem, but the solution should be ambiguous.

An example of a TAT using a cartoon drawing in which the respondent suggests a dialogue in which the characters might engage is provided in Exhibit 7.5. This TAT is a purposely ambiguous illustration of an everyday occurrence. The two office workers are shown in a situation and the respondent is asked what the woman might be talking about. This setting could be used for discussions about the organization's management, store personnel, particular software products, and so on.

Exploratory Research in Science and in Practice

Misuses of Exploratory and Qualitative Research

Any research tool can be misapplied. Exploratory research cannot take the place of conclusive, confirmatory research. Thus, since many qualitative tools are best applied in exploratory design, they are likewise limited in the ability to draw conclusive inferences—test hypotheses. One of the biggest drawbacks is the subjectivity that comes along with "interpretation." In fact, sometimes the term interpretive research is used synonymously with qualitative research. When only one researcher interprets the meaning of what a single person said in a depth interview or similar technique, one should be very cautious before major business decisions are made based on these results. Is the result replicable? **Replication** means that the same results and conclusions will be drawn if the study is repeated by different researchers with different respondents following the same methods. In other words, would the same conclusion be reached based on another researcher's interpretation?

Indeed, some qualitative research methodologies were generally frowned upon for years based on a few early and public misapplications during what became known as the "motivational research" era. While many of the ideas produced during this time had some merit, as can sometimes be the case, too few researchers did too much interpretation of too few respondents. Compounding this, managers were quick to act on the results, believing that the results peaked inside one's subliminal consciousness and therefore held some type of extra power. Thus, often the research was flawed based on poor interpretation, and the decision process was flawed because the deciders acted prematurely. As examples, projective techniques and depth interviews were frequently used in the late 1950s and early 1960s, producing some interesting and occasionally bizarre reasons for consumers' purchasing behavior:

- A woman is very serious when she bakes a cake because unconsciously she is going through the symbolic act of giving birth.
- A man buys a convertible as a substitute mistress and a safer (and potentially cheaper) way of committing adultery.
- Men who wear suspenders are reacting to an unresolved castration complex.[31]

About two decades later, researchers for the McCann-Erickson advertising agency interviewed low-income women using a form of TAT involving story completion regarding attitudes toward insecticides. Themes noted included:

- The joy of victory over roaches (watching them die or seeing them dead)
- Using the roach as a metaphor through which women can take out their hostility toward men (women generally referred to roaches as "he" instead of "she" in their stories).[32]

Certainly, some useful findings resulted. Even today, we have the Pillsbury Doughboy as evidence that useful ideas were produced. In many of these cases, interpretations were either misleading or too ambitious (taken too far). However, many companies became frustrated when decisions based upon motivational research approaches proved poor. Thus, researchers moved away from qualitative tools during the late 1960s and 1970s. Today, however, qualitative tools have won acceptance once again as researchers realize they have greater power in discovering insights that would be difficult to capture in typical survey research (which is limited as an exploratory tool).

Scientific Decision Processes

Objectivity and replicability are two characteristics of scientific inquiry. Are focus groups objective and replicable? Would three different researchers all interpret focus group data identically? How should a facial expression or nod of the head be interpreted? Have subjects fully grasped the idea or concept behind a nonexistent product? Have respondents overstated their satisfaction because they think their supervisor will read the report and recognize them from their comments? Many of these questions are reduced to a matter of opinion that may vary from researcher to researcher and from one respondent group to another. Therefore, a focus group, or a depth interview, or TAT alone does not best represent a complete scientific inquiry.

However, if the thoughts discovered through these techniques survive preliminary evaluations and are developed into research hypotheses, they can be further tested. These tests may involve survey research or an experiment testing an idea very specifically (for example, if a certain advertising slogan is more effective than another). Thus, exploratory research approaches using qualitative research tools are very much a part of scientific inquiry. However, before making a scientific decision, a research project should include a confirmatory study using objective tools and an adequate sample in terms of both size and how well it represents a population.

replication

The same interpretation will be drawn if the study is repeated by different researchers with different respondents following the same methods.

But is a scientific decision approach always used or needed? In practice, many business decisions are based solely on the results of focus group interviews or some other exploratory result. The primary reasons for this are (1) time, (2) money, and (3) emotion.

Time

Sometimes, researchers simply are not given enough time to follow up on exploratory research results. Companies feel an increasingly urgent need to get new products to the market faster. Thus, a seemingly good idea generated in a focus group (like Clear, Vanilla, or Cherry Dr Pepper) is simply not tested with a more conclusive study. The risk of delaying a decision may be seen as greater than the risk of proceeding without completing the scientific process. Thus, although the researcher may warn against it, there may be logical reasons for such action. The decision makers should be aware, though, that the conclusions drawn from exploratory research designs are just that—exploratory. Thus, there is less likelihood of good results from the decision than if the research process had involved further testing.

Money

Similarly, researchers sometimes do not follow up on exploratory research results because they believe the cost is too high. Realize that tens of thousands of dollars may have already been spent on qualitative research. Managers who are unfamiliar with research will be very tempted to wonder, "Why do I need yet another study?" and "What did I spend all that money for?" Thus, they choose to proceed based only on exploratory results. Again, the researcher has fulfilled the professional obligation as long as the tentative nature of any ideas derived from exploratory research has been relayed through the research report.

Again, this isn't always a bad approach. If the decision itself does not involve a great deal of risk or if it can be reversed easily, the best course of action may be to proceed to implementation instead of investing more money in confirmatory research. Remember, research shouldn't be performed if it will cost more than it will return.

Emotion

Time, money, and emotion are all related. Decision makers sometimes become so anxious to have something resolved, or they get so excited about some novel discovery resulting from a focus group interview, that they may act rashly. Perhaps some of the ideas produced during the motivational research era sounded so enticing that decision makers got caught up in the emotion of the moment and proceeded without the proper amount of testing. Thus, as in life, when we fall in love with something, we are prone to act irrationally. The chances of emotion interfering in this way are lessened, but not reduced, by making sure multiple decision makers are involved in the decision process.

In conclusion, we began this section by suggesting that exploratory, qualitative research cannot take the place of a confirmatory study. However, a confirmatory study cannot take the place of an exploratory, qualitative study either. While confirmatory studies are best for testing specific ideas, a qualitative study is far better suited to developing ideas and practical theories.

:: SUMMARY

1. List and understand the differences between qualitative research and quantitative research. The chapter emphasized that any argument about the overall superiority of qualitative versus quantitative research is misplaced. Rather, each approach has advantages and disadvantages that make it appropriate in certain situations. The presence or absence of numbers is not the key factor discriminating between qualitative and quantitative research. Qualitative research relies more on researchers' subjective interpretations of text or other visual material. In contrast,

the numbers produced in quantitative research are objective in the sense that they don't change simply because someone else computed them. Thus, we expect quantitative research to have intersubjective certifiability, while qualitative research may not. Qualitative research typically involves small samples while quantitative research usually uses large samples. Qualitative procedures are generally more flexible and produce deeper and more elaborate explanations than quantitative research.

2. Understand the role of qualitative research in exploratory research designs. The high degree of flexibility that goes along with most qualitative techniques makes it very useful in exploratory research designs. Therefore, exploratory research designs most often involve some qualitative research technique.

3. Describe the basic qualitative research orientations. Phenomenology is a philosophical approach to studying human experiences based on the idea that human experience itself is inherently subjective and determined by the context within which a person experiences something. It lends itself well to conversational research. Ethnography represents ways of studying cultures through methods that include high involvement with that culture. Participant-observation is a common ethnographic approach. Grounded theory represents inductive qualitative investigation in which the researcher continually poses questions about a respondent's discourse in an effort to derive a deep explanation of their behavior. Collages are sometimes used to develop grounded theory. Case studies simply are documented histories of a particular person, group, organization, or event.

4. Prepare a focus group interview outline. A focus group outline should begin with introductory comments followed by a very general opening question that does not lead the respondent. More specific questions should be listed until a blunt question directly pertaining to the study objective is included. However, a skilled moderator can often lead the group without having to explicitly state these questions. It should conclude with debriefing comments and a chance for question-and-answers with respondents.

5. Recognize technological advances in the application of qualitative research approaches. Videoconferencing and online chat rooms are more economical ways of trying to do much the same as traditional focus group interviews. Some companies have even established a focus blog that is a source for continuous commentary on a company. While they are certainly cost advantageous, there is less control over who participates.

6. Recognize common qualitative research tools and know the advantages and limitations of their use. The most common qualitative research tools include the focus group interview and the depth interview. The focus group has some cost advantage per respondent because it would take 10 times as long to conduct the interview portion(s) of a series of depth interviews compared to one focus group. However, the depth interview is more appropriate for discussing sensitive topics.

7. Know the risks associated with acting on only exploratory results. Companies do make decisions using only exploratory research. There are several explanations for this behavior. The researcher's job is to make sure that decision makers understand the increased risk that comes along with basing a decision only on exploratory research results.

∶∶KEY TERMS AND CONCEPTS

:: QUESTIONS FOR REVIEW AND CRITICAL THINKING

1. Define qualitative and quantitative research. Compare and contrast the two approaches.
2. Why do exploratory research designs rely so much on qualitative research techniques?
3. Why do causal designs rely so much on quantitative research techniques?
4. What are the basic orientations of qualitative research?
5. Of the four basic orientations of qualitative research, which do you think is most appropriate for a qualitative approach designed to better define a business situation prior to conducting confirmatory research?
6. What type of exploratory research would you suggest in the following situations?
   a. A product manager suggests development of a nontobacco cigarette blended from wheat, cocoa, and citrus.
   b. A research project has the purpose of evaluating potential names for a corporate spin-off.
   c. A human resource manager must determine the most important benefits of an employee health plan.
   d. An advertiser wishes to identify the symbolism associated with cigar smoking.
7. What are the key differences between a focus group interview and a depth interview?

8. 'NET Visit some websites for large companies like Honda, Qantas Airlines, Target, Tesco, and Marriott. Is there any evidence that they are using their Internet sites in some way to conduct a continuous online focus blog or intermittent online focus groups?
9. What is laddering? How might it be used in trying to understand which fast-food restaurant customers prefer?
10. Comment on the following remark by a business consultant: "Qualitative exploration is a tool of research and a stimulant to thinking. In and by itself, however, it does not constitute business research."
11. ETHICS A researcher tells a manager of a wine company that he has some "cool focus group results" suggesting that respondents like the idea of a screw cap to top wine bottles. Even before the decision maker sees the report, the manager begins purchasing screw caps and the new bottling equipment. Comment on this situation.
12. A packaged goods manufacturer receives many thousands of customer letters a year. Some are complaints, some are compliments. They cover a broad range of topics. Are these letters a possible source for exploratory research? Why or why not?

:: RESEARCH ACTIVITIES

1. 'NET How might the following organizations use an Internet chat room for exploratory research?
   a. A provider of health benefits
   b. A computer software manufacturer
   c. A video game manufacturer
2. Go back to the opening vignette. What if Vans approached you to do a focus group interview that explored the idea of offering casual attire (off-board) aimed at their primary segment (skateboarders) and offering casual attire for male retirees like Samuel Teel? How would you recommend the focus group(s) proceed? Prepare a focus group outline(s) to accomplish this task.

3. Interview two people about their exercise behavior. In one interview, try to use a semistructured approach by preparing questions ahead of time and trying to have the respondent complete answers for these questions. With the other, try a conversational approach. What are the main themes that emerge in each? Which approach do you think was more insightful? Do you think there were any "sensitive" topics that a respondent was not completely forthcoming about?

Disaster and Consumer Value

CASE 7.1

In February 2009, bushfires raced across the Australian state of Victoria. This terrible tragedy resulted in the loss of over 300 lives, Australia's highest ever loss of life from a bushfire. In addition, more than 2,000 homes were destroyed and insurance losses are estimated to exceed $2 billion.[33] While rebuilding will take years, at some point after these disasters, it is time to get back to business. But major catastrophic events are likely to leave permanent changes on consumers and employees in the affected areas.

Suppose you are approached by the owner of several full-service wine stores in Victoria. It is January 2010, and they want to get back to business. But they are uncertain about whether they should simply maintain the same positioning they had previous to the bushfires. They would like to have a report from you within 60 days.

Questions

1. How could each orientation of qualitative research be used here?
2. What qualitative research tool(s) would you recommend be used and why?
3. Where would you conduct any interviews and with whom would you conduct them?
4. ETHICS Are there ethical issues that you should be sensitive to in this process? Explain.
5. What issues would arise in conducting a focus group interview in this situation?
6. Prepare a focus group outline.

Edward Jones

CASE 7.2

Edward Jones is one of the largest investment firms in the United States, with over 4,000 branch offices in this country, Canada, and the United Kingdom. It is the only major brokerage firm that exclusively targets individual investors and small businesses, and it has nearly 6 million clients.

Edward Jones' philosophy is to offer personalized services to individual clients starting with a one-on-one interview. During the interview, investment representatives seek to identify each client's specific goals for investing. Richard G. Miller, one such representative, says that he needs to thoroughly understand what a client wants before he can build an investment strategy for that person. His initial conversation starts with, "Hey, how are you?" Gregory L. Starry, another representative, confirms the Edward Jones philosophy: "Most of my day is spent talking with and meeting clients [rather than placing stock trades]."

Only after learning these goals do the representatives design an investment strategy that will provide a client with income, growth, and safety. Each client's goals also evolve over time. Young people are focused on earning enough money to make a down payment on their first home or to buy a car. Clients in the 35 to 45 age range are concerned about getting their children through school and about their own retirement. Those in retirement want to make sure that they have an adequate income level. Miller notes, "It's not the timing in the market, but the time in the market" that will help clients achieve their goals.

Questions

1. Many people in minority groups, including African Americans, Hispanic Americans, Asian Americans, and Native Americans, do not invest. What exploratory research should Edward Jones do to develop business with these minority markets?
2. Another group with low investment activity includes those who stopped their education at the high school level. What factors should Edward Jones representatives consider in designing focus groups with these potential clients?

Secondary Data Research in a Digital Age

LEARNING OUTCOMES

After studying this chapter, you should be able to

1. Discuss the advantages and disadvantages of secondary data
2. Define types of secondary data analysis conducted by business research managers
3. Identify various internal and proprietary sources of secondary data
4. Give examples of various external sources of secondary data
5. Describe the impact of single-source data and globalization on secondary data research

Chapter Vignette:

Business Facts on a Grand Scale

A key problem that faces any business research manager is the need to constantly capture relevant data about customers, competitors, and/or market characteristics. The use of secondary data (i.e., data that has been collected previously for other purposes) has exploded with the advent of large-scale electronic information sources and the web. One company that has taken full advantage of integrating various business related information sources is Nielsen Claritas.

Prior to its merge with The Nielsen Company, Claritas (which in Latin means "brightness") had a 40-year history of collecting and integrating business-related data from difference sources. Its products include (1) PRIZM, which provides market segmentation information based upon consumer behavior and geographic location; (2) Consumer Point, a target marketing analysis solution for different industry spaces; and (3) Business-Facts, which provides accurate business data for market support and strategic planning.

Business-Facts holds great promise as a secondary data source for existing companies. Using Standard Industrial Classification (SIC) and North American Industry Classification (NAICS)[1] codes developed through the Census Bureau, characteristics on business ownership, location, employment, and sales are available for 10 major industrial groupings. Data and employee counts within the Business-Facts system represent over

13 million businesses. Examples of these industry groups include construction, manufacturing, and retail sales establishments across the United States. Since business information can become quickly obsolete, Nielsen Claritas spends millions of dollars each year to verify business information on a quarterly basis.

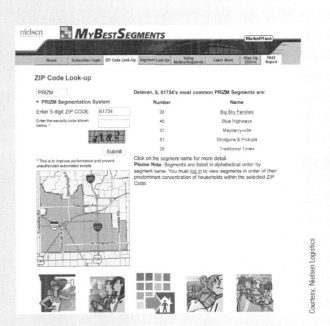

Courtesy, Nielsen Logistics

The advantages of knowing broadly both the characteristics and location of major customer groups (or potential competitors) are very real. Using a sophisticated statistical modeling approach, Nielsen Claritas can link your customers to your existing or proposed locations, in a fashion such that the information is as timely and applicable as possible.

All of the information sources within Nielsen Claritas add value to business users by satisfying two very critical needs. First, Nielsen Claritas has expertise in linking different data streams into a cohesive system. This allows users to answer through secondary data sources critical existing business questions. Secondly, their information systems are geographically based, so that businesses can query data to a common point on the globe.

Truly, the integration and utilization of secondary data sources by Nielsen Claritas has put business research "on the map"—both literally and figuratively!

Introduction

secondary data

Data that have been previously collected for some purpose other than the one at hand.

Business researchers are always working under time and budget constraints. So, they are wise to ask if the data needed to examine the research questions already exists. If so, the analysis can proceed quickly, efficiently, and at minimum cost. Therefore, research projects should begin with **secondary data**, which are gathered and recorded by someone else prior to, and for purposes other than, the current project. Secondary data usually are already assembled. They require no access to respondents or subjects.

Advantages of Secondary Data

"If I have seen farther than others, it is because I have stood on the shoulders of giants."

—ISAAC NEWTON

The primary advantage of secondary data is their availability. Obtaining secondary data is almost always faster and less expensive than acquiring primary data. This is particularly true when researchers use electronic retrieval to access data stored digitally. In many situations, collecting secondary data is instantaneous and free.

Consider the money and time saved by researchers who obtained updated population estimates for a town since the 2010 Census. Instead of doing the fieldwork themselves, researchers could acquire estimates from a firm dealing in demographic information or from sources such as Nielsen Claritas or PCensus. As in this example, the use of secondary data eliminates many of the activities normally associated with primary data collection, such as sampling and data processing.

Secondary data are essential in instances when data simply cannot be obtained using primary data collection procedures. For example, a manufacturer of farm implements could not duplicate the information in the Census of Agriculture due to the sheer amount of information and the fact that much of the information (for example, amount of taxes paid) might not be provided to a private firm. Similarly, in India researchers use census estimates to track sensitive topics like child labor rates, which would be simply overwhelming for a private organization to undertake.

Disadvantages of Secondary Data

An inherent disadvantage of secondary data is that they were not designed to meet the researchers' specific needs. Thus, researchers must ask how pertinent the data are to their particular project. To evaluate secondary data, researchers should ask questions such as these:

- Is the subject matter consistent with our problem definition?
- Do the data apply to the population of interest?
- Do the data apply to the time period of interest?
- Do the secondary data appear in the correct units of measurement?
- Do the data cover the subject of interest in adequate detail?

Even when secondary information is available, it can be inadequate. Consider the following typical situations:

- A researcher interested in forklift trucks finds that the secondary data on the subject are included in a broader, less pertinent category encompassing all industrial trucks and tractors. Furthermore, the data were collected five years earlier.

The data in the online survey provide qualitative and quantitative data based upon responses from students around the world. While some of these data are centered on university experiences and attitudes, several data variables are similar to the kinds of data gathered from public opinion research. For example, take a look at some basic results (such as how many people strongly agree) on a few of the items in the online survey related to how a person's job affects them outside of work. Then, do a Google search on terms like "work tension opinions" and "work stress study." Look at the linked documents. Do the results obtained from the online survey appear consistent with other opinion study results?

The next set of items concerns how much your current job affects what you do when you are away from work. For each question, choose the response that best describes how your current job has impact on:

	Strong Negative Impact	Negative Impact	Mild Negative Impact	Mild Positive Impact	Positive Impact	Strong Positive Impact
your mental and physical state away from work	○	○	○	○	○	○
your participation in home activities	○	○	○	○	○	○
concern for your health	○	○	○	○	○	○
your personal development	○	○	○	○	○	○
your performance in school	○	○	○	○	○	○
your social life	○	○	○	○	○	○

Close

Courtesy of Qualtrics.com

- An investigator who wishes to study individuals earning more than $100,000 per year finds the top category in a secondary study reported at $75,000 or more per year.
- A brewery that wishes to compare its per-barrel advertising expenditures with those of competitors finds that the units of measurement differ because some report point-of-purchase expenditures with advertising and others do not.
- Data from a previous warranty card study show where consumers prefer to purchase the product but provide no reasons why.

While it is wonderful to be able to access secondary data quickly and cheaply, a researcher needs to be careful that it accurately addresses the research issues. Secondary data often do not adequately satisfy research needs because of (1) variation in definitions of terms, (2) the use of different units of measurement, (3) inadequate information to verify the data's validity, and (4) data that are too old.

Every primary researcher has the right to define the terms or concepts under investigation to satisfy the purpose of his or her primary investigation. This practice provides little solace, however, to the investigator of the African-American market who finds secondary data reported as "percent nonwhite." Variances in terms or variable classifications should be scrutinized to determine whether differences are important. The populations of interest must be described in comparable terms. Researchers frequently encounter secondary data that report on a population of interest that is similar but not directly comparable to their population of interest. For example, Arbitron reports its television audience estimates by geographical areas known as ADIs (Areas of Dominant Influence). An ADI is a geographic area consisting of all counties in which the home market commercial television stations receive a preponderance of total viewing hours. This unique population of interest is used exclusively to report television audiences. The geographic areas used in the census of population, such as Metropolitan Statistical Areas, are not comparable to ADIs.

Units of measurement may cause problems if they do not conform exactly to a researcher's needs as well. For example, lumber shipments in millions of board feet are quite different from billions of ton-miles of lumber shipped on freight cars. Head-of-household income is not the same unit of measure as total family income. Often the objective of the original primary study may dictate that the data be summarized, rounded, or reported. When that happens, even if the original units of measurement were comparable, aggregated or adjusted units of measurement are not suitable in the secondary study.

When secondary data are reported in a format that does not exactly meet the researcher's needs, data conversion may be necessary. **Data conversion** (also called *data transformation*) is the process of changing the original form of data to a format more suitable for achieving a stated research

data conversion

The process of changing the original form of the data to a format suitable to achieve the research objective; also called data transformation.

objective. For example, sales for food products may be reported in pounds, cases, or dollars. An estimate of dollars per pound may be used to convert dollar volume data to pounds or another suitable format.

Another disadvantage of secondary data is that the user has no control over their validity—a topic we will discuss in more detail later. For now, think of this as representing data accuracy or trustworthiness. Although timely and pertinent secondary data may fit the researcher's requirements, the data could be inaccurate. The research methods used to collect the data may have somehow introduced bias to the data. For example, media often publish data from surveys to identify the characteristics of their subscribers or viewers. These data will sometimes exclude derogatory data from their reports. Good researchers avoid data with a high likelihood of bias or for which the overall accuracy cannot be determined.

Investigators are naturally more prone to accept data from reliable sources such as the U.S. government. Nevertheless, the researcher must assess the reputation of the organization that gathers the data and critically assess the research design to determine whether the research was correctly implemented. Unfortunately, such evaluation may be impossible without full information that explains how the original research was conducted.

Finally, data must be current to be useful. While technology today allows much faster access to data, our rapidly changing environment also means information quickly becomes outdated. Because the purpose of most studies is to use current data to predict the future, secondary data must be timely to be useful.

cross-checks

The comparison of data from one source with data from another source to determine the similarity of independent projects.

Researchers should verify the accuracy of the data whenever possible. **Cross-checks** of data from multiple sources, similar to what Nielsen Claritas does with its Business-Facts database, should be made to determine the similarity of independent projects. When the data are not consistent, researchers should attempt to identify reasons for the differences or to determine which data are most likely to be correct. If the accuracy of the data cannot be established, the researcher must determine whether using the data is worth the risk. Exhibit 8.1 illustrates a series of questions that should be asked to evaluate secondary data before they are used.

Typical Objectives for Secondary Data Research Designs

It would be impossible to identify all the purposes of research using secondary data. However, some common business problems that can be addressed with secondary research designs are useful. Exhibit 8.2 shows three general categories of research objectives: fact-finding, model building, and database marketing.

Fact-Finding

The simplest form of secondary data research is fact-finding. A restaurant serving breakfast might be interested in knowing what new products are likely to entice consumers. Secondary data available from National Eating Trends, a service of the NPD Group, show that the most potential may be in menu items customers can eat on the go.[2] According to data from the survey of eating trends, the increased prevalence of nutrition and calorie counts on menus has not significantly affected consumer choices. In addition, while overall restaurant sales dropped during the economic downturn of 2009 and 2010, fast casual restaurants such as Chili's have seen their sales go up. Another research firm, Market Facts, says almost half of consumers say they would pay extra for cheese. These simple facts would interest a researcher who was investigating today's dining market.

Identification of Consumer Behavior for a Product Category

A typical objective for a secondary research study might be to uncover all available information about consumption patterns for a particular product category or to identify demographic trends that affect an industry. For example, a company called Servigistics offers software that will scan

EXHIBIT **8.1**
Evaluating Secondary Data

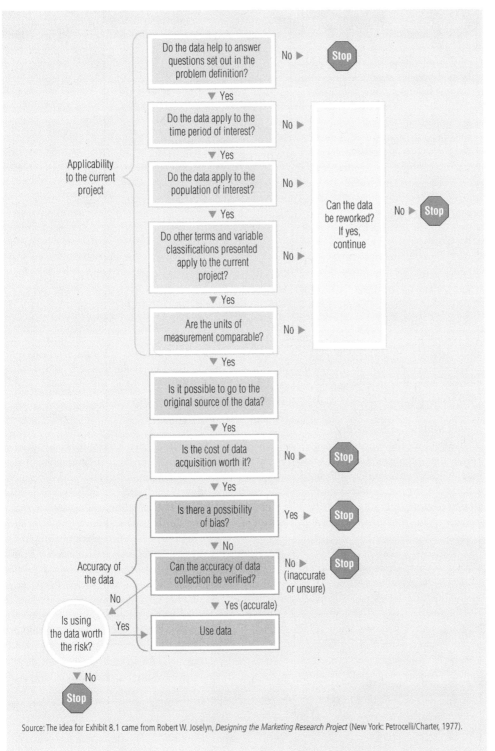

Source: The idea for Exhibit 8.1 came from Robert W. Joselyn, *Designing the Marketing Research Project* (New York: Petrocelli/Charter, 1977).

a company's own parts inventory data and compare it with marketing objectives and competitors' prices to evaluate whether the company should adjust prices for its parts. Kia Motors tried using this service in place of the usual method of marking up cost by a set fraction. By considering secondary data including internal inventory data and external data about competitors' prices, it was able to make service parts a more profitable segment of its business.[3] This example illustrates

© Cengage Learning 2013

EXHIBIT 8.2

Common Research Objectives for Secondary Data Studies

Broad Objective	Specific Research Example
Fact-finding	Identifying consumption patterns Tracking trends
Model building	Estimating market potential Forecasting sales Selecting trade areas and sites
Database marketing	Enhancing customer databases Developing prospect lists

the wealth of factual information about consumption and behavior patterns that can be obtained by carefully collecting and analyzing secondary data.

Trend Analysis

Business researchers are challenged to constantly watch for trends in the marketplace and the environment. **Market tracking** is the observation and analysis of trends in industry volume and brand share over time. Scanner research services and other organizations provide facts about sales volume to support this work.

Almost every large consumer goods company routinely investigates brand and product category sales volume using secondary data. This type of analysis typically involves comparisons with competitors' sales or with the company's own sales in comparable time periods. It also involves industry comparisons among different geographic areas. Exhibit 8.3 shows information available from secondary sources regarding the largest retail store chains in Europe.

ENVIRONMENTAL SCANNING

In many instances, the purpose of fact-finding is simply to study the environment to identify trends. Environmental scanning entails information gathering and fact-finding designed to detect indications of environmental changes in their initial stages of development. The Internet can be used for environmental scanning; however, there are other means, such as periodic review of contemporary publications and reports. For example, environmental scanning has shown many researchers that consumer demand in China is skyrocketing. In the case of beauty products such as cosmetics, Chinese authorities in the early 1990s stopped discouraging the use of makeup, and sales of these products took off—hitting $524 million in 2005. Sales continue to skyrocket, as the total Chinese market for cosmetics and toiletries was RMB 133.24 billion ($19.51 billion) in 2009. The market is up over 11 percent from 2008 despite the economic conditions. Companies including Procter & Gamble, L'Oréal, and Shiseido have captured a sizable share of this market by realizing the potential and developing products to get into the Chinese market early.[4]

A number of online information services, such as Factiva and LexisNexis, routinely collect news stories about industries, product lines, and other topics of interest that have been specified by the researcher. In addition, push technology is an Internet information

market tracking

The observation and analysis of trends in industry volume and brand share over time.

● ● ● ● ● ● ●

Secondary data shows which restaurants have seen increases in sales.

Does It Matter?

Secondary data, but for its name, may seem to lack power compared to primary data. However, with secondary data, researchers can test research questions that would be difficult to examine any other way. For example, what firms are the market leaders in their industry? What matters when it comes to firm performance? Does customer satisfaction ultimately lead to superior firm performance? Given that firm performance is a property of the company and not of its customers or employees, the researcher cannot directly capture this with surveys. Therefore, researchers turn to secondary data to try to isolate controllable variables that drive firm performance.

Basic research addresses this issue by tapping into secondary data sources such as the Nielsen database, Compustat, and the American Consumer Satisfaction Index (the ACSI). What should companies emphasize? Advertising, services, value, or satisfaction? Statistical models using secondary data suggest

Carrefour, the second largest retailer in the world, has the recipe for success.

that advertising, satisfaction, and services all play a role. But, as an industry becomes more competitive, services and value come to the top in shaping a firm's stock value. Thus, what matters? It seems like firms should allocate scarce resources toward increasing services and greater value. That's a recipe for success.

Sources: Grewal, P., M. Chandrashkaran and A. V. Citrin, "Customer Satisfaction Heterogeneity and Shareholder Value," *Journal of Marketing Research*, 47 (August 2010), 612–626. Fang, E., R. W. Palmatier and J. B. Steencamp, "Effect of Service Transition Strategies on Firm Value," *Journal of Marketing*, 72 (September 2008), 1–14. Luo, X. and C. Homburg, "Neglected Outcomes of Consumer Satisfaction," *Journal of Marketing*, 71 (April 2007), 133–149.

EXHIBIT 8.3

2011 Largest Retail Chains in Europe

Rank	Store Name	Home Country	Type of Store
1	WalMart	United States	Discount Store
2	Carrefour	France	Hypermarket/Supercenter/Superstore
3	Metro AG	Germany	Cash & Carry/Warehouse Club
4	Tesco plc	U. K.	Hypermarket/Supercenter/Superstore
5	Schwarz Untemehmens	Germany	Discount Store

2011 Largest European Retail Chains—Complete List of Biggest Europe Retailers
Source: From http://retailindustry.about.com/od/largesteuropeanretailers/a/largest_european_largest_retail_chains-2011-world_rankings_europes-biggest-retailers.htm, accessed May 12, 2011.

technology that automatically delivers content to the researcher's or manager's desktop. Push technology uses "electronic smart agents," custom software that filters, sorts, prioritizes, and stores information for later viewing.[5] This service frees the researcher from doing the searching. The true value of push technology is that the researcher who is scanning the environment can specify the kinds of news and information he or she wants, have it delivered to his or her computer quickly, and view it at leisure.

Model Building

The second general objective for secondary research, model building, is more complicated than simple fact-finding. **Model building** involves specifying relationships between two or more variables, perhaps extending to the development of descriptive or predictive equations, a technique that is used by Nielsen Claritas routinely to add value to their secondary data. Models need not include complicated mathematics, though. In fact, decision makers often prefer simple models that everyone can readily understand over complex models that are difficult to comprehend. For example, market share is company sales divided by industry sales. Although some may not think of this simple calculation as a model, it represents a mathematical model of a basic relationship.

model building

The use of secondary data to help specify relationships between two or more variables; can involve the development of descriptive or predictive equations.

We will illustrate model building by discussing three common objectives that can be satisfied with secondary research: estimating market potential, forecasting sales, and selecting potential facility or expansion sites.

Estimating Market Potential for Geographic Areas

Business researchers often estimate their company's market potential using secondary data. In many cases exact figures may be published by a trade association or another source. However, when the desired information is unavailable, the researcher may estimate market potential by transforming secondary data from two or more sources. For example, managers may find secondary data about market potential for a country or other large geographic area, but this information may not be broken down into smaller geographical areas, such as by metropolitan area, or in terms unique to the company, such as sales territory. In this type of situation, researchers often need to make projections for the geographic area of interest.

Suppose a Belgian beer company is looking for opportunities to expand sales by exporting or investing in other countries. Managers decide to begin by estimating market potential in several potential target markets. Secondary research uncovered data for per capita beer consumption in numerous sources including reports from Data Monitor, a company that catalogs commercial statistics by country. Population estimates are also available in several places including the census bureau and through the CIA (see **www.cia.gov** to access the World Factbook). Exhibit 8.4 illustrates the main findings compiled.

The trade area market potential for the Czech Republic in 2012 is found by multiplying the country's population estimate[6] by the per capita beer consumption:

$$10,190,000 \ people \times 160 \ liters/person = 1,630,400,000 \ liters$$

That's over a bottle a day per person. To get a sense of the expected sales volume, the marketer would have to multiply this amount by the price per liter at which beer typically sells. Although the Czech Republic may be an attractive market, greater overall volume might be offered by other markets with larger overall populations. As Exhibit 8.4 reveals, China offers the largest potential market for beer sales in the world.[7] Brazil and the U.S. also display relatively high total beer consumption. Although those countries aren't known so much for beer consumption, the sheer size of the markets makes them attractive targets for the brewery.

Of course, the calculated market potential for each country in Exhibit 8.4 is a rough estimate. One obvious problem is that not everyone in a country will be of beer-drinking age. If the researcher can get statistics for each country's projected adult population, the estimate will be closer. This illustrates one of the weaknesses of secondary data. Also, you might want to consider whether each country is experiencing growth or decline in the demand for beer to estimate whether

EXHIBIT 8.4

Market Potential for Select Geographic Areas by Country

Country	2012 Population Estimate (thousands)	Annual per Capita Beer Consumption (liters)	Market Potential Estimate (k liters)
United States	315,000	85	26,775,000
Germany	81,000	105	8,505,000
Australia	22,000	107	2,354,000
Brazil	205,000	55	11,275,000
China	1,400,000	25	35,000,000
Czech Republic	10,190	160	1,630,400

Sources: https://www.cia.gov/library/publications/the-world-factbook/index.html, accessed April 4, 2010; http://www.just-drinks.com, accessed April 4, 2011.

consumption habits are likely to be different in 2012. For example, beer consumption is barely growing in Europe and Japan, but it is expanding in Latin America (at about 4 percent a year) and even faster in China (by at least 6 percent a year).[8] Perhaps this information will encourage you to investigate market potential in additional countries where more growth is expected.

Forecasting Sales

Sales forecasting is the process of predicting sales totals over a specific time period. Accurate sales forecasts, especially for products in mature, stable markets, frequently come from secondary data research that identifies trends and extrapolates past performance into the future. Business researchers often use internal company sales records to project sales. A rudimentary model would multiply past sales volume by an expected growth rate. A researcher might investigate a secondary source and find that industry sales normally grow about 10 percent per year; multiplying company sales volume by 10 percent would give a basic sales forecast.

Exhibit 8.5 illustrates trend projection using a moving average projection of growth rates. Average ticket prices for a major-league baseball game are secondary data from Team Marketing Report (**http://www.teammarketing.com**). The moving average is the sum of growth rates for the past three years divided by 3 (number of years). The resulting number is a forecast of the percentage increase in ticket price for the coming year. Using the three-year average growth rate of 1.9 percent for the 2009, 2010, and 2011 sales periods, we can forecast the average ticket price for 2012 as follows:

$$\$26.92 + (\$26.92 \times .019) = \$27.43$$

A major league baseball team is probably more interested in financial metrics like revenue. Using the ticket price for any season, one can compute average ticket sales revenue for any

Year	Average Ticket Price ($)	Percentage Rate of Growth (Decline) from Previous Year	3-Year Moving Average Rate of Growth (Decline)
1996	11.20	5.2%	3.5%
1997	12.36	10.4%	5.8%
1998	13.59	10.0%	8.5%
1999	14.91	9.7%	10.0%
2000	16.67	11.8%	10.5%
2001	18.99	13.9%	11.8%
2002	18.30	−3.6%	7.4%
2003	19.01	3.9%	4.7%
2004	19.82	4.3%	1.5%
2005	21.17	6.8%	5.0%
2006	22.21	4.9%	5.3%
2007	22.70	2.2%	4.6%
2008	25.43	12.0%	6.4%
2009	26.21	3.0%	5.7%
2010	26.60	1.5%	5.5%
2011	26.92	1.2%	1.9%

EXHIBIT **8.5**

Secondary Data for Major League Baseball Ticket Prices with Moving Average

© Cengage Learning 2013

upcoming season by multiplying the average major league attendance projection times the number of home games (81) times the average ticket price. For the year 2011, the estimated attendance using the three-year moving average is 31,006. Thus, the estimated revenue for a typical team is:

$$31,006 \text{ tickets/game} \times 81 \text{ games} \times \$26.92 \text{ per ticket} = \$67,609,203$$

Moving average forecasting is best suited to a static environment. More dynamic situations make other sales forecasting techniques more appropriate.

Often, more sophisticated forecasting approaches are used. We'll discuss other forecasting methods later in the book but simple moving averages like the three-year moving average are often applied in practice.

Analysis of Trade Areas and Sites

site analysis techniques

Techniques that use secondary data to select the best location for retail or wholesale operations.

index of retail saturation

A calculation that describes the relationship between retail demand and supply.

Managers routinely examine trade areas and use **site analysis techniques** to select the best locations for retail or wholesale operations. Secondary data research helps managers make these site selection decisions. Some organizations, especially franchisers, have developed special computer software based on analytical models to select sites for retail outlets. The researcher must obtain the appropriate secondary data for analysis with the computer software.

The **index of retail saturation** offers one way to investigate retail sites and to describe the relationship between retail demand and supply.[9] It is easy to calculate once the appropriate secondary data are obtained:

$$\text{Index of retail saturation} = \frac{\text{Local market potential (demand)}}{\text{Local market retailing space}}$$

For example, Exhibit 8.6 shows the relevant secondary data for shoe store sales in a five-mile radius surrounding a Florida shopping center. These types of data can be purchased from vendors of market information such as Urban Decision Systems. First, to estimate local market potential (demand), we multiply population by annual per capita shoe sales. This estimate, line 3 in Exhibit 8.6, goes in the numerator to calculate the index of retail saturation:

$$\text{Index of retail saturation} = \frac{\$14,249,000}{94,000} = 152$$

The retailer can compare this index figure with those of other areas to determine which sites have the greatest market potential with the least amount of retail competition. An index value above 200 is considered to indicate exceptional opportunities.

EXHIBIT 8.6

Secondary Data for Calculating an Index of Retail Saturation

1. Population	261,7852
2. Annual per capita shoe sales	$54.43
3. Local market potential (line 1 × line 2)	$14,249,000
4. Square feet of retail space used to sell shoes	94,000 sq. ft.
5. Index of retail saturation (line 3/line 4)	152

© Cengage Learning 2013

Data Mining

Large corporations' decision support systems often contain millions or even hundreds of millions of records of data. These complex data volumes are too large to be understood by managers. Consider, for example, Capital One, a consumer lending company with nearly 50 million customer accounts, including credit cards and auto loans. Suppose the company collects data on customer purchases, and each customer makes five transactions in a month, or 60 per year. With 50 million

Mining Data from Blogs

One way to find out what people are thinking these days is to read what they are posting on their blogs. But with tens of millions of blogs available on the Internet, there is no way to read them all. One solution: data-mining software designed for the blogosphere.

Umbria Communications, based in Boulder, Colorado, offers a program called Buzz Report, which searches 13 million blogs, looking for messages related to particular products and trends. Marketers can buy the service to find out what people are saying about their new products, or they can explore unmet needs in areas they might consider serving. Not only does Buzz Report identify relevant blogs, but it also has a language processor that can identify positive and negative messages and analyze word choices and spelling to estimate the writer's age range and sex. The company's CEO, Howard Kaushansky, says the program can even recognize sarcasm.

PR NewsFoto/Sprint

Most of Umbria's clients are large makers of consumer products, including Sprint and Electronic Arts. U.S. Cellular used Buzz Report to learn that teenage users of cell phones are particularly worried about using more than their allotted minutes, fearing that parents would take the extra amount from their allowance. Such knowledge is useful for developing new service plans and marketing messages.

Sources: Based on Finn, Bridget, "Mining Blogs for Marketing Insight," *Business 2.0*, (September 1, 2005), http://money.cnn.com/magazines/business2/business2_archive/2005/09/01/8356522/index.htm, accessed August 4, 2011; Martin, Justin, "Blogging for Dollars," *Fortune Small Business* (January 20, 2006), http://money.cnn.com/magazines/fsb/fsb_archive/2005/12/01/8365363/index.htm, accessed August 4, 2011.

customers and decades of data (the company was founded in 1988), it's easy to see how record counts quickly grow beyond the comfort zone for most humans.[10]

Two points about data volume are important to keep in mind. First, relevant data are often in independent and unrelated files. Second, the number of distinct pieces of information each data record contains is often large. When the number of distinct pieces of information contained in each data record and data volume grows too large, end users don't have the capacity to make sense of it all. Data mining helps clarify the underlying meaning of the data.

The term **data mining** refers to the use of powerful computers to dig through volumes of data to discover patterns about an organization's customers and products. As seen in the Research Snapshot "Mining Data from Blogs," this can even apply to Internet content from blogs. It is a broad term that applies to many different forms of analysis. For example, **neural networks** are a form of artificial intelligence in which a computer is programmed to mimic the way that human brains process information. One computer expert put it this way:

> *A neural network learns pretty much the way a human being does. Suppose you say "big" and show a child an elephant, and then you say "small" and show her a poodle. You repeat this process with a house and a giraffe as examples of "big" and then a grain of sand and an ant as examples of "small." Pretty soon she will figure it out and tell you that a truck is "big" and a needle is "small." Neural networks can similarly generalize by looking at examples.*[11]

Market-basket analysis is a form of data mining that analyzes anonymous point-of-sale transaction databases to identify coinciding purchases or relationships between products purchased and other retail shopping information.[12] Consider this example about patterns in customer purchases: Osco Drugs mined its databases provided by checkout scanners and found that when men go to its drugstores to buy diapers in the evening between 6:00 p.m. and 8:00 p.m., they sometimes walk out with a six-pack of beer as well. Knowing this behavioral pattern, supermarket managers may consider laying out their stores so that these items are closer together.[13]

Customer discovery is a data-mining application that similarly involves mining data to look for patterns that can increase the value of customers. For example, Macy's commissioned data-mining techniques looking for patterns of relationships among the huge volumes of previous sales records. In 2011, Macy's sent out millions of catalogs. Not every customer got the same catalog though and in fact, tens of thousands of version of the catalog were carefully tailored to specific customers.[14] Female customers 30 years of age will see more handbags, accessories, shoes, and women's clothing than will a middle-aged man. Further, if her individual records show purchases of baby clothing,

data mining

The use of powerful computers to dig through volumes of data to discover patterns about an organization's customers and products; applies to many different forms of analysis.

neural networks

A form of artificial intelligence in which a computer is programmed to mimic the way that human brains process information.

market-basket analysis

A form of data mining that analyzes anonymous point-of-sale transaction databases to identify coinciding purchases or relationships between products purchased and other retail shopping information.

customer discovery

Involves mining data to look for patterns identifying who is likely to be a valuable customer.

she'll probably see lots of things for toddlers. The end result is that the customer sees more purchase possibilities that have a high probability of addressing some current need or desire.

When a company knows the identity of the customer who makes repeated purchases from the same organization, an analysis can be made of sequences of purchases. The use of data mining to detect sequence patterns is a popular application among direct marketers, such as catalog retailers. A catalog merchant has information for each customer, revealing the sets of products that the customer buys in every purchase order. A sequence detection function can then be used to discover the set of purchases that frequently precedes the purchase of, say, a microwave oven. As another example, a sequence of insurance claims could lead to the identification of frequently occurring medical procedures performed on patients, which in turn could be used to detect cases of medical fraud.

Data mining requires sophisticated computer resources, and it is expensive. That's why companies like DataMind, IBM, Oracle, Information Builders, and Acxiom Corporation offer data-mining services. Customers send the databases they want analyzed and let the data-mining company do the "number crunching."

Database Marketing and Customer Relationship Management

database marketing

The use of customer databases to promote one-to-one relationships with customers and create precisely targeted promotions.

CRM (customer relationship management) systems are decision support systems that manage the interactions between an organization and its customers. A CRM maintains customer databases containing customers' names, addresses, phone numbers, past purchases, responses to past promotional offers, and other relevant data such as demographic and financial data. **Database marketing** is the practice of using CRM databases to develop one-to-one relationships and precisely targeted promotional efforts with individual customers. For example, a fruit catalog company CRM contains a database of previous customers, including what purchases they made during the Christmas holidays. Each year the company sends last year's gift list to customers to help them send the same gifts to their friends and relatives.

Because database marketing requires vast amounts of CRM data compiled from numerous sources, secondary data are often acquired for the exclusive purpose of developing or enhancing databases. The transaction record, which often lists the item purchased, its value, customer name, address, and zip code, is the building block for many databases. This may be supplemented with data customers provide directly, such as data on a warranty card, and by secondary data purchased from third parties. For example, credit services may sell databases about applications for loans, credit card payment history, and other financial data. Several companies, such as Infogroup (with its sales and marketing data services) and Nielsen Claritas (with PRIZM), collect primary data and then sell demographic data that can be related to small geographic areas, such as those with a certain zip code. (Remember that when the vendor collects the data, they are primary data, but when the database marketer incorporates the data into his or her database, they are secondary data.)

Now that some of the purposes of secondary data analysis have been addressed, we turn to a discussion of the sources of secondary data.

Sources of Secondary Data

internal and proprietary data

Secondary data that originate inside the organization.

Secondary data can be classified as either internal to the organization or external. Modern information technology makes this distinction seem somewhat simplistic. Some accounting documents are indisputably internal records of the organization. Researchers in another organization cannot have access to them. Clearly, a book published by the federal government and located at a public library is external to the company. However, in today's world of electronic data interchange, the data that appear in a book published by the federal government may also be purchased from an online information vendor for instantaneous access and subsequently stored in a company's decision support system.

Internal data should be defined as data that originated in the organization, or data created, recorded, or generated by the organization. **Internal and proprietary data** is perhaps a more descriptive term.

Sources of Internal and Proprietary Data

Most organizations routinely gather, record, and store internal data to help them solve future problems. An organization's accounting system can usually provide a wealth of information. Routine documents such as sales invoices allow external financial reporting, which in turn can be a source of data for further analysis. If the data are properly coded into a modular database in the accounting system, the researcher may be able to conduct more detailed analysis using the decision support system. Sales information can be broken down by account or by product and region; information related to orders received, back orders, and unfilled orders can be identified; and sales can be forecast on the basis of past data. Other useful sources of internal data include salespeople's call reports, customer complaints, service records, warranty card returns, and other records.

Researchers frequently aggregate or disaggregate internal data. For example, a computer service firm used internal secondary data to analyze sales over the previous three years, categorizing business by industry, product, purchase level, and so on. The company discovered that 60 percent of its customers represented only 2 percent of its business and that nearly all of these customers came through telephone directory advertising. This simple investigation of internal records showed that, in effect, the firm was paying to attract customers it did not want.

Internet technology is making it easier to research internal and proprietary data. Often companies set up intranets so that employees can use web tools to store and share data within the organization. And just as Google's search software lets people search the entire World Wide Web, Google is offering the enterprise search, which is essentially the same technology in a version that searches a corporate intranet. The enterprise search considers not only how often a particular document has been viewed but also the history of the user's past search patterns, such as how often that user has looked at particular documents and for how long. In addition, other companies have purchased specialized software, such as Autonomy, which searches internal sources plus such external sources as news and government websites.[15]

External Data: The Distribution System

External data are generated or recorded by an entity other than the researcher's organization. The government, newspapers and journals, trade associations, and other organizations create or produce information. Traditionally, this information has been in published form, perhaps available from a public library, trade association, or government agency. Today, however, computerized data archives and electronic data interchange make external data as accessible as internal data. Exhibit 8.7 illustrates some traditional and some modern ways of distributing information.

external data
Data created, recorded, or generated by an entity other than the researcher's organization.

Information As a Product and Its Distribution Channels

Because secondary data have value, they can be bought and sold like other products. And just as bottles of perfume or plumbers' wrenches may be distributed in many ways, secondary data also flow through various channels of distribution. Many users, such as Fortune 500 corporations, purchase documents and computerized census data directly from the government. However, many small companies get census data from a library or another intermediary or vendor of secondary information.

Libraries

Traditionally, libraries' vast storehouses of information have served as a bridge between users and producers of secondary data. The library staff deals directly with the creators of information, such as the federal government, and intermediate distributors of information, such as abstracting and indexing services. The user need only locate the appropriate secondary data on the library shelves. Libraries provide collections of books, journals, newspapers, and so on for reading and reference. They also stock many bibliographies, abstracts, guides, directories, and indexes, as well as offer access to basic databases.

Information as a Product and
Its Distribution Channels

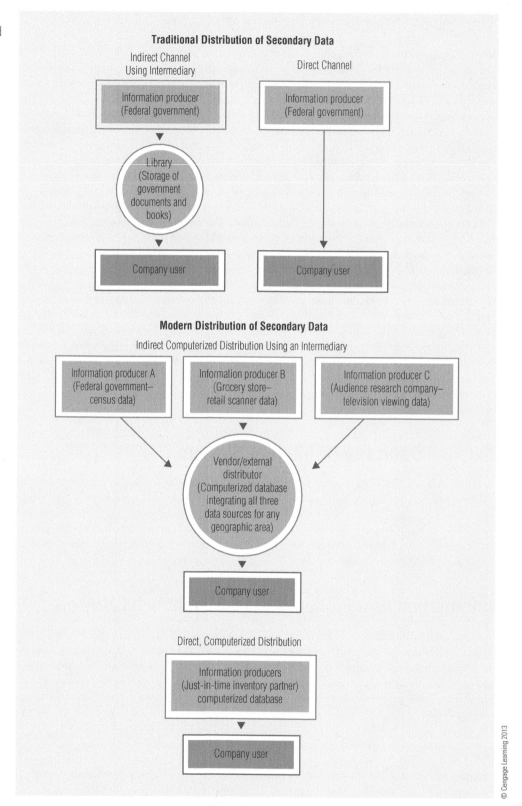

Traditional Distribution of Secondary Data

Indirect Channel
Using Intermediary

Direct Channel

Information producer
(Federal government)

Information producer
(Federal government)

Library
(Storage of
government
documents and
books)

Company user

Company user

Modern Distribution of Secondary Data

Indirect Computerized Distribution Using an Intermediary

Information producer A
(Federal government—
census data)

Information producer B
(Grocery store—
retail scanner data)

Information producer C
(Audience research company—
television viewing data)

Vendor/external
distributor
(Computerized database
integrating all three
data sources for any
geographic area)

Company user

Direct, Computerized Distribution

Information producers
(Just-in-time inventory partner)
computerized database

Company user

The word library typically connotes a public or university facility. However, many major corporations and government agencies also have libraries. A corporate librarian's advice on sources of industry information or the United Nations librarian's help in finding statistics about international markets can be invaluable.

The Internet

Today, of course, much secondary data is conveniently available over the Internet. Its creation has added an international dimension to the acquisition of secondary data. For example, Library Spot, at **http://www.libraryspot.com**, provides links to online libraries, including law libraries, medical libraries, and music libraries. Its reference desk features links to calendars, dictionaries, encyclopedias, maps, and other sources typically found at a traditional library's reference desk.

Exhibit 8.8 lists some of the more popular Internet addresses where secondary data may be found.

EXHIBIT **8.8**

Selected Internet Sites for Secondary Data

Name	Description	URL
Yahoo!	Portal that serves as a gateway to all kinds of sites on the web.	http://www.yahoo.com
CEOexpress	The 80/20 rule applied to the Internet. A series of links designed by a busy executive for busy executives.	http://www.ceoexpress.com
The New York Public Library Home Page	Library resources and links available online.	http://www.nypl.org
Census Bureau	Demographic information from the U.S. Census Bureau	http://www.census.gov
Statistical Abstract of the United States	Highlights from the primary reference book for government statistics.	http://www.census.gov/statab/www
FedWorld	Central access gateway to United States government information	http://www.fedworld.gov
Advertising Age magazine	Provides content on marketing media, advertising, and public relations.	http://www.adage.com
Inc.com	*Inc.* magazine's resources for growing a small business.	http://www.inc.com
The Wall Street Journal Online	Provides a continually updated view of business news around the world.	http://online.wsj.com
CNN Money	Provides business news, information on managing a business and managing money, and other business data.	http://money.cnn.com
NAICS—North American Industry Classification System	Describes the new classification system that replaced the SIC system.	http://www.census.gov/epcd/www/naics.html
MapQuest	Allows users to enter an address and zip code and see a map.	http://www.mapquest.com
Brint.com: The BizTech Network	Business and technology portal and global network for e-business, information, technology, and knowledge management.	http://www.brint.com

© Cengage Learning 2013

Vendors

The information age offers many channels besides libraries through which to access data. Many external producers make secondary data available directly from the organizations that produce the data or through intermediaries, which are often called vendors. Vendors such as Factiva now allow managers to access thousands of external databases via desktop computers and telecommunications systems. Hoover's (**http://www.hoovers.com**) specializes in providing information about thousands of companies' financial situations and operations.

Producers

Classifying external secondary data by the nature of the producer of information yields five basic sources: publishers of books and periodicals, government sources, media sources, trade association sources, and commercial sources. The following section discusses each type of secondary data source.

BOOKS AND PERIODICALS

"The man who does not read good books has no advantage over the man who cannot read them."

—MARK TWAIN

Some researchers consider books and periodicals found in a library to be the quintessential secondary data source. A researcher who finds books on a topic of interest obviously is off to a good start.

Professional journals, such as the Journal of Marketing, Journal of Management, Journal of the Academy of Marketing Science, The Journal of Business Research, Journal of Advertising Research, American Demographics, and The Public Opinion Quarterly, as well as commercial business periodicals such as the Wall Street Journal, Fortune, and BusinessWeek, contain much useful material. Sales and Marketing Management's Survey of Buying Power is a particularly useful source of information about markets. To locate data in periodicals, indexing services such as the ABI/INFORM, Business Periodicals Index, and Wall Street Journal Index are very useful. Guides to data sources also are helpful. For example, the American Statistical Index and Business Information Sources are very valuable sources. Most university libraries provide access to at least some of these databases.

GOVERNMENT SOURCES

Government agencies produce data prolifically. Most of the data published by the federal government can be counted on for accuracy and quality of investigation. Most students are familiar with the U.S. Census of Population, which provides a wealth of data.

The Census of Population is only one of many resources that the government provides. Banks and savings and loan companies rely heavily on the Federal Reserve Bulletin and the Economic Report of the President for data relating to research on financial and economic conditions. Builders and contractors use the information in the Current Housing Reports and American Housing Survey for their research. The Statistical Abstract of the United States is an extremely valuable source of information about the social, political, and economic organizations of the United States. It abstracts data available in hundreds of other government publications and serves as a convenient reference to more specific statistical data. FedWorld (**http://www.fedworld.gov**) provides a central access gateway to government information. FedWorld is administered by the National Technical Information Service (NTIS) and manages a comprehensive inventory of federal government information.

State, county, and local government agencies can also be useful sources of information. Many state governments publish state economic models and forecasts, and many cities have metropolitan planning agencies that provide data about the population, economy, transportation system, and so on. These are similar to federal government data but are more current and are structured to suit local needs.

Many cities and states publish information on the Internet. Many search engines have directory entries that allow easy navigation to a particular state's website. A researcher using Yahoo!, for example, needs only to click Regional Information to find numerous paths to information about states.

MEDIA SOURCES

Information on a broad range of subjects is available from broadcast and print media. CNN Financial News and BusinessWeek are valuable sources for information on the economy and many industries. Media frequently commission research studies about various aspects of Americans' lives, such as financial affairs, and make reports of survey findings available to potential advertisers free of charge.

What's That Buzzing Sound?

Bees aren't the only creatures that buzz. Consumers do too and more and more they create that buzz online. Just think about it, the Internet is filled with billions of consumer conversations. Obviously, these billions of data points contain a lot of useful information. But, a lot of it is useless too. How can a firm make sense of this? One solution: data-mining software designed for the blogosphere.

Buzzmetrics, a part of Nielsen Online, serves firms by monitoring Internet conversations, letting firms know whether conversation about their brand is up or down on any given time period. Want to know if a Super Bowl ad had any impact? The buzz an ad creates from the time it becomes public is a good indicator. If there is no buzz, there was probably not much sizzle in terms of market effectiveness. Is Dancing with the Stars still popular? If people aren't talking about it online then that show

too may be losing its sizzle. For large brands, companies like Buzzmetrics monitor thousands of websites for brand mentions and whether those mentions are positive or negative. Thus, secondary data can provide a buzz that can come with or without a sting based on whether the conversations spread good or bad news about the brand.

Sources: Hargrave, S., "Ears to the Ground," *New Media Age*, (January 17, 2008), 21. Notarantonio, E. M., "The Effectiveness of a Buzz Marketing Approach Compared to Traditional Advertising: An Exploration,"*Journal of Promotion Management*, 15 (Oct–Dec 2009), 455–464. Alahnah, M. and D. Khazanchi, "The Importance of Buzz," *Marketing Research*, 22 (Summer 2010), 20–25.

Data about the readers of magazines and the audiences for broadcast media typically are profiled in media kits and advertisements.

Information about special-interest topics may also be available. Hispanic Business reports that the number of Hispanic-owned companies in the United States is expected to grow at a rate of 55 percent between 2004 and 2010, reaching 3.2 million firms, with revenue growth for the period of 70 percent. According to the magazine, most of these firms are located in 20 states, with over half in California and Florida. For researchers willing to pay a modest $85, Hispanic Business offers a more detailed report about Hispanic-owned businesses.[16]

Data such as these are plentiful because the media like to show that their vehicles are viewed or heard by advertisers' target markets. These types of data should be evaluated carefully, however, because often they cover only limited aspects of a topic. Nevertheless, they can be quite valuable for research, and they are generally available free of charge.

TRADE ASSOCIATION SOURCES

Trade associations, such as the Food Marketing Institute or the American Petroleum Institute, serve the information needs of a particular industry. The trade association collects data on a number of topics of specific interest to firms, especially data on market size and market trends. Association members have a source of information that is particularly germane to their industry questions. For example, the Newspaper Advertising Bureau (NAB) has catalogued and listed in its computer the specialized sections that are currently popular in newspapers. The NAB has surveyed all daily, Sunday, and weekend newspapers in the United States and Canada on their editorial content and has stored this information, along with data on rates, circulation, and mechanical requirements, in its computer for advertisers' use.

COMMERCIAL SOURCES

Numerous firms specialize in selling and/or publishing information. For example, the Polk Company publishes information on the automotive field, such as average car values and new-car purchase rates by zip code. Many of these organizations offer information in published formats and as CD-ROM or Internet databases. The following discussion of several of these firms provides a sampling of the diverse data that are available.

Market Share Data. A number of syndicated services supply either wholesale or retail sales volume data based on product movement. Information Resources, Inc., collects market share data using Universal Product Codes (UPC) and optical scanning at retail store checkouts. INFOSCAN is a syndicated store tracking service that collects scanner data weekly from more than 32,000 supermarket, drug, and mass merchandiser outlets across the United States. Sales in France, Germany, Greece, Italy, the Netherlands, Spain, and the United Kingdom also are tracked by INFOSCAN.

Although it is best known for its television rating operations, Nielsen also has a scanner-based marketing and sales information service called ScanTrack. This service gathers sales and marketing data from a sample of more than 4,800 stores representing more than 800 retailers in 50 major U.S. markets. As part of Nielsen's Retail Measurement Service, auditors visit the stores at regular intervals to track promotions to customers, retail inventories, displays, brand distribution, out-of-stock conditions, and other retail activity. Scanner data allow researchers to monitor sales data before, during, and after changes in advertising frequency, price changes, distribution of free samples, and similar marketing tactics.

Walmart operates its own in-store scanner system called RetailLink. Key suppliers can have online access to relevant data free of charge.[17] The Market Share Reporter is produced each year, made available for sale, and provides market share data for most industries.

Many primary data investigations use scanner data to measure the results of experimental manipulations such as altering advertising copy. For example, scanning systems combined with consumer panels are used to create electronic test-markets. Systems based on UPCs (bar codes) and similar technology have been implemented in factories, warehouses, and transportation companies to research inventory levels, shipments, and the like.

Demographic and Census Updates. A number of firms, such as CACI Marketing Systems and Urban Information Systems, offer computerized U.S. census files and updates of these data broken down by small geographic areas, such as zip codes. Many of these research suppliers provide in-depth information on minority customers and other market segments.

Consumer Attitude and Public Opinion Research. Many research firms offer specialized syndicated services that report findings from attitude research and opinion polls. For example, Yankelovich provides custom research, tailored for specific projects, and several syndicated services. Yankelovich's public opinion research studies, such as the voter and public attitude surveys that appear in Time and other news magazines, are a source of secondary data. One of the firm's services is the Yankelovich MONITOR, a syndicated annual census of changing social values and an analysis of how they can affect consumer marketing. The MONITOR charts the growth and spread of new social values, characterizes the types of customers who support the new values and those who continue to support traditional values, and outlines the ways in which people's values affect purchasing behavior.

Harris Interactive is another public opinion research firm that provides syndicated and custom research for business. One of its services is its ABC News/Harris survey. This survey, released three times per week, monitors the pulse of the American public on topics such as inflation, unemployment, energy, attitudes toward the president, elections, and so on.

Consumption and Purchase Behavior Data. NPD's National Eating Trends (NET) is the most detailed database available on consumption patterns and trends for more than 4,000 food and beverage products. This is a syndicated source of data about the types of meals people eat and when and how they eat them. The data, called diary panel data, are based on records of meals and diaries kept by a group of households that have agreed to record their consumption behavior over an extended period of time.

National Family Opinion (NFO), Marketing Research Corporation of America (MRCA), and many other syndicated sources sell diary panel data about consumption and purchase behavior. Since the advent of scanner data, diary panels are more commonly used to record purchases of apparel, hardware, home furnishings, jewelry, and other durable goods, rather than purchases of nondurable consumer packaged goods. More recently, services have been tracking consumer behavior online, collecting data about sites visited and purchases made over the Internet.

Advertising Research. Advertisers can purchase readership and audience data from a number of firms. W. R. Simmons and Associates measures magazine audiences; Arbitron measures radio audiences; and Nielsen Media Measurement estimates television audience ratings. By specializing in collecting and selling audience information on a continuing basis, these commercial sources provide a valuable service to their subscribers.

Other syndicated services provide assistance in measuring magazine readership and magazine advertising effectiveness. Affinity's American Magazine Study (AMS) provides insight into magazine readership and reader profiles. Simmons National Consumer Study (NCS) assesses consumer attitudes, behaviors, and brand preferences. Combined, these organizations have created Affinity AMS Experian Simmons to provide a complete data base regarding magazine readership.

Burke Marketing Research provides a service that measures the extent to which respondents recall television commercials aired the night before. It provides product category norms, or average DAR (day-after recall) scores, and DAR scores for other products.

An individual advertiser would be unable to monitor every minute of every television program before deciding on the appropriate ones in which to place advertising. However, numerous clients, agencies, television networks, and advertisers can purchase the Nielsen television ratings service.

Single-Source Data-Integrated Information

The Nielsen Company offers data from both its television meters and scanner operations. The integration of these two types of data helps marketers investigate the impact of television advertising on retail sales. In other ways as well, users of data find that merging two or more diverse types of data into a single database offers many advantages.

PRIZM by Nielsen Claritas and other syndicated databases report product purchase behavior, media usage, demographic characteristics, lifestyle variables, and business activity by geographic area such as zip code. Although such data are often called geodemographic, they cover such a broad range of phenomena that no one name is a good description. These data use small geographic areas as the unit of analysis.

The data and information industry uses the term **single-source data** for diverse types of data offered by a single company. Exhibit 8.9 identifies three major marketers of single-source data.

single-source data

Diverse types of data offered by a single company; usually integrated on the basis of a common variable such as geographic area or store.

CACI Marketing Systems http://www.caci.co.uk	Provides industry-specific marketing services, such as customer profiling and segmentation, custom target analysis, emographic data reports and maps, and site evaluation and selection. CACI offers demographics and data on businesses, lifestyles, consumer spending, purchase potential, shopping centers, traffic volumes, and other statistics.
PRIZM by Nielsen Claritas http://www.claritas.com/ MyBestSegments/Default.jsp	PRIZM, which stands for Potential Rating Index for Zip Markets, is based on the "birds-of-a-feather" assumption that people live near others who are like themselves. PRIZM combines census data, consumer surveys about shopping and lifestyle, and purchase data to identify market segments. Colorful names such as Young Suburbia, Shot Guns, and Pickups describe 40 segments that can be identified by zip code.
GfK MRI Survey of the American Consumer™ http://www.gfkmri.com/	Provides "the most reliable and comprehensive consumer marketing and media database available." Research covers media choices, demographics, lifestyles and attitudes, and product usage of almost 6,000 products.

EXHIBIT **8.9**

Examples of Single-Source Databases

© Cengage Learning 2013

Sources for Global Research

As business has become more global, so has the secondary data industry. The Japan Management Association Research Institute, Japan's largest provider of secondary research data to government and industry, maintains an office in San Diego. The Institute's goal is to help U.S. firms access its enormous store of data about Japan to develop and plan their business there. The office in

SNAPSHOT

Around the World of Data

With the Internet, we can quickly go around the world and find data. Many countries have websites that summarize basic characteristics with data tables. Here are just a few of the many websites that make finding data about different parts of the world easier:

© Michael Newman/PhotoEdit

- United States
  http://www.fedworld.gov
- South Africa
  http://www.statssa.gov.za
- Australia
  http://www.nla.gov.au/oz/stats.html
- Japan
  http://www.stat.go.jp

- U.K.
  http://www.statistics.gov.uk
- France
  http://www.insee.fr
- South America
  http://www.internetworldstats.com/south.htm
- Norway
  http://www.ssb.no
- United Nations
  http://www.un.org/esa

© Cengage Learning 2013

San Diego provides translators and acts as an intermediary between Japanese researchers and U.S. clients.

Secondary data compiled outside the United States have the same limitations as domestic secondary data. However, international researchers should watch for certain pitfalls that frequently are associated with foreign data and cross-cultural research. First, data may simply be unavailable in certain countries. Second, the accuracy of some data may be called into question. This is especially likely with official statistics that may be adjusted for the political purposes of foreign governments. Finally, although economic terminology may be standardized, various countries use different definitions and accounting and recording practices for many economic concepts. For example, different countries may measure disposable personal income in radically different ways. International researchers should take extra care to investigate the comparability of data among countries. The Research Snapshot "Around the World of Data" provides some of the many website locations for data from around the world.

The U.S. government and other organizations compile databases that may aid international secondary data needs. For example, the website for the delegation of the European Union to the United States (**http://www.eurunion.org**) reports on historical and current activity in the European Union providing a comprehensive reference guide to information about laws and regulations. It profiles in detail each European Union member state, investment opportunities, sources of grants and other funding, and other information about business resources.

The U.S. government offers a wealth of data about foreign countries. The CIA's World Factbook and the National Trade Data Bank (NTDB) are especially useful. Both can be accessed using the Internet. The NTDB, the U.S. government's most comprehensive source of world trade data, illustrates what is available.

The NTDB was established by the Omnibus Trade and Competitiveness Act of 1988.[18] Its purpose was to provide "reasonable public access, including electronic access" to an export promotion data system that was centralized, inexpensive, and easy to use.

The U.S. Department of Commerce has the responsibility for operating and maintaining the NTDB and works with federal agencies that collect and distribute trade information to keep the NTDB up-to-date. The NTDB has been published monthly on CD-ROM since 1990. Over one thousand public and university libraries offer access to the NTDB through the Federal Depository Library Program.

The NTDB consists of 133 separate trade- and business-related programs (databases). By using it, small- and medium-sized companies get immediate access to information that until now only Fortune 500 companies could afford.

Topics in the NTDB include export opportunities by industry, country, and product; foreign companies or importers looking for specific products; how-to market guides; demographic, political, and socioeconomic conditions in hundreds of countries; and much more. NTDB offers one-stop shopping for trade information from more than 20 federal sources. You do not need to know which federal agency produces the information: All you need to do is consult NTDB.

Some of the specific information that can be obtained from the NTDB is listed in Exhibit 8.10.

EXHIBIT **8.10**

Examples of Information Contained in the NTDB

Agricultural commodity production and trade

Basic export information

Calendars of trade fairs and exhibitions

Capital markets and export financing

Country reports on economic and social policies and trade practices

Energy production, supply, and inventories

Exchange rates

Export licensing information

Guides to doing business in foreign countries

International trade terms directory

How-to guides

International trade regulations/agreements

International trade agreements

Labor, employment, and productivity

Maritime and shipping information

Market research reports

Overseas contacts

Overseas and domestic industry information

Price indexes

Small business information

State exports

State trade contacts

Trade opportunities

U.S. export regulations

U.S. import and export statistics by country and commodity

U.S. international transactions

World Factbook

World minerals production

∴ SUMMARY

1. **Discuss the advantages and disadvantages of secondary data.** Secondary data are data that have been gathered and recorded previously by someone else for purposes other than those of the current researcher. The chief advantage of secondary data is that they are almost always less expensive to obtain than primary data. Generally they can be obtained rapidly and may provide information not otherwise available to the researcher. The disadvantage of secondary data is that they were not intended specifically to meet the researcher's needs. The researcher must examine secondary data for accuracy, bias, and soundness. One way to do this is to cross-check various available sources.

2. **Define types of secondary data analysis conducted by business research managers.** Secondary research designs address many common business research problems. There are three general categories of secondary research objectives: fact-finding, model building, and database marketing. A typical fact-finding study might seek to uncover all available information about consumption patterns for a particular product category or to identify business trends that affect an industry. Model building is more complicated; it involves specifying relationships between two or more variables. The practice of database marketing, which involves maintaining customer databases with customers' names, addresses, phone numbers, past purchases, responses to past promotional offers, and other relevant data such as demographic and financial data, is increasingly being supported by business research efforts.

3. **Identify various internal and proprietary sources of secondary data.** Managers often get data from internal proprietary sources such as accounting records. Data mining is the use of powerful computers to dig through volumes of data to discover patterns about an organization's customers and products. It is a broad term that applies to many different forms of analysis.

4. **Give examples of various external sources of secondary data.** External data are generated or recorded by another entity. The government, newspaper and journal publishers, trade associations, and other organizations create or produce information. Traditionally this information has been distributed in published form, either directly from producer to researcher, or indirectly through intermediaries such as public libraries. Modern computerized data archives, electronic data interchange, and the Internet have changed the distribution of external data, making them almost as accessible as internal data. Push technology is a term referring to an Internet information technology that automatically delivers content to the researcher's or manager's desktop. This service helps in environmental scanning.

5. **Describe the impact of single-source data and globalization on secondary data research.** The marketing of multiple types of related data by single-source suppliers has radically changed the nature of secondary data research. Businesses can measure promotional efforts and related buyer behavior by detailed customer characteristics. As business has become more global, so has the secondary data industry. International researchers should watch for pitfalls that can be associated with foreign data and cross-cultural research, such as problems with the availability and reliability of data.

∴ KEY TERMS AND CONCEPTS

cross-checks, *162*
customer discovery, *169*
data conversion, *161*
data mining, *169*
database marketing, *170*

external data, *171*
index of retail saturation, *168*
internal and proprietary data, *170*
market tracking, *164*
market-basket analysis, *169*

model building, *165*
neural networks, *169*
secondary data, *160*
single-source data, *177*
site analysis techniques, *168*

:: QUESTIONS FOR REVIEW AND CRITICAL THINKING

1. Secondary data have been called the first line of attack for business researchers. Discuss this description.
2. Suppose you wish to learn about the size of the soft-drink market, particularly root beer sales, growth patterns, and market shares. Indicate probable sources for these secondary data.
3. What is push technology?
4. Identify some typical research objectives for secondary data studies.
5. How might a researcher doing a job for a company such as Pulte Homes (**http://www.pultehomes.com**) or David Weekley Homes (**http://www.davidweekley.com**) use secondary data and data mining?
6. What would be a source for the following data?
   a. Population, average income, and employment rates for Oregon
   b. Maps of U.S. counties and cities
   c. Trends in automobile ownership
   d. Divorce trends in the United States
   e. Median weekly earnings of full-time, salaried workers for the previous five years
   f. Annual sales of the top 10 fast-food companies
   g. Top 10 websites ranked by number of unique visitors
   h. Attendance at professional sports events

7. Suppose you are a business research consultant and a client comes to your office and says, "I must have the latest information on the supply of and demand for Maine potatoes within the next 24 hours." What would you do?
8. Find the following data in the Survey of Current Business:
   a. U.S. gross domestic product for the second quarter of 2008 and the first quarter of 2011
   b. Exports of goods and services for the second quarter of 2008 and the first quarter of 2011
   c. Imports of goods and services for the second quarter of 2008 and the first quarter of 2011
9. ETHICS A newspaper reporter finds data in a study that surveyed children that reports a high percentage of children can match cartoon characters with the products they represent. For instance, they can match cereal with Captain Crunch and Ronald McDonald with a Big Mac. The reporter used this to write a story about the need to place limits on the use of cartoon characters. However, the study also provided data suggesting that matching the cartoon character and the product did not lead to significantly higher consumption. Would this be a proper use of secondary data?

:: RESEARCH ACTIVITIES

1. Use secondary data to learn the size of the U.S. golf market and to profile the typical golfer.
2. 'NET Where could a researcher working for the U.S. Marine Corps (**http://www.marines.com**) find information that would identify the most productive areas of the United States in which to recruit? What would you recommend?
3. 'NET POPClocks estimate the U.S. and world populations. Go to the Census Bureau home page (**http://www.census.gov**), navigate to the population section, and find today's estimate of the U.S. and world populations.
4. 'NET Try to find the U.S. market share for the following companies within 30 minutes:
   a. Home Depot
   b. Burger King
   c. Marlboro
   d. Was this a difficult task? If so, why do you think it is this difficult?
5. 'NET Use the Internet to learn what you can about Indonesia.
   a. Check the corruption index for Indonesia at **http://www.transparency.org**.
   b. What additional kinds of information are available from the following sources?

   - Go to **http://freetheworld.com/member.html** and view info for Indonesia.
   - Visit the CIA's World Factbook at **https://www.cia.gov/library/publications/the-world-factbook/index.html**.
   - Go to Google, Yahoo! Search, or another search engine, and use "Indonesia" as a search word.
6. 'NET Go to Statistics Norway at **http://www.ssb.no**. What data, if any, can you obtain in English? What languages can be used to search this website? What databases might be of interest to the business researcher?
7. 'NET Go to Statistics Canada at **http://www.statcan.gc.ca**. What languages can be used to search this website? What databases might be of interest to the business researcher?
8. 'NET Suppose you were working for a company that wanted to start a business selling handmade acoustic guitars that are reproductions of classic vintage guitars. Pricing is a big part of the decision. Secondary information is available via the Internet. Use eBay (**http://ebay.com**) to identify four key brands of acoustic guitars by studying the vintage acoustic guitars listed for sale. Since the company wishes to charge premium prices, they will model after the most expensive brand. What brand seems to be associated with the highest prices?

Demand for Gas Guzzlers

CASE 8.1

In fall 2005, Hurricanes Katrina and Rita churning in the Gulf of Mexico damaged oil rigs and refineries, contributing to a spike in oil prices. Many observers expressed confidence that those events were the long-expected trigger that would kill off demand for SUVs and other gas-guzzling vehicles.[19] They were only partly right.

In the months leading up to the hurricanes, sales of SUVs had already been falling, according to data from Automotive News. Automakers had been shifting ad dollars away from these products. CNW Market Research said that in August 2005, consumers had for the first time placed fuel economy ahead of performance when ranking factors for choosing a new vehicle. When gas prices approached three dollars a gallon in September 2005, marketers felt sure that fuel economy would remain a top concern. Advertisers began creating more ads featuring vehicles' gas mileage.

But by the end of the year, attitudes were shifting again. The National Automobile Dealers Association surveyed consumers visiting its website for information about car purchases, and it learned they ranked price as most important, followed by make and model, then performance. Fuel economy ranked last, with 3 percent considering it most important and 11 percent considering it least important. What's a carmaker to do? General Motors gathers data from the shoppers who visit websites such as **http://www.kbb.com** to look up information, and it is analyzing the data to identify the price of fuel at which car buyers adjust their priorities.

Questions

1. From the standpoint of an automobile company, what sources of information in this article offer secondary data?
2. Suggest two or three other sources of data that might be of interest to auto companies interested in forecasting demand.
3. Online or at your library, look for information about recent trends in SUV purchases. Report what you learned, and forecast whether SUV sales are likely to recover or continue their decline. What role do gas prices play in your forecast?

CHAPTER 1

Data and Statistics

BLOOMBERG BUSINESSWEEK*
NEW YORK, NEW YORK

With a global circulation of more than 1 million, *Bloomberg Businessweek* is one of the most widely read business magazines in the world. Bloomberg's 1700 reporters in 145 service bureaus around the world enable *Bloomberg Businessweek* to deliver a variety of articles of interest to the global business and economic community. Along with feature articles on current topics, the magazine contains articles on international business, economic analysis, information processing, and science and technology. Information in the feature articles and the regular sections helps readers stay abreast of current developments and assess the impact of those developments on business and economic conditions.

Most issues of *Bloomberg Businessweek,* formerly *BusinessWeek,* provide an in-depth report on a topic of current interest. Often, the in-depth reports contain statistical facts and summaries that help the reader understand the business and economic information. Examples of articles and reports include the impact of businesses moving important work to cloud computing, the crisis facing the U.S. Postal Service, and why the debt crisis is even worse than we think. In addition, *Bloomberg Businessweek* provides a variety of statistics about the state of the economy, including production indexes, stock prices, mutual funds, and interest rates.

Bloomberg Businessweek also uses statistics and statistical information in managing its own business. For example, an annual survey of subscribers helps the company learn about subscriber demographics, reading habits, likely purchases, lifestyles, and so on. *Bloomberg Businessweek* managers use statistical summaries from the survey to provide better services to subscribers and advertisers. One recent North American subscriber survey indicated that 90% of *Bloomberg Businessweek*

Bloomberg Businessweek uses statistical facts and summaries in many of its articles. © Kyodo/Photoshot.

subscribers use a personal computer at home and that 64% of *Bloomberg Businessweek* subscribers are involved with computer purchases at work. Such statistics alert *Bloomberg Businessweek* managers to subscriber interest in articles about new developments in computers. The results of the subscriber survey are also made available to potential advertisers. The high percentage of subscribers using personal computers at home and the high percentage of subscribers involved with computer purchases at work would be an incentive for a computer manufacturer to consider advertising in *Bloomberg Businessweek*.

In this chapter, we discuss the types of data available for statistical analysis and describe how the data are obtained. We introduce descriptive statistics and statistical inference as ways of converting data into meaningful and easily interpreted statistical information.

---

*The authors are indebted to Charlene Trentham, Research Manager, for providing this Statistics in Practice.

Frequently, we see the following types of statements in newspapers and magazines:

- The median price for an existing single-family home is $186,000, up 7.6% from a year earlier (*The Wall Street Journal,* November 8, 2012).
- Women account for 14.1% of the executive officers in Fortune 500 companies (*The Wall Street Journal,* April 30, 2012).

- The average annual cost for a college education is $17,100 for public, in-state universities and $38,600 for private universities (*Money Magazine,* March 2012).
- A Yahoo Finance survey reported 51% of workers say the key to getting ahead is internal politics, while 27% say the key to getting ahead is hard work (*USA Today,* September 29, 2012).
- The median age of a first marriage is 29 for men and 26 for women (Associated Press, December 25, 2011).
- The percentage of U.S. workers getting less than six hours of sleep per night is 30% (*The Wall Street Journal,* August 4, 2012).
- The average credit card debt is $5,204 per person (PRWeb website, April 5, 2012).

The numerical facts in the preceding statements ($186,000, 7.6%, 14.1%, $17,100, $38,600, 51%, 27%, 29, 26, 30%, and $5,204) are called **statistics**. In this usage, the term statistics refers to numerical facts such as averages, medians, percentages, and maximums that help us understand a variety of business and economic situations. However, as you will see, the field, or subject, of statistics involves much more than numerical facts. In a broader sense, statistics is the art and science of collecting, analyzing, presenting, and interpreting data. Particularly in business and economics, the information provided by collecting, analyzing, presenting, and interpreting data gives managers and decision makers a better understanding of the business and economic environment and thus enables them to make more informed and better decisions. In this text, we emphasize the use of statistics for business and economic decision making.

Chapter 1 begins with some illustrations of the applications of statistics in business and economics. In Section 1.2 we define the term *data* and introduce the concept of a data set. This section also introduces key terms such as *variables* and *observations,* discusses the difference between quantitative and categorical data, and illustrates the uses of cross-sectional and time series data. Section 1.3 discusses how data can be obtained from existing sources or through survey and experimental studies designed to obtain new data. The important role that the Internet now plays in obtaining data is also highlighted. The uses of data in developing descriptive statistics and in making statistical inferences are described in Sections 1.4 and 1.5. The last three sections of Chapter 1 provide the role of the computer in statistical analysis, an introduction to data mining, and a discussion of ethical guidelines for statistical practice. A chapter-ending appendix includes an introduction to the add-in StatTools which can be used to extend the statistical options for users of Microsoft Excel.

Applications in Business and Economics

In today's global business and economic environment, anyone can access vast amounts of statistical information. The most successful managers and decision makers understand the information and know how to use it effectively. In this section, we provide examples that illustrate some of the uses of statistics in business and economics.

Accounting

Public accounting firms use statistical sampling procedures when conducting audits for their clients. For instance, suppose an accounting firm wants to determine whether the amount of accounts receivable shown on a client's balance sheet fairly represents the actual amount of accounts receivable. Usually the large number of individual accounts receivable makes reviewing and validating every account too time-consuming and expensive. As common practice in such situations, the audit staff selects a subset of the accounts called a sample.

After reviewing the accuracy of the sampled accounts, the auditors draw a conclusion as to whether the accounts receivable amount shown on the client's balance sheet is acceptable.

Finance

Financial analysts use a variety of statistical information to guide their investment recommendations. In the case of stocks, analysts review financial data such as price/earnings ratios and dividend yields. By comparing the information for an individual stock with information about the stock market averages, an analyst can begin to draw a conclusion as to whether the stock is a good investment. For example, *The Wall Street Journal* (March 19, 2012) reported that the average dividend yield for the S&P 500 companies was 2.2%. Microsoft showed a dividend yield of 2.42%. In this case, the statistical information on dividend yield indicates a higher dividend yield for Microsoft than the average dividend yield for the S&P 500 companies. This and other information about Microsoft would help the analyst make an informed buy, sell, or hold recommendation for Microsoft stock.

Marketing

Electronic scanners at retail checkout counters collect data for a variety of marketing research applications. For example, data suppliers such as ACNielsen and Information Resources, Inc., purchase point-of-sale scanner data from grocery stores, process the data, and then sell statistical summaries of the data to manufacturers. Manufacturers spend hundreds of thousands of dollars per product category to obtain this type of scanner data. Manufacturers also purchase data and statistical summaries on promotional activities such as special pricing and the use of in-store displays. Brand managers can review the scanner statistics and the promotional activity statistics to gain a better understanding of the relationship between promotional activities and sales. Such analyses often prove helpful in establishing future marketing strategies for the various products.

Production

Today's emphasis on quality makes quality control an important application of statistics in production. A variety of statistical quality control charts are used to monitor the output of a production process. In particular, an *x*-bar chart can be used to monitor the average output. Suppose, for example, that a machine fills containers with 12 ounces of a soft drink. Periodically, a production worker selects a sample of containers and computes the average number of ounces in the sample. This average, or *x*-bar value, is plotted on an *x*-bar chart. A plotted value above the chart's upper control limit indicates overfilling, and a plotted value below the chart's lower control limit indicates underfilling. The process is termed "in control" and allowed to continue as long as the plotted *x*-bar values fall between the chart's upper and lower control limits. Properly interpreted, an *x*-bar chart can help determine when adjustments are necessary to correct a production process.

Economics

Economists frequently provide forecasts about the future of the economy or some aspect of it. They use a variety of statistical information in making such forecasts. For instance, in forecasting inflation rates, economists use statistical information on such indicators as the Producer Price Index, the unemployment rate, and manufacturing capacity utilization. Often these statistical indicators are entered into computerized forecasting models that predict inflation rates.

Information Systems

Information systems administrators are responsible for the day-to-day operation of an organization's computer networks. A variety of statistical information helps administrators assess the performance of computer networks, including local area networks (LANs), wide area networks (WANs), network segments, intranets, and other data communication systems. Statistics such as the mean number of users on the system, the proportion of time any component of the system is down, and the proportion of bandwidth utilized at various times of the day are examples of statistical information that help the system administrator better understand and manage the computer network.

Applications of statistics such as those described in this section are an integral part of this text. Such examples provide an overview of the breadth of statistical applications. To supplement these examples, practitioners in the fields of business and economics provided chapter-opening Statistics in Practice articles that introduce the material covered in each chapter. The Statistics in Practice applications show the importance of statistics in a wide variety of business and economic situations.

Data

Data are the facts and figures collected, analyzed, and summarized for presentation and interpretation. All the data collected in a particular study are referred to as the **data set** for the study. Table 1.1 shows a data set containing information for 60 nations that participate in the World Trade Organization. The World Trade Organization encourages the free flow of international trade and provides a forum for resolving trade dispute.

Elements, Variables, and Observations

Elements are the entities on which data are collected. Each nation listed in Table 1.1 is an element with the nation or element name shown in the first column. With 60 nations, the data set contains 60 elements.

A **variable** is a characteristic of interest for the elements. The data set in Table 1.1 includes the following five variables:

- WTO Status: The nation's membership status in the World Trade Organization; this can be either as a member or an observer.
- Per Capita GDP ($): The total output of the nation divided by the number of people in the nation; this is commonly used to compare economic productivity of the nations.
- Trade Deficit ($1000s): The difference between total dollar value of the nation's imports and total dollar value of the nation's exports.
- Fitch Rating: The nation's sovereign credit rating as appraised by the Fitch Group[1]; the credit ratings range from a high of AAA to a low of F and can be modified by + or −.
- Fitch Outlook: An indication of the direction the credit rating is likely to move over the upcoming two years; the outlook can be negative, stable, or positive.

Measurements collected on each variable for every element in a study provide the data. The set of measurements obtained for a particular element is called an **observation**. Referring to Table 1.1, we see that the first observation contains the following measurements:

---

[1]The Fitch Group is one of three nationally recognized statistical rating organizations designated by the U.S. Securities and Exchange Commission. The other two are Standard and Poor's and Moody's investor service.

TABLE 1.1   DATA SET FOR 60 NATIONS IN THE WORLD TRADE ORGANIZATION

Nations

Data sets such as Nations are available on the website for this text.

Nation	WTO Status	Per Capita GDP ($)	Trade Deficit ($1000s)	Fitch Rating	Fitch Outlook
Armenia	Member	5,400	2,673,359	BB−	Stable
Australia	Member	40,800	−33,304,157	AAA	Stable
Austria	Member	41,700	12,796,558	AAA	Stable
Azerbaijan	Observer	5,400	−16,747,320	BBB−	Positive
Bahrain	Member	27,300	3,102,665	BBB	Stable
Belgium	Member	37,600	−14,930,833	AA+	Negative
Brazil	Member	11,600	−29,796,166	BBB	Stable
Bulgaria	Member	13,500	4,049,237	BBB−	Positive
Canada	Member	40,300	−1,611,380	AAA	Stable
Cape Verde	Member	4,000	874,459	B+	Stable
Chile	Member	16,100	−14,558,218	A+	Stable
China	Member	8,400	−156,705,311	A+	Stable
Colombia	Member	10,100	−1,561,199	BBB−	Stable
Costa Rica	Member	11,500	5,807,509	BB+	Stable
Croatia	Member	18,300	8,108,103	BBB−	Negative
Cyprus	Member	29,100	6,623,337	BBB	Negative
Czech Republic	Member	25,900	−10,749,467	A+	Positive
Denmark	Member	40,200	−15,057,343	AAA	Stable
Ecuador	Member	8,300	1,993,819	B−	Stable
Egypt	Member	6,500	28,486,933	BB	Negative
El Salvador	Member	7,600	5,019,363	BB	Stable
Estonia	Member	20,200	802,234	A+	Stable
France	Member	35,000	118,841,542	AAA	Stable
Georgia	Member	5,400	4,398,153	B+	Positive
Germany	Member	37,900	−213,367,685	AAA	Stable
Hungary	Member	19,600	−9,421,301	BBB−	Negative
Iceland	Member	38,000	−504,939	BB+	Stable
Ireland	Member	39,500	−59,093,323	BBB+	Negative
Israel	Member	31,000	6,722,291	A	Stable
Italy	Member	30,100	33,568,668	A+	Negative
Japan	Member	34,300	31,675,424	AA	Negative
Kazakhstan	Observer	13,000	−33,220,437	BBB	Positive
Kenya	Member	1,700	9,174,198	B+	Stable
Latvia	Member	15,400	2,448,053	BBB−	Positive
Lebanon	Observer	15,600	13,715,550	B	Stable
Lithuania	Member	18,700	3,359,641	BBB	Positive
Malaysia	Member	15,600	−39,420,064	A−	Stable
Mexico	Member	15,100	1,288,112	BBB	Stable
Peru	Member	10,000	−7,888,993	BBB	Stable
Philippines	Member	4,100	15,667,209	BB+	Stable
Poland	Member	20,100	19,552,976	A−	Stable
Portugal	Member	23,200	21,060,508	BBB−	Negative
South Korea	Member	31,700	−37,509,141	A+	Stable
Romania	Member	12,300	13,323,709	BBB−	Stable
Russia	Observer	16,700	−151,400,000	BBB	Positive
Rwanda	Member	1,300	939,222	B	Stable
Serbia	Observer	10,700	8,275,693	BB−	Stable
Seychelles	Observer	24,700	666,026	B	Stable
Singapore	Member	59,900	−27,110,421	AAA	Stable
Slovakia	Member	23,400	−2,110,626	A+	Stable
Slovenia	Member	29,100	2,310,617	AA−	Negative
South Africa	Member	11,000	3,321,801	BBB+	Stable

Sweden	Member	40,600	−10,903,251	AAA	Stable
Switzerland	Member	43,400	−27,197,873	AAA	Stable
Thailand	Member	9,700	2,049,669	BBB	Stable
Turkey	Member	14,600	71,612,947	BB+	Positive
UK	Member	35,900	162,316,831	AAA	Negative
Uruguay	Member	15,400	2,662,628	BB	Positive
USA	Member	48,100	784,438,559	AAA	Stable
Zambia	Member	1,600	−1,805,198	B+	Stable

Member, 5,400, 2,673,359, BB−, and Stable. The second observation contains the following measurements: Member, 40,800, −33,304,157, AAA, and Stable, and so on. A data set with 60 elements contains 60 observations.

Scales of Measurement

Data collection requires one of the following scales of measurement: nominal, ordinal, interval, or ratio. The scale of measurement determines the amount of information contained in the data and indicates the most appropriate data summarization and statistical analyses.

When the data for a variable consist of labels or names used to identify an attribute of the element, the scale of measurement is considered a **nominal scale**. For example, referring to the data in Table 1.1, the scale of measurement for the WTO Status variable is nominal because the data "member" and "observer" are labels used to identify the status category for the nation. In cases where the scale of measurement is nominal, a numerical code as well as a nonnumerical label may be used. For example, to facilitate data collection and to prepare the data for entry into a computer database, we might use a numerical code for WTO Status variable by letting 1 denote a member nation in the World Trade Organization and 2 denote an observer nation. The scale of measurement is nominal even though the data appear as numerical values.

The scale of measurement for a variable is considered an **ordinal scale** if the data exhibit the properties of nominal data and in addition, the order or rank of the data is meaningful. For example, referring to the data in Table 1.1, the scale of measurement for the Fitch Rating is ordinal because the rating labels which range from AAA to F can be rank ordered from best credit rating AAA to poorest credit rating F. The rating letters provide the labels similar to nominal data, but in addition, the data can also be ranked or ordered based on the credit rating, which makes the measurement scale ordinal. Ordinal data can also be recorded by a numerical code, for example, your class rank in school.

The scale of measurement for a variable is an **interval scale** if the data have all the properties of ordinal data and the interval between values is expressed in terms of a fixed unit of measure. Interval data are always numeric. College admission SAT scores are an example of interval-scaled data. For example, three students with SAT math scores of 620, 550, and 470 can be ranked or ordered in terms of best performance to poorest performance in math. In addition, the differences between the scores are meaningful. For instance, student 1 scored $620 - 550 = 70$ points more than student 2, while student 2 scored $550 - 470 = 80$ points more than student 3.

The scale of measurement for a variable is a **ratio scale** if the data have all the properties of interval data and the ratio of two values is meaningful. Variables such as distance, height, weight, and time use the ratio scale of measurement. This scale requires that a zero value be included to indicate that nothing exists for the variable at the zero point.

For example, consider the cost of an automobile. A zero value for the cost would indicate that the automobile has no cost and is free. In addition, if we compare the cost of $30,000 for one automobile to the cost of $15,000 for a second automobile, the ratio property shows that the first automobile is $30,000/$15,000 = 2 times, or twice, the cost of the second automobile.

Categorical and Quantitative Data

Data can be classified as either categorical or quantitative. Data that can be grouped by specific categories are referred to as **categorical data**. Categorical data use either the nominal or ordinal scale of measurement. Data that use numeric values to indicate how much or how many are referred to as **quantitative data**. Quantitative data are obtained using either the interval or ratio scale of measurement.

The statistical method appropriate for summarizing data depends upon whether the data are categorical or quantitative.

A **categorical variable** is a variable with categorical data, and a **quantitative variable** is a variable with quantitative data. The statistical analysis appropriate for a particular variable depends upon whether the variable is categorical or quantitative. If the variable is categorical, the statistical analysis is limited. We can summarize categorical data by counting the number of observations in each category or by computing the proportion of the observations in each category. However, even when the categorical data are identified by a numerical code, arithmetic operations such as addition, subtraction, multiplication, and division do not provide meaningful results. Section 2.1 discusses ways for summarizing categorical data.

Arithmetic operations provide meaningful results for quantitative variables. For example, quantitative data may be added and then divided by the number of observations to compute the average value. This average is usually meaningful and easily interpreted. In general, more alternatives for statistical analysis are possible when data are quantitative. Section 2.2 and Chapter 3 provide ways of summarizing quantitative data.

Cross-Sectional and Time Series Data

For purposes of statistical analysis, distinguishing between cross-sectional data and time series data is important. **Cross-sectional data** are data collected at the same or approximately the same point in time. The data in Table 1.1 are cross-sectional because they describe the five variables for the 60 World Trade Organization nations at the same point in time. **Time series data** are data collected over several time periods. For example, the time series in Figure 1.1 shows the U.S. average price per gallon of conventional regular gasoline between 2007 and 2012. Note that gasoline prices peaked in the summer of 2008 and then dropped sharply in the fall of 2008. Since 2008, the average price per gallon has continued to climb steadily, approaching an all-time high again in 2012.

Graphs of time series data are frequently found in business and economic publications. Such graphs help analysts understand what happened in the past, identify any trends over time, and project future values for the time series. The graphs of time series data can take on a variety of forms, as shown in Figure 1.2. With a little study, these graphs are usually easy to understand and interpret. For example, Panel (A) in Figure 1.2 is a graph that shows the Dow Jones Industrial Average Index from 2002 to 2012. In April 2002, the popular stock market index was near 10,000. Over the next five years the index rose to its all-time high of slightly over 14,000 in October 2007. However, notice the sharp decline in the time series after the high in 2007. By March 2009, poor economic conditions had caused the Dow Jones Industrial Average Index to return to the 7000 level. This was a scary and discouraging period for investors. However, by late 2009, the index was showing a recovery by reaching 10,000. The index has climbed steadily and was above 13,000 in early 2012.

FIGURE 1.1   U.S. AVERAGE PRICE PER GALLON FOR CONVENTIONAL
REGULAR GASOLINE

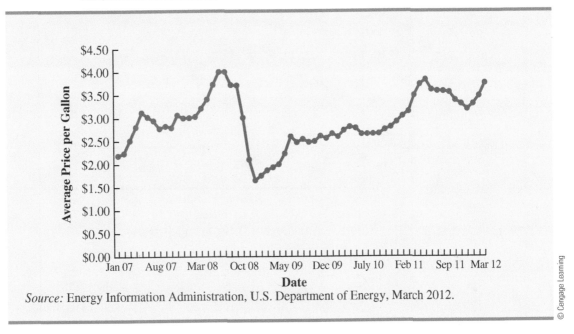

Source: Energy Information Administration, U.S. Department of Energy, March 2012.

The graph in Panel (B) shows the net income of McDonald's Inc. from 2005 to 2011. The declining economic conditions in 2008 and 2009 were actually beneficial to McDonald's as the company's net income rose to all-time highs. The growth in McDonald's net income showed that the company was thriving during the economic downturn as people were cutting back on the more expensive sit-down restaurants and seeking less-expensive alternatives offered by McDonald's. McDonald's net income continued to new all-time highs in 2010 and 2011.

Panel (C) shows the time series for the occupancy rate of hotels in South Florida over a one-year period. The highest occupancy rates, 95% and 98%, occur during the months of February and March when the climate of South Florida is attractive to tourists. In fact, January to April of each year is typically the high-occupancy season for South Florida hotels. On the other hand, note the low occupancy rates during the months of August to October, with the lowest occupancy rate of 50% occurring in September. High temperatures and the hurricane season are the primary reasons for the drop in hotel occupancy during this period.

NOTES AND COMMENTS

1. An observation is the set of measurements obtained for each element in a data set. Hence, the number of observations is always the same as the number of elements. The number of measurements obtained for each element equals the number of variables. Hence, the total number of data items can be determined by multiplying the number of observations by the number of variables.

2. Quantitative data may be discrete or continuous. Quantitative data that measure how many (e.g., number of calls received in 5 minutes) are discrete. Quantitative data that measure how much (e.g., weight or time) are continuous because no separation occurs between the possible data values.

FIGURE 1.2   A VARIETY OF GRAPHS OF TIME SERIES DATA

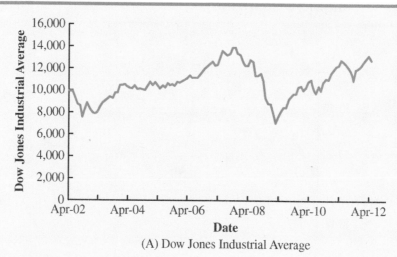

(A) Dow Jones Industrial Average

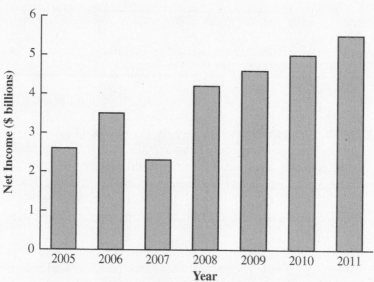

(B) Net Income for McDonald's Inc.

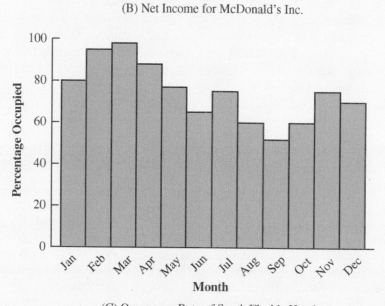

(C) Occupancy Rate of South Florida Hotels

1.3 Data Sources

Data can be obtained from existing sources or from surveys and experimental studies designed to collect new data.

Existing Sources

In some cases, data needed for a particular application already exist. Companies maintain a variety of databases about their employees, customers, and business operations. Data on employee salaries, ages, and years of experience can usually be obtained from internal personnel records. Other internal records contain data on sales, advertising expenditures, distribution costs, inventory levels, and production quantities. Most companies also maintain detailed data about their customers. Table 1.2 shows some of the data commonly available from internal company records.

Organizations that specialize in collecting and maintaining data make available substantial amounts of business and economic data. Companies access these external data sources through leasing arrangements or by purchase. Dun & Bradstreet, Bloomberg, and Dow Jones & Company are three firms that provide extensive business database services to clients. ACNielsen and Information Resources, Inc., built successful businesses collecting and processing data that they sell to advertisers and product manufacturers.

Data are also available from a variety of industry associations and special interest organizations. The Travel Industry Association of America maintains travel-related information such as the number of tourists and travel expenditures by states. Such data would be of interest to firms and individuals in the travel industry. The Graduate Management Admission Council maintains data on test scores, student characteristics, and graduate management education programs. Most of the data from these types of sources are available to qualified users at a modest cost.

The Internet is an important source of data and statistical information. Almost all companies maintain websites that provide general information about the company as well as data on sales, number of employees, number of products, product prices, and product specifications. In addition, a number of companies now specialize in making information available over the Internet. As a result, one can obtain access to stock quotes, meal prices at restaurants, salary data, and an almost infinite variety of information.

Government agencies are another important source of existing data. For instance, the U.S. Department of Labor maintains considerable data on employment rates, wage rates, size of the labor force, and union membership. Table 1.3 lists selected governmental agencies

TABLE 1.2 EXAMPLES OF DATA AVAILABLE FROM INTERNAL COMPANY RECORDS

Source	Some of the Data Typically Available
Employee records	Name, address, social security number, salary, number of vacation days, number of sick days, and bonus
Production records	Part or product number, quantity produced, direct labor cost, and materials cost
Inventory records	Part or product number, number of units on hand, reorder level, economic order quantity, and discount schedule
Sales records	Product number, sales volume, sales volume by region, and sales volume by customer type
Credit records	Customer name, address, phone number, credit limit, and accounts receivable balance
Customer profile	Age, gender, income level, household size, address, and preferences

TABLE 1.3   EXAMPLES OF DATA AVAILABLE FROM SELECTED GOVERNMENT AGENCIES

Government Agency	Some of the Data Available
Census Bureau	Population data, number of households, and household income
Federal Reserve Board	Data on the money supply, installment credit, exchange rates, and discount rates
Office of Management and Budget	Data on revenue, expenditures, and debt of the federal government
Department of Commerce	Data on business activity, value of shipments by industry, level of profits by industry, and growing and declining industries
Bureau of Labor Statistics	Consumer spending, hourly earnings, unemployment rate, safety records, and international statistics

and some of the data they provide. Most government agencies that collect and process data also make the results available through a website. Figure 1.3 shows the homepage for the U.S. Bureau of Labor Statistics website.

Statistical Studies

The largest experimental statistical study ever conducted is believed to be the 1954 Public Health Service experiment for the Salk polio vaccine. Nearly 2 million children in grades 1, 2, and 3 were selected from throughout the United States.

Sometimes the data needed for a particular application are not available through existing sources. In such cases, the data can often be obtained by conducting a statistical study. Statistical studies can be classified as either *experimental* or *observational*.

In an experimental study, a variable of interest is first identified. Then one or more other variables are identified and controlled so that data can be obtained about how they influence the variable of interest. For example, a pharmaceutical firm might be interested in conducting an experiment to learn how a new drug affects blood pressure. Blood pressure is the variable of interest in the study. The dosage level of the new drug is another variable

FIGURE 1.3   U.S. BUREAU OF LABOR STATISTICS HOMEPAGE

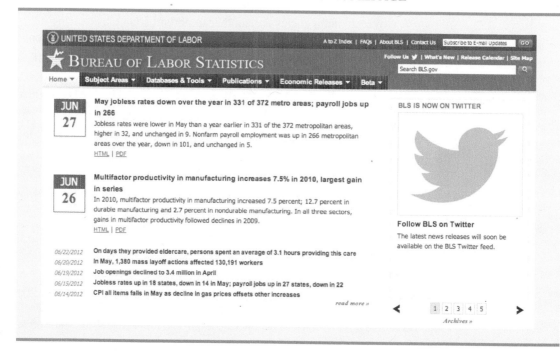

that is hoped to have a causal effect on blood pressure. To obtain data about the effect of the new drug, researchers select a sample of individuals. The dosage level of the new drug is controlled, as different groups of individuals are given different dosage levels. Before and after data on blood pressure are collected for each group. Statistical analysis of the experimental data can help determine how the new drug affects blood pressure.

Studies of smokers and nonsmokers are observational studies because researchers do not determine or control who will smoke and who will not smoke.

Nonexperimental, or observational, statistical studies make no attempt to control the variables of interest. A survey is perhaps the most common type of observational study. For instance, in a personal interview survey, research questions are first identified. Then a questionnaire is designed and administered to a sample of individuals. Some restaurants use observational studies to obtain data about customer opinions on the quality of food, quality of service, atmosphere, and so on. A customer opinion questionnaire used by Chops City Grill in Naples, Florida, is shown in Figure 1.4. Note that the customers who fill out the questionnaire are asked to provide ratings for 12 variables, including overall experience, greeting by hostess, manager (table visit), overall service, and so on. The response categories of excellent, good, average, fair, and poor provide categorical data that enable Chops City Grill management to maintain high standards for the restaurant's food and service.

Anyone wanting to use data and statistical analysis as aids to decision making must be aware of the time and cost required to obtain the data. The use of existing data sources is desirable when data must be obtained in a relatively short period of time. If important data are not readily available from an existing source, the additional time and cost involved in obtaining the data must be taken into account. In all cases, the decision maker should

FIGURE 1.4   CUSTOMER OPINION QUESTIONNAIRE USED BY CHOPS CITY GRILL RESTAURANT IN NAPLES, FLORIDA

Chop/s
CITY GRILL

Date: _____   Server Name: _____

*O*ur customers are our top priority. Please take a moment to fill out our survey card, so we can better serve your needs. You may return this card to the front desk or return by mail. Thank you!

SERVICE SURVEY	Excellent	Good	Average	Fair	Poor
Overall Experience	❑	❑	❑	❑	❑
Greeting by Hostess	❑	❑	❑	❑	❑
Manager (Table Visit)	❑	❑	❑	❑	❑
Overall Service	❑	❑	❑	❑	❑
Professionalism	❑	❑	❑	❑	❑
Menu Knowledge	❑	❑	❑	❑	❑
Friendliness	❑	❑	❑	❑	❑
Wine Selection	❑	❑	❑	❑	❑
Menu Selection	❑	❑	❑	❑	❑
Food Quality	❑	❑	❑	❑	❑
Food Presentation	❑	❑	❑	❑	❑
Value for $ Spent	❑	❑	❑	❑	❑

What comments could you give us to improve our restaurant?

_____

_____

Thank you, we appreciate your comments. —The staff of Chops City Grill.

consider the contribution of the statistical analysis to the decision-making process. The cost of data acquisition and the subsequent statistical analysis should not exceed the savings generated by using the information to make a better decision.

Data Acquisition Errors

Managers should always be aware of the possibility of data errors in statistical studies. Using erroneous data can be worse than not using any data at all. An error in data acquisition occurs whenever the data value obtained is not equal to the true or actual value that would be obtained with a correct procedure. Such errors can occur in a number of ways. For example, an interviewer might make a recording error, such as a transposition in writing the age of a 24-year-old person as 42, or the person answering an interview question might misinterpret the question and provide an incorrect response.

Experienced data analysts take great care in collecting and recording data to ensure that errors are not made. Special procedures can be used to check for internal consistency of the data. For instance, such procedures would indicate that the analyst should review the accuracy of data for a respondent shown to be 22 years of age but reporting 20 years of work experience. Data analysts also review data with unusually large and small values, called outliers, which are candidates for possible data errors. In Chapter 3 we present some of the methods statisticians use to identify outliers.

Errors often occur during data acquisition. Blindly using any data that happen to be available or using data that were acquired with little care can result in misleading information and bad decisions. Thus, taking steps to acquire accurate data can help ensure reliable and valuable decision-making information.

1.4 Descriptive Statistics

Most of the statistical information in newspapers, magazines, company reports, and other publications consists of data that are summarized and presented in a form that is easy for the reader to understand. Such summaries of data, which may be tabular, graphical, or numerical, are referred to as **descriptive statistics**.

Refer to the data set in Table 1.1 showing data for 60 nations that participate in the World Trade Organization. Methods of descriptive statistics can be used to summarize these data. For example, consider the variable Fitch Outlook that indicates the direction the nation's credit rating is likely to move over the next two years. The Fitch Outlook is recorded as being negative, stable, or positive. A tabular summary of the data showing the number of nations with each of the Fitch Outlook ratings is shown in Table 1.4. A graphical summary of the same data, called a bar chart, is shown in Figure 1.5. These types of summaries make the data easier to interpret. Referring to Table 1.4 and Figure 1.5, we can see that the majority of Fitch Outlook credit ratings are stable, with 65% of the nations

TABLE 1.4   FREQUENCIES AND PERCENT FREQUENCIES FOR THE FITCH CREDIT RATING OUTLOOK OF 60 NATIONS

Fitch Outlook	Frequency	Percent Frequency (%)
Positive	10	16.7
Stable	39	65.0
Negative	11	18.3

FIGURE 1.5 BAR CHART FOR THE FITCH CREDIT RATING OUTLOOK FOR 60 NATIONS

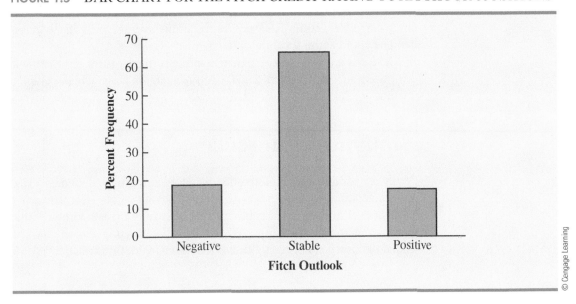

having this rating. Negative and positive outlook credit ratings are similar, with slightly more nations having a negative outlook (18.3%) than a positive outlook (16.7%).

A graphical summary of the data for quantitative variable Per Capita GDP in Table 1.1, called a histogram, is provided in Figure 1.6. Using the histogram, it is easy to see that Per Capita GDP for the 60 nations ranges from $0 to $60,000, with the highest concentration between $10,000 and $20,000. Only one nation had a Per Capita GDP exceeding $50,000.

In addition to tabular and graphical displays, numerical descriptive statistics are used to summarize data. The most common numerical measure is the average, or mean. Using

FIGURE 1.6 HISTOGRAM OF PER CAPITA GDP FOR 60 NATIONS

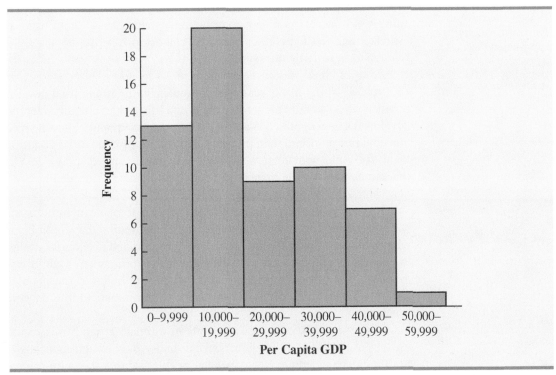

the data on Per Capita GDP for the 60 nations in Table 1.1, we can compute the average by adding Per Capita GDP for all 60 nations and dividing the total by 60. Doing so provides an average Per Capita GDP of $21,387. This average provides a measure of the central tendency, or central location of the data.

There is a great deal of interest in effective methods for developing and presenting descriptive statistics. Chapters 2 and 3 devote attention to the tabular, graphical, and numerical methods of descriptive statistics.

1.5   Statistical Inference

Many situations require information about a large group of elements (individuals, companies, voters, households, products, customers, and so on). But, because of time, cost, and other considerations, data can be collected from only a small portion of the group. The larger group of elements in a particular study is called the **population**, and the smaller group is called the **sample**. Formally, we use the following definitions.

POPULATION

A population is the set of all elements of interest in a particular study.

SAMPLE

A sample is a subset of the population.

The U.S. government conducts a census every 10 years. Market research firms conduct sample surveys every day.

The process of conducting a survey to collect data for the entire population is called a **census**. The process of conducting a survey to collect data for a sample is called a **sample survey**. As one of its major contributions, statistics uses data from a sample to make estimates and test hypotheses about the characteristics of a population through a process referred to as **statistical inference**.

As an example of statistical inference, let us consider the study conducted by Norris Electronics. Norris manufactures a high-intensity lightbulb used in a variety of electrical products. In an attempt to increase the useful life of the lightbulb, the product design group developed a new lightbulb filament. In this case, the population is defined as all lightbulbs that could be produced with the new filament. To evaluate the advantages of the new filament, 200 bulbs with the new filament were manufactured and tested. Data collected from this sample showed the number of hours each lightbulb operated before filament burnout. See Table 1.5.

Suppose Norris wants to use the sample data to make an inference about the average hours of useful life for the population of all lightbulbs that could be produced with the new filament. Adding the 200 values in Table 1.5 and dividing the total by 200 provides the sample average lifetime for the lightbulbs: 76 hours. We can use this sample result to estimate that the average lifetime for the lightbulbs in the population is 76 hours. Figure 1.7 provides a graphical summary of the statistical inference process for Norris Electronics.

Whenever statisticians use a sample to estimate a population characteristic of interest, they usually provide a statement of the quality, or precision, associated with the estimate. For the Norris example, the statistician might state that the point estimate of the average

TABLE 1.5 **HOURS UNTIL BURNOUT FOR A SAMPLE OF 200 LIGHTBULBS FOR THE NORRIS ELECTRONICS EXAMPLE**

107	73	68	97	76	79	94	59	98	57
54	65	71	70	84	88	62	61	79	98
66	62	79	86	68	74	61	82	65	98
62	116	65	88	64	79	78	79	77	86
74	85	73	80	68	78	89	72	58	69
92	78	88	77	103	88	63	68	88	81
75	90	62	89	71	71	74	70	74	70
65	81	75	62	94	71	85	84	83	63
81	62	79	83	93	61	65	62	92	65
83	70	70	81	77	72	84	67	59	58
78	66	66	94	77	63	66	75	68	76
90	78	71	101	78	43	59	67	61	71
96	75	64	76	72	77	74	65	82	86
66	86	96	89	81	71	85	99	59	92
68	72	77	60	87	84	75	77	51	45
85	67	87	80	84	93	69	76	89	75
83	68	72	67	92	89	82	96	77	102
74	91	76	83	66	68	61	73	72	76
73	77	79	94	63	59	62	71	81	65
73	63	63	89	82	64	85	92	64	73

WEB file

Norris

© Cengage Learning

FIGURE 1.7 **THE PROCESS OF STATISTICAL INFERENCE FOR THE NORRIS ELECTRONICS EXAMPLE**

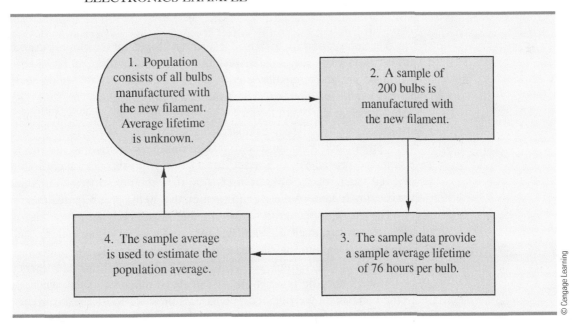

© Cengage Learning

lifetime for the population of new lightbulbs is 76 hours with a margin of error of ± 4 hours. Thus, an interval estimate of the average lifetime for all lightbulbs produced with the new filament is 72 hours to 80 hours. The statistician can also state how confident he or she is that the interval from 72 hours to 80 hours contains the population average.

Computers and Statistical Analysis

Statisticians frequently use computer software to perform the statistical computations required with large amounts of data. For example, computing the average lifetime for the 200 lightbulbs in the Norris Electronics example (see Table 1.5) would be quite tedious without a computer. To facilitate computer usage, many of the data sets in this book are available on the website that accompanies the text. The data files may be downloaded in either Minitab or Excel formats. In addition, the Excel add-in StatTools can be downloaded from the website. End-of-chapter appendixes cover the step-by-step procedures for using Minitab, Excel, and the Excel add-in StatTools to implement the statistical techniques presented in the chapter.

Minitab and Excel data sets and the Excel add-in StatTools are available on the website for this text.

Data Mining

With the aid of magnetic card readers, bar code scanners, and point-of-sale terminals, most organizations obtain large amounts of data on a daily basis. And, even for a small local restaurant that uses touch screen monitors to enter orders and handle billing, the amount of data collected can be substantial. For large retail companies, the sheer volume of data collected is hard to conceptualize, and figuring out how to effectively use these data to improve profitability is a challenge. Mass retailers such as Walmart capture data on 20 to 30 million transactions every day, telecommunication companies such as France Telecom and AT&T generate over 300 million call records per day, and Visa processes 6800 payment transactions per second or approximately 600 million transactions per day. Storing and managing the transaction data is a substantial undertaking.

The term *data warehousing* is used to refer to the process of capturing, storing, and maintaining the data. Computing power and data collection tools have reached the point where it is now feasible to store and retrieve extremely large quantities of data in seconds. Analysis of the data in the warehouse may result in decisions that will lead to new strategies and higher profits for the organization.

The subject of **data mining** deals with methods for developing useful decision-making information from large databases. Using a combination of procedures from statistics, mathematics, and computer science, analysts "mine the data" in the warehouse to convert it into useful information, hence the name *data mining*. Dr. Kurt Thearling, a leading practitioner in the field, defines data mining as "the automated extraction of predictive information from (large) databases." The two key words in Dr. Thearling's definition are "automated" and "predictive." Data mining systems that are the most effective use automated procedures to extract information from the data using only the most general or even vague queries by the user. And data mining software automates the process of uncovering hidden predictive information that in the past required hands-on analysis.

The major applications of data mining have been made by companies with a strong consumer focus, such as retail businesses, financial organizations, and communication companies. Data mining has been successfully used to help retailers such as Amazon and Barnes & Noble determine one or more related products that customers who have already purchased a specific product are also likely to purchase. Then, when a customer logs on to the company's website and purchases a product, the website uses pop-ups to alert the customer about additional products that the customer is likely to purchase. In another application, data mining may be used to identify customers who are likely to spend more than $20 on a particular shopping trip. These customers may then be identified as the ones to receive special e-mail or regular mail discount offers to encourage them to make their next shopping trip before the discount termination date.

Data mining is a technology that relies heavily on statistical methodology such as multiple regression, logistic regression, and correlation. But it takes a creative integration of all

*Statistical methods play
an important role in data
mining, both in terms of
discovering relationships
in the data and predicting
future outcomes. However,
a thorough coverage of
data mining and the use
of statistics in data mining
are outside the scope of
this text.*

these methods and computer science technologies involving artificial intelligence and machine learning to make data mining effective. A substantial investment in time and money is required to implement commercial data mining software packages developed by firms such as Oracle, Teradata, and SAS. The statistical concepts introduced in this text will be helpful in understanding the statistical methodology used by data mining software packages and enable you to better understand the statistical information that is developed.

Because statistical models play an important role in developing predictive models in data mining, many of the concerns that statisticians deal with in developing statistical models are also applicable. For instance, a concern in any statistical study involves the issue of model reliability. Finding a statistical model that works well for a particular sample of data does not necessarily mean that it can be reliably applied to other data. One of the common statistical approaches to evaluating model reliability is to divide the sample data set into two parts: a training data set and a test data set. If the model developed using the training data is able to accurately predict values in the test data, we say that the model is reliable. One advantage that data mining has over classical statistics is that the enormous amount of data available allows the data mining software to partition the data set so that a model developed for the training data set may be tested for reliability on other data. In this sense, the partitioning of the data set allows data mining to develop models and relationships and then quickly observe if they are repeatable and valid with new and different data. On the other hand, a warning for data mining applications is that with so much data available, there is a danger of overfitting the model to the point that misleading associations and cause/effect conclusions appear to exist. Careful interpretation of data mining results and additional testing will help avoid this pitfall.

1.8 Ethical Guidelines for Statistical Practice

Ethical behavior is something we should strive for in all that we do. Ethical issues arise in statistics because of the important role statistics plays in the collection, analysis, presentation, and interpretation of data. In a statistical study, unethical behavior can take a variety of forms including improper sampling, inappropriate analysis of the data, development of misleading graphs, use of inappropriate summary statistics, and/or a biased interpretation of the statistical results.

As you begin to do your own statistical work, we encourage you to be fair, thorough, objective, and neutral as you collect data, conduct analyses, make oral presentations, and present written reports containing information developed. As a consumer of statistics, you should also be aware of the possibility of unethical statistical behavior by others. When you see statistics in newspapers, on television, on the Internet, and so on, it is a good idea to view the information with some skepticism, always being aware of the source as well as the purpose and objectivity of the statistics provided.

The American Statistical Association, the nation's leading professional organization for statistics and statisticians, developed the report "Ethical Guidelines for Statistical Practice"[2] to help statistical practitioners make and communicate ethical decisions and assist students in learning how to perform statistical work responsibly. The report contains 67 guidelines organized into eight topic areas: Professionalism; Responsibilities to Funders, Clients, and Employers; Responsibilities in Publications and Testimony; Responsibilities to Research Subjects; Responsibilities to Research Team Colleagues; Responsibilities to Other Statisticians or Statistical Practitioners; Responsibilities Regarding Allegations of Misconduct; and Responsibilities of Employers Including Organizations, Individuals, Attorneys, or Other Clients Employing Statistical Practitioners.

---

[2]American Statistical Association, "Ethical Guidelines for Statistical Practice," 1999.

One of the ethical guidelines in the professionalism area addresses the issue of running multiple tests until a desired result is obtained. Let us consider an example. In Section 1.5 we discussed a statistical study conducted by Norris Electronics involving a sample of 200 high-intensity lightbulbs manufactured with a new filament. The average lifetime for the sample, 76 hours, provided an estimate of the average lifetime for all lightbulbs produced with the new filament. However, consider this. Because Norris selected a sample of bulbs, it is reasonable to assume that another sample would have provided a different average lifetime.

Suppose Norris's management had hoped the sample results would enable them to claim that the average lifetime for the new lightbulbs was 80 hours or more. Suppose further that Norris's management decides to continue the study by manufacturing and testing repeated samples of 200 lightbulbs with the new filament until a sample mean of 80 hours or more is obtained. If the study is repeated enough times, a sample may eventually be obtained—by chance alone—that would provide the desired result and enable Norris to make such a claim. In this case, consumers would be misled into thinking the new product is better than it actually is. Clearly, this type of behavior is unethical and represents a gross misuse of statistics in practice.

Several ethical guidelines in the responsibilities and publications and testimony area deal with issues involving the handling of data. For instance, a statistician must account for all data considered in a study and explain the sample(s) actually used. In the Norris Electronics study the average lifetime for the 200 bulbs in the original sample is 76 hours; this is considerably less than the 80 hours or more that management hoped to obtain. Suppose now that after reviewing the results showing a 76 hour average lifetime, Norris discards all the observations with 70 or fewer hours until burnout, allegedly because these bulbs contain imperfections caused by startup problems in the manufacturing process. After discarding these lightbulbs, the average lifetime for the remaining lightbulbs in the sample turns out to be 82 hours. Would you be suspicious of Norris's claim that the lifetime for their lightbulbs is 82 hours?

If the Norris lightbulbs showing 70 or fewer hours until burnout were discarded to simply provide an average lifetime of 82 hours, there is no question that discarding the lightbulbs with 70 or fewer hours until burnout is unethical. But, even if the discarded lightbulbs contain imperfections due to startup problems in the manufacturing process—and, as a result, should not have been included in the analysis—the statistician who conducted the study must account for all the data that were considered and explain how the sample actually used was obtained. To do otherwise is potentially misleading and would constitute unethical behavior on the part of both the company and the statistician.

A guideline in the shared values section of the American Statistical Association report states that statistical practitioners should avoid any tendency to slant statistical work toward predetermined outcomes. This type of unethical practice is often observed when unrepresentative samples are used to make claims. For instance, in many areas of the country smoking is not permitted in restaurants. Suppose, however, a lobbyist for the tobacco industry interviews people in restaurants where smoking is permitted in order to estimate the percentage of people who are in favor of allowing smoking in restaurants. The sample results show that 90% of the people interviewed are in favor of allowing smoking in restaurants. Based upon these sample results, the lobbyist claims that 90% of all people who eat in restaurants are in favor of permitting smoking in restaurants. In this case we would argue that only sampling persons eating in restaurants that allow smoking has biased the results. If only the final results of such a study are reported, readers unfamiliar with the details of the study (i.e., that the sample was collected only in restaurants allowing smoking) can be misled.

The scope of the American Statistical Association's report is broad and includes ethical guidelines that are appropriate not only for a statistician, but also for consumers of statistical information. We encourage you to read the report to obtain a better perspective of ethical issues as you continue your study of statistics and to gain the background for determining how to ensure that ethical standards are met when you start to use statistics in practice.

Summary

Statistics is the art and science of collecting, analyzing, presenting, and interpreting data. Nearly every college student majoring in business or economics is required to take a course in statistics. We began the chapter by describing typical statistical applications for business and economics.

Data consist of the facts and figures that are collected and analyzed. Four scales of measurement used to obtain data on a particular variable include nominal, ordinal, interval, and ratio. The scale of measurement for a variable is nominal when the data are labels or names used to identify an attribute of an element. The scale is ordinal if the data demonstrate the properties of nominal data and the order or rank of the data is meaningful. The scale is interval if the data demonstrate the properties of ordinal data and the interval between values is expressed in terms of a fixed unit of measure. Finally, the scale of measurement is ratio if the data show all the properties of interval data and the ratio of two values is meaningful.

For purposes of statistical analysis, data can be classified as categorical or quantitative. Categorical data use labels or names to identify an attribute of each element. Categorical data use either the nominal or ordinal scale of measurement and may be nonnumeric or numeric. Quantitative data are numeric values that indicate how much or how many. Quantitative data use either the interval or ratio scale of measurement. Ordinary arithmetic operations are meaningful only if the data are quantitative. Therefore, statistical computations used for quantitative data are not always appropriate for categorical data.

In Sections 1.4 and 1.5 we introduced the topics of descriptive statistics and statistical inference. Descriptive statistics are the tabular, graphical, and numerical methods used to summarize data. The process of statistical inference uses data obtained from a sample to make estimates or test hypotheses about the characteristics of a population. The last three sections of the chapter provide information on the role of computers in statistical analysis, an introduction to the relative new field of data mining, and a summary of ethical guidelines for statistical practice.

Glossary

Statistics The art and science of collecting, analyzing, presenting, and interpreting data.
Data The facts and figures collected, analyzed, and summarized for presentation and interpretation.
Data set All the data collected in a particular study.
Elements The entities on which data are collected.
Variable A characteristic of interest for the elements.
Observation The set of measurements obtained for a particular element.
Nominal scale The scale of measurement for a variable when the data are labels or names used to identify an attribute of an element. Nominal data may be nonnumeric or numeric.
Ordinal scale The scale of measurement for a variable if the data exhibit the properties of nominal data and the order or rank of the data is meaningful. Ordinal data may be nonnumeric or numeric.
Interval scale The scale of measurement for a variable if the data demonstrate the properties of ordinal data and the interval between values is expressed in terms of a fixed unit of measure. Interval data are always numeric.
Ratio scale The scale of measurement for a variable if the data demonstrate all the properties of interval data and the ratio of two values is meaningful. Ratio data are always numeric.

Categorical data Labels or names used to identify an attribute of each element. Categorical data use either the nominal or ordinal scale of measurement and may be nonnumeric or numeric.

Quantitative data Numeric values that indicate how much or how many of something. Quantitative data are obtained using either the interval or ratio scale of measurement.

Categorical variable A variable with categorical data.

Quantitative variable A variable with quantitative data.

Cross-sectional data Data collected at the same or approximately the same point in time.

Time series data Data collected over several time periods.

Descriptive statistics Tabular, graphical, and numerical summaries of data.

Population The set of all elements of interest in a particular study.

Sample A subset of the population.

Census A survey to collect data on the entire population.

Sample survey A survey to collect data on a sample.

Statistical inference The process of using data obtained from a sample to make estimates or test hypotheses about the characteristics of a population.

Data mining The process of using procedures from statistics and computer science to extract useful information from extremely large databases.

Supplementary Exercises

1. Discuss the differences between statistics as numerical facts and statistics as a discipline or field of study.

2. The U.S. Department of Energy provides fuel economy information for a variety of motor vehicles. A sample of 10 automobiles is shown in Table 1.6 (Fuel Economy website, February 22, 2008). Data show the size of the automobile (compact, midsize, or large), the number of cylinders in the engine, the city driving miles per gallon, the highway driving miles per gallon, and the recommended fuel (diesel, premium, or regular).
   a. How many elements are in this data set?
   b. How many variables are in this data set?
   c. Which variables are categorical and which variables are quantitative?
   d. What type of measurement scale is used for each of the variables?

3. Refer to Table 1.6.
   a. What is the average miles per gallon for city driving?
   b. On average, how much higher is the miles per gallon for highway driving as compared to city driving?

TABLE 1.6   FUEL ECONOMY INFORMATION FOR 10 AUTOMOBILES

Car	Size	Cylinders	City MPG	Highway MPG	Fuel
Audi A8	Large	12	13	19	Premium
BMW 328Xi	Compact	6	17	25	Premium
Cadillac CTS	Midsize	6	16	25	Regular
Chrysler 300	Large	8	13	18	Premium
Ford Focus	Compact	4	24	33	Regular
Hyundai Elantra	Midsize	4	25	33	Regular
Jeep Grand Cherokee	Midsize	6	17	26	Diesel
Pontiac G6	Compact	6	15	22	Regular
Toyota Camry	Midsize	4	21	31	Regular
Volkswagen Jetta	Compact	5	21	29	Regular

© Cengage Learning

TABLE 1.7   DATA FOR EIGHT CORDLESS TELEPHONES

Brand	Model	Price ($)	Overall Score	Voice Quality	Handset on Base	Talk Time (Hours)
AT&T	CL84100	60	73	Excellent	Yes	7
AT&T	TL92271	80	70	Very Good	No	7
Panasonic	4773B	100	78	Very Good	Yes	13
Panasonic	6592T	70	72	Very Good	No	13
Uniden	D2997	45	70	Very Good	No	10
Uniden	D1788	80	73	Very Good	Yes	7
Vtech	DS6521	60	72	Excellent	No	7
Vtech	CS6649	50	72	Very Good	Yes	7

© Cengage Learning

   c. What percentage of the cars have four-cylinder engines?
   d. What percentage of the cars use regular fuel?

4. Table 1.7 shows data for eight cordless telephones (*Consumer Reports,* November 2012). The Overall Score, a measure of the overall quality for the cordless telephone, ranges from 0 to 100. Voice Quality has possible ratings of poor, fair, good, very good, and excellent. Talk Time is the manufacturer's claim of how long the handset can be used when it is fully charged.
   a. How many elements are in this data set?
   b. For the variables Price, Overall Score, Voice Quality, Handset on Base, and Talk Time, which variables are categorical and which variables are quantitative?
   c. What scale of measurement is used for each variable?

5. Refer to the data set in Table 1.7.
   a. What is the average price for the cordless telephones?
   b. What is the average talk time for the cordless telephones?
   c. What percentage of the cordless telephones has a voice quality of excellent?
   d. What percentage of the cordless telephones has a handset on the base?

6. J.D. Power and Associates surveys new automobile owners to learn about the quality of recently purchased vehicles. The following questions were asked in the *J.D. Power Initial Quality Survey,* May 2012.
   a. Did you purchase or lease the vehicle?
   b. What price did you pay?
   c. What is the overall attractiveness of your vehicle's exterior? (Unacceptable, Average, Outstanding, or Truly Exceptional)
   d. What is your average miles-per-gallon?
   e. What is your overall rating of your new vehicle? (1- to 10-point scale with 1 unacceptable and 10 truly exceptional)
   Comment on whether each question provides categorical or quantitative data.

7. The Kroger Company is one of the largest grocery retailers in the United States, with over 2000 grocery stores across the country. Kroger uses an online customer opinion questionnaire to obtain performance data about its products and services and learn about what motivates its customers (Kroger website, April 2012). In the survey, Kroger customers were asked if they would be willing to pay more for products that had each of the following four characteristics. The four questions were: Would you pay more for

     products that have a brand name?
     products that are environmentally friendly?
     products that are organic?
     products that have been recommended by others?

For each question, the customers had the option of responding Yes if they would pay more or No if they would not pay more.

    a.   Are the data collected by Kroger in this example categorical or quantitative?

    b.   What measurement scale is used?

8.   The *FinancialTimes*/Harris Poll is a monthly online poll of adults from six countries in Europe and the United States. A January poll included 1015 adults in the United States. One of the questions asked was, "How would you rate the Federal Bank in handling the credit problems in the financial markets?" Possible responses were Excellent, Good, Fair, Bad, and Terrible (Harris Interactive website, January 2008).

    a.   What was the sample size for this survey?

    b.   Are the data categorical or quantitative?

    c.   Would it make more sense to use averages or percentages as a summary of the data for this question?

    d.   Of the respondents in the United States, 10% said the Federal Bank is doing a good job. How many individuals provided this response?

9.   The Commerce Department reported receiving the following applications for the Malcolm Baldrige National Quality Award: 23 from large manufacturing firms, 18 from large service firms, and 30 from small businesses.

    a.   Is type of business a categorical or quantitative variable?

    b.   What percentage of the applications came from small businesses?

10.   The Bureau of Transportation Statistics Omnibus Household Survey is conducted annually and serves as an information source for the U.S. Department of Transportation. In one part of the survey the person being interviewed was asked to respond to the following statement: "Drivers of motor vehicles should be allowed to talk on a hand-held cell phone while driving." Possible responses were strongly agree, somewhat agree, somewhat disagree, and strongly disagree. Forty-four respondents said that they strongly agree with this statement, 130 said that they somewhat agree, 165 said they somewhat disagree, and 741 said they strongly disagree with this statement (Bureau of Transportation website, August 2010).

    a.   Do the responses for this statement provide categorical or quantitative data?

    b.   Would it make more sense to use averages or percentages as a summary of the responses for this statement?

    c.   What percentage of respondents strongly agree with allowing drivers of motor vehicles to talk on a hand-held cell phone while driving?

    d.   Do the results indicate general support for or against allowing drivers of motor vehicles to talk on a hand-held cell phone while driving?

11.   J.D. Power and Associates conducts vehicle quality surveys to provide automobile manufacturers with consumer satisfaction information about their products (Vehicle Quality Survey, January 2010). Using a sample of vehicle owners from recent vehicle purchase records, the survey asks the owners a variety of questions about their new vehicles, such as those shown below. For each question, state whether the data collected are categorical or quantitative and indicate the measurement scale being used.

    a.   What price did you pay for the vehicle?

    b.   How did you pay for the vehicle? (Cash, Lease, or Finance)

    c.   How likely would you be to recommend this vehicle to a friend? (Definitely Not, Probably Not, Probably Will, and Definitely Will)

    d.   What is the current mileage?

    e.   What is your overall rating of your new vehicle? A 10-point scale, ranging from 1 for unacceptable to 10 for truly exceptional, was used.

12.   The Hawaii Visitors Bureau collects data on visitors to Hawaii. The following questions were among 16 asked in a questionnaire handed out to passengers during incoming airline flights.

    •   This trip to Hawaii is my: 1st, 2nd, 3rd, 4th, etc.

    •   The primary reason for this trip is: (10 categories, including vacation, convention, honeymoon)

- Where I plan to stay: (11 categories, including hotel, apartment, relatives, camping)
- Total days in Hawaii

a. What is the population being studied?

b. Is the use of a questionnaire a good way to reach the population of passengers on incoming airline flights?

c. Comment on each of the four questions in terms of whether it will provide categorical or quantitative data.

SELF test

13. Figure 1.8 provides a bar chart showing the amount of federal spending for the years 2004 to 2010 (Congressional Budget Office website, May 15, 2011).

a. What is the variable of interest?

b. Are the data categorical or quantitative?

c. Are the data time series or cross-sectional?

d. Comment on the trend in federal spending over time.

14. The following data show the number of rental cars in service for three rental car companies: Hertz, Avis, and Dollar. The data are for the years 2007–2010 and are in thousands of vehicles (Auto Rental News website, May 15, 2011).

	Cars in Service (1000s)			
Company	**2007**	**2008**	**2009**	**2010**
Hertz	327	311	286	290
Dollar	167	140	106	108
Avis	204	220	300	270

a. Construct a time series graph for the years 2007 to 2010 showing the number of rental cars in service for each company. Show the time series for all three companies on the same graph.

b. Comment on who appears to be the market share leader and how the market shares are changing over time.

c. Construct a bar chart showing rental cars in service for 2010. Is this chart based on cross-sectional or time series data?

FIGURE 1.8 FEDERAL SPENDING

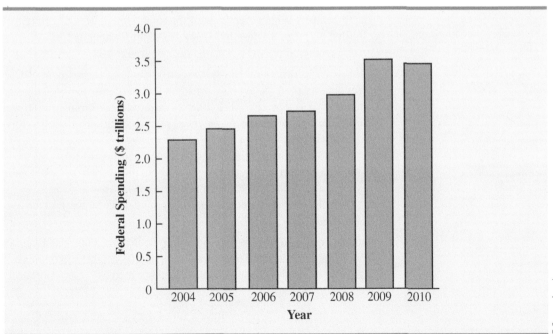

FIGURE 1.9   NUMBER OF RECREATIONAL BOATING ACCIDENTS

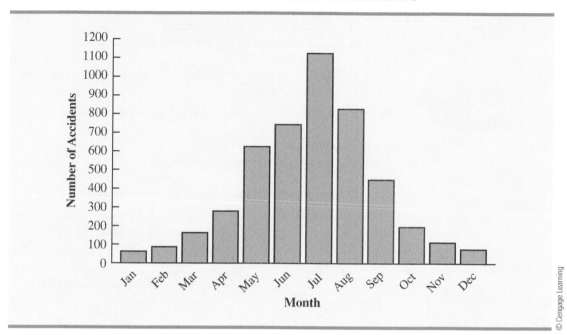

15. Every year, the U.S. Coast Guard collects data and compiles statistics on reported rec-reational boating accidents. These statistics are derived from accident reports that are filed by the owners/operators of recreational vessels involved in accidents. In 2009, 4730 recreational boating accident reports were filed. Figure 1.9 provides a bar chart summariz-ing the number of accident reports that were filed each month (U.S. Coast Guard's Boating Safety Division website, August 2010).
a.   Are the data categorical or quantitative?
b.   Are the data time series or cross-sectional?
c.   In what month were the most accident reports filed? Approximately how many?
d.   There were 61 accident reports filed in January and 76 accident reports filed in December. What percentage of the total number of accident reports for the year was filed in these two months? Does this seem reasonable?
e.   Comment on the overall shape of the bar graph.

16. The Energy Information Administration of the U.S. Department of Energy provided time series data for the U.S. average price per gallon of conventional regular gasoline between January 2007 and March 2012 (Energy Information Administration website, April 2012). Use the Internet to obtain the average price per gallon of conventional regular gasoline since March 2012.
a.   Extend the graph of the time series shown in Figure 1.1.
b.   What interpretations can you make about the average price per gallon of conventional regular gasoline since March 2012?
c.   Does the time series continue to show a summer increase in the average price per gal-lon? Explain.

17. A manager of a large corporation recommends a $10,000 raise be given to keep a valued subordinate from moving to another company. What internal and external sources of data might be used to decide whether such a salary increase is appropriate?

18. A random telephone survey of 1021 adults (aged 18 and older) was conducted by Opinion Research Corporation on behalf of CompleteTax, an online tax preparation and e-filing service. The survey results showed that 684 of those surveyed planned to file their taxes electronically (CompleteTax Tax Prep Survey 2010).

    a. Develop a descriptive statistic that can be used to estimate the percentage of all taxpayers who file electronically.

    b. The survey reported that the most frequently used method for preparing the tax return is to hire an accountant or professional tax preparer. If 60% of the people surveyed had their tax return prepared this way, how many people used an accountant or professional tax preparer?

    c. Other methods that the person filing the return often used include manual preparation, use of an online tax service, and use of a software tax program. Would the data for the method for preparing the tax return be considered categorical or quantitative?

19. A *Bloomberg Businessweek* North American subscriber study collected data from a sample of 2861 subscribers. Fifty-nine percent of the respondents indicated an annual income of $75,000 or more, and 50% reported having an American Express credit card.

    a. What is the population of interest in this study?

    b. Is annual income a categorical or quantitative variable?

    c. Is ownership of an American Express card a categorical or quantitative variable?

    d. Does this study involve cross-sectional or time series data?

    e. Describe any statistical inferences *Bloomberg Businessweek* might make on the basis of the survey.

20. A survey of 131 investment managers in *Barron's* Big Money poll revealed the following:

    - 43% of managers classified themselves as bullish or very bullish on the stock market.
    - The average expected return over the next 12 months for equities was 11.2%.
    - 21% selected health care as the sector most likely to lead the market in the next 12 months.
    - When asked to estimate how long it would take for technology and telecom stocks to resume sustainable growth, the managers' average response was 2.5 years.

    a. Cite two descriptive statistics.

    b. Make an inference about the population of all investment managers concerning the average return expected on equities over the next 12 months.

    c. Make an inference about the length of time it will take for technology and telecom stocks to resume sustainable growth.

21. A seven-year medical research study reported that women whose mothers took the drug DES during pregnancy were twice as likely to develop tissue abnormalities that might lead to cancer as were women whose mothers did not take the drug.

    a. This study compared two populations. What were the populations?

    b. Do you suppose the data were obtained in a survey or an experiment?

    c. For the population of women whose mothers took the drug DES during pregnancy, a sample of 3980 women showed that 63 developed tissue abnormalities that might lead to cancer. Provide a descriptive statistic that could be used to estimate the number of women out of 1000 in this population who have tissue abnormalities.

    d. For the population of women whose mothers did not take the drug DES during pregnancy, what is the estimate of the number of women out of 1000 who would be expected to have tissue abnormalities?

    e. Medical studies often use a relatively large sample (in this case, 3980). Why?

22. The Nielsen Company surveyed consumers in 47 markets from Europe, Asia-Pacific, the Americas, and the Middle East to determine which factors are most important in determining where they buy groceries. Using a scale of 1 (low) to 5 (high), the highest rated factor was *good value for money,* with an average point score of 4.32. The second highest rated factor was *better selection of high-quality brands and products,* with an average point score of 3.78, and the lowest rated factor was *uses recyclable bags and packaging,* with an average point score of 2.71 (Nielsen website, February 24, 2008). Suppose that you have been hired by a grocery store chain to conduct a similar study to determine what factors customers at the chain's stores in Charlotte, North Carolina, think are most important in determining where they buy groceries.
     a. What is the population for the survey that you will be conducting?
     b. How would you collect the data for this study?

23. Pew Research Center is a nonpartisan polling organization that provides information about issues, attitudes, and trends shaping America. In a recent poll, Pew researchers found that 47% of American adult respondents reported getting at least some local news on their cell phone or tablet computer (Pew Research website, May 14, 2011). Further findings showed that 42% of respondents who own cell phones or tablet computers use those devices to check local weather reports and 37% use the devices to find local restaurants or other businesses.
     a. One statistic concerned using cell phones or tablet computers for local news. What population is that finding applicable to?
     b. Another statistic concerned using cell phones or tablet computers to check local weather reports and to find local restaurants. What population is this finding applicable to?
     c. Do you think the Pew researchers conducted a census or a sample survey to obtain their results? Why?
     d. If you were a restaurant owner, would you find these results interesting? Why? How could you take advantage of this information?

24. A sample of midterm grades for five students showed the following results: 72, 65, 82, 90, 76. Which of the following statements are correct, and which should be challenged as being too generalized?
     a. The average midterm grade for the sample of five students is 77.
     b. The average midterm grade for all students who took the exam is 77.
     c. An estimate of the average midterm grade for all students who took the exam is 77.
     d. More than half of the students who take this exam will score between 70 and 85.
     e. If five other students are included in the sample, their grades will be between 65 and 90.

25. Table 1.8 shows a data set containing information for 25 of the shadow stocks tracked by the American Association of Individual Investors. Shadow stocks are common stocks of smaller companies that are not closely followed by Wall Street analysts. The data set is also on the website that accompanies the text in the file named Shadow02.
     a. How many variables are in the data set?
     b. Which of the variables are categorical and which are quantitative?
     c. For the Exchange variable, show the frequency and the percent frequency for AMEX, NYSE, and OTC. Construct a bar graph similar to Figure 1.5 for the Exchange variable.
     d. Show the frequency distribution for the Gross Profit Margin using the five intervals: 0–14.9, 15–29.9, 30–44.9, 45–59.9, and 60–74.9. Construct a histogram similar to Figure 1.6.
     e. What is the average price/earnings ratio?

TABLE 1.8   DATA SET FOR 25 SHADOW STOCKS

Company	Exchange	Ticker Symbol	Market Cap ($ millions)	Price/ Earnings Ratio	Gross Profit Margin (%)
DeWolfe Companies	AMEX	DWL	36.4	8.4	36.7
North Coast Energy	OTC	NCEB	52.5	6.2	59.3
Hansen Natural Corp.	OTC	HANS	41.1	14.6	44.8
MarineMax, Inc.	NYSE	HZO	111.5	7.2	23.8
Nanometrics Incorporated	OTC	NANO	228.6	38.0	53.3
TeamStaff, Inc.	OTC	TSTF	92.1	33.5	4.1
Environmental Tectonics	AMEX	ETC	51.1	35.8	35.9
Measurement Specialties	AMEX	MSS	101.8	26.8	37.6
SEMCO Energy, Inc.	NYSE	SEN	193.4	18.7	23.6
Party City Corporation	OTC	PCTY	97.2	15.9	36.4
Embrex, Inc.	OTC	EMBX	136.5	18.9	59.5
Tech/Ops Sevcon, Inc.	AMEX	TO	23.2	20.7	35.7
ARCADIS NV	OTC	ARCAF	173.4	8.8	9.6
Qiao Xing Universal Tele.	OTC	XING	64.3	22.1	30.8
Energy West Incorporated	OTC	EWST	29.1	9.7	16.3
Barnwell Industries, Inc.	AMEX	BRN	27.3	7.4	73.4
Innodata Corporation	OTC	INOD	66.1	11.0	29.6
Medical Action Industries	OTC	MDCI	137.1	26.9	30.6
Instrumentarium Corp.	OTC	INMRY	240.9	3.6	52.1
Petroleum Development	OTC	PETD	95.9	6.1	19.4
Drexler Technology Corp.	OTC	DRXR	233.6	45.6	53.6
Gerber Childrenswear Inc.	NYSE	GCW	126.9	7.9	25.8
Gaiam, Inc.	OTC	GAIA	295.5	68.2	60.7
Artesian Resources Corp.	OTC	ARTNA	62.8	20.5	45.5
York Water Company	OTC	YORW	92.2	22.9	74.2

© Cengage Learning

WEB file

Shadow02

Appendix   An Introduction to StatTools

StatTools is a professional add-in that expands the statistical capabilities available with Microsoft Excel. StatTools software can be downloaded from the website that accompanies this text.

Excel does not contain statistical functions or data analysis tools to perform all the statistical procedures discussed in the text. StatTools is a Microsoft Excel statistics add-in that extends the range of statistical and graphical options for Excel users. Most chapters include a chapter appendix that shows the steps required to accomplish a statistical procedure using StatTools. For those students who want to make more extensive use of the software, StatTools offers an excellent Help facility. The StatTools Help system includes detailed explanations of the statistical and data analysis options available, as well as descriptions and definitions of the types of output provided.

Getting Started with StatTools

StatTools software may be downloaded and installed on your computer by accessing the website that accompanies this text. After downloading and installing the software, perform the following steps to use StatTools as an Excel add-in.

Step 1. Click the **Start** button on the taskbar and then point to **All Programs**
Step 2. Point to the folder entitled **Palisade Decision Tools**
Step 3. Click **StatTools for Excel**

FIGURE 1.10   THE STATTOOLS - DATA SET MANAGER DIALOG BOX

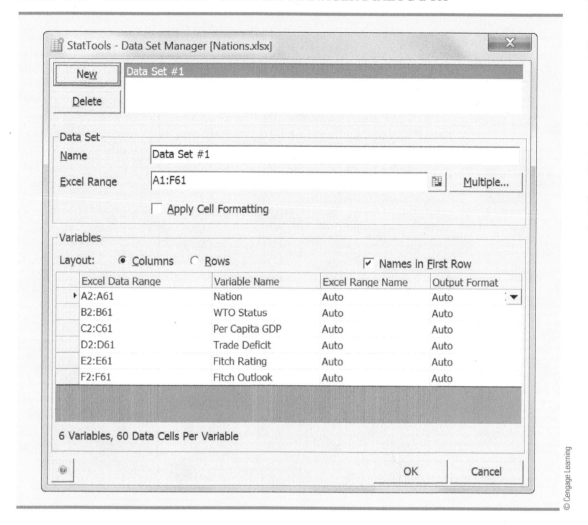

These steps will open Excel and add the StatTools tab next to the Add-Ins tab on the Excel Ribbon. Alternately, if you are already working in Excel, these steps will make StatTools available.

Using StatTools

Nations

Before conducting any statistical analysis, we must create a StatTools data set using the StatTools Data Set Manager. Let us use the Excel worksheet for the 60 nations in the World Trade Organization data set in Table 1.1 to show how this is done. The following steps show how to create a StatTools data set for this application.

Step 1. Open the Excel file named Nations
Step 2. Select any cell in the data set (for example, cell A1)
Step 3. Click the **StatTools** tab on the Ribbon
Step 4. In the **Data** group, click **Data Set Manager**
Step 5. When StatTools asks if you want to add the range $A$1:$F$61 as a new StatTools data set, click **Yes**
Step 6. When the StatTools - Data Set Manager dialog box appears, click **OK**

Figure 1.10 shows the StatTools - Data Set Manager dialog box that appears in step 6. By default, the name of the new StatTools data set is Data Set #1. You can replace the name

FIGURE 1.11   THE STATTOOLS - APPLICATION SETTINGS DIALOG BOX

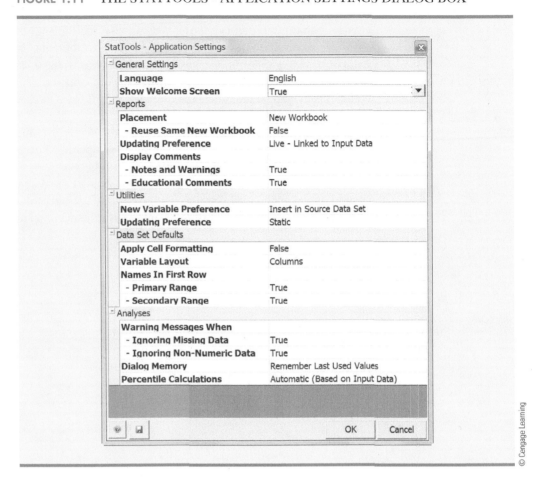

Data Set #1 in step 6 with a more descriptive name. And, if you select the Apply Cell Format option, the column labels will be highlighted in blue and the entire data set will have outside and inside borders. You can select the Data Set Manager at any time in your analysis to make these types of changes.

Recommended Application Settings

StatTools allows the user to specify some of the application settings that control such things as where statistical output is displayed and how calculations are performed. The following steps show how to access the StatTools - Application Settings dialog box.

Step 1. Click the **StatTools** tab on the Ribbon
Step 2. In the **Tools Group**, click **Utilities**
Step 3. Choose **Application Settings** from the list of options

Figure 1.11 shows that the StatTools - Application Settings dialog box has five sections: General Settings; Reports; Utilities; Data Set Defaults; and Analyses. Let us show how to make changes in the Reports section of the dialog box.

Figure 1.11 shows that the Placement option currently selected is **New Workbook**. Using this option, the StatTools output will be placed in a new workbook. But suppose you would like to place the StatTools output in the current (active) workbook. If you click the words **New Workbook**, a downward-pointing arrow will appear to the right. Clicking this arrow will display a list of all the placement options, including **Active Workbook**; we recommend using this option. Figure 1.11 also shows that the Updating

Preferences option in the Reports section is currently **Live - Linked to Input Data**. With live updating, anytime one or more data values are changed StatTools will automatically change the output previously produced; we also recommend using this option. Note that there are two options available under Display Comments: **Notes and Warnings** and **Educational Comments**. Because these options provide useful notes and information regarding the output, we recommend using both options. Thus, to include educational comments as part of the StatTools output you will have to change the value of False for Educational Comments to True.

The StatTools - Settings dialog box contains numerous other features that enable you to customize the way that you want StatTools to operate. You can learn more about these features by selecting the Help option located in the Tools group, or by clicking the Help icon located in the lower left-hand corner of the dialog box. When you have finished making changes in the application settings, click OK at the bottom of the dialog box and then click Yes when StatTools asks you if you want to save the new application settings.

CHAPTER 2

Descriptive Statistics: Tabular and Graphical Displays

CONTENTS

COLGATE-PALMOLIVE COMPANY*
NEW YORK, NEW YORK

The Colgate-Palmolive Company started as a small soap and candle shop in New York City in 1806. Today, Colgate-Palmolive employs more than 40,000 people working in more than 200 countries and territories around the world. Although best known for its brand names of Colgate, Palmolive, and Fab, the company also markets Mennen, Hill's Science Diet, and Hill's Prescription Diet products.

The Colgate-Palmolive Company uses statistics in its quality assurance program for home laundry detergent products. One concern is customer satisfaction with the quantity of detergent in a carton. Every carton in each size category is filled with the same amount of detergent by weight, but the volume of detergent is affected by the density of the detergent powder. For instance, if the powder density is on the heavy side, a smaller volume of detergent is needed to reach the carton's specified weight. As a result, the carton may appear to be underfilled when opened by the consumer.

To control the problem of heavy detergent powder, limits are placed on the acceptable range of powder density. Statistical samples are taken periodically, and the density of each powder sample is measured. Data summaries are then provided for operating personnel so that corrective action can be taken if necessary to keep the density within the desired quality specifications.

A frequency distribution for the densities of 150 samples taken over a one-week period and a histogram are shown in the accompanying table and figure. Density levels above .40 are unacceptably high. The frequency distribution and histogram show that the operation is meeting its quality guidelines with all of the densities less than or equal to .40. Managers viewing these statistical summaries would be pleased with the quality of the detergent production process.

In this chapter, you will learn about tabular and graphical methods of descriptive statistics such as frequency distributions, bar charts, histograms, stem-and-leaf displays, crosstabulations, and others. The goal of

*The authors are indebted to William R. Fowle, Manager of Quality Assurance, Colgate-Palmolive Company, for providing this Statistics in Practice.

The Colgate-Palmolive Company uses statistical summaries to help maintain the quality of its products. © Kurt Brady/Alamy.

these methods is to summarize data so that the data can be easily understood and interpreted.

Frequency Distribution of Density Data

Density	Frequency
.29–.30	30
.31–.32	75
.33–.34	32
.35–.36	9
.37–.38	3
.39–.40	1
Total	150

Histogram of Density Data

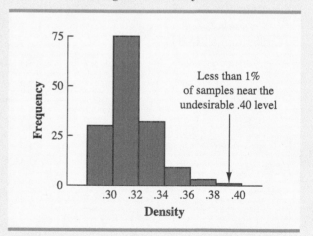

As indicated in Chapter 1, data can be classified as either categorical or quantitative. **Categorical data** use labels or names to identify categories of like items, and **quantitative data** are numerical values that indicate how much or how many. This chapter introduces the use of tabular and graphical displays for summarizing both categorical and quantitative data. Tabular and graphical displays can be found in annual reports, newspaper articles, and research studies. Everyone is exposed to these types of presentations. Hence, it is important to understand how they are constructed and how they should be interpreted.

We begin with a discussion of the use of tablular and graphical displays to summarize the data for a single variable. This is followed by a discussion of the use of tabular and graphical displays to summarize the data for two variables in a way that reveals the relationship between the two variables. **Data visualization** is a term often used to describe the use of graphical displays to summarize and present information about a data set. The last section of this chapter provides an introduction to data visualization and provides guidelines for creating effective graphical displays.

Modern statistical software packages provide extensive capabilities for summarizing data and preparing visual presentations. Minitab and Excel are two packages that are widely available. In the chapter appendixes, we show some of their capabilities.

2.1 Summarizing Data for a Categorical Variable

Frequency Distribution

We begin the discussion of how tabular and graphical displays can be used to summarize categorical data with the definition of a **frequency distribution**.

> **FREQUENCY DISTRIBUTION**
>
> A frequency distribution is a tabular summary of data showing the number (frequency) of observations in each of several nonoverlapping categories or classes.

Let us use the following example to demonstrate the construction and interpretation of a frequency distribution for categorical data. Coca-Cola, Diet Coke, Dr. Pepper, Pepsi, and Sprite are five popular soft drinks. Assume that the data in Table 2.1 show the soft drink selected in a sample of 50 soft drink purchases.

TABLE 2.1   DATA FROM A SAMPLE OF 50 SOFT DRINK PURCHASES

SoftDrink

Coca-Cola	Coca-Cola	Coca-Cola	Sprite	Coca-Cola
Diet Coke	Dr. Pepper	Diet Coke	Dr. Pepper	Diet Coke
Pepsi	Sprite	Coca-Cola	Pepsi	Pepsi
Diet Coke	Coca-Cola	Sprite	Diet Coke	Pepsi
Coca-Cola	Diet Coke	Pepsi	Pepsi	Pepsi
Coca-Cola	Coca-Cola	Coca-Cola	Coca-Cola	Pepsi
Dr. Pepper	Coca-Cola	Coca-Cola	Coca-Cola	Coca-Cola
Diet Coke	Sprite	Coca-Cola	Coca-Cola	Dr. Pepper
Pepsi	Coca-Cola	Pepsi	Pepsi	Pepsi
Pepsi	Diet Coke	Coca-Cola	Dr. Pepper	Sprite

TABLE 2.2

FREQUENCY
DISTRIBUTION OF
SOFT DRINK
PURCHASES

Soft Drink	Frequency
Coca-Cola	19
Diet Coke	8
Dr. Pepper	5
Pepsi	13
Sprite	5
Total	50

To develop a frequency distribution for these data, we count the number of times each soft drink appears in Table 2.1. Coca-Cola appears 19 times, Diet Coke appears 8 times, Dr. Pepper appears 5 times, Pepsi appears 13 times, and Sprite appears 5 times. These counts are summarized in the frequency distribution in Table 2.2.

This frequency distribution provides a summary of how the 50 soft drink purchases are distributed across the five soft drinks. This summary offers more insight than the original data shown in Table 2.1. Viewing the frequency distribution, we see that Coca-Cola is the leader, Pepsi is second, Diet Coke is third, and Sprite and Dr. Pepper are tied for fourth. The frequency distribution summarizes information about the popularity of the five soft drinks.

Relative Frequency and Percent Frequency Distributions

A frequency distribution shows the number (frequency) of observations in each of several nonoverlapping classes. However, we are often interested in the proportion, or percentage, of observations in each class. The *relative frequency* of a class equals the fraction or proportion of observations belonging to a class. For a data set with n observations, the relative frequency of each class can be determined as follows:

RELATIVE FREQUENCY

$$\text{Relative frequency of a class} = \frac{\text{Frequency of the class}}{n} \qquad (2.1)$$

The *percent frequency* of a class is the relative frequency multiplied by 100.

A **relative frequency distribution** gives a tabular summary of data showing the relative frequency for each class. A **percent frequency distribution** summarizes the percent frequency of the data for each class. Table 2.3 shows a relative frequency distribution and a percent frequency distribution for the soft drink data. In Table 2.3 we see that the relative frequency for Coca-Cola is 19/50 = .38, the relative frequency for Diet Coke is 8/50 = .16, and so on. From the percent frequency distribution, we see that 38% of the purchases were Coca-Cola, 16% of the purchases were Diet Coke, and so on. We can also note that 38% + 26% + 16% = 80% of the purchases were for the top three soft drinks.

Bar Charts and Pie Charts

A **bar chart** is a graphical display for depicting categorical data summarized in a frequency, relative frequency, or percent frequency distribution. On one axis of the chart (usually the horizontal axis), we specify the labels that are used for the classes (categories). A frequency, relative frequency, or percent frequency scale can be used for the other axis of the chart

TABLE 2.3 RELATIVE FREQUENCY AND PERCENT FREQUENCY DISTRIBUTIONS
OF SOFT DRINK PURCHASES

Soft Drink	Relative Frequency	Percent Frequency
Coca-Cola	.38	38
Diet Coke	.16	16
Dr. Pepper	.10	10
Pepsi	.26	26
Sprite	.10	10
Total	1.00	100

FIGURE 2.1   BAR CHART OF SOFT DRINK PURCHASES

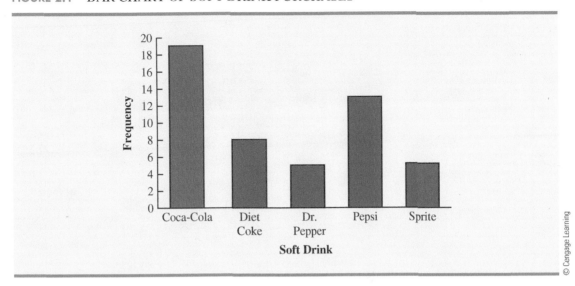

In quality control applications, bar charts are used to identify the most important causes of problems. When the bars are arranged in descending order of height from left to right with the most frequently occurring cause appearing first, the bar chart is called a Pareto *diagram. This diagram is named for its founder, Vilfredo Pareto, an Italian economist.*

(usually the vertical axis). Then, using a bar of fixed width drawn above each class label, we extend the length of the bar until we reach the frequency, relative frequency, or percent frequency of the class. For categorical data, the bars should be separated to emphasize the fact that each category is separate. Figure 2.1 shows a bar chart of the frequency distribution for the 50 soft drink purchases. Note how the graphical display shows Coca-Cola, Pepsi, and Diet Coke to be the most preferred brands.

The **pie chart** provides another graphical display for presenting relative frequency and percent frequency distributions for categorical data. To construct a pie chart, we first draw a circle to represent all the data. Then we use the relative frequencies to subdivide the circle into sectors, or parts, that correspond to the relative frequency for each class. For example, because a circle contains 360 degrees and Coca-Cola shows a relative frequency of .38, the sector of the pie chart labeled Coca-Cola consists of .38(360) = 136.8 degrees. The sector of the pie chart labeled Diet Coke consists of .16(360) = 57.6 degrees. Similar calculations for the other classes yield the pie chart in Figure 2.2.

FIGURE 2.2   PIE CHART OF SOFT DRINK PURCHASES

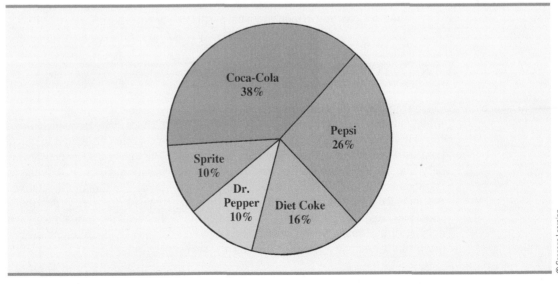

FIGURE 2.3 THREE-DIMENSIONAL PIE CHART OF SOFT DRINK PURCHASES

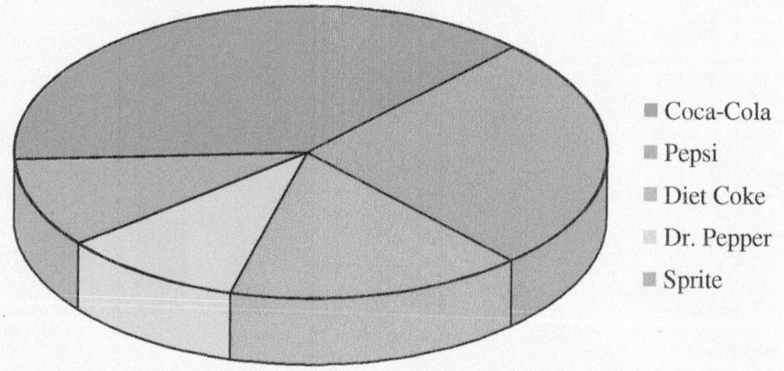

■ Coca-Cola
■ Pepsi
■ Diet Coke
■ Dr. Pepper
■ Sprite

© Cengage Learning

The numerical values shown for each sector can be frequencies, relative frequencies, or percent frequencies.

Numerous options involving the use of colors, shading, legends, text font, and three-dimensional perspectives are available to enhance the visual appearance of bar and pie charts. When used carefully, such options can provide a more effective display. But this is not always the case. For instance, consider the three-dimensional pie chart for the soft drink data shown in Figure 2.3. Compare it to the simpler presentation shown in Figure 2.2. The three-dimensional perspective adds no new understanding. In fact, because you have to view the three-dimensional pie chart in Figure 2.3 at an angle rather than straight overhead, it can be more difficult to visualize. The use of a legend in Figure 2.3 also forces your eyes to shift back and forth between the key and the chart. The simpler chart shown in Figure 2.2, which shows the percentages and classes directly on the pie, is more effective.

In general, pie charts are not the best way to present percentages for comparison. Research has shown that people are much better at accurately judging differences in length rather than differences in angles (or slices). When making such comparisons, we recommend you use a bar chart similar to Figure 2.1. In Section 2.5 we provide additional guidelines for creating effective visual displays.

NOTES AND COMMENTS

1. Often the number of classes in a frequency distribution is the same as the number of categories found in the data, as is the case for the soft drink purchase data in this section. The data involve only five soft drinks, and a separate frequency distribution class was defined for each one. Data that included all soft drinks would require many categories, most of which would have a small number of purchases. Most statisticians recommend that classes with smaller frequencies be grouped into an aggregate class called "other." Classes with frequencies of 5% or less would most often be treated in this fashion.

2. The sum of the frequencies in any frequency distribution always equals the number of observations. The sum of the relative frequencies in any relative frequency distribution always equals 1.00, and the sum of the percentages in a percent frequency distribution always equals 100.

Exercises

Methods

1. The response to a question has three alternatives: A, B, and C. A sample of 120 responses provides 60 A, 24 B, and 36 C. Show the frequency and relative frequency distributions.

2. A partial relative frequency distribution is given.

Class	Relative Frequency
A	.22
B	.18
C	.40
D	

   a. What is the relative frequency of class D?
   b. The total sample size is 200. What is the frequency of class D?
   c. Show the frequency distribution.
   d. Show the percent frequency distribution.

3. A questionnaire provides 58 Yes, 42 No, and 20 no-opinion answers.
   a. In the construction of a pie chart, how many degrees would be in the section of the pie showing the Yes answers?
   b. How many degrees would be in the section of the pie showing the No answers?
   c. Construct a pie chart.
   d. Construct a bar chart.

Applications

Syndicated

4. For the 2010–2011 viewing season, the top five syndicated programs were *Wheel of Fortune* (WoF), *Two and Half Men* (THM), *Jeopardy* (Jep), *Judge Judy* (JJ), and the *Oprah Winfrey Show* (OWS) (Nielsen Media Research website, April 16, 2012). Data indicating the preferred shows for a sample of 50 viewers follow.

WoF	Jep	JJ	Jep	THM
THM	WoF	OWS	Jep	THM
Jep	OWS	WoF	WoF	WoF
WoF	THM	OWS	THM	WoF
THM	JJ	JJ	Jep	THM
OWS	OWS	JJ	JJ	Jep
JJ	WoF	THM	WoF	WoF
THM	THM	WoF	JJ	JJ
Jep	THM	WoF	Jep	Jep
WoF	THM	OWS	OWS	Jep

   a. Are these data categorical or quantitative?
   b. Provide frequency and percent frequency distributions.
   c. Construct a bar chart and a pie chart.
   d. On the basis of the sample, which television show has the largest viewing audience? Which one is second?

5. In alphabetical order, the six most common last names in the United States are Brown, Johnson, Jones, Miller, Smith, and Williams (*The World Almanac,* 2012). Assume that a sample of 50 individuals with one of these last names provided the following data.

2012Names

Brown	Williams	Williams	Williams	Brown
Smith	Jones	Smith	Johnson	Smith
Miller	Smith	Brown	Williams	Johnson
Johnson	Smith	Smith	Johnson	Brown
Williams	Miller	Johnson	Williams	Johnson
Williams	Johnson	Jones	Smith	Brown
Johnson	Smith	Smith	Brown	Jones
Jones	Jones	Smith	Smith	Miller
Miller	Jones	Williams	Miller	Smith
Jones	Johnson	Brown	Johnson	Miller

Summarize the data by constructing the following:

a. Relative and percent frequency distributions

b. A bar chart

c. A pie chart

d. Based on these data, what are the three most common last names?

6. Nielsen Media Research provided the list of the 25 top-rated single shows in television history (*The World Almanac*, 2012). The following data show the television network that produced each of these 25 top-rated shows.

2012Networks

CBS	CBS	NBC	FOX	CBS
CBS	NBC	NBC	NBC	ABC
ABC	NBC	ABC	ABC	NBC
CBS	NBC	CBS	ABC	NBC
NBC	CBS	CBS	ABC	CBS

a. Construct a frequency distribution, percent frequency distribution, and bar chart for the data.

b. Which network or networks have done the best in terms of presenting top-rated television shows? Compare the performance of ABC, CBS, and NBC.

7. The Canmark Research Center Airport Customer Satisfaction Survey uses an online questionnaire to provide airlines and airports with customer satisfaction ratings for all aspects of the customers' flight experience (airportsurvey website, July, 2012). After completing a flight, customers receive an e-mail asking them to go to the website and rate a variety of factors, including the reservation process, the check-in process, luggage policy, cleanliness of gate area, service by flight attendants, food/beverage selection, on-time arrival, and so on. A five-point scale, with Excellent (E), Very Good (V), Good (G), Fair (F), and Poor (P), is used to record customer ratings. Assume that passengers on a Delta Airlines flight from Myrtle Beach, South Carolina, to Atlanta, Georgia, provided the following ratings for the question, "Please rate the airline based on your overall experience with this flight." The sample ratings are shown below.

AirSurvey

E	E	G	V	V	E	V	V	V	E
E	G	V	E	E	V	E	E	E	V
V	V	V	F	V	E	V	E	G	E
G	E	V	E	V	E	V	V	V	V
E	E	V	V	E	P	E	V	P	V

a. Use a percent frequency distribution and a bar chart to summarize these data. What do these summaries indicate about the overall customer satisfaction with the Delta flight?

b. The online survey questionnaire enabled respondents to explain any aspect of the flight that failed to meet expectations. Would this be helpful information to a manager looking for ways to improve the overall customer satisfaction on Delta flights? Explain.

8.   Data for a sample of 55 members of the Baseball Hall of Fame in Cooperstown, New York, are shown here. Each observation indicates the primary position played by the Hall of Famers: pitcher (P), catcher (H), 1st base (1), 2nd base (2), 3rd base (3), shortstop (S), left field (L), center field (C), and right field (R).

BaseballHall

L	P	C	H	2	P	R	1	S	S	1	L	P	R	P
P	P	P	R	C	S	L	R	P	C	C	P	P	R	P
2	3	P	H	L	P	1	C	P	P	P	S	1	L	R
R	1	2	H	S	3	H	2	L	P					

   a.   Construct frequency and relative frequency distributions to summarize the data.
   b.   What position provides the most Hall of Famers?
   c.   What position provides the fewest Hall of Famers?
   d.   What outfield position (L, C, or R) provides the most Hall of Famers?
   e.   Compare infielders (1, 2, 3, and S) to outfielders (L, C, and R).

9.   The Pew Research Center's Social & Demographic Trends project found that 46% of U.S. adults would rather live in a different type of community than the one where they are living now (Pew Research Center, January 29, 2009). The national survey of 2260 adults asked: "Where do you live now?" and "What do you consider to be the ideal community?" Response options were City (C), Suburb (S), Small Town (T), or Rural (R). A representative portion of this survey for a sample of 100 respondents is as follows.

Where do you live now?

LivingArea

S	T	R	C	R	R	T	C	S	T	C	S	C	S	T
S	S	C	S	S	T	T	C	C	S	T	C	S	T	C
T	R	S	S	T	C	S	C	T	C	T	C	T	C	R
C	C	R	T	C	S	S	T	S	C	C	C	R	S	C
S	S	C	C	S	C	R	T	T	T	C	R	T	C	R
C	T	R	R	C	T	C	C	R	T	T	R	S	R	T
T	S	S	S	S	S	C	C	R	T					

What do you consider to be the ideal community?

S	C	R	R	R	S	T	S	S	T	T	S	C	S	T
C	C	R	T	R	S	T	T	S	S	C	C	T	T	S
S	R	C	S	C	C	S	C	R	C	T	S	R	R	R
C	T	S	T	T	T	R	R	S	C	C	R	R	S	S
S	T	C	T	T	C	R	T	T	T	C	T	T	R	R
C	S	R	T	C	T	C	C	T	T	T	R	C	R	T
T	C	S	S	C	S	T	S	S	R					

   a.   Provide a percent frequency distribution for each question.
   b.   Construct a bar chart for each question.
   c.   Where are most adults living now?
   d.   Where do most adults consider the ideal community?
   e.   What changes in living areas would you expect to see if people moved from where they currently live to their ideal community?

10.   Virtual Tourist provides ratings for hotels throughout the world. Ratings provided by 649 guests at the Sheraton Anaheim Hotel, located near the Disneyland Resort in Anaheim, California, can be found in the file HotelRatings (Virtual Tourist website, February 25, 2013). Possible responses were Excellent, Very Good, Average, Poor, and Terrible.
   a.   Construct a frequency distribution.
   b.   Construct a percent frequency distribution.
   c.   Construct a bar chart for the percent frequency distribution.
   d.   Comment on how guests rate their stay at the Sheraton Anaheim Hotel.
   e.   Results for 1679 guests who stayed at Disney's Grand Californian provided the following frequency distribution.

HotelRatings

Rating	Frequency
Excellent	807
Very Good	521
Average	200
Poor	107
Terrible	44

Compare the ratings for Disney's Grand Californian with the results obtained for the Sheraton Anaheim Hotel.

2.2 Summarizing Data for a Quantitative Variable

Frequency Distribution

TABLE 2.4

YEAR-END AUDIT TIMES (IN DAYS)

12	14	19	18
15	15	18	17
20	27	22	23
22	21	33	28
14	18	16	13

© Cengage Learning

As defined in Section 2.1, a frequency distribution is a tabular summary of data showing the number (frequency) of observations in each of several nonoverlapping categories or classes. This definition holds for quantitative as well as categorical data. However, with quantitative data we must be more careful in defining the nonoverlapping classes to be used in the frequency distribution.

For example, consider the quantitative data in Table 2.4. These data show the time in days required to complete year-end audits for a sample of 20 clients of Sanderson and Clifford, a small public accounting firm. The three steps necessary to define the classes for a frequency distribution with quantitative data are

1. Determine the number of nonoverlapping classes.
2. Determine the width of each class.
3. Determine the class limits.

Audit

Let us demonstrate these steps by developing a frequency distribution for the audit time data in Table 2.4.

Number of classes Classes are formed by specifying ranges that will be used to group the data. As a general guideline, we recommend using between 5 and 20 classes. For a small number of data items, as few as five or six classes may be used to summarize the data. For a larger number of data items, a larger number of classes is usually required. The goal is to use enough classes to show the variation in the data, but not so many classes that some contain only a few data items. Because the number of data items in Table 2.4 is relatively small ($n = 20$), we chose to develop a frequency distribution with five classes.

Making the classes the same width reduces the chance of inappropriate interpretations by the user.

Width of the classes The second step in constructing a frequency distribution for quantitative data is to choose a width for the classes. As a general guideline, we recommend that the width be the same for each class. Thus the choices of the number of classes and the width of classes are not independent decisions. A larger number of classes means a smaller class width, and vice versa. To determine an approximate class width, we begin by identifying the largest and smallest data values. Then, with the desired number of classes specified, we can use the following expression to determine the approximate class width.

$$\text{Approximate class width} = \frac{\text{Largest data value} - \text{Smallest data value}}{\text{Number of classes}} \quad (2.2)$$

The approximate class width given by equation (2.2) can be rounded to a more convenient value based on the preference of the person developing the frequency distribution. For example, an approximate class width of 9.28 might be rounded to 10 simply because 10 is a more convenient class width to use in presenting a frequency distribution.

For the data involving the year-end audit times, the largest data value is 33 and the smallest data value is 12. Because we decided to summarize the data with five classes, using equation (2.2) provides an approximate class width of $(33 - 12)/5 = 4.2$. We therefore decided to round up and use a class width of five days in the frequency distribution.

No single frequency distribution is best for a data set. Different people may construct different, but equally acceptable, frequency distributions. The goal is to reveal the natural grouping and variation in the data.

In practice, the number of classes and the appropriate class width are determined by trial and error. Once a possible number of classes is chosen, equation (2.2) is used to find the approximate class width. The process can be repeated for a different number of classes. Ultimately, the analyst uses judgment to determine the combination of the number of classes and class width that provides the best frequency distribution for summarizing the data.

For the audit time data in Table 2.4, after deciding to use five classes, each with a width of five days, the next task is to specify the class limits for each of the classes.

Class limits Class limits must be chosen so that each data item belongs to one and only one class. The *lower class limit* identifies the smallest possible data value assigned to the class. The *upper class limit* identifies the largest possible data value assigned to the class. In developing frequency distributions for categorical data, we did not need to specify class limits because each data item naturally fell into a separate class. But with quantitative data, such as the audit times in Table 2.4, class limits are necessary to determine where each data value belongs.

TABLE 2.5

FREQUENCY DISTRIBUTION FOR THE AUDIT TIME DATA

Audit Time (days)	Frequency
10–14	4
15–19	8
20–24	5
25–29	2
30–34	1
Total	20

Using the audit time data in Table 2.4, we selected 10 days as the lower class limit and 14 days as the upper class limit for the first class. This class is denoted 10–14 in Table 2.5. The smallest data value, 12, is included in the 10–14 class. We then selected 15 days as the lower class limit and 19 days as the upper class limit of the next class. We continued defining the lower and upper class limits to obtain a total of five classes: 10–14, 15–19, 20–24, 25–29, and 30–34. The largest data value, 33, is included in the 30–34 class. The difference between the lower class limits of adjacent classes is the class width. Using the first two lower class limits of 10 and 15, we see that the class width is $15 - 10 = 5$.

With the number of classes, class width, and class limits determined, a frequency distribution can be obtained by counting the number of data values belonging to each class. For example, the data in Table 2.4 show that four values—12, 14, 14, and 13— belong to the 10–14 class. Thus, the frequency for the 10–14 class is 4. Continuing this counting process for the 15–19, 20–24, 25–29, and 30–34 classes provides the frequency distribution in Table 2.5. Using this frequency distribution, we can observe the following:

1. The most frequently occurring audit times are in the class of 15–19 days. Eight of the 20 audit times belong to this class.
2. Only one audit required 30 or more days.

Other conclusions are possible, depending on the interests of the person viewing the frequency distribution. The value of a frequency distribution is that it provides insights about the data that are not easily obtained by viewing the data in their original unorganized form.

Class midpoint In some applications, we want to know the midpoints of the classes in a frequency distribution for quantitative data. The **class midpoint** is the value halfway between the lower and upper class limits. For the audit time data, the five class midpoints are 12, 17, 22, 27, and 32.

Relative Frequency and Percent Frequency Distributions

We define the relative frequency and percent frequency distributions for quantitative data in the same manner as for categorical data. First, recall that the relative frequency is the proportion

TABLE 2.6   RELATIVE FREQUENCY AND PERCENT FREQUENCY DISTRIBUTIONS FOR THE AUDIT TIME DATA

Audit Time (days)	Relative Frequency	Percent Frequency
10–14	.20	20
15–19	.40	40
20–24	.25	25
25–29	.10	10
30–34	.05	5
Total	1.00	100

© Cengage Learning

of the observations belonging to a class. With n observations,

$$\text{Relative frequency of class} = \frac{\text{Frequency of the class}}{n}$$

The percent frequency of a class is the relative frequency multiplied by 100.

Based on the class frequencies in Table 2.5 and with $n = 20$, Table 2.6 shows the relative frequency distribution and percent frequency distribution for the audit time data. Note that .40 of the audits, or 40%, required from 15 to 19 days. Only .05 of the audits, or 5%, required 30 or more days. Again, additional interpretations and insights can be obtained by using Table 2.6.

Dot Plot

One of the simplest graphical summaries of data is a **dot plot**. A horizontal axis shows the range for the data. Each data value is represented by a dot placed above the axis. Figure 2.4 is the dot plot for the audit time data in Table 2.4. The three dots located above 18 on the horizontal axis indicate that an audit time of 18 days occurred three times. Dot plots show the details of the data and are useful for comparing the distribution of the data for two or more variables.

Histogram

A common graphical display of quantitative data is a **histogram**. This graphical display can be prepared for data previously summarized in either a frequency, relative frequency, or percent frequency distribution. A histogram is constructed by placing the variable of interest on the horizontal axis and the frequency, relative frequency, or percent frequency on the vertical axis. The frequency, relative frequency, or percent frequency of each class is shown by drawing a rectangle whose base is determined by the class limits on the horizontal axis and whose height is the corresponding frequency, relative frequency, or percent frequency.

FIGURE 2.4   DOT PLOT FOR THE AUDIT TIME DATA

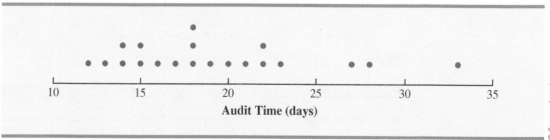

© Cengage Learning

FIGURE 2.5   HISTOGRAM FOR THE AUDIT TIME DATA

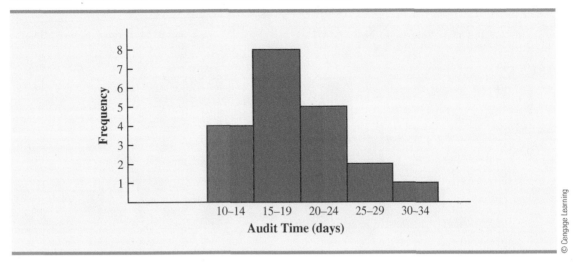

Figure 2.5 is a histogram for the audit time data. Note that the class with the greatest frequency is shown by the rectangle appearing above the class of 15–19 days. The height of the rectangle shows that the frequency of this class is 8. A histogram for the relative or percent frequency distribution of these data would look the same as the histogram in Figure 2.5 with the exception that the vertical axis would be labeled with relative or percent frequency values.

As Figure 2.5 shows, the adjacent rectangles of a histogram touch one another. Unlike a bar graph, a histogram contains no natural separation between the rectangles of adjacent classes. This format is the usual convention for histograms. Because the classes for the audit time data are stated as 10–14, 15–19, 20–24, 25–29, and 30–34, one-unit spaces of 14 to 15, 19 to 20, 24 to 25, and 29 to 30 would seem to be needed between the classes. These spaces are eliminated when constructing a histogram. Eliminating the spaces between classes in a histogram for the audit time data helps show that all values between the lower limit of the first class and the upper limit of the last class are possible.

One of the most important uses of a histogram is to provide information about the shape, or form, of a distribution. Figure 2.6 contains four histograms constructed from relative frequency distributions. Panel A shows the histogram for a set of data moderately skewed to the left. A histogram is said to be skewed to the left if its tail extends farther to the left. This histogram is typical for exam scores, with no scores above 100%, most of the scores above 70%, and only a few really low scores. Panel B shows the histogram for a set of data moderately skewed to the right. A histogram is said to be skewed to the right if its tail extends farther to the right. An example of this type of histogram would be for data such as housing prices; a few expensive houses create the skewness in the right tail.

Panel C shows a symmetric histogram. In a symmetric histogram, the left tail mirrors the shape of the right tail. Histograms for data found in applications are never perfectly symmetric, but the histogram for many applications may be roughly symmetric. Data for SAT scores, heights and weights of people, and so on lead to histograms that are roughly symmetric. Panel D shows a histogram highly skewed to the right. This histogram was constructed from data on the amount of customer purchases over one day at a women's apparel store. Data from applications in business and economics often lead to histograms that are skewed to the right. For instance, data on housing prices, salaries, purchase amounts, and so on often result in histograms skewed to the right.

FIGURE 2.6   HISTOGRAMS SHOWING DIFFERING LEVELS OF SKEWNESS

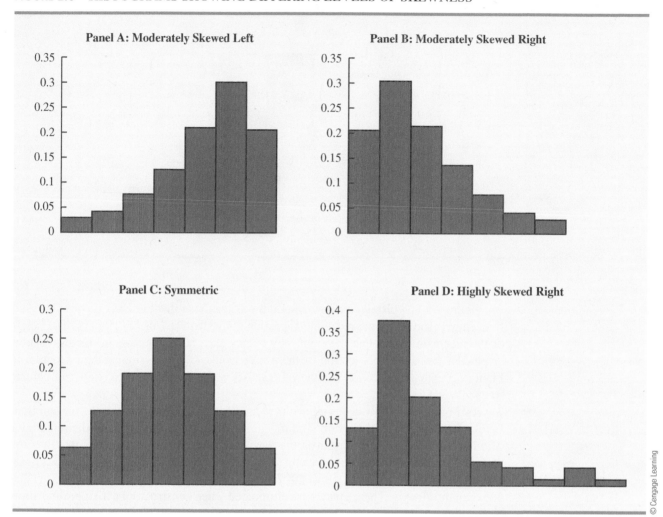

Cumulative Distributions

A variation of the frequency distribution that provides another tabular summary of quantitative data is the **cumulative frequency distribution**. The cumulative frequency distribution uses the number of classes, class widths, and class limits developed for the frequency distribution. However, rather than showing the frequency of each class, the cumulative frequency distribution shows the number of data items with values *less than or equal to the upper class limit* of each class. The first two columns of Table 2.7 provide the cumulative frequency distribution for the audit time data.

To understand how the cumulative frequencies are determined, consider the class with the description "less than or equal to 24." The cumulative frequency for this class is simply the sum of the frequencies for all classes with data values less than or equal to 24. For the frequency distribution in Table 2.5, the sum of the frequencies for classes 10–14, 15–19, and 20–24 indicates that $4 + 8 + 5 = 17$ data values are less than or equal to 24. Hence, the cumulative frequency for this class is 17. In addition, the cumulative frequency distribution in Table 2.7 shows that four audits were completed in 14 days or less and 19 audits were completed in 29 days or less.

TABLE 2.7   CUMULATIVE FREQUENCY, CUMULATIVE RELATIVE FREQUENCY, AND CUMULATIVE PERCENT FREQUENCY DISTRIBUTIONS FOR THE AUDIT TIME DATA

Audit Time (days)	Cumulative Frequency	Cumulative Relative Frequency	Cumulative Percent Frequency
Less than or equal to 14	4	.20	20
Less than or equal to 19	12	.60	60
Less than or equal to 24	17	.85	85
Less than or equal to 29	19	.95	95
Less than or equal to 34	20	1.00	100

As a final point, we note that a **cumulative relative frequency distribution** shows the proportion of data items, and a **cumulative percent frequency distribution** shows the percentage of data items with values less than or equal to the upper limit of each class. The cumulative relative frequency distribution can be computed either by summing the relative frequencies in the relative frequency distribution or by dividing the cumulative frequencies by the total number of items. Using the latter approach, we found the cumulative relative frequencies in column 3 of Table 2.7 by dividing the cumulative frequencies in column 2 by the total number of items ($n = 20$). The cumulative percent frequencies were again computed by multiplying the relative frequencies by 100. The cumulative relative and percent frequency distributions show that .85 of the audits, or 85%, were completed in 24 days or less, .95 of the audits, or 95%, were completed in 29 days or less, and so on.

Stem-and-Leaf Display

A **stem-and-leaf display** is a graphical display used to show simultaneously the rank order and shape of a distribution of data. To illustrate the use of a stem-and-leaf display, consider the data in Table 2.8. These data result from a 150-question aptitude test given to 50 individuals recently interviewed for a position at Haskens Manufacturing. The data indicate the number of questions answered correctly.

To develop a stem-and-leaf display, we first arrange the leading digits of each data value to the left of a vertical line. To the right of the vertical line, we record the last digit for each data value. Based on the top row of data in Table 2.8 (112, 72, 69, 97, and 107),

TABLE 2.8   NUMBER OF QUESTIONS ANSWERED CORRECTLY ON AN APTITUDE TEST

WEB file

ApTest

112	72	69	97	107
73	92	76	86	73
126	128	118	127	124
82	104	132	134	83
92	108	96	100	92
115	76	91	102	81
95	141	81	80	106
84	119	113	98	75
68	98	115	106	95
100	85	94	106	119

the first five entries in constructing a stem-and-leaf display would be as follows:

```
 6 | 9
 7 | 2
 8 |
 9 | 7
10 | 7
11 | 2
12 |
13 |
14 |
```

For example, the data value 112 shows the leading digits 11 to the left of the line and the last digit 2 to the right of the line. Similarly, the data value 72 shows the leading digit 7 to the left of the line and last digit 2 to the right of the line. Continuing to place the last digit of each data value on the line corresponding to its leading digit(s) provides the following:

```
 6 | 9  8
 7 | 2  3  6  3  6  5
 8 | 6  2  3  1  1  0  4  5
 9 | 7  2  2  6  2  1  5  8  8  5  4
10 | 7  4  8  0  2  6  6  0  6
11 | 2  8  5  9  3  5  9
12 | 6  8  7  4
13 | 2  4
14 | 1
```

With this organization of the data, sorting the digits on each line into rank order is simple. Doing so provides the stem-and-leaf display shown here.

```
 6 | 8  9
 7 | 2  3  3  5  6  6
 8 | 0  1  1  2  3  4  5  6
 9 | 1  2  2  2  4  5  5  6  7  8  8
10 | 0  0  2  4  6  6  6  7  8
11 | 2  3  5  5  8  9  9
12 | 4  6  7  8
13 | 2  4
14 | 1
```

The numbers to the left of the vertical line (6, 7, 8, 9, 10, 11, 12, 13, and 14) form the *stem,* and each digit to the right of the vertical line is a *leaf.* For example, consider the first row with a stem value of 6 and leaves of 8 and 9.

$$6 \mid 8 \quad 9$$

This row indicates that two data values have a first digit of six. The leaves show that the data values are 68 and 69. Similarly, the second row

$$7 \mid 2 \quad 3 \quad 3 \quad 5 \quad 6 \quad 6$$

indicates that six data values have a first digit of seven. The leaves show that the data values are 72, 73, 73, 75, 76, and 76.

To focus on the shape indicated by the stem-and-leaf display, let us use a rectangle to contain the leaves of each stem. Doing so, we obtain the following:

```
 6 | 8  9
 7 | 2  3  3  5  6  6
 8 | 0  1  1  2  3  4  5  6
 9 | 1  2  2  2  4  5  5  6  7  8  8
10 | 0  0  2  4  6  6  6  7  8
11 | 2  3  5  5  8  9  9
12 | 4  6  7  8
13 | 2  4
14 | 1
```

Rotating this page counterclockwise onto its side provides a picture of the data that is similar to a histogram with classes of 60–69, 70–79, 80–89, and so on.

Although the stem-and-leaf display may appear to offer the same information as a histogram, it has two primary advantages.

1. The stem-and-leaf display is easier to construct by hand.
2. Within a class interval, the stem-and-leaf display provides more information than the histogram because the stem-and-leaf shows the actual data.

Just as a frequency distribution or histogram has no absolute number of classes, neither does a stem-and-leaf display have an absolute number of rows or stems. If we believe that our original stem-and-leaf display condensed the data too much, we can easily stretch the display by using two or more stems for each leading digit. For example, to use two stems for each leading digit, we would place all data values ending in 0, 1, 2, 3, and 4 in one row and all values ending in 5, 6, 7, 8, and 9 in a second row. The following stretched stem-and-leaf display illustrates this approach.

In a stretched stem-and-leaf display, whenever a stem value is stated twice, the first value corresponds to leaf values of 0–4, and the second value corresponds to leaf values of 5–9.

```
 6 | 8  9
 7 | 2  3  3
 7 | 5  6  6
 8 | 0  1  1  2  3  4
 8 | 5  6
 9 | 1  2  2  2  4
 9 | 5  5  6  7  8  8
10 | 0  0  2  4
10 | 6  6  6  7  8
11 | 2  3
11 | 5  5  8  9  9
12 | 4
12 | 6  7  8
13 | 2  4
13 |
14 | 1
```

Note that values 72, 73, and 73 have leaves in the 0–4 range and are shown with the first stem value of 7. The values 75, 76, and 76 have leaves in the 5–9 range and are shown with the second stem value of 7. This stretched stem-and-leaf display is similar to a frequency distribution with intervals of 65–69, 70–74, 75–79, and so on.

The preceding example showed a stem-and-leaf display for data with as many as three digits. Stem-and-leaf displays for data with more than three digits are possible. For example, consider the following data on the number of hamburgers sold by a fast-food restaurant for each of 15 weeks.

1565	1852	1644	1766	1888	1912	2044	1812
1790	1679	2008	1852	1967	1954	1733	

A stem-and-leaf display of these data follows.

Leaf unit = 10

```
15 | 6
16 | 4  7
17 | 3  6  9
18 | 1  5  5  8
19 | 1  5  6
20 | 0  4
```

A single digit is used to define each leaf in a stem-and-leaf display. The leaf unit indicates how to multiply the stem-and-leaf numbers in order to approximate the original data. Leaf units may be 100, 10, 1, 0.1, and so on.

Note that a single digit is used to define each leaf and that only the first three digits of each data value have been used to construct the display. At the top of the display we have specified Leaf unit = 10. To illustrate how to interpret the values in the display, consider the first stem, 15, and its associated leaf, 6. Combining these numbers, we obtain 156. To reconstruct an approximation of the original data value, we must multiply this number by 10, the value of the *leaf unit*. Thus, $156 \times 10 = 1560$ is an approximation of the original data value used to construct the stem-and-leaf display. Although it is not possible to reconstruct the exact data value from this stem-and-leaf display, the convention of using a single digit for each leaf enables stem-and-leaf displays to be constructed for data having a large number of digits. For stem-and-leaf displays where the leaf unit is not shown, the leaf unit is assumed to equal 1.

NOTES AND COMMENTS

1. A bar chart and a histogram are essentially the same thing; both are graphical presentations of the data in a frequency distribution. A histogram is just a bar chart with no separation between bars. For some discrete quantitative data, a separation between bars is also appropriate. Consider, for example, the number of classes in which a college student is enrolled. The data may assume only integer values. Intermediate values such as 1.5, 2.73, and so on are not possible. With continuous quantitative data, however, such as the audit times in Table 2.4, a separation between bars is not appropriate.

2. The appropriate values for the class limits with quantitative data depend on the level of accuracy of the data. For instance, with the audit time data of Table 2.4 the limits used were integer values. If the data were rounded to the nearest tenth of a day (e.g., 12.3, 14.4, and so on), then the limits would be stated in tenths of days. For instance, the first class would be 10.0–14.9. If the data were recorded to the nearest hundredth of a day (e.g., 12.34, 14.45, and so on), the limits would be stated in hundredths of days. For instance, the first class would be 10.00–14.99.

3. An *open-end* class requires only a lower class limit or an upper class limit. For example, in the audit time data of Table 2.4, suppose two of the audits had taken 58 and 65 days. Rather than continue with the classes of width 5 with classes 35–39, 40–44, 45–49, and so on, we could simplify the frequency distribution to show an open-end class of "35 or more." This class would have a frequency of 2. Most often the open-end class appears at the upper end of the distribution. Sometimes an open-end class appears at the lower end of the distribution, and occasionally such classes appear at both ends.

4. The last entry in a cumulative frequency distribution always equals the total number of observations. The last entry in a cumulative relative frequency distribution always equals 1.00 and the last entry in a cumulative percent frequency distribution always equals 100.

Exercises

Methods

11. Consider the following data.

WEB file
Frequency

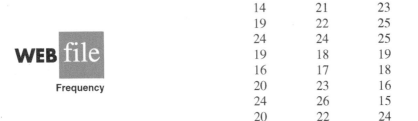

14	21	23	21	16
19	22	25	16	16
24	24	25	19	16
19	18	19	21	12
16	17	18	23	25
20	23	16	20	19
24	26	15	22	24
20	22	24	22	20

   a. Develop a frequency distribution using classes of 12–14, 15–17, 18–20, 21–23, and 24–26.
   b. Develop a relative frequency distribution and a percent frequency distribution using the classes in part (a).

12. Consider the following frequency distribution.

SELF test

Class	Frequency
10–19	10
20–29	14
30–39	17
40–49	7
50–59	2

   Construct a cumulative frequency distribution and a cumulative relative frequency distribution.

13. Construct a histogram for the data in exercise 12.

14. Consider the following data.

8.9	10.2	11.5	7.8	10.0	12.2	13.5	14.1	10.0	12.2
6.8	9.5	11.5	11.2	14.9	7.5	10.0	6.0	15.8	11.5

   a. Construct a dot plot.
   b. Construct a frequency distribution.
   c. Construct a percent frequency distribution.

15. Construct a stem-and-leaf display for the following data.

SELF test

11.3	9.6	10.4	7.5	8.3	10.5	10.0
9.3	8.1	7.7	7.5	8.4	6.3	8.8

16. Construct a stem-and-leaf display for the following data. Use a leaf unit of 10.

1161	1206	1478	1300	1604	1725	1361	1422
1221	1378	1623	1426	1557	1730	1706	1689

Applications

17. A doctor's office staff studied the waiting times for patients who arrive at the office with a request for emergency service. The following data with waiting times in minutes were collected over a one-month period.

SELF test

2 5 10 12 4 4 5 17 11 8 9 8 12 21 6 8 7 13 18 3

   Use classes of 0–4, 5–9, and so on in the following:
   a. Show the frequency distribution.
   b. Show the relative frequency distribution.

    c.   Show the cumulative frequency distribution.

    d.   Show the cumulative relative frequency distribution.

    e.   What proportion of patients needing emergency service wait 9 minutes or less?

18.   CBSSports.com developed the Total Player Ratings system to rate players in the National Basketball Association (NBA) based upon various offensive and defensive statistics. The following data show the average number of points scored per game (PPG) for 50 players with the highest ratings for a portion of the 2012–2013 NBA season. (CBSSports.com website, February 25, 2013).

NBAPlayerPts

27.0	28.8	26.4	27.1	22.9	28.4	19.2	21.0	20.8	17.6
21.1	19.2	21.2	15.5	17.2	16.7	17.6	18.5	18.3	18.3
23.3	16.4	18.9	16.5	17.0	11.7	15.7	18.0	17.7	14.6
15.7	17.2	18.2	17.5	13.6	16.3	16.2	13.6	17.1	16.7
17.0	17.3	17.5	14.0	16.9	16.3	15.1	12.3	18.7	14.6

Use classes with number of points per game of 10–11.9, 12–13.9, 14–15.9, and so on.

    a.   Show the frequency distribution.

    b.   Show the relative frequency distribution.

    c.   Show the cumulative percent frequency distribution.

    d.   Develop a histogram for the average number of points scored per game.

    e.   Do the data appear to be skewed? Explain.

    f.   What percentage of the players averaged at least 20 points per game?

19.   Based on the tons handled in a year, the ports listed below are the 25 busiest ports in the United States (*The 2013 World Almanac*).

Ports

Port	Tons Handled (Millions)	Port	Tons Handled (Millions)
Baltimore	39.6	Norfolk Harbor	41.6
Baton Rouge	55.5	Pascagoula	37.3
Beaumont	77.0	Philadelphia	34.0
Corpus Christi	73.7	Pittsburgh	33.8
Duluth-Superior	36.6	Plaquemines	55.8
Houston	227.1	Port Arthur	30.2
Hunnington	61.5	Savannah	34.7
Lake Charles	54.6	South Louisiana	236.3
Long Beach	75.4	St. Louis	30.8
Los Angeles	62.4	Tampa	34.2
Mobile	55.7	Texas City	56.6
New Orleans	72.4	Valdez	31.9
New York	139.2		

    a.   What is the largest number of tons handled? What is the smallest number of tons handled?

    b.   Using a class width of 25, develop a frequency distribution of the data starting with 25–49.9, 50–74.9, 75–99.9 and so on.

    c.   Prepare a histogram. Interpret the histogram.

20.   The London School of Economics and the Harvard Business School conducted a study of how chief executive officers (CEOs) spend their day. The study found that CEOs spend on average about 18 hours per week in meetings, not including conference calls, business

meals, and public events (*The Wall Street Journal,* February 14, 2012). Shown below is the time spent per week in meetings (hours) for a sample of 25 CEOs.

CEOTime

14	15	18	23	15
19	20	13	15	23
23	21	15	20	21
16	15	18	18	19
19	22	23	21	12

a. What is the least amount of time spent per week on meetings? The highest?
b. Use a class width of two hours to prepare a frequency distribution and a percent frequency distribution for the data.
c. Prepare a histogram and comment on the shape of the distribution.

21. *Fortune* provides a list of America's largest corporations based on annual revenue. Shown below are the 50 largest corporations, with annual revenue expressed in billions of dollars (*CNN Money* website, January 15, 2010).

LargeCorp

Corporation	Revenue	Corporation	Revenue
Amerisource Bergen	71	Lowe's	48
Archer Daniels Midland	70	Marathon Oil	74
AT&T	124	McKesson	102
Bank of America	113	Medco Health	51
Berkshire Hathaway	108	MetLife	55
Boeing	61	Microsoft	60
Cardinal Health	91	Morgan Stanley	62
Caterpillar	51	Pepsico	43
Chevron	263	Pfizer	48
Citigroup	112	Procter & Gamble	84
ConocoPhillips	231	Safeway	44
Costco Wholesale	72	Sears Holdings	47
CVS Caremark	87	State Farm Insurance	61
Dell	61	Sunoco	52
Dow Chemical	58	Target	65
ExxonMobil	443	Time Warner	47
Ford Motors	146	United Parcel Service	51
General Electric	149	United Technologies	59
Goldman Sachs	54	UnitedHealth Group	81
Hewlett-Packard	118	Valero Energy	118
Home Depot	71	Verizon	97
IBM	104	Walgreen	59
JPMorgan Chase	101	Walmart	406
Johnson & Johnson	64	WellPoint	61
Kroger	76	Wells Fargo	52

Summarize the data by constructing the following:
a. A frequency distribution (classes 0–49, 50–99, 100–149, and so on).
b. A relative frequency distribution.
c. A cumulative frequency distribution.
d. A cumulative relative frequency distribution.
e. What do these distributions tell you about the annual revenue of the largest corporations in America?
f. Show a histogram. Comment on the shape of the distribution.
g. What is the largest corporation in America and what is its annual revenue?

22. *Entrepreneur* magazine ranks franchises using performance measures such as growth rate, number of locations, startup costs, and financial stability. The number of locations for the top 20 U.S. franchises follow (*The World Almanac,* 2012).

Franchise

Franchise	No. U.S. Locations	Franchise	No. U.S. Locations
Hampton Inns	1864	Jan-Pro Franchising Intl. Inc.	12,394
ampm	3183	Hardee's	1901
McDonald's	32,805	Pizza Hut Inc.	13,281
7-Eleven Inc.	37,496	Kumon Math & Reading Centers	25,199
Supercuts	2130	Dunkin' Donuts	9947
Days Inn	1877	KFC Corp.	16,224
Vanguard Cleaning Systems	2155	Jazzercise Inc.	7683
		Anytime Fitness	1618
Servpro	1572	Matco Tools	1431
Subway	34,871	Stratus Building Solutions	5018
Denny's Inc.	1668		

Use classes 0–4999, 5000–9999, 10,000–14,999, and so forth to answer the following questions.

a. Construct a frequency distribution and a percent frequency distribution of the number of U.S. locations for these top-ranked franchises.

b. Construct a histogram of these data.

c. Comment on the shape of the distribution.

23. The *Nielsen Home Technology Report* provided information about home technology and its usage. The following data are the hours of personal computer usage during one week for a sample of 50 persons.

Computer

4.1	1.5	10.4	5.9	3.4	5.7	1.6	6.1	3.0	3.7
3.1	4.8	2.0	14.8	5.4	4.2	3.9	4.1	11.1	3.5
4.1	4.1	8.8	5.6	4.3	3.3	7.1	10.3	6.2	7.6
10.8	2.8	9.5	12.9	12.1	0.7	4.0	9.2	4.4	5.7
7.2	6.1	5.7	5.9	4.7	3.9	3.7	3.1	6.1	3.1

Summarize the data by constructing the following:

a. A frequency distribution (use a class width of three hours)

b. A relative frequency distribution

c. A histogram

d. Comment on what the data indicate about personal computer usage at home.

24. *Money* magazine listed top career opportunities for work that is enjoyable, pays well, and will still be around 10 years from now (*Money,* November 2009). Shown below are 20 top career opportunities, with the median pay and top pay for workers with two to seven years of experience in the field. Data are shown in thousands of dollars.

Careers

Career	Median Pay	Top Pay
Account Executive	81	157
Certified Public Accountant	74	138
Computer Security Consultant	100	138
Director of Communications	78	135
Financial Analyst	80	109
Finance Director	121	214
Financial Research Analyst	66	155
Hotel General Manager	77	146
Human Resources Manager	72	111
Investment Banking	106	221
IT Business Analyst	83	119
IT Project Manager	99	140

Career	Median Pay	Top Pay
Marketing Manager	77	126
Quality-Assurance Manager	80	122
Sales Representative	67	125
Senior Internal Auditor	76	106
Software Developer	79	116
Software Program Manager	110	152
Systems Engineer	87	130
Technical Writer	67	100

Develop a stem-and-leaf display for both the median pay and the top pay. Comment on what you learn about the pay for these careers.

25. A psychologist developed a new test of adult intelligence. The test was administered to 20 individuals, and the following data were obtained.

114	99	131	124	117	102	106	127	119	115
98	104	144	151	132	106	125	122	118	118

Construct a stem-and-leaf display for the data.

26. The 2011 Cincinnati Flying Pig Half-Marathon (13.1 miles) had 10,897 finishers (Cincinnati Flying Pig Marathon website). The following data show the ages for a sample of 40 half-marathoners.

Marathon

49	33	40	37	56
44	46	57	55	32
50	52	43	64	40
46	24	30	37	43
31	43	50	36	61
27	44	35	31	43
52	43	66	31	50
72	26	59	21	47

a. Construct a stretched stem-and-leaf display.
b. What age group had the largest number of runners?
c. What age occurred most frequently?

2.3 Summarizing Data for Two Variables Using Tables

Thus far in this chapter, we have focused on using tabular and graphical displays to summarize the data for a single categorical or quantitative variable. Often a manager or decision maker needs to summarize the data for two variables in order to reveal the relationship—if any—between the variables. In this section, we show how to construct a tabular summary of the data for two variables.

Crosstabulation

A **crosstabulation** is a tabular summary of data for two variables. Although both variables can be either categorical or quantitative, crosstabulations in which one variable is categorical and the other variable is quantitative are just as common. We will illustrate this latter case by considering the following application based on data from Zagat's Restaurant Review. Data showing the quality rating and the typical meal price were collected for a sample of

TABLE 2.9   QUALITY RATING AND MEAL PRICE DATA FOR 300 LOS ANGELES
RESTAURANTS

Restaurant

Restaurant	Quality Rating	Meal Price ($)
1	Good	18
2	Very Good	22
3	Good	28
4	Excellent	38
5	Very Good	33
6	Good	28
7	Very Good	19
8	Very Good	11
9	Very Good	23
10	Good	13
.	.	.
.	.	.
.	.	.

© Cengage Learning

300 restaurants in the Los Angeles area. Table 2.9 shows the data for the first 10 restaurants. Quality rating is a categorical variable with rating categories of good, very good, and excellent. Meal price is a quantitative variable that ranges from $10 to $49.

A crosstabulation of the data for this application is shown in Table 2.10. The labels shown in the margins of the table define the categories (classes) for the two variables. In the left margin, the row labels (good, very good, and excellent) correspond to the three rating categories for the quality rating variable. In the top margin, the column labels ($10–19, $20–29, $30–39, and $40–49) show that the meal price data have been grouped into four classes. Because each restaurant in the sample provides a quality rating and a meal price, each restaurant is associated with a cell appearing in one of the rows and one of the columns of the crosstabulation. For example, Table 2.9 shows restaurant 5 as having a very good quality rating and a meal price of $33. This restaurant belongs to the cell in row 2 and column 3 of the crosstabulation shown in Table 2.10. In constructing a crosstabulation, we simply count the number of restaurants that belong to each of the cells.

Grouping the data for a quantitative variable enables us to treat the quantitative variable as if it were a categorical variable when creating a crosstabulation.

Although four classes of the meal price variable were used to construct the crosstabulation shown in Table 2.10, the crosstabulation of quality rating and meal price could have been developed using fewer or more classes for the meal price variable. The issues involved in deciding how to group the data for a quantitative variable in a crosstabulation are similar to the issues involved in deciding the number of classes to use when constructing a frequency distribution for a quantitative variable. For this application, four classes of meal price were considered a reasonable number of classes to reveal any relationship between quality rating and meal price.

TABLE 2.10   CROSSTABULATION OF QUALITY RATING AND MEAL PRICE DATA
FOR 300 LOS ANGELES RESTAURANTS

Quality Rating	Meal Price				
	$10–19	$20–29	$30–39	$40–49	Total
Good	42	40	2	0	84
Very Good	34	64	46	6	150
Excellent	2	14	28	22	66
Total	78	118	76	28	300

© Cengage Learning

In reviewing Table 2.10, we see that the greatest number of restaurants in the sample (64) have a very good rating and a meal price in the $20–29 range. Only two restaurants have an excellent rating and a meal price in the $10–19 range. Similar interpretations of the other frequencies can be made. In addition, note that the right and bottom margins of the crosstabulation provide the frequency distributions for quality rating and meal price separately. From the frequency distribution in the right margin, we see that data on quality ratings show 84 restaurants with a good quality rating, 150 restaurants with a very good quality rating, and 66 restaurants with an excellent quality rating. Similarly, the bottom margin shows the frequency distribution for the meal price variable.

Dividing the totals in the right margin of the crosstabulation by the total for that column provides a relative and percent frequency distribution for the quality rating variable.

Quality Rating	Relative Frequency	Percent Frequency
Good	.28	28
Very Good	.50	50
Excellent	.22	22
Total	1.00	100

From the percent frequency distribution we see that 28% of the restaurants were rated good, 50% were rated very good, and 22% were rated excellent.

Dividing the totals in the bottom row of the crosstabulation by the total for that row provides a relative and percent frequency distribution for the meal price variable.

Meal Price	Relative Frequency	Percent Frequency
$10–19	.26	26
$20–29	.39	39
$30–39	.25	25
$40–49	.09	9
Total	1.00	100

Note that the sum of the values in the relative frequency column do not add exactly to 1.00 and the sum of the values in the percent frequency distribution do not add exactly to 100; the reason is that the values being summed are rounded. From the percent frequency distribution we see that 26% of the meal prices are in the lowest price class ($10–19), 39% are in the next higher class, and so on.

The frequency and relative frequency distributions constructed from the margins of a crosstabulation provide information about each of the variables individually, but they do not shed any light on the relationship between the variables. The primary value of a crosstabulation lies in the insight it offers about the relationship between the variables. A review of the crosstabulation in Table 2.10 reveals that restaurants with higher meal prices received higher quality ratings than restaurants with lower meal prices.

Converting the entries in a crosstabulation into row percentages or column percentages can provide more insight into the relationship between the two variables. For row percentages, the results of dividing each frequency in Table 2.10 by its corresponding row total are shown in Table 2.11. Each row of Table 2.11 is a percent frequency distribution of meal price for one of the quality rating categories. Of the restaurants with the lowest quality rating (good), we see that the greatest percentages are for the less expensive restaurants (50% have $10–19 meal prices and 47.6% have $20–29 meal prices). Of the restaurants with the highest quality rating (excellent), we see that the greatest

TABLE 2.11   ROW PERCENTAGES FOR EACH QUALITY RATING CATEGORY

Quality Rating	Meal Price $10–19	$20–29	$30–39	$40–49	Total
Good	50.0	47.6	2.4	0.0	100
Very Good	22.7	42.7	30.6	4.0	100
Excellent	3.0	21.2	42.4	33.4	100

© Cengage Learning

percentages are for the more expensive restaurants (42.4% have $30–39 meal prices and 33.4% have $40–49 meal prices). Thus, we continue to see that restaurants with higher meal prices received higher quality ratings.

Crosstabulations are widely used to investigate the relationship between two variables. In practice, the final reports for many statistical studies include a large number of crosstabulations. In the Los Angeles restaurant survey, the crosstabulation is based on one categorical variable (quality rating) and one quantitative variable (meal price). Crosstabulations can also be developed when both variables are categorical and when both variables are quantitative. When quantitative variables are used, however, we must first create classes for the values of the variable. For instance, in the restaurant example we grouped the meal prices into four classes ($10–19, $20–29, $30–39, and $40–49).

Simpson's Paradox

The data in two or more crosstabulations are often combined or aggregated to produce a summary crosstabulation showing how two variables are related. In such cases, conclusions drawn from two or more separate crosstabulations can be reversed when the data are aggregated into a single crosstabulation. The reversal of conclusions based on aggregate and unaggregated data is called **Simpson's paradox**. To provide an illustration of Simpson's paradox we consider an example involving the analysis of verdicts for two judges in two different courts.

Judges Ron Luckett and Dennis Kendall presided over cases in Common Pleas Court and Municipal Court during the past three years. Some of the verdicts they rendered were appealed. In most of these cases the appeals court upheld the original verdicts, but in some cases those verdicts were reversed. For each judge a crosstabulation was developed based upon two variables: Verdict (upheld or reversed) and Type of Court (Common Pleas and Municipal). Suppose that the two crosstabulations were then combined by aggregating the type of court data. The resulting aggregated crosstabulation contains two variables: Verdict (upheld or reversed) and Judge (Luckett or Kendall). This crosstabulation shows the number of appeals in which the verdict was upheld and the number in which the verdict was reversed for both judges. The following crosstabulation shows these results along with the column percentages in parentheses next to each value.

Verdict	Judge Luckett	Kendall	Total
Upheld	129 (86%)	110 (88%)	239
Reversed	21 (14%)	15 (12%)	36
Total (%)	150 (100%)	125 (100%)	275

A review of the column percentages shows that 86% of the verdicts were upheld for Judge Luckett, while 88% of the verdicts were upheld for Judge Kendall. From this aggregated crosstabulation, we conclude that Judge Kendall is doing the better job because a greater percentage of Judge Kendall's verdicts are being upheld.

The following unaggregated crosstabulations show the cases tried by Judge Luckett and Judge Kendall in each court; column percentages are shown in parentheses next to each value.

Judge Luckett

Verdict	Common Pleas	Municipal Court	Total
Upheld	29 (91%)	100 (85%)	129
Reversed	3 (9%)	18 (15%)	21
Total (%)	32 (100%)	118 (100%)	150

Judge Kendall

Verdict	Common Pleas	Municipal Court	Total
Upheld	90 (90%)	20 (80%)	110
Reversed	10 (10%)	5 (20%)	15
Total (%)	100 (100%)	25 (100%)	125

From the crosstabulation and column percentages for Judge Luckett, we see that the verdicts were upheld in 91% of the Common Pleas Court cases and in 85% of the Municipal Court cases. From the crosstabulation and column percentages for Judge Kendall, we see that the verdicts were upheld in 90% of the Common Pleas Court cases and in 80% of the Municipal Court cases. Thus, when we unaggregate the data, we see that Judge Luckett has a better record because a greater percentage of Judge Luckett's verdicts are being upheld in both courts. This result contradicts the conclusion we reached with the aggregated data crosstabulation that showed Judge Kendall had the better record. This reversal of conclusions based on aggregated and unaggregated data illustrates Simpson's paradox.

The original crosstabulation was obtained by aggregating the data in the separate crosstabulations for the two courts. Note that for both judges the percentage of appeals that resulted in reversals was much higher in Municipal Court than in Common Pleas Court. Because Judge Luckett tried a much higher percentage of his cases in Municipal Court, the aggregated data favored Judge Kendall. When we look at the crosstabulations for the two courts separately, however, Judge Luckett shows the better record. Thus, for the original crosstabulation, we see that the *type of court* is a hidden variable that cannot be ignored when evaluating the records of the two judges.

Because of the possibility of Simpson's paradox, realize that the conclusion or interpretation may be reversed depending upon whether you are viewing unaggregated or aggregate crosstabulation data. Before drawing a conclusion, you may want to investigate whether the aggregate or unaggregate form of the crosstabulation provides the better insight and conclusion. Especially when the crosstabulation involves aggregated data, you should investigate whether a hidden variable could affect the results such that separate or unaggregated crosstabulations provide a different and possibly better insight and conclusion.

Exercises

Methods

27. The following data are for 30 observations involving two categorical variables, *x* and *y*. The categories for *x* are A, B, and C; the categories for *y* are 1 and 2.

Crosstab

Observation	x	y	Observation	x	y
1	A	1	16	B	2
2	B	1	17	C	1
3	B	1	18	B	1
4	C	2	19	C	1
5	B	1	20	B	1
6	C	2	21	C	2
7	B	1	22	B	1
8	C	2	23	C	2
9	A	1	24	A	1
10	B	1	25	B	1
11	A	1	26	C	2
12	B	1	27	C	2
13	C	2	28	A	1
14	C	2	29	B	1
15	C	2	30	B	2

a. Develop a crosstabulation for the data, with *x* as the row variable and *y* as the column variable.
b. Compute the row percentages.
c. Compute the column percentages.
d. What is the relationship, if any, between *x* and *y*?

28. The following observations are for two quantitative variables, *x* and *y*.

Crosstab2

Observation	x	y	Observation	x	y
1	28	72	11	13	98
2	17	99	12	84	21
3	52	58	13	59	32
4	79	34	14	17	81
5	37	60	15	70	34
6	71	22	16	47	64
7	37	77	17	35	68
8	27	85	18	62	67
9	64	45	19	30	39
10	53	47	20	43	28

a. Develop a crosstabulation for the data, with *x* as the row variable and *y* as the column variable. For *x* use classes of 10–29, 30–49, and so on; for *y* use classes of 40–59, 60–79, and so on.
b. Compute the row percentages.
c. Compute the column percentages.
d. What is the relationship, if any, between *x* and *y*?

Applications

29. The Daytona 500 is a 500-mile automobile race held annually at the Daytona International Speedway in Daytona Beach, Florida. The following crosstabulation shows the automobile make by average speed of the 25 winners from 1988 to 2012 (*The 2013 World Almanac*).
a. Compute the row percentages.
b. What percentage of winners driving a Chevrolet won with an average speed of at least 150 miles per hour?

| | Average Speed in Miles per Hour | | | | | |
Make	130–139.9	140–149.9	150–159.9	160–169.9	170–179.9	Total
Buick	1					1
Chevrolet	3	5	4	3	1	16
Dodge		2				2
Ford	2	1	2	1		6
Total	6	8	6	4	1	25

    c.   Compute the column percentages.

    d.   What percentage of winning average speeds 160–169.9 miles per hour were Chevrolets?

30.   The following crosstabulation shows the average speed of the 25 winners by year of the Daytona 500 automobile race (*The 2013 World Almanac*).

| | Year | | | | | |
Average Speed	1988–1992	1993–1997	1998–2002	2003–2007	2008–2012	Total
130–139.9	1			2	3	6
140–149.9	2	2	1	2	1	8
150–159.9		3	1	1	1	6
160–169.9	2		2			4
170–179.9			1			1
Total	5	5	5	5	5	25

    a.   Calculate the row percentages.

    b.   What is the apparent relationship between average winning speed and year? What might be the cause of this apparent relationship?

31.   Recently, management at Oak Tree Golf Course received a few complaints about the condition of the greens. Several players complained that the greens are too fast. Rather than react to the comments of just a few, the Golf Association conducted a survey of 100 male and 100 female golfers. The survey results are summarized here.

Male Golfers

| | Greens Condition | |
Handicap	Too Fast	Fine
Under 15	10	40
15 or more	25	25

Female Golfers

| | Greens Condition | |
Handicap	Too Fast	Fine
Under 15	1	9
15 or more	39	51

    a.   Combine these two crosstabulations into one with Male and Female as the row labels and Too Fast and Fine as the column labels. Which group shows the highest percentage saying that the greens are too fast?

    b.   Refer to the initial crosstabulations. For those players with low handicaps (better players), which group (male or female) shows the highest percentage saying the greens are too fast?

    c.   Refer to the initial crosstabulations. For those players with higher handicaps, which group (male or female) shows the highest percentage saying the greens are too fast?

    d.   What conclusions can you draw about the preferences of men and women concerning the speed of the greens? Are the conclusions you draw from part (a) as compared with parts (b) and (c) consistent? Explain any apparent inconsistencies.

32. Table 2.12 shows a data set containing information for 45 mutual funds that are part of the *Morningstar Funds 500* for 2008. The data set includes the following five variables:

TABLE 2.12   FINANCIAL DATA FOR A SAMPLE OF 45 MUTUAL FUNDS

Fund Name	Fund Type	Net Asset Value ($)	5-Year Average Return (%)	Expense Ratio (%)	Morningstar Rank
Amer Cent Inc & Growth Inv	DE	28.88	12.39	0.67	2-Star
American Century Intl Disc	IE	14.37	30.53	1.41	3-Star
American Century Tax-Free Bond	FI	10.73	3.34	0.49	4-Star
American Century Ultra	DE	24.94	10.88	0.99	3-Star
Ariel	DE	46.39	11.32	1.03	2-Star
Artisan Intl Val	IE	25.52	24.95	1.23	3-Star
Artisan Small Cap	DE	16.92	15.67	1.18	3-Star
Baron Asset	DE	50.67	16.77	1.31	5-Star
Brandywine	DE	36.58	18.14	1.08	4-Star
Brown Cap Small	DE	35.73	15.85	1.20	4-Star
Buffalo Mid Cap	DE	15.29	17.25	1.02	3-Star
Delafield	DE	24.32	17.77	1.32	4-Star
DFA U.S. Micro Cap	DE	13.47	17.23	0.53	3-Star
Dodge & Cox Income	FI	12.51	4.31	0.44	4-Star
Fairholme	DE	31.86	18.23	1.00	5-Star
Fidelity Contrafund	DE	73.11	17.99	0.89	5-Star
Fidelity Municipal Income	FI	12.58	4.41	0.45	5-Star
Fidelity Overseas	IE	48.39	23.46	0.90	4-Star
Fidelity Sel Electronics	DE	45.60	13.50	0.89	3-Star
Fidelity Sh-Term Bond	FI	8.60	2.76	0.45	3-Star
Fidelity	DE	39.85	14.40	0.56	4-Star
FPA New Income	FI	10.95	4.63	0.62	3-Star
Gabelli Asset AAA	DE	49.81	16.70	1.36	4-Star
Greenspring	DE	23.59	12.46	1.07	3-Star
Janus	DE	32.26	12.81	0.90	3-Star
Janus Worldwide	IE	54.83	12.31	0.86	2-Star
Kalmar Gr Val Sm Cp	DE	15.30	15.31	1.32	3-Star
Managers Freemont Bond	FI	10.56	5.14	0.60	5-Star
Marsico 21st Century	DE	17.44	15.16	1.31	5-Star
Mathews Pacific Tiger	IE	27.86	32.70	1.16	3-Star
Meridan Value	DE	31.92	15.33	1.08	4-Star
Oakmark I	DE	40.37	9.51	1.05	2-Star
PIMCO Emerg Mkts Bd D	FI	10.68	13.57	1.25	3-Star
RS Value A	DE	26.27	23.68	1.36	4-Star
T. Rowe Price Latin Am	IE	53.89	51.10	1.24	4-Star
T. Rowe Price Mid Val	DE	22.46	16.91	0.80	4-Star
Templeton Growth A	IE	24.07	15.91	1.01	3-Star
Thornburg Value A	DE	37.53	15.46	1.27	4-Star
USAA Income	FI	12.10	4.31	0.62	3-Star
Vanguard Equity-Inc	DE	24.42	13.41	0.29	4-Star
Vanguard Global Equity	IE	23.71	21.77	0.64	5-Star
Vanguard GNMA	FI	10.37	4.25	0.21	5-Star
Vanguard Sht-Tm TE	FI	15.68	2.37	0.16	3-Star
Vanguard Sm Cp Idx	DE	32.58	17.01	0.23	3-Star
Wasatch Sm Cp Growth	DE	35.41	13.98	1.19	4-Star

MutualFunds

© Cengage Learning

Fund Type: The type of fund, labeled DE (Domestic Equity), IE (International Equity), and FI (Fixed Income)

Net Asset Value ($): The closing price per share

5-Year Average Return (%): The average annual return for the fund over the past 5 years

Expense Ratio (%): The percentage of assets deducted each fiscal year for fund expenses

Morningstar Rank: The risk adjusted star rating for each fund; Morningstar ranks go from a low of 1-Star to a high of 5-Stars

    a. Prepare a crosstabulation of the data on Fund Type (rows) and the average annual return over the past 5 years (columns). Use classes of 0–9.99, 10–19.99, 20–29.99, 30–39.99, 40–49.99, and 50–59.99 for the 5-Year Average Return (%).

    b. Prepare a frequency distribution for the data on Fund Type.

    c. Prepare a frequency distribution for the data on 5-Year Average Return (%).

    d. How has the crosstabulation helped in preparing the frequency distributions in parts (b) and (c)?

    e. What conclusions can you draw about the fund type and the average return over the past 5 years?

33. Refer to the data in Table 2.12.

    a. Prepare a crosstabulation of the data on Fund Type (rows) and the Expense Ratio (%) (columns). Use classes of .25–.49, .50–.74, .75–.99, 1.00–1.24, and 1.25–1.49 for Expense Ratio (%).

    b. Prepare a percent frequency distribution for Expense Ratio (%).

    c. What conclusions can you draw about fund type and the expense ratio?

34. The file named BankFail contains a list of 492 banks that failed from 2000–2012 (Federal Deposit Insurance Corporation website, March 9, 2013). The file contains the name of the bank, city, state, and year of failure.

    a. Construct a crosstabulation with state as the rows and year as the columns.

    b. Which three states have had the most failed banks?

    c. Give the frequency distribution of bank failures by year. Comment on what appears to be happening with bank failures over time.

BankFail

35. The U.S. Department of Energy's Fuel Economy Guide provides fuel efficiency data for cars and trucks (Fuel Economy website, September 8, 2012). A portion of the data for 149 compact, midsize, and large cars is shown in Table 2.13. The data set contains the following variables:

Size: Compact, Midsize, and Large

Displacement: Engine size in liters

Cylinders: Number of cylinders in the engine

TABLE 2.13   FUEL EFFICIENCY DATA FOR 311 CARS

WEB file

FuelData2012

Car	Size	Displacement	Cylinders	Drive	Fuel Type	City MPG	Hwy MPG
1	Compact	2.0	4	F	P	22	30
2	Compact	2.0	4	A	P	21	29
3	Compact	2.0	4	A	P	21	31
•	•	•	•	•	•	•	•
•	•	•	•	•	•	•	•
•	•	•	•	•	•	•	•
94	Midsize	3.5	6	A	R	17	25
95	Midsize	2.5	4	F	R	23	33
•	•	•	•	•	•	•	•
•	•	•	•	•	•	•	•
•	•	•	•	•	•	•	•
148	Large	6.7	12	R	P	11	18
149	Large	6.7	12	R	P	11	18

Drive: All wheel (A), front wheel (F), and rear wheel (R)

Fuel Type: Premium (P) or regular (R) fuel

City MPG: Fuel efficiency rating for city driving in terms of miles per gallon

Hwy MPG: Fuel efficiency rating for highway driving in terms of miles per gallon

The complete data set is contained in the file named FuelData2012.

a. Prepare a crosstabulation of the data on Size (rows) and Hwy MPG (columns). Use classes of 15–19, 20–24, 25–29, 30–34, 35–39, and 40–44 for Hwy MPG.
b. Comment on the relationship beween Size and Hwy MPG.
c. Prepare a crosstabulation of the data on Drive (rows) and City MPG (columns). Use classes of 10–14, 15–19, 20–24, 25–29, 30–34, 35–39, and 40–44 for City MPG.
d. Comment on the relationship between Drive and City MPG.
e. Prepare a crosstabulation of the data on Fuel Type (rows) and City MPG (columns). Use classes of 10–14, 15–19, 20–24, 25–29, 30–34, 35–39, and 40–44 for City MPG.
f. Comment on the relationship between Fuel Type and City MPG.

2.4   Summarizing Data for Two Variables Using Graphical Displays

In the previous section we showed how a crosstabulation can be used to summarize the data for two variables and help reveal the relationship between the variables. In most cases, a graphical display is more useful for recognizing patterns and trends in the data.

In this section, we introduce a variety of graphical displays for exploring the relationships between two variables. Displaying data in creative ways can lead to powerful insights and allow us to make "common-sense inferences" based on our ability to visually compare, contrast, and recognize patterns. We begin with a discussion of scatter diagrams and trendlines.

Scatter Diagram and Trendline

A **scatter diagram** is a graphical display of the relationship between two quantitative variables, and a **trendline** is a line that provides an approximation of the relationship. As an illustration, consider the advertising/sales relationship for a stereo and sound equipment store in San Francisco. On 10 occasions during the past three months, the store used weekend television commercials to promote sales at its stores. The managers want to investigate whether a relationship exists between the number of commercials shown and sales at the store during the following week. Sample data for the 10 weeks with sales in hundreds of dollars are shown in Table 2.14.

TABLE 2.14   SAMPLE DATA FOR THE STEREO AND SOUND EQUIPMENT STORE

WEB file

Stereo

Week	Number of Commercials x	Sales ($100s) y
1	2	50
2	5	57
3	1	41
4	3	54
5	4	54
6	1	38
7	5	63
8	3	48
9	4	59
10	2	46

FIGURE 2.7   SCATTER DIAGRAM AND TRENDLINE FOR THE STEREO AND SOUND
EQUIPMENT STORE

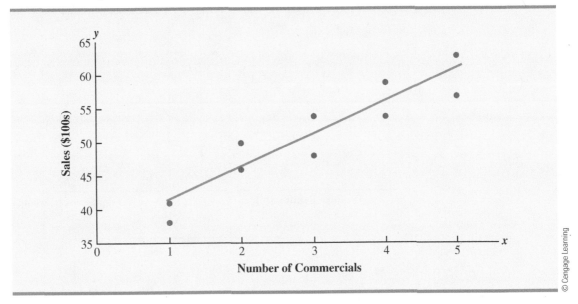

Figure 2.7 shows the scatter diagram and the trendline[1] for the data in Table 2.14. The number of commercials (x) is shown on the horizontal axis and the sales (y) are shown on the vertical axis. For week 1, $x = 2$ and $y = 50$. A point with those coordinates is plotted on the scatter diagram. Similar points are plotted for the other nine weeks. Note that during two of the weeks one commercial was shown, during two of the weeks two commercials were shown, and so on.

The scatter diagram in Figure 2.7 indicates a positive relationship between the number of commercials and sales. Higher sales are associated with a higher number of commercials. The relationship is not perfect in that all points are not on a straight line. However, the general pattern of the points and the trendline suggest that the overall relationship is positive.

Some general scatter diagram patterns and the types of relationships they suggest are shown in Figure 2.8. The top left panel depicts a positive relationship similar to the one for the number of commercials and sales example. In the top right panel, the scatter diagram shows no apparent relationship between the variables. The bottom panel depicts a negative relationship where y tends to decrease as x increases.

Side-by-Side and Stacked Bar Charts

In Section 2.1 we said that a bar chart is a graphical display for depicting categorical data summarized in a frequency, relative frequency, or percent frequency distribution. Side-by-side bar charts and stacked bar charts are extensions of basic bar charts that are used to display and compare two variables. By displaying two variables on the same chart, we may better understand the relationship between the variables.

A **side-by-side bar chart** is a graphical display for depicting multiple bar charts on the same display. To illustrate the construction of a side-by-side chart, recall the application involving the quality rating and meal price data for a sample of 300 restaurants located in the Los Angeles area. Quality rating is a categorical variable with rating categories of good, very good, and excellent. Meal price is a quantitative variable that ranges from $10 to $49. The crosstabulation displayed in Table 2.10 shows that the data for meal price were

---

[1]The equation of the trendline is $y = 36.15 + 4.95x$. The slope of the trendline is 4.95 and the y-intercept (the point where the trendline intersects the y-axis) is 36.15. We will discuss in detail the interpretation of the slope and y-intercept for a linear trendline in Chapter 12 when we study simple linear regression.

FIGURE 2.8   TYPES OF RELATIONSHIPS DEPICTED BY SCATTER DIAGRAMS

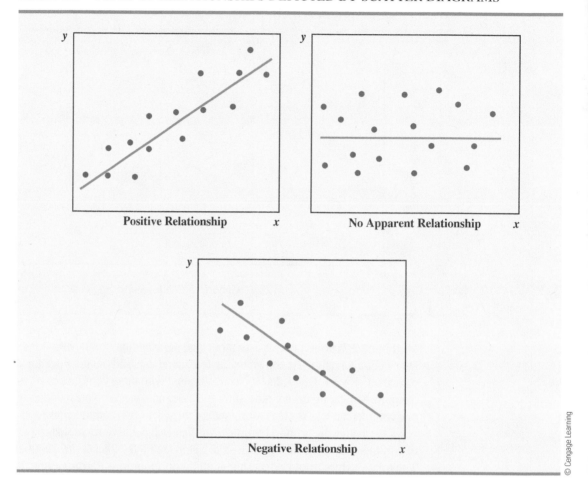

grouped into four classes: \$10–19, \$20–29, \$30–39, and \$40–49. We will use these classes to construct a side-by-side bar chart.

Figure 2.9 shows a side-by-side chart for the restaurant data. The color of each bar indicates the quality rating (blue = good, red = very good, and green = excellent). Each bar is constructed by extending the bar to the point on the vertical axis that represents the frequency

FIGURE 2.9   SIDE-BY-SIDE BAR CHART FOR THE QUALITY AND MEAL PRICE DATA

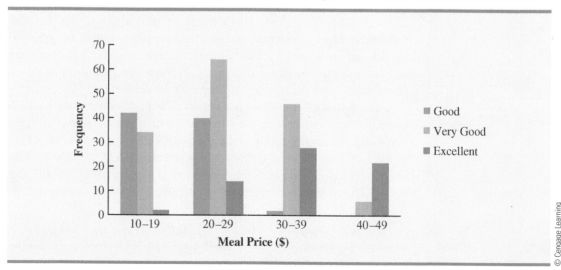

with which that quality rating occurred for each of the meal price categories. Placing each meal price category's quality rating frequency adjacent to one another allows us to quickly determine how a particular meal price category is rated. We see that the lowest meal price category ($10–$19) received mostly good and very good ratings, but very few excellent ratings. The highest price category ($40–49), however, shows a much different result. This meal price category received mostly excellent ratings, some very good ratings, but no good ratings.

Figure 2.9 also provides a good sense of the relationship between meal price and quality rating. Notice that as the price increases (left to right), the height of the blue bars decreases and the height of the green bars generally increases. This indicates that as price increases, the quality rating tends to be better. The very good rating, as expected, tends to be more prominent in the middle price categories as indicated by the dominance of the red bars in the middle of the chart.

Stacked bar charts are another way to display and compare two variables on the same display. A **stacked bar chart** is a bar chart in which each bar is broken into rectangular segments of a different color showing the relative frequency of each class in a manner similar to a pie chart. To illustrate a stacked bar chart we will use the quality rating and meal price data summarized in the crosstabulation shown in Table 2.10.

We can convert the frequency data in Table 2.10 into column percentages by dividing each element in a particular column by the total for that column. For instance, 42 of the 78 restaurants with a meal price in the $10–19 range had a good quality rating. In other words, (42/78)100 or 53.8% of the 78 restaurants had a good rating. Table 2.15 shows the column percentages for each meal price category. Using the data in Table 2.15 we constructed the stacked bar chart shown in Figure 2.10. Because the stacked bar chart is based on

TABLE 2.15   COLUMN PERCENTAGES FOR EACH MEAL PRICE CATEGORY

	Meal Price			
Quality Rating	**$10–19**	**$20–29**	**$30–39**	**$40–49**
Good	53.8%	33.9%	2.6%	0.0%
Very Good	43.6	54.2	60.5	21.4
Excellent	2.6	11.9	36.8	78.6
Total	100.0%	100.0%	100.0%	100.0%

© Cengage Learning

FIGURE 2.10   STACKED BAR CHART FOR QUALITY RATING AND MEAL PRICE DATA

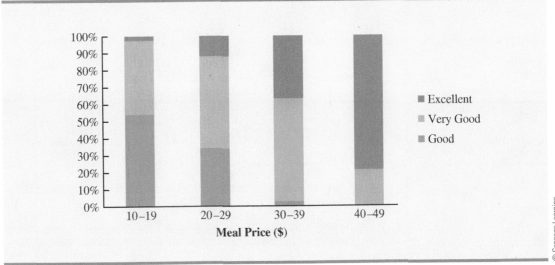

© Cengage Learning

percentages, Figure 2.10 shows even more clearly than Figure 2.9 the relationship between the variables. As we move from the low price category ($10–19) to the high price category ($40–49), the length of the blue bars decreases and the length of the green bars increases.

NOTE AND COMMENT

A stacked bar chart can also be used to display frequencies rather than percentage frequencies. In this case, the different color segments of each bar represent the contribution to the total for that bar, rather than the percentage contribution.

Exercises

Methods

Scatter

36. The following 20 observations are for two quantitative variables, x and y.

Observation	x	y	Observation	x	y
1	−22	22	11	−37	48
2	−33	49	12	34	−29
3	2	8	13	9	−18
4	29	−16	14	−33	31
5	−13	10	15	20	−16
6	21	−28	16	−3	14
7	−13	27	17	−15	18
8	−23	35	18	12	17
9	14	−5	19	−20	−11
10	3	−3	20	−7	−22

    a. Develop a scatter diagram for the relationship between x and y.
    b. What is the relationship, if any, between x and y?

37. Consider the following data on two categorical variables. The first variable, x, can take on values A, B, C, or D. The second variable, y, can take on values I or II. The following table gives the frequency with which each combination occurs.

	y	
x	**I**	**II**
A	143	857
B	200	800
C	321	679
D	420	580

    a. Construct a side-by-side bar chart with x on the horizontal axis.
    b. Comment on the relationship between x and y.

38. The following crosstabulation summarizes the data for two categorical variables, x and y. The variable x can take on values low, medium, or high and the variable y can take on values yes or no.

x	Yes	No	Total
Low	20	10	30
Medium	15	35	50
High	20	5	25
Total	55	50	105

a.   Compute the row percentages.
b.   Construct a stacked percent frequency bar chart with x on the horizontal axis.

Applications

39.   A study on driving speed (miles per hour) and fuel efficiency (miles per gallon) for midsize automobiles resulted in the following data:

Driving Speed	30 50 40 55 30 25 60 25 50 55
Fuel Efficiency	28 25 25 23 30 32 21 35 26 25

a.   Construct a scatter diagram with driving speed on the horizontal axis and fuel efficiency on the vertical axis.
b.   Comment on any apparent relationship between these two variables.

40.   The Current Results website lists the average annual high and low temperatures (degrees Fahrenheit) and average annual snowfall (inches) for 51 major U.S. cities, based on data from 1981 to 2010. The data are contained in the file *Snow*. For example, the average low temperature for Columbus, Ohio, is 44 degrees and the average annual snowfall is 27.5 inches.
   a.   Construct a scatter diagram with the average annual low temperature on the horizontal axis and the average annual snowfall on the vertical axis.
   b.   Does there appear to be any relationship between these two variables?
   c.   Based on the scatter diagram, comment on any data points that seem to be unusual.

41.   People often wait until middle age to worry about having a healthy heart. However, recent studies have shown that earlier monitoring of risk factors such as blood pressure can be very beneficial (*The Wall Street Journal*, January 10, 2012). Having higher than normal blood pressure, a condition known as hypertension, is a major risk factor for heart disease. Suppose a large sample of individuals of various ages and gender was selected and that each individual's blood pressure was measured to determine if they have hypertension. For the sample data, the following table shows the percentage of individuals with hypertension.

Age	Male	Female
20–34	11.0%	9.0%
35–44	24.0%	19.0%
45–54	39.0%	37.0%
55–64	57.0%	56.0%
65–74	62.0%	64.0%
75+	73.30%	79.0%

a. Develop a side-by-side bar chart with age on the horizontal axis, the percentage of individuals with hypertension on the vertical axis, and side-by-side bars based on gender.
b. What does the display you developed in part (a), indicate about hypertension and age?
c. Comment on differences by gender.

42. Smartphones are advanced mobile phones with Internet, photo, and music and video capability (The Pew Research Center, Internet & American Life Project, 2011). The following survey results show smartphone ownership by age.

Smartphones

Age Category	Smartphone (%)	Other Cell Phone (%)	No Cell Phone (%)
18–24	49	46	5
25–34	58	35	7
35–44	44	45	11
45–54	28	58	14
55–64	22	59	19
65+	11	45	44

a. Construct a stacked bar chart to display the above survey data on type of mobile phone ownership. Use age category as the variable on the horizontal axis.
b. Comment on the relationship between age and smartphone ownership.
c. How would you expect the results of this survey to be different if conducted in 2021?

43. The Northwest regional manager of an outdoor equipment retailer conducted a study to determine how managers at three store locations are using their time. A summary of the results is shown in the following table.

ManagerTime

	Percentage of Manager's Work Week Spent on			
Store Location	Meetings	Reports	Customers	Idle
Bend	18	11	52	19
Portland	52	11	24	13
Seattle	32	17	37	14

a. Create a stacked bar chart with store location on the horizontal axis and percentage of time spent on each task on the vertical axis.
b. Create a side-by-side bar chart with store location on the horizontal axis and side-by-side bars of the percentage of time spent on each task.
c. Which type of bar chart (stacked or side-by-side) do you prefer for these data? Why?

2.5 Data Visualization: Best Practices in Creating Effective Graphical Displays

Data visualization is a term used to describe the use of graphical displays to summarize and present information about a data set. The goal of data visualization is to communicate as effectively and clearly as possible, the key information about the data. In this section, we provide guidelines for creating an effective graphical display, discuss how to select an appropriate type of display given the purpose of the study, illustrate the use of data dashboards, and show how the Cincinnati Zoo and Botanical Garden uses data visualization techniques to improve decision making.

TABLE 2.16   PLANNED AND ACTUAL SALES BY SALES REGION ($1000s)

WEB file

PlannedActual

Sales Region	Planned Sales ($1000s)	Actual Sales ($1000s)
Northeast	540	447
Northwest	420	447
Southeast	575	556
Southwest	360	341

© Cengage Learning

Creating Effective Graphical Displays

The data presented in Table 2.16 show the forecasted or planned value of sales ($1000s) and the actual value of sales ($1000s) by sales region in the United States for Gustin Chemical for the past year. Note that there are two quantitative variables (planned sales and actual sales) and one categorical variable (sales region). Suppose we would like to develop a graphical display that would enable management of Gustin Chemical to visualize how each sales region did relative to planned sales and simultaneously enable management to visualize sales performance across regions.

Figure 2.11 shows a side-by-side bar chart of the planned versus actual sales data. Note how this bar chart makes it very easy to compare the planned versus actual sales in a region, as well as across regions. This graphical display is simple, contains a title, is well labeled, and uses distinct colors to represent the two types of sales. Note also that the scale of the vertical axis begins at zero. The four sales regions are separated by space so that it is clear that they are distinct, whereas the planned versus actual sales values are side-by-side for easy comparison within each region. The side-by-side bar chart in Figure 2.11 makes it easy to see that the Southwest region is the lowest in both planned and actual sales and that the Northwest region slightly exceeded its planned sales.

Creating an effective graphical display is as much art as it is science. By following the general guidelines listed below you can increase the likelihood that your display will effectively convey the key information in the data.

- Give the display a clear and concise title.
- Keep the display simple. Do not use three dimensions when two dimensions are sufficient.

FIGURE 2.11   SIDE-BY-SIDE BAR CHART FOR PLANNED VERSUS ACTUAL SALES

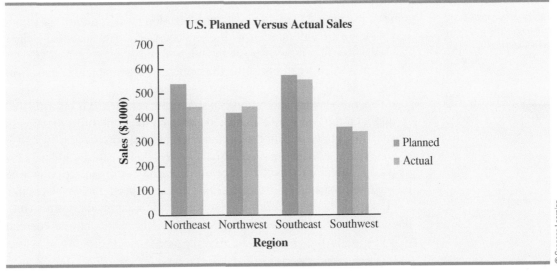

© Cengage Learning

- Clearly label each axis and provide the units of measure.
- If color is used to distinguish categories, make sure the colors are distinct.
- If multiple colors or line types are used, use a legend to define how they are used and place the legend close to the representation of the data.

Choosing the Type of Graphical Display

In this chapter we discussed a variety of graphical displays, including bar charts, pie charts, dot plots, histograms, stem-and-leaf plots, scatter diagrams, side-by-side bar charts, and stacked bar charts. Each of these types of displays was developed for a specific purpose. In order to provide guidelines for choosing the appropriate type of graphical display, we now provide a summary of the types of graphical displays categorized by their purpose. We note that some types of graphical displays may be used effectively for multiple purposes.

Displays Used to Show the Distribution of Data

- Bar Chart—Used to show the frequency distribution and relative frequency distribution for categorical data
- Pie Chart—Used to show the relative frequency and percent frequency for categorical data
- Dot Plot—Used to show the distribution for quantitative data over the entire range of the data
- Histogram—Used to show the frequency distribution for quantitative data over a set of class intervals
- Stem-and-Leaf Display—Used to show both the rank order and shape of the distribution for quantitative data

Displays Used to Make Comparisons

- Side-by-Side Bar Chart—Used to compare two variables
- Stacked Bar Charts—Used to compare the relative frequency or percent frequency of two categorical variables

Displays Used to Show Relationships

- Scatter diagram—Used to show the relationship between two quantitative variables
- Trendline—Used to approximate the relationship of data in a scatter diagram

Data Dashboards

Data dashboards are also referred to as digital dashboards.

One of the most widely used data visualization tools is a **data dashboard**. If you drive a car, you are already familiar with the concept of a data dashboard. In an automobile, the car's dashboard contains gauges and other visual displays that provide the key information that is important when operating the vehicle. For example, the gauges used to display the car's speed, fuel level, engine temperature, and oil level are critical to ensure safe and efficient operation of the automobile. In some new vehicles, this information is even displayed visually on the windshield to provide an even more effective display for the driver. Data dashboards play a similar role for managerial decision making.

A data dashboard is a set of visual displays that organizes and presents information that is used to monitor the performance of a company or organization in a manner that is easy to read, understand, and interpret. Just as a car's speed, fuel level, engine temperature, and oil level are important information to monitor in a car, every business has key performance indicators (KPIs)[2] that need to be monitored to assess how a company is performing.

---

[2] Key performance indicators are sometimes referred to as Key Performance Metrics (KPMs).

Examples of KPIs are inventory on hand, daily sales, percentage of on-time deliveries, and sales revenue per quarter. A data dashboard should provide timely summary information (potentially from various sources) on KPIs that is important to the user, and it should do so in a manner that informs rather than overwhelms its user.

To illustrate the use of a data dashboard in decision making, we will discuss an application involving the Grogan Oil Company. Grogan has offices located in three cities in Texas: Austin (its headquarters), Houston, and Dallas. Grogan's Information Technology (IT) call center, located in the Austin office, handles calls from employees regarding computer-related problems involving software, Internet, and e-mail issues. For example, if a Grogan employee in Dallas has a computer software problem, the employee can call the IT call center for assistance.

The data dashboard shown in Figure 2.12 was developed to monitor the performance of the call center. This data dashboard combines several displays to monitor the call center's KPIs. The data presented are for the current shift, which started at 8:00 A.M. The stacked bar chart in the upper left-hand corner shows the call volume for each type of problem (software, Internet, or e-mail) over time. This chart shows that call volume is heavier during the first few hours of the shift, calls concerning e-mail issues appear to decrease over time, and volume of calls regarding software issues is highest at midmorning. The pie chart in the upper

FIGURE 2.12   GROGAN OIL INFORMATION TECHNOLOGY CALL CENTER DATA DASHBOARD

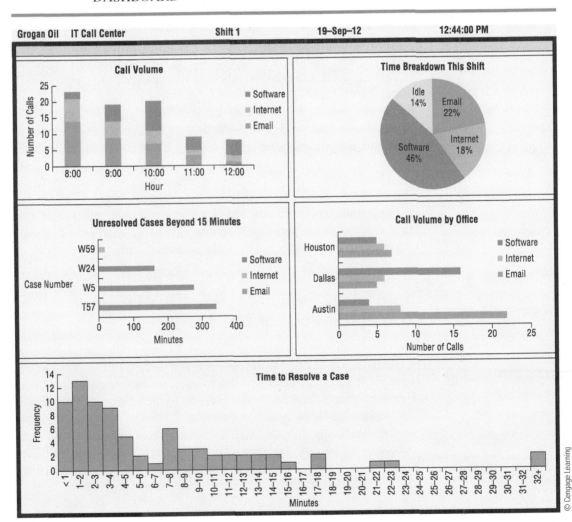

right-hand corner of the dashboard shows the percentage of time that call-center employees spent on each type of problem or not working on a call (idle). Both of these charts are important displays in determining optimal staffing levels. For instance, knowing the call mix and how stressed the system is—as measured by percentage of idle time—can help the IT manager make sure there are enough call center employees available with the right level of expertise.

The side-by-side bar chart below the pie chart shows the call volume by type of problem for each of Grogan's offices. This allows the IT manager to quickly identify if there is a particular type of problem by location. For example, it appears that the office in Austin is reporting a relatively high number of issues with e-mail. If the source of the problem can be identified quickly, then the problem for many might be resolved quickly. Also, note that a relatively high number of software problems are coming from the Dallas office. The higher call volume in this case was simply due to the fact that the Dallas office is currently installing new software, and this has resulted in more calls to the IT call center. Because the IT manager was alerted to this by the Dallas office last week, the IT manager knew there would be an increase in calls coming from the Dallas office and was able to increase staffing levels to handle the expected increase in calls.

For each unresolved case that was received more than 15 minutes ago, the bar chart shown in the middle left-hand side of the data dashboard displays the length of time that each of these cases has been unresolved. This chart enables Grogan to quickly monitor the key problem cases and decide whether additional resources may be needed to resolve them. The worst case, T57, has been unresolved for over 300 minutes and is actually left over from the previous shift. Finally, the histogram at the bottom shows the distribution of the time to resolve the problem for all resolved cases for the current shift.

The Grogan Oil data dashboard illustrates the use of a dashboard at the operational level. The data dashboard is updated in real time and used for operational decisions such as staffing levels. Data dashboards may also be used at the tactical and strategic levels of management. For example, a logistics manager might monitor KPIs for on-time performance and cost for its third-party carriers. This could assist in tactical decisions such as transportation mode and carrier selection. At the highest level, a more strategic dashboard would allow upper management to quickly assess the financial health of the company by monitoring more aggregate financial, service level, and capacity utilization information.

The guidelines for good data visualization discussed previously apply to the individual charts in a data dashboard, as well as to the entire dashboard. In addition to those guidelines, it is important to minimize the need for screen scrolling, avoid unnecessary use of color or three-dimensional displays, and use borders between charts to improve readability. As with individual charts, simpler is almost always better.

Data Visualization in Practice: Cincinnati Zoo and Botanical Garden[3]

The Cincinnati Zoo and Botanical Garden, located in Cincinnati, Ohio, is the second oldest zoo in the world. In order to improve decision making by becoming more data-driven, management decided they needed to link together the different facets of their business and provide nontechnical managers and executives an intuitive way to better understand their data. A complicating factor is that when the zoo is busy, managers are expected to be on the grounds interacting with guests, checking on operations, and anticipating issues as they arise or before they become a problem. Therefore, being able to monitor what is happening on a real-time basis was a key factor in deciding what to do. Zoo management concluded that a data visualization strategy was needed to address the problem.

---

[3] The authors are indebted to John Lucas of the Cincinnati Zoo and Botanical Garden for providing this application.

FIGURE 2.13 DATA DASHBOARD FOR THE CINCINNATI ZOO

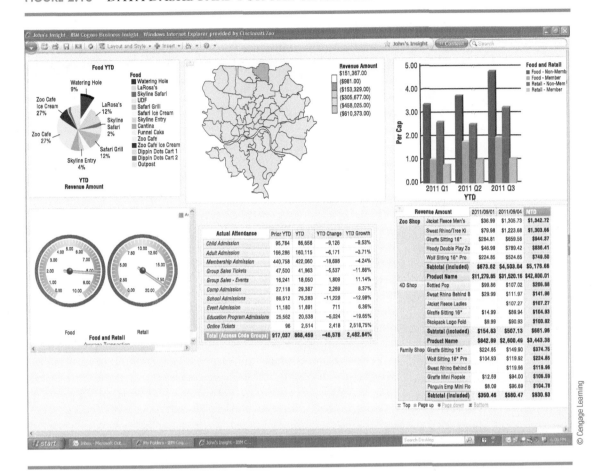

Because of its ease of use, real-time updating capability, and iPad compatibility, the Cincinnati Zoo decided to implement its data visualization strategy using IBM's Cognos advanced data visualization software. Using this software, the Cincinnati Zoo developed the data dashboard shown in Figure 2.13 to enable zoo management to track the following key performance indicators:

- Item Analysis (sales volumes and sales dollars by location within the zoo)
- Geo Analytics (using maps and displays of where the day's visitors are spending their time at the zoo)
- Customer Spending
- Cashier Sales Performance
- Sales and Attendance Data versus Weather Patterns
- Performance of the zoo's Loyalty Rewards Program

An iPad mobile application was also developed to enable the zoo's managers to be out on the grounds and still see and anticipate what is occurring on a real-time basis. The Cincinnati Zoo's iPad data dashboard, shown in Figure 2.14, provides managers with access to the following information:

- Real-time attendance data, including what "types" of guests are coming to the zoo
- Real-time analysis showing which items are selling the fastest inside the zoo
- Real-time geographical representation of where the zoo's visitors live

FIGURE 2.14   THE CINCINNATI ZOO iPAD DATA DASHBOARD

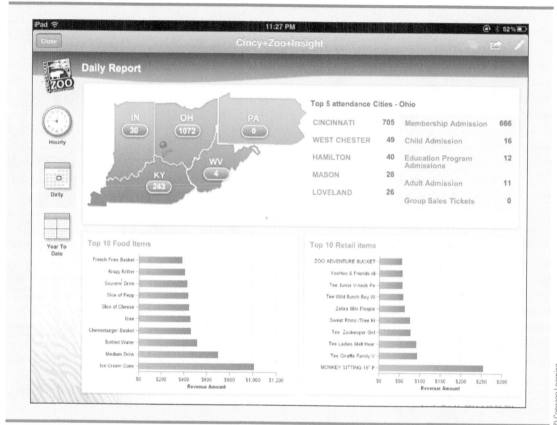

Having access to the data shown in Figures 2.13 and 2.14 allows the zoo managers to make better decisions on staffing levels within the zoo, which items to stock based upon weather and other conditions, and how to better target its advertising based on geodemographics.

The impact that data visualization has had on the zoo has been significant. Within the first year of use, the system has been directly responsible for revenue growth of over $500,000, increased visitation to the zoo, enhanced customer service, and reduced marketing costs.

NOTES AND COMMENTS

1. A variety of software is available for data visualization. Among the more popular packages are Cognos, JMP, Spotfire, and Tableau.
2. Radar charts and bubble charts are two other commonly used charts for displaying relationships between multiple variables. However, many experts in data visualization recommend against using these charts because they can be overcomplicated. Instead, the use of simpler displays such as bar charts and scatter diagrams is recommended.
3. A very powerful tool for visualizing geographic data is a Geographic Information System (GIS).

A GIS uses color, symbols, and text on a map to help you understand how variables are distributed geographically. For example, a company interested in trying to locate a new distribution center might wish to better understand how the demand for its product varies throughout the United States. A GIS can be used to map the demand where red regions indicate high demand, blue lower demand, and no color for regions where the product is not sold. Locations closer to red high-demand regions might be good candidate sites for further consideration.

Summary

A set of data, even if modest in size, is often difficult to interpret directly in the form in which it is gathered. Tabular and graphical displays can be used to summarize and present data so that patterns are revealed and the data are more easily interpreted. Frequency distributions, relative frequency distributions, percent frequency distributions, bar charts, and pie charts were presented as tabular and graphical displays for summarizing the data for a single categorical variable. Frequency distributions, relative frequency distributions, percent frequency distributions, histograms, cumulative frequency distributions, cumulative relative frequency distributions, cumulative percent frequency distributions, and stem-and-leaf displays were presented as ways of summarizing the data for a single quantitative variable.

A crosstabulation was presented as a tabular display for summarizing the data for two variables and a scatter diagram was introduced as a graphical display for summarizing the data for two quantitative variables. We also showed that side-by-side bar charts and stacked bar charts are just extensions of basic bar charts that can be used to display and compare two categorical variables. Guidelines for creating effective graphical displays and how to choose the most appropriate type of display were discussed. Data dashboards were introduced to illustrate how a set of visual displays can be developed that organizes and presents information that is used to monitor a company's performance in a manner that is easy to read, understand, and interpret. Figure 2.15 provides a summary of the tabular and graphical methods presented in this chapter.

FIGURE 2.15   TABULAR AND GRAPHICAL DISPLAYS FOR SUMMARIZING DATA

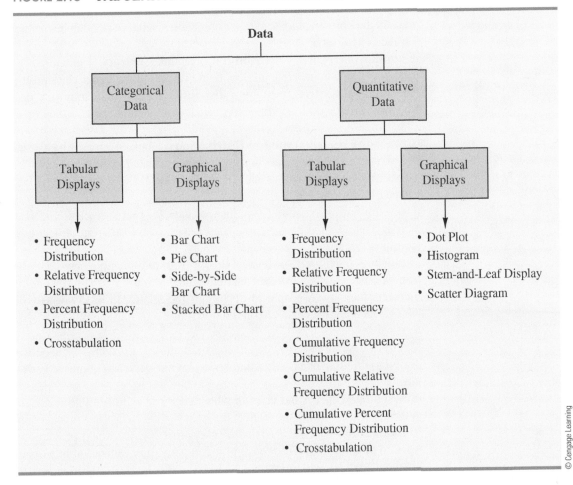

© Cengage Learning

With large data sets, computer software packages are essential in constructing tabular and graphical summaries of data. In the chapter appendixes, we show how Minitab, Excel, and StatTools can be used for this purpose.

Glossary

Categorical data Labels or names used to identify categories of like items.

Quantitative data Numerical values that indicate how much or how many.

Data visualization A term used to describe the use of graphical displays to summarize and present information about a data set.

Frequency distribution A tabular summary of data showing the number (frequency) of observations in each of several nonoverlapping categories or classes.

Relative frequency distribution A tabular summary of data showing the fraction or proportion of observations in each of several nonoverlapping categories or classes.

Percent frequency distribution A tabular summary of data showing the percentage of observations in each of several nonoverlapping classes.

Bar chart A graphical device for depicting categorical data that have been summarized in a frequency, relative frequency, or percent frequency distribution.

Pie chart A graphical device for presenting data summaries based on subdivision of a circle into sectors that correspond to the relative frequency for each class.

Class midpoint The value halfway between the lower and upper class limits.

Dot plot A graphical device that summarizes data by the number of dots above each data value on the horizontal axis.

Histogram A graphical display of a frequency distribution, relative frequency distribution, or percent frequency distribution of quantitative data constructed by placing the class intervals on the horizontal axis and the frequencies, relative frequencies, or percent frequencies on the vertical axis.

Cumulative frequency distribution A tabular summary of quantitative data showing the number of data values that are less than or equal to the upper class limit of each class.

Cumulative relative frequency distribution A tabular summary of quantitative data showing the fraction or proportion of data values that are less than or equal to the upper class limit of each class.

Cumulative percent frequency distribution A tabular summary of quantitative data showing the percentage of data values that are less than or equal to the upper class limit of each class.

Stem-and-leaf display A graphical display used to show simultaneously the rank order and shape of a distribution of data.

Crosstabulation A tabular summary of data for two variables. The classes for one variable are represented by the rows; the classes for the other variable are represented by the columns.

Simpson's paradox Conclusions drawn from two or more separate crosstabulations that can be reversed when the data are aggregated into a single crosstabulation.

Scatter diagram A graphical display of the relationship between two quantitative variables. One variable is shown on the horizontal axis and the other variable is shown on the vertical axis.

Trendline A line that provides an approximation of the relationship between two variables.

Side-by-side bar chart A graphical display for depicting multiple bar charts on the same display.

Stacked bar chart A bar chart in which each bar is broken into rectangular segments of a different color showing the relative frequency of each class in a manner similar to a pie chart.

Data dashboard A set of visual displays that organizes and presents information that is used to monitor the performance of a company or organization in a manner that is easy to read, understand, and interpret.

Key Formulas

Relative Frequency

$$\frac{\text{Frequency of the class}}{n} \qquad (2.1)$$

Approximate Class Width

$$\frac{\text{Largest data value} - \text{Smallest data value}}{\text{Number of classes}} \qquad (2.2)$$

Supplementary Exercises

44. Approximately 1.5 million high school students take the SAT each year and nearly 80% of the college and universities without open admissions policies use SAT scores in making admission decisions (College Board, March 2009). The current version of the SAT includes three parts: reading comprehension, mathematics, and writing. A perfect combined score for all three parts is 2400. A sample of SAT scores for the combined three-part SAT are as follows:

NewSAT

1665	1525	1355	1645	1780
1275	2135	1280	1060	1585
1650	1560	1150	1485	1990
1590	1880	1420	1755	1375
1475	1680	1440	1260	1730
1490	1560	940	1390	1175

a. Show a frequency distribution and histogram. Begin with the first class starting at 800 and use a class width of 200.
b. Comment on the shape of the distribution.
c. What other observations can be made about the SAT scores based on the tabular and graphical summaries?

45. The Pittsburgh Steelers defeated the Arizona Cardinals 27 to 23 in professional football's 43rd Super Bowl. With this win, its sixth championship, the Pittsburgh Steelers became the team with the most wins in the 43-year history of the event (*Tampa Tribune*, February 2,

SuperBowl

Super Bowl	State	Won By Points	Super Bowl	State	Won By Points	Super Bowl	State	Won By Points
1	CA	25	16	MI	5	31	LA	14
2	FL	19	17	CA	10	32	CA	7
3	FL	9	18	FL	19	33	FL	15
4	LA	16	19	CA	22	34	GA	7
5	FL	3	20	LA	36	35	FL	27
6	FL	21	21	CA	19	36	LA	3
7	CA	7	22	CA	32	37	CA	27
8	TX	17	23	FL	4	38	TX	3
9	LA	10	24	LA	45	39	FL	3
10	FL	4	25	FL	1	40	MI	11
11	CA	18	26	MN	13	41	FL	12
12	LA	17	27	CA	35	42	AZ	3
13	FL	4	28	GA	17	43	FL	4
14	CA	12	29	FL	23			
15	LA	17	30	AZ	10			

2009). The Super Bowl has been played in eight different states: Arizona (AZ), California (CA), Florida (FL), Georgia (GA), Louisiana (LA), Michigan (MI), Minnesota (MN), and Texas (TX). Data in the table show the state where the Super Bowls were played and the point margin of victory for the winning team.

a. Show a frequency distribution and bar chart for the state where the Super Bowl was played.

b. What conclusions can you draw from your summary in part (a)? What percentage of Super Bowls were played in the states of Florida or California? What percentage of Super Bowls were played in northern or cold-weather states?

c. Show a stretched stem-and-leaf display for the point margin of victory for the winning team. Show a histogram.

d. What conclusions can you draw from your summary in part (c)? What percentage of Super Bowls have been close games with the margin of victory less than 5 points? What percentage of Super Bowls have been won by 20 or more points?

e. The closest Super Bowl occurred when the New York Giants beat the Buffalo Bills. Where was this game played and what was the winning margin of victory? The biggest point margin in Super Bowl history occurred when the San Francisco 49ers beat the Denver Broncos. Where was this game played and what was the winning margin of victory?

46. Data showing the population by state in millions of people follow (*The World Almanac*, 2012).

WEB file

2012Population

State	Population	State	Population	State	Population
Alabama	4.8	Louisiana	4.5	Ohio	11.5
Alaska	0.7	Maine	1.3	Oklahoma	3.8
Arizona	6.4	Maryland	5.8	Oregon	4.3
Arkansas	2.9	Massachusetts	6.5	Pennsylvania	12.7
California	37.3	Michigan	9.9	Rhode Island	1.0
Colorado	5.0	Minnesota	5.3	South Carolina	4.6
Connecticut	3.6	Mississippi	3.0	South Dakota	0.8
Delaware	0.9	Missouri	6.0	Tennessee	6.3
Florida	18.8	Montana	0.9	Texas	25.1
Georgia	9.7	Nebraska	1.8	Utah	2.8
Hawaii	1.4	Nevada	2.7	Vermont	0.6
Idaho	1.6	New Hampshire	1.3	Virginia	8.0
Illinois	12.8	New Jersey	8.8	Washington	6.7
Indiana	6.5	New Mexico	2.0	West Virginia	1.9
Iowa	3.0	New York	19.4	Wisconsin	5.7
Kansas	2.9	North Carolina	9.5	Wyoming	0.6
Kentucky	4.3	North Dakota	0.7		

a. Develop a frequency distribution, a percent frequency distribution, and a histogram. Use a class width of 2.5 million.

b. Does there appear to be any skewness in the distribution? Explain.

c. What observations can you make about the population of the 50 states?

47. A startup company's ability to gain funding is a key to success. The funds raised (in millions of dollars) by 50 startup companies appear below (*The Wall Street Journal*, March 10, 2011).

StartUps

81	61	103	166	168
80	51	130	77	78
69	119	81	60	20
73	50	110	21	60
192	18	54	49	63

91	272	58	54	40
47	24	57	78	78
154	72	38	131	52
48	118	40	49	55
54	112	129	156	31

a. Construct a stem-and-leaf display.

b. Comment on the display.

48. Consumer complaints are frequently reported to the Better Business Bureau. In 2011, the industries with the most complaints to the Better Business Bureau were banks, cable and satellite television companies, collection agencies, cellular phone providers, and new car dealerships (*USA Today,* April 16, 2012). The results for a sample of 200 complaints are contained in the file BBB.

a. Show the frequency and percent frequency of complaints by industry.

b. Construct a bar chart of the percent frequency distribution.

c. Which industry had the highest number of complaints?

d. Comment on the percentage frequency distribution for complaints.

49. Dividend yield is the annual dividend paid by a company expressed as a percentage of the price of the stock (Dividend/Stock Price × 100). The dividend yield for the Dow Jones Industrial Average companies is shown in Table 2.17 (*The Wall Street Journal,* June 8, 2009).

a. Construct a frequency distribution and percent frequency distribution.

b. Construct a histogram.

c. Comment on the shape of the distribution.

d. What do the tabular and graphical summaries indicate about the dividend yields among the Dow Jones Industrial Average companies?

e. What company has the highest dividend yield? If the stock for this company currently sells for $14 per share and you purchase 500 shares, how much dividend income will this investment generate in one year?

50. The U.S Census Bureau estimates the characteristics of the U.S. population through a survey the bureau administers every 10 years. Below is a crosstabulation of age versus education level of achievement (U.S. Census Bureau website, March 9, 2013).

TABLE 2.17 DIVIDEND YIELD FOR DOW JONES INDUSTRIAL AVERAGE COMPANIES

Company	Dividend Yield %	Company	Dividend Yield %
3M	3.6	IBM	2.1
Alcoa	1.3	Intel	3.4
American Express	2.9	JPMorgan Chase	0.5
AT&T	6.6	Johnson & Johnson	3.6
Bank of America	0.4	Kraft Foods	4.4
Boeing	3.8	McDonald's	3.4
Caterpillar	4.7	Merck	5.5
Chevron	3.9	Microsoft	2.5
Cisco Systems	0.0	Pfizer	4.2
Coca-Cola	3.3	Procter & Gamble	3.4
DuPont	5.8	Travelers	3.0
ExxonMobil	2.4	United Technologies	2.9
General Electric	9.2	Verizon	6.3
Hewlett-Packard	0.9	Wal-Mart Stores	2.2
Home Depot	3.9	Walt Disney	1.5

Age	Below High School	High School Graduate	Some College No Degree	Associate's Degree	Bachelor's Degree	Advanced Degree	Total
25–34	4766	11,175	7765	3903	9860	3657	41,126
35–44	4732	11,568	6593	4166	8858	4530	40,447
45–54	4616	14,559	7413	4705	8434	4616	44,343
55–64	3681	11,079	6123	3256	6583	4637	35,359
65–74	3563	7418	3290	1383	2955	2326	20,935
75 & older	4344	6639	2472	812	2101	1289	17,657
Total	25,702	62,438	33,656	18,225	38,791	21,055	199,867

    a.   Calculate the row percentages.

    b.   Calculate the column percentages. Compare the percent frequency distributions for a Bachelor's Degree versus an Advanced Degree.

51.   Western University has only one women's softball scholarship remaining for the coming year. The final two players that Western is considering are Allison Fealey and Emily Janson. The coaching staff has concluded that the speed and defensive skills are virtually identical for the two players, and that the final decision will be based on which player has the best batting average. Crosstabulations of each player's batting performance in their junior and senior years of high school are as follows:

	Allison Fealey				Emily Janson	
Outcome	Junior	Senior		Outcome	Junior	Senior
Hit	15	75		Hit	70	35
No Hit	25	175		No Hit	130	85
Total At-Bats	40	250		Total At Bats	200	120

A player's batting average is computed by dividing the number of hits a player has by the total number of at-bats. Batting averages are represented as a decimal number with three places after the decimal.

    a.   Calculate the batting average for each player in her junior year. Then calculate the batting average of each player in her senior year. Using this analysis, which player should be awarded the scholarship? Explain.

    b.   Combine or aggregate the data for the junior and senior years into one crosstabulation as follows:

	Player	
Outcome	Fealey	Janson
Hit		
No Hit		
Total At-Bats		

Calculate each player's batting average for the combined two years. Using this analysis, which player should be awarded the scholarship? Explain.

    c.   Are the recommendations you made in parts (a) and (b) consistent? Explain any apparent inconsistencies.

52. *Fortune* magazine publishes an annual survey of the best companies to work for. The data in the file named FortuneBest shows the rank, company name, the size of the company, and the percentage job growth for full-time employees for the coming year for 98 companies (*Fortune* magazine website, February 25, 2013).

   a. Construct a crosstabulation with Job Growth (%) as the row variable and Size as the column variable. Use classes of -10 to -1, 0–9, 10–19 and so on for Growth Rate (%).

   b. Show the frequency distribution for Job Growth (%) and the frequency distribution for Size.

   c. Using the crosstabulation constructed in part (a), develop a crosstabulation showing column percentages.

   d. Using the crosstabulation constructed in part (a), develop a crosstabulation showing row percentages.

   e. Comment on the relationship between the percentage job growth for full-time employees and the size of the company.

53. Table 2.18 shows a portion of the data for a sample of 103 private colleges and universities. The complete data set is contained in the file named Colleges. The data include the name of the college or university, the year the institution was founded, the tuition and fees (not including room and board) for the most recent academic year, and the percentage of full-time, first-time bachelor's degree-seeking undergraduate students who obtain their degree in six years or less (*The World Almanac*, 2012)

   a. Construct a crosstabulation with Year Founded as the row variable and Tuition & Fees as the column variable. Use classes starting with 1600 and ending with 2000 in increments of 50 for Year Founded. For Tuition & Fees, use classes starting with 1 and ending with 45,000 in increments of 5000.

   b. Compute the row percentages for the crosstabulation in part (a).

   c. What relationship, if any, do you notice between Year Founded and Tuition & Fees?

54. Refer to the data set in Table 2.18.

   a. Construct a crosstabulation with Year Founded as the row variable and % Graduate as the column variable. Use classes starting with 1600 and ending with 2000 in increments of 50 for Year Founded. For % Graduate, use classes starting with 35% and ending with 100% in increments of 5%.

   b. Compute the row percentages for your crosstabulation in part (a).

   c. Comment on any relationship between the variables.

55. Refer to the data set in Table 2.18.

   a. Construct a scatter diagram to show the relationship between Year Founded and Tuition & Fees.

   b. Comment on any relationship between the variables.

TABLE 2.18   DATA FOR A SAMPLE OF PRIVATE COLLEGES AND UNIVERSITIES

School	Year Founded	Tuition & Fees	% Graduate
American University	1893	$36,697	79.00
Baylor University	1845	$29,754	70.00
Belmont University	1951	$23,680	68.00
.	.	.	.
.	.	.	.
.	.	.	.
Wofford College	1854	$31,710	82.00
Xavier University	1831	$29,970	79.00
Yale University	1701	$38,300	98.00

56. Refer to the data set in Table 2.18.
    a. Prepare a scatter diagram to show the relationship between Tuition & Fees and % Graduate.
    b. Comment on any relationship between the variables.

57. Google has changed its strategy with regard to how much and over which media it invests in advertising. The following table shows Google's marketing budget in millions of dollars for 2008 and 2011 (*The Wall Street Journal,* March 27, 2012).

	2008	2011
Internet	26.0	123.3
Newspaper, etc.	4.0	20.7
Television	0.0	69.3

   a. Construct a side-by-side bar chart with year as the variable on the horizontal axis. Comment on any trend in the display.
   b. Convert the above table to percentage allocation for each year. Construct a stacked bar chart with year as the variable on the horizontal axis.
   c. Is the display in part (a) or part (b) more insightful? Explain.

58. A zoo has categorized its visitors into three categories: member, school, and general. The member category refers to visitors who pay an annual fee to support the zoo. Members receive certain benefits such as discounts on merchandise and trips planned by the zoo. The school category includes faculty and students from day care and elementary and secondary schools; these visitors generally receive a discounted rate. The general category includes all other visitors. The zoo has been concerned about a recent drop in attendance. To help better understand attendance and membership, a zoo staff member has collected the following data:

Zoo

		Attendance		
Visitor Category	2008	2009	2010	2011
General	153,713	158,704	163,433	169,106
Member	115,523	104,795	98,437	81,217
School	82,885	79,876	81,970	81,290
Total	352,121	343,375	343,840	331,613

   a. Construct a bar chart of total attendance over time. Comment on any trend in the data.
   b. Construct a side-by-side bar chart showing attendance by visitor category with year as the variable on the horizontal axis.
   c. Comment on what is happening to zoo attendance based on the charts from parts (a) and (b).

Case Problem 1   Pelican Stores

Pelican Stores, a division of National Clothing, is a chain of women's apparel stores operating throughout the country. The chain recently ran a promotion in which discount coupons were sent to customers of other National Clothing stores. Data collected for a sample of 100 in-store credit card transactions at Pelican Stores during one day while the promotion was running are contained in the file named PelicanStores. Table 2.19 shows a portion of the data set. The Proprietary Card method of payment refers to charges made using a National Clothing charge card. Customers who made a purchase using a discount coupon are referred to as promotional customers and customers who made a purchase but did not use a discount coupon are referred to as regular customers. Because the promotional coupons were not

TABLE 2.19   DATA FOR A SAMPLE OF 100 CREDIT CARD PURCHASES AT PELICAN STORES

Customer	Type of Customer	Items	Net Sales	Method of Payment	Gender	Marital Status	Age
1	Regular	1	39.50	Discover	Male	Married	32
2	Promotional	1	102.40	Proprietary Card	Female	Married	36
3	Regular	1	22.50	Proprietary Card	Female	Married	32
4	Promotional	5	100.40	Proprietary Card	Female	Married	28
5	Regular	2	54.00	MasterCard	Female	Married	34
.	.	.	.	.	.	.	.
.	.	.	.	.	.	.	.
96	Regular	1	39.50	MasterCard	Female	Married	44
97	Promotional	9	253.00	Proprietary Card	Female	Married	30
98	Promotional	10	287.59	Proprietary Card	Female	Married	52
99	Promotional	2	47.60	Proprietary Card	Female	Married	30
100	Promotional	1	28.44	Proprietary Card	Female	Married	44

PelicanStores

© Cengage Learning

sent to regular Pelican Stores customers, management considers the sales made to people presenting the promotional coupons as sales it would not otherwise make. Of course, Pelican also hopes that the promotional customers will continue to shop at its stores.

Most of the variables shown in Table 2.19 are self-explanatory, but two of the variables require some clarification.

Items   The total number of items purchased
Net Sales   The total amount ($) charged to the credit card

Pelican's management would like to use this sample data to learn about its customer base and to evaluate the promotion involving discount coupons.

Managerial Report

Use the tabular and graphical methods of descriptive statistics to help management develop a customer profile and to evaluate the promotional campaign. At a minimum, your report should include the following:

1. Percent frequency distribution for key variables.
2. A bar chart or pie chart showing the number of customer purchases attributable to the method of payment.
3. A crosstabulation of type of customer (regular or promotional) versus net sales. Comment on any similarities or differences present.
4. A scatter diagram to explore the relationship between net sales and customer age.

Case Problem 2   Motion Picture Industry

The motion picture industry is a competitive business. More than 50 studios produce a total of 300 to 400 new motion pictures each year, and the financial success of each motion picture varies considerably. The opening weekend gross sales ($millions), the total gross sales ($millions), the number of theaters the movie was shown in, and the number of weeks the motion picture was in release are common variables used to measure the success of a motion picture. Data collected for the top 100 motion pictures produced in 2011 are

TABLE 2.20 PERFORMANCE DATA FOR 10 MOTION PICTURES

Motion Picture	Opening Gross Sales ($millions)	Total Gross Sales ($millions)	Number of Theaters	Weeks in Release
Harry Potter and the Deathly Hallows Part 2	169.19	381.01	4375	19
Transformers: Dark of the Moon	97.85	352.39	4088	15
The Twilight Saga: Breaking Dawn Part 1	138.12	281.29	4066	14
The Hangover Part II	85.95	254.46	3675	16
Pirates of the Caribbean: On Stranger Tides	90.15	241.07	4164	19
Fast Five	86.20	209.84	3793	15
Mission: Impossible— Ghost Protocol	12.79	208.55	3555	13
Cars 2	66.14	191.45	4115	25
Sherlock Holmes: A Game of Shadows	39.64	186.59	3703	13
Thor	65.72	181.03	3963	16

contained in the file named 2011Movies (Box Office Mojo, March 17, 2012). Table 2.20 shows the data for the first 10 motion pictures in this file.

Managerial Report

Use the tabular and graphical methods of descriptive statistics to learn how these variables contribute to the success of a motion picture. Include the following in your report.

1. Tabular and graphical summaries for each of the four variables along with a discussion of what each summary tells us about the motion picture industry.
2. A scatter diagram to explore the relationship between Total Gross Sales and Opening Weekend Gross Sales. Discuss.
3. A scatter diagram to explore the relationship between Total Gross Sales and Number of Theaters. Discuss.
4. A scatter diagram to explore the relationship between Total Gross Sales and Number of Weeks in Release. Discuss.

Appendix 2.1 Using Minitab for Tabular and Graphical Presentations

Minitab offers extensive capabilities for constructing tabular and graphical summaries of data. In this appendix we show how Minitab can be used to construct several graphical summaries and the tabular summary of a crosstabulation. The graphical methods presented include the dot plot, the histogram, the stem-and-leaf display, and the scatter diagram.

Dot Plot

Audit

We use the audit time data in Table 2.4 to demonstrate. The data are in column C1 of a Minitab worksheet. The following steps will generate a dot plot.

> **Step 1.** Select the **Graph** menu and choose **Dotplot**
> **Step 2.** Select **One Y, Simple** and click **OK**
> **Step 3.** When the Dotplot-One Y, Simple dialog box appears:
> > Enter C1 in the **Graph Variables** box
> > Click **OK**

Histogram

Audit

We show how to construct a histogram with frequencies on the vertical axis using the audit time data in Table 2.4. The data are in column C1 of a Minitab worksheet. The following steps will generate a histogram for audit times.

> **Step 1.** Select the **Graph** menu
> **Step 2.** Choose **Histogram**
> **Step 3.** When the Histograms dialog box appears:
> > Choose **Simple** and click **OK**
> **Step 4.** When the Histogram-Simple dialog box appears:
> > Enter C1 in the **Graph Variables** box
> > Click **OK**
> **Step 5.** When the Histogram appears:*
> > Position the mouse pointer over any one of the bars
> > Double-click
> **Step 6.** When the Edit Bars dialog box appears:
> > Click the **Binning** tab
> > Select **Cutpoint** for Interval Type
> > Select **Midpoint/Cutpoint positions** for Interval Definition
> > Enter 10:35/5 in the **Midpoint/Cutpoint positions** box
> > Click **OK**

Note that Minitab also provides the option of scaling the *x*-axis so that the numerical values appear at the midpoints of the histogram rectangles. If this option is desired, modify step 6 to include Select **Midpoint** for Interval Type and Enter 12:32/5 in the **Midpoint/ Cutpoint positions** box. These steps provide the same histogram with the midpoints of the histogram rectangles labeled 12, 17, 22, 27, and 32.

Stem-and-Leaf Display

ApTest

We use the aptitude test data in Table 2.8 to demonstrate the construction of a stem-and-leaf display. The data are in column C1 of a Minitab worksheet. The following steps will generate the stretched stem-and-leaf display shown in Section 2.3.

> **Step 1.** Select the **Graph** menu
> **Step 2.** Choose **Stem-and-Leaf**
> **Step 3.** When the Stem-and-Leaf dialog box appears:
> > Enter C1 in the **Graph Variables** box
> > Click **OK**

---

*Steps 5 and 6 are optional but are shown here to demonstrate user flexibility in displaying the histogram. The entry 10:35/5 in step 6 indicates that 10 is the starting value for the histogram, 35 is the ending value for the histogram, and 5 is the class width.

Scatter Diagram

Stereo

We use the stereo and sound equipment store data in Table 2.14 to demonstrate the construction of a scatter diagram. The weeks are numbered from 1 to 10 in column C1, the data for number of commercials are in column C2, and the data for sales are in column C3 of a Minitab worksheet. The following steps will generate the scatter diagram shown in Figure 2.7.

> **Step 1.** Select the **Graph** menu
> **Step 2.** Choose **Scatterplot**
> **Step 3.** Select **Simple** and click **OK**
> **Step 4.** When the Scatterplot-Simple dialog box appears:
> > Enter C3 under **Y variables** and C2 under **X variables**
> > Click **OK**

Crosstabulation

Restaurant

We use the data from Zagat's restaurant review, part of which is shown in Table 2.9, to demonstrate. The restaurants are numbered from 1 to 300 in column C1 of the Minitab worksheet. The quality ratings are in column C2, and the meal prices are in column C3.

Minitab can only create a crosstabulation for qualitative variables and meal price is a quantitative variable. So we need to first code the meal price data by specifying the class to which each meal price belongs. The following steps will code the meal price data to create four classes of meal price in column C4: $10–19, $20–29, $30–39, and $40–49.

> **Step 1.** Select the **Data** menu
> **Step 2.** Choose **Code**
> **Step 3.** Choose **Numeric to Text**
> **Step 4.** When the Code-Numeric to Text dialog box appears:
> > Enter C3 in the **Code data from columns** box
> > Enter C4 in the **Store coded data in columns** box
> > Enter 10:19 in the first **Original values** box and $10–19 in the adjacent **New** box
> > Enter 20:29 in the second **Original values** box and $20–29 in the adjacent **New** box
> > Enter 30:39 in the third **Original values** box and $30–39 in the adjacent **New** box
> > Enter 40:49 in the fourth **Original values** box and $40–49 in the adjacent **New** box
> > Click **OK**

For each meal price in column C3 the associated meal price category will now appear in column C4. We can now develop a crosstabulation for quality rating and the meal price categories by using the data in columns C2 and C4. The following steps will create a crosstabulation containing the same information as shown in Table 2.10.

> **Step 1.** Select the **Stat** menu
> **Step 2.** Choose **Tables**
> **Step 3.** Choose **Cross Tabulation and Chi-Square**
> **Step 4.** When the Cross Tabulation and Chi-Square dialog box appears:
> > Enter C2 in the **For rows** box and C4 in the **For columns** box
> > Select **Counts** under Display
> > Click **OK**

Appendix 2.2   Using Excel for Tabular and Graphical Presentations

Excel offers extensive capabilities for constructing tabular and graphical summaries of data. In this appendix, we show how Excel can be used to construct a frequency distribution, relative frequency distribution, percent frequency distribution, bar chart, pie chart, histogram, scatter diagram, crosstabulation, side-by-side bar chart, and stacked bar chart.

Using Excel to Construct a Frequency Distribution, a Relative Frequency Distribution, and a Percent Frequency Distribution

WEB file

SoftDrink

We can use Excel's Recommended PivotTables tool to construct a frequency distribution for the sample of 50 soft drink purchases. Open the file named SoftDrink. The data are in cell A2:A51 and a label is in cell A1.

The following steps describe how to use Excel's Recommended PivotTables tool to construct a frequency distribution for the sample of 50 soft drink purchases.

Step 1. Select any cell in the data set (cells A1:A51)
Step 2. Click **Insert** on the Ribbon
Step 3. In the **Tables Group** choose **Recommended PivotTables**; a preview showing the frequency distribution appears
Step 4. Click **OK**; the frequency distribution will appear in a new worksheet

The worksheet in Figure 2.16 shows the frequency distribution for the 50 soft drink purchases created using these steps. Also shown is the PivotTable Fields dialog box, a key component of every PivotTable report. We will discuss the use of the PivotTable Fields dialog box later in this appendix.

Editing options You can easily change the column headings in the frequency distribution output. For instance, to change the current heading in cell A3 (Row Labels) to "Soft Drink" click in cell A3 and type "Soft Drink"; to change the current heading in cell B3 (Count of Brand Purchases) to "Frequency," click in cell B3 and type "Frequency"; and to change the current heading in A9 (Grand Total) to "Total," click in cell A9 and type "Total." The foreground and background worksheets shown in Figure 2.17 contain the revised headings; in addition, the label "Relative Frequency" was entered into cell C3 and the label "Percent Frequency" was added into cell D3 to illustrate how to compute relative and percent frequency distributions.

Enter functions and formulas Refer to Figure 2.17 as we describe how to create the relative and percent frequency distributions for the soft drink purchases. The formula worksheet is in the background and the value worksheet is in the foreground. To compute the relative frequency for Coca-Cola using equation (2.1), we entered the formula =B4/$B$9 into cell C4; the result, 0.38, is the relative frequency for Coca-Cola. Copying cell C4 to cells C5:C8 computes the relative frequencies for each of the other soft drinks. To compute the percent frequency for Coca-Cola, we entered the formula =C4*100 into cell D4. The result, 38, indicates that 38% of the soft drink purchases were Coca-Cola. Copying cell D4 to cells D5:D8 computes the percent frequencies for each of the other soft drinks. To compute the total of the relative frequencies, we entered the formula =SUM(C4:C8) into cell C9. And to compute the total of the percent frequencies we copied cell C9 to cell C10.

FIGURE 2.16   FREQUENCY DISTRIBUTION OF SOFT DRINK PURCHASES
CONSTRUCTED USING EXCEL'S RECOMMENDED PIVOTTABLES TOOL

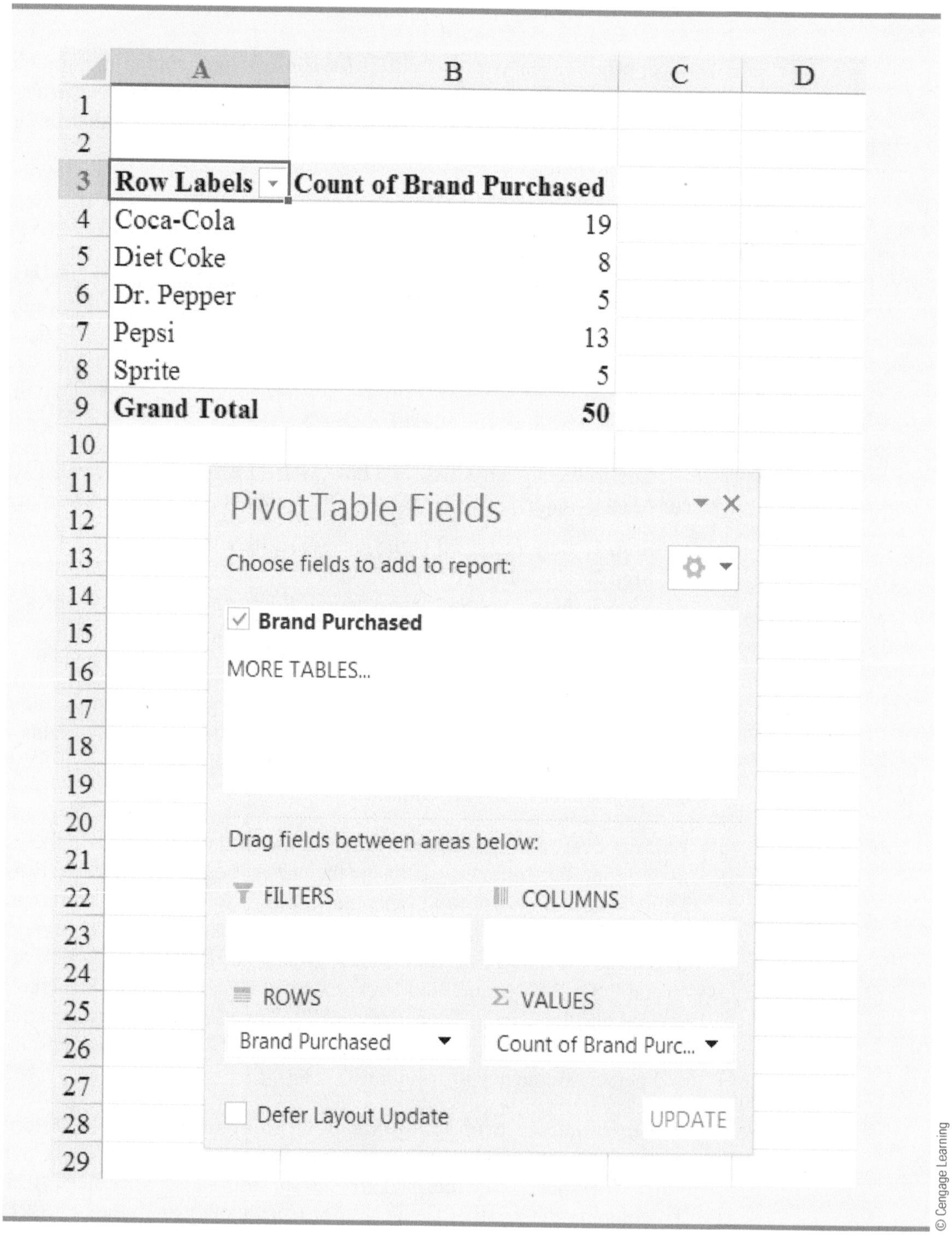

	A	B	C	D
1				
2				
3	**Row Labels** ▾	**Count of Brand Purchased**		
4	Coca-Cola	19		
5	Diet Coke	8		
6	Dr. Pepper	5		
7	Pepsi	13		
8	Sprite	5		
9	**Grand Total**	**50**		
10				

PivotTable Fields   ▾ ✕

Choose fields to add to report: ⚙ ▾

☑ **Brand Purchased**

MORE TABLES...

Drag fields between areas below:

▼ FILTERS   ▥ COLUMNS

≡ ROWS   Σ VALUES

Brand Purchased ▾   Count of Brand Purc... ▾

☐ Defer Layout Update   UPDATE

© Cengage Learning

Using Excel to Construct a Bar Chart and a Pie Chart

SoftDrink

We can use Excel's Recommended Charts tool to construct a bar chart and a pie chart for the sample of 50 soft drink purchases. Open the file named SoftDrink. The data are in cell A2:A51 and a label is in cell A1.

The following steps describe how to use Excel's Recommended Charts tool to construct a bar chart for the sample of 50 soft drink purchases.

FIGURE 2.17   RELATIVE FREQUENCY AND PERCENT FREQUENCY DISTRIBUTIONS OF SOFT DRINK PURCHASES CONSTRUCTED USING EXCEL FUNCTIONS

	A	B	C	D	E
1					
2					
3	**Soft Drink**	**Frequency**	**Relative Frequency**	**Percent Frequency**	
4	Coca-Cola	19	=B4/$B$9	=C4*100	
5	Diet Coke	8	=B5/$B$9	=C5*100	
6	Dr. Pepper	5	=B6/$B$9	=C6*100	
7	Pepsi	13	=B7/$B$9	=C7*100	
8	Sprite	5	=B8/$B$9	=C8*100	
9	**Total**	**50**	=SUM(C4:C8)	=SUM(D4:D8)	

	A	B	C	D	E
1					
2					
3	**Soft Drink**	**Frequency**	**Relative Frequency**	**Percent Frequency**	
4	Coca-Cola	19	0.38	38	
5	Diet Coke	8	0.16	16	
6	Dr. Pepper	5	0.1	10	
7	Pepsi	13	0.26	26	
8	Sprite	5	0.1	10	
9	**Total**	**50**	1	100	

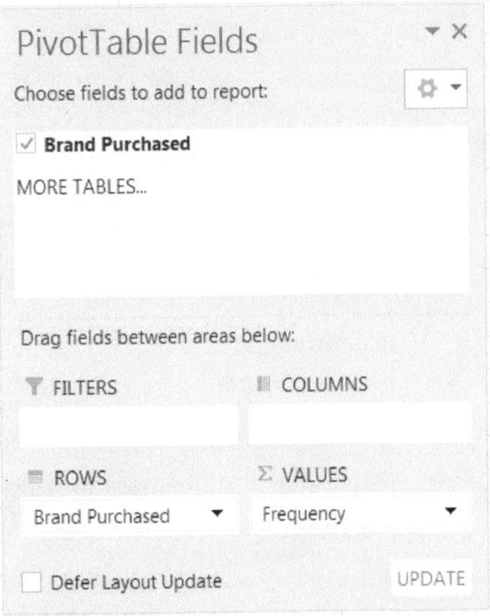

PivotTable Fields

Choose fields to add to report:

☑ **Brand Purchased**

MORE TABLES…

Drag fields between areas below:

▼ FILTERS   ‖ COLUMNS

≡ ROWS   Σ VALUES

Brand Purchased ▼   Frequency ▼

☐ Defer Layout Update   UPDATE

Step 1. Select any cell in the data set (cells A1:A51)

Step 2. Click **Insert** on the Ribbon

Step 3. In the **Charts Group** choose **Recommended Charts**; a preview showing the chart appears

Step 4. Click **OK**; the bar chart will appear in a new worksheet

Excel refers to the bar chart in Figure 2.18 as a Clustered Column chart.

The worksheet in Figure 2.18 shows the bar chart for the 50 soft drink purchases created using these steps. Also shown are the frequency distribution and PivotTable Fields dialog box that were created by Excel in order to construct the bar chart. Thus, using Excel's

FIGURE 2.18   BAR CHART OF SOFT DRINK PURCHASES CONSTRUCTED USING EXCEL'S RECOMMENDED CHARTS TOOL

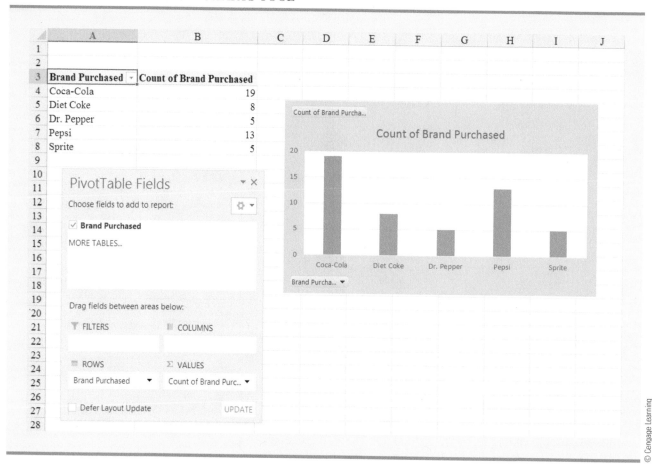

Recommended Charts tool you can construct a bar chart and a frequency distribution at the same time.

Editing options You can easily edit the bar chart to display a different chart title and add axis titles. For instance, suppose you would like to use "Bar Chart of Soft Drink Purchases" as the chart title and insert "Soft Drink" for the horizontal axis title and "Frequency" for the vertical axis title.

> **Step 1**. Click the **Chart Title** and replace it with **Bar Chart of Soft Drink Purchases**
>
> **Step 2.** Click the **Chart Elements** button ⊞ (located next to the top right corner of the chart)
>
> **Step 3.** When the list of chart elements appears:
> Click **Axis Titles** (creates placeholders for the axis titles)
>
> **Step 4**. Click the **Horizontal (Category) Axis Title** and replace it with **Soft Drink**
>
> **Step 5.** Click the **Vertical (Value) Axis Title** and replace it with **Frequency**

The edited bar chart is shown in Figure 2.19.

Creating a pie chart To display a pie chart, select the bar chart (by clicking anywhere in the chart) to display three tabs (**Analyze, Design**, and **Format**) located on the Ribbon under the heading **PivotChart Tools**. Click the **Design Tab** and choose the **Change Chart Type** option to display the Change Chart Type dialog box. Click the **Pie** option and then **OK** to display a pie chart of the soft drink purchases.

FIGURE 2.19   EDITED BAR CHART OF SOFT DRINK PURCHASES CONSTRUCTED USING EXCEL'S RECOMMENDED CHARTS TOOL

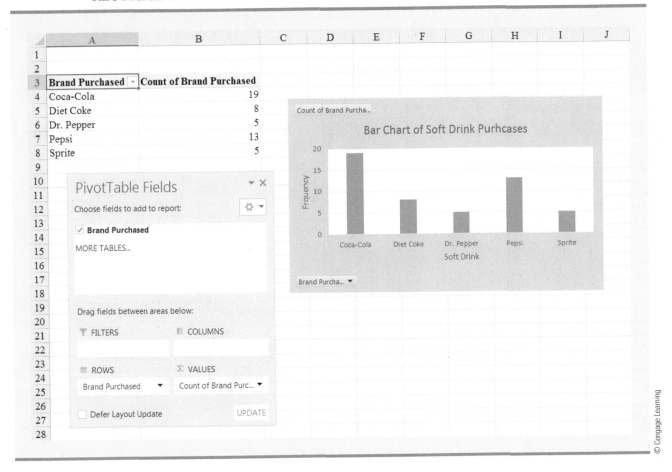

Using Excel to Construct a Frequency Distribution

Audit

Previously we illustrated how to use Excel's Recommended PivotTables tool to construct a frequency distribution. We can also use Excel's PivotTable tool directly to construct a frequency distribution. We illustrate this here for the audit time data. Open the file named Audit. The data are in cells A2:A21 and a label is in cell A1.

The following steps describe how to use Excel's PivotTable tool to construct a frequency distribution for the audit time data. When using Excel's PivotTable tool, each column of data is referred to as a field. Thus, for the audit time example, the data appearing in cells A2:A21 and the label in cell A1 are referred to as the Audit Time field.

Step 1. Select any cell in the data set (cells A1:A21)
Step 2. Click **Insert** on the Ribbon
Step 3. In the **Tables Group** choose **PivotTable**
Step 4. When the **Create PivotTable** dialog box appears:
      Click **OK**; a PivotTable and PivotTable Fields dialog box will appear in a new worksheet
Step 5. In the **PivotTable Fields** dialog box:
      Drag the **Audit Time** field to the **Rows** area
      Drag the **Audit Time** field to the **Values** area
Step 6. Click on **Sum of Audit Time** in the **Values** area

FIGURE 2.20   PIVOTTABLE FIELD LIST AND INITIAL PIVOTTABLE USED TO CONSTRUCT A FREQUENCY DISTRIBUTION FOR THE AUDIT TIME DATA

	A	B	C	D	E	F	G	H
1								
2								
3	**Row Labels** ▾	**Count of Audit Time**						
4	12	1						
5	13	1						
6	14	2						
7	15	2						
8	16	1						
9	17	1						
10	18	3						
11	19	1						
12	20	1						
13	21	1						
14	22	2						
15	23	1						
16	27	1						
17	28	1						
18	33	1						
19	**Grand Total**	**20**						
20								
21								
22								
23								

PivotTable Fields   ▾ ✕

Choose fields to add to report: ⚙ ▾

☑ **Audit Time**

MORE TABLES...

Drag fields between areas below:

▼ FILTERS   ‖‖ COLUMNS

☰ ROWS   Σ VALUES

Audit Time   ▾   Count of Audit Time ▾

☐ Defer Layout Update   UPDATE

Step 7. Click **Value Field Settings** from the list of options that appears

Step 8. When the Value Field Settings dialog box appears:

     Under **Summarize value field by**, choose **Count**

     Click **OK**

Figure 2.20 shows the resulting PivotTable Fields list and the corresponding PivotTable. To construct the frequency distribution shown in Table 2.5, we must group the rows containing the audit times. The resulting steps accomplish this.

Step 1. Right-click cell A4 in the PivotTable or any other cell containing an audit time

Step 2. Choose **Group** from the list of options that appears

Step 3. When the Grouping dialog box appears:

     Enter 10 in the **Starting at** box

     Enter 34 in the **Ending at** box

     Enter 5 in the **By** box

     Click **OK**

Figure 2.21 shows the completed PivotTable Fields list and the corresponding PivotTable. We see that with the exception of the column headings, the PivotTable provides the same information as the frequency distribution shown in Table 2.5.

Editing options You can easily change the labels in the PivotTable to match the labels in Table 2.5. For instance, to change the current heading in cell A3 (Row Labels) to "Audit

FIGURE 2.21   FREQUENCY DISTRIBUTION FOR THE AUDIT TIME DATA CONSTRUCTED USING EXCEL'S PIVOTTABLE TOOL

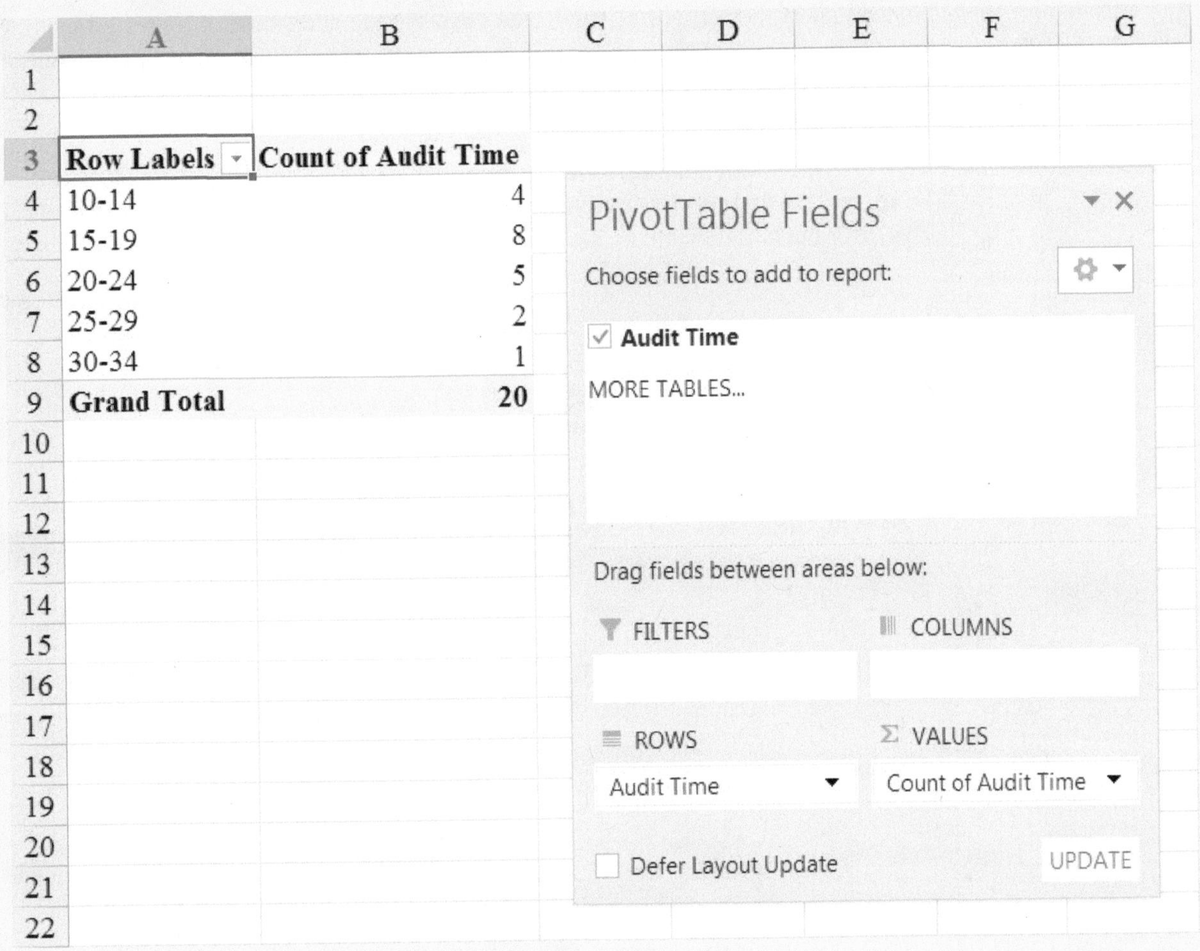

	A	B	C	D	E	F	G
1							
2							
3	**Row Labels** ⏷	**Count of Audit Time**					
4	10-14	4					
5	15-19	8					
6	20-24	5					
7	25-29	2					
8	30-34	1					
9	**Grand Total**	**20**					

PivotTable Fields ⏷ ✕

Choose fields to add to report: ⚙ ▾

☑ **Audit Time**

MORE TABLES...

Drag fields between areas below:

▼ FILTERS   ▥ COLUMNS

≡ ROWS   Σ VALUES

Audit Time ▾   Count of Audit Time ▾

☐ Defer Layout Update   UPDATE

The same Excel procedures we followed in the first section of this appendix can now be used to develop relative and percent frequency distributions, if desired.

Time (days)," click in cell A3 and type "Audit Time (days)"; to change the current heading in cell B3 (Count of Audit Time) to "Frequency," click in cell B3 and type "Frequency"; and to change the current heading in A9 (Grand Total) to "Total," click in cell A9 and type "Total."

Using Excel's Recommended Charts Tool to Construct a Histogram

In Figure 2.21 we showed the results of using Excel's PivotTable tool to construct a frequency distribution for the audit time data. We will use these results to illustrate how Excel's Recommended Charts tool can be used to construct a histogram for depicting quantitative data summarized in a frequency distribution. Refer to Figure 2.21 as we describe the steps involved.

The following steps describe how to use Excel's Recommended Charts tool to construct a histogram for the audit time data.

Step 1. Select any cell in the PivotTable report (cells A3:B9 in Figure 2.21)
Step 2. Click **Insert** on the Ribbon

Step 3. In the **Charts Group** choose **Recommended Charts**; a preview showing the chart appears

Step 4. Click **OK**

Excel refers to the bar chart in Figure 2.22 as a Clustered Column chart.

The worksheet in Figure 2.22 shows the chart for the audit time data created using these steps. With the exception of the gaps separating the bars, this resembles the histogram for the audit time data shown in Figure 2.5. We can easily edit this chart to remove the gaps between the bars and enter more descriptive axis labels and chart heading.

Editing options In addition to removing the gaps between the bars, suppose you would like to use "Histogram for Audit Time Data" as the chart title and insert "Audit Time (days)" for the horizontal axis title and "Frequency" for the vertical axis title.

Step 1. Right-click any bar in the chart and choose **Format Data Series** from the list of options that appear

Step 2. When the Format Data Series dialog box appears:

Go to the **Series Options** section

Set the **Gap Width** to 0

Click the **Close** button × at the top right of the dialog box

Step 3. Click the **Chart Title** and replace it with **Histogram for Audit Time Data**

Step 4. Click the **Chart Elements** button + (located next to the top right corner of the chart)

FIGURE 2.22   INITIAL CHART USED TO CONSTRUCT A HISTOGRAM FOR THE AUDIT TIME DATA

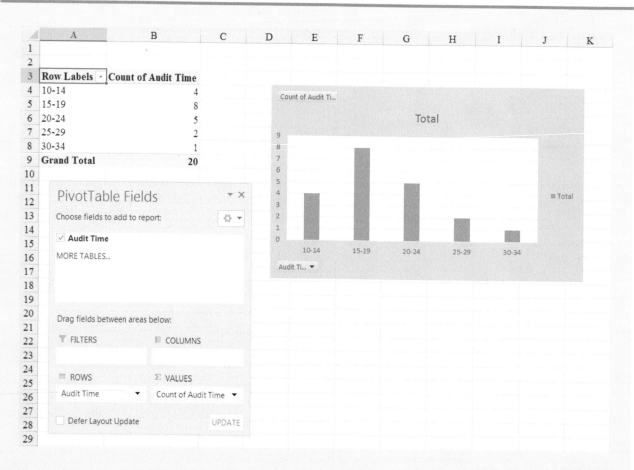

FIGURE 2.23   HISTOGRAM FOR THE AUDIT TIME DATA CREATED USING EXCEL'S RECOMMENDED CHARTS TOOL

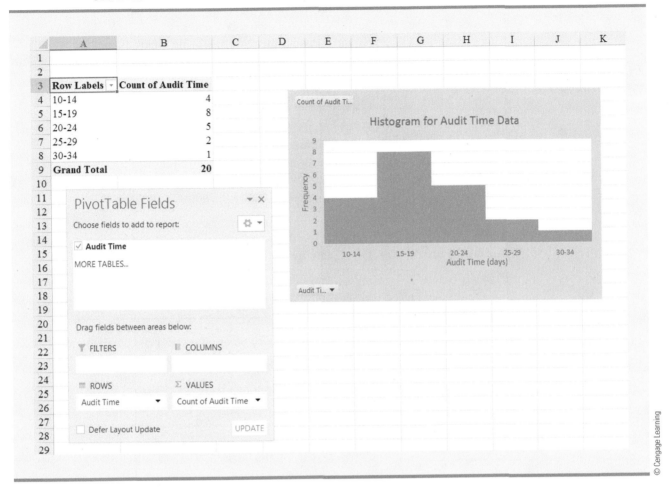

Step 5. When the list of chart elements appears:
   Click **Axis Titles** (creates placeholders for the axis titles)
   Click **Legends** to remove the check in the Legends box
Step 6. Click the **Horizontal (Category) Axis Title** and replace it with **Audit Time (days)**
Step 7. Click the **Vertical (Value) Axis Title** and replace it with **Frequency**

The edited histogram for the audit time is shown in Figure 2.23.

Using Excel's PivotTable Tool to Construct a Crosstabulation

Restaurant

Excel's PivotTable tool can be used to summarize the data for two or more variables simultaneously. We will illustrate the use of Excel's PivotTable tool by showing how to develop a crosstabulation of quality ratings and meal prices for the sample of 300 restaurants located in the Los Angeles area. Open the webfile Restaurant. The data are in cells B2:C301 and labels are in column A and cells B1:C1.

Each of the three columns in the Restaurant data set labeled, Restaurant, Quality Rating, and Meal Price ($), is considered a field by Excel. Fields may be chosen to represent rows, columns, or values in the PivotTable. The following steps describe how to use Excel's PivotTable tool to construct a crosstabulation of quality ratings and meal prices.

Step 1. Select cell A1 or any cell in the data set

Step 2. Click **Insert** on the Ribbon

Step 3. In the **Tables Group** choose **PivotTable**

Step 4. When the Create PivotTable dialog box appears:

Click **OK** and a PivotTable and PivotTable Fields dialog box will appear in a new worksheet

Step 5. In the **PivotTable Fields** dialog box:

Drag the **Quality Rating** field to the **Rows** area

Drag the **Meal Price** field to the **Columns** area

Drag the **Restaurant** field to the **Values** area

Step 6. Click on **Sum of Restaurant** in the **Values** area

Step 7. Click **Value Field Settings** from the list of options that appears

Step 8. When the Value Field Settings dialog box appears:

Under **Summarize value field by**, choose **Count**

Click **OK**

Figure 2.24 shows the PivotTable Fields list and the corresponding PivotTable created following the above steps. For readability, columns H:AC have been hidden.

Editing options   To complete the PivotTable we need to group the rows containing the meal prices and place the rows for quality rating in the proper order. The following steps accomplish this.

Step 1. Right-click cell B4 in the PivotTable or any other cell containing meal prices

Step 2. Choose **Group** from the list of options that appears

FIGURE 2.24   INITIAL PIVOTTABLE FIELDS DIALOG BOX AND PIVOTTABLE FOR THE RESTAURANT DATA

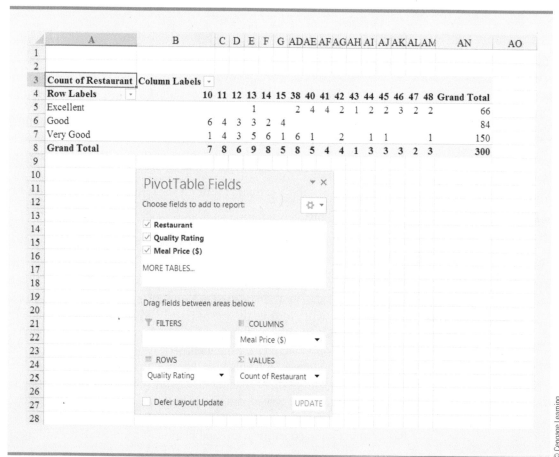

FIGURE 2.25   FINAL PIVOTTABLE FOR THE RESTAURANT DATA

	A	B	C	D	E	F	G
1							
2							
3	**Count of Restaurant**	**Column Labels** ▾					
4	**Row Labels** ▾	**10-19**	**20-29**	**30-39**	**40-49**	**Grand Total**	
5	Good		42	40	2		84
6	Very Good		34	64	46	6	150
7	Excellent		2	14	28	22	66
8	**Grand Total**		78	118	76	28	300
9							

PivotTable Fields   ▾ ✕

Choose fields to add to report: ⚙ ▾

☑ **Restaurant**
☑ **Quality Rating**
☑ **Meal Price ($)**

MORE TABLES...

Drag fields between areas below:

▼ FILTERS   ▥ COLUMNS
                   Meal Price ($)   ▼

▤ ROWS   Σ VALUES
Quality Rating ▼ Count of Restaurant ▼

☐ Defer Layout Update   UPDATE

© Cengage Learning

Step 3. When the Grouping dialog box appears:
　　　　Enter 10 in the **Starting at** box
　　　　Enter 49 in the **Ending at** box
　　　　Enter 10 in the **By** box
　　　　Click **OK**
Step 4. Right click on **Excellent** in cell A5
Step 5. Choose **Move** and click **Move "Excellent" to End**

The final PivotTable is shown in Figure 2.25. Note that it provides the same information as the crosstabulation shown in Table 2.10.

Using Excel's Charts Tool to Construct a Scatter Diagram and a Trendline

WEB file

Stereo

We can use Excel's Charts tool to construct a scatter diagram and a trendline for the stereo and sound equipment store data. Open the file named Stereo. The data are in cells B2:C11 and the labels are in column A and cells B1:C1.

　　The following steps describe how to use Excel's Charts tool to construct a scatter diagram from the data in the worksheet.

Step 1. Select cells B1:C11
Step 2. Click the **Insert** tab on the Ribbon
Step 3. In the **Charts Group**, click **Insert Scatter (X,Y)** or **Bubble Chart** ⬚ ▾

FIGURE 2.26   INITIAL SCATTER DIAGRAM FOR THE STEREO AND SOUND EQUIPMENT STORE USING EXCEL'S RECOMMENDED CHARTS TOOL

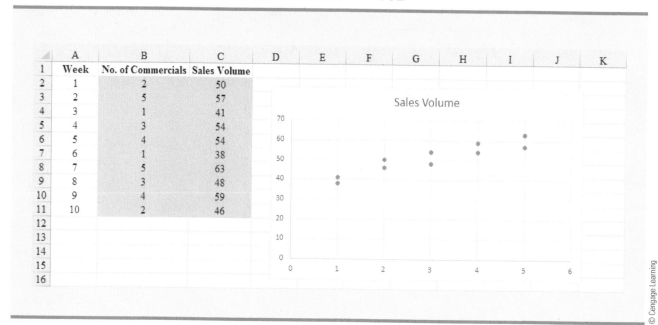

Step 4. When the list of scatter diagram subtypes appears:
Click **Scatter** (the chart in the upper left corner)

The worksheet in Figure 2.26 shows the scatter diagram produced using these steps.

Editing options You can easily edit the scatter diagram to display a different chart title, add axis titles, and display the trendline. For instance, suppose you would like to use "Scatter Diagram for the Stereo and Sound Equipment Store" as the chart title and insert "Number of Commercials" for the horizontal axis title and "Sales ($1000s)" for the vertical axis title.

Step 1. Click the **Chart Title** and replace it with **Scatter Diagram for the Stereo and Sound Equipment Store**
Step 2. Click the **Chart Elements** button ⊞ (located next to the top right corner of the chart)
Step 3. When the list of chart elements appears:
Click **Axis Titles** (creates placeholders for the axis titles)
Click **Gridlines** (to deselect the Gridlines option)
Click **Trendline**
Step 4. Click the **Horizontal (Value) Axis Title** and replace it with **Number of Commercials**
Step 5. Click the **Vertical (Value) Axis Title** and replace it with **Sales ($1000s)**
Step 6. To change the trendline from a dashed line to a solid line, right-click on the trendline and select the **Format Trendline** option
Step 7. When the Format Trendline dialog box appears:
Select the **Fill & Line** option ◇
In the **Dash type** box, select **Solid**
Close the Format Trendline dialog box

The edited scatter diagram and trendline are shown in Figure 2.27.

FIGURE 2.27   EDITED SCATTER DIAGRAM AND TRENDLINE FOR THE STEREO AND SOUND EQUIPMENT STORE USING EXCEL'S RECOMMENDED CHARTS TOOL

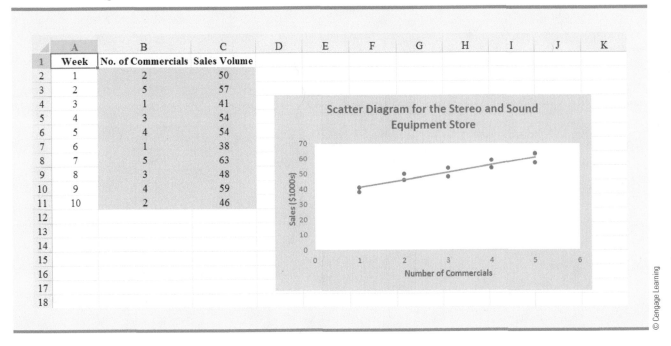

Using Excel's Recommended Charts Tool to Construct Side-by-Side and Stacked Bar Charts

In Figure 2.25 we showed the results of using Excel's PivotTable tool to construct a frequency distribution for the sample of 300 restaurants in the Los Angeles area. We will use these results to illustrate how Excel's Recommended Charts tool can be used to construct side-by-side and stacked bar charts for the restaurant data using the Pivot-Table output.

The following steps describe how to use Excel's Recommended Charts tool to construct a side-by-side bar chart for the restaurant data using the PivotTable tool output shown in Figure 2.25.

Step 1. Select any cell in the PivotTable report (cells A3:F8 in Figure 2.25)
Step 2. Click **Insert** on the Ribbon
Step 3. In the **Charts Group** choose **Recommended Charts**; a preview showing a bar chart with quality rating on the horizontal axis appears
Step 4. Click **OK**
Step 5. Click **Design** on the Ribbon (located below the PivotCharts Tools heading)
Step 6. In the **Data Group** choose **Switch Row/Column**; a bar chart with meal price on the horizontal axis appears

Excel refers to the bar chart in Figure 2.28 as a Clustered Column chart.

The worksheet in Figure 2.28 shows the side-by-side chart for the restaurant data created using these steps.

Editing options We can easily edit the side-by-side bar chart to enter a chart heading and axis labels. Suppose you would like to use "Side-by-Side Bar Chart" as the chart title, insert "Meal Price ($)" for the horizontal axis title, and insert "Frequency" for the vertical axis title.

FIGURE 2.28   SIDE-BY-SIDE CHART FOR THE RESTAURANT DATA CONSTRUCTED USING EXCEL'S RECOMMENDED CHARTS TOOL

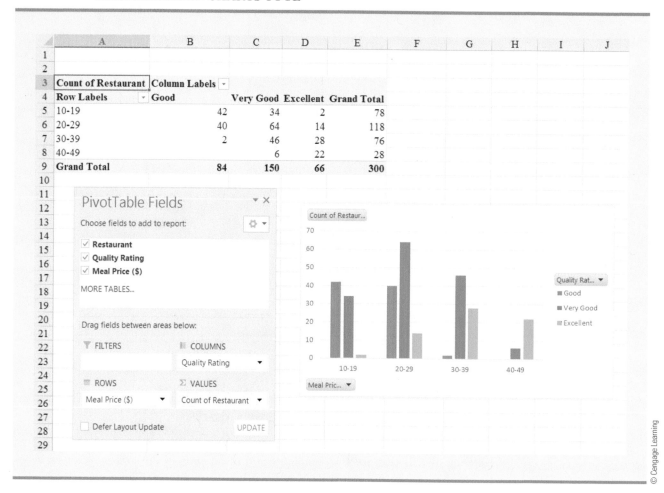

Step 1. Click the **Chart Elements** button ⊞ (located next to the top right corner of the chart)

Step 2. When the list of chart elements appears:
   Click **Chart Title** (creates placeholder for the chart title)
   Click **Axis Titles** (creates placeholders for the axis titles)

Step 3. Click the **Chart Title** and replace it with **Side-by-Side Bar Chart**

Step 4. Click the **Horizontal (Category) Axis Title** and replace it with **Meal Price ($)**

Step 5. Click the **Vertical (Value) Axis Title** and replace it with **Frequency**

The edited side-by-side chart is shown in Figure 2.29.

You can easily change the side-by-side bar chart to a stacked bar chart using the following steps.

Step 1. Click **Design** on the Ribbon

Step 2. In the **Type Group** click **Change Chart Type**

Step 3. When the Change Chart Type dialog box appears:
   Select the **Stacked Columns** option
   Click **OK**

Once you have created a side-by-side bar chart or a stacked bar chart, you can easily switch back and forth between the two chart types by reapplying steps 7 and 8.

FIGURE 2.29   EDITED SIDE-BY-SIDE CHART FOR THE RESTAURANT DATA CONSTRUCTED USING EXCEL'S RECOMMENDED CHARTS TOOL

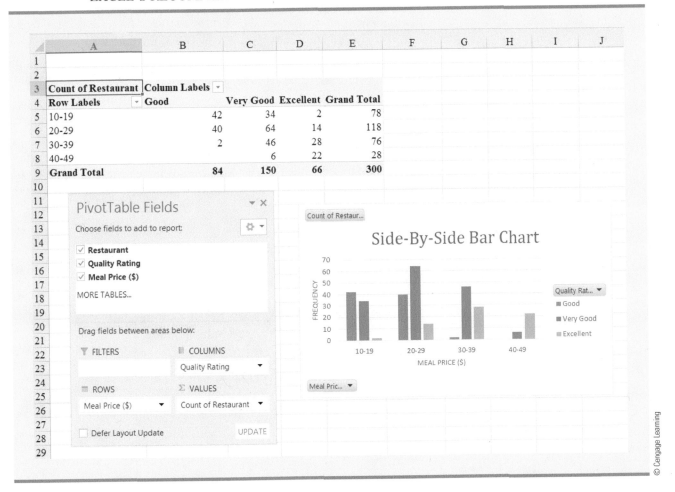

Appendix 2.3 Using StatTools for Tabular and Graphical Presentations

In this appendix we show how StatTools can be used to construct a histogram and a scatter diagram.

Histogram

We use the audit time data in Table 2.4 to illustrate. Begin by using the Data Set Manager to create a StatTools data set for these data using the procedure described in the appendix in Chapter 1. The following steps will generate a histogram.

Audit

Step 1. Click the **StatTools** tab on the Ribbon
Step 2. In the **Analyses Group,** click **Summary Graphs**
Step 3. Choose the **Histogram** option
Step 4. When the StatTools - Histogram dialog box appears:
　　In the **Variables** section, select **Audit Time**
　　In the **Options** section,
　　　Enter 5 in the **Number of Bins** box
　　　Enter 9.5 in the **Histogram Minimum** box

Enter 34.5 in the **Histogram Maximum** box
Choose **Categorical** in the **X-Axis** box
Choose **Frequency** in the **Y-Axis** box
Click **OK**

A histogram for the audit time data similar to the histogram shown in Figure 2.5 will appear. The only difference is the histogram developed using StatTools shows the class midpoints on the horizontal axis.

Scatter Diagram

Stereo

We use the stereo and sound equipment data in Table 2.14 to demonstrate the construction of a scatter diagram. Begin by using the Data Set Manager to create a StatTools data set for these data using the procedure described in the appendix in Chapter 1. The following steps will generate a scatter diagram.

Step 1. Click the **StatTools** tab on the Ribbon
Step 2. In the **Analyses Group,** click **Summary Graphs**
Step 3. Choose the **Scatterplot** option
Step 4. When the StatTools - Scatterplot dialog box appears:
      In the **Variables** section,
        In the column labeled **X**, select **No. of Commercials**
        In the column labeled **Y**, select **Sales Volume**
      Click **OK**

A scatter diagram similar to the one shown in Figure 2.26 will appear.

CHAPTER 3

Descriptive Statistics: Numerical Measures

CONTENTS

SMALL FRY DESIGN*
SANTA ANA, CALIFORNIA

Founded in 1997, Small Fry Design is a toy and accessory company that designs and imports products for infants. The company's product line includes teddy bears, mobiles, musical toys, rattles, and security blankets and features high-quality soft toy designs with an emphasis on color, texture, and sound. The products are designed in the United States and manufactured in China.

Small Fry Design uses independent representatives to sell the products to infant furnishing retailers, children's accessory and apparel stores, gift shops, upscale department stores, and major catalog companies. Currently, Small Fry Design products are distributed in more than 1000 retail outlets throughout the United States.

Cash flow management is one of the most critical activities in the day-to-day operation of this company. Ensuring sufficient incoming cash to meet both current and ongoing debt obligations can mean the difference between business success and failure. A critical factor in cash flow management is the analysis and control of accounts receivable. By measuring the average age and dollar value of outstanding invoices, management can predict cash availability and monitor changes in the status of accounts receivable. The company set the following goals: The average age for outstanding invoices should not exceed 45 days, and the dollar value of invoices more than 60 days old should not exceed 5% of the dollar value of all accounts receivable.

In a recent summary of accounts receivable status, the following descriptive statistics were provided for the age of outstanding invoices:

Mean	40 days
Median	35 days
Mode	31 days

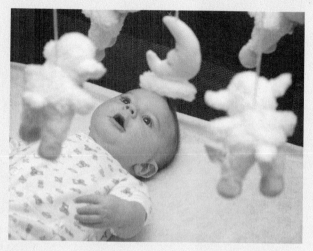

Small Fry Design uses descriptive statistics to monitor its accounts receivable and incoming cash flow. © Robert Dant/Alamy

Interpretation of these statistics shows that the mean or average age of an invoice is 40 days. The median shows that half of the invoices remain outstanding 35 days or more. The mode of 31 days, the most frequent invoice age, indicates that the most common length of time an invoice is outstanding is 31 days. The statistical summary also showed that only 3% of the dollar value of all accounts receivable was more than 60 days old. Based on the statistical information, management was satisfied that accounts receivable and incoming cash flow were under control.

In this chapter, you will learn how to compute and interpret some of the statistical measures used by Small Fry Design. In addition to the mean, median, and mode, you will learn about other descriptive statistics such as the range, variance, standard deviation, percentiles, and correlation. These numerical measures will assist in the understanding and interpretation of data.

*The authors are indebted to John A. McCarthy, President of Small Fry Design, for providing this Statistics in Practice.

In Chapter 2 we discussed tabular and graphical presentations used to summarize data. In this chapter, we present several numerical measures that provide additional alternatives for summarizing data.

We start by developing numerical summary measures for data sets consisting of a single variable. When a data set contains more than one variable, the same numerical measures can be computed separately for each variable. However, in the two-variable case, we will also develop measures of the relationship between the variables.

Numerical measures of location, dispersion, shape, and association are introduced. If the measures are computed for data from a sample, they are called **sample statistics**. If the measures are computed for data from a population, they are called **population parameters**. In statistical inference, a sample statistic is referred to as the **point estimator** of the corresponding population parameter. In Chapter 7 we will discuss in more detail the process of point estimation.

In the three chapter appendixes, we show how Minitab, Excel, and StatTools can be used to compute the numerical measures described in the chapter.

Measures of Location

Mean

The mean is sometimes referred to as the arithmetic mean.

Perhaps the most important measure of location is the **mean**, or average value, for a variable. The mean provides a measure of central location for the data. If the data are for a sample, the mean is denoted by $\bar{x}$; if the data are for a population, the mean is denoted by the Greek letter μ.

In statistical formulas, it is customary to denote the value of variable x for the first observation by x_1, the value of variable x for the second observation by x_2, and so on. In general, the value of variable x for the ith observation is denoted by x_i. For a sample with n observations, the formula for the sample mean is as follows.

The sample mean $\bar{x}$ is a sample statistic.

SAMPLE MEAN

$$\bar{x} = \frac{\sum x_i}{n} \tag{3.1}$$

In the preceding formula, the numerator is the sum of the values of the n observations. That is,

$$\sum x_i = x_1 + x_2 + \cdots + x_n$$

The Greek letter $\sum$ is the summation sign.

To illustrate the computation of a sample mean, let us consider the following class size data for a sample of five college classes.

$$46 \quad 54 \quad 42 \quad 46 \quad 32$$

We use the notation x_1, x_2, x_3, x_4, x_5 to represent the number of students in each of the five classes.

$$x_1 = 46 \qquad x_2 = 54 \qquad x_3 = 42 \qquad x_4 = 46 \qquad x_5 = 32$$

Hence, to compute the sample mean, we can write

$$\bar{x} = \frac{\sum x_i}{n} = \frac{x_1 + x_2 + x_3 + x_4 + x_5}{5} = \frac{46 + 54 + 42 + 46 + 32}{5} = 44$$

The sample mean class size is 44 students.

To provide a visual perspective of the mean and to show how it can be influenced by extreme values, consider the dot plot for the class size data shown in Figure 3.1. Treating the horizontal axis used to create the dot plot as a long narrow board in which each of the

FIGURE 3.1   THE MEAN AS THE CENTER OF BALANCE FOR THE DOT PLOT OF THE
CLASSROOM SIZE DATA

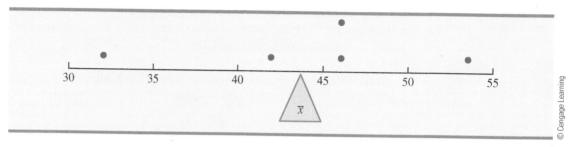

dots has the same fixed weight, the mean is the point at which we would place a fulcrum or
pivot point under the board in order to balance the dot plot. This is the same principle by
which a see-saw on a playground works, the only difference being that the see-saw is
pivoted in the middle so that as one end goes up, the other end goes down. In the dot plot
we are locating the pivot point based upon the location of the dots. Now consider what happens to the balance if we increase the largest value from 54 to 114. We will have to move
the fulcrum under the new dot plot in a positive direction in order to reestablish balance.
To determine how far we would have to shift the fulcrum, we simply compute the sample
mean for the revised class size data.

$$\bar{x} = \frac{\Sigma x_i}{n} = \frac{x_1 + x_2 + x_3 + x_4 + x_5}{5} = \frac{46 + 114 + 42 + 46 + 32}{5} = \frac{280}{5} = 56$$

Thus, the mean for the revised class size data is 56, an increase of 12 students. In other
words, we have to shift the balance point 12 units to the right to establish balance under the
new dot plot.

Another illustration of the computation of a sample mean is given in the following situation. Suppose that a college placement office sent a questionnaire to a sample of business
school graduates requesting information on monthly starting salaries. Table 3.1 shows the
collected data. The mean monthly starting salary for the sample of 12 business college
graduates is computed as

$$\bar{x} = \frac{\Sigma x_i}{n} = \frac{x_1 + x_2 + \cdots + x_{12}}{12}$$

$$= \frac{3850 + 3950 + \cdots + 3880}{12}$$

$$= \frac{47,280}{12} = 3940$$

TABLE 3.1   MONTHLY STARTING SALARIES FOR A SAMPLE OF 12 BUSINESS SCHOOL
GRADUATES

WEB file

2012StartSalary

Graduate	Monthly Starting Salary ($)	Graduate	Monthly Starting Salary ($)
1	3850	7	3890
2	3950	8	4130
3	4050	9	3940
4	3880	10	4325
5	3755	11	3920
6	3710	12	3880

Equation (3.1) shows how the mean is computed for a sample with n observations. The formula for computing the mean of a population remains the same, but we use different notation to indicate that we are working with the entire population. The number of observations in a population is denoted by N and the symbol for a population mean is μ.

The sample mean $\bar{x}$ is a point estimator of the population mean μ.

POPULATION MEAN

$$\mu = \frac{\sum x_i}{N} \qquad (3.2)$$

Weighted Mean

In the formulas for the sample mean and population mean, each x_i is given equal importance or weight. For instance, the formula for the sample mean can be written as follows:

$$\bar{x} = \frac{\sum x_i}{n} = \frac{1}{n}\left(\sum x_i\right) = \frac{1}{n}(x_1 + x_2 + \cdots + x_n) = \frac{1}{n}(x_1) + \frac{1}{n}(x_2) + \cdots + \frac{1}{n}(x_n)$$

This shows that each observation in the sample is given a weight of $1/n$. Although this practice is most common, in some instances the mean is computed by giving each observation a weight that reflects its relative importance. A mean computed in this manner is referred to as a **weighted mean**. The weighted mean is computed as follows.

WEIGHTED MEAN

$$\bar{x} = \frac{\sum w_i x_i}{\sum w_i} \qquad (3.3)$$

where

$$w_i = \text{weight for observation } i$$

When the data are from a sample, equation (3.3) provides the weighted sample mean. If the data are from a population, μ replaces $\bar{x}$ and equation (3.3) provides the weighted population mean.

As an example of the need for a weighted mean, consider the following sample of five purchases of a raw material over the past three months.

Purchase	Cost per Pound ($)	Number of Pounds
1	3.00	1200
2	3.40	500
3	2.80	2750
4	2.90	1000
5	3.25	800

Note that the cost per pound varies from $2.80 to $3.40, and the quantity purchased varies from 500 to 2750 pounds. Suppose that a manager wanted to know the mean cost per pound of the raw material. Because the quantities ordered vary, we must use the formula for a weighted mean. The five cost-per-pound data values are $x_1 = 3.00$, $x_2 = 3.40$, $x_3 = 2.80$, $x_4 = 2.90$, and $x_5 = 3.25$. The weighted mean cost per pound is found by weighting each cost by its corresponding quantity. For this example, the weights are $w_1 = 1200$, $w_2 = 500$, $w_3 = 2750$, $w_4 = 1000$, and $w_5 = 800$. Based on equation (3.3), the weighted mean is calculated as follows:

$$\bar{x} = \frac{1200(3.00) + 500(3.40) + 2750(2.80) + 1000(2.90) + 800(3.25)}{1200 + 500 + 2750 + 1000 + 800}$$

$$= \frac{18{,}500}{6250} = 2.96$$

Thus, the weighted mean computation shows that the mean cost per pound for the raw material is $2.96. Note that using equation (3.1) rather than the weighted mean formula in equation (3.3) would provide misleading results. In this case, the sample mean of the five cost-per-pound values is $(3.00 + 3.40 + 2.80 + 2.90 + 3.25)/5 = 15.35/5 = \$3.07$, which overstates the actual mean cost per pound purchased.

The choice of weights for a particular weighted mean computation depends upon the application. An example that is well known to college students is the computation of a grade point average (GPA). In this computation, the data values generally used are 4 for an A grade, 3 for a B grade, 2 for a C grade, 1 for a D grade, and 0 for an F grade. The weights are the number of credit hours earned for each grade. Exercise 16 at the end of this section provides an example of this weighted mean computation. In other weighted mean computations, quantities such as pounds, dollars, or volume are frequently used as weights. In any case, when observations vary in importance, the analyst must choose the weight that best reflects the importance of each observation in the determination of the mean.

Median

The **median** is another measure of central location. The median is the value in the middle when the data are arranged in ascending order (smallest value to largest value). With an odd number of observations, the median is the middle value. An even number of observations has no single middle value. In this case, we follow convention and define the median as the average of the values for the middle two observations. For convenience the definition of the median is restated as follows.

MEDIAN

Arrange the data in ascending order (smallest value to largest value).

(a) For an odd number of observations, the median is the middle value.
(b) For an even number of observations, the median is the average of the two middle values.

Let us apply this definition to compute the median class size for the sample of five college classes. Arranging the data in ascending order provides the following list.

32   42   46   46   54

Because $n = 5$ is odd, the median is the middle value. Thus the median class size is 46 students. Even though this data set contains two observations with values of 46, each observation is treated separately when we arrange the data in ascending order.

Suppose we also compute the median starting salary for the 12 business college graduates in Table 3.1. We first arrange the data in ascending order.

3710 3755 3850 3880 3880 3890 3920 3940 3950 4050 4130 4325

Middle Two Values

Because $n = 12$ is even, we identify the middle two values: 3890 and 3920. The median is the average of these values.

$$\text{Median} = \frac{3890 + 3920}{2} = 3905$$

The procedure we used to compute the median depends upon whether there is an odd number of observations or an even number of observations. Let us now describe a more conceptual and visual approach using the monthly starting salary for the 12 business college graduates. As before, we begin by arranging the data in ascending order.

3710 3755 3850 3880 3880 3890 3920 3940 3950 4050 4130 4325

Once the data are in ascending order, we trim pairs of extreme high and low values until no further pairs of values can be trimmed without completely eliminating all the data. For instance, after trimming the lowest observation (3710) and the highest observation (4325) we obtain a new data set with 10 observations.

3710 3755 3850 3880 3880 3890 3920 3940 3950 4050 4130 4325

We then trim the next lowest remaining value (3755) and the next highest remaining value (4130) to produce a new data set with eight observations.

3710 3755 3850 3880 3880 3890 3920 3940 3950 4050 4130 4325

Continuing this process we obtain the following results.

3710 3755 3850 3880 3880 3890 3920 3940 3950 4050 4130 4325
3710 3755 3850 3880 3880 3890 3920 3940 3950 4050 4130 4325
3710 3755 3850 3880 3880 3890 3920 3940 3950 4050 4130 4325

At this point no further trimming is possible without eliminating all the data. So, the median is just the average of the remaining two values. When there is an even number of observations, the trimming process will always result in two remaining values, and the average of these values will be the median. When there is an odd number of observations, the trimming process will always result in one final value, and this value will be the median. Thus, this method works whether the number of observations is odd or even.

The median is the measure of location most often reported for annual income and property value data because a few extremely large incomes or property values can inflate the mean. In such cases, the median is the preferred measure of central location.

Although the mean is the more commonly used measure of central location, in some situations the median is preferred. The mean is influenced by extremely small and large data values. For instance, suppose that the highest paid graduate (see Table 3.1) had a starting salary of $10,000 per month (maybe the individual's family owns the company). If we change the highest monthly starting salary in Table 3.1 from $4325 to $10,000 and re-compute the mean, the sample mean changes from $3940 to $4413. The median of $3905, however, is unchanged, because $3890 and $3920 are still the middle two values. With the extremely high starting salary included, the median provides a better measure of central location than the mean. We can generalize to say that whenever a data set contains extreme values, the median is often the preferred measure of central location.

Geometric Mean

The **geometric mean** is a measure of location that is calculated by finding the nth root of the product of n values. The general formula for the geometric mean, denoted $\bar{x}_g$, follows.

GEOMETRIC MEAN

$$\bar{x}_g = \sqrt[n]{(x_1)(x_2)\cdots(x_n)} = [(x_1)(x_2)\cdots(x_n)]^{1/n} \qquad (3.4)$$

The geometric mean is often used in analyzing growth rates in financial data. In these types of situations the arithmetic mean or average value will provide misleading results.

To illustrate the use of the geometric mean, consider Table 3.2, which shows the percentage annual returns, or growth rates, for a mutual fund over the past 10 years. Suppose we want to compute how much $100 invested in the fund at the beginning of year 1 would be worth at the end of year 10. Let's start by computing the balance in the fund at the end of year 1. Because the percentage annual return for year 1 was -22.1%, the balance in the fund at the end of year 1 would be

$$\$100 - .221(\$100) = \$100(1 - .221) = \$100(.779) = \$77.90$$

The growth factor for each year is 1 plus .01 times the percentage return. A growth factor less than 1 indicates negative growth, while a growth factor greater than 1 indicates positive growth. The growth factor cannot be less than zero.

Note that .779 is identified as the growth factor for year 1 in Table 3.2. This result shows that we can compute the balance at the end of year 1 by multiplying the value invested in the fund at the beginning of year 1 times the growth factor for year 1.

The balance in the fund at the end of year 1, $77.90, now becomes the beginning balance in year 2. So, with a percentage annual return for year 2 of 28.7%, the balance at the end of year 2 would be

$$\$77.90 + .287(\$77.90) = \$77.90(1 + .287) = \$77.90(1.287) = \$100.2573$$

Note that 1.287 is the growth factor for year 2. And, by substituting $100(.779) for $77.90 we see that the balance in the fund at the end of year 2 is

$$\$100(.779)(1.287) = \$100.2573$$

In other words, the balance at the end of year 2 is just the initial investment at the beginning of year 1 times the product of the first two growth factors. This result can be generalized to

TABLE 3.2   PERCENTAGE ANNUAL RETURNS AND GROWTH FACTORS FOR THE MUTUAL FUND DATA

Year	Return (%)	Growth Factor
1	−22.1	0.779
2	28.7	1.287
3	10.9	1.109
4	4.9	1.049
5	15.8	1.158
6	5.5	1.055
7	−37.0	0.630
8	26.5	1.265
9	15.1	1.151
10	2.1	1.021

show that the balance at the end of year 10 is the initial investment times the product of all 10 growth factors.

$$\$100\big[(.779)(1.287)(1.109)(1.049)(1.158)(1.055)(.630)(1.265)(1.151)(1.021)\big] =$$

$$\$100(1.334493) = \$133.4493$$

The nth root can be computed using most calculators or by using the POWER function in Excel. For instance, using Excel, the 10th root of 1.334493 = POWER (1.334493,1/10) or 1.029275.

So, a \$100 investment in the fund at the beginning of year 1 would be worth \$133.4493 at the end of year 10. Note that the product of the 10 growth factors is 1.334493. Thus, we can compute the balance at the end of year 10 for any amount of money invested at the beginning of year 1 by multiplying the value of the initial investment times 1.334493. For instance, an initial investment of \$2500 at the beginning of year 1 would be worth \$2500(1.334493) or approximately \$3336 at the end of year 10.

But what was the mean percentage annual return or mean rate of growth for this investment over the 10-year period? Let us see how the geometric mean of the 10 growth factors can be used to answer to this question. Because the product of the 10 growth factors is 1.334493, the geometric mean is the 10th root of 1.334493 or

$$\bar{x}_g = \sqrt[10]{1.334493} = 1.029275$$

The geometric mean tells us that annual returns grew at an average annual rate of $(1.029275 - 1)100\%$ or 2.9275%. In other words, with an average annual growth rate of 2.9275%, a \$100 investment in the fund at the beginning of year 1 would grow to $\$100(1.029275)^{10} = \$133.4493$ at the end of 10 years.

It is important to understand that the arithmetic mean of the percentage annual returns does not provide the mean annual growth rate for this investment. The sum of the 10 annual percentage returns in Table 3.2 is 50.4. Thus, the arithmetic mean of the 10 percentage annual returns is 50.4/10 = 5.04%. A broker might try to convince you to invest in this fund by stating that the mean annual percentage return was 5.04%. Such a statement is not only misleading, it is inaccurate. A mean annual percentage return of 5.04% corresponds to an average growth factor of 1.0504. So, if the average growth factor were really 1.0504, \$100 invested in the fund at the beginning of year 1 would have grown to $\$100(1.0504)^{10} = \$163.51$ at the end of 10 years. But, using the 10 annual percentage returns in Table 3.2, we showed that an initial \$100 investment is worth \$133.45 at the end of 10 years. The broker's claim that the mean annual percentage return is 5.04% grossly overstates the true growth for this mutual fund. The problem is that the sample mean is only appropriate for an additive process. For a multiplicative process, such as applications involving growth rates, the geometric mean is the appropriate measure of location.

While the applications of the geometric mean to problems in finance, investments, and banking are particularly common, the geometric mean should be applied any time you want to determine the mean rate of change over several successive periods. Other common applications include changes in populations of species, crop yields, pollution levels, and birth and death rates. Also note that the geometric mean can be applied to changes that occur over any number of successive periods of any length. In addition to annual changes, the geometric mean is often applied to find the mean rate of change over quarters, months, weeks, and even days.

Mode

Another measure of location is the **mode**. The mode is defined as follows.

MODE

The mode is the value that occurs with greatest frequency.

To illustrate the identification of the mode, consider the sample of five class sizes. The only value that occurs more than once is 46. Because this value, occurring with a frequency of 2, has the greatest frequency, it is the mode. As another illustration, consider the sample of starting salaries for the business school graduates. The only monthly starting salary that occurs more than once is $3880. Because this value has the greatest frequency, it is the mode.

Situations can arise for which the greatest frequency occurs at two or more different values. In these instances more than one mode exists. If the data contain exactly two modes, we say that the data are *bimodal*. If data contain more than two modes, we say that the data are *multimodal*. In multimodal cases the mode is almost never reported because listing three or more modes would not be particularly helpful in describing a location for the data.

Percentiles

A **percentile** provides information about how the data are spread over the interval from the smallest value to the largest value. For data that do not contain numerous repeated values, the *p*th percentile divides the data into two parts. Approximately *p* percent of the observations have values less than the *p*th percentile; approximately $(100 - p)$ percent of the observations have values greater than the *p*th percentile. The *p*th percentile is formally defined as follows.

PERCENTILE

The *p*th percentile is a value such that *at least p* percent of the observations are less than or equal to this value and *at least* $(100 - p)$ percent of the observations are greater than or equal to this value.

Colleges and universities frequently report admission test scores in terms of percentiles. For instance, suppose an applicant obtains a raw score of 54 on the verbal portion of an admission test. How this student performed in relation to other students taking the same test may not be readily apparent. However, if the raw score of 54 corresponds to the 70th percentile, we know that approximately 70% of the students scored lower than this individual and approximately 30% of the students scored higher than this individual.

The following procedure can be used to compute the *p*th percentile.

CALCULATING THE *p*TH PERCENTILE

Step 1. Arrange the data in ascending order (smallest value to largest value).
Step 2. Compute an index *i*

Following these steps makes it easy to calculate percentiles.

$$i = \left(\frac{p}{100}\right)n$$

where *p* is the percentile of interest and *n* is the number of observations.
Step 3. (a) If *i* is *not an integer, round up.* The next integer *greater* than *i* denotes the position of the *p*th percentile.
   (b) If *i is an integer,* the *p*th percentile is the average of the values in positions *i* and $i + 1$.

As an illustration of this procedure, let us determine the 85th percentile for the starting salary data in Table 3.1.

Step 1. Arrange the data in ascending order.

3710 3755 3850 3880 3880 3890 3920 3940 3950 4050 4130 4325

Step 2.

$$i = \left(\frac{p}{100}\right)n = \left(\frac{85}{100}\right)12 = 10.2$$

Step 3. Because i is not an integer, *round up*. The position of the 85th percentile is the next integer greater than 10.2, the 11th position.

Returning to the data, we see that the 85th percentile is the data value in the 11th position, or 4130.

As another illustration of this procedure, let us consider the calculation of the 50th percentile for the starting salary data. Applying step 2, we obtain

$$i = \left(\frac{50}{100}\right)12 = 6$$

Because i is an integer, step 3(b) states that the 50th percentile is the average of the sixth and seventh data values; thus the 50th percentile is $(3890 + 3920)/2 = 3905$. Note that the *50th percentile is also the median.*

Quartiles

Quartiles are just specific percentiles; thus, the steps for computing percentiles can be applied directly in the computation of quartiles.

It is often desirable to divide data into four parts, with each part containing approximately one-fourth, or 25% of the observations. The division points are referred to as the **quartiles** and are defined as

Q_1 = first quartile, or 25th percentile

Q_2 = second quartile, or 50th percentile (also the median)

Q_3 = third quartile, or 75th percentile.

To compute the quartiles for the starting salary data, we begin by arranging the data in ascending order.

3710 3755 3850 3880 3880 3890 3920 3940 3950 4050 4130 4325

We already identified Q_2, the second quartile (median), as 3905. The computations of quartiles Q_1 and Q_3 require the use of the rule for finding the 25th and 75th percentiles. These calculations follow.

For Q_1,

$$i = \left(\frac{p}{100}\right)n = \left(\frac{25}{100}\right)12 = 3$$

Because i is an integer, step 3(b) indicates that the first quartile, or 25th percentile, is the average of the third and fourth data values; thus, $Q_1 = (3850 + 3880)/2 = 3865$.

For Q_3,

$$i = \left(\frac{p}{100}\right)n = \left(\frac{75}{100}\right)12 = 9$$

Again, because i is an integer, step 3(b) indicates that the third quartile, or 75th percentile, is the average of the ninth and tenth data values; thus, $Q_3 = (3950 + 4050)/2 = 4000$.

The quartiles divide the starting salary data into four parts, with each part containing 25% of the observations.

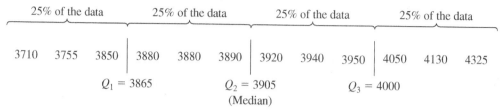

25% of the data	25% of the data	25% of the data	25% of the data

| 3710 | 3755 | 3850 | 3880 | 3880 | 3890 | 3920 | 3940 | 3950 | 4050 | 4130 | 4325 |

$Q_1 = 3865$ $Q_2 = 3905$ $Q_3 = 4000$
                          (Median)

We defined the quartiles as the 25th, 50th, and 75th percentiles. Thus, we computed the quartiles in the same way as percentiles. However, other conventions are sometimes used to compute quartiles, and the actual values reported for quartiles may vary slightly depending on the convention used. Nevertheless, the objective of all procedures for computing quartiles is to divide the data into four equal parts.

NOTES AND COMMENTS

1. It is better to use the median than the mean as a measure of central location when a data set contains extreme values. Another measure that is sometimes used when extreme values are present is the trimmed mean. The trimmed mean is obtained by deleting a percentage of the smallest and largest values from a data set and then computing the mean of the remaining values. For example, the 5% trimmed mean is obtained by removing the smallest 5% and the largest 5% of the data values and then computing the mean of the remaining values. Using the sample with $n = 12$ starting salaries, $0.05(12) = 0.6$. Rounding this value to 1 indicates that the 5% trimmed mean is obtained by removing the smallest data value and the largest data value and then computing the mean of the remaining 10 values. For the starting salary data, the 5% trimmed mean is 3924.50.

2. Other commonly used percentiles are the quintiles (the 20th, 40th, 60th, and 80th percentiles) and the deciles (the 10th, 20th, 30th, 40th, 50th, 60th, 70th, 80th, and 90th percentiles).

Exercises

Methods

1. Consider a sample with data values of 10, 20, 12, 17, and 16. Compute the mean and median.
2. Consider a sample with data values of 10, 20, 21, 17, 16, and 12. Compute the mean and median.
3. Consider the following data and corresponding weights.

x_i	Weight (w_i)
3.2	6
2.0	3
2.5	2
5.0	8

a. Compute the weighted mean.
b. Compute the sample mean of the four data values without weighting. Note the difference in the results provided by the two computations.

4.   Consider the following data.

Period	Rate of Return (%)
1	−6.0
2	−8.0
3	−4.0
4	2.0
5	5.4

What is the mean growth rate over these five periods?

5.   Consider a sample with data values of 27, 25, 20, 15, 30, 34, 28, and 25. Compute the 20th, 25th, 65th, and 75th percentiles.

6.   Consider a sample with data values of 53, 55, 70, 58, 64, 57, 53, 69, 57, 68, and 53. Compute the mean, median, and mode.

Applications

7.   The average number of minutes Americans commute to work is 27.7 minutes (*Sterling's Best Places*, April 13, 2012). The average commute time in minutes for 48 cities are as follows:

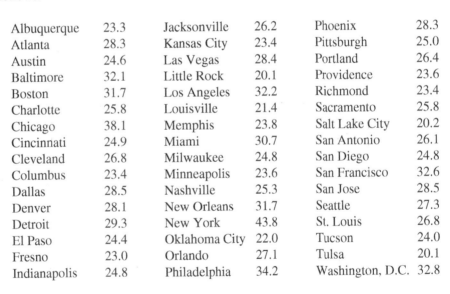

Albuquerque	23.3	Jacksonville	26.2	Phoenix	28.3
Atlanta	28.3	Kansas City	23.4	Pittsburgh	25.0
Austin	24.6	Las Vegas	28.4	Portland	26.4
Baltimore	32.1	Little Rock	20.1	Providence	23.6
Boston	31.7	Los Angeles	32.2	Richmond	23.4
Charlotte	25.8	Louisville	21.4	Sacramento	25.8
Chicago	38.1	Memphis	23.8	Salt Lake City	20.2
Cincinnati	24.9	Miami	30.7	San Antonio	26.1
Cleveland	26.8	Milwaukee	24.8	San Diego	24.8
Columbus	23.4	Minneapolis	23.6	San Francisco	32.6
Dallas	28.5	Nashville	25.3	San Jose	28.5
Denver	28.1	New Orleans	31.7	Seattle	27.3
Detroit	29.3	New York	43.8	St. Louis	26.8
El Paso	24.4	Oklahoma City	22.0	Tucson	24.0
Fresno	23.0	Orlando	27.1	Tulsa	20.1
Indianapolis	24.8	Philadelphia	34.2	Washington, D.C.	32.8

WEB file

CommuteTime

a.   What is the mean commute time for these 48 cities?
b.   Compute the median commute time.
c.   Compute the mode.
d.   Compute the third quartile.

8.   During the 2007–2008 NCAA college basketball season, men's basketball teams attempted an all-time high number of 3-point shots, averaging 19.07 shots per game (Associated Press Sports, January 24, 2009). In an attempt to discourage so many 3-point shots and encourage more inside play, the NCAA rules committee moved the 3-point line back from 19 feet, 9 inches to 20 feet, 9 inches at the beginning of the 2008–2009 basketball season. Shown in the following table are the 3-point shots taken and the 3-point shots made for a sample of 19 NCAA basketball games during the 2008–2009 season.

3Points

3-Point Shots	Shots Made	3-Point Shots	Shots Made
23	4	17	7
20	6	19	10
17	5	22	7
18	8	25	11
13	4	15	6
16	4	10	5
8	5	11	3
19	8	25	8
28	5	23	7
21	7		

a. What is the mean number of 3-point shots taken per game?

b. What is the mean number of 3-point shots made per game?

c. Using the closer 3-point line, players were making 35.2% of their shots. What percentage of shots were players making from the new 3-point line?

d. What was the impact of the NCAA rules change that moved the 3-point line back to 20 feet, 9 inches for the 2008–2009 season? Would you agree with the Associated Press Sports article that stated, "Moving back the 3-point line hasn't changed the game dramatically"? Explain.

9. Endowment income is a critical part of the annual budgets at colleges and universities. A study by the National Association of College and University Business Officers reported that the 435 colleges and universities surveyed held a total of $413 billion in endowments. The 10 wealthiest universities are shown below (*The Wall Street Journal,* January 27, 2009). Amounts are in billion of dollars.

University	Endowment ($billion)	University	Endowment ($billion)
Columbia	7.2	Princeton	16.4
Harvard	36.6	Stanford	17.2
M.I.T.	10.1	Texas	16.1
Michigan	7.6	Texas A&M	6.7
Northwestern	7.2	Yale	22.9

a. What is the mean endowment for these universities?

b. What is the median endowment?

c. What is the mode endowment?

d. Compute the first and third quartiles.

e. What is the total endowment at these 10 universities? These universities represent 2.3% of the 435 colleges and universities surveyed. What percentage of the total $413 billion in endowments is held by these 10 universities?

f. *The Wall Street Journal* reported that over a recent five-month period, a downturn in the economy has caused endowments to decline 23%. What is the estimate of the dollar amount of the decline in the total endowments held by these 10 universities? Given this situation, what are some of the steps you would expect university administrators to be considering?

10. Over a nine-month period, OutdoorGearLab tested hardshell jackets designed for ice climbing, mountaineering, and backpacking. Based on the breathability, durability, versatility,

JacketRatings

features, mobility, and weight of each jacket, an overall rating ranging from 0 (lowest) to 100 (highest) was assigned to each jacket tested. The following data show the results for 20 top-of-the line jackets (OutdoorGearLab website, February 27, 2013).

42	66	67	71	78	62	61	76	71	67
61	64	61	54	83	63	68	69	81	53

a.   Compute the mean, median, and mode.
b.   Compute the first and third quartiles.
c.   Compute and interpret the 90th percentile.

11.   According to the National Education Association (NEA), teachers generally spend more than 40 hours each week working on instructional duties (NEA website, April 2012). The following data show the number of hours worked per week for a sample of 13 high school science teachers and a sample of 11 high school English teachers.

High School Science Teachers: 53 56 54 54 55 58 49 61 54 54 52 53 54
High School English Teachers: 52 47 50 46 47 48 49 46 55 44 47

a.   What is the median number of hours worked per week for the sample of 13 high school science teachers?
b.   What is the median number of hours worked per week for the sample of 11 high school English teachers?
c.   Which group has the highest median number of hours worked per week? What is the difference between the median number of hours worked per week?

BigBangTheory

12.   *The Big Bang Theory*, a situation comedy featuring Johnny Galecki, Jim Parsons, and Kaley Cuoco, is one of the most watched programs on network television. The first two episodes for the 2011–2012 season premiered on September 22, 2011; the first episode attracted 14.1 million viewers and the second episode attracted 14.7 million viewers. The following table shows the number of viewers in millions for the first 21 episodes of the 2011–2012 season (*The Big Bang Theory* website, April 17, 2012).

Air Date	Viewers (millions)	Air Date	Viewers (millions)
September 22, 2011	14.1	January 12, 2012	16.1
September 22, 2011	14.7	January 19, 2012	15.8
September 29, 2011	14.6	January 26, 2012	16.1
October 6, 2011	13.6	February 2, 2012	16.5
October 13, 2011	13.6	February 9, 2012	16.2
October 20, 2011	14.9	February 16, 2012	15.7
October 27, 2011	14.5	February 23, 2012	16.2
November 3, 2011	16.0	March 8, 2012	15.0
November 10, 2011	15.9	March 29, 2012	14.0
November 17, 2011	15.1	April 5, 2012	13.3
December 8, 2011	14.0		

a.   Compute the minimum and maximum number of viewers.
b.   Compute the mean, median, and mode.
c.   Compute the first and third quartiles.
d.   Has viewership grown or declined over the 2011–2012 season? Discuss.

13. In automobile mileage and gasoline-consumption testing, 13 automobiles were road tested for 300 miles in both city and highway driving conditions. The following data were recorded for miles-per-gallon performance.

City: 16.2 16.7 15.9 14.4 13.2 15.3 16.8 16.0 16.1 15.3 15.2 15.3 16.2
Highway: 19.4 20.6 18.3 18.6 19.2 17.4 17.2 18.6 19.0 21.1 19.4 18.5 18.7

Use the mean, median, and mode to make a statement about the difference in performance for city and highway driving.

14. The data contained in the file named StateUnemp show the unemployment rate in March 2011 and the unemployment rate in March 2012 for every state and the District of Columbia (Bureau of Labor Statistics website, April 20, 2012). To compare unemployment rates in March 2011 with unemployment rates in March 2012, compute the first quartile, the median, and the third quartile for the March 2011 unemployment data and the March 2012 unemployment data. What do these statistics suggest about the change in unemployment rates across the states?

StateUnemp

15. Martinez Auto Supplies has retail stores located in eight cities in California. The price they charge for a particular product in each city varies because of differing competitive conditions. For instance, the price they charge for a case of a popular brand of motor oil in each city follows. Also shown are the number of cases that Martinez Auto sold last quarter in each city.

City	Price ($)	Sales (cases)
Bakersfield	34.99	501
Los Angeles	38.99	1425
Modesto	36.00	294
Oakland	33.59	882
Sacramento	40.99	715
San Diego	38.59	1088
San Francisco	39.59	1644
San Jose	37.99	819

Compute the average sales price per case for this product during the last quarter.

16. The grade point average for college students is based on a weighted mean computation. For most colleges, the grades are given the following data values: A (4), B (3), C (2), D (1), and F (0). After 60 credit hours of course work, a student at State University earned 9 credit hours of A, 15 credit hours of B, 33 credit hours of C, and 3 credit hours of D.
a. Compute the student's grade point average.
b. Students at State University must maintain a 2.5 grade point average for their first 60 credit hours of course work in order to be admitted to the business college. Will this student be admitted?

17. Morningstar tracks the total return for a large number of mutual funds. The following table shows the total return and the number of funds for four categories of mutual funds (*Morningstar Funds 500*, 2008).

Type of Fund	Number of Funds	Total Return (%)
Domestic Equity	9191	4.65
International Equity	2621	18.15
Specialty Stock	1419	11.36
Hybrid	2900	6.75

a. Using the number of funds as weights, compute the weighted average total return for the mutual funds covered by Morningstar.

b. Is there any difficulty associated with using the "number of funds" as the weights in computing the weighted average total return for Morningstar in part (a)? Discuss. What else might be used for weights?

c. Suppose you had invested $10,000 in mutual funds at the beginning of 2007 and diversified the investment by placing $2000 in Domestic Equity funds, $4000 in International Equity funds, $3000 in Specialty Stock funds, and $1000 in Hybrid funds. What is the expected return on the portfolio?

18. Based on a survey of 425 master's programs in business administration, *U.S. News & World Report* ranked the Indiana University Kelley Business School as the 20th best business program in the country (*America's Best Graduate Schools,* 2009). The ranking was based in part on surveys of business school deans and corporate recruiters. Each survey respondent was asked to rate the overall academic quality of the master's program on a scale from 1 "marginal" to 5 "outstanding." Use the sample of responses shown below to compute the weighted mean score for the business school deans and the corporate recruiters. Discuss.

Quality Assessment	Business School Deans	Corporate Recruiters
5	44	31
4	66	34
3	60	43
2	10	12
1	0	0

19. Annual revenue for Corning Supplies grew by 5.5% in 2007; 1.1% in 2008; −3.5% in 2009; −1.1% in 2010; and 1.8% in 2011. What is the mean growth annual rate over this period?

20. Suppose that at the beginning of 2004 you invested $10,000 in the Stivers mutual fund and $5,000 in the Trippi mutual fund. The value of each investment at the end of each subsequent year is provided in the table below. Which mutual fund performed better?

Year	Stivers	Trippi
2004	11,000	5,600
2005	12,000	6,300
2006	13,000	6,900
2007	14,000	7,600
2008	15,000	8,500
2009	16,000	9,200
2010	17,000	9,900
2011	18,000	10,600

21. If an asset declines in value from $5,000 to $3,500 over nine years, what is the mean annual growth rate in the asset's value over these nine years?

22. The current value of a company is $25 million. If the value of the company six year ago was $10 million, what is the company's mean annual growth rate over the past six years?

3.2 Measures of Variability

The variability in the delivery time creates uncertainty for production scheduling. Methods in this section help measure and understand variability.

In addition to measures of location, it is often desirable to consider measures of variability, or dispersion. For example, suppose that you are a purchasing agent for a large manufacturing firm and that you regularly place orders with two different suppliers. After several months of operation, you find that the mean number of days required to fill orders is 10 days for both of the suppliers. The histograms summarizing the number of working days required to fill orders from the suppliers are shown in Figure 3.2. Although the mean number of days is 10 for both suppliers, do the two suppliers demonstrate the same degree of reliability in terms of making deliveries on schedule? Note the dispersion, or variability, in delivery times indicated by the histograms. Which supplier would you prefer?

For most firms, receiving materials and supplies on schedule is important. The 7- or 8-day deliveries shown for J.C. Clark Distributors might be viewed favorably; however, a few of the slow 13- to 15-day deliveries could be disastrous in terms of keeping a workforce busy and production on schedule. This example illustrates a situation in which the variability in the delivery times may be an overriding consideration in selecting a supplier. For most purchasing agents, the lower variability shown for Dawson Supply, Inc., would make Dawson the preferred supplier.

We turn now to a discussion of some commonly used measures of variability.

Range

The simplest measure of variability is the **range**.

RANGE

$$\text{Range} = \text{Largest value} - \text{Smallest value}$$

Let us refer to the data on starting salaries for business school graduates in Table 3.1. The largest starting salary is 4325 and the smallest is 3710. The range is $4325 - 3710 = 615$.

FIGURE 3.2   HISTORICAL DATA SHOWING THE NUMBER OF DAYS REQUIRED TO FILL ORDERS

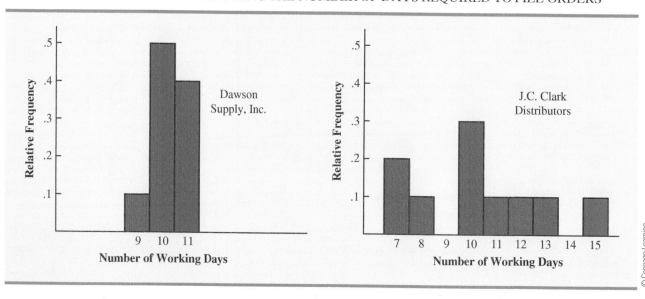

Although the range is the easiest of the measures of variability to compute, it is seldom used as the only measure. The reason is that the range is based on only two of the observations and thus is highly influenced by extreme values. Suppose the highest paid graduate received a starting salary of $10,000 per month. In this case, the range would be $10,000 - 3710 = 6290$ rather than 615. This large value for the range would not be especially descriptive of the variability in the data because 11 of the 12 starting salaries are closely grouped between 3710 and 4130.

Interquartile Range

A measure of variability that overcomes the dependency on extreme values is the **interquartile range (IQR)**. This measure of variability is the difference between the third quartile, Q_3, and the first quartile, Q_1. In other words, the interquartile range is the range for the middle 50% of the data.

INTERQUARTILE RANGE

$$IQR = Q_3 - Q_1 \tag{3.5}$$

For the data on monthly starting salaries, the quartiles are $Q_3 = 4000$ and $Q_1 = 3865$. Thus, the interquartile range is $4000 - 3865 = 135$.

Variance

The **variance** is a measure of variability that utilizes all the data. The variance is based on the difference between the value of each observation (x_i) and the mean. The difference between each x_i and the mean ($\bar{x}$ for a sample, μ for a population) is called a *deviation about the mean*. For a sample, a deviation about the mean is written ($x_i - \bar{x}$); for a population, it is written ($x_i - \mu$). In the computation of the variance, the deviations about the mean are *squared*.

If the data are for a population, the average of the squared deviations is called the *population variance*. The population variance is denoted by the Greek symbol σ^2. For a population of N observations and with μ denoting the population mean, the definition of the population variance is as follows.

POPULATION VARIANCE

$$\sigma^2 = \frac{\Sigma(x_i - \mu)^2}{N} \tag{3.6}$$

In most statistical applications, the data being analyzed are for a sample. When we compute a sample variance, we are often interested in using it to estimate the population variance σ^2. Although a detailed explanation is beyond the scope of this text, it can be shown that if the sum of the squared deviations about the sample mean is divided by $n - 1$, and not n, the resulting sample variance provides an unbiased estimate of the population variance. For this reason, the *sample variance,* denoted by s^2, is defined as follows.

The sample variance s^2 is a point estimator of the population variance σ^2.

SAMPLE VARIANCE

$$s^2 = \frac{\Sigma(x_i - \bar{x})^2}{n - 1} \tag{3.7}$$

TABLE 3.3 COMPUTATION OF DEVIATIONS AND SQUARED DEVIATIONS ABOUT THE MEAN FOR THE CLASS SIZE DATA

Number of Students in Class (x_i)	Mean Class Size ($\bar{x}$)	Deviation About the Mean ($x_i - \bar{x}$)	Squared Deviation About the Mean ($x_i - \bar{x})^2$
46	44	2	4
54	44	10	100
42	44	−2	4
46	44	2	4
32	44	−12	144
		0	256
		$\Sigma(x_i - \bar{x})$	$\Sigma(x_i - \bar{x})^2$

To illustrate the computation of the sample variance, we will use the data on class size for the sample of five college classes as presented in Section 3.1. A summary of the data, including the computation of the deviations about the mean and the squared deviations about the mean, is shown in Table 3.3. The sum of squared deviations about the mean is $\Sigma(x_i - \bar{x})^2 = 256$. Hence, with $n - 1 = 4$, the sample variance is

$$s^2 = \frac{\Sigma(x_i - \bar{x})^2}{n - 1} = \frac{256}{4} = 64$$

Before moving on, let us note that the units associated with the sample variance often cause confusion. Because the values being summed in the variance calculation, $(x_i - \bar{x})^2$, are squared, the units associated with the sample variance are also *squared*. For instance, the sample variance for the class size data is $s^2 = 64$ (students)^2. The squared units associated with variance make it difficult to develop an intuitive understanding and interpretation of the numerical value of the variance. We recommend that you think of the variance as a measure useful in comparing the amount of variability for two or more variables. In a comparison of the variables, the one with the largest variance shows the most variability. Further interpretation of the value of the variance may not be necessary.

The variance is useful in comparing the variability of two or more variables.

As another illustration of computing a sample variance, consider the starting salaries listed in Table 3.1 for the 12 business school graduates. In Section 3.1, we showed that the sample mean starting salary was 3940. The computation of the sample variance ($s^2 = 27,440.91$) is shown in Table 3.4.

In Tables 3.3 and 3.4 we show both the sum of the deviations about the mean and the sum of the squared deviations about the mean. For any data set, the sum of the deviations about the mean will *always equal zero*. Note that in Tables 3.3 and 3.4, $\Sigma(x_i - \bar{x}) = 0$. The positive deviations and negative deviations cancel each other, causing the sum of the deviations about the mean to equal zero.

Standard Deviation

The **standard deviation** is defined to be the positive square root of the variance. Following the notation we adopted for a sample variance and a population variance, we use s to denote the sample standard deviation and σ to denote the population standard deviation. The standard deviation is derived from the variance in the following way.

TABLE 3.4 COMPUTATION OF THE SAMPLE VARIANCE FOR THE STARTING SALARY DATA

Monthly Salary (x_i)	Sample Mean $(\bar{x})$	Deviation About the Mean $(x_i - \bar{x})$	Squared Deviation About the Mean $(x_i - \bar{x})^2$
3850	3940	−90	8,100
3950	3940	10	100
4050	3940	110	12,100
3880	3940	−60	3,600
3755	3940	−185	34,225
3710	3940	−230	52,900
3890	3940	−50	2,500
4130	3940	190	36,100
3940	3940	0	0
4325	3940	385	148,225
3920	3940	−20	400
3880	3940	−60	3,600
		0	301,850
		$\sum(x_i - \bar{x})$	$\sum(x_i - \bar{x})^2$

Using equation (3.7),

$$s^2 = \frac{\sum(x_i - \bar{x})^2}{n - 1} = \frac{301,850}{11} = 27,440.91$$

© Cengage Learning

STANDARD DEVIATION

The sample standard deviation s is a point estimator of the population standard deviation σ.

$$\text{Sample standard deviation} = s = \sqrt{s^2} \qquad (3.8)$$

$$\text{Population standard deviation} = \sigma = \sqrt{\sigma^2} \qquad (3.9)$$

Recall that the sample variance for the sample of class sizes in five college classes is $s^2 = 64$. Thus, the sample standard deviation is $s = \sqrt{64} = 8$. For the data on starting salaries, the sample standard deviation is $s = \sqrt{27,440.91} = 165.65$.

The standard deviation is easier to interpret than the variance because the standard deviation is measured in the same units as the data.

What is gained by converting the variance to its corresponding standard deviation? Recall that the units associated with the variance are squared. For example, the sample variance for the starting salary data of business school graduates is $s^2 = 27,440.91$ (dollars)^2. Because the standard deviation is the square root of the variance, the units of the variance, dollars squared, are converted to dollars in the standard deviation. Thus, the standard deviation of the starting salary data is $165.65. In other words, the standard deviation is measured in the same units as the original data. For this reason the standard deviation is more easily compared to the mean and other statistics that are measured in the same units as the original data.

Coefficient of Variation

The coefficient of variation is a relative measure of variability; it measures the standard deviation relative to the mean.

In some situations we may be interested in a descriptive statistic that indicates how large the standard deviation is relative to the mean. This measure is called the **coefficient of variation** and is usually expressed as a percentage.

COEFFICIENT OF VARIATION

$$\left(\frac{\text{Standard deviation}}{\text{Mean}} \times 100\right)\%$$ (3.10)

For the class size data, we found a sample mean of 44 and a sample standard deviation of 8. The coefficient of variation is $[(8/44) \times 100]\% = 18.2\%$. In words, the coefficient of variation tells us that the sample standard deviation is 18.2% of the value of the sample mean. For the starting salary data with a sample mean of 3940 and a sample standard deviation of 165.65, the coefficient of variation, $[(165.65/3940) \times 100]\% = 4.2\%$, tells us the sample standard deviation is only 4.2% of the value of the sample mean. In general, the coefficient of variation is a useful statistic for comparing the variability of variables that have different standard deviations and different means.

NOTES AND COMMENTS

1. Statistical software packages and spreadsheets can be used to develop the descriptive statistics presented in this chapter. After the data are entered into a worksheet, a few simple commands can be used to generate the desired output. In three chapter-ending appendixes we show how Minitab, Excel, and StatTools can be used to develop descriptive statistics.

2. The standard deviation is a commonly used measure of the risk associated with investing in stock and stock funds (*Morningstar* website, July 21, 2012). It provides a measure of how monthly returns fluctuate around the long-run average return.

3. Rounding the value of the sample mean $\bar{x}$ and the values of the squared deviations $(x_i - \bar{x})^2$

may introduce errors when a calculator is used in the computation of the variance and standard deviation. To reduce rounding errors, we recommend carrying at least six significant digits during intermediate calculations. The resulting variance or standard deviation can then be rounded to fewer digits.

4. An alternative formula for the computation of the sample variance is

$$s^2 = \frac{\sum x_i^2 - n\bar{x}^2}{n - 1}$$

where $\sum x_i^2 = x_1^2 + x_2^2 + \cdots + x_n^2$.

Exercises

Methods

23. Consider a sample with data values of 10, 20, 12, 17, and 16. Compute the range and interquartile range.

24. Consider a sample with data values of 10, 20, 12, 17, and 16. Compute the variance and standard deviation.

SELF test 25. Consider a sample with data values of 27, 25, 20, 15, 30, 34, 28, and 25. Compute the range, interquartile range, variance, and standard deviation.

Applications

SELF test 26. A bowler's scores for six games were 182, 168, 184, 190, 170, and 174. Using these data as a sample, compute the following descriptive statistics:
   a. Range   c. Standard deviation
   b. Variance   d. Coefficient of variation

27. The results of a search to find the least expensive round-trip flights to Atlanta and Salt Lake City from 14 major U.S. cities are shown in the following table. The departure date was June 20, 2012, and the return date was June 27, 2012.

Flights

Departure City	Round-Trip Cost ($)	
	Atlanta	Salt Lake City
Cincinnati	340.10	570.10
New York	321.60	354.60
Chicago	291.60	465.60
Denver	339.60	219.60
Los Angeles	359.60	311.60
Seattle	384.60	297.60
Detroit	309.60	471.60
Philadelphia	415.60	618.40
Washington, D.C.	293.60	513.60
Miami	249.60	523.20
San Francisco	539.60	381.60
Las Vegas	455.60	159.60
Phoenix	359.60	267.60
Dallas	333.90	458.60

a. Compute the mean price for a round-trip flight into Atlanta and the mean price for a round-trip flight into Salt Lake City. Is Atlanta less expensive to fly into than Salt Lake City? If so, what could explain this difference?

b. Compute the range, variance, and standard deviation for the two samples. What does this information tell you about the prices for flights into these two cities?

28. The Australian Open is the first of the four Grand Slam professional tennis events held each year. Victoria Azarenka beat Maria Sharapova to win the 2012 Australian Open women's title (*Washington Post*, January 27, 2012). During the tournament Ms. Azarenka's serve speed reached 178 kilometers per hour. A list of the 20 Women's Singles serve speed leaders for the 2012 Australian Open is provided below.

AustralianOpen

Player	Serve Speed (km/h)	Player	Serve Speed (km/h)
S. Williams	191	G. Arn	179
S. Lisicki	190	V. Azarenka	178
M. Keys	187	A. Ivanovic	178
L. Hradecka	187	P. Kvitova	178
J. Gajdosova	187	M. Krajicek	178
J. Hampton	181	V. Dushevina	178
B. Mattek-Sands	181	S. Stosur	178
F. Schiavone	179	S. Cirstea	177
P. Parmentier	179	M. Barthel	177
N. Petrova	179	P. Ormaechea	177

a. Compute the mean, variance, and standard deviation for the serve speeds.

b. A similar sample of the 20 Women's Singles serve speed leaders for the 2011 Wimbledon tournament showed a sample mean serve speed of 182.5 kilometers per hour. The variance and standard deviation were 33.3 and 5.77, respectively. Discuss any difference between the serve speeds in the Australian Open and the Wimbledon women's tournaments.

29. The *Los Angeles Times* regularly reports the air quality index for various areas of Southern California. A sample of air quality index values for Pomona provided the following data: 28, 42, 58, 48, 45, 55, 60, 49, and 50.
    a. Compute the range and interquartile range.
    b. Compute the sample variance and sample standard deviation.
    c. A sample of air quality index readings for Anaheim provided a sample mean of 48.5, a sample variance of 136, and a sample standard deviation of 11.66. What comparisons can you make between the air quality in Pomona and that in Anaheim on the basis of these descriptive statistics?

30. The following data were used to construct the histograms of the number of days required to fill orders for Dawson Supply, Inc., and J.C. Clark Distributors (see Figure 3.2).

Dawson Supply Days for Delivery:	11	10	9	10	11	11	10	11	10	10
Clark Distributors Days for Delivery:	8	10	13	7	10	11	10	7	15	12

    Use the range and standard deviation to support the previous observation that Dawson Supply provides the more consistent and reliable delivery times.

31. The results of Accounting Principals' latest Workonomix survey indicate the average American worker spends $1092 on coffee annually (*The Consumerist*, January 20, 2012). To determine if there are any differences in coffee expenditures by age group, samples of 10 consumers were selected for three age groups (18–34, 35–44, and 45 and Older). The dollar amount each consumer in the sample spent last year on coffee is provided below.

Coffee

18–34	35–44	45 and Older
1355	969	1135
115	434	956
1456	1792	400
2045	1500	1374
1621	1277	1244
994	1056	825
1937	1922	763
1200	1350	1192
1567	1586	1305
1390	1415	1510

    a. Compute the mean, variance, and standard deviation for the each of these three samples.
    b. What observations can be made based on these data?

Advertising

32. *Advertising Age* annually compiles a list of the 100 companies that spend the most on advertising. Consumer-goods company Procter & Gamble has often topped the list, spending billions of dollars annually (*Advertising Age* website, March 12, 2013). Consider the data found in the file Advertising. It contains annual advertising expenditures for a sample of 20 companies in the automotive sector and 20 companies in the department store sector.
    a. What is the mean advertising spend for each sector?
    b. What is the standard deviation for each sector?
    c. What is the range of advertising spend for each sector?
    d. What is the interquartile range for each sector?
    e. Based on this sample and your answers to parts (a) to (d), comment on any differences in the advertising spending in the automotive companies versus the department store companies.

33. Scores turned in by an amateur golfer at the Bonita Fairways Golf Course in Bonita Springs, Florida, during 2011 and 2012 are as follows:

2011 Season:	74	78	79	77	75	73	75	77
2012 Season:	71	70	75	77	85	80	71	79

a. Use the mean and standard deviation to evaluate the golfer's performance over the two-year period.
b. What is the primary difference in performance between 2011 and 2012? What improvement, if any, can be seen in the 2012 scores?

34. The following times were recorded by the quarter-mile and mile runners of a university track team (times are in minutes).

Quarter-Mile Times:	.92	.98	1.04	.90	.99
Mile Times:	4.52	4.35	4.60	4.70	4.50

After viewing this sample of running times, one of the coaches commented that the quarter-milers turned in the more consistent times. Use the standard deviation and the coefficient of variation to summarize the variability in the data. Does the use of the coefficient of variation indicate that the coach's statement should be qualified?

Measures of Distribution Shape, Relative Location, and Detecting Outliers

We have described several measures of location and variability for data. In addition, it is often important to have a measure of the shape of a distribution. In Chapter 2 we noted that a histogram provides a graphical display showing the shape of a distribution. An important numerical measure of the shape of a distribution is called **skewness**.

Distribution Shape

Figure 3.3 shows four histograms constructed from relative frequency distributions. The histograms in Panels A and B are moderately skewed. The one in Panel A is skewed to the left; its skewness is −.85. The histogram in Panel B is skewed to the right; its skewness is +.85. The histogram in Panel C is symmetric; its skewness is zero. The histogram in Panel D is highly skewed to the right; its skewness is 1.62. The formula used to compute skewness is somewhat complex.[1] However, the skewness can easily be computed using statistical software. For data skewed to the left, the skewness is negative; for data skewed to the right, the skewness is positive. If the data are symmetric, the skewness is zero.

For a symmetric distribution, the mean and the median are equal. When the data are positively skewed, the mean will usually be greater than the median; when the data are negatively skewed, the mean will usually be less than the median. The data used to construct the histogram in Panel D are customer purchases at a women's apparel store. The mean purchase amount is $77.60 and the median purchase amount is $59.70. The relatively few large purchase amounts tend to increase the mean, while the median remains unaffected by the large purchase amounts. The median provides the preferred measure of location when the data are highly skewed.

z-Scores

In addition to measures of location, variability, and shape, we are also interested in the relative location of values within a data set. Measures of relative location help us determine how far a particular value is from the mean.

---

[1]The formula for the skewness of sample data:

$$\text{Skewness} = \frac{n}{(n-1)(n-2)} \Sigma \left(\frac{x_i - \bar{x}}{s} \right)^3$$

FIGURE 3.3   HISTOGRAMS SHOWING THE SKEWNESS FOR FOUR DISTRIBUTIONS

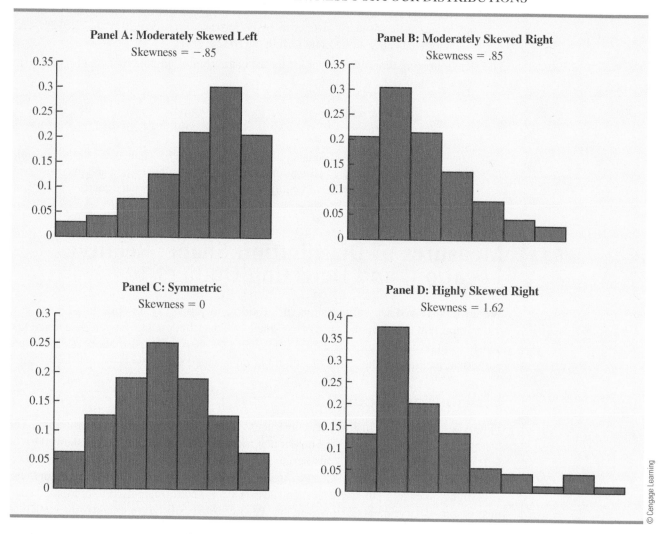

By using both the mean and standard deviation, we can determine the relative location of any observation. Suppose we have a sample of n observations, with the values denoted by $x_1, x_2, \ldots, x_n$. In addition, assume that the sample mean, $\bar{x}$, and the sample standard deviation, s, are already computed. Associated with each value, x_i, is another value called its **z-score**. Equation (3.11) shows how the z-score is computed for each x_i.

z-SCORE

$$z_i = \frac{x_i - \bar{x}}{s} \qquad \text{(3.11)}$$

where

z_i = the z-score for x_i
$\bar{x}$ = the sample mean
s = the sample standard deviation

TABLE 3.5   z-SCORES FOR THE CLASS SIZE DATA

Number of Students in Class (x_i)	Deviation About the Mean ($x_i - \bar{x}$)	z-Score $\left(\dfrac{x_i - \bar{x}}{s}\right)$
46	2	2/8 = .25
54	10	10/8 = 1.25
42	−2	−2/8 = −.25
46	2	2/8 = .25
32	−12	−12/8 = −1.50

© Cengage Learning

The z-score is often called the *standardized value*. The z-score, z_i, can be interpreted as the *number of standard deviations x_i is from the mean $\bar{x}$*. For example, $z_1 = 1.2$ would indicate that x_1 is 1.2 standard deviations greater than the sample mean. Similarly, $z_2 = -.5$ would indicate that x_2 is .5, or 1/2, standard deviation less than the sample mean. A z-score greater than zero occurs for observations with a value greater than the mean, and a z-score less than zero occurs for observations with a value less than the mean. A z-score of zero indicates that the value of the observation is equal to the mean.

The z-score for any observation can be interpreted as a measure of the relative location of the observation in a data set. Thus, observations in two different data sets with the same z-score can be said to have the same relative location in terms of being the same number of standard deviations from the mean.

The process of converting a value for a variable to a z-score is often referred to as a z transformation.

The z-scores for the class size data from Section 3.1 are computed in Table 3.5. Recall the previously computed sample mean, $\bar{x} = 44$, and sample standard deviation, $s = 8$. The z-score of −1.50 for the fifth observation shows it is farthest from the mean; it is 1.50 standard deviations below the mean. Figure 3.4 provides a dot plot of the class size data with a graphical representation of the associated z-scores on the axis below.

Chebyshev's Theorem

Chebyshev's theorem enables us to make statements about the proportion of data values that must be within a specified number of standard deviations of the mean.

FIGURE 3.4   DOT PLOT SHOWING CLASS SIZE DATA AND z-SCORES

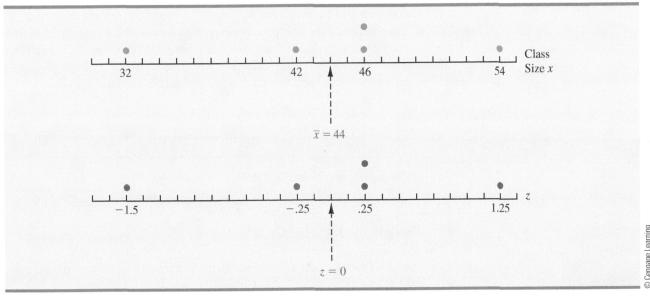

© Cengage Learning

CHEBYSHEV'S THEOREM

At least $(1 - 1/z^2)$ of the data values must be within z standard deviations of the mean, where z is any value greater than 1.

Some of the implications of this theorem, with $z = 2, 3,$ and 4 standard deviations, follow.

- At least .75, or 75%, of the data values must be within $z = 2$ standard deviations of the mean.
- At least .89, or 89%, of the data values must be within $z = 3$ standard deviations of the mean.
- At least .94, or 94%, of the data values must be within $z = 4$ standard deviations of the mean.

For an example using Chebyshev's theorem, suppose that the midterm test scores for 100 students in a college business statistics course had a mean of 70 and a standard deviation of 5. How many students had test scores between 60 and 80? How many students had test scores between 58 and 82?

For the test scores between 60 and 80, we note that 60 is two standard deviations below the mean and 80 is two standard deviations above the mean. Using Chebyshev's theorem, we see that at least .75, or at least 75%, of the observations must have values within two standard deviations of the mean. Thus, at least 75% of the students must have scored between 60 and 80.

Chebyshev's theorem requires $z > 1$; but z need not be an integer.

For the test scores between 58 and 82, we see that $(58 - 70)/5 = -2.4$ indicates 58 is 2.4 standard deviations below the mean and that $(82 - 70)/5 = +2.4$ indicates 82 is 2.4 standard deviations above the mean. Applying Chebyshev's theorem with $z = 2.4$, we have

$$\left(1 - \frac{1}{z^2}\right) = \left(1 - \frac{1}{(2.4)^2}\right) = .826$$

At least 82.6% of the students must have test scores between 58 and 82.

Empirical Rule

The empirical rule is based on the normal probability distribution, which will be discussed in Chapter 6. The normal distribution is used extensively throughout the text.

One of the advantages of Chebyshev's theorem is that it applies to any data set regardless of the shape of the distribution of the data. Indeed, it could be used with any of the distributions in Figure 3.3. In many practical applications, however, data sets exhibit a symmetric mound-shaped or bell-shaped distribution like the one shown in Figure 3.5. When the data are believed to approximate this distribution, the **empirical rule** can be used to determine the percentage of data values that must be within a specified number of standard deviations of the mean.

EMPIRICAL RULE

For data having a bell-shaped distribution:

- Approximately 68% of the data values will be within one standard deviation of the mean.
- Approximately 95% of the data values will be within two standard deviations of the mean.
- Almost all of the data values will be within three standard deviations of the mean.

FIGURE 3.5   A SYMMETRIC MOUND-SHAPED OR BELL-SHAPED DISTRIBUTION

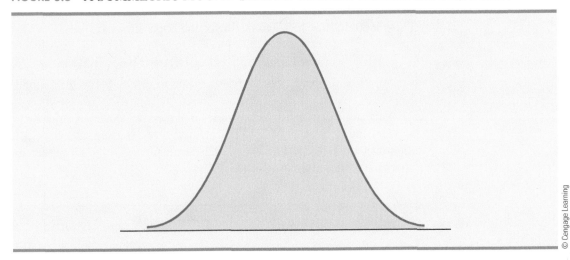

For example, liquid detergent cartons are filled automatically on a production line. Filling weights frequently have a bell-shaped distribution. If the mean filling weight is 16 ounces and the standard deviation is .25 ounces, we can use the empirical rule to draw the following conclusions.

- Approximately 68% of the filled cartons will have weights between 15.75 and 16.25 ounces (within one standard deviation of the mean).
- Approximately 95% of the filled cartons will have weights between 15.50 and 16.50 ounces (within two standard deviations of the mean).
- Almost all filled cartons will have weights between 15.25 and 16.75 ounces (within three standard deviations of the mean).

Detecting Outliers

Sometimes a data set will have one or more observations with unusually large or unusually small values. These extreme values are called **outliers**. Experienced statisticians take steps to identify outliers and then review each one carefully. An outlier may be a data value that has been incorrectly recorded. If so, it can be corrected before further analysis. An outlier may also be from an observation that was incorrectly included in the data set; if so, it can be removed. Finally, an outlier may be an unusual data value that has been recorded correctly and belongs in the data set. In such cases it should remain.

It is a good idea to check for outliers before making decisions based on data analysis. Errors are often made in recording data and entering data into the computer. Outliers should not necessarily be deleted, but their accuracy and appropriateness should be verified.

Standardized values (z-scores) can be used to identify outliers. Recall that the empirical rule allows us to conclude that for data with a bell-shaped distribution, almost all the data values will be within three standard deviations of the mean. Hence, in using z-scores to identify outliers, we recommend treating any data value with a z-score less than −3 or greater than +3 as an outlier. Such data values can then be reviewed for accuracy and to determine whether they belong in the data set.

Refer to the z-scores for the class size data in Table 3.5. The z-score of −1.50 shows the fifth class size is farthest from the mean. However, this standardized value is well within the −3 to +3 guideline for outliers. Thus, the z-scores do not indicate that outliers are present in the class size data.

Another approach to identifying outliers is based upon the values of the first and third quartiles (Q_1 and Q_3) and the interquartile range (IQR). Using this method, we first compute the following lower and upper limits:

$$\text{Lower Limit} = Q_1 - 1.5(\text{IQR})$$
$$\text{Upper Limit} = Q_3 + 1.5(\text{IQR})$$

The approach that uses the first and third quartiles and the IQR to identify outliers does not necessarily provide the same results as the approach based upon a z-score less than −3 or greater than +3. Either or both procedures may be used.

An observation is classified as an outlier if its value is less than the lower limit or greater than the upper limit. For the monthly starting salary data shown in Table 3.1, $Q_1 = 3465$, $Q_3 = 3600$, IQR = 135, and the lower and upper limits are

$$\text{Lower Limit} = Q_1 - 1.5(\text{IQR}) = 3465 - 1.5(135) = 3262.5$$
$$\text{Upper Limit} = Q_3 + 1.5(\text{IQR}) = 3600 + 1.5(135) = 3802.5$$

Looking at the data in Table 3.1 we see that there are no observations with a starting salary less than the lower limit of 3262.5. But, there is one starting salary, 3925, that is greater than the upper limit of 3802.5. Thus, 3925 is considered to be an outlier using this alternate approach to identifying outliers.

NOTES AND COMMENTS

1. Chebyshev's theorem is applicable for any data set and can be used to state the minimum number of data values that will be within a certain number of standard deviations of the mean. If the data are known to be approximately bell-shaped, more can be said. For instance, the empirical rule allows us to say that *approximately* 95% of the data values will be within two standard deviations of the mean; Chebyshev's theorem allows us to conclude only that at least 75% of the data values will be in that interval.

2. Before analyzing a data set, statisticians usually make a variety of checks to ensure the validity of data. In a large study it is not uncommon for errors to be made in recording data values or in entering the values into a computer. Identifying outliers is one tool used to check the validity of the data.

Exercises

Methods

35. Consider a sample with data values of 10, 20, 12, 17, and 16. Compute the z-score for each of the five observations.

36. Consider a sample with a mean of 500 and a standard deviation of 100. What are the z-scores for the following data values: 520, 650, 500, 450, and 280?

37. Consider a sample with a mean of 30 and a standard deviation of 5. Use Chebyshev's theorem to determine the percentage of the data within each of the following ranges:
    a. 20 to 40
    b. 15 to 45
    c. 22 to 38
    d. 18 to 42
    e. 12 to 48

38. Suppose the data have a bell-shaped distribution with a mean of 30 and a standard deviation of 5. Use the empirical rule to determine the percentage of data within each of the following ranges:
    a. 20 to 40
    b. 15 to 45
    c. 25 to 35

Applications

39. The results of a national survey showed that on average, adults sleep 6.9 hours per night. Suppose that the standard deviation is 1.2 hours.
    a. Use Chebyshev's theorem to calculate the percentage of individuals who sleep between 4.5 and 9.3 hours.

b.   Use Chebyshev's theorem to calculate the percentage of individuals who sleep between 3.9 and 9.9 hours.

c.   Assume that the number of hours of sleep follows a bell-shaped distribution. Use the empirical rule to calculate the percentage of individuals who sleep between 4.5 and 9.3 hours per day. How does this result compare to the value that you obtained using Chebyshev's theorem in part (a)?

40.   The Energy Information Administration reported that the mean retail price per gallon of regular grade gasoline was $3.43 (Energy Information Administration, July 2012). Suppose that the standard deviation was $.10 and that the retail price per gallon has a bell-shaped distribution.

a.   What percentage of regular grade gasoline sold between $3.33 and $3.53 per gallon?

b.   What percentage of regular grade gasoline sold between $3.33 and $3.63 per gallon?

c.   What percentage of regular grade gasoline sold for more than $3.63 per gallon?

41.   The national average for the math portion of the College Board's SAT test is 515 (*The World Almanac*, 2009). The College Board periodically rescales the test scores such that the standard deviation is approximately 100. Answer the following questions using a bell-shaped distribution and the empirical rule for the math test scores.

a.   What percentage of students have an SAT math score greater than 615?

b.   What percentage of students have an SAT math score greater than 715?

c.   What percentage of students have an SAT math score between 415 and 515?

d.   What percentage of students have an SAT math score between 315 and 615?

42.   Many families in California are using backyard structures for home offices, art studios, and hobby areas as well as for additional storage. Suppose that the mean price for a customized wooden, shingled backyard structure is $3100. Assume that the standard deviation is $1200.

a.   What is the z-score for a backyard structure costing $2300?

b.   What is the z-score for a backyard structure costing $4900?

c.   Interpret the z-scores in parts (a) and (b). Comment on whether either should be considered an outlier.

d.   If the cost for a backyard shed-office combination built in Albany, California, is $13,000, should this structure be considered an outlier? Explain.

43.   Florida Power & Light (FP&L) Company has enjoyed a reputation for quickly fixing its electric system after storms. However, during the hurricane seasons of 2004 and 2005, a new reality was that the company's historical approach to emergency electric system repairs was no longer good enough (*The Wall Street Journal*, January 16, 2006). Data showing the days required to restore electric service after seven hurricanes during 2004 and 2005 follow.

Hurricane	Days to Restore Service
Charley	13
Frances	12
Jeanne	8
Dennis	3
Katrina	8
Rita	2
Wilma	18

Based on this sample of seven, compute the following descriptive statistics:

a.   Mean, median, and mode

b.   Range and standard deviation

c.   Should Wilma be considered an outlier in terms of the days required to restore electric service?

d.   The seven hurricanes resulted in 10 million service interruptions to customers. Do the statistics show that FP&L should consider updating its approach to emergency electric system repairs? Discuss.

44.   A sample of 10 NCAA college basketball game scores provided the following data.

NCAA

Winning Team	Points	Losing Team	Points	Winning Margin
Arizona	90	Oregon	66	24
Duke	85	Georgetown	66	19
Florida State	75	Wake Forest	70	5
Kansas	78	Colorado	57	21
Kentucky	71	Notre Dame	63	8
Louisville	65	Tennessee	62	3
Oklahoma State	72	Texas	66	6
Purdue	76	Michigan State	70	6
Stanford	77	Southern Cal	67	10
Wisconsin	76	Illinois	56	20

a.   Compute the mean and standard deviation for the points scored by the winning team.
b.   Assume that the points scored by the winning teams for all NCAA games follow a bell-shaped distribution. Using the mean and standard deviation found in part (a), estimate the percentage of all NCAA games in which the winning team scores 84 or more points. Estimate the percentage of NCAA games in which the winning team scores more than 90 points.
c.   Compute the mean and standard deviation for the winning margin. Do the data contain outliers? Explain.

45.   The Associated Press Team Marketing Report listed the Dallas Cowboys as the team with the highest ticket prices in the National Football League (*USA Today,* October 20, 2009). Data showing the average ticket price for a sample of 14 teams in the National Football League are as follows.

NFLTickets

Team	Ticket Price	Team	Ticket Price
Atlanta Falcons	72	Green Bay Packers	63
Buffalo Bills	51	Indianapolis Colts	83
Carolina Panthers	63	New Orleans Saints	62
Chicago Bears	88	New York Jets	87
Cleveland Browns	55	Pittsburgh Steelers	67
Dallas Cowboys	160	Seattle Seahawks	61
Denver Broncos	77	Tennessee Titans	61

a.   What is the mean ticket price?
b.   The previous year, the mean ticket price was $72.20. What was the percentage increase in the mean ticket price for the one-year period?
c.   Compute the median ticket price.
d.   Compute the first and third quartiles.
e.   Compute the standard deviation.
f.   What is the z-score for the Dallas Cowboys ticket price? Should this price be considered an outlier? Explain.

3.4   Five-Number Summaries and Box Plots

Summary statistics and easy-to-draw graphs based on summary statistics can be used to quickly summarize large quantities of data. In this section we show how five-number summaries and box plots can be developed to identify several characteristics of a large data set.

Five-Number Summary

In a **five-number summary**, five numbers are used to summarize the data:

1. Smallest value
2. First quartile (Q_1)
3. Median (Q_2)
4. Third quartile (Q_3)
5. Largest value

To develop a five-number summary we first arrange the data in ascending order. We then identify the smallest value, the three quartiles, and the largest value. For the monthly starting salary data in Table 3.1 we obtain the following results.

$$3710 \quad 3755 \quad 3850 \; \Big| \; 3880 \quad 3880 \quad 3890 \; \Big| \; 3920 \quad 3940 \quad 3950 \; \Big| \; 4050 \quad 4130 \quad 4325$$

$$Q_1 = 3865 \qquad\qquad Q_2 = 3905 \qquad\qquad Q_3 = 4000$$
$$\text{(Median)}$$

We showed how to compute the median, 3905, and the quartiles, $Q_1 = 3865$ and $Q_3 = 4000$, in Section 3.1. Reviewing the data shows that the smallest value is 3710 and the largest value is 4325. Thus the five-number summary for the monthly starting salary data is 3710, 3865, 3905, 4000, 4325. Approximately one-fourth, or 25%, of the observations are between adjacent numbers in a five-number summary.

Box Plot

A **box plot** is a graphical summary of data that is based on a five-number summary. A key to the development of a box plot is the computation of the interquartile range, IQR $= Q_3 - Q_1$. Figure 3.6 shows a box plot for the monthly starting salary data. The steps used to construct the box plot follow.

Box plots provide a convenient visual display of several characteristics of a data set.

1. A box is drawn with the ends of the box located at the first and third quartiles. For the monthly starting salary data, $Q_1 = 3865$ and $Q_3 = 4000$. This box contains the middle 50% of the data.
2. A vertical line is drawn in the box at the location of the median (3905 for the monthly starting salary data).
3. By using the interquartile range, IQR $= Q_3 - Q_1$, *limits* are located at 1.5(IQR) below Q_1 and 1.5(IQR) above Q_3. For the monthly starting salary data, IQR $= Q_3 - Q_1 = 4000 - 3865 = 135$. Thus, the limits are $3865 - 1.5(135) = 3662.5$ and $4000 + 1.5(135) = 4202.5$. Data outside these limits are considered *outliers*.

FIGURE 3.6 BOX PLOT OF THE MONTHLY STARTING SALARY DATA WITH LINES SHOWING THE LOWER AND UPPER LIMITS

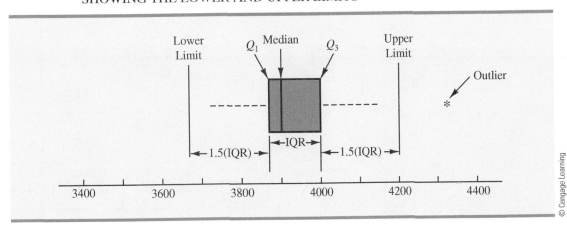

FIGURE 3.7   BOX PLOT OF THE MONTHLY STARTING SALARY DATA

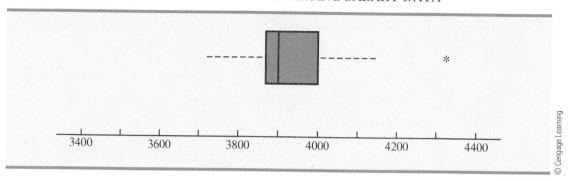

4. The dashed lines in Figure 3.6 are called *whiskers*. The whiskers are drawn from the ends of the box to the smallest and largest values *inside the limits* computed in step 3. Thus, the whiskers end at salary values of 3710 and 4130.
5. Finally, the location of each outlier is shown with the symbol *. In Figure 3.6 we see one outlier, 4325.

In Figure 3.6 we included lines showing the location of the upper and lower limits. These lines were drawn to show how the limits are computed and where they are located. Although the limits are always computed, generally they are not drawn on the box plots. Figure 3.7 shows the usual appearance of a box plot for the monthly starting salary data.

In order to compare monthly starting salaries for business school graduates by major, a sample of 111 recent graduates was selected. The major and the monthly starting salary were recorded for each graduate. Figure 3.8 shows the Minitab box plots for accounting, finance, information systems, management, and marketing majors. Note that the major is shown on the horizontal axis and each box plot is shown vertically above the corresponding major. Displaying box plots in this manner is an excellent graphical technique for making comparisons among two or more groups.

What observations can you make about monthly starting salaries by major using the box plots in Figure 3.8? Specifically, we note the following:

• The higher salaries are in accounting; the lower salaries are in management and marketing.

FIGURE 3.8   MINITAB BOX PLOTS OF MONTHLY STARTING SALARY BY MAJOR

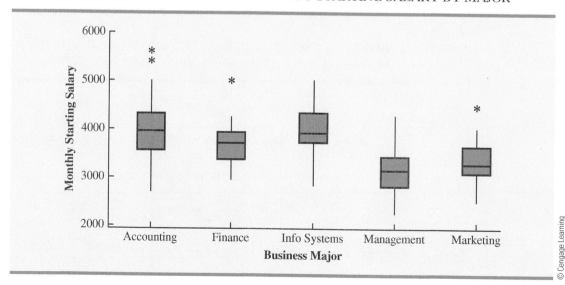

- Based on the medians, accounting and information systems have similar and higher median salaries. Finance is next with management and marketing showing lower median salaries.
- High salary outliers exist for accounting, finance, and marketing majors.
- Finance salaries appear to have the least variation, while accounting salaries appear to have the most variation.

Perhaps you can see additional interpretations based on these box plots.

NOTE AND COMMENT

In Appendix 3.1, we show how to construct a box plot for the starting salary data using Minitab. The box plot obtained looks like the one in Figure 3.7, but turned on its side.

Exercises

Methods

46. Consider a sample with data values of 27, 25, 20, 15, 30, 34, 28, and 25. Provide the five-number summary for the data.

47. Show the box plot for the data in exercise 46.

48. Show the five-number summary and the box plot for the following data: 5, 15, 18, 10, 8, 12, 16, 10, 6.

49. A data set has a first quartile of 42 and a third quartile of 50. Compute the lower and upper limits for the corresponding box plot. Should a data value of 65 be considered an outlier?

Applications

50. Naples, Florida, hosts a half-marathon (13.1-mile race) in January each year. The event attracts top runners from throughout the United States as well as from around the world. In January 2009, 22 men and 31 women entered the 19–24 age class. Finish times in minutes are as follows (*Naples Daily News,* January 19, 2009). Times are shown in order of finish.

Runners

Finish	Men	Women	Finish	Men	Women	Finish	Men	Women
1	65.30	109.03	11	109.05	123.88	21	143.83	136.75
2	66.27	111.22	12	110.23	125.78	22	148.70	138.20
3	66.52	111.65	13	112.90	129.52	23		139.00
4	66.85	111.93	14	113.52	129.87	24		147.18
5	70.87	114.38	15	120.95	130.72	25		147.35
6	87.18	118.33	16	127.98	131.67	26		147.50
7	96.45	121.25	17	128.40	132.03	27		147.75
8	98.52	122.08	18	130.90	133.20	28		153.88
9	100.52	122.48	19	131.80	133.50	29		154.83
10	108.18	122.62	20	138.63	136.57	30		189.27
						31		189.28

a. George Towett of Marietta, Georgia, finished in first place for the men and Lauren Wald of Gainesville, Florida, finished in first place for the women. Compare the first-place finish times for men and women. If the 53 men and women runners had competed as one group, in what place would Lauren have finished?

b. What is the median time for men and women runners? Compare men and women runners based on their median times.

c. Provide a five-number summary for both the men and the women.

d. Are there outliers in either group?

e. Show the box plots for the two groups. Did men or women have the most variation in finish times? Explain.

SELF test

51. Annual sales, in millions of dollars, for 21 pharmaceutical companies follow.

8408	1374	1872	8879	2459	11413
608	14138	6452	1850	2818	1356
10498	7478	4019	4341	739	2127
3653	5794	8305			

a. Provide a five-number summary.

b. Compute the lower and upper limits.

c. Do the data contain any outliers?

d. Johnson & Johnson's sales are the largest on the list at $14,138 million. Suppose a data entry error (a transposition) had been made and the sales had been entered as $41,138 million. Would the method of detecting outliers in part (c) identify this problem and allow for correction of the data entry error?

e. Show a box plot.

52. *Consumer Reports* provided overall customer satisfaction scores for AT&T, Sprint, T-Mobile, and Verizon cell-phone services in major metropolitan areas throughout the United States. The rating for each service reflects the overall customer satisfaction considering a variety of factors such as cost, connectivity problems, dropped calls, static interference, and customer support. A satisfaction scale from 0 to 100 was used with 0 indicating completely dissatisfied

WEB file

CellService

Metropolitan Area	AT&T	Sprint	T-Mobile	Verizon
Atlanta	70	66	71	79
Boston	69	64	74	76
Chicago	71	65	70	77
Dallas	75	65	74	78
Denver	71	67	73	77
Detroit	73	65	77	79
Jacksonville	73	64	75	81
Las Vegas	72	68	74	81
Los Angeles	66	65	68	78
Miami	68	69	73	80
Minneapolis	68	66	75	77
Philadelphia	72	66	71	78
Phoenix	68	66	76	81
San Antonio	75	65	75	80
San Diego	69	68	72	79
San Francisco	66	69	73	75
Seattle	68	67	74	77
St. Louis	74	66	74	79
Tampa	73	63	73	79
Washington	72	68	71	76

and 100 indicating completely satisfied. The ratings for the four cell-phone services in 20 metropolitan areas are as shown (*Consumer Reports*, January 2009).

a. Consider T-Mobile first. What is the median rating?
b. Develop a five-number summary for the T-Mobile service.
c. Are there outliers for T-Mobile? Explain.
d. Repeat parts (b) and (c) for the other three cell-phone services.
e. Show the box plots for the four cell-phone services on one graph. Discuss what a comparison of the box plots tells about the four services. Which service did *Consumer Reports* recommend as being best in terms of overall customer satisfaction?

53. The Philadelphia Phillies defeated the Tampa Bay Rays 4 to 3 to win the 2008 major league baseball World Series. Earlier in the major league baseball playoffs, the Philadelphia Phillies defeated the Los Angeles Dodgers to win the National League Championship, while the Tampa Bay Rays defeated the Boston Red Sox to win the American League Championship. The file MLBSalaries contains the salaries for the 28 players on each of these four teams (*USA Today* Salary Database, October 2008). The data, shown in thousands of dollars, have been ordered from the highest salary to the lowest salary for each team.

MLBSalaries

a. Analyze the salaries for the World Champion Philadelphia Phillies. What is the total payroll for the team? What is the median salary? What is the five-number summary?
b. Were there salary outliers for the Philadelphia Phillies? If so, how many and what were the salary amounts?
c. What is the total payroll for each of the other three teams? Develop the five-number summary for each team and identify any outliers.
d. Show the box plots of the salaries for all four teams. What are your interpretations? Of these four teams, does it appear that the team with the higher salaries won the league championships and the World Series?

BorderCrossings

54. The Bureau of Transportation Statistics keeps track of all border crossings through ports of entry along the U.S.-Canadian and U.S.-Mexican borders. The Web file BorderCrossings contains data on the number of personal vehicle crossings (rounded to the nearest 1000) at the 50 busiest ports of entry during the month of August (U.S. Department of Transportation website, February 28, 2013).

a. What are the mean and median number of crossings for these ports of entry?
b. What are the first and third quartiles?
c. Provide a five-number summary.
d. Do the data contain any outliers? Show a box plot.

3.5 Measures of Association Between Two Variables

Thus far we have examined numerical methods used to summarize the data for *one variable at a time*. Often a manager or decision maker is interested in the *relationship between two variables*. In this section we present covariance and correlation as descriptive measures of the relationship between two variables.

We begin by reconsidering the application concerning a stereo and sound equipment store in San Francisco as presented in Section 2.4. The store's manager wants to determine the relationship between the number of weekend television commercials shown and the sales at the store during the following week. Sample data with sales expressed in hundreds of dollars are provided in Table 3.6. It shows 10 observations (*n* = 10), one for each week. The scatter diagram in Figure 3.9 shows a positive relationship, with higher sales (*y*) associated with a greater number of commercials (*x*). In fact, the scatter diagram suggests that

TABLE 3.6   SAMPLE DATA FOR THE STEREO AND SOUND EQUIPMENT STORE

Week	Number of Commercials x	Sales Volume ($100s) y
1	2	50
2	5	57
3	1	41
4	3	54
5	4	54
6	1	38
7	5	63
8	3	48
9	4	59
10	2	46

a straight line could be used as an approximation of the relationship. In the following discussion, we introduce **covariance** as a descriptive measure of the linear association between two variables.

Covariance

For a sample of size n with the observations (x_1, y_1), (x_2, y_2), and so on, the sample covariance is defined as follows.

SAMPLE COVARIANCE

$$s_{xy} = \frac{\Sigma(x_i - \bar{x})(y_i - \bar{y})}{n - 1} \tag{3.12}$$

FIGURE 3.9   SCATTER DIAGRAM FOR THE STEREO AND SOUND EQUIPMENT STORE

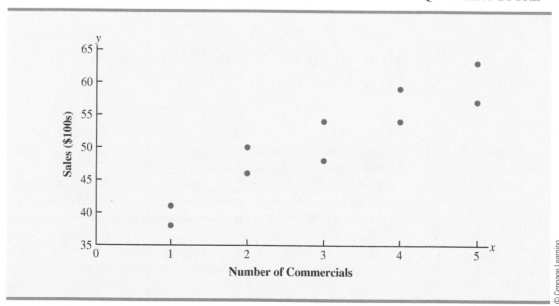

This formula pairs each x_i with a y_i. We then sum the products obtained by multiplying the deviation of each x_i from its sample mean $\bar{x}$ by the deviation of the corresponding y_i from its sample mean $\bar{y}$; this sum is then divided by $n - 1$.

To measure the strength of the linear relationship between the number of commercials x and the sales volume y in the stereo and sound equipment store problem, we use equation (3.12) to compute the sample covariance. The calculations in Table 3.7 show the computation of $\Sigma(x_i - \bar{x})(y_i - \bar{y})$. Note that $\bar{x} = 30/10 = 3$ and $\bar{y} = 510/10 = 51$. Using equation (3.12), we obtain a sample covariance of

$$s_{xy} = \frac{\Sigma(x_i - \bar{x})(y_i - \bar{y})}{n - 1} = \frac{99}{9} = 11$$

The formula for computing the covariance of a population of size N is similar to equation (3.12), but we use different notation to indicate that we are working with the entire population.

POPULATION COVARIANCE

$$\sigma_{xy} = \frac{\Sigma(x_i - \mu_x)(y_i - \mu_y)}{N}$$

(3.13)

In equation (3.13) we use the notation μ_x for the population mean of the variable x and μ_y for the population mean of the variable y. The population covariance σ_{xy} is defined for a population of size N.

TABLE 3.7   CALCULATIONS FOR THE SAMPLE COVARIANCE

x_i	y_i	$x_i - \bar{x}$	$y_i - \bar{y}$	$(x_i - \bar{x})(y_i - \bar{y})$
2	50	−1	−1	1
5	57	2	6	12
1	41	−2	−10	20
3	54	0	3	0
4	54	1	3	3
1	38	−2	−13	26
5	63	2	12	24
3	48	0	−3	0
4	59	1	8	8
2	46	−1	−5	5
Totals 30	510	0	0	99

$$s_{xy} = \frac{\Sigma(x_i - \bar{x})(y_i - \bar{y})}{n - 1} = \frac{99}{10 - 1} = 11$$

FIGURE 3.10   PARTITIONED SCATTER DIAGRAM FOR THE STEREO AND SOUND
EQUIPMENT STORE

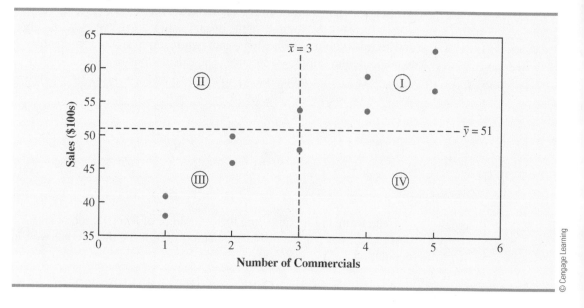

Interpretation of the Covariance

To aid in the interpretation of the sample covariance, consider Figure 3.10. It is the same as the scatter diagram of Figure 3.9 with a vertical dashed line at $\bar{x} = 3$ and a horizontal dashed line at $\bar{y} = 51$. The lines divide the graph into four quadrants. Points in quadrant I correspond to x_i greater than $\bar{x}$ and y_i greater than $\bar{y}$, points in quadrant II correspond to x_i less than $\bar{x}$ and y_i greater than $\bar{y}$, and so on. Thus, the value of $(x_i - \bar{x})(y_i - \bar{y})$ must be positive for points in quadrant I, negative for points in quadrant II, positive for points in quadrant III, and negative for points in quadrant IV.

The covariance is a measure of the linear association between two variables.

If the value of s_{xy} is positive, the points with the greatest influence on s_{xy} must be in quadrants I and III. Hence, a positive value for s_{xy} indicates a positive linear association between x and y; that is, as the value of x increases, the value of y increases. If the value of s_{xy} is negative, however, the points with the greatest influence on s_{xy} are in quadrants II and IV. Hence, a negative value for s_{xy} indicates a negative linear association between x and y; that is, as the value of x increases, the value of y decreases. Finally, if the points are evenly distributed across all four quadrants, the value of s_{xy} will be close to zero, indicating no linear association between x and y. Figure 3.11 shows the values of s_{xy} that can be expected with three different types of scatter diagrams.

Referring again to Figure 3.10, we see that the scatter diagram for the stereo and sound equipment store follows the pattern in the top panel of Figure 3.11. As we should expect, the value of the sample covariance indicates a positive linear relationship with $s_{xy} = 11$.

From the preceding discussion, it might appear that a large positive value for the covariance indicates a strong positive linear relationship and that a large negative value indicates a strong negative linear relationship. However, one problem with using covariance as a measure of the strength of the linear relationship is that the value of the covariance depends on the units of measurement for x and y. For example, suppose we are interested in the relationship between height x and weight y for individuals. Clearly the strength of the relationship should be the same whether we measure height in feet or inches. Measuring the height in inches, however, gives us much larger numerical values for $(x_i - \bar{x})$ than when we measure height in feet. Thus, with

FIGURE 3.11 INTERPRETATION OF SAMPLE COVARIANCE

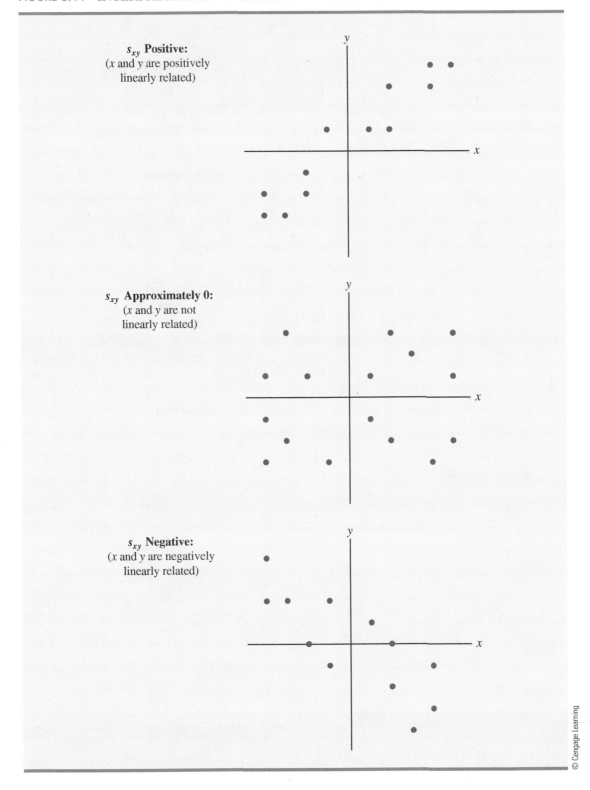

height measured in inches, we would obtain a larger value for the numerator $\sum(x_i - \bar{x})$ $(y_i - \bar{y})$ in equation (3.12)—and hence a larger covariance—when in fact the relationship does not change. A measure of the relationship between two variables that is not affected by the units of measurement for x and y is the **correlation coefficient**.

Correlation Coefficient

For sample data, the Pearson product moment correlation coefficient is defined as follows.

PEARSON PRODUCT MOMENT CORRELATION COEFFICIENT: SAMPLE DATA

$$r_{xy} = \frac{s_{xy}}{s_x s_y} \tag{3.14}$$

where

$$r_{xy} = \text{sample correlation coefficient}$$
$$s_{xy} = \text{sample covariance}$$
$$s_x = \text{sample standard deviation of } x$$
$$s_y = \text{sample standard deviation of } y$$

Equation (3.14) shows that the Pearson product moment correlation coefficient for sample data (commonly referred to more simply as the *sample correlation coefficient*) is computed by dividing the sample covariance by the product of the sample standard deviation of x and the sample standard deviation of y.

Let us now compute the sample correlation coefficient for the stereo and sound equipment store. Using the data in Table 3.6, we can compute the sample standard deviations for the two variables:

$$s_x = \sqrt{\frac{\Sigma(x_i - \bar{x})^2}{n - 1}} = \sqrt{\frac{20}{9}} = 1.49$$

$$s_y = \sqrt{\frac{\Sigma(y_i - \bar{y})^2}{n - 1}} = \sqrt{\frac{566}{9}} = 7.93$$

Now, because $s_{xy} = 11$, the sample correlation coefficient equals

$$r_{xy} = \frac{s_{xy}}{s_x s_y} = \frac{11}{(1.49)(7.93)} = .93$$

The formula for computing the correlation coefficient for a population, denoted by the Greek letter ρ_{xy} (rho, pronounced "row"), follows.

PEARSON PRODUCT MOMENT CORRELATION COEFFICIENT: POPULATION DATA

The sample correlation coefficient r_{xy} is a point estimator of the population correlation coefficient ρ_{xy}.

$$\rho_{xy} = \frac{\sigma_{xy}}{\sigma_x \sigma_y} \tag{3.15}$$

where

$$\rho_{xy} = \text{population correlation coefficient}$$
$$\sigma_{xy} = \text{population covariance}$$
$$\sigma_x = \text{population standard deviation for } x$$
$$\sigma_y = \text{population standard deviation for } y$$

FIGURE 3.12   SCATTER DIAGRAM DEPICTING A PERFECT POSITIVE LINEAR
RELATIONSHIP

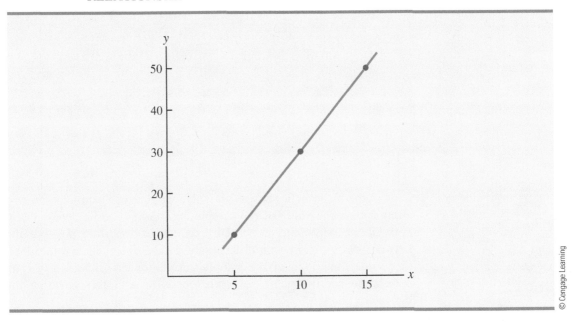

The sample correlation coefficient r_{xy} provides an estimate of the population correlation
coefficient ρ_{xy}.

Interpretation of the Correlation Coefficient

First let us consider a simple example that illustrates the concept of a perfect positive linear
relationship. The scatter diagram in Figure 3.12 depicts the relationship between x and y
based on the following sample data.

x_i	y_i
5	10
10	30
15	50

The straight line drawn through each of the three points shows a perfect linear relationship between x and y. In order to apply equation (3.14) to compute the sample correlation we must first compute s_{xy}, s_x, and s_y. Some of the computations are shown in Table 3.8.
Using the results in this table, we find

$$s_{xy} = \frac{\Sigma(x_i - \bar{x})(y_i - \bar{y})}{n - 1} = \frac{200}{2} = 100$$

$$s_x = \sqrt{\frac{\Sigma(x_i - \bar{x})^2}{n - 1}} = \sqrt{\frac{50}{2}} = 5$$

$$s_y = \sqrt{\frac{\Sigma(y_i - \bar{y})^2}{n - 1}} = \sqrt{\frac{800}{2}} = 20$$

$$r_{xy} = \frac{s_{xy}}{s_x s_y} = \frac{100}{5(20)} = 1$$

Thus, we see that the value of the sample correlation coefficient is 1.

TABLE 3.8   COMPUTATIONS USED IN CALCULATING THE SAMPLE
CORRELATION COEFFICIENT

	x_i	y_i	$x_i - \bar{x}$	$(x_i - \bar{x})^2$	$y_i - \bar{y}$	$(y_i - \bar{y})^2$	$(x_i - \bar{x})(y_i - \bar{y})$
	5	10	−5	25	−20	400	100
	10	30	0	0	0	0	0
	15	50	5	25	20	400	100
Totals	30	90	0	50	0	800	200

$\bar{x} = 10$ $\bar{y} = 30$

The correlation coefficient ranges from −1 to +1. Values close to −1 or +1 indicate a strong linear relationship. The closer the correlation is to zero, the weaker the relationship.

In general, it can be shown that if all the points in a data set fall on a positively sloped straight line, the value of the sample correlation coefficient is +1; that is, a sample correlation coefficient of +1 corresponds to a perfect positive linear relationship between x and y. Moreover, if the points in the data set fall on a straight line having negative slope, the value of the sample correlation coefficient is −1; that is, a sample correlation coefficient of −1 corresponds to a perfect negative linear relationship between x and y.

Let us now suppose that a certain data set indicates a positive linear relationship between x and y but that the relationship is not perfect. The value of r_{xy} will be less than 1, indicating that the points in the scatter diagram are not all on a straight line. As the points deviate more and more from a perfect positive linear relationship, the value of r_{xy} becomes smaller and smaller. A value of r_{xy} equal to zero indicates no linear relationship between x and y, and values of r_{xy} near zero indicate a weak linear relationship.

For the data involving the stereo and sound equipment store, $r_{xy} = .93$. Therefore, we conclude that a strong positive linear relationship occurs between the number of commercials and sales. More specifically, an increase in the number of commercials is associated with an increase in sales.

In closing, we note that correlation provides a measure of linear association and not necessarily causation. A high correlation between two variables does not mean that changes in one variable will cause changes in the other variable. For example, we may find that the quality rating and the typical meal price of restaurants are positively correlated. However, simply increasing the meal price at a restaurant will not cause the quality rating to increase.

NOTE AND COMMENT

Because the correlation coefficient measures only the strength of the linear relationship between two quantitative variables, it is possible for the correlation coefficient to be near zero, suggesting no linear relationship, when the relationship between the two variables is nonlinear. For example, the following scatter diagram shows the relationship between the amount spent by a small retail store for environmental control (heating and cooling) and the daily high outside temperature over 100 days.

The sample correlation coefficient for these data is $r_{xy} = -.007$ and indicates there is no linear relationship between the two variables. However, the scatter diagram provides strong visual evidence of a nonlinear relationship. That is, we can see that as the daily high outside temperature increases, the money spent on environmental control first decreases as less heating is required and then increases as greater cooling is required.

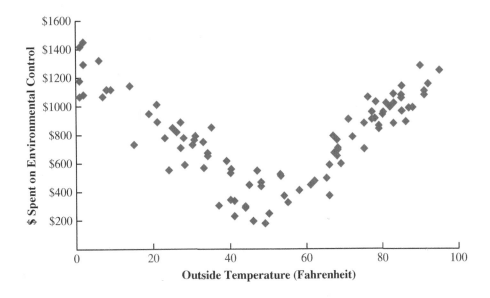

Exercises

Methods

55. Five observations taken for two variables follow.

x_i	4	6	11	3	16
y_i	50	50	40	60	30

a. Develop a scatter diagram with x on the horizontal axis.
b. What does the scatter diagram developed in part (a) indicate about the relationship between the two variables?
c. Compute and interpret the sample covariance.
d. Compute and interpret the sample correlation coefficient.

56. Five observations taken for two variables follow.

x_i	6	11	15	21	27
y_i	6	9	6	17	12

a. Develop a scatter diagram for these data.
b. What does the scatter diagram indicate about a relationship between x and y?
c. Compute and interpret the sample covariance.
d. Compute and interpret the sample correlation coefficient.

Applications

57. Ten major college football bowl games were played in January 2010, with the University of Alabama beating the University of Texas 37 to 21 to become the national champion of college football. The results of the 10 bowl games follow (*USA Today,* January 8, 2010).

BowlGames

Bowl Game	Score	Predicted Point Margin	Actual Point Margin
Outback	Auburn 38 Northwestern 35	5	3
Gator	Florida State 33 West Virginia 21	1	12
Capital One	Penn State 19 LSU 17	3	2
Rose	Ohio State 26 Oregon 17	−2	9
Sugar	Florida 51 Cincinnati 24	14	27
Cotton	Mississippi State 21 Oklahoma State 7	3	14
Alamo	Texas Tech 41 Michigan State 31	9	10
Fiesta	Boise State 17 TCU 10	−4	7
Orange	Iowa 24 Georgia Tech 14	−3	10
Championship	Alabama 37 Texas 21	4	16

The predicted winning point margin was based on Las Vegas betting odds approximately one week before the bowl games were played. For example, Auburn was predicted to beat Northwestern in the Outback Bowl by five points. The actual winning point margin for Auburn was three points. A negative predicted winning point margin means that the team that won the bowl game was an underdog and expected to lose. For example, in the Rose Bowl, Ohio State was a two-point underdog to Oregon and ended up winning by nine points.

a. Develop a scatter diagram with predicted point margin on the horizontal axis.
b. What is the relationship between predicted and actual point margins?
c. Compute and interpret the sample covariance.
d. Compute the sample correlation coefficient. What does this value indicate about the relationship between the Las Vegas predicted point margin and the actual point margin in college football bowl games?

58. A department of transportation's study on driving speed and miles per gallon for midsize automobiles resulted in the following data:

Speed (Miles per Hour)	30	50	40	55	30	25	60	25	50	55
Miles per Gallon	28	25	25	23	30	32	21	35	26	25

Compute and interpret the sample correlation coefficient.

59. At the beginning of 2009, the economic downturn resulted in the loss of jobs and an increase in delinquent loans for housing. The national unemployment rate was 6.5% and the

Housing

Metro Area	Jobless Rate (%)	Delinquent Loan (%)	Metro Area	Jobless Rate (%)	Delinquent Loan (%)
Atlanta	7.1	7.02	New York	6.2	5.78
Boston	5.2	5.31	Orange County	6.3	6.08
Charlotte	7.8	5.38	Orlando	7.0	10.05
Chicago	7.8	5.40	Philadelphia	6.2	4.75
Dallas	5.8	5.00	Phoenix	5.5	7.22
Denver	5.8	4.07	Portland	6.5	3.79
Detroit	9.3	6.53	Raleigh	6.0	3.62
Houston	5.7	5.57	Sacramento	8.3	9.24
Jacksonville	7.3	6.99	St. Louis	7.5	4.40
Las Vegas	7.6	11.12	San Diego	7.1	6.91
Los Angeles	8.2	7.56	San Francisco	6.8	5.57
Miami	7.1	12.11	Seattle	5.5	3.87
Minneapolis	6.3	4.39	Tampa	7.5	8.42
Nashville	6.6	4.78			

percentage of delinquent loans was 6.12% (*The Wall Street Journal,* January 27, 2009). In projecting where the real estate market was headed in the coming year, economists studied the relationship between the jobless rate and the percentage of delinquent loans. The expectation was that if the jobless rate continued to increase, there would also be an increase in the percentage of delinquent loans. The data below show the jobless rate and the delinquent loan percentage for 27 major real estate markets.

a. Compute the correlation coefficient. Is there a positive correlation between the jobless rate and the percentage of delinquent housing loans? What is your interpretation?
b. Show a scatter diagram of the relationship between jobless rate and the percentage of delinquent housing loans.

Russell

60. The Russell 1000 is a stock market index consisting of the largest U.S. companies. The Dow Jones Industrial Average is based on 30 large companies. The file Russell gives the annual percentage returns for each of these stock indexes for the years 1988 to 2012 (1stock1 website).
a. Plot these percentage returns using a scatter plot.
b. Compute the sample mean and standard deviation for each index.
c. Compute the sample correlation.
d. Discuss similarities and differences in these two indexes.

61. The daily high and low temperatures for 14 cities around the world are shown (The Weather Channel, April 22, 2009).

WorldTemp

City	High	Low	City	High	Low
Athens	68	50	London	67	45
Beijing	70	49	Moscow	44	29
Berlin	65	44	Paris	69	44
Cairo	96	64	Rio de Janeiro	76	69
Dublin	57	46	Rome	69	51
Geneva	70	45	Tokyo	70	58
Hong Kong	80	73	Toronto	44	39

a. What is the sample mean high temperature?
b. What is the sample mean low temperature?
c. What is the correlation between the high and low temperatures? Discuss.

3.6 Data Dashboards: Adding Numerical Measures to Improve Effectiveness

In Section 2.5 we provided an introduction to data visualization, a term used to describe the use of graphical displays to summarize and present information about a data set. The goal of data visualization is to communicate key information about the data as effectively and clearly as possible. One of the most widely used data visualization tools is a data dashboard, a set of visual displays that organizes and presents information that is used to monitor the performance of a company or organization in a manner that is easy to read, understand, and interpret. In this section we extend the discussion of data dashboards to show how the addition of numerical measures can improve the overall effectiveness of the display.

The addition of numerical measures, such as the mean and standard deviation of key performance indicators (KPIs), to a data dashboard is critical because numerical measures often provide benchmarks or goals by which KPIs are evaluated. In addition, graphical displays that include numerical measures as components of the display are also frequently

FIGURE 3.13   INITIAL GROGAN OIL INFORMATION TECHNOLOGY CALL CENTER DATA DASHBOARD

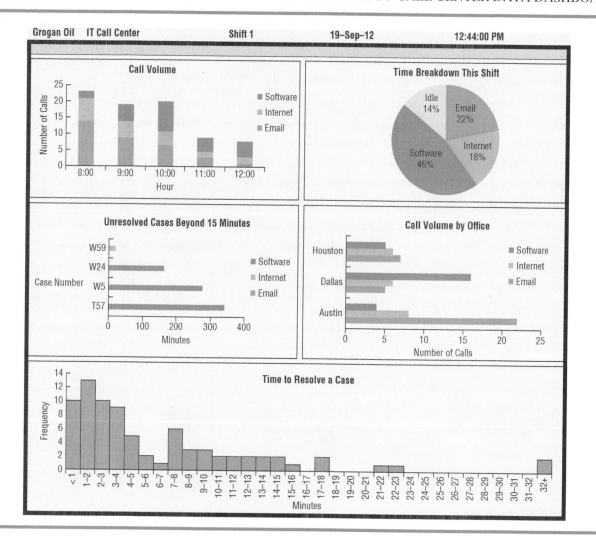

included in data dashboards. We must keep in mind that the purpose of a data dashboard is to provide information on the KPIs in a manner that is easy to read, understand, and interpret. Adding numerical measures and graphs that utilize numerical measures can help us accomplish these objectives.

To illustrate the use of numerical measures in a data dashboard, recall the Grogan Oil Company application that we used in Section 2.5 to introduce the concept of a data dashboard. Grogan Oil has offices located in three cities in Texas: Austin (its headquarters), Houston, and Dallas. Grogan's Information Technology (IT) call center, located in the Austin office, handles calls regarding computer-related problems (software, Internet, and e-mail) from employees in the three offices. Figure 3.13 shows the data dashboard that Grogan developed to monitor the performance of the call center. The key components of this dashboard are as follows:

- The stacked bar chart in the upper left corner of the dashboard shows the call volume for each type of problem (software, Internet, or e-mail) over time.
- The pie chart in the upper right corner of the dashboard shows the percentage of time that call center employees spent on each type of problem or not working on a call (idle).
- For each unresolved case that was received more than 15 minutes ago, the bar chart shown in the middle left portion of the dashboard shows the length of time that each of these cases has been unresolved.

- The bar chart in the middle right portion of the dashboard shows the call volume by office (Houston, Dallas, Austin) for each type of problem.
- The histogram at the bottom of the dashboard shows the distribution of the time to resolve a case for all resolved cases for the current shift.

In order to gain additional insight into the performance of the call center, Grogan's IT manager has decided to expand the current dashboard by adding box plots for the time required to resolve calls received for each type of problem (e-mail, Internet, and software). In addition, a graph showing the time to resolve individual cases has been added in the lower left portion of the dashboard. Finally, the IT manager added a display of summary statistics for each type of problem and summary statistics for each of the first few hours of the shift. The updated dashboard is shown in Figure 3.14.

The IT call center has set a target performance level or benchmark of 10 minutes for the mean time to resolve a case. Furthermore, the center has decided it is undesirable for the time to resolve a case to exceed 15 minutes. To reflect these benchmarks, a black horizontal line at the mean target value of 10 minutes and a red horizontal line at the maximum acceptable level of 15 minutes have been added to both the graph showing the time to resolve cases and the box plots of the time required to resolve calls received for each type of problem.

The summary statistics in the dashboard in Figure 3.14 show that the mean time to resolve an e-mail case is 4.6 minutes, the mean time to resolve an Internet case is 5.4 minutes, and the mean time to resolve a software case is 5.2 minutes. Thus, the mean time to resolve each type of case is better than the target mean (10 minutes).

Reviewing the box plots, we see that the box associated with the e-mail cases is "larger" than the boxes associated with the other two types of cases. The summary statistics also show that the standard deviation of the time to resolve e-mail cases is larger than the standard deviations of the times to resolve the other types of cases. This leads us to take a closer look at the e-mail cases in the two new graphs. The box plot for the e-mail cases has a whisker that extends beyond 15 minutes and an outlier well beyond 15 minutes. The graph of the time to resolve individual cases (in the lower left position of the dashboard) shows that this is because of two calls on e-mail cases during the 9:00 hour that took longer than the target maximum time (15 minutes) to resolve. This analysis may lead the IT call center manager to further investigate why resolution times are more variable for e-mail cases than for Internet or software cases. Based on this analysis, the IT manager may also decide to investigate the circumstances that led to inordinately long resolution times for the two e-mail cases that took longer than 15 minutes to resolve.

The graph of the time to resolve individual cases also shows that most calls received during the first hour of the shift were resolved relatively quickly; the graph also shows that the time to resolve cases increased gradually throughout the morning. This could be due to a tendency for complex problems to arise later in the shift or possibly to the backlog of calls that accumulates over time. Although the summary statistics suggest that cases submitted during the 9:00 hour take the longest to resolve, the graph of time to resolve individual cases shows that two time-consuming e-mail cases and one time-consuming software case were reported during that hour, and this may explain why the mean time to resolve cases during the 9.00 hour is larger than during any other hour of the shift. Overall, reported cases have generally been resolved in 15 minutes or less during this shift.

Drilling down refers to functionality in interactive data dashboards that allows the user to access information and analyses at an increasingly detailed level.

Dashboards such as the Grogan Oil data dashboard are often interactive. For instance, when a manager uses a mouse or a touch screen monitor to position the cursor over the display or point to something on the display, additional information, such as the time to resolve the problem, the time the call was received, and the individual and/or the location that reported the problem, may appear. Clicking on the individual item may also take the user to a new level of analysis at the individual case level.

FIGURE 3.14   UPDATED GROGAN OIL INFORMATION TECHNOLOGY CALL CENTER DATA DASHBOARD

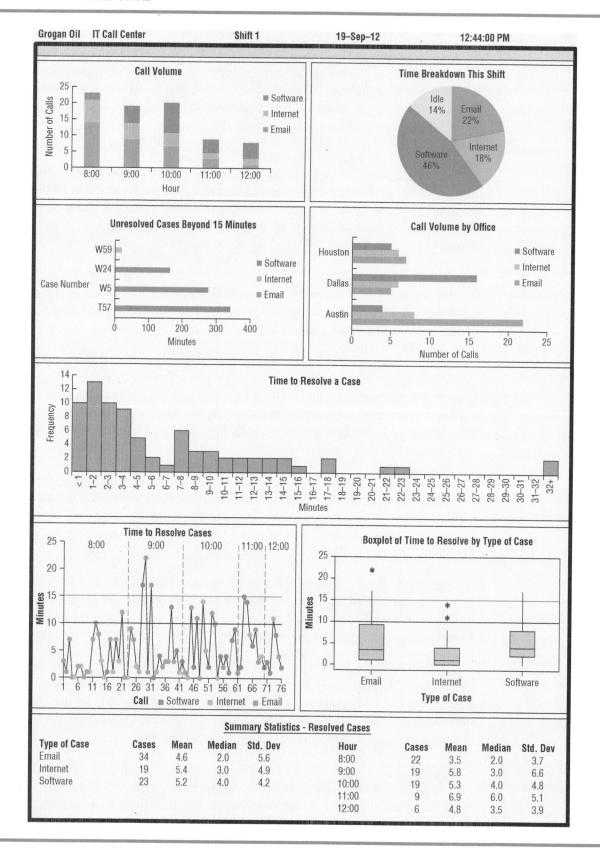

Summary

In this chapter we introduced several descriptive statistics that can be used to summarize the location, variability, and shape of a data distribution. Unlike the tabular and graphical displays introduced in Chapter 2, the measures introduced in this chapter summarize the data in terms of numerical values. When the numerical values obtained are for a sample, they are called sample statistics. When the numerical values obtained are for a population, they are called population parameters. Some of the notation used for sample statistics and population parameters follows.

In statistical inference, a sample statistic is referred to as a point estimator of the population parameter.

	Sample Statistic	Population Parameter
Mean	$\bar{x}$	μ
Variance	s^2	σ^2
Standard deviation	s	σ
Covariance	s_{xy}	σ_{xy}
Correlation	r_{xy}	ρ_{xy}

As measures of location, we defined the mean, median, mode, weighted mean, geometric mean, percentiles, and quartiles. Next, we presented the range, interquartile range, variance, standard deviation, and coefficient of variation as measures of variability or dispersion. Our primary measure of the shape of a data distribution was the skewness. Negative values of skewness indicate a data distribution skewed to the left, and positive values of skewness indicate a data distribution skewed to the right. We then described how the mean and standard deviation could be used, applying Chebyshev's theorem and the empirical rule, to provide more information about the distribution of data and to identify outliers.

In Section 3.4 we showed how to develop a five-number summary and a box plot to provide simultaneous information about the location, variability, and shape of the distribution. In Section 3.5 we introduced covariance and the correlation coefficient as measures of association between two variables. In the final section, we showed how adding numerical measures can improve the effectiveness of data dashboards.

The descriptive statistics we discussed can be developed using statistical software packages and spreadsheets. In the chapter-ending appendixes we show how to use Minitab, Excel, and StatTools to develop the descriptive statistics introduced in this chapter.

Glossary

Sample statistic A numerical value used as a summary measure for a sample (e.g., the sample mean, $\bar{x}$, the sample variance, s^2, and the sample standard deviation, s).
Population parameter A numerical value used as a summary measure for a population (e.g., the population mean, μ, the population variance, σ^2, and the population standard deviation, σ).
Point estimator A sample statistic, such as $\bar{x}$, s^2, and s, used to estimate the corresponding population parameter.
Mean A measure of central location computed by summing the data values and dividing by the number of observations.
Weighted mean The mean obtained by assigning each observation a weight that reflects its importance.
Median A measure of central location provided by the value in the middle when the data are arranged in ascending order.
Geometric mean A measure of location that is calculated by finding the nth root of the product of n values.

Mode A measure of location, defined as the value that occurs with greatest frequency.

Percentile A value such that at least p percent of the observations are less than or equal to this value and at least $(100 - p)$ percent of the observations are greater than or equal to this value. The 50th percentile is the median.

Quartiles The 25th, 50th, and 75th percentiles, referred to as the first quartile, the second quartile (median), and third quartile, respectively. The quartiles can be used to divide a data set into four parts, with each part containing approximately 25% of the data.

Range A measure of variability, defined to be the largest value minus the smallest value.

Interquartile range (IQR) A measure of variability, defined to be the difference between the third and first quartiles.

Variance A measure of variability based on the squared deviations of the data values about the mean.

Standard deviation A measure of variability computed by taking the positive square root of the variance.

Coefficient of variation A measure of relative variability computed by dividing the standard deviation by the mean and multiplying by 100.

Skewness A measure of the shape of a data distribution. Data skewed to the left result in negative skewness; a symmetric data distribution results in zero skewness; and data skewed to the right result in positive skewness.

z-score A value computed by dividing the deviation about the mean $(x_i - \bar{x})$ by the standard deviation s. A z-score is referred to as a standardized value and denotes the number of standard deviations x_i is from the mean.

Chebyshev's theorem A theorem that can be used to make statements about the proportion of data values that must be within a specified number of standard deviations of the mean.

Empirical rule A rule that can be used to compute the percentage of data values that must be within one, two, and three standard deviations of the mean for data that exhibit a bell-shaped distribution.

Outlier An unusually small or unusually large data value.

Five-number summary A technique that uses five numbers to summarize the data: smallest value, first quartile, median, third quartile, and largest value.

Box plot A graphical summary of data based on a five-number summary.

Covariance A measure of linear association between two variables. Positive values indicate a positive relationship; negative values indicate a negative relationship.

Correlation coefficient A measure of linear association between two variables that takes on values between -1 and $+1$. Values near $+1$ indicate a strong positive linear relationship; values near -1 indicate a strong negative linear relationship; and values near zero indicate the lack of a linear relationship.

Key Formulas

Sample Mean

$$\bar{x} = \frac{\sum x_i}{n} \tag{3.1}$$

Population Mean

$$\mu = \frac{\sum x_i}{N} \tag{3.2}$$

Weighted Mean

$$\bar{x} = \frac{\sum w_i x_i}{w_i} \tag{3.3}$$

Geometric Mean

$$\bar{x}_g = \sqrt[n]{(x_1)(x_2)\cdots(x_n)} = [(x_1)(x_2)\cdots(x_n)]^{1/n} \tag{3.4}$$

Interquartile Range

$$\text{IQR} = Q_3 - Q_1 \tag{3.5}$$

Population Variance

$$\sigma^2 = \frac{\sum(x_i - \mu)^2}{N} \tag{3.6}$$

Sample Variance

$$s^2 = \frac{\sum(x_i - \bar{x})^2}{n - 1} \tag{3.7}$$

Standard Deviation

$$\text{Sample standard deviation} = s = \sqrt{s^2} \tag{3.8}$$

$$\text{Population standard deviation} = \sigma = \sqrt{\sigma^2} \tag{3.9}$$

Coefficient of Variation

$$\left(\frac{\text{Standard deviation}}{\text{Mean}} \times 100 \right)\% \tag{3.10}$$

z-Score

$$z_i = \frac{x_i - \bar{x}}{s} \tag{3.11}$$

Sample Covariance

$$s_{xy} = \frac{\sum(x_i - \bar{x})(y_i - \bar{y})}{n - 1} \tag{3.12}$$

Population Covariance

$$\sigma_{xy} = \frac{\sum(x_i - \mu_x)(y_i - \mu_y)}{N} \tag{3.13}$$

Pearson Product Moment Correlation Coefficient: Sample Data

$$r_{xy} = \frac{s_{xy}}{s_x s_y} \tag{3.14}$$

Pearson Product Moment Correlation Coefficient: Population Data

$$\rho_{xy} = \frac{\sigma_{xy}}{\sigma_x \sigma_y} \tag{3.15}$$

Supplementary Exercises

62. The average number of times Americans dine out in a week fell from 4.0 in 2008 to 3.8 in 2012 (Zagat.com, April 1, 2012). The number of times a sample of 20 families dined out last week provides the following data.

6	1	5	3	7	3	0	3	1	3
4	1	2	4	1	0	5	6	3	1

 a. Compute the mean and median.
 b. Compute the first and third quartiles.
 c. Compute the range and interquartile range.
 d. Compute the variance and standard deviation.
 e. The skewness measure for these data is 0.34. Comment on the shape of this distribution. Is it the shape you would expect? Why or why not?
 f. Do the data contain outliers?

WEB file

Coaches

63. *USA Today* reports that NCAA colleges and universities are paying higher salaries to a newly recruited football coach compared to what they paid their previous football coach. (*USA Today*, February 12, 2013). The annual base salaries for the previous head football coach and the new head football coach at 23 schools are given in the file Coaches.

 a. Determine the median annual salary for a previous head football coach and a new head football coach.
 b. Compute the range for salaries for both previous and new head football coaches.
 c. Compute the standard deviation for salaries for both previous and new head football coaches.
 d. Based on your answers to a-c, comment on any differences between the annual base salary a school pays a new head football coach compared to what it paid its pervious head football coach.

64. The average waiting time for a patient at an El Paso physician's office is just over 29 minutes, well above the national average of 21 minutes. In fact, El Paso has the longest physician's office waiting times in the United States (*El Paso Times,* January 8, 2012). In order to address the issue of long patient wait times, some physicians' offices are using wait tracking systems to notify patients of expected wait times. Patients can adjust their arrival times based on this information and spend less time in waiting rooms. The following data show wait times (minutes) for a sample of patients at offices that do not have an office tracking system and wait times for a sample of patients at offices with an office tracking system.

 a. What are the mean and median patient wait times for offices with a wait tracking system? What are the mean and median patient wait times for offices without a wait tracking system?

WEB file

WaitTracking

Without Wait Tracking System	With Wait Tracking System
24	31
67	11
17	14
20	18
31	12
44	37
12	9
23	13
16	12
37	15

b. What are the variance and standard deviation of patient wait times for offices with a wait tracking system? What are the variance and standard deviation of patient wait times for visits to offices without a wait tracking system?

c. Do offices with a wait tracking system have shorter patient wait times than offices without a wait tracking system? Explain.

d. Considering only offices without a wait tracking system, what is the z-score for the tenth patient in the sample?

e. Considering only offices with a wait tracking system, what is the z-score for the sixth patient in the sample? How does this z-score compare with the z-score you calculated for part (d)?

f. Based on z-scores, do the data for offices without a wait tracking system contain any outliers? Based on z-scores, do the data for offices with a wait tracking system contain any outliers?

Sleep

65. U.S. companies lose $63.2 billion per year from workers with insomnia. Workers lose an average of 7.8 days of productivity per year due to lack of sleep (*Wall Street Journal*, January 23, 2013). The following data show the number of hours of sleep attained during a recent night for a sample of 20 workers.

6	5	10	5	6	9	9	5	9	5
8	7	8	6	9	8	9	6	10	8

a. What is the mean number of hours of sleep for this sample?
b. What is the variance? Standard deviation?

Smartphone

66. A study of smartphone users shows that 68% of smartphone use occurs at home and a user spends an average of 410 minutes per month using a smartphone to interact with other people (*Harvard Business Review*, January–February 2013). Consider the following data indicating the number of minutes in a month spent interacting with others via a smartphone for a sample of 50 smartphone users.

353	458	404	394	416
437	430	369	448	430
431	469	446	387	445
354	468	422	402	360
444	424	441	357	435
461	407	470	413	351
464	374	417	460	352
445	387	468	368	430
384	367	436	390	464
405	372	401	388	367

a. What is the mean number of minutes spent interacting with others for this sample? How does it compare to the mean reported in the study?
b. What is the standard deviation for this sample?
c. Are there any outliers in this sample?

67. Public transportation and the automobile are two methods an employee can use to get to work each day. Samples of times recorded for each method are shown. Times are in minutes.

Public Transportation:	28	29	32	37	33	25	29	32	41	34
Automobile:	29	31	33	32	34	30	31	32	35	33

a. Compute the sample mean time to get to work for each method.
b. Compute the sample standard deviation for each method.

c. On the basis of your results from parts (a) and (b), which method of transportation should be preferred? Explain.

d. Develop a box plot for each method. Does a comparison of the box plots support your conclusion in part (c)?

68. Consumers borrow money for many different reasons, including the purchase of a home, car, and appliances, to remodel, or to help pay for college. Approximately 75% of U.S. households carry some debt (*Wall Street Journal,* February 25, 2013). Consider the amount of household debt in the sample of 25 households shown below.

WEB file

Debt

122,231	69,402	52,055	131,176	59,423
125,409	142,762	72,576	58,458	18,927
59,025	131,934	148,782	57,380	124,831
116,128	107,320	79,649	110,354	53,880
60,370	68,140	94,513	97,544	72,140

a. What is the median amount of household debt?
b. Provide a five-number summary of this sample data.
c. What is the mean household debt for this sample?
d. Does this sample contain any outliers?
e. Would you prefer to use the mean or the median when describing household debt? Why?

69. The U.S. Census Bureau's American Community Survey reported the percentage of children under 18 years of age who had lived below the poverty level during the previous 12 months (U.S. Census Bureau website, August 2008). The region of the country, Northeast (NE), Southeast (SE), Midwest (MW), Southwest (SW), and West (W), and the percentage of children under 18 who had lived below the poverty level are shown for each state.
a. What is the median poverty level percentage for the 50 states?
b. What are the first and third quartiles? What is your interpretation of the quartiles?

WEB file

PovertyLevel

State	Region	Poverty %	State	Region	Poverty %
Alabama	SE	23.0	Montana	W	17.3
Alaska	W	15.1	Nebraska	MW	14.4
Arizona	SW	19.5	Nevada	W	13.9
Arkansas	SE	24.3	New Hampshire	NE	9.6
California	W	18.1	New Jersey	NE	11.8
Colorado	W	15.7	New Mexico	SW	25.6
Connecticut	NE	11.0	New York	NE	20.0
Delaware	NE	15.8	North Carolina	SE	20.2
Florida	SE	17.5	North Dakota	MW	13.0
Georgia	SE	20.2	Ohio	MW	18.7
Hawaii	W	11.4	Oklahoma	SW	24.3
Idaho	W	15.1	Oregon	W	16.8
Illinois	MW	17.1	Pennsylvania	NE	16.9
Indiana	MW	17.9	Rhode Island	NE	15.1
Iowa	MW	13.7	South Carolina	SE	22.1
Kansas	MW	15.6	South Dakota	MW	16.8
Kentucky	SE	22.8	Tennessee	SE	22.7
Louisiana	SE	27.8	Texas	SW	23.9
Maine	NE	17.6	Utah	W	11.9
Maryland	NE	9.7	Vermont	NE	13.2
Massachusetts	NE	12.4	Virginia	SE	12.2
Michigan	MW	18.3	Washington	W	15.4
Minnesota	MW	12.2	West Virginia	SE	25.2
Mississippi	SE	29.5	Wisconsin	MW	14.9
Missouri	MW	18.6	Wyoming	W	12.0

c. Show a box plot for the data. Interpret the box plot in terms of what it tells you about the level of poverty for children in the United States. Are any states considered outliers? Discuss.

d. Identify the states in the lower quartile. What is your interpretation of this group and what region or regions are represented most in the lower quartile?

70. *Travel + Leisure* magazine presented its annual list of the 500 best hotels in the world (*Travel + Leisure,* January 2009). The magazine provides a rating for each hotel along with a brief description that includes the size of the hotel, amenities, and the cost per night for a double room. A sample of 12 of the top-rated hotels in the United States follows.

Travel

Hotel	Location	Rooms	Cost/Night
Boulders Resort & Spa	Phoenix, AZ	220	499
Disney's Wilderness Lodge	Orlando, FL	727	340
Four Seasons Hotel Beverly Hills	Los Angeles, CA	285	585
Four Seasons Hotel	Boston, MA	273	495
Hay-Adams	Washington, DC	145	495
Inn on Biltmore Estate	Asheville, NC	213	279
Loews Ventana Canyon Resort	Phoenix, AZ	398	279
Mauna Lani Bay Hotel	Island of Hawaii	343	455
Montage Laguna Beach	Laguna Beach, CA	250	595
Sofitel Water Tower	Chicago, IL	414	367
St. Regis Monarch Beach	Dana Point, CA	400	675
The Broadmoor	Colorado Springs, CO	700	420

a. What is the mean number of rooms?

b. What is the mean cost per night for a double room?

c. Develop a scatter diagram with the number of rooms on the horizontal axis and the cost per night on the vertical axis. Does there appear to be a relationship between the number of rooms and the cost per night? Discuss.

d. What is the sample correlation coefficient? What does it tell you about the relationship between the number of rooms and the cost per night for a double room? Does this appear reasonable? Discuss.

71. Morningstar tracks the performance of a large number of companies and publishes an evaluation of each. Along with a variety of financial data, Morningstar includes a Fair Value estimate for the price that should be paid for a share of the company's common stock. Data for 30 companies are available in the file named FairValue. The data include the Fair Value estimate per share of common stock, the most recent price per share, and the earning per share for the company (*Morningstar Stocks 500,* 2008).

FairValue

a. Develop a scatter diagram for the Fair Value and Share Price data with Share Price on the horizontal axis. What is the sample correlation coefficient, and what can you say about the relationship between the variables?

b. Develop a scatter diagram for the Fair Value and Earnings per Share data with Earnings per Share on the horizontal axis. What is the sample correlation coefficient, and what can you say about the relationship between the variables?

72. Does a major league baseball team's record during spring training indicate how the team will play during the regular season? Over the last six years, the correlation coefficient between a team's winning percentage in spring training and its winning percentage in the regular season is .18 (*The Wall Street Journal,* March 30, 2009). Shown are the winning percentages for the 14 American League teams during the 2008 season.

SpringTraining

Team	Spring Training	Regular Season	Team	Spring Training	Regular Season
Baltimore Orioles	.407	.422	Minnesota Twins	.500	.540
Boston Red Sox	.429	.586	New York Yankees	.577	.549
Chicago White Sox	.417	.546	Oakland A's	.692	.466
Cleveland Indians	.569	.500	Seattle Mariners	.500	.377
Detroit Tigers	.569	.457	Tampa Bay Rays	.731	.599
Kansas City Royals	.533	.463	Texas Rangers	.643	.488
Los Angeles Angels	.724	.617	Toronto Blue Jays	.448	.531

    a.   What is the correlation coefficient between the spring training and the regular season winning percentages?

    b.   What is your conclusion about a team's record during spring training indicating how the team will play during the regular season? What are some of the reasons why this occurs? Discuss.

73.   The days to maturity for a sample of five money market funds are shown here. The dollar amounts invested in the funds are provided. Use the weighted mean to determine the mean number of days to maturity for dollars invested in these five money market funds.

Days to Maturity	Dollar Value ($millions)
20	20
12	30
7	10
5	15
6	10

74.   Automobiles traveling on a road with a posted speed limit of 55 miles per hour are checked for speed by a state police radar system. Following is a frequency distribution of speeds.

Speed (miles per hour)	Frequency
45–49	10
50–54	40
55–59	150
60–64	175
65–69	75
70–74	15
75–79	10
Total	475

    a.   What is the mean speed of the automobiles traveling on this road?

    b.   Compute the variance and the standard deviation.

75.   The Panama Railroad Company was established in 1850 to construct a railroad across the isthmus that would allow fast and easy access between the Atlantic and Pacific Oceans. The following table (*The Big Ditch*, Mauer and Yu, 2011) provides annual returns for Panama Railroad stock from 1853 through 1880.

Year	Return on Panama Railroad Company Stock (%)
1853	−1
1854	−9
1855	19
1856	2
1857	3
1858	36
1859	21
1860	16
1861	−5
1862	43
1863	44
1864	48
1865	7
1866	11
1867	23
1868	20
1869	−11
1870	−51
1871	−42
1872	39
1873	42
1874	12
1875	26
1876	9
1877	−6
1878	25
1879	31
1880	30

PanamaRailroad

a.   Create a graph of the annual returns on the stock. The New York Stock Exchange earned an annual average return of 8.4% from 1853 through 1880. Can you tell from the graph if the Panama Railroad Company stock outperformed the New York Stock Exchange?

b.   Calculate the mean annual return on Panama Railroad Company stock from 1853 through 1880. Did the stock outperform the New York Stock Exchange over the same period?

Case Problem 1   Pelican Stores

Pelican Stores, a division of National Clothing, is a chain of women's apparel stores operating throughout the country. The chain recently ran a promotion in which discount coupons were sent to customers of other National Clothing stores. Data collected for a sample of 100 in-store credit card transactions at Pelican Stores during one day while the promotion was running are contained in the file named PelicanStores. Table 3.9 shows a portion of the data set. The proprietary card method of payment refers to charges made using a National Clothing charge card. Customers who made a purchase using a discount coupon are referred to as promotional customers and customers who made a purchase but did not use a discount coupon are referred to as regular customers. Because the promotional coupons were not sent to regular Pelican Stores customers, management considers the sales made to people presenting the promotional coupons as sales it would not otherwise make. Of course, Pelican also hopes that the promotional customers will continue to shop at its stores.

TABLE 3.9 SAMPLE OF 100 CREDIT CARD PURCHASES AT PELICAN STORES

PelicanStores

Customer	Type of Customer	Items	Net Sales	Method of Payment	Gender	Marital Status	Age
1	Regular	1	39.50	Discover	Male	Married	32
2	Promotional	1	102.40	Proprietary Card	Female	Married	36
3	Regular	1	22.50	Proprietary Card	Female	Married	32
4	Promotional	5	100.40	Proprietary Card	Female	Married	28
5	Regular	2	54.00	MasterCard	Female	Married	34
6	Regular	1	44.50	MasterCard	Female	Married	44
7	Promotional	2	78.00	Proprietary Card	Female	Married	30
8	Regular	1	22.50	Visa	Female	Married	40
9	Promotional	2	56.52	Proprietary Card	Female	Married	46
10	Regular	1	44.50	Proprietary Card	Female	Married	36
.	.	.	.	.	.	.	.
.	.	.	.	.	.	.	.
.	.	.	.	.	.	.	.
96	Regular	1	39.50	MasterCard	Female	Married	44
97	Promotional	9	253.00	Proprietary Card	Female	Married	30
98	Promotional	10	287.59	Proprietary Card	Female	Married	52
99	Promotional	2	47.60	Proprietary Card	Female	Married	30
100	Promotional	1	28.44	Proprietary Card	Female	Married	44

© Cengage Learning

Most of the variables shown in Table 3.9 are self-explanatory, but two of the variables require some clarification.

Items   The total number of items purchased

Net Sales   The total amount ($) charged to the credit card

Pelican's management would like to use this sample data to learn about its customer base and to evaluate the promotion involving discount coupons.

Managerial Report

Use the methods of descriptive statistics presented in this chapter to summarize the data and comment on your findings. At a minimum, your report should include the following:

1. Descriptive statistics on net sales and descriptive statistics on net sales by various classifications of customers.
2. Descriptive statistics concerning the relationship between age and net sales.

Case Problem 2   Motion Picture Industry

The motion picture industry is a competitive business. More than 50 studios produce several hundred new motion pictures each year, and the financial success of the motion pictures varies considerably. The opening weekend gross sales, the total gross sales, the number of theaters the movie was shown in, and the number of weeks the motion picture was in release are common variables used to measure the success of a motion picture. Data on the top 100 grossing motion pictures released in 2011 (Box Office Mojo website, March 17, 2012) are contained in a file named 2011Movies. Table 3.10 shows the data for the first 10 motion pictures in this file. Note that some movies, such as *War Horse,* were released late in 2011 and continued to run in 2012.

TABLE 3.10   PERFORMANCE DATA FOR 10 MOTION PICTURES

2011Movies

Motion Picture	Opening Gross Sales ($millions)	Total Gross Sales ($millions)	Number of Theaters	Weeks in Release
Harry Potter and the Deathly Hallows Part 2	169.19	381.01	4375	19
Transformers: Dark of the Moon	97.85	352.39	4088	15
The Twilight Saga: Breaking Dawn Part 1	138.12	281.29	4066	14
The Hangover Part II	85.95	254.46	3675	16
Pirates of the Caribbean: On Stranger Tides	90.15	241.07	4164	19
Fast Five	86.20	209.84	3793	15
Mission: Impossible—Ghost Protocol	12.79	208.55	3555	13
Cars 2	66.14	191.45	4115	25
Sherlock Holmes: A Game of Shadows	39.64	186.59	3703	13
Thor	65.72	181.03	3963	16

Managerial Report

Use the numerical methods of descriptive statistics presented in this chapter to learn how these variables contribute to the success of a motion picture. Include the following in your report:

1. Descriptive statistics for each of the four variables along with a discussion of what the descriptive statistics tell us about the motion picture industry.
2. What motion pictures, if any, should be considered high-performance outliers? Explain.
3. Descriptive statistics showing the relationship between total gross sales and each of the other variables. Discuss.

Case Problem 3   Business Schools of Asia-Pacific

Asian

The pursuit of a higher education degree in business is now international. A survey shows that more and more Asians choose the master of business administration (MBA) degree route to corporate success. As a result, the number of applicants for MBA courses at Asia-Pacific schools continues to increase.

Across the region, thousands of Asians show an increasing willingness to temporarily shelve their careers and spend two years in pursuit of a theoretical business qualification. Courses in these schools are notoriously tough and include economics, banking, marketing, behavioral sciences, labor relations, decision making, strategic thinking, business law, and more. The data set in Table 3.11 shows some of the characteristics of the leading Asia-Pacific business schools.

Managerial Report

Use the methods of descriptive statistics to summarize the data in Table 3.11. Discuss your findings.

1. Include a summary for each variable in the data set. Make comments and interpretations based on maximums and minimums, as well as the appropriate means and

TABLE 3.11 DATA FOR 25 ASIA-PACIFIC BUSINESS SCHOOLS

Business School	Full-Time Enrollment	Students per Faculty	Local Tuition ($)	Foreign Tuition ($)	Age	% Foreign	GMAT	English Test	Work Experience	Starting Salary ($)
Melbourne Business School	200	5	24,420	29,600	28	47	Yes	No	Yes	71,400
University of New South Wales (Sydney)	228	4	19,993	32,582	29	28	Yes	No	Yes	65,200
Indian Institute of Management (Ahmedabad)	392	5	4,300	4,300	22	0	No	No	No	7,100
Chinese University of Hong Kong	90	5	11,140	11,140	29	10	Yes	No	No	31,000
International University of Japan (Niigata)	126	4	33,060	33,060	28	60	Yes	Yes	No	87,000
Asian Institute of Management (Manila)	389	5	7,562	9,000	25	50	Yes	No	Yes	22,800
Indian Institute of Management (Bangalore)	380	5	3,935	16,000	23	1	Yes	No	No	7,500
National University of Singapore	147	6	6,146	7,170	29	51	Yes	Yes	Yes	43,300
Indian Institute of Management (Calcutta)	463	8	2,880	16,000	23	0	No	No	No	7,400
Australian National University (Canberra)	42	2	20,300	20,300	30	80	Yes	Yes	Yes	46,600
Nanyang Technological University (Singapore)	50	5	8,500	8,500	32	20	Yes	No	Yes	49,300
University of Queensland (Brisbane)	138	17	16,000	22,800	32	26	No	No	Yes	49,600
Hong Kong University of Science and Technology	60	2	11,513	11,513	26	37	Yes	No	Yes	34,000
Macquarie Graduate School of Management (Sydney)	12	8	17,172	19,778	34	27	No	No	Yes	60,100
Chulalongkorn University (Bangkok)	200	7	17,355	17,355	25	6	Yes	No	Yes	17,600
Monash Mt. Eliza Business School (Melbourne)	350	13	16,200	22,500	30	30	Yes	Yes	Yes	52,500
Asian Institute of Management (Bangkok)	300	10	18,200	18,200	29	90	No	Yes	Yes	25,000
University of Adelaide	20	19	16,426	23,100	30	10	No	No	Yes	66,000
Massey University (Palmerston North, New Zealand)	30	15	13,106	21,625	37	35	No	Yes	Yes	41,400
Royal Melbourne Institute of Technology Business Graduate School	30	7	13,880	17,765	32	30	No	Yes	Yes	48,900
Jamnalal Bajaj Institute of Management Studies (Mumbai)	240	9	1,000	1,000	24	0	No	No	Yes	7,000
Curtin Institute of Technology (Perth)	98	15	9,475	19,097	29	43	Yes	No	Yes	55,000
Lahore University of Management Sciences	70	14	11,250	26,300	23	2.5	No	No	No	7,500
Universiti Sains Malaysia (Penang)	30	5	2,260	2,260	32	15	No	Yes	Yes	16,000
De La Salle University (Manila)	44	17	3,300	3,600	28	3.5	Yes	No	Yes	13,100

proportions. What new insights do these descriptive statistics provide concerning Asia-Pacific business schools?

2. Summarize the data to compare the following:
   a. Any difference between local and foreign tuition costs.
   b. Any difference between mean starting salaries for schools requiring and not requiring work experience.
   c. Any difference between starting salaries for schools requiring and not requiring English tests.
3. Do starting salaries appear to be related to tuition?
4. Present any additional graphical and numerical summaries that will be beneficial in communicating the data in Table 3.11 to others.

Case Problem 4   Heavenly Chocolates Website Transactions

Heavenly Chocolates manufactures and sells quality chocolate products at its plant and retail store located in Saratoga Springs, New York. Two years ago the company developed a website and began selling its products over the Internet. Website sales have exceeded the company's expectations, and management is now considering strategies to increase sales even further. To learn more about the website customers, a sample of 50 Heavenly Chocolate transactions was selected from the previous month's sales. Data showing the day of the week each transaction was made, the type of browser the customer used, the time spent on the website, the number of website pages viewed, and the amount spent by each of the 50 customers are contained in the file named Shoppers. A portion of the data are shown in Table 3.12.

Heavenly Chocolates would like to use the sample data to determine if online shoppers who spend more time and view more pages also spend more money during their visit to the website. The company would also like to investigate the effect that the day of the week and the type of browser have on sales.

TABLE 3.12   A SAMPLE OF 50 HEAVENLY CHOCOLATES WEBSITE TRANSACTIONS

Shoppers

Customer	Day	Browser	Time (min)	Pages Viewed	Amount Spent ($)
1	Mon	Internet Explorer	12.0	4	54.52
2	Wed	Other	19.5	6	94.90
3	Mon	Internet Explorer	8.5	4	26.68
4	Tue	Firefox	11.4	2	44.73
5	Wed	Internet Explorer	11.3	4	66.27
6	Sat	Firefox	10.5	6	67.80
7	Sun	Internet Explorer	11.4	2	36.04
.	.	.	.	.	.
.	.	.	.	.	.
.	.	.	.	.	.
48	Fri	Internet Explorer	9.7	5	103.15
49	Mon	Other	7.3	6	52.15
50	Fri	Internet Explorer	13.4	3	98.75

Managerial Report

Use the methods of descriptive statistics to learn about the customers who visit the Heavenly Chocolates website. Include the following in your report.

1. Graphical and numerical summaries for the length of time the shopper spends on the website, the number of pages viewed, and the mean amount spent per transaction. Discuss what you learn about Heavenly Cholcolates' online shoppers from these numerical summaries.
2. Summarize the frequency, the total dollars spent, and the mean amount spent per transaction for each day of week. What observations can you make about Hevenly Chocolates' business based on the day of the week? Discuss.
3. Summarize the frequency, the total dollars spent, and the mean amount spent per transaction for each type of browser. What observations can you make about Heavenly Chocolate's business based on the type of browser? Discuss.
4. Develop a scatter diagram and compute the sample correlation coefficient to explore the relationship between the time spent on the website and the dollar amount spent. Use the horizontal axis for the time spent on the website. Discuss.
5. Develop a scatter diagram and compute the sample correlation coefficient to explore the relationship between the the number of website pages viewed and the amount spent. Use the horizontal axis for the number of website pages viewed. Discuss.
6. Develop a scatter diagram and compute the sample correlation coefficient to explore the relationship between the time spent on the website and the number of pages viewed. Use the horizontal axis to represent the number of pages viewed. Discuss.

Case Problem 5   African Elephant Populations

Although millions of elephants once roamed across Africa, by the mid-1980s elephant populations in African nations had been devastated by poaching. Elephants are important to African ecosystems. In tropical forests, elephants create clearings in the canopy that encourage new tree growth. In savannas, elephants reduce bush cover to create an environment that is favorable to browsing and grazing animals. In addition, the seeds of many plant species depend on passing through an elephant's digestive tract before germination.

The status of the elephant now varies greatly across the continent; in some nations, strong measures have been taken to effectively protect elephant populations, while in other nations the elephant populations remain in danger due to poaching for meat and ivory, loss of habitat, and conflict with humans. Table 3.13 shows elephant populations for several African nations in 1979, 1989, and 2007 (Lemieux and Clarke, "The International Ban on Ivory Sales and Its Effects on Elephant Poaching in Africa," *British Journal of Criminology,* 49(4), 2009).

The David Sheldrick Wildlife Trust was established in 1977 to honor the memory of naturalist David Leslie William Sheldrick, who founded Warden of Tsavo East National Park in Kenya and headed the Planning Unit of the Wildlife Conservation and Management Department in that country. Management of the Sheldrick Trust would like to know what these data indicate about elephant populations in various African countries since 1979.

Managerial Report

Use methods of descriptive statistics to summarize the data and comment on changes in elephant populations in African nations since 1979. At a minimum your report should include the following.

1. The mean annual change in elephant population for each country in the 10 years from 1979 to 1989, and a discussion of which countries saw the largest changes in elephant population over this 10-year period.

TABLE 3.13   ELEPHANT POPULATIONS FOR SEVERAL AFRICAN NATIONS IN 1979, 1989, AND 2007

Country	Elephant population 1979	1989	2007
Angola	12,400	12,400	2,530
Botswana	20,000	51,000	175,487
Cameroon	16,200	21,200	15,387
Cen African Rep	63,000	19,000	3,334
Chad	15,000	3,100	6,435
Congo	10,800	70,000	22,102
Dem Rep of Congo	377,700	85,000	23,714
Gabon	13,400	76,000	70,637
Kenya	65,000	19,000	31,636
Mozambique	54,800	18,600	26,088
Somalia	24,300	6,000	70
Sudan	134,000	4,000	300
Tanzania	316,300	80,000	167,003
Zambia	150,000	41,000	29,231
Zimbabwe	30,000	43,000	99,107

AfricanElephants

© Cengage Learning

2. The mean annual change in elephant population for each country from 1989 to 2007, and a discussion of which countries saw the largest changes in elephant population over this 18-year period.
3. A comparison of your results from parts 1 and 2, and a discussion of the conclusions you can draw from this comparison.

Appendix 3.1   Descriptive Statistics Using Minitab

In this appendix, we describe how Minitab can be used to compute a variety of descriptive statistics and display box plots. We then show how Minitab can be used to obtain covariance and correlation measures for two variables.

Descriptive Statistics

2012StartSalary

Table 3.1 provided the starting salaries for 12 business school graduates. These data are in column C2 of the file 2012StartSalary. The following steps can be used to generate descriptive statistics for the starting salary data.

Step 1. Select the **Stat** menu
Step 2. Choose **Basic Statistics**
Step 3. Choose **Display Descriptive Statistics**
Step 4. When the Display Descriptive Statistics dialog box appears:
        Enter C2 in the **Variables** box
        Click **OK**

Figure 3.15 shows the descriptive statistics obtained using Minitab. Definitions of the headings follow.

N	number of data values	Minimum	minimum data value
N*	number of missing data values	Q1	first quartile
Mean	mean	Median	median
SE Mean	standard error of mean	Q3	third quartile
StDev	standard deviation	Maximum	maximum data value

FIGURE 3.15 DESCRIPTIVE STATISTICS PROVIDED BY MINITAB

N	N*	Mean	SEMean	StDev
12	0	3940.0	47.8	165.7
Minimum	Q1	Median	Q3	Maximum
3710.0	4025.0	3905.0	4025.0	4325.0

The label SE Mean refers to the *standard error of the mean*. It is computed by dividing the standard deviation by the square root of N. The interpretation and use of this measure are discussed in Chapter 7 when we introduce the topics of sampling and sampling distributions.

The ten descriptive statistics shown in Figure 3.15 are the default descriptive statistics selected automatically by Minitab. These descriptive statistics are of interest to the majority of users. However, Minitab provides 15 additional descriptive statistics that may be selected depending upon the preferences of the user. The variance, coefficient of variation, range, interquartile range, mode, and skewness are among the additional descriptive statistics available. To select one or more of these additional descriptive statistics, modify step 4 as follows.

Step 4. When the Display Descriptive Statistics dialog box appears:
        Enter C2 in the **Variables** box
        Click **Statistics**
        Select the **descriptive statistics** you wish to obtain or
            choose **All** to obtain all 25 descriptive statistics
        Click **OK**
        Click **OK**

Finally, note that Minitab's quartiles $Q_1 = 3857.5$ and $Q_3 = 4025.0$ are slightly different from the quartiles $Q_1 = 3865$ and $Q_3 = 4000$ computed in Section 3.1. The different conventions* used to identify the quartiles explain this variation. Hence, the values of Q_1 and Q_3 provided by one convention may not be identical to the values of Q_1 and Q_3 provided by another convention. Any differences tend to be negligible, however, and the results provided should not mislead the user in making the usual interpretations associated with quartiles.

Box Plot

The following steps use the file 2012StartSalary to generate the box plot for the starting salary data.

Step 1. Select the **Graph** menu
Step 2. Choose **Boxplot**
Step 3. Under the heading **OneY** select **Simple** and click **OK**
Step 4. When the Boxplot-One Y, Simple dialog box appears:
        Enter C2 in the **Graph variables** box
        Click **OK**

Covariance and Correlation

Stereo

Table 3.6 provided the number of commercials and the sales volume for a stereo and sound equipment store. These data are available in the file Stereo, with the number of commercials in column C2 and the sales volume in column C3. The following steps show how Minitab can be used to compute the covariance for the two variables.

---

*With the n observations arranged in ascending order (smallest value to largest value), Minitab uses the positions given by $(n + 1)/4$ and $3(n + 1)/4$ to locate Q_1 and Q_3, respectively. When a position is fractional, Minitab interpolates between the two adjacent ordered data values to determine the corresponding quartile.

Step 1. Select the **Stat** menu
Step 2. Choose **Basic Statistics**
Step 3. Choose **Covariance**
Step 4. When the Covariance dialog box appears:
        Enter C2 C3 in the **Variables** box
        Click **OK**

To obtain the correlation coefficient for the number of commercials and the sales volume, only one change is necessary in the preceding procedure. In step 3, choose the **Correlation** option.

Appendix 3.2 Descriptive Statistics Using Excel

Excel can be used to generate the descriptive statistics discussed in this chapter. We show how Excel can be used to generate several measures of location and variability for a single variable and to generate the covariance and correlation coefficient as measures of association between two variables.

Using Excel Functions

2012StartSalary

Stereo

Excel provides functions for computing the mean, median, mode, sample variance, and sample standard deviation. We illustrate the use of these Excel functions by computing the mean, median, mode, sample variance, and sample standard deviation for the starting salary data in Table 3.1. Refer to Figure 3.16 as we describe the steps involved. The data are entered in column B.

Excel's AVERAGE function can be used to compute the mean by entering the following formula into cell E1:

$$=\text{AVERAGE}(B2{:}B13)$$

FIGURE 3.16   USING EXCEL FUNCTIONS FOR COMPUTING THE MEAN, MEDIAN, MODE, VARIANCE, AND STANDARD DEVIATION

	A	B	C	D	E
1	Graduate	Starting Salary		Mean	=AVERAGE(B2:B13)
2	1	3850		Median	=MEDIAN(B2:B13)
3	2	3950		Mode	=MODE(B2:B13)
4	3	4050		Variance	=VAR.S(B2:B13)
5	4	3880		Standard Deviation	=STDEV.S(B2:B13)
6	5	3755			
7	6	3710			
8	7	3890			
9	8	4130			
10	9	3940			
11	10	4325			
12	11	3920			
13	12	3880			

	A	B	C	D	E
1	Graduate	Starting Salary		Mean	3940
2	1	3850		Median	3905
3	2	3950		Mode	3880
4	3	4050		Variance	27440.91
5	4	3880		Standard Deviation	165.653
6	5	3755			
7	6	3710			
8	7	3890			
9	8	4130			
10	9	3940			
11	10	4325			
12	11	3920			
13	12	3880			

FIGURE 3.17   USING EXCEL FUNCTIONS FOR COMPUTING THE COVARIANCE AND CORRELATION

	A	B	C	D	E	F	G
1	Week	No. of Commercials	Sales Volume		Sample Covariance	=COVARIANCE.S(B2:B11,C2:C11)	
2	1	2	50		Sample Correlation	=CORREL(B2:B11,C2:C11)	
3	2	5	57				
4	3	1	41				
5	4	3	54				
6	5	4	54				
7	6	1	38				
8	7	5	63				
9	8	3	48				
10	9	4	59				
11	10	2	46				
12							

	A	B	C	D	E	F
1	Week	No. of Commercials	Sales Volume		Sample Covariance	11
2	1	2	50		Sample Correlation	0.930491
3	2	5	57			
4	3	1	41			
5	4	3	54			
6	5	4	54			
7	6	1	38			
8	7	5	63			
9	8	3	48			
10	9	4	59			
11	10	2	46			
12						

To find the variance, standard deviation, and covariance for population data, follow the same steps but use the VAR.P, STDEV.P, and COV.P functions.

Similarly, the formulas =MEDIAN(B2:B13), =MODE.SNGL(B2:B13), =VAR.S(B2:B13), and =STDEV.S(B2:B13) are entered into cells E2:E5, respectively, to compute the median, mode, variance, and standard deviation for this sample. The worksheet in the foreground shows that the values computed using the Excel functions are the same as we computed earlier in the chapter.

Excel also provides functions that can be used to compute the sample covariance and the sample correlation coefficient. We show here how these functions can be used to compute the sample covariance and the sample correlation coefficient for the stereo and sound equipment store data in Table 3.6. Refer to Figure 3.17 as we present the steps involved.

Excel's sample covariance function, COVARIANCE.S, can be used to compute the sample covariance by entering the following formula into cell F1:

$$=COVARIANCE.S(B2:B11,C2:C11)$$

Similarly, the formula =CORREL(B2:B11,C2:C11) is entered into cell F2 to compute the sample correlation coefficient. The worksheet in the foreground shows the values computed using the Excel functions. Note that the value of the sample covariance (11) is the same as computed using equation (3.12). And the value of the sample correlation coefficient (.93) is the same as computed using equation (3.14).

Using Excel's Descriptive Statistics Tool

As we already demonstrated, Excel provides statistical functions to compute descriptive statistics for a data set. These functions can be used to compute one statistic at a time (e.g., mean, variance, etc.). Excel also provides a variety of Data Analysis Tools. One of these tools, called Descriptive Statistics, allows the user to compute a variety of descriptive statistics at once. We show here how it can be used to compute descriptive statistics for the starting salary data in Table 3.1.

WEB file

2012StartSalary

Step 1. Click the **Data** tab on the Ribbon
Step 2. In the **Analysis** group, click **Data Analysis**
Step 3. When the Data Analysis dialog box appears:
  Choose **Descriptive Statistics**
  Click **OK**

FIGURE 3.18 EXCEL'S DESCRIPTIVE STATISTICS TOOL OUTPUT

	A	B	C	D	E	F
1	Graduate	**Monthly Starting Salary ($)**		*Monthly Starting Salary ($)*		
2	1	3850				
3	2	3950		Mean	3940	
4	3	4050		Standard Error	47.82	
5	4	3880		Median	3905	
6	5	3755		Mode	3880	
7	6	3710		Standard Deviation	165.65	
8	7	3890		Sample Variance	27440.91	
9	8	4130		Kurtosis	1.72	
10	9	3940		Skewness	1.09	
11	10	4325		Range	615	
12	11	3920		Minimum	3710	
13	12	3880		Maximum	4325	
14				Sum	47280	
15				Count	12	
16						

© Cengage Learning

Step 4. When the Descriptive Statistics dialog box appears:

Enter B1:B13 in the **Input Range** box

Select **Grouped By Columns**

Select **Labels in First Row**

Select **Output Range**

Enter D1 in the **Output Range** box (to identify the upper left-hand corner of the section of the worksheet where the descriptive statistics will appear)

Select **Summary statistics**

Click **OK**

Cells D1:E15 of Figure 3.18 show the descriptive statistics provided by Excel. The boldface entries are the descriptive statistics we covered in this chapter. The descriptive statistics that are not boldface are either covered subsequently in the text or discussed in more advanced texts.

NOTES AND COMMENTS

If the **Analysis** tab doesn't appear on your ribbon or if the **Data Analysis** option doesn't appear in the **Data Analysis** tab, you need to activate the **Data Analysis ToolPak** by following these three steps:

1. Click the **File** tab, then click **Options**, and then click the **Add-Ins** category.

2. In the **Manage** box, click **Excel Add-ins**, and then click **Go**. The **Add-Ins** dialog box will then appear.

3. In the **Add-Ins available** box, select the check-box next to the **Data Analysis ToolPak** add-in and click **OK**.

The **Analysis** tab will now be available with the **Data Analysis** option.

Appendix 3.3   Descriptive Statistics Using StatTools

In this appendix, we describe how StatTools can be used to compute a variety of descriptive statistics and also display box plots. We then show how StatTools can be used to obtain covariance and correlation measures for two variables.

Descriptive Statistics

WEB file

2012StartSalary

We use the starting salary data in Table 3.1 to illustrate. Begin by using the Data Set Manager to create a StatTools data set for these data using the procedure described in the appendix in Chapter 1. The following steps will generate a variety of descriptive statistics.

Step 1. Click the **StatTools** tab on the Ribbon
Step 2. In the **Analyses Group,** click **Summary Statistics**
Step 3. Choose the **One-Variable Summary** option
Step 4. When the One-Variable Summary Statistics dialog box appears:
　　　　　In the **Variables** section, select **Starting Salary**
　　　　　Click **OK**

A variety of descriptive statistics as shown in Figure 3.18 will appear.

Box Plots

WEB file

2012StartSalary

We use the starting salary data in Table 3.1 to illustrate. Begin by using the Data Set Manager to create a StatTools data set for these data using the procedure described in the appendix in Chapter 1. The following steps will create a box plot for these data.

Step 1. Click the **StatTools** tab on the Ribbon
Step 2. In the **Analyses Group,** click **Summary Graphs**
Step 3. Choose the **Box-Whisker Plot** option
Step 4. When the StatTools - Box-Whisker Plot dialog box appears:
　　　　　In the Variables section, select **Starting Salary**
　　　　　Click **OK**

In its box plots, StatTools defines any value that is at least 1.5 IQR, but less than 3 IQR outside the box as a mild outlier, and any value that is at least 3 IRQ outside the box as an extreme outlier. The symbol □ is used to identify a mild outlier, the symbol ■ is used to signify an extreme outlier, and x is used to identify the mean.

Covariance and Correlation

We use the stereo and sound equipment data in Table 3.6 to demonstrate the computation of the sample covariance and the sample correlation coefficient. Begin by using the Data Set Manager to create a StatTools data set for these data using the procedure described in the appendix in Chapter 1. The following steps will provide the sample covariance and sample correlation coefficient.

Stereo

Step 1. Click the **StatTools** tab on the Ribbon

Step 2. In the **Analyses Group,** click **Summary Statistics**

Step 3. Choose the **Correlation and Covariance** option

Step 4. When the StatTools - Correlation and Covariance dialog box appears:

In the **Variables** section:

Select **No. of Commercials**

Select **Sales Volume**

In the **Tables to Create** section:

Select **Table of Correlations**

Select **Table of Covariances**

In the **Table Structure** section select **Symmetric**

Click **OK**

A table showing the correlation coefficient and the covariance will appear.